PESTS OF LANDSCAPE TREES AND SHRUBS: AN INTEGRATED PEST MANAGEMENT GUIDE

Second Edition

PESTS
of
LANDSCAPE
TREES
and
SHRUBS

An Integrated Pest Management Guide

SECOND EDITION

Steve H. Dreistadt
Writer

Jack Kelly Clark
Principal Photographer

Mary Louise Flint
Technical Editor

IPM EDUCATION AND PUBLICATIONS
STATEWIDE INTEGRATED PEST MANAGEMENT PROGRAM
UNIVERSITY OF CALIFORNIA

AGRICULTURE AND NATURAL RESOURCES
PUBLICATION 3359

2004

PRECAUTIONS FOR USING PESTICIDES

Pesticides are poisonous and must be used with caution. READ THE LABEL BEFORE OPENING A PESTICIDE CONTAINER. Follow all label precautions and directions, including requirements for protective equipment. Use a pesticide only on the plants or site specified on the label or in published University of California recommendations. Apply pesticides at the rates specified on the label or at lower rates if suggested in this publication. In California, all agricultural uses of pesticides must be reported, including use in many non-farm situations, such as cemeteries, golf courses, parks, roadsides, and commercial plant production including nurseries. Contact your county agricultural commissioner for further details. Laws, regulations, and information concerning pesticides change frequently, so be sure the publication you are using is up-to-date.

Legal Responsibility. The user is legally responsible for any damage due to misuse of pesticides. Responsibility extends to effects caused by drift, runoff, or residues.

Transportation. Do not ship or carry pesticides together with food or feed in a way that allows contamination of the edible items. Never transport pesticides in a closed passenger vehicle or in a closed cab.

Storage. Keep pesticides in original containers until used. Store them in a locked cabinet, building, or fenced area where they are not accessible to children, unauthorized persons, pets, or livestock. DO NOT store pesticides with foods, feed, fertilizers, or other materials that may become contaminated by the pesticides.

Container Disposal. Consult the pesticide label, the County Department of Agriculture, or the local waste disposal authorities for instructions on disposing of pesticide containers. Dispose of empty containers carefully. Never reuse them. Make sure empty containers are not accessible to children or animals. Never dispose of containers where they may contaminate water supplies or natural waterways. Offer empty containers for recycling if available. Home use pesticide containers can be thrown in the trash only if they are completely empty.

Protection of Nonpest Animals and Plants. Many pesticides are toxic to useful or desirable animals, including honey bees, natural enemies, fish, domestic animals, and birds. Certain rodenticides may pose a special hazard to animals that eat poisoned rodents. Plants may also be damaged by misapplied pesticides. Take precautions to protect nonpest species from direct exposure to pesticides and from contamination due to drift, runoff, or residues.

Permit Requirements. Certain pesticides require a permit from the county agricultural commissioner before possession or use.

Plant Injury. Certain chemicals may cause injury to plants (phytotoxicity) under certain conditions. Always consult the label for limitations. Before applying any pesticide, take into account the stage of plant development, the soil type and condition, the temperature, moisture, and wind. Injury may also result from the use of incompatible materials.

Personal Safety. Follow label directions carefully. Avoid splashing, spilling, leaks, spray drift, and contamination of clothing. NEVER eat, smoke, drink, or chew while using pesticides. Provide for emergency medical care IN ADVANCE as required by regulation.

Worker Protection Standards. Federal Worker Protection Standards require pesticide safety training for all employees working in agricultural fields, greenhouses, and nurseries that have been treated with pesticides, including pesticide training for employees who don't work directly with pesticides.

ISBN 1-879906-61-9

Library of Congress Control Number 2003103905

©2004 by the Regents of the University of California Division of Agriculture and Natural Resources.

For information about ordering this publication and/or a free catalog, contact

University of California
Agriculture and Natural Resources
Communication Services
6701 San Pablo Avenue, 2nd Floor
Oakland, California 94608-1239

Telephone 1-800-994-8849
(510) 642-2431

FAX (510) 643-5470
E-mail: danrcs@ucdavis.edu
Visit the ANR Communication Services Web site at http://anrcatalog.ucdavis.edu

Publication 3359

This publication has been peer reviewed for technical accuracy by University of California scientists and other qualified professionals. This review process was managed by the ANR Associate Editor for Pest Management.

Contributors and Acknowledgments

TECHNICAL ADVISORS

Laurence R. Costello, *UC Cooperative Extension, San Mateo and San Francisco Counties*

James A. Downer, *UC Cooperative Extension, Ventura County*

Clyde L. Elmore, *Weed Science Program, UC Davis*

Donald R. Hodel, *UC Cooperative Extension, Los Angeles County*

John N. Kabashima, *UC Cooperative Extension, Orange County*

Edward J. Perry, *UC Cooperative Extension, Stanislaus County*

Robert D. Raabe, *Division of Environmental Science, Policy, and Management, UC Berkeley*

Pavel Svihra, *UC Cooperative Extension, Marin County*

Cheryl A. Wilen, *UC Cooperative Extension and UC IPM Program, San Diego, Los Angeles, and Orange Counties*

CONTRIBUTORS AND PRINCIPAL REVIEWERS

David H. Adams, *California Department of Forestry and Fire Protection*

Michael Baefsky, *Baefsky & Associates*

Bethallyn Black, *UC Cooperative Extension, Contra Costa County*

Heather Costa, *Department of Entomology, UC Riverside*

Laurence R. Costello, *UC Cooperative Extension, San Mateo and San Francisco Counties*

Dean R. Donaldson, *UC Cooperative Extension, Napa County*

James A. Downer, *UC Cooperative Extension, Ventura County*

Lester E. Ehler, *Department of Entomology, UC Davis*

Clyde L. Elmore, *Weed Science Program, UC Davis*

Richard W. Harris, *Department of Environmental Horticulture, UC Davis*

Donald R. Hodel, *UC Cooperative Extension, Los Angeles County*

Chuck A. Ingels, *UC Cooperative Extension, Sacramento County*

John N. Kabashima, *UC Cooperative Extension, Orange County*

John F. Karlik, *UC Cooperative Extension, Kern County*

John Lichter, *Tree Associates*

Timothy D. Paine, *Department of Entomology, UC Riverside*

Edward J. Perry, *UC Cooperative Extension, Stanislaus County*

Dennis R. Pittenger, *UC Cooperative Extension, Central Coast and South Region, and Botany and Plant Sciences Department, UC Riverside*

Robert D. Raabe, *Division of Environmental Science, Policy, and Management, UC Berkeley*

Pavel Svihra, *UC Cooperative Extension, Marin County*

Cheryl A. Wilen, *UC Cooperative Extension and UC IPM Program, San Diego, Los Angeles, and Orange Counties*

Ellen M. Zagory, *Davis Arboretum, UC Davis*

ADDITIONAL TECHNICAL ADVISORS FOR THE FIRST EDITION

Pamela S. Bone, *Horticulture Advisor*

Richard Cowles, *Assistant Scientist, Connecticut Agricultural Experiment Station*

Carlton S. Koehler, *Extension Entomologist Emeritus, UC Berkeley*

Arthur H. McCain, *Extension Plant Pathologist Emeritus, UC Berkeley*

REVIEWERS

David H. Adams, Edith B. Allen, Michael Baefsky, J. Ole Becker, Walter J. Bentley, Alison M. Berry, Bethallyn Black, Pamela S. Bone, Patrick Brown, Robert L. Bugg, David W. Burger, Kathleen Campbell, Donald A. Cooksey, Heather Costa, Laurence R. Costello, Cheryl Covert, Richard Cowles, David W. Cudney, Kent M. Daane, Donald L. Dahlsten, Jerry Davidson, Joseph DiTomaso, Linda L. Dodge, Dean R. Donaldson, James A. Downer, Lester E. Ehler, Thomas D. Eichlin, Clyde L. Elmore, Lynn Epstein, Richard Y. Evans, Donald M. Ferrin, Mary Louise Flint, Debbie Flower, Matteo Garbelotto, Rosser W. Garrison, Pamela M. Geisel, Raymond J. Gill, Deborah D. Giraud, David A. Grantz, Marcella E. Grebus, Walter D. Gubler, Bruce Hagen, Susan E. Halbert, Richard W. Harris, Janet S. Hartin, Janine Hasey, Michael J. Henry, Gary W. Hickman, Raymond L. Hix, Mark S. Hoddle, Donald R. Hodel, Chuck A. Ingels, John N. Kabashima, John F. Karlik, Harry K. Kaya, Carlton S. Koehler, Steven T. Koike, W. Thomas Lanini, Vincent Lazaneo, Michelle LeStrange, Vernard R. Lewis, John Lichter, James D. MacDonald, Armand R. Maggenti, Michael V. McKenry, Gregory E. McPherson, John A. Menge, Roland D. Meyer, Jocelyn G. Millar, Richard H. Molinar, Robert F. Norris, Patrick J. O'Connor-Marer, Timothy D. Paine, Michael P. Parrella, Edward J. Perry, Dennis R. Pittenger, Antoon T. Ploeg, Dan Pratt, Alexander H. Purcell, Robert D. Raabe, Richard A. Redak, David M. Rizzo, Phillip A. Roberts, William Roltsch, Robin L. Rosetta, Dave A. Shaw, Andrew J. Storer, Larry L. Strand, Pavel Svihra, Beth L. Teviotdale, Timothy Tidwell, Steven A. Tjosvold, Diane E. Ullman, Baldo Villegas, Becky B. Westerdahl, Karen Wikler, Cheryl A. Wilen, Frank P. Wong, David L. Wood, Laosheng Wu, Ellen M. Zagory, Robert L. Zuparko

SPECIAL THANKS

Matthew Blua, Margaret A. Brush, Linda Farrar Bybee, Bob Cordrey, Don Cox, John Debenedictis, Mach T. Fukada, Sal Genito, Patricia Gouveia, Darren Haver, Carole Hinkle, Christine Joshel, Andrea Joyce, Greg Kareofalas, Ann I. King, Shawn King, Bruce C. Kirkpatrick, John LaFlour, Robert F. Luck, Jennifer Manson-Hing, Nelda Matheny, Doug McCreary, John McKnight, Richard S. Melnicoe, Laura Merrill, Mike Miller, Eric T. Natwick, Julie P. Newman, Kenneth Nunes, Barbara L. P. Ohlendorf, Loren R. Oki, Gale Perez, Mitch Poole, Cheryl A. Reynolds, Steve Ries, Karen L. Robb, Celeste Rusconi, Kay Ryugo, Dave Shelter, Glen Struckman, Mac Takeda, Lucy Tolmach, Doug E. Walker, Edward Weber, Stuart Wooley, Heather Yaffee, Roger T. Zerillo

This book was produced under the auspices of the University of California Statewide Integrated Pest Management (IPM) Program, Richard Roush, James M. Lyons, and Frank G. Zalom, Directors, and prepared by IPM Education and Publications of the Statewide IPM Program at the University of California, Davis, Mary Louise Flint, Director.

PRODUCTION

Design and production: Seventeenth Street Studios
Drawings: Valerie Winemiller, David Kidd
Editor: Stephen W. Barnett
Proofreading: Mary Rogers, Jason Joseph
Index: Richard Evans, Infodex Indexing Services

Contents

CHAPTER ONE

What's in This Book

THIS BOOK is for landscape professionals, home gardeners, and pest managers interested in woody ornamental plants. Its purpose is to encourage maintenance of healthy landscapes through integrated pest management (IPM).

Methods include selecting plants that are well adapted to the environment and resistant to pests, as well as adopting appropriate cultural practices and biological, mechanical, and physical controls. Pesticides are also essential in many integrated pest management programs, but this book generally does not make specific recommendations because availability and appropriate and legal uses of pesticides frequently change. Where pesticides are mentioned, less toxic materials, such as insecticidal soap, narrow-range or horticultural oil, microbials, and botanicals are emphasized because they generally are more compatible with IPM programs. Your local Cooperative Extension office, other experts, or University publications such as the *UCIPM Pest Notes* available online at www.ipm.ucdavis.edu can provide more specific and current information on pesticides.

Chapter 2 describes how to develop an IPM program. Landscape design, planting, and cultural care activities that prevent and minimize damage to woody

landscape plants are detailed in Chapter 3. Subsequent chapters cover pest identification, biology, monitoring, and management. Pests include insects, mites, and snails and slugs (Chapter 4), plant pathogens (Chapter 5), weeds (Chapter 7), and nematodes (Chapter 8). Abiotic or noninfectious disorders are discussed in Chapter 6.

Vertebrate pests are covered in *Wildlife Pest Control Around Gardens and Homes* (Salmon and Lickliter 1984) and several *UCIPM Pest Notes. Pest Notes* include those on California ground squirrel, cliff swallows, house mouse, pocket gophers, rabbits, and voles (meadow mice) as listed in the Suggested Reading and online at www.ipm.ucdavis.edu

If you are uncertain of the cause of a problem and don't know which chapter to go to for solutions, two tables are provided at the back of the book (Chapter 9) to help with diagnosis. The section "Problem-Solving Guide" briefly summarizes damage symptoms that can occur on many woody landscape plants and directs readers to sections of the book that discuss common causes of these problems. The "Tree and Shrub Pest Tables" are more extensive and are organized according to host plants. They list the common problems of over 200 genera or species of trees and shrubs occurring in California and other western landscapes.

The *UC Guide to Solving Garden and Landscape Problems* (Flint et al. 2000) is another good source of information with hundreds of color photographs. For identification and biology of pests affecting herbaceous ornamentals and flowers, consult publications such as *Integrated Pest Management for Floriculture and Nurseries* (Dreistadt 2001). Commercial ornamental growers can consult that publication and *Floriculture and Ornamental Nurseries Pest Management Guidelines* (Raabe et al. 2002) for management recommendations. Home fruit and vegetable garden pest management is discussed in *Pests of the Garden and Small Farm* (Flint 1998) and several *UCIPM Pest Notes*.

A list of references, suggested reading, a glossary, an index, and information on ordering UC IPM publications are provided at the back of the book.

Designing an IPM Program

Landscape professionals and home gardeners have many opportunities to prevent or minimize serious pest problems. This ecological approach to avoiding unacceptable pest presence and damage is called integrated pest management (IPM).

Integrated pest management is a strategy that avoids or prevents pest damage with minimum adverse impact on human health, the environment, and nontarget organisms. To apply IPM, managers use knowledge of plant and pest biology to take actions that reduce the environment's suitability for pest establishment and population increase. IPM employs careful monitoring techniques and combinations of biological, chemical, cultural, mechanical, and physical (also called environmental) control. Pesticides are used only if monitoring reveals that they are needed. If pesticides are necessary, they are chosen and applied in a way that avoids disrupting other IPM practices.

Which Organisms Are Pests?

Many types of organisms can damage trees and shrubs or otherwise be undesirable inhabitants of landscapes. Landscapes are also damaged by abiotic disorders caused by adverse environmental conditions and inappropriate cultural practices. Abiotic factors and pest organisms often work in combination to damage plants.

Common pests include insects, mites, mollusks, nematodes, pathogens, vertebrates, and weeds. However, in each of these groups there are many related species that are beneficial or do not harm desirable plants; in fact, the great majority of organisms in the landscape are desirable components of the ecosystem.

Even the presence of organisms with the potential to become pests may not be cause for concern. For example, many fungi and other microorganisms that can cause disease are continually present in the environment; they usually become damaging only when conditions are favorable for disease development or unfavorable for plant growth, such as when poor cultural practices weaken a plant. Insects, mites, and nematodes that can cause damage when they are abundant can be harmless or even beneficial when their numbers are low; the presence of a few of these plant-feeding pests provides food to maintain natural enemies that help to prevent outbreaks.

Organisms are pests primarily because they compete with, feed on, or infect desirable organisms. Some organisms are pests because of their excrement or by-products, such as sticky aphid honeydew. Pests reduce landscape quality and function, and range in severity from problems that are merely annoying or unattractive to organisms that threaten the survival of desirable plants.

Many states and countries impose quarantines to prevent the introduction of exotic pests, species that do not occur within the jurisdiction imposing the quarantine. Quarantines may prohibit the movement across borders of potentially infested plants, such as nursery stock. To avoid quarantines or induce other jurisdictions to remove their quarantines, agricultural authorities may implement pest eradication programs, such as those targeting exotic gypsy moths or fruit flies inadvertently introduced into suburban landscapes.

Organisms that are harmless in landscapes sometimes become pests if they move to nearby gardens or crops. For example, the bacterium *Xylella fastidiosa* apparently does not seriously damage many ornamental plants in which it occurs, but it causes the serious Pierce's disease of grapes, and a different strain damages oleander as discussed in the section "Bacterial Leaf Scorch and Oleander Scorch." *Xylella fastidiosa* is vectored by certain leafhoppers, and Pierce's disease is controlled partly by replacing nearby noncrop host plants with alternative plant species that do not host the bacterium. Similarly, beet curly top virus (vectored by certain leafhopper species different from those that spread Pierce's disease) is a serious pathogen of beans, melons, peppers, spinach, and tomatoes. The virus can persist without causing symptoms in some ornamentals such as certain buckwheat, ceanothus, and willow species. Avoid using landscape, hedgerow, and insectary plant species that host serous pests of nearby crops.

The extent to which insects, fungi, weeds, and other organisms are landscape pests depends mostly on how much they interfere with the specific purposes for which plants are grown. Location, plant vigor, the species of plant-feeding organisms present, and the attitude and knowledge of people using the landscape also influence whether certain organisms are a pest problem.

IPM Program Components

Effective, environmentally sound pest management requires considerable forethought, knowledge, and observation. Most landscape pest problems can be avoided by taking several steps: choose pest-resistant cultivars and species that are well adapted to local conditions, correctly prepare sites before planting, use proper planting techniques, and provide appropriate cultural care to create optimal conditions for plant growth.

Take action to prevent problems in established landscapes. If you wait until a tree or shrub is nearly dead or heavily damaged by pests, the only options might be to spray it with a fast-acting pesticide, which normally does not permanently correct the problem, or to replace the plant. Plan for possible problems before they occur. Learn the potential pest problems and damage symptoms of plants in your landscape areas by reviewing the section "Tree and Shrub Pest Tables" at the back of this book and by consulting other resources and experts. Talk to Cooperative Extension advisors, master gardeners, knowledgeable homeowners, garden centers with a certified nurseryperson, and landscape professionals in your area to learn of their experience with local growing conditions and particular plant species.

Examine valued plants regularly for pests, damage, and inappropriate cultural practices; keep records of any problems you encounter. Learn to recognize when a plant appears abnormal or when pest abundance or damage is approaching levels that require control. Select control methods that are effective under your growing conditions and least likely to cause adverse effects on the environment. Often, more than one method can

Landscape planners can choose from among many plant species and cultivars, choices that will minimize or promote pest problems. For example, rose cultivars resistant to pests such as black spot and powdery mildew are good choices when planting roses in landscapes.

be employed to give the most reliable control. Five components are key to successful integrated pest management (Figure 2-1):

- prevention
- pest and symptom identification
- regular surveying for pests and problems
- action thresholds and guidelines
- appropriate management methods

PREVENTION

Prevention is the most important component of IPM. Most pest problems can be avoided by careful landscape design, thoughtful plant selection, good site preparation, proper planting, and appropriate cultural practices such as irrigating and mulching. Applying recommended cultural practices is probably the single best way to avoid problems. Irrigation, fertilization, pruning, and other plant care practices are directly linked to many pest problems. Many insect and disease pests and

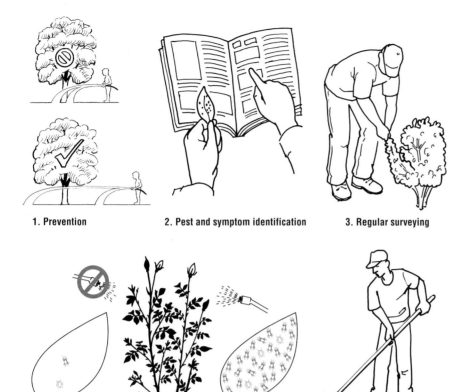

1. Prevention   2. Pest and symptom identification   3. Regular surveying

4. Thresholds   5. Appropriate management

FIGURE 2-1. The major components of integrated pest management

1. Prevention, such as selecting plants well-adapted for that location, proper planting, and ongoing practices such as applying and maintaining mulch and providing appropriate cultural care, such as not irrigating established plants around the root crown, which promotes root rot pathogens;

2. Correct pest identification and diagnosis of the cause of plant damage symptoms;

3. Regular surveying of valued plants for damage, pests, and conditions that contribute to problems, such as inappropriate cultural practices;

4. Action thresholds and guidelines, which entail tolerating some level of pests and damage that does not threaten plants' long-term survival; and

5. Appropriate management, including a combination of biological, chemical, mechanical, and physical controls where needed, such as hoeing weeds.

abiotic disorders are caused by inappropriate irrigation (most commonly watering too frequently) or other maintenance practices that are not appropriate for the specific plants and conditions at that location. If the symptoms caused by poor cultural practices are incorrectly blamed on pathogens or insect pests, then unwarranted pesticide applications might be made, which can contaminate the environment and harm beneficial organisms. Plant health and survival will not be improved if the true causes of the problems are not remedied. Plants will continue to decline and may die prematurely while time and effort are wasted on ineffective actions.

Chapter 3 summarizes cultural practices essential for maintaining healthy plants and preventing pest problems. Also review the section "Tree and Shrub Pest Tables" at the back of this book to learn the specific pests to which your plants are susceptible. Seek advice from Cooperative Extension advisors and other experts. Consult additional resources such as those listed in Suggested Reading.

PEST AND SYMPTOM IDENTIFICATION

Many pests, or the damage caused by them, look similar, especially to the untrained eye. Some pests can be easily confused with beneficial or innocuous organisms. Frequently, people blame damage symptoms on insects or other organisms that happen to be on the plant at the time symptoms are observed when, in fact, those organisms are not causing the problem. The pest causing the damage may have left the site or may be hard to detect, such as pathogens within the roots or the plant's water-conducting vessels. Symptoms caused by factors other than pests, such as overwatering, unfavorable soil conditions, pesticide toxicity, air pollution, or choosing the wrong plant for that location, can be incorrectly blamed on insects, mites, or pathogens. Similar-looking symptoms may have very different causes; spotted leaves, for example, may result from abiotic disorders or disease-causing microorganisms as well as from certain insects. Plants also are frequently subject to more than one disor-

der or pest problem at a time. Diagnosing the specific causes that produce certain symptoms can be a challenge.

Proper pest identification is essential for choosing the right control actions. Even closely related species often require different management strategies, and some species require no action at all. Accurate identification of the cause of plant problems depends on a combination of experience, knowledge, observation, and available resources. The first step is to learn the cultural and environmental conditions required by each plant and to check that these are being adequately provided. Look for sometimes subtle differences between the appearance of unhealthy plants and healthy plants of the same species. Patterns in the symptoms may provide clues to the cause. Obtain information about the recent history of affected plants, environmental conditions, the site, and cultural practices. Use appropriate tools, including a soil sampling tube, pocket knife, hand lens or binoculars, sample collecting containers (plastic bags or vials), and reference material like this book.

The descriptions and photographs in this book will help you recognize many common pests of woody ornamental plants in California, other western states, and the United States. However, because of the broad scope of this book and because new plant and pest species are often introduced from elsewhere, some of the pests you may encounter are not pictured or described here. Consult *Abiotic Disorders of Landscape Plants: A Diagnostic Guide* (Costello et al. 2003), the *UC Guide to Solving Garden and Landscape Problems* (Flint et al. 2000), and other references at the back of this book for additional information. Other excellent publications on western landscapes include *Insects and Diseases of Woody Plants of the Central Rockies* (Cranshaw et al. 2000), *Landscape Plant Problems* (Byther et al. 2000), *Pacific Northwest Landscape Integrated Pest Management (IPM) Manual* (Bobbitt et al. 2002), and *Pests of the West* (Cranshaw 1988). *Insects That Feed on Trees and Shrubs* (Johnson and Lyon 1988) and *Diseases of Trees and Shrubs* (Sinclair, Lyon, and Johnson 1987) are especially useful publications of national scope.

Some pest problems can only be diagnosed reliably by experienced professionals; do not hesitate to seek their help. Your Cooperative Extension advisor, qualified horticultural consultant, certified arborist, or certified nurseryperson may be able to make an identification or direct you to professional diagnostic services.

REGULAR SURVEYING FOR PESTS

Go out to the landscape on a regular basis and systematically check for pests, damage symptoms, and conditions and practices that can damage plants. Develop a routine that is adequate and efficient for the areas under your management. Although sophisticated sampling programs and monitoring techniques have been developed for use in agricultural crops and a few major landscape pests, monitoring in most landscape situations is a less formal process.

Learn the problems that commonly occur in your area on each species of plant that you manage so that you know what to monitor for and where to look on and around the plant. Learn to recognize the stages of common pests and to distinguish them from beneficial organisms. Check regularly for damage and adequate cultural care. Frequency of inspection varies with the season, potential problems, plant value, and resources. Weekly inspections may be needed for certain plants during times of the year when problems can develop quickly. Time invested in monitoring can avoid plant damage and reduce the extent of any necessary management actions. If problems are not detected until they become more obvious, your manage-

ment options may be limited to pesticide use or replacing the plant.

Examine plants in a systematic manner. For example, start with any buds or flowers, then inspect succulent new growth, younger leaves, older leaves, main stems, the trunk, and the basal root crown. Be sure to examine both the upper and lower surfaces of leaves and temporarily remove soil to inspect the basal trunk. If problems such as root crown rot or vascular wilt disease are suspected, consider shaving off a thin slice of bark to inspect a portion of the cambial layer and wood just beneath cambium. In addition to inspecting them close-up, examine plants from a distance for subtle changes in canopy density and foliage color in comparison with surrounding plants and your knowledge of how healthy plants should appear. Use a predetermined pattern of inspection to collect information in the same manner each time, allowing you to compare results among inspection dates. Examine plants in locations with different environmental conditions, such as both sunny and shady sites. Check soil compaction and moisture conditions, for example by using a soil probe or tube.

Keep written monitoring records. Suggested monitoring forms are provided in this book for insects and weeds. Some

Proper identification is essential. Some people may mistake this large hover fly (*Scaeva pyrastri*) larva for a caterpillar, but this beneficial insect eats aphids, not plants.

Examine valued plants regularly for pests, damage, and inappropriate cultural practices. Keep records of any problems that you encounter. Examine plants in a systematic manner, inspect all plant parts that may be infested or show symptoms, and view plants both close up and from afar.

If problems such as root crown rot or vascular wilt disease are suspected, remove soil from around the root crown and shave off a thin slice of bark. Inspect a portion of the cambium and wood for decayed or discolored tissue.

professional landscape managers enter these records into a computer and summarize and analyze them using a database or statistical software program. Professional managers of large numbers of plants can evaluate and compare the effectiveness of management practices in their situation by conducting field trials as discussed in publications such as *IPM in Practice* (Flint and Gouveia 2001).

Compare monitoring results from different dates to determine if problems are increasing or decreasing, whether control action is needed, and how effective were previous management activities. Record the date, specific location, host plant, pests, natural enemies, description of procedures, who sampled, and counts or results. Note pest management activities, such as any pesticide applications. Record other actions and weather that may influence pests. For example, the reproductive and feeding rates of most insects and mites increase with increasing temperature; monitoring temperature and time in units called degree-days helps when managing certain pests. Information available through the World Wide Web (the Web) at www.ipm.ucdavis.edu allows ready use of these tools. Degree-days and other specific monitoring methods are discussed in each section on particular pests.

ACTION THRESHOLDS AND GUIDELINES

A certain number of pest individuals and some amount of damage usually can be tolerated; this concept is fundamental to integrated pest management. The difficulty is in determining the action threshold—the point at which some action must be taken to prevent unacceptable damage.

Researchers have developed control action thresholds or guidelines for some pests in agriculture, especially insects and mites. Crops are grown for profit, so control action thresholds in agriculture are based largely on economic criteria; action is warranted when it will improve crop quality or yield and provide increased revenue that exceeds the extra cost of management.

Few formalized control action guidelines have been developed for pests on landscape trees and shrubs. There are several reasons for this, including a lack of research. However, the most important factor is the difficulty in defining what level of pests or damage is intolerable. Although the death of an attractive plant can be an economic loss to the property owner, the most common landscape pests are those that are annoying to some people or that make plants unsightly;

many of these pests do not seriously damage or kill the plant. Even when dealing with pests that have the potential to threaten plant health or survival, people are often bothered by pests or their damage at levels well below those that threaten the plant. The pest population or damage level when action must be taken to deter undesirable damage to ornamental plants often depends on people's attitudes and is commonly referred to as the "aesthetic threshold."

Aesthetic tolerance varies with the attitude and knowledge of people using the landscape. For example, certain annual plants growing wild as ground covers are tolerated or enjoyed by one segment of the public, while another group considers them weeds and insists on bare soil beneath shrubs. Defining an aesthetic threshold that people can agree on is difficult and subjective. Damage that is acceptable on out-of-the-way plants may not be tolerable on prominent plants. Organisms such as gall-forming insects and mites or a few leaf-chewing caterpillars may cause no real harm to plants but can be annoying or even frightening to some people.

Despite the lack of numerical action guidelines for most landscape trees and shrubs, you will find recommendations throughout this book to help you determine whether actions may be needed and the best time to take action to avoid or reduce specific pest problems. Many plants are more vulnerable to pest damage at certain times in their development—especially during the first year or two after establishment or during certain seasons. These differences in susceptibility mean that the control action guidelines also differ over the growing season and as the plant develops. Other conditions affect a plant's ability to tolerate pest damage; for example, plants weakened by water stress, weed competition, root disease, adverse soil conditions, or injury must be more carefully protected because they are less tolerant of additional stresses or more pests.

Timing of actions is often critical for effective management. For example, once symptoms become apparent, it is often

People's aesthetic tolerance for pest damage varies. The yellow leaf blotches on this Chinese lantern are caused by abutilon mosaic virus. This virus causes no apparent harm to plants, and propagators deliberately select infected plants because many people like these variegated abutilon cultivars.

too late to control many plant diseases effectively. Sometimes the pest life stage that damages plants is not the life stage susceptible to control action. Many times the appropriate action is not to apply pesticide but to use cultural practices such as irrigating or pruning. If you are limited to methods that take several days or months to provide control or that kill a smaller fraction of the pests, you have to allow for more lead time than you would with faster-acting measures.

How To Establish Thresholds. Establish thresholds for highly valued or problem-prone plants by systematically monitoring landscapes, keeping good records, and judging the health and quality of plants in comparison with pest scouting and control records. Thresholds should be quantitative or numerical to be useful. For example, thresholds could be based on the percent of plants or leaves found to be damaged or infested during visual inspection or the number of pests dislodged per branch beat sample (a monitoring technique discussed in Chapter 4). Suggested numerical thresholds are provided for a few pests, such as in the sections "Aphids" and "Elm Leaf Beetle."

Control action guidelines or thresholds are helpful only when used with accurate pest identification and careful

monitoring. Keep records of pests, how you determined when to treat, and the results of management activities. These records will help you to develop and refine action guidelines that work best for your situation in the future.

Experiment over time to develop thresholds appropriate for your situation. Be flexible in adjusting thresholds and adapting monitoring techniques and management methods as appropriate.

MANAGEMENT METHODS

Integrated pest managers must consider the interrelation of cultural practices, environmental conditions, and the biology of plants, pests, and beneficial organisms in order to provide healthy landscapes. Primary methods used specifically for pest management are biological, chemical, cultural, mechanical, and physical control.

Before applying these methods, determine whether action is needed and likely to be effective. If it is too late for control to be effective or if the problem is minor or does not threaten plant health, consider taking no action or applying other methods. When action is needed, whenever possible use more than one method in combination to provide more effective control. Methods are summarized below and detailed in later chapters.

Cultural Control. Cultural controls are modifications of normal plant care activities that reduce or avoid pest problems as detailed in Chapter 3. Some landscape designs, and selecting resistant species and cultivars, can minimize pest problems. Plant properly and irrigate, prune, and otherwise care for plants appropriately. Providing plants with proper cultural care is the single most important component of pest management. Many problems that threaten plant survival are caused by inappropriate cultural practices such as irrigating too frequently. Good care can prevent many pests from adversely affecting plants. For certain problems, such as root diseases and most wood-boring insects, cultural control is often the only effective method.

Mechanical Control. Mechanical controls use labor, materials not usually considered to be pesticides, and machinery to reduce pest abundance directly. For example, control weeds with mulch, mowing, weed eaters, flamers, and hand-pulling where appropriate (see Chapter 7). Install copper bands around trunks and planting areas to exclude snails and slugs. Apply sticky material around trunks to prevent canopies from being infested by ants, flightless weevils, and snails. Clip and dispose of foliage infested with insects that feed in groups, such as tentmaking caterpillars. Hand-pick snails or leaves infested with insects or disease. Prune out or rake up foliage and twigs infected with disease, such as leaf spots and anthracnose, to prevent pathogen propagules from spreading and infecting healthy plant tissue.

Physical Control. Physical controls (also called environmental controls) indirectly suppress or prevent pests by altering temperature, light, and humidity. Control black scale and possibly some other scale species by thinning plant canopies in hot areas of California, thereby increasing scale mortality due to heat exposure. Control certain foliar diseases by thinning the plant canopy or cutting back nearby plants to improve

Prevent weeds and improve plant growth by applying and maintaining an attractive and effective mulch.

A raspberry horntail larva is tunneling inside this wilted rose shoot. This pest is easily managed with mechanical control, the pruning off of wilted shoots below any noticeable damage.

Biological control has been used most successfully to control pest insects and mites. This bigeyed bug nymph (*Geocoris* sp.) is feeding on a moth egg, preventing a plant-chewing caterpillar from hatching.

air circulation and reduce humidity. Apply white interior (not exterior) latex paint, diluted 50% with water, to trunks of young or heavily pruned woody plants to reduce light exposure and prevent sunburn or sunscald and to avoid attack by wood-boring insects that are attracted to injured trunks. Improving aeration and drainage of soil will prevent many abiotic and pathogen problems caused by adverse soil conditions and unhealthy roots.

Biological Control. Biological control is the intentional use of beneficial organisms to control pests. Pathogens, parasites, and predators are the primary beneficials used in biological control, as detailed in publications such as *Natural Enemies Handbook* (Flint and Dreistadt 1998). Biological control has been used most successfully to control pest insects and mites, as discussed in Chapter 4. Under certain circumstances, biological control is also effective against nematodes, plant diseases, snails, and weeds.

For example, adverse environmental conditions or ants that tend honeydew-producing pests can prevent parasites and predators from controlling certain pests. Control honeydew-seeking ants, reduce dust, and avoid persistent pesticides to enhance the effectiveness of natural enemies of certain insect and mite pests. Plant a diversity of flowering and nonflowering species to provide habitat and food for beneficial predators and parasites. Periodically releasing commercially available natural enemies may control target pests under certain circumstances, but conserving resident natural enemies is usually a more economical and effective strategy. Avoid cultivating soil deeply to prevent burying weed seeds where they are protected from decay microorganisms or cannot be reached by seed-eating insects and small vertebrates. As with other methods, biological control is most effective when integrated with other strategies, such as applying selective pesticides instead of broad-spectrum pesticides that kill natural enemies.

Chemical Control. Pesticides are chemicals that control, prevent, or repel pests or mitigate the problems they cause. You can quickly obtain temporary control of certain pests if you choose the correct pesticide and apply it at the right time in an appropriate manner. Follow all label directions—if you use an incorrect pesticide, the wrong rate, or improper application methods, you can do more harm than good.

Consider alternatives before using a pesticide; cultural practices and other alternatives often provide more long-lasting control. Incorrect pesticide use can damage plants or natural enemies. Before using a pesticide, understand its relative toxicity, mode of action, persistence, and safe and legal use. Read the information later in this chapter and consult publications such as *The Safe and Effective Use of Pesticides* (O'Connor-Marer 2000) and *Pesticides: Theory and Application* (Ware 1983) for more information.

If you use a pesticide, combine its use with nonchemical control methods. Respect pesticides for their hazards; many pesticides are poisonous to other living things besides the pest you wish to control. Use the least hazardous pesticide where possible. Avoid broad-spectrum, persistent pesticides when possible or apply them in a selective manner as discussed below. Read the label carefully before you buy the pesticide so you will understand its hazard, and be certain it is registered and appropriate for use on the plants or site where it will be applied. Read the label again before using it and follow all the precautions and application directions.

Types of Pesticides. Pesticides are categorized several ways, most commonly according to the type of organism controlled. Insecticides control insects. Miticides or acaricides control mites. Herbicides control weeds. Fungicides control disease-causing fungi. Molluscicides control snails and slugs. Rodenticides control mice and other rodents. Batericides control bacteria.

Mode of action (*see* "Pesticide Resistance") and chemical class (for example, carbamate or organophosphate) are other classification systems. Pesticides are also categorized by the source of the material, such as botanicals, which are extracted from plants. Inorganic pesticides like sulfur and copper are refined from minerals. Synthetic pesticides such as organophosphates and chlorinated hydrocarbons are manufactured from petroleum.

The chapters in this book concentrate on biological, IPM-compatible, organically acceptable, and reduced-risk pesticides. Characteristics such as acute toxicity to people and beneficial organisms, persistence, and the types of pests they control are summarized for some common pesticides in Tables 2-1, 2-2, 4-6 (in the chapter Insects, Mites, and Snails and Slugs), Tables 5-3 and 5-4 (Diseases), and Tables 7-11 and 7-12 (Weeds). For more specific pesticide recommendations, consult publications such as *UCIPM Pest Notes,* which are cited in the text, listed in Suggested Reading, and available at www.ipm.ucdavis.edu using the Internet. Commercial growers can consult publications such as the *Floricul-*

ture and Ornamental Nurseries Pest Management Guidelines (Raabe et al. 2002).

Reduced-risk Pesticides. Reduced-risk pesticides have received accelerated registration approval by the U.S. Environmental Protection Agency because they have one or more desirable characteristics, including:

- better worker safety
- low toxicity to nontarget organisms
- reduced potential for groundwater contamination
- low application rates
- less potential for development of pest resistance
- greater compatibility with IPM

Some reduced-risk and IPM-compatible pesticides are available only for use by professional applicators. Their availability is limited in part because using these relatively new pesticides effectively often requires more knowledge and skill than do older, broad-spectrum pesticides.

Pesticides Are Toxic. All pesticides are toxic (poisonous) in some way. The degree of acute (immediate) toxicity ranges from slight to extreme (Tables 2-1, 2-2). Hazard is the risk of danger from pesticides. The distinction between toxicity and hazard is important. Toxicity is the capability of a substance to cause injury or death. Hazard or risk is a function of two factors—toxicity and potential exposure to the toxic substance. Toxic substances pose a relatively low hazard if their use can minimize or avoid exposure to people and other nontarget organisms. For example, some toxic compounds are used in low concentrations and enclosed in containers with a bait. Pests are attracted to feed by entering the container openings, which are small enough to exclude children and pets. These enclosed baits, such as "ant stakes," minimize nontarget exposure, thereby greatly reducing risk.

Pesticides sold in the United States must have a signal word on their label indicating potential hazard of immediate or acute injury. Signal words are CAUTION (the least hazardous), WARNING,

and DANGER (the latter the most hazardous, often including a skull and crossbones and also labeled POISON). Hazard is estimated primarily by assessing potential exposure and performing toxicity studies on laboratory mammals that are affected similarly to people. Toxicity is assessed through several means of exposure, such as oral (ingestion), inhalation (breathing), and dermal (through skin). Toxicity is reported as the amount in milligrams (mg) of toxic material per kilogram (kg) of animal body weight or liter (L) of air that is lethal to 50% of the test animals. The lethal dose (LD_{50}) or lethal concentration (LC_{50}) and corresponding signal words are listed in Table 2-1. The lower the LD_{50} or LC_{50}, the greater the acute toxicity.

Broad-spectrum pesticides can sometimes be used selectively. Spot spraying an area encircling the trunk (bark banding) kills elm leaf beetle larvae as they crawl down to pupate around the tree base. Wear a washable hat when spraying overhead.

Some pesticides are suspected of causing long-term health effects, but this information is not provided on the label. A Material Safety Data Sheet (MSDS) detailing potential hazards is available for each pesticide. The MSDS for most potentially hazardous substances can be obtained from the University of California MSDS Management System at www.ucmsds.com using the World Wide Web. Obtain and read the MSDS for more information.

The most hazardous pesticides (DANGER or POISON) generally are available only to certified applicators. These pesticides require special training and equipment and generally should not be used in ways or places where people or pets may be exposed. Employers must ensure that workers who apply, handle, or mix pesticides have been properly trained. Federal Worker Protection Standards also require pesticide safety training for all employees working in agricultural fields, greenhouses, and nurseries that have been treated with pesticides, including employees who do not work directly with pesticides.

Pesticide Selectivity. Selective pesticides are toxic only to the target organism and related species, in contrast with broad-spectrum pesticides, which kill many different species. For example, certain strains of *Bacillus thuringiensis* (Bt) kill only moth and butterfly larvae, while many synthetic insecticides kill both caterpillars and their natural enemies. Use selective pesticides where possible because they are generally less damaging to nontarget organisms and are safer for use around people.

In addition to describing the inherent toxicity of a pesticide, selectivity also refers to the manner of use. Broad-spectrum pesticides sometimes can be used selectively by modifying application timing, equipment, and method. For example, dormant season application of narrow-range oil to kill scale insects may reduce the impact on natural enemies in comparison with a foliar season spraying, because the beneficials tend to be inactive during the winter or are not present in the treatment area. Pesticides for ant or rodent control can be mixed with bait and enclosed in a container that prevents most nontarget organisms from being exposed to the pesticides. Spot treatments, such as insecticide bark banding instead of spraying the whole plant canopy, help control elm leaf beetle without killing predators and parasites that live on leaves. Selective application methods and pesticides are discussed in the chapters on diseases, insects, and weeds.

Pesticide Persistence. The length of time after application during which a pesticide remains active is called persistence. Persistence is important in determining how long a pesticide controls the target pest. Persistence may also influence the extent to which a pesticide can harm beneficial organisms. Longer persistence sometimes may be desirable. For example, a more persistent preemergent herbicide (as listed in Table 7-11) suppresses weed seedlings longer, providing desirable plants with more time to grow larger and become established without having to compete for moisture and nutrients. Conversely, a more persistent insecticide can be undesirable to suppress pests because of its longer-lasting toxicity to natural enemies or other effects in the environment.

Pests often become temporarily abundant before natural enemies become common enough to provide control. Most predators and parasites also are more sensitive to pesticides than are pests. If a persistent insecticide is applied to control a pest that has temporarily escaped biological control, its residues can continue to kill natural enemies that migrate in after spraying, long after the insecticide has ceased to kill the pests. Therefore, persistent residues can prevent natural enemies from providing biological control, leading to another outbreak or resurgence of the pest population.

Pesticide Toxicity to Natural Enemies. Pesticides can severely disrupt biological control. Natural enemies often are more susceptible to pesticides than are pests due to many ecological and physiological factors. In comparison with most pests, natural enemies are more active searchers, which results in greater contact with more treated surfaces. Natural enemies require pests as hosts, so few predators and parasites will be present after spraying reduces pest numbers; pests therefore get a head start in reproducing and natural enemy populations will lag behind until sufficient numbers of pests again develop to attract natural enemies and support their reproduction. Plants produce toxic secondary chemicals in their leaves and wood to ward off plant-feeding herbivores; pests have evolved physiological systems to detoxify and protect themselves from plant chemicals. These same chemical defenses help pests to develop pesticide resistance; natural enemies often lack

TABLE 2-1.

Pesticide Toxicity Categories.

HAZARD INDICATORS	I. DANGER	II. WARNING	III. CAUTION
oral LD_{50}	up to 50 mg/kg	>50–500 mg/kg	>500 mg/kg
approximate lethal oral dose	≤1 teaspoon[1]	>1 teaspoon to 2 tablespoons[1]	>2 tablespoons or >1 oz[1]
inhalation LC_{50}	up to 0.2 mg/L	>0.2–2 mg/L	>2 mg/L
dermal LD_{50}	up to 200 mg/kg	>200–2,000 mg/kg	>2,000 mg/kg
eye effects	corrosive	persistent irritation	reversible irritation
skin effects	corrosive	severe irritation	moderate irritation

See the text for an explanation and the definition of abbreviations.

1. The probable lethal oral dose for a 170-lb. human.

TABLE 2-2.

Approximate Oral LD$_{50}$ Values for Some Pesticides.

CHEMICAL	LD$_{50}$	TYPE
2,4-D	400	herbicide
abamectin or avermectins	300	insecticide, miticide
acephate	900	insecticide
aspirin (acetylsalicyclic acid)[1]	1,000	analgesic
azadirachtin	>5,000	insecticide
B. thuringiensis	>15,000	insecticide
benefin	>5,000	herbicide
benomyl	>10,000	fungicide
bensulide	900	herbicide
bentazon	1,100	herbicide
bifenthrin	60	insecticide, miticide
bromoxynil	440	herbicide
captan	9,000	fungicide
carbaryl	260	insecticide
chlorothalonil	>10,000	fungicide
chlorpyrifos	160	insecticide
cinnamaldehyde	2,220	fungicide, insecticide, miticide
clethodim	1,630	herbicide
copper hydroxide	1,000	fungicide
copper sulfate	500	fungicide
cyfluthrin	1,100	insecticide
cypermethrin	250	insecticide
DCPA	>3,000	herbicide
diazinon	300	miticide, insecticide
dicamba	1,700	herbicide
dichlobenil	4,460	herbicide
dicofol	900	miticide
diflubenzuron	40,000	insecticide
dimethoate	300	miticide
diquat	230	herbicide
dithiopyr	>5,000	herbicide
EPTC	1,600	herbicide
esfenvalerate	460	insecticide
fatty acids, pelargonic acid	>5,000	herbicide
fluazifop-p-butyl	4,100	herbicide

CHEMICAL	LD$_{50}$	TYPE
fluvalinate	270	insecticide, miticide
glufosinate	2,170	herbicide
glyphosate	4,300	herbicide
imidacloprid	450	insecticide
iron phosphate	5,000	molluscicide
isoxaben	>10,000	herbicide
lime sulfur or calcium polysulfide	700	fungicide
malathion	1,400	insecticide
MCPA	1,160	herbicide
metaldehyde	450	molluscicide
napropamide	>4,600	herbicide
nicotine	50	insecticide
norflurazon	>8,000	herbicide
oil, narrow-range	>4,300	insecticide, miticide
oryzalin	>10,000	herbicide
oxadiazon	>5,000	herbicide
oxydemeton-methyl	130	insecticide
oxyfluorfen	>5,000	herbicide
paraquat	150	herbicide
pendimethalin	2,500	herbicide
permethrin	1,100	insecticide
prodiamine	>5,000	herbicide
pyrethrins, pyrethrum	1,500	insecticide
resmethrin	1,250	insecticide
ryania	1,200	insecticide
sabadilla	4,000	insecticide
sethoxydim	3,000	herbicide
simazine	5,000	herbicide
soap, insecticidal	>16,900	insecticide, miticide
spinosad	>5,000	insecticide, miticide
sulfur	>5,000	fungicide, miticide
table salt (sodium chloride)[1]	3,000	food additive
triclopyr	700	herbicide
trifluralin	>5,000	herbicide

LD$_{50}$ values are in milligrams of chemical per kilogram of body weight, usually determined from oral rat studies. Lower LD$_{50}$ values indicate higher toxicity; for example, acephate (900) is more acutely toxic than narrow-range oil (4,300). Most values are for the pesticide active ingredient; actual toxicity varies depending on the pesticide formulation. LD$_{50}$ values are only one of several considerations when selecting a pesticide. Laws, regulations, and information concerning pesticides change frequently. Certain of these materials may not be registered (legal) for use in your situation. Certain of these materials are available only to professional applicators or are listed only for comparison. Consult a current label and the local department of agriculture for details on legal pesticide use.

> indicates that the LD$_{50}$ value is higher than the number listed.

1. Not pesticides; provided for acute toxicity comparison.

Sources: Ahrens 1994, Extension Toxicology Network
http://ace.orst.edu/info/extoxnet, Ware 1983.

these chemical-protection systems because natural enemies' food (the pests) commonly lack poisonous chemicals.

In addition to immediately killing natural enemies that are present at the time of spraying (contact toxicity), many pesticides leave persistent residues (residual toxicity) that kill predators or parasites that migrate in long after spraying. Even if beneficial organisms survive an application, low levels of pesticide residues can have adverse sublethal effects on natural enemy longevity, fecundity, and ability to locate and kill pests. Insecticides with little or no persistence or residual toxicity to natural enemies as listed in Tables 4-4 and 4-6 are frequently preferable when controlling landscape pests.

Pesticides Can Damage Plants. Phytotoxicity is the ability of materials to injure plants. Herbicides are designed to kill plants, so they can injure or kill desirable species if they are applied improperly or drift onto nontarget plants. Insecticides, fungicides, and other chemicals such as fertilizers can also cause phytotoxicity. Plant injury from pesticides usually occurs because pesticides have been used carelessly or in a manner contrary to the label. Common mistakes are applying excess amounts, allowing spray to drift, failing to obey label precautions, treating plants or a site not listed on the label, or using a sprayer contaminated with herbicides to apply other materials. Environmental stress, such as drought, heat, or wind, or sensitivity of particular plant cultivars can influence whether and how severely phytotoxicity develops from exposure to pesticides.

Because herbicides are made specifically to kill plants, they pose the greatest risk of unintended damage to desirable plant species. Each kind of herbicide causes characteristic damage symptoms as discussed for some common herbicides in Chapter 6 in the section "Pesticides and Phytotoxicity."

Narrow-range oil, insecticidal soap, and other pesticides also can damage certain plants under specific conditions. Pesticide labels often list sensitive plants to avoid spraying. When in doubt as to whether the plant species is sensitive to a pesticide, spray a small out-of-the-way area of the plant and observe it for at least several days for any signs of damage before spraying it further.

Pesticides Can Contaminate Water. Creeks and rivers are being contaminated with pesticides. These pesticides not only threaten aquatic life, but they can also affect the quality of our drinking water. The organophosphates chlorpyrifos and diazinon have been primary water contaminants, and these insecticides have been withdrawn from sale for most home and garden uses. Herbicides and certain other insecticides also have the potential to cause environmental harm, including carbaryl, malathion, and pyrethroids. Use all pesticides with caution.

Pesticides reach creeks and rivers through household drains and storm drains (Figure 2-2). When you apply a pesticide, some of the material may move to other locations. Rain and irrigation runoff from landscapes flow down the streets through gutters into storm drains. The storm drain runoff flows through pipes directly into our creeks, lakes, rivers, or the ocean. Sewers run from drains within the home and carry wastewater from sinks and toilets to treatment

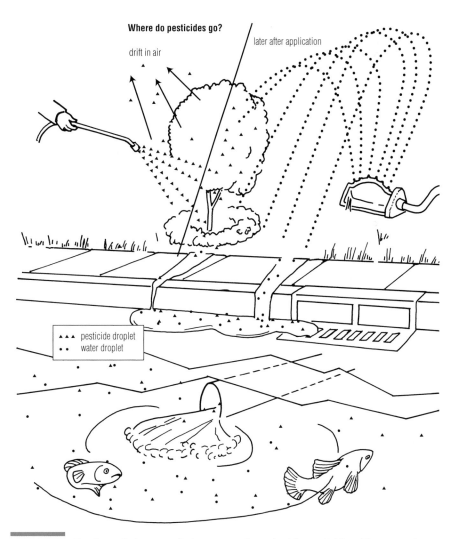

Where do pesticides go?

drift in air

later after application

▲▲▲ pesticide droplet
• • water droplet

FIGURE 2-2. Creeks and rivers are being contaminated with pesticides. These pesticides not only threaten aquatic life, but they also affect the quality of our drinking water. Do not allow soil or water to move into storm drains from areas recently treated with pesticides. Do not dump unwanted pesticides down the sink or into storm drains. Do not dispose of pesticide containers in the garbage unless they are completely empty, home-use product containers.

plants. Wastewater treatment plants remove organic solids and disinfect pathogens before discharging water into rivers or the ocean, but wastewater treatment plants do not detoxify pesticides, thus releasing pesticide residue into waterways. The Federal Clean Water Act requires local water agencies to develop plans to manage water-discharged contaminants (called the Total Maximum Daily Load, or TMDL). These plans may impose restrictions on water users and those who have water runoff from their property, such as golf courses and nurseries. In addition to environmental problems, the financial costs of remedying water contamination are paid through taxes, water use fees, and (indirectly) by increased prices for products and services provided by commercial and industrial water users.

Never pour pesticides down the sink or into curbside storm drains. Do not allow soil or water to move into storm drains from areas recently treated with pesticides. Use alternatives to pesticides whenever possible. If you must use pesticides, follow all instructions on the product label for proper use. Be sure to store and dispose of all pesticides properly. For more information on pesticides and water quality, including reference to agencies, organizations, and research addressing these problems, go to the pesticides and water quality information on the Web at www.ipm.ucdavis.edu or the pesticide leaching and runoff risk information at www.pw.ucr.edu

Pesticide Resistance. Many insects and pathogens and some weeds have developed resistance to certain pesticides. Resistance occurs when a pest population is no longer controlled by pesticides that previously provided control (Figure 2-3). A different type of pesticide or some other control measure must be substituted to control that pest. Pest resistance may not be a significant problem in most landscapes, but the extent of this problem in landscapes is not known. Resistance is a serious problem in certain crops and commercial ornamental production. Certain pests that develop resis-

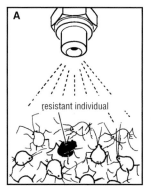

FIGURE 2-3. Resistance to pesticides develops through genetic selection in populations of pests, including insects, mites, pathogens, and weeds. A. Certain individuals in a pest population are naturally less susceptible to a pesticide than other individuals. B. These less-susceptible pest biotypes are more likely to survive an application and to produce progeny that are also less susceptible. C. After repeated applications over several generations, the pest population consists primarily of resistant or less-susceptible individuals. Applying the same pesticide, or other chemicals with the same mode of action, is no longer effective.

tance in these situations can be introduced into landscapes, such as on new plantings from nurseries.

Take as many steps as possible to avoid creating resistant pests (Table 2-3). Delay pesticide resistance by using biological, cultural, mechanical, and physical controls whenever possible. When pesticides are applied, chose selective materials, use them in combination with alternatives, and make spot applications whenever possible. If pests are frequently sprayed, avoid repeatedly applying pesticides in the same chemical class or those with the same mode of action. Unless otherwise directed on the labeling, consider switching to a pesticide with a different mode of action about every 2 to 3 pest generations in situations where pests are frequently sprayed. To identify pesticide classes or modes of action so you can select pesticides for rotation, consult Table 4-6 (in the chapter Insects, Mites, and Snails and Slugs), Tables 5-3 and 5-4 (Diseases), and Tables 7-11 and 7-12 (Weeds).

Choose the Correct Pesticide. Make sure you have correctly identified the pest and have considered nonchemical alternatives before you purchase or apply a pesticide. Read the label carefully before deciding which pesticide to purchase and apply. Do not use a pesticide unless the host plant or location to be sprayed is listed on the label.

The oral LD_{50} values for some common pesticides are listed in Table 2-2. Although pesticides with a high LD_{50} are less acutely toxic than those with a low LD_{50}, a high LD_{50} does not necessarily mean that a pesticide is "safe." Certain formulations of some pesticides with a relatively high LD_{50}, like sulfur and glyphosate, can be very irritating to the eyes, lungs, or skin. Others may cause acute or chronic diseases after long-term exposure despite relatively low toxicity. Pesticides that have a low toxicity to people can be very toxic to beneficial organisms.

Read the precautionary statement on the label. Consider hazards to humans, pets, desirable plants, beneficial organisms, wildlife, and the rest of the environment. Note the signal word and choose the least toxic pesticide available for the job. For potential chronic effects, consult the Material Safety Data Sheet on that pesticide, such as those available from the UC Material Safety Data Sheet Management System at www.ucmsds.com on the Web. Purchase only the amount of pesticide you expect to use up within a few months; proper disposal of unused pesticide may be difficult.

Transport Pesticides Safely. Do not carry pesticides in the passenger compartment of any vehicle. Do not carry pesticides in the same compartment as food or drink. Make sure that containers can-

TABLE 2-3.

Take Steps to Avoid Pesticide Resistance.

- Monitor landscapes or plants before treating and identify specifically which pest species are present.
- Evaluate whether pesticide application is truly warranted.
- Minimize the amount and frequency of applications and the extent of area treated, for example, by spot-spraying only locations and plant parts where target pests occur.
- Use biological, cultural, mechanical, and physical control alternatives whenever possible.
- If pesticides are applied frequently, rotate pesticides by making sequential applications of pesticides that have a different mode of action.
- If control results are unsatisfactory, reexamine the effectiveness of your techniques, evaluate whether your expectations are realistic, and reconsider using alternative methods. Consider sending samples to a laboratory that can test for pesticide resistance if resistance is suspected.

not fall or be knocked over, such as by tying them down or carrying them in an attached compartment. Protect glass bottles by wrapping them in paper to reduce the chance of breakage if they fall over or crash together. Protect bags from damage by sharp objects. Protect containers from moisture. Do not leave pesticides unattended unless they are in a locked container.

Store Pesticides Safely. Store pesticides only in the original labeled container. Never store pesticides in soft-drink bottles or other food or drink containers. Store pesticides in a locked and labeled area or cabinet that is out of reach of children and pets. Do not store pesticides near beverages, clothing, feed, food, or rags. Protect stored pesticides from moisture and extreme heat or cold. Be sure the storage area is well ventilated to prevent the accumulation of toxic fumes. Check pesticide containers periodically for leakage or corrosion.

Use Appropriate Application Equipment. Pesticide application equipment ranges from simple devices, such as a hand pump spray bottle, to power-driven machines. Consult Tables 2-4 to 2-6 for help in choosing the proper equipment. For more details see *The Safe and Effective Use of Pesticides* (O'Connor-Marer 2000).

Check Equipment Before Use. Fill the sprayer with clean water and operate it before use. Look for leaking connections, hoses, and tanks, and worn or plugged nozzles. Repair or replace faulty equipment before use.

Mix Pesticides Properly. Pesticides are in their most hazardous form when you mix and handle the concentrated material. Choose an outdoor or open location with good light and ventilation. Read the label carefully and make sure that you are upwind before you open the container. Wear any safety equipment listed on the label, such as plastic or rubber gloves and tightly woven clothing with long sleeves and pant legs worn outside of (not tucked into) gloves and boots. Wear eye protection (which shields the brow, eyes, and temples) even if it is not listed on the label. It is also a good idea to wear a rubber apron while mixing pesticides. Do not wear leather gloves or boots; wear rubber or neoprene unless otherwise designated on the label. Keep the container below eye level when pouring pesticide. Mix only the amount needed to complete the immediate job. Use measuring tools specifically reserved for this purpose. Label those tools for use only with pesticides. Triple rinse all pesticide-contaminated measuring tools and empty containers and pour the rinsings into the spray tank before filling the sprayer to its final level.

Clean any Spills Immediately. Wear protective equipment when cleaning any spills. Sweep or shovel any spilled pesticide dust or powder into a container, such as a plastic bag. Absorb liquid spills with sand, sawdust, or cat litter, then shovel it into a container. Dispose of any spilled pesticide and contaminated substances at a hazardous materials disposal site. Do not allow any wash water to enter sewer systems, storm drains, or bodies of water. Special absorptive materials are available that allow pesticide spilled on an otherwise clean surface to be collected and put back into the spray tank where it dissolves and can be sprayed; this avoids the expense of disposing of spilled pesticide and cleaning material as a hazardous waste. Report all spills to the local county department of agriculture, which can provide information and assistance.

Dispose of Containers Properly. Consult the pesticide label, the county department of agriculture, or the local waste disposal authorities for instructions on disposing of pesticide containers. Some communities have special collections or drop-off points where small amounts of household hazardous waste, such as pesticides, can be disposed of occasionally. The best method is to purchase only the amount of pesticide that will soon be used; use up all the material as directed on the label so that no pesticides in need of disposal are left over.

Some pesticide vendors and manufacturers accept empty pesticide containers for recycling; offer empty containers for recycling if available. Many empty containers can be disposed of in a sanitary landfill if containers have been properly rinsed (triple rinsed) and, where required, inspected by the county department of agriculture.

Home-use pesticide containers can be thrown in the trash only if they are completely empty. Never dispose of unwanted pesticides in the trash. Do not dump unwanted pesticides down a sink; sewage treatment plants are not designed to process pesticides. Never dump pesticides into a storm drain; storm drains usually flow directly into creeks, rivers,

TABLE 2-4.

Selection Guide for Nonpowered and Hand-Operated Application Equipment for Liquid Pesticides.

	TYPE	USES	SUITABLE FORMULATIONS	COMMENTS
	Aerosol can	Insect control on house or patio plants, small areas.	Liquids must dissolve in solvent; some dusts are available.	Very convenient. High cost per unit of active ingredient. Good for spot applications. Proper disposal may be a problem as some pesticide may unavoidably remain in the container.
	Hose-end sprayer	Home garden and small landscaped areas. Used for insect, pathogen, and weed control, where water pressure is sufficient.	All formulations. Wettable powders and emulsifiable concentrates require frequent shaking.	Convenient and low-cost way of applying pesticides to small outdoor areas. Cannot spray straight up. Install an anti-siphon device on the hose-end connector to prevent pesticide from being sucked into the water line if water pressure drops. Disadvantages include poor spray coverage, nozzle clogging, and inaccurate metering of the active ingredient due to variable water pressure. Low purchase price can be negated by the waste and environmental contamination from excessively high spray volume.
	Trigger pump sprayer	Indoor plants and small home yard areas. Used for insect, pathogen, and weed control on relatively small areas.	Liquid-soluble formulations best.	Low cost and easy to use. Good for spot applications.
	Trombone sprayer or slide sprayer	Used for treating shrubs and medium-sized trees up to about 25 feet tall.	All formulations. Wettable powders and emulsifiable concentrates require frequent mixing.	Applies a uniform concentration of active ingredient if properly mixed. Relatively easy to clean and maintain. Moderately priced. Effort required to maintain pressure by continually operating a push-pull slide handle. Requires practice to obtain uniform spray coverage.
	Compressed air sprayers	Many commercial and homeowner applications. Can develop fairly high pressures. Used for insect, weed and pathogen control.	All formulations. Wettable powders and emulsifiable concentrates require frequent shaking.	Good overall sprayer for many types of applications. Relatively inexpensive. Needs thorough cleaning and regular servicing to keep sprayer in good working condition and to prevent corrosion of parts.
	Backpack sprayers	Same uses as compressed air sprayers.	All formulations. Wettable powders and emulsifiable concentrates require frequent shaking.	Durable and easy to use. Requires periodic maintenance. May be heavy for long periods of use.
	Wick applicators	Used for applying herbicides to emerged weeds. Landscape and agricultural uses.	Only water-soluble herbicides.	Simple and easy to use. Clean frequently. Avoids drift onto desirable plants.

Once used with herbicides, do not use the sprayer for other pesticides.

Adapted from O'Connor-Marer 2000.

TABLE 2-5.

Selection Guide for Powered Liquid Pesticide Application Equipment.

	TYPE	USES	SUITABLE FORMULATIONS	COMMENTS
	Powered backpack sprayer	Landscape, right-of-way, aquatic, forest, and agricultural applications.	All. Some may require agitation.	Applies a uniform concentration of active ingredient. May be heavy for long periods of use. Requires frequent maintenance. Generally too expensive for individual home garden use.
	Controlled droplet applicator	Used for application of herbicides (such as systemics) and some insecticides. Some are hand-held while others are mounted on spray brooms. May also be used with air blast sprayers. Produces uniform droplet sizes.	Usually water-soluble formulations.	Plastic parts may break if handled carelessly.
	Low-pressure sprayer	Very common type of sprayer used in commercial applications for insect, pathogen, and weed control. Used with mounted spray brooms or hand-held equipment.	All. Equipment may include agitator.	Useful for larger areas. Powered by own motor or external power source. Frequent cleaning and servicing is required. Expensive.
	High-pressure hydraulic sprayer	Landscape, right-of-way, and agricultural applications. Use on dense foliage and large trees and shrubs.	All. Equipment may include agitator.	Useful for larger areas. Important to clean and service equipment frequently. Requires own motor or external power source. Abrasive pesticides may cause rapid wear of pumps and nozzles. Expensive.

Once used with herbicides, do not use the sprayer for other pesticides.

Adapted from O'Connor-Marer 2000.

TABLE 2-6.

Selection Guide for Dust and Granule Application Equipment.

	TYPE	USES	SUITABLE FORMULATIONS	COMMENTS
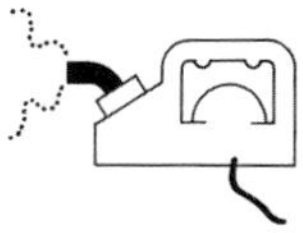	Mechanical dust applicator	For landscape and small agricultural uses.	Dusts.	May have bellows to disperse dust. Requires care to avoid drift. Do not breathe dust.
	Hand-operated granule applicator	Landscape, aquatic, and some agricultural areas.	Granules or pellets.	Suitable for small areas. Easy to use. Inexpensive. Can be difficult to uniformly apply an accurately metered amount of active ingredient.
	Mechanically driven granule applicator	Turf and other landscape areas. Also commonly used in agricultural areas.	Granules or pellets.	Requires accurate calibration.
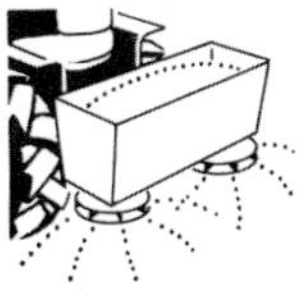	Powered granule applicator	Large landscape applications applications (e.g., golf courses).	Granules or pellets.	Some units may have blowers to disperse granules. Others may distribute granules along a boom. Frequent servicing and cleaning is required.

Once used with herbicides, do not use the sprayer for other pesticides.

Adapted from O'Connor-Marer 2000.

or the ocean without any treatment of the discharge.

Rinse empty containers three times (triple rinse them) immediately after emptying them and before you finish filling the spray tank. First drain the empty container into the spray tank for at least 30 seconds. Next, fill the container about one-quarter full with clean water, close the container, and gently shake or roll it to rinse all interior surfaces. Drain the rinse material into the spray tank and continue to let the material drain for at least 30 seconds after the container is mostly empty and has begun to drip. Repeat this rinse procedure two more times, then fill the spray tank to the proper level. Punch holes in the empty container so it cannot inadvertently be reused for other purposes (do not puncture sealed, pressured containers).

Use Effective Methods. Proper methods and timing are critical for effective pesticide application. Spraying is the most common application method, and spot spraying (spraying only small areas) is preferable when effective. Baits for ants or rodents and wick or wiper applicators for herbicides are examples of other methods that are more effective or preferred in certain situations.

Certain systemic pesticides can be applied to soil beneath plants or injected or implanted into tree trunks or roots to control certain pests, primarily insects that chew foliage or suck plant juices. These methods can minimize environmental contamination in comparison with spraying foliage. When using systemics, whenever possible make a soil application instead of spraying foliage or injecting or implanting trees (Figure 2-4). Systemic insecticides, including injections and implants, are not effective against most wood-boring pests such as bark beetles and clearwing moths. Non-chemical methods (such as proper plant care) are the only effective control for most wood-boring pests.

Correct timing of control is vital. For example, *Bacillus thuringiensis* (Bt) must be applied to cover foliage thoroughly when young caterpillars are actively feeding or it

will not be effective. Application of oil during the dormant season (after leaves have dropped) to kill scale insects and overwintering stages of some mites and aphids may provide better control than foliar season spraying. Less spray volume is needed because leaves are not present and timing is less critical than during the foliar season, when applications must coincide with the activity of young crawlers, which must be monitored closely.

Many fungicides act only as protectants and must be applied before infection takes place. Most fungicides protect undamaged tissue, but they do not cure tissue once it becomes infected. Some herbicides must be applied before weeds emerge; others are effective only when emerged weeds are actively growing. Certain pesticides are less effective if mixed with alkaline water, so check whether water pH should be adjusted to approximately 5.5 to 6.5 before preparing any spray mix.

Apply pesticides at the correct time and in the proper manner (according to label directions) or your effort is wasted, the environment is needlessly contaminated, and target pests are not controlled.

Injecting or Implanting Pesticides. Make an application to soil whenever possible instead of injecting or implanting trees with systemic pesticides (Figure 2-4). Soil application is possible even if trees are mostly surrounded by pavement, if permitted on the product label; the pesticide can be applied to soil immediately adjacent to the trunk, or to nearby bare soil, lawn, or planting beds where most absorbing tree roots usually occur. Disadvantages of injecting or implanting trunks or roots include the difficulty of repeatedly placing insecticide at the proper depth. Injecting or implanting trunks or roots injures trees and creates wounds that can provide entry sites for pests. Especially avoid methods that cause large wounds, such as implants placed in holes drilled in trunks. Do not implant or inject roots or trunks more than once a year.

Avoid methods that use the same device (such as drills or needles) to contact internal parts of more than one tree unless tools are cleaned and sterilized before moving to the next plant. Contaminated tools can mechanically spread certain pathogens from one tree to another, including

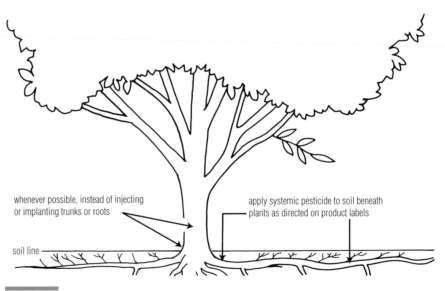

FIGURE 2-4. When applying systemic pesticides to trees, make an application to soil whenever possible as directed on product labels instead of injecting or implanting trees with pesticide. Injecting or implanting trunks or roots injures trees and creates wounds that can provide entry sites for pests. Unless tools that contact internal parts of trees are cleaned and disinfected when treating multiple trees, contaminated tools can mechanically spread certain bacterial, fungal, and viral pathogens from one tree to another.

bacteria (such as slime flux or wetwood), fungi (canker stain of sycamore, Dutch elm disease, and Fusarium wilt), and certain viruses. Whenever working on plants known or suspected of being susceptible to mechanically transmissible pathogens, clean and disinfect tools before working on each new plant to reduce the chance of spreading pathogens. Before chemical disinfection, remove all plant material and scrub any plant sap from tools or equipment that penetrate bark. Bleach, and to a lesser extent, certain other materials, can be effective disinfectants if applied to debris-free tools as discussed in the section "Disinfectants" in the Diseases chapter. Depending on the disinfectant, at least 1 to 2 minutes of disinfectant contact time between contaminated uses may be required for reliable disinfection. Consider rotating work among several tools, using a freshly disinfected tool while the most recently used tools are being soaked in disinfectant.

Apply Pesticides Safely. Read the label instructions again and follow them exactly before applying pesticides. It is illegal and may be dangerous to disregard label instructions. From the area to be treated, clear any people, pets, and items such as pet food containers and toys that should not become contaminated. Wear protective clothing, including eye protection, gloves, and any protective equipment listed on the label. Never apply pesticides when it is windy or raining. Avoid drift over water and do not fill, drain, or rinse equipment near water. Provide buffer zones when spraying near water. Do not apply more pesticide than is indicated on the label.

All people who mix, apply, or otherwise handle pesticides at work must be trained by their employer. Employers must maintain written evidence of this training. Many people using pesticides as part of their job must also be licensed or certified by passing an examination administered by the state and then attending continuing education courses, or they must work under the supervision of a licensed or certified applicator.

Federal Worker Protection Standards also require pesticide safety training for all employees working in agricultural fields, greenhouses, and nurseries that have been treated with pesticides, including employees who do not work directly with pesticides. Contact the local county department of agriculture to determine the legal requirements before handling any pesticides in connection with your employment.

Be Properly Certified or Licensed. Most people who apply pesticides as part of their job in California must be certified or licensed by the California Department of Pesticide Regulation (DPR), or their work must be supervised by a certified or licensed person. Certification is also required for anyone in the landscape maintenance business who applies pesticide, even if they only occasionally apply pesticide as part of a landscape maintenance business. Anyone in California who presents themselves as an authority, or offers a recommendation, on any agricultural use of a pest control product or technique must be licensed as a pest control adviser. "Agricultural use" is legally defined to include many nonfarm situations, such as cemeteries, golf courses, parks, roadsides, and commercial nurseries. Certification and licensing includes knowing information in study guides produced by the University of California, passing examinations administered by DPR, and attending regular pest control continuing education.

Homeowners, farmers, and other individuals using nonrestricted pesticides on their own private property or property they control, and in many instances government and university employees, are not required to be certified. No pest control adviser license is required to give pest management advice for nonagricultural uses, including residential yard and garden use. Master gardeners and retail nursery employees do not need any license to advise homeowners on landscape pest management.

For more information on pesticide and pest management certification and licensing, consult resources such as *The Safe*

and Effective Use of Pesticides (O'Connor-Marer 2000), *IPM in Practice* (Flint and Gouveia 2001), and the California Department of Pesticide Regulation's Web site at www.cdpr.ca.gov

Wear Protective Clothing. Always wear at least as much protective clothing as specified on the pesticide label (Figure 2-5). Always wear protective eyewear that covers the brow and temple when applying or handling pesticides, even if no eyewear is specified on the label. Minimize your exposure to pesticides, even if the material has a high LD_{50} (Table 2-2). Unless otherwise specified on the label, rubber or neoprene gloves and boots, eye protection, and a washable hat, long pants, and a long-sleeved shirt that are laundered after each use are the minimum protective clothing that should be worn, even when applying "safe" materials such as oil or soap. A rubber or neoprene apron provides additional protection.

FIGURE 2-5. **Minimize your exposure to pesticides. Unless otherwise stated on the label, wear rubber or neoprene gloves and boots, eye protection that covers the brows and temples, and long pants, long-sleeved shirt, and a hat that can be washed after each use. It is also a good idea to wear a rubber or neoprene apron.**

CHAPTER THREE

Growing Healthy Trees and Shrubs

SELECTING AN appropriate plant for each location and providing its basic growth requirements are the most important aspects of pest management. If plants are well adapted to local conditions, the environment is conducive to good growth, and proper care is provided, plants are healthier and more aesthetically pleasing. Plants relatively free of other stresses typically are also more tolerant of pests. Plants that are stressed from adverse environmental conditions or a lack of proper care may be damaged by even a small number of pests. The purpose of an integrated pest management program is not to kill every pest, but to prevent major outbreaks and cultivate healthy plants that can tolerate some pests and provide the benefits people desire.

This chapter summarizes basic care of woody plants to minimize pests and grow healthy landscapes. For more information, consult *Abiotic Disorders of Landscape Plants: A Diagnostic Guide* (Costello et al. 2003), *Arboriculture: Integrated Management of Landscape Trees, Shrubs, and Vines* (Harris, Clark, and Matheny 1999), *Plant Health Care for Woody Ornamentals* (Lloyd 1997), and other publications listed in the Suggested Reading.

Growth Requirements

Plants are living organisms that require carbon dioxide, energy, oxygen, and water. Energy is provided by oxidation of food (primarily sugars and starches) during the process of respiration. Unlike animals, most plants produce their own food using solar energy. This food-producing process, called photosynthesis, occurs in green tissue, primarily leaves. Plants need essential elements, carbon dioxide, and appropriate light, temperatures, and water to carry out photosynthesis.

People modify the landscape environment and affect the availability of resources that plants need. Water and oxygen availability to roots is affected by aeration, drainage, irrigation, and changes in the composition, density, grade, structure, and texture of soil. For example, plants often become unhealthy when people irrigate too frequently, which restricts oxygen availability to roots. Nutrient availability to plants may be increased by fertilizing, applying amendments and mulches that add organic matter, or by allowing fallen leaves to remain and decompose. Nutrient deficiency symptoms in plants usually are not

23

21

Plants are living organisms that require energy, carbon dioxide, oxygen, nutrients, water, and adequate space for growth. Providing plants with a good growing environment and proper cultural care are the most critical aspects of pest management.

the result of insufficient nutrients in soil; instead, symptoms usually occur because people inadvertently create adverse soil conditions, injure roots, or restrict root growth, which prevents roots from absorbing the available nutrients and water. Temperature and light vary naturally according to weather, but they can be manipulated locally by pruning, adding or removing plants, modifying structures or pavement, and by planting at a suitable location. Depending on their type and location, mulches or ground covers can increase or decrease soil temperatures or light around plants.

All the basic requirements for growth must be properly maintained for plants to have maximum resistance to damage from pests such as insects and pathogens. Failing to provide an appropriate environment and adequate care increases the likelihood that pests will injure or kill plants. Most plants are particularly vulnerable to damage during certain stages of their growth or under specific environmental conditions; under other circum-

stances or at other times, plants are relatively resistant or can tolerate more pests or damage.

Plant Development and Seasonal Growth

Trees and woody shrubs are perennial plants; they live for many years. Deciduous woody perennials typically drop leaves in the fall before entering winter dormancy and regrow foliage in the spring. However, some species like the California buckeye adapt to drought by dropping leaves during hot, dry weather and regrowing foliage after the winter rainfall begins. Evergreen trees and shrubs retain some foliage year around. They still exhibit seasonal changes in growth, flowering, foliage production, and leaf fall. For example, evergreen conifers typically drop their oldest needles in the fall while retaining their youngest needles, those produced during the last several years. Most broadleaf evergreens drop older foliage during spring.

Perennial plants are alive all year. Although deciduous perennials may be without leaves for several months each year, tissues beneath bark and in roots are still living. Improper watering, excessive light, extreme temperatures, drying winds, and other adverse conditions can damage plants even when they are dormant.

Changes in temperature, moisture, and especially in the amount and length of daylight induce seasonal changes in plant growth and appearance, such as flowering or leaf flush and growth (Figure 3-1). Pest abundance and damage are also linked to this seasonal cycle of plant growth, as illustrated by examples in the section "Pruning and Pest Management," Figure 3-8, the Chapter 4 section "Degree-Day Monitoring," and Tables 4-20 and 5-1. Cultural activities to improve plant health and actions to prevent and manage pests must be properly timed to be effective.

Design a Pest-Tolerant Landscape

Effective pest management begins before the landscape is planted. Design landscapes to provide an optimal living environment for plants. Minimize pest problems by selecting relatively pest-resistant species and cultivars that are well adapted to local conditions. Group the plants that have similar cultural requirements.

Determine the Expectations. Before preparing and planting the site, decide what aesthetics and functions (such as shading and visual screening) are desired and how much time, money, and other resources will be budgeted. If the desires are for high visual appeal, very few pests, and almost no plant damage, more effort and inputs will be required to develop and maintain the landscape so that it meets these expectations. Be aware that inadequate site preparation, improper planting, selecting pest-prone cultivars, planting species not adapted to local conditions, or employing inappropriate cultural practices can cause landscapes to perform poorly regardless of pest control efforts.

CHOOSE A GOOD LOCATION

Consider drainage, soil characteristics, water quality and availability, and other conditions before selecting a planting site and the species to grow there. Assess how much light and heat occur at that location based on climate, exposure, and the influence of nearby structures, pavement, and plants. Determine proximity to pavement, structures, overhead lines, and underground utilities that may be damaged by growing limbs or roots.

Select species suited to the site's conditions by matching the plant to the location. Examine the space available for growth and learn about the mature size of candidate plants. Give limbs and roots plenty of room to grow and use only

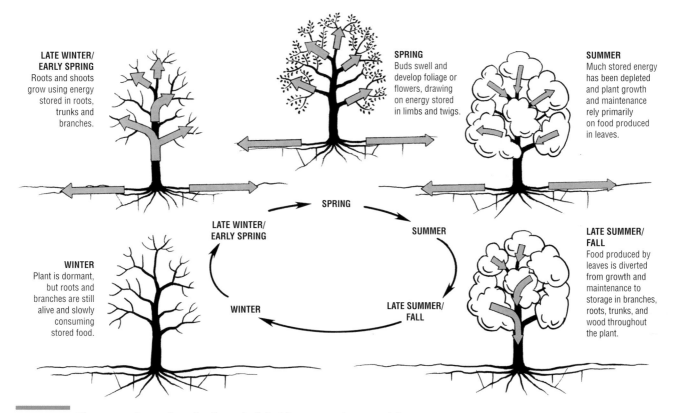

LATE WINTER/ EARLY SPRING
Roots and shoots grow using energy stored in roots, trunks and branches.

SPRING
Buds swell and develop foliage or flowers, drawing on energy stored in limbs and twigs.

SUMMER
Much stored energy has been depleted and plant growth and maintenance rely primarily on food produced in leaves.

WINTER
Plant is dormant, but roots and branches are still alive and slowly consuming stored food.

LATE SUMMER/ FALL
Food produced by leaves is diverted from growth and maintenance to storage in branches, roots, trunks, and wood throughout the plant.

LATE WINTER/ EARLY SPRING → SPRING → SUMMER → LATE SUMMER/ FALL → WINTER →

FIGURE 3-1. The seasonal growth cycle of a typical deciduous, woody perennial. Wide arrows indicate the direction of major energy flow in the form of carbohydrates.

plants that will fit at maturity. Most small trees should be placed at least 6 feet from structures and at least 3 feet from any paved area; larger trees may need to be placed even farther away. Look for overhead obstacles. Do not plant tall-growing species beneath utility lines. Utility companies are required to prune trees that grow into overhead lines, which can severely disfigure trees and promote decay, structural failure, and insect attacks, and increase utility costs. For more information, consult resources such as *SelecTree: A Tree Selection Guide* (Reimer and Mark 2001) and *Trees Under Power Lines* (Costello et al. 1989) or go to Web sites such as http://selectree.calpoly.edu

PROVIDE FOR ROOTS

Healthy roots are vital to plant survival. Nutrients, oxygen, and water are absorbed by root tips and their associated mycorrhizae (see below). Roots produce compounds essential to the plant, store food, and support the aboveground plant structure.

Good design minimizes pest problems. For example, this close spacing of plants shades out weeds.

Determine whether the location is adequate for good plant growth. If the tree in this photo is retained, the site probably should be modified to provide more space for trunk and root growth as the plant matures.

Damage appearing on aboveground parts often occurs because roots have been smothered, cut, crushed, poisoned, overwatered, underwatered, or otherwise cared for improperly. Excessively wet conditions and soil compaction are probably the most common landscape problems. Insects and diseases that attack trunks, limbs, or foliage also can cause more serious damage if roots are unhealthy.

Roots are often neglected because they grow underground and are not seen. Provide roots with proper soil conditions and adequate space. Examine the surrounding soil for barriers to root growth before planting. After the first few years of growth, lateral (horizontally growing) roots of healthy plants often extend well beyond the canopy or drip line to a distance equivalent to two to three times or more the diameter of the drip line. Woody dicotyledonous plants may also have heart (structural) roots that grow downward and can help anchor the tree, and absorbing roots with concentrations of root hairs that take up water from the soil. Often about 90% of woody plant roots grow in the top 3 feet of soil, most in the top 1 foot (Figure 3-2). Actual root systems can vary greatly, depending in part on cultural practices, plant species, and soil conditions.

Properly preparing the planting area is important for future root development. Typically the prepared planting area should be at least 2 to 3 times the diameter of the root ball, but no deeper than the bottom of the root ball, as discussed in this chapter in the section "Planting Properly." Additionally, breaking up hardpans or compacted soils deeper than 3 feet before planting can improve plant growth by increasing drainage and facilitating development of sinker roots, which in some species grow near the trunk and deep into the soil. Although it can be an expensive task, breaking up hardpan can be especially beneficial in arid areas where hard layers often form near the soil surface.

CONSIDER MYCORRHIZAE

Most healthy trees have beneficial fungi growing in or on their absorbing roots; the symbiotic (mutually beneficial) association between a mycorrhizal fungus and the plant is called a mycorrhizae. There are hundreds of different species of mycorrhizal fungi. Some are generalists that associate with many plant species, while other fungi and plants are specialized associates. Mycorrhizal root tips are a primary location where plants absorb nutrients and water. Mycorrhizae can increase growth rates and improve the drought tolerance of plants, and may also help protect plants from pathogenic nematodes and soil microorganisms. Many trees grow poorly and die in the absence of mycorrhizae, especially if plants are stressed from other environmental conditions.

Endomycorrhizae occur mostly within roots, so colonized roots appear normal. *Ectomycorrhizae* form a sheath or mantle around short lateral roots, so colonized roots are often devoid of root hairs and may appear swollen. Mushrooms growing out of the ground near conifers may be the reproductive structures of certain mycorrhizal fungi. However, spores of the

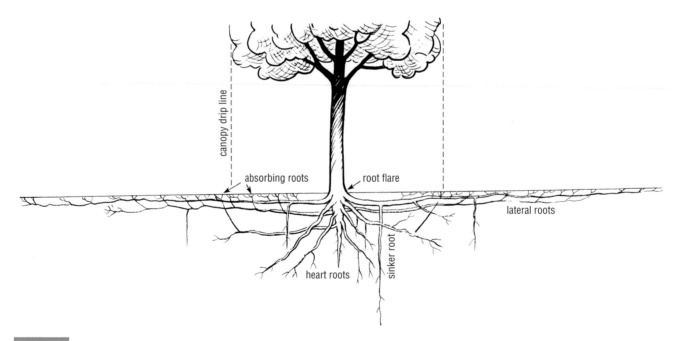

FIGURE 3-2. Healthy roots are vital to plant survival. Woody plants have several different types of roots and typically about 90% of roots grow in the upper 3 feet of soil. Up to about 70% of roots are in the top 1 foot. Because roots need air, even more of a tree's roots are near the surface if soils are compacted or waterlogged. Conversely, drought-adapted species and trees in deep or well-drained soil have more of their roots growing deeper below ground than shown here. Roots typically extend beyond the tree canopy drip line. Actual root systems can vary greatly, depending in part on cultural practices, soil conditions, and the species of plant. For example, unlike the central taproot of many dicotyledonous plants, monocots such as bamboo, palm, and yucca have thread- or ropelike roots that spread laterally to form a fibrous mat near the soil surface.

most common types of endomycorrhizae (arbuscular mycorrhizae) are produced in soil next to roots and are microscopic.

Mycorrhizae are common in soils where the plant species with which they associate have grown previously. They disperse in soil, on roots of host plants, or by spores that can be windblown or occur in litter on the soil. Inoculating plants with appropriate mycorrhizal fungi benefits forest conifer seedlings, revegetation of low-quality disturbed soils (such as reclaimed surface mines), and certain plants in nurseries. However, mycorrhizal fungi may not improve growth if plants are fertilized and regularly irrigated. Commercial mycorrhizal inoculants are available, but their quality varies. There is no research showing that applying mycorrhizal inoculants is beneficial in most fertilized and irrigated urban landscapes. Exceptions might be obligately mycorrhizal plants such as conifers and oaks that will receive little fertilization or irrigation and are planted in constructed or highly disturbed soils.

Mycorrhizal fungi are already present in most soils and often naturally colonize nursery plants grown in organic media. Promote mycorrhizal growth and development by providing plants with appropriate growing conditions. Prevent soil compaction and changes in soil grade or drainage. Avoid overwatering or underwatering and do not overfertilize, particularly with phosphorus or quick-release synthetic formulations. Apply organic mulch as detailed in Chapter 7 to moderate soil temperatures and conserve moisture around plants. Avoid fumigating soils or contaminating soils with toxic materials, which kill beneficial fungi.

CHOOSE THE RIGHT TREE OR SHRUB

Proper plant selection is one of the best ways to avoid pest problems. Problems often occur because plants are poorly suited to local conditions. Each plant species or cultivar grows best under specific environmental conditions and is affected by local soil, temperature, sunlight, and water. Some plants tolerate a wide range of conditions while other species survive only within a narrow range. Many of the plants that thrive in the eastern states or other areas of the world with summer rainfall do not do well in most of California unless they are irrigated regularly. Likewise, a plant that does well along California's coast may grow poorly in the warmer, drier interior valleys. Plants poorly adapted to their planting sites are more likely to perform poorly or die due to environmental stress and pests.

Learn which species or cultivars are adapted to local conditions. For example, look in nearby parks or botanical gardens and choose from among plants performing well there. Many local park agencies and public utilities will provide a list of trees recommended for planting in that community. Seek advice from local experts such as Cooperative Extension advisors, certified arborists, or certified nurserypersons. Consult publications listed in Suggested Reading. Guidelines for plant selection are also available on the Web, such as at http://selectree.calpoly.edu

Soil. Determine the key chemical and physical properties of the soil where you plan to plant as discussed in the section "Prepare the Site." Many California soils are alkaline, compacted, and poorly drained, especially in urban areas. Local Cooperative Extension personnel, certified arborists, and nursery professionals may know the common soil types in your area. Consider having soils tested by a laboratory for bulk density, organic matter, pH, salinity, and texture as discussed in the Chapter 6 sections "pH" and "Salinity." Learn which plants tolerate local soil conditions and choose from among those species and cultivars. If necessary for that site, aerate, change grade, provide for surface drainage, or install drain pipe or drain tile before planting. Seek professional advice on which measures are appropriate for your situation.

Water. Choose plants that thrive within the water limitations at the site. Most species in California will need some irrigation during plant establishment. If species that are adapted to summer rainfall are planted, they will need regular irrigation throughout their life or they will perform poorly and be plagued with problems. If drought-adapted species are planted in areas provided with irrigation (such as in lawns), watering may need to be modified because frequent summer irrigation can damage or kill drought-adapted plants.

Consider water quality in addition to irrigation frequency and quantity. For example, certain plants grow poorly if water mineral content is high, as it is in some irrigation well water. Consult sections such as "Boron" and "Salinity" in Chapter 6 for more information.

Climate. Most landscape plants are adapted to either summer drought or summer rainfall. Summer rainfall-adapted species are generally those native to the eastern United States, northern Europe, or eastern Asia, where summer rainfall occurs. Most of California has a Mediterranean climate. Winters are cool and wet, summers are hot and dry, and much of the

Choose plants by looking to see what species or cultivars are doing well in that neighborhood or in nearby parks or botanical gardens. This blue-flowering ceanothus and yellow-flowered flannel bush in the University of California's Davis Arboretum are well adapted to dry areas of central and southern California.

state receives little or no precipitation from late spring through early fall. Californians should consider planting native California species or exotics from other parts of the world that also have a Mediterranean climate (Figure 3-3); these species should require significant irrigation only during establishment and perhaps during years when rainfall is below normal. Be aware that some of these plants are dormant or do not have lush foliage during summer, so expectations for their appearance should differ in comparison with frequently irrigated species that are adapted to summer rainfall.

California encompasses many different climate zones. Within each climate zone are microclimates where conditions vary over distances ranging from several miles (for example, due to hills and valleys) or within a few feet (because of buildings, pavement, and surrounding vegetation). Even native plants must be matched to local site conditions and provided with the cultural care to which they are adapted. For example, Monterey pine and Monterey cypress from the coast and giant sequoia from the Sierra do poorly in hot, dry, interior areas of the state regardless of how much water they are given. For more information on selecting drought-adapted and native California plants, see the Suggested Reading.

Cold, Heat, Light, and Wind. Consider the local climate and the environmental conditions expected at the site. Determine the direct and reflected light conditions, range of temperatures, and windiness at the site and choose species that tolerate those conditions. For example, species especially susceptible to mechanical injury or moisture stress from hot or cold winds should be planted where they will be sheltered from prevailing winds.

Light, temperature, and wind can vary dramatically in urban areas between locations only a few feet apart due to the influence of buildings, pavement, and surrounding vegetation. Wind dehydrates and tatters leaves and breaks limbs. Too much or too little sunlight causes foliage of susceptible species to discolor, die, and drop. Excess cold or heat or light that converts to heat when it contacts surfaces, cause cracked and sunken bark. These wounds promote wood-boring insects, bark cankers, and decay fungi. For more discussion, see the sections "Extreme Temperatures," "Sunburn and Sunscald," "Sunlight," and "Wind" in Chapter 6.

Select Healthy Plants. Choose good-quality nursery stock (Table 3-1). Investment in better-quality plants can pay great dividends in lower maintenance costs and better performance. Avoid improperly pruned trees. Nurseries sometimes clip the main terminal to produce more compact lateral growth that appears attractive when plants are young; improper pruning of young trees can lead to serious structural problems once the plants mature. Consult resources such as *Training Young Trees for Structure and Form* (Costello 1999).

Check roots in container-grown plants. Feel below the soil surface or use a hose to wash away topsoil close to the trunk (this soil can be replaced); examine smaller plants by temporarily removing them from the container. Avoid plants with major

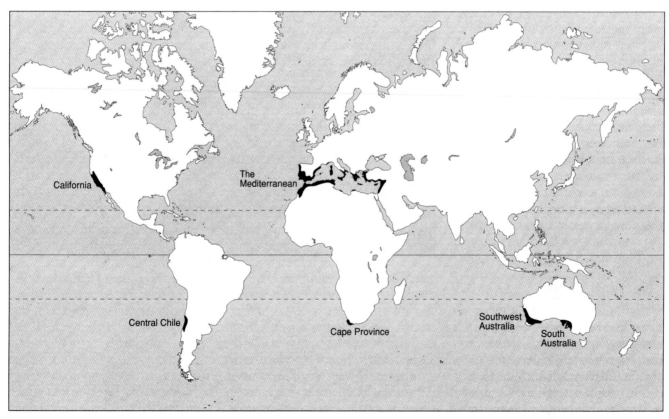

FIGURE 3-3. Central and southern California have a Mediterranean climate: cool, moist winters and hot, dry summers. Native plants and species from other Mediterranean regions labeled on the map are generally better adapted to California climates.

roots that are kinked or circling near the trunk; these will eventually become girdled by their own root system and grow poorly, break off, or die. Trees and shrubs in containers should be well-rooted in the soil mix. When the trunk is carefully lifted, both the trunk and root ball should move as one; if the trunk can be raised 1 or 2 inches before the container moves, roots may be poorly developed or extensively circling. Smaller roots circling the container periphery can be spread or cut before planting, but if larger roots or roots near the trunk are kinked, reject the plant. If possible, select trees that are not staked and have a noticeably tapered trunk; they will have sturdier trunks.

Root and crown rots, such as Phytophthora root rot, may develop in certain susceptible nursery plants and lead to poor growth and death after transplanting. Avoid plants infested with insects or diseases that may cause problems in landscapes. See Table 3-1 for a summary nursery plant selection checklist. Consult *Arboriculture: Integrated Management of Landscape Trees, Shrubs, and Vines* (Harris, Clark, and Matheny 1999) and *Specification Guidelines for Container-Grown Trees* (Harris et al. 2002) in the Suggested Reading for more detailed suggestions.

TABLE 3–1.

Nursery Tree and Shrub Selection Checklist.

LOOK FOR:	AVOID:
☐ Species or cultivars well adapted to heat, light, soil, water, wind, and other environmental conditions where they will be planted.	☐ Species or cultivars poorly adapted to local environmental conditions.
☐ A plant that at maturity will fit into the space provided for roots and branches.	☐ Plants that at maturity will be too large for the available space.
☐ Pest-resistant species or cultivars, where available.	☐ Species or cultivars prone to pest problems.
☐ Roots and crown area free of galls, insects, rots, and wounds.	☐ Injured, distorted, diseased, or girdled trunks, roots, or crown area.
☐ Large roots, root crown (collar), and trunk that are not kinked and main roots that do not circle the trunk.	☐ Encircling or kinked roots or a root mass too small in comparison with aboveground plant parts.
☐ Roots that are not a solid mass or are too small in comparison with aboveground parts.	☐ Discolored, distorted, or undersized foliage.
☐ Good overall appearance, color, leaf size, and vigor.	☐ Trees without tapered trunks and that lack a single, relatively straight central leader.
☐ Branches distributed radially around and vertically along the trunk.	☐ Trees with large branches close together on the trunk.
☐ A tree with a tapered trunk and a single, relatively straight central leader.	☐ Tree trunks that can't stand without being staked.
☐ A trunk that is without wounds and that can stand without being staked.	

Adapted from: *Arboriculture: Integrated Management of Landscape Trees, Shrubs, and Vines* (Harris, Clark, and Matheny 1999) and *Specification Guidelines for Container-Grown Trees* (Harris et al. 2002).

When selecting new plants, avoid specimens like this with major roots that are kinked or circling the container.

Reject container-grown plants with poor structure, like this kinked, circling, or girdling root next to the trunk in the crown area.

Pest Resistance. In some cases, pest-resistant cultivars or species can be selected that otherwise perform and look similar to susceptible plants. Avoid planting species or cultivars known to be prone to serious problems in your area. Do not replant in locations where plants have been killed or severely damaged by pathogens unless you select a species or cultivar highly resistant to that cause of disease. Do not plant species highly susceptible to root and crown diseases in poorly drained, compacted soils. Improve drainage or plant high, such as on a mound or soil berm.

Consult Table 3-2 and the appropriate sections in the text for resistant species or cultivars before selecting plants. Tables of species resistant or susceptible to *Armillaria, Phytophthora,* and *Verticillium* serve as a guide for selecting plants to avoid these diseases. Resistance is not

TABLE 3-2.

Pest-Resistant Alternative Species or Cultivars for Common Problems on Woody Landscape Plants.

HOST PLANT	PEST	RESISTANT OR LESS-SUSCEPTIBLE ALTERNATIVES
many species	Armillaria root rot	Table 5-14, page 262
many species	broadleaf mistletoes	page 338
many species	crown gall	page 258
many species	nematodes	Plants not listed in Table 8-1, page 346
many species	Phytophthora root rot	Table 5-15, page 265
many species	Verticillium wilt	Table 5-7, page 232
acacia	acacia psyllid	Table 4-13, page 114
alder	flatheaded alder borer	black alder, page 181
ash	anthracnose	Moraine or Raywood, page 223, Table 5-6
birch	bronze birch borer	non-white-barked birch, e.g., *Betula alleghaniensis, B. lenta,* or *B. nigra,* page 180
box elder	boxelder bug	male box elder, page 153
ceanothus	ceanothus stem gall moth	Table 4-17, page 165
crape myrtle	powdery mildew	Table 5-9, page 236
cypress	cypress canker	Table 5-13, page 254
cypress	cypress tip miner	Table 4-18, page 167
dogwood	anthracnose	Table 5-6, page 223
elm, Chinese	anthracnose	Drake cultivar, pages 225, 255
elm	Dutch elm disease	hackberry, zelkova, resistant elms, Table 5-8, page 234
elm	elm leaf beetle	hackberry, zelkova, resistant elms, Table 5-8, pages 85, 235
elm	European elm scale	hackberry, zelkova, page 144
eucalyptus	longhorned borer	Table 4-14, pages 118, 183
eucalyptus	tortoise beetle	Table 4-14, pages 90, 118

HOST PLANT	PEST	RESISTANT OR LESS-SUSCEPTIBLE ALTERNATIVES
eucalyptus	redgum lerp psyllid	Table 4-14, page 117
euonymus	euonymus scale	*Euonymus alata,* page 135
euonymus	powdery mildew	variegated cultivars
fuchsia	fuchsia gall mite	Table 4-26, page 205
juniper	cypress tip miner	Table 4-18, page 167
juniper	juniper twig girdler	Hollywood or twisted Chinese juniper, page 195
pear, ornamental	fire blight	Bradford, Capital, and Red Spire cultivars, page 229
pepper tree	peppertree psyllid	page 116
pine	Nantucket pine tip moth	Table 4-19, page 170
pine	pitch canker	Table 5-11, page 251
pine	Sequoia pitch moth	Table 4-24, page 191
poplar	Cytospora canker	Easter, Nor, Mighty Mo, and Platte poplar hybrids, page 250
privet	anthracnose	Amur, Ibota, and Regal, Table 5-6, page 223
rhododendron	root weevils	Table 4-11, pages 92, 96
rose	certain petal chewing beetles, such as hoplia beetle and rose curculio	red roses and other cultivars with darker-colored petals
rose	powdery mildew	Simplicity and Meidiland series, many glossy-leafed hybrid tea, grandiflora, and *Rosa rugosa* cultivars, page 236
sycamore and London plane	anthracnose	Bloodgood, Columbia, and Liberty cultivars, Table 5-6, page 223
sycamore and London plane	powdery mildew	Columbia, Liberty, and Yarwood cultivars, page 236

Resistance is not the same as immunity. Plants may become affected by problems to which they are resistant if plants are stressed because of poor cultural care or other factors.

the same as immunity. Plants may become affected by problems to which they are resistant if plants are stressed because of poor cultural care or other factors. New plant cultivars and better information are constantly being developed; consult a knowledgeable Cooperative Extension advisor, certified arborist, or certified nurseryperson for assistance in selecting pest-resistant plants.

Plant Compatibility. Group together plants having compatible growth characteristics and similar needs for irrigation and other cultural care. For example, some ground cover and turf species can spread rapidly and overgrow nearby shrubs and young trees. Turf and trees have different soil moisture and irrigation requirements. Grow incompatible species apart from each other or separate them with structures, pavement, or headers, which are wood, plastic, metal, or concrete barriers extending well below ground (Figure 7-4).

Site Preparation and Planting

Properly prepare the soil and control weeds before planting as discussed in Chapter 7. Especially with perennial species, it is easier and more effective to control weeds if you take action before planting.

PREPARE THE SITE

Many urban soils exhibit slow water infiltration (drain slowly), often because they are compacted, naturally contain impervious layers (hardpan), or have high clay content. To help learn about local soil and its possible effects on root health, examine nearby plants, observing their species and maturity. Note how well they are growing and the frequency and type of irrigation they receive.

Digging, collecting soil cores, or conducting a percolation test as discussed below help to assess soil and drainage at

a site. If poor drainage or other adverse soil conditions are found, determine the cause and identify appropriate remedies. Appropriate plant selection is one option. However, especially where slow drainage is the problem, drainage usually must be improved if young trees and shrubs are to grow well in a poorly drained landscape.

In poorly drained soils it may be necessary to loosen compacted topsoil or to break up or penetrate hardpan if impervious layers occur within about 1½ to 2 feet of the surface. Use a backhoe, jackhammer, pick axe, powered auger, or deep ripping to penetrate hardpan. Compacted soil can be loosened with deep ripping or plowing, or possibly by rototilling or using a digging fork or shovel before planting. Mix different soil layers well after loosening soil to provide a relatively uniform soil texture and to minimize distinct boundaries between layers. If it is not possible to break through hardpan or to loosen heavily compacted soil, planting on a soil berm or raised bed 1 to 2 feet tall may provide adequate aeration and drainage for good plant growth.

Assess Drainage. One method to assess infiltration rate (drainage) of topsoil is to perform a percolation test (Figure 3-4). Dig a 12-inch-deep hole the width of a spade. Roughen the bottom and sides to eliminate any smeared, packed soil. Fill the hole to the top with water at least once and soak the surrounding surface with a sprinkler or hose so that the soil around the hole becomes saturated with water. Wait 24 hours, refill the hole with water, and observe how long it takes for all the water to drain. If all the water is gone within 1 hour, drainage (infiltration) may be too fast. If any water remains after 24 hours, drainage is probably too slow. A desirable rate of soil drainage for many landscapes is about 1 to 2 inches per hour (roughly 6 to 12 hours are required to drain a 12-inch hole).

It is usually desirable to know the drainage and water-holding characteristics of soil deeper than 1 foot, except possibly when growing turfgrass or very short,

Shrubs and trees have different irrigation requirements than turf. Use sidewalks, driveways, or headers to separate plants and irrigate them differently according to their cultural needs.

FIGURE 3-4. Many urban soils exhibit slow water infiltration (slow drainage). Wet soil that drains slowly can damage roots and make plants susceptible to root rot pathogens. One method to assess infiltration rate of topsoil is to conduct a percolation test. Dig a 12-inch-deep hole the width of a spade. Roughen the bottom and sides to eliminate any smeared, packed soil. Fill the hole to the top with water at least once and soak the surrounding surface so that soil around the hole becomes saturated with water. Wait 24 hours, refill the hole with water, and observe how long it takes for all the water to drain. If any water remains after 24 hours, drainage probably is too slow. A desirable rate of soil drainage for many landscapes is about 1 to 2 inches per hour (roughly 6 to 12 hours are required to drain a 12 inch hole).

roughen sides and bottom of hole

12" depth

width of spade

Digging, feeling soil, and observing how quickly water drains when poured into a hole are among the techniques for assessing soil conditions. Investigation may reveal that the planting location or method, the species grown, or a combination of factors may need to be modified to allow landscape plants to perform as desired.

shallow-rooted plants. The National Resource Conservation Service publishes useful soil survey maps that are available from the federal government and many public libraries. Developers, local public works departments, and realtors may also have copies.

Use a soil sampling tube or dig a 1-foot-deep hole and compare your topsoil with survey maps to reveal whether your soil matches the maps. If the topsoil differs from published surveys (for example, because it has been disturbed), deeper soils may also differ. It may be feasible to investigate soil types by digging down 3 feet or deeper using a spade, although considerable effort may be required. An auger (either hand or powered) can remove soil for inspection up to 6 feet or more below ground.

Consulting with a knowledgeable expert via phone may be adequate to learn more about your soil. University Cooperative Extension advisors, master gardeners, and private consultants such as certified arborists may be knowledgeable

about local soils. However, it is often desirable to have an expert visit the site, and it may still be necessary to dig or core at that site to identify the extent of any soil disturbance.

PREPARE THE SOIL

Before planting, mark out a planting space that is at least two to three times the diameter of the root ball. Preparing an even a larger planting space can greatly benefit trees. If needed, loosen the soil within this area. However, in the center of the hole where the plant will be placed, loosen soil only to the depth of about 2 inches less than the root ball so the root crown can be planted slightly high on firm or settled soil.

Determine whether soil has chemical or physical deficiencies before deciding whether to amend it. Adding gypsum (calcium sulfate) then leaching heavily with water low in salts may improve soils that are sodic (high in exchangeable sodium), but a soil test is needed to determine if gypsum additions would be help-

ful. Species like azaleas and camellias are adapted to well-drained, acidic soils; they will do poorly in alkaline, poorly drained soils unless acidifying amendments (such as elemental sulfur) are added and drainage is improved before planting. For more information on soil problems, see Chapter 6, especially the sections "Iron," "Nutrient Deficiencies," "pH," and "Salinity;" contact your local university Cooperative Extension; or consult related publications in the Suggested Reading, such as *Western Fertilizer Handbook* (California Fertilizer Association 1998).

Mixing organic matter into the soil before planting trees and large shrubs has not been shown to yield consistent benefits. Adding organic amendments is controversial, in part because it can create topsoil with different water-holding capacity than sublayers, causing poor root development. Amending the entire potential root zone of trees is generally not practical, and amending soils around established plants will damage roots. Conversely, adding peat or well-composted organic matter may improve soil texture (tilth), increase water-holding capacity in sandy soils, and help to improve drainage of clay soils. If organic matter is added to soil, it should be well decomposed or well composted and should constitute no more than about 20% of the soil volume in the upper 12 inches of soil or the anticipated rooting zone of the mature plant. Thoroughly mix the organic matter into the topsoil. If mixing in organic matter, evaluate whether adding a modest amount of nitrogen fertilizer is appropriate to compensate for a temporary reduction in nitrogen availability to plants that can occur as soil microorganisms further decompose the organic matter. Because organic matter will gradually decompose and cause plants and soil to settle, planting on a berm or a mound is an especially good idea in soil amended with organic matter.

Provide for necessary irrigation. Properly designed and maintained low-volume systems (such as drip emitters) conserve water, reduce weed growth, and help to avoid certain disease problems.

PLANT PROPERLY

Site preparation (Figure 3-5) and the timing of planting are essential for helping new plants become well established. Late fall (especially) through early spring are generally good times to plant in most of California; avoid planting during hot summer weather. Depending on conditions and preparations needed at that site, weed control and other work may need to begin well before planting.

Planting too deeply or not deeply enough are common problems. Planting too deeply favors root and crown diseases to which young plants are especially susceptible. Planting trees and shrubs too shallowly can make them unstable and lead to root damage from exposure and excessive drying.

Dig a shallow hole in the center of the prepared soil area and set the plant on firm or well-settled ground in the center of the hole. In most situations plant the root crown about 2 inches higher than soil level. Planting "high" is especially important if the soil is compacted, will

drain poorly, has been loosened deeper than the root ball, or if the soil is highly amended so the plant is likely to settle as organic matter decays. Avoid planting in a depression or low-lying area (Figure 5-3). However, planting 1 to 2 inches below the surrounding surface may be acceptable in sandy soils.

Place the plant in the hole and position the main stem perpendicular to the ground. Cut any wires or rope around the root ball and pull them away. Remove any burlap or other root wrapping. If the plant has a container, remove the container and any nursery stake before planting. Check for roots that circle the container and gently spread or cut them before planting. Cut any broken or encircling roots that are too large to spread. Do not use the plant if it is extensively

rootbound with major roots kinked or encircling the trunk or root ball; the plant will perform poorly and may die sooner than normal.

Backfill the hole with native soil after properly positioning the plant and preparing the roots. Do not cover container soil with field soil, as the difference in texture can prevent water penetration into the container soil where all the roots are located initially. Loosen the periphery of the container soil and mix it with native soil to minimize a distinct layer between the two types of soil. Settle soil near the trunk after planting, such as by pressing down gently with your shoe, then watering thoroughly to eliminate air holes; don't stamp soil down too hard before watering and don't press down on soil at all after watering or you may overpack soil.

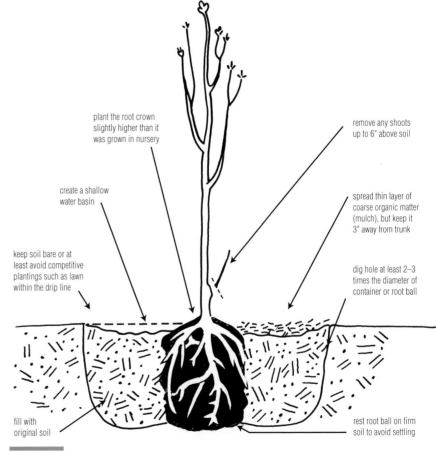

plant the root crown slightly higher than it was grown in nursery

create a shallow water basin

keep soil bare or at least avoid competitive plantings such as lawn within the drip line

fill with original soil

remove any shoots up to 6" above soil

spread thin layer of coarse organic matter (mulch), but keep it 3" away from trunk

dig hole at least 2–3 times the diameter of container or root ball

rest root ball on firm soil to avoid settling

FIGURE 3-5. Plant new trees properly. Prepare an area at least two to three times the diameter of the root ball. Place the root ball on firm or well-settled ground in the center of the hole, in most instances positioned so that the root crown is about 2 inches higher than the surrounding soil. Stake trees only if needed, using two stakes. Apply mulch over the entire prepared area, but keep organic mulch and landscape fabrics about 3 inches away from the trunk or apply organic mulch thinly in this area. Adapted from Hickman and Svihra 2001.

Keep an area 2 feet in diameter or larger free of turf or other vegetation around the trunk of young woody plants. Apply 3 to 4 inches of organic mulch over the entire prepared area, except possibly when plants are flood-irrigated within a basin, which can cause organic mulch to float. Keep mulch about 3 inches away from the stem or trunk or apply it thinly near trunks to avoid problems such as excess moisture where the trunk and roots meet (which can promote disease) and to minimize cover for small vertebrates (which may chew tender bark).

Remove any labels or tree tags, stakes, and trunk wrapping or protective tape that came with the new plant. Tags, stakes, or wrapping material can restrict trunk growth and seriously injure young plants. Prevent sunburn or sunscald by applying white *interior* latex paint, diluted 50% with water, to the trunk. Nursery plants are commonly grown close together so their trunks are shaded; planting in the landscape exposes tender bark to sun damage unless trunks are also shaded in the landscape. Make sure young plants are appropriately irrigated after planting. Consult publications such as *Planting Landscape Trees* (Hickman and Svihra 2001) for more details on proper planting.

STAKING

Stake trees during the first year or so after planting only if needed to protect or support the trunk or anchor the root ball (such as at windy sites). At the time of planting, remove any nursery stake that came with the container and restake the plant if staking is appropriate. Do not fasten trunks firmly; they must be allowed to flex some with the wind in order to develop stem strength.

Use two stakes in most situations and tie the trunk at just one level so the trunk is free to flex below the tie as well as above it. Three stakes may be appropriate in very windy locations. Some innovative single staking systems that provide support and allow trunks to flex are also suitable for use. When using two stakes at windy locations, orient the stakes so they and the trunk form a line perpendicular to the direction of prevailing winds, so the trunk is not blown directly towards either stake. At locations with south or west exposure where bark sunburn may be a problem, consider locating one of the stakes southwest or west of the trunk to help shade the bark unless stakes should be otherwise located because of prevailing winds. Stakes should be tall enough to be easily seen, and they should be located near the edge of the root ball, about 6 to 8 inches from the trunk. After tying the trunk, cut the stakes off just above the ties so that stakes do not rub against limbs or the trunk.

To determine the proper staking height of trunks that cannot stand upright without support, hold the lower part of the trunk in one hand, bend the top of the trunk to one side, then release the top. Locate the first tie about 6 inches above the lowest level at which the trunk can be held and still return upright after the top is deflected. The second tie should be located immediately above the first. Trunks should not be tied within 2 feet of the tip of the leader to avoid deforming growth.

Ties should be belt-like straps with a broad surface that forms a loose loop around the trunk, contacting the trunk without cutting into bark. Ties should be made of a flexible or elastic material, such as polyethylene tape or rubber tubing (old bicycle tubes can be cut and split open lengthwise). The preferred staking method is to use two ties, each about 18 inches long, attached to opposite posts. Circle each tie around the trunk and attach both ends to the same stake (Figure 3-6) or cross or overlap the ends to form a figure eight. Remove any stakes after a year or so; if the trunk is then unable to stand alone, determine the cause and if possible remedy the problem before restaking. Consult *Staking Landscape Trees* (Harris, Leiser, and Davis 1982) or *Arboriculture: Integrated Management of Landscape Trees, Shrubs, and Vines* (Harris, Clark, and Matheny 1999) for more details.

CARE FOR YOUNG TREES AND SHRUBS

Learn the cultural requirements of plants under local conditions. Water, fertilize (where appropriate), and prune young

Planting too shallowly or allowing drainage water or irrigation to wash away soil leads to root damage from exposure and excessive drying.

FIGURE 3-6. Stake trees only if needed to protect or support the trunk or anchor the root ball. Use two stakes in most situations and tie the trunk at just one level so the trunk is free to flex above and below the tie. Orient the stakes and the trunk so they form an imaginary line perpendicular to the direction of prevailing winds, so the trunk is not blown directly towards either stake.

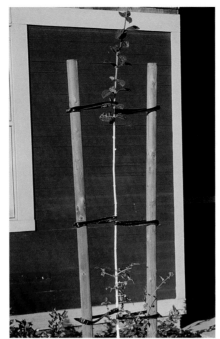

Ties were left on this young tree too long, causing wood to grow around the top tie. The branch at the right has a canker from rubbing a stake that is too tall, too close, and should be removed.

Trunks must be allowed to flex with the wind in order to develop stem strength. Too many ties (shown here) or not removing the nursery stake that came with the container are common problems of newly planted trees.

Prevent sunburn or sunscald on bark by applying white *interior* latex paint diluted 50% with water to young trunks. If you must plant trees in lawn, keep a 2-foot-diameter or larger area around the trunk free of turf or other vegetation.

plants correctly. Proper cultural care is critical to keeping trees healthy and minimizing pest damage. If pests or damage do appear, reevaluate cultural practices to determine whether improper care has contributed to the problem. Proper cultural care alone may provide the solution. Other activities, such as pesticide applications, may be of little benefit to plants if cultural care is inadequate.

Keep soil moist but not soggy in the root ball and for several feet outwards around newly planted trees and shrubs. Proper irrigation frequency depends on the plant, soil, and weather. For about the first 2 months, new spring plantings may need to be irrigated almost daily during hot, dry weather because their roots are confined to the small volume of soil that was the old soil ball in the container. Water the root ball directly during early establishment of new plants because water often does not move easily from surrounding soil into the root ball. However, do not allow water to puddle around the base of the trunk (the root crown or collar) and minimize direct wetting of the trunk.

Allow the surface and upper topsoil to dry between waterings, but be sure soil several inches below the surface is remaining moist, especially in the original root ball. Until you learn how irrigation practices affect subsurface soil moisture in that situation, periodically dig a shallow hole or use a soil tube or moisture indicator probe to check subsurface moisture levels. As roots grow into the surrounding native soil, apply water at increasing distances away from the trunk and keep the root crown area dry. After the initial establishment period, gradually increase the interval between irrigations and encourage good root growth through infrequent, thorough soakings around the canopy drip line (Figure 5-2). Avoid frequent sprinkling that only wets the surface; this encourages undesirable shallow root growth.

Fertilize woody plants sparingly or not at all during their first growing season in the landscape. Exceptions include mixing a modest amount of nitrogen into soil before planting if soil is amended with organic matter. Nitrogen is usually the only nutri-

ent to which woody plants respond in most soils. Exceptions may include soils such as sand that are especially low in nutrients and woody monocots such as palms, which often benefit from addition of several nutrients as discussed later. If young plants will be fertilized, avoid applying too much. Do not incorporate quick-release fertilizers into the planting hole.

Avoid pruning during the first year after planting, except to remove damaged or diseased branches. During the next 4 or 5 years of growth, prune young woody plants if needed to encourage good structure; establishing a central leader or dominant main terminal is especially important. Hire a professional such as a certified arborist to prune trees or consult resources such as the video *Training Young Trees for Structure and Form* (Costello 1999). Avoid excessive pruning, which can ruin tree structure and retard overall growth by removing food-producing foliage. Leave some temporary, short branches along the trunk or main stem during the first few years; these protect tender bark from injuries and sunburn, improve trunk growth and strength, and nourish the tree.

Prevent weeds, turf, and ground covers from growing near the trunk of young trees and shrubs. Nearby plants can seriously retard young woody plant growth. Apply and maintain 3 to 4 inches of mulch over a 2-foot-diameter or larger area beneath new trees and shrubs. Benefits of mulching include reduced weed competition, retained soil moisture, increased soil microbial activity, improved soil structure, and moderated root-zone temperatures.

Water Management

Poor water management is probably the biggest problem suffered by landscape trees and shrubs. Each species has a different range of maximum and minimum water necessary for good growth and for simply surviving. Learn the water requirements of plants at each location. Be aware that irrigating too frequently is often the original cause of nutritional deficiency symptoms and root rots. Monitor soil moisture around the plant's root zone and adjust irrigation according to need. Maintain adequate but not excessive water in the soil to ensure plant survival and good growth. Dig up and examine small roots to become familiar with their appearance. Healthy root tips are generally cream colored and firm; unhealthy roots are often dark, water-soaked, and soft. Excess water can cause fine roots to decay and slough off when dug from the soil.

WATER AND PEST PROBLEMS

Too much or too little water damages or kills plants (Tables 3-3 and 3-4). Insufficient water causes leaves to droop, drop, yellow, or wilt. Drought stress promotes certain pest insects and pathogens, sunburn or sunscald, shoot and branch dieback, bark cracking, and cankers. For example, the *Botryosphaeria* fungus commonly causes cankers and branch dieback on drought-stressed giant sequoia planted outside its native range; other species can

TABLE 3-3.

Common Problems Associated with Underwatering Woody Landscape Plants.

DAMAGE SYMPTOMS	CAUSE	MANAGEMENT
bark cracking	abiotic disorder	pages 34, 273
bark or branch cankers	abiotic disorder Botryosphaeria canker cypress canker Cytospora canker	pages 34, 250 page 255 page 254 page 250
bark weeping or resin exudation	abiotic disorder bacteria Botryosphaeria canker wood-boring insect	pages 34, 273 page 245 page 255 page 171
bark with holes or sawdust	wood-boring insect	page 171
leaves bleached or stippled	mites sucking insects	page 197 pages 152–160
leaves drop prematurely	abiotic disorder	pages 34, 273–274
leaves spotted	abiotic disorder	pages 34, 223
shoot or branch dieback	abiotic disorder Botryosphaeria canker wood-boring insect	pages 34, 273–274 page 255 page 171

Abiotic disorders are noninfectious plant diseases induced by adverse environmental conditions as discussed in Chapter 6. Some of these symptoms can also be due to other causes not listed here.

also become infected. Monterey and Leyland cypress planted in hot, dry locations are highly susceptible to cypress canker disease and insect attack; few Monterey cypress survive to maturity in California when they are not planted in the cool, moist coastal areas they prefer.

Mites and some leaf-chewing and leaf-sucking insects are more damaging to plants receiving insufficient moisture. Most wood-boring insects such as bark beetles, flatheaded and longhorned beetles, and clearwing moths primarily attack plants stressed from drought or other unfavorable conditions. Prevent damage through proper plant care; once trees and shrubs become severely infested by borers, they do poorly and usually die. When these pests appear on plants, prune out and dispose of infested limbs and apply cultural practices that can improve plant vigor.

Overwatering (usually the result of watering too frequently) and poor water placement are more common problems in landscapes than underwatering. Excess water encourages germination of weed seeds and excludes oxygen from soil that tree and shrub roots need to

survive. Water dripping, ponding, or spraying near the basal trunk of trees and shrubs, and soggy soil around the root collar, are primary causes of root and crown diseases due to pathogens such as *Dematophora* and *Phytophthora*. These disease-causing fungi are present in many soils, but usually become damaging only when wet conditions favor them.

Poor water placement promotes other diseases in addition to root and crown rots. Splashing water spreads fungal spores and wets foliage, promoting foliar and fruit diseases such as anthracnose, brown rot, leaf spots, and rusts. Minimize or prevent many foliar diseases by using low-volume drip irrigation or mini-sprinklers instead of overhead sprinkling.

The seasonal timing of irrigation also is important in disease development. For example, oak root fungus (*Armillaria mellea*) is present on dead or living roots in many soils and becomes active when soils are warm and moist. Because California's rainfall occurs during the winter when soils are cool, oaks growing in dry summer soils usually escape damage. However, when people frequently water native oaks during the summer, or alter

TABLE 3-4.

Common Problems Associated with Overwatering or Poor Water Placement.

DAMAGE SYMPTOMS	CAUSE	MANAGEMENT
branch cankers	anthracnose diseases	pages 232, 250
branches die back	abiotic disorder root and crown diseases	pages 34, 273–274 page 262
foliage yellows or wilts	abiotic disorder root and crown diseases vascular wilt diseases	pages 34, 273–274 page 262 pages 232–234
fruit spotted or discolored	fungal diseases	pages 223–228
leaves drop prematurely	abiotic disorder anthracnose diseases root and crown diseases	pages 34, 273–274 page 223 page 262
leaves spotted or discolored	bacterial and fungal pathogens	page 223

Abiotic disorders are noninfectious plant diseases induced by adverse environmental conditions as discussed in Chapter 6. Some of these symptoms can also be due to other causes not listed here.

Poor water placement, such as this prolonged wetting of the basal trunk, promotes diseases such as Dematophora and Phytophthora root rots. If irrigation basins are used, instead of a hole as shown here, plant on a central mound so the root collar is kept dry.

soils through compaction or changes in grade, moist roots and warm soils coincide, predisposing oaks and many other species to infection and death by the *Armillaria* fungus.

Drought-adapted plants such as oaks and certain eucalyptus may benefit from deep, supplemental water at 1- or 2-month intervals during the summer, especially during years of abnormally low rainfall. Supplemental irrigation may also be appropriate if trees have been injured, for example, by cutting roots. Be aware that certain eucalyptus species and non-native oaks are not drought-adapted and require more frequent irrigation when planted in California. For species

adapted to summer drought, irrigation should be provided to simulate natural patterns and applied mostly during the normal rainy season, if needed, tapering off during the dry season. Apply water around and beyond the drip line, not near the trunk where the root collar should remain dry (Figure 5-2).

IRRIGATION

Irrigation is required to maintain most urban landscapes in California, where rainless weather prevails throughout much of the growing season. Early morning or just before dawn is generally the best time to irrigate. Irrigating around dawn reduces water loss from

evaporation while minimizing the length of time when foliage is wet, thereby discouraging the development of certain foliar diseases. Predawn irrigation improves sprinkler efficiency and the uniformity of water distribution because there is generally less wind and more water pressure. Irrigating during late evening or night can minimize evaporation, but avoid overhead sprinkling then if foliar diseases are a problem because leaves will remain wet longer in comparison with irrigating around dawn.

The appropriate irrigation frequency and the volume of water to apply during each watering varies greatly according to many factors. Considerations include moisture demand by plants, microclimate, root depth, drainage patterns, irrigation system type and efficiency, and soil texture, structure, and depth.

Rooting depth varies according to plant age, type, species, soil, and moisture conditions. Plants generally have more shallow roots when they are young or receive relatively frequent and light irrigations or are growing in compacted or poorly drained soils. Roots are usually deeper in older plants, as well as in plants growing in well-aerated soils with good drainage and less-frequent but deep irrigation. However, about 90% of tree and shrub roots are usually in the top 3 feet of soil (Figure 3-2).

Water demand or loss depend on the environment and plant species. Water lost through a combination of evaporation from soil and transpiration by plants is called evapotranspiration (ET). A plant's demand for water increases when weather is sunny, hot, and windy and when humidity is low. However, many broadleaves can temporarily stop transpiring and limit their water loss under extreme conditions. More-exposed plants and those growing near pavement or other heat-absorbing and light-reflecting surfaces typically require more water than the same plant growing where it is sheltered.

Several terms are used to describe how soil affects the air and water that are available to plant roots. *Texture* is the relative

proportion of different sizes of soil particles, including sand (the largest soil
particles), silt (intermediate sizes), and
clay (the smallest particles). *Structure* is
the arrangement of these soil particles.
Pore spaces are the voids between soil
particles, which fill with air or water or
both. *Field capacity* is the amount of
water that can be held in pore spaces by
capillary action after excess water has
moved down and passed beyond topsoil
by the force of gravity. *Capillary action*
results from a combination of the natural attraction of water molecules to the
surface of soil particles and the attraction of water molecules to each other.
Because of this attraction between soil
and water, only a portion of the water in
soil—the *available water*—can actually
be extracted by plants. The *wilting point*
occurs when plants have extracted all
the available water. Loam soils (clay,
sand, and silt combined) that are not
compacted generally provide the best
combination of available water (Table
3-5) and adequate oxygen for roots
(Figure 3-7): they provide a range of
pore sizes, with the smaller pores holding moisture while the larger pores drain
and allow air to enter the soil. For more
information on soil and irrigation, consult publications such as *Water Management* (Hartin and Faber 2002).

Estimating Irrigation Needs. Schedule
irrigation by observing plants or monitoring soil moisture or evapotranspiration. These techniques all assume plants
are correctly planted, well-rooted, and
have been growing well. Combine more
than one method for the best results.

Observe Plants. Examine plants regularly
for symptoms of water stress. Early
drought-stress symptoms exhibited by
broadleaf plants include wilting of leaves
and normally shiny green foliage that becomes faded, dull, or grayish. Growing
tips may wilt in the afternoon and recover
during evening or by the next morning.
As drought stress becomes more severe,
plants may not recover from wilt. As
symptoms progress, leaf margins or inte-
riors turn yellow or brown, foliage dies and

drops, and twigs, branches, and eventually
the entire plant may die. Certain plants
may exhibit symptoms first because they
are more isolated and exposed, are planted
on higher ground, or are less-drought-
tolerant species. Inspect these plants more
frequently and use them as indicators of
drought stress and irrigation need.

Monitor Soil Moisture. Schedule irrigation
by monitoring soil moisture. The frequency of monitoring varies greatly, depending on the factors discussed above.
Soil around young plants during hot
weather may need to be monitored daily;
every few weeks may be adequate when
monitoring around mature trees during
more favorable weather. Sample soil from
the root zone in several different areas of
the landscape to assess overall irrigation

needs and determine whether water is
being applied deeply and uniformly
enough.

Monitor soil moisture by digging a
shallow hole with a trowel or other small
digging tool that minimizes root injury.
Alternatively, use an auger, soil probe, or
soil sampling tube, such as those pictured
in Chapter 8 for sampling nematodes.
Examine soil moisture in the rooting
zone to a depth of about 1 foot.

Soil lightens in color when it is dry.
Also, consult guidelines for estimating
soil texture and moisture by how soil
feels and molds in your hand, such as
the table in *Water Management* (Hartin
and Faber 2002). For example, medium-
and fine-textured soils such as loam and
clay can be molded, rolled, or squeezed
into a ball when wet. If soil does not

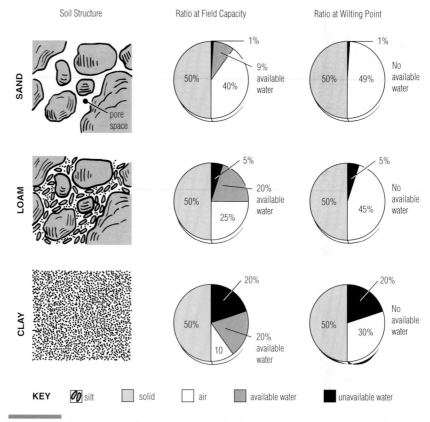

FIGURE 3-7. The amount of air and water available to plant roots varies depending on
soil texture (particle sizes) and structure (particle arrangement). Sandy soils have large
pore spaces that contain large amounts of air, but large spaces allow water to drain
quickly. Clay soils have many small pore spaces that retain water, but much of this water
is too tightly held to be available to roots. Small pore spaces drain poorly (slowly) and
often provide insufficient space for oxygen needed by roots. Silt particles are intermediate in size between clay and sand. Loam soils are a reasonably balanced mixture of sand,
silt, and clay that are not compacted. Loam soils generally provide the best balance between water-holding ability and aeration.

mold, it is too dry. If soil molds into a ball but does not crumble when rubbed, it is too wet. If the soil can be molded and crumbles when rubbed, the moisture content is probably suitable, except that sandy soil crumbles even when moist.

A more accurate way to monitor soil moisture is to install a tensiometer or other reliable soil moisture sensor. A tensiometer is a closed tube containing a porous, water-filled cup at the bottom. The tube is buried so that its bottom is in contact with the water film surrounding soil particles in the root zone, perhaps about 1 to 2 feet deep. As the soil dries, water is sucked out of the cup, creating a vacuum, which is measured by a gauge. The entire unit can be secured below ground. Some tensiometers can be wired into irrigation system controls to trigger watering automatically when needed.

Irrigation in commercial landscapes can also be scheduled using other devices not discussed here, including capacitance sensors, electrical-resistance blocks (gypsum blocks), and neutron probes. For discussion of these, consult publications such as *Arboriculture: Integrated Management of Landscape Trees, Shrubs, and Vines* (Harris, Clark, and Matheny 1999).

Monitor Evapotranspiration. Irrigation can be scheduled by monitoring evaporation of water from soil surfaces and transpiration from plants. These water losses combined are called evapotranspiration (ET) and are commonly expressed in inches per day. *Reference ET* (ET_o) is the amount of water used by well-watered cool-season turfgrass, which typically requires more water than trees and

Basin irrigation is often used in dry locations that do not have an installed irrigation system. However, it may be best to avoid basins around trunks, except for about the first year after planting. Continually enlarge any basin to encourage lateral root growth as the tree matures. Break basins down during the rainy season to prevent waterlogging.

This drip system, which will be covered with organic mulch, helps conserve water. Low-volume irrigation also reduces soil compaction, salinity, and weed growth problems associated with sprinklers.

Early symptoms of drought stress include temporary wilting of foliage during the day, as with these pittosporum terminals. However, irrigating too frequently also causes wilting by damaging roots. Investigate the true cause of any injury so you can apply the correct remedy.

TABLE 3-5.

Approximate Amounts of Available Water When Soils Are at Field Capacity.

SOIL TEXTURE	INCHES OF AVAILABLE WATER PER FOOT OF SOIL
sand	0.5–1.0
sandy loam	1.0–1.5
clay loam	1.5–2.0
clay	1.5–2.0

Monitor soil moisture at regular intervals to help determine the frequency and amount of irrigation. This Oakfield soil tube has just been withdrawn from the ground after collecting soil up to 1 foot deep. The tube's side is cut away for easy removal of a soil core for examination to determine the depths where soil is moist.

shrubs. After they are established, most woody landscape plants perform well by irrigating them with about 50 to 60% of ET_o. During years of average rainfall, providing even 30% of reference ET appears to be adequate for many established woody plants.

A standard recommendation is to irrigate established woody landscapes when evapotranspiration monitoring indicates that about 50% of available soil water has been used. For example, assume most woody plant roots are in the upper 2 feet of a loam soil. At field capacity (after irrigation and initial drainage), loam soil contains about 1.5 inches of available water per foot (see Table 3-5), or a total of 3 inches of available water in the upper 2 feet. Thus, irrigation would occur when ET accumulates to about 1.5 inches (50% of available water, or a proportion equal to 0.5). If a typical summer reference ET is 0.2 inches per day, many woody plants would need about 0.1 inches of water per day ($ET_o \times 0.5$). Therefore, about 1.5 inches of water should be applied after about 15 days (1.5 inches = 15 days × 0.1 inches of water per day). Woody plants growing within turfgrass areas often receive adequate water if the turf is well watered.

Historical and current (real-time) reference ET values for many locations are available from universities or government agencies, such as the California Irrigation Management Information System (CIMIS). CIMIS reports ET_o at sites throughout California and disseminates this information through many sources, including the World Wide Web site at www.ipm.ucdavis.edu maintained by the University of California Statewide IPM Program.

Evaporation outdoors can be monitored onsite by regularly measuring water loss from a shallow pan. Automated evaporation pans use a sensor to monitor water level and send that information to a data logger or automated control system. Computer software programs are also available for predicting ET. Some irrigation controllers can access historical ET_o data or current reference ET information gathered onsite or online and use these data to schedule irrigation automatically.

Public agencies or managers of commercial landscapes may benefit from modified methods of irrigating based on ET. For example, estimated ET values have been published for specific plant species or for plants similar to those being grown. These guidelines can be helpful, but this "landscape coefficient" method of scheduling irrigation based on plant factors is controversial because there is no research documenting the different irrigation needs for most plant species in landscapes.

For more information, consult the California Department of Water Resources Web site at www.owue.water.ca.gov/landscape/pubs/pubs.cfm or publications such as *Determining Daily Reference Evapotranspiration* (Snyder, Pruitt, and Shaw 1987) or *Evapotranspiration and Irrigation Water Requirements* (Jensen, Burman, and Allen 1990).

IRRIGATION METHODS

Basin, sprinkler, and low-volume soaker or drip irrigation systems are common in landscapes. A basin is formed by creating a berm of soil several inches high that encompasses the drip line of the young tree or shrub bed. Water is provided within the berm by installing an irrigation head, using a hose or tank truck, or (after plant establishment) by relying on runoff or precipitation. Do not irrigate so frequently that topsoil within berms is constantly wet. Plant on a central mound or slope soil within any berm away from the plant's root collar. Break down berms during prolonged rainy weather to prevent water from ponding around the trunk (see Figure 5-2). If berms are used beyond the first year or two after planting, gradually move the berm further from trunks to increase the area of irrigated soil.

Sprinklers irrigate the soil and also wash dust from plants and increase humidity in landscapes. However, sprinklers may distribute water unevenly and waste water, especially in windy conditions. They can compact the surface of bare soil, increase weed germination and growth, and promote certain foliar dis-

Weather monitoring stations provide plant care and pest management decision-making information, such as evapotranspiration (ET) and insect development degree-days (DD). For example, many woody landscapes perform well in California when irrigated with water amounts equaling about 50% of reference ET. Up-to-date reference ET is readily available, such as on the World Wide Web at www.ipm.ucdavis.edu

Planting species that require little irrigation, as shown here, is one method of conserving water. Even when woody species requiring more water are grown in California landscapes, research finds that increasing the interval between irrigations often improves plant health and wastes less water.

eases by splashing fungal spores and wetting foliage. In comparison with low-volume irrigation systems, sprinkler irrigation of trees and shrubs is less efficient because water is dispersed widely, making it suitable only for relatively large plantings with uniform water needs.

Low-volume systems emit water directly on or below the soil surface using porous hoses, drippers, or emitter nozzles. Low-volume systems can be more expensive to install than sprinklers and may require more maintenance and more skill to use, especially in developing appropriate irrigation schedules. Be aware that it can be difficult to monitor and maintain systems installed below-ground or beneath mulch. When using a low-volume system, shrubs in dry areas may need to be occasionally washed of dust to keep them healthy. Yet low-volume irrigation systems provide many benefits.

They waste comparatively little water and reduce or avoid compaction, salinity, and extensive weed growth associated with sprinkler irrigation.

For more information, consult publications such as *Drip Irrigation in the Home Landscape* (Schwankl and Prichard 1999), *Water Conservation Tips for the Home Lawn and Garden* (Geisel and Unruh 2001), and *Water Management* (Hartin and Faber 2002).

CONSERVE WATER IN LANDSCAPES

Conserve water by installing an efficient drip or low-output sprinkler irrigation system. Maintain and operate irrigation equipment properly. Irrigate only when needed; monitor evapotranspiration, plants, or soil moisture as discussed above to help you decide when to irrigate. Modify irrigation throughout the

year to match plants' seasonal changes in irrigation needs.

Avoid runoff by improving soil permeability (drainage). To avoid runoff, cycle irrigation systems on and off in several short but closely spaced periods instead of irrigating continuously for one long period. Regularly inspect systems to ensure they are applying water to the desired area, in appropriate amounts, and with a proper interval between irrigations.

Choose species that are tolerant of the heat, exposure, soil, and moisture conditions at the site. Group together plants with similar water requirements. Use plant species adapted to the local climate. Many California natives and plants from other areas of the world with a Mediterranean climate require little or no irrigation once they become established.

Fertilizing Woody Plants

About sixteen elements are required for plant growth; they usually occur naturally in sufficient quantities. Carbon, hydrogen, and oxygen are the most common and are provided to plants by air and water. The remaining are mineral elements in soil that are absorbed by plant roots. The most important mineral nutrients (those required in the greatest amounts) are the six macronutrients (Table 3-6). Although there are many fertilizer recommendations for landscape plants, adding fertilizer to established woody plants is not necessary in most situations.

Nutrient deficiency symptoms in landscape plants usually are not due to a deficiency of nutrients in soil. Inadequate nitrogen, phosphorus, and potassium are especially rare in established woody landscapes, except in containers or planter boxes, fruit and nut trees, woody monocots such as palms, and certain atypical soil types. Most nutrient disorder symptoms (such as iron or nitrogen deficiency)

TABLE 3-6.

Mineral Nutrients Essential for Plant Growth.

MACRONUTRIENTS	MICRONUTRIENTS
nitrogen (N)	iron (Fe)
potassium (K)	chlorine (Cl)
calcium (Ca)	manganese (Mn)
phosphorus (P)	zinc (Zn)
magnesium (Mg)	boron (B)
sulfur (S)	copper (Cu)
	molybdenum (Mo)
	nickel (Ni)[1]

Nutrients are listed in decreasing order of their abundance as commonly found in dry-weight plant tissue. Consult Chapter 6 for descriptions and pictures of nutrient deficiency symptoms and recommended remedies.

1. Plants may need minute quantities of nickel, making it the seventeenth "essential" element; not listed here are carbon, hydrogen, and oxygen, which are provided by air and water.

result from other causes, especially adverse soil conditions and anything that injures roots or restricts root growth, inhibiting plants' ability to absorb nutrients. Common causes of deficiency symptoms include high pH, inappropriate irrigation (usually irrigating too frequently), physical injury to roots, poor drainage, and root decay pathogens. With a few exceptions, fertilization of established woody plants is not recommended unless insufficient soil nutrients has definitely been diagnosed as the cause of unhealthy plants.

Nitrogen is the most commonly applied fertilizer. It is available in various organic and inorganic forms, as discussed in Chapter 6. Current research indicates that nitrogen should not be routinely applied to woody landscapes. Exceptions are containers or planter boxes, fruit and nut trees, some woody monocots such as palms, plants growing in very sandy soils, and possibly young trees and shrubs where increased growth is desired. As with other nutrient deficiencies, when established woody plants exhibit nitrogen deficiency symptoms, the cause usually is not a lack of nitrogen in soil. Symptoms resembling nitrogen deficiency can be caused by anything that impairs root growth or health.

Consult Chapter 6 for descriptions and pictures of nutrient deficiency symptoms and the recommended remedies.

Be aware that adding nutrients will not improve the appearance of foliage damaged by other causes. Improper or excessive fertilization damages plants, is detrimental to soil chemistry and microorganisms, and can pollute ground and surface water. Excess fertilization with nitrogen can cause pest problems, increase maintenance (such as the need for more frequent pruning), and shorten a plant's life span.

FERTILIZATION AND PESTS

Fertilize only as needed and only if other problems have been eliminated as the cause of poor growth. Some abiotic disorders, such as mineral deficiencies that cause undersized, discolored, or distorted foliage, can be remedied by adding nutrients.

Avoid overfertilization, especially with high-nitrogen fertilizers. Overfertilization promotes excess foliage that undesirably shades the inner canopy and understory plants. Fertilization results in the need for more frequent pruning, increases a plant's demand for other resources such as irrigation water, and can shorten a plant's life by causing it to outgrow available space. Rapid growth from excess fertilizer can cause bark to crack, allowing entry of fungi. Excessive fertilizer kills roots and "burns" or kills foliage. Application of nitrogen late in the growing season may delay dormancy in deciduous plants; if cold weather occurs early, plants can be damaged.

Too much fertilizer also promotes excessive succulent foliage, which can increase populations of pests, such as mites, aphids, and psyllids, which prefer new growth. Cypress bark moth larvae in natural situations feed primarily on Monterey cypress cones. In landscapes, they often infest trunks and limbs because landscape cypresses are fertilized and watered to promote rapid growth, resulting in thin bark susceptible to bark moth attack. Fertilizing oaks may promote distorted terminals. These "witches' brooms" are caused by a powdery mildew fungus, which readily infects and damages succulent new growth formed during the dry season in response to fertilization and excess irrigation. Do not fertilize pines that exhibit cankers or rosaceous plants infected with fire blight as fertilization increases plant susceptibility to these diseases.

WHEN TO FERTILIZE

Most woody landscape plants should not be routinely fertilized. Nutrients in most situations should be provided only selectively in response to identified needs. As long as woody plants exhibit normal leaf size and color and desired growth, nutrients are probably adequate. When deficiency symptoms do occur, the cause usually is not due to insufficient nutrients in soil.

The major exceptions are fruit and nut trees grown for their yield, many woody monocots, and certain unique situations, such as plants grown in containers or sandy soils. For example, with woody monocots such as palms, it may be best to apply modest amounts of potassium and magnesium in combination or a special palm fertilizer at regular intervals. True nutrient deficiencies are common in these species when grown in California and the southwestern United States, and palm foliage damaged by deficiencies takes years to be replaced by new growth. Young trees and shrubs, especially those growing in infertile soil, may grow more quickly after fertilization (primarily in response to nitrogen), and people often desire young plants to grow rapidly. Certain species poorly adapted to local soils may also benefit from some specific nutrients; however, avoid planting these and consider replacing them with plants better adapted to local conditions.

NUTRIENT DEFICIENCIES

Deficiencies cause foliage to discolor, fade, distort, or become spotted, sometimes in a characteristic pattern that can be used to identify the cause. Fewer leaves, flowers, and fruit may be produced and they may develop later than normal and remain undersized if plants are deficient. More severely deficient plants become stunted and exhibit dieback. Learn to recognize symptoms of nutrient deficiency as summarized in Table 6-2; nitrogen and iron deficiency symptoms are the most common.

Be aware that deficiency symptoms in established woody plants usually are not due to inadequate nutrients in soil. Fruit and nut trees and woody moncots, especially palms, are major exceptions. Deficiency symptoms are usually caused by adverse soil conditions or anything that injures roots or restricts root growth. Symptoms resembling nutrient deficiencies also have other causes, including injury caused by certain herbicides or plant pathogens.

Diagnose the actual cause of symptoms by investigating whether soil conditions are adverse or roots are unhealthy. Learn

This Catalina ironwood (*Lyonothamnus floribundus*) has chlorotic and necrotic leaves symptomatic of severe iron and nitrogen deficiencies. However, highly alkaline soil and unhealthy roots are the actual causes of this damage. Fertilization is unlikely to improve foliage appearance, and the plant will not perform well unless soil conditions are improved.

whether the situation is among those relatively few instances where nutrients may truly be deficient. Consider laboratory testing of soil and symptomatic foliage to help diagnose the cause.

Common nutrient deficiencies, their symptoms, and proper diagnosis and remedies are discussed in Chapter 6. More detailed discussions are presented in *Abiotic Disorders of Landscape Plants: A Diagnostic Guide* (Costello et al. 2003), *Fertilizing Landscape Trees* (Perry and Hickman 2001), and *Western Fertilizer Handbook* (California Fertilizer Association 1998) listed in the Suggested Reading.

Pruning

Woody plant parts are commonly removed to direct plant growth and improve performance. However, improper pruning damages plants and causes pest

problems. The International Society of Arboriculture, National Arborists Association, and other tree care organizations publish pruning standards to help ensure that trees are kept attractive, healthy, and safe. Tree pruning should often be done by professionals. For example, only qualified arborists should prune large trees or those near power lines.

REASONS FOR PRUNING

Prune landscape plants to remove damaged or diseased wood, to induce strong structure in young plants, and to maintain mature plant health and structure. Enhancing flowering or fruiting, improving appearance or form, and controlling size are other common reasons to prune. Closely spaced groups of naturally growing plants may be "self-pruning" because lower and inner branches become shaded, weaken, die, and drop. Many landscape trees grown more in the open need to be pruned to obtain the desired spacing of main branches vertically and radially around the trunk. Properly pruning young plants during their first few years of growth is vital so that structural problems are minimized as plants mature. Removing branches also provides more light to the plants below and reduces wind resistance, avoiding deformities or breakage. Obstruction of views or interference with utility lines are also remedied by pruning plants that grow too large for the space provided.

Minimize pruning requirements by selecting species that mature to a size appropriate for that location. Where plants are too large, consider replacing them with lower-growing species. Select plants that have been well cared for and correctly pruned in the nursery as summarized in Table 3-1.

PRUNING AND PEST MANAGEMENT

Proper pruning can control or prevent certain pests. Correctly prune plants when they are young to minimize the need to remove large limbs later, thereby avoiding large pruning wounds. Remove damaged or diseased limbs. Consider pruning out pests confined to a small portion of the plant. Where appropriate, prune to increase air circulation within the canopy, which reduces humidity and the incidence of certain foliar diseases.

Trees do not "heal" wounds the way people do. Although cuts can eventually be closed by new growth, the wound is forever contained (compartmentalized) within the tree. Avoid unnecessary pruning because wounds are entry sites for decay, disease organisms, and termites, which can remain active inside trees even after wounds have closed. Excessive or unnecessary pruning stimulates succulent new growth. This new growth may be more susceptible to pests or may develop into limbs with poor structural strength.

Do not prune too much too soon. Plants store energy in their trunk and limbs (in addition to roots) and sufficient photosynthetic surface (primarily foliage) is required to manufacture enough food. Topping trees or otherwise removing excess wood in one season stimulates production of vigorous,

dense growth, which is susceptible to breakage and shades interior branches. Removing too much foliage exposes previously shaded bark, causing sunburn or sunscald. Sunburned bark leads to cankers or attack by fungi and wood-boring insects.

Pruning off and disposing of declining or dead limbs that are infested with wood-boring pests removes developing insects before they can emerge and attack other parts of the plant or nearby plants. However, pruning must be properly timed to avoid the adult insect's flight season because adults are attracted to fresh wounds where they feed or lay eggs or introduce plant pathogens. For example, prune eucalyptus during December or January (in southern California) or from November through March (in northern California) to avoid attracting eucalyptus longhorned borers, which fly during the other times of the year. Prune elms only during the late fall and winter, when the bark beetles that spread Dutch elm disease are not active. Avoid pruning plants susceptible to powdery mildew during the dry season. Pruning stimulates succulent new growth, which

is susceptible to powdery mildew fungi during dry weather. Tables 4-20 and 5-1 list insects and diseases, respectively, that can be managed by pruning.

Keep pruning cuts as small as possible to promote more rapid wound closure. Make pruning cuts correctly, just outside the branch bark ridge and branch collar as illustrated in Figure 3-9.

Keep pruning tools clean. Contaminated tools may spread bacterial gall of oleander and olive or fire blight of plants in the rose family, such as fruit trees. In situations where pathogens can be mechanically spread during pruning, sterilize tools before each cut as discussed in the section "Disinfectants" in Chapter 5.

WHEN TO PRUNE

The best time to prune depends on the age and species of the plant, condition of the host, purpose of pruning, and time of year (Figure 3-8, Tables 4-20, and 5-1). Remove hazardous branches whenever they appear. Remove damaged branches and branches with included bark (where two limbs meet at a narrow angle, causing bark to become

Certain tree care activities, such as pruning large trees, should be performed only by a competent professional. The best assurance of getting quality advice or tree work is to hire an arborist who is certified by the International Society of Arboriculture (ISA) or registered with the American Society of Consulting Arborists (ASCA).

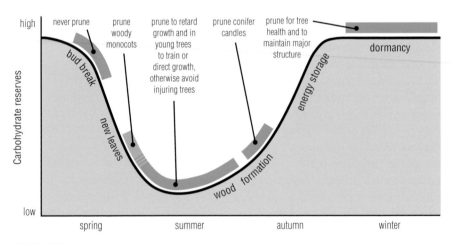

FIGURE 3-8. Carbohydrate reserves (energy storage) in plants vary with the season and the extent to which stored carbohydrate is lost in plant parts that are removed. To promote plant health and direct woody growth as desired, pruning should usually be timed according to the annual variation in stored carbohydrates as shown here. For example, winter dormancy is often the optimal pruning time for deciduous plants because they better tolerate the energy lost in pruned parts when carbohydrate reserves in remaining plant parts are at their maximum. For broadleaf evergreens, pruning just before their normal growth season (pruning during late dormancy, usually in late winter or early spring) minimizes dwarfing. See Tables 4-20 and 5-1 for the recommended pruning times to control certain pests affecting specific plant species.

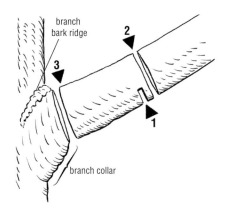

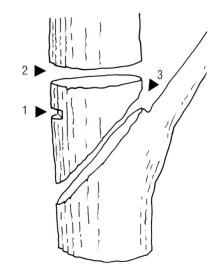

FIGURE 3-9. Remove a branch by making the pruning cut just outside the branch bark ridge and branch collar as indicated by the number 3. When removing a limb larger than about 2 inches in diameter, make three cuts in the order indicated. Make the first cut from below, about one-fourth of the way through the limb and 1 or 2 feet from the trunk. Make the second cut about 2 inches beyond the first cut, cutting from above until the limb drops. Make a final cut at number 3.

FIGURE 3-10. Drop crotch pruning removes an upper limb back to a lower lateral. This technique should be used instead of topping, a poor pruning practice that leaves stubs. When cutting large limbs, use the 3-cut method as shown here and in Figure 3-9 to avoid tearing bark.

embedded in the crotch, resulting in weakly attached limbs). Prune to improve structure and shape, especially when plants are young. Development of a single dominant leader should be encouraged in most cases, and this leader tip should not be pruned. Suppress (subdue) branches that compete with the main leader and that have a branch diameter that is about one-half or more than that of the trunk, such as by thinning or heading it back to a smaller branch (called drop crotch pruning) (Figure 3-10). If many branches should be removed, reduce excessive shoot growth and dwarfing by spreading pruning over several years. Young trees are often pruned during midsummer to direct development of good structure because regrowth then is often more predictable and less vigorous. Avoid pruning deciduous plants when buds are breaking or early in the season when leaves are expanding. Minimize dwarfing of evergreen species by pruning just before their normal growth season, usually in the spring.

HOW TO PRUNE

Heading and thinning are the two primary types of pruning cuts; each promotes a different plant response. Heading removes part of a branch terminal back to a bud or a smaller branch. Pinching, tip pruning, shearing, stubbing, and topping are all types of heading cuts. Heading stimulates new growth from buds just below the cut. The resulting foliage and shoots are often dense, may be weakly attached to the old branches, and may break off easily. In some cases, a headed branch dies or produces only weak sprouts.

A thinning cut removes a branch at its point of attachment (Figure 3-9) or shortens it to a lateral large enough to assume the terminal role. Compared with a heading cut, growth near the pruning site is less vigorous after a thinning cut; thinning cuts promote more evenly distributed growth throughout the plant. Thinning cuts are more selective and time-consuming, but they result in stronger structure and retain more of the plant's natural shape. The extra time initially required for thinning cuts is

generally rewarded over the long term by avoiding the time and expense of attempting to remedy problems and potential hazards caused by poor pruning practices.

The location of the pruning cut in relation to the branch attachment influences the size of the wound, extent of callusing, and potential decay. Make most pruning cuts just outside the branch collar and branch bark ridge (Figure 3-9). Do not cut flush with the main limb or trunk and do not leave stubs. Cutting just outside the branch bark ridge reduces the wound size, reduces the exposure of trunk tissue to infection, and preserves the attachment zone, which is most resistant to decay and contains tissue best able to close over the wound after a cut.

Pruning shears or loppers can be used for small-diameter cuts. A scissors-type or bypass pruner makes cleaner cuts than anvil shears. Do not use hedge shears to prune trees. Use a pruning saw when cutting branches greater than about $1/2$ to 1 inch in diameter. On branches larger than about 2 inches in diameter, avoid tearing bark or splitting the wood by making three cuts, as illustrated in Figure 3-9.

When pruning young trees during their first few years of growth, leave temporary branches along the trunk to nourish, strengthen, shade, and protect the lower trunk from injury; keep these temporary branches less than about 12 inches long. Remove the largest temporary branches during dormant season pruning each year during the first 4 or 5 years of a tree's growth. The remaining branches should then provide the maturing tree's structure.

Tree seals or paints provide no benefit when applied to pruning cuts or other wounds. Wound dressings are not recommended and may be detrimental to tree health.

Organizations such as the International Society of Arboriculture and the National Arborists Association provide pruning guidelines for professional tree care. Other information sources include

This black walnut was topped, encouraging growth of branches weakly attached below the cut on both limbs. A major limb was also removed below the first main branch crotch, leaving a large wound, which closes slowly and has developed decay.

the demonstration video *Training Young Trees for Structure and Form* (Costello 1999) and the publications *Plant Health Care for Woody Ornamentals* (Lloyd 1997) and *Woody Landscape Plants* (Hodel and Pittenger 2002). If you are not certain about proper pruning techniques, it may be best to hire a certified or registered arborist.

AVOID TOPPING TREES

Topping (also called dehorning, coat or hat racking, or stubbing) is the drastic heading of large branches in mature trees. Main limbs are often sheared as with a hedge, leaving stubs. Topping is a poor pruning practice sometimes used to shorten tall trees, remove hazardous or diseased limbs, or to prevent interference with overhead utility lines.

Topping broadleaves and conifers ruins their conformation, while topping palms will kill them. Drastic pruning is rarely justified simply because trees are believed to be too tall. Removing extensive canopy may not leave enough foliage to manufacture sufficient food and may cause roots to die and the tree to decline. The large wounds left by

topping often fail to close and are susceptible to internal decay and attack by wood-boring insects. Topping encourages growth of branches weakly attached below the cut, which become susceptible to wind breakage.

When it is necessary to reduce the size of a tree's canopy (crown reduction), instead of topping, selectively remove upper limbs back to lower lateral branches (drop crotch pruning). This proper method (Figure 3-10) is more time-consuming and expensive, but it avoids future expense from improper pruning and provides a more attractive, healthier, and safer tree. Where trees are repeatedly pruned because they grow too tall, replace them with lower-growing species.

Injuries, Hazards, and Protecting Landscapes

Prevent injuries to trees and shrubs. Wounds attract boring insects, serve as entry sites for disease-causing organisms, and can lead to limb, trunk, or root failure and tree death. Plant injury occurs when people cut roots, improperly stake young trees, inject or implant trunks, make pruning wounds, and operate equipment or vehicles that strike bark or compact soil over roots. Deer, gophers, rabbits, mice, and other animals chew bark and wood. Drought, frost, hail, ice, lightning, and snow are among the environmental conditions that can injure landscapes.

Make pruning cuts properly, just outside the branch bark ridge and branch collar (Figure 3-9). Keep weed trimmers and lawn mowers away from trunks. Choose plants that are well adapted to local environmental conditions so they are less likely to be damaged by moisture or temperature extremes. Provide proper cultural care so plants are less likely to be injured and better able to tolerate damage. Protect plants during construction as discussed below.

The lower left pine was topped to prevent damage to power lines. Terminals are dying back and bark beetles are attacking the tree, which died 3 months after this photograph was taken. Do not plant tall-growing species beneath overhead utility lines.

Wounds, such as these made to implant insecticide in a tulip tree trunk, provide entry sites for bacterial wetwood and other disease-causing organisms. Unless tools (such as drills or needles) are cleaned and sterilized before moving to the next plant, pathogens may be spread mechanically by equipment that contacts internal parts of more than one tree.

Protect trees from likely injury by installing barriers to keep vehicle bumpers away from trunks.

PROTECT TREES DURING CONSTRUCTION

Protect trees or they may decline, become hazardous, or die quickly or later as a result of construction-related damage. Forests, oak woodlands, and urban lots are often developed because mature trees make these sites desirable to people. However, in constructing homes and roads and while installing amenities, trees are often killed outright or their lives are greatly shortened. Stress resulting from construction-related damage can increase a tree's susceptibility to many pests. Negligent or thoughtless activities wound limbs, roots, and trunks. Injuring roots by crushing or cutting them or by compacting soil are very serious problems that are often caused by construction. Wet soil is especially susceptible to compaction by heavy equipment. Compaction or changes in soil grade or drainage deprive roots of water or oxygen. Changes belowground promote root and crown diseases and predispose trees to attack by bark beetles and other wood-boring insects. Adverse effects may not become apparent until several years after the injury or stress.

Consider tree preservation during the planning stage of development projects. Consult a certified arborist or other tree care professional for help in protecting trees. Check county or city ordinances before working around mature trees as they may be city-owned or protected by ordinances.

Fence off individual trees or groups of trees around the drip line or beyond to provide tree protection zones that prevent equipment and activities from damaging roots and trunks. Most roots are near the soil surface and many extend much farther than the tree canopy spread (Figure 3-2). If soil must be driven on or temporarily used to store heavy materials, apply and maintain a thick layer of mulch to reduce soil compaction. Minimize changes in soil grade and drainage; compaction and changes in soil contour alter surface and subsurface water flow on which established vegetation may depend.

In areas that will include both landscape and paving (such as commercial parking lots where shade trees will be planted), consider using special structural soil mixes. These specially engineered soil mixes can be compacted to the legal density required to ensure pavement integrity while still providing the air- and water-holding properties vital for root growth.

Do not place fill around trunks. If the grade must be elevated, construct a stone or concrete well around each trunk. Before placing the fill, installing a drainage system on top of the existing soil may help provide oxygen and appropriate water to established roots once the original soil level is covered. If grade must be lowered, construct retaining walls to preserve as much of the original grade, roots, and soil as possible, at least within the drip line of established trees. If soil is undisturbed on one side, removing soil on the other side halfway between the trunk and drip line may allow the tree to survive if adequate cultural care is provided. If grade must be lowered near trunks, consider removing these plants as they are likely to become diseased and hazardous, and eventually die.

At construction sites, fence off trees around the drip line or beyond to prevent equipment and activities from damaging roots or trunks.

Minimize trenching near trees; digging damages roots.

Be realistic in assessing which trees are worth saving and are likely to survive construction. Remove trees that are likely to die rather than leaving them to become a hazardous and expensive problem after sites are occupied; trees can be left to protect other trees during construction, then removed soon afterward. Remove declining or severely injured trees. Consider removing trees if the drainage, root zone, or soil grade will be seriously disturbed or if species with incompatible cultural needs will be planted nearby.

Remove and dispose of all recently dead wood and dying trees. Wood-boring beetles may emerge from recently dead wood and attack nearby healthy trees unless wood is properly handled, such as removing bark to promote drying or solarizing it beneath clear plastic tarps as discussed in Chapter 4 in the section "Bark Beetles." Apply urea or borax (sodium tetraborate decahydrate) to freshly cut pine stumps in areas where pines grow naturally. This helps prevent infection by airborne spores of annosus root disease that can spread from stumps through roots to nearby living conifers.

Avoid crushing or cutting roots, especially those larger than about 2 inches in diameter. Trench for utilities away from roots, combine utilities in a single trench, and consider tunneling beneath roots to minimize cutting them. Instead of digging around roots, use hydro-excavation or pneumatic-excavation techniques. Locate septic systems away from trees; chemicals used in these systems may leach and damage roots or roots may infiltrate the systems and cause damage.

Use partially permeable materials (like bricks instead of concrete) if extensive areas near trunks must be paved. Use caution when applying wood preservatives; they may kill nearby vegetation through direct contact or by leaching. Be aware of fire hazards from natural or planted vegetation around buildings. Use good judgment by planting with species with compatible water requirements in an existing landscape. Irrigation of turf and other new landscape plants can weaken and possibly kill nearby established plants that are adapted to summer drought. For more information, consult Table 7-2 and publications in the Suggested Reading, including *Compatible Plants Under and Around Oaks* (Hagen, Coate, and Keater 1991), *Living Among the Oaks* (Johnson undated), *Protecting Trees When Building on Forested Land* (Koehler et al. 1983), and *Trees and Development* (Matheny and Clark 1998).

MINIMIZE FIRE HAZARDS

Fire is a serious hazard throughout much of California where hot, dry weather often prevails. All plants will burn if conditions are suitable, but appropriate plant selection and maintenance dramatically reduce the likelihood that vegetation fires will burn structures. Structure type, building materials, topography, and other factors are also important, but only landscape plants are discussed here.

Large plants provide more fuel than small plants, and they present a greater fire hazard the closer they are to structures. Prevent large plants from contacting structures or overhanging roofs. In some areas prone to brush fires, laws require a vegetation-free area around structures; consult local fire officials.

Provide plants with proper cultural care, especially appropriate irrigation, to improve plant resistance to fire. Even drought-adapted species may benefit from watering every 1 to 2 months during the dry season, and the increased moisture may decrease their flammability. Prune lower limbs to provide a fuel break between the ground and tree canopies. Prune out dead branches and remove dead or dying plants. Thin crowns by pruning limbs that form bridges between tall plants. Avoid grouping together a progression of shorter to taller plants near structures; these provide a fuel "ladder," allowing a ground fire to reach the tree canopies where fire can readily spread from one tree to the next. Minimize the buildup of litter (leaves, bark, etc.) around trees.

Unwatered landscapes generally increase the risk of fire, except for succulent ground covers (such as ice plant) and groves of cleanly maintained trees. In unirrigated landscapes in fire-prone locations, minimize the use of plants that contain flammable resins and oils, such as many broadleaf evergreens and certain conifers such as junipers. Consider using cacti, yuccas, and similar species that retain water during dry periods and are more fire resistant. Other drought-adapted plants can be more fire resistant if properly maintained (Table 3-7). For more information, consult *A Property Owner's Guide to Reducing Wildfire Threat* (Farnham 1995), *How Can We Live with Wildland Fire?* (Adams, Huntsinger, and Wright 1998), or the UC Forest Products Laboratory Web site at www.ucfpl.ucop.edu

TABLE 3-7.

Drought-Adapted and Relatively Fire-Resistant Shrubs and Trees.

COMMON NAME	SCIENTIFIC NAME
SHRUBS	
artemisia	*Artemisia* spp.
Carmel creeper	*Ceanothus griseus* var. *horizontalis*
holly-leafed cherry laurel	*Prunus ilicifolia*
hopseed bush	*Dodonaea viscosa*
Italian buckthorn	*Rhamnus alaternus*
lemonade berry	*Rhus integrifolia, R. ovata*
manzanita	*Arctostaphylos* spp.
oleander[1]	*Nerium oleander*
rock rose[1]	*Cistus crispus, C. salviifolius*
toyon	*Heteromeles arbutifolia*
TREES	
Brazilian pepper tree	*Schinus terebinthifolius*
California bay laurel	*Umbellularia californica*
California buckeye	*Aesculus californica*
California pepper tree	*Schinus molle*
carob	*Ceratonia siliqua*
coast live oak	*Quercus agrifolia*

All plants will burn if conditions are suitable, but these species resist fire if properly maintained.

1. Keep these plants pruned low.

A 1991 fire in Oakland and Berkeley, California, killed 25 people and destroyed over 3,000 houses. Appropriate plant selection and maintenance dramatically reduce the likelihood that vegetation fires will burn structures.

Any one of these signs—mushrooms around the trunk, brackets or conks on bark, or damaged bark—can indicate a hazardous tree.

RECOGNIZE HAZARDOUS TREES

Damaged or unhealthy trees that may drop limbs or fall over (fail) are hazardous. In more natural settings, dead or declining trees provide benefits such as wildlife habitat and recycled nutrients. In urban or recreational areas, hazardous trees can injure people and damage property.

Prevent injuries to roots and above-ground parts. Examine trees regularly to see that they are receiving proper cultural care and are not hazardous. Table 3-8 lists some signs to look for that can indicate that trees may be hazardous. Be aware that some hazards are difficult to detect, such as internal decay or unhealthy roots. If trees are located where their failure could cause injury or damage property, have trees regularly inspected by a competent expert, such as an arborist who is certified by the International Society of Arboriculture (ISA) or registered with the American Society of Consulting Arborists (ASCA). Also see publications such as *Evaluation of Hazard Trees in Urban Areas* (Matheny and Clark 1991) and *Recognizing Tree Hazards* (Costello, Hagen, and Jones 1999) listed in the Suggested Reading.

TABLE 3-8.

Some Warning Signs That Trees May Be Hazardous.

- brackets, conks, mushrooms, or other decay fruiting bodies growing on bark or out of the tree base
- cankers or wounds in bark or wood
- cavities on the main trunk or at the tree base
- cracks in the main trunk or at crotches (where limbs fork)
- dead or dying limbs
- fissures in soil near the base of trees
- trunks that lean or tilt instead of growing upright

Some hazards are difficult to detect. Have a competent plant care professional inspect regularly for potential hazards if trees are located where their failure could cause injury or damage property.

CHAPTER FOUR

Insects, Mites, and Snails and Slugs

M ANY INSECTS, mites, and other invertebrates live on and around landscape trees and shrubs. Some are pests because they annoy us or injure ornamentals, but most are innocuous or beneficial and should not be destroyed. Many invertebrates are necessary food for birds and other wildlife that live in urban areas. Some invertebrates are valuable parasites or predators that destroy pests. Others are scavengers that break down organic matter so that nutrients are available for plant growth. Insects, including honey bees, are essential for pollinating plants so that seeds and fruit are produced. Many invertebrates are neither damaging nor clearly beneficial, but removing them disrupts the natural relationships among organisms and may lead to problems.

This chapter discusses common species that sometimes become pests. Some level of invertebrate pests can usually be tolerated without harm to landscape plants. When control is appropriate, selective methods are often available and preferable.

Damage

Invertebrate pests are a very diverse group. Most of them damage plants through their feeding, but few other generalizations can be made. The damage is determined by many factors, including plant age, part affected, species, and location; the size and stage of the pest; and the nature and extent of any other stresses on the plant.

The type of feeding damage depends on the pest's mouthparts. Invertebrates generally have chewing or sucking mouthparts. Beetles, caterpillars, snails and slugs, and other invertebrates with chewing mouthparts commonly cause identifiable holes in flowers, fruit, leaves, or twigs. Sometimes they cut

Insects with chewing mouthparts, like this California oakworm, make distinct holes in fruit, leaves, or stems.

Sucking pests, like this adult southern green stink bug (*Nezara viridula*), insert their tubular mouthparts into plants, causing plant parts to discolor, distort, or drop.

parts completely from plants. Some insects with chewing mouthparts feed hidden inside trunks and limbs. These boring pests include bark beetles, clearwing moth larvae, and flatheaded and roundheaded borers. Weevil larvae and some other insects chew on roots. These insects that feed inside plant tissue or chew on roots can cause discolored or wilted leaves and other symptoms of plant decline that may be confused with diseases or cultural problems.

Pests with tubular sucking mouthparts feed on plant fluids and never cut away pieces of tissue. Sucking insects and mites cause buds, fruit, or leaves to discolor, distort, or drop. Sucking pests include aphids, leafhoppers, mites, scales, thrips, and true bugs.

Life Cycles

Most invertebrates begin life as an egg, which hatches into an immature form called a nymph or larva. Immature insects and mites grow by periodically forming a new outer skin or exoskeleton (molting) and shedding their old skin. In addition to the change in size, insects may modify their shape with each successive molt, a process known as metamorphosis.

Insects, the most common invertebrate pests, can be divided into two major groups depending on their type of metamorphosis. Species with complete metamorphosis undergo major changes in form between the immature stages and adult. This metamorphosis occurs within the nonfeeding pupal stage (Figure 4-1). Species that undergo complete metamorphosis, such as beetles and butterflies, often have different feeding habits during their immature and adult stages. Their immatures are called larvae. In groups such as butterflies, moths, and flies, only the larval stage causes damage; the adults consume only nectar and water. Many beetles chew plant parts as both larvae and adults. One stage typically is more damaging than the other, in part because larvae and adults often feed on different parts of the plant.

Insects in the other major group undergo gradual or incomplete metamorphosis. They have no pupal stage. Homoptera (such as aphids, mealybugs, and scales) and true bugs have incomplete metamorphosis. Their immatures are called nymphs. Nymphs differ from adults primarily in size, lack of wings, and color (Figure 4-2).

The development of mites is similar to the gradual metamorphosis of insects; however, the stage that hatches out of

the egg usually has six legs and is normally called a larva. Later-stage immatures (nymphs) and adults usually have eight legs, but otherwise look similar to mite larvae.

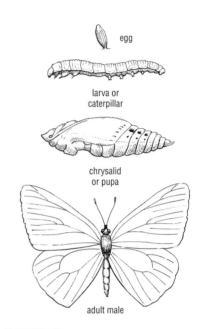

FIGURE 4-1. Insects with complete metamorphosis develop through four life stages: egg, larva, pupa, and adult. Each stage has a radically different appearance. Most moths and butterflies go through 4 or 5 molts during the larval stage. In butterflies and moths, the larva is also called a caterpillar; the pupa of some species is also called a chrysalid or chrysalis.

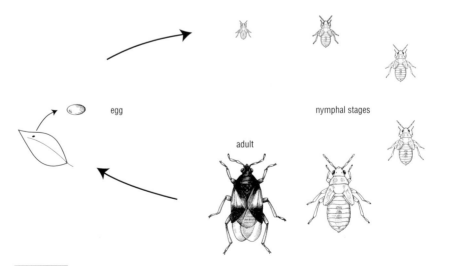

FIGURE 4-2. Insects with incomplete metamorphosis develop through three life stages: egg, nymph, and adult. Nymphs resemble adults, except for color, size, and the lack of wings. The minute pirate bug (*Orius* species) illustrated here is a beneficial predator on aphids, psyllids, thrips, mites, and insect eggs. Adapted from drawings by Celeste Green in Smith and Hagen 1956.

Thresholds

The presence of a few invertebrates and some amount of damage often does not threaten plant health and usually can be tolerated. Few quantitative thresholds have been established for landscape pests, in part because of the lack of research and variation in people's tolerance for pests. Example thresholds are provided for aphid honeydew, defoliating caterpillars, and elm leaf beetle in the sections on those pests. Approximate thresholds can be developed over the long term by regularly monitoring plants and keeping and evaluating records, as discussed in Chapter 2. One strategy is to focus efforts on problems where reasonable control actions can be effective. Recognize that in many instances by the time problems become obvious, there is no effective cure; tolerating damage, waiting (possibly months) until pests develop to a stage vulnerable to control, or in some instances replacing plants, may be the only options.

Monitoring and Diagnosing Problems

Regularly inspect valued plants to determine what invertebrate species are present and to get a general idea of their relative abundance. Insect and mite populations can increase rapidly; regular monitoring or sampling allows you to recognize developing problems and take action at the proper time. Once pest populations are high and damage becomes extensive, your management options become more limited or infeasible because you did not act early.

Proper identification of pest and natural enemy species is essential for successful pest management. One approach is to identify the host plant, then use the "Tree and Shrub Pest Tables" at the end of this book to help diagnose the problem. Alternatively, if you know what kind of pest you have (for example, caterpillars or scale insects), you can go to that section of the book and use the photographs and descriptions to help identify common species. Because of the broad scope of this book and because new species are frequently introduced from other places, not all possible landscape pests are included in this book. Take pests or damaged plant parts you cannot identify to a local Cooperative Extension or department of agriculture office, a certified nurseryperson, or pest management expert. Consult other published or online resources, such as those listed in the Suggested Reading and World Wide Web Sites at the back of this book.

After identifying the invertebrates on your plants, learn about their biology and potential damage. You may find that some species, while present near the damage or symptoms, are actually innocuous or beneficial. Even those species that cause damage can usually be tolerated at moderate levels without seriously threatening plant health.

Monitor or scout for pests or damage at regular intervals by inspecting a number of leaves, shoots, branches, or terminals or by using other techniques (Table 4-1) instead of or in addition to inspecting plant parts. Select an appropriate monitoring method based on knowledge of pest biology, the goals of your monitoring, and available resources.

Specialized techniques and equipment are often useful for monitoring. Sticky traps, branch beating, and degree-day (temperature) monitoring are discussed here; other methods are detailed in the sections on individual pests. For more

TABLE 4-1.

Insect and Mite Monitoring Methods.

METHOD	INVERTEBRATE SPECIES
visual inspection of plant parts	Most exposed-feeding species, including evidence of parasitism and predation. Monitoring tiny pests requires a hand lens.
branch beating	Most exposed, readily dislodged species, especially the adults, including green and brown lacewings, lady beetles, leaf beetles, leafhoppers, mites, non-webbing caterpillars, psyllids, thrips, true bugs, and weevils.
sticky traps	Adults of many insects, including leafhoppers, parasitoids, psyllids, thrips, whiteflies, and winged aphids.
double-sided sticky tape	Scale and mealybug crawlers.
burlap trunk bands	Adult weevils, gypsy moth larvae.
trap boards	Certain ground-dwelling invertebrates, including snails, slugs, and adult weevils.
pheromone traps	Adults of certain moths and scales, including California red scale, clearwing moths, fruittree leafroller, gypsy moth, Nantucket pine tip moth, omnivorous looper, and San Jose scale.
pitfall traps	Adult weevils, ground-dwelling spiders, predaceous ground beetles.
timed counts	Pest individuals that are relatively large and obvious, such as caterpillars, and that occur at relatively low density so they are not observed faster than they can be counted.
honeydew monitoring	Aphids.
frass dropping	Non-webbing caterpillars.
degree-day monitoring	Species for which researchers have determined development thresholds and rates, including elm leaf beetle, California red scale, San Jose scale, and Nantucket pine tip moth.

information on special tools and how to sample, consult publications such as *IPM in Practice* (Flint and Gouveia 2001) and *Integrated Pest Management for Floriculture and Nurseries* (Dreistadt 2001).

Sampling. Instead of simply scouting to detect the presence of pests or damage, professional managers of commercial and public landscapes and anyone responsible for highly valued or problem-prone plants can benefit from a more sophisticated monitoring technique called sampling. Sampling is quantitative monitoring that counts the number (or presence-absence) of pests per plant part (such as 1-foot-branch terminals) or per monitoring device (such as a trap). The average number (or percentage infested) is then calculated for all samples for each sample date. Compare the results of samples taken on several different dates to help decide if action is needed, when and where to implement controls, and to evaluate the effectiveness of management actions.

Keep good written records when sampling. Write down a description of your methods and sample the same way every time to make the results comparable among sample dates and from year to year. Record the number of samples (plant parts, traps, etc.) inspected. Write down the date, specific location, host plant and pests sampled, who sampled, and the results or counts from your samples. Record what management action you took and when you took it. Use appropriate tools, such as a 10-power hand lens, to help identify small insects and mites.

Presence-Absence Sampling. An alternative to counting each individual insect is to determine the percent of samples with pests or damage. This presence-absence sampling is quicker than counting each individual. However, presence- absence sampling is generally less precise, except in instances where researchers have determined the relationship between the percentage of samples infested and actual insect densities, as discussed in the section "Elm Leaf Beetle."

Conduct presence-absence sampling by inspecting each sample and recording whether it is damaged or infested with one or more pests. As soon as you discover damage or pests, move on to inspect the next sample. Calculate and record the percent of infested or damaged samples:

$$\text{Percentage of samples infested} = \frac{\text{Number of samples infested}}{\text{Number of samples inspected}} \times 100$$

Yellow Sticky Traps. Bright yellow (about 550–600 nm wavelength light) is highly attractive to adults of many insects. Adult leafhoppers, parasitoids, psyllids, thrips, whiteflies, winged aphids, and certain other pests and beneficial parasitoids can be monitored with yellow sticky traps (Table 4-1). While extremely useful in enclosures such as conservatories or greenhouses, it can be difficult to know the importance of insects trapped outdoors. Catching many adults may indicate they are abundant on nearby plants or that they are migrating in and will soon become abundant. Alternatively, the insects may have flown or been blown from a distance or may be species that do not attack valued nearby plants. If trapping outdoors, determine whether captured insects are species of concern, such as by having them authori-

tatively identified, then saving them for comparison to future trap catches. Alternatively, use a hand lens or binocular dissecting microscope to compare key characters (such as wing vein pattern and body markings) of trapped insects to those of winged specimens collected from valued, nearby infested plants.

When trapping, hang several bright yellow cards covered with clear sticky material near plants to detect the adults and get a rough estimate of changes in their numbers. Inspect trap cards about weekly whenever adults may be present. Carefully identify insects in traps before taking action, since many of them may be harmless or beneficial. Even large numbers of pest species in traps does not necessarily indicate that control action is needed. There are no specific guidelines for when treatment is warranted in landscapes based on the number of insects caught in traps. However, regular trapping for certain pests can help experienced users determine whether pest abundance is changing or remaining about the same. Evaluating trap catches can help in determining treatment timing and the effectiveness of previous management actions. By orienting traps in different directions and comparing the relative numbers caught on different surfaces, the direction from which pests are arriving can be determined, helping to locate nearby sources of pests.

Adult psyllids are caught in this clear plastic container lid coated with a thin film of viscous STP motor oil additive and clipped to a yellow surface that attracts insects. Monitoring helps to manage topiary eugenia because pest populations are reduced by shearing plants at about 3-week intervals when sticky traps show egg-laying adult psyllids are abundant.

When trapping outdoors, it may be adequate to visually compare the number of insects per trap, rather than count each individual. If you are counting large numbers of trapped insects, research shows that for many pests, it is not necessary to examine the entire trap; counting the insects in a vertical, 1-inch-wide strip on both sides of the card gives results that are representative of the entire trap. For example, when using 3-by-5-inch cards, count only the insects in a 1-by-5-inch vertical column on both sides of each card, then multiply your results by 3 to get a good estimate of the overall number of insects in each trap. When using traps to detect pest presence or when sampling less-abundant species, it is best to examine the entire trap.

Rectangular yellow cardboard or plastic traps that are sticky on both sides (each 3 by 5 inches or larger) are available from most well-stocked garden supply stores and are relatively inexpensive if purchased in quantity, such as by mail order. Traps also can be homemade and reused by periodically cleaning them and reapplying sticky material. Yellow wood, metal, or plastic boards or disks, such as clear plastic 4-inch-diameter cottage cheese container lids painted bright yellow (e.g., with Rustoleum Yellow No. 659), can be coated with clear polybutene sticky material (for example, Tanglefoot). These adhesives must be washed off using commercial solvents before recoating traps for reuse, so reusing these traps can be time-consuming and messy. Alternatively, you can coat the bright yellow surface of homemade traps with a thin film of STP motor oil additive. This is viscous enough to snare adults of relatively small, weak insects (such as aphids, psyllids, and whiteflies), but generally allows larger, stronger insects (such as large bees, flies, and wasps) to escape. Trap adhesive can also be composed of one part petroleum jelly (e.g., Vaseline) or mineral oil mixed with one part household detergent; however, some insects more easily escape this material and it may drip off boards under hot conditions unless applied thinly.

Because catches will vary somewhat depending on the trap, it is important to use the same trap type and method throughout the season so that results are comparable among dates. Periodic cleaning or replacement of traps is essential to maintain the sticky surface. For more information, consult *Sticky Trap Monitoring of Insect Pests* (Dreistadt, Newman, and Robb 1998) or *Integrated Pest Management for Floriculture and Nurseries* (Dreistadt 2001).

Branch Beating. Branch beating samples invertebrates that are readily dislodged from foliage, as listed in Table 4-1. Sample by holding a special beating tray, sheet, or a clipboard with a white sheet of paper beneath the branch as a collecting surface. Shake the branch or hit it two or three times with a padded stick. Use the same size collecting surface and the same number of beats or shakes per branch each time you sample so that results are comparable between locations or over time. Monitor about the same time of day on each date, preferably in the morning when temperatures are cool and invertebrates are less active.

Beat two to four branches from different parts of each of several plants on each

Detect and monitor certain pest and beneficial species by branch beating to dislodge insects onto a collecting surface. This technique is effective for adults and sometimes immatures of many species, including green and brown lacewings, lady beetles, leaf beetles, leafhoppers, mites, psyllids, thrips, and true bugs.

sample date. Count and record separately the number of individuals of each pest species and beneficial species that are dislodged in each sample. Total the insects counted and divide this sum by the number of branches beaten to determine the average insect density. If insect densities are relatively high, consider dividing your collecting surface into equal-sized subunits. Count only the insects on one or several representative subunits. Estimate the number of insects on the entire collecting surface by dividing your count by the number of subunits examined and then multiplying by the total number of subunits on the collecting surface.

Degree-Day Monitoring. The growth rate of plants and invertebrates is closely related to temperature; generally, the higher the temperature, the more rapid the development. Because of variation in weather, calendar dates are not a good guide for carrying out management actions. Measuring the amount of heat accumulated over time provides a physiological time scale that is biologically more useful than calendar days. The unit used to measure physiological time is the degree-day (DD). One degree-day is defined as 1 degree above the threshold temperature maintained for a full day.

The lower threshold temperature is the temperature below which no development or activity occurs. Pests do not feed, grow, or reproduce unless temperatures are above this threshold. Development also slows and eventually stops if temperatures are too warm, so an upper threshold is sometimes used in calculating degree-days. Each plant and invertebrate species has a specific lower and upper development threshold. The lower development threshold and the number of degree-days required to complete each life stage must be known in order to use degree-days for pest management. Researchers have determined the threshold temperature and developmental times for some important pests.

Degree-days for each day are estimated by subtracting the threshold temperature from the average daily temperature for that date as in Table 4-2. Computerized "sine wave" calculation methods are also available; these are recommended because they provide more accurate estimates. Degree-day monitoring tells you when to take action, but monitoring temperatures does not tell you whether control action is needed; you must still monitor plants to decide whether thresholds are exceeded. Degree-day monitoring tells you when pests will reach susceptible life stages. If pests are abundant, monitoring degree-days helps eliminate the guesswork otherwise required to determine when to time a control action.

For example, elm leaf beetles do not develop below about 51.8°F. First- and second-instar larvae of first-generation elm leaf beetle are most abundant in California at about 700 degree-days above 51.8°F accumulated from 1 March. If populations are high and damage is anticipated, a foliar insecticide applied at about 700 degree-days will catch susceptible larvae at their greatest abundance.

Current temperatures and easy-to-use point-and-click software for calculating degree-days and timing control actions for certain pests can be obtained from the Internet, such as at the University of California Statewide IPM Program at www.ipm.ucdavis.edu on the World Wide Web. Portable, compact electronic temperature recorders that calculate and display degree-days are also available. Information on using degree-days for decision-making is discussed later in sections on specific pests, including elm leaf beetle, Nantucket pine tip moth, and several species of scales.

Management

Integrated pest management (IPM) is a strategy for preventing and minimizing pest damage. IPM employs various tactics, including biological, cultural, chemical, mechanical, and physical controls. Effective pest management begins when you select plants that are well adapted to their location and properly plant and care for them. As detailed in Chapter 3, by providing proper cultural care, such as appropriate pruning and watering, you keep landscape plants vigorous so they are less likely to be attacked by certain pests and are better able to tolerate any damage. Summaries of mechanical and physical controls, and broader overviews of biological and selective chemical controls, are provided below. Consult the individual pest sections for more information.

MECHANICAL CONTROL

Mechanical controls use labor or nonpesticidal materials to control pests. For example, install copper bands around trunks and planting areas to exclude snails and slugs. Apply sticky barriers on trunks to prevent canopies from being infested by ants, weevils, and certain other flightless invertebrates. When only a small part of a plant is infested, clip and dispose of infested foliage, such as shoots harboring tentmaking caterpillars or other insects that feed in groups. Hand-pick snails or leaves infested with insects.

Sticky Barriers. Ants, flightless weevils, snails, and certain other invertebrates (such as gypsy moth larvae in the East) can be managed by encircling trunks with a band of sticky material (for example, Tanglefoot). Prune branches to eliminate bridges to the ground, structures, and any touching plants that are not also banded. Wrap the trunk with a collar of fabric tree wrap, heavy paper, or tape such as masking tape, then coat the wrap with the sticky material to protect young or sensitive trees from possible bark injury and to facilitate removal. If bark is not smooth, use a pliable wrap and wedge it snugly into cracks and crevices. To avoid restricting trunk growth, periodically replace bands and do not wrap trunks tightly. Increase the persistence of sticky material by applying it higher above the ground, which reduces dust and dirt contamination and decreases sprinkler wash-off. Avoid applying sticky material to horizontal surfaces where birds may roost.

TABLE 4-2.

Approximating Degree-Days (DD) Manually.

1. Add the daily minimum and maximum temperature (from Day 1 below) and divide by 2 to get the average daily temperature.	$\dfrac{41°F + 64°F}{2} = 53°F$
2. Subtract the lower threshold temperature (for example, about 52°F for elm leaf beetle) from the average daily temperature. The result is the approximate number of degree-days accumulated that day.	$53°F - 52°F = 1\ DD$

3. Add up the degree-days accumulated for each day until you reach the sum when specific actions are recommended. For example, elm leaf beetle development each year begins March 1 (Day 1). Starting then, degree-days are calculated each day and added to the degree-days from previous days. When the cumulative degree-day total reaches 700 (on day 71 in this example) control action (if warranted) is taken, as discussed in the section "Elm Leaf Beetle."

	Temperature, °F			
DAY	MIN.	MAX.	AVG.	DD
1	41	64	53	1
2	48	62	55	3
3	48	60	54	2
•	•	•	•	•
•	•	•	•	•
•	•	•	•	•
70	51	80	66	14
71	49	79	64	12
	CUMULATIVE TOTAL			700

This "manual" method of estimating degree-days becomes significantly inaccurate when temperatures are near the threshold; for example, when the high temperature is above the lower threshold, but the mean is below the threshold, no degree-days accumulate using the manual method even though degree-day accumulation and insect development actually does occur. Computerized estimates are more accurate and are available on the Internet at www.ipm.ucdavis.edu or by using electronic temperature recorders that calculate and display degree-days.

Apply sticky material around trunks to prevent canopies from being infested by ants, flightless weevils, and snails. Apply the sticky barrier over wrapping to protect young or sensitive trees from possible bark injury and to facilitate removal. This is an example of mechanical pest control.

A barrier band about 2 to 6 inches wide should be adequate in most situations. Check the sticky material at least every 1 to 2 weeks and stir it with a stick to prevent the surface from becoming clogged with debris or dead insects that allow ants to cross. Periodically remove and relocate any wrap to inspect for and minimize injury to bark.

PHYSICAL CONTROL

Physical or environmental controls suppress or prevent pests by altering temperature, light, and humidity. For example, control black scale and possibly other soft scales by thinning plant canopies in hot areas of California, thereby increasing scale mortality due to heat exposure. Apply white interior (not exterior) latex paint, diluted 50% with water, to trunks of young or heavily pruned woody plants to reduce or prevent sunburn or sunscald, thereby avoiding attack by certain wood-boring insects such as flatheaded and round-headed borers that are attracted to injured trunks. Spraying foliage with a forceful stream of water to dislodge and kill aphids could be considered mechan-

ical control; but when the underside of mite-infested foliage is regularly wetted during hot weather the reduction in spider mite populations is apparently due to increased humidity (physical control), which improves the reproduction and survival of predatory mites.

BIOLOGICAL CONTROL

Biological control—the action of predators, parasites, and pathogens to control pests and reduce damage—is very important in the management of invertebrates. Augmentation, conservation, and importation (classical biological control) are three tactics for using natural enemies. Classical biological control is the importation, release, and establishment of exotic natural enemies of pests. Conservation is the use of management practices that preserve naturally occurring beneficial organisms. Augmentation is the manipulation of pests or natural enemies to make biological control more effective.

Obtain a colorful *Natural Enemies Are Your Allies!* poster (Flint and Clark 1990) and display it so you and others can become familiar with common beneficial species. For more details, consult *Natural Enemies Handbook* (Flint and Dreistadt 1998).

Obtain a colorful *Natural Enemies Are Your Allies!* poster (Flint and Clark 1990) and display it so you and others can become familiar with common beneficial species.

Importation, or Classical. Importation is used primarily against pests that have been introduced from elsewhere. Many organisms that are not pests in their native habitat become unusually abundant when they arrive in a new area without their natural controls. Importation is often called classical biological control because many people first became aware of biological control as a result of the spectacularly successful importation project for cottony cushion scale. Many insects that were formerly widespread pests in California landscapes are now partially or completely controlled by introduced natural enemies (Table 4-3), except where these natural enemies are disrupted, such as by pesticide applications or honeydew-seeking ants.

Natural enemy importation requires several steps. Researchers go to the pest's native habitat, collect and study the natural enemies that kill the pest there, and then ship promising natural enemies back for testing. Natural enemies are held and studied in an approved quarantine facility to exclude potential contaminants and prevent their escape until studies confirm that the natural enemy will have minimal negative impact in the new country of release. Natural enemies found to be promising are introduced into the new environment so they are reassociated with the pest. If they become established, these introduced natural enemies may reduce their host to a low enough level so that it is no longer a pest.

Introduction of exotic natural enemies from foreign countries by law must be done only by qualified university or government scientists. However, it is important for landscape managers to recognize imported natural enemies and conserve them whenever possible. Because classical biological control can provide long-term benefits over a large area and is conducted by agencies and institutions funded through taxes, support from growers, pest control professionals, and the general public is critical to the continued success of classical biological control.

TABLE 4-3.

Woody Landscape Pests Substantially to Completely Controlled by Natural Enemies.

PEST COMMON NAME	PEST SCIENTIFIC NAME	INTRODUCED NATURAL ENEMIES (PARASITIC WASPS EXCEPT WHERE NOTED)	SEE PAGE
acacia psyllid	*Acizzia uncatoides*	*Diomus pumilio*,[1] *Anthocoris nemoralis*[2]	64, 114, 120
ash whitefly	*Siphoninus phillyreae*	*Encarsia inaron, Clitostethus arcuatus*[1]	121, 125
bayberry whitefly	*Parabemisia myricae*	*Encarsia* spp., *Eretmocerus* spp.	
black scale	*Saissetia oleae*	many species, including *Metaphycus bartletii, Metaphycus helvolus, Scutellista caerulea* (=*S. cyanea*)	136
bluegum psyllid	*Ctenarytaina eucalypti*	*Psyllaephagus pilosus*	116
brown soft scale	*Coccus hesperidum*	*Chilocorus* spp.,[1] *Metaphycus luteolus, Metaphycus* spp., *Microterys nietneri, Rhizobius lophanthae*[1]	137, 147
California red scale	*Aonidiella aurantii*	*Chilocorus* spp.,[1] *Aphytis melinus, Aphytis* spp., *Comperiella bifasciata, Rhizobius lophanthae*[1]	131, 147
citricola scale	*Coccus pseudomagnoliarum*	*Coccophagus lycimnia, Coccophagus scutellaris, Metaphycus flavus, Metaphycus luteolus*	138
citrophilus mealybug	*Pseudococcus calceolariae*	*Coccophagus gurneyi, Hungariella* (=*Tetracnemoides*) *pretiosa*	
citrus mealybug	*Planococcus citri*	*Leptomastix dactylopii, Leptomastidea abnormis, Cryptolaemus montrouzieri*[1]	127, 129
citrus whitefly	*Dialeurodes citri*	*Encarsia* spp.	122
Comstock mealybug	*Pseudococcus comstocki*	*Allotropa convexifrons, Allotropa burrelli, Pseudaphycus malinus*	
cottony cushion scale	*Icerya purchase*	*Rodolia cardinalis*,[1] *Cryptochaetum iceryae*[3]	142
dictyospermum scale	*Chrysomphalus dictyospermi*	*Aphytis* spp.	
elm aphid	*Tinocallis platani*	*Trioxys tenuicaudus*	
eucalyptus longhorned borer	*Phoracantha semipunctata*[4]	*Avetianella longoi, Syngaster lepidus*	183
eucalyptus snout beetle	*Gonipterus scutellatus*	*Anaphes nitens*	
eugenia psyllid	*Trioza eugeniae*	*Tamarixia* sp.	59, 115
European elm scale	*Gossyparia spuria*	*Baryscapus* (=*Trichomasthus*) *coeruleus*	
filbert aphid	*Myzocallis coryli*	*Trioxys pallidus*	
linden aphid	*Eucallipterus tiliae*	*Trioxys curvicaudus*	
longtailed mealybug	*Pseudococcus longispinus*	*Anarhopus sydneyensis, Arhopoideus peregrinus*	127
Nantucket pine tip moth	*Rhyacionia frustrana*	*Campoplex frustranae*	170
nigra scale	*Parasaissetia nigra*	*Metaphycus helvolus*	
obscure scale	*Melanaspis obscura*	*Encarsia aurantii*	134
olive scale	*Parlatoria oleae*	*Aphytis maculicornis, Coccophagoides utilis*	
peppertree psyllid	*Calophya rubra*	*Tamarixia* sp.	116
purple scale	*Lepidosaphes beckii*	*Aphytis lepidosaphes, Chilocorus* spp.,[1] *Rhizobius lophanthae*[1]	147
San Jose scale	*Diaspidiotus* (=*Quadraspidiotus*) *pernicious*	*Encarsia* (=*Prospaltella*) *perniciosi*	132
walnut aphid	*Chromaphis juglandicola*	*Trioxys pallidus*	
woolly whitefly	*Aleurothrixus floccosus*	*Amitus spiniferus, Cales noacki*	124

These pests are reported as substantially to completely controlled by natural enemies introduced for classical biological control in California except where disrupted, such as by pesticide applications or honeydew-seeking ants.

1. lady beetle
2. pirate bug
3. parasitic fly
4. A more recently introduced longhorned borer (*Phoracantha recurva*) is apparently less well controlled by parasites.

Is Biological Control "Safe"? One of the great benefits of biological control methods is their relative safety for human health and the environment. Most negative impacts from exotic species have been caused by undesirable organisms contaminating imported goods, by travelers carrying in pest-infested fruit, and from introduced ornamentals that escape cultivation and become weeds. These ill-advised or illegal importations are not part of biological control.

Negative impacts have occurred from poorly conceived, quasi-biological control importations of predaceous vertebrates like frogs, mongooses, and certain fish, often conducted by nonscientists. To avoid these problems, biological control researchers follow government quarantine regulations and work mostly with relatively host-specific natural enemies. Biological control provides great benefits. The environmental and public health risks from careful and well-conceived biological control projects are relatively low.

Conservation and Enhancement. Preserve resident natural enemies whenever you can by choosing cultural, mechanical, or selective chemical controls that do not interfere with or kill beneficial species. Most pests are attacked by a complex of natural enemies, and their conservation is the primary way to successfully use biological control in landscapes. Ant control, habitat manipulation, and pesticide management are key conservation strategies.

Pesticide Management. In comparison with their effect on pest species, pesticides often kill a higher proportion of predators and parasites. In addition to immediately killing natural enemies that are present at the time of spraying (contact toxicity), many pesticides leave residues on foliage that kill predators or parasites that migrate in after spraying (residual toxicity). Even if beneficial organisms survive an application, low levels of pesticide residues can interfere with natural enemies' abilities to reproduce and to locate and kill pests.

Biological control's importance often becomes apparent when broad-spectrum, persistent pesticides cause problems such as secondary pest outbreaks or pest resurgence. A secondary outbreak occurs when pesticides applied against a target pest kill natural enemies of other species, causing the formerly innocuous species to become a pest (Figure 4-3). Target pest resurgence occurs when spraying reduces the number of pests, but causes an even greater destruction of the pest's natural enemies. The resulting unfavorable ratio of pests to natural enemies permits a rapid increase or resurgence of the primary pest population.

Eliminate or reduce the use of broad-spectrum, persistent pesticides whenever possible. Carbamates, organophosphates, and pyrethroids are especially toxic to natural enemies (Table 4-4). When pesticides are used, apply them in a selective manner (such as spot applications), time

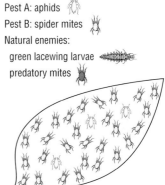
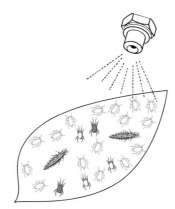

Pest A: aphids
Pest B: spider mites
Natural enemies:
  green lacewing larvae
  predatory mites

A pesticide applied to control pest A also kills natural enemies that are controlling pest B.

Released from the control exerted by natural enemies, pest B builds up to economically damaging levels.

FIGURE 4-3. Killing natural enemies often results in secondary outbreaks of insects and mites. For example, spider mites are often present on plants at low densities but become excessively abundant and cause damage when pesticides applied against other species kill the natural enemies of the spider mites. Here a pesticide applied to kill aphids (Pest A) not only killed aphids but also killed predaceous green lacewing larvae and predatory mites, leading to a secondary outbreak of spider mites (Pest B). Insecticides applied during hot weather appear to have the greatest effect on mites, sometimes causing dramatic mite outbreaks within a few days after spraying.

TABLE 4-4.

Relative Toxicity to Natural Enemies of Certain Insecticide Groups.

| INSECTICIDE | TOXICITY[1] | |
	DIRECT CONTACT	RESIDUAL CONTACT
microbials	no	no
botanicals	yes/no[2]	no
oil, soap	yes	no
IGRs,[3] imidacloprid	yes/no[2]	yes/no[2]
carbamates, organophosphates	yes	yes
pyrethroids	yes	yes

See Table 4-6 for information about specific pesticides.

1. Direct contact toxicity is killing within several hours from spraying the beneficial or its habitat. Residual contact toxicity is killing or sublethal affects (such as reduced reproduction or impaired ability to locate and kill pests) due to residues that persist.

2. Toxicity depends on the specific material and the species and life stage of the natural enemy.

3. IGRs are insect growth regulators.

applications to minimize impacts on natural enemies (such as dormant season applications), and choose insecticides that
are more specific in the types of invertebrates they kill. Wherever possible, rely
on low-persistence insecticides (such as
insecticidal soap and narrow-range oil) or
selective materials (such as *Bacillus
thuringiensis*). See Table 4-6 in the section
"Pesticides" for a list of some common insecticides, the pests they control, and
their toxicity.

Ant Control. Ants are beneficial as con-
sumers of weed seeds, predators of many
insect pests, soil builders, and nutrient
cyclers. Certain species (such as fire ants)
attack people and pets or are direct pests
of crops, feeding on nuts or fruit. The
Argentine ant and certain other species are
pests primarily because they feed on honeydew produced by aphids, soft scales,
whiteflies, mealybugs, and some other
Homoptera; these ants protect Homoptera
from predators and parasites that might
otherwise control these pests. Ants sometimes move these honeydew-producing
insects from plant to plant. Where natural
enemies are present, if ants are controlled,
populations of many pests will gradually
(over several generations of pests) be reduced as natural enemies become more
abundant. Ant control methods include
cultivation, barriers, and insecticide baits
around the base of plants. See the section
"Ants" in this chapter for identification
and management of pest species.

Habitat Manipulation. Good management
of plants and landscaped areas can enhance natural enemy effectiveness, although this has not been well researched
and there are few specific recommendations for landscapes and gardens. Reduce
dust, for example, by planting ground
covers and windbreaks. Dust can interfere
with natural enemies and may cause outbreaks of pests such as spider mites. Plant
a variety of species to improve certain biological controls by providing natural enemies with nectar, pollen, and shelter
throughout the growing season.

Flowering species can serve as insectary plants by providing natural enemies

	Moisture*	Jan.	Feb.	Mar.	Apr.	May	June	July	Aug.	Sept.	Oct.	Nov.	Dec.
Willow species	W	■	■	■									
Ceanothus spp.	D			■									
Redbud	D-I			■	■								
Mule fat	I-W				■								
Yarrow species	D-I					■	■	■					
Coffeeberry	D-I					■	■						
Hollyleaf cherry	I					■	■						
Soapbark tree	I						■						
Buckwheat species	D						■	■	■	■	■		
Elderberry species	I-W					■	■						
Toyon	D						■	■					
Creeping boobyalla	I							■					
Bottletree	I								■	■	■		
Narrowleaf milkweed	D-I						■	■					
Coyote brush	D-I										■	■	■

*Moisture requirements:
dry (D)   dry to intermediate (D-I)   intermediate (I)   intermediate to wet (I-W)   wet (W)

FIGURE 4-4. Darkened cells show the flowering periods of some perennial insectary
plants that, when used in the right combination, can provide nectar and pollen for
natural enemies sequentially throughout the year in California. Consult resources such
as Chapter 9 to identify plants that are alternate hosts of pests that can damage your
landscape and avoid using those as insectary plants.

with nectar and pollen (Figure 4-4). Adult
parasites and the adult stage of many insects with predaceous larvae (such as
green lacewings and syrphid flies) feed
only on pollen and nectar. Even if pests
are abundant for the predaceous and parasitic stages, many beneficials will do
poorly unless flowering or nectar plants
are available to adult natural enemies.
Growing a variety of diverse plant species
or certain insectary plants can provide
natural enemies with food and shelter and
increase the fecundity, longevity, and population density of beneficials.

Pruning management can conserve
parasite populations of certain pests such
as psyllids and whiteflies. For example,
eugenia psyllid is partially controlled by
an introduced *Tamarixia* sp., but parasites developing within older psyllid
nymphs are removed if plants are regularly sheared, as with eugenia managed as
topiary plants. Leaving prunings as
mulch near plants for at least 3 weeks
allows many parasites to complete their
development and emerge, while most
psyllids on cut foliage will die (Figure
4-5). Alternate pruning (pruning half of
the plants or only one-half of a single
plant this month and trimming the rest a
month or more later) is recommended for

some whitefly-infested plants such as citrus. Many whiteflies prefer to lay eggs on
the succulent new growth that develops
after pruning. Alternate pruning provides
refuges for whitefly parasitoids, allowing
parasites to emerge from older growth on
untrimmed terminals and attack whiteflies infesting the new growth of nearby,
recently trimmed plants.

Augmentation. When resident natural
enemies are insufficient, their populations
can be increased (augmented) in certain
situations through the purchase and release of commercially available beneficial
species. Natural enemy releases are most
likely to be effective in situations similar to
those where researchers or pest managers
have previously demonstrated success.
This includes situations where certain levels of pests and damage can be tolerated.
Augmentation may be more effective for
perennial plants of relatively high value.
Avoid using pesticides that may harm beneficials in systems where natural enemies
are released. Desperate situations where
pests or damage are already abundant are
not good opportunities for augmentation.

Inoculation and inundation are two
tactics for augmenting natural enemies.
In inoculative releases, pest populations

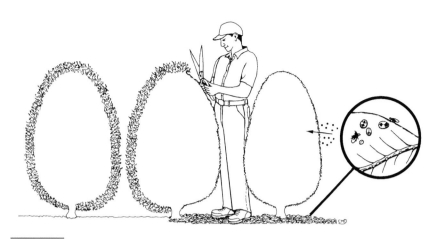

FIGURE 4-5. Pruning management conserves parasites of certain pests such as psyllids and whiteflies. Here, clippings from eugenia bushes are left as mulch on the ground for at least 3 weeks. This allows parasites to complete their development and return to the shrubs as adults that parasitize other psyllid nymphs by laying eggs in them. Most psyllids on cut foliage will die. Illustration by Christine M. Dewees from Dreistadt and Dahlsten 2001.

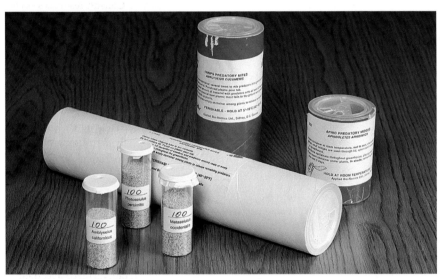

Many natural enemies are available for purchase and release, but there has been relatively little research on their use in landscapes. Conserving resident parasites and predators is usually the most effective strategy.

Releasing Natural Enemies Effectively. There has been relatively little research on how to effectively release commercially available natural enemies in landscapes. Most research and use is in field or orchard crops (such as citrus) and plants grown in greenhouses, and much of the information below has been extrapolated from those situations.

Take steps to increase the likelihood that natural enemy releases will be effective. Accurately identify the pest and its life stages. Learn about the biology of the pest and its natural enemies. Most parasitic insects attack only certain stages of their host; release the appropriate natural enemy species when the pest is in its vulnerable life stage. Some parasites lay their eggs in one host life stage, but the parasite does not kill its host and emerge until the host has developed to another stage. For example, the holes in mature female scales are often caused by parasites that attacked and laid their eggs in the host when it was immature. The pest life stage that can be effectively controlled with natural enemies may also be different from the pest stage that damages plants. For example, *Trichogramma* species wasps kill only moth and butterfly eggs; they are not effective against caterpillars. *Trichogramma* must be released when moths or butterflies are laying eggs, before plant-damaging caterpillars become abundant.

Anticipate pest problems and plan releases ahead of time. Begin making releases before pests are too abundant or intolerable damage is imminent. Avoid applying broad-spectrum or persistent pesticides, or, if they are used, use them as spot sprays. Be prepared to tolerate some pests and possible damage since pests must be present to provide food for natural enemies. Remember that natural enemies are living organisms that require water, food, and shelter. Natural enemies may be adversely affected by extreme conditions such as high temperatures. Keep them in a cool place and release them at night or early in the day if conditions are hot.

Effectively releasing natural enemies requires knowledge, practice, and

are low and relatively few natural enemies are released. The progeny of these predators or parasites, not the same individuals released, are expected to eventually provide biological control. Releasing the mealybug destroyer lady beetle (*Cryptolaemus montrouzieri*) in the spring to control mealybugs is an example of inoculative release. The mealybug destroyer is effective in killing mealybug species that feed openly on foliage or bark, but it overwinters poorly in California and often needs to be reintroduced to target areas in the spring. Inoculation can be used in combination with certain pesticides, such as by reducing high spider mite populations with an oil or soap spray, then introducing predatory mites a day or so later before pest mites become abundant.

Inundative releases involve large numbers of natural enemies, often released several times over a growing season. The natural enemies released, and possibly their progeny, are expected to provide biological control. Periodically releasing *Trichogramma* species (parasitic wasps) to kill moth eggs or introducing lady beetles ("ladybugs") to suppress aphids are examples of inundative biological control.

imagination. Releases often fail because information or experience was inadequate, the wrong species was released, the timing was incorrect, or pesticides were applied. Obtain beneficials from a quality supplier; the quality of commercially available natural enemies is not regulated and sometimes may be poor. Some of the natural enemy species that are sold are available because they are the easiest and most economical to produce and sell, not because they are the most effective species. Available natural enemies may not always be able to keep pest populations below acceptable damage thresholds. In some cases, the value of the plants and availability of alternatives may not justify the cost and effort of releasing natural enemies. Common pests for which natural enemies can be purchased and released are listed in Table 4-5, which also includes beneficial nematodes and bacteria that are discussed in the section "Microbial and Biological Insecticides." Specific strategies for augmentative releases are discussed in the sections on that particular pest.

The convergent lady beetle (*Hippodamia convergens*) is probably the most widely sold natural enemy. Natural populations of these lady beetles, sometimes called "ladybugs," are important aphid predators, as discussed in the section "Aphids."

Releases of preying mantids are not recommended. Preying mantids feed indiscriminately on pest and beneficial species, including other mantids and honey bees. Although preying mantids are fascinating creatures to study and care for as pets, their release is unlikely to provide effective pest control.

TYPES OF NATURAL ENEMIES

Three primary groups of natural enemies are used in biological pest control: pathogens, parasites, and predators. Many natural enemies, including most parasites, pathogens, and some predators, attack only one or several closely related pest species. For example, syrphid fly larvae and the convergent lady beetle feed primarily on aphids. Other more specialized

natural enemies are discussed in the individual pest sections.

Pathogens. Pathogens are microorganisms including bacteria, fungi, certain nematodes, protozoa, and viruses that infect and kill the host. Populations of aphids, caterpillars, certain mites, and other invertebrates are sometimes drastically reduced by naturally occurring pathogens; although special conditions, such as prolonged high humidity or dense pest populations, are often required. Certain pathogens are commercially available as biological or microbial pesticides and are discussed later in this chapter in the section "Microbial and Biological Insecticides." These include *Bacillus thuringiensis*, entomopathogenic nematodes, and microorganism by-products such as avermectins and spinosyns.

Parasites. A parasite is an organism that lives and feeds in or on a larger host. Insect parasites (more precisely called par-

asitoids) are smaller than their host and develop inside, or attached to the outside, of the host's body. Often only the immature stage of the parasite feeds on the host, and it kills only one host individual during its development (see Figure 4-6). However, adult females of certain parasites (such as many wasps that attack scales and whiteflies) feed on their hosts. Pest mortality resulting from this host feeding by adults can be an easily overlooked but important source of biological control in addition to the host mortality caused by parasitism.

Most parasitic insects are either flies (Diptera) or wasps (Hymenoptera). The most common parasitic flies are in the family Tachinidae. Adult tachinids often resemble house flies, and their larvae are maggots that feed inside their host.

Parasitic Hymenoptera occur in over three dozen families. Aphelinidae is one of the most important, with about 1,000 known species of tiny wasps that attack aphids, mealybugs, psyllids, scales, and

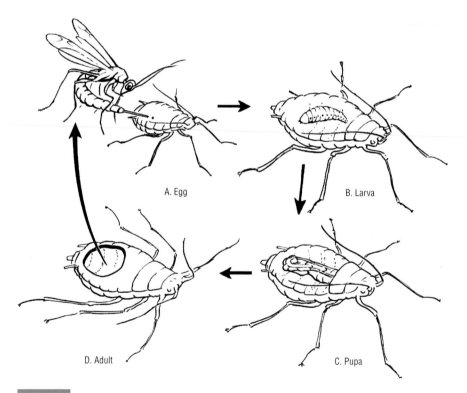

FIGURE 4-6. In many cases, only the immature stage of a parasite feeds on the host, as illustrated here with a species that attacks aphids. *A.* An adult parasite lays an egg inside a live aphid. *B.* The egg hatches into a parasite larva that grows as it feeds on the aphid's insides. *C.* After killing the aphid, the parasite pupates. *D.* The wasp chews a hole and emerges from the dead aphid, then flies off to find and parasitize other aphids.

TABLE 4-5.

Some Woody Landscape Invertebrate Pests That Have Commercially Available Natural Enemies.

| PEST TARGETED | NATURAL ENEMIES | | SEE PAGE |
	COMMON NAMES	SCIENTIFIC NAME	
aphids	lacewings	*Chrysoperla* spp.	63
	lady beetle	*Hippodamia convergens*	110
carpenterworm	entomopathogenic nematodes	*Steinernema carpocapsae*	69, 194
caterpillars	egg parasites	*Trichogramma* spp.	73
	microbial insecticide	*Bacillus thuringiensis* ssp. *kurstaki*	68, 75
	nuclear polyhedrosis viruses	several host-specific species	
clearwing moth larvae	entomopathogenic nematodes	*Steinernema carpocapsae*	69, 190–191
elm leaf beetle	microbial insecticide	*Bacillus thuringiensis* ssp. *tenebrionis*	68, 89–90
Japanese beetle[1]	entomopathogenic nematodes	*Heterorhabditis bacteriophora* *Steinernema glaseri*	69, 98
mealybugs	citrus mealybug parasite	*Leptomastix dactylopii* and others	127
	lacewings	*Chrysoperla* spp.	63
	mealybug destroyer	*Cryptolaemus montrouzieri*	129
	predatory mites	*Neoseiulus* (=*Amblyseius*), *Metaseiulus*, and *Phytoseiulus* spp.	202–203
scale insects	predaceous lady beetle	*Rhyzobius* (=*Lindorus*) *lophanthae*	147
	red scale parasite	*Aphytis melinus*	131
	soft scale parasites	*Metaphycus helvolus, Microterys flavus*	136–137
snail, brown garden	predatory snail[2]	*Rumina decollata*[2]	207
spider mites	lacewings	*Chrysoperla* spp.	63
	predatory lady beetle	*Stethorus punctillum*	202
	predatory mites	*Neoseiulus* (=*Amblyseius*), *Metaseiulus*, and *Phytoseiulus* spp.	202–203
thrips	lacewings	*Chrysoperla* spp.	63
	pirate bug	*Orius tristicolor*	159
	predatory mites	*Neoseiulus* (=*Amblyseius*) and *Euseius* spp.	159, 202–203
weevils, root or soil-dwelling	entomopathogenic nematodes	*Steinernema carpocapsae, Heterorhabditis bacteriophora*	63, 96
whiteflies	lacewings	*Chrysoperla* spp.	63
	predaceous lady beetle	*Delphastus pusillus*	125
	parasitic wasps	*Eretmocerus* and *Encarsia* spp.	123–125

Release of natural enemies has been consistently successful in controlling pests in relatively few situations. Other natural enemies are commercially available; only the better-studied species are listed here. See Suppliers for additional species and sources of natural enemies.

1. In the western United States, take suspected Japanese beetles to a Cooperative Extension or department of agriculture office; officials will take action to prevent this pest from becoming established.

2. Legal for release only in certain areas of southern and central California.

whiteflies. The Encyrtidae family includes over 3,000 species that attack primarily scales and mealybugs, but also beetles, bugs, cockroaches, flies, and moths. Braconidae and Ichneumonidae are often large wasps, but they do not sting people. These groups include about 5,000 species in North America that commonly parasitize beetle, caterpillar, and sawfly larvae and pupae. Aphidiidae attack aphids. Trichogrammatidae parasitize insect eggs. Wasps in the family Eulophidae attack beetles, caterpillars, flies, scales, and thrips.

Predators. Immature predators (and in certain groups, also the adults) kill and feed on several to many other individual prey during their lifetimes. Some predators are specialized and feed on only one or a few closely related species, but many predators are more generalized and feed on a variety of similar types of organisms. These "general predators" feed opportunistically on currently abundant prey and can be important in suppressing pest populations. Some species are predaceous only during their immature stage, while others are predaceous as both adults and immatures. Depending on the species, adult predators also (or only) feed on pollen, nectar, and honeydew.

Predators important in the control of insect pests include beetles (in the insect order Coleoptera), bugs (Hemiptera), flies (Diptera), lacewings (Neuroptera), and wasps (Hymenoptera). Spiders (Class Araneae, order Arachnida) are also important predators of insects. Mites in the family Phytoseiidae are very important in the control of pest mites and certain insects.

Encourage general predators by maintaining landscapes with diverse plant species. Tolerate low populations of plant-feeding insects and mites so that some food is always available for predators. Avoid using pesticides that adversely affect natural enemies and treat only heavily infested spots instead of entire plants. Encourage general predators so that if pest outbreaks do develop, the

predators will already be present to help provide control. Because they depend on specific prey, more specialized predators (and many parasites and pathogens) may not provide much control until pest populations become abundant. Once outbreaks develop, these more specialized natural enemies may rapidly increase in abundance and are more often responsible for reducing high pest populations than are more general predators.

Birds and Other Vertebrates

Insects are important food for many birds, mammals, reptiles, and amphibians. Some birds feed almost exclusively on insects, and many species that normally feed on seeds or other plant parts rely on insects to feed their nestlings. Caterpillars are apparently the pests most commonly fed upon by many birds. Populations of desirable birds can be increased by growing a mixture of trees, shrubs, and ground covers of different size, species, and density and by providing water and supplemental food. Many species of insect-eating birds nest in cavities in dead trees. Dead and dying trees can rarely be left in urban landscapes because they are hazardous and may fall; a practical alternative is to provide nesting boxes or bird houses. The value of dead and dying trees as wildlife habitat should be assessed along with the hazard when considering tree removal.

Spiders

Spiders are very common invertebrates. Unlike insects, which have six legs and three main body parts, spiders have eight legs, two main body parts, and are classified in the arachnid group along with mites. Most spiders feed entirely on insects, commonly capturing prey in webs

All spiders are predaceous, usually feeding on insects. This adult funnel weaver spider (*Hololena nedra*, Agelenidae family), is a sit-and-wait predator that captures insects that blunder into its webbing.

or stalking them across the ground or vegetation and pouncing on them. Spiders seek to avoid people, and most are harmless to humans.

Mites

Although some mites feed on plants and can become pests, many species of mites are predators of pest mites and insects. Mites often go unnoticed because they are tiny and natural controls frequently keep their populations low. Mites, unlike insects, do not have antennae, segmented bodies, or wings. Most predaceous mites are long-legged, pear-shaped, and shiny. Many are translucent, although after feeding they often take on the color of their host and may be bright red, yellow, or green. Predaceous mite eggs are colorless and oblong, compared with the eggs of plant-feeding mites, which are commonly spherical and colored to opaque. One way to distinguish plant-feeding mites from predaceous species is to closely observe them on your plants with a good hand lens. Predaceous species appear more active than plant-feeding species; they stop only to feed. In comparison with pest mites, predaceous mites are often larger and do not occur in large groups. See the section "Mites" near the end of this chapter for photographs and more information.

Lacewings and Dustywings

Lacewing and dustywing larvae are flattened, tapered at the tail, and have distinct legs. Their long, curved mandibles are used for grasping prey. The larvae resemble tiny alligators; lacewing larvae are sometimes called aphidlions because they often feed voraciously on aphids. However, they also feed on a wide variety of other small insects, including leafhoppers, mealybugs, whiteflies, caterpillars, psyllids, and insect eggs. The less commonly seen dustywings feed on mites and virtually any tiny insect they can capture.

Adult lacewings have large, lacy-veined wings. Depending on the species, adults may feed on insects or only on honeydew, nectar, and pollen. The green lacewings (*Chrysopa* and *Chrysoperla* spp., family Chrysopidae), have green, slender bodies and green wings with netlike veins. Adult brown lacewings (such as the *Hemerobius* species, family Hemerobiidae) resemble green lacewings, except that brown lacewings are typically about half as large and brown. Adult dustywings (Coniopterygidae) resemble lacewings, except whitish powder covers their wings, obscuring the vein pattern. Green lacewings lay their oblong green to gray eggs on slender stalks, either singly or in groups. Stalks help protect the eggs from predators and from their cannibalistic siblings. Brown lacewings' oblong eggs are laid singly on plants and resemble syrphid eggs. Dustywings pupate in an inconspicuous, flat, white silken cocoon, often on the underside of leaves.

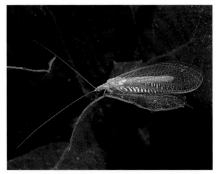

This adult green lacewing (*Chrysoperla* sp.) is named for its green body and wings with netlike veins. Adult brown lacewings look similar but are usually about one half as large and are brownish.

Green lacewings lay their oblong eggs on slender stalks. Depending on the species, eggs are laid singly or in groups, as shown here for *Chrysopa nigricornis*.

A green lacewing (*Chrysoperla carnea*) pupating, or changing from larva to adult, within a loosely woven silken cocoon.

This alligatorlike green lacewing larva (*Chrysoperla rufilabris*) is grasping a rose aphid with it mandibles. Lacewings' varied prey includes caterpillars, leafhoppers, mealybugs, psyllids, whiteflies, and insect eggs.

Brown lacewing eggs, such as this *Hemerobius* sp., are oblong and are laid singly on their side on plants without any attaching stalk. Although brown lacewing eggs resemble syrphid eggs, brown lacewing eggs have a tiny knob projecting at one end and have a relatively smooth surface. In comparison, syrphid eggs lack a terminal knob and appear to have fibers or lines crisscrossing the egg surface.

GREEN LACEWING

egg   larva   pupa   adult

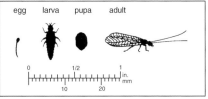

BROWN LACEWING

adult

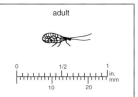

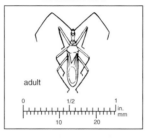

An adult assassin bug (*Zelus renardii*) eating a lygus bug. Both nymphs and adults prey on a wide variety of insects.

An adult flower bug or pirate bug (*Anthocoris nemoralis*) feeding on an acacia psyllid nymph. These tiny predators consume mites, insect eggs, and various small, soft-bodied pests.

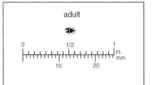

MINUTE PIRATE BUG

adult

ASSASSIN BUG

adult

An adult syrphid, commonly called a flower fly or hover fly, requires pollen to reproduce. It is sometimes mistaken for a honey bee; syrphid flies cannot sting.

SYRPHID

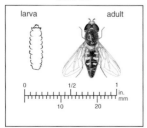

larva   adult

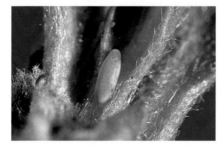

Syrphid fly eggs are elongate-oval, have a reticulated surface, and are laid singly near aphid colonies.

Assassin Bugs

Assassin bugs (family Reduviidae) are oval or elongate. Most are black and reddish or brown. Assassin bugs have a long, narrow head with an extended, needlelike beak and are larger and have longer legs than most other predaceous bugs. They feed on most insect species and often can be observed near flowers waiting for prey.

Pirate Bugs

Pirate bugs (family Anthocoridae), including species sometimes called minute pirate bugs, are small, oval insects. The adults of many species are black or purplish with white markings and have a triangular head. As with most true bugs, adults have a triangle or X-shaped pattern on the back caused by the folding of their half-dark and half-clear wings. The small nymphs are commonly yellowish or reddish brown and may be overlooked in monitoring. *Orius* and *Anthocoris* are two common genera. Adults and nymphs commonly feed on aphids, mites, thrips, psyllids, and insect eggs.

Predaceous Flies

Larvae of many flies prey on soft-bodied insects, such as aphids, mealybugs, and some scales. Predaceous groups include aphid flies (family Chamaemyiidae), predatory gall midges (Cecidomyiidae), and syrphid flies (Syrphidae). Larvae are maggotlike and can be green, yellow, brown, orangish, or whitish. Syrphids, also known as hover flies or flower flies, are probably the most common predaceous flies. Adult syrphids resemble honey bees but do not sting. They are often seen feeding on flower nectar. Adult aphid flies are small and chunky; gall midges are small, slender, and delicate.

Lady Beetles

Adults and larvae of lady beetles (family Coccinellidae) are predators of pest mites and most soft-bodied or sessile (immobile) insects, including aphids, mealybugs, scales, and whiteflies. Over 500 different species occur in the United States. The convergent lady beetle (*Hippodamia convergens*) and many other orangish lady beetle species feed primarily on whatever species of aphids are abundant. Certain species such as multicolored Asian lady beetle feed on a variety of pests, including aphids, psyllids, and scales. The vedalia beetle (*Rodolia cardinalis*) feeds on only one species, the cottony cushion scale (*Icerya purchasi*). Other species of lady beetles specialize on mites or certain insects. For photographs and more information on specific lady beetles, see the sections in this chapter "Aphids," "Mealybugs," "Mites," "Psyllids," and "Scales."

Predaceous Ground Beetles

Predaceous ground beetle (family Carabidae) adults are commonly black or dark reddish, although some species are brilliantly colored or iridescent. They dwell on the ground and are most active at night. Adults have long legs and are fast runners. Larvae dwell in litter or the soil, are elongate, and have a large head with distinct mandibles. Carabids feed on snails, slugs, root-feeding insects, and insect larvae and pupae.

Soldier Beetles

Adult soldier beetles (family Cantharidae) are long, narrow beetles, usually red or orange with black, gray, or brown wing covers. Adults are often observed on flowers. The dark, flattened larvae are predaceous, as are the adults of many species. They feed on aphids and the eggs and larvae of beetles, moths, and butterflies.

This adult predaceous ground beetle (*Calosoma* sp.) stalks its prey on soil or in litter.

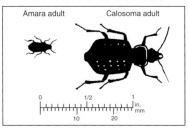

PREDACEOUS GROUND BEETLES

Amara adult   Calosoma adult

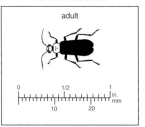

SOLDIER BEETLE

adult

Adult soldier beetles are long and narrow, often with an orangish head and thorax and dark wing covers. They eat aphids and the eggs and larvae of beetles and moths.

PESTICIDES

Pesticides are substances applied to kill or repel pests or control pest damage. They can provide a quick but temporary reduction in pest populations. Many pesticides of low toxicity to humans and pets are available, including insecticidal soap, narrow-range oil, botanicals, and microbial insecticides. These selective, less toxic, or less persistent pesticides can reduce, delay, or prevent future outbreaks (pest resurgence) or outbreaks of other potential pests (secondary pest outbreaks), in part because they are not as harmful as other pesticides to natural enemies. If an application needs to be made, whenever possible choose a pesticide with little or no contact or residual toxicity to natural enemies (Table 4-6).

Some pests develop resistance to pesticides so that spraying becomes less effective. Resistance develops because the genetic makeup of some individuals in a pest population happens to make them less susceptible to pesticides. These tolerant individuals are more likely to survive an application and produce descendants. Repeated applications over several generations eventually result in a pest population composed primarily of tolerant or resistant individuals, as discussed and illustrated in the section "Pesticide Resistance" in Chapter 2.

Pesticides sometimes damage plants (cause phytotoxicity), especially if plants lack proper cultural care, environmental conditions are extreme, or pesticides are used carelessly, as discussed in the section "Pesticides and Phytotoxicity" in

TABLE 4-6.

Toxicity to Invertebrates of Some Insecticides and Acaricides.

PESTICIDE COMMON NAME (TRADE NAME)	CLASS	ACTIVITY AGAINST INVERTEBRATES	EFFECT ON NATURAL ENEMIES	
			IMMEDIATE IMPACT	DURATION OF IMPACT
abamectin, avermectins (Avid[1])	M	moderate: mites, leafminers	predatory mites: high; many insects: low	predatory mites and affected insects: long
acephate (Orthene)	OP	broad: insects and beneficial mites	high	intermediate
azadirachtin (Azatin[1], Bioneem, Neemazad[1])	B, IGR	broad: insects and beneficial mites	moderate	short
Bacillus thuringiensis ssp. *kurstaki* (Caterpillar Killer, Dipel, WormKiller)	M	narrow: caterpillars	none	none
Bacillus thuringiensis ssp. *tenebrionis*	M	narrow: leaf beetles	none	none
Beauveria bassiana (BotaniGard[1])	M	narrow: some soft-bodied predators	low	short
bifenthrin (Attain[1], Talstar[1], Ortho Rose & Flower Insect Killer)	P	broad: insects and beneficial mites	high	long
carbaryl (Garden Tech Sevin, Sevin, XLR Plus[1])	C	broad: insects and beneficial mites	high	long
chlorpyrifos (Dursban[1])	OP	broad: insects and beneficial mites	high	intermediate
cinnamaldehyde (Cinnamite[1])	B	intermediate: aphids, thrips and mites	low	short
copper bands	CON	narrow: snails and slugs	none	none
cyfluthrin (Bayer Advanced Garden Lawn & Garden Multi-Insect Killer, Tempo[1])	P	broad: insects and beneficial mites	high	intermediate
cypermethrin (Cynoff[1], Raid)	P	broad: insects and beneficial mites	high	intermediate
diazinon[1]	OP	broad: insects and beneficial mites	high	intermediate to long
dicofol (Kelthane[1])	CH	narrow: pest mites and beneficial mites	beneficial mites: high	beneficial mites: long
diflubenzuron (Dimilin[1])	IGR	intermediate: immature stage insects	moderate to low	short

PESTICIDE COMMON NAME (TRADE NAME)	CLASS	ACTIVITY AGAINST INVERTEBRATES	EFFECT ON NATURAL ENEMIES	
			IMMEDIATE IMPACT	DURATION OF IMPACT
dimethoate (Cygon[1])	OP	broad: insects and beneficial mites	high	long
fipronil[2]	CH	broad: chewing and sucking insects	moderate to low	short to intermediate
fluvalinate (Mavrik[1])	P	broad: insects and mites	high	long
hydramethylnon[2]	IGR	intermediate: immature stage insects	moderate to low	short
imidacloprid (Bayer Advanced Garden Tree & Shrub Insect Control, Marathon[1], Merit[1])	N	intermediate: mostly sucking insects, some chewing pests	low on many, exceptions include vedalia lady beetle	short to intermediate
malathion	OP	broad: insects and beneficial mites	high	intermediate
metaldehyde (Deadline)	A	narrow: pest snails and slugs and beneficial snails	decollate snail: high; insects and mites: low	decollate snail: variable; insects and mites: short
neem oil (Neem Concentrate, Triact[1])	B, CON	intermediate: mostly soft-bodied insects	moderate	short
oil, narrow-range (SunSpray)	CON	broad: exposed insects and mites	moderate to high	short to none
oxydemeton-methyl (Metasystox-R[1])	OP	narrow: sucking insects and mites high; insects: low	beneficial mites: insects: short to none	mites: intermediate
permethrin (Ambush[1], Pounce[1], Pramex[1])	P	broad: insects and beneficial mites	high	long
pyrethrins (pyrethrum); pyrethrins + piperonyl butoxide (Pyrenone[1])	B	broad: insects	high	short
resmethrin	P	broad: insects and beneficial mites	high	intermediate
rotenone	B	narrow: aphids and some soft scales	moderate to none	short to none
sabadilla[1]	B	narrow: citrus thrips	low to none	short to none
insecticidal soap (M-Pede[1], Safer)	CON	broad: insects and beneficial mites	moderate	short to none
spinosad (Conserve[1], Monterey Garden Insect Spray)	M	intermediate: caterpillars, katydids, leafminers, thrips	adult parasitic wasps: high; predators: low	intermediate
sticky materials	CON	narrow: trunk climbing insects and snails	moderate to none	long to none
sulfur	IO	narrow: mites and citrus thrips	beneficial mites and certain parasitic wasps: moderate	mites and certain parasitic wasps: intermediate

Immediate impact on natural enemies is the killing of natural enemies resulting from spraying the pest or its habitat, commonly called contact toxicity. Duration of impact on natural enemies refers to persistent residues that kill natural enemies that migrate in and contact previously treated areas, commonly called residual toxicity. Stated toxicities should be used only as a general guide. Actual impact of specific chemicals depends in part on concentration, exposure, environmental conditions, formulation, and the species and life stage of the organism. Laws, regulations, and information concerning pesticides change frequently. Certain of these materials may not be registered (legal) for use in your situation. Consult a current label and the local department of agriculture for details on legal pesticide use.

1. May be available only to professional applicators.

2. Often used at very low rates, mixed with bait, which minimizes exposure and hazard.

Sources: Croft 1990, Hassan et al. 1994, Jepson 1989, Ohr et al. 2002, *Pesticide Wise* www.pw.ucr.edu, Ware 1983.

KEY

A	acetaldehyde
B	botanical
C	carbamate
CH	chlorinated hydrocarbon
CON	contact including smothering or barrier effect
IGR	insect growth regulator
IO	inorganic
M	microbial
N	chloronicotinyl nitroguanidine
OP	organophosphate
P	pyrethroid

Chapter 6. Check the label for plant species that should not be sprayed with that material. Before spraying a plant with a new pesticide, consider spraying a small portion of it and examining it for damage during the following week before spraying the rest of the plant.

Understand the relative toxicity, mode of action, persistence, and safe and legal use of pesticides. You can then more favorably manage natural enemies in the landscape and avoid other potential problems. For more discussion on using pesticides effectively and minimizing their hazards, see Chapter 2 and publications such as *The Safe and Effective Use of Pesticides* (O'Connor-Marer 2000).

Microbial and Biological Insecticides.

Microbial pesticides, including products sometimes called biologicals, are naturally occurring pathogens or their by-products that are commercially produced for pest control. Most microbials affect only a certain group or several related groups of pests. Most of these commercial products present little or no toxicity to humans. Many have low toxicity to beneficial insects or significantly lower toxicity to natural enemies than broad-spectrum, persistent pesticides. Abamectin, *Bacillus thuringiensis*, *Beauveria bassiana*, entomopathogenic nematodes, and spinosyns are discussed here.

Abamectin. Abamectin is a mixture of several avermectins, which are compounds derived from the soil bacterium *Streptomyces avermitilis.* Commercial abamectin is a fermentation product of this bacterium. It acts as an insecticide and miticide that affects the nervous system of invertebrates and paralyzes them. It controls several pests, including leaf beetles, leafminers, mites, and thrips. Abamectin has some translaminar activity (is absorbed short distances into leaves). It has a short residual toxicity of several days or less. Certain abamectin products may be available only to professional applicators.

Bacillus thuringiensis. Bacillus thuringiensis, or Bt, is a group of naturally occurring

bacteria that cause disease in certain insects. Bts are produced commercially by a fermentation process similar to brewing beer. Different *Bacillus thuringiensis* subspecies (ssp.) are available for controlling different pests. *Bacillus thuringiensis* ssp. *kurstaki* is the most commonly used microbial insecticide; it kills moth and butterfly larvae that eat sprayed foliage. Bt ssp. *tenebrionis* (Btt) primarily kills leaf beetles. Bt ssp. *israelensis* (Bti) is applied to water to kill mosquito and black fly larvae and to soil to kill fungus gnat larvae.

Bt does not affect humans or most beneficial species. To be effective, it must be eaten by the pest (Figure 4-7), so

thorough spray coverage is critical. Bt may need to be applied several times at intervals because it degrades quickly, and often not all of the individuals in a pest population are in a Bt-susceptible stage at the same time.

Beauveria bassiana. Beauveria bassiana is a fungus that can control aphids, thrips, whiteflies, and certain other insects. It may be available only to professional applicators, and its use is recommended mostly in conservatories, greenhouses, and crops, not in landscapes. Excellent spray coverage and multiple applications are required to achieve control.

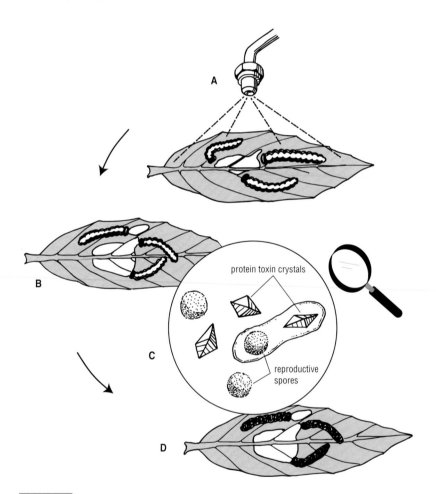

protein toxin crystals

reproductive spores

FIGURE 4-7. The most commonly used *Bacillus thuringiensis* (Bt ssp. *kurstaki*) controls moth and butterfly larvae. *A.* Bt must be sprayed during warm, dry conditions to thoroughly cover foliage where young caterpillars are actively feeding. *B.* Within about 1 day of consuming treated foliage, caterpillars become infected, relatively inactive, and stop feeding. *C.* An enlarged view of Bt in the gut of a caterpillar. The natural bacteria are rod-shaped and contain reproductive spores and protein toxin crystals (endotoxins), but the spores and protein crystals are separate components in some commercial Bt formulations, and these separate components and one whole bacterium (greatly enlarged) are shown here. *D.* Within several days of ingesting Bt, caterpillars darken and die, and their carcasses eventually decompose into a dark, liquidy, putrid mass.

Entomopathogenic Nematodes. Nematodes are tiny (usually microscopic) roundworms. Pest species feed on plants, as discussed in Chapter 8. Nematodes that kill insects are beneficial. They are called entomopathogenic nematodes because invertebrate hosts are killed by the nematode in combination with associated bacteria, usually within several days of infection (Figure 4-8).

Many insects are susceptible to entomopathogenic nematodes. *Heterorhabditis* and *Steinernema* species (families Heterorhabditidae and Steinernematidae, respectively) entomopathogenic nematodes are commercially available for application primarily against soil-dwelling insects (including armyworms, cutworms, root or soil-dwelling weevils, white grubs, and wireworms) and certain boring pests (such as carpenterworms and clearwing moth larvae). Application methods include squirting a water solution of nematodes into borer tunnel openings or drenching the soil beneath infested plants when pest larvae or pupae are present. When drenching, soil temperatures should be at least 60°F. Keep soil moist (well irrigated) but not soggy before application and for 2 weeks afterward.

Heterorhabditis bacteriophora and *Steinernema carpocapsae* are the most commonly sold nematodes, available mostly through the mail. Obtaining a relatively fresh product, such as by ordering directly from nematode producers or a primary distributor, is critical. See Suppliers for sources of beneficial nematodes. Nematodes are perishable, so store them under cool, dark conditions. Nematodes can be mixed and applied in combination with certain other materials, such as insecticidal soap and *Bacillus thuringiensis*. In addition to applying nematodes in conventional sprayers, nematodes can also be applied through irrigation systems as long as they are not mixed with fungicides or other potentially toxic materials. Irrigation water should be well aerated to provide nematodes with adequate oxygen. Each batch of nematodes should not be immersed for longer than about 24 hours before application.

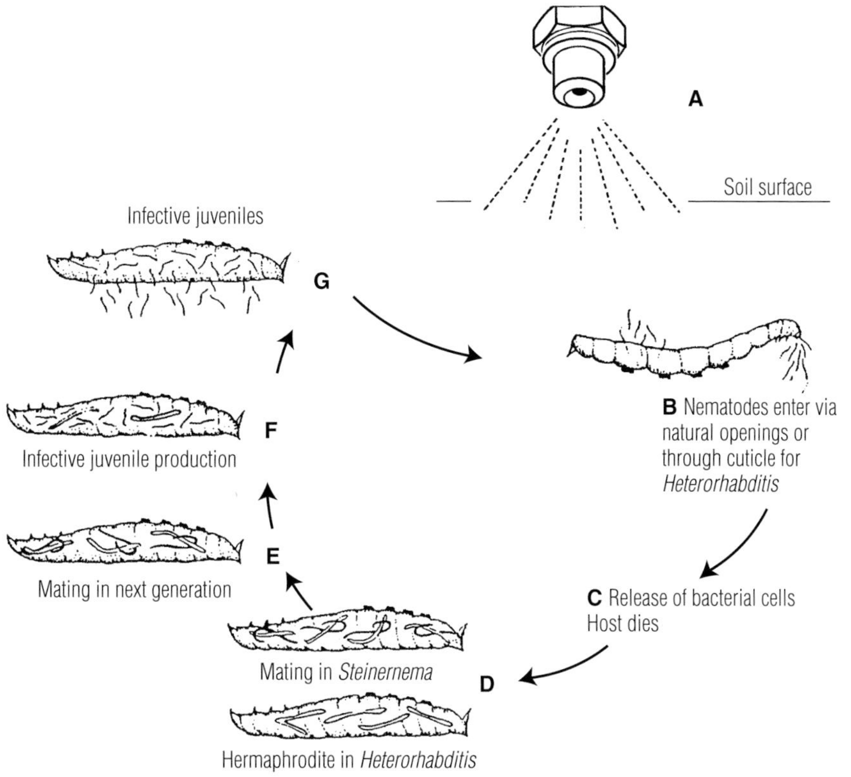

Spinosyns. The spinosyns are produced by fermentation of by-products from the bacterium *Saccharopolyspora spinosa* (Actinomycetes). Spinosyns are toxic to most caterpillars, fly larvae, thrips, and certain species of beetles and wasps. They are quick-acting, both on contact and when eaten by insects. They have some translaminar activity (are absorbed short distances into leaves), have relatively short residual activity, and degrade rapidly. One of the most effective microbials, spinosyns have relatively low toxicity to people, but can be highly toxic to certain natural enemies.

Botanicals. Botanical pesticides are derived from plants. Most botanicals are of low toxicity to humans; however, nicotine sulfate is a notable exception. Some, such as rotenone, can be highly irritating to eyes, skin, and (if inhaled) lungs. Botanicals are effective against many exposed-feeding insects. They break down rapidly after application, which makes them relatively safe for the environment and natural enemies of pests. Most botanicals have only contact toxicity, provide little or no residual control, and must be applied precisely when and where pests are present to be effective.

Azadirachtin, cinnamaldehyde (also called cinnamic aldehyde), citrus oils (limonenes), and pyrethrins (pyrethrum) are among the available botanicals. Natural cinnamaldehyde is derived from the bark of several *Cinnamomum* species trees, which are the source of the food

FIGURE 4-8. Life cycle of beneficial nematodes. A. Infective-stage nematodes are applied to soil. B. The nematodes seek a host and enter it. C. Once inside, the host is killed by nematodes and mutualistic bacteria carried by the nematodes. D. Nematodes feed, grow, mature, and reproduce. The initial development of nematodes in the host differs because there are no separate male and female nematodes in the first generation of *Heterorhabditis*, which are hermaphrodites. E. All generations of *Steinernema* and subsequent generations of *Heterorhabditis* in the host produce both males and females. F. Females produce infective-stage juvenile nematodes inside the dead host. G. Infective nematodes exit and seek hosts. Nematodes persist in media and in dead hosts and, under suitable conditions, can provide residual control. The entire life cycle from infection of the host to release of the new infective generation takes 7 to 14 days. Adapted from Kaya 1993.

spice cinnamon. The cinnamaldehyde used in pesticides is synthesized and applied to control exposed eggs of mites and certain insects and fungi, as discussed in Chapter 5. Limonene (d-limonene) is a contact insecticide extracted and refined from citrus fruit peels. Pyrethrins are derived from chrysanthemum flowers grown in Africa and South America. Pyrethrins are very fast-acting in knocking down and paralyzing insects, but insects often recover unless a petroleum-derived synergist (piperonyl butoxide, or PBO) is added to increase pyrethrins' effectiveness. Certain products combine pyrethrins with other active ingredients, such as insecticidal soap or oil.

Azadirachtin is extracted from the seeds of the neem tree. Neem extracts are toxic to a wide range of invertebrate pests and deter certain pests from feeding or laying eggs for a short period after treating plants. Neem oils can kill exposed, soft-bodied insects and mites on contact and can control certain pathogens such as powdery mildew and rust. The active ingredient, azadirachtin, is slow-acting as an insect growth regulator that kills immature insects when they attempt to molt to their next life stage.

Read the labels of botanicals carefully before use and observe all recommended precautions; for example, rotenone is extremely toxic to fish and must be used with great care near water. Insects and fish metabolize rotenone into breakdown products that are highly toxic to them.

Inorganics. Inorganic insecticides are elements or salts usually refined from minerals. Sulfur, probably the first effective pesticide discovered, is primarily used to control plant fungal diseases, as discussed in Chapter 5, but it also controls mites. Do not treat plants labeled as susceptible to damage by sulfur and do not apply it during very hot or humid weather. Sulfur can irritate the skin and is harmful if inhaled, so wear protective equipment and appropriate clothing during mixing and application.

Insect Growth Regulators. Insect growth regulators (IGRs) control certain

pests by inhibiting or mimicking insect hormones. For example, certain IGRs prevent insects from molting to their next life stage, thereby causing insects to die. IGRs are relatively selective (because they may kill only immature insects, not adults) and can be relatively slow-acting. IGRs include the azadirachtin discussed in the section "Botanicals," above; the synthetic hydramethylnon, used in certain ant baits; and diflubenzuron, which is sprayed to control caterpillars.

Insecticidal Soaps. Insecticide soaps are salts of fatty acids made from animal fat (such as fish oil or lard) or plant oils (including coconut, cottonseed, and palm). Insecticidal soap is effective against mites and soft-bodied insects including aphids, thrips, immature scales, and leafhoppers. Insecticidal soap has low toxicity to humans and wildlife, but can damage some plants, especially species with hairy leaves. Soaps may not be as effective as horticultural oils, but they can be combined with other active ingredients, such as pyrethrins. Soaps are easily applied as spot treatments using a hand-pump sprayer; good coverage is essential. Before treating a plant, consider making a test application to a portion of the foliage and observing it for damage over several days before spraying it further. Do not treat water-stressed plants or spray when it is expected to be hot, windy, or humid. Early morning or late afternoon may be the best application times.

Oils. Narrow-range or horticultural oils, also called supreme or superior oil, are highly refined petroleum products manufactured specifically to control pests on plants. In addition to the botanical neem oil, other plant-derived oils, such as those made from cottonseed, may also be available. In comparison with motor oils or many other petroleum products, narrow-range oils have low toxicity to humans and most wildlife. Some products may irritate skin and, as with all pesticides, should be kept away from eyes.

Oil smothers insects by clogging spiracles, the tiny openings in insect bodies

through which they breathe. Narrow-range oil apparently also disrupts cell membranes, interfering with normal metabolic activities. Oils are effective against exposed eggs and soft-bodied immature and adult pests, including aphids, mealybugs, scales, and whiteflies.

Oils formerly were applied only to leafless deciduous trees during the winter as "dormant oil" or delayed dormant sprays. Delayed dormant season sprays are applied before leaves flush but after buds have begun to swell in the spring. Oil at this time controls aphid eggs, mites, scales, and other pests overwintering on bark. Foliar season sprays of narrow-range oils are now a popular and effective way to control many exposed-feeding invertebrates. However, dormant season or delayed dormant applications are still very useful against certain pests and in comparison with foliar sprays may require fewer gallons and may have less impact on some natural enemies.

Narrow-range oils will not damage most plants when applied as directed as a foliar spray during the spring or summer. However, check the label and avoid spraying plants identified as susceptible to foliar damage, such as some arborvitae, juniper, maple, and blue spruce. For example, oil will remove the bluish tinge from blue spruce foliage, although the plants' health is not actually impaired.

Do not apply oil (or any other pesticide) when plants are drought-stressed, when it is windy, or when temperatures are over 90°F or below freezing. Do not spray oil when the relative humidity is expected to be above 90% for 48 hours, and avoid spraying oil when it is very foggy. High humidity reduces the evaporation of oil, increasing its effectiveness against pests and also increasing the likelihood of phytotoxicity. For summer or dormant season applications, use only oils that say "supreme" or "superior" or "narrow-range" on the label. These have a minimum unsulfonated residue (UR) of 92 and a minimum percent paraffin (% Cp) of 60%, characteristics that make an oil relatively safe for plants. Use pressurized application equipment. Thorough spray coverage is essential. For more details on effectively using oils see *Managing Insects and Mites with Spray Oils* (Davidson et al. 1991).

Synthetics. Acephate, chlorpyrifos, diazinon, and malathion (all organophosphates); carbaryl (a carbamate); and pyrethroids are commonly used synthetic insecticides. Organophosphates and carbamates inhibit cholinesterase, an important enzyme in the nervous system. Because all insects and mammals use cholinesterase to regulate nerve activity, these pesticides can adversely affect nontarget organisms. Pets and people may be harmed if they are exposed to a large enough dose, such as from careless use or accidents. Some of these materials are contaminating urban surface water at levels hazardous to aquatic life, as discussed in Chapter 2 in the section "Pesticides Can Contaminate Water."

Most organophosphates and carbamates kill a wide variety of pests that are directly sprayed or that touch or eat treated foliage. They also kill many natural enemies and promote the development of resistance. Carbaryl is especially toxic to honey bees and can cause mite outbreaks, in part because it kills spider mite natural enemies. Avoid using these materials if less-toxic materials or nonchemical alternatives are available.

Pyrethroids. Pyrethroids are synthesized from petroleum in a way that makes them chemically similar to naturally occurring pyrethrin insecticides. Pyrethroids, such as fluvalinate and permethrin, are more persistent and more toxic to pests than natural botanicals. Most pyrethroids have relatively low toxicity to humans and other mammals. However, like many synthetic pesticides, pyrethroids can be very toxic to natural enemies (see Table 4-6) and pests may readily develop resistance to them, so try to avoid their use in landscapes.

FOLIAGE-FEEDING CATERPILLARS

Caterpillars are the larval stage of moths or butterflies (order Lepidoptera). Do not confuse them with the immature stages of other caterpillarlike insects covered elsewhere in this book, including beetles and sawflies (which also feed on foliage) or fly larvae, such as syrphids (which are beneficial aphid predators). Hundreds of different leaf-chewing caterpillars feed on landscape plants, but most are so uncommon that they are not pests. Many species are important food for birds or mature into attractive butterflies.

DAMAGE

Some caterpillars fold or roll leaves together with silk to form shelters. Others feed on leaves beneath a canopy of silk, sometimes creating dense "nests" or "tents" in foliage. Many species chew irregular holes in flowers, fruit, or leaves; tunnel within foliage; or devour entire leaves or flowers. This damage can be unsightly, but it often looks more serious than it is. The importance of the injury depends on the age, species, and health of the plant and the level of aesthetic quality desired for that location. A relatively small number of caterpillars can retard the growth of plants that are young or already stressed from other causes, such as a lack of proper cultural care. Severe defoliation, especially during consecutive years, may cause branch dieback or kill entire plants. However, most otherwise healthy mature trees and shrubs tolerate extensive feeding by caterpillars, especially later in the growing season, with little or no loss in plant growth or vigor.

IDENTIFICATION AND BIOLOGY

After mating, the female moth or butterfly lays her eggs singly or in a mass on the host plant. These eggs hatch after several days, except in the case of species that spend the winter in the egg stage. The emerging larvae move singly or in groups to feeding sites on the plant. In addition to three pairs of legs on the thorax (the area immediately behind the head), caterpillars have pairs of round or fleshy leglike tubercles (called prolegs) on at least some segments of the abdomen, but there are no prolegs on at least the first two abdominal segments. Legs and the presence and location of prolegs distinguish caterpillar larvae from similar-appearing larvae of beetles, flies, and sawflies, as illustrated in Figure 4-9.

Most caterpillars eat voraciously and grow rapidly, shedding old skins three to five times before entering a nonactive pupal stage (Figure 4-1); some species pupate within silken cocoons. Most species pupate in a characteristic location, such as in litter beneath a tree, on leaves, or the trunk. The adult moth or butterfly emerges from the pupal case

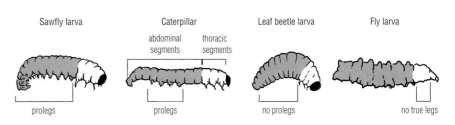

FIGURE 4-9. Caterpillars can be distinguished from larvae of beetles, sawflies, and true flies by the number and arrangement of their appendages. Caterpillars and larvae of beetles and sawflies have three pairs of true legs, one pair on each thoracic segment. Most sawfly larvae also have fleshy protuberances or leglike appendages (called prolegs) on all of their abdominal segments, but there are exceptions, as discussed in the section "Sawflies" later in this chapter. Caterpillars have prolegs on some abdominal segments, but never on their first two abdominal segments. Beetle larvae have true legs, but no prolegs. Fly larvae (such as predatory syrphids) have no true legs. Fly larvae can have either smooth bodies or fleshy protuberances, which can be just on their abdomen or on both their abdomen and thorax.

after several days to several months, depending on the species and season. Some common caterpillar pests, such as the fruittree leafroller and most tussock moths, have one generation per year. Other species have several generations annually and can cause damage throughout the growing season.

CONTROL ACTION THRESHOLDS

Most plants tolerate feeding by moderate populations of caterpillars, and control is not needed merely because caterpillars are present. No thresholds have been established for caterpillar numbers or damage on most landscape plants, although action guidelines have been suggested for the California oakworm. Suggested control action thresholds for healthy, mature, deciduous plants in landscapes are approximately 20% defoliation in the spring and 30 to 40% in the summer. In the fall, it is generally inappropriate to control insects feeding on deciduous plant leaves regardless of damage levels, since the leaves will be shed soon. A 30% defoliation level may warrant control on conifers. Tolerance for injury varies among locations and host plants. Some people are bothered by observing insects or damage that does not actually threaten plant health. Monitor plants as discussed below and use that information to develop and modify action thresholds that are appropriate for your situation.

Identify the species present and learn about their biology before taking action. Some caterpillars have only one generation per year, and it may be too late for control to be effective once mature caterpillars or their damage are observed. Keep thorough records of your insect or damage monitoring. Record the location, date, and specific reason why pests were considered a problem. Adjust your thresholds based on experience or special circumstances, such as weakened plants that are less tolerant of defoliation. Some pesticides may also adversely affect weakened plants.

MONITORING

The first step toward preventing unacceptable damage is to learn how to rec-ognize infestations early. Plants with a history of damage or that are prone to certain pests may need to be monitored every week for certain pest life stages during critical parts of the year. Monitoring is necessary to determine whether populations warrant control, to time management efforts so that they are effective, and (after taking action) to assess the effectiveness of your management. Monitoring provides only a relative measure of insect abundance; for example, it alerts you to whether insect numbers are going up or down. Choose a sampling method appropriate to your host plant and pest situation and be consistent in your method so that results are comparable among sample data. Several sampling methods are available.

Sweep Net Shake or Branch Beating.

Sweep net or branch beat samples are appropriate for caterpillars that are easily dislodged from foliage. Neither technique is effective for species that web themselves in leaves. Insert new growth flushes into a standard sweep net and shake vigorously. Alternatively, hold a light-colored tray, framed cloth, or clipboard beneath foliage and shake or beat the branch a fixed number of times (such as once or twice) to dislodge insects. Shaking or beating branches from each of about four locations per plant on each of about four plants may be adequate for sampling at each location. Empty the samples onto a clean surface and record the number of larvae collected per branch or shake sample (total number of larvae divided by the number of branches sampled).

Timed Counts.

Timed counts can be used to monitor any type of caterpillar that can easily be observed in foliage. Inspect foliage and record the number of caterpillars, rolled leaves, or webbing "nests" seen in 1 or 2 minutes. Pull apart rolled leaves or webbing and count them only if they contain live caterpillars. Make several timed searches on different plants or on different parts of the same large plant. To keep track of time while counting insects, time your counts with an alarm watch or work with a second person who can time and record. Timed counts are not useful if populations are so high that the number of insects recorded is limited by how quickly each can be seen and counted.

Visual Inspection.

A common method for sampling foliage-chewing insects is to visually inspect a set number of randomly selected leaves or growth terminals for caterpillars or their eggs. Record the number of insects found on each leaf or terminal. Determine the average number of insects per sample by adding up the total number of insects found and dividing by the number of samples inspected.

Foliage may also be inspected for damage instead of, or in addition to, counting insects. Record the number of chewed or skeletonized leaves or terminals and the total number of leaves or terminals sampled. To obtain a more exact estimate of damage, assign each sample a damage rating from 0 to 10, where 0 equals no damage, 1 equals about 10% damage, 2 is about 20% damage, and so on. About 30 samples at each site may be adequate. Take the average of all samples to estimate overall damage at that location. For insects that occur in groups, such as fall webworms or tent caterpillars, a timed count or whole plant count is more useful because of the clumped distribution.

Damage sampling indicates past insect activity. Insect populations may change rapidly because of factors such as weather or natural enemies, so make sure that the damaging life stages susceptible to treatment are still abundant before using damage as the basis for your control actions.

Pheromone-Baited Traps.

Traps are commercially available for monitoring adults of many Lepidoptera, including American plum borer, certain armyworms, clearwing moths, cutworms, gypsy moth, leafrollers, loopers, and Nantucket pine tip moth. Traps typically consist of a sticky surface and a dispenser containing a pheromone (sex attractant) to lure adults of one sex (usually the male). Because both sexes are active around the same time, traps can be used to determine when females are laying eggs and to time control actions. Unless that species overwinters as eggs, larvae will be present beginning about 1 week after adult moths are trapped. Because the rate of development is related to heat, monitoring temperatures in degree-days is the most reliable method for determining the time to hatching. Although traps can indicate when to take action for some pests, traps do not reliably indicate numbers of an insect in landscapes. Therefore, traps should not be used for deciding whether control action is needed.

No specific trapping recommendations have been developed for landscape plants. However, to determine when specific moths are active in an area, hang one trap at chest height in each of two host trees spaced at least several hundred feet apart. Deploy traps during the season when adults are expected and check them about once a week. Reapply sticky material or replace the traps when they are no longer sticky. Pheromone dispensers may need to be replaced about once monthly, especially if the weather has been hot. Check with trap distributors for specific recommendations.

Frass Collection. Fecal pellets (frass) are monitored by researchers and occasionally by pest managers to estimate density and damage by caterpillars, including the California oakworm and gypsy moth.

Caterpillars excrete characteristic droppings, which drop from plants. Pellets increase in size as the larvae grow, and pellets are generally produced in greater amounts with an increase in the number of larvae or an increase in temperature, which causes caterpillars to feed faster.

To monitor frass, place several light-colored sticky cards, shallow trays, or cups beneath the canopy at regular intervals, such as for 24 hours once each week during spring when no rain or sprinkler irrigation is expected. Use the same number of sticky cards or the same size and number of cups on each sample date. Compare dropping density on cards or total frass volume in cups among sample dates.

Initially, you may want to conduct both frass monitoring and foliage inspection, then with experience, frass monitoring alone to estimate caterpillar density and damage, in order to determine whether most caterpillars are early instars (most susceptible to *Bacillus thuringiensis*) or older caterpillars, and to help in deciding whether control is warranted. Fecal trap monitoring is not useful for sampling tent-making and leaf-rolling caterpillars, because little of their frass falls to the ground.

MANAGEMENT

Cultural Controls. Proper cultural care allows landscapes to tolerate moderate levels of defoliation without harm to the plants. Provide irrigation if appropriate, depending on soil type, location, and plant species. Protect roots and trunks from damage. Prune trees properly when needed.

Biological Controls. Predators, parasites, and natural outbreaks of disease sometimes kill enough caterpillars to control populations. Predators include assassin bugs, bigeyed bugs, birds, damsel bugs, ground beetles, lacewing larvae, pirate bugs, and spiders. Mice and other small mammals feed on pupae on the ground and near the soil surface. Many caterpillar eggs are destroyed by tiny parasitic wasps, such as *Trichogramma* species. Most larvae are attacked by one or more larger species of wasp. For example, redhumped caterpillars are often controlled by two species of parasitic wasps.

Caterpillars are often killed by diseases caused by naturally occurring bacteria, fungi, or viruses. Caterpillars killed by viruses and bacteria may turn dark and their bodies may become soft and limp. These carcasses hanging limply from foliage or twigs and eventually degenerate into a sack of liquefied contents. When broken, they release more viral particles or bacterial spores that infect other caterpillars that eat contaminated foliage. Such disease outbreaks can rapidly reduce populations under favorable conditions, although

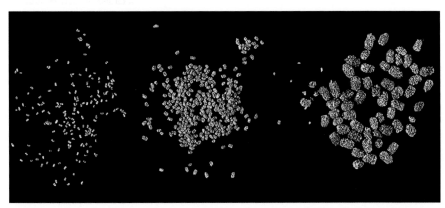

This frass was collected to monitor the California oakworm. These three piles of caterpillar droppings (from left to right) were produced by the smallest larvae (first instars), third instars, and fifth-instar larvae. Pellets average 0.3, 0.6, and 1.4 mm long, respectively. *Bacillus thuringiensis* (Bt) will be more effective if foliage is sprayed when most droppings are the smaller sizes because smaller droppings are produced by the youngest oakworms, which are most susceptible to Bt.

This parasitic wasp (*Hyposoter* sp.) is laying an egg in a caterpillar. Because most parasites feed hidden within their host, this important biological control is easily overlooked. Look carefully for evidence of natural enemy activity, including disease-killed caterpillars, pupae or eggs with holes from which parasites emerged, and unhatched eggs that are darker than normal, indicating they may contain parasites.

These white cocoons were made by larvae of an *Apanteles* sp. wasp that emerged to pupate after feeding inside and killing redhumped caterpillars.

Naturally occurring pathogens often control caterpillars, as shown by the two silverspotted tiger moth caterpillars (*Lophocampa =Halysidota argentata*) hanging beneath this Monterey pine twig. A healthy larva is on top.

outbreaks are difficult to predict and may not occur until caterpillar populations have become high.

You get the greatest benefit from natural enemies if you avoid the use of insecticides that destroy them. For instance, among materials used for control of caterpillars, the biological insecticide *Bacillus thuringiensis* (subspecies *kurstaki* and *aizawai*) leaves most natural enemies unharmed because it kills only Lepidoptera larvae.

When monitoring for pests, also look closely for the presence of predators, parasites, and other evidence of biological control; record this information. Evidence of natural enemy activity includes disease-killed caterpillars; pupae or eggs with holes from which parasites emerged; unhatched eggs that are darker than normal, indicating that they may contain parasites; or hatched caterpillar eggs with no evidence of caterpillars or damage. If you have an increasing number of pests but also many natural enemies, wait a few days before using insecticides. Monitor again to determine whether pest populations have declined or natural enemies are increasing to levels that may soon cause pest numbers to decline. Although selective insecticides such as *Bacillus thuringiensis* may not provide such rapid insect control as broad-spectrum sprays, where natural enemies are active, better long-term control is

provided by using methods that conserve natural enemies.

Mass Releases of Trichogramma Wasps. *Trichogramma* are tiny stingless wasps that attack the eggs of many moths and butterflies. Adults are about $1/25$ inch long or smaller. Although they often occur naturally on plants infested with caterpillar eggs, several species are available by mail from commercial insectaries (see Suppliers for publications listing vendors). University researchers have successfully used *Trichogramma* releases to control a few agricultural pests that lay exposed eggs, including omnivorous leafroller (*Platynota stultana*), loopers, and tomato fruitworm. Although some of these same pest species occur on ornamentals, no research has demonstrated the effectiveness of *Trichogramma* releases against pests in landscapes. *Trichogramma* released for controlling pest caterpillars may also kill nearby eggs of innocuous or desirable species of moths and butterflies.

Commercial insectaries claim to sell several species, including *Trichogramma pretiosum*, *T. platneri*, and *T. minutum*. However, *Trichogramma* are extremely difficult to reliably identify to species. Only certain *Trichogramma* species may be adapted for specific situations. Based on research against *Amorbia cunea* and omnivorous looper in southern California avocado and citrus orchards, weekly releases each of

10,000 or more *Trichogramma platneri* per 20-foot tree over a period of 3 weeks or longer may be effective if releases coincide with peak moth egg-laying.

Commercial suppliers of *Trichogramma* normally ship the parasite in the form of parasitized moth eggs glued to a piece of cardboard. The wasps, which complete their immature stage within the moth eggs, should emerge as adults soon after the shipment arrives. *Trichogramma* are more likely to be effective if they are allowed to emerge in containers very lightly streaked with honey diluted with water and permitted to feed for 24 hours before release. Using clear containers covered with tightly woven cloth allows you to observe the tiny wasps and permits some air flow while preventing their escape prior to release.

Trichogramma must be released in large numbers just before or at the peak of pest egg-laying for any likelihood of effectiveness. Monitor plants regularly to determine when adults or moth eggs first appear, then order *Trichogramma*. Consider using pheromone-baited traps that are available for some pest species to indicate when egg-laying moths are active.

Physical Controls. Many species, such as the fall webworm, mimosa webworm, redhumped caterpillar, spiny elm caterpillar, and tent caterpillars, feed in groups, which in some species are evidenced by silken webbing on foliage. Clip and dispose of infested foliage; a pole pruner (a blade on the end of a telescoping pole) or ladder may be needed for this. Alternatively, tents and the caterpillars inside can be removed by twirling or scrubbing the webbing into a ball using a toilet brush or similar tool attached to a telescoping pole, then squashing the larvae or discarding the brush. Effective physical control may require monitoring to identify infestations while the caterpillars are still young, because some group-feeding species disperse as the larvae mature. Clipping or removal methods are best done on cool, rainy, or overcast days when young caterpillars remain in tents or inactive groups. Heavily infested plants can be sprayed if necessary, preferably with a selective insecticide, then monitored during subsequent seasons when populations are lower and physical control is more practical.

Some caterpillars, such as gypsy moth and tussock moths, overwinter in obvious egg masses on bark or other objects. After leaves have dropped, inspect the bark and area around susceptible plants. Scrape any egg masses into a bucket of soapy water and dispose of them.

Microbial and Biological Insecticides.
Microbial and biological insecticides are almost ideal pesticides from an environmental and safety point of view. *Bacillus thuringiensis* subspecies *kurstaki* (Bt) is the most important microbial insecticide. Entomopathogenic nematodes can be used to control ground-dwelling larvae and pupae of armyworms and cutworms attacking certain low-growing ornamentals. Spinosyns are highly effective against caterpillars. Because they are expensive to produce and difficult to handle, certain viruses toxic only to one pest species are used mostly for a few crop pests (such as codling moth) or in certain government-managed programs (such as against gypsy moths).

Bacillus thuringiensis. When eaten, the Bt bacterium destroys caterpillars' digestive system and causes larvae to stop feeding within about a day. Most infected cater-

pillars die within a few days (Figure 4-7). *Bacillus thuringiensis* is effective against most leaf-eating caterpillars when larvae are young. Larvae of hawk moths (family Sphingidae), inchworms or measuring worms (Geometridae), and whites and sulfur butterflies (Pieridae) are highly susceptible to Bt during all larvae stages. Because many caterpillars are not pest species and may be ecologically important (such as food for birds), apply Bt only to individual plants infested with damaging levels of pest caterpillars. Desirable butterflies will not be affected if their larval food plants are not sprayed.

Unlike broad-spectrum insecticides that kill on contact, caterpillars must eat sprayed foliage in order to be killed. Proper timing and thorough spray coverage is therefore very important for effective application, so monitor caterpillar populations before treatment. Use a high-pressure sprayer (or hire a professional applicator) to provide adequate spray penetration when treating leafrolling and tentmaking species. Apply *Bacillus thuringiensis* during warm, dry weather when caterpillars are feeding actively. Because sunlight quickly decomposes Bt on foliage, most caterpillars hatching after the application are not affected. A second application about 7 to 10 days after the first may be required. Follow label directions for mixing and applying.

Narrow-Range Oil.
Spraying trees during the dormant season with specially refined narrow-range or horticultural oils, also labeled "superior" or "supreme," kills overwintering eggs of fruittree leafroller, gypsy moths, tent caterpillars, tussock moths, and other caterpillars on bark, thereby substantially lowering summer populations of these pests. The primary reason for applying oil during the dormant season is to control scales or overwintering eggs of aphids and mites; high caterpillar populations the previous spring or summer may also warrant a dormant season oil spray. See the section on scale insects later in this chapter for more information on dormant season oil treatments.

Other Pesticides. If more toxic pesticides than the ones discussed above are needed, confine treatments to those plants or portions of plants that are infested. Time treatments to coincide with the pest's most vulnerable life stage—usually the newly hatched larvae. Some synthetic pesticides such as organophosphates, carbamates, or pyrethroids rapidly reduce populations of most caterpillar species. However, these broad-spectrum insecticides also kill beneficial organisms, may cause outbreaks of other pests such as mites, and are contaminating urban surface waters. Avoid using these pesticides if nonchemical alternatives or less-toxic materials are available (see Table 4-6). Use of these materials is rarely justified for caterpillar control in landscapes. Do not apply broad-spectrum insecticides to flowering plants if honey bees are present.

In addition to microbials and oil, some "organically acceptable" insecticides such as pyrethrins are available. Check labels to determine whether these materials are registered for ornamentals and what pests are likely to be controlled. For specific insecticide recommendations see publications such as *California Oakworm Pest Notes* (Gouveia, Ohlendorf, and Flint 2000), *Fruittree Leafroller on Ornamental and Fruit Trees Pest Notes* (Bentley et al. 2000), and *Redhumped Caterpillar Pest Notes* (Rice and Van Steenwyk 2000).

California Oakworm
Phryganidia californica

The California oakworm (family Dioptidae) is one of many species of caterpillars that feed on oaks in California; it is especially numerous in some years in the San Francisco Bay Area and Monterey Bay region. Fruittree leafroller, tent caterpillars, and tussock moths are other common oak-feeding caterpillars, so properly distinguish the species before taking any action.

The California oakworm adult is a uniform tan to gray moth, distinguished by its prominent wing veins. The tiny round eggs are laid in groups of about two or three dozen on twigs or leaves. The eggs

The adult male (left) and female (right) of the California oakworm are tan to grayish moths with prominent wing veins, as seen here on coast live oak.

CALIFORNIA OAKWORM

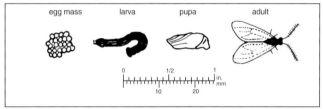

egg mass   larva   pupa   adult

C. S. KOEHLER

California oakworm eggs are whitish when laid but develop red centers that become pinkish to brownish gray before hatching. See the chapter introduction for a photograph of a larva.

California oakworm pupae usually occur on oak bark. Instead of producing an adult moth, oakworm pupae are often parasitized by *Brachymeria ovata*. This stout black chalcid wasp with yellow-banded legs can greatly reduce the number of oakworms in subsequent generations.

are white when laid, but develop red centers that become pinkish to brownish gray before hatching. The young larvae are yellowish green with dark stripes on their sides and have overly large brown heads. Mature larvae are variable in color, commonly dark with prominent lengthwise yellow or olive stripes. Pupae are white or yellow with black markings and are found on bark or suspended from limbs, leaves, or objects near trees.

Two generations per year typically occur in northern California; a third generation sometimes occurs in southern California and in northern California in years of uncommonly warm, dry winters. Oakworms overwinter as young larvae on the lower leaf surface. Young larvae skeletonize the lower leaf surface, while mature larvae chew all the way through the leaf. Overwintering larvae in northern California mature about May or early June, when defoliation on live oaks may become extensive. Large populations of the spring generation generally do not occur on deciduous oaks because these trees drop their leaves in the fall, causing the overwintering generation larvae and eggs to die. The spring-generation larvae produce moths often seen fluttering around oaks in the late afternoon in June and July. These adults lay eggs that hatch into larvae that may cause noticeable defoliation in July through September. Second-generation moths are present in October and November when they lay eggs that hatch into the overwintering larvae. Development in southern California is more variable, and moths may appear almost any time from March through November.

Thresholds. Healthy oaks tolerate extensive defoliation without serious harm. Well-cared for oaks not otherwise subject to serious stress survive being totally defoliated. If trees need protection from defoliation because they are stressed or of especially high aesthetic value, regularly inspect foliage for larvae and spray only when caterpillars are abundant. No thresholds have been established, but some guidelines have been suggested: If more than 8 to 10 larvae greater than ¼ inch long are observed after inspecting 25 young (lighter green) shoots, defoliation may become apparent on untreated oaks. A density of 25 California oakmoth larvae per 100 twigs has also been suggested as the population density that may warrant control action to prevent annoying levels of defoliation. Frass monitoring has occasionally been used for oakworm monitoring, as discussed earlier in the section "Frass Collection" earlier in this chapter. Because California oakworms are generally more abundant in the west part of the tree canopy, concentrate any monitoring in the west side of trees to provide an earlier and more sensitive measure of their feeding.

Management. Predators, parasites, and natural outbreaks of disease (oakworm nuclear polyhedrosis virus) sometimes kill enough oakworms to control populations. The spined soldier bug (*Podisus maculiventris*) is reportedly the most important oakworm predator. Other predators include assassin bugs, bigeyed bugs, birds, damsel bugs, ground beetles, lacewing larvae, pirate bugs, spiders, and small mammals. Two pupal parasites, *Brachymeria ovata* (Chalcididae) and *Itoplectis behrensii* (Ichneumonidae), are the most important oakworm parasites. Oakworm larvae are also attacked by two tachinid flies, *Actia flavipes* and *Hyphantrophaga* (=*Zenillia*) *virillis*.

Bacillus thuringiensis is most effective against young larvae, but because young oakworms only scrape the lower leaf surface, spraying is less effective at that stage unless you thoroughly treat the underside of leaves. It can be more effective to thoroughly treat foliage when larvae are first observed to be chewing completely through the leaf or chewing at the leaf edge. Alternatively, diflubenzuron and spinosad are highly effective insecticides with relatively low toxicity to most natural enemies. Homeowners generally lack the equipment and experience to effectively treat large trees. When hiring a professional applicator, discuss the specific pesticide to be applied and insist on use of an IPM-compatible one. For more information, see *California Oakworm Pest Notes* (Gouveia, Ohlendorf, and Flint 2000).

Tussock Moths

Many tussock moths (family Lymantriidae), especially *Orgyia* species, occur throughout the United States. One or more kinds of tussock moths can feed at least occasionally on most species of deciduous and evergreen trees.

Adults are hairy, brownish to white moths. Females of some species are flightless because they are heavily laden with eggs or their wings are reduced to small pads (vestigial wings). Females produce a sex pheromone that attracts the night-flying males. After mating, females lay their tiny whitish eggs in a mass of several hundred, covered with hairs from the female's body. In species that overwinter as eggs, eggs hatch in the spring into tiny dark caterpillars, which may travel on the wind. Full-grown caterpillars have prominent hairs that protrude, sometimes in tufts, from colored tubercles along their body. These hairs readily detach from the larvae and are often irritating to human skin. Pupation occurs on or near the host plant.

The western tussock moth (*Orgyia vetusta*) occurs from southern California to British Columbia. Its hosts include fruit and nut trees, hawthorn, manzanita, oak, pyracantha, toyon, walnut, and willow. Mature caterpillars are gray and have numerous bright red, blue, and yellow spots from which gray to white hairs radiate. They have four dense white tufts of hair on the back, two black tufts on the head, and a black and a white tuft

The western tussock moth larva has brightly colored spots and dense tufts of hairs. Tussock moths rarely become abundant enough in landscapes to warrant control.

Tussock moth cocoons occur near or on host plants, such as on this coast live oak leaf.

WESTERN TUSSOCK MOTH

egg mass   larva

0   1/2   1
||||||||||||||||||||||| in.
||||||||||||||||||||||| mm
  10   20

at the rear. After emerging from the overwintering eggs and feeding during the spring, the larvae pupate on the bark of the trunk or main limbs. Cocoons are a tan brown. Adults emerge from late spring through early summer. Males are brown with gray markings. The western tussock moth usually has one generation per year, although in southern California two generations may occur. Second-generation larvae are present from about late August to October, and adults lay the overwintering eggs in September and October.

Rusty tussock moth (*Orgyia antiqua*) occurs throughout the United States on many different deciduous and evergreen plants. Its hairy, blackish larvae have three projecting tufts of black hair, two in front and one at the rear, and four orangish tufts along the back.

The Douglas-fir tussock moth (*Orgyia pseudotsugata*) occurs only in the western states, primarily on Douglas fir and true firs. It also has two tufts of black hair in front and one at the rear, but lighter-colored tufts of hair along the back, red spots on top, and an orange stripe along each side distinguish its mature larvae from those of the rusty tussock moth.

Whitemarked tussock moth (*Orgyia leucostigma*) occurs mostly in the eastern states. Its larvae are yellowish along the sides with a bright orangish red head.

Naturally occurring diseases and parasites often keep tussock moth populations at low levels. For example, a tiny, purplish, black parasitic wasp (*Telenomus californicus*) kills many western tussock moth eggs. *Bacillus thuringiensis* controls tussock moth larvae, especially if applied when young larvae are the predominant stage present.

Redhumped Caterpillar
Schizura concinna

The redhumped caterpillar (family Notodontidae) feeds on a variety of hosts throughout the United States, including aspen, birch, cottonwood, fruit and nut trees, liquidambar, poplar, redbud, walnut, and willow. In California, high populations are usually found only in the inland valleys. Adult moths are reddish brown or gray and first appear about early May. After mating, the females lay pearly white, spherical eggs in masses of 25 to 100 on the underside of leaves. The larvae are yellow or reddish and have dark lines and projections along their bodies. The fourth segment behind the head is red and distinctly humped with two black projections. Larvae feed in groups, particularly when young. They consume the entire leaf, except for the major vein, and often feed only on a single branch. The insect overwinters as reddish brown pupae in the soil or in organic debris on the ground and has one to three generations per year.

Redhumped caterpillar populations are often controlled by two species of wasps, *Hyposoter fugitivus* (Ichneumonidae) and *Apanteles schizurae* (Braconidae). The female wasps lay their eggs in caterpillars, and the wasp larvae hatch and feed inside. After killing the caterpillars, the *Apanteles* parasite larvae emerge and pupate in whitish, silken cocoons in groups that may be seen on leaves near dead caterpillars. *Hyposoter* pupae are oblong and mottled black or purplish. Parasite numbers can increase quickly, causing caterpillar populations to crash. Conserve these parasites by avoiding the use of broad-spectrum pesticides. Plant flowering species near host trees so that adult parasites have nectar to feed on (Figure 4-4). Adult parasitoids live longer and

Older redhumped caterpillar larvae have two black projections on the distinctly reddish and enlarged fourth segment behind their head. This species usually does not cause serious damage in landscapes. Where it is undesirable, clip off infestations while larvae are feeding in groups.

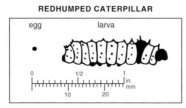

REDHUMPED CATERPILLAR

egg   larva

0   1/2   1 in.
            mm
      10   20

Hatched redhumped caterpillar eggs (upper right), unhatched eggs (below), and young larvae. Because parasites often control this species, if damage cannot be tolerated, apply only selective insecticides such as Bt.

can parasitize and kill more caterpillars when provided with nectar. Prune out and dispose of infestations that are on a limited portion of the plant. Apply *Bacillus thuringiensis* if spraying is necessary. For more information, consult *Redhumped Caterpillar Pest Notes* (Rice and Van Steenwyk 2000).

Omnivorous Looper
Sabulodes aegrotata
(=S. caberata)

The omnivorous looper (family Geometridae) occurs in the western states on several dozen plant species including acacia, box elder, California buckeye, chestnut, citrus, elm, eucalyptus, fruit trees, ginkgo, magnolia, maple, pepper tree, and willow. Young larvae are pale yellow and feed on the leaf surface, leaving a characteristic brown membrane. Older larvae are yellow to pale green or pink, with dark brown, black, or green lines along the sides and a gold-colored head. They eat through the entire leaf, often leaving only the midrib and larger veins.

In addition to the three pairs of legs behind the head, loopers have two additional prolegs near the rear (see Figure 4-9), allowing them to travel in the characteristic looping manner. Larvae feed singly on the edge of leaves or shoots, or singly or in groups between two leaves tied with silk. After about 6 weeks, the larvae form pearly white to brown pupae, usually found in webbing between leaves. The adults that emerge are tan with a narrow black band across the middle of the wing and are active at night. The barrel-shaped eggs are laid in clusters of 3 to 80 on the underside of leaves. The eggs have a ring of tiny projections around one end and, after about 2 days, change from pale green to a shiny, reddish brown. The insect has up to five generations each year; all stages may be found whenever foliage is present. One or more applications of *Bacillus thuringiensis* can provide control when larvae are present.

Fruittree Leafroller
Archips argyrospila

The fruittree leafroller (family Tortricidae) occurs throughout the United States on many hosts, including aspen, box elder, buckeye, citrus, cottonwood, elm, fruit and nut trees, hawthorn, locust, maple, oak, poplar, rose, and willow. The larvae feed only in the spring on new leaves, giving foliage a ragged or curled appearance. Unusually high populations can defoliate trees and understory plants and cover them with silken threads.

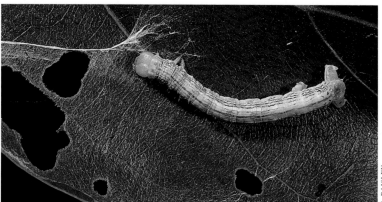

Omnivorous looper larvae have leglike appendages (prolegs) near their rears, as shown here, which allows them to travel in a characteristic looping manner. They eat through the entire leaf, often leaving only the midrib and larger veins, but they rarely cause serious harm to woody landscapes.

Some species of caterpillars tie foliage together with silken threads and feed inside. This fruittree leafroller, taken out of its leafroll, is distinguished by its shiny black head. When especially abundant, this species can entirely defoliate large trees.

The fruittree leafroller overwinters in irregular, flat masses of eggs on twigs and small branches. Egg masses are coated with a dark gray or brown cement, which later turns white and becomes perforated as the larvae emerge. Larvae hatch in the spring, usually coincident with the flush of new leaves. Young caterpillars are green with a black, shiny head. They tie or roll leaves or blossoms together with silken threads and feed inside the nest. The caterpillars wriggle vigorously and often drop to the ground on a silken thread when disturbed. They frequently move to other leaves and construct a new nest, eventually pupating inside a nest or

The fruittree leafroller lays its irregular flat egg masses on twigs and small branches. The lower egg mass shows exit holes left by emerged larvae. A dormant season oil application to bark can control this pest.

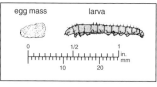

FRUITTREE LEAFROLLER

egg mass   larva

0   1/2   1 in.
||||||||||||||||||||||||| mm
        10   20

on bark in thin brown cocoons. The dark brown to yellowish tan, patterned moths emerge about 8 to 12 days after pupation. These adults soon mate and lay their over-wintering eggs. The fruittree leafroller has one generation per year.

Pheromone-baited traps are commercially available for determining when moths are flying, usually in May or June. Traps may be useful for deciding whether leafrollers will be locally abundant the next spring. Traps for egg-laying adults do not help to time applications against the resulting larvae because this species overwinters as eggs. If fruittree leafroller damage has been a problem, apply oil in January or February to thoroughly cover limbs and small twigs infested with overwintering eggs. Alternatively, monitor several egg masses in spring when leaves begin to flush and apply *Bacillus thuringiensis* when about 25 to 50% of eggs have hatched. Repeat an application if necessary when most eggs have hatched. If larger larvae in rolled leaves are abundant, use high-pressure application equipment so that the insecticide penetrates into rolled foliage. For more information, consult *Fruittree Leafroller on Ornamental and Fruit Trees Pest Notes* (Bentley et al. 2000).

Spiny Elm Caterpillar
Nymphalis antiopa

The spiny elm caterpillar (family Nymphalidae) feeds on elm, poplar, and willow throughout the United States. It causes ragged, chewed leaves, often on a single branch, which may be entirely defoliated. The group-feeding larvae produce dark fecal pellets. At maturity, larvae are mostly black with a row of orange to brown spots down the back and rows of tiny white dots on each segment. The most distinctive larval feature is the row of black spines around each segment, which may be mildly irritating to human skin.

Larvae form black, brown, or gray pupae from which strikingly beautiful butterflies emerge. The adult, known as the mourning cloak butterfly, is mostly brownish black to purple. Adult wing margins are often ragged and have yellow bands bordered inwardly by blue spots.

The tiny eggs are orange or pink to brown, and are almost cylindrical with eight longitudinal ribs. They are laid in masses of several dozen on leaves, limbs, or twigs. Spiny elm caterpillars have about two generations per year, but in southern California, both adults and larvae may be observed during almost any month.

Spiny elm caterpillar larvae do not harm the tree and no control is needed. Clip and dispose of the infested branch if caterpillars cannot be tolerated.

Tent Caterpillars
Malacosoma spp.

Tent caterpillars (family Lasiocampidae) feed on deciduous trees and shrubs throughout the United States. Depending on the species, their hosts include ash, birch, fruit and nut trees, madrone, oak, poplar, redbud, toyon, and willow. Adults are hairy, medium-sized, day-flying moths, usually dull brown, yellow, or gray in color. Tent caterpillars overwinter in pale gray to dark brown eggs encircling small twigs or as eggs laid in a flat mass on bark. The larvae hatch and begin feeding in the spring, and some species form silken webs on foliage. After feeding, tent caterpillars spin silken cocoons in folded leaves, on bark, or in litter. Adults emerge in mid-summer. Tent caterpillars have one generation per year.

Western tent caterpillar (*Malacosoma californicum*) larvae are reddish brown with some blue spots and are covered with tufts of orange to white hairs. They

Spiny elm caterpillars are mostly black with distinctive spines and a row of orangish spots down the back. Larval feeding does not harm the tree, and caterpillars mature into attractive morning cloak butterflies. Clip and dispose of the infested branch if caterpillars cannot be tolerated.

Western tent caterpillars are mostly reddish brown. Their dark frass or droppings are visible here, caught in silken webbing they have made on coast live oak leaves.

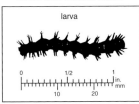

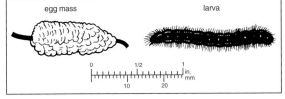

spin large silken webs in which the larvae do most of their feeding.

The Pacific tent caterpillar (*M. constrictum*) looks very similar to *M. californicum*, except more blue is visible and the larvae usually feed only on oaks. Pacific tent caterpillars produce small tents a few inches wide. Larvae feed openly, in groups when they are young, and usually enter the tent only to molt.

Forest tent caterpillar (*M. disstria*) larvae are mostly dark blue, with wavy reddish brown lines and distinct white, keyhole-shaped markings down the back. Larvae feed in groups without making any webbing.

Inspect plants regularly, and when larvae are young, prune out tents or clip and dispose of infested branches if this can be done without cutting major limbs. *Bacillus thuringiensis* provides control if high-pressure spray equipment is used so that insecticide penetrates any webbing. Also thoroughly spray foliage around any webbing, as these leaves will be enclosed in webbing and consumed as the caterpillar tents are expanded.

Fall Webworm
Hyphantria cunea

The fall webworm (family Arctiidae) is one of several tentmaking species in the United States. Its tents are formed over the foliage toward the outer portions of the tree, while the nests of the tent caterpillars (*Malacosoma* spp.) are usually formed around the juncture of branches. The hosts of fall webworm include aspen, birch, cottonwood, elm, fruit and nut trees, liquidambar, maple, mulberry, poplar, sycamore, and willow. Its feeding damage is rarely severe, and the presence of silken tents is its primary effect.

Adult moths emerge in the late spring or early summer and are mostly white, sometimes with black wing spots. In June or July, the females lay globular white or yellow eggs in large masses beneath leaves. These eggs hatch in about 10 days, and the larvae feed in silken tents until late summer or early fall. While feeding, the larvae enlarge their tents to include more leaves and shoots. Mature larvae are yellowish brown or gray with longitudinal stripes and have long white or black hairs arising from black and orange projections along the body. Fall webworms overwinter in dark brown cocoons, usually attached to the tree trunk or in organic debris on the ground. Fall webworm produces one or two generations per year.

Regularly inspect host plants for silken tents during late spring and summer. Prune out or "scrub" and dispose of caterpillar-infested tents as soon as they appear, as discussed above in the section "Physical Controls." If nests are abundant and cannot be pruned or tolerated, apply *Bacillus thuringiensis* with a high-pressure sprayer to penetrate webbed foliage. Also thoroughly spray foliage around tents, as these leaves will be enclosed in webbing and consumed as the caterpillar tents are expanded. Inspect plants again the season after treating; populations should be lower then and any remaining colonies can be pruned out.

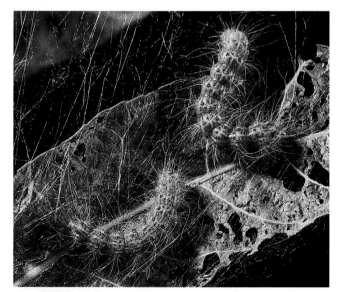

Fall webworms and their chewing damage are shown within this silken webbing on willow. Inspect hosts regularly and clip off webbed foliage before colonies become abundant.

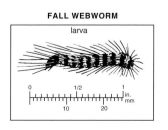

FALL WEBWORM

larva

0   1/2   1 in.
mm
10   20

Fall webworm nests, as shown here on Lombardy poplar, are typically formed over outer foliage. This distinguishes them from tent caterpillars, which usually make nests around branch junctures.

Mimosa Webworm
Homadaula anisocentra

The mimosa webworm (family Plutellidae) was inadvertently introduced from China and occurs throughout the United States. In California, it is a pest primarily in the Sacramento Valley. It feeds on *Albizia* species (also called mimosa), and especially on honey locust. Young larvae commonly feed in groups, covering foliage with silk and causing leaves to turn brown and die. Mature larvae vary from gray to blackish brown, have five longitudinal white stripes on the body, and commonly feed singly. They can move rapidly when alarmed and may drop from the foliage on a silken thread when disturbed. The adults are small, silvery gray moths with stippled black dots on their wings. They emerge in the late spring from whitish overwintering cocoons, on the trunk or in organic debris beneath host trees. After mating, females deposit pearly gray to pink eggs singly on foliage or on webbing formed by feeding larvae. The mimosa webworm usually has two generations per year.

Inspect plants for silken webbing and chewed or brown leaves and prune out and dispose of infested foliage while caterpillars are still young and feeding in groups. Apply *Bacillus thuringiensis* when young larvae are abundant if damage cannot be tolerated.

Gypsy Moth
Lymantria dispar

The gypsy moth (family Lymantriidae) was introduced from Europe. It is the most serious caterpillar pest of deciduous trees in the northeastern states and has spread south and to the Midwest. Scattered infestations have been discovered in the West, where they are the target of eradication programs. Larvae prefer alder, basswood, some poplars and flowering fruit trees, willows, and especially oaks, but high populations

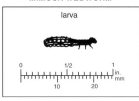

MIMOSA WEBWORM

larva

will feed on many other plants. In the western United States, report suspected gypsy moths to the county department of agriculture (in California) or other agricultural agency officials.

Mature gypsy moth larvae are dark, and rows of blue dots near the front and red dots toward the rear may be visible along the back at the base of tufts of dark hairs. Mature larvae feed at night, then crawl down the trunk to hide during the day in bark crevices or litter on the ground. This behavior allows populations to be monitored by wrapping a folded burlap band around host tree trunks and checking beneath it during spring days for hiding larvae. Larvae can be scraped into a bucket of soapy water or otherwise destroyed, which may provide some control. Larvae feed for about one and a half months during the spring, then form large, dark, oblong pupae. Pupation occurs on or near the host plant, commonly in leaf litter, bark crevices, or on manmade objects.

Adults emerge from the pupae in about 10 days. Female moths are whitish with inverted dark V-patterns on their wings. Gypsy moth females in the East

do not fly, but females of the Asian gypsy moth strain do fly and are sometimes introduced, especially in the West. Male gypsy moths are brownish and tan with wavy black bands on their wings. Gypsy moths overwinter as immatures in masses of eggs laid on bark or objects near host plants. If laid on manmade items, egg masses may be inadvertently transported on vehicles or outdoor equipment, introducing this pest into new locations.

Commercially available sticky traps baited with pheromone to attract males are used to monitor populations. *Bacillus thuringiensis* provides control if applied to thoroughly cover foliage when young caterpillars are predominant. The number of larvae infesting foliage can also be reduced as discussed earlier in this chapter in the section "Sticky Barriers." A 12-inch-wide strip of burlap folded in half lengthwise and tied loosely to encircle trunks (and placed above any sticky band) provides a shelter where all gypsy moth life stages may be found; check bands daily and squash any gypsy moths or scrape them into a bucket of water with bleach or soap.

SAWFLIES

Sawflies are not true flies; they are in the order Hymenoptera, which includes ants, bees, and wasps. Sawflies are named for the adult female's sawlike abdominal ap-

Mature gypsy moth larvae are hairy, with a row of 5 pairs of blue spots and 6 pairs of red spots on their backs. In the western United States, report suspected gypsy moths to your county department of agriculture (in California) or other agricultural officials.

pendage used for inserting eggs into plant tissue. Larvae of most conifer-feeding sawflies (family Diprionidae) feed externally on young conifer shoots or needles and resemble caterpillars (Lepidoptera larvae). Stem sawflies (family Cephidae) bore in plants, such as the raspberry horntail miner of caneberries and roses discussed in the section "Twig, Branch, And Trunk Boring Insects" later in this chapter.

Sawflies in the family Tenthredinidae are probably the most common sawflies found in landscapes. They are a diverse group with different species that feed openly, in leaf and stem mines, or in galls. Tenthredinids feed mostly on or in broadleaf plants, including alder, birch, fruit trees, poplar, oak, rose, and willow. A few species, such as the cypress sawfly, feed on evergreens. Tenthredinids include the pear sawfly and roseslugs discussed below and the willow gall sawflies discussed later in the section "Gall Makers."

DAMAGE

Most conifer sawflies cause chewed needles or buds; a few mine in shoots and cause tip dieback. Broadleaf-feeding species cause more variable damage. Some skeletonize or chew holes in leaves; others mine tissue, causing winding, discolored tunnels. Different species roll leaves, web foliage, or cause plant galls. Sawflies in forests in the western states rarely cause serious damage, but high populations retard plant growth and occasionally kill trees in landscapes and tree plantations.

IDENTIFICATION AND BIOLOGY

Adult sawflies have two pairs of wings and are dark, wasplike, somewhat flattened insects, usually ½ inch long or shorter. They have a relatively wide abdomen, which is broadly attached to the thorax, in contrast to most other adult hymenopterans, which have a narrow "waist" between the thorax and abdomen. Most exposed-feeding larvae (the pearslug is an exception) have six or more prolegs on the abdomen (see Figure 4-9) and one large "eye" on each side of the head. This distinguishes them

from butterfly caterpillars, which have five or fewer prolegs, always lack legs on at least the first two segments of the abdomen, and have a group of small eyespots but no large eyes.

Most sawflies in California overwinter as eggs in foliage or as pupae in litter. Depending on the species, they have from one to several generations per year.

Conifer Sawflies
Neodiprion spp.

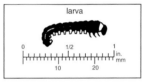

Over two dozen *Neodiprion* species sawflies are native to the United States. In the eastern states, several foreign species that feed on conifers have also been introduced, including the European pine sawfly (*Neodiprion sertifer*) and the European spruce sawfly (*Gilpinia hercyniae*). The cypress sawfly also infests certain conifers, as discussed below.

Pines are the most common hosts of *Neodiprion* species; arborvitae, cypress, fir, hemlock, juniper, larch, and spruce are also fed upon, especially in the East. Most conifer sawfly adults are yellowish brown to black with yellowish legs. Females lay eggs in niches carved in needles. Larvae are commonly yellowish or greenish and develop dark stripes or spots as they mature. Young larvae often feed several to a needle with their heads pointed away from the twig. Older larvae

may wrap their bodies around the needle on which they are feeding.

Several webspinning sawflies (*Acantholyda* spp., family Pamphiliidae), occur on Monterey pine and other conifers in California. These sawflies spin nests or silken webs on foliage and feed inside in groups or singly. Unlike most free-feeding sawflies, these webspinning species have no prolegs and instead have a pair of three-segmented appendages on the last segment of the body. They pupate in an earthen cell in the ground.

Pear Sawfly
Caliroa cerasi

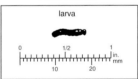

The pear sawfly, commonly called the pearslug, occurs throughout the United States. Larvae skeletonize the leaf surface of most fruit trees, especially cherry and pear, and occasionally other plants such as ash and hawthorn. Larvae are dark olive

CONIFER SAWFLY

larva

0   1/2   1
|‖‖‖‖‖‖‖‖‖‖‖‖‖‖‖‖‖‖‖‖‖‖| in.
      10   20   mm

PEAR SAWFLY

larva

0   1/2   1
|‖‖‖‖‖‖‖‖‖‖‖‖‖‖‖‖‖‖‖‖‖‖| in.
      10   20   mm

Young conifer sawflies, like these *Neodiprion fulviceps* larvae, often feed several to a needle with their heads pointed away from the twig. Unlike caterpillars and leaf beetle larvae, appendages (prolegs) can be seen on each abdominal segment on most species of sawflies.

Pear sawfly larvae skeletonize leaves; their dark, slimy coating gives them a sluglike appearance, except during the last instar, when they lack this coating. Pear sawfly larvae can be washed from plants with a forceful stream of water.

green and covered with slime, so they resemble slugs. Adults are shiny black with dark wings. There are generally two generations per year, and larvae are most abundant in the mid to late spring and again in mid to late summer.

Roseslugs

Roseslug larvae skeletonize the leaf surface and may chew entirely through foliage, leaving behind just the large leaf veins. Larvae grow up to about ¾ inch long and are yellowish green with a brown head. Take care to distinguish roseslugs from beneficial syrphid larvae that feed on rose aphids. Roseslugs occur near chewed leaves, while syrphids occur among aphids, where they can be observed eating insects, not

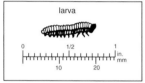

BRISTLY ROSESLUG

larva

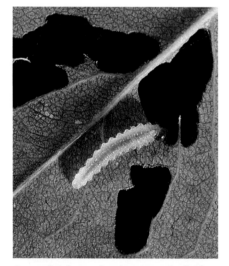

A roseslug larva chewing a rose leaf. Although many sawfly larvae resemble moth larvae, applying *Bacillus thuringiensis* will not control roseslugs. If intolerable, they can be controlled with almost any contact insecticide applied to achieve good spray coverage, including insecticidal soap, narrow-range oil, or neem oil.

chewing leaves. Syrphid larvae have no true legs, while similar-looking larvae of leaf beetles, moth larvae, and roseslugs all have 3 pairs of abdominal legs (see Figure 4-9). Depending on the species, roseslug larvae pupate in cocoons on leaves, in organic debris beneath plants, in a cell in twigs, or in the stub end of cut roses. Adults are stout, broad-waisted, mostly black wasps with yellow or orange markings. Females lay small eggs in leaf tissue.

At least three species of sawflies are occasional pests of roses throughout the United States. These include bristly roseslug (*Cladius difformis*), coiled or curled rose sawfly (*Allantus cinctus*), and the American, European, or common roseslug (*Endelomyia aethiops*), officially named "roseslug." Bristly roseslug in California has several generations per year and occurs mainly in coastal or cool areas. Its larvae are pale green with many hairlike bristles. Roseslug and curled rose sawfly larvae do not have many distinct bristles or hairs. However, curled rose sawfly larvae have rows of pale dots and pale tubercles (short projections more stout than hairs), and larvae often coil their bodies while feeding.

Cypress Sawfly
Susana cupressi

About one-half dozen *Susana* species sawflies feed on broad-needled conifers in the western United States. The most important species in California, primarily in the south, is the cypress sawfly. Cypress sawfly primarily damages cypress, but reportedly also feeds on arborvitae and juniper. Adult wasps are black and yellow. Larvae are grayish green with rows of whitish dots. The cypress sawfly spends the winter in a cocoon in the soil and has one generation per year.

MANAGEMENT OF SAWFLIES
Healthy trees and shrubs tolerate moderate defoliation without significant loss in growth, flowering, or fruit yield. Nat-

ural enemies are responsible for keeping most sawfly populations low and can cause outbreak populations to soon decline. Parasitic wasps, insectivorous birds and small mammals, predaceous beetles, or fungal and viral diseases commonly kill sawflies. In the eastern states some sawflies in forests have been managed by introducing and augmenting sawfly parasites and insect-specific viruses. Sawflies in the western states are mostly native species and rarely damage forest trees. There has not been sufficient research in landscapes or Christmas-tree plantations to allow recommendations on effectively using natural enemies.

Clip off infested foliage if larvae are on a small portion of the plant. Pearslugs and some other sawfly larvae that feed openly can be washed from plants with a forceful stream of water.

Most sawfly larvae that chew foliage are relatively easy to control if sprayed with almost any insecticide applied to achieve good spray coverage, including insecticidal soap, narrow-range oil, or neem oil. Broad-spectrum, persistent insecticides should be avoided because of their adverse affect on natural enemies. Be aware that sprays of virtually any insecticide sometimes damage blossoms. Although some larvae resemble caterpillars, sawflies are not controlled by *Bacillus thuringiensis*.

LEAF BEETLES AND FLEA BEETLES

Hundreds of species of leaf beetles and flea beetles (family Chrysomelidae) occur in the United States. Only a few are common pests in landscapes, although new species are periodically introduced, such as the viburnum leaf beetle (*Pyrrhalta viburni*) from Europe that now occurs in eastern Canada and the United States at least in the Northeast. Elm leaf beetle and eucalyptus tortoise beetle are primary landscape pests in this group. Other species of leaf beetles are sometimes abundant enough to be pests on various other hosts, including alder, aspen, cottonwood, coyote brush, hypericum, poplar, and willow.

DAMAGE

Leaf beetle adults and larvae scrape the surface or chew holes in leaves. Similar damage may be caused by larvae of some moths, butterflies, or sawflies, by adult weevils, or by adult and immature grasshoppers, katydids, snails, and slugs. Damaged leaves may turn yellow or brown and drop prematurely. High populations of leaf beetle cover leaves with their dark droppings and can skeletonize or defoliate entire plants. Repeated defoliation causes plants to decline, become susceptible to other problems, and in rare cases die. However, otherwise healthy deciduous plants tolerate extensive skeletonization or defoliation. Larvae of some species feed on roots, but these are not known to seriously damage established woody plants.

IDENTIFICATION AND BIOLOGY

Most adult leaf beetles are less than ⅓ inch long, oval, blunt, and have threadlike antennae. The smallest species, flea beetles, are metallic in color and often jump away when disturbed. Larger species may be colorful or blend with the colors of their host and usually drop when disturbed. Both adults and larvae of many species feed on leaves, while other species, including cucumber beetles (*Diabrotica* spp.), have larvae that feed on roots but cause no known damage to woody plants. Larvae of a few chrysomelids feed in stems or mine leaves. Larvae of openly-feeding species are caterpillarlike, but unlike caterpillars and sawflies, they lack prolegs (see Figure 4-9). Many species feed in groups when young, then feed individually as they mature. Most leaf beetles pupate on the ground or attached to foliage or bark. Most overwinter as adults in debris or protected places, such as bark crevices or inside buildings. Each species usually feeds only on a few closely related plants.

MANAGEMENT

No thresholds have been established for leaf beetle numbers or damage on most landscape plants; tolerance varies among individuals and location. Suggested control action thresholds for leaf beetle damage to healthy, mature deciduous landscape plants are approximately 30 to 40% defoliation in the spring or summer. In the fall, it is generally inappropriate to control leaf beetles on deciduous plants regardless of damage levels, since the leaves will be shed soon. Leaf beetle damage or larvae can be monitored by regularly inspecting leaves, as discussed for foliage-feeding caterpillars. Degree-day monitoring is useful for timing control actions against elm leaf beetle.

Provide proper cultural care to keep plants vigorous and better able to tolerate some defoliation. Many deciduous landscape plants, such as American and European elms, are adapted to frequent summer rainfall and require regular irrigation when grown in areas with summer drought. Consider replacing especially problem-prone trees with pest-resistant species or cultivars.

A microbial insecticide, *Bacillus thuringiensis* subspecies *tenebrionis*, controls some leaf beetles, including elm leaf beetle and cottonwood leaf beetle. Broad-spectrum insecticides may also be applied, but spaying foliage with these adversely affects natural enemies and may cause outbreaks of other pests such as mites.

Elm Leaf Beetle
Xanthogaleruca (=Pyrrhalta) luteola

Elm leaf beetle feeds on elms and occasionally on zelkova throughout the United States. European elm species are most susceptible to damage, and American and Siberian elm are less preferred. Most Chinese (evergreen) elm, zelkova, and many newer elm cultivars are infrequently fed upon. Larvae skeletonize the leaf surface, while adults eat through the leaf, often in a shothole pattern. High

beetle populations can entirely defoliate trees, eliminating shade, reducing aesthetic value, and causing premature leaf drop. Repeated extensive defoliation weakens elms, causing trees to decline.

IDENTIFICATION AND BIOLOGY

Adults are olive-green with a black longitudinal stripe along each margin and down the center of their back. Females lay yellowish to gray eggs in double rows of about 5 to 25 on the underside of leaves. Newly hatched larvae are black. Mature larvae are a dull yellow or greenish. Third-instar larvae have dense rows of tiny dark tubercles that resemble two black stripes, one along each side. After feeding in the canopy for several weeks, mature larvae crawl down the tree trunk and form bright yellowish pupae around the tree

An elm leaf beetle adult, egg mass, and first-instar larva. Certain elms are rarely damaged by elm leaf beetle or Dutch elm disease, and these pest-resistant elms are good choices for landscapes.

Several third-instar (mature) elm leaf beetle larvae on the lower surface of an English elm leaf they have skeletonized. Adult feeding, one hole chewed through the leaf, is visible at the left.

base. After about 10 days, adult beetles emerge and fly to the canopy to feed and lay eggs. Elm leaf beetle has at least one generation per year in northern California and one to three generations per year in central and southern California. Adults commonly overwinter in bark crevices, buildings, litter, and woodpiles.

MONITORING AND THRESHOLDS

Elm leaf beetle populations fluctuate dramatically from year to year. Few if any elms require treatment every year. When beetles are present, healthy elms can tolerate substantial defoliation. Suggested thresholds are about 40% defoliation (portion of leaf area chewed or leaves dropped prematurely). If damage is less tolerable (for example, if elms are otherwise unhealthy), 20% defoliation is a suggested threshold.

Evaluate the need and effective timing for treatment using one or more of several methods, depending on the planned control method and your resources available for monitoring. Some practices may require professional help. As summarized in Tables 4-7 and 4-8, key methods include visually inspecting leaves for eggs or larvae during spring, monitoring temperature using degree-days, and inspect-

ing leaves during late summer to early fall to assess program effectiveness and help decide whether control actions may be needed the next season. For more details, consult *Elm Leaf Beetle Pest Notes* (Dreistadt, Dahlsten, and Lawson 2001).

When using foliar sprays, insecticide bark bands, or systemic insecticide ap-

Curled elm leaf beetle prepupae and yellowish pupae around the base of an English elm. Before they crawl down from the canopy, these can be controlled by spot-spraying bark with a small amount of persistent insecticide.

plied during spring, visually inspect leaves for eggs or larvae at about weekly intervals during the period when the first generation of those stages are expected to be most abundant, as summarized in Table 4-7. In general, monitor earlier if spraying trees because you are targeting early-instar larvae. If trees are bark banded, take action later, before the earliest third instars crawl down the trunk. Because beetle development varies dramatically from year to year depending on weather, degree-days (discussed below) are the best way to determine the optimal time to monitor and apply treatments.

If insecticide injection is planned, monitor during spring for eggs and young larvae to determine whether treatment is warranted. If an application of a soil systemic insecticide is planned, the optimal treatment time is before beetles are present on leaves and before knowing whether beetles will be abundant enough to warrant control during the current or next generation of insects. Use several criteria to help decide if a preventive, soil-applied insecticide is warranted (Table 4-8). For example, inspect elms during late summer to early fall; if beetles and damage are low, especially on untreated elms, it is unlikely

TABLE 4-7.

Timing of Elm Leaf Beetle Monitoring and Management.

ACTION	WHEN	WHEN, IF MONITORING DEGREE-DAYS DD (F)	
		FIRST GENERATION	SECOND GENERATION
sample eggs once a week[1]	for several weeks after first-generation eggs appear in spring; repeat during second generation	329–689	1,535–1,895
Btt[2] applied about twice at 7- to 10-day intervals	first and second instars present in spring	550–800	not recommended
single foliar spray	peak density of first and second instars combined	700	not recommended
bark banding or trunk spray	before earliest third instars crawl down trunk	700	2,000
systemic insecticide applied to soil	during late winter or early spring[3]		
systemic insecticide implant or injection	as soon as possible during spring if egg sampling during 329–689 DD indicates thresholds are exceeded		

Actions are listed in chronological order, except for systemic insecticide use. Degree-days (DD) are accumulated above 51.8°F from 1 March. See the UC Statewide IPM Program's Web site at www.ipm.ucdavis.edu for more information.

1. This technique is for professionals managing large numbers of elms and using egg presence-absence sampling to predict treatment need.

2. *Bacillus thuringiensis* ssp. *tenebrionis*.

3. See Table 4-8 for decision-making criteria.

that insecticide application will be needed next season.

Although it has not been scientifically demonstrated, relatively warm and wet winters are believed to reduce the likelihood that beetles will be a problem in California the following spring. Wet winters can increase overwintering mortality of beetles from insect pathogenic fungi. Warm winters may cause many "hibernating" beetles to starve to death because warmer weather increases the rate at which these insects consume their stored energy (e.g., body fat), increasing the likelihood that beetles become weakened or starve before elm leaves appear in spring. If elm leaf beetle damage was low the previous fall and the winter is warm and wet, avoid preventive insecticide application the subsequent spring.

Degree-Day Monitoring. Because insect activity and growth rate depend on temperature, measuring heat over time provides a physiological time scale called degree-days that is more useful than calendar days for timing insect monitoring and control. The lower threshold for elm leaf beetle is 51.8°F. When temperatures are cooler, this pest does not feed, grow, or reproduce. To predict the peak abundance of each life stage, degree-days above 51.8°F are accumulated for elm leaf beetle each season beginning March 1 (Tables 4-2, 4-9). If populations are high and damage is anticipated, treatment options include injecting elms as soon as need is predicted (based on monitoring eggs) or applying a trunk spray or foliar spray at about 700 degree-days (Tables 4-7, 4-9).

Temperatures for many locations and relatively easy to use degree-day calculation tools are available from the UC Statewide IPM Program at www.ipm.ucdavis.edu on the World Wide Web. Alternatively, dedicated devices can record temperatures and calculate degree-days.

Presence-Absence Sampling for Professionals. The percentage of one-foot branch terminals infested with elm leaf beetle eggs can be used to determine the need for foliar spraying or spring application of systemic insecticide. This presence-absence monitoring can be useful for professionals managing many elms. Although time-consuming, it can save substantial amounts of treatment time and money by directing control actions only to locations where they are needed and by helping managers to confidently avoid unwarranted treatments.

Monitor degree-days to determine when to sample (Table 4-7). Begin sampling of first-generation eggs at about 329 degree-days (above 51.8°F accumulated since March 1). Continue sampling weekly until the percent of branches with eggs peaks then falls, until about 689 degree-days have accumulated (which is well after the predicted peak egg time), or until thresholds are exceeded on any one sample date, whichever comes first. If egg presence-absence is monitored in the second generation, monitor weekly during about 1,535 to 1,895 degree-days. This will usually mean sampling a maximum of four or five times per generation.

Use a pole pruner to clip two or more 1-foot terminals from each of 8 locations in the lower canopy of each sample tree. Examine the leaves on each sample and record whether eggs are present or absent. Once you observe the first eggs on a sample, there is no need to examine it further; record it as infested and move on to inspect the next terminal. To determine the percentage of samples (terminals) infested, divide the number of samples infested by the total number of samples inspected and multiply by 100. Table 4-10 summarizes the number of trees and terminals per tree that should

TABLE 4-8.

Criteria To Help Decide Whether Preventive Systemic Insecticide May Be Warranted For Elm Leaf Beetle Control.

CRITERIA	AVOID TREATMENT	TREATMENT MAY BE WARRANTED
beetle populations and damage the previous late summer or early fall	low population or damage	high population or damage
tree treated the previous season	yes	no
overwintering weather	wetter or warmer than average or both	drier or colder than average or both

TABLE 4-9.

Time of Peak Abundance (Mean ± Standard Deviation) of Elm Leaf Eggs and Larvae in Northern California Based on Degree-Day (DD) Monitoring.

FIRST GENERATION	DD (F)
eggs	509 ±95
first-instar larvae	635 ±112
second-instar larvae	794 ±162
third-instar larvae	857 ±167
SECOND GENERATION	**DD (F)**
eggs	1,715 ±167
first-instar larvae	1,962 ±131
second-instar larvae	2,055 ±158
third-instar larvae	2,129 ±162

Degree-days are accumulated above 51.8°F from 1 March. See the UC Statewide IPM Program's Web site at www.ipm.ucdavis.edu for more information. Adapted from Dahlsten et al. 1993.

TABLE 4-10.

▬▬▬▬

Suggested Number of Terminals to Inspect for Elm Leaf Beetle Egg Presence-Absence in Different-Sized Groups of English Elms.

TOTAL TREES	NUMBER OF TREES SAMPLED	SAMPLES PER TREE	SAMPLES PER LOCATION WITHIN TREES	TOTAL SAMPLES	% OF TOTAL TREES SAMPLED
3	3	40	5	120	100%
4	4	32	4	128	100%
5	5	32	4	160	100%
6	6	24	3	144	100%
7	6	24	3	144	86%
8	7	24	3	168	88%
9–15	8	16	2	128	89–53%
16–21	9	16	2	144	56–43%
22–30	10	16	2	160	45–33%
40	12	16	2	192	30%
50	15	16	2	240	30%
60	15	16	2	240	25%

Sample at least 25% of the trees, and 3 or more trees, at each site. Randomly select the trees to be sampled, then sample those same trees each week. Inspect a minimum of 120 total samples (1-foot terminals) per site. Collect 2 to 5 terminals from each location within each sample tree. Locations within each tree should be on the north, east, south, and west sides of the tree, in both the inner canopy (from trunk halfway to the drip line) and the outer canopy. Adapted from Dahlsten et al. 1993.

be inspected to confidently predict the likelihood of defoliation on untreated English elms.

Using a threshold of 40% defoliation, treatment is warranted when over 45% of branch terminals have beetle eggs during the week when egg density is at its maximum during the first generation. If the preferred threshold is 20% defoliation, treatment is warranted when over 30% of branch terminals are egg-infested during the first generation. In the less common situation where treatment is based on second-generation eggs, the treatment threshold is about 30% of terminals infested.

MANAGEMENT

Plant trees that resist both Dutch elm disease and elm leaf beetle, such as Frontier and Prospector elms and most Chinese elms (except for Dynasty, which is highly susceptible to elm leaf beetle). Avoid planting European trees such as English elm or Scotch elm and consider

replacing these and other species that are especially susceptible to both Dutch elm disease and elm leaf beetle. Consult Table 5-8 in the section "Dutch Elm Disease" for a list of pest-resistant and susceptible elms.

Provide elms with proper irrigation, especially American and European elms, which are adapted to summer rainfall. Protect trees from injury, such as by avoiding changes in grade and drainage around established trees. Control elm leaf beetle with an integrated program that includes good tree care, bark bands, and (if populations are high) selective or low residual toxicity insecticides that conserve natural enemies. For current information on management including insecticides, consult the most recent *Elm Leaf Beetle Pest Notes* (Dreistadt, Dahlsten, and Lawson 2001).

Biological Control. Several introduced and native natural enemies kill elm leaf beetles but generally do not provide ade-

quate control by themselves. The most important natural enemy in California is a small black tachinid fly (*Erynniopsis antennata*) that emerges from mature beetle larvae. Its black to reddish, cylinder- or teardrop-shaped pupae occur at the tree base among the bright yellow beetle pupae. It overwinters in adult beetles and emerges in spring, although this is not obvious. Consult *Natural Enemies Handbook* (Flint and Dreistadt 1998) for more information, including an illustration of this species' life cycle.

Baryscapus (=*Tetrastichus*) *brevistigma*, a tiny wasp, leaves one or more small round holes in beetle pupae that it emerges from around the tree base; this species is uncommon in California but may be important in the eastern United States. An egg parasite (*Baryscapus gallerucae*) occurs in California and at least some portions of the Midwest (at least from Ohio to Oklahoma). It leaves round holes when it emerges from beetle eggs, which remain golden. When beetle larvae have emerged, the egg shell is whitish with ragged holes. Conserve these natural enemies by avoiding foliar applications of broad-spectrum insecticides; use less-toxic methods, such as narrow-range oil, *Bacillus thuringiensis* subspecies *tenebrionis*, and insecticide bark bands in an integrated program to obtain maximum benefits from biological control.

Bark Banding. Bark banding is an inexpensive and environmentally sound technique that involves spraying the tree trunk with an insecticide. Use a hand pump sprayer or hydraulic sprayer at low pressure to spray a band of bark several feet wide around the first main branch crotch. Apply the product to bark at the rate labeled for elm bark beetles or other wood-boring insects. If bark spraying is not listed on the label of the commercial products available for home landscape use, it will be necessary to have the trunk application done by a licensed pesticide applicator. Do not use the rate labeled for foliar applications because this rate will not be effective as a trunk banding treatment. Carbaryl or certain pyrethroids (e.g., fluvalinate) are effective. About ½ gallon of dilute material is applied on each large tree. Larvae are killed by the insecticide when they crawl down to pupate around the tree base after feeding in the canopy. By reducing the number of elm leaf beetles that pupate and emerge as adults, bark banding reduces damage by later beetle generations, especially when done to all nearby elms.

Inspect foliage weekly from late April through June and band when mature larvae are first observed on leaves, before they begin to crawl down the trunk. Alternatively, monitor local temperatures and use a degree-day method to time the application in California. Spray at about 700 degree-days above 51.8°F accumulated since March 1, as discussed in the section "Degree-Day Monitoring" earlier in this chapter.

A single application to bark each spring can kill most beetle larvae that crawl over the treated bark all season long. If rain occurs after application, if trunks are wetted by sprinklers, or if a less-persistent material is used, regularly inspect around the base of trees throughout the season. If many beetles have changed from greenish prepupae (the stage killed by banding) to bright yellowish pupae (unaffected beetles), another application may be warranted.

Bark banding alone does not provide satisfactory control in many situations. Treatment of a single or few trees is unlikely to be as effective as banding all nearby trees in a neighborhood, because adult beetles can fly between treated and untreated trees. Not all beetles crawl down the trunk to pupate; some drop to the ground from branches or pupate in upper branch crotches or bark crevices. Because overwintering adults fly to the canopy and lay eggs, first-generation beetle populations or damage are not reduced by that season's banding. Study of Siberian elms (*Ulmus pumila*) in northern California found good control during the first season of banding, but beetles were not controlled during the first year on English elm and Scotch elm. This is because Siberian elms are less susceptible to elm leaf beetle and are not as seriously damaged by the

A close-up of elm leaf beetle prepupae (left) and pupae (center) and pupae of the elm leaf beetle parasite *Erynniopsis antennata* (right).

An adult *Erynniopsis antennata* and two second-instar elm leaf beetle larvae. In many locations, this tachinid fly is the most important natural enemy of elm leaf beetle.

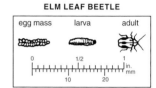

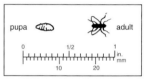

Two black second-instar elm leaf beetle larvae killed by *Bacillus thuringiensis* subspecies *tenebrionis* and a healthy green larva.

first generation of beetles in comparison to the more susceptible elms. Little or no control should be expected during the first year when banding the more susceptible species; banding all nearby elms over several consecutive years can provide control after the first year of treatment.

Systemic Insecticides. In years when populations are expected to be high, elm leaf beetle feeding can be controlled with certain insecticides that move within plant tissue, including abamectin and imidacloprid. Some formulations of these materials can be sprayed onto the tree foliage, but soil applications (if labeled for this method of application) and tree injections minimize environmental contamination and may be more effective than foliar sprays.

When using systemic insecticides, to avoid tree injury and spread of pathogens, consider using a soil application instead of injecting or implanting trees whenever possible. Especially avoid methods that cause large wounds, such as implants placed in holes drilled in trunks. Do not implant or inject roots or trunks more than once a year. It is usually not necessary to treat 2 years in a row using this method. See the section "Injecting or Implanting Pesticides" in Chapter 2 and "Systemic Insecticides" earlier in this chapter for more information.

A major disadvantage of certain uses of systemic insecticide is that treatment is made in late winter before beetles appear in spring, before knowing whether insects and damage will be abundant enough to warrant control action. Consult the suggested criteria for help in deciding whether preventive treatment is warranted (Table 4-8).

Foliar Sprays. Several foliar insecticide sprays are available for elm leaf beetle. Foliar spraying may be appropriate to supplement banding during the first year or two of treatment or when early-season beetle populations are high. The low toxicity insecticides azadirachtin or *Bacillus thuringiensis* ssp. *tenebrionis* (Btt) are good choices in an integrated pest management program. They can be combined with narrow-range oil to kill beetle eggs and other elm pests such as scales. More broad-spectrum, persistent materials, such as pyrethroids, are also available for foliar application, but they are generally not recommended because of their negative impact on natural enemies and their potential for environmental impacts in urban settings. Carefully time all foliar applications to target first- and second-instar larvae. Because specialized equipment is required to spray the tops of large elm trees, it is best to hire a professional applicator.

Bacillus thuringiensis ssp. *tenebrionis* (Btt) kills young beetle larvae and is the only truly selective insecticide available. Btt is not toxic to people and most nontarget organisms, including natural enemies of the elm leaf beetle. However, Btt may not be available (registered) for use in California. Bt subspecies labeled for moth and butterfly caterpillars or mosquito larvae are not effective against elm leaf beetle.

To obtain control, foliage throughout the tree must be thoroughly sprayed with Btt during warm, dry weather when young larvae are actively feeding. Because only a portion of the beetle population is in the susceptible stages at any one time and Btt breaks down within several days, at least two applications at an interval of about 7 to 10 days may be necessary, beginning when young larvae are first observed feeding.

Eucalyptus Tortoise Beetle
Trachymela sloanei

The eucalyptus tortoise beetle, also called bluegum leaf beetle, was discovered infesting eucalyptus in southern California in 1998. Because adults readily fly, it is expected to spread to most locations where eucalyptus occur. Adults and larvae chew semicircular or irregular notches along leaf edges and can remove most of a leaf's surface, leaving only the midvein. Adults also clip off young terminals. Heavy feeding can cause trees to

become sparsely foliated when beetles are abundant. The *Eucalyptus* species preferences of this pest have not been well documented, but certain species are known to be preferred or avoided, as summarized and compared with other major eucalyptus pests in Table 4-14 in the section "Redgum Lerp Psyllid."

Eucalyptus tortoise beetle adults are hemispherical and brown with darker mottled spots. Adults are about ¼ to

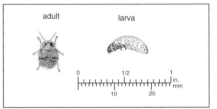

EUCALYPTUS TORTOISE BEETLE

Eucalyptus tortoise beetle larvae have a green to reddish abdomen with a black head and black prothoracic shield behind their head. If the cause of chewed eucalyptus leaves is not obvious, look under loose tree bark, where tortoise beetle adults, egg masses, larvae, and possibly pupae can be observed and collected for identification.

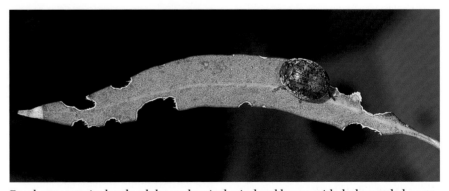

Eucalyptus tortoise beetle adults are hemispherical and brown with dark, mottled spots. Adults and larvae chew semicircular or irregular notches along leaf edges. Egg parasites are being introduced in an effort to provide biological control of this leaf beetle.

⅜ inch long and superficially resemble a large lady beetle. Females oviposit about 5 to 40 or more pinkish brown to dark purplish eggs, which occur in an irregular group under loose eucalyptus bark. Larvae have a red to green abdomen, and their head and prothoracic shield (top and sides of the first segment behind the head) are black. Three pairs of true legs and no prolegs on the abdomen distinguish leaf beetle larvae from immatures of other caterpillarlike insects (Figure 4-9). Larvae develop through four immature stages before pupating in the soil or litter around the base of host trees or beneath loose bark adhering to trees. At warm temperatures, development time from egg to adult may be as short as 5 weeks. There are several generations each year from late winter through fall.

Eucalyptus tortoise beetle can readily be distinguished from the other eucalyptus defoliator reported in California, the eucalyptus snout beetle (*Gonipterus scutellatus*). Eucalyptus snout beetle adults are reddish brown weevils with an elongate head, as opposed to the hemispherical shape of the tortoise beetle. The legless weevil larvae are yellowish green with a slimy coating. Because eucalyptus snout beetle is under good biological control from an introduced egg parasite (*Anaphes nitens*), the snout beetle is now uncommon and no longer a pest.

The cause of clipped, notched, or scraped eucalyptus leaves may not be obvious because most tortoise beetle adults and larvae hide under loose bark during the day and feed primarily at night. Also, individuals may be concentrated high in the tree. If no leaf-feeding adults or larvae are observed on foliage, inspect beneath loose bark where adults, egg masses, larvae, and possibly pupae can be observed and collected for identification.

Trachymela sloanei is not normally a pest in its native home of Australia, presumably because natural enemies there keep beetle populations low. University of California scientists have introduced a tiny egg parasite (*Enoggera reticulata*) from Australia into California in an effort to control the beetle. This parasite

searches under eucalyptus bark and in cracks and fissures, laying one of its eggs in each leaf beetle egg. The parasite larva feeds inside, turning the host egg reddish orange, often with black spots. An adult parasite then emerges to seek and attack more beetle eggs. In addition to beetle eggs killed by parasite larvae, adult female parasites feed on the eggs, which kills many additional beetle eggs.

Protect trees from injury and provide eucalyptus with good cultural care, especially appropriate irrigation. Before taking any other actions, consult the sections "Eucalyptus Longhorned Borers" and "Eucalyptus Redgum Lerp Psyllid" later in this chapter. Consider the impact of controls on other eucalyptus pests, such as the potential of insecticides to disrupt biological control of the bluegum psyllid and eucalyptus snout beetle. For more information, consult *Eucalyptus Tortoise Beetle Pest Notes* (Millar et al. 2003).

Cottonwood Leaf Beetle
Chrysomela scripta

The cottonwood leaf beetle feeds on cottonwood and willow. Several other related *Altica, Calligrapha, Chrysomela, Plagiodera,* and *Pyrrhalta* species throughout the United States also feed on alder, aspen, cottonwood, poplar, or willow. Adult cottonwood leaf beetles are grayish, orangish, or yellowish with variable black spots and stripes on the back.

Females lay yellowish eggs in clusters of about 25 on the lower leaf surface. The young, black larvae feed in groups on the lower leaf surface. Mature larvae are yellowish, grayish, or reddish, often with rows of black tubercles. There are several generations per year.

Provide regular, deep irrigation for hosts planted in areas with hot, dry summers. Protect plants from injury, such as by avoiding compaction or other soil disturbances around roots. Vigorous host plants tolerate moderate leaf beetle feeding, and control is generally not warranted. If populations are not tolerable, foliar or systemic insecticides as discussed above for elm leaf beetle may provide control.

Klamathweed Beetle
Chrysolina quadrigemina

The Klamathweed beetle was deliberately introduced into California during the 1940s to control *Hypericum perforatum*, a toxic rangeland weed. The beetle largely eliminated Klamathweed from several million acres, and each year saves ranchers millions of dollars in otherwise lost grazing land and poisoned livestock. However, certain other *Hypericum*

COTTONWOOD LEAF BEETLE

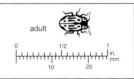

Adults, eggs, and larval chewing damage of the California willow leaf beetle (*Plagiodera californica*). Black larval frass covers part of the chewed underside of the left willow leaf. This species resembles another pest, the imported willow leaf beetle (*P. versicolora*).

Klamathweed beetle adults are metallic dark brown to bluish green. This important biological control agent of rangeland Klamath weed sometimes defoliates hypericum ground covers.

KLAMATHWEED BEETLE

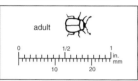

species that subsequently became popular ground covers and shrubs in landscapes, especially *H. calycinum*, can be severely defoliated by this leaf beetle. The metallic bluish green to brown adults feed on foliage the year around, except during the hot, dry summer. Eggs are laid from fall through spring singly or in clusters on leaves where the grayish larvae feed. Larvae pupate just beneath the soil surface. Damage occurs during the spring, when plants produce most of their growth flush.

Insecticidal soap or another insecticide, applied when larvae or adults are feeding, can provide control. Removing litter accumulated beneath plants in hot areas may reduce the survival of adult beetles that rest there during the summer. Keeping soil beneath plants moist during the spring may increase disease and mortality of immature beetles that pupate near the soil surface. Applying parasitic nematodes to soil beneath plants, as discussed below for weevils, may provide control if applications are made when most beetles are pupating, before adults emerge. Pupation often occurs during April and May, but populations vary, so monitor plants to determine when to treat; pupation occurs after mature larvae are observed on foliage.

WEEVILS

Many weevils, also called snout beetles (family Curculionidae), feed on landscape plants. Weevils are the most diverse group of beetles; over 1,000 species occur in California alone.

DAMAGE

Adult weevils generally feed on aboveground plant parts. They cause leaves or flowers to appear notched or ragged, and leaves or needles may be clipped from twigs. This adult feeding is the primary damage caused by live oak weevils (*Deporaus glastinus*), pine needle weevils (*Scythropus* spp.), and Fuller rose beetle. Unless populations are high, this damage does not harm established woody plants and can be ignored. Rose curculio and the oak-feeding filbert weevil feed on aboveground plant parts during both their adult and larval stages. Although sometimes bothersome, damage from these species does not threaten plant health.

Larvae of the yucca weevil (*Scyphophorus yuccae*) tunnel under bark, in the base of green flowers, and in the basal heart of the plant, causing yuccas to decline and possibly die. Soil-dwelling larvae of several other weevil species seriously damage roots

Adult weevils characteristically chew irregular notches in leaf edges, such as on this viburnum. Collecting and identifying the species of weevils present is important because weevils that primarily chew foliage are relatively harmless in landscapes. However, species such as black vine weevil (photo top) can seriously damage roots during larval feeding.

and girdle plants near the soil surface. These root-feeding species cause a general decline and sometimes the death of young host plants in landscapes and nursery containers. Weevils whose larvae are damaging root-feeders include black vine weevil (*Otiorhynchus sulcatus*), cribrate weevil (*O. cribricollis*), whitefringed beetles (*Naupactus =Graphognathus* spp.), and woods weevil (*Nemocestes incomptus*).

IDENTIFICATION AND BIOLOGY

Adult weevils have the head elongated into a snout and have elbowed and clubbed antennae. Many weevils are flightless because their wing covers are fused. Females may feed for an extended period before laying eggs, and many species produce viable eggs without mating. Larvae of most species are whitish grubs that feed hidden within plant parts or on roots in the soil.

Black Vine Weevil
Otiorhynchus sulcatus

Black vine weevil is the most important of the approximately 16 *Otiorhynchus* species that have been introduced into the United States. Adult black vine weevils feed on yew (*Taxus* spp.), broadleaf evergreens such as azalea and rhododendron, and many different herbaceous and perennial plants. Other major hosts include euonymus, grape, hemlock, liquidambar, viburnum, and strawberry. Adults are stocky, dark, about $\frac{3}{8}$ to $\frac{1}{2}$ inch long, and have sparse, fine yellowish patches of hairs on their wing covers. They resemble cribrate weevil (*O. cribricollis*), another species that feeds on many hosts and is also common in California. In comparison with black vine weevil, cribrate weevil is usually smaller (about $\frac{5}{16}$ inch long) and has differently shaped front tibia (Figure 4-10).

Black vine weevil occurs throughout the United States and has one generation per year. In California, adults emerge from pupae in the soil and feed during the night from March through September. Larvae are the most damaging stage

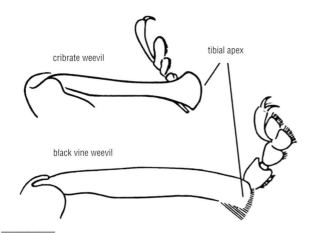

FIGURE 4-10. Characters for distinguishing black vine weevil from cribrate weevil. The first tibia (the longest segment of the first pair of legs) of cribrate weevil is distinctly wider near its apex (the end nearest the tarsi or "feet") in comparison with the width of the rest of that segment. The apex of the first tibia of black vine weevil is rounded. Black vine weevil can also be distinguished because it has sparse, fine yellowish patches of hairs on its wing covers, while cribrate weevil lacks fine yellowish patches of hairs. Adapted from Garrison 1993.

An adult black vine weevil chewing a euonymus leaf edge. Black vine weevil can be a severe pest of certain shrubs and young trees because its soil-dwelling larvae can extensively chew roots and girdle basal stems.

of this weevil, causing damage primarily in nurseries or on young landscape plants. Larvae feed on roots and bark near the soil surface. Most feeding and damage occurs in the fall and spring. Even a few weevils or slight foliage damage may warrant control actions to prevent larvae from developing and causing damage to young plants; mature plants tolerate more extensive feeding. Monitoring and management of black vine weevil and other species is discussed below.

Conifer Twig Weevils
Pissodes spp.

Conifer twig weevils feed on Douglas fir, fir, pine, and spruce throughout the United States. The most important species, the white pine weevil (*Pissodes strobi*) feeds on shoots and needles of pines and spruce as both larvae and adults. White pine weevil can severely distort terminals and stunt plant growth. Most of the more than two dozen other *Pissodes* spp. are rarely, if ever, serious pests. Only the adults of most of these other species, such as the Monterey pine weevil (*Pissodes radiatae*), feed on foliage;

this foliage damage is minor. Larvae of Monterey pine weevil and most other *Pissodes* spp. attack primarily conifers that are already dying or injured. These larvae feed on roots and the trunk near the soil; this feeding can cause unsightly cankers on bark. Because other causes can produce similar damage symptoms and most *Pissodes* spp. are secondary pests, consult the Diseases chapter, Table 5-12, for a summary of insects and pathogens affecting pines.

Filbert Weevils and Acorn Worms

Oak acorns are commonly infested with larvae of filbert weevils (*Curculio* spp.), the filbertworm (*Cydia latiferreana* =*Melissopus latiferreanus*, family Tortricidae), or an acorn moth (*Valentinia glandulella*, family Blastobasidae). The moth larvae also sometimes damage other nuts, including almond and chestnut. Although harmless to trees, these larvae kill the seeds. Natural oak regeneration may be reduced by the feeding of these larvae, but this has not been demonstrated. The number of acorns

and acorn-feeding insects varies dramatically from year to year due to many factors. In comparison with these insects, oak seedling mortality (from other causes) and the loss of older trees (such as from development) are probably more important factors influencing the number of oaks.

The major concern is that larval feeding kills acorns that people collect for planting. Another concern is drippy oak and drippy nut disease, which occurs when insect-damaged oak tissue (such as acorns) becomes colonized by *Erwinia quercina* bacteria. A clear to brownish ooze develops in bacterial-colonized tissue, causing a sticky mess on cars, sidewalks, and other surfaces beneath affected oaks. Although annoying, drippy oak apparently does not threaten tree health. For more information, see the Chapter 5 section "Drippy Oak and Drippy Nut Disease."

Acorn moths and filbertworms are larvae of small moths, which are commonly bronze, coppery, or reddish brown. Larvae are light brown to whitish with a darker head and have three pairs of true legs. Filbert weevils are brown beetles with a long thin snout. Larvae are light brownish, yellow, or white. Filbert weevil larvae have no obvious legs, are relatively inactive, and may curl into a C shape if disturbed.

Filbert weevils drill a small hole and insert their eggs into acorns on the tree. The female moths oviposit on nuts, and the emerging larvae bore inside. The moth and weevil larvae feed and develop through several instars inside each acorn. After the oak seed drop, larvae chew a hole in the acorn and exit to pupate overwinter in the soil, or they remain inside the nut and pupate. Insects emerge as adults in late spring to early summer, and the females seek acorns and lay eggs. Filbertworms and filbert weevils have one generation per year.

No methods have been demonstrated as effective for controlling these insects in the field, and no controls are recommended. If acorns are collected for planting, separate good acorns from the bad and dispose of those that are damaged. One efficient sorting method is to place acorns in a tub of water and discard those that float. Larval feeding creates air pockets in nuts, causing insect-damaged acorns to float. Other methods are to feel and visually inspect each nut. Acorns that are unusually lightweight or deform easily when squeezed are often not viable. One or more small exit holes may be visible in insect-damaged nuts.

An adult filbert weevil. The acorn has a hole chewed by a weevil larva, which emerged to pupate in soil. Filbert weevils do not damage established oaks; no methods have been demonstrated to control these weevils. If collecting acorns, inspect and discard damaged nuts before storing or planting them.

Fuller Rose Beetle
Asynonychus godmani (=Pantomorus cervinus)

Fuller rose beetle is found in the southern and western states on many hosts, including acacia, box elder, citrus, oak, photinia, *Rhaphiolepis*, rose, toyon, and *Prunus* and *Pyrus* species. These brown weevils lay their tiny eggs in organic matter on the soil or on branches, leaves, or fruit. The emerging larvae enter the soil and feed on roots for 6 to 10 months. Most adults emerge between June and November, but a few can emerge from pupae during each month of the year. The foliage- or blossom-feeding adults, not larvae on roots, are the damaging stage of this weevil, so low populations of adults of this species can be ignored.

FULLER ROSE BEETLE

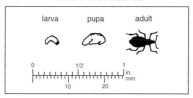

Rose Curculios
Merhynchites spp.

Rose curculios are red to black snout beetles about 1/4 inch long. The legless larvae are pale orange to whitish and up to 1/4 inch long. Rose curculio larvae feed in flower buds, often killing buds before they open. Adults chew ragged holes in rose petals and make circular holes in flower buds and stems. If rose curculios are numerous, terminal shoots may be killed in addition to flower buds.

Stem feeding below buds by these weevils can cause terminals to bend over, injury that may be confused with damage caused by raspberry horntail larvae (*Hartigia cressoni*) mining in canes. Weevil larvae resemble larvae of the rose midge (*Dasineura rhodophaga*).

However, rose midges grow only up to 1/16 inch long, are more slender, are uncommon in California (reported only in Sonoma County), and also are rarely pests in Oregon and Washington State.

Hand-pick adult weevils, especially if few in number. Adults drop from the plant when disturbed, so they can be collected by gently shaking canes over a tray or a bucket of soapy water. Prune out and dispose of damaged buds and finished flowers, which will remove larvae and help reduce future problems as well as improve plant appearance. Entomopathogenic nematodes applied to soil in late winter or early spring where mature larvae or pupae are overwintering may provide some control. A broad-spectrum, persistent insecticide can be applied to kill adults if the infestation is severe.

MONITORING WEEVILS
Regularly inspect the foliage, buds, and flowers of host plants for evidence of weevil feeding. Damage was likely

These rose curculios chew blossoms and buds. Their larvae feed in flower buds, often killing buds before they open. Hand-pick adult weevils, especially if few in number. Clip and dispose of damaged buds and finished blossoms to remove larvae and reduce future populations of this pest.

ROSE CURCULIO

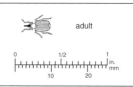

caused by weevils if needles are clipped or notched or jagged-edged leaves are observed, but no slime trails from snails or slugs and no leaf-feeding caterpillars, katydids, or other insects are found on foliage. Monitor plants as discussed below to determine whether nocturnal adults of soil-dwelling weevils are present. Decide on the need for and timing of control actions based on the extent of observed damage and on the presence and abundance of adults. For species such as the Fuller rose beetle that are damaging only when adults are abundant, conduct control actions only if the apparent damage is intolerable or if it was high the previous season. For weevils such as *Graphognathus* spp., *Nemocestes* spp., and *Otiorhynchus* spp. that cause damage primarily in the larval stage, even a few adults or low levels of foliage feeding warrant further investigation and possible control actions to prevent damage to young plants that tolerate relatively little damage to roots.

Monitoring Nocturnal Adults. Several methods are available to determine whether the night-feeding adult weevils are present. About 1 or 2 hours after dark, sweep foliage with a net or hold a tray, clipboard, or framed cloth beneath a branch and beat or shake it to dislodge any weevils. Sample several branches on each of several susceptible plants.

As an alternative to foliage sampling at night, adults such as *Graphognathus* spp., *Nemocestes* spp., and *Otiorhynchus* spp. weevils can be trapped by taking advantage of their behavior, which is to seek shelter during the day. Burlap bands wrapped around trunks are an effective monitoring method in landscapes. Pitfall traps may be best in nurseries, but they can also be useful in landscapes. Trap boards, though apparently a less-effective method, can also be used.

Monitor weevils by banding trunks with a strip of burlap (approximately 3 by 4 feet) folded lengthwise several times, then wrapped snugly around the base of each plant. Once or twice a week, gently remove the trunk wrap,

carefully unfold it, count and record the number of weevils, then dispose of them. Corrugated plastic tree wrap or corrugated cardboard with the smooth paper removed on one side may also be wrapped around trunks with the corrugated side placed against the bark.

Weevils may also be captured using a pitfall trap constructed from a several-inch-deep, wide-mouthed plastic cup or dish and a funnel or smaller tapered cup. Cut off most of the funnel's spout or the bottom of the smaller cup and snugly insert it into the larger cup with the hole pointed down. A single plastic cup may be used if the sides are regularly lubricated (such as with oil or silicon spray) to prevent the beetles from climbing out. Bury your trap so its top is flush with, or slightly below, the soil surface (Figure 4-11). Drill small holes in the bottom of the cup so that water can drain out. Alternatively, keep irrigation

water out by covering each trap with an inverted gallon pot after first cutting legs into the rim. Bury one or more traps as close to the trunk as possible beneath the canopy of each of several host plants. Check each trap about weekly, and record the total number of weevils caught in all traps. Do not be surprised to find a variety of ground-dwelling creatures in your pitfall traps or trunk wraps, including beneficial predaceous carabid beetles. Release these predators as they help to control weevils.

Alternatively, small boards (about 10 by 10 inches) can be placed on the ground to serve as daytime refuges for adult black vine weevils and certain other weevils in landscapes. Place one or more trap boards beneath each of several host plants. Inspect the underside of the trap boards and the ground beneath them during the day when beetles are resting.

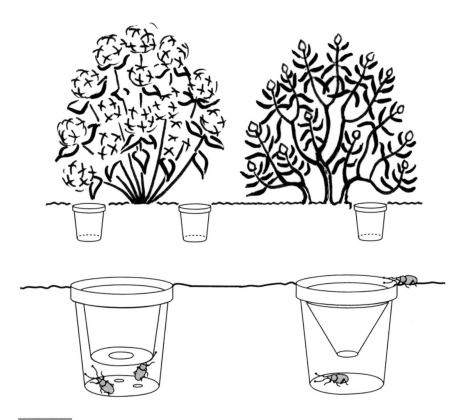

FIGURE 4-11. Pitfall traps can be used to monitor for adults of many soil-dwelling weevil species. Traps are constructed from a funnel (at bottom right), or smaller cup with a hole in its bottom (left), fit inside another cup that is buried in the soil near plants so that beetles walking on the soil surface fall into it.

MANAGEMENT OF SOIL-DWELLING WEEVILS

Plant less-susceptible species to avoid weevil damage. Many rhododendron hybrids resist damage from *Otiorhynchus* and *Nemocestes* species weevils (Table 4-11). Provide proper cultural care and a good growing environment, especially appropriate irrigation and good soil conditions for roots, to keep plants vigorous and better able to tolerate damage.

TABLE 4-11.

Hybrid Rhododendrons Resistant to Feeding Injury by Adult Root Weevils.

RHODODENDRON HYBRID	RATING
P. J. Mezzitt	100
Jock	92
Sapphire	90
Rose Elf	89
Cilpimense	88
Lucky Strike	83
Exbury Naomi	81
Virginia Richards	81
Cowslip	80
Luscombei	80
Vanessa	80
Oceanlake	80
Dora Amateis	79
Crest	79
Rainbow	76
Point Defiance	76
Naomi	76
Pilgrim	76
Letty Edwards	76
Odee Wright	76
Moonstone	73
Lady Clementine Mitford	72
Candi	72
Graf Zeppelin	71
Snow Lady	71
Loderi Pink Diamond	71
Faggetter's Favourite	70

Ranked from highly (100 rating) to moderately resistant (70) to *Sciopithes obscures, Otiorhynchus sulcatus, O. singularis, Nemocestes incomptus,* and *Dyslobus* spp. *Source:* Antonelli and Campbell 1984.

If plants have only one or a few trunks, flightless weevils such as the Fuller rose beetle and black vine weevil can be prevented from feeding on foliage by trimming branches that provide a bridge to other plants or the ground, then applying a several-inch-wide band of sticky material to trunks, as discussed and illustrated earlier in this chapter in the section "Sticky Barriers." Persistent trapping year-round as discussed under monitoring may significantly reduce weevil populations in some situations.

Soil-dwelling immature stages can be controlled with commercially available parasitic nematodes (such as *Heterorhabditis bacteriophora* or *Steinernema carpocapsae*) or by applying certain broad-spectrum insecticides to soil as labeled. Apply nematodes (see Suppliers for sources) when weevil larvae or pupae are expected to be present. Apply nematodes in mid-summer to fall or before adults emerge in the spring; about mid-March for most weevil species in northern California. In hot areas, apply nematodes in the early morning or evening. Soil must be warm (at least 60°F) and moist (well irrigated) but not soggy before application and for 2 weeks afterwards.

A persistent insecticide may also be applied to foliage to control adults, but monitor weevil populations beginning early in the spring before spraying. If you can tolerate some foliage damage, do not spray until 4 or 5 weeks after first detecting feeding damage or weevils; few if any weevils will have laid eggs by then because snout beetles must feed for about a month before they start laying eggs. If adult feeding cannot be tolerated, spray about a week after first detecting adults or damage. The most effective time to make a single application to foliage is as soon as your regular sampling for adults indicates that weevil populations have peaked and begun to decline. If weevil emergence is prolonged, a second foliar spray may be warranted about 3 to 4 weeks after the first application.

WHITE GRUBS AND SCARAB BEETLES

Certain scarab beetles (family Scarabaeidae) and their larvae (called white grubs) are occasional pests in western landscapes, feeding on flowers or fruit as adults or chewing roots during their larval stage. Adults are medium to large, dull to brightly colored and metallic beetles with antennae that terminate in an oval club composed of several thin leaflike plates (lamellae). The soil-dwelling larvae are commonly robust, wrinkly, and yellowish to dirty white, with well-developed legs and an enlarged

A healthy black vine weevil pupa and larva (left) and two darker-colored pupae and a larva infected with *Steinernema feltiae* nematodes (right).

Scarabs, such as this *Pleocoma* species, are called rain beetles because they emerge from pupae in soil after precipitation in fall. Adults are harmless, but larvae are root-feeders that sometimes damage young woody plants.

abdomen. When disturbed, larvae tend to curl into a C shape.

Pests of woody landscapes include hoplia beetles (*Hoplia* spp.), June beetles (including *Cotinus, Phobetus,* and *Polyphylla* spp.), and rain beetles (*Pleocoma* spp.). Other scarabs primarily damage turfgrass roots, such as *Cyclocephala* species chafers. Many species of scarabs are harmless or beneficial, including those that feed on (and help to decompose) animal dung or compost. Because larvae live underground or hidden in organic debris and adults of many species are nocturnal, many people observe scarabs only when adults are drawn to lights at night.

Certain species, including Japanese beetle (*Popillia japonica*) and Asiatic garden beetle or oriental beetle (*Maladera castanea*) that are problems in the eastern United States and overseas, do not occur in California. However, such exotic scarabs are occasionally introduced in the West, for example as larvae infesting roots of imported nursery containers. Larvae of many white grubs can be identified to genus or species by examining the arrangement of hairs and bare areas on their raster (the underside of their last abdominal segment) and comparing this pattern to illustrations in publications such as *Handbook of Turfgrass Insect Pests* (Brandenburg and Villani 1995). If you find unfamiliar scarabs, have them identified by a knowledgeable person, such as an agricultural agency entomologist.

Hoplia Beetles

Several *Hoplia* species occasionally damage woody plants. Pest species in California include *Hoplia oregona*, which feeds on developing grape clusters, and *Hoplia callipyge,* which chews holes in flowers of various species, most notably rose. Hoplia beetles are about ¼ inch long and reddish brown with silvery or coppery scales, making them appear iridescent in sunlight. *Hoplia callipyge* is primarily a problem in the Central Valley from Sacramento south to Bakersfield. It prefers feeding on petals of light-colored roses (white, pink, apricot, and yellow) but does not damage leaves. Larvae are root feeders but apparently do not feed on rose roots. There is only one generation per year and damage is usually confined to about a 2- to 4-week period in spring, ranging from mid-March to May depending on location and weather.

Where they have been a problem, inspect rose blossoms regularly for hoplia beetles during spring. Inspect mostly light-colored flowers. Hand-pick adult weevils, especially if few in number. Adults drop from the plant when disturbed, so they can be collected by gently shaking canes over a tray or a bucket of soapy water. Alternatively, clip off infested rose blooms into a bag or container, cover it to prevent beetle escape, then dispose of them. Insecticide sprays should not be necessary in most landscape situations. Sprays often are not very effective and sometimes damage young blossoms or young foliage. Consult *Hoplia Beetle Pest Notes* (Perry 2002) for more information.

RAIN BEETLE

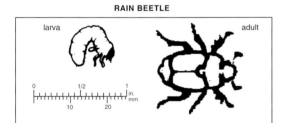

larva   adult

HOPLIA BEETLE

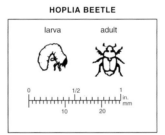

larva   adult

Most scarab larvae are dirty white to yellowish with well-developed legs and enlarged abdomens. Larvae of the tenlined June beetle (*Polyphylla decemlineata*) can girdle roots on small fruit and nut trees and ornamentals such as black locust, privet, and wisteria. Adults are mostly brown with longitudinal white stripes on their wing covers.

An adult hoplia beetle and its feeding damage on rose petals. Hoplia beetles cause only aesthetic damage in landscapes. Larvae are not pests of rose roots and adults do not chew leaves. Adults apparently prefer light-colored blossoms, so concentrate monitoring and hand-picking adults on apricot, pink, white, and yellow rose blossoms. Sprays are often not very effective.

Japanese Beetle

Popillia japonica

Japanese beetle is established throughout the northeastern United States. It is occasionally found and eradicated in California and elsewhere in the western United States. In the West, report suspected Japanese beetles to the county department of agriculture or other agricultural officials.

Japanese beetle is primarily a pest of turf, but adults feed on many different species including woody ornamentals such as American chestnut, apple, black walnut, crab apple, elm, grape, Japanese maple, linden, *Prunus* spp., and rose. The most serious damage is caused by larvae feeding on roots of grasses and herbaceous species. Most damage to woody ornamentals is from adults feeding on foliage, flowers, and fruit. Adults chew out tissue between the veins, leaving a lacy skeleton of damaged leaves. Although this damage is unsightly, vigorous plants tolerate extensive defoliation. Beetles also congregate on individual fruit or blossoms, which they eat.

IDENTIFICATION AND BIOLOGY

Adult beetles are mostly a shiny metallic green with coppery brown wing covers and tufts of short, whitish hairs along their sides. Larvae are plump, whitish grubs. They are distinguished from several other species of lawn-feeding grubs by differences in their anal hairs, as illustrated in publications such as *Handbook of Turfgrass Insect Pests* (Brandenburg and Villani 1995).

In the northeastern United States, adults are present from about June through September; they lay eggs in moist soil or turf near where they feed on foliage, flowers, and fruit. Most of the life cycle is spent as larvae in soil, which pupate underground, primarily during May and June, before emerging as adults. Females produce a sex pheromone that attracts males. Adults tend to be active during warm, sunny weather, when they congregate on hosts to feed and mate.

MANAGEMENT

Established woody plants tolerate extensive defoliation and are unlikely to be seriously harmed by beetle feeding. Many cultivars and species of woody ornamentals are rarely or never attacked. If you live where Japanese beetle is established, obtain information on nonhosts from a local Cooperative Extension office or a well-informed nursery person and consider planting these species.

The most effective control is against larvae in soil. Parasitic nematodes kill immature Japanese beetles if applied to turf and to warm, moist soil around ornamentals, as discussed for weevil larvae. *Heterorhabditis bacteriophora, H. megidis,* and *Steinernema glaseri* appear more effective against Japanese beetle than *Steinernema carpocapsae.* May or early June is probably the best time to apply nematodes; most Japanese beetles are then in the more susceptible late larval instar or pupal stages. Later in the season (about July), systemic insecticide (imidacloprid) applied to soil when adults are laying eggs can be highly effective against early instar larvae.

Milky disease, or *Paenibacillus* (=*Bacillus*) *popilliae,* occurs in many soils in the eastern United States. It infects and kills immature beetles before adults emerge, naturally helping to control populations, without killing earthworms and other beneficial organisms in the soil. However, there is little or no information showing that applying additional *P. popilliae* to soil increases beetle control.

Commercially available traps designed for Japanese beetle can capture many adults, although the extent to which traps provide control is debatable. Traps do indicate when adult beetles are active so that you know when to take action against them. When monitoring with traps, they should probably be located away from rather than near susceptible ornamentals. Broad-spectrum, persistent foliar insecticides can be applied to protect foliage and flowers when adults are active, but this is generally not warranted on woody ornamentals unless they are of very high aesthetic value, such as with rose blossoms. Broad-spectrum materials kill natural enemies, and spraying foliage may cause outbreaks of other pests. Knocking or beating adults from branches onto a sheet or tray and disposing of them in a bucket of soapy water

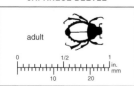

JAPANESE BEETLE

adult

0   1/2   1 in.
         mm
  10   20

Adult Japanese beetles are mostly shiny metallic green with coppery brown wing covers and tufts of short whitish hairs along the side. One beetle shown here has two white eggs of a tachinid parasite (*Hyperecteina aldrichi*) on its thorax. In the western United States, report suspected Japanese beetles to the county department of agriculture or other agricultural officials.

may provide control on shrubs or small trees if done daily during the cool morning from June through September. In infested areas, it is best to plan ahead and control larvae in turf and soil around ornamentals before adults emerge.

CRICKETS, GRASSHOPPERS, AND KATYDIDS

Various species of crickets, grasshoppers, and katydids (order Orthoptera) chew holes or notch the edge of leaves. Though often observed, they rarely cause serious damage to established woody plants. Apple, citrus, pear, and stone fruits are among the many hosts on which these insects nibble. For more information, see publications such as *Grasshoppers Pest Notes* (Flint 2002).

Because of their relatively large size and humanoid appearance, Jerusalem crickets (*Stenopelmatus* spp., family Stenopelmatidae) may be the orthopterans most commonly brought by homeowners to entomologists for identification. They are given many common names, including "niñas de la tierra" (children of the earth) and sand crickets. They also are sometimes called potato bugs because they are occasional pests of potatoes, but the name "potato bug" is confusing because it is applied to several different invertebrates, including Colorado potato beetle, pill bugs, sow bugs,

and Jerusalem crickets, none of which are in the order Hemiptera (Heteroptera), which is the only group entomologists consider to be true bugs.

Jerusalem crickets are easily recognized by their bald round head, fat orangish abdomen with black rings, spiny hind legs, and a lack of wings. They molt (shed their skin and grow larger) up to about ten times during their life span, which can be up to about 2 years. These insects are harmless to woody plants and only occasional damage turf and vegetables. They live in soil, feeding mostly on nonwoody roots and succulent tubers, and may be important food for certain vertebrate predators. They are most often seen by gardeners turning the soil or aboveground after heavy irrigation, at night, and during mild twilight weather.

ANTS

Ants (family Formicidae) are in the order Hymenoptera, along with bees and wasps. There are over 12,000 ant species in the world, including over 200 species in California. Many ants are beneficial, for instance, they improve soil and can be important natural enemies of insect pests.

About a dozen ant species in California are commonly pests. Pest species can tunnel in wood (carpenter ants) or chew bark or plant parts (fire ants, pavement ants). Ants are a pest in landscapes primarily when they feed on

honeydew excreted by homopteran insects, including aphids, mealybugs, soft scales, and whiteflies. Ants protect these honeydew-producing insects from predators and parasites that might otherwise control the pests. Ants can also disrupt the biological control of some non-honeydew-producing pests, such as mites and armored scales, especially if these pests occur on the same plants as honeydew-producing species. Ants also protect nectar-producing oak gall wasps (certain cynipids in the genera *Andricus, Disholcaspis,* and *Dryocosmus*) from their invertebrate natural enemies. Ants can disrupt augmentative biological control, such as by preying on released lacewing eggs or moth eggs containing *Trichogramma* wasps. If ants are abundant near structures, such as on homopteran-infested landscapes, ants are more likely to be a nuisance by coming indoors. Where they occur, introduced fire ants are a serious problem. Red imported fire ants can severely sting people and pets, damage equipment and property, and cause great ecological harm to native wildlife including birds, invertebrates, and mammals.

IDENTIFICATION AND BIOLOGY

Ants are sometimes confused with termites. Ants have a narrow constriction between the thorax and abdomen, their antennae are distinctly elbowed, and winged ants have hind wings that are much shorter than the forewings. Termites have a broad waist, antennae that

Jerusalem crickets are commonly brought to entomologists for identification, but they are harmless to woody plants. They live underground, feeding on succulent tubers and nonwoody roots.

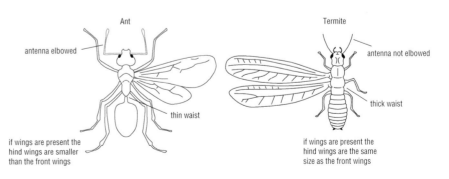

FIGURE 4-12. Ants are distinguished from termites by their narrow waist, elbowed antennae, and (if wings are present) hind wings that are much shorter than the forewings. Termites have beaded antennae, a broad waist, and wings (if present) that are of equal length.

False or small honey ants (*Prenolepis imparis*) are tending woolly aphids on this shamel ash. This species resembles Argentine ant, but in comparison it is a relatively minor pest, in part because false honey ants are active mostly during cool weather (about 45° to 60°F) and are dormant during dry, warm weather.

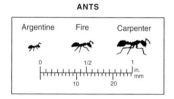

are not elbowed, and equal-length wings (see Figure 4-12). It can be very helpful to identify the particular ant species present as their biology and management often differs. To identify ants to species, you must magnify them and count the number and arrangement of antennal segments and observe the number of nodes (projections) on the petiole, which is the first (narrow) segment of the abdomen. To identify common species, consult publications such as *A Key to the Most Common and/or Economically Important Ants of California* (Haney, Philips, and Wagner 1983) or *Key to Identifying Common Household Ants* (Reynolds et al. 2001) at www.ipm.ucdavis.edu/ TOOLS/ANTKEY on the Web.

Adult ants are divided into three social classes: winged males that occur only during the mating season, queens that spend most of their time in the nest laying eggs, and workers, which are sterile

females. Queens develop wings during the brief mating season, which is usually the only time they and the males are observed, often in large swarms outside of the nest. Most ants are wingless workers that spend their time digging tunnels, defending the colony from natural enemies, foraging for food outside the nest, or caring for the tiny, pale, grublike immatures in the nest. Most ants nest underground or beneath rocks, buildings, or other objects where the tiny elliptical eggs are laid.

An important aspect of ant (and termite) biology is food sharing (trophallaxis). As each ant meets another from its nest, they exchange a tiny droplet containing food and colony communication chemicals. Trophallaxis transports nutrients to nest-bound ants (such as immatures and queens) and directs workers to nearby food sources. As discussed below, baits take advantage of this food-sharing behavior to spread insecticide throughout the colony and poison ants in their nests.

Argentine Ant
Linepithema humile

The Argentine ant (formerly named *Iridomyrmex humilis*) is a common honeydew-feeding species in California and the southern states. The small workers are uniformly dark brown and travel in characteristic trails on bark or the ground. Argentine ants nest in moist soil and can quickly relocate nests in response to changes in food and weather. Colony size varies, often numbering in the thousands. Unlike many social hymenopterans that have only one queen per nest, each Argentine ant colony may have many queens that contribute to this species' high reproductive capability. The winged reproductive males and females are about twice as long as workers and are rarely observed above ground, except sometimes in the spring. Argentine ant populations increase greatly in mid-summer and early fall. Take control action (such as applying

barriers or insecticide baits) beginning in late winter or early spring, before ants and the pests they tend become abundant. Sweet baits are most attractive to Argentine ants.

Carpenter Ants
Camponotus spp.

Carpenter ants nest underground or in wood, sometimes in structures or the interior of living trees. Carpenter ants do not eat wood, but their tunneling weakens limbs, which may drop. Carpenter ants feed on insects, honeydew, and plant sap. Columns of these relatively large, black or dark reddish ants may be observed foraging from nests. Wood borings may also accumulate beneath nest entrances.

Help prevent carpenter ants and termites from attacking trees by providing plants with proper cultural care. Prune plants properly when needed and prevent injuries to trunks and limbs, as detailed in Chapter 3. Consult *Carpenter Ants Pest Notes* (Rust and Klotz 2000) for more information.

Pavement Ant
Tetramorium caespitum

This species is named for its behavior of often nesting in or under cracks in pavement. They also nest in lawns, near foundations, or under objects on the ground such as boards, bricks, stones, and wood. Pavement ants occur in Pacific Coast states and throughout the eastern United States. Workers are relatively slow-moving, light to dark brown, and about ⅛ inch long. They resemble Argentine ants in size and color, but pavement ants have 2 distinct petiole nodes while Argentine ants have only 1 node.

Pavement ants prefer sweet liquids such as honeydew and they also prey on insects. They often nest near water, so populations can be reduced by improving soil drainage, repairing leaky irrigation systems, and reducing the frequency between irrigations to the extent this is compatible with healthy plant growth. Sweet baits placed near nests and trails are effective if using insecticides.

Velvety Tree Ant
Liometopum occidentale

Velvety tree ant occurs in California and the Southwest. It is ¹⁄₁₀ to ¹⁄₄ inch long, with a glistening, velvety-black abdomen covered with fine hairs, red thorax, and brownish-black head. Velvety tree ants are often observed in ant trails on limbs and trunks of decaying trees because they nest inside decaying trees or in nearby soil. They feed primarily on honeydew and insects and usually do not damage landscapes. Because they are attracted to certain proteinaceous food and sweet liquids, their presence can be annoying at picnics and when occasionally drawn indoors. To reduce annoying populations, protect trees from injuries that can lead to wood decay, prune off dead limbs, and replace dead or potentially

hazardous hollow trees in which velvety tree ants nest.

Native Fire Ants
Solenopsis spp.

Several native *Solenopsis* species in the southern and western United States are important predators of insects; most species rarely injure plants. However, some ants, such as the southern or California fire ant (*Solenopsis xyloni*) nest in mounds around trees and shrubs and can inflict painful bites or stings on people and pets. The southern fire ant also girdles and kills young trees by feeding on bark. If fire ants nest in landscapes, consider applying insecticide baits (such as growth regulators) according to label directions. Be aware that the introduced red imported fire ant (discussed below) differs from native species (Table 4-12) and requires special attention. Fire ants are primarily attracted to insecticides formulated with protein baits.

Red Imported Fire Ant
Solenopsis wagneri (=*S. invicta*)

The red imported fire ant is a widespread severe pest throughout the southern United States. It has recently been introduced into southern California, where it is a more aggressive and prolific pest than native fire ants. Red imported fire ant has a painful sting that can severely injure people or animals attacked by swarming ants. A single sting can be life-threatening to the small percentage of people who are allergic. Although primarily predators of insects and other invertebrates and therefore beneficial in certain situations, fire ants also feed on seeds, tend honeydew-producing insects, and sometimes feed on plants, such as by stripping bark from young trees and shrubs.

The red imported fire ant can be distinguished from other ants in California by the great variability in the size of worker ants. These workers of very differing size can be observed together in the same trail.

The velvety tree ant has a reddish thorax and a black abdomen covered with fine hairs. This species is rarely a serious pest. However, because they often nest in decayed wood, trails of velvety tree ants on bark may indicate that trees should be inspected for potential hazards, such as dead or hollow limbs that should be pruned off.

Southern fire ants exposed in their nests, revealing pale pupae and larvae, winged reproductives, and worker ants. Their yellowish red head and thorax and dark brown abdomen distinguish southern fire ant workers from workers of harvester ants and other fire ant species found in California.

TABLE 4-12.

Characteristics Helpful in Distinguishing Three Species of Fire Ants Found in California.

CHARACTERISTIC	COMMON NAME, *SOLENOPSIS* SPECIES		
	DESERT FIRE ANT, *S. AUREA*	RED IMPORTED FIRE ANT, *S. XYLONI*	SOUTHERN FIRE ANT, *S. WAGNERI*
worker length	≤ $\frac{1}{8}$ inch	$\frac{1}{12}$–$\frac{1}{4}$ inch	$\frac{1}{12}$–$\frac{1}{5}$ inch
worker color	golden yellow	uniformly dark reddish brown	yellowish red head, dark brown to black abdomen
location	deserts	irrigated or moist locations	coastal, inland
mound	variable; often use other ants' nest	usually domed mounds	irregular, low craters

Positive ant species identification requires expert knowledge or reference to appropriate technical publications and an examination under magnification of certain physical characteristics, including the number of antennal segments and projections (nodes) on top of the abdomen. In California, report suspected red imported fire ants to the county department of agriculture.

Size, color, and location help to distinguish the red imported fire ant from native California fire ants (Table 4-12). The red imported fire ants may also be confused with harvester ants, which are also called red ants. However, workers of the California harvester ant (*Pogonomyrmex californicus*) are uniformly red, more robust (stout) than fire ants, and uniformly sized, about ¼ inch long. Red imported fire ants are more aggressive than native species and will readily run up any object that touches their mound.

Fire ants are spread long distances primarily by people moving ant-infested soil. Inspect incoming soil and container plants to avoid introducing fire ant colonies, especially if material is arriving from areas known to be infested. In areas where they are not established, do not attempt to control red imported fire ants yourself. In California, report suspected red imported fire ant infestations to agricultural officials by telephoning 1-888-4FIREANT toll free. For more information, consult *Red Imported Fire Ant Pest Notes* (Greenberg, Klotz, and Kabashima 2001) or the www.fireant.ca.gov Web site.

MANAGEMENT OF ANTS

Tolerate most ant species outdoors whenever possible because many ants are ecologically beneficial. Control ants when they are direct pests (such as aggressive species that sting or damage plants) or are tending bothersome honeydew-producing Homoptera. Depending on the situation, controlling honeydew-feeding ants sometimes allows natural enemies to gradually become abundant enough to control certain pests. Inspect trees and shrubs for ants in spring, when honeydew-producing insects such as aphids appear. Trails of ants descending plants infested with Homoptera may be tending the honeydew-producing species.

Where ants are a nuisance by coming indoors, this problem may be reduced by controlling ant-tended Homoptera in gardens and landscapes near structures. Keeping debris (such as organic litter or mulch), vegetation, and water (such as irrigation) from contacting foundations and walls may also reduce indoor ant problems. Consult *Ants Pest Notes* (Rust and Klotz 2000) for more information on managing ants indoors.

Barriers. Deny ants access to plant canopies by pruning branches that provide a bridge between buildings, other plants, or the ground, and by applying sticky material or other barriers to trunks. A narrow band of sticky material (such as Tanglefoot) applied over a wrapping to protect bark is the most popular technique as discussed and illustrated earlier in this chapter in the section "Sticky Barriers." Other effective barriers may include slippery materials such as Teflon. Slippery sprays or tapes (if available) may exclude ants from relatively smooth surfaces if bark can be wrapped snugly enough to prevent ants from passing through gaps between the barrier and bark.

Commercially available plastic tape or strips containing a low percentage of insecticide such as permethrin can be highly effective at excluding ants for several months or longer. Because they are repellant (over very short distances), in comparison with sticky or slippery barriers, pyrethroid-impregnated barriers do not need to fit so tightly.

Insecticides. Avoid surface sprays and acutely toxic insecticides such as organophosphates and pyrethroids for ant control. Certain insecticides cause environmental problems, such as by moving after application and contaminating runoff water that flows into streams and rivers. Sprays kill only foraging workers and most are not very persistent outdoors, so ants that were protected in nests underground will soon appear.

Baits (insecticide mixed with an attractant) are the preferred chemical method for ant control. Effective bait insecticides are slow-acting, so that before they die, workers will spread the toxicant among many other ants during food sharing. Boric acid, fipronil, and hydramethylnon are examples of insecticides used in ant baits. Although baits act slowly (requiring users to be patient), baits can be much more effective than sprays. Sprays only kill foraging workers, while ant baits are carried back to their nests, where reproductive queens and the entire colony can be killed.

For the most effective and economical ant control, treat in late winter or early spring when ant populations are lowest. Place bait near nests or on ant trails beneath plants. Baits can be solids or liquids that are applied in stations (enclosures) or solid granules that are broadcast. Bait stations can be preferable to broadcasting granules, in part because ants communicate the location of food sources and recruit large numbers of ants to feed and consume the pesticide in bait stations. Some active ingredients (hydramethylnon) quickly break down in sunlight, so apply them late during the day and in shaded areas when broadcasting granules.

Bait effectiveness varies with ant species, availability of alternative food, active ingredient, and the type of bait. For example, fire ants are primarily attracted to baits containing fats, proteins, and oils, so solid baits such as proteins are usually most attractive to these ants. Sweet baits attract most species that become problems indoors, including Argentine ant, odorous house ant, pavement ant, and thief ant. Protein baits can also be attractive to Argentine ants, such as in spring when colonies are producing young, which consume proteinaceous solids.

Determine which bait to use by placing out a small quantity of each of two or more different types of baits and observing which is preferred by the ants. Slight changes in formulation can alter the effectiveness of bait products. Too high a concentration of active ingredient or certain preservatives mixed with some products can dramatically reduce product effectiveness. For example, boric acid mixed in 10 to 25% sucrose and 75 to 90% water controls liquid-feeding ants, but only when baits contain 0.5 to 1% boric acid. Consult the latest *Ants Pest Notes* (Rust and Klotz 2000) for more information.

Argentine ants are collecting this slow-acting insecticide bait. Baits are the most effective ant control because before they die, worker ants carry the toxicant to their nest and spread it among other ants during food sharing. Because baits and ants' preference for them vary, place out a small quantity of each of two or more different types of baits and observe which is preferred by the ants.

APHIDS

Aphids (family Aphididae) are small, soft-bodied insects that suck plant juices. Over 200 species are occasional or frequent pests of landscape or agricultural plants.

DAMAGE

Feeding by high aphid populations can slow plant growth or cause leaves to yellow, curl, or drop early. Some species distort stems or fruit or cause galls on roots, leaves, or stems. Aphids are important pests of many annual crops because they transmit certain viruses that cause plant diseases, but this is usually not a problem in landscape trees and shrubs.

Landscape plants commonly tolerate extensive feeding by aphids, and established woody plants are not killed by them. The whitish cast skins aphids produce may be unsightly, but the most bothersome aspect of aphids in landscapes is the honeydew they produce. Honeydew is sugary water excreted by many homopterans that ingest phloem sap. It is harmless to plants, except if it becomes so abundant that extensive black sooty mold grows on it, reducing light reaching foliage to the extent that it slows plant growth. Copious honeydew and sooty mold create a sticky and unsightly mess on trees, sidewalks, automobiles, and other surfaces beneath the plant.

IDENTIFICATION AND BIOLOGY

Many aphids are difficult to distinguish to species; fortunately, identification to species is often not necessary before determining how to manage them. Exceptions are that it can be very helpful to know whether your pest species is host specific. Host-specific aphids attack only one species or a few closely related plant species and cannot spread to other plant species. Host-specific aphids commonly overwinter as eggs on their deciduous hosts. Controls, such as dormant or delayed dormant oil sprays or a soil-applied systemic insecticide in late winter, need only be directed at that host. Conversely, polyphagous aphid species migrate among hosts, may feed and reproduce throughout the year, and often lack a dormant season egg stage in much of California where winters are mild. Most aphids on woody ornamentals, including gall-making and woolly aphids, are host-specific.

Aphids often feed in dense groups on leaves or stems and do not rapidly disperse when disturbed. Adults are usually 1/8 inch or less in length and are pear-shaped with long legs and antennae. They vary from green, yellow, white, brown, or red to black. Some species, such as the woolly aphids, are covered with a waxy, white to grayish coating. Adult aphids may be winged or wingless. A pair of tubelike projections (cornicles) near the hind end of the body distinguishes most aphids from other insects. Gall-making and woolly aphids are the exception, as many of these have no distinct cornicles.

During warm weather, aphids may go through a complete generation in less than 2 weeks. The outgrown and shed aphid skins from successive molts may dot foliage as small white flecks, often persisting long after aphids have left the plant. There are many generations per year and populations can increase rapidly, especially under conditions of moderate temperatures. Extreme temperatures may retard aphid growth and reproduction. Throughout most of the year, adult aphids (either winged or wingless) give birth to live young without mating (Figure 4-13). Aphids may produce overwintering eggs, primarily in species that are host-specific on deciduous plants or those that occur in locations with cold winters.

APHIDS WITH MANY HOSTS

A few species of aphids can infest many different herbaceous and woody plant species. These pests with broad host ranges include bean aphid, green peach aphid, and melon aphid.

Shiny, sticky honeydew coats these flowering plum leaves infested with the waterlily aphid (*Rhopalosiphum nymphaeae*).

Blackish sooty mold on California bay infested with California laurel aphids. Sooty mold does not damage plants, but if it is extensive it may slow plant growth by reducing photosynthesis.

APHIDS

winged adult
wingless adult and nymph
parasite adult

0   1/2   1   in.
                        mm
    10   20

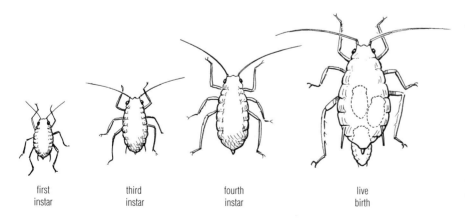

first
instar

third
instar

fourth
instar

live
birth

FIGURE 4-13. During most of the growing season, aphids reproduce asexually, giving live birth to nymphs without laying eggs. Metamorphosis is incomplete, and adults are often wingless.

Bean Aphid
Aphis fabae

Hosts of the bean aphid include elderberry, euonymus, jacaranda, pyracantha, viburnum, and many herbaceous plants. Aphids are dark olive green to black with black appendages. As with melon aphid, they can occur in dense colonies, sometimes with both green and black individuals.

Green Peach Aphid
Myzus persicae

The green peach aphid is one of the most common species nationwide. It is green, yellow, or reddish, with black on the top of the head and thorax of winged adults. It feeds on a large variety of woody and herbaceous landscape plants, including *Prunus* species such as flowering plum. Because succulent foliage on some of its host plants is available year-round in mild-winter areas, this insect can have up to two dozen generations per year, and overwintering eggs are produced only in cold-winter areas.

Melon Aphid, or Cotton Aphid
Aphis gossypii

Hosts of the melon aphid, also called cotton aphid, include apple, camellia, crape myrtle, euonymus, *Prunus* species, willow, and many herbaceous plants. It feeds and reproduces all year long in areas of California with mild winters where hosts are available. Melon aphids are commonly blackish or dark green, but pale yellow to whitish forms also occur.

HOST-SPECIFIC APHIDS

Although many aphids look similar, most species on woody landscape plants feed on only one or several closely related plant species and cannot spread to plants of another species. Host-specific species include the linden aphid (*Eucallipterus tiliae*), Norway maple aphid (*Periphyllus lyropictus*), oleander aphid (*Aphis nerii*), tuliptree aphid (*Illinoia liriodendri*), and birch aphids (such as *Callipterinella calliptera, Betulaphis brevipilosa,* and *Euceraphis betulae*). The rose aphid (*Macrosiphum rosae*) may spend part of the summer on nearby herbaceous plants, but it usually occurs on roses whenever succulent tissue is present. Woolly aphids and galling species are also host specific.

Crapemyrtle Aphid
Sarucallis (=Tinocallis) kahawaluokalani

The crapemyrtle aphid is occasionally so abundant on crape myrtle that plants may be defoliated. This aphid is mostly yellowish green, except for winged adults that have distinctive black marks on the abdomen, wings, and tips of the antennae.

Giant Conifer Aphids
Cinara spp.

Giant conifer aphids commonly occur on fir, pine, and spruce. They are among the largest aphids, up to ⅕ inch long. At first glance they are sometimes mistaken for ticks, but ticks have eight legs and no antennae, while aphids have two long, slender antennae and six legs. Giant conifer aphids have especially long legs and occur individually or in large colonies on foliage and bark. The purplish or black body may be covered with gray powder. Colonies on deodar cedar often infest only a single limb. These aphids may shift their bodies in unison when disturbed, apparently in response to an alarm pheromone they secrete. There are several dozen *Cinara* species and each species is specific to one or a

Melon or cotton aphids are smaller than many other aphid species. They are commonly green to blackish, but pale yellow to whitish forms also occur. Unlike most aphids that feed only on a few closely related plants, this species infests many different hosts.

few conifer species, but more than one aphid species may occur on the same plant. Giant conifer aphids give birth to live nymphs year-round in mild-winter climates, but overwinter as eggs where winters are severe.

Oleander Aphid
Aphis nerii

Oleander aphids are bright yellow or orangish with black appendages. They primarily infest oleander, but occasionally occur on certain other plants including milkweeds (*Asclepias* spp.) and vinca. Dense colonies can infest growing terminals, unopened flower buds, and foliage, especially when leaves are young and succulent or old and senescing. Biological control is sometimes quite effective in controlling the oleander aphid, but cultural practices such as regular pruning and frequent irrigation greatly reduce the effectiveness of natural enemies. *Lysiphlebus testaceipes* is the most important biological control agent in at least some

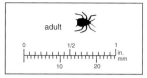

Giant conifer aphids are among the largest aphids. At first glance they are sometimes mistaken for ticks, but ticks have eight legs and no antennae, while aphids have two long, slender antennae and six legs. This bow-legged fir aphid (*Cinara curvipes*) occurs on fir, spruce, and deodar cedar, often in large colonies.

Oleander aphids are yellowish with black appendages. Their most important biological control agents are tiny parasitic wasps, which cause parasitized aphids to become swollen mummies. Avoid regular pruning and irrigation of oleander. These practices stimulate succulent plant growth, which increases aphid reproduction and survival and decrease the effectiveness of biological control.

parts of California. Larvae of this braconid wasp feed inside aphids, causing parasitized aphids to become papery, swollen, light brown to tan mummies. Generalist predators such as lacewings, lady beetles, and syrphid larvae also prey on oleander aphid. But in comparison with the biological control of other aphid species, predators may be less important because oleander aphids consume and store toxic plant compounds and can secrete these noxious chemicals when attacked by predators.

Poplar Gall Aphids
Pemphigus spp.

Several species of aphids cause apparently harmless galls on cottonwood or poplar leaves. Aphids with similar biology and damage include the lettuce root aphid (*Pemphigus bursarius*) and the poplar petiolegall aphid (*P. populitransversus*). The lettuce root aphid occurs throughout North America and much of the world and is believed to be the most common poplar-galling aphid in California. The poplar petiolegall aphid is reported only east of the Rocky Mountains. Feeding by these aphids on poplar trees stimulates plant tissue to form a hollow gall around the aphid on leaves or leaf petioles. The enclosed aphid gives birth to about 100 to 250 waxy, grayish nymphs, many of which develop wings and migrate up to several miles to feed on their alternate hosts. Alternate hosts are mostly in the family Compositae, including many weeds and lettuce (*Lactuca* spp.) for lettuce root aphid, and *Brassica* species such as cabbage for the poplar petiolegall aphid. These aphids feed on the basal stems and roots of their alternate hosts, then in the fall fly back to poplars where both females and males are produced; these mate, and females lay overwintering eggs. These aphids can be significant pests on their vegetable crop alternate hosts, but the aphids are harmless to poplar and no control is recommended on trees.

This gall on a poplar leaf petiole has been opened to reveal the waxy, grayish poplar gall aphids inside. These galls are harmless to poplar, but this aphid can damage its alternate hosts, primarily lettuce.

Woolly apple aphids produced the white waxy material on this pyracantha stem. Bean aphids, both black and green forms, infest the plant tips.

Woolly Aphids

Woolly aphids cover themselves with white waxy material similar to that secreted by some adelgids and mealybugs. Some species feed in groups and cause gall-like swellings on bark or curled leaves. Many species alternate generations among plant species or different parts of the same plant. Migratory woolly aphids include poplar gall aphid and ash leaf curl aphids. The life cycles of most woolly aphids are poorly known. Some species feed on roots, especially during the winter, making them difficult to study and manage. The same species of aphid may look different depending on the host plant, season, and the part of the plant it is feeding on. As with most aphids infesting woody ornamentals, these are aesthetic pests and no control is needed to protect the survival of otherwise healthy trees. Where intolerable, they are difficult to manage without using systemic insecticide.

The woolly apple aphid (*Eriosoma lanigerum*) occurs on apple, cotoneaster, elm, hawthorn, and pyracantha leaves and bark and sometimes causes gall-like swellings on bark. On American elm, woolly apple aphid feeds and reproduces in bark crevices during late winter and early spring, where it causes globular bark swellings. A subsequent generation migrates to leaf buds, causing new foliage to curl. Later generations migrate from elm to apple or other hosts. At least one other *Eriosoma* species that distorts American elm bark and leaves migrates to different hosts than woolly apple aphid.

At least five species of woolly oak aphids (*Stegophylla* species) occur in the United States and are known only on oaks. *Stegophylla essigi*, *S. quercicola*, and *S. quercifolia* are reported in California, where they curl leaves and produce copious flocculent wax on oak leaves and shoots. Their hosts include coast live oak, interior live oak, and valley oak.

An Asian woolly hackberry aphid (*Shivaphis celti*) has been introduced into the southeastern United States and California. It produces copious honeydew and small, roundish, waxy tufts on the underside of hackberry leaves, especially on *Celtis sinensis* in California. This species overwinters as eggs on hackberry terminals and becomes most abundant during late summer.

Ash Leaf Curl Aphids

At least two *Prociphilus* species aphids infest ash leaves. Infestations cause leaves to curl, distort, form "pseudo-galls," and drop prematurely. The aphids excrete copious honeydew and flocculent waxy material, making a mess beneath trees and promoting the growth of dark sooty mold. Abundant winged ash aphids can be a nuisance when they migrate among bark, foliage, or roots, especially in the fall.

Certain ash species and cultivars appear to be less susceptible to ash aphids, but there are no research-based recommendations that identify resistant ash.

The manzanita leaf gall aphid (*Tamalia coweni*) caused these leaves to swell into harmless pod-shaped galls. This aphid feeds only on manzanita and is prevalent on new growth, such as that stimulated by frequently irrigating and shearing plants.

Their biology and identification has not been well studied, and the number of ash aphid species is uncertain. Some ash aphids have been called *Prociphilus californica*, but this is not a valid name.

Prociphilus fraxinifolii (sometimes called leafcurl ash aphid) infests ash leaves from spring through fall and overwinters as immatures on ash roots and eggs on bark. *Prociphilus fraxinifolii* is apparently the common pest in southern California. In the Pacific Northwest, *P. americanus* reportedly is the more abundant species. *Prociphilus americanus* infests ash leaves only during spring; winged stages migrate to spend summer through winter on roots of conifers, such as true firs. *Prociphilus americanus* will leave ash (migrate to conifers) during spring, so no treatment of any kind is recommended if *P. americanus* can be identified as the species infesting landscapes. Winged aphids of both species may emerge from roots during fall to mate. Root-feeding by *Prociphilus* species apparently does not harm trees in landscapes. Root-feeding can damage small plants in

Ash leaves curled by woolly aphids (*Prociphilus* sp.). Woolly aphids can be difficult to manage, in part because many species have a complex life history, migrating between leaves and roots, sometimes among different hosts.

These round, gray California laurel aphids (*Euthoracaphis umbellulariae*) are sometimes mistaken for immature whiteflies or scale insects. They occur on the underside of California bay, often in rows along veins. Camphor tree and sassafras are occasionally infested. Even high populations apparently do not harm trees and can be ignored.

nurseries, and roots are the source of migrating aphids that infest leaves.

THRESHOLDS FOR APHIDS

Low numbers of aphids are beneficial by producing honeydew that attracts and feeds adults of many beneficial species that are parasitic or predaceous on pests. Even very high aphid populations rarely, if ever, seriously harm or kill established woody plants. Even though they have no noticeable affect on plant health, aphids can be very bothersome to people at moderate levels when they produce large amounts of honeydew. Tolerance for honeydew varies among people and according to the species and location of plants. You can establish approximate action thresholds by monitoring aphids or honeydew, then comparing your results to when aphids or honeydew become a problem. Monitor during subsequent seasons and take action if aphids or honeydew approach this previously bothersome level.

MONITORING APHIDS

Monitor aphids and their natural enemies by visually inspecting 5 to 10 or more leaves, new growth tips, or 1-foot branch terminals on each of several plants. Aphids commonly occur on the lower leaf surface; clipping leaves may facilitate their inspection. Inspect foliage every 1 or 2 weeks during the period when aphids may be a problem. Professionals can benefit from actually counting and recording separately the number of aphids, parasitized aphids, and predators on each sample. Total the number of aphids and natural enemies and divide by the number of samples inspected. Compare these numbers among sample weeks and years to evaluate control efficacy or establish thresholds, as discussed in the section "Honeydew Monitoring," below.

Inspect trunks for columns of ants, as ant trails on bark often indicate that plant juice-sucking insects are abundant on plants. Most ants will feed on honeydew, and some species of ants aggressively tend Homoptera, chasing away natural enemies that would otherwise help to control these pests.

Winged aphids can be monitored using yellow sticky cards. While extremely useful in greenhouses, it can be difficult to know the importance of insects trapped outdoors, especially with aphids, where most reproductive adults are wingless. See the section "Sticky Traps" earlier in this chapter for suggestions on using this monitoring method.

Honeydew Monitoring. Honeydew production is the primary problem caused by aphids, and monitoring honeydew provides direct measure of this damage. When managing street trees or other situations where substantial resources are spent on control, monitoring honeydew helps managers to establish thresholds, time control actions, and evaluate treatment efficacy.

Honeydew can be efficiently monitored using water-sensitive paper or cards. These cards are often used for monitoring insecticide droplets and calibrating sprayers, and they include bright yellow cards that produce distinct blue dots upon contact with honeydew or water (see Suppliers). Attach the cards to a stiff background and place the cards beneath plants. Cards can be suspended several inches beneath branches of trees using a bent wire coat hanger. Begin monitoring before honeydew typically becomes a problem, usually in the spring. Use about four cards per tree, such as one beneath the lower, outer canopy of each quadrant. Monitor several plants that have had honeydew problems. Place the cards beneath plants for the same period about once each week, such as from 11 A.M. to 3 P.M. on a day of typical weather when no rain or overhead irrigation is anticipated. Handle the cards with forceps or gloves because they will change color from the moisture in your skin.

Label and save the cards from each monitoring date, such as by attaching them to sheets of paper stored in a 3-ring binder. When honeydew becomes intolerable (such as when complaints are received), note the approximate droplet density measured during that week and during previous weeks. Monitor honeydew next season and take control action if honeydew density approaches the level that was previously found to be intolerable. Visually compare cards among sample dates before and after control actions to assess the effectiveness of management efforts.

In situations where honeydew has been a chronic problem, some professionals have found it useful to establish more quantitative treatment thresholds. Average droplet density per area of card is determined for each of the several monitoring dates just before and after honeydew becomes intolerable. All drops can be counted, or drops can be counted and averaged from several sub-areas of each card (such as counting drops in three representative 1-sq-cm areas per card, then using the average of these numbers). The overall average droplet density from all cards is calculated for each week (such as 4 drops/sq cm) to provide a quantitative threshold for treatment during subsequent years.

To save time, instead of counting drops on all cards, you can estimate honeydew density by visually comparing each card to reference cards with previously determined droplet densities (such as one card averaging 1 drop/sq cm, another with 2 drops/sq cm, and so forth in increasing increments to about 10 drops/sq cm if using a total of ten reference cards). For each card, record the average that appears closest to the appropriate reference card. Add up all of these averages and divide the sum by the total number of cards to estimate the overall average honeydew density on that monitoring date. In some street tree situations, the complaint threshold for aphid honeydew collected during the 4-hour monitoring period has been found to range from 2 to 8 drops/sq cm. Thresholds acceptable for your situation may be different.

MANAGEMENT OF APHIDS

Many natural enemies help to control aphids. These predators and parasites may not always appear in sufficient numbers until after aphids become abundant; however, their preservation is an essential part of a long-term IPM program for aphids. If aphids or honeydew cannot be tolerated and insecticide applications are deemed necessary, choose materials that are least toxic to natural enemies. Treat only in spots where aphids are most abundant to preserve natural enemies elsewhere. Insecticidal soap and narrow-range oil kill aphids and other insects on contact. In comparison to other materials (Table 4-6), they have low residual toxicity to natural enemies that move onto

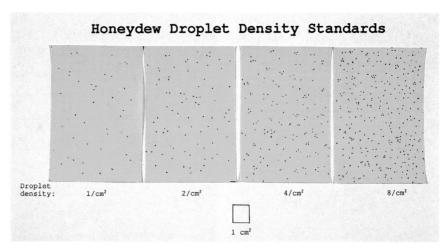

Honeydew Droplet Density Standards

Droplet density: 1/cm²   2/cm²   4/cm²   8/cm²

1 cm²

If monitoring honeydew, save water-sensitive cards exhibiting a range of droplet densities, as shown here. During subsequent monitoring, instead of counting drops on cards, estimate honeydew density by visually comparing each card to reference cards such as these.

plants after sprayings. Certain systemic insecticides can be highly effective. Use baits or sticky barriers to control honeydew-seeking ants because ants can disrupt biological controls by protecting aphids from their natural enemies. A forceful stream of water dislodges aphids from small plants, and many of these aphids will die. Wash plants early in the day so they dry before night.

Populations of most aphids are highest on plant parts with high nitrogen levels, such as new growth or foliage that will soon drop. Minimize fertilization, pruning, and other cultural practices that stimulate succulent plant growth because succulent growth increases aphid reproduction and survival. Conversely, at least some predators (such as lacewings attacking oleander aphids) survive better when plants grow slowly or are not producing new growth.

Do not irrigate too frequently (over-irrigate), as excess water can stimulate succulent growth. Avoid applying nitrogen to established woody plants unless plants are definitely known to be deficient due to a lack of available nutrients. Be aware that most nutrient deficiencies are actually caused by unhealthy roots and poor soil conditions. If fertilizing, do not use more than necessary and use slow-release materials.

Severe aphid infestations on only a portion of the plant may be pruned out.

Water-sensitive paper placed at intervals (for several hours about weekly) beneath trees is an efficient method of monitoring insect honeydew. Where substantial resources are spent on control, monitoring honeydew helps to establish thresholds, time control actions, and evaluate treatment efficacy.

The introduced multicolored Asian lady beetle preys on aphids, psyllids, scales, and various other insects. Its highly variable markings range from 19 large dark spots, to fewer, smaller, or no spots on its wing covers, which can be orange, red, or yellow.

A convergent lady beetle (*Hippodamia convergens*) eating a green peach aphid. This aphid predator is named for the two converging white bars behind the adult's head; individuals vary in the number of black spots and some have no spots.

Lady beetles lay their oblong, orangish eggs on their ends in a group. These resemble eggs of plant-feeding leaf beetles, but leaf beetle eggs are distinctly swollen near their base, while lady beetle eggs are widest in their middle.

In a futile effort to repel the *Metasyrphus* species syrphid larva grasping it, a rose aphid is secreting a droplet of noxious liquid from its cornicle. See the section "Predaceous Flies" earlier in this chapter for a photograph of an adult.

Pruning is especially appropriate for *Cinara* species if they are infesting only a few branches, or for gall-making species. Thinning especially dense inner tree canopy foliage may lower aphid numbers but may also stimulate new growth flushes, which aphids favor. Consult the most current *Aphids Pest Notes* (Flint 2000) for more management information.

Biological Controls. Adult lady beetles and soldier beetles and the larvae of lady beetles, lacewings, and certain flies (aphid flies, predaceous midges, and syrphids) are common aphid predators. Many small wasps, including *Aphelinus, Aphidius, Ephedrus, Praon,* and *Trioxys* species, are also important aphid natural enemies. These parasites reproduce by laying their eggs in aphids. The immature wasp feeds inside and kills its host, causing the aphid to "mummify," or become slightly puffy and turn tan or black. A round hole can be observed where the adult parasite has chewed its way out of the aphid mummy (Figure 4-6). As an example, *Aphelinus mali* is a tiny wasp that often causes populations of the woolly apple aphid to crash.

Many predators and parasites are aided in their search for aphids by the presence of honeydew, which attracts them and also provides a food source. Plant nectar-producing flowers to further increase the food supply for adult lacewings, parasitic wasps, and syrphid flies (Figure 4-4). Avoid using persistent, broad-spectrum, contact insecticides. These provide only temporary aphid control and are likely to kill more of the active natural enemies in comparison with the more sessile aphids; aphid populations may resurge after an application and become more of a problem than before they were sprayed. Use barriers and insecticide baits to control ants, which may prevent predators and parasites from controlling pests.

Aphids are very susceptible to fungal disease when the weather is humid. Look for dead aphids that have turned reddish or brown and have a fuzzy, shriveled texture, unlike the smooth, bloated mummies formed when aphids are parasitized. Fungus-killed aphids sometimes have fine, whitish mycelium growing over their surfaces.

Resident natural enemies frequently provide sufficient biological control of aphids. Some managers supplement these populations on small plants by releasing commercially available aphid predators; there is little information on their effectiveness. In many situations, conserving resident beneficials is likely to be more effective and economical than releasing purchased species.

The convergent lady beetle (*Hippodamia convergens*) is commonly sold for release to control aphids (see Suppliers). Although resident lady beetles are important predators, the commercial *Hippodamia* are collected in the Sierra Nevada where they overwinter in large aggregations. After overwintering, beetles inherently fly, and most will soon leave the site where they are released, even if food is plentiful.

Releasing sufficient numbers of lady beetles can temporarily reduce aphid numbers on small plants. There is little research-based information on how many beetles to release and how often,

Orange gall midge larvae (*Aphidoletes* sp.) are feeding on willow aphids (*Chaitophorus* sp.). The black, shriveled aphids have already been consumed.

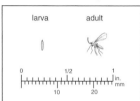

APHIDOLETES

larva   adult

An orange convergent lady beetle pupa and several larvae among whitish cast skins of aphids.

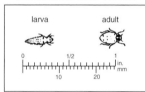

CONVERGENT LADY BEETLE

larva   adult

Aphid mummies, the crusty skins of aphids killed by parasitic wasps, are commonly tan or black. After a parasite larva consumes the aphid and pupates inside, the adult wasp chews a round hole and emerges to seek other aphids and lay eggs in them.

Rose aphids vary in color from green to red. However, the orangish, fuzzy aphids seen here have been killed by a naturally occurring fungal disease.

but one study found that controlling aphids on roses can require 1,000 or more beetles per shrub released at 1- to 2-week intervals. Purchased lady beetles are often thirsty, so spraying them with sugar water before release may increase their survival. If beetles are stored in the refrigerator (do not freeze them) and some are released periodically, warm beetles weekly to room temperature and feed them very dilute sugar water, such as misting them using a trigger-pump spray bottle. Wetting plants first and releasing beetles on the ground near the trunk and under plants in the late evening when it is cooler may reduce beetle dispersal.

Chrysoperla (=*Chrysopa*) species green lacewings (such as *C. carnea, C. comanche,* and *C. rufilabris*) can be purchased as oblong, green to grayish eggs or as tiny alligatorlike larvae (see Suppliers). Although lacewing larvae are voracious aphid predators, releasing them for aphid control has given mixed results.

Insecticides. Aphids on established trees and shrubs rarely, if ever, require control to protect the plant's health or survival. If

aphids or their honeydew are intolerable, insecticidal soap, narrow-range oil, or neem oil, or one of these in combination with pyrethrins, provides temporary control if applied to thoroughly cover infested foliage. They provide no residual control, so applications may need to be repeated. Because aphid predators and parasites often become abundant only after aphids are numerous, applying nonpersistent insecticides like soap or oil may provide more effective long-term control because they do not kill natural enemies that migrate in after the spray. These and other insecticides with only contact activity are generally ineffective in preventing damage from aphids that gall or distort foliage or produce extensive waxiness.

Oil applied during the delayed dormant season kills overwintering aphid eggs and may require a smaller volume of spray than treating leafy plants. Treatments will not give complete control and probably are not justified for aphid control alone if plants are large enough to require a professional applicator in order to obtain thorough coverage. If aphids were a problem the previous season and the pest species is known to overwinter as eggs on bark rather than on alternate hosts, apply narrow-range oil after buds have swollen but before they burst into leaf.

Several organophosphate, carbamate, pyrethroid, and other broad-spectrum insecticides can be applied to foliage and generally will kill a higher percentage of the aphids than oils and soaps. However, these can reduce long-term control by killing natural enemies, and some of these are a source of pollution in creeks and rivers. Carbaryl (Sevin) is not very effective against aphids; some insecticides are ineffective because populations of some species, such as the green peach aphid, have developed resistance to them.

Systemic insecticides applied by implants or injection may control aphids without directly affecting natural enemies. At least one effective material (imidacloprid) can be applied to soil beneath plants, where it is absorbed by roots and transported to leaves. Because efficacy is delayed, it may be most effective in California if applied during late winter or early spring, about 1 month before aphids typically are a problem. Systemic insecticides can also be injected or implanted into trunks or roots; this also avoids the environmental contamination of sprays and may be quicker-acting than soil application, but injections and implants injure trunks or roots and may spread pathogens. Do not inject or implant trees more than once a year. See the section "Injecting or Implanting Pesticides" in Chapter 2 for more discussion.

ADELGIDS

Adelgids (family Adelgidae) are small aphidlike insects that suck plant juices. They feed only on conifers, including Douglas fir, fir, hemlock, larch, pine, and spruce. There are about 14 adelgid species in the United States in two genera (*Pineus* and *Adelges*).

Adelgids cause white cottony tufts on the bark, branches, twigs, needles, or cones of their host plants. Cone-shaped galls or swollen twigs may also appear on infested spruce or fir. High adelgid populations cause yellowing and early drop of needles and drooping and dieback of terminals. The galls on spruce can be unsightly but are unlikely to seriously harm trees. High populations of the non-gall-forming stages can retard or kill trees, although vigorous plants tolerate moderate adelgid populations.

IDENTIFICATION AND BIOLOGY

Most adelgid species alternate generations between two different conifers. Adelgids commonly form galls on spruce, which are considered the primary host on which these insects undergo sexual reproduction and overwinter. Pines are the alternate host for *Pineus* species adelgids. *Adelges* species feed on Douglas fir, fir, hemlock, or larch as their alternate host. Adelgids on their alternate hosts are recognized by the cottony white or grayish material secreted by colonies of females on the trunk, limbs, cones, twigs, or needles. Heavily infested trees may seem covered with snow. The adelgids themselves are beneath this material and are small, dark, soft-bodied insects, and somewhat pear-shaped, like aphids.

Most adelgids have a complex life history similar to that of the species detailed below. The conifer species serving as the primary or secondary host is not known for all adelgids, and some populations apparently do not migrate between hosts. The insects can look different depending on the host, and a single species can have several different kinds of egg-laying adults. Most species overwinter as eggs

under cottony masses or as early-stage immatures under bark or bud scales.

Cooley Spruce Gall Adelgid
Adelges cooleyi

The Cooley spruce gall adelgid occurs throughout the United States. It alternates generations between spruce and Douglas fir. Females or nymphs on spruce overwinter under buds or bark. These move to the base of needles in the spring, where they suck plant juices, which can cause tissue to distort or form a gall that eventually encloses the insects. The galls are from ½ to 3 inches long and are light green to purple. About mid-summer, the nymphs emerge and molt into winged adults. The empty galls harden, turn brown, and may persist for years. Galls on spruce in California are seldom seen, except along the north coast or in mountainous areas.

The emerged adults feed and reproduce on spruce or migrate to Douglas fir. Adults that migrate settle on needles, shoots, or cones. They give birth to wingless nymphs and produce white cottony tufts. This generation overwinters on Douglas fir and can damage trees in the spring when feeding resumes and high populations cause needles to be-

The settled nymph (bottom, with waxy margins) and several active first instars of Cooley spruce gall adelgid are less than 1/20 inch long. Adelgids are morphologically variable insects, often having 6 or more different adult forms in the same species. In comparison with aphids, adelgids are usually smaller, lack obvious cornicles, and occur only on conifers.

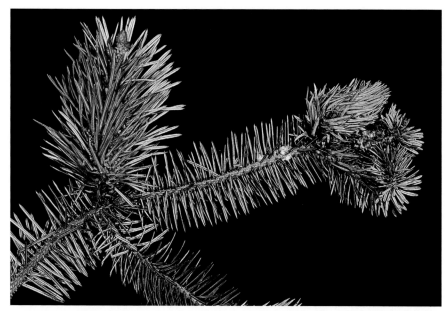

Cooley spruce gall adelgids are causing new spruce terminals to become thick and short (right). The brown terminal is a previous year's shoot that was killed by adelgids. Clip and dispose of these galls to restore plant aesthetic quality. Pruning may provide some control if infested foliage is clipped when the galls are relatively young and still green.

Pine bark adelgids produce a whitish gray material on pine bark.

come distorted, spotted, and drop prematurely. Some of these adelgids develop wings and migrate back to spruce to feed and reproduce. Feeding by the ensuing nymphs can cause galling, and the insect's 2-year life cycle begins again.

Pine Bark Adelgids
Pineus spp.

The pine bark adelgid (*Pineus strobi*) is also called the pine bark aphid. It and two similar but less common species, the pine leaf adelgid (*P. pinifoliae*) and *P. similis*, occur throughout the United States. Most pine bark adelgids form harmless but sometimes unsightly galls on spruce. Their alternate hosts are pine, or pine and spruce in the case of *P. pinifoliae*. Adult females are purplish black, soft-bodied insects. Females and yellowish pink masses of eggs occur in cottony, wax-covered colonies on pine. Crawlers resemble tiny pepper grains on the cottony egg masses. The adelgids overwinter as eggs and have several generations per year.

MANAGEMENT OF ADELGIDS

Many predators feed on adelgids, including lacewings, the small maggotlike larvae of aphid flies (family Chamaemyiidae) and predaceous midges (Cecidomyiidae), and several species of small dark lady beetles. Predators are especially important in natural forests, where most adelgids are uncommon. Except for the balsam woolly adelgid (*Adelges piceae*), a serious pest of fir in the Northwest and Northeast, there has been little research on adelgid natural enemies, especially in landscapes.

Replace some spruce or the alternate hosts with other (nonconifer) species to reduce adelgid populations that alternate hosts. A forceful stream of water directed at the cottony masses on conifers, especially on trunks, dislodges and kills many adelgids. High populations, especially on young trees, can be controlled by applying insecticidal soap, narrow-range oil, or another broad-spectrum insecticide in the spring when crawlers are abundant. Oil may cause spruce foliage to change color, and carbaryl can cause an increase in mite populations unless a miticide is added. Insecticide sprays

are more effective when a wetting agent is added and applications are made with high-pressure equipment so that the spray penetrates the insects' waxy secretions. Certain systemic insecticides may also be effective.

On spruce, to restore the plant's aesthetic quality and provide some control, break off or clip and dispose of infested foliage when the galls are green and before the insects have emerged. Avoid excess fertilization and quick-release formulations, which can promote adelgid populations. No other control is needed to protect plant health or survival. Insecticide sprays are not effective in preventing galls unless application is correctly timed, based on careful and frequent monitoring. Examine the base of terminal buds and locate overwintering females. Inspect females regularly during late winter and spring to determine when they begin to increase greatly in size and start to produce waxy strands. This development time is just before bud sheaths loosen and females lay eggs. Thorough spraying then with insecticidal soap, oil, or other insecticides can provide control.

PSYLLIDS

Psyllids (family Psyllidae) resemble miniature cicadas and are sometimes called jumping plantlice. Over 100 species occur on both native and introduced landscape plants in the United States, but each kind of psyllid feeds on only one plant or closely related species. For example, the boxwood psyllid (*Psylla buxi*) occurs only on boxwood, causing terminal leaves to become cupped. Over two dozen *Psylla* species occur on willow, mostly in the western United States. In the eastern United States, about a dozen species of *Pachypsylla* occur only on hackberry, causing various types of leaf galls.

DAMAGE

Psyllids suck phloem sap. All produce honeydew as a sticky liquid, and some secrete a pale wax or honeydew in pelletized or crystallized form. Honeydew promotes blackish sooty mold growth. Infested leaves may drop prematurely. High populations reduce plant growth or cause terminals to distort, discolor, or die back. A few species cause galls on leaves or buds. Many native shrubs planted as ornamentals, such as manzanita and sugarbush or lemonade berry, can host native psyllid species. These are hardly ever problems and, even if psyllids are abundant, most plants tolerate extensive psyllid feeding. Several introduced plants support exotic psyllids that can be pests.

IDENTIFICATION AND BIOLOGY

Adults hold their wings rooflike over their bodies and at maturity are commonly about 1/10 inch long. In comparison with aphids, psyllids have shorter antenna, strong jumping legs, and no cornicles. Psyllids also lack the dark spot found near the front tip of aphid forewings. Do not confuse psyllids with similar-looking psocids, which feed on fungi, including sooty mold growing on psyllid honeydew. Mature psyllids commonly jump when disturbed, while psocids run or fly away. Unlike psyllids,

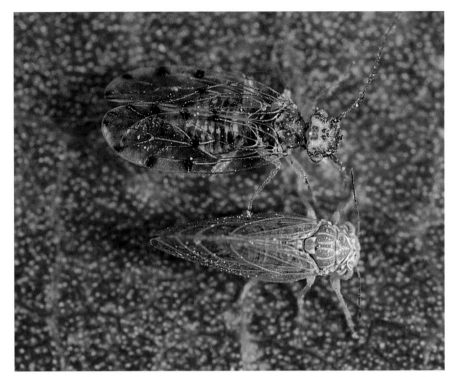

An adult psocid (on top) has longer antennae, a more narrow "neck," or separation between head and thorax, and chewing mouthparts (not visible here) in comparison with adult psyllids, which have tubular, sucking mouthparts. Psocids, which do not damage plants, may be confused with adult psyllids, such as the acacia psyllid shown below it. See the section "Pirate Bugs" for a photograph of an acacia psyllid nymph.

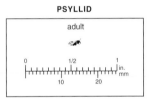

PSYLLID

adult

0   1/2   1 in.
10   20   mm

psocids have a distinctly swollen, bulbous area in front of the head between the widely spaced antennae, which can be distinguished with a hand lens. Psocids also lack sucking mouthparts and do not damage plants.

Psyllids on deciduous trees overwinter as eggs or young nymphs in or around bud scales. Nymphs emerge in the spring and feed on developing buds, flowers, and new leaves. On evergreen plants in mild-climate areas, all stages may be found year-round. Populations are usually highest when new plant growth is abundant, but high temperatures may reduce populations of some species. Consult *Psyllids Pest Notes* (Dreistadt and Dahlsten 2001) for more information.

Acacia Psyllid
Acizzia (=Psylla) uncatoides

Acacia psyllid was accidentally introduced from Australia or New Zealand in the 1950s and occurs in Arizona, California, and Hawaii. The small adults are mostly green or brownish. They often appear darker during cooler weather. The tiny eggs and the orange to green, flattened nymphs are found primarily on growing tips, new leaves, or flower buds. Psyllids are most abundant in the spring when temperatures warm and host plants produce new growth flushes. All stages and reproduction occur throughout the year.

Avoid planting susceptible acacia species (see Table 4-13) and consider replacing problem acacias. Acacia psyllid is often kept under control by natural enemies, including a small black lady beetle (*Diomus pumilio*) introduced from Australia and a purplish pirate bug (*Anthocoris nemoralis*).

During the months of March through June, avoid practices that stimulate psyllid-preferred new growth, including fertilizing, irrigating, and pruning. Whenever possible, conduct any needed cultural practices from July through November. Natural enemies often do not become effective (abundant) until late spring, after psyllid populations have increased and weather warms. Tolerate psyllids until predators provide control, or temporarily reduce high populations with spot applications of soap or oil. See the section "Management of Psyllids," below, for more discussion.

Eugenia Psyllid
Trioza eugeniae

The eugenia psyllid was introduced into California from Australia in 1988. Adults are mostly dark brown with a white band around the abdomen. The tiny golden eggs are laid primarily along the edges of young leaves, where the yellowish crawlers with orange-red eyes settle and feed. As it forms a feeding pit, the nymph resembles a soft scale insect and appears flat when viewed from the lower leaf surface. Populations are highest when new foliage is produced in the winter and spring, but reproduction and all psyllid stages occur year-round.

A parasitic wasp (*Tamarixia* sp.) introduced from Australia provides partial biological control of this pest. However, especially in cooler areas near the California coast, parasite populations often do not increase quickly enough in spring to provide satisfactory control. If eugenia are regularly sheared (such as with topiary plants or neat hedges), well-timed pruning of new growth in combination with parasite conservation can be especially effective in managing psyllids infesting eugenia topiary plantings. Prune terminals after maximum spring growth appears or about 3 weeks after the first peak in adult psyllid density (as determined weekly by branch beating, foliage inspection, or sticky traps, as discussed

TABLE 4-13.

Resistance of *Acacia* species to the Acacia Psyllid in Northern California.

NOT INFESTED OR SLIGHTLY INFESTED (<0.5 NYMPHS/TIP)
albida, armata, aspera, baileyana,[1] *cardiophylla, collettioides, craspedocarpa, dealbata, gerardii, giraffae, karoo, podalyriifolia, pravissima*

SLIGHTLY TO MODERATELY INFESTED (0.5–1.1 NYMPHS/TIP)
cultriformis, cunninghami, cyanophylla, decurrens, iteaphylla, mearnsii, robusta, triptera

MODERATELY TO SEVERELY INFESTED (>2 NYMPHS/TIP)
cyclops, implexa, longifolia, melanoxylon, obtusata, pendula, penninervis, retinodes, salingna, spectobilis

1. Infested by the baileyana psyllid *(Acizzia acaciaebaileyanae).*
Source: Koehler, Moore, and Coate 1983.

The adult eugenia psyllid has a white band around its dark brown abdomen. Yellow sticky traps can be used to efficiently monitor these adults to time control actions.

Tiny golden eugenia psyllid eggs cause the edges of new eugenia leaves to glisten. This pest can be controlled by well-timed shearing and leaving clippings as mulch beneath plants so that parasitic wasps can emerge.

in the section "Monitoring Psyllids," below). Leave eugenia clippings as mulch near the shrubs for at least 3 weeks to allow parasites within psyllid nymphs to complete their development and emerge (Figure 4-5). Eugenia psyllid eggs and nymphs on the cut foliage will die. Consider shearing eugenia tips at about 3-week intervals (and leaving clippings on-site) throughout the period of new plant growth or as long as adult psyllids are abundant. In addition to providing direct control, shearing terminals is the only way of eliminating damaged foliage (aside from waiting for old leaves to drop). Insecticide may also provide some control, as discussed in the section "Management of Psyllids."

Eugenia psyllid nymphs feed in pits on the leaf underside, causing the upper side of foliage to redden and distort.

Peppertree Psyllid
Calophya rubra

The peppertree psyllid was accidentally introduced into California from South America in about 1984. It feeds only on the California pepper tree (*Schinus molle*). Adults are greenish or tan and somewhat pear-shaped. Females deposit their tiny eggs on growing tips throughout the year. The orangish nymphs feed on any succulent plant part, causing the plant to form a pit around where each nymph settles. One psyllid generation requires only a few weeks during warm weather. Reproduction and all life stages occur throughout the year.

An introduced *Tamarixia* species wasp apparently has reduced peppertree psyllid abundance and foliage distortion. Parasite larvae feed and pupate inside psyllid nymphs. Adult parasites leave a roundish emergence hole in dead nymphs that can be observed from the underside of leaves. Avoid using contact foliar insecticides on pepper trees as they are not very effective at controlling psyllids and can substantially disrupt biological control.

Improve pepper tree health and tolerance to psyllids and other damage by providing proper cultural care. Pepper trees are adapted to well-drained, sandy soil and summer drought. Planting trees in heavy clay soils or in summer-watered landscapes, such as lawns, promotes root disease and causes trees to decline and die. Avoid psyllid problems entirely by planting other species. For example, Australian willow myrtle or peppermint tree (*Agonis flexuosa*), desert willow (*Pittosporum phillyraeoides*), and Australian willow (*Geijera parviflora*) are relatively drought-tolerant and have a weeping appearance but are not affected by the peppertree psyllid.

Except for conserving parasites, generally no control is needed in southern California and in warmer inland areas. In cooler areas such as coastal northern California, parasites appear to be less effective. When adults are abundant and terminals are growing (usually winter),

Feeding by the peppertree psyllid nymph pits and distorts California pepper tree foliage. This injury is relatively harmless to pepper trees and is not obvious unless plants are closely inspected. Excess irrigation and poor soil drainage are the primary problems that threaten pepper tree survival.

a systemic insecticide can provide longer control, as discussed in the section "Management of Psyllids," below.

Eucalyptus Psyllids

At least eight species of eucalyptus psyllids have been introduced into California from Australia. Each feeds on only certain species of eucalyptus. Redgum lerp psyllid is discussed separately below.

The lemongum psyllid (*Cryptoneossa triangula*) and spottedgum lerp psyllid (*Eucalyptolyma maideni*) are abundant only on *Eucalyptus citriodora* and *E. maculata*. Both species can occur together on the same plants. Spottedgum lerp psyllid nymphs construct a cornucopia- or funnel-shaped covering with openings that resemble skeletal ribs. These coverings (lerps) are composed of crystallized honeydew and wax. Each lerp may harbor several nymphs, which may be observed moving in and out from beneath their coverings. Lemongum psyllids do not construct any covering. They are free-living, but often occur beneath the coverings formed by spottedgum lerp psyllid.

Bluegum psyllid (*Ctenarytaina eucalypti*) primarily infests *Eucalyptus pul-*

Spottedgum lerp psyllid nymphs secrete an elongate, funnel-shaped, fluted cover. They can be abundant on *Eucalyptus citriodora* and *E. maculata*.

verulenta and juvenile foliage of *Eucalyptus globulus*. This species does not produce hardened covers but can secrete extensive wax and honeydew. Bluegum psyllid is now under good biological control by an introduced parasitic wasp (*Psyllaephagus pilosus*, family Encyrtidae). Pairs of adult bluegum psyllids mate tail-to-tail and may resemble a grayish moth, unless examined more closely. Their pale eggs and orangish, gray, or green nymphs occur among flocculent wax on leaves and terminals.

An introduced encyrtid wasp (*Psyllaephagus pilosus*) leaves round emergence holes in nymphs that it kills. Bluegum psyllids are effectively controlled by this parasite, so eucalyptus should not be treated for this pest.

Psyllids have three life stages: eggs, nymph (left), and adult. At top right is a cover made by a nymph of these redgum lerp psyllids.

A redgum lerp psyllid cover with a parasite emergence hole is flipped over here to reveal a dead, mummified psyllid nymph, also with a parasite emergence hole. Inspecting beneath nearby lerps would reveal that some of the psyllid nymphs underneath them are parasitized. After feeding inside as a larva, the redgum lerp psyllid parasite (*Psyllaephagus bliteus*) pupates and emerges as a shiny greenish wasp with yellow legs.

Eucalyptus are attacked by several other important insects. Learn how management efforts may affect these other introduced pests before taking any actions against eucalyptus psyllids. In particular, consult the sections "Eucalyptus Longhorned Borers" and "Eucalyptus Tortoise Beetle."

Redgum Lerp Psyllid
Glycaspis brimblecombei

The redgum lerp psyllid was discovered in Los Angeles in 1998 and has spread throughout most of California. This Australian native also occurs in Florida and Mexico and may eventually infest much of the southern United States where susceptible eucalyptus are grown. High populations of redgum lerp psyllid secrete copious honeydew and cause premature leaf drop. Extensive defoliation weakens trees, can increase tree susceptibility to wood-boring pests such as longhorned beetles, and may contribute to the premature death of highly susceptible species. Abundant yellow jackets feeding on honeydew may annoy or threaten people in some locations. Redgum lerp

psyllid infests over two dozen *Eucalyptus* species, especially *Eucalyptus camaldulensis, E. rudis,* and *E. tereticornis.* Certain *Eucalyptus* species are avoided by this psyllid or psyllid populations do not build to bothersome levels (Table 4-14).

Redgum lerp psyllid nymphs form a cover called a "lerp," which makes nymphs resemble armored scales. Lerps are small white, hemispherical caps on leaves. Lerps grow up to about $\frac{1}{8}$ inch in diameter and $\frac{1}{12}$ inch tall. The nymph underneath each lerp is yellow or brownish and looks similar to a wingless aphid. Nymphs enlarge their lerp as they grow or move and form a new covering. Adults are about $\frac{1}{8}$ inch long, slender, and light green with orangish and yellow blotches. They differ from other psyllids in California in that redgum lerp psyllid adults have relatively long forward projections (genal cones) on each side of their head below their eyes. Females lay tiny, yellowish, ovoid eggs singly or in scattered groups.

Females prefer to lay eggs on succulent leaves and young shoots, so population increases often follow the production of new plant growth. However, all psyllid life stages can occur on both new and mature foliage. Development time from

TABLE 4-14.

Approximate Relative Susceptibility of *Eucalyptus* (Gum) Species to Several Introduced Pests in California.

COMMON NAME OF GUM	*EUCALYPTUS* SPECIES	LONGHORNED BORERS[1]	REDGUM LERP PSYLLID[2]	TORTOISE BEETLE[3]
Australian beech	polyanthemos	—	L	L
blue	globulus	M	I L[4]	M
desert	rudis	—	M	I
dollar leaf	cinerea	—	L	—
flooded	grandis	I	I	M
forest red	tereticornis	—	M	—
gray ironbark	paniculata	—	L	—
hybrid	trabutii	L	—	—
Karri	diversicolor	M	I	—
lemon	citriodora	L	I[5]	L
long flowered	macandra	—	I	—
manna	viminalis	M	I	M
mountain	dalrympleana	L	—	—
narrow leaved	spathulata	—	L	—
Nichol's willow leaved	nicholii	—	I	—
red flowering	ficifolia	—	L	L
red ironbark	sideroxylon	L	I L	L
river red	camaldulensis	L	M	M
round leaved/red flowered	platypus/nutans	M	I L	—
shining	nitens	M	M I	—
silver	crenulata	—	—	L
silver dollar	pulverulenta	—	L[4]	—
spotted	maculata	—	—[5]	L
sugar	cladocalyx	L	I L	—
swamp mahogany	robusta	L	L	—
Sydney blue	saligna	M	L	—
white ironbark	leucoxylon	—	I	—

KEY

—   information not available

M   more or most susceptible

I   intermediate susceptibility

L   less or least susceptible or reportedly not attacked

1. This column reports susceptibility to *Phoracantha semipunctata*, which is believed to be similar to the susceptibility to *P. recurva*.

2. *Glycaspis brimblecombei*.

3. *Trachymela sloanei*.

4. Susceptible to bluegum psyllid (*Ctenarytaina eucalypti*), but this psyllid is generally under good biological control.

5. Susceptible to lemongum lerp psyllid (*Cryptoneossa triangula*) and spottedgum psyllid (*Eucalyptolyma maideni*).

Adapted partly from: Brennan et al. 2001, Hanks et al. 1995.

egg to adult varies from several weeks during warm weather to several months during prolonged cool temperatures. This insect has several generations each year, and in mild coastal areas, all stages can be present throughout the year. However, because some nymphs form multiple lerps, leaving old whitish covers empty, the number of lerps on leaves is not a good indication of the actual number of insects present.

MONITORING PSYLLIDS

Because psyllid damage is primarily aesthetic, tolerance varies among people and with the species and location of plants. Set thresholds appropriate to your local situation by monitoring insect populations or honeydew and recording when psyllids become a problem. During subsequent seasons, take control action if populations or damage approach the levels that you previously found to be intolerable. Keep in mind that foliar damage is caused primarily by nymphs. However, for effective treatment timing, you must monitor adults or eggs and spray to kill eggs or newly hatched nymphs before damage occurs. Therefore, you must base your decision on the adult populations occurring several weeks before damage became intolerable. You may discover an annual cycle to psyllid abundance; population increases are typically associated with the availability of tender new growth.

Quantitative monitoring to time control action and evaluate efficacy can be very useful in situations where psyllids are very damaging or substantial resources are devoted to managing them. One approach is to monitor psyllids on foliage near the ground by visually inspecting and counting the insects on 4 to 8 or more leaves, new growth tips, or branch terminals on each of several plants. Leaves should be of the same age at each sampling. Use a hand lens or microscope and clip samples to facilitate their inspection. Because counting the small immature psyllids is tedious, counting only adults is an efficient alternative.

Adult psyllids are easily monitored with yellow sticky traps or, on low branches, by beating foliage to dislodge insects. Consult the sections "Yellow Sticky Traps" and "Branch Beating" earlier in this chapter for more information on these techniques. Sticky traps are best for monitoring around tall trees or when the most important natural enemies are parasites (because parasitic wasps can also be monitored with yellow traps). Branch beating may be best for some species like acacia psyllid because it allows important predators to also be monitored. When sampling, count and record separately the number of adult (winged) psyllids and psyllid-feeding predators (dislodged by beating) or parasites (caught in yellow sticky traps). Be sure that you distinguish psyllids from psocids, as discussed above. Sample every 1 or 2 weeks beginning before psyllids become a problem, typically in the spring. Sample until plants stop producing new growth or psyllid populations decline.

MANAGEMENT OF PSYLLIDS

Plant species is a primary determinant of whether psyllids will be a problem. Choose species that are well adapted to the location. Consider replacing problem-prone plants with more pest-resistant species (Tables 4-13, 4-14). Discourage excessive flushes of succulent foliage that promote increased psyllid populations; for example, do not irrigate too frequently and avoid fertilizing established woody plants. Unless well-timed and repeated as discussed above for eugenia psyllid, minimize shearing or trimming terminals to provide a smooth, dense canopy surface for ornamental purposes. Shearing stimulates new growth preferred by psyllids.

Lady beetles, lacewing larvae, small predaceous bugs, and parasitic wasps are important in controlling psyllids. University researchers are introducing new beneficial species that attack psyllids that are currently pests. Because beneficials often do not become abundant until after

psyllids are common and weather has warmed, supplemental control may be desirable, even for those species with effective natural enemies.

Psyllids are difficult to control effectively with sprays because most species reproduce all year and have many annual generations. Limit use of insecticides to situations where psyllids and their damage cannot be tolerated. Many species rarely warrant insecticide treatment.

Azadirachtin, horticultural oil (an insecticide labeled narrow-range, superior, or supreme oil), insecticidal soap (potassium salts of fatty acids), or neem oil can provide temporary control of psyllids that are directly contacted by the spray. Infested new growth must be thoroughly covered with the insecticide spray. The low toxicity and short persistence of these "organically acceptable" materials does not kill natural enemies that migrate in after the spray has dried, so application of these materials early in the season before natural enemies build up on (and migrate from) nearby unsprayed plants is compatible with later-season biological control. However, an additional treatment may be necessary within several weeks if psyllid populations rebound and the plants produce a new growth flush. These sprays have very limited effectiveness against lerp psyllid species that feed beneath covers.

Time any sprays to kill eggs and young nymphs before damage or psyllids become abundant. Monitor when susceptible new growth or adult psyllids or both become abundant, as discussed above. Treat soon after a sharp increase in adult numbers is observed on sticky traps or in beat samples, or when significant numbers of eggs are observed on leaves and shoots. Continue monitoring after treatment. If natural enemies as well as psyllids become abundant, delay reapplication and monitor again later to determine whether populations have declined and spraying can be avoided.

Systemic insecticides are the most practical, effective materials for control-

An adult lady beetle (*Diomus pumilio*) feeding on acacia psyllid eggs. Introduction of this 1/12-inch-long predator and a small pirate bug have greatly reduced acacia psyllid populations.

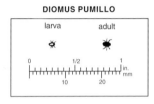

DIOMUS PUMILLO

larva   adult

A multicolored Asian lady beetle larva (top) and an adult beetle that just emerged from the pupal case next to it. This species and other generalist predators can be abundant on psyllid-infested eucalyptus. However, predators do not control this pest, so tiny parasites that feed as wasp larvae hidden within their hosts are being introduced in an effort to provide effective biological control.

ling psyllids that infest large trees. Imidacloprid has the advantage of being formulated into products that can be applied to soil, thus avoiding the plant injury that occurs when trunks are injected or implanted, as discussed in Chapter 2 in the section "Injecting or Implanting Pesticides." Consult *Eucalyptus Redgum Lerp Psyllid Pest Notes* (Dahlsten et al. 2003) and *Psyllids Pest Notes* (Dreistadt and Dahlsten 2001) for more information.

Management of Redgum Lerp Psyllid. Plant resistant species to prevent redgum lerp psyllid from being a problem, as only a few species become highly infested (Table 4-14). Minimize tree stress by providing eucalyptus with proper cultural care and protecting trees from injury. Drought stress and high nitrogen apparently increase redgum lerp psyllid populations. Consider providing trees with supplemental water during periods of prolonged drought, such as during summer and fall in much of Cali-

fornia. Avoid fertilizing eucalyptus. Use slow-release nutrient formulations if other plants near the drip line of eucalyptus require fertilization.

Consider pruning off limbs that overhang surfaces where dripping honeydew is especially intolerable. Be aware that pruning can stimulate new growth of succulent foliage preferred by psyllids. Except for dead or hazardous branches, which should be removed whenever they appear, prune eucalyptus only during December or January (in southern California) or November through March (in northern California).

Redgum lerp psyllid is attacked by many predators including multicolored Asian lady beetle (*Harmonia axyridis*) and other coccinellids, minute pirate bugs (*Anthocoris* spp.), larvae of lacewings and syrphid flies, spiders, and small birds. Native predators do not provide adequate biological control, but whenever possible select management efforts that have the least adverse effect on these beneficial species.

At least one psyllid-specific parasitic wasp (*Psyllaephagus bliteus*) has been introduced from Australia. Adult *P. bliteus* are about 1/12 inch long encyrtid wasps with metallic green bodies and yellowish legs. Females oviposit on young nymphs. After feeding as larvae, wasps pupate and emerge from beneath larger lerps, leaving a roundish emergence hole in parasitized nymphs and their lerps. *Psyllaephagus bliteus* is established in much of California and apparently is reducing psyllid populations in at least some locations.

Before taking any action, consult the sections "Eucalyptus Longhorned Borers" and "Eucalyptus Tortoise Beetle" in this chapter. Consider the impact of controls on other eucalyptus pests, such as the potential of insecticides to disrupt biological control of the bluegum psyllid and eucalyptus snout beetle. A systemic insecticide (imidacloprid) has provided control in some situations, but other users find results to be disappointing. For more information, consult the most current *Eucalyptus Redgum Lerp Psyllid Pest Notes* (Dahlsten et al. 2003).

WHITEFLIES

Whiteflies (family Aleyrodidae) are not true flies, but are related to psyllids and aphids in the order Homoptera. Many different species of whiteflies occur on landscape plants, but most are uncommon because of natural controls such as parasites and predators.

Whiteflies are most often pests in greenhouses, interior plantscapes, and outdoors in mild-winter areas. They suck phloem sap, and high populations cause leaves to yellow, shrivel, and drop prematurely. The honeydew excreted by nymphs collects dust and leads to sooty mold growth. Honeydew attracts ants, which disrupt the biological control of whiteflies and other pests.

IDENTIFICATION AND BIOLOGY

Whiteflies usually occur in groups on the underside of leaves. They derive their name from the mealy white wax covering the adult's wings and body. Adults are shaped like a tiny moth or house fly, and most species are very similar in appearance. They have yellowish bodies and whitish wings, and some species have dark wing markings. Tiny oblong eggs are usually laid on the underside of leaves. Eggs hatch into barely visible, oblong, yellowish nymphs or crawlers. Crawlers wander for a few hours, then insert their mouthparts into plant tissue and remain settled until adulthood. After the first molt, the semitransparent nymphs become flattened, oval, may become covered with waxy secretions, and resemble tiny scale insects. Most species have several annual generations, with all stages present year-round on evergreen hosts in areas with mild winters. The time required for whiteflies to complete a single generation can vary from several months during the winter to a few weeks in the summer.

Whitefly metamorphosis differs from most Homoptera because mature nymphs become temporarily inactive during the last instar. This stage is commonly called a pupa, even though whiteflies have incomplete metamorphosis and do not have a true pupal stage. The appearance of these pupae, the location and pattern of egg laying, and the species of host plant help distinguish whitefly species. Pupae are usually pale-colored and relatively translucent, but depending on the species pupae may be smooth or covered with filaments, curly whitish to transparent wax, or a combination of filaments and wax. For species with a clear pupal cover, the yellow to black, sometimes patterned insect body helps to identify the whitefly. Most adult whiteflies leave a T-shaped slit in the pupal case from which they emerged; parasites generally leave a small rounded hole in the top of the nymph.

Several of the most common whitefly species in landscapes are described and pictured here. For additional species, consult publications such as *Integrated Pest Management for Floriculture and Nurseries* (Dreistadt 2001) and *Whiteflies Pest Notes* (Flint 2002).

MONITORING

Inspect the underside of shriveled and yellow foliage and nearby healthy leaves for whiteflies. Most species prefer to feed on new plant growth. A cloud of tiny mothlike adults appears when you shake heavily infested foliage. Yellow sticky traps are useful for detecting the presence of adult whiteflies and for estimating seasonal changes in their abundance, as discussed at the beginning of this chapter.

Adult whiteflies are difficult to identify to species. Pupae are used to distinguish among most whitefly species. For example, these ash whitefly pupae have a characteristic broad band of wax down the back and a fringe of tiny tubes, each with a liquid droplet at the end.

Ash Whitefly
Siphoninus phillyreae

Ash whitefly occurs in the southwestern United States on hosts that include ash, citrus, pear, pomegranate, redbud, and toyon. Mature ash whitefly nymphs have a broad band of whitish wax extending lengthwise down the back and a fringe of tiny tubes around the periphery of the body. A tiny liquid droplet collects on the end of each tube.

Soon after its discovery in southern California in 1988, host plants became heavily infested. Enormous numbers of adults become active on warm days. Ash whitefly is now rarely a pest because it is under good biological control by two introduced natural enemies: a tiny black and yellowish parasitic wasp (*Encarsia inaron*) and a small, mostly brownish lady beetle (*Clitostethus arcuatus*). Conserve these natural enemies by controlling ants and dust and by avoiding the use of broad-spectrum, persistent insecticides. Tolerate local outbreaks; they are likely to be temporary because natural enemies will soon provide control.

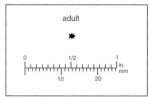

WHITEFLY

pupa   adult

0   1/2   1 in.
|||||||||||||||||||||||| mm
    10   20

CLITOSTETHUS ARCUATUS

adult

0   1/2   1 in.
|||||||||||||||||||||||| mm
    10   20

Crown whitefly occurs in California on oak and chestnut. Nymphs blacken as they mature. Pupae have broad, white, waxy plates spreading from their sides. The similar Stanford whitefly (*Tetraleurodes stanfordi*) occurs on oaks and chinquapin (*Chrysolepis* spp.). These whiteflies are apparently harmless and no control is needed.

Citrus Whitefly
Dialeurodes citri

Citrus whitefly eggs are laid randomly on the underside of full-sized leaves. Pupae lack a visible waxy covering and have a distinct Y-shaped mark on the back. This insect occurs in the southern states and California, primarily on citrus but sometimes on other plants including ash, ficus, and pomegranate. Populations are usually low because of effective natural enemies, especially *Encarsia* species parasites. No special control should be necessary in landscapes, except to avoid harming natural enemies. Where it is a problem, consult publications such as *Integrated Pest Management for Citrus* (UCIPM 1991) and the most recent *Citrus Pest Management Guidelines* (Ohr et al. 2002).

Crown Whitefly
Aleuroplatus coronata

Crown whitefly occurs in California on oak and chestnut. Adults appear only during the spring and may become a nuisance on warm days when enormous numbers may emerge, resembling swirling snowflakes. These adults soon disappear and can be ignored because they do no apparent damage to plants. Tiny white to pink eggs are attached by a

short stalk to the lower leaf surface. Nymphs and pupae are oval-shaped and black, but become mostly covered with broad, white waxy plates that spread out from the insects' sides, somewhat resembling a minute crown. Crown whitefly overwinters as a pupa and has one generation per year. Although high populations can be unsightly, generally no control is recommended.

Giant Whitefly
Aleurodicus dugesii

The introduced giant whitefly is a pest in the southern United States and in California at least in the south. It is named for its relatively large size. Giant whitefly attacks over 60 plant species, including aralia, begonia, giant bird of paradise, hibiscus, mulberry, orchid tree, xylosma, and various vegetables.

After emerging from pupal cases, most adults remain on the leaf where they emerged, laying eggs until they die. Many adults will remain on a dying or fallen leaf and perish as the leaf dries. This clustering tendency allows a relatively large number of whiteflies to be destroyed by

removing relatively few leaves. Monitoring to detect infestations early is extremely critical. Early detection allows new infestations to be largely eliminated by hand-picking and bagging foliage for disposal before whiteflies disperse.

Directing a strong stream of water to the underside of infested leaves (syringing) also is highly effective. Syringing performed as well or better than chemical treatments in a University of California study. Contact insecticides have difficulty reaching whiteflies in part because of the abundant wax they produce. Syringing improves plant appearance by removing honeydew and has much less negative effect on biological control than applying pesticides does.

At least three species of introduced parasitic wasps have become established on giant whitefly in southern California: *Encarsiella noyessi* (family Aphelinidae), *Entedononecremnus krauteri* (Eulophidae), and *Idioporus affinis* (Pteromalidae). It is hoped that natural enemies will eventually provide effective biological control, as they have against certain other introduced whiteflies. Conserve these natural enemies whenever possible, such as by avoiding application of broad-spectrum, persistent insecticides. Because this may be a quarantined pest, if suspected giant whiteflies are found outside areas known to be infested, report this to the county department of agriculture (in California) or other agricultural officials. For more information consult *Giant Whitefly Pest Notes* (Bellows, Kabashima, and Robb 2000).

Greenhouse Whitefly
Trialeurodes vaporariorum

Greenhouse whitefly eggs are whitish yellow when laid and turn dark black, green, or gray before nymphs emerge. The tiny eggs are sometimes laid in circles or half circles or are grouped or scattered on the undersurface of leaves. Pupae have a transparent cover and are oblong with vertical sides. A fringe of filaments protrude around the perimeter of the upper edge of the last instar nymph, or "pupa." Greenhouse whitefly is a pest throughout the United States primarily on annuals, especially vegetables and flowers, but it can occur on some woody landscape species, including avocado, fuchsia, gardenia, lantana, and redbud.

Conserve important natural enemies of the greenhouse whitefly by controlling dust and ants and avoiding the use of broad-spectrum insecticides. If whitefly populations are high and cannot be tolerated, apply insecticidal soap or narrow-range oil. *Encarsia formosa* and other parasitic wasps are important greenhouse whitefly natural enemies. Female *Encarsia* feed on all nymphal stages except the last instar and lay eggs in third- and fourth-instar whiteflies. Eggs hatch into larvae that feed inside and kill the whitefly. Parasitized nymphs resemble brownish or black scales, in contrast to the whitish or yellowish green color of healthy whitefly nymphs. *Encarsia* adults chew a round hole in whiteflies and leave black deposits in the host, in contrast to the mostly clear skin left by emerging whiteflies. *Encarsia formosa* is sold through the mail and is effective when released in warm, humid greenhouses; however, there is no information demonstrating that releases control greenhouse whitefly in landscapes.

Beardlike wax strands beneath leaves and blackish sooty mold caused by giant whitefly nymphs infesting hibiscus. Because this pest spreads slowly, infestations can be controlled by carefully monitoring hosts and promptly disposing of infested leaves where giant whiteflies are first found.

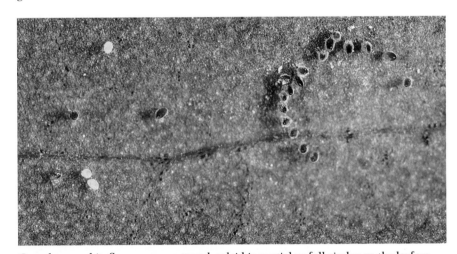

Greenhouse whitefly eggs are scattered or laid in partial or full circles on the leaf underside.

Greenhouse whitefly pupae have long, waxy filaments on top (submarginal filaments) and a short, marginal, waxy fringe.

Greenhouse whitefly pupae turn black when parasitized by *Encarsia formosa*, in comparison with a white or yellowish unparasitized pupa (right) and empty pupal case from which a whitefly emerged (lower left).

Silverleaf Whitefly
Bemisia argentifolii

Silverleaf whitefly has apparently displaced an almost identical-looking species, sweetpotato whitefly (*Bemisia tabaci*). Silverleaf whitefly can be a severe pest in greenhouses and outdoors in warm locations such as the interior areas of California. Herbaceous species are most severely affected, but some woody ornamentals can be heavily infested, including citrus, crape myrtle, hibiscus, lantana, orchid tree (*Bauhinia* spp.), rose, and willow.

Discolored and distorted foliage, copious honeydew, sooty mold, and premature defoliation are common damage symptoms. Some hosts become stunted or develop silvery foliage, apparently because silverleaf whitefly saliva is toxic to some plants. Nymphs and pupae are round to oval and yellowish. Unlike most other common species, they do not produce whitish waxy material and they have few or no tiny filaments, or setae, protruding from around their edge.

Adults are attracted to yellow sticky traps, which are used primarily for monitoring populations. Control is difficult, and university scientists have been introducing natural enemies in an effort to provide biological control. Various introduced and native *Encarsia* and *Eretmocerus* species wasps may help control silverleaf whitefly in certain situations. Spraying lower leaf surfaces with a forceful stream of water daily during warm weather can provide control. Soap or oil applied to thoroughly cover lower leaf surfaces temporarily reduces populations.

Silverleaf whitefly nymphs produce little or no whitish wax. Pupae have no obvious marginal waxy fringe, but sometimes short filaments arise from their top.

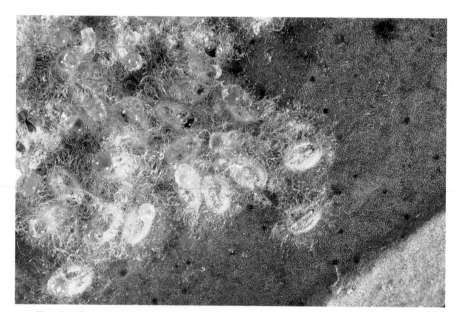

Woolly whitefly nymphs and pupae are covered with fluffy, waxy filaments. This species occurs on eugenia and citrus in California and states along the Gulf of Mexico, but it is usually well controlled by introduced parasites.

Woolly Whitefly
Aleurothrixus floccosus

Woolly whitefly eggs are laid in circles or partial circles on the lower surface of mostly full-sized leaves. Nymphs and pupae are covered with fluffy, waxy filaments. Woolly whitefly occurs in Gulf states and California, mostly on citrus and eugenia and usually at low densities.

Parasitic wasps (especially *Amitus spiniferus* and *Cales noacki*) provide complete biological control of woolly whitefly in California unless disrupted by ants, dust, or pesticides. Conserve these natural enemies and avoid spraying broad-spectrum insecticides. A bright reddish fungus (*Aschersonia aleyrodis*) has been reported in Florida as effective in controlling the woolly whitefly and some other whiteflies under warm, moist conditions.

MANAGEMENT OF WHITEFLIES

Most whitefly species are satisfactorily controlled by natural enemies, unless

Yellow sticky traps are a good way to detect adult whiteflies and adults of certain other insects. Covering traps with clear plastic preserves insects before collecting traps. Comparing the number of insects in traps over time helps to determine whether pest populations are increasing, decreasing, or remaining about the same.

Parasitized whitefly nymphs commonly darken and develop round emergence holes (left). Adult whiteflies leave a characteristic ragged or T-shaped slit (right), as shown here for ash whitefly.

these beneficials are disrupted by ants, dust, or insecticide sprays. For example, introduced biological control agents now control several former ornamental pests, including ash whitefly, bayberry whitefly (*Parabemisia myricae*), citrus whitefly, and woolly whitefly (*Aleurothrixus floccosus*). Bigeyed bugs, dustywings, lacewings, lady beetles, and pirate bugs are important native predators. Parasitic wasps, such as *Amitus, Encarsia,* and *Eretmocerus* species, control many species of whiteflies. Conserve these natural enemies. Control ants by using enclosed insecticide baits or sticky material barriers, as discussed in the section "Ants" earlier in this chapter. Plant ground covers to reduce dust, which interferes with natural enemies. When managing many whitefly-infested plants, trim only a portion of the plants at a time. Mature foliage provides a refuge for natural enemies, which can migrate to attack whiteflies that are more common on new growth. Some natural enemies of whiteflies are also commercially available. A parasitic wasp (*Encarsia formosa*) is effective in controlling greenhouse whitefly when released in greenhouses, but it has not been shown to be effective when released outdoors.

A forceful stream of water applied to plant surfaces (syringing) washes away honeydew, which is often the most both-ersome aspect of whiteflies. Regularly syringing small plants can control certain species such as giant whitefly. An insecticidal soap or narrow-range oil spray can provide temporary control; however, whiteflies are difficult to manage with insecticides. Thorough coverage on the underside of leaves is essential. Applications made primarily to the upper leaf surface kill many beneficial insects while missing whiteflies and thus do more harm than good. Broad-spectrum, persistent sprays are generally not recommended. They are often more toxic to the actively searching beneficial insects than to whiteflies, which settle on the lower leaf surface where they are somewhat protected from insecticides. Whiteflies also have developed resistance to many broad-spectrum insecticides. Certain systemic insecticides may be effective for when extreme populations are intolerable.

Adult whiteflies are attracted to bright yellow surfaces. Sticky yellow traps are used primarily for monitoring adult populations during the time of year when adults are active. Standard-sized or extra-large sticky traps may also help to reduce colonization of uninfested plants by adult whiteflies where many traps can be deployed around smaller, relatively isolated hosts. Traps will not help to control immature whiteflies already on plants.

Small lady beetles are important whitefly predators. This *Delphastus pusillus* is feeding on a silverleaf whitefly nymph.

An adult wasp (*Encarsia formosa*) parasitizing a greenhouse whitefly nymph. These tiny adult parasites are easily overlooked. Whitefly pupae that are differently colored (parasitized) or have round holes are the most obvious signs of parasite presence.

Watch for the availability of special highly attractive traps being developed for species such as the silverleaf whitefly.

MEALYBUGS

Several hundred species of mealybugs (family Pseudococcidae) occur in the United States, and most plants are susceptible to one or more species. Some species, like the citrus mealybug and obscure mealybug, occur on many different hosts throughout mild-winter areas.

Mealybugs tend to congregate in large numbers, forming white, cottony masses on plants. High populations slow plant growth and cause premature leaf or fruit drop and twig dieback. Honeydew production and black sooty mold are the primary damage caused by most mealybugs. A few species (such as pink hibiscus mealybug) have saliva that is toxic to plants, and some mealybugs transmit viruses that damage certain crops. Low populations of most species do not harm plants. High populations can cause plant decline, and young plants may be killed.

IDENTIFICATION AND BIOLOGY

Most adult female mealybugs are wingless, soft-bodied, grayish insects about $1/20$ to $1/5$ inch long. They are usually elongate and segmented, and may have wax filaments radiating from their body, especially at the tail. Most females can move slowly and are covered with whitish mealy or cottony wax. The cypress bark mealybug is somewhat atypical; it looks more like a scale insect than a mealybug.

Adelgids, cottony cushion scales, and woolly aphids may sometimes be confused with mealybugs because they also produce a whitish, waxy material. The white, fluted egg sac of cottony cushion scales erupts from the female's body, which is usually bright orange, red, yellow, or brownish. Underneath the loose, cottony, waxy covering, the bodies of most aphids and adelgids appear pear-shaped. Some of the aphids or adelgids in a colony may have wings, while only male mealybugs and scales have wings and males are rarely seen. Male mealybugs are tiny and delicate; their body is commonly yellow or red with two long whitish tail filaments.

Most female mealybugs lay tiny yellow eggs in a mass intermixed with white wax called an ovisac. Mealybug nymphs are oblong, whitish, yellowish, or reddish and may or may not be covered with waxy filaments. Most species feed on branches, twigs, or leaves, often in groups in protected places such as crevices or where foliage touches. Depending on the species, host, and climate, they may overwinter only as eggs or females, or as all stages. Most mealybugs have several generations each year.

Many mealybugs superficially resemble each other, and records of which species attack what hosts are often unreliable. For example, until recently it was not known that Madeira mealybug (*Phenacoccus madeirensis*) is widespread in North America because this species was often misidentified as Mexican

Large numbers of mealybugs, like these on mimosa, can form white, cottony masses.

Most mealybugs are elongate, grayish or powdery white, and segmented. Many species have wax filaments radiating from their body, especially at the tail, as with these obscure mealybugs on grape.

mealybug (*Phenacoccus gossypii*). Obscure mealybug (*Pseudococcus viburni*) has been given several incorrect names (including *Pseudococcus affinis* and *P. obscurus*) and has often been confused with grape mealybug (*Pseudococcus maritimus*). New species become introduced, such as pink hibiscus mealybug and vine mealybug. It can be helpful to have mealybugs correctly identified to species. Some have very effective natural enemies, while others apparently do not. Certain species move among many plant species, while management efforts for others can be narrowly focused on their relatively few hosts. For help with identification, submit specimens to an expert or consult publications such as *Mealybugs in California Vineyards* (Godfrey et al. 2002).

Cypress Bark Mealybug and Cedar or Cypress Scales

The cypress bark mealybug (*Ehrhornia cupressi*), sometimes called cypress bark scale, occurs beneath bark plates and in bark crevices on cedar, cypress, and juniper in Pacific Coast states. Populations are usually innocuous in natural areas, but it can be a serious pest of Monterey cypress in urban areas. Foliage on infested plants becomes yellow and red and eventually may die. Heavy populations cause dieback at the treetop, which gradually extends down the tree and may kill it.

Cypress bark mealybug nymphs and adults are round and bright red or orangish. They are surrounded by a ring of white wax. They do not move after settling as crawlers, and they have one generation per year.

Incense cedar scale, or Monterey cypress scale, (*Xylococculus macrocarpae*, family Margarodidae) during its preadult female stage closely resembles the cypress bark mealybug. Both species occur on incense cedar, Monterey cypress, and some related *Cupressus* and *Juniperus* species

conifers. Incense cedar scale also causes foliage discoloring and dieback, especially on young plants growing at shaded locations. However, incense cedar scale usually is common only in stands of native trees, not in urban areas. Cypress bark mealybug and incense cedar scale both have a very different appearance from minute cypress scale, which is discussed later in the section "Armored Scales." All three of these organisms are sometimes called "cypress scale" even though they are in separate insect families with differing biology.

Obscure Mealybug
Pseudococcus viburni (=*P. affinis* =*P. obscurus*)

The obscure mealybug occurs in warm areas of the United States on many hosts, including cactus, camellia, fruit trees, gardenia, magnolia, oak, oleander, palm, pine, walnut, willow, and yew. The light gray to white adults are covered with a powdery wax and have distinct filaments around the body. All stages occur year-round on bark, twigs, and leaves. One generation requires about 6 weeks during warm weather, and there are four to five annual generations.

Longtailed Mealybug
Pseudococcus longispinus

In areas with mild winters, the long-tailed mealybug can occur on many hosts, including cactus, ficus, fuchsia, gardenia, hibiscus, jasmine, oleander, and palm. It is most commonly a pest on nursery stock and indoor ornamentals. It is distinguished by its two tail filaments, which are longer than its body. Its biology also differs from most species because it gives live birth to nymphs; therefore no egg masses are found in longtailed mealybug colonies. Several parasitic wasps (including *Acerophagus notativentris, Anarhopus sydneyensis,* and

A bark plate on Monterey cypress has been removed to reveal these cypress bark mealybugs. Unlike most mealybugs, this species is round, bright red or orangish, and surrounded by white wax. The preadult female stage of incense cedar scale closely resembles this mealybug, but incense cedar scale is not common on urban conifers.

Arhopoideus peregrinus) often keep long-tailed mealybug populations at low levels outdoors.

Citrus Mealybug
Planococcus citri

Citrus mealybug is a pest of citrus in coastal California, where it also occurs on ficus, fuchsia, gardenia, rose, and certain other ornamentals. It infests many additional hosts in greenhouses and indoor ornamental plantings. It has short, waxy filaments of about equal length all around its margin; one grayish or dark, longitudinal stripe may be visible down its back. Outdoors, citrus mealybug populations are often controlled by several important natural enemies including two parasitic wasps (*Leptomastix dactylopii* and *Leptomastidea abnormis*) and the mealybug destroyer lady beetle.

At least one parasite (*Leptomastix dactylopii*), effective only against the citrus mealybug, is commercially available. This yellowish brown wasp lays its eggs in late-instar nymphs and adult mealybugs, preferring hosts in warm, sunny, humid environments. At warm temperatures, *Leptomastix* can complete one generation in about 3 weeks. It has been released in combination with the mealybug destroyer to successfully control citrus mealybug in greenhouses.

Leptomastix was reportedly effective when several hundred parasites were released on each shrub infested with citrus mealybug in interior plantscapes that were not previously sprayed with persistent insecticides. There is no available information on its effectiveness when released in outdoor landscapes.

Vine Mealybug
Planococcus ficus

Vine mealybug, also called grape vine mealybug, is a relatively new pest in interior and desert areas of California. Its hosts include apple, avocado, citrus, date palm, ficus, grape, mesquite, pomegranate, and willow. It produces copious honeydew and transmits virus in certain crops such as grapes. In addition to infesting aboveground parts, vine mealybug feeds on roots, where it may be tended by ants, which is not apparent because both the mealybugs and ants are underground.

Vine mealybugs are soft, oval, flat, distinctly segmented, and have a pinkish body. They are covered with white, powdery wax that extends into filaments along the body margin and posterior end. At maturity, vine mealybug is slightly smaller than the similar-looking grape mealybug and obscure mealybug. However, the waxy filaments that protrude from the body of the vine mealybug are shorter than those on these *Pseudococcus* species, and vine mealybug does not possess long terminal filaments as with longtailed mealybug.

Pink Hibiscus Mealybug
Maconellicoccus hirsutus

The pink hibiscus mealybug became established in Imperial County in southern California in 1999. It occurs in many warm regions, including Florida, Hawaii, the Caribbean, and parts of Africa, Asia, and Australia. It has the potential to spread throughout much of the southern United States. If suspected pink hibiscus mealybugs are found in areas where this pest is not known to occur, report this to the county department of agriculture (in California) or other agricultural agency officials.

Pink hibiscus mealybug feeds on over 200 species of plants, including hibiscus, ficus, grevillea, mulberry, natal plum, oleander, orchid tree, palm, and rose. Hosts also include avocado, citrus, grape, and vegetables such as beans, cabbage, cucumber, lettuce, pepper, and tomato. As with other mealybugs, this pest produces sticky honeydew, which attracts ants and causes blackish sooty mold growth. Additionally, pink hibiscus mealybug saliva is toxic to plants. Feeding causes bunching, crinkling, curling, or twisting of leaves and terminals. Flowers and fruit can distort or fail to develop. Plants can become stunted overall, and heavily infested young plants can be killed.

Depending on the host, this mealybug can feed on bark, fruit, leaves, shoots, and roots, although populations in California have not been found on roots. Colonies are composed of females and males. The tiny adult males are reddish brown and have one pair of wings and two long waxy "tails," but males are not easily observed. Females grow up to about 1/8 inch long. Their body is pink, and when crushed it exudes pink fluid. Females may also appear to be purplish or dark brown, but most commonly are whitish because of their covering of powdery wax. This species can be distinguished from many other mealybugs because pink hibiscus mealybug lacks wax strands or filaments extending from

Deformed leaves and thickened twigs of hibiscus infested with pink hibiscus mealybug. This pest injects saliva that is toxic to plants. Introduced parasites are apparently providing good biological control, and spraying this mealybug is not recommended in California landscapes.

the margin of its body. Eggs are laid in wax-covered clusters (egg sacs), and the emerging nymphs develop through 3 or 4 instars. Under warm conditions one generation may be completed in about a month and there are several generations each year.

Several species of tiny ($<\frac{1}{12}$ inch long) parasitic wasps that attack only mealybugs have been introduced into California, the Caribbean, and Hawaii, and they significantly control this pest. Female parasites lay their eggs inside mealybugs, where a wasp larva feeds inside and eventually kills the pest. *Anagyrus kamali*, the most important species in California, can complete one generation in less than 3 weeks when temperatures are warm. Mealybugs parasitized by *A. kamali* become puffy mummies with a hardened exterior. After the wasp larvae matures and pupates inside, each mummy develops a hole where the adult wasp emerges to seek and parasitize other mealybugs. In addition to parasitizing mealybugs, female *Anagyrus kamali* puncture mealybugs with their ovipositors and feed on the exuding fluid. Unlike mummified mealybugs killed by parasitization, mealybug mortality from this host feeding is not easily recognized.

The mealybug destroyer (*Cryptolaemus montrouzieri*) feeds on all stages of pink hibiscus mealybug when released into infestations. It is not know whether this lady beetle provides substantial control or whether releasing commercially available mealybug destroyers would be beneficial.

MANAGEMENT OF MEALYBUGS

Provide proper cultural care so that plants are vigorous and can tolerate moderate mealybug feeding without being damaged. Use good sanitation methods to avoid spreading mealybugs to uninfested plants. First-instar nymphs (crawlers) disperse by walking, are carried by wind, and spread as contaminants on objects such as pruning tools that cut infested plants and then are used to cut other plants.

Naturally occurring predators and parasites provide good control of many mealybug species, unless these beneficials are disrupted. Conserve natural enemies by controlling ants, reducing dust, and avoiding use of persistent pesticides. Control ants that tend mealybugs by placing enclosed pesticide baits such as ant stakes at the base of infested plants or trim branches to eliminate ant bridges and apply barriers such as sticky material to trunks, as discussed in the section "Ants" earlier in this chapter. Once disruptions are stopped, several months (several insect generations) may be required before natural enemies provide control, so be patient or make spot applications of insecticides that have minimal impacts on predators and parasites.

Avoid using broad-spectrum, persistent contact sprays such as carbamates, organophosphates, and pyrethroids. Contact sprays are often not very effective because mealybugs are protected by a waxy coating and they feed within protected plant parts. Insecticidal soap, narrow-range oil, or a forceful stream of water can be applied to somewhat reduce populations with minimal harm to

Mealybug destroyer larvae are covered with waxy white curls and look like mealybugs. This one is feeding on orangish grape mealybug (*Pseudococcus maritimus*) eggs laid within a cottony sac.

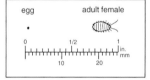

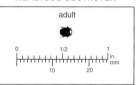

natural enemies that may migrate in later. Certain systemic insecticides can be effective if conserving natural enemies does not provide sufficient control. Populations of cypress bark mealybug can be reduced by thoroughly spraying infested bark with narrow-range oil in August and again in September; however, dense foliage makes it difficult to thoroughly spray bark.

Mealybug Destroyer. The mealybug destroyer (*Cryptolaemus montrouzieri*) is an important predator of the citrus mealybug and other exposed species. This small, mostly blackish lady beetle has a reddish brown head and tail. Mealybug destroyer larvae are covered with waxy white curls and resemble mealybugs, except that the lady beetle larvae are larger and more active. Both adult and larval lady beetles feed on all mealybug stages. The beetle has about four generations per year and lays its eggs into mealybug egg masses.

This adult mealybug destroyer is an important predator of exposed mealybug species.

The mealybug destroyer survives poorly over the winter in California and cold areas and may need to be reintroduced locally in the spring to provide control. Some citrus growers purchase *Cryptolaemus* from commercial suppliers and release them in the spring. Adult mealybug destroyers may not reproduce or provide control unless mealybugs are relatively abundant, so releasing them on localized "hot spots" is most likely to be effective. There is no research showing whether this is effective in landscapes.

Ground Mealybugs
Rhizoecus spp.

Ground mealybugs commonly live in the soil and feed on the roots of many different plants, including abutilon, acacia, boxwood, citrus, grape, palm, pine, *Prunus* spp., spruce, and syringa. Several native and introduced ground mealybug species occur throughout the United States; *Rhizoecus falcifer* is apparently the most common in California. High populations can cause a general decline of a plant and can kill young plants. Ground mealybugs may be covered with white wax and their short antennae and legs may be visible, but they do not have obvious filaments along their sides and tail.

Minimize ground mealybug damage by providing adequate summer and fall irrigation to prevent drought stress. If populations are extremely high, a soil-applied insecticide may be effective. Some insect growth regulators can be applied to control ground mealybugs; check pesticide labels for permitted uses. Insecticidal soap in warm water poured on soil around small plants as labeled may reduce ground mealybug populations.

The ground mealybug does not have obvious filaments along its sides or tail. It feeds on basal stems and roots.

SCALES

Scale insects (over one dozen families in the order Homoptera) are common and damaging pests. They are easily overlooked because they are small and immobile for much of their lives and do not resemble most other insects.

DAMAGE

Scales feed by sucking plant juices, and some may inject toxic saliva into plants. When numerous, some species weaken a plant and cause it to grow slowly. Infested plants appear water stressed, leaves turn yellow, and foliage and fruit may become black from sooty mold or may drop prematurely. Branches or other plant parts that remain heavily infested die; if they die quickly, the dead brownish leaves may remain on branches, giving them a scorched appearance. Several years of severe infestations may kill young plants.

The importance of infestations depends on the scale species, the plant species and cultivar, environmental factors, and natural enemies. Populations of some scales can increase dramatically within a few months, especially when honeydew-seeking ants protect scales from their natural enemies. Plants are not harmed by a few scales, and even high populations of certain species apparently do not damage plants. However, scale-infested plants may become sticky from honeydew and foliage may blacken from the resulting sooty mold growth. Sticky and blackened foliage may be bothersome to people even when scale populations are not harming the plant.

IDENTIFICATION AND BIOLOGY

Adult female scales of most species are circular to oval, wingless, and lack a separate head or other easily recognizable body parts. Adult males are tiny, delicate, white to yellow insects with one pair of wings and a long tail filament. Adult males are rarely seen in many species, do not feed as adults, and live only a few hours. Females of many scale species reproduce without mating.

Eggs are commonly protected beneath the cover of the female. The newly hatched scale nymphs, called crawlers, emerge and walk along branches or are spread by the wind or inadvertently by people or animals. Scale crawlers are usually pale yellow to orange and about the size of a period. Within 1 to a few days, crawlers settle and insert their strawlike mouthparts to feed on plant juices. After settling, armored scales secrete a waxy covering and remain on the same plant part for the rest of their lives (Figure 4-14); nymphs of soft scale species can move a little, usually from foliage to bark before leaves drop in the fall.

It is often very helpful to have an expert positively identify the scale species present. Many obvious species are rarely, if ever, damaging pests on most hosts, while others are serious pests of certain plants. About one dozen scale families contain at least a few species important in landscapes. Scales in different families can vary greatly in appearance and biology. Most scale species are either armored scales (family Diaspididae) or soft scales (Coccidae). The following discussion and photographs and the "Tree and Shrub Pest Tables" at the end of this book will help you to identify and manage common scales on landscape plants. Most of the species discussed here occur throughout the United States. Color photographs and descriptions for some scale species not detailed here may be found in publications such as *Insects That Feed on Trees and Shrubs* (Johnson and Lyon 1982), *Pests of the Garden and Small Farm* (Flint 1998), *The Scale Insects of California*

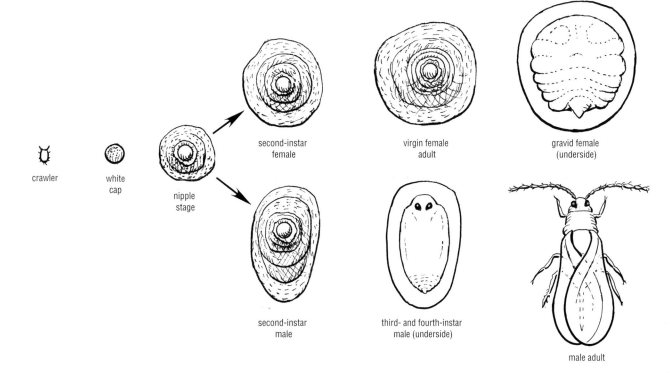

crawler

white cap

nipple stage

second-instar female

virgin female adult

gravid female (underside)

second-instar male

third- and fourth-instar male (underside)

male adult

FIGURE 4-14. Life cycle of a typical armored scale, California red scale. Eggs hatch into tiny crawlers that soon settle and secrete a cottony (white cap) cover and later a more solid cover (the nipple stage). After the first molt, males begin to develop an elongated scale cover whereas female covers remain round. Females molt three times. The final stage is the mated, or gravid, female, a rounded scale cover with a legless, wingless, immobile female beneath. Males molt four times. They develop eyespots, which can be seen when scale covers are turned over in the third and fourth instar. The adult male has legs, two wings, and is easily overlooked.

(Gill 1988, 1993, 1997), and *Scales Pest Notes* (Dreistadt et al. 2001) listed in the Suggested Reading.

ARMORED SCALES

Most armored scales (family Diaspididae) are less than 1/8 inch long and have a platelike shell. This cover usually can be removed to reveal the actual scale body underneath. Armored scale covers often have concentric rings, which form as each nymphal stage secretes an enlargement to its cover. Covers often have a different colored, slight protuberance (exuviae, or "nipple") formed from the covering of the first-instar nymph. The life cycle of a typical armored scale is illustrated in Figure 4-14. Armored scales, such as the greedy, oystershell, and San Jose scale, do not excrete honeydew. Once the crawler stage settles to feed, armored scales generally lose their legs and cannot move. Most armored scale species have several generations each year.

California Red Scale
Aonidiella aurantii

California red scale, and the similar yellow scale (*Aonidiella citrina*), are serious pests only on citrus, where heavy infestations over several years can cause branch dieback, plant decline, and eventually the death of citrus. California red scale prefers broadleaf evergreens and can be found (but is rarely a pest) on many plants, including acacia, boxwood, eugenia, euonymus, magnolia, mulberry, palm, podocarpus, privet, and rose.

The minute yellow crawlers emerge from beneath females and settle in small depressions on fruit, leaves, or twigs. They begin feeding and secrete cottony filaments to form a circular cover. As the scales grow, they develop a more solid cover with a nipple near the center. Midway through the second instar, females and males begin to look different (as

Aphytis melinus is an important parasite of California red scale.

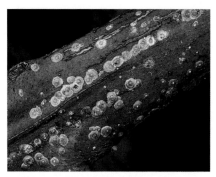

Female California red scales are round with concentric rings on their cover. Although present on many plants, this species is rarely a pest except on citrus.

illustrated in Figure 4-14). All stages overwinter, although cold weather often kills the early instars. Red scale has two to five generations per year.

Oil effectively controls California red scale if plants are thoroughly sprayed. On citrus, July through September is the best period to spray to minimize adverse effects on parasites and possible spotting of fruit. Spray deciduous plants, if needed, during the dormant season; alternatively, spray the late winter–early spring generation of crawlers based on monitoring with sticky tape traps. Pheromone-baited traps for males can also be used to time controls when managing a large number of high-value plants, as detailed in *Citrus Pest Management Guidelines* (Ohr et al. 2002) and *Integrated Pest Management for Citrus* (UCIPM 1991).

Biological Control. Several tiny, yellow to brownish parasitic wasps attack California red scale, including *Aphytis melinus*, *Aphytis lingnanensis*, *Encarsia perniciosi*, and *Comperiella bifasciata*. *Rhyzobius lophanthae* and *Chilocorus orbus* are important predaceous lady beetles. For more information on these parasitoids, consult publications such as *Life Stages of California Red Scale and Its Parasitoids* (Forster, Luck, and Grafton-Cardwell 1995).

Aphytis melinus, the most important parasite, kills scales by puncturing them and feeding on the exuding fluid or by laying an egg under the scale cover, where the immature parasite feeds. *Aphytis* leaves a flat and dehydrated scale body beneath the scale cover where the parasite's cast skin and fecal pellets may be observed. The adult wasp may emerge through a small, round exit hole in the scale cover or push out from beneath the scale cover, so that parasitized scales often slough off. Naturally occurring populations of *Aphytis* are more effective in controlling California red scale in south coastal areas than in the Central Valley of California. The female scales susceptible to parasitization by *Aphytis* are more continuously present in mild-climate areas than in hot areas where there is less overlapping of scale life stages.

Releasing commercially available *Aphytis melinus* (see Suppliers) can reduce red scale populations in citrus orchards if dust and ants are controlled and broad-spectrum, persistent insecticides are not applied. *Aphytis* are released at intervals when the adult virgin females are present; these have a wide, gray margin extending beyond the insect body, and the scale cover and body can be readily separated. The effectiveness of releases in landscapes has not been researched. Consult publications such as *Natural Enemies Handbook* (Flint and Dreistadt 1998) and the most recent *Citrus Pest Management Guidelines* (Ohr et al. 2002) for more information.

Cycad Scale
Furchadaspis zamiae

Cycad scale infests cycad or sago palm (*Cycas* and *Zamia* spp.) and bird of paradise in California and the southern United States. High populations cause severe mottling or yellowing of foliage, stunt growth, and can eventually kill these expensive and slow-growing plants. Females are oval to oblong and moderately convex. Scales occur on the underside and base of fronds and on the basal trunk. Cycad scale most closely resembles oleander scale. Both species occur on bird of paradise and cycad, but oleander scale does not harm plants. Cycad scale is white or whitish with yellow, while oleander scale is mostly tan. Submit samples to an expert for identification if it is uncertain whether the species present is cycad scale, which warrants control action.

San Jose Scale
Diaspidiotus (=Quadraspidiotus) perniciosus

San Jose scale has many hosts including acacia, aspen, citrus, cottonwood, fruit trees, maple, mulberry, poplar, pyracantha, walnut, and willow. However, it usually is a serious pest only on nut trees and stone fruits, where high populations over several years can cause gradual decline and sometimes death of plants. Heavy scale infestations can be recognized on deciduous plants by the brown foliage that remains on infested branches after plants have dropped their leaves in the fall.

Yellowing of fronds may indicate a cycad scale infestation. Distinguish cycad scale from oleander scale, which both occur on cycads or sago palms. Oleander scale is innocuous, while cycad scale can seriously damage or slowly kill cycads.

Mature females have a smooth, yellow body beneath the round, grayish cover. San Jose scale looks like olive scale (*Parlatoria oleae*), which is found on many of the same hosts, except that the female olive scale's body beneath its cover is purple. Olive scale is under good biological control and is rarely a pest unless its effective natural enemies are disrupted. Walnut scale, *Diaspidiotus (=Quadraspidiotus) juglansregiae*, also resembles San Jose scale, except that under its cover, the margin of the walnut scale female's yellow body has indentations. Walnut scale is usually a serious pest only on ash, birch, and walnut.

After settling on bark, San Jose scale crawlers secrete a white, waxy covering (called the white cap) and sometimes cause a red halo to form on young wood or fruit where they feed. After about a week, a band of dark wax appears around the periphery of the white cap, marking the beginning of the black cap stage, in which most San Jose scales overwinter.

Scales resume growth and molt in the spring; females and males then become distinguishable, as illustrated in Figure 4-14. Males begin emerging in March and April. Females mature then and produce a sex pheromone, which attracts flying males. About a month after mating, eggs laid by females begin hatching into crawlers. These usually first appear in May. The scale has two to five generations per year.

The twicestabbed lady beetle (*Chilocorus orbus*), a dark, pinhead-sized nitidulid beetle (*Cybocephalus californicus*), and tiny parasitic wasps, including *Aphytis* and *Encarsia* species, are important natural enemies of San Jose scale. Apply narrow-range oil during the delayed dormant season if a pesticide application is necessary on deciduous plants. Oil or other insecticides may also be applied when crawlers are abundant (about May), but this disrupts natural enemies. If spraying is necessary during the foliage season, monitor scale crawlers beginning in April with double-sided sticky tape. Spray 2 to 3 weeks after the bright yellow, pinpoint-sized scale crawlers are first observed on the tapes.

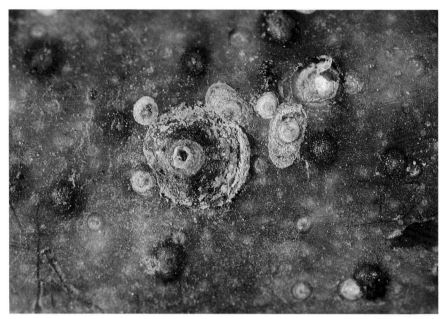

The cover of armored scale females typically is circular, while immature male scales have an elongate cover, as shown here in San Jose scale. Also visible are tiny round immature scales prior to their first molt, called white cap and black cap stages.

Alternatively, on high-value trees, use pheromone traps and degree-day monitoring to time applications, as described in *Almond Pest Management Guidelines* (Teviotdale et al. 2002) or *Integrated Pest Management for Almonds* (Strand 2002).

Greedy Scale
Hemiberlesia rapax
and Latania Scale
Hemiberlesia lataniae

Greedy scale is so named because of its many hosts, including acacia, bay, boxwood, ceanothus, fruit trees, holly, ivy, laurel, magnolia, manzanita, palm, pepper tree, pittosporum, pyracantha, redbud, strawberry tree, and willow. Latania scale has a similarly broad host list and in California may be the more common of these two species. The scales occur on leaves, stems, and fruit. Though sometimes unsightly, these species rarely, if ever, cause serious damage to plants, except possibly in certain crops such as kiwifruit.

Females are circular, convex, and gray, tan, or white. Distinct concentric rings

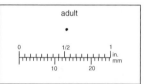

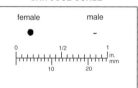

Greedy scales are usually tan with an off-center yellow or brown nipple, like these infesting acacia.

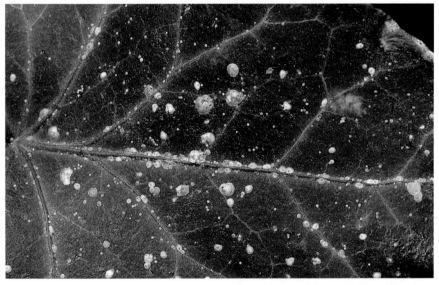

These oleander scales infesting ivy are tan to yellow and flat. They are lighter colored and less globular than greedy scale. Although obvious, this species is harmless to plants.

such as wood-boring insects. Obscure scale has been found and eradicated in southern California, but it has become well-established in Sacramento. If suspected obscure scales are found in areas where this pest is not known to occur, report this to the county department of agriculture (in California) or other agricultural agency officials.

Obscure scale occurs on bark or under loose bark. Its common name was given because scale covers are the color of bark, making this species hard to observe. Obscure scales are slightly convex, circular to oval, and gray with an off-center "nipple." The body underneath is pale, often pinkish or yellowish. Obscure scale overwinters as first or second instars. Males and females mature and mate during spring or early summer. Crawlers emerge from beneath females over a prolonged period from about June through September. This species has one generation per year.

Obscure scale is very difficult to control by spraying insecticide, in part because young scales often develop in groups protected under bark or beneath covers of old scales. Natural enemies are abundant and apparently control obscure scale in natural tree stands in the East, but biological control is often ineffective on preferred hosts in urban areas. University of California researchers introduced an aphelinid scale parasite (*Encarsia aurantii*) into Sacramento from Texas. This tiny, dark, yellowish wasp has gradually reduced obscure scale populations and is providing biological control in California.

often form on the cover as the scales grow. It is difficult to distinguish between greedy and latania scale without microscopic examination by an expert. These species also resemble oleander scale and olive scale, but the waxy covering of female *Hemiberlesia* is more conical and the small dark "nipple" spot is to one side of the center.

Prune out heavily infested branches. Apply oil if necessary during the dormant season or when monitoring indicates that crawlers are active in the spring.

Obscure Scale
Melanaspis obscura

Obscure scale can occur on many woody plants, most commonly on chestnut, oaks, and pecan. In urban areas of the eastern and southern United States it is a serious pest of certain oaks and sometimes pecan. High populations kill small branches and cause decline, which increases tree susceptibility to other pests

Oleander Scale
Aspidiotus nerii

Oleander scale, also called ivy scale or white scale, is probably the most common armored scale species infesting landscapes. While often abundant and unsightly, it rarely, if ever, causes serious harm to plants. It prefers aucuba, cycad or sago palm, ivy, oleander, and olive. Its many other hosts include acacia, bay, boxwood, holly, ivy, laurel, magnolia, manzanita, maple, mulberry, pepper tree, redbud, yew, and yucca. Oleander scale is tan to yellow and flat, but otherwise appears very similar to greedy scale. Oleander scale is lighter colored, less globular, and the brown nipple is more nearly centered on the cover in comparison to greedy scale. Scales are found on bark, foliage, and fruit. Several generations occur each year.

No control is needed to protect plant health. If unsightly, prune out heavily infested branches. Oil can be applied during the dormant season or when monitoring indicates that crawlers are active in the spring.

Oystershell Scale
Lepidosaphes ulmi

Oystershell scale feeds on about 150 plant species, including alder, apple, ash, aspen, box elder, boxwood, ceanothus, cottonwood, fruit trees, holly, maple, poplar, sycamore, and walnut. It is especially common on certain poplars and native willows in riparian areas, and it damages many ornamentals in the Midwest and eastern United States. In California, oystershell scale usually is not a serious pest, but it sometimes damages deciduous fruit and nut trees and preferred ornamentals. High populations over several years can kill twigs and branches on young trees and cause stunted growth and decline of mature plants.

Mature, gray to dark brown, elongated scales resemble miniature oysters and are found on bark, usually in clusters. Oystershell scale does not attack citrus, which may be infested with a similar-looking species, purple scale (Lepidosaphes beckii). Oystershell scale overwinters as whitish eggs, about 50 to 150 of which can be found under the cover of mature females. Crawlers emerge in the spring after buds have burst and walk across the bark for several hours before settling to feed. Oystershell scale usually has one generation per year in northern California and two generations in southern California.

Prune out heavily infested branches. An oil spray, if necessary, is apparently most effective if applied when monitoring indicates that crawlers are active in the spring.

Euonymus Scale
Unaspis euonymi

When abundant, euonymus scale is a serious pest of certain Euonymus species plants, causing severe yellowing, stunting, premature leaf drop, and sometimes the gradual death of plants. Yellowish or brownish spots on euonymus leaves indicate a euonymus scale infestation. The immature male is felty or fuzzy white and elongated with three longitudinal ridges. The female is wider, oystershell-shaped, slightly convex, and brown to black. Both sexes have brownish yellow areas on the narrow end of their covers. Scales overwinter as mature females. Eggs develop beneath these scales and, in spring, hatch into orangish crawlers, which emerge over a several-week period. Euonymus scale has two or three annual generations.

Replace, and do not plant, Euonymus japonica. It is extremely susceptible to euonymus scale. Euonymus kiautschovica (=E. sieboldiana) tolerates scales. Euonymus alata remains nearly scale-free even when heavy infestations occur on nearby susceptible hosts. Narrow-range oil controls euonymus scale if foliage and shoots are thoroughly sprayed; time any application by monitoring crawlers. One annual application during several consecutive years may be necessary to reduce high populations.

A predaceous lady beetle (Chilocorus kuwanae) has been introduced into California for euonymus scale control. In the eastern United States this predator appears to often control euonymus scale. Chilocorus kuwanae resembles the twice-stabbed lady beetle (Chilocorus orbus =C. stigma) pictured in the section "Management of Scales," below. Both predators are shiny black with two reddish spots. However, the spots of C. kuwanae tend to

Oystershell scale females on Lombardy poplar bark. This species does not attack citrus, which may be infested with a similar-looking species, purple scale.

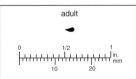

OYSTERSHELL SCALE

adult

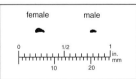

EUONYMUS SCALE

female   male

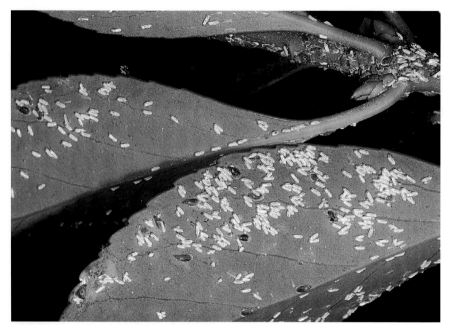

Euonymus scale males are elongated and white, females are wider and darker, and nymphs are tiny and yellowish. This species is a serious pest of *Euonymus japonica*, but certain *Euonymus* species are rarely attacked or are not damaged by this scale.

be deep red, somewhat rectangular, and are located near the center of each wing cover. In contrast, spots of *C. stigma* tend to be more yellowish orange, round, and located more forward toward the head of the beetle. Larvae are brownish with black spines. Whenever they are present, conserve these predators, such as by avoiding applications of broad-spectrum, persistent insecticides.

Minute Cypress Scale
Carulaspis minima

Minute cypress scale, also called cypress scale, can occur on almost any conifer. Be aware that the name cypress scale is also applied to at least two other very different insects, as discussed earlier in the section "Cypress Bark Mealybug and Cedar or Cypress Scales."

Minute cypress scale is most common on arborvitae, cypress, and juniper but usually is a serious pest only on Italian cypress (*Cupressus sempervirens*) and in nurseries. Infestations can cause foliage to turn yellow or brown and die, result-

ing in limb death. Other pests beside these scales, such as the juniper twig girdler and cypress tip miner, may cause the foliage of junipers and other conifers to turn yellow or brown and die, so use a hand lens to inspect discolored foliage for scales. The mature female is circular, convex, and whitish with a yellow center. The tiny male is elongate, oval, felty with longitudinal ridges, and is yellow on the terminal of its mostly whitish cover. This scale has one to two generations per year. Apply oil if necessary or use another insecticide on oil-sensitive species when monitoring indicates that crawlers are active in the spring.

SOFT SCALES

Female soft scales (family Coccidae) may be smooth or cottony and usually are ¼ inch long or shorter. The scale's surface is the actual body wall of the insect and cannot be removed. Most immature soft scales retain their barely visible legs and antennae after settling and are able to move very slowly. Soft scales, including black and brown soft scale, are prolific honeydew excreters. Most species have only one generation per year.

Black Scale
Saissetia oleae

Black scale is probably the most damaging soft scale in California. It is especially abundant away from the coast and where ants are present. Among the black scale's many hosts are aspen, bay, citrus, cottonwood, coyote brush, fruit trees, holly, maple, mayten, oleander, olive, palm, pepper tree, pistachio, poplar, privet, and strawberry tree. Adult female black scales are about ⅕ inch in diameter, dome-shaped, and dark brown or black. Each female produces hundreds of pearly white to reddish orange eggs beneath her hard shell body, mainly during May and June. The tiny emerging crawlers are light brown. Crawlers settle and feed mostly on leaves. During the late second instar, a ridge develops on the scale's back and later expands into an H-shape. After the second molt, young scales migrate to twigs, where they become dark mottled gray and leathery. Once egg laying starts, the scales become darker and harder and the H-shaped ridge may become difficult to see. Black scale has two generations per year along the coast and one generation in inland California.

Parasitic wasps, especially *Coccophagus* species and *Metaphycus* species such as *Metaphycus helvolus*, kill young black scales by laying eggs in them or by feeding on their body fluids. Parasite activity can be recognized with a hand lens by inspecting scale covers for the round exit hole chewed by the emerging adult parasite. *Scutellista caerulea* and *C. cyanea* emerge from mature scales after the larvae feed as egg predators underneath female scales.

Commercially available *Metaphycus* can be released when young scales with an H-shaped ridge are present, but there is little research on the effectiveness of parasite releases in landscapes. Monitor for scale crawlers using double-sided sticky tape and begin making any *Metaphycus* releases after crawler activity declines and young nymphs begin to settle and feed.

Based on use in citrus and greenhouses, releases should be made when first- and second-instar scales are common; these are the young, flattened, brownish or yellow stages. Consult the beginning of this chapter for general guidelines on effectively introducing natural enemies.

Conserve resident and introduced natural enemies by controlling ants, reducing dust, and avoiding broad-spectrum, persistent insecticides. Prune off heavily infested parts if most scales are limited to only a portion of the plant. Also prune to open up tree canopies in warm-climate areas such as the Central Valley of California. This increases heat mortality and helps control black scale. Narrow-range oil controls black scale; spray deciduous plants during the dormant season if needed, or time a foliar application by monitoring crawlers.

Black scales have a characteristic H-shape on the back. The feature is most visible here on the flattened, brownish nymphs in the center. The dark, bulbous black scales are adult females.

Brown soft scale has several generations per year, so different-sized life stages commonly occur at the same time. Shown here are tiny yellow crawlers, yellow first instars, and orangish to dark brown females.

Brown Soft Scale
Coccus hesperidum

Its copious honeydew and the resulting sooty mold can be very annoying, but brown soft scale seldom causes serious damage to landscapes. Brown soft scale prefers broadleaf evergreens, but may occur on most any plant except grasses. Hosts include aspen, citrus, cottonwood, fruit trees, holly, manzanita, palm, poplar, strawberry tree, and willow. Immature scales are a mottled yellow brown and are rounded. Nymphs are found primarily on leaves and then move back onto twigs to mature. Mature females are yellow to dark brown, somewhat flattened, and look similar to citricola scale (see below). Brown soft scale has three to five annual generations, which overlap so that multiple life stages are usually present at once. Populations are usually highest from mid-summer to early fall.

The wasp *Metaphycus luteolus* is an important parasite of brown soft scale, leaving one to several exit holes in larger nymphs or mature scales. Immature scales are also parasitized by several *Coccophagus* species wasps. The small, ob-

long scales parasitized by *Coccophagus* are black, in contrast to the normal yellowish color of brown soft scale nymphs. At least one small, mostly black lady beetle (*Chilocorus cacti*) also preys on brown soft scale. Control honeydew-seeking ants and conserve beneficials. Prune out heavily infested branches. Apply oil if necessary during the dormant season or when monitoring indicates that crawlers are active in the spring.

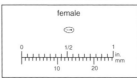

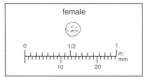

BROWN SOFT SCALE

female

0   1/2   1 in.
        mm
   10   20

BLACK SCALE

female

0   1/2   1 in.
        mm
   10   20

These calico scale females on box elder are typically mottled white and black or brown. The low populations of this scale found on most hosts are not damaging.

Citricola scale females are larger and grayer than similar-looking mature brown soft scales. Maturing citricola scales are all about the same size because the insect has only one generation per year. Note the tiny crawlers on the branch.

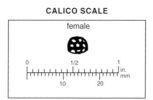

CALICO SCALE

female

0   1/2   1   in.
mm
10   20

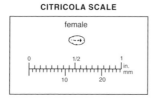

CITRICOLA SCALE

female

0   1/2   1   in.
mm
10   20

Calico Scale
Eulecanium cerasorum

Calico scale occurs on many deciduous trees, usually on plants and plant parts that are well-shaded. Hosts include box elder, liquidambar, maple, stone fruits, and walnut. Low populations found on many hosts are not damaging, but preferred hosts such as liquidambar in California may decline if highly infested over several years.

The mature female is relatively large, globular, and has a typical white and brown or black mottled "calico" pattern. Scales begin to mature on twigs in late winter. The tiny crawlers emerge in early spring and move onto leaves. Before leaves drop in fall, scales move back onto twigs to overwinter.

Calico scale nymphs are covered with thick, elevated, waxy plates. Nymphs are larger and more elongated than frosted scale nymphs, which are flat. Unlike calico scale, the mature frosted scale has a frostlike or powdery covering in spring that weathers away by early summer. Both scales have one generation per year.

Calico scale populations are rarely abundant enough to warrant control. If populations cannot be tolerated, apply narrow-range oil after leaf drop but before mid-January, when scales begin to mature and become less susceptible to treatment. Oil or another insecticide can be applied when monitoring shows that crawlers are numerous in late spring or early summer, but spraying then may be more disruptive of natural enemies.

Citricola Scale
Coccus pseudomagnoliarum

Citricola scale is common and a pest only on citrus and hackberry. Insignificant numbers are reported to occasionally occur on certain other hosts including elm, pomegranate, and walnut. In California it is most common in the Central Valley, where high populations over several years can cause decline of citrus and hackberry and reduced fruit on citrus. The scales are mottled dark brown to gray. Citricola scale may be confused with brown soft scale, but the mature brown soft scale is smaller and yellow or dark brown, not gray. Citricola scale has only one generation per year, so most individuals are about the same size. Because brown soft scale has several generations per year, different-sized life stages commonly occur at the same time.

Citricola scale is well controlled by parasitoids in south coastal California, but not in California's Central Valley. Conserve natural enemies where they are present. Crawler density peaks in northern California at about 635 degree-days above 51.8°F accumulated from 1 March. If applying oil, spray after this time, during about July through early September, after monitoring indicates that most crawlers have emerged and settled. Alternatively, hackberry can be sprayed with oil after leaves drop during the dormant season.

Green Shield Scale
Pulvinaria psidii

Green shield scale is a relatively new species in California. This Asian native has also become established in the Caribbean, eastern United States, and Hawaii. Its hosts include anthurium, aralia, begonia, camellia, croton, eugenia, ficus, hibiscus, gardenia, pittosporum, plumeria, *Schefflera*, *Schinus*, and *Syzygium*. Heavy infestations produce copious honeydew and extensive sooty mold growth, and mature females cover plants with flocculent white egg sacs.

The green, yellowish, or brownish female scale is about ⅛ to ⅙ inch long, and several times longer than this when a cottony egg sac is produced. Unlike most other species of scales, which settle and feed in one spot soon after emerging from eggs, immature green shield scales are relatively mobile. They can feed in one spot for days, then slowly crawl to infest adjoining plants.

The mealybug destroyer appears to be an important predator of green shield scale. Some species of native parasites are also attacking this pest. Green shield scale infestations are often tended by Argentine ants, which carry scales from one plant to another, attack parasites, and can prevent biological control organisms from becoming abundant. Green shield scale may be quarantined, prohibiting nurseries from shipping plants unless they are pest-free. In areas where this pest is not known to occur, report suspected green shield scales to the county department of agriculture or other agricultural officials.

Lecanium Scales
Parthenolecanium spp.

At least five lecanium scale species occur in California. European fruit lecanium (*Parthenolecanium corni*), also called brown apricot scale, is the most common and may actually be a complex of more than one species. It feeds on a few evergreen species and many deciduous ornamentals, including alder, aspen, cottonwood, coyote brush, elm, fruit trees, pistachio, poplar, toyon, and

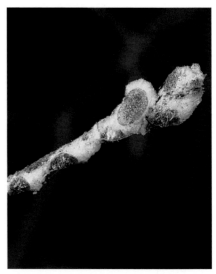

Mature female green shield scales are convex and oval. As shown here, eggs develop in a flocculent waxy mass beneath females. Report this pest to the county department of agriculture (in California) or other agricultural agency officials if green shield scale is found where it is not known to occur.

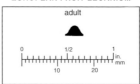

EUROPEAN FRUIT LECANIUM

adult

0   1/2   1 in.
10   20   mm

This oak lecanium scale resembles European fruit lecanium and frosted scale. A reddish brown scale-feeding lady beetle (*Chilocorus bipustulatus*), which resembles its hosts, is visible atop the two left-most scales. Close examination would reveal that the lady beetle has three lighter spots on each wing cover.

walnut. European fruit lecanium is often innocuous, but very high populations sometimes develop on many ornamentals, and the resulting honeydew and sooty mold become very annoying and can make fruit unmarketable.

Frosted scale (*P. pruinosum*), sometimes called globose scale, is usually a pest only on walnuts. Insignificant populations occur on many other deciduous trees, including ash, birch, elm, fruit trees, laurel, locust, pistachio, rose, and sycamore. Oak lecanium (*P. quercifex*) occurs on oak and other Fagaceae. If abundant on oaks, it can weaken trees and kill twigs and branches.

Female lecanium scales have a shiny, dark brown, oval-domed shell, often with several ridges along the back. The scales' life cycles are similar, except that unlike other lecanium, the frosted scale female produces a white, waxy, frostlike cover in spring that weathers away by early summer. In spring, the female produces hundreds of ovoid, translucent white eggs beneath its cover. The yellow to brown nymphs emerge from May to July and feed on twigs and leaves. They have one generation per year.

Conserve natural enemies by avoiding persistent pesticides and control ants and dust. Prune out heavily infested branches. Depending on the host, recommended times for oil application, if necessary, are during the early dormant season (before mid-January), delayed dormant season (as buds begin to swell), or when monitoring in the spring indicates that the peak density of crawlers has definitely passed and most crawlers have settled.

Kuno Scale
Eulecanium (=Lecanium) kunoensis

Kuno scale is usually a minor pest, but damaging populations sometimes occur on *Prunus* species and stone fruit such as plum. Hosts where Kuno scale rarely becomes a problem include cotoneaster,

pyracantha, rose, walnut, and other woody species in the family Rosaceae. Females are almost spherical, resembling rows of beads on stems. Females are dark and shiny brown during most of the year, except that they are yellow and orangish with black bands and blotches during a short period prior to egg production in late spring. Crawlers migrate to leaves, where nymphs develop during summer. Before leaf drop, nymphs migrate to twigs to overwinter. Nymphs are yellow or brown, flattened, and with a fringe of marginal wax. Elongate, translucent male cocoons are prevalent on twigs. Originally from Asia, Kuno scale occurs in the San Francisco Bay Area and Sacramento Valley of California. It has one generation per year. If applying oil, spray during the period from late dormant season until bud swell.

Irregular Pine Scale
Toumeyella pinicola

Irregular pine scale is probably the most serious soft scale pest of pines in California. High populations cause yellow

foliage, seriously weaken trees, kill branches, and sometimes kill young pines. Irregular pine scale infests at least eight pine species, especially Monterey pine (*Pinus radiata*). At least one other *Toumeyella* species in California and several other *Toumeyella* species in the eastern United States infest pines, and in the field they cannot be distinguished from this species. Monterey pine scale (*Physokermes insignicola*) also resembles this species. Monterey pine scale is more spherical, less irregular, and darker. Monterey pine scale causes little or no damage to plants and is reported only on Bishop pine (*P. muricata*) and Monterey pine in California, mostly in the San Francisco Bay region. Because other causes can produce similar damage symptoms, consult Table 5-12 in the chapter Diseases and the "Tree and Shrub Pest Tables" at the end of this book for help in distinguishing among pests affecting pines.

IRREGULAR PINE SCALE

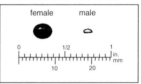

Irregular pine scale males look like grains of rice on these Monterey pine needles. Brownish females encrusted with sooty mold infest the twig; one dead female has parasite emergence holes. Monterey pine scale (*Physokermes insignicola*) looks very similar but it is uniformly spherical and black.

Irregular pine scale overwinters as females on pine branches, typically in blackened and honeydew-encrusted colonies on 1- or 2-year-old shoots. The yellowish, gray, and brown female is robust, dimpled, and irregularly circular. The late-instar immature male scale is elongate and flattened with a raised central ridge. Male nymphs resemble grains of rice and may be observed in large numbers on needles. Females produce crawlers that are distinctly flattened, oval, orange to yellow, and visible as they move over shoots and needles. Crawlers appear from February through May in southern California and from late April through June in the San Francisco Bay Area. One generation occurs each year.

If populations are damaging, monitor crawlers with sticky tape or inspect foliage weekly with a hand lens beginning in February in southern California or in April in northern California. Apply oil when crawlers first become abundant and spray again about 3 weeks later if populations are especially high. Some more-persistent insecticides (such as carbaryl) to which a commercial spreader-sticker has been added are effective but may cause a spider mite outbreak unless a miticide is also added.

Tuliptree Scale
Toumeyella liriodendri

Tuliptree scale is widespread in the eastern United States. In California it has been spreading throughout the San Francisco Bay Area. A long-term project to eradicate it from Alameda and Santa Clara Counties was unsuccessful. In addition to producing copious honeydew, tuliptree scale is a serious pest that causes limb dieback, decline, and sometimes the death of tulip tree (also called tulip poplar) and deciduous magnolias. It sometimes infests other hosts, including gardenia and linden. Tuliptree scale most resembles lecanium scales and an eastern United States species, magnolia scale (Neolecanium cornuparvum). In addition to color differences, these can be distin-

guished because tuliptree scale females are alive throughout the summer (liquid will exude when their body is squashed), while lecanium females mature earlier and by late June are dead and dried out.

Females are large (about ⅓ inch), irregularly hemispherical, and variably colored. Females usually are brown or gray and have irregular black blotches and green, orange, pink, red, or yellow markings. Tuliptree scale overwinters on twigs as nymphs, which mature in late spring to early summer. Males emerge from elongate cocoons. Unlike lecanium scales, mature females do not produce a large mass of eggs under their body. Eggs hatch within the female's body, and crawlers emerge from beneath females for a prolonged period from late summer to late fall. If applying oil, spray overwintering nymphs during late winter or spray during about September after most crawlers have emerged.

Wax Scales
Ceroplastes spp.

About one dozen species of wax scale occur in the United States. Species such

as barnacle scale (Ceroplastes cirripediformis), Chinese wax scale (C. sinensis), and tortoise wax scale (C. cistudiformis) can occur on many different hosts, but populations are usually innocuous and rarely, if ever, threaten plant health. Infestations occasionally create a gooey mess by excreting copious honeydew. In California, Chinese wax scale is sometimes a pest along the South Coast and in the San Francisco Bay Area on Australian willow, Escallonia, and mayten. Occasionally it is abundant on other hosts, including California bay laurel, citrus, coyote brush, holly, Mahonia, and pepper tree. In southern California, barnacle scale is an occasional pest, primarily on gardenia.

Females are hemispherical and covered with thick oily wax. Their predominant color is pale gray, as with honey bee wax or uncolored candles. Mature females have waxy ridges or dark-colored indentations or speckles, which help to distinguish among species. Males are absent or rare. There is apparently one generation per year. Chinese wax scale crawlers are most abundant during fall, but some active first instars may be present anytime from fall through winter.

Wax scales (Ceroplastes spp.) are hemispherical and mostly pale. They are occasional pests of various ornamentals. These mature females were killed by parasites, as evidenced by the round emergence holes.

Black predominates on some vedalia, while some others have more red. This predator is the most important natural enemy of cottony cushion scale at interior California locations. A parasitic fly predominates near the coast.

Cottony cushion scale females and nymphs encrust this grevillea bark. This species can occur on many hosts, but it is usually at very low densities because of effective natural enemies.

COTTONY CUSHION SCALE

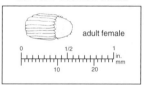

VEDALIA

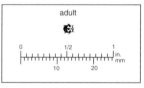

OTHER COMMON SCALES

Several important scales occur in insect families other than the armored and soft scales. Species discussed here include felt scales (family Eriococcidae), pit scales (Asterolecaniidae), and woolly sac scales (Margarodidae).

Cottony Cushion Scale
Icerya purchasi

Cottony cushion scale (family Margarodidae) can occur on many woody plants, including acacia, boxwood, citrus, magnolia, nandina, olive, pittosporum, and rose. It usually is not a pest because most populations are well controlled by effective natural enemies unless biological control is disrupted, for example, by application of certain insecticides. An exception is *Cocculus laurifolius*, which often is highly infested with cottony cushion scale, especially when grown away from the coast, because scale-feeding lady beetles avoid this plant.

The cottony cushion scale female is bright orange, red, yellow, or brown. It is distinguished by its elongated, fluted,

white cottony egg sac, which contains from 600 to 800 eggs. Eggs hatch in a few days during warm weather, but take up to two months to hatch in winter. Crawlers are red with dark legs and antennae. First- and second-instar nymphs settle on twigs and leaves, usually along veins. The third instar is covered with a thick, yellow, cottony secretion, which disappears after it molts. The minute, red, winged male is rarely seen; it seeks a secluded place on the tree or ground to form a loose, white cocoon. Cottony cushion scale has several generations per year.

The vedalia beetle (*Rodolia cardinalis*) is the most famous natural enemy of cottony cushion scale. This red and black lady beetle was introduced from Australia in the 1880s and helped save California's fledgling citrus industry from destruction by the prolific scales. Adult beetles feed on scales, and females lay their eggs underneath the scale or attached to scale egg sacs. The young reddish beetle larvae feed on scale eggs; more mature larvae feed on all scale stages. For photographs of each life stage of vedalia and cottony cushion scale, consult *Stages of the Cottony Cushion Scale*

(Icerya purchasi) *and its Natural Enemy, the Vedalia Beetle* (Rodolia cardinalis) (Grafton-Cardwell 2002).

The other important natural enemy, a parasitic fly (*Cryptochaetum iceryae*, family Cryptochaetidae), deposits its eggs inside the scale body. The larvae feed within the scale; later their dark, oblong pupal cases may be seen there. This fly produces up to eight generations per year. *Cryptochaetum* apparently is the most important natural enemy of cottony cushion scale in coastal California, while vedalia predominates in inland areas.

Conserve natural enemies by controlling ants and dust and by avoiding use of broad-spectrum, persistent insecticides. Imidacloprid and certain insect growth regulators may also have a severe adverse effect on beneficial vedalia. If scales cannot be tolerated until natural enemies become abundant, apply narrow-range oil to deciduous hosts during the dormant season or spray foliage when the tiny reddish scale crawlers are active. See *Cottony Cushion Scale Pest Notes* (Ohlendorf and Flint 1998) for more information.

Sycamore Scale
Stomacoccus platani

Sycamore scale (family Margarodidae) occurs only on sycamore. It can be a serious pest that causes bark roughening, extensive leaf damage, and premature leaf drop that stresses trees. Premature leaf drop is messy and eliminates tree amenities such as summer shade. Infested leaves have numerous small yellow spots. Expanding leaves infested during spring become distorted and stunted and may turn brown, die, and drop. Premature leaf drop can also be caused by an anthracnose fungus (*Apiognomonia veneta*). Anthracnose can be distinguished by the browning it causes along leaf veins, often including large portions of leaves. Anthracnose does not cause the tiny circular spots characteristic of sycamore scale.

Leaf symptoms readily identify this pest. Cottony wax, especially on bark, is another obvious indicator of infestations. The insects themselves are tiny (<$\frac{1}{12}$ inch long), and adults and settled nymphs do not resemble most other scales. Sycamore scale nymphs are brown or yellow and elliptical, resembling insect eggs. Adults greatly resemble brown or yellow thrips nymphs. Mature females produce cottony white tufts covering yellowish eggs. Male cocoons and waxy strands secreted by some nymphs also appear cottony. During fall, some nymphs move to trunks and limbs and overwinter on and beneath bark plates. Nymphs resume development during about January, and at maturity each female produces about 50 to 100 eggs beneath prominent wax strands. Crawlers

Sycamore scale severely spots and often distorts sycamore leaves. Leaf bud break is the most effective time to treat for this pest, not after leaves mature and become damaged, as shown here.

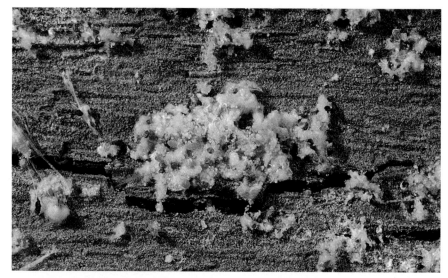

Orangish sycamore scale nymphs and eggs in cottony material on the underside of a sycamore bark plate.

emerge from eggs and move from bark to feed on leaf buds coincident with bud break. All stages can occur on foliage whenever leaves are present. Some scales also develop on bark or move between leaves and bark during summer. Sycamore scale has several overlapping generations per year.

Lady beetles often occur under loose bark feeding on sycamore scale. Most common are the twicestabbed lady beetle (a black predator with two red spots)

and *Exochomus quadripustulatus* (which is black with four orange to yellow blotches).

Sycamore scale damage is most obvious during the late spring, when leaves may be severely damaged. Foliar sprays are not recommended because it is difficult to spray the underside of leaves thoroughly where scales feed. The lower leaf surface of native *Platanus racemosa* has dense mats of tiny hairs, which entwine scales and repel liquids. If scales were abundant the previous season and damage cannot be tolerated, apply 1% narrow-range oil, insecticidal soap, or another insecticide during the delayed dormant season. Inspect trees regularly beginning in late December and spray at bud break; scales are in the highly susceptible immature stage at bud break. Applying oil too late, after buds open and before leaves fully flush, may cause phytotoxicity and is less effective. Thoroughly spray branch tips and use a high-pressure sprayer to reach scales under the bark plates on trunks and large limbs. For more information consult *Sycamore Scale Pest Notes* (Ohlendorf and Flint 2000).

European Elm Scale
Gossyparia spuria

European elm scale (family Eriococcidae) is a pest only on elm, especially Chinese elm (*Ulmus parvifolia*). It can be a serious problem, causing extensive leaf yellowing, plant decline, and death of small branches, in addition to copious, annoying honeydew.

The conspicuous mature female is a dark red, brown, or purple oval surrounded by a white cottony wax fringe on the sides of the body. Females encrust bark at the crotches of twigs and on the lower surface of limbs. Scales overwinter as yellow to brown second-instar nymphs on bark. The immature male in the spring looks like a tiny, elongate, whitish cocoon. Females appear during late winter to early spring and mature during late spring to early summer, when crawlers begin emerging. Nymphs settle and feed on the underside of leaves before returning to bark in the fall. The insect has one generation per year.

Keep trees healthy so they tolerate feeding by scales and other insects. American and European elms are adapted to frequent summer rains; provide adequate irrigation in areas of prolonged summer drought. Several introduced parasites, primarily *Baryscapus* (=*Trichomasthus*) *coeruleus* and *Coccophagus insidiator*, attack European elm scale at some locations in California. If parasites are present, as evidenced by round emergence holes in mature female scales, increase the effectiveness of biological control by controlling honeydew-seeking ants.

European elm scale can be controlled on smaller or individual trees by using a hydraulic sprayer to thoroughly apply a forceful stream of water to twigs, branches, and crevices from at least three directions. Spray after the soft-bodied females have begun maturing in spring, but before elm leaves unfold to obstruct the water. Foliage usually begins pushing out when the clusters of seeds (fruit) have matured and start to drop. If populations are intolerable later, narrow-range oil can be applied in spring or early summer, as timed by monitoring for when crawler abundance declines after it has peaked. Because female scale density peaks in northern California at about 540 degree-days above 51.8°F accumulated from 1 March, begin once-a-week monitoring of crawlers by about 400 degree-days if oil spray is planned. The systemic insecticide imidacloprid also provides control.

Oak Pit Scales
Asterolecanium spp.

Oak pit scales (family Asterolecaniidae) can be serious pests of oaks. Least pit scale (*Asterolecanium minus*) and drab pit scale (*A. quercicola*) in California prefer native valley oak (*Quercus lobata*) and blue oak (*Q. douglasii*) and also occur on coast live oak (*Q. agrifolia*) and California black oak (*Q. kelloggii*). Golden oak scale (*A. variolosum*) prefers English oak (*Q. robur*) and also occurs on California black oak.

Heavy pit scale infestations cause branch dieback, distorted terminal re-

Purplish, white-fringed, mature female European elm scales on Chinese elm tended by Argentine ants. At some locations, introduced parasites help to control this scale if ants are controlled.

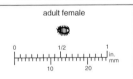

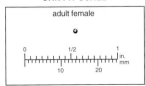

growth, severe tree decline, and eventually death of some oaks. High pit scale populations can also be associated with severe infection by twig branch dieback fungus (*Diplodia quercina*). Pit scale feeding causes ring-shaped depressions in bark. Dead twigs and brown leaves that do not drop are apparent in winter on infested deciduous oaks. Mature scales resemble armored scales. They are brown, gold, or green, flattened, circular, immobile insects about the size of the head of a pin. Crawlers emerge from beneath the female from April through October, primarily in April through June. When scales are abundant, their feeding pits coalesce, giving twigs a roughened, dimpled appearance.

Narrow-range oil provides control if applied to cover all bark and branch tips thoroughly in the delayed dormant season, just before buds open. To get control after leaves have fully flushed, combine oil with a compatible botanical, organophosphate, or carbamate insecticide and apply it with high-pressure commercial spray equipment. Make this spray when inspection with a hand lens or monitoring with double-sided sticky tape indicates that crawlers are abundant (about April to June). One annual application during several consecutive years may be necessary to reduce high populations to a low level. Certain systemic insecticides may also control this pest. See *Oak Pit Scales Pest Notes* (Geisel and Perry 2000) for more information.

MONITORING OF SCALES

Regularly monitor scales if valued plants host scale species that can cause significant damage. Inspect plants for crawlers, mature females, or scale-associated ants. Pheromone traps for adult males, in combination with degree-day monitoring, can be used to time California red scale and San Jose scale controls when managing many high-value plants. For certain scale species, degree-day (temperature monitoring) models are available to estimate when female scales are likely to mature and crawlers are expected to be most abundant. Examine portions of the plant (leaves, fruit, or 1-foot branch terminal

Golden oak scale and pits made by scales that have dropped from this California black oak twig. Some scales have parasite emergence holes.

segments) where mature females occur, as described for each species. Note that dead scales from previous generations may remain on the plant. Distinguish live scales from dead scales, for example, by appearance, by squishing them to see if liquid exudes, or by turning them over or looking beneath them.

Inspect trunks for columns of ants, which may indicate a soft scale infestation. If the descending ants have swollen, almost translucent abdomens, they may be feeding on honeydew produced by scales or other insects that suck plant juices.

Consider using quantitative sampling if plants are especially valued or substantial resources will be devoted to managing scales. For example, count and record the number of mature female scales on each of 4 to 8 shoots on each of several plants. Also record the number of parasitized scales, which can be recognized by one or more holes chewed in the scale cover by the emerging adult parasites or by the darker color of parasitized nymphs. Estimate the average number of parasitized and unparasitized live scales per sample by totaling the number of insects counted, and dividing by the number of samples inspected.

Compare the average scale density on your samples to the density during previous years to determine whether scales are increasing and to evaluate whether any treatment during the last year was effective. Compare your samples from the same year to see if the percentage of parasitized scales is increasing.

An alternative to counting each scale is determining the percentage of samples (such as branch terminals) with scales. This presence-absence sampling is quicker but less precise than counting each scale, and it is difficult to estimate parasitism.

Sticky tape traps and degree-day monitoring help to efficiently determine the proper time to treat, but these and some other methods (such as looking for ants and scale presence) do not tell you if control is needed (whether scales are abundant enough to cause problems). The need for treatment can be indicated by intolerably abundant honeydew, high numbers of viable and nonparasitized scales, and plant dieback or decline.

Sticky Tape Traps. If insecticide application is needed, apply oil during the dormant season where possible. If application is necessary during the spring or summer, use sticky tape traps to monitor and effectively time a foliar insecticide application against crawlers, which are the stage most susceptible to insecticides.

Choose several twigs or small branches for monitoring on each of two or more plants. Before crawlers begin to emerge in the spring, tightly encircle each twig or branch with transparent tape that is sticky on both sides (this tape is available at stationery stores). Double over the loose end of the tape several times so you can pull the end to easily unwind it. Place

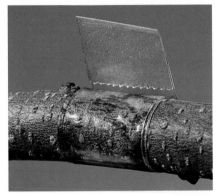

Wrap double-sided sticky tape tightly around twigs to monitor when scale crawlers are active. Double over the end so you can grasp and easily unwrap tapes to check them.

a tag or flagging near each tape so you can readily find it. Change the tapes at regular intervals, about weekly. After removing the old tape, wrap the twig at the same location with fresh tape. Preserve the old sticky tapes by sandwiching them between a sheet of white paper and clear plastic, such as an overhead projector acetate or a plastic bag. Label the tapes with the date, location, and host plant from which they were collected.

Scale crawlers get stuck on the tapes and appear as yellow or orange specks. Examine the tapes with a hand lens to distinguish the crawlers (which are round or oblong, orangish, and have very short appendages) from pollen and dust. Use a hand lens to examine the crawlers beneath mature female scales on bark or foliage to be certain of crawler appearance. Other tiny creatures, including mites, may also be caught in the tapes.

Visually compare the tapes collected on each sample date. If a spring or summer foliar insecticide application is planned, unless another time is recommended for that species, spray after crawler production has peaked and definitely begun to decline, which is soon after most crawlers have settled.

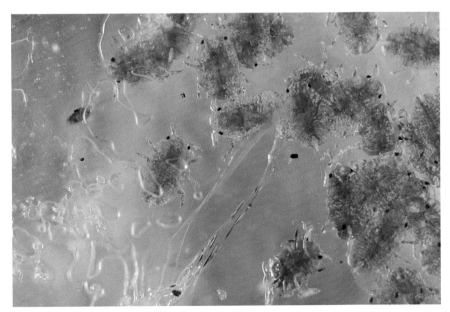

An enlargement of European fruit lecanium scale crawlers caught in a sticky tape trap. Many scales are most effectively controlled if plants are sprayed after monitoring shows that crawler abundance has clearly peaked and begun to decline, which is soon after most crawlers have settled.

MANAGEMENT OF SCALES

Biological control and applying certain insecticides are the primary tactics for managing many scale species. Appropriate plant selection can also avoid many scale problems. Many scales are highly host specific, sometimes damaging only certain species and not other species or cultivars in the same plant genus. Scales that can infest many different plants often damage only one or a few of those host species. Selective pruning can reduce infestations if high populations are limited only to certain parts of the plant. In areas with hot summers, pruning to open canopies can reduce populations of some species, such as black scale and citricola scale, by increasing insect mortality from heat exposure. For additional information on scales, including suggested insecticides, consult the most current *Scales Pest Notes* (Dreistadt et al. 2001).

Biological Control. Scales are often controlled by natural enemies. These include many *Chilocorus, Hyperaspis,* and *Rhyzobius* species lady beetles that can easily be overlooked because many are tiny, colored and shaped like scales, or feed beneath scales. Over 100 *Hyperaspis* species in North America feed on Homoptera. Adults are tiny (usually ≤$^1/_{10}$ inch) shiny lady beetles, often black with several red, orange, or yellow spots on the back. Other species include *Rhyzobius lophanthae,* a lady beetle that has a reddish head and underside and a grayish back densely covered with tiny hairs. The twicestabbed lady beetle (*Chilocorus orbus*) is shiny black with two red spots on its back, and reddish underneath. The larvae of many predaceous lady beetles, especially their early instars, occur hidden underneath female scales feeding on scale eggs and crawlers.

Many parasitic wasps are important natural enemies, including species of *Aphytis, Coccophagus, Encarsia,* and *Metaphycus.* Estimate parasite activity by checking scale covers for the round exit holes made by emerging adult parasites and flip armored scale covers and examine beneath them for immature parasitoids. Plant flowering species near scale-infested trees and shrubs to help nourish adult parasites and augment natural enemies (Figure 4-4). Adult parasitic wasps live longer, lay more eggs, and kill more scales when they have nectar or honeydew to feed on. Natural enemies are commercially available for release against black scale and California red scale (see below). However, conserving resident natural enemies is a more efficient and longer-lasting strategy.

Avoid using broad-spectrum, persistent insecticides for scales or other pests because these disrupt natural enemies. Apply narrow-range oil instead, preferably during the dormant season. To enhance the biological control of scales, prevent excessive dust and control honeydew-seeking ants, as discussed in the section "Ants" earlier in this chapter.

Insecticides. Dormant season applications of specially refined narrow-range oils, labeled "supreme" or "superior" oil, are effective against many scales on landscape plants. Avoid oils called dormant oil or dormant oil emulsions, which are more likely to injure plants. When applied as a delayed dormant spray, just before buds break, narrow-range oil treatment also kills a portion of overwintering mite, aphid, and caterpillar eggs on bark. Do not spray oils when plants are drought-stressed or if temperatures are anticipated to soon be over 90° or under 32°F.

Narrow-range oils are also effective in spring or summer against scale eggs and crawlers. A foliage season application may require more spray volume than a dormant season spray to deciduous plants because foliage as well as bark must be thoroughly covered. Do not apply oil to the foliage of sensitive plant species, as identified in *Managing Insects and Mites with Spray Oils* (Davidson et al. 1991).

In addition to narrow-range oil, insecticidal soap and several carbamate, organophosphate, and pyrethroid insecticides and other materials that may be available only to professional applicators are registered as foliar sprays for scale control. Monitor scale crawlers to

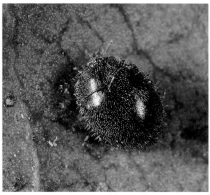

An adult *Rhyzobius lophanthae* on the underside of a toyon leaf infested with European fruit lecanium scale nymphs. During their larval stage, many scale-feeding lady beetles feed hidden beneath the scale's body.

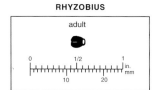

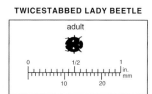

The adult twicestabbed lady beetle (*Chilocorus orbus* =*C. stigma*), has two reddish spots on its shiny black body. An almost identical lady beetle (*Chilocorus kuwanae*) has been introduced to help control euonymus scale. The spots of *C. kuwanae* tend to be rectangular and near the center of the wing covers. Spots on *C. orbus* are more roundish and occur somewhat forward of the wing cover's midpoint.

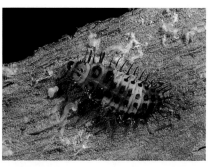

A twicestabbed lady beetle larva feeding on sycamore scale eggs and nymphs on the underside of a sycamore bark plate.

effectively time any spray during spring or summer, as discussed in the section "Sticky Tape Traps." Foliar sprays of the more broad-spectrum, persistent insecticides cause more disruption of biological control than oil or soap because persistent residues kill natural enemies migrating in after the application (Table 4-6). Certain systemic insecticides (imidacloprid) are effective against honeydew-excreting (phloem-feeding) scales such as European elm scale and soft scales, but imidacloprid does not control armored scales. Systemics can be applied into trunks or limbs or onto soil beneath plants; soil application of a systemic is preferred whenever possible because it avoids tree damage, as discussed in Chapter 2 in the section "Injecting or Implanting Pesticides." See *Scales Pest Notes* (Dreistadt et al. 2001) for more information.

Leafhopper feeding sometimes causes foliage to become bleached or stippled. This damage is usually harmless to plants. For example, rose leafhopper (*Edwardsiana rosae*) fed on these leaves, but it does not feed on rose blossoms (not shown).

Leafhoppers have one or more long rows of spines along the entire length of the hind tibia (their longest leg segment). Spines are most obvious in nymphs because they are not covered by wings. However, leg spines are apparent in this side view of an adult leafhopper on myoporum.

LEAFHOPPERS AND SHARPSHOOTERS

Leafhoppers (family Cicadellidae) include species that are called sharpshooters. Several hundred species of plant juice-sucking leafhoppers inhabit landscapes, but most never become pests, in part because most species feed on only one or several closely related plant species. Leafhopper feeding causes leaves to appear stippled, pale, or brown, and shoots may curl and die. Some leafhopper species transmit plant diseases, but this is important mostly in crop plants. Some species secrete liquid that causes chalky residue on plants, or they produce sticky honeydew on which foliage-blackening sooty mold grows.

Most adult leafhoppers are slender and ¼ inch long, or shorter. Glassy-winged sharpshooter and a few other species can be up to about ½ inch long. Some species are brightly colored, while others blend with their host plant. One or more long rows of spines on their hind legs and characters on their head distinguish leafhoppers from most other insects they resemble (Table 4-15). Leafhoppers are active insects that walk rapidly sideways or readily jump when disturbed. Adults and nymphs and their pale cast skins are usually found on the underside of leaves.

Females insert their tiny eggs in tender plant tissue. The wingless nymphs that emerge molt four or five times and mature in about 2 to 7 weeks. Leafhoppers overwinter as eggs on or in leaves or twigs or as adults in protected places such as bark crevices. Most species have two or more generations each year.

With certain exceptions, such as glassy-winged sharpshooter, ignore

LEAFHOPPER

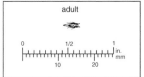

these insects in most situations because most leafhoppers do not cause serious harm to woody landscape plants. Where bothersome, insecticidal soap or narrow-range oil can be applied to infested foliage to suppress high populations of leafhopper nymphs; thorough coverage of leaf undersides is important. It can be very difficult to effectively control adults, and generally no control is recommended.

Glassy-Winged Sharpshooter and Smoke-Tree Sharpshooter

Glassy-winged sharpshooter (*Homalodisca coagulata*) was inadvertently introduced into southern California in the early 1990s. It closely resembles a native species, the smoke-tree sharpshooter (*Homalodisca lacerta*). Both species occur on many different plants, with glassy-winged sharpshooter adults feeding on over 300 plant species and able to reproduce (lay eggs) in about 100 species. Hosts include acacia, ash, azalea, blackberry, camellia, citrus, coyote brush, crape myrtle, elm, eucalyptus, eugenia, euonymus, grape, hibiscus, locust, mulberry, oak, oleander, olive, and walnut. Sharpshooter feeding rarely causes significant damage to plants, although very high populations may reduce citrus yield. Abundant sharpshooters excrete copious, misty liquid (sharpshooter rain) that makes leaves and fruit appear whitewashed and creates a nuisance on vehicles and surfaces beneath infested trees.

The serious problem associated primarily with glassy-winged sharpshooter is that it spreads a disease-causing bacterium (*Xylella fastidiosa*) from one plant to another. This pathogen is also vectored by certain other leafhoppers, including blue-green sharpshooter (*Graphocephala atropunctata*) and smoke-tree sharpshooter, but glassy-winged sharpshooter is a much more important vector because it is highly

TABLE 4-15.

Characters Helpful for Distinguishing among Certain Homoptera.

COMMON NAME (FAMILY)	ATTACHMENT OF SHORT ANTENNAE	BODY	PROTHORAX ENLARGED	OCELLI[1]	HIND TIBIAL SPINES[2]
cicadas (Cicadidae)	in front of or between the eyes[3]	≥1 inch long	no[4]	3	rows of spines along length
leafhoppers (Cicadellidae)	in front of or between the eyes[3]	usually ≤½ inch long, rounded, elongate	no	2 or none	1 or more long rows of small spines along entire length
planthoppers (many)	below eyes on side of head[5]	in U.S. usually ≤½ inch long, flattened, broad	no[6]	2 or none	several large spines
spittlebugs (Cercopidae)	in front of or between the eyes[3]	usually ≤½ inch long, rounded, elongate	no	2 or none	1 or 2 stout spines along length and a whorl of many terminal spines
treehoppers (Membracidae)	in front of or between the eyes[3]	≤½ inch long, flattened, broad	yes[7]	2 or none	rows of spines along length

1. Small beadlike or colored spots, which are light receptors on the head between or above the larger true eyes.

2. The tibia is usually the longest leg segment, that between the femur and the terminal tarsi, or "feet."

3. Antennae attached in front of the lowest point of the eye (as seen from the side) and between the eyes (as seen from the front).

4. Prothorax (area just behind the head) often prominent but does not extend over the abdomen or head.

5. Antennae attached below the eyes: behind the lowest point of the eye (as seen from the side) and definitely under the eyes (as seen from the front).

6. Head typically has enlargements, ridges, or projections (often snoutlike) in front of the eyes.

7. Greatly enlarged prothorax projects backward over the abdomen (and in some species also projects forward or above), so that treehoppers appear humpbacked or resemble a thorn or roughening on plants.

mobile, can feed on tough plant parts such as woody stems, and infests many different plant species. Strains of *Xylella fastidiosa* cause lethal plant diseases such as Pierce's disease of grape, oleander leaf scorch, and almond leaf scorch. Although the relationships among leafhopper species, host plants, and pathogenic *Xylella* are not fully understood, it is known that the strain of *X. fastidiosa* that causes oleander leaf scorch will not cause Pierce's disease.

Glassy-winged sharpshooter adults are about ½ inch long and dark brownish with whitish and yellow spots. They closely resemble smoke-tree sharpshooters, but the head of the smoke-tree sharpshooter is covered with wavy, light-colored lines, not the light spots found on glassy-winged sharpshooter. Immature glassy-winged sharpshooters develop through several stages (instars) and resemble small adults, except the immatures are wingless, uniformly olive gray, and have prominent bulging red eyes. Smoke-tree sharpshooter nymphs appear very similar but have blue eyes. Females lay eggs in a cluster of about one dozen eggs within the lower surface of leaves. Eggs initially resemble a greenish blister on the leaf, which females cover with a white chalky secretion. Eggs turn brown as they mature and leave a permanent brown to gray scar in leaf tissue after nymphs emerge.

Presently there is no cure for any of the diseases caused by *Xylella fastidiosa*. Management relies on quarantines to stop the spread of glassy-winged sharpshooters and prevent infested plants such as nursery crops from being moved from infested areas to other locations where glassy-winged sharpshooter does not occur. Glassy-winged sharpshooter occurs in the southern United States and in California at least in the south. Report suspected glassy-winged sharpshooters to the county department of agriculture (in California) or other agricultural agency officials if you find this insect outside areas it is known to infest.

GLASSY-WINGED SHARPSHOOTER

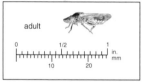

These glassy-winged sharpshooter eggs in leaves are easily overlooked. White, chalky wax around eggs (as shown here) or a yellow leaf blister (not shown) are signs of this leafhopper's eggs. After hatching, eggs leave a permanent brown blister in leaves.

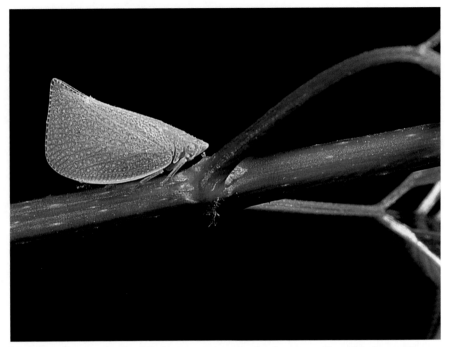

Glassy-winged sharpshooter (bottom) is much larger than most leafhoppers, such as the blue-green sharpshooter (top). Because it is the important vector of lethal plant diseases, report suspected glassy-winged sharpshooters to the county department of agriculture (in California) or other agricultural agency officials if you find this insect outside of areas it is known to infest.

Most planthoppers are harmless curiosities in the landscape, such as this Australian torpedo bug (*Siphanta acuta*, family Flatidae), which occurs on various plants in coastal California.

In infested areas where sharpshooter excretions are intolerable, a systemic insecticide (such as imidacloprid) can be applied to soil beneath plants. Various foliar insecticides are available, but these require more reapplication and are more toxic to tiny egg-parasitic beneficial wasps (*Gonatocerus* spp.) that are being introduced to reduce sharpshooter populations. For more information, consult the section "Bacterial Leaf Scorch and Oleander Leaf Scorch" in Chapter 5, publications such as *Oleander Leaf Scorch Pest Notes* (Wilen et al. 2000) and *Glassy-Winged Sharpshooter Pest Notes* (Phillips, Wilen, and Varela 2001), or http://danr.ucop.edu/news/MediaKit/GWSS.shtml on the Web.

Twospotted Leafhopper
Sophonia rufofascia

The twospotted leafhopper was inadvertently introduced into Hawaii and southern California. It feeds on more than 200 plant species and has become especially common on guava in southern California. Other hosts include abutilon, avocado, cape honeysuckle, camellia, citrus, eugenia, fern, ficus, fuchsia, gardenia, hibiscus, hydrangea, lantana, mock orange, pittosporum, rose, and wisteria. Depending on the host species, plants may be unaffected or they may be severely damaged by leafhopper feeding. Leaves may distort or develop prominent yellowing between veins. Plants can become stunted overall. In severe infestations, leaves develop large brown or black dead patches and plants may die. Damage may not become apparent until several weeks after initial feeding, at which time leafhoppers may have moved, so that sometimes no live insects are present when damage is first recognized.

Adult twospotted leafhoppers are light green to pale yellow and about 1/5 inch long. Down the center of their back is a dark stripe that is variably bordered by shades of pink or red. Adults have two prominent eye spots near their rear, one on the tip of each forewing. Because its real eyes are the same color as the body, the leafhopper appears to be moving backwards when walking. Nymphs are green to translucent yellow with two dark spots near their rear. Nymphs produce clear cast skins that have two dark spots. Cast skins can remain attached to the plant for long periods, resembling pale leafhoppers. Most live stages occur on new growth on the underside of terminal leaves.

In an effort to provide biological control, leafhopper parasites are being introduced into the United States from China, where this leafhopper is native. The systemic insecticide imidacloprid can provide some control. If suspected twospotted leafhoppers are found outside areas where this insect is known to occur, report it to the county department of agriculture (in California) or other agricultural agency officials.

PLANTHOPPERS

Planthoppers occasionally are pests, but usually they are merely a curiosity in landscapes. Planthoppers (superfamily Fulgoroidea) in the United States occur in about one dozen families (such as Acanaloniidae, Delphacidae, Flatidae, Fulgoridae, and Issidae) and include hundreds of species in California. The location of the antennae (below each eye on the sides of the head) distinguishes planthoppers from most other Homoptera they resemble (Table 4-15).

TREEHOPPERS

Treehoppers (family Membracidae) suck plant juices. This feeding damage is slight, although the honeydew produced by treehoppers supports the growth of sooty mold, which may blacken leaves and twigs when treehoppers become numerous. Treehoppers injure plants primarily by making numerous small slits or crescentlike punctures in bark where they lay their eggs. These egg punctures cause bark to appear roughened, and twigs may die back. Mature woody plants tolerate extensive egg-laying damage, but the growth of heavily infested younger plants may be retarded.

Treehopper adults are commonly greenish to brown and ½ inch long or shorter. They have an expanded hood covering the body, which may be formed into hornlike projections. This enlarged prothorax distinguishes treehoppers from most other Homoptera they resemble (Table 4-15). Nymphs have numerous spines on the back of the abdomen, and both immatures and adults readily jump.

The oak treehopper (*Platycotis vittata*) is common in the spring throughout the United States on the lower branches of deciduous and live oaks and occasionally on birch, chestnut, or other broadleaf trees. Egg-laying wounds from abundant leafhoppers can cause noticeable twig dieback, but leafhopper damage does not threaten tree health. Adults are olive green to bronze with reddish bands and their surface is covered with tiny pits. They often scurry to the opposite side of the twig or leaf when approached. Females usually remain with their eggs and the nymphs after they emerge. The nymphs are black with yellow and red markings. The spring generation is colorful and usually gregarious; individuals typically aggregate in rows on twigs.

The buffalo treehopper (*Stictocephala bisonia*) is common in landscapes throughout the United States. Its hosts include ash, elm, fruit trees, hawthorn, locust, poplar, and many herbaceous plants. Adults are bright green or yellowish with a yellowish underside. Nymphs are green with prominent spines on the back.

If treehopper populations were high on deciduous trees the previous season and damage cannot be tolerated, narrow-range oil can be applied to thoroughly cover terminals during the dormant season to kill overwintering eggs. For species known to feed on many different plants, removing some of the alternate hosts may reduce treehopper populations feeding on more-valued plants. High populations of nymphs and adults may be reduced by spraying exposed insects with insecticidal soap, narrow-range oil, or another insecticide.

Oak treehopper adults feeding on coast live oak. Tiny bark punctures are visible where eggs were laid. These bark punctures and some resulting twig dieback are this insect's only damage and can usually be tolerated.

OAK TREEHOPPER

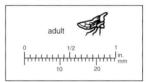

SPITTLEBUGS

Spittlebugs, or froghoppers, (family Cercopidae) suck plant juices. They occur throughout the United States and can at least occasionally be found on almost any plant. Heavy infestations distort plant tissue and slow plant growth, but this is primarily a problem on herbaceous species. The obvious and occasionally abundant masses of white foam on cones, foliage, or stems may be annoying, but spittlebugs do not seriously harm established woody plants.

Adult spittlebugs are inconspicuous, often brownish insects, about ¼ inch long. They readily jump or fly when disturbed and resemble leafhoppers, but spittlebugs lack the long rows of spines found along the hind tibia of leafhoppers (Table 4-15). Females lay small eggs in rows in hidden parts of the plant, such as the sheath between leaves and stems. The presence of immature spittlebugs is readily recognized by the frothy white mass that nymphs surround themselves with on plant tissue where they feed. Nymphs undergo about five molts and may be orange, yellow, or green. More than one nymph may be found in a single spittle mass.

The meadow spittlebug (*Philaenus spumarius*) is found throughout the United States. It feeds primarily on herbaceous plants, but also occurs on conifers and young woody deciduous plants. Adults are robust and tan, black, or mottled brownish. Females lay white to brown eggs in rows at plant nodes. Nymphs are yellow to green and are hidden beneath a foaming mass of spittle.

The western pine spittlebug (*Aphrophora permutata*) is one of several *Aphrophora* species that feed on conifers

The white, frothy material on this rose bud petiole conceals an immature spittlebug sucking on plant tissue. If bothersome, a forceful stream of water will wash away spittlebugs.

Cicadas, such as this *Platypedia* species, are periodically abundant throughout much of the eastern and midwestern United States. In California, these noisy insects are relatively uncommon and are not pests.

and nearby herbaceous plants. It is especially common on Monterey pine and other pines in coastal California areas. Other hosts also include Douglas fir, fir, hemlock, spruce, and various broadleaves. Pine spittlebugs' tiny, pale yellow to purple, eggs are laid in a row on pine needles or may be partially or completely embedded in needles. Nymphs are dark greenish, brown, or black, sometimes with lighter spots or a pink abdomen. Adults are brownish orange to dark brown and may have an indistinct diagonal white line across the back. Overwintering occurs as eggs, and pine spittlebugs have one or two generations per year in California.

Ignore spittlebugs on woody plants or wash nymphs off with a forceful stream of water. Spittlebugs are more likely to become abundant on woody plants when they migrate from nearby herbaceous species. Cut infested weeds or wash spittlebugs off these alternate hosts in the spring, before the insects mature and can spread.

CICADAS

Cicadas (family Cicadidae), sometimes called locusts, are among the loudest insects. Males attract females by producing high-frequency vibrations that people can hear for long distances. Noisy cicadas are periodically abundant throughout much of the eastern and midwestern United States, but they are relatively uncommon in California. Aside from the noise, damage occurs when the egg-laying adults are abundant. Females are relatively large (up to 1 to 2 inches) and insert numerous eggs into terminals of trees and shrubs, often causing plant tips to die back. The emerging nymphs drop to soil and feed on woody plant roots. This root feeding does not seriously harm most plants, in part because cicadas feed and grow very slowly, taking at least several years, and in some species 13 to 17 years, to complete their nymphal development.

Cicadas do not cause noticeable plant damage in California so no control is needed. In the East, no control is known or recommended, other than pruning out and disposing of damaged or egg-infested terminals if plants are small enough to make this feasible. Local populations of the same species often emerge at about the same time, sometimes making cicadas very abundant for a short period. However, adults will mate and die within about 1 month. Depending on the number of local species and their development rates, intervals of several years will often pass before cicadas become abundant again in that location.

TRUE BUGS

Boxelder bugs, chinch bugs, lace bugs, lygus bugs, and plant bugs are in the order Hemiptera, the only group of insects that entomologists call "bugs;" they are also known as "true bugs." More than 600 true bug species occur just in California. Many are aquatic or semiaquatic, and most of these are predaceous. Many terrestrial true bugs feed on plants, although some species such as assassin bugs, bigeyed bugs, damsel bugs, and pirate bugs are important predators.

DAMAGE

Plant-feeding true bugs suck juices from leaves, fruit, or nuts. A pale white or yellow stippling forms around feeding sites, and plant tissue may become distorted. True bugs do not seriously harm established woody plants; however, activities of some species can be undesirable: for instance, lace bugs leave dark specks of excrement on the underside of leaves. Large numbers of boxelder bugs (and occasionally other species like assassin bugs) can be a nuisance when they enter houses to overwinter.

IDENTIFICATION AND BIOLOGY

Bugs usually have thickened forewings with membranous tips. When they rest, the dissimilar parts of their folded wings overlap. Nearly all true bugs can be recognized by the characteristic triangle or X-shape on the back formed by their folded wings. Hemipterans have sucking mouthparts, which on plant-feeding species point downward, perpendicular to the plane of the insect's body. The mouthparts of predaceous bugs can be extended forward when attacking other insects. Depending on the species, eggs are laid exposed on foliage or bark or inserted in plant tissue. The flightless nymphs gradually change to winged adults without any pupal stage (Figure 4-2).

MANAGEMENT

True bugs rarely cause serious harm to established woody plants. Provide proper cultural care so that plants are vigorous. Damaged foliage can be pruned out. Consider replacing especially susceptible plants with resistant species. Spraying for bugs is generally not recommended. Extreme populations may be reduced by applying an insecticide to foliage when nymphs are abundant in the spring; systemic insecticides may be the most effective. No treatment will restore stippled foliage, which remains until replaced by new growth. Seal exterior cracks in houses and screen windows and doors to prevent bugs from entering buildings, as discussed in publications such as *Conenose Bugs Pest Notes* (Greenberg and Klotz 2002).

Ash Plant Bugs
Tropidosteptes spp.

Ash plant bugs (family Miridae) occur throughout the United States. They usually damage only ash but may occasionally feed on nearby plants if ash becomes heavily infested and defoliated. *Tropidosteptes illitus* and *T. pacificus* are pests in the West, especially in the warm interior valleys of California. *Tropidosteptes illitus* nymphs are light brown, and adults are yellow and brown or black. *Tropidosteptes pacificus* adults are brown, and the nymphs are green with black

spots. Nymphs and adults suck plant juices from ash flowers, leaves, seeds, and twigs, but ash plant bug damage usually is observed only as leaf bleaching or stippling. Tiny, dark spots of excrement may be visible on foliage. Extreme infestations can defoliate trees, although severe defoliation of ash is more often due to other causes such as anthracnose fungus or drought stress.

Ash plant bugs overwinter as eggs in twig bark. Eggs hatch in February or March, and the nymphs feed until they mature in April or May. The adults feed until June or July, when they lay eggs. Ash plant bugs have one or two generations per year.

Trees apparently tolerate ash plant bug damage; it is rarely severe enough to cause defoliation or warrant control. If damage cannot be tolerated, and insecticide such as narrow-range oil or soap may be applied to thoroughly cover leaf undersides infested with nymphs in the spring.

Boxelder Bugs
Boisea spp.

Boxelder bugs (family Rhopalidae) occur throughout the United States. They sometimes are incorrectly called boxelder beetles. Boxelder bug (*Boisea trivittata*) and western boxelder bug (*B. rubrolineata*) are the most common species. Boxelder bugs usually become abundant only on female box elder trees (*Acer negundo*), but they can occur on other hosts, including maple and fruit and nut trees. Boxelder bug feeding sometimes discolors, distorts, or stipples some leaves, but this is harmless to trees. Feeding may cause minor damage to stone fruits like apricot and plum, and occasionally significant damage to commercial nut crops, if bug populations are high.

Boxelder bugs are a pest primarily because high populations in and around buildings annoy people. The bugs cause no actual damage to structures or their contents. In the fall, adults often aggregate in large numbers on sunny surfaces,

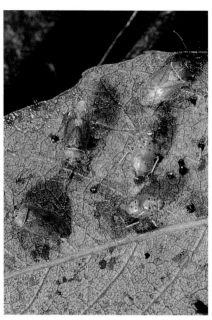

Brown adults and green nymphs of the Pacific ash plant bug (*Tropidosteptes pacificus*) leave varnishlike excrement on the underside of ash leaves. Trees usually tolerate plant bug damage; it is rarely severe enough to cause defoliation or warrant control. Defoliated ash is more commonly caused by anthracnose or drought.

ASH PLANT BUG
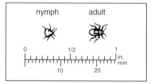

LYGUS BUG
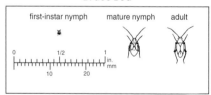

BOXELDER BUG
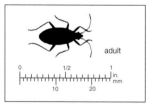

LACE BUG
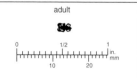

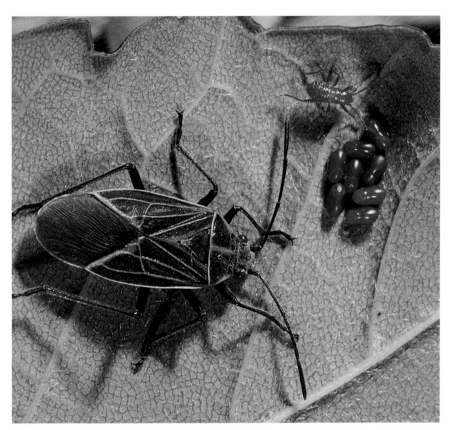

Boxelder bugs like this adult, nymph, and eggs are most common on female (pod-bearing) box elder trees. Three lengthwise red lines (down the middle and on each margin) on their pronotum distinguish boxelder bug adults from most other bugs they resemble.

such as the south side of trees or buildings. Swarms of adults then fly to sheltered places to overwinter, often entering homes through cracks, crevices, and unscreened windows.

Boxelder bugs are grayish brown to black with conspicuous red lines on the body. Females lay oblong red or orange eggs in the spring in bark crevices or on foliage. Nymphs are gray and bright red, and develop black marks as they mature. Boxelder bugs have one or two generations per year. They are sometimes confused with various species that feed on other plants, including bordered plant bug (*Largus cinctus*, family Largidae), small milkweed bug (*Lygaeus kalmii*, Lygaeidae), and squash bugs (*Anasa* spp., Coreidae). In addition to their bright red abdomen and reddish wing margins, boxelder bugs are distinguished from these other bugs by the lengthwise red lines (down the middle and on each margin) on their pronotum.

Replace, and do not plant, the pod-bearing female box elder trees; they support high boxelder bug populations. Eliminate debris and litter near homes, especially around foundations, to reduce the shelter that boxelder bugs need to successfully overwinter. Vacuum up bugs that enter the home. Seal exterior cracks in the house and screen windows and doors to prevent bugs from entering the home, as discussed in publications such as *Conenose Bugs Pest Notes* (Greenberg and Klotz 2002). No pesticides are recommended.

Chinch Bugs

Chinch bugs (family Lygaeidae) damage the leaves, fruit, and flowers of some landscape trees, but they are primarily pests of herbaceous plants. *Blissus* species are the most common pests. The

adults are small, slender, and up to 1/2 inch long. They are black, gray, purple, or reddish bugs with reddish or yellowish brown legs. Wings may be white with brown spots or brown with white tips.

Replanting turf or other nearby herbaceous plants with species less preferred by chinch bugs can reduce populations that may build up and move to attack woody ornamentals. Tolerate damage or manage nearby herbaceous vegetation to reduce movement, as discussed below for lygus bugs.

Lace Bugs
Corythucha spp.

Many kinds of lace bugs (family Tingidae) feed on landscape plants throughout the United States. *Corythucha* species are common, and each species feeds on only one or a few closely related plants, including alder, ash, birch, ceanothus, coyote brush, fruit trees, photinia, poplar, sycamore, toyon, walnut, and willow. Leaf stippling caused by lace bugs usually appears late in the summer and can be distinguished from feeding by mites by the dark specks of excrement that lace bugs deposit on the underside of leaves. Greenhouse thrips and certain other insects also produce both leaf stippling and dark excrement, so you must examine the lower leaf surface for insects to distinguish these pests. Although highly visible, even extensive lace bug stippling does not threaten landscape plants' health.

Most adult lace bugs are flat and about 1/8 inch long. The body is concealed beneath an expanded lacelike or reticulated thorax and forewings. Females insert tiny eggs partly in plant tissue, often hidden under excrement. The wingless nymphs commonly have body spines. All stages occur in groups on the underside of leaves. Most species overwinter as adults under bark plates and have several generations per year.

Tolerate lace bug damage, as it does not seriously harm plants. Provide adequate irrigation and other care to im-

Adults and a nymph of the California Christmas berry tingid (*Corythucha incurvata*), a common lace bug species on toyon. Although leaf stippling from lace bugs can be prominent, this feeding is harmless to established woody plants.

Bleached foliage caused by lace bugs feeding on photinia. Other true bugs, leafhoppers, thrips, and mites cause similar leaf stippling. Look carefully for the insects or mites themselves to diagnose the cause of this damage.

prove plant vigor. Prune out damaged foliage, as insecticides do not restore undamaged appearance. Narrow-range oil or pyrethrins can be applied to lower leaf surfaces infested by adults and nymphs to lower their abundance. A pyrethroid spray or certain systemic insecticides early in the season can be more effective, but pesticide application is generally not warranted or recommended for lace bugs in landscapes. Consult *Lace Bugs Pest Notes* (Dreistadt and Perry 2000) for more information.

Lygus Bugs
Lygus spp.

Lygus bugs (family Miridae), also called tarnished plant bugs, feed on many different broadleaf plants. Hosts include rose, *Prunus* species, the fruit of trees, and numerous herbaceous plants. At least 3 *Lygus* species occur in California, where the western tarnished plant bug (*Lygus hesperus*) is the most common. Adults are green, straw yellow, or brown with a conspicuous yellow or pale green triangle on the back. Nymphs are greenish and resemble aphids, but lygus

nymphs lack cornicles (a rear pair of tubular projections), usually have red-tipped antennae, and move faster than aphids. Lygus bug eggs are inserted into plant tissue and are not easily observed.

Lygus occasionally cause distorted or malformed leaves and terminals. Lygus bug feeding also causes discolored bumps or depressions on fruit, but without the white pithy areas beneath that are characteristic of stink bug feeding. Lygus bugs are most likely to damage fruit when nearby herbaceous vegetation on which they feed dries up or is cut, prompting the bugs to move into trees.

Control is generally not recommended on woody ornamental plants. If damage cannot be tolerated, reduce movement by controlling weeds and reducing nearby herbaceous vegetation before young fruit appear on trees. Alternatively, keep nearby vegetation lush so that bugs are not induced to move.

Stink Bugs

Stink bugs (family Pentatomidae) are shield-shaped with a large scutellum, or triangle, on their backs. They are wider

The adult western tarnished plant bug (*Lygus hesperus*) **has a distinct yellow or pale triangle behind its head. Lygus bugs usually damage only herbaceous plants, but they can cause discolored bumps or depressions on fruit.**

than most other true bugs and are so named because of the offensive-smelling chemical some species give off when disturbed. Stink bug eggs are barrel-shaped with distinct circular lids and are usually laid in groups of 10 or more on leaf surfaces.

Most stink bugs are pests of vegetable or herbaceous plants. Some are beneficial predators, including *Perillus* and *Podisus* species such as twospotted stink bug (*Perillus bioculatus*). The consperse stink bug (*Euschistus consperus*) attacks stone fruit and pear trees, causing discolored depressions, blemishes, or dark pinpricks on fruit. Damaged areas beneath spots on fruit become white and pithy but remain firm as fruit ripen. Except for fruit, woody plants are not harmed by stink bug feeding and control is generally not recommended. If damage cannot be tolerated, manage nearby herbaceous vegetation to reduce movement, as discussed above for lygus bugs.

THRIPS

Thrips (order Thysanoptera) are tiny, slender insects that feed on tissue surfaces with their sucking mouthparts. Species discussed here are in the family Thripidae unless stated otherwise. Most species of thrips feed in flowers, buds, or other hidden areas of growing plant parts such as central terminals. Most thrips are relatively harmless to plants, and some are beneficial predators.

DAMAGE

Thrips feeding can stunt growth and cause leaves to become stippled, papery, and distorted. Infested terminals may discolor, become tightly rolled, and drop leaves prematurely. Thrips can cause dead spots or blotches to appear on flowers, and high populations of some species cover the lower surface of leaves with black, varnishlike specks of excrement. Feeding damage often first appears in one location, then slowly spreads over the plant. Pear thrips (*Taeniothrips inconsequens*), an exotic species introduced into the northeastern United States, causes somewhat unusual damage by tattering sugar maple foliage and defoliating entire large trees, greatly retarding production of sugar maple syrup. Although thrips infestations reduce the aesthetic quality of certain landscape plants, thrips rarely cause serious damage or kill woody plants. Certain species vector viruses, but this usually damages only herbaceous plants in commercial production.

IDENTIFICATION AND BIOLOGY

Adults are narrow, less than 1/20 inch long, and have long fringes on the margins of their wings. Adults are commonly yellowish or blackish and shiny. Females lay tiny eggs within leaf tissue or in the curled or distorted foliage caused by feeding nymphs and adults. Nymphs (also called larvae) are translucent white to yellowish. Depending mostly on the species, pupae can occur on plants where active stages feed, or mature nymphs may drop and pupate near the soil surface. Thrips have several generations per year. Certain thrips species are beneficial predators that feed only on other insects and mites. Beneficial species include black hunter thrips (*Leptothrips mali*, family Phlaeothripidae) and the sixspotted thrips (*Scolothrips sexmaculatus*). Consult *Natural Enemies Handbook* (Flint and Dreistadt 1998) and *Thrips Pest Notes* (Dreistadt and Phillips 2001) for more information on distinguishing among thrips species.

Unless blemished fruit cannot be tolerated, this consperse stink bug and related species do not harm woody plants. Some stink bugs are beneficial predators. At left are the tops of white stink bug eggs, which are barrel-shaped if viewed from the side.

STINK BUG

| egg mass | early-instar nymph | late-instar nymph | adult |

0   1/2   1 in.
mm
10   20

Citrus Thrips
Scirtothrips citri

Citrus thrips can occur on most fruit trees, California pepper tree, and pomegranate. It usually causes damage only on citrus, where it scars the rind surface but does not damage the fruit inside.

Bleaching and stippling on viburnum foliage infested with greenhouse thrips. Because this sluggish thrips feeds openly on the underside of leaves, it is controlled by thorough coverage with insecticidal soap or oil. However, no treatment will restore already-damaged foliage.

Toyon thrips (*Rhyncothrips ilex*) feeding distorted these toyon terminals, but plant health is not seriously impaired. Keeping soil bare beneath plants may help to reduce this damage, apparently because bare soil reduces survival of toyon thrips pupae.

Flower thrips (discussed below) can occur on the same plants and are difficult to distinguish from citrus thrips. Flower thrips often (but not always) have a dark abdomen, while adult citrus thrips is entirely yellowish. A citrus thrips infestation is indicated by the yellow to brownish scabby feeding scars that form on fruit, often in a ring on the rind around the citrus stem.

Dustywings, lacewings, and predaceous mites such as *Euseius tularensis* are important predators of citrus thrips. *Euseius* nymphs and adults are shiny, translucent to tan, tiny, pear-shaped mites. This predator often remains unnoticed because it is small and most abundant on the underside of leaves in the interior area of trees. Do not spray for citrus thrips unless you are marketing fruit; thrips damage does not harm trees or the internal fruit quality. If you do spray, cosmetic damage can be reduced by spraying only the outside of the canopy, where thrips are most abundant as described in *Citrus Pest Management Guidelines* (Ohr et al. 2002).

Cuban Laurel Thrips
Gynaikothrips ficorum

Cuban laurel thrips (family Phlaeothripidae) occurs in Gulf Coast states, Hawaii, and in southern California, where it is especially abundant on Indian laurel fig (*Ficus microcarpa*). All thrips stages occur year-round in tightly rolled, podlike leaf terminals of *Ficus* species. Adults are black, nymphs are yellow, and eggs are white. Thrips populations are highest from about October through December, and galled foliage is formed from midsummer through fall. This elongate pod galling by thrips differs from leaf blister galls caused by the ficus gall wasp discussed later.

Cuban laurel thrips do not seriously harm ficus, so no control is needed if distorted foliage can be tolerated. Several predators occur in galls, most commonly green lacewing larvae and adults and nymphs of a pirate bug (*Macrotracheliella nigra*), which is dark reddish brown to black and less than ⅛ inch long. Pruning and disposing of infested

terminals can provide effective control. Winter may be the best time to prune off tips because more galled tissue generally does not form until next summer and relatively few thrips can survive the winter outside of the protection provided by the rolled leaves.

Flower Thrips
Frankliniella spp.

Flower thrips occur throughout the United States and overwinter as adults in debris or on herbaceous plants. Western flower thrips (*Frankliniella occidentalis*) is the most common pest species. Adults are mostly yellowish with a brown or blackish abdomen. Flower thrips feed primarily on herbaceous plants, but high populations occasionally damage continuously- or late-blossoming flowers on woody plants such as roses. This aesthetic damage is of concern on exhibition blooms and in greenhouse production, but damage is usually not important to woody plants and control is

Thrips are tiny, slender insects that have many fine fringes on their wings. The adult western flower thrips shown here is mostly yellowish, often with a darker abdomen.

Rolled, podlike *Ficus microcarpa* terminals caused by Cuban laurel thrips feeding. Conserving natural enemies and pruning off galled terminals during winter can provide good control.

High populations of greenhouse thrips bleach foliage and produce black excrement specks. This species can be controlled with contact sprays of oil or insecticidal soap because, unlike most thrips species, greenhouse thrips feed openly on leaves.

Greenhouse Thrips
Heliothrips haemorrhoidalis

Greenhouse thrips occurs on many landscape plants throughout the United States. It usually is a pest only on broadleaf evergreens, especially azalea and rhododendron. Other hosts include avocado, laurel (English and Grecian), photinia, and toyon. Adults are mostly black, except for the tip of the abdomen, which is reddish brown. Unlike most thrips species, greenhouse thrips feeds openly on leaves in dense colonies of adults and immatures. This species is relatively sluggish, so damage often begins in one area and only gradually spreads throughout the entire plant. Greenhouse thrips has five to seven annual generations in California.

Where practical, frequent spraying of infested surfaces with a forceful stream of water controls greenhouse thrips. Populations can also be controlled by thoroughly spraying insecticide on the

generally not recommended in landscapes. Even with plants of extremely high aesthetic value such as commercial rose blossoms, study finds that most rose cultivars are not noticeably blemished by one or two thrips per rose bud. In commercial production of herbaceous ornamentals and certain row crops, western flower thrips is a serious pest because it is the primary vector of impatiens necrotic wilt virus and tomato spotted wilt virus.

A yellow and black *Thripobius semiluteus* adult (center left) and black pupae of this parasite among yellowish greenhouse thrips nymphs.

Predators, including this adult pirate bug (*Orius tristicolor*), help control many thrips species.

An adult predatory mite (*Euseius tularensis*) is eating this yellow citrus thrips nymph. Predatory mites are important biological control agents primarily of pest mites, but predaceous mites also feed on many different tiny soft-bodied insects and insect eggs.

underside of leaves when insects and damage first appear. Insecticidal soap, oil, or pyrethrins are recommended sprays because they are less disruptive of natural enemies. These beneficials include a predatory thrips (*Franklinothrips vespiformis*, family Aeolothripidae), which feeds on avocado and greenhouse thrips, and a parasitic wasp (*Thripobius semiluteus*), which attacks only greenhouse thrips.

Thripobius releases in greenhouses and southern California avocado orchards have been effective in controlling greenhouse thrips. The tiny wasp lays its eggs in young thrips nymphs, which become swollen around the head as they mature. About 2 weeks before the wasp's emergence, parasitized nymphs turn black, in contrast to the yellow color of unparasitized nymphs. Unlike healthy black mature thrips, the black parasitized nymphs are smaller and do not move. The commercial availability of *Thripobius* is uncertain, and no specific release recommendations or information on effectiveness have been developed for landscapes. For more information, consult *Natural Enemies Handbook* (Flint and Dreistadt 1998).

MANAGEMENT OF THRIPS

Healthy woody plants usually tolerate thrips damage, which is mostly aesthetic.

Provide proper cultural care to keep plants vigorous. Prune and destroy injured and infested terminals when managing a few small specimen plants. Avoid shearing plants. Shearing—clipping the surface of dense foliage to maintain an even surface on formal hedges—stimulates susceptible new growth. New growth increases populations of Cuban laurel thrips and other species, resulting in more damage. Prune by cutting plants just above growing points such as branch crotches and nodes instead of shearing off terminals.

Resident populations of predaceous arthropods, including predatory thrips, predaceous mites, pirate bugs, and spiders, help to control plant-feeding thrips. Some natural enemies of thrips may be commercially available, including several *Neoseiulus* (=*Amblyseius*) species of mites and at least one pirate bug (*Orius tristicolor*). Little or no research has been conducted on the effectiveness of releasing additional thrips predators or parasites in landscapes. Conserving naturally occurring populations of beneficials by controlling dust and avoiding persistent pesticides is the most important way to encourage biological control of thrips.

Most thrips are difficult to control effectively with insecticides because they reproduce year-round in areas of

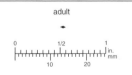

THRIPS

adult

0   1/2   1
|||||||||||||||||| in.
        10   20   mm

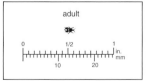

MINUTE PIRATE BUG

adult

0   1/2   1
|||||||||||||||||| in.
        10   20   mm

California with mild winters and are protected from sprays by leaf curls or other plant parts that surround them. Spraying also kills natural enemies. Insecticides generally are not recommended. If treated, certain microbial-derived insecticides available only to professional applicators and certain systemic insecticides are most likely to be effective if applied before damage becomes extensive. Consult *Thrips Pest Notes* (Dreistadt and Phillips 2001) for more information.

Monitor plants for thrips before any treatment to be certain that thrips are present. Damage remains after insect populations have declined or disappeared. Monitor for thrips by branch beating or shaking foliage or flowers onto a sheet of paper and counting the thrips. Adult populations can be monitored using bright yellow sticky traps, as discussed earlier in this chapter. Blue sticky traps are most effective against western flower thrips and possibly other species, but thrips are more difficult to discern in blue traps. Identify thrips in traps to confirm they are species damaging to your plants before taking any action.

GALL MAKERS

Galls are distorted, sometimes colorful swellings in plant tissue. There are many potential causes for galls, including nematodes, parasitic plants, and pathogens (Table 4-16). Secretions of certain plant-feeding insects and mites also induce distorted growth in plant tissue. These unusual growths may be found on branches, flowers, leaves, trunks, or twigs. Galls are caused by many different invertebrates, including those discussed elsewhere in this book: adelgids on spruce, aphids (on poplar, cottonwood, and manzanita), and gall mites or eriophyids (on many hosts including aspen, alder, beech, cottonwood, elm, fuchsia, linden, maple, poplar, and walnut). Ceanothus stem gall moth, ficus gall wasp, gall midge flies, oak cynipid gall wasps, and willow gall sawflies are discussed here.

Gall development is poorly understood, but larval secretions apparently induce abnormal growth of cells in the plant. Many galls harbor a single, legless larva. Other galls may harbor several larvae, some of which may be different species that are predators or parasites of the gall maker.

Most galls are not known to harm trees. Prune and dispose of galls if they are annoying. This may provide control of some species if pruning is done when the immatures are in plant tissue and before the adults begin to emerge.

Ficus Gall Wasp
Josephiella microcarpae

This leaf galling chalcid wasp (family Agaonidae) was discovered in southern California in 1997 infesting Indian laurel fig (*Ficus microcarpa* =*F. nitida* =*F. retusa*). It also occurs in Hawaii, the Canary Islands, and Southeast Asia. Gall wasp larvae cause brown, green, or reddish swellings or warty blisters on leaves that can cause Indian laurel leaves to turn yellow, curl, and drop prematurely. This damage differs from the elongate podgalls caused by Cuban laurel thrips discussed earlier. Tree health and survival appears not to be seriously threatened by leaf galls, but infestations are aesthetically undesirable. Because young leaves are especially susceptible, new growth stimulated by recent pruning and frequently pruned Indian laurel (such as topiary plants) can be extensively damaged.

Adult ficus gall wasps are dark brown with pale yellow appendages, but these $^1/_{10}$-inch-long wasps are easily overlooked. The tiny females lay one to several eggs per leaf in young terminals. Larvae feed inside, causing expanding leaves to develop warty blisters that are conspicuous on both the upper and lower leaf surfaces. Galls range in size from about $^1/_{20}$ to $^2/_3$ inch in diameter, and each typically contains several pale wasp larvae. Larvae pupate inside galled leaves both on trees and on the ground.

Warty blisters are conspicuous on both the upper and lower leaf surfaces of Indian laurel infested with ficus gall wasps. This pest infests only *Ficus microcarpa* and appears not to seriously threaten plant health. However, new growth stimulated by pruning apparently attracts the egg-laying gall wasps, so frequently or recently pruned plants can become extensively galled.

TABLE 4-16.

Common Causes of Plant Galls and Characteristics for Distinguishing Them.

CAUSE	PLANT PARTS AFFECTED	DISTINGUISHING CHARACTERISTICS
crown gall	basal stem, root crown; uncommon on more aerial parts	Surface same color as healthy plant tissue; swellings cannot be rubbed off of plant; surface as firm as and same color as surrounding ungalled tissue. On woody hosts, when cut with a knife, crown galls are softer than normal wood and lack the typical pattern of annual growth rings.
fasciation, bacterial or other causes	crown, stems, foliage, buds	Plant often becomes extensively distorted, and secondary decay may be present. Bacterial fasciation often develops under wet conditions.
insects that bore, mine, or chew inside plant tissue	roots, stems, foliage	Cast skins, emergence holes, frass, tunnels, or the insects themselves (often maggotlike) may be observed in and around galls. Common groups are larvae of beetles, cynipid wasps, gall midges, moths, and sawflies. Certain insects are secondary, attracted to galls originally formed due to other causes.
woolly aphids	roots, bark, foliage	Whitish flocculent material around galls during certain times of the year; aphids or cast skins commonly visible.
nitrogen-fixing beneficial bacteria	roots	Galls easily rub off of roots; a thumbnail can easily be pressed into galls. They occur only on plants in certain groups, especially legumes.
ectomycorrhizae	roots	Roots appear more forked than nonmycorrhizal roots; forms a microscopic, white, brown, yellow, or black fungal sheath or threadlike mold growth around the outside of feeder roots and adjacent soil, which may be too small to be visible to the naked eye; when sectioned and examined under a microscope, intercellular fungus growth can be observed between epidermal and cortical cells of roots.
root knot nematodes	roots	Surface of galls is as firm as surrounding ungalled tissue; swellings cannot be rubbed off; cutting into gall may reveal pinhead-sized, shiny, white female nematodes inside, which look like tiny, pear-shaped pearls that are visible if galls are inspected through a hand lens.
fungal leaf galls	foliage, stems	Fungi, including *Exobasidium* and *Taphrina* spp., hosts include azalea, California buckeye, certain stone fruits, and oaks.
eriophyid or tarsonemid mites	buds, stems, foliage	Tiny mites, cast skins, or excrement occur in and around distorted tissue. A microscope may be needed to discern mites.
sucking insects	buds, stems, terminals	Thrips, aphids, bugs, or other insects or their cast skins or excrement are present. Sucking insects commonly feed on new growth, which later distorts.
broadleaf mistletoes	branches, trunks	Leafy green parasitic plant causes bark and wood to swell where mistletoe attaches to its host.

The emerging adult chews a round exit hole, which is visible in old leaf galls.

This pest is highly host specific. Entirely avoid damage by planting other *Ficus* species, including creeping fig (*F. pumila*), Moreton Bay fig (*F. macrophylla*), rubber plant (*F. elastica*), and weeping Chinese banyon (*F. benjamina*). If planting Indian laurel, consider using Green Gem; observations indicate it may be less susceptible than some other *F. microcarpa* cultivars. Pruning, bagging, and disposing of young infested leaves helps to reduce local gall wasp populations and removes damaged tissue, but is time consuming. Severe pruning detracts from plant appearance and can stimulate excess succulent new growth, which attracts egg-laying gall wasps if unmanaged Indian laurel are nearby. Promptly raking and disposing of fallen leaves may help to reduce infestations by removing some wasp pupae before they emerge as adults. Where damage is intolerable, certain systemic insecticides may help to prevent damage.

Oak Gall Wasps

Hundreds of species of gall wasps (family Cynipidae) occur in the United States. Galls caused by these hymenopterans are especially abundant and varied on oak. The size, shape, and color of the galls vary greatly depending on the species of wasp and the part of the host plant where the egg is laid. Certain cynipid gall wasps in the genera *Andricus, Dishol-caspis,* and *Dryocosmus* also induce plants to secrete copious sticky nectar.

An oak stem gall made by *Callirhytis perdens* wasp larvae in California black oak. Although sometimes unsightly, galls are generally harmless to oaks.

Oak galls are diverse and often quite attractive. These pink spined turban galls (made by *Antron douglasii* wasps) and reddish oak cone galls (made by *Andricus kingi*) occur on the underside of valley oak leaves.

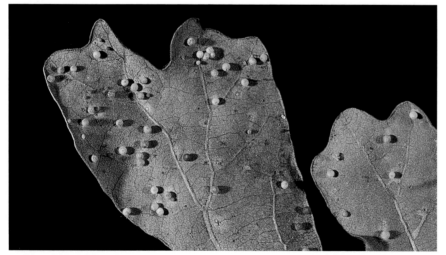

The jumping oak gall wasp (*Neuroterus saltatorius*) causes discolored spots on the upper side, and these seedlike deformations on the underside, of leaves of various oaks, especially valley oak. Galls drop from leaves in summer. Huge numbers of galls may be seen hopping an inch or more above the ground because of movement by a tiny wasp larva inside each gall.

Adult cynipids are small, stout, shiny insects. They have very few wing veins, and the body is usually purple or black. The female deposits an egg in plant tissue, which may hatch within days or up to several months later. A gall begins forming several weeks or months after egg laying, and one or more white larvae feed inside on the distorted tissue.

Many oak gall wasps exhibit a complex life history, often alternating between one sexual and one asexual generation each year. The appearance of galls and wasps may vary with the season and the part of the plant attacked. Most cynipid species occur on just one or several related host species. Species identifications are more easily based on their galls than on descriptions of the tiny wasps.

Gall wasps do not seriously damage oaks. Plant vigor, variations in plant chemicals such as tannins, and natural enemies influence the abundance of cynipids and their galls. Gall wasps are killed by a complex of fungi and competing insects (primarily moth larvae and other wasps), parasites, and predators that live within galls. Cynipids are also preyed upon by various small insectivorous birds, woodpeckers, and rodents and other small mammals. In most situations, no controls have been shown to be effective and no management is necessary.

Certain gall wasps contribute to annoying problems, such as leaf scorch or messy dripping as discussed in Chapter 5 in the section "Drippy Oak and Drippy Nut Disease." If nectar producing gall wasps are the problem (such as certain *Andricus*, *Disholcaspis*, or *Dryocosmus* species), control ants that help protect these gall wasps from their invertebrate natural enemies. Ant control can gradually (over several years) help to dramatically reduce nectar-inducing gall wasp populations by allowing gall wasp competitors and parasites to become more abundant.

Twohorned Oak Gall Wasp
Dryocosmus dubiosus

The twohorned oak gall wasp infests coast live oak and interior live oak. Leaf margins beyond each gall often discolor and die. High populations of gall wasp cause extensive leaf scorching, and some infested leaves drop prematurely. Although aesthetically undesirable, these oak gall wasps do not seriously threaten tree health.

Damage from twohorned oak galls is often confused with damage from other causes, such as oak twig blight fungi and oak branch dieback (discussed in Chapter 5) or twig girdlers (discussed in the section "Flatheaded Borers" in this chapter). However, these other pests cause the entire leaf to die, and they kill many adjacent leaves in a group. Twohorned oak gall wasps kill only portions of each leaf. Each leaf remains partly green, and discolored leaves will be on the same twig as unaffected leaves.

This tiny wasp has two generations per year. The first generation develops during late winter or early spring from eggs laid in catkins. Affected flower parts turn reddish or brown, but this innocuous galling is easily overlooked unless the small galls are cut to reveal pale larvae feeding inside. Second-generation eggs are laid during spring in veins of very young new leaves. Several weeks later, infested leaves develop brown, 1/8-inch-diameter, oblong galls with a protuberance near each end, hence the name "twohorned." Larvae pupate overwinter in galls, then adults emerge from galls on the leaf or galls that have dropped.

Gall wasp abundance varies naturally from year to year, although these population fluctuations may not be obvious because live oaks retain scorched foliage for the several-year life span of each leaf. Environmental conditions, foliage quality (such as tannin concentration), fungi that infect wasp larvae, and parasitic

Disholcaspis washingtonensis induced these brown, round growths on valley oak twigs. This oak cynipid and certain other gall wasps cause plants to secrete sticky nectar, which attracts ants. This sticky malady is discussed in Chapter 5 in the section "Drippy Oak and Drippy Nut Disease."

Young oak apple galls are green. Galls turn reddish or brown, then black after the tiny California gallfly (*Andricus californicus*) wasps inside mature and leave the galls.

OAK CONE GALL

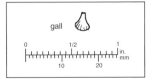

gall

0   1/2   1
|||||||||||||||||||||| in.
          mm
    10   20

JUMPING OAK GALL

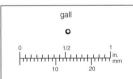

gall

o

0   1/2   1
|||||||||||||||||||||| in.
          mm
    10   20

SPINED TURBAN OAK GALL

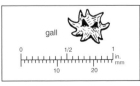

gall

0   1/2   1
|||||||||||||||||||||| in.
          mm
    10   20

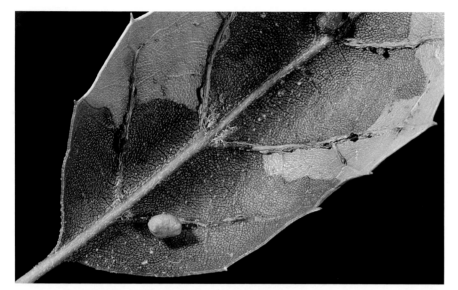

A twohorned oak gall on the underside of a coast live oak leaf vein. Portions of the leaf above and to the right of this gall were killed by gall wasps, but this cause of oak leaf scorch is not obvious because those galls have dropped.

Coast live oak leaf margins killed by twohorned oak galls. Other pests, such as twig blight fungi or twig girdler beetles, are frequently misdiagnosed as the cause of dead oak leaves. These other pests cause the entire leaf to die, and leaves are entirely killed in groups. Twohorned oak gall wasps kill only portions of each leaf, and partly brown leaves will be on the same twig as unaffected leaves.

wasps (including *Torymus* spp. chalcids) affect gall wasp abundance.

Provide oaks with proper environmental conditions and good cultural care. No other management is recommended because gall wasps can be very difficult to control, and they do not seriously harm oaks. If damage is intolera-ble, limited research indicates that some leaf galling species may be reduced by certain insecticides with systemic or translaminar (leaf-penetrating) activity applied in late winter to spring, or by a broad-spectrum, persistent insecticide foliar spray when second-generation adults are ovipositing. Time any foliar spraying to coincide with leaf bud break or the early expansion of new leaves. For more precise timing to improve spray ef-ficacy, clip terminals containing galled flower parts (swollen, brown or red sta-minate aments), hold them in a venti-lated (screen-covered) container at temperatures experienced by the oaks, and spray terminals as soon as the first small black cynipid adults emerge. How-ever, gall wasps are unlikely to be well controlled by any single treatment, and broad-spectrum foliar sprays should be avoided because they can induce out-breaks of other oak pests.

Gall Midges

Hundreds of species of gall midges (fam-ily Cecidomyiidae), also called gall gnats or gall flies, occur in the United States. Each gall-forming species feeds inside only one or a few related hosts, including coyote brush, dogwood, Douglas fir, honey locust, oak, pine, and willow. Not all of these dipteran species form galls. The larvae of some of these midges feed on fungi or dead organic matter. Larvae of the aphid midge (*Aphidoletes aphidimyza*) and other species are important predators of small insects or mites.

Adult gall midges are tiny, delicate flies, often with long, slender antennae. They lay their minute eggs on foliage. Eggs hatch into tiny white, yellowish, reddish, or orange maggots, which in gall-making species bore into plant tissue and feed inside the galls that form. Most species have several annual generations.

Honeylocust Pod Gall Midge
Dasineura gleditchiae

Feeding by larvae of the honeylocust pod gall midge causes honey locust (*Gleditsia triacanthos*) leaflets to form brown, green, or reddish galls. Each distorted leaflet contains one to several small pinkish white maggots. Heavily infested foliage turns brown and drops prematurely, leaving parts of branches leafless. Galls are most apparent early in the growing season; by mid-summer egg-laying ceases and plants often continue to produce new leaves that no longer develop galls.

This midge overwinters as pupae or mature larvae in soil. In California, adults can emerge as early as February, and the insects become most abundant during spring. Eggs must be laid on succulent new terminals in order for larvae to feed and cause galls. Mature larvae drop or crawl to pupate near the soil surface. This fly has about six generations per year.

Several species of parasitic and predaceous wasps feed on this pest. Biological control may be why honeylocust pod gall midge is rarely a problem in the eastern United States (where this insect is native) and why damage appears to have declined in California since this pest was introduced in the 1970s. Because the honeylocust pod gall midge has many generations from late winter through early summer and larvae in galls are protected from sprays, this insect is not easily controlled with insecticides. Research in nurseries found that narrow-range oil sprayed to thoroughly cover terminals at intervals during about March and April can substantially reduce damage on small plants, apparently by killing eggs of early-generation gall midges.

Established trees are rarely, if ever, killed, so damage, while unsightly, can be tolerated. Consider planting alternative species or cultivars in landscapes where the plant aesthetic value is high. The Shademaster cultivar of honey locust appears less susceptible. Black locust and other *Robinia* species are not attacked by this midge, but *Robinia* species may be attacked by other galling midges, including a different *Dasineura* species and *Obolodiplosis robiniae*. Where damage cannot be tolerated, avoid the Sunburst honey locust, which has bright yellow spring foliage. Sunburst is very sensitive to gall midge damage and defoliates in response to drought or temperature changes as well as gall midge damage.

Distorted terminals infested with honeylocust pod gall midge larvae, which infest only *Gleditsia* species. Shademaster honey locust is less susceptible than Sunburst.

Swollen stems infested with ceanothus stem gall moth larvae causing dieback (bottom) and stunted terminal growth (top). If intolerable, prune off galled shoots or replace susceptible plants with ceanothus species resistant to stem gall moths.

Ceanothus Stem Gall Moth
Periploca ceanothiella

The ceanothus stem gall moth (family Cosmopterigidae) probably occurs throughout the United States wherever *Ceanothus* species plants occur, but the moth is apparently a pest only in California. The small, dark moths lay eggs on buds and flowers; eggs hatch into tunneling larvae. The spindle-shaped swellings on stems caused by the larvae stunt plant growth and reduce blooming. Overwintering is as larvae in galls. Adults emerge during the spring and early summer. They have one generation per year. Prune and dispose of galled shoots. Where galling cannot be tolerated, plant less-susceptible *Ceanothus* species and consider replacing shrubs most susceptible to the ceanothus stem gall moth (see Table 4-17).

Willow Gall Sawflies
Pontania pacifica

Several dozen different sawflies, primarily *Euura* and *Pontania* species (family Tenthredinidae), induce galls on the foliage, terminals, or twigs of various willow species throughout the United States. Adults are stout, broad-waisted wasps. Their larvae are yellow to whitish maggots. Willow galls are also caused by other pests, including the willow beaked-gall midge (*Mayetiola rigidae*) and an eriophyid mite (*Vasates laevigatae*).

The willow leaf gall sawfly (*Pontania pacifica*) is a common species infesting *Salix lasiolepis* in California and the Pacific Northwest. Willow leaf gall sawfly males are shiny black, and females are dull reddish. Females insert their eggs in young willow leaves. This induces formation of reddish berrylike galls on foliage. One larva develops in each of these galls, which are globular or elongate and about ⅓ inch long. Mature larvae emerge from the galls and pupate on the ground. This insect apparently has several generations per year.

Willow leaf gall sawflies do not harm plants. No controls are recommended or known. The larvae of several wasps, and at least one weevil and moth, feed on the sawfly larvae or on the gall tissue, causing the sawflies to die. A wasp (*Eurytoma* sp.) appears especially important in controlling willow leaf gall sawfly populations in California.

TABLE 4-17.

Relative Susceptibility of *Ceanothus* Species and Cultivars to the Ceanothus Stem Gall Moth.

NOT INFESTED
americanus, Blue Cloud, *cuneatus, foliosus, gloriosus, gloriosus exaltatus, impressus, insularis, jepsonii*, Lester Rowntree, *masonii, megacarpus, papillosus, parryi, prostratus, purpureus, ramulosus fascicularis, rigidus Albus, spinosus, verroucosus*

LIGHTLY INFESTED
aboreus, Concha, *diversifolius, integerrimus, lemmonii, leucodermis, lobbianus oliganthus*, Mary Lake, Mountain Haze, Royal Blue, Sierra Blue, Treasure Island

MODERATELY INFESTED
cyaneus, Marie Simon, Ray Hartman, *thyrsiflorus*

SEVERELY INFESTED
griseus, griseus horizontalis

Source: Munro 1963.

Willow leaf gall sawfly larvae feed within these reddish, berrylike galls. Several dozen *Euura* and *Pontania* species sawflies cause harmless galls such as these on foliage, terminals, or twigs of various willows.

FOLIAGE MINERS

Many kinds of non-gall-forming insects feed inside succulent plant tissue, including some species of beetles, flies, moths, and sawflies. The larvae of several different families of small moths are the most common foliage-mining pests in landscapes. These insects feed inside of leaves, needles, shoots, or buds and include casebearers, leafminers, tipminers, and shield bearers. Larval stages of some species also feed externally and skeletonize the surface of buds, leaves, or other plant parts. Mature larvae may pupate inside leaves or in cocoons on foliage or bark.

Several hundred miner species feed in foliage of woody plants in the United States. Each kind feeds on only one or several closely related plants. The host species and characteristic form of the larva's damage help to identify the insect species. The cypress tip miner, Nantucket pine tip moth, oak ribbed casemaker, and shield bearers are discussed here.

Foliage-mining insects cause off-color patches, sinuous trails, or holes in leaves. Portions of a leaf or patches of foliage may turn yellow or brown and die back. Tiny larvae may be seen dropping from foliage on silken threads. Severe infestations can slow plant growth, but established woody plants tolerate extensive foliage mining and are rarely, if ever, killed by these insects.

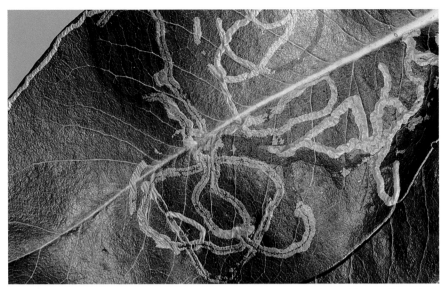

Sinuous trails caused by the madrone leaf miner (*Marmara arbutiella*). A yellowish moth larva is visible in its mine at the right edge of the leaf. This leaf tunneling is harmless to plants.

This juniper is brown because cypress tip miner larvae are feeding inside foliage. Planting less-susceptible junipers virtually eliminates tip miner problems.

CYPRESS TIP MINER

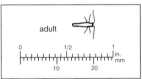

Provide proper cultural care to keep plants vigorous. Prune out and dispose of foliage infested with immature leafminers to restore the plant's aesthetic appearance and provide some control. Plant resistant species or cultivars to avoid damage by some foliage miners. Other species can be effectively controlled by natural enemies; conserve these beneficials by avoiding broad-spectrum, persistent insecticide sprays.

Cypress and Arborvitae Foliage Miners
Argyresthia spp.

The cypress tip miner (*A. cupressella*) is the most common of several *Argyresthia* species that are pests of arborvitae, cypress, juniper, and redwood in the western United States, mostly along the Pacific Coast. Several arborvitae leafminers, especially *A. thuiella*, infest arborvitae and eastern red cedar in the East. Infested foliage turns yellow in early winter and brown by late winter or early spring, then recovers its green color during the spring and summer. Although unsightly, even severe infestations proba-

This silvery tan adult cypress tip miner emerged from the silken cocoon at the base of the dead twiglet. If damage is intolerable and control is planned, carefully monitor foliage for new cocoons and adults such as this. Spraying will not be effective unless it is very well timed, based on regular monitoring.

bly do not kill plants. Do not confuse damage with that caused by insects discussed in the sections "Minute Cypress Scale" and "Juniper Twig Girdler."

The adult tip miners are silvery tan moths. The moths appear from March through May in southern California, during April and May in northern California, from May to June in Oregon, and from mid-June to mid-July in the East. Females lay scalelike eggs on green tips. These hatch into yellow or green larvae, which feed in branch tips until late winter or spring. The larvae then spin slender, white, silken cocoons between the twiglets. The moth has one generation per year.

Where damage cannot be tolerated, consider replacing plants especially susceptible to the cypress tip miner (see Table 4-18). High populations of, and damage from, cypress tip miner can be reduced on established plantings by applying a broad-spectrum, persistent insecticide when adult moths are active. Beginning in early spring, examine foliage tips for the cocoons. When these appear, vigorously shake foliage and watch to see if silvery tan, tiny moths fly up then settle back on the foliage. One application to foliage can be made when a large number of tip moths appear, between March and May, in California. This reduces foliage browning next season.

TABLE 4-18.

Susceptibility of Juniper (*Juniperus* spp.) Cultivars and Other Cupressaceae in California to the Cypress Tip Miner.

LEAST SUSCEPTIBLE, ½ TO 2½ TIP MINERS
Juniperus chinensis Kaizuka, *J. scopuloru* Erecta Glauca, *J. chinensis sargentii* Glauca, *Thuja plicata*
MODERATELY SUSCEPTIBLE, 5 TO 8 TIP MINERS
J. chinensis Pfitzerana Aurea, *J. sabina* Arcadia, *J. sabina* Tamariscifolia, *J. virginiana* Prostrata
MORE SUSCEPTIBLE, 13 TO 19 TIP MINERS
Chamaecyparis lawsoniana Allumii, *J. chinensis* Pfitzerana, *J. chinensis* Robust Green, *J. virginiana* Cupressifolia
MOST SUSCEPTIBLE, ABOUT 40 TIP MINERS
Thuja occidentalis

Numbers are tip miner larvae per 100 grams (3.5 oz) of foliage.

Source: Koehler and Moore 1983.

Oak ribbed casemaker first-instar larvae leave round webbing as they change from feeding inside to feeding on the underside of leaves. The white pupal cocoons are elongate with distinct longitudinal ribs.

Oak and Birch Casemakers and Skeletonizers
Bucculatrix spp.

The oak ribbed casemaker (*Bucculatrix albertiella*, family Lyonetiidae) is probably the most common leafminer on deciduous and live oaks throughout California. Its common name refers to its white, cigar-shaped cocoons, which have distinct longitudinal ribs. Several similar *Bucculatrix* species occur in the eastern states, including the oak leaf skeletonizer (*B. ainsliella*) on oak and chestnut, the birch skeletonizer (*B. canadensisella*) on birch, and *Bucculatrix pomifoliella*, which infests hawthorn and flowering fruit trees, especially apple, crabapple, and cherry.

Bucculatrix cocoons occur on host tree bark, leaves, and nearby plants and ob-

Brown patches on coast live oak caused by oak ribbed casemaker larvae feeding inside and under the leaf. No control is recommended, as this insect is apparently harmless to trees.

OAK RIBBED CASEMAKER

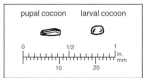

jects. Adults are mottled white, brown, and black. First-instar larvae mine inside the leaf. Later instars feed externally on the lower leaf surface. Damaged foliage between leaf veins appears translucent. Mature larvae are olive green with rows of pale spots. There are two generations per year for each species, one each in the spring and summer, except for *B. canadensisella*, which has one generation.

No control is generally warranted for *Bucculatrix* in landscapes. Intolerable populations may be reduced by a foliar insecticide application that thoroughly covers the lower leaf surface when larvae are observed feeding there. However, spraying broad-spectrum, persistent insecticides can induce outbreaks of other invertebrate pests.

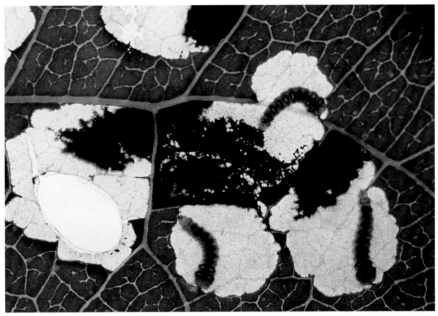

Cottonwood shield bearer larvae (*Coptodisca* sp.) feeding in poplar leaf mines. No control is recommended or demonstrated to be effective on landscape trees.

Shield Bearers
Coptodisca spp.

Larvae of more than one dozen species of shield bearers (family Heliozelidae) feed entirely within the leaves of plants. Hosts include apple, cottonwood, crape myrtle, oak, madrone, manzanita, poplar, and strawberry tree. At maturity, each shield bearer larva cuts a round or oval area of mined foliage from the leaf approximately ¼ inch long. This portion of the leaf drops to the ground or is carried by the larva and fastened to bark, then the insect pupates inside this elliptical case. High populations of shield bearers cause leaves to develop numerous holes ≤ ¼ inch in diameter. Infested leaves may become partially necrotic and drop prematurely. However, plants tolerate even abundant leafminers and no control is necessary in most landscapes. An exception may be the tupelo leafminer, a severe defoliator of sour gum (*Nyssa*) in the eastern United States.

The madrone shield bearer (*Coptodisca arbutiella*) attacks the foliage of madrone, manzanita, and strawberry tree in Pacific Coast states. The ⅕-inch-long, silvery female moth emerges in the early spring and lays eggs in leaves. Eggs apparently remain inactive until the fall, when they

hatch and the larvae begin mining. In the late winter, the mature black larva cuts an elliptical disk of foliage from the leaf, inside which the larva pupates. The madrone shield bearer has one generation per year. Certain species, such as the resplendent shield bearer (*Coptodisca splendoriferella*) on apple, have two generations per year. The cottonwood or poplar shield bearer is an apparently undescribed species that can be abundant on *Populus* species in the western United States.

No effective controls have been documented for most shield bearers in landscapes. Pick and dispose of infested leaves on small plants if damage cannot be tolerated. Spraying for shield bearers is not recommended. Much of their life cycle is spent within plant tissue protected from insecticides. Spraying disrupts the parasites that may help to limit shield bearer outbreaks to a short duration.

Elliptical holes in manzanita foliage caused by the madrone shield bearer. This harmless damage occurs when each mature larva cuts and carries away a portion of the leaf to pupate inside.

POPLAR SHIELD BEARER

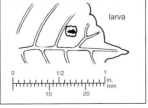

larva

0   1/2   1 in.
            mm
   10   20

NANTUCKET PINE TIP MOTH

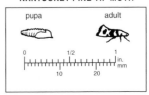

pupa   adult

0   1/2   1 in.
            mm
   10   20

The adult Nantucket pine tip moth is reddish brown with silver-gray markings. If attempting control by pruning or spraying, monitoring adults with pheromone traps to time actions will greatly improve control efficacy.

A Nantucket pine tip moth pupa exposed in the terminal where it fed as a larva. An ichneumonid wasp was introduced to parasitize these pupae, and it has improved the vigor and appearance of pines susceptible to tip moth.

Pine Tip Moths
Rhyacionia spp.

About two dozen *Rhyacionia* species feed on pine terminals in the United States. Pine tip moths in California are pests primarily in the south, and mostly on Monterey pine, especially when it is planted away from the coast.

Nantucket pine tip moth (*Rhyacionia frustrana*) is the major pest species in California and much of the southern United States, attacking most pine species with two or three needles per bundle. In California, the Monterey pine tip moth (*R. pasadenana*) also infests these same pines, primarily near the coast. Ponderosa pine tip moth (*R. zozana*) damages various species of young pines grown in the open in the Pacific Northwest and inland California, primarily in nurseries and plantations. The European pine tip moth (*R. buoliana*) is the most common pine tip moth pest from coast to coast in the northern United States, but it is not reported to occur in California.

Dead shoots very noticeable from a distance are the most obvious symptom of infestation; shoots may be brown or reddish. Silk webbing and boring frass are visible during close inspection of infested terminals. Tip moth damage to the central growing terminal can significantly alter tree shape, causing crooked or forked stems and reducing the marketability of Christmas trees. Because other causes can produce similar damage symptoms, consult Table 5-12 in the chapter Diseases and "Tree and Shrub Pest Tables" at the end of this book for help in distinguishing among insects and pathogens affecting pines.

Adult pine tip moths are reddish brown with silver-gray markings. They begin emerging in southern California in January. After mating, the female lays tiny eggs singly on the new growth tips. The eggs hatch in 1 to 2 weeks, and the young larvae feed on or in the base of needles or buds. More-mature larvae are yellow to pale brown with a dark head. They cover shoot tips with webbing, which becomes covered with pitch as the larvae bore into the shoots and feed for 3 to 4 weeks. Summer-generation larvae pupate in the tips; overwintering pupae commonly occur in the litter. The number of annual generations for Nantucket pine tip moth range from one in Massa-chusetts to about four in the southern United States, including southern California. Monterey pine tip moth and Ponderosa pine tip moth have one or possibly two generations each year.

Management. Do not plant pine species particularly susceptible to the pine tip moths if little or no damage can be tolerated (see Table 4-19). Consider replacing susceptible species like Monterey pine if their performance is unacceptable in the landscape. Alternatively, tolerate damage; pines appear to be less affected as they mature. Provide trees with proper cultural care, especially appropriate irrigation, to increase their tolerance to damage. An introduced ichneumonid wasp (*Campoplex frustranae*) parasitizes Nantucket pine tip moth pupae and has reduced moth populations in many locations in southern California and the eastern United States, resulting in improved vigor and appearance of infested pines.

Prune infested tips from October through January to prevent overwintering moths from emerging. If high-value pines must be pruned during other times, monitor adults with pheromone-baited traps and prune between the peaks representing each generation of

TABLE 4-19.

Relative Susceptibility of Pines (*Pinus* spp.) in California to the Nantucket Pine Tip Moth.

NOT INFESTED
amandii, attenuata, bungeana, canariensis, caribaea, coulteri, edulis, gerardiana, monophylla, montezumae, mugo, nigra, palustris, pinaster, pinea, thunbergiana, torreyana
UNDER 25% OF TIPS INFESTED
flexilis, halepensis, jeffreyi, oocarpa, ponderosa, rigida, taeda
ABOUT 30–40% OF TIPS INFESTED
brutia, cembroides, muricata, patula, pseudostrobus, roxburghii, sabiniana, sylvestris
ABOUT 50–85% OF TIPS INFESTED
contorta, densiflora, echinata, glabra, insularis, radiata, resinosa, virginiana

Source: Scriven and Luck 1980.

moth flights. Remove and dispose of clipped foliage to eliminate developing larvae and pupae on pruned tips.

High populations of Nantucket pine tip moth can be reduced by applying a broad-spectrum insecticide to foliage to kill young larvae soon after moths are observed flying during each generation and before larvae enter tissue. However, pines tolerate extensive tip moth feeding, and natural enemies often provide acceptable control in landscapes. The repeated spraying necessary to provide good control usually is not justified unless trees are of especially high aesthetic value, such as in nurseries or Christmas tree plantations. Insecticide applications kill natural enemies, which can provide substantial biological control. Spraying broad-spectrum insecticides for tip moth during warm weather can also cause spider mite outbreaks, so monitor treated plants for this problem.

Monitoring High-Value Pines. Spraying or pruning between flight periods are more effective if they are timed by monitoring moth flights from January through September. Because insect activity varies with weather, quantitative monitoring to effectively time controls can be warranted when managing large numbers of susceptible pines.

Hang one trap (baited with tip moth pheromone) chest high in the outer canopy of each of two trees at least 50 feet apart. On properties with extensive pine plantings, deploy additional traps at approximately 500-foot intervals. Inspect each trap daily. Remove any debris and count, record, and remove any moths in the traps. Replace traps when the sticky surface becomes dirty and replace the pheromone lure about every 4 weeks or as recommended by suppliers. If pruning or spraying a persistent insecticide is planned, do so 10 to 14 days after the beginning of an overall decline in the number of first-generation moths caught. Spray or prune about 1 week after the peak number of each subsequent generation of moths, a total of up to four times per year in southern California. If sprayings are planned, thorough coverage of all branch tips and the treetop with a pyrethroid or other persistent insecticide is important.

The most precise and effective control timing uses degree-day monitoring and moth traps. Where damage cannot be tolerated, spray or prune at about 1,233 degree-days after the beginning of each moth generation, using a lower development threshold temperature of 42°F and an upper threshold of 99°F. The first generation begins in the spring when the first moth is caught. Subsequent generations start when moth catches first begin increasing after a dramatic decline in numbers from the previous peak.

TWIG, BRANCH, AND TRUNK BORING INSECTS

The adult or larval stages of certain insects bore in wood, xylem, or phloem tissues beneath bark. Holes in bark, stains or oozing liquid on trunks or limbs, and sawdustlike powder in bark crevices and around trunks are common damage symptoms caused by borers. Foliage may discolor or drop prematurely because of borer activity. Wood-boring insects can become serious landscape pests because they weaken limbs and trunks and can kill branches or entire plants. However, many wood borers are secondary pests that develop because trees lack proper care or are injured or dying from other causes.

Boring insects discussed in this book include bark beetles, carpenter ants, carpenterworm, clearwing moths, flatheaded borers, juniper twig girdler, roundheaded borers, and termites. For information on wood-infesting insects that are not discussed here, see publications such as *Carpenter Bees Pest Notes* (Ohlendorf 2000), *Wood Wasps and Horntails Pest Notes* (Mussen 2000), and *Wood Preservation* (Marer and Grimes 1992).

MANAGEMENT OF WOOD BORERS

Prevention is the most effective method of managing wood-boring insects; in many instances it is the only available control. Plant only species well adapted for the conditions at that location. Prepare the site, plant properly, and protect tree roots and trunks from injuries, as discussed in Chapter 3. Protect trees from sunburn or sunscald and other abiotic disorders as detailed in Chapter 6. Learn the cultural requirements of plants and provide proper care to keep them growing vigorously. Healthy plants are less likely to be attacked and are better able to survive the damage from a few boring insects. Appropriate irrigation is particularly important; plants are seriously damaged by irrigating too frequently or by providing too little water.

Irrigate near the outer portion of the canopy, not near the trunk.

Remove hazardous limbs whenever they appear, but otherwise avoid pruning during the host's growing season when egg-laying adult borers may be attracted to fresh tree wounds, as summarized in Table 4-20. Prune out and dispose of borers restricted to a few limbs and remove and dispose of dying trees to prevent boring insects from emerging and attacking other nearby trees. Replace old, declining trees so that future generations may enjoy mature trees.

Do not pile unseasoned, freshly cut wood near woody landscape plants. Freshly cut wood or trees that are dying or recently dead provide an abundant breeding source for many wood-boring pests. Solarize recently cut wood to exclude attacking beetles and to kill any beetles already infesting the wood. Seal wood beneath heavy clear plastic tarps in a sunny location for several months through the warm season; after this time, any emerged borers will have died and the dry wood will no longer be suitable for most borers. Tightly seal the tarp edges (such as with soil) to prevent any insects from escaping. Instead of one large pile, use several smaller wood piles to promote quicker drying.

Except for pruning and general cultural practices that improve tree vigor,

A sapsucker (*Sphyrapicus varius*) caused these horizontal rows of holes in spruce bark. Do not confuse woodpecker feeding with damage from boring insects.

TABLE 4-20.

Pruning To Control Wood-Boring Insects.

HOST PLANT	DAMAGE SYMPTOMS	PEST SPECIES	WHEN TO PRUNE
alder, apricot, ash, birch, cherry, oak, peach, plum, poplar, sycamore, willow[1]	dying limbs, rough bark, sawdustlike frass	**clearwing moths** (e.g., *Paranthrene, Podosesia,* and *Synanthedon* spp.)	fall through early winter (but avoid any pruning if possible)
alder, white[2]	D-shape holes in bark, sudden mid-summer branch death	**flatheaded borer** (*Agrilus burkei*)	fall through March (also remove bleeding, externally stained limbs)
birch[2]	D-shape holes in bark, branches die back	**bronze birch borer** (*Agrilus anxius*)	fall through April
elms[1]	foliage yellows, limbs die back, plant dies	**European elm bark beetle** (*Scolytus multistriatus*)	November through February
eucalyptus[2]	foliage off-color and light-green to yellowish, branches die, broad galleries beneath bark	**eucalyptus longhorned borers** (*Phoracantha* spp.)	December or January (in southern California), November through March (in northern California)
juniper[2]	scattered dying or dead branches, entire plant is never dead	**juniper twig girdler** (*Periploca nigra*)	fall through April
many deciduous trees[2]	BB-shot-sized holes in bark, limbs decline or die	**shothole borer** (*Scolytus rugulosus*)	summer and fall
many[2]	branches die back, entire plant may be killed	**Pacific flatheaded borer** (*Chrysobothris mali*)	fall through February
pines[2]	pitchy masses 1 to several inches in diameter on limbs or trunk	**Pitch moths** (e.g., *Synanthedon sequoia*)	October to February (alternatively, excise pitch masses and kill immature insects)
many, including fruit trees, oak, and pine[1]	pitch tubes, sawdustlike frass, foliage yellows, limbs or top die back	**Bark beetles** (e.g., *Dendroctonus, Ips,* and *Scolytus* spp.)	November through February

Bury, chip, debark, solarize (by tightly sealing under clear plastic in a sunny location), or otherwise properly dispose of pruned wood. Diseases controlled by pruning are listed in Table 5-1.

Adapted from Svihra 1994.

1. Properly timed pruning reduces the likelihood that plants will become infested. Pruning is of uncertain benefit to already-infested plants but may reduce infestation of nearby hosts.

2. Properly timed pruning reduces the likelihood that plants will become infested. Timed pruning also removes and kills immature insects before pests emerge as adults and reinfest plants.

little can be done to control most boring insects beneath bark once trees have been attacked. Insecticides will not kill the wood-boring stages of most insects.

With certain borers, especially valuable trees may be protected from further attack by a well-timed insecticide application. However, unless trees are monitored regularly so that borer activity and attack can be detected early, and the type of boring insect is identified so an effective treatment method can be selected, pesticide use is likely to be too late and ineffective. Do not substitute insecticide applications for proper cultural care. Borers are attracted to trees that are already unhealthy from other causes, and relying only on insecticide can allow trees to die from those other causes unless the growing environment and cultural practices are improved.

BARK BEETLES

Bark beetles (family Scolytidae) are common conifer pests. Some species attack woody nonconiferous plants. Several hundred species occur in the United States.

DAMAGE

Some species live in cones or roots, but most bark beetles mine between the bark and sapwood (the phloem-cambial region) on twigs, branches, or trunks of trees. This boring activity often starts a flow of tree pitch or sawdustlike boring particles called frass. Frass created by boring higher in the tree may drop and be visible in lower bark crevices, on the ground, or in spiderwebs. Bark beetles commonly attack trees weakened by other factors, such as drought stress, disease, injuries, or lack of proper cultural care. Infestation by *Ips* beetles and certain *Dendroctonus* and *Scolytus* species indicates that trees are seriously unhealthy and likely to decline or die. Because other causes can produce similar damage symptoms, consult Table 5-12 in the chapter Diseases for a summary of insects and pathogens affecting pines.

IDENTIFICATION AND BIOLOGY

Adults are small, cylindrical, hard-bodied beetles about the size of rice grains. Most species are dark red, brown, or black. Their antennae are elbowed and the outer segments are enlarged and clublike. When viewed from above, the head is partly or completely hidden by the thorax. They have strong, scooplike jaws (mandibles) for boring.

Small, oval, whitish eggs are laid in the tunnel that is constructed by adults at the interface of the bark and wood. After the eggs hatch, mining larvae form branching tunnels. Larvae of most species are cream or white, robust, grub-like, and may have a dark head. At first the larval mines are very small, but they gradually increase in diameter as the larvae grow. Pupae are usually whitish and occur within or beneath bark. A buckshot pattern of holes may be apparent where the new adults have emerged. Emerging adults may disperse to attack other trees rather than laying eggs on the same tree that they emerged from.

The species of tree attacked and the location of damage on bark helps in identifying the bark beetle species present. For example, engraver beetles usually attack pines beginning near the treetop, while red turpentine beetle attacks pine trunks near the ground. Peeling off a portion of infested bark also aids in identifying the

beetle species present by revealing beetle tunnels (Figure 4-15). For example, *Dendroctonus* species adults usually pack at least part of their egg-laying tunnel with boring dust; these packed adult galleries distinguish *Dendroctonus* species from engraver beetles, which maintain open adult tunnels. Larval galleries of all species are packed with frass. For more information, see publications such as *Bark Beetles Pest Notes* (Dahlsten, Dreistadt, and Paine 2000).

Boring by adult bark beetles often results in pitch tubes; this one was caused by red turpentine beetle attacking Monterey pine. Pines tolerate boring by a few red turpentine beetles, but attack often indicates that pines need improved growing conditions and better cultural care.

C. S. KOEHLER

Sawdustlike frass in lower bark crevices, spiderwebs, or on the ground indicate that bark beetles are feeding in this tree.

Centipedelike pattern: European elm bark beetle egg galleries

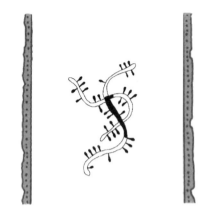

Winding mazelike egg galleries in pine: *Dendroctonus* spp. e.g., Western pine beetle

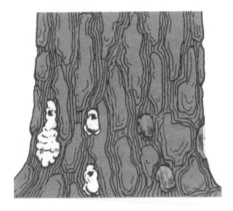

Frass and pitch tubes on bark exterior at base of tree: many bark beetles, e.g., Red turpentine beetle

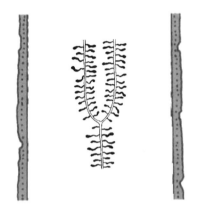

Tuning-fork pattern of egg galleries: *Ips* spp., e.g., Fivespined engraver beetle

FIGURE 4-15. Bark beetle adults bore a tunnel or gallery in which they lay eggs at the interface between bark and wood. Larvae hatch and bore side tunnels. Tunnels packed with frass (excrement) are shown in black, while open portions of galleries are white. The location of pitch tubes (e.g., height above ground), the pattern of adult and larval galleries, and whether adult tunnels are open versus filled with frass, help to identify the species of bark beetles. Illustrations by C. M. Dewees, A. Child, and D. Kidd from Dahlsten, Dreistadt, and Paine (2000) and Marer, Grimes, and Cromwell (1995).

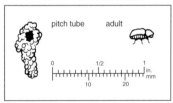

RED TURPENTINE BEETLE

This red turpentine beetle resembles adults of other species of bark beetles, except that red turpentine beetle is somewhat larger than most other species.

Red Turpentine Beetle
Dendroctonus valens

The red turpentine beetle occurs in the Midwest and western United States. Black turpentine beetle (*D. terebrans*) is a pest in the southern and eastern United States with virtually the same biology and management. These turpentine beetles bore into the base of pine and, on rare occasions, spruce and fir trees. Beetle presence is indicated by pinkish brown to white pitch tubes, a mixture of pitch and beetle boring dust that appears on the lower trunk. Reddish or white granular material or brown frass may accumulate at the tree base or in bark crevices.

Red turpentine beetle is usually not a serious pest. Vigorous trees can survive a few red turpentine beetles boring, and only a small area of the tree cambium may die. Weakened trees attacked by this beetle may die, especially Monterey pines, usually because they are under stress from a combination of other factors in addition to beetles.

Red turpentine beetle adults are reddish brown and larger than most other bark beetles. Pairs of male and female beetles bore through the bark together. They usually attack the trunk no more than 6 to 8 feet above ground. Pitch tubes observed higher on the trunk are probably caused by other species of beetles or, if pitch blobs are much larger, by clearwing moths as discussed below in the section "Pitch Moths."

Red turpentine beetle adults excavate a gallery ½ to 1 inch wide and a few inches to several feet long in the phloem tissue beneath the bark. The female lays 100 or more white eggs along the side of this groove; these hatch into white larvae with brown heads. When fully grown in 2 or more months, the larvae are about ⅜ inch long and collectively will have killed a few square inches to more than a square foot in the phloem-cambial area. The beetle overwinters beneath bark and may have several generations each year.

Western Pine Beetle
Dendroctonus brevicomis

Western pine beetle attacks pines stressed from old age, severe drought, root rot, or other injuries. More-vigorous trees may be attacked and killed due to the large numbers of beetles that emerge from dying trees and attack apparently healthy pines nearby. Inconspicuous pitch tubes and boring dust appear on the main trunk of successfully attacked trees, often on the main trunk well above ground. Adult galleries are much-branched and run both laterally and longitudinally, crossing other galleries in a mazelike pattern. *Dendroctonus* spp. bark beetles pack at least part of the central egg-laying gallery with frass.

Larvae of most bark beetles are small pale grubs, as with these California fivespined ips (*Ips paraconfusus*) larvae exposed in their tunnels in wood just beneath bark. Trees infested by *Ips* species beetles are often killed. Usually the trees were severely stressed and unhealthy before beetles attacked them.

Engraver Beetles
Ips spp.

Engraver beetles (including *Ips mexicanus, I. paraconfusus,* and *I. pini*) are important pests of pines and spruce, especially Monterey pine planted outside its native coastal range. When pines are infested, their tops fade from their normal bright green color to lighter green, then to tan, red, and brown; this fading may occur within a few weeks or over several months or longer. In contrast to the normal shedding of interior needles, this fading extends to the branch tips and gradually progresses down from the treetop. The treetop, and sometimes the whole tree, dies.

The adults are dark brown, cylindrical beetles. *Ips* are distinguished from other bark beetles by the conspicuous cavity on the wing covers (elytra) at the rear of the body. There are three to six spines on each lateral margin of this cavity, depending on the species. *Ips* beetles prefer to bore at the treetops, although Monterey pine is often attacked along the entire trunk. Males attack first and produce an attractant that draws other attacking male and female beetles of the same species. Engraver beetles also breed in freshly cut pine wood or trimmed branches. When bark is removed, galleries can be observed in the cambium, where adults lay their eggs and larvae bore (Figure 4-15). The pattern of boring in wood can help identify the pest species. The wishbone-shaped central gallery made by adult *Ips* spp. is largely free of frass. As with all bark beetles, the larval galleries radiating from the central tunnel are packed with frass.

In southern California, beetles can attack any time of year; in colder areas, beetles overwinter beneath the bark and begin to emerge in the late winter or spring. *Ips* have two to four generations per year depending on location.

Cedar and Cypress Bark Beetles
Phloeosinus spp.

Several *Phloeosinus* bark beetles attack arborvitae, *Chamaecyparis,* cypress, and redwoods in the western United States, especially in Pacific Coast states. Arborvitae, cedar, cypress, and juniper are common hosts in the East. Cedar and cypress bark beetles kill twigs, resulting in dead

Cypress bark beetle feeding caused these dead terminals or flagging. This twig damage does not threaten tree survival and no control is recommended.

tips or "flags" hanging on the tree. This twig damage does not threaten tree survival. Beetles also attack the limbs and trunk of stressed or injured trees, which may become girdled and die; vigorous trees are rarely, if ever, attacked.

Phloeosinus are the only species of bark beetles commonly found in arborvitae, *Chamaecyparis*, coast redwood, and cypress. Adults are small, reddish brown to black beetles. The wing covers are roughened and are convex with short, stout, sawtoothlike spines at the posterior end. Adults feed by mining twigs for a distance of about 6 inches back from their tips. The egg-laying female is attracted to the trunk and major limbs of unhealthy and declining trees. It bores through the bark and, depending on the species, tunnels parallel or perpendicular to the grain at the interface of the bark and wood. The eggs laid in these tunnels hatch into larvae that tunnel across the grain. When the bark is peeled back, these adult and larval engravings resemble a centipede on both the inner bark surface and on the wood. Pupation occurs in enlarged chambers at the ends of the larval tunnels. Adults emerge any time of the year, primarily in late spring and again in late summer to early fall, when most of the twig mining occurs.

Shothole Borer
Scolytus rugulosus

The shothole borer bark beetle attacks the limbs and trunks of many broadleaf species throughout the United States. Hosts include English laurel, fruit trees, and hawthorn. When trees are first attacked, holes in bark (bored by the newly arriving adults) often exude clear to brownish sap. The numerous tiny holes in bark (without exuding sap) made by emerging adults (after larvae feed and mature) resemble holes made by buckshot and give rise to this insect's common name.

The dark brown or black cylindrical adults attack trees weakened by root diseases, sunburn, insufficient irrigation, or infestations of other pests. Adults first appear from April through June and may be found crawling on bark. After boring a tiny hole through the bark, the mated female excavates a tunnel about 1 to 1¼ inch long in the cambium just beneath the bark and deposits her eggs along this tunnel. Beetles overwinter as immature stages beneath the bark and have two or more generations per year. Although the beetles typically attack weakened or injured trees, high populations may then move to attack nearby healthy limbs or trunks.

European Elm Bark Beetle
Scolytus multistriatus

The European elm bark beetle was accidentally introduced from Europe and occurs throughout the United States. This beetle and the native elm bark beetle (*Hylurgopinus rufipes*), which has similar biology and management but occurs only in eastern states, spread the Dutch elm disease fungus and are serious pests of elms. Although *Scolytus multistriatus* occurs throughout California, the Dutch elm disease fungus in California is limited to the San Francisco Bay Area and around Sacramento, as discussed in the Chapter 5 section "Dutch Elm Disease."

The adult European elm bark beetle is shiny dark brown to black. It lays its eggs in the limbs and trunk of injured or weakened elms or recently cut elm wood. Before doing so, it may fly to other elms to feed on twig bark, occasionally causing twigs to die and drop. If the adult emerges from infected elm wood, its body is contaminated with Dutch elm disease spores. The beetle then infects the healthy elms with the Dutch elm disease fungus during feeding.

After feeding, the female bores through the bark of a dead or dying elm and makes a straight tunnel 1 to 2 inches long parallel to the grain of the wood, except that on Chinese elm the gallery is more meandering. It lays several dozen eggs along this gallery. These hatch into larvae, each of which bores a tunnel at right angles to the parent gallery. This tunneling is at the juncture of the bark

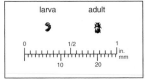

SHOTHOLE BORER

larva   adult

0   1/2   1   in.
|''''|''''|''''|''''| mm
       10   20

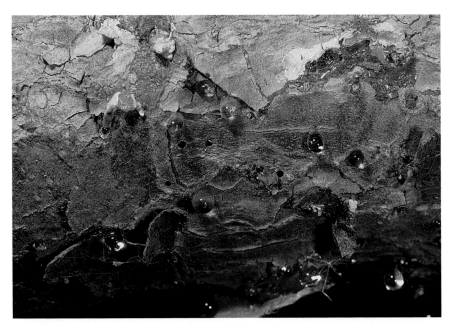

Small holes in bark, some weeping sap, indicate that bark beetles are feeding inside.

and sapwood, and when these are separated, both appear engraved with a distinctive centipedelike pattern. The beetle overwinters as larvae, pupae, or adults beneath bark. The European elm bark beetle has about two generations each year, depending on location.

Oak Bark Beetles
Pseudopityophthorus spp.

Several bark beetle species attack oaks throughout the United States. The western oak bark beetle (*Pseudopityophthorus pubipennis*) is common in Pacific Coast states. It attacks live oaks (such as *Quercus agrifolia*), tanbark oak, and California buckeye. It often occurs in combination with oak ambrosia beetles discussed below. In the eastern United States, *Pseudopityophthorus* spp. may occur in beech, birch, chestnut, hickory, and maple, as well as oaks. Bleeding or frothy material may bubble from tiny holes in the trunk or limbs of infested trees. Alternatively, bark beetle holes may be dry and surrounded by a pile of fine reddish boring dust. Severely infested trees can become hazardous and may die or fail.

Oak bark beetles usually attack injured, dying, or dead trees. They can also attack lower limbs and the trunk of apparently healthy trees, such as when large numbers reproduce in and emerge from nearby firewood. For example, large numbers emerge from oaks dying from *Phytophthora ramorum*, as discussed in the Chapter 5 section "Sudden Oak Death."

Adult oak bark beetles are cylindrical, dark reddish brown to black, and about 1/10 inch long. The adults bore through the bark to its junction with the sapwood and create two horizontal tunnels that are not plugged with frass, one on each side of the entrance hole. Eggs are laid along these lateral tunnels. After hatching, each whitish larva tunnels perpendicular to the adult gallery. The mature larvae bore to just beneath the bark surface and pupate. The new adults gnaw through the bark, creating many tiny

shot holes in the bark when they emerge. The beetles overwinter beneath bark and develop through two or more overlapping generations each year.

Ambrosia Beetles

Ambrosia beetles and bark beetles resemble each other physically (all are Scolytidae), but their biology differs, as summarized in Table 4-21. Certain bark beetle species are relatively aggressive and will mass attack apparently healthy trees after emerging in large numbers from nearby dying trees in which they reproduced. Ambrosia beetles are considered to be less serious pests, attacking mostly dead, dying, or severely stressed trees.

Oak Ambrosia Beetles
Monarthrum spp.

Oak ambrosia beetles occur in severely weakened and recently killed trees. For example, oak ambrosia beetles and the western oak bark beetle (*Pseudopityophthorus pubipennis*) reproduce in large numbers in true oaks (*Quercus* spp.) and tanbark oak (*Lithocarpus densiflorus*) dying

The female European elm bark beetle bores a linear tunnel where bark meets wood. The frass-filled side tunnels were made by larvae. European elm bark beetle is the primary vector of Dutch elm disease.

TABLE 4-21.

Differences between Bark Beetles and Ambrosia Beetles.

BARK BEETLES	AMBROSIA BEETLES
tunnel primarily in cambium, just beneath bark	bore at least several inches deep into wood
feed mostly on plant tissue	primarily eat fungi, which develop in wood from spores introduced on beetle bodies
tunnels are at least partly packed with excrement (frass)	tunnels are kept open
frass is mostly pink or reddish, the color of cambial tissue	frass is mostly whitish, the color of sapwood or heartwood
after pupating, each new adult chews an individual emergence hole in bark	new adults exit trees using tunnels created by their parents, so there are relatively few bark holes per beetle

Ambrosia beetles and bark beetles physically resemble each other during all life stages (all are Scolytidae).

Ambrosia beetle frass is the whitish color of sapwood or heartwood where the beetles tunnel and introduce fungi, which they eat. Oak ambrosia beetles, such as *Monarthrum scutellare* shown here, reproduce in large numbers in California oaks dying from sudden oak death (*Phytophthora ramorum*) or other causes. Provide trees with a good growing environment and proper cultural care to reduce their risk of becoming infested with borers.

from sudden oak death (*Phytophthora ramorum*), discussed in Chapter 5. Nearly all coast live oaks that die following infection with *P. ramorum* have been colonized by these beetles before dying. Infested trunks or limbs become hazardous, and even large-diameter trunks can fail (fall).

Monarthrum scutellare and to a lesser extent *M. dentiger* are the common oak ambrosia beetles in California. Adults are elongate, cylindrical, and dark brown. *Monarthrum scutellare* adults are about ⅛ inch long, while adults of *M. dentiger* are about ¹⁄₁₆ inch long. Males bore about 2 inches deep into sapwood beginning in March. A female arrives, mates, and introduces spores of an ambrosia fungus (*Monilia* sp.) on which beetles feed. Both sexes excavate several

longer galleries for laying eggs in heartwood. Larvae develop over a several-month period, pupate, then emerge as adults. In northern California oak ambrosia beetles have about two generations per year. Most first-generation adults fly during about March, and the next generation emerges in about September. Because beetles develop at different rates and from eggs laid at various times, some adults may be flying anytime from about March through October.

Asian Ambrosia Beetle
Xylosandrus crassiusculus

The introduced Asian ambrosia beetle occurs in Oregon and the southeastern United States westward to Texas. If suspected Asian bark beetles are found in California or other areas where they are not known to occur, contact the county department of agriculture (in California) or other agricultural agency officials.

The Asian bark beetle attacks young woody trunks more aggressively than most native ambrosia beetles. Its broad host range includes cherry, crape myrtle, elm, ficus, golden rain tree, liquidambar, magnolia, oak, pecan, persimmon, plum, and redbud.

This species is recognizable in the field because of its distinctive frass. Unlike the sawdustlike powder or scattered excrement granules from most scolytids, Asian ambrosia beetle produces solidified frass pinnacles or spines that resemble short round toothpicks protruding from bark. Because these fragile structures dissolve in water, such as when trunks receive sprinkler irrigation, protruding frass is readily washed away and may not be observed. It is thus possible to be unaware of an infestation of Asian ambrosia beetles until the tree suddenly dies.

MANAGEMENT OF BARK BEETLES

Prevent ambrosia and bark beetle infestations by following the recommendations presented above in the section "Management of Wood Borers." Keep plants

healthy and protect them from damage, as discussed in Chapters 3 and 6. Provide proper care to keep trees growing vigorously. Appropriate irrigation is particularly important; plants are often seriously damaged by too much or too little water. Irrigate near the outer portion of the canopy, not near the trunk.

Prune off infested limbs during November through February. Remove and dispose of dying trees so that boring insects do not emerge and attack other nearby trees. Do not pile unseasoned, freshly cut wood near woody landscape plants, as beetles can breed or emerge from there. Solarize recently cut wood for at least several months by tightly sealing it beneath clear plastic in a sunny location.

Replace old, declining trees so that future generations may enjoy mature trees. Plant resistant species where bark beetles have been a problem. *Ips* and red turpentine beetle do not attack redwoods and atlas or deodar cedar.

Except for pruning limbs and general cultural practices that improve tree vigor, nothing can be done to control boring larvae beneath bark once trees have been attacked. Systemic insecticides applied to soil or injected into roots or trunks do not control or prevent attack by bark beetles. Especially valuable trees may be protected from further bark beetle attacks by spraying bark with a persistent insecticide in the spring and perhaps again later, but do not substitute insecticide applications for proper cultural care. Unless trees are monitored regularly so that beetle attack can be detected early, any spraying is likely to be too late and ineffective. Bark must be sprayed before adults land and bore tunnels or spraying will not be effective in preventing egg laying. As demonstrated by cut Christmas trees, conifers can remain green long after they have irreversibly begun to die or are already dead. If treating for red turpentine beetle, spray only the lower 10 feet of the trunk as this species only attacks around the tree base. For more specific recommendations see the most recent *Bark Beetles Pest Notes* (Dahlsten, Dreistadt, and Paine 2000).

FLATHEADED BORERS

Most woody landscape plants can be attacked by flatheaded borers (family Buprestidae), also known as metallic wood borers. Injury by flatheaded borers can cause sap to exude and form a wet spot around affected bark. Portions of the bark may crack and die. Limbs or entire trees, especially young trees, may be killed. Most flatheaded borers do not attack vigorous plants.

Adult flatheaded borers can be the color of bark (brown to grayish) or metallic and shiny (black, blue, coppery, or green). Their streamlined bodies are flattened, elongate or oval, and typically have longitudinal grooves on the wing covers. Females lay their eggs in bark crevices or wounds. After hatching, the larvae bore tunnels beneath the bark and sometimes into the wood. Tunnels are often winding and filled with frass. Larvae of many species are broad and flat in the front and narrow and tapered toward the rear.

Pacific Flatheaded Borer and Flatheaded Appletree Borer

Both the Pacific flatheaded borer (*Chrysobothris mali*) and flatheaded appletree borer (*Chrysobothris femorata*) are attracted to diseased, stressed, or injured trunks or limbs of more than 70 woody landscape plants including ceanothus, cotoneaster, fruit trees, manzanita, maple, mayten, oak, *Rhaphiolepis*, rose, sycamore, toyon, and willow. The flatheaded appletree borer is found throughout the United States and is especially abundant in the East. The Pacific flatheaded borer occurs only in western states.

The adult Pacific flatheaded borer has a dark bronze or gray body and mottled coppery wing covers. The flatheaded appletree borer is greenish blue to grayish bronze. Adult beetles may feed at the

The adult Pacific flatheaded borer is dark bronze, gray, or a mottled coppery color.

Flatheaded borer larvae are usually broad and flat in the front and narrow and tapered toward the rear, as with this Pacific flatheaded borer.

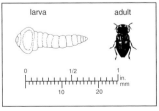

PACIFIC FLATHEADED BORER

larva   adult

0   1/2   1 in.
                        mm
        10   20

Rough, broken bark on a young apple tree trunk caused by Pacific flatheaded borer larvae. Protecting trees from injury and providing good cultural care are the primary controls for borers.

base of twigs and partially defoliate young trees. Females lay their eggs in bark wounds caused by disease or injuries such as sunburn or sunscald, pruning cuts, staking wounds, or the area where rootstock and scion are grafted. Larvae excavate just beneath bark in the cambial area and may bore deeper into wood as they mature. Sap, which is sometimes frothy white, may exude around boring sites, and bark may become cracked. Mature larvae are pale yellow. The thorax is enlarged just behind the head. Larvae form creamy white to dark pupae just under the bark surface in the spring. Adults emerge and fly from April through August. Both species have one generation per year.

MANAGEMENT OF FLATHEADED BORERS

Prevention, as detailed above in the section "Management of Wood Borers," is the most effective strategy for flatheaded borers. Correctly plant species that are well adapted to that location. Provide proper cultural care to keep trees vigorous. Protect trees from injuries and prevent sunburn and other damage from abiotic causes, as discussed in Chapters 3 and 6. Prune out and dispose of dying limbs where borers breed, but prune during the time of year adult borers are not active, as listed in Table 4-20. Promptly remove dead trees. Do not pile freshly cut wood near trees. Solarize logs beneath clear plastic in the sun to prevent beetles from emerging from cut wood and attacking nearby plants.

Larvae of some of the larger, shallow boring species sometimes can be killed by inserting a sharp wire and probing tunnels. This method is practical only in a small infestation, and it is often difficult to know whether the wire has penetrated the tunnel far enough to reach and kill the larva.

Insecticide sprays are not effective against larvae beneath bark. Applying systemic insecticide or spraying foliage and bark with persistent insecticide in spring can help to control certain species, as discussed below, in part because adults will contact plants and sometimes chew a small (often unnoticeable) amount of foliage before ovipositing. Do not substitute insecticide for proper tree care. Borers are attracted to trees that are unhealthy from other causes, and trees may still die unless the growing environment and cultural practices are improved.

Bronze Birch Borer
Agrilus anxius

Bronze birch borer is a pest only of birch. This native of the eastern United States was discovered in California in 1992 and now occurs at least in the area of Marin and Sonoma Counties. Many other *Agrilus* species infesting landscapes have similar biology and management, including the bronze poplar borer (*Agrilus liragus*), which infests virtually any *Populus* species, and emerald ash borer (*Agrilus planipennis*), which was introduced from Asia and occurs at least in the midwestern United States and in Ontario, Canada. Foliage of borer-infested trees turns pale green, yellow, and then brown. Leaves drop prematurely and scattered limbs die. Swollen ridges develop on branches and the trunk where larvae tunnel beneath bark. Liquid oozes from bark, creating stained blotches. Severely infested birch die prematurely.

Adults are dark metallic, coppery beetles about ⅜ to ½ inch long. They emerge in northern California beginning in April, leaving a characteristic D-shaped, smooth-edged hole in bark. Adults cause inconspicuous chewing on leaf edges of alder, birch, and poplar. Adults mate mostly in the southwest canopy of birch, then lay tiny eggs on sunny birch bark. Larvae chew through bark and feed in phloem and xylem tissue, packing frass (excrement) behind them in tunnels. Mature larvae tunnel in the outer sapwood, where they overwinter. In spring, larvae resume feeding, construct an oblong chamber beneath bark, pupate, then emerge as adults.

Bark exhibiting swollen ridges was cut with a wood chisel, then peeled back to reveal these winding galleries. Chiseling into these ridges would reveal bronze birch borer larvae feeding in frass-packed tunnels in phloem-xylem tissue. Prevention is the most critical management strategy for borers.

BRONZE BIRCH BORER

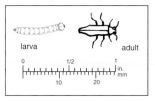

Management of Bronze Birch Borer. Prevention is the most critical management strategy. Provide a good growing environment and proper cultural practices, as summarized in Table 4-22. Birch require more water than most other trees, so good soil conditions, healthy roots, and appropriate irrigation are especially critical. Some common practices can be detrimental, such as routine fertilization, which can increase birch's demand for water, thereby increasing tree stress. Birch typically have an especially short life span in California, particularly in hot, dry interior areas. Avoid planting white-barked birch species, which are especially susceptible to borers. Consider planting

TABLE 4-22.

Bronze Birch Borer Management Methods.

• Do not plant birch where they will be exposed to heat stress, such as the south and west sides of buildings.
• Avoid planting white-barked birch species (e.g., *Betula jacquemontii*, *B. pendula*), which are especially susceptible to bronze birch borer.
• If planting birch, consider using *B. alleghaniensis*, *B. lenta*, or *B. nigra*. Borers attack all birch, but these species appear to be less susceptible in California.
• Plant at the most suitable location, such as the east side of buildings where heat stress is typically less severe.
• Apply mulch to retain soil moisture and keep roots cooler.
• Provide sufficient irrigation, such as deep watering about every 1 to 2 weeks during prolonged dry weather.
• Do not fertilize birch unless nutrient deficiency has been confidently diagnosed as the cause of poor growth.
• Regularly inspect birch for bark swelling and wet stains from April through September; promptly prune off these borer-infested limbs and remove hazardous limbs whenever they appear. Otherwise, do not prune birch from April through August, the season when adult borers fly and are attracted to fresh pruning wounds.
• Promptly remove dead and dying birch. Chip the wood or cut it into logs and solarize it under clear plastic to prevent adults from emerging and infesting nearby birch.

Adapted from Svihra and Duckles 1999.

Wet spots and dark staining on this alder trunk are characteristic of flatheaded borer damage. Because alder are adapted to moist, well-drained soils, they frequently become infested with borers when planted in arid western landscapes.

FLATHEADED ALDER BORER

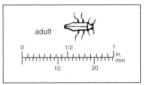

other species that are well-adapted to local conditions.

Regularly monitor birches from mid-April through summer, looking for bark swelling and stains. Prune off and dispose of any infested branches before mid-September. Except for removing hazardous and borer-infested limbs whenever they appear, prune birches during fall through March when adult bronze birch borers are not flying.

If the critical cultural and environmental practices summarized in Table 4-22 have been followed and bronze birch borer is a local problem, spraying birch thoroughly about twice (once each during April and again about late May) with pyrethroid can kill adults and larvae hatching from eggs before larvae bore into wood. A professional applicator usually must be hired to apply the proper material using equipment that provides good spray coverage. Soil application of the systemic insecticide imidacloprid may provide some control if trees are relatively healthy and contain only a few or no borers. For example, treatment can be warranted where nearby birch are an infested source of borers. Severely infested trees will die regardless of treatment. Instead of applying pesticide, promptly remove birch that are highly infested, dying, or dead. Chip the wood or cut and solarize it under plastic to prevent borers form emerging to attack other birch. Plant replacement species that are adapted to local conditions.

Flatheaded Alder Borer
Agrilus burkei

The flatheaded alder borer attacks only alders in the western United States, primarily white alder (*Alnus rhombifolia*) in poorly irrigated landscapes. Wet spots, dark staining, and gnarled, ridged growth often appear on the bark of infested hosts. Adult emergence holes, often D-shaped and about ⅛ inch in diameter, are left in bark. Infested limbs die and trees can be killed.

The metallic blue adult of the flatheaded alder borer emerges from infested alders in April and May. The adult feeds on foliage, although the slight damage it causes is usually not apparent. In the late spring, the female lays whitish egg masses on the trunk and main branches of alders, especially stressed or declining trees. Several days later, the larvae emerge through the bottom of the egg mass and bore into the bark, making long winding tunnels through cambial tissue. Pupation occurs beneath the bark in late winter. There is one generation each year.

Management of Alder Borers. Provide proper cultural care and protect trees from injury, as discussed above in "Management of Wood Borers." Provide white alders with frequent irrigation throughout their lives if planted where drought prevails; these trees are native to sites near permanent water. Alders grow poorly in western landscapes where summer drought prevails, and trees become very susceptible to borer attack. Do not plant alders unless you can provide adequate water. Consider replacing problem trees and planting more borer-resistant species, such as black alder (*Alnus glutinosa*). During late summer or fall, when adult beetles are not active, prune out and dispose of all branches showing bleeding, swelling, dieback, or other evidence of larval infestation. Avoid pruning hosts for at least a month before and during the season when adults are active. Do not prune white alder anytime between March and the end of May as egg-laying adult beetles are apparently attracted to recent pruning wounds.

Properly timed insecticide sprays may reduce beetle attacks, but do not substitute insecticide applications for proper cultural care or trees are still likely to die. If an application is planned, beginning the first of April inspect leaves for adult feeding holes and look for adult beetles during mid to late afternoon by examining foliage and branch beating. Foliage and wood can be thoroughly sprayed with a persistent insecticide when adults are active, usually one time about mid-April and again about 3 to 4 weeks later.

Oak Twig Girdler
Agrilus angelicus

Oak twig girdler is a flatheaded borer that attacks true oaks and tanbark oak throughout California and Oregon, especially live oaks in southern California. This species' biology differs from many other *Agrilus* species infesting landscapes, such as the twolined chestnut borer (*Agrilus bilineatus*), which attacks chestnut and oak in the eastern United States, and the bronze birch borer and flatheaded alder borer discussed above. Unlike the tunneling in large limbs or trunks due to these others, oak twig girdler infests only small twigs. Although its damage can be unsightly, oak twig girdler does not significantly harm trees.

The adult beetle is dark brownish copper. It emerges around June in coastal areas and in May further inland. The tiny eggs are laid singly on the bark of young twigs. The whitish larva bores through the bark and spends 3 to 6 months chewing a linear mine several inches long in the direction of older twigs. It then begins to girdle or mine spirally around the twig, causing terminal foliage to die and turn brown. During the next season, it extends its mine a foot or more down the branch, causing more extensive patches of foliage to die. It bores into the center of the branch, then mines back out toward the terminal it has killed and pupates in wood near the surface of the twig. About 24 months after being laid as an egg, the adult gnaws through the bark and emerges.

An oak twig girdler infestation is first indicated by scattered patches of whitish brown leaves throughout the canopy. Leaves are dead, but have not been chewed and exhibit no surface scraping. These symptoms of twig girdler damage may be confused with oak twig blight and branch dieback diseases discussed in chapter 5. To distinguish the twig girdler from disease, peel back the bark of the larger twig at the junction of live and dead foliage. A flattened, spiral tunnel, possibly containing coarse, dark brown frass and a larva, should be visible in oaks infested by twig girdler.

If a broadly oval (in twig cross-section), frass-filled tunnel is found down the center of twigs, this may belong to the round-headed oak twig borer (*Styloxus fulleri*), a less-common species. Adults are greenish brown longhorned borers. Adults and the yellowish larvae can be up to ½ to ¾ inches long. This species does not significantly harm oaks, but it can be managed as described for oak twig girdler.

Management of Oak Twig Girdler. Provide trees with proper cultural care and appropriate environmental conditions to greatly reduce the likelihood they will be damaged by borers. Native California oaks are adapted to summer drought; avoid planting turf or irrigated ground covers under them, as frequent irriga-

This cross-section of a coast live oak branch exposes a frass-filled tunnel and brown wood killed by an oak twig girdler. Because scattered canopy dieback has many potential causes, cut under bark at the junction between dead and green leaves and look for tunnels and frass to help distinguish oak twig girdler from other causes, such as twig blight fungi.

tions during warm weather make the oaks susceptible to oak root disease. However, drought-weakened trees are especially prone to twig girdler attack, and urbanization often reduces the natural availability of soil moisture. It may be appropriate to irrigate urban oaks once every 1 to 2 months during the warm dry season. Allow the water to soak deeply into the soil. Irrigate near the outer part of the canopy, not close to the trunk.

Prune infested branches to restore the oak's aesthetic quality. At least six species of parasitic wasps attack oak twig girdler; however, their importance in biological control has not been documented. Because damage by this pest does not affect tree survival and spraying kills natural enemies, no further management is necessary. Where twig girdling has been extensive and damage cannot be tolerated on trees of high aesthetic value, adults and eggs in California may be killed by one insecticide application to outer canopy foliage in about early June on the coast or about early May inland. Precise timing is very important because, except for the few weeks as adults and eggs, these borers spend most of their two-year life cycle as larvae beneath bark and are protected from insecticides. To better time an application, monitor for adults by branch beating. Alternatively, enclose several infested branches with flexible screening on at least two locations on the sunny or warmer part of the canopy in the spring. Every few days, vigorously shake the caged foliage, then inspect the cage for dislodged beetles. Make a single application of a persistent insecticide when adult borers are first observed.

LONGHORNED BORERS

Most species of trees are attacked by one or more species of longhorned beetles (family Cerambycidae), also called round-headed borers. Most longhorned borers are relatively innocuous, reproducing in injured or stressed trees. Important introduced species include eucalyptus longhorned borers and the Asian longhorned beetle. Other common longhorned beetles include *Ergates, Necydalis, Prionus,* and *Saperda* species. For example, the poplar borer (*Saperda calcarata*) attacks aspen, cottonwood, poplar, and willow. Adults are robust, elongate, grayish green beetles with yellow stripes and spots on the back. Other *Saperda* species attack apple, ash, basswood, cotoneaster, hawthorn, linden, and poplar.

DAMAGE

Holes in bark and stains or oozing liquid on limbs or trunks are common symptoms of roundheaded borer damage. Foliage may discolor and wilt, limbs may die back, and branches or entire plants may be killed. However, roundheaded borers attack mostly damaged or dying plants. Vigorous trees are rarely attacked. Most species of longhorned borers found in landscapes do not threaten tree health.

IDENTIFICATION AND BIOLOGY

Adult roundheaded borers are medium to large, elongate, cylindrical beetles that are often brightly colored. Because they have long antennae, they are sometimes called longhorned beetles. Adult females of most species lay eggs in bark crevices. The larvae bore beneath the bark and sometimes into the wood on tree limbs, trunks, and main roots. Roundheaded borer larvae are creamy white, elongate, and cylindrical in cross-section.

MANAGEMENT

Plant species that are well adapted to each location, provide proper cultural care, and protect trees from injuries, as discussed in Chapters 3 and 6. Remove dead limbs during the season when adult borers are not active. Promptly remove dead or dying trees. Do not store freshly cut wood near trees or solarize wood beneath clear plastic in the sun to prevent beetles from emerging from wood and attacking nearby plants. Prevention, as discussed above in the section "Management of Wood Borers," is the primary strategy for avoiding attack by most roundheaded borer species. Pesticide spraying of bark has not been found to be effective.

Larvae of some of the larger, shallow-boring species sometimes can be killed by inserting a sharp wire and probing tunnels. This method is practical only in a small infestation, and it is often difficult to know whether the wire has penetrated the tunnel far enough to reach and kill the larva.

Eucalyptus Longhorned Borers
Phoracantha spp.

Two closely related species of longhorned borers attack eucalyptus in California. *Phoracantha semipunctata* was introduced into southern California in the 1980s. It rapidly became a pest, killing large numbers of eucalyptus trees. In 1995, a second species (*P. recurva*) was discovered in southern California. Both borers and their host trees are native to Australia. Attacked trees may produce copious amounts of resin, and the tree-tops, branches, or entire trees may be killed. Resprouting may occur from the tree base. Certain species resist longhorned borer attacks, including *Eucalyptus camaldulensis, E. cladocalyx, E. robusta, E. sideroxylon,* and *E. trabutii*, while others are more susceptible, as summarized and compared to other eucalyptus pests in Table 4-14 in the section "Eucalyptus

Two longhorned borer species attack eucalyptus in California. In comparison with the mostly dark wing covers of *Phoracantha semipunctata* (photo left), the more recently introduced *Phoracantha recurva* (right) has dark brown areas primarily limited to the rear third of its wing covers.

Redgum Lerp Psyllid." Trees that receive proper cultural care, especially appropriate irrigation, are not readily attacked.

The adults are shiny blackish brown with yellow to cream-colored areas on the wing covers. The antennae are as long as or longer than the body, and the antennae of the male have prominent spines. Several nights after emerging and mating, the female begins laying eggs in groups of 3 to 30 under loose bark of eucalyptus trees. Females may live from one to several months and lay up to 300 eggs, which hatch in 10 to 14 days. The larva sometimes leaves a distinct dark trail, ¼ inch to several inches long, on the bark before boring into the living cambial tissue beneath bark. The gallery formed by each large, dirty white to yellow larva widens as the insect feeds. A single gallery can ex-

tend several feet and can girdle a tree. Larvae require about 70 days to develop in fresh logs and up to 180 days in dry logs. During the spring and summer, the beetle requires 3 to 4 months to complete its life cycle, but in the fall and winter it may require up to 9 months.

Management of Eucalyptus Borers. Prevent borers by caring for and protecting trees, as discussed in Chapters 3 and 6 and above in the section "Management of Wood Borers." If planting eucalyptus, consider choosing the species based on tree resistance or susceptibility to longhorned borers and other key pests as summarized in Table 4-14. Before taking any control action, consult the sections "Eucalyptus Redgum Lerp Psyllid" and "Eucalyptus Tortoise Beetle" earlier in

this chapter. Consider the impact of controls on other eucalyptus pests, such as the potential of insecticides to disrupt biological control of the bluegum psyllid and eucalyptus snout beetle.

Several larval parasites and an egg parasite of eucalyptus borers have been introduced from Australia. By reducing beetle populations to a lower level, natural enemies have helped reduce borer damage because vigorous trees can survive a few attacks. The most important parasite is *Avetianella longoi* (family Encyrtidae), a ¹⁄₁₆-inch-long, host-specific wasp that lays its eggs within the eggs of the beetles. Parasitized eggs develop brown shells through which the body and dark eye spots of developing wasps can be observed. *Avetianella longoi* disperses rapidly and efficiently finds borer eggs. This wasp has become widely established in California, typically attacking and killing over 90% of *P. semipunctata* eggs in the field. However, research indicates that it is less effective against the more recently introduced *P. recurva*. Conserve parasites by avoiding spraying eucalyptus bark or foliage with broad-spectrum, persistent insecticides.

Map the location of high-value trees and inspect them regularly for stress, such as damage from *Armillaria* or *Phytophthora* root rots. Stress symptoms include a sparse canopy, leaf color changes (usually yellowing), and sprouting from inactive buds on the main trunk. Appropriate irrigation greatly reduces or eliminates eucalyptus longhorned borer attacks. Consider providing supplemental water about once a month during prolonged dry periods, particularly if seasonal rainfall has been below normal. Irrigate around the outer canopy, not near the trunk. Avoid frequent watering, as this promotes root disease.

Prune dead branches and remove dead trees immediately; conduct other pruning during December and January (in southern California) and November through March (in northern California) when adult beetles are inactive. Eucalyptus logs, such as firewood, and dead branches and trees are the primary beetle breeding sites. Bury or, where per-

P. SVIHRA

A mature eucalyptus longhorned borer larva exposed in wood. Appropriate irrigation greatly reduces longhorned borer attacks on eucalyptus. Natural enemies have also been introduced by University of California scientists to help reduce populations of this pest.

EUCALYPTUS LONGHORNED BORER

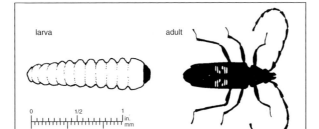

larva

adult

0   1/2   1
|⊢⊢⊢⊢⊢⊢⊢⊢⊢⊢⊢⊢⊢⊢⊢| in.
   10   20   mm

mitted, burn dead wood. Alternatively, remove the bark from felled logs or seal the wood in a sunny location under an ultraviolet-resistant, clear polyethylene tarp for at least 6 months. This prevents new beetles from attacking or resident beetles from emerging and flying to nearby living eucalyptus. For more information, consult *Eucalyptus Longhorned Borers Pest Notes* (Paine, Millar, and Dreistadt 2000).

Asian Longhorned Beetle
Anoplophora glabripennis

Asian longhorned beetle infestations occur in the eastern United States, where thousands of infested trees have been cut down. This pest has been intercepted at many American entry ports, including in California, Oregon, and Washington State, where it arrives from Asia in untreated wood products, such as shipping crates and pallets. If suspected Asian longhorned borers are found, report this to the county department of agriculture (in California) or other agricultural agency officials.

Unlike most longhorned borers, which are innocuous species that reproduce in dying wood, Asian longhorned beetle aggressively attacks apparently healthy trees. It can infest many broadleaves, including ash, birch, elm, locust, maple, mulberry, poplar, and willow. Liquid oozing from bark, sawdustlike boring frass on bark or around trunks, and dying trees limbs where larvae feed are characteristics of infestations. Asian longhorned beetle adults produce relatively large, smooth-edged holes about ½ inch in diameter in wood when they emerge from pupae. Adults range from about ¾ to 1¼ inches long and have very long antennae with alternating bands of black and white. Their body is smooth, shiny, and black with many irregular white blotches. Their legs are black and bluish white. Asian longhorned beetle can be distinguished from several native species by color differences, as summarized in Table 4-23, but submit any borers suspected of being this species to an expert for identification.

CLEARWING MOTHS

Over 100 species of clearwing moths (family Sesiidae) occur in the United States. Several are important wood-boring pests in landscapes. Hosts include alder, ash, aspen, birch, cottonwood, Douglas fir, oak, olive, pine, poplar, stone fruit trees, sycamore, and willow.

Clearwing moth larvae feed beneath the bark, sometimes destroying the plant's food- and water-conducting tissue. With some species, such as those attacking sycamore and pine, feeding is tolerated by trees and apparently causes no serious harm. Most other mature trees can tolerate feeding by a few borers. When populations are high, feeding by larvae of certain species causes girdling and dieback of plant parts so that limbs may drop and entire plants may die. The presence of clearwing moths often indicates that trees lack appropriate cultural care or have otherwise been injured.

This banded alder borer (*Rosalia funebris*) is one of several native species that resemble the introduced Asian long-horned beetle. Also called the California laurel borer, this species is not a significant pest. Banded alder borer larvae feed in declining broadleaf trees, including ash, California bay laurel, and willow. Adults have a pale thorax with one large black spot. Their wing covers have several broad bands that are black and pale (gray, light bluish, or white). Their coloration differs from the Asian longhorned borer, which has a about 20 whitish spots on its shiny black body.

TABLE 4-23.

Characteristics for Distinguishing the Asian Longhorned Beetle from Some Native Longhorned Borers.

DISTINGUISHING CHARACTERS	COMMON NAME (SCIENTIFIC NAME)
Thorax entirely black. Antennae black-and-white banded. Wing covers do not have distinct white dot at base (where wings meet thorax), though wing covers have many irregular white blotches. Overall appearance smooth and shiny.	Asian longhorned beetle (*Anoplophora glabripennis*)
Thorax whitish with one large black spot. Wing covers have several broad bands that are black and whitish.	banded alder borer (*Rosalia funebris*)
Thorax has white bands. Antenna all black.	cottonwood borer (*Plectrodera scalator*)
Wing covers have distinct white dot where they meet thorax. Overall appearance bumpy, rough, and dull-colored.	Oregon fir sawyer (*Monochamus oregonensis*)
Wing covers have distinct white dot where they meet thorax.	whitespotted pine sawyer (*Monochamus scutellatus*)

Report suspected Asian longhorned beetles to the county department of agriculture (in California) or other agricultural agency officials. Most longhorned borers are innocuous species that inhabit declining trees, but Asian longhorned beetle is an aggressive pest of apparently healthy trees.

Frass around tunnel entrances and gnarled bark produced by ash borer larvae infesting Raywood ash.

Clearwing moth larvae are usually whitish to pink with a reddish brown head, as with this sycamore borer larva. Examining the pattern of hooks beneath their prolegs can distinguish clearwings from some other larvae, as discussed in the section "American Plum Borer."

Scattered dead branches may indicate a clearwing moth infestation. Infestation by clearwing moths often indicates that trees lack appropriate cultural care or have otherwise been injured.

IDENTIFICATION AND BIOLOGY

Copious sawdustlike frass on bark or around trunks, dying limbs, and rough or gnarled bark are key signs that trees are infested with wood-boring insects. Clearwing moth larvae have a dark brown head and whitish to pink bodies up to 1½ inches long. Mature larvae or mobile pupae leave an empty brown pupal case that can often be observed protruding from bark or lying on soil around the tree base, except for peachtree borer, which pupates in soil.

Clearwing moth adults are recognized by their narrow, mostly clear wings and, on the male, the many fine hairlike projections along the antennae. Unlike some similar-appearing species of tiger moths (Arctiidae) and hawk moths (Sphingidae), clearwing moths have interlocking forewings and hind wings. They are day-flying moths that resemble paper wasps with a broad waist. The two sexes usually have different amounts of clear wing area and are differently colored, often with yellow, orange, or red on black.

Adult moths may feed on nectar and live about 1 week. Soon after emerging from the host tree, female moths emit a pheromone that attracts the males. After mating, the female deposits her eggs in cracks, crevices, or rough areas on bark. Within several days, eggs hatch into larvae, which bore in the bark, cambium, or heartwood.

American plum borer (discussed below) and clearwings attack some of the same hosts (such as fruit trees, olive, and sycamore), but some of the cultural and physical controls differ for managing these pests. Before taking control action, it can be helpful to distinguish between these pests, such as by using a hand lens to examine the arrangement of small hooks on the bottom of larval prolegs (Figure 4-16).

American Hornet Moth
Sesia tibialis

American hornet moth closely resembles western poplar clearwing discussed below, and it infests many of the same plants. Hosts include aspen, cottonwood, poplar, and willow. It ranges from New England to Pacific coast states. American hornet moth is mostly blackish blue with some brown, orange, or yellow.

Ash Borer
Podosesia syringae

Larvae of the ash borer, also known as the lilac or lilac-ash borer, mine the wood of ash, olive, privet, and syringa (also called lilac). This clearwing moth occurs throughout the United States, but it varies in appearance and behavior depending on location. In the East, there are also two similar species (*Podosesia aureocincta* and *P. syringae*). In the West, the male ash borer resembles a paper wasp. It has very long brownish legs and a black body with narrow yellow bands. In California, the ash borer occurs primarily in the Central Valley, where it attacks the tree trunk and small limbs, mostly within about 5 to 10 feet of the ground. Infestations most often occur at sites on the tree where bark has been injured, such as by improper staking, lawn mowers, string trimmers, or previous generations of *Podosesia*.

Throughout the United States, adult *P. syringae* emerge from April to early June and deposit eggs on the bark of host trees. The boring larva is creamy white with a brown head. It periodically returns to the bark surface to expel sawdustlike frass, which accumulates around the exit hole. There is one generation per year.

The redbelted clearwing (*Synanthedon culiciformis*) is a similar species that is common around Sacramento, California. It infests red and white ash and also occurs in birch and alder. The adult is mostly brownish black with an orangish red band on the anterior of the abdomen. Its biology and management is similar to that of the ash borer.

Provide trees proper cultural care and protect them from injury, as detailed in Chapters 3 and 6. A persistent insecticide applied to bark when moths are active can prevent further attacks. If spraying is necessary, time the application using pheromone traps, as discussed below. Nematodes squirted into tunnels may kill boring larvae, but their effectiveness against ash borer has not been documented.

Peachtree Borer
Synanthedon exitiosa

The peachtree borer attacks all stone fruit trees, including apricot, cherry, peach, and plum. Adults are mostly bluish black. Males have narrow yellow bands on the abdomen; females have a single orange band. Virtually all larval tunneling occurs within a few inches of the ground near the base of the main trunk, after which larvae emerge and pupate in soil. Keeping soil bare around the tree base, especially in California's Central Valley, can increase peachtree borer egg and larval mortality due to dryness and heat.

Monitor for peachtree borers by inspecting the basal trunk for reddish brown frass, as seen here. Keeping soil bare around the tree base, especially in California's Central Valley, can increase peachtree borer egg and larval mortality from dryness and heat.

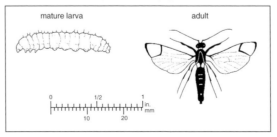

PEACHTREE BORER

mature larva   adult

Sycamore Borer
Synanthedon resplendens

The sycamore borer occurs in the Southwest. It is prevalent in sycamore and also infests ceanothus and oak. Adults emerge from May through July after overwintering as larvae or pupae in tunnels in bark. Adults resemble yellow-jacket wasps. The male is mostly yellow with a brownish black head and black bands on the body. Its legs are yellow, except for black along the margins on the portions nearest to the body. The wings are mostly clear with orangish to yellow margins. Adults display wasplike behavior by intermittently running while rapidly fluttering their wings.

Sycamores tolerate extensive boring by this insect, and generally no control is recommended.

Rough bark and sawdustlike frass in crevices and around the tree base due to a sycamore borer infestation. Sycamore trees tolerate even very high populations of clearwing moths without apparent threat to tree health.

A western poplar clearwing pupal cast skin (lower left) and a frass-covered larval tunnel entrance on a young poplar trunk. Regularly inspecting trunks for new pupal skins and fresh frass are key methods for timing control actions and evaluating treatment effectiveness.

Western Poplar Clearwing
Paranthrene robiniae

The western poplar clearwing, also called the locust clearwing, is a native moth found throughout warm, low-elevation sites in the West. In southern California and the Central Valley of California it is a pest of birch, poplar, and willow, usually in stressed trees. The adult moth greatly resembles a hornet or vespid wasp. The forewings are an opaque pale orange to brownish; the hind wings are clear. The thorax is black with a yellow hind border and the abdomen is yellow with three broad black bands. The body of the desert form of this insect is entirely pale yellow. The insect requires 1 or 2 years to complete a generation.

MONITORING CLEARWING MOTHS

Time any direct control actions and assess treatment effectiveness by using pheromone-baited traps, bark inspection for frass or pupal cases or the reopening of plugged tunnels, or a combination of these methods. Monitor to determine adult emergence by regularly inspecting trunks for fresh clearwing moth pupal cases protruding from bark, in tree crotches, and around the base of trees. Because old pupal cases can persist for months, remove these when found and monitor frequently with care during spring and summer to ensure that any pupal cases observed are new. This trunk inspection method does not work with peachtree borer because larvae drop from tunnels and pupate in soil around tree bases.

Ash borer, sycamore borer, western poplar clearwing, and other clearwing moth larvae that expel sawdustlike frass from bark surface openings can be monitored from spring through fall by brushing away the frass and plugging tunnel entrances with rope putty or grafting wax. Spraying the plug with brightly colored paint will make it easier to relocate that spot for monitoring. Check the plug 1 week later. If the plug is gone, a larva is still feeding beneath the bark. This

method can be used to determine whether an application of nematodes or probing tunnels with wire has killed larvae, as discussed below.

Pheromone Traps. Pheromones are available to attract adult male ash borers and some other species, including two

species with similar biology and management that occur only in the East: the rhododendron borer (*Synanthedon rhododendri*) infesting rhododendron and occasionally azalea and laurel, and the oak borer (*Paranthrene simulans*) attacking oak and elm. Pheromone-baited traps are useful for capturing moths for species identification and for determining when egg-laying adults are active to effectively time insecticide applications to kill adults. Pheromone-baited traps are generally not useful for estimating population densities, in part because a trap's attractiveness to a particular species varies depending on the blend of volatile compounds and type of dispenser used.

When the weather warms in the spring, hang a trap about shoulder high on each of two or more trees spaced at least several hundred feet apart. Because moths may be attracted from great distances, traps need not be located in infested trees, but may be placed where they are more

Placing a clearwing moth pheromone lure in a wing-type trap. Pheromone traps are a critical tool for timing the spraying of trunks to kill ovipositing adults.

Adult clearwing moths. *A.* Sycamore borer male. *B.* Sycamore borer female. *C.* Western poplar clearwing male. *D.* Western poplar clearwing female. *E.* Sequoia pitch moth female. *F.* Ash borer male from the western U.S. *G.* Ash borer male from the eastern U.S. *H.* Douglas-fir pitch moth male. *I.* Peachtree borer male from the eastern U.S. *J.* Peachtree borer female from the eastern U.S. *K.* Pitch mass borer (*Synanthedon pini*) from the eastern U.S. *L.* Peachtree borer male from the western U.S. *M.* Redbelted clearwing male. *N.* Oak borer (*Paranthrene simulans*) from the eastern U.S.

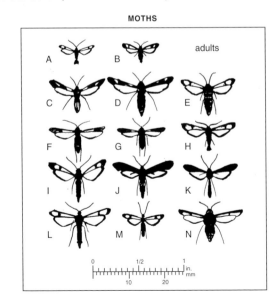

A cluster of white cocoons left by *Apanteles* species wasps that killed a sycamore borer larva.

Larvae of clearwing moth species that maintain a tunnel open to the outside can be controlled by squirting in certain commercially available species of insect-killing nematodes.

convenient to monitor. Once each week, check traps for moths and identify whether any are a species that might attack your plants. Replace traps or the pheromone dispenser as needed or as recommended by your supplier.

Although clearwing moths may be captured in traps almost any time during the growing season, each species typically flies in numbers during only a few weeks or months each year. Ash borer and redbelted clearwings adults in California fly from April through July. Peachtree borer, sycamore borer, and western poplar clearwing adults are active primarily from May through July. In southern California, western poplar clearwings adults have also been found in November and February through May. Male moths emerge first and fly primarily around dusk. Females are ready to mate and lay eggs almost immediately after they emerge.

When using pheromone traps to time spraying, it is important to correctly distinguish the adults of the species that are a pest of your plants from the adults of other clearwing moth species that may be caught. To identify insects, use the adult descriptions and photographs in this publication, consult photographs in the *Clearwing Moth Pest Notes* (Dreistadt and Perry 2000) at www.ipm.ucdavis.edu on

the Web, or take the trap containing your moths to your county Cooperative Extension office. Save the identified moths for comparison when additional moths are captured.

MANAGEMENT OF CLEARWING MOTHS

Mature woody plants usually tolerate and can recover from the attack of a few clearwing moth larvae. However, the presence of this pest is a good indicator that plants require extra cultural care. Many species prefer to attack plants that are newly planted, have been injured, or are poorly cared for. Prevention is the best strategy. Protect roots and limbs from injuries and provide good cultural care, as detailed in Chapters 3 and 6. Prune and dispose of infested and dying limbs. Heavier infestations may warrant treatment with insecticides or beneficial nematodes. Use selective methods whenever possible to help preserve natural enemies, including woodpeckers and parasitic wasps that attack most species of clearwing moths. As discussed in the section "Pitch Moths," clearwing moths infesting conifers have somewhat different management than that discussed below for clearwings attacking broadleaves.

Cultural Control. Make sure trees receive appropriate irrigation. Provide good soil conditions. Protect roots, trunks, and limbs from injury. Keep weed trimmers and lawn mowers away from trunks, for example, by maintaining a several-foot-wide area around trunks free of turf and other vegetation. Stake young trees only if needed to protect or support the trunk or anchor the root ball during the first year or so after planting. Avoid pruning live branches unless necessary to develop tree structure or remove severely infested, dying, or hazardous limbs. Except for hazardous limbs that should be removed whenever they appear, prune only during fall through early winter to minimize the chance of attracting egg-laying moths.

Physical Control. Kill peachtree borers and possibly larvae of other clearwing species by carefully using a knife or stiff wire to probe the trunk during spring or fall where gummy frass exudes from bark. It is difficult to know whether the larva has actually been killed by being punctured or crushed. Reinspect trunks in a week and again probe tunnels if fresh gum exudate is observed, indicating that a live larva is present. Minimize injuries to bark when probing tunnels. Do not create large wounds in cambial tissue. Where peachtree borer is a problem, remove suckers and keep vegetation and mulch away from the base of the tree. Bare soil around trunks increases the likelihood that any tunneling will be observed. In the Central Valley of California, bare soil around trunks increases heat and dryness. This reduces survival of borer eggs and larvae and can prevent peachtree borer from becoming a pest.

Biological Control. Clearwing moths are killed by various parasites and predators, including small *Apanteles* spp. braconid wasps. For example, *Apanteles paranthrenidis* often parasitizes western poplar clearwing larvae. Larvae parasitized by *Apanteles* spp. have many small, oblong maggots (parasite larvae) or white cocoons (pupae) adhering to their bodies. A minute blackish brown wasp emerges from each cocoon after the larva dies. The importance of parasites and predators in reducing clearwing moth populations has not been documented, but avoid disrupting natural enemies whenever possible, for example, by not spraying trees that tolerate borers (sycamores) and by using physical controls (for peachtree borer) and preventive cultural methods (for all species).

Nematodes. Larvae of clearwing moth species that maintain a tunnel open to the outside can be controlled with certain species of insect-parasitic nematodes (*Steinernema carpocapsae* and *S. feltiae*), which usually must be mail-ordered. These nematodes carry mutualistic bacteria, and together they kill the host insect. Nematodes have been shown to control the peachtree borer, redbelted clearwing, sycamore borer, western poplar clearwing, and the dogwood

borer (*Synanthedon scitula*), an eastern species. See the section "Entomopathogenic Nematodes" earlier in this chapter for discussion on biology and proper handling of nematodes.

Apply nematodes with a hand-pump or squeeze bottle applicator or 20-ounce oil can at a concentration of 1,000,000 or more invasive-stage nematodes per ounce of distilled water. First clear the tunnel entrance, then insert the applicator nozzle as far as possible into each gallery. Inject the suspension until the gallery is filled or liquid runs out another hole, then plug the tunnel entrances with rope putty or grafting wax. Agitate the applicator frequently to keep nematodes suspended in the liquid. Adding 2 percent red or orange latex pigment marks treated tunnels. Nematodes can also be sprayed onto bark, but spraying is less effective because nematodes are killed by light and exposure on dry surfaces.

Applications may be made during warm weather (at least 60°F) from spring through fall. Application is most effective when larvae are feeding most actively and tunnel openings are largest. Nematode-treated larvae continue to feed and push frass from their tunnels for about 1 week before dying. A second application 1 or 2 weeks after the first increases the likelihood that borers become infected. Alternatively, monitor tunnels 1 week after application, check that the opening of each gallery is plugged, replug any that have been opened, then spray the plugged openings with bright-colored paint. Wait another week and check to see if these plugs are intact. If the gallery opening is no longer plugged or covered with paint, the larva has not died. Retreat the gallery.

Insecticides. Attack by some borer species, including the ash borer, sycamore borer, and western poplar clearwing, can be prevented by applying a persistent insecticide (such as a carbamate or pyrethroid) to the trunk when egg-laying adults are active. A professional applicator may be required to make effective applications. Proper timing is critical or spraying is not effective. Insecticides have not been found to be effective against the sequoia pitch moth.

If a pheromone is available for the clearwing borer of concern, use pheromone-baited traps to properly time applications. Spray bark and branch crotches with an insecticide on the trunk and lower limbs 10 to 14 days after catching the first pest moth. If moths continue to be caught for longer than about 3 to 4 weeks after the application, spray again. Systemic insecticide injections, implants, or soil application have not been shown to control clearwing borer larvae and are not recommended. For more information, see the most recent *Clearwing Moth Pest Notes* (Dreistadt and Perry 2000).

Pitch Moths

Conifers are attacked by several *Synanthedon* species pitch moths. The sequoia pitch moth (*Synanthedon sequoiae*) is found in pines throughout California, primarily in Monterey pine in urban areas of northern California. The Douglas-fir pitch moth (*S. novaroensis*) infests pines, spruce, and Douglas fir from northern California to Alaska. Pitch mass borer (*S. pini*) infests white pines and spruce in the central and eastern United States. Larvae cause very little injury to cambium and wood. Damage from these clearwings is primarily aesthetic and generally does not harm trees. All the *Synanthedon* pine borers have biology and management as described below for sequoia pitch moth.

In the central and eastern United States, Zimmerman pine moth (*Dioryctria zimmermani*, family Pyralidae) also causes pitch masses on branch crotches. Additionally, it commonly causes branch dieback, most often in upper limbs. Pitch mass removal as described below can help to manage it. However, Zimmerman pine moth has a somewhat different biology, overwintering as young larvae in a cocoon on bark and often initially feeding around branch tips, causing tip dieback resembling that discussed earlier in the section "Pine Tip Moths."

Pitch moth infestations are recognized by the unsightly masses of gummy white,

Sequoia pitch moth larvae cause unsightly but generally harmless gummy masses on pine bark. Scraping away or prying off masses is the only way to eliminate unsightly pitch, and if done to all nearby trees it helps control the pest if the insect underneath is killed.

Sequoia pitch moth larvae are easily overlooked because their pink to gray color closely resembles the color of pitch. If pitch masses are simply scraped away without actually locating and killing or disposing of the larva or pupa, the insect can survive and cause a new pitch mass to develop at that site.

yellow, or pink pitch on the trunk and limbs. Pitch masses may be from one to several inches in diameter and protrude from the bark. People unfamiliar with the damage sometimes confuse pitch moth masses with bark beetle pitch tubes. Bark beetle pitch tubes are usually less than ½ inch in diameter and typically have a distinct round hole in the center made by an adult beetle. Bark beetle pitch tubes often resemble the end of a large gummy drinking straw protruding from bark. Sequoia pitch moth masses are much larger and vary in shape from roundish to elongate oval. Other causes such as canker fungi can cause pines to ooze, but pitch from other fungal infections rarely protrudes in masses from bark as with boring insects. Consult Table 5-12 in the chapter Diseases for a summary of insects and pathogens affecting pines.

The adult sequoia pitch moth's wings have bluish black margins with some yellow at the base. The male's head and thorax are brownish black, except for some yellow along the sides. The abdomen is broadly banded yellow. The legs are mostly bright yellow. Instead of yellow, the markings on the Douglas-fir pitch moth are bright orange. Adult pitch moths are active in the summer, when the females lay their eggs on bark, especially around pruning wounds and other injury sites on bark. The dirty white or creamy larvae excavate shallow cavities just below the bark and typically do not girdle the trunk or limb. Larvae pupate in a brown, paperlike case, which can often be found protruding from the pitch masses.

Management of Sequoia Pitch Moth.
Pines vary greatly in their susceptibility to sequoia pitch moth, based on tree species and cultural practices. Consider planting only less-susceptible pines where sequoia pitch moth has been a problem (Table 4-24). Provide trees with proper cultural care and protect them from injury, as detailed in Chapters 3 and 6. Moths are attracted to lay eggs on bark near pruning wounds and other injury sites. If conifers must be pruned, prune only from October through January so that injuries begin closing before the egg-laying female pitch moths appear in the spring.

Scraping away or prying off resinous pitch is the only direct method of controlling pitch masses and larvae, except possibly for pruning off smaller branches. If resin masses are carefully excised, larvae or pupae can be found and killed. Properly removing pitch masses from all nearby trees, along with appropriate cultural practices, can reduce reinfestations and control local clearwing moth populations. Once the borer is removed, sap flow will slow and the wound will close.

Larvae are easily overlooked because their color closely resembles the color of pitch. Young larvae (those found in smaller, pinkish masses) typically occur below the bark surface within a small cavity they chew in inner bark. Pupae and older, larger larvae occur in grayish pitch masses. These older insects are usually found near the surface of the mass, somewhat outward from the bark cavity they created when younger. If pitch masses are simply scraped away without actually locating and killing or disposing of the larva or pupa, the insect

TABLE 4-24.

Relative Susceptibility of Pines (*Pinus* spp.) to Sequoia Pitch Moth.

MOST SUSCEPTIBLE
Afghan, Allepo, Brutia, Calabrian, and Mondel (*Pinus brutia, P. eldarica,* and *P. halepensis*)[1], Bishop (*P. muricata*), Japanese black (*P. thunbergiana*), Mexican (*P. patula*), Monterey (*P. radiata*), ponderosa (*P. ponderosa*), shore or beach (*P. contorta*)
LEAST SUSCEPTIBLE
Canary Island (*P. canariensis*), Italian stone (*P. pinea*)

Pines are more susceptible to pitch moths if pruned or otherwise injured.

1. Various common names, spellings, and scientific names are used for these closely related European natives. The correct names and taxonomic distinctions are uncertain. Their susceptibility to pine tip moths apparently varies, but many are quite susceptible.

Adapted from Frankie, Fraser, and Barthell 1986.

Extensive gumming from American plum borer larvae in the cambium of a young tree. Avoiding bark wounds is the most critical management strategy for this pest. Larvae can enter cambium only through existing injuries.

AMERICAN PLUM BORER

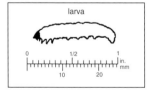

can survive and cause a new pitch mass to develop at that site. Pupae or older larvae can survive in discarded pitch masses unless insects are crushed or bagged and disposed of away from trees. No other control except minimizing injuries is recommended, as pines apparently are not seriously harmed by this insect. Insecticide applications have been found not to be effective. For more information and photographs, consult the latest *Sequoia Pitch Moth Pest Notes* (Svihra and Dreistadt 2000).

OTHER BORING MOTHS

In addition to clearwing moths, larvae of various other moths can be boring pests in landscape plants, including species discussed earlier in the sections "Ceanothus Stem Gall Moth" and "Foliage Miners." American plum borer, carpenterworm, and juniper twig girdler are discussed below.

American Plum Borer
Euzophera semifuneralis

American plum borer (family Pyralidae) is a serious pest of many deciduous trees, including fruit and nut trees, mountain ash, olive, and sycamore. Adults are highly attracted to lay eggs in bark wounds around main branch crotches, the lower trunk, or root crown. Larvae bore in cambium, where their feeding causes extensive gumming, reddish orange frass, and webbing. This girdling weakens limbs, which often fail during windy conditions, and sometimes kills young trees.

Adults are gray moths with brown and black wing markings. Larvae are dull green, pinkish, or white. Both are up to about 1 inch long. Overwintering is as pupae in bark crevices or damaged wood on trees. Adults emerge and mate and females lay eggs beginning in about April. American plum borer has 3 to 4 generations per year.

American plum borer attacks some of the same hosts as certain clearwing moths, but it has cultural and physical controls that differ from those for clearwings. Before taking control action, it can be helpful to distinguish among these pests, such as by using a hand lens to examine the arrangement of small hooks on the bottom of larval prolegs (Figure 4-16).

Avoiding bark wounds is the most critical management strategy for American plum borer. Larvae can enter cambium only through relatively fresh bark wounds. Pruning cuts, other physical injuries such as from sunburn or weed trimmers, and wood-damaging pathogens such as bacterial galls and canker fungi make trees highly susceptible to infestation. Therefore, protective measures such as painting lower trunks with interior white latex diluted 50% with water may reduce borer-susceptible bark injuries, as discussed in the Chapter 6 section "Sunburn and Sunscald."

Where damage is unavoidable or already present, such as from an existing borer infestation, on valuable trees, a persistent insecticide can be applied from about 1 foot above the main lower branch

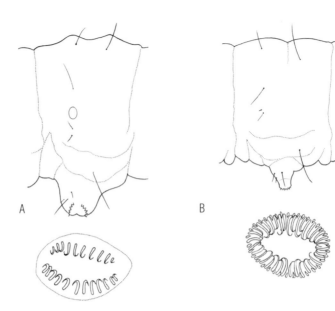

FIGURE 4-16. Distinguish American plum borer larvae from clearwing moth larvae by using a hand lens to examine the crochet pattern (arrangement of small hooks) on the bottom of the prolegs on their fourth abdominal segment: *A.* Clearwing larva have crochets in two transverse rows (rows are oriented perpendicular to the insect's body length). *B.* American plum borer crochets are more dense and form a complete circle or oval. The plum borer's prolegs are also more narrow than clearwing prolegs when compared with the width of their abdominal segment. Distinguishing these larvae can be important because they infest some of the same plants (e.g., fruit trees, olive, sycamore) but some of the cultural and physical controls for them are different. Adapted from Peterson 1956.

crotch to the soil line. Peak egg-laying during the first generation is an optimal treatment time. One or two reapplications at about 6-week intervals or during peak flight in later generations may also be warranted. To increase treatment effectiveness, time application by using pheromone-baited traps to monitor adult flights, which coincide with egg-laying.

Carpenterworm
Prionoxystus robiniae

The carpenterworm (family Cossidae) is a pest of deciduous trees throughout the United States. Hosts include ash, aspen, cottonwood, elm, locust, oak, poplar, and willow. Sawdustlike frass around the tree base and discolored or bleeding limbs or trunks can indicate carpenterworm feeding. The bark of attacked trees becomes irregular and gnarled. Vigorous trees can apparently tolerate some carpenterworms. Continued attacks over several

CARPENTERWORM

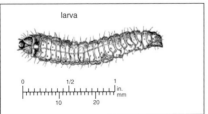

larva

years can cause branch dieback and make trees hazardous and prone to fail.

IDENTIFICATION AND BIOLOGY

The adult is a large (≤1¾ inch long), mottled grayish moth. The male has orange to red margins on the front of the hind wings. Adults emerge in the evening during the spring and early summer. After mating, the female lays small, ovoid eggs in clumps of about two to six on roughened areas of the bark. Eggs change from a dirty white or greenish when first laid to dark brown before hatching. The newly hatched larva immediately bores through the bark and does most of its feeding in the heartwood. Its ½-inch-diameter gallery is mostly vertical and 6 to 10 inches long. Larvae occasionally come to the surface of the trunk or limb to clear their tunnels, spilling frass onto the trunk or ground. The large, mature larva is white or pinkish with a dark head and has brown spots at the base of groups of prominent hairs. It forms a shiny dark brown pupa, which has a double row of spines. Mature pupae wriggle to the surface of the bark where the adults emerge, leaving the empty pupal skins protruding about two-thirds of the way out of the bark. Carpenterworms require 2 to 4 years to complete one generation; most of this time is spent as wood-boring larvae.

MANAGEMENT

Provide trees with proper cultural care and protect them from injuries, as detailed in Chapters 3 and 6. Appropriate irrigation is especially important; for example, California native oaks are adapted to summer drought and are stressed or killed from frequent nearby irrigation. Trees are better able to tolerate a few carpenterworms if they are kept vigorous. If trees are heavily infested and may be hazardous, have them inspected by a professional arborist or other tree care expert and consider removing and replacing trees.

Entomopathogenic nematodes injected into tunnel openings, as described above for clearwing moths, can provide biological control. Nematodes can also be sprayed onto bark, but bark application will be less effective than applying nematodes into tunnel openings. Larvae can sometimes be killed by inserting a sharp wire and probing tunnels. This method is practical only in a small infestation, and it is often difficult to know whether the wire has penetrated the tunnel far enough to reach and kill the larva. After probing with wire or applying nematodes, plug, mark, and monitor tunnel openings and retreat where needed, as discussed above with physical controls in the section "Management of Clearwing Moths." Insecticides are not effective against larvae beneath bark. Carefully monitoring bark at least once a week beginning in late winter, then promptly spraying bark with persistent insecticide when the first new pupal case appears, can kill emerging and egg-laying adults. However, because of carpenterworm's prolonged life cycle and varying development rates among individuals, it will be necessary to inspect bark repeatedly and respray at intervals over a period of about 4 years. Do not spray trees unless you will definitely devote the extraordinary resources required over the long term, including improving cultural care and the tree's growing environment, to reduce the likelihood that trees will become reinfested. For more information, consult publications such as *Carpenterworm Pest Notes* (Geisel 2003).

Despite their large size (up to 1¾ inches) carpenterworm adults are easily overlooked because their mottled gray coloring blends with bark. Inspecting trunks for resting adults and fresh pupal cases are key monitoring methods for diagnosing this cause of wood boring and for timing certain control actions.

Juniper Twig Girdler
Periploca nigra

The juniper twig girdler (family Cosmopterigidae) occurs throughout the United States. It apparently is a pest of juniper only in California, primarily in the south and the warm interior valleys.

DAMAGE

The smaller limbs of infested junipers become yellow, then turn brown and die. This branch "flagging" is most apparent in the late summer and causes a checkerboard of green and brown limbs and retarded plant growth. Twig girdler feeding does not kill entire juniper plants.

Do not confuse twig girdler damage with that caused by disease or other juniper pests, such as those discussed earlier in this chapter's sections "Cypress and Arborvitae Foliage Miners" and "Minute Cypress Scale." Look for larvae and tunnels under twig bark to confirm the presence of this insect. Dying juniper branches may also be caused by mice or root rot fungi. Bark chewed away in bands from lower parts of branches is symptomatic of rodent feeding. If you do not find insect damage or rodent chewing, the dieback

Juniper twig girdler caused these scattered dead canopy patches. Foliage miners, scale insects, various pathogens, and dog urine can cause similar symptoms, so be sure to correctly diagnose the cause of damage before taking any action.

may be caused by soil fungi, which thrive when soil moisture is high for prolonged periods. Twig dieback at the edges of plantings may be the result of dog urine, which can be diagnosed by the characteristic odor.

IDENTIFICATION AND BIOLOGY

The small, shiny, brownish black twig girdler moth is not often observed; it flies primarily from May through June in the

San Francisco Bay Area and March through May in southern California. The adult female lays tiny, shiny eggs on the woody stems of juniper. The eggs hatch into larvae, which tunnel in the stems for about 8 or 9 months. To confirm twig girdler damage, peel the bark from the area of the branch between dead or dying and living tissue. Inspect the wood for the characteristic girdling tunnels and the presence of larvae. The mature larva is cream-colored with a brown head. By the time the larva matures, it often has girdled the twig, although the twig may live for several years before dying. The shiny black to brown pupa occurs beneath bark. The adult emerges in the spring, and there is a single generation per year.

MANAGEMENT

To improve plant appearance, prune out and dispose of affected branches. Tam juniper (*Juniperus sabina* 'Tamariscifolia') is extremely susceptible to damage. Avoid planting this and consider replacing existing plantings with junipers resistant to this twig girdler, such as Hollywood juniper or twisted Chinese juniper (*J. chinensis* 'Kaizuka' or 'Torulosa'). Pfitzer junipers (*J. chinensis* 'Pfitzerana') are attacked, but in comparison with Tam junipers, many Pfitzer are less heavily damaged by juniper twig girdler.

If damage cannot be tolerated, it can be reduced by thoroughly spraying

The wilting of this rose shoot, which will die and turn brown, was caused by a raspberry horntail larva feeding inside. Inspect roses during spring and prune off infested shoots below any noticeable damage.

foliage with a pyrethroid or other broad-spectrum, persistent insecticide twice annually. Insecticide kills adult moths and prevents them from laying eggs, but boring larvae are not affected. Spraying does not restore the appearance of damaged foliage, which remains brown until new growth occurs. In southern California, spray in late March and early May; in northern California, spray in early June and mid-July.

Raspberry Horntail
Hartigia cressoni

Drooping or "flagging" young rose shoots in spring (despite healthy roots and adequate moisture) are commonly due to sawfly larvae (family Cephidae) boring in canes. Raspberry horntail occurs in the western United States, while another species (*H. trimaculata*) with similar biology and damage occurs in the East. Damage is usually severe only in rose, but caneberries (including blackberry and raspberry) are also hosts. The larvae are white or yellowish, segmented, and up to 1 inch long. The black with yellow adults are about ½-inch-long wasps with thick waists.

Inspect canes for drooping or dead tips during April through June. A small dark or reddish spot or oviposition scar where an adult laid an egg can often be observed in canes several inches below the flower bud. Prune off and dispose of infested terminals. Make cuts in healthy pith below any noticeable oviposition scar or hole or any stem swelling (which indicates a larva inside). No insecticide spraying is recommended.

Termites

Trees sometimes are infested by termites (order Isoptera), including dampwood termites (*Zootermopsis* spp., family Termopsidae), drywood termites (*Incisitermes* spp., Kalotermitidae), and subterranean termites (*Reticulitermes* spp., Rhinotermi-

tidae). Termites enter trees through existing wounds and chew tunnels in dead wood. Signs of termite infestation include flights of winged stages in fall or spring, tunnels in wood, dark or blistered wood, and wood surfaces that are thin or easily punctured with a knife or screwdriver.

Although highly damaging to wooden structures, termites provide great ecological benefits by improving soils and decomposing dead wood so that nutrients become available for new plant growth. Termites are not the primary cause of tree damage and they do not attack living cambium or sapwood.

Termites are social insects that form large colonies containing several types of individuals that perform different tasks. Their biology and life history resembles that of ants; exceptions include that termite workers can be either females or males and their food is wood and other plant material. Unlike ants, termites have a broad waist, antennae that are not elbowed, and equal-length wings (see Figure 4-12).

Preventing wounds to trees, as discussed in Chapters 3 and 6, is the most critical method for avoiding termite infestations. Prune properly when needed, such as by removing dead limbs during a time of year when doing so will not attract other boring pests of that plant as summarized in Table 4-20. Provide proper cultural care to keep trees vigorous. Keeping mulch (both organic and inorganic materials) at least several inches away from trunks and building foundations, may reduce the likelihood of termite infestations. Because internal decay or an injury that causes dead wood can make limbs or trunks hazardous (likely to fail), a termite infestation indicates that trees should be inspected by a certified arborist or other tree care professional to determine whether any remedies are appropriate, such as tree trimming or removal.

Spraying surfaces with insecticide is not effective against termites in trees. There is no research demonstrating that drilling holes and injecting insecticide controls termites infesting trees in California. Treating termites will not remedy

A western subterranean termite (*Reticulitermes hesperus*) soldier (lower left) and workers shown close up. Termites enter trees through existing wounds, so protecting plants from injury and providing proper cultural care are the primary methods for avoiding termites in trees.

Stippled, bleached rose foliage caused by twospotted spider mites feeding on the underside of leaflets. Because pests such as leafhoppers produce similar damage, determine the cause before taking action. Spider mite outbreaks are often induced by drought stress or pesticides sprayed against other pests.

the problem that trees with dead wood or wounds may be hazardous. For information on termite biology, identification, and control in structures, consult publications such as *Termites Pest Notes* (Lewis 2001) and *Drywood Termites Pest Notes* (Lewis 2002).

MITES

Mites are common in landscapes, but in most situations they are not serious pests. Some are plant feeders, but many are beneficial predators. Mites are not insects but arachnids, belonging to the same class as spiders and ticks. Mites often go unnoticed because they are tiny and natural controls such as weather and predators frequently keep their populations low. Their damage to plants can usually be observed before you notice the mites themselves.

DAMAGE

Pest mites puncture plant cells with their mouthparts, then suck the exuding fluid. This causes leaves to appear stippled or flecked with pale dots where tiny areas of leaf tissue have been killed. Mite feeding on fruit appears as a silvery or brownish sheen called russeting. Some mites cover leaves, shoots, or flowers with large amounts of fine webbing; other species cause plant tissues to become distorted, thickened, or galled. Prolonged heavy infestations slow plant growth, cause leaves or fruit to drop prematurely, and may kill young plants. Severe infestations often result because natural controls such as predators are disrupted by pesticide applications or excessive dust. Vigorous plants tolerate extensive stippling or tissue distortion with little or no loss in plant growth or fruit yield.

IDENTIFICATION AND BIOLOGY

Mites, unlike insects, do not have antennae, segmented bodies, or wings. Most mites pass through an egg stage, a six-legged larval stage, and two eight-legged nymphal stages before becoming an eight-legged adult (Figure 4-17). Mites overwinter as adult females or eggs on bark or in litter. In most of California and the southern United States, all stages of mites can be present year-round on evergreen plants. At moderate temperatures,

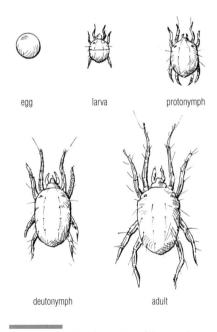

egg larva protonymph

deutonymph adult

FIGURE 4-17. Spider mites, false spider mites, and predatory phytoseiid species develop through five life stages. Eggs hatch, producing six-legged larvae. The two nymphal stages and adults have eight legs. At moderate temperatures, some species can complete one generation in 1 or 2 weeks.

Inspect foliage with a hand lens when mite presence is suspected. Hold the lens close to your eye and move the object being viewed until it is in focus.

slightly larger than spider mites and false spider mites, but individuals of all these groups are only about 1/50 inch long. Eriophyids and tarsonemids are about one-fourth the size of spider mites. Because of their tiny size and diversity, most mites can be positively identified to the species level only by an expert. Determining what taxonomic family mites are in is usually sufficient because mites within these groups commonly have a similar life cycle and management.

Spider Mites

Many species of spider mites (family Tetranychidae) occur in landscapes. Spider mites include the pine and spruce mites, red mites, and various *Oligonychus* species. In California, twospotted spider mite (*Tetranychus urticae*) and Pacific spider mite (*Tetranychus pacificus*) may be the most common pest species. They feed on many nonconiferous plants including azalea, fuchsia, maple, rose, and fruit and nut trees, such as almond, citrus, pear, and walnut.

Spider mite adults have eight legs and tiny globular or spherical bodies that are translucent or colored. Immatures and adults are yellowish or greenish with irregular dark blotches on the sides of the body. Overwintering females may lack blotches and are often red to orange. Most tetranychid mites have long bristles on their body and produce silken webbing from which the name spider mite is derived. Eggs are translucent and spherical and resemble tiny drops on the leaf. Colonies are most abundant in pockets on the underside of leaves during summer and, especially in the case of Pacific spider mite, are surrounded by webbing when populations are high. Pacific spider mites occur on both sides of leaves, while twospotted mites occur more on the leaf underside. For more information, see publications such as *Spider Mites Pest Notes* (Ohlendorf and Flint 2000).

Twospotted spider mites are yellowish or greenish with irregular dark blotches on the sides of their body. Eggs are spherical and translucent.

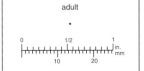

some species can complete a generation in 1 or 2 weeks.

If stippled or distorted plants are observed, inspect damaged foliage and nearby healthy plant parts with a hand lens to determine if mites are present. Stippled and distorted foliage can be caused by other pests, including lace bugs, plant bugs, and thrips. However, these other pests do not make webbing, often leave specks of dark excrement on lower leaf surfaces, and may be observed around the damage. Many mites prefer the lower leaf surface, so remove and turn some leaves over and inspect them. You can also sample spider mites and predaceous mites by branch beating, holding a sheet of paper beneath the plant and tapping the foliage sharply. Inspect the paper for any dislodged mites; to the naked eye they resemble moving specks. Some of these mites may be beneficial predators helping to control pest mites.

The most common pest groups are the spider mites and red mites (family Tetranychidae), false spider mites (Tenuipalpidae), gall mites or eriophyid mites (Eriophyidae), and cyclamen and broad mites (Tarsonemidae). Common predatory mites are in the family Phytoseiidae. Predaceous mites are often

Red Mites

Several species of red mites occur in landscapes, including citrus red mite (*Panonychus citri*), European red mite (*Panonychus ulmi*), and southern red mite (*Oligonychus ilicis*). Citrus red mite occurs on many plants, especially on citrus in the southern United States and California. The European red mite occurs throughout the United States, especially on apple and *Prunus* species such as stone fruits. European red mite is less common on ash, elm, locust, rose, and other plants. Southern red mite occurs throughout the United States, most commonly on broadleaf evergreens such as azalea, camellia, holly, and rhododendron.

These mites closely resemble each other. Adults and nymphs are mostly red with irregular dark blotches. They are oval, globular, and pinpoint-sized or smaller. Unlike many other tetranychids, red mites commonly produce little or no webbing. Citrus red mite females deposit eggs on both sides of leaves; European and southern red mite eggs are usually on the lower leaf surface. The tiny red egg of these species has a distinct whitish, vertical stalk; the citrus red mite egg also has 10 to 12 threads radiating from the tip of this stalk to the leaf surface. Hot weather reduces citrus and southern red mite populations. Southern red mite populations are promoted by cooler weather. One generation of these species requires about 2 weeks when temperatures are moderate.

An adult male and egg of southern red mite on an azalea leaf. This species is most common on broadleaf evergreens and thrives under cool conditions.

European red mite eggs shown close up on a leaf. Citrus red mite eggs look similar, except that they have 10 to 12 threads radiating from the tip of the vertical stalk protruding from each egg.

Persea Mite
Oligonychus perseae

Persea mite is an introduced pest of avocado. It can infest foliage of many other plants, including acacia, apple, bamboo, liquidambar, persimmon, rose, stone fruits, and willow. Small purplish to brown dead spots develop on the underside of infested leaves, initially near veins. Each spot is covered with fine silvery webbing. Spots usually appear yellow on the upper leaf surface. These spots can coalesce, causing irregular blotches (on broadleaf plants) or discolored streaks (on monocots such as bamboo). Highly infested leaves drop prematurely.

Adults and immatures are oval shaped, slightly flattened, and elongated. Their bodies are yellow to green, often with several tiny dark spots on the abdomen. The semispherical eggs are pale yellow and develop red eye spots as they mature. Populations increase in late winter and generally peak during mid-summer. Populations decline during hot conditions (>90°F). One generation develops in less than 2 weeks during warm temperatures or more than 1 month if weather is cool.

Numerous predators feed on persea mite, including black hunter thrips, sixspotted thrips, native *Euseius* and *Galendromus* species predaceous mites, and

Persea mite causes this characteristic chlorotic leaf mottling on many hosts. On bamboo, almost identical damage is caused by several bamboo mites (*Schizotetranychus* species). As with most spider mites, controls include adequate irrigation, washing leaf undersides, applying contact sprays such as oil or soap, and conserving (and possibly releasing) predaceous mites.

Spruce spider mite webbing on male (pollen-producing) cones and the base of ponderosa pine needles. In California, spruce spider mite is usually most abundant in the spring and fall; reproduction stops under prolonged high temperatures.

the spider mite destroyer lady beetle. Commercially available predaceous mites, including *Galendromus annectens*, *G. helveolus*, and *Neoseiulus californicus*, have helped control persea mite in some situations when released at monthly intervals during about late March through August.

Consider applying whitewash to protect trunks from sunburn if plants are defoliating due to mite infestations. Good cultural practices and spraying the underside of leaves with insecticidal soap, narrow-range oil, or a forceful stream of water, provide control, as discussed below.

Pine and Spruce Spider Mites
Oligonychus spp.

Several spider mites cause conifer foliage to become discolored or stippled bronze, reddish, or yellow. *Oligonychus subnudus* and *O. milleri* occur on pines, especially Monterey pine in western states. The spruce spider mite (*O. ununguis*) can occur on virtually any conifer throughout the United States, including arborvitae, *Chamaecyparis*, Douglas fir, fir, giant sequoia, juniper, redwood, spruce, and occasionally pine. Depending in part on the host plant and mite species, these mites can be green, pink, or brown. *Oligonychus ununguis* produces webbing, especially around the base of needles. Neither *O. subnudus* nor *O. milleri* produce obvious webbing. These mites overwinter as eggs or motile stages. Nymphs and adults are readily dispersed by wind. *Oligonychus subnudus* is most common in spring. In California, *O. ununguis* is usually most abundant in the spring and fall; populations stop reproducing under prolonged high temperatures. *Oligonychus milleri* can be abundant anytime from spring through fall. Feeding on young foliage may not produce obvious damage until months or a year later, when foliage matures. Therefore, the effectiveness of any current treatment (such as thoroughly covering foliage with narrow-range oil or insecticidal soap) will not become apparent until the following season.

Sycamore Spider Mite
Oligonychus platani

The sycamore mite is common in hot, dry areas of California and the southwestern United States. This green to black mite feeds on the upper surface of sycamore leaves and other hosts including loquat, oak, and pyracantha. Many other *Oligonychus* species, which are commonly brown or reddish, feed on the upper surface of broadleaf plants.

False Spider Mites

False spider mites (family Tenuipalpidae), also called flat mites, include privet mite (*Brevipalpus obovatus*) and various other *Brevipalpus* and *Tenuipalpus* species. The biology and damage of false spider mites resembles that of spider mites, except that tenuipalpids produce no silk webbing. Most false spider mites are orange to red with dark spots. Their bodies are somewhat more flattened than spider mites or red mites and their eggs are oval. False spider mite damage includes faint brown flecks or large chlorotic areas on the upper leaf surface, brown areas on the lower leaf surface, and stunted plant growth.

MANAGEMENT OF SPIDER MITES AND FALSE SPIDER MITES

Mite damage is usually not as serious as it looks. Plants tolerate extensive leaf stippling or distorted tissue without being seriously harmed. Citrus, for example, one of the best-studied trees, generally tolerates an average of 8 citrus red mites per leaf without reductions in tree growth or yield. When mites are abundant, the most important actions are to conserve and augment natural enemies and to provide proper cultural care to keep plants vigorous.

Avoid using broad-spectrum pesticides to prevent disrupting important biological controls. Some organophosphates, pyrethroids, and carbaryl can increase spider mite populations even though the labels may say they control mites. These pesticides kill mite predators and can induce physiological changes in mites or host plants. Insecticides applied for other pests during hot weather appear to have the greatest effect on mites, sometimes causing dramatic outbreaks within a few days. If spraying is necessary, use selective miticides (also called acaricides) or materials with a low residual toxicity, such as narrow-range

oil or insecticidal soap (Table 4-6). The release of commercially available predaceous mites may be helpful in some situations, such as after reducing the number of pest mites with a soap or oil application.

Provide plants with adequate irrigation to prevent stress. Plants that are drought-stressed may be more likely to experience mite outbreaks and are less able to tolerate pest feeding. Regular sprinkling of foliage helps control some mites. Sprinkling reduces dust that interferes with some predators, can alleviate drought stress that promotes mite outbreaks, dislodges some mites, and may enhance reproduction of predaceous mites or promote development of mite-killing fungal diseases.

Spider mite populations can be reduced with a forceful stream of water directed at the lower leaf surfaces. Spider mites are not controlled by many insecticides, and some of the most effective miticides are available only by hiring a professional applicator. If rapid control of high populations of spider mites or red mites is necessary, insecticidal soap or narrow-range oil may be thoroughly sprayed on infested foliage, usually the

underside of leaves. For example, thorough application of narrow-range oil applied at ½ to 1% active ingredient is very effective against twospotted spider mite and has relatively low toxicity to predatory mites. Sulfur is very effective in reducing populations of some spider mites, but this dust can disrupt predaceous mites.

Control dust and ants; they also disrupt natural enemies. Plant ground covers or other herbaceous plants to reduce dust and provide habitat for some overwintering predaceous mites. Ants protect honeydew-producing insects from natural enemies and can disrupt predators that feed on mites on the same plants. Control ants by placing ant stakes or other enclosed pesticide baits at the tree base or by trimming branches to eliminate ant bridges and applying sticky material barriers to tree trunks.

High foliar nitrogen levels can favor outbreaks of some mites by increasing their reproduction and allowing their populations to grow more rapidly than their natural enemies. Do not apply nitrogen unless fertilization is truly necessary, avoid excess rates, and use less-soluble forms. Urea-based "time

Predaceous mites are the most important natural enemies of plant-feeding mites. Shown here are two elongate western predatory mites, with a spider mite (center) and spider mite eggs.

Phytoseiulus persimilis eating a twospotted spider mite egg. A spider mite nymph and more eggs are to its left. *Phytoseiulus persimilis* and other predatory species can be purchased for release, but their is little information on the effectiveness of releasing them in landscapes.

A spider mite destroyer lady beetle eating a European red mite. These pinhead-sized predators are easily overlooked.

SPIDER MITE DESTROYER

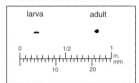

The predaceous mite egg, such as this of *Galendromus annectens* (photo bottom) is colorless and oblong. The plant-feeding spider mite egg (top) is commonly spherical and colored to opaque.

release" formulations and most organic fertilizers generally release nitrogen more slowly.

Biological Control. Natural enemies frequently provide adequate control of mites with little outside assistance. The most important natural enemies of plant-feeding mites are predaceous mites, including *Euseius tularensis*, *E. hibisci*, *Neoseiulus californicus*, *Phytoseiulus persimilis*, and the western predatory mite (*Metaseiulus occidentalis*). These predators are commonly found on the underside of leaves in the interior of trees. Other important predators include the spider mite destroyer lady beetle (*Stethorus picipes*), the sixspotted thrips (*Scolothrips sexmaculatus*), and brown and green lacewings. Mite outbreaks often occur because natural enemies have been disrupted. Avoid using broad-spectrum pesticides for mites and other pests.

Naturally occurring viral diseases sometimes control mites. For example, when citrus red mite populations reach about 3 or 4 mites per leaf, populations are often rapidly reduced by a viral disease harmless to people. Virus-infected mites walk stiffly, curl up, then die of di-

arrhea. In dry weather, the dead mites quickly dry up and blow away, and under humid conditions, they leave reddish brown to black watery spots on leaves or fruit.

Most predaceous mites are long-legged, pear-shaped, shiny, and fast-moving. Many are translucent, although after feeding they often take on the color of their host and may be bright red, yellow, or green. Predaceous mite eggs are colorless and oblong in comparison with the eggs of most plant-feeding mites, which are commonly spherical and colored to opaque. One way to distinguish plant-feeding mites from predaceous species is to observe mites closely with a good hand lens. Predaceous species appear more active and move faster than plant-feeding species; the predators stop only to feed.

Many predaceous mites feed not only on all stages of plant-feeding mites, but also on insects such as thrips and scale crawlers or on pollen and fungi. *Phytoseiulus persimilis*, an orangish predator, and the light-colored western predatory mite are commercially available (see Table 4-25) and can be released to control Pacific spider mite, twospotted mite, and some other species if resident predators are insufficient. However, few recommendations have been developed for releasing predaceous mites in landscapes. It is more efficient to conserve resident natural enemies by controlling dust, ants, and avoiding applications of broad-spectrum, persistent pesticides. If releasing predators, do so in combination with these other techniques.

Broad Mites and Cyclamen Mite

Tarsonemids are primarily pests of herbaceous ornamentals in greenhouses or outdoors in humid growing areas. Tarsonemids usually feed hidden within protected plant parts such as flowers or terminal buds. They cause stunting and distortion of terminal shoots and leaves. Leaf margins often become thickened, leathery, brownish, and downward-cupped. Broad mites have a tapered body that is widest between their second pair of legs and more narrow toward the rear. Cyclamen mites have sides that are more nearly parallel, not sharply tapered.

Gall Mites or Eriophyid Mites

Aceria, Eriophyes, Phytoptus, Trisetacus, and *Vasates* species are among the many eriophyids that can infest landscapes. Eriophyids cause damage such as blistered leaves or galled twigs on many hosts, including alder, aspen, beech, elm, fuchsia, grape, linden, maple, walnut, and willow. Eriophyids are named for a primary type of damage they cause, such as blister mites, bud mites, gall mites, and rust mites. For example, fuchsia gall mite distorts fuchsia blossoms. The cottonwood gall mite (*Eriophyes parapopuli*) causes dark, warty, woody swellings on twigs near the buds of cottonwoods and poplars throughout the United States. Pale felty or hairy patches on tissue

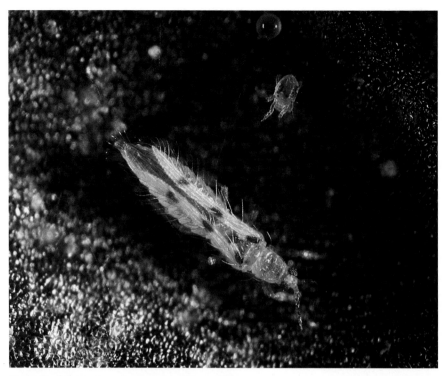

Sixspotted thrips is an important mite predator. This natural enemy is named for the three dark spots on each wing.

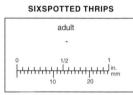

SIXSPOTTED THRIPS

TABLE 4-25.

Some Commercially Available Predatory Mites.

PREDATOR	COMMENTS
Galendromus (=Metaseiulus) occidentalis, western predatory mite	Light-colored mite that tolerates hot climates if relative humidity is ≥50%. Some pesticide-tolerant strains are available. Often released against *Tetranychus* species. Eggs are commonly colored pale salmon.
Iphiseius (=Amblyseius) degenerans	Continues to reproduce under short day length, and its eggs tolerate relatively low humidity. Also used to control western flower thrips.
Neoseiulus (=Amblyseius) californicus	Commonly used in greenhouses. It tolerates temperatures up to 85° to 90°F but needs relative humidity ≥65%. It persists well when pest populations are low.
Phytoseiulus longipes	Looks like *P. persimilis,* but will tolerate lower relative humidity (≥40%) at 70°F. At higher temperatures, it requires more humidity than *P. persimilis.*
Phytoseiulus persimilis	Orangish general predator active at 60–90% relative humidity and 70° to 100°F. A strain that tolerates temperatures over 100°F is available. Often released against *Tetranychus* species.

Few specific recommendations have been developed for releasing predaceous mites in landscapes. If releasing predators, do so in combination with other techniques, such as good cultural practices and avoiding use of broad-spectrum, persistent insecticides and miticides.

Sources: Easterbrook 1992; Fan and Petitt 1994; Osborne, Ehler, and Nechols 1985.

Eriophyids are wormlike or wedge-shaped with four legs, which appear to be coming out of their head. These are greatly enlarged pearleaf blister mites (*Phytoptus pyri*).

Walnut purse gall mites, or pouch gall mites, (*Eriophyes brachytarsus*) caused these harmless growths on California black walnut leaves.

Live oak erineum mites feed in yellow to orange felty masses in depressions on the underside of these coast live oak leaves; the top of infested leaves looks blistered. Oak leaf blister fungus (*Taphrina caerulescens*) also galls leaves and produces spore masses that resemble erineum mite damage. However, *Taphrina* spores can occur on either leaf surface, while the felty colonies of erineum mites usually occur only on the underside of oak leaves.

called erineum are distorted leaf growths induced by the feeding of eriophyid mites called erineum mites.

Adult and immature eriophyid mites have four legs, which appear to be coming out of the head. They are carrot-shaped or wedge-shaped, or wormlike, and commonly are yellow, pinkish, or white. Eriophyids are minute and can be just barely seen with a 10× hand lens; a microscope

is required to clearly distinguish them. One method is to place infested plant tissue in a container with 90% ethyl alcohol. Shake this for about 10 seconds so tissue is thoroughly coated and eriophyids are killed and dislodged. At a magnification of about 25 to 30×, examine the fluid for pale, elongate eriophyids.

No controls are recommended for most eriophyid mites. Eriophyids cause

aesthetic damage and may reduce fruit yield, but most do not seriously harm woody landscape plants and can be tolerated. If gall mites have been intolerable, narrow-range oil or wettable sulfur spray thoroughly applied to terminals just before bud break can reduce populations of some species. Do not apply oil within about 2 months after spraying sulfur.

Live Oak Erineum Mite
Eriophyes mackiei

The live oak erineum mite, also called the coast live oak erineum mite, causes green to brown raised blisters on the leaves of live oak species in California. Hosts include *Quercus agrifolia*, *Q. chrysolepis*, *Q. vaccinifolia,* and *Q. wislizenii*. The mites occur in yellow to orange felty masses in depressions on the underside of blistered leaves, which may become curled or grossly distorted. This damage is harmless to oaks, and no control is known or needed.

Oak leaf blister fungus (*Taphrina coerulescens*) causes similar blisters on oak leaves. *Taphrina* also produces masses of pale spores on leaf surfaces that resemble the felty mass caused by erineum mites. However, *Taphrina* spores (asci) can occur on either leaf surface while the felty colonies of erineum mites usually occur only on the underside of oak leaves. Microscopic examination may be required to confidently distinguish between erineum mites and *Taphrina* spores. The minute eriophyid mites can barely be seem with a 10× hand lens. A dissecting binocular microscope is required to clearly distinguish whether eriophyid mites are present.

Fuchsia Gall Mite
Aculops fuchsiae

Fuchsia gall mite was accidentally introduced from South America in the 1980s. This mite causes leaves and shoots to become thickened and distorted, sometimes forming irregular galls. Fuchsia gall mites occur on growing tips year-round and in flowers during the blooming period. Because fuchsias grow best where summers are cool, this mite is a particular problem in coastal California.

To reduce problems with fuchsia gall mite, plant only resistant fuchsias (Table 4-26) and consider replacing susceptible fuchsia. Prune or pinch off and destroy infested terminals. If damage cannot be tolerated, pruning may be followed with two applications of a miticide, applied 2 to 3 weeks apart. Soap or oil sprays provide some control, but in comparison with exposed-feeding pests, are less effective than synthetic miticides against eriophyid mites enclosed in distorted plant tissue.

Fuchsia gall mites caused these *Fuchsia magellanica* leaves to thicken and distort. Growing resistant fuchsia cultivars may be the only way to avoid the frequent tip pruning and pesticide application often needed to control this pest.

TABLE 4-26.

Susceptibility of *Fuchsia* Species and Cultivars to Fuchsia Gall Mite Damage in California.

LOW SUSCEPTIBILITY OR RESISTANT[1]
Baby Chang, Chance Encounter, Cinnabarina, *boliviana, minutiflora, microphylla* ssp. *Hindalgensis, radicans, thymifolia, tincta, venusta,* Isis, Mendocino Mini, Miniature Jewels, Ocean Mist, Space Shuttle

MODERATE SUSCEPTIBILITY[2]
Dollar Princess, Englander, *aborescens, denticulata, gehrigeri, macrophylla, procumbens, triphylla,* Golden West, Lena, Macchu Picchu, Pink Marshmallow, Postijon, Psychedelic

HIGH SUSCEPTIBILITY[3]
Angel's Flight, Bicentennial, Capri, China Doll, Christy, Dark Eyes, Display, Firebird, First Love, *magellanica,* Golden Anne, Jingle Bells, Kaleidoscope, Kathy Louise, Lisa, Louise Emershaw, Manrinka, Novella, Papoose Raspberry, South Gate, Stardust, Swingtime, Tinker Bell Troubadour, Vienna Waltz, Voodoo, Westergeist

1. No control needed.
2. Merely pruning off galled tissue whenever it occurs provides adequate control.
3. Pruning galled tissue followed by spraying may be necessary every several weeks to provide high aesthetic quality.

Sources: Koehler, Allen, and Costello 1985; Costello, Koehler, and Allen 1987.

SNAILS AND SLUGS

Snails and slugs are mollusks with similar biology and structure, except that snails have a conspicuous spiral shell. Snails and slugs glide along on a muscular "foot." This muscle constantly secretes mucus, which later dries to form the silvery "slime trail" that is a clue to the presence of these pests.

DAMAGE

Snails and slugs feed on many species of plants. They chew irregular holes with smooth edges in leaves and can clip succulent plant parts. They can also chew fruit and young plant bark. Because they prefer succulent foliage near the ground, they are primarily a pest of seedlings, herbaceous plants, and other low-growing vegetation. The brown garden snail (*Helix aspersa*) is a frequently observed species that was introduced from Europe because some people consider it to be a culinary delicacy. Brown garden snail now occurs in Pacific Coast states and many scattered locations in the eastern and southern

Snails and slugs are primarily pests of seedlings and low-growing herbaceous plants, but they also chew fruit and young woody plant bark. The brown garden snail and its damage are shown here on citrus.

Brown garden snail eggs are about ⅕ inch long, pale to dark orange or brown, and round or teardrop-shaped with a protuberance at one end. Eggs and most feeding damage occur in damp locations, such as on plants near the drip irrigation hose shown here. If applying baits, make only spot applications in moist locations, preferably in areas shaded from the sun.

United States. The strategies described here for its management are effective against most other snails and slugs in landscapes.

IDENTIFICATION AND BIOLOGY

Dried silvery trails on and around foliage, as well as chewed plants, indicate snail and slug activity. Search protected places as described below to find snails and slugs during the day or inspect plants at night using a flashlight. Snails and slugs are most active during mild, damp periods during the night and early morning. In mild-winter areas such as southern California and coastal locations, snails are active throughout the year. During cold weather, snails and slugs hibernate in the topsoil. During hot, dry periods, snails seal themselves off with a parchmentlike membrane and often attach themselves to tree trunks, fences, or walls. Adult brown garden snails lay spherical to teardrop-shaped eggs that range from brown, yellow, to white. Mature snails deposit several to 2 dozen or more eggs at a time in a loosely clumped group in sheltered locations on the soil surface or in a slight depression.

MANAGEMENT

Use a combination of methods to control snails and slugs. High snail and slug populations are promoted by wet, humid conditions. Avoid watering too frequently and irrigate early in the day so surfaces dry by evening. Reduce the places around susceptible plants where snails and slugs can hide during the day. Snail harborage includes boards, debris, dense ground covers such as ivy, leafy branches growing near the ground, stones, and weedy areas around tree trunks. Reducing these hiding places allows fewer snails and slugs to survive. The survivors congregate in the remaining shelters, where they are more easily located and controlled.

During the rainy season, or year-round in well-irrigated locations, regularly inspect for snails and slugs hiding in shelter that cannot be eliminated, such as low ledges under fences or decks and near the ground on walls adjacent to vegetation. Hand-picking can be effective (wearing rubber gloves may be desirable). Wooden squares about 12 inches on a side, raised off the ground by 1-inch runners, can be used to monitor and trap snails. Place one or two trap boards beneath each tree or group of shrubs. Check the boards and other hiding places every evening the first week, every second evening the second week, every 3 to 4 days the third week, and weekly thereafter. Crush or dispose of these pests.

Containers of beer also attract slugs, and to a lesser extent, snails. Use relatively flat containers, about the dimensions of an 8-ounce can of tuna. Fill the cans with beer and bury them with their tops about level with the soil surface or place traps on benches or in beds. Beer becomes less attractive to slugs after several days so it should be replaced at least twice a week. If the plants are sprinkler-irrigated, keep water out by covering each trap with an inverted gallon pot after first cutting legs in the pot's rim so the snails and slugs have access to the trap. Because snails and slugs caught in beer traps are killed, other monitoring methods may be better where decollate snails are common predators or are being introduced, as discussed below.

Barriers. Copper flashing or screen can be placed around planting beds and trunks to exclude snails and slugs. Other barrier materials have been investigated, including diatomaceous earth, wood ashes, and sand. Though effective in limited circumstances, these barriers do not provide long-term control.

Use a 6-inch vertical copper screen buried several inches deep in the ground to prevent slugs from crawling through the soil beneath it. Prune lower branches that touch the ground or other objects and apply a copper barrier or other trunk treatment to keep snails out of trees. Copper foil (for example, Snail-Barr) can be wrapped around planting boxes, headers, or trunks to repel snails for several years. When banding trunks, wrap the copper foil around the trunk, tab side down, and cut it to allow an 8-inch overlap. Attach one end or the middle of the band to the trunk with one staple oriented parallel to the trunk. Overlap and fasten the ends with one or two large paper clips to allow the copper band to slide as the trunk grows. Bend the tabs out at a 90° angle from the trunk. The bands may need to be cleaned occasionally.

Instead of copper bands, Bordeaux mixture (a copper sulfate and hydrated lime mixture) can be brushed on trunks to repel snails. One treatment should last about a year and can be prepared as discussed in *Bordeaux Mixture Pest Notes* (Donaldson, Olson, and Raabe 2002). Sticky material applied to trunks to exclude ants and flightless species of weevils can also help to exclude snails and slugs, as discussed and illustrated earlier in this chapter in the section "Sticky Barriers."

Biological Controls. Snails and slugs have many natural enemies, including ground beetles, pathogens, snakes, and birds. These agents alone may not provide effective control, but avoid the use of broad-spectrum pesticides to help improve natural enemies' contribution to pest control. The predatory decollate snail (*Rumina decollata*) consumes young to half-grown brown garden snails and has been very effective in controlling

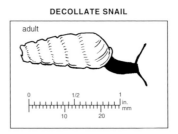

DECOLLATE SNAIL

adult

Snails and slugs are repelled by copper. Copper foil or screen wrapped around planting boxes, headers, or trunks can prevent mollusks from crossing for up to several years.

A predatory species, the decollate snail, can effectively control brown garden snails in southern California. However, it is illegal to import it into other areas of the state because it attacks ecologically important native snails and slugs.

snails in citrus orchards. However, because they also feed on succulent young plants to a limited degree, decollate snail releases may not be desirable in herbaceous ornamentals or newly planted landscapes.

Decollate snail is native to North Africa and southern Europe and was introduced in southern California in the 1970s. Do not release this natural enemy in the San Francisco Bay Area or northern California. Decollate snail introductions in California are currently permitted only in certain counties in central and southern California. Releases in other areas are illegal because they might decimate native snail and slug populations of ecological importance in natural areas. Check with your local wildlife protection agency to determine if decollate snail introductions are permitted in your area. For more information on releasing decollate snails, see *Citrus Pest Management Guidelines* (Ohr et al. 2002) or *Integrated Pest Management for Citrus* (UCIPM 1991).

Pesticide Baits. Baits can provide effective, temporary control of snails and slugs, but they may not be necessary where the recommended integrated program of reducing hiding places, using barriers, and biological control has been employed. Baits are toxic to the decollate snail, and certain materials may poison pets.

The time of any baiting is critical; it should be during a cool, damp period—when snails are most active—before dry, warm weather begins. If the soil surface is dry, irrigate before applying bait to promote snail activity. Make spot applications of bait instead of widespread applications. Apply bait in a narrow strip around sprinklers or in other moist and protected locations. Plant-eating snails and slugs are drawn to these locations, but predaceous snails are less affected than when bait is widely dispersed because decollate snails are not as mobile as other species. Do not make molluscicide applications if heavy rain is expected soon, and avoid irrigating overhead for several days after application, as baits decompose upon exposure to excessive moisture. Certain molluscicides are decomposed by sunlight. Several active ingredients with different characteristics and mixed with various attractants are available as snail and slug baits. For more information, consult *Snails and Slugs Pest Notes* (Flint 2003).

Diseases

MICROORGANISMS and environmental stresses can cause disease symptoms on any plant part. Diseased roots may be enlarged, stunted, or rotted. Sap may drip from infected branches or trunks. Leaves or stems may become spotted, stunted, swollen, discolored, distorted, or wilted, or they may die. The severity of symptoms expressed by affected plants depends on the interaction among the plant, its environment, and the pest or causal agents (Figure 5-1). Biotic or living causal agents include mistletoes (discussed in Chapter 7), nematodes or tiny roundworms (Chapter 8), as well as the bacteria, fungi, phytoplasmas, and viruses discussed in this chapter. Nonliving (noninfectious or abiotic) causes such as overwatering or underwatering, toxins, and environmental stresses that can lead to disease are discussed in Chapter 6.

Disease diagnosis is often difficult. Symptoms of different diseases may be similar to each other, or they may be difficult to distinguish from other causes, such as mechanical injury or damage by certain insects. The organisms or noninfectious conditions causing disease are often not visible to the naked eye and may not be readily apparent at the time disease symptoms develop. Disease symptoms are often variable, and there are often several contributing factors. Professional help and laboratory tests are frequently needed to positively identify the cause of a disease.

Some common pathogens affecting woody ornamentals are discussed in this chapter. Diseases are grouped according to affected plants parts and similar types of pathogens, as summarized in the table of contents.

Types of Pathogens

Microorganisms that are causal agents of disease are called pathogens. Fungi, bacteria, phytoplasmas, viruses, and nematodes (see Chapter 8) are the most common pathogens that cause plant disease. However, many bacteria, fungi, and nematodes are beneficial; they attack and kill pests or feed on dead organic matter and help to decompose dead plants and animals so that nutrients become available for plant growth.

Fungi. Pathogenic fungi cause many different symptoms, including flower blight, heart rots, root rots, leaf spots, wilts, curled leaves, dieback, enlargements, and stunted or dead plants. Fungi are usually composed of fine, threadlike structures (hyphae) that form a network or mass (mycelium) growing on or through their host. Fungi spread mainly through tiny, seedlike structures called spores. They also can spread by sclerotia, other resting structures, and rhizomorphs. Rhizomorphs are rootlike or cordlike masses of hyphae that can contaminate soil and plant parts. Sclerotia are compact masses of hyphae that can persist for relatively long periods.

Fungal spores can be spread by wind, water, soil movement, machinery, insects, or other things with which they come in contact, such as birds and other animals, including humans. Sclerotia, rhizomorphs, and some types of spores may survive for long periods in or on plants or soil. When and where conditions such as temperature, moisture, and the presence of a host plant are suitable for growth, they can infect plants. If they are large enough to be seen with the naked eye or a hand lens, signs such as mycelium, masses of spores, and spore-forming structures help in identifying fungi. Signs include visible mildews and sooty molds (fungal mycelia and spores) and rusts (orangish spores). Mushrooms (spore-producing structures) also demonstrate that fungi are present, but many of these are beneficial or innocuous species, as discussed in Chapter 3 in the section "Mycorrhizae" and publications such as *Mushrooms and Other Nuisance Fungi in Lawns Pest Notes* (Le Strange, Frate, and Davis 2002).

Bacteria. Bacteria are microscopic, one-celled organisms that feed in or on plants or other organic matter. Common symptoms of disease resulting from bacterial infection are shoot blight, leaf spots, soft rots, scabs, wilts, cankers, and galls on branches, twigs, stems, and roots. Unlike fungi, plant pathogenic bacteria generally do not produce spores that can survive adverse environmental conditions; they must usually remain in contact with a host plant or plant debris to survive. Plant-infecting bacteria generally require warmth and moisture to multiply and are usually not a problem during dry summer weather, except where there is

overhead irrigation. Bacteria are commonly spread by splashing water, but are also dispersed by insects or by moving infested plants, soil, or equipment. Bacteria cannot penetrate plant tissue directly and must enter plants through natural openings or wounds.

Viruses. Viruses are noncellular submicroscopic particles that can infect plants and lead to stunting, discoloring, or deformation of leaves, stems, fruit, or entire plants. Viruses rarely kill woody plants, and some infected plants exhibit no symptoms. Viruses require a living host cell in which to reproduce and generally do not survive for very long outside of living tissue. Many viruses are spread by aphids, leafhoppers (including sharpshooters), or other plant-feeding insects. Some viruses are spread by nematodes, infected plants or seeds, or plant parts used during propagation, such as with budding or grafting. A few can be spread mechanically, such as tobacco mosaic virus. Once a plant is infected by a virus, it usually remains infected during its entire life. There is no treatment to cure virus-infected plants in landscapes.

Check plants regularly for stress symptoms, improper cultural care, and disease symptoms and signs.

Phytoplasmas. Phytoplasmas, formerly called mycoplasmas, are minute organisms smaller than bacteria. They are often spread by leafhoppers, and many are called "yellows" because leaf chlorosis is a common damage symptom.

Monitoring and Diagnosing Diseases

All infectious diseases involve a complex interaction among the host plant, pathogen, and the environment (Figure 5-1). Disease symptoms and damage are influenced by the disease-producing ability of the causal organism, the plant's genetic characteristics, and the stage of growth and vigor of the host plant. Environmental conditions such as humidity, temperature, and other stresses on the plant influence disease development. If conditions are poor for pathogen development and plants are otherwise healthy, many pathogens have little or no effect on their host. The same pathogen can be devastating when conditions are favorable for the pathogen or when host plants are stressed and predisposed to infection or disease development.

It is often too late to provide effective control once disease symptoms appear or become severe. Learn what diseases the plant species in your location are prone to, and if possible prevent the conditions that allow those diseases to develop. The "Tree and Shrub Pest Tables" at the back of this book list common diseases in California organized according to the landscape plants they affect. Checking for conditions that promote disease (overwatering, soil compaction, injuries, and so on) is often more important than looking for disease symptoms. Action may be required before damage becomes apparent.

Check plants regularly, at least monthly, for symptoms of stress, improper cultural care, and disease symptoms and signs. Monitoring highly susceptible plants at least weekly or even daily during certain times of the year

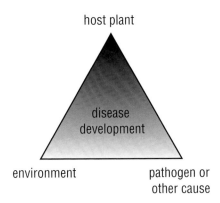

host plant

disease
development

environment   pathogen or
                   other cause

FIGURE 5-1. The disease triangle. Disease results from complex interactions among a susceptible host plant, an environment favorable for disease development, and virulent pathogens. Time (such as season or duration of disease-favoring conditions) is also a factor. This disease-development interaction is sometimes illustrated as a pyramid with time represented as a fourth axis.

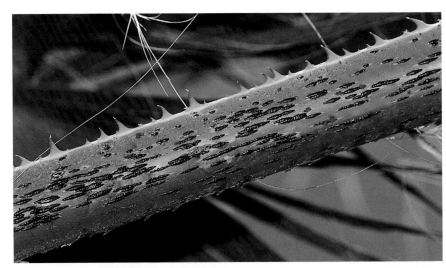

These black, greasy fruiting bodies of *Sphaerodothis neowashingtoniae* on California fan palm are called diamond scale because they resemble scale insects. This fungus causes severe chlorosis and death of palm fronds. The damage can be confused with that caused by certain insects and noninfectious disorders such as nutrient deficiency.

may be necessary to allow prompt management actions for certain quickly developing pathogens. Record when disease outbreaks are observed. Note the current and past environmental factors that may have contributed to the problem, including humidity, temperature, pesticide use, injuries, soil conditions such as drainage, and the presence of free water. Rain, dew, irrigation, and other water sources are especially important because many pathogens require water for germination of spores and infection.

Compare symptoms that appear in the field with the illustrations and descriptions in this chapter, which are grouped according to the portion of the plant where symptoms most often appear. Consult the "Problem-Solving Guide" and "Tree and Shrub Pest Tables" at the end of this book for lists of common damage symptoms and their causes. Examine as many affected plants or parts of the same plant as possible. Look for disease signs (actual structures of the pathogens, such as mushrooms or rust pustules) and symptoms (outward expressions by host plants that they are unhealthy, such as chlorosis or wilting). Examine several plants if possible with different stages of disease to determine how symptoms

Examining plants from a distance helps to reveal problems. The hackberry trees on the left side of the street have yellow, sparse foliage and dead terminals at the treetops. In comparison, hackberry trees of the same age across the street appear healthy.

change as the disease progresses. Plant parts in the early stage of disease development often show more characteristic symptoms; secondary organisms or other factors that obscure symptoms may later become involved. Do not rely on a single symptom; the observation of several different symptoms is usually needed to identify a disease-producing agent. Examine plants both close-up and from a distance and look at all affected plant parts, as discussed in Chapter 2 in the section "Regular Surveying for Pests." Some aboveground symptoms like wilt and twig dieback can be caused by root diseases. Even though these symptoms often first appear at the top of the plant or on terminal parts, when these symptoms occur you should expose and inspect the root crown and roots if possible to see if they are diseased.

A notebook, hand lens, pocket knife, and shovel are essential for diagnosing many diseases. A soil-sampling tube and plastic bags and an ice chest for preserving samples frequently are useful. It is often not possible to identify diseases with certainty in the field. Many can be confirmed only through special laboratory techniques performed on the diseased plants, surrounding soil, or nearby apparently healthy plant tissue. Contact the Cooperative Extension office in your county for a list of private laboratories that test for diseases.

Disease Management

Prevention is the most important method of disease management; for many diseases, prevention is the only effective option. Learn the cultural and environmental requirements of your plants and provide them with proper care. Pathogens frequently kill plants that are poorly cared for, so keep valued plants vigorous. Avoid conditions stressful to plants. Stresses include soil that is kept continually too wet, too dry, or compacted; overfertilization; and improper pruning, especially at bud break or during early growth flush; and repeated insect defoliation. Physical damage to roots and trunks, changes in soil grade, excessive herbicides or salts, use of injections or implants, and planting species that are poorly adapted for local conditions also cause stress. Most pathogens require specific conditions to spread and infect plants. Learn the conditions that promote diseases common to your plants and avoid creating those situations. Read Chapters 3 and 6 in this book to learn how to care for plants to prevent disease.

Resistant Plants. The species or cultivars planted often determine whether certain diseases are likely to develop or can be avoided. Some species or cultivars are highly susceptible to disease. Avoid

Prevent conditions that are stressful to plants. Paving around established trees reduces oxygen and moisture availability to roots and changes temperatures, affecting aboveground plant parts.

growing highly susceptible plants unless they will be provided with much extra care. Resistant cultivars usually are not seriously damaged if they do become infected. However, resistance is not the same as immunity. Plants may become affected by problems to which they are resistant if plants are stressed because of poor cultural care or other factors.

Landscape plants that are resistant to certain insects and diseases, including anthracnose, root rots, powdery mildew, and vascular wilts, are listed in Table 3-2. Be aware that plants resistant to certain pests may be susceptible to other maladies. Check with the Cooperative Extension office in your county or a certified nurseryperson for the most recent recommendations and use the information provided here to choose resistant

species and cultivars that are well suited to local conditions. If you select a more susceptible cultivar because of other preferred horticultural characteristics, be prepared to accept disease damage or devote the effort and resources required to manage it. When plants are placed in locations where soil or other environmental conditions are inappropriate for their growth, certain problems develop regardless of how much care plants are given, such as cypress canker, which infects certain cypress species, and Botryosphaeria canker of giant sequoia, which develops when these plants are grown in hot interior areas of California. The only effective strategy for some problems is to replace and avoid growing certain plants in inappropriate locations.

Quality Planting Material. Many diseases can be transmitted by nursery stock, transplants, or seeds. Select certified virus-free nursery stock when available. Before purchasing plants from outside the local area or moving plants across county lines, contact the local county department of agriculture to learn whether any quarantines restrict or prohibit plant movement to avoid introducing exotic pests. Examine young plants for symptoms of root disease, crown gall, and virus diseases before purchasing and planting. Expose roots to be sure they are not diseased or excessively kinked or restricted by the planting container. Examine bark for wounds and galls. Avoid plants that have been improperly pruned, as they are unlikely to develop good structure. See Table 3-1 for a checklist of what to look for when purchasing nursery stock. A relatively small initial investment in higher quality plants can pay great dividends in improved aesthetic quality, lower maintenance costs, and less disease.

Planting Site and Design. Select plants that are adapted for your location. Some species require full sun while others do well in shady areas. Some diseases, such as powdery mildews, are more prevalent in shady areas; sunburn occurs when sensitive plants are planted at bright sites.

Improve poorly drained soils before planting to avoid root diseases. Group plants according to their water requirements; do not plant drought-adapted species near plants requiring frequent watering. Do not plant grass or other water-demanding ground covers around the trunks of trees and shrubs that are adapted to a Mediterranean climate where they naturally receive only winter rainfall (such as much of California); use compatible plants, keep the soil bare, or apply mulch. Keep any mulch thin around the trunk or about 3 to 4 inches back from the trunk to avoid promoting crown diseases. When replanting after removing diseased trees or shrubs, use species resistant to the disease-producing agent that occurred there if resistant plants are available. See Chapters 2 and 3 for more discussion on landscape design and planting to prevent disease development.

Many fungal diseases are caused or aggravated by poor irrigation practices. Do not allow water to pond around trunks; this promotes development of root and crown rots.

Mulch. Mulching, as discussed in Chapter 7, is a recommended technique to control weeds and improve plant growth, such as by conserving soil moisture, thereby allowing an increase in the time between irrigations. One common question is whether fresh mulch prepared from trees killed by plant pathogens can spread the disease when applied beneath other plants. This potentially is a problem, but probably is of little importance in most situations. For example, finely chopping organic matter contaminated with *Armillaria* or *Phytophthora* and leaving it in a loose pile or allowing it to dry for 2 weeks can eliminate the material's ability to infect plants. Finely chopping organic matter and adequately composting it will kill virtually all insects and nematodes, most plant pathogens, and many weeds. However, because it can be difficult to adequately heat (by composting) all material to the temperature desired to kill pathogens, certain mulches are not recommended in some situations, as discussed elsewhere in this chapter. Because most plant pathogens affect only certain host plants, this potential problem can be entirely eliminated by knowing the source of mulch and not applying it beneath plants that could become infected by pathogens it might contain, especially if the organic material has not been finely chipped and thoroughly dried or well composted.

Irrigation and Fertilization. Provide adequate water for your plants, as discussed in Chapter 3. Be aware that overwatering (applying too much water or watering too frequently, especially when drainage is poor) is the most common cause of plant disease. Irrigating during the wrong time of year promotes the development of certain root diseases. Where foliar pathogens are a problem, avoid overhead watering if feasible or water early in the day or before sunrise so foliage can dry quickly.

Many people assume that unhealthy plants will benefit from fertilization, but most established woody landscapes do not require added fertilizer. Fertilization can promote certain disease-producing organisms (such as fire blight and certain canker pathogens). Nutrient deficiency symptoms in most woody landscape plants are due to unhealthy roots or adverse soil conditions (often caused by inappropriate irrigation), which prevent plants from absorbing available nutrients. With a few exceptions such as fruit trees and woody monocots, avoid routine fertilization. Determine the actual cause of unhealthy plants before taking action. Use laboratory soil or plant tissue tests, where available, to determine the nutrient needs when maintaining many plants or especially valued specimens, as discussed in Chapter 6.

Learn the pattern of moisture your plant is adapted to and provide proper watering. Most plants native to the eastern United States, northern Europe, and eastern Asia require summer irrigation or rainfall. Conversely, except during establishment, avoid summer irrigation of plants adapted to summer drought, such as California oaks and many other native California plants. During years of below-normal rainfall, if supplemental water is needed, these species should generally be irrigated during the normal rainy season. Irrigation at about 1- or 2-month intervals during the dry season may also be appropriate for drought-adapted species in disturbed urban soils, as discussed in Chapter 3. The specific amount and frequency of water needed varies greatly, depending in part on plant species, soil conditions, and the local environment.

FIGURE 5-2. Do not water established trees and shrubs near their trunks, as this promotes root and crown disease. Water plants when needed around the drip line and beyond. Adjust sprinklers or install deflectors to prevent wetting of trunk bases. Move drip emitters away from the base of the trunk after plants are established.

Irrigate when needed near the drip line, not around the trunk (Figure 5-2). Do not let water stand around trunks. If you have irrigation water basins around trunks, break down the mounded soil during the rainy season so that water can drain away. Provide good soil drainage by gently grading soil surfaces, installing subsurface drains or sumps, breaking up compacted soil layers, or sloping the base of compacted subsoils before planting. Instead of planting in a low-lying area, plant in raised beds or on a berm, mound, or ridge of soil (Figure 5-3). Prevent soil compaction, for example, by avoiding traffic under plants, especially when soil is wet.

If plants become damaged by root rot, reduce irrigation. Surface drains can be installed in established landscapes. It may help if the irrigation method is changed from flooding or sprinklers to a drip system. Temporarily remove soil near the base of diseased plants to expose roots and promote drying. Roots some distance away from the trunk are the most functional. Protect newly exposed tissue from direct sun or excessive temperature changes. After drying, cover roots to the same level with the same soil, which has been air dried. Do not wet or compact the earth. Alternatively, for plants adapted to a Mediterranean climate, cover roots around the crown with pea gravel, which provides good drainage

and aeration. Thinning dense lower canopies and eliminating weeds or ground covers beneath plants may help some by reducing humidity beneath plants. Once severe damage symptoms appear, little can be done to save the plant. Remove and dispose of dying trees, which may become hazardous. Correct any soil or water conditions that promote disease and replant with resistant species.

Pruning. Consider pruning and disposing of localized areas of diseased plant tissue as soon as they appear. Pruning to remove infected tissue can stop or slow the spread of certain pathogens, as summarized in Table 5-1. Make pruning cuts in healthy tissue, well below the diseased or infected area. Dispose of diseased prunings away from susceptible plants. Removing some branches, especially in the lower canopy, can reduce the incidence of certain diseases, such as brown rot of stone fruit, by improving air flow and reducing the movement of spores from the ground to the canopy. See Chapter 3 for more discussion on proper pruning.

Sanitation. Rake away and dispose of pathogen-infected plant parts that drop, and prune infected wood as discussed above to help control certain pathogens. Clean soil particles and plant parts off shoes and garden tools and wash your hands before moving to another area

FIGURE 5-3. Avoid planting in a hole or a low-lying area, except when planting in sandy soils. Plant in raised beds or on a ridge or mound of soil several inches high and several feet across in areas where drainage is poor or soil is highly amended and plants will settle as organic matter in the soil decomposes.

after working with diseased plants. Keep implements clean to avoid spreading contaminated soil or pathogens from infected plants. In certain situations, consider sterilizing pruning shears and other equipment with a commercial disinfectant after working on or around plants suspected of pathogen infection.

Disinfectants. Sterilizing pruning shears, tools used to inject or implant pesticides into trunks or roots, and other equipment that contacts internal parts of plants can reduce the likelihood of new infections by pathogens that spread mechanically. Disinfecting pruning shears between cuts is recommended when working on plants infected with fungi that cause Fusarium wilt and pink rot of palms, pitch canker, and sycamore canker stain. Disinfection is also recommended by some experts when pruning plants infected with bacterial gall, fire blight, oleander leaf scorch, and certain other pathogens. The recommended disinfection frequency varies from relatively often (such as after each cut or whenever tools contact discolored plant tissue or exudate from infected plants) to less often (such as when moving between plants).

There is disagreement on the specific situations where disinfecting tools is important in the field, in part because the risk of pathogen spread varies depending on the season and disinfection method. The benefit from disinfecting tools while pruning also depends on the extent to which pathogen propagules contaminate plant surfaces. Even if tools are sterile, pathogens on plant surfaces may sometimes be introduced into wounds when plants are cut during pruning.

Disinfectant efficacy has been relatively well studied for fire blight bacteria. Bleach (sodium hypochlorite) is the only consistently reliable disinfectant for fire blight, and a disinfectant's effectiveness for fire blight provides guidance on its relative effectiveness against other pathogens. Certain other materials are somewhat effective and can be substituted if tool and clothing damage from bleach must be avoided (Table 5-2).

Before chemical disinfection, remove plant material and scrub any plant sap from cutting blades and other tools as these contaminants reduce the effectiveness of disinfectants. Bleach (and to a lesser extent, certain other materials) is effective if squirted onto debris-free tools. Mix a solution of 1 part household bleach with 9 parts of water. At least 1 to 2 minutes of disinfectant contact time between contaminated uses may be required for reliable tool disinfection using other materials. Consider rotating work among several tools, using a freshly disinfected tool while the most recently used tools are being soaked in disinfectant. Promptly rinse, dry, and oil metal equipment and tools following treat-

Localized areas of diseased tissue can be pruned off, and certain modified hand pruners slowly drip disinfectant over blades to help sterilize tools, as shown here. However, there is disagreement on when disinfecting tools is important in the field. For fire blight, at least 1 to 2 minutes of disinfectant contact time between contaminated uses may be required for reliable tool disinfection when using materials other than household bleach.

These white *Ganoderma* species basidiocarps or conks are a sign of disease. However, decay pathogens such as white-mottled heart rot (*G. applanatum*) are usually secondary pests that infect injured or stressed trees.

ments such as bleach that promote rust. Wear proper eye and skin protective equipment when using disinfectants.

Weed and Insect Control. Control weeds, turf, and ground covers near trunks of plants adapted to summer drought by properly using mulch, drought-tolerant plantings, or by maintaining bare soil. Infrequent or light-to-moderate damage by foliage-feeding insects can be tolerated by many landscape plants. However, repeated heavy insect damage that occurs more than once in a growing season or during consecutive years, such as total loss of

TABLE 5-1.

Pathogens That May Be Managed By Pruning.

DISEASE COMMON NAME	SCIENTIFIC NAME	HOSTS	PRUNING METHOD AND TIMING
bacterial blight and canker	*Pseudomonas syringae*	*Prunus* spp.	Prune diseased branches back at least 6 inches into healthy-appearing tissue during dry summer weather.
bacterial gall	*Pseudomonas syringae* pv. *savastanoi*	oleander, olive	Prune and dispose of infected tissue during the dry season. Briefly flame the cut margins with a propane torch.
brown rot or blossom and twig blight	*Monilinia* spp.	*Prunus* spp.	Prune infected branches during winter. Thin canopy to increase air circulation.
Chinese elm anthracnose	*Stegophora ulmea*	Chinese elm	Prune infected branches to the next healthy lateral. Excise small cankers on the trunk and major limbs before they become large by cutting about ½ inch into healthy wood.
cypress canker	*Seiridium cardinale*	See Table 5-13	During hot, dry weather promptly prune dying branches at least 6 inches below any apparent cankers.
Dutch elm disease	*Ophiostoma* spp.	See Table 5-8	If tree is otherwise vigorous and healthy and symptoms are limited to one or a few limbs, promptly prune at least 10 feet back into healthy wood. If more extensive, promptly remove entire tree.
Eutypa canker	*Eutypa lata*	apricot, cherry, grape	Prune at least 1 foot below visible infection. Prune stone fruits during July or August and prune grape late in the dormant season. Immediately flame the cut surface for 5-10 seconds with a propane torch or apply fungicide.
fire blight	*Erwinia amylovora*	apple, crabapple, pear, pyracantha, quince, and others	Prune diseased branches back at least 6 inches into healthy-appearing tissue and remove and dispose of all infected tissue.[2]
leaf gall	*Exobasidium vaccinii*	azalea	Remove galled tissue during summer.
mistletoe, leafy	*Phoradendron* spp.	many deciduous species	Cut infected limbs at least 1 foot below mistletoe attachment point.
oak branch dieback[1]	*Diplodia quercina*	oaks	Prune diseased and dead branches from November through January.
oak twig blight[1]	*Cryptocline cinerescens* and *Discula quercina*	oaks	If infection is limited to a relatively small proportion of the plant canopy, prune in healthy wood below infected twigs during dry weather in the summer or fall.
pitch canker	*Fusarium circinatum*	See Table 5-11	If tree is lightly infected and relatively isolated from other infestations, promptly remove and dispose of infected terminals by cutting well below visibly infected wood. Remove and properly dispose of severely infected conifers.[2]
powdery mildew[1]	*Podosphaera leucotricha*	apple	Prune and dispose of infected shoot tips.
Septoria leaf spot[1]	*Septoria* spp.	many hosts	On deciduous hosts, prune and dispose of infected wood in the fall after leaves drop.
silver leaf	*Chondrostereum purpureum*	*Prunus* spp.	Prune infected branches during late spring to early fall. Make cuts in healthy wood.[2]
shot hole	*Wilsonomyces carpophilus*	*Prunus* spp.	Prune and dispose of infected tissue as soon as it appears. After leaf drop, inspect plants carefully and prune varnished appearing (infected) buds and twigs with lesions.
sycamore anthracnose[1]	*Apiognomonia veneta* or *Discula platani*	See Table 5-6	Prune into previous year's growth to remove and dispose of infected twigs.

TABLE 5-1.

Pathogens That May Be Managed By Pruning *(continued)*.

DISEASE			
COMMON NAME	**SCIENTIFIC NAME**	**HOSTS**	**PRUNING METHOD AND TIMING**
sycamore canker or canker stain	*Ceratocystis fimbriata* f. sp. *platani*	*Platanus* species	Prune sycamore and London plane only during dry weather in December and January. When a tree is found to be infected, remove and dispose of it promptly.[2]
western gall rust	*Endocronartium harknessii*	2- and 3-needle pines in the western U.S.	Prune and dispose of infected branches during October to January, before spring.

Pruning usually is more effective when combined with other methods as discussed in the section on that pathogen elsewhere in this book. Dispose of infected material away from healthy trees.

1. Pruning for these diseases and possibly others is practical only on shrubs and small trees.

2. Carefully clean and sterilize tools before reuse (before making another cut) if they contact discolored tissue or resinous wood.

Adapted from Svihra 1994.

foliage, should be prevented as this can weaken plants and increase their susceptibility to disease.

Soil Solarization. Some soil pathogens can be destroyed or their populations can be reduced by solarization before planting. Cover moist, bare soil with clear plastic for at least 4 to 6 weeks during the sunny, dry part of the year to reduce pathogen numbers near the soil surface, as detailed in Chapter 7. Because solarization is normally effective only to a depth of about 1 foot, this method is primarily used for annual and shallow-rooted plants.

Biological Control. Many naturally occurring organisms kill or retard the growth of pathogens. However, despite their importance, little is known on how to manipulate most of these beneficial microorganisms. For example, suppressive soils contain microorganisms that improve plant growth when added to certain types of pathogen-infested soil. Unfortunately, there are no general recommendations on effectively using suppressive soils in landscapes.

An increasing number of beneficial microorganisms or their by-products are commercially available for use in preventing disease. These include *Ampelomyces quisqualis,* for preventing powdery mildew, and strobilurins, which are effective against many patho-

TABLE 5-2.

Effectiveness of Selected Disinfectants for Preventing Transmission of Fire Blight Bacteria on Cutting Blades.

EFFECTIVE[1]
≥0.5% sodium hypochlorite (≥10% Clorox bleach)

LESS EFFECTIVE[2]
alcohol, isopropyl (undiluted 70–99% rubbing alcohol)[3] pine oil (≥20% Pine-Sol) soap, phenols, alcohol, and other compounds mixed (≥20% Lysol)[3,4]

LEAST EFFECTIVE[5]
dimethyl benzyl ammonium chloride and dimethyl ethylbenzyl ammonium chloride (e.g., Greenshield, Physan) trisodium phosphate (T.S.P. saturated solution or diluted up to 5%)[4]

NOT EFFECTIVE
copper, fixed (cupric hydroxide, 53% metallic copper) streptomycin sulfate (21%)

Plant care professionals and persons conducting pest management for hire should use only disinfectants that are registered pesticides and must employ them as directed on the label.

1. Spraying a debris-free tool or quickly dipping it in ≥10% bleach (≥0.5% sodium hypochlorite) entirely disinfests it of fire blight bacteria. For home use, mix a solution of 1 part household bleach (5% sodium hypochlorite) with 9 parts of water, e.g., 1 cup bleach diluted with 9 cups of water. Bleach can severely damage clothing and metal tools.

2. Soaking debris-free tools for a least 1 minute is the most effective method of using these

disinfectants. Spraying a debris-free tool with this material or quickly dipping the tool in disinfectant is less effective.

3. Lysol concentrated disinfectant, not Lysol cleanser.

4. May cause some rust damage to metal tools.

5. Soaking debris-free tools in these materials for a least 1 minute may disinfect tools, but is not always effective. Spraying or quickly dipping tools with these materials is less effective.

Adapted from Teviotdale 1991, 1992; Teviotdale, Wiley, and Harper 1991.

genic fungi. Crown gall can be prevented from developing in nurseries by dipping roots for 30 seconds in a protective suspension of the biological con-

trol agent *Agrobacterium tumefaciens* 'K-84' or *A. tumefaciens* 'K-1026'. Formerly called *Agrobacterium radiobacter*, these are nonpathogenic strains of the

Many microorganisms are beneficial or innocuous, such as this slime mold (*Fuligo septica*) that occurs in decaying organic matter. If mushrooms or other fungal structures are aesthetically objectionable in mulch (this species is called dog vomit fungus) rake them or (during their gelatinous phase) spray slime molds with a forceful stream of water. Reduce irrigation frequency and periodically mix or stir mulch to reduce fungal development.

A. tumefaciens bacterium that causes crown gall. Consult the specific pathogen sections later in this chapter and *Natural Enemies Handbook* (Flint and Dreistadt 1998) for more information.

Beneficial Microorganisms. Many soil-dwelling microorganisms improve plant growth in ways other than their ability to control pathogens. Many fungi and bacteria break down organic and certain inorganic materials in soil so that nutrients become available for new plant growth. Mycorrhizae are beneficial associations between plant roots and fungi, as discussed in Chapter 3. They improve plants' ability to absorb nutrients, may aid in water uptake, and apparently increase plants' tolerance to drought. Soil-dwelling bacteria convert nitrogen-containing materials into forms that plants can use. Some species of nitrogen-fixing bacteria form nodules on roots, especially roots of plants in the legume family. Determine whether symptoms such as galls on roots are the result of beneficial or harmful organisms before taking control action.

Fungicides and Bactericides. With careful cultural management, at least some cultivars of most landscape plants can be grown at a high level of aesthetic quality with little or no pesticide application. Growing species well-adapted to local conditions, selecting cultivars resistant to disease, and employing cultural and environmental management practices that prevent diseases are generally the most effective strategies; many disease-producing organisms cannot be effectively controlled once plants become infected and symptoms develop or become severe.

Synthetic and organically acceptable pesticides are available to control certain plant pathogens, primarily foliage-infecting fungi. However, because each bactericide or fungicide is effective only against certain types of pathogens, accurate identification of the cause of problems is critical to effective pesticide use. All pesticides for pathogen control also require careful timing to be effective. Many fungicides and most bactericides prevent only the infection of healthy, spray-covered tissue and do not

act systemically to kill pathogens in existing lesions; these are called protectants. Where needed, protectant, or preventive, fungicides should be applied before plants become infected or show symptoms. Curatives (also called eradicants) can kill an existing infection if they are applied at the earliest stages of infection. Repeated applications may be necessary to protect new growth or during prolonged periods that favor disease development. In many landscape situations, fungicides will not effectively control certain types of plant pathogens, such as root rot and vascular wilt pathogens. Even for diseases that are potentially manageable with pesticides (primarily fungal diseases of blossoms, fruit, and leaves), pesticides are infrequently used on large trees because of the application expense, potential for spray drift, and difficulty of achieving good spray coverage.

Several types of fungicides (and a few bactericides) are available for disease control in landscapes, as directed on the product labels. Copper, oil, soap, and sulfur are probably the mostly widely used products on shrubs (such as roses) and small trees (especially fruit trees) in landscapes. Synthetic fungicides include chlorothalonil (an aromatic hydrocarbon) and several sterol biosynthesis inhibitors (myclobutanil, triadimefon, and triforine), which are marketed under various trade (commercial) names. Certain fungicides are available only to professional applicators.

Often, synthetic fungicides are easier to apply, more effective, provide control at lower rates, and are less likely to damage some plants than most "organically acceptable" materials. However, many synthetic fungicides attack pathogens at only one biochemical site (called a single-site mode of action). In comparison with copper, sulfur, and other pesticides that have a multi-site mode of action, pathogenic microorganisms are more likely to develop resistance to bactericides and fungicides with a single-site mode of action, rendering those materials ineffective in certain situations.

Some pest managers or their clients prefer to use organically acceptable pesticides when spraying even though organic regulations apply only to crops. In comparison with synthetic fungicides, many of these "more natural" products, such as botanicals and mycopesticides, are less effective when used alone, but they can work well in IPM programs when combined with cultural practices and environmental modifications. Fungicides organically acceptable in California include botanicals, inorganics, myco-fungicides, oils, and soaps (Table 5-3). Pathogen control is a relatively new use for antitranspirants, bicarbonates, horticultural oil, neem oil, and soaps, some of which are primarily applied to control powdery mildew. Oils and soaps are most often used to control insects and mites, as discussed in Chapter 4. Proper timing of application (usually when symptoms first appear) and thorough spray coverage are especially critical when applying most fungicides.

Botanicals. Plant-derived fungicides include botanical oils such as jojoba and neem oil. Cinnamaldehyde (also called cinnamic aldehyde) discussed in the section "Powdery Mildew" in this chapter, is also plant-derived, but the product used in pesticides is synthesized. Neem oil is extracted from seeds of the tropical neem tree. It is mostly a curative foliar spray, but also has some short-term protectant properties. Neem oil helps to control foliar pathogens, primarily powdery mildew and rusts, on many plants that are small enough to be thoroughly sprayed.

Inorganics. Inorganics include bicarbonates (discussed in the section "Powdery Mildew"), coppers, lime sulfur (calcium polysulfide), and sulfur alone. These have no systemic activity and should be used primarily as protectants. Sulfur is probably the oldest known effective fungicide. Although primarily used against powdery mildews, it is also effective against certain other pathogens, such as rusts and scabs, and it can control mites. Sulfur's effectiveness increases

with increasing temperature, but plant damage may result if temperatures exceed about 85°F. As with other protectants, repeated applications are generally necessary to prevent infection of new growth and to renew deposits removed by rain or irrigation. Thorough plant coverage is needed to obtain control.

Sulfur is available in several forms, including combinations with other ingredients such as soaps. Elemental sulfur is applied as a dust, such as by lightly shaking it from a container onto small plants in the evening or in the morning when they are slightly moist with morning dew. Sulfur is also available as a wettable powder or flowable liquid that is finely ground and mixed with a wetting agent so it readily disperses in water. Micronized sulfur (also called flotation or colloidal sulfur) consists of tiny uniform particles. Before application, it is diluted with water. Micronized or wettable sulfurs often provide better coverage and easier handling than sulfur dust for control of pathogens and mites.

Lime sulfur (calcium polysulfide) is best used as a protectant dormant spray on deciduous plants, such as for peach leaf curl or rose diseases. It also has curative action against certain pathogens, such as powdery mildew. However, lime sulfur can be quite phytotoxic to leaves, and the residue on foliage from certain formulations can be unsightly. Lime sulfur can damage foliage if temperatures exceed about 85°F, and certain plants are affected even below that temperature. Be particularly careful about wearing proper safety equipment when mixing or applying lime sulfur, especially protective eyewear that also shields the brow and temples.

Several types of fungicides have copper as their active ingredient. Fixed copper fungicides include cupric hydroxide, copper oxychloride, and various copper sulfates. Fixed copper fungicides are easier to prepare than Bordeaux (discussed below) and they prevent many of the same foliar bacterial and fungal diseases (Table 5-3). To be effective in preventing infection by certain pathogens such as peach leaf curl, the fixed copper compound must contain

at least 50% copper. Copper fungicides resist weathering because they are only slightly soluble in water and have an ionic attraction to plant surfaces. Although copper compounds are relatively insoluble, small amounts must dissolve to be effective, and this copper can damage plants, especially during cool, wet spring weather. Therefore, most copper fungicides are "fixed coppers," compounds formulated to minimize the amount of copper that dissolves, thereby releasing (dissolving) only the tiniest amounts of copper needed to prevent infection by bacteria and fungi while reducing the risk of phytotoxicity from overexposing plants to copper.

Many copper compounds can leave a visible, sometimes unsightly residue on plants. Copper salts of fatty and rosin acids (also called copper octanoate, copper soaps, or organic copper) control aerial fungi while avoiding the visible residue that commonly results from Bordeaux mixture and fixed coppers.

Bordeaux Mixture. Bordeaux mixture is the oldest copper formulation used as a fungicide. It is named after a famous grape-growing region, where it was discovered in the 1800s by a scientist investigating control of downy mildew threatening French vineyards. Bordeaux mixture is a variable combination of bluestone (copper sulfate) and lime (calcium hydroxide) that must be mixed in a particular way and used soon after preparation. Bordeaux is highly effective at preventing plant infection by many bacteria and fungi. Bordeaux mixture adheres well to plants and persists through extensive rain, making it an excellent choice for pathogen control in California from fall through spring. However, Bordeaux applied to foliage during hot weather or immediately before rain may cause leaves to yellow and drop prematurely. Bordeaux also colors sprayed plants blue and may discolor painted surfaces. If Bordeaux mixture is applied in spring after deciduous plants break dormancy, reduce the risk of phytotoxicity by using a more dilute formula. Alternatively, use fixed copper fungicides when tender plant parts are present. Fixed coppers are more commonly applied in landscapes than Bordeaux, but they are less persistent and do not withstand winter rains as well as Bordeaux mix.

Bordeaux is not easy to prepare and must be mixed fresh shortly before application. Commercially available premixed Bordeaux is less effective and is not recommended. Always wear appropriate personal protective (safety) equipment when mixing and applying Bordeaux, especially eye protection. Triple-rinse the spray equipment when you finish spraying; Bordeaux is corrosive to metal parts. Consult *Bordeaux Mixture Pest Notes* (Donaldson, Olson, and Raabe 2000) for information on preparing and using Bordeaux.

Oils. Certain petroleum-derived and botanical oils can eradicate slight to moderate powdery mildew infections, providing good control. The botanical neem oil is also effective on certain other fungi (Table 5-3). Oils are sometimes formulated into products with other active ingredients, but unless otherwise stated on the label they should not be combined with sulfur or applied within 2 weeks (or longer on certain plants) of applying sulfur due to the risk of phytotoxicity. In addition to neem, other plant-derived oils may be available, such as jojoba oil, which is quite effective at curing powdery mildew. Some botanical oils for home use are not required to be registered as pesticides, and relatively little may be known about their efficacy in comparison with oils registered as pesticides. Botanical oils are also more likely to cause phytotoxicity than petroleum-based narrow-range, supreme, or superior oils.

Mycopesticides. Mycopesticides are commercially available beneficial microorganisms or their by-products that control plant pathogens. They are also called mycofungicides because the most common products target pathogenic fungi. Technically, the name excludes other types of beneficial organisms (such as the bacterium *Agrobacterium,* discussed below) because *myco* is Latin for "fungi."

Mycopesticides have little or no toxicity to nontarget organisms and people. However, there is relatively little information on the efficacy of most of these products in landscapes. In comparison with conventional synthetic pesticides, mycopesticides often require more knowledge and more careful application to use them effectively, and they may be less effective unless used in combination with cultural practices and environmental modifications. Watch for the availability of new products. Currently most mycopesticides are available only through distributors that sell to professional applicators.

The protectants *Agrobacterium tumefaciens* (=*A. radiobacter*) 'K-84' and 'K-1026' are applied to roots before planting, as discussed below in the section "Crown Gall." *Ampelomyces quisqualis* is discussed in the section "Powdery Mildew." *Bacillus subtilis* is a naturally occurring microorganism labeled as a foliar spray for vegetables; for fire blight, powdery mildew, and scab on apple and pear; for gray mold and powdery mildew on grape; and for walnut blight.

Strobilurins. Strobilurins are natural antifungal compounds produced by certain wood decay fungi, including *Strobilurus tenacellus* and *Oudemansiella mucida.* Strobilurins are classified as QoI fungicides because they inhibit (I) fungal respiration at the quinol oxidizing (Qo) site. Strobilurins (such as azoxystrobin and trifloxystrobin) have both curative and protectant efficacy against certain pathogens, but they should be used primarily as protectants because their systemic movement is limited. Because they are very site-specific in their mode of action, certain pathogens have become resistant to them. Any strobilurin use should be limited and alternated with other fungicides with different modes of action, as discussed in Chapter 2 in the section "Pesticide Resistance."

Synthetic Bactericides and Fungicides. Petroleum-derived pesticides include certain oils, cinnamaldehyde, strobilurins that occur naturally but are manufactured for use as pesticides, and the ma-

terials discussed below. Certain synthetic fungicides have systemic activity, so they can control pathogens on plant parts that are not actually covered with spray. Certain materials are both curative and protectant, although most of these are best used only as protectants because they are most effective if applied before pathogen infection or significant disease development. As identified in Table 5-4, some synthetics are "multisite;" they affect more than one type of a pathogen's metabolic processes and therefore are less likely to promote resistance. Others are "single-site;" they have one mode of action, causing them to become ineffective in certain situations because some pathogens have developed resistance to them.

Chlorothalonil. Chlorothalonil is a chlorinated aromatic hydrocarbon that is effective in preventing many fungal disease, but it has little or moderate activity against powdery mildews and no activity against downy mildews. It works by binding fungal proteins, inhibiting spore germination and preventing fungi from infecting plants. As with other protectant fungicides, chlorothalonil needs to be reapplied to plants as it is washed off by rain and irrigation or breaks down. To protect new growth, it needs to be reapplied after new tissue emerges.

EBDC fungicides. Ethylene-bis-dithiocarbamate (EBDC) fungicides include mancozeb and maneb. These protectants resemble chlorothalonil in activity and are used against a wide range of foliar fungal pathogens. EBDCs are not effective against powdery mildews, but they can prevent downy mildew infections.

Fosetyl-al. This organic phosphate fungicide (which is not the same as organophosphate insecticides) is systemic and moves upwards and downwards in the plant, unlike other systemics that usually only move upwards or outwards in the xylem. It is both a protectant and curative and controls fire blight, certain foliar-infecting fungi, and *Phytophthora* and *Pythium* species.

TABLE 5-3.

Selected Botanicals, Inorganics, and Mycopesticides for Pathogen Control.

PESTICIDE (TRADE NAME EXAMPLES)	CURES OR PROTECTS	TYPE	PATHOGENS TARGETED
Agrobacterium tumefaciens =A. radiobacter (Galltrol-A, Nogall)	P	M	crown gall on many hosts, excluding grapes
Ampelomyces quisqualis[1] (AQ-10)	P[2]	M	powdery mildew on grape, rose, and other hosts
Bacillus subtilis[1] (Serenade)	P[2]	M	fire blight, powdery mildew, and scab on apple and pear; powdery mildew on grape; and walnut blight
Bordeaux mixture[3]	P	I	anthracnose, bacterial blight and canker, bacterial and fungal leaf spots, and fire blight on many hosts
copper, fixed, including copper hydroxide (Kocide, Nu-Cop)	P	I	anthracnose, bacterial and fungal leaf spots, fire blight, and others on many hosts
copper, organic or soap (Camelot, Concern Copper Soap)	P	I, S	leaf spots, rusts, and others on many hosts
copper sulfate (Microcop, Phyton 27)	P	I	leaf spots, rusts, and others on many hosts
cinnamaldehyde[1,3] (Cinnacure, Cinnamite, No Mas)	C	B	powdery mildew on rose and certain other hosts
jojoba oil[1,3] (E-Rase)	C	B	powdery mildew on rose and many ornamentals
lime sulfur[3]	P[4]	I	powdery mildew, rusts, and scabs on fruit trees, rose, and certain small trees; peach leaf curl
neem oil (Powdery Mildew Killer, Triact)	C	B	black spot, powdery mildews, and rusts on many hosts
potassium bicarbonate[3] (Armicarb, Kaligreen)	P	I	powdery mildew on shrubs such as grape and rose
soap (M-Pede, Safer)	C	S	powdery mildew on many hosts
sulfur[3] (Bonide Sulfur Plant Fungicide, Green Light Wettable Dusting Sulfur, Safer Garden Fungicide)	P	I	black spot, powdery mildew, rusts, and scabs on fruit trees, roses, and other hosts

KEY

C	curative or eradicant	B	botanical
P	protectant or preventive	I	inorganic
		I, S	copper octanoate or copper salts of fatty and rosin acids
		M	mycopesticide
		S	soap, potassium salts of fatty acids

In comparison with synthetic fungicides (Table 5-4), some of these products are less effective if used alone, but they can work well if applied in an integrated program that includes cultural and environmental controls. All copper and sulfur compounds, and probably all the oils, have multisite modes of action, meaning that they affect two or more biochemical sites in a pathogen. In comparison with the single-site mode of action materials listed in Table 5-4, all these products (including the mycopesticides) are believed to have a low potential for promoting pathogen resistance. Often, materials are for use only on certain landscape plants and are effective only against certain pathogen species, such as some species of anthracnose, powdery mildew, or rust, but not others. Laws, regulations, and information concerning pesticides change frequently. Certain of these materials may not be registered (legal) for use in your situation, or are available only to professional applicators. Consult a current label and the local department of agriculture for details on legal pesticide use.

1. Provide some control, but in comparison to certain other materials (e.g., certain oils or sulfur for powdery mildews) are not as effective.

2. Products are applied as if they are protectants, although technically they may be curative by killing or parasitizing pathogenic fungi.

3. In comparison with other materials, are more likely to cause phytotoxicity to foliage under certain conditions.

4. Primarily applied as protectant during the dormant season, but can also have curative action against certain pathogens.

TABLE 5-4.

Selected Synthetic Bactericides and Fungicides for Pathogen Control.

PESTICIDE (TRADE NAME EXAMPLES)	CURES OR PROTECTS	CLASS[1]	SITE[2]	PATHOGENS TARGETED
azoxystrobin (Heritage), trifloxystrobin (Compass)	P[3,4]	S	single	anthracnose, black spot, downy mildew, leaf spots, powdery mildews, rusts, scabs, and certain others on many species of shrubs and small trees
chlorothalonil (Bravado, Daconil, Ortho Garden Disease Control)	P	AR	multi	black spot, leaf spots, rust, and others on many shrub and small trees
fenarimol (Rubigan A. S.), myclobutanil (Eagle, Immunox), triadimefon[5] (Bayleton, Green Light Fungaway), triforine (Ortho Rose Pride)	C, P	SI	single	black spot and other leaf spots, powdery mildews, rusts, and scabs on certain shrubs and small trees
fosetyl-al (Aliette)	P[3]	OP	multi	bacterial blight, downy mildew on rose, fire blight, and Pythium and Phytophthora root rots on certain shrubs and small trees
mancozeb (Dithane), maneb (Penncozeb)	P	EBDC	multi	black spot, Botrytis blight, leaf spots, petal blights, rust, and others on certain shrubs and small trees including azalea, camellia, crabapple, dogwood, rhododendron, and rose
oil (JMS Stylet Oil, Sunspray)	C	O	multi	powdery mildew on certain hosts including roses
thiophanate-methyl (Cavalier, Cleary's 3336, Zyban)	P[3]	BE	single	black spot, leaf spots, Ovulinia petal blight, powdery mildews, scabs, and others on many trees and shrubs

KEY

C	curative or eradicant	AR	(chlorinated) aromatic	
P	protectant or preventive	BE	benzimidazole or thiophanate[1]	
		EBDC	Ethylene-bis-dithiocarbamate	
		O	narrow-range, supreme, or superior petroleum oil	
		OP	organic phosphate	
		SI	sterol inhibitors, also called demethylation (DMI) inhibitors	
		S	strobilurins, also called Qo inhibitors (QoI)	

1. Bactericides and fungicides belonging to the same chemical class have the same mode of action, so pathogens that develop resistance to one of these pesticides typically are resistant to all pesticides in that class. Because they have the same mode of action, benzimidazole and thiophanate are grouped together here.

2. "Single" materials are active against only one of a pathogen's biochemical sites (called a single-site mode of action). "Multi" materials affect two or more biochemical sites in a pathogen. Pathogens are more likely to develop resistance to pesticides with a single-site mode of action, rendering those materials ineffective in certain situations.

3. Can also have some curative efficacy, but are best applied as protectants, before plant infection and significant disease development.

4. Test for efficacy in your situation before further use; these are relatively new products for woody landscapes.

5. In comparison with other materials, is more likely to cause phytotoxicity to foliage under certain conditions.

Often materials are for use only on certain plants and are effective only against certain pathogen species, such as some species of anthracnose, powdery mildew, or rust, but not others. Laws, regulations, and information concerning pesticides change frequently. Certain of these materials may not be registered (legal) for use in your situation, or are available only to professionals applicators. Consult a current label and the local department of agriculture for details on legal pesticide use.

Benzimidazoles. Thiophanate-methyl is a systemic benzimidazole fungicide that has both protectant and curative activity. It inhibits fungal cell division. Benzimidazoles control many plant pathogenic fungi, but do not control downy mildews or *Phytophthora* and *Pythium* species. Certain fungi have developed resistance to benzimidazoles, which are ineffective against certain pathogen populations, especially Botrytis blights and powdery mildews.

Sterol Biosynthesis Inhibitors. This large class of site-specific fungicides includes fenarimol, myclobutanil, propiconazole, triadimefon, and triforine. These fungicides inhibit fungal sterol synthesis and are effective against mycelium, preventing the proper formation of cell membranes. They are called SI (sterol-inhibiting), SBI (sterol biosynthesis inhibitor), or DMI (sterol demethylation inhibitor) fungicides. SI inhibitors have protectant and curative properties for many fungi, but are not effective against *Phytophthora* or *Pythium* species. Resistance to SI fungicides has developed in certain pathogens.

SYMPTOMS ON FLOWERS, LEAVES, TWIGS, AND STEMS

Many pathogens and environmental conditions cause leaves or twigs to discolor or wilt. Some of these diseases, such as sooty mold, many leaf spots, and certain powdery mildews, are aesthetically displeasing but usually do not cause serious, long-term harm to plants. On the other hand, symptoms on leaves and stems can also be caused by pests (such as wilt and root pathogens and wood-boring insects) that affect the plant's water- and nutrient-conducting tissue; plants with these problems often die. Leaf spots (Table 5-5), cankers (Table 5-10), galls (Table 4-16), and other symptoms can have many different causes. It is important to correctly identify the cause of your unhealthy plants before taking action.

LEAF SPOTS

Leaves can develop discolored blotches, spots, or holes and can die and drop prematurely due to foliar infection by various different pathogens, commonly fungi and occasionally bacteria that spread and infect when plants are wet. Discolored, dying leaves can also be due to other maladies and pests discussed elsewhere in this book, including adverse growing conditions, certain insects, inappropriate cultural practices, and virtually anything that makes limbs or roots unhealthy (Table 5-5). Anthracnose, Entomosporium leaf spot, scabs, Septoria leaf spot, and shot hole are common leaf spotting fungi discussed below.

Anthracnose

Anthracnose, often called bud, leaf, shoot, or twig blight, is a group of diseases resulting from various fungi, including *Colletotrichum*, *Cryptocline*, *Discula*, *Gloeosporium*, *Glomerella*,

TABLE 5-5.

Selected Causes of Leaf Spots.

CAUSE	COMMENTS	SEE PAGE
air pollution	Aggravates other causes if air quality is poor.	293
anthracnose	Many hosts, promoted by moisture during new growth.	223
bacterial blight	Dieback, cankers, and oozing twigs may be associated symptoms.	245
chewing or boring insects	Insects present usually help to identify.	71, 171
Entomosporium leaf spot	Plants in Pomoideae group of the Rosaceae are affected.	227
eriophyid mites	Tiny elongate mites may barely be seen with a hand lens.	203
leaf blisters	California buckeye and oak leaves affected by *Taphrina* fungi if spring is moist.	204
mineral deficiency or toxicity	Some produce characteristic pattern helpful in identifying the cause.	40, 274, 280
pesticide injury	Commonly herbicides, but other pesticides can be the cause.	284
rusts	Orangish or yellowish spore masses, usually on leaf underside or on branches or stems.	240
scabs	Dark, circular, scabby or velvety spots on many hosts.	227
scale insects	Unlike disease causes, scales can usually be scraped off.	130
Septoria leaf spot	Spots mostly older leaves; cankers may develop on poplars.	227
shot hole	Almond, apricot, plum, and other *Prunus* species are affected.	226
spider mites and red mites	May be webbing, foliage speckling, or tiny mites present.	197
sucking insects	May be dark excrement of thrips, lace bugs, or plant bugs.	152–160
sunburn	Yellow or brown area beginning between leaf veins.	288
viruses	Streaked, discolored, or distorted foliage.	268
water deficiency	May begin as yellow or brown area between leaf veins.	34, 273

Gnomonia, *Marssonina*, *Mycosphaerella*, and *Stegophora* species. Anthracnose pathogens infect trees and shrubs throughout the United States. Damage is most severe in areas where prolonged spring rains occur during new growth.

DAMAGE

Anthracnose damage is commonly limited to conspicuous spots or irregular dead areas on leaves and twigs, which may cause foliage to become distorted and drop prematurely. Anthracnose does not seriously harm plants unless defoliation occurs repeatedly or branch dieback or cankering is extensive. Twigs and branches can die on the more susceptible hosts, including some species of ash, elm, dogwood, oak, and sycamore. Cankers—dead areas that may or may

Sycamore anthracnose (*Apiognomonia veneta* or *Discula platani*) kills sycamore shoots and causes leaf tissue to die beginning along veins. Bloodgood sycamore are resistant to anthracnose.

Terminal dieback and partly killed Modesto ash leaves due to ash anthracnose (*Discula fraxinea*). This pathogen can be avoided by selecting another species or cultivar because anthracnose affects only flowering ash (*Fraxinus ornus*) and Modesto ash (*F. velutina* var. *glabra*).

Black leaf spots on Chinese elm leaves caused by Chinese elm anthracnose (*Stegophora ulmea*). This is a problem in California near the coast, where anthracnose cankers on bark can cause limb dieback.

Midvein necrosis of coast live oak leaf infected with oak anthracnose, possibly *Gloeosporium quercuum*.

not be surrounded by callus tissue—can form on twigs or small branches, causing them to become girdled and die. The resulting regrowth from lateral buds can give trees a gnarled or crooked appearance. Chinese elm anthracnose, also called black leaf spot, is one of the most serious anthracnose diseases. It produces especially large cankers, which can weaken, girdle, or kill limbs and trunks, as discussed in the section on canker diseases in this chapter. Dogwood anthracnose cankers frequently affect the lower branches first, causing lower branch dieback and sometimes death of the entire tree.

IDENTIFICATION AND BIOLOGY

Small tan, brown, black, or tarlike spots appear on infected leaves of some hosts, including oak or walnut. Dead leaf areas may be more irregular on other hosts such as ash, birch, elm, or redbud. Maple and sycamore anthracnose lesions typically develop around the major leaf veins. If leaves are very young when infected, they may become curled and distorted, with only a portion of each leaf dying. Affected leaves may look like they have been damaged by frost. Infected dogwood leaves and flower bracts often develop large brownish lesions with well-defined dark discolored margins that may be purple or grayish. Anthracnose-infected leaves usually drop prematurely, but completely blighted leaves may persist on the tree through the winter on some hosts such as dogwood.

Anthracnose fungi overwinter primarily in lesions or cankers on infected twigs on the tree (Figure 5-4). On evergreen species such as California bay, Chinese elm, and live oaks, the fungus can occur year-round on leaves. Spores are produced in the spring and are spread to new growth by splashing rain and windborne rain. If it is moist during the new growth season, these spores germinate and infect new twigs and foliage. More spores are produced and are readily spread to nearby young foliage by raindrops or overhead irrigation.

MANAGEMENT

In areas where prolonged spring rains or foggy conditions are common, plant resistant species and avoid planting especially susceptible species, such as those listed in Table 5-6.

TABLE 5-6.

Relative Susceptibility of Selected Landscape Trees to Anthracnose.

SUSCEPTIBLE	RESISTANT OR LESS SUSCEPTIBLE
Ash (*Fraxinus* spp.) Modesto (*F. velutina* 'Modesto')	Moraine (*F. holotricha* 'Moraine') Raywood (*F. oxycarpa* 'Raywood')
Dogwood (*Cornus* spp.) flowering (*C. florida*): many cultivars Chinese Kousa (*C. kousa* 'Chinensis') Pacific (*C. nuttallii*)	flowering: Spring Grove, Sunset Kousa (*C. kousa*): many cultivars bunchberry (*C. canadensis*) Carnelian cherry (*C. mas*) Japanese cornel (*C. officinalis*)
Chinese elm (*Ulmus parvifolia*)[1] Evergreen, True Green	Drake
Privet (*Ligustrum* spp.)[2] Common privet (*L. vulgare*)	Amur (*L. amurense*) Ibota (*L. obtusifolium*) Regal (*L. obtusifolium* 'Regelianum')
Sycamore (*Platanus* spp.) London plane (*P. acerifolia*): Yarwood[3] American sycamore (*P. occidentalis*) California sycamore (*P. racemosa*)	London plane: Bloodgood, Columbia, Liberty

1. All cultivars appear resistant in warm interior areas of California where Chinese elm anthracnose is uncommon.

2. *Glomerella cingulata* severely blights and cankers common privet in the eastern United States. It infects other hosts in California but is not common or does not occur on privet.

3. Yarwood is largely undamaged by anthracnose if pollarded regularly.

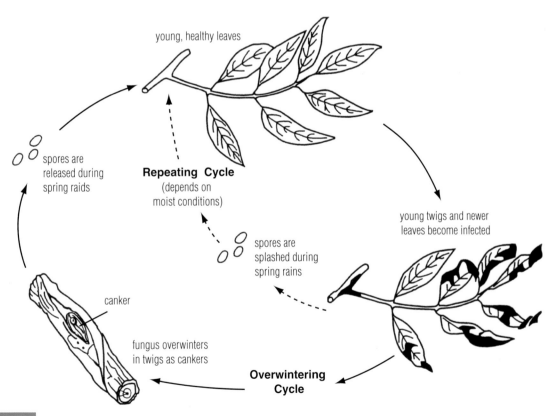

FIGURE 5-4. Anthracnose disease cycle illustrated with *Discula fraxinea* infecting Modesto ash. By V. Winemiller from Gouveia, Ohlendorf, and Flint 1999.

Prevent sprinklers from wetting foliage, as wetting leaves promotes anthracnose. Prune and dispose of infected twigs during the fall or winter where practical (such as on small trees) to help control anthracnose. For example, although highly susceptible to anthracnose, Yarwood London plane is usually undamaged if pollarded regularly because overwintering infections are pruned off. Rake up and dispose of fallen leaves during the growing season and during fall. Do not use mulch around hosts of anthracnose if the material contains leaves or flowers from plants susceptible to that same anthracnose. Increasing sunlight and air circulation (for example, by pruning nearby plants that provide shade) and avoiding drought stress can reduce the severity of anthracnose infecting dogwood and possibly other hosts.

Fungicides have not been found to be effective in controlling anthracnose on elm, oak, or sycamore in California, but certain fungicides help to prevent anthracnose on dogwood and Modesto ash if thoroughly sprayed on all new growth as buds begin to open in the spring. If moist weather prevails, additional applications may be needed at intervals of about 2 weeks to protect newly exposed growth. Repeated fungicide applications for anthracnose control usually are not appropriate on other hosts. See *Anthracnose Pest Notes* (Gouveia, Ohlendorf, and Flint 1999) for specific fungicide recommendations.

Shot Hole
Wilsonomyces carpophilus

Shot hole, also called coryneum blight, affects *Prunus* species such as almond, Catalina cherry, peach, and plum. Apricot is especially susceptible. It causes discolored spots on buds, leaves, shoots, and fruit. Lesions on fruit can become rough and corky or scabby. Holes can appear in affected leaves, and foliage may drop prematurely. Concentric lesions may develop on branches. Severe mineral deficiency, injuries, insects, chemical damage, and viruses can cause similar leaf symptoms on some *Prunus* species such as Japanese flowering cherry (Table 5-5). However, most holes in leaves are caused by chewing insects (see Chapter 4).

Shot hole first appears in the spring as reddish, purplish, or brown spots about $\frac{1}{10}$ inch in diameter on new buds, leaves, and shoots. The spots expand and their centers turn brown. Tiny dark specks, visible only with a hand lens, form in the brown centers, especially on buds; these dark specks, the spores of the fungus, help to distinguish shot hole from other diseases. Spots on young leaves have a narrow, light green or yellow margin, and their centers often fall out as leaves expand, leaving holes. Leaves may fall from the tree. Fruit spotting may occur, usually on the upper surface.

The disease is most severe following warm, wet winters and when wet weather is prolonged in the spring after leaves develop. The fungus survives the dormant season inside infected buds and in twig lesions. Spores are spread by splashing rain or irrigation water, which also promote spore germination.

MANAGEMENT

Sprinklers or overhead irrigation that wets foliage increase the severity of shot hole. Use low-volume, drip irrigation systems instead. Alternatively, keep water pressure low, redirect nozzles, use sprinkler deflectors, and prune lower branches to prevent foliage from getting wet.

Prune and dispose of infected tissue as soon as it appears. After leaf drop, inspect plants carefully and prune varnished-appearing (infected) buds and twigs with lesions. Diligent sanitation and water management can provide adequate control where the incidence of shot hole is low. Bordeaux mixture or fixed copper can be applied where disease incidence or plant aesthetic value is high. When applying a copper-containing compound, make one application of a material that is at least 50% copper after leaf drop (to avoid phytotoxicity) and before fall rains begin. Additional treatment in late winter before buds swell or between full bloom and petal fall or both times may be necessary on severely infected apricot or if prolonged wet weather occurs in the spring. Some synthetic fungicides are also effective and avoid potential copper damage to fruit.

Discolored, scabby spots on fruit and holes in these apricot leaves are characteristic of shot hole fungus, which is promoted by moisture. Other causes of similar holes in *Prunus* species leaves include severe mineral deficiency, insects, injuries, and viruses.

Septoria Leaf Spot

Septoria spp.

Several dozen *Septoria* species occur in the United States, each on a different group of closely related hosts. *Septoria* causes round or angular, flecked, sunken, or irregular spots on mostly older leaves. Aspen, azalea, cottonwood, hebe, and poplar are commonly infected. Some *Septoria* species are the conidial stages of *Mycosphaerella* species, such as *Septoria populicola* (also called *Mycosphaerella populicola*), which causes leaf spots and cankers (Septoria canker) on the branches of certain severely infected *Populus* species.

The biology and management of *Septoria* is similar to that of anthracnose, as discussed above. Prune and dispose of infected wood in the fall after leaves drop from deciduous hosts. Reduce splashing water and humidity if possible.

Entomosporium causes reddish spots, sometimes surrounded by a yellow halo; spots darken and enlarge as leaves mature, like these on rhaphiolepis. Switching from overhead sprinkling to drip irrigation greatly reduces this problem in many situations.

Entomosporium Leaf Spot

Entomosporium mespili

Entomosporium spots the leaves of most plants in the Pomoideae group of the rose family. This pathogen was formerly called *Entomosporium maculatum,* and during one phase of its development it is named *Diplocarpon mespili.* Hosts of Entomosporium leaf spot include apple, crabapple, evergreen pear, hawthorn, loquat, pear, photinia, pyracantha, quince, *Rhaphiolepis,* serviceberry, and toyon.

Tiny reddish spots, sometimes surrounded by a dark red, purple, or yellow halo, appear on the leaves of infected plants. These spots darken and enlarge as the leaves mature. Spore-forming bodies eventually appear in the center of the spots; these cream-colored specks may appear to be covered with a glossy membrane, beneath which white masses of spores are visible.

Fungi infecting deciduous plants overwinter mainly as spores or mycelia within tissue on fallen leaves. On ever-green hosts, the fungi may remain on leaves year-round. Fungi are spread from infected tissue or contaminated leaf litter to healthy leaves by splashing raindrops or overhead irrigation. The pathogens are most severe during wet weather, especially when it coincides with new plant growth.

Remove and dispose of spotted leaves that are on plants or have fallen. Do not water overhead, as this spreads the fungus spores and favors infection. Consider removing ground covers beneath infected shrubs and mulching or maintaining bare soil instead. Where the problem is severe, a copper fungicide or certain other materials can greatly reduce damage if thoroughly sprayed on plants before they are damaged.

Scabs

Venturia spp.

Fungal scabs include over one dozen *Venturia* species, which during their conidial (asexual) stage are given other generic names including *Fusicladium* and *Spilocaea.* Fungal scabs affect many hosts in

Leaf veins limit the spread of the Septoria leaf spot fungus (*Mycosphaerella populorum*), so some of these dead patches on poplar have angular edges.

Circular, scabby spots on toyon leaves caused by *Spilocaea photinicola*. This malady is favored by wet spring weather. It apparently does not threaten plant health and little can be done to prevent this disease when weather favors its development in landscapes.

Oak twig blight caused scattered patches of dead leaves on current-season growth of this coast live oak. Other pathogens and certain insects cause similar damage, so correctly determine the cause before attempting any control.

California, including apple, loquat, manzanita, olive, pear, photinia, pyracantha, *Rhamnus*, toyon, and willow. Maple and poplar are additional important hosts in the Midwest and northeastern United States. Olive green to black, circular, scabby or velvety spots appear on infected leaves, which may yellow or redden and drop prematurely. Scabby spots, often more sunken, may appear on fruit, which may crack or shrivel and drop. Shoots may die back if disease is severe.

Scab fungi on deciduous hosts overwinter primarily on fallen leaves; on evergreen hosts the pathogen persists on fruit and leaves on the plant as well as on fallen leaves. Spores develop on infected tissue and are forcibly discharged into the air, usually in the spring. Airborne spores infect host leaves and fruit when they are wet. Mild temperatures and high humidity promote disease development, which is arrested by hot, dry weather.

Remove and dispose of fallen leaves in the fall. Fall foliar fertilizer (urea) applications on deciduous hosts hasten leaf drop and promote leaf decomposition, reducing the number of spores in spring. Avoid overhead sprinkling or irrigate early in the day so that foliage dries more quickly. Prune branches to thin canopies, which improves air circu-

lation and reduces humidity. Sulfur applied about weekly to foliage during the rainy season before disease develops, or some synthetic fungicides, may prevent the disease, but chemical control is generally not warranted except where the disease is severe on apple or pear fruit. See publications such as *Apple Scab Pest Notes* (Ohlendorf and Flint 2001) for more information.

Oak Branch and Twig Death

Oak branches or twigs (and their leaves) can die from many causes, including Armillaria root rot, oak twig girdler, Phytophthora root rot, and sudden oak death. Oak leaves can also be partly or entirely killed by anthracnose fungi, certain gall wasps, and other maladies as summarized in the "Tree and Shrub Pest Tables" at the end of this book.

Oak branch dieback and oak twig blight are similar fungal diseases that are discussed below. Oak branch dieback kills larger woody plant parts (small branches), while oak twig blight usually affects only twigs. Entire large limbs are rarely, if ever, killed by either malady,

while *Armillaria* and *Phytophthora* species will kill large limbs or entire trees.

Oak twig blight is associated with wetter years and oak pit scale, while oak branch dieback is more prevalent during and after periods of drought. Both diseases may become more prevalent when trees are stressed from environmental conditions. Often certain oaks will exhibit damage from either oak branch dieback or oak twig blight while nearby oaks appear unaffected. Differences in oaks' ability to withstand stressful conditions can be influenced by the extent to which nearby human activities injure trees, especially by altering the belowground (root zone) environment.

Oak Branch Dieback
Diplodia quercina

Oak branch dieback occurs on several oak species in California, including black oak, coast live oak, English oak, and valley oak. It causes leaves to turn tan or brown and to wilt on some oak species. Infected small branches die in scattered patches throughout the tree canopy. If the bark is peeled back, infected wood is usually dark brown to black.

Prevent branch dieback by protecting trees from injury and providing proper cultural care. Drought stress appears to contribute greatly to this disease. Even drought-adapted species may require supplemental irrigation if rainfall has been below normal. However, irrigation of native oaks should generally be done during the normal rainy season to supplement inadequate natural rainfall. Oaks in disturbed urban soils may also benefit from irrigation around the drip line (not near the trunk) at about 1- or 2-month intervals during the dry season. The specific amount and frequency of irrigation varies greatly, depending on factors such as environmental and soil conditions. Frequent irrigation during the dry season promotes serious oak root diseases, such as Armillaria root rot discussed later in this chapter.

Prune diseased and dead branches from November through January; new infections are least likely to occur during that time. Fungicides generally do not provide effective control. The disease is not likely to be a problem in most years, and control is usually not needed, especially if trees are cared for properly. For more information, consult *Twig Blight and Branch Dieback of Oaks in California* (Costello, Hecht-Poinar, and Parmeter 1989).

Oak Twig Blight
Cryptocline cinerescens and *Discula quercina*

Oak twig blight affects primarily coast live oak, but it may also occur on other oak species. It is sporadic in occurrence and is caused by two fungi, *Cryptocline cinerescens* and *Discula quercina*. Leaves and twigs from the current season's growth turn white or tan and remain on the tree, often in scattered patches throughout the tree canopy. Oak twig blight has been found to be more severe on trees infested with oak pit scale and is apparently more prevalent during years with greater rainfall.

Provide infected trees with adequate cultural care, especially appropriate watering. Avoid irrigating native oaks during the dry season; irrigate during the winter if needed because rainfall has been below normal. Proper pruning may help to control the disease, but this may be feasible only for a few small or specimen trees with limited infections. Prune infected twigs during dry weather in the summer or fall; make pruning cuts properly (Figure 3-9) in tissue below infected twigs. Some systemic fungicides provide control if applied within 1 week after pruning. Fungicides alone are not as effective. Dead twigs and leaves remain on the tree for 2 or 3 years, and the tree's appearance does not improve until these drop or are pruned out.

Fire Blight
Erwinia amylovora

Fire blight is caused by a bacterium that infects only plants in the pome tribe of the rose family. Pear and quince are extremely susceptible. Apple, crabapple, and pyracantha are frequently damaged. Other hosts include cotoneaster, hawthorn, loquat, mountain ash (*Sorbus* spp.), serviceberry, spirea, and toyon.

DAMAGE

Fire blight causes a sudden wilting, shriveling, and blackening or browning of shoots, blossoms, and fruit. Rapid infection of extensive portions of the plant gives it a scorched appearance, hence the name "fire blight." Dead leaves remain attached when twigs are killed quickly. Cankers can form on twigs and branches, which die back. Prolonged serious infections can kill some plants, such as pear.

IDENTIFICATION AND BIOLOGY

Fire blight bacteria infect new growth through flowers during the spring (Figure 5-5). During warm, wet, or humid weather, brownish droplets containing the bacteria ooze from around cankers if infected limbs are left unpruned in trees

though the winter. These bacteria are spread to flowers by many species of flying or crawling insects. Once flowers are infected, bees and splashing water can spread the bacteria from one flower to another. Infection occurs through the blossoms and slowly spreads throughout twigs and terminal branches. The bacteria overwinter in plant tissue around cracked, sunken cankers in bark. Diagnose fire blight by peeling back bark around cankers and newly infected twigs and branches; inspect the wood, which turns reddish brown when newly infected. Once tissue dies (which can happen quickly) it turns black.

MANAGEMENT

Manage fire blight by growing resistant cultivars and maintaining plants in an appropriate range of vigor. Regularly inspect host plants for infections. Use good sanitation and remove blighted wood. If fire blight has previously been a problem, consider applying fungicide during blossoming.

Plant cultivars such as Prairie Fire crabapple and Bradford or Chanticleer ornamental pear, which are less susceptible to fire blight than some other ornamental pome trees. Capitol and Red Spire in California are also less susceptible, but they are reported as susceptible to fire blight in some places in the eastern United States. Avoid Aristocrat, which is highly susceptible. Avoid excess irrigation and overfertilization of infected plants. Vigorously growing shoots are most severely infected, so conditions that favor rapid plant growth can increase the severity of damage.

Eliminate fire blight by pruning diseased branches back at least 8 to 12 inches into healthy-appearing tissue and removing and disposing of all infected tissue. It may be necessary to make cuts even further back into apparently healthy tissue when pruning major branches or making cuts during about May and June, when blight bacteria are moving rapidly. If fire blight occurs on the trunk or a major limb, the wood sometimes can be saved by scraping off bark down to the cambium in infected areas (i.e., removing

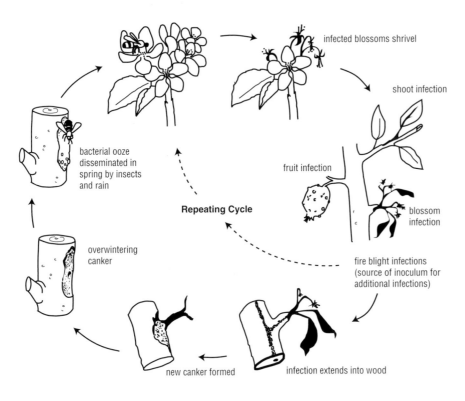

FIGURE 5-5. Fire blight disease cycle. The pathogen persists in infected wood. It infects new growth through flowers during the spring when the bacteria are spread by insects or splashing water. By V. Winemiller from Ohlendorf and Flint 1999.

Fire blight caused this pear blossom and terminal to suddenly wilt, blacken, and die. Most susceptible ornamental species have certain cultivars that are resistant to fire blight.

both inner and outer bark). Look for and remove any long, narrow infections that may extend beyond the canker margin. Prune when plants are dry to minimize the risk of mechanically spreading the bacteria. Consider disinfecting tools by dipping them in a solution of ≥10% bleach (about 0.5% sodium hypochloride produced by diluting 1 part bleach in 9 parts water) or possibly another commercial disinfectant (Table 5-2) whenever tools come into direct contact with diseased tissue and periodically throughout pruning, especially if conditions are damp. Dry and oil tools after use to minimize rust.

A very weak (about ½%) Bordeaux mixture, other copper fungicide, or certain synthetic fungicides applied several times as blossoms open can reduce the incidence of new infections but will not eliminate existing infections. Make the first application when the first blossoms

appear and the average temperature [(minimum + maximum)/2] over a 24-hour period exceeds 60° F. Repeat the application at 4- to 5-day intervals throughout bloom if conditions are humid or rainy. Fungicide treatments after bloom are not effective. Depending on conditions, fungicidal control may require as many as 12 applications per season on pear. Such frequent applications are rarely, if ever, warranted in landscapes. The copper fungicides themselves can cause scarring or russetting of fruit and the risk of phytotoxicity increases as fruits enlarge. For more information, consult *Fire Blight Pest Notes* (Ohlendorf and Flint 1999) or *Integrated Pest Management for Apples and Pears* (Ohlendorf 1999).

Bacterial Leaf Scorch and Oleander Leaf Scorch
Xylella fastidiosa

Scorch of oleander in California is caused by *Xylella fastidiosa*, a xylem-infecting bacterium spread by certain leafhoppers. It has been reported in southern California and some other southwestern states and it is spreading. Other strains of *Xylella fastidiosa* are the cause of Pierce's disease in grapes, almond leaf scorch, and *Xylella*-related maladies in other crops; the strain of *X. fastidiosa* that causes oleander leaf scorch does not cause Pierce's disease or these other crop maladies.

Ash, elm, maple, mulberry, oak, and sycamore are among the landscape plants exhibiting leaf scorch and branch and twig dieback from *Xylella* bacteria in the eastern United States. Liquidambar, olive, and ornamental plum are among the plants in California that may develop leaf scorch and dieback due to infection by *Xylella* bacteria. The relationships among species of leafhopper vectors, host plants, and pathogenic *Xylella* strains are not fully understood. The strain of *X. fastidiosa* that causes oleander scorch may infect and cause symptoms in certain other plants in California, such as those in the same family (Apocynaceae), including periwinkle (*Vinca* sp.). Various strains of *X. fastidiosa* (including the strain damaging oleander) can also occur in certain plant species without causing symptoms in those hosts.

DAMAGE

Margins or tips of scorch-infected leaves turn yellow, brown, dry out, and eventually die. Initially only portions of individual leaves and scattered parts of plants appear affected. Symptoms can appear at any time of the year but develop most rapidly when weather becomes warm. Where different cultivars are planted together, such as oleanders of different flower color, initial symptoms may be more severe on certain cultivars than others. Some infected plants survive only 1 to 2 years after first showing symptoms, while other oleanders can survive for 3 to 5 years and possibly longer.

IDENTIFICATION AND BIOLOGY

Glassy-winged sharpshooter (*Homalodisca coagulata*) is the primary vector of oleander leaf scorch. Blue-green sharpshooter (*Graphocephala atropunctata*), smoke tree sharpshooter (*Homalodisca lacerta*), and possibly other leafhopper species can also spread *Xylella fastidiosa*. These leafhoppers, some of which are called sharpshooters, spread the bacteria when they move after feeding on infected plants to feed on healthy host plants. The bacteria introduced by infective sharpshooters spread and reproduce in xylem tissue, damaging or eventually killing susceptible, infected hosts.

An ELISA test for confirming presence of *Xylella fastidiosa* is available from some diagnostic laboratories. Managers of large numbers of oleanders or other host plants in areas where the pathogen has not been reported may find ELISA testing useful for reliably distinguishing oleander scorch damage from other causes of similar symptoms, including pesticide phytotoxicity, salt burn, severe drought, or dieback caused by *Phoma exigua*. The cause of damage may also be distinguished by applying remedies for these

Yellow, brown, dying leaf margins are symptoms of bacterial leaf scorch vectored by leafhoppers and infecting this oleander. A laboratory ELISA test can distinguish this pathogen from causes of similar damage, including phytotoxicity, salt burn, and severe drought.

other potential causes and observing whether plants improve. For example, providing adequate irrigation relieves drought stress, and sprinkling plants and leaching soil with water low in salts reduces salt toxicity symptoms, but these methods do not restore plants damaged by oleander scorch.

MANAGEMENT

There is no known cure for *Xylella*-infected plants. Some oleander cultivars appear to succumb more slowly that others, so it may be possible to develop scorch-resistant oleanders. Consider gradually replacing extensive oleander plantings with a mixture of nonhost plants, especially if this disease occurs in your area. Consult *Oleander Leaf Scorch Pest Notes* (Wilen et al. 2000) for other management suggestions.

Severely pruning oleanders and disposing of infected plant parts may temporarily suppress symptoms in some infected oleanders and regrowth may initially appear healthy. However, pruning will not cure the disease and symptoms and damage will reappear. To avoid spreading pathogens on infested tools,

clean debris from tools after using them on each plant, then thoroughly spray tools with disinfectant or soak tools in disinfectant for 1 minute or more, as discussed earlier (Table 5-2).

Controlling leafhoppers as discussed in the chapter "Insects, Mites, and Snails and Slugs" may help slow pathogen spread, but control actions must be repeated and at most may be only partially effective. Eliminate weeds, which can host leafhopper-vectored pathogens and leafhoppers that can migrate to crops or landscape plants. Where possible, avoid planting alternative hosts of the leafhopper species that vector *Xylella fastidiosa*. Because these leafhoppers have broad ornamental hosts ranges (for example, glassy-winged sharpshooter hosts include eucalyptus and oaks, and blue-green sharpshooter feeds on many shrubs and grasses), it may not be feasible to manage these leafhoppers by eliminating host plants until more is known about this problem.

Pesticide spraying by homeowners will not prevent oleander scorch, and applications by homeowners are not recommended. Systemic insecticides are unlikely to protect individual plants from infection, especially where leafhoppers are abundant. When managing large groups of valued oleanders, certain systemic insecticides applied to control leafhoppers may slow the rate of pathogen spread if all nearby hosts are treated before oleander become infected, insecticide is periodically reapplied, and infected plants are promptly removed as they appear. Infection-delaying treatments may be worth considering only when combined with a program to replace oleanders with alternative, nonhost plants. Treatments are relatively expensive and are rarely warranted in comparison with the value of oleanders in low-maintenance landscapes. For more information, consult publications such as *Oleander Leaf Scorch Pest Notes* (Wilen et al. 2000) and *Glassy-Winged Sharpshooter Pest Notes* (Phillips, Wilen, and Varela 2001) and Web sites such as http://danr.ucop.edu/news/MediaKit/ GWSS.shtml

Verticillium Wilt
Verticillium dahliae

Many deciduous trees, shrubs, and herbaceous plants are susceptible to infection by Verticillium wilt fungi. Common hosts include ash, camphor, Chinese pistache, fuchsia, hebe, maple, olive, pepper tree, and rose.

DAMAGE

Verticillium wilt, along with Fusarium wilt and Dutch elm disease, discussed in the next sections, and sycamore canker stain, discussed in the section "Canker Diseases," affect a plant's vascular system, the network of phloem and xylem tissue that transports nutrients, food, and water among plant parts. By interfering mainly with xylem tissue, these vascular wilt diseases cause foliage to turn faded green, yellow, or brown, and wilt in scattered portions of the canopy or on scattered branches.

Shoots and branches die, often beginning on one side of the plant, and entire plants may die.

Small plants may or may not die from Verticillium wilt in a single season, but in larger plants the disease spreads slowly. Mature trees may take many years to die and may suddenly recover if conditions become favorable for plant growth and poor for disease development.

IDENTIFICATION AND BIOLOGY

The survival structures of the Verticillium wilt fungus (microsclerotia) reside in the soil. When it is cool and roots are present, microsclerotia germinate and hyphae grow. Hyphae infect susceptible plants through roots, then spread upward in the current year's growth, blocking the plant's ability to transport nutrients and water. In some but not all plants, peeling back the bark on newly infected branches may reveal dark streaks following the wood grain. Depending on the plant species, the stains are dark gray, black, brownish, or greenish. A laboratory cul-

Dark staining, which is visible when stem and trunk tissue is cut in cross-section, is characteristic of Verticillium wilt and certain other vascular wilt diseases.

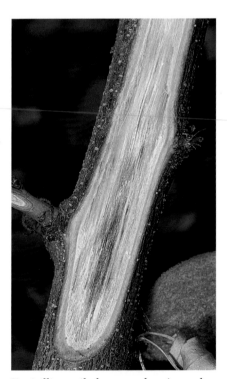

Verticillium wilt damages plants' vascular tissue; peeling back the bark on newly infected branches may reveal dark stains following the grain, as seen on this almond wood.

Brown, dead foliage in scattered patches on one side of a Japanese maple due to Verticillium wilt.

ture from newly infected wood is often required to confirm the presence of Verticillium wilt fungus. Infection can occur during the spring but does not become apparent until warm weather, when plants are more stressed.

MANAGEMENT

Keep plants vigorous by providing for their cultural requirements. Provide infected trees with proper irrigation, modest amounts of slow-release fertilizer, and other appropriate care to promote new growth and increase their chances of survival. Chronic branch dieback may develop in surviving trees; prune any dead wood. Regularly inspect for possible hazards: affected trees may need to be removed. Where Verticillium wilt has been a problem, plant only resistant species, such as those listed in Table 5-7.

Solarization can reduce *Verticillium* and *Fusarium* fungi in the upper few inches of soil in areas with sunny weather. This may help during the establishment of young woody plants, but because roots of perennial plants eventually grow outside the treated zone, this method is most effective for annual plants. When solarizing before replanting, cover bare, moist soil with clear plastic for about 4 to 6 weeks during warm, sunny weather, as discussed in the section "Solarization" in Chapter 7.

Fusarium Wilt
Fusarium oxysporum

Fusarium wilt affects relatively few woody ornamental species but can kill certain hosts, including albizia, date palm, hebe, and pyracantha. Most forms of *Fusarium oxysporum* attack only herbaceous plants. Fusarium wilt symptoms often appear first on one side of a plant. Older leaves usually die first in infected plants, commonly followed by death of the entire plant. Cutting into infected wood may reveal that vascular tissue has turned brown, often all the way from the shoot to the soil line.

TABLE 5-7.

Landscape Trees and Shrubs Resistant to Verticillium Wilt.

COMMON NAME	SCIENTIFIC NAME
apple and crabapple	*Malus* spp.[1]
arborvitae	*Thuja* spp.
beech	*Fagus* spp.
birch	*Betula* spp.
box and boxwood	*Buxus* spp.
California bay	*Umbellularia californica*
citrus	*Citrus* spp.
cedar	*Thuja* spp.
dogwood	*Cornus* spp.
eucalyptus	*Eucalyptus* spp.
European mountain ash	*Sorbus aucuparia*
fig, edible	*Ficus carica*
fir	*Abies* spp.
hawthorn	*Crataegus* spp.
holly	*Ilex* spp.
honey locust	*Gleditsia* spp.
hornbeam	*Carpinus* spp.
katsura tree	*Cercidiphyllum japonicum*
linden	*Tilia* spp.
manzanita	*Arctostaphylos* spp.
mulberry	*Morus* spp.
oak	*Quercus* spp.
oleander	*Nerium oleander*
pine	*Pinus* spp.
palms	All genera
pear	*Pyrus* spp.[1]
pyracantha	*Pyracantha* spp.
spruce	*Picea* spp.
sweet gum	*Liquidambar styraciflua*
sycamore, plane tree	*Platanus* spp.
walnut	*Juglans* spp.
western sycamore	*Platanus racemosa*
willow	*Salix* spp.

This list provides a guideline only; there is no guarantee that these plants will not be affected. New pathogen strains develop or are introduced. Disease incidence is greatly influenced by cultural care and environmental conditions.

1. Apple, pear, and quince are susceptible to European strains of *Verticillium albo-atrum* not reported in California.

Adapted from Farr et al. 1989; McCain, Raabe, and Wilhelm 1981.

Fusarium species are divided into various special forms (*forma specialis,* or f. sp.), subspecies or populations that are physiologically distinct but morphologically indistinguishable. Each f. sp. of *Fusarium* is specific to certain hosts and does not spread to infect plants in other genera. Several f. sp. of *F. oxysporum* and other *Fusarium* spp. (including *F. lateritium* and *F. solani*) cause non-wilt diseases, including root rot of Douglas fir and pines, especially in the Pacific Northwest, and branch cankers and twig dieback of many deciduous woody hosts, mostly in the eastern United States.

Fusarium wilt results from infection through roots by hyphae that germinate from long-lasting survival structures (chlamydospores) in the soil. Avoid this problem by replanting at that site using species from different genera than plants previously infected there by *Fusarium.* Provide proper cultural care and management, as described above for Verticillium wilt. Avoid using undecayed organic amendments and excessive fertilizer, especially urea, which may promote development of *Fusarium.*

Fusarium Wilt of Palms

Fusarium oxysporum f. sp. *canariensis* is highly pathogenic to Canary Island date palm (*Phoenix canariensis*). Only *Phoenix* species in landscapes have been reported infected in California. New growth is often stunted. Fronds on *Fusarium*-infected palms die more rapidly and more extensively than normal. Older, lower fronds die first, sometimes so rapidly that only a few surviving fronds remain, forming a green spike at the top of the tree. Fusarium wilt often causes vascular discoloring and the pinnae or spines often are dead on one side of the frond while the other side is alive. Vascular discoloring can be observed on the wet and clean surface of cut fronds. A *Dothiorella* species also causes one-sided frond death and vascular browning. Only a laboratory test on a section of

partially alive rachis (the central frond axis or stem) can confirm *Fusarium* presence. *Fusarium*-infected palms also become very susceptible to certain other pathogens, especially pink rot, as discussed later.

Fusarium-infected palms will die. Promptly remove and dispose of infected trees to reduce pathogen spread to nearby palms. Remove as much of the root ball as possible if there are other susceptible palms nearby. Plant only pathogen-free palms. The fungus can persist in soil for many years. Do not plant date palms where Fusarium wilt has been a problem; consider avoiding all palms at that site.

Fusarium oxysporum spreads by contaminated pruning tools, movement of infected plants and infested soil, and root contact among nearby susceptible palms. Assume that every palm is a source of the fungus. Clean pruning tools and other equipment that may contact infected tissue, then sterilize them with bleach, as discussed earlier in the sanitation section, before moving to work on another palm. Avoid using climbing spikes on palms. Clean and sterilize climbing spikes after each tree if they are used. Do not use chain saws on date palms because sterilizing chain saws is impractical. Use reciprocating power saws or hand tools because these can be readily sterilized. Do not transport soil from around palms to other sites where palms grow.

Provide palms with optimal growing conditions, including appropriate water and nutrients. Ensure proper nutrition, such as by applying special palm fertilizers or magnesium and potassium where needed; palms are often deficient in these minerals.

Dutch Elm Disease

Dutch elm disease fungus in California killed about 3,000 elms in the San Francisco Bay Area from 1975 to 1990 and fewer elms in the Sacramento area; millions of elms have been killed in the

Midwest and eastern states since 1930. The disease is caused by a complex of closely related *Ophiostoma* species fungi, including *Ophiostoma* (=*Ceratocystis*) *ulmi* and *O. novo-umli.*

The symptoms of Dutch elm disease usually appear first in only one portion of the canopy, resulting in yellow or wilting foliage. The dead leaves curl and turn brown but remain on branches. Peeling back the bark reveals brown to blackish streaks in the wood, which appear as dark concentric rings when infected branches are cut in cross-section. Do not confuse disease symptoms with the leaf discoloring caused by the elm leaf beetle. Elm leaf beetle chews holes and skeletonizes leaves, which may then become discolored, often giving the tree a brown appearance when viewed from some distance. Elms suspected of being infected with Dutch elm disease in California should be reported to the county department of agriculture for confirmation of the disease.

Dutch elm disease is spread long distances primarily by the European elm bark beetle (see Chapter 4). Beetles emerge from dead or dying trees or from elm logs infected with the fungus, carrying spores that infect healthy trees when the adult beetles feed in the crotch of young twigs. People inadvertently assist this spread by moving infected elm logs to disease-free areas and by storing wood from infected trees. The fungi can also spread from infected elms through root grafts to nearby elms.

MANAGEMENT

American and European elm species are adapted to summer rainfall. Maintain tree vigor by providing adequate summer irrigation in areas with summer drought. Prune elms only from late fall through winter to avoid creating fresh wounds that attract disease-spreading elm bark beetles, which fly during the spring and summer. Bury or (where permitted) burn freshly cut elm wood. Alternatively, seal elm logs tightly under clear plastic in the sun through the warm season and for at least 7 months, after which they are no longer suitable for beetle breeding. For more information on elm bark beetle control, see Chapter 4.

Plant resistant species to avoid Dutch elm disease (Table 5-8). Hackberry and hornbeam resemble elms but are not attacked by Dutch elm disease or elm leaf beetle. Certain elms are less often affected than other elms, and new resistant elm hybrids have been developed and are available in nurseries. When planting elms, use these species instead of highly susceptible American and European elms.

Contact local agricultural or forestry agency officials if elms are suspected of being infected with Dutch elm disease fungus. Remove infected elms immediately to eliminate them as a source of the fungus, which otherwise will spread to nearby elms. Digging a 2-foot deep trench around infected trees may prevent the fungus from being spread by root grafts to nearby elms.

Promptly removing recently diseased limbs may be an alternative in areas where quarantine regulations do not require the removal of the entire tree. This "therapeutic pruning" can be effective only if done immediately during the first season when disease symptoms first appear on a tree. Symptoms must be limited to one or a few limbs, and at least 10 feet of healthy wood (free of visible disease streaking) must separate the infected wood from the pruning point on the main trunk. The trees must be otherwise vigorous and healthy.

No fungicides have been demonstrated to be effective against Dutch elm disease in California. Based on use in the eastern United States, injection of certain fungicides (propiconazole, thiabendazole) by a competent, professional applicator can prevent Dutch elm disease infection, and some recently infected trees may survive if properly treated while less than 5 to 10% of the canopy is symptomatic. Fungicides are effective only when combined with the prompt pruning out of infected limbs and the removal of nearby dying and dead elms.

TABLE 5-8.

Susceptibility of Elms (*Ulmus* spp.) and Elm Substitutes to Dutch Elm Disease (DED) and Elm Leaf Beetle (ELB).

TREE		SUSCEPTIBILITY	
COMMON NAME	SCIENTIFIC NAME	DED	ELB
American elm	*Ulmus americana*	HS	S
English elm	*U. procera*	HS	HS
Scotch elm	*U. glabra*	HS	HS
Chinese elm[1]	*U. parvifolia*	MR	R
'Dynasty' Chinese elm[1]	*U. parvifolia* selection	MR	HS
'Liberty' group American elms[2]	*U. americana* selections	MR	S[3]
Siberian elm	*U. pumila*	MR	S
zelkova	*Zelkova serrata*	MR	R
'Frontier' elm	*U. carpinifolia* × *U. parvifolia*	R	MR[4]
'Homestead' elm	complex hybrid including *U. carpinifolia, U. hollandica,* and *U. pumila*	R	S
'New Horizon' and 'Valley Forge' American elms[2]	*U. americana* selections	R	S[2]
'Pioneer' elm	*U. glabra* × *U. carpinifolia*	R	S
'Prospector' elm	*U. wilsoniana* selection	R	R
hackberry	*Celtis* spp.	NS	NS
hornbeam	*Carpinus* spp.	NS	NS

KEY

HS	Highly susceptible	R	Resistant
S	Susceptible	NS	Not susceptible
MR	Moderately resistant		

1. Dynasty cultivar is highly susceptible to ELB, unlike most Chinese elms (e.g., Allee, Athena, Drake, Evergreen, and Green, True Green), which are resistant to elm leaf beetle. For susceptibility to elm anthracnose, See Table 5-5.

2. American elm selections resistant to DED have exibited poor growth structure when grown in California.

3. Generally susceptible to elm leaf beetle, but certain selections exhibit some resistance.

4. Reported susceptibility to elm leaf beetle ranges from susceptible to resistant, possibly due to location, genetic variability among plants, or misidentification of elms.

Consider fungicide treatment only if Dutch elm disease has been discovered infecting nearby elms. Do not inject trees with fungicide more frequently than recommended on the product label (no more than once every 2 to 3 years for some products); injection itself can damage trees. Do not use fungicide alone, as it has limited effectiveness and experience indicates that fungicide can be helpful only if combined with proper pruning and tree care. Fungicide is not effective if Dutch elm disease infection occurs in the main trunk, if trees were systemically infected through root contact with infected nearby elms, or if elms show symptoms of advanced infections; these trees should be removed promptly. Failing to remove infected trees increases the risk that nearby elms will become infected and die. The prompt detection and removal of dead and dying elms is the most effective method for managing the disease.

Some euonymus cultivars are highly susceptible to powdery mildew, which develops in white patches on infected leaves and may cause premature leaf drop.

Powdery Mildew

Many landscape plants are susceptible to one or more species of powdery mildew fungi. Common hosts include apple, crape myrtle, euonymus, rose, stone fruits, and sycamore. *Microsphaera*, *Podosphaera*, *Phyllactinia*, and *Uncinula* species are some of the more common powdery mildew fungi infecting woody plants.

DAMAGE

Some powdery mildews are unlikely to seriously harm certain plants, while others grow extensively into tissue and significantly impact their hosts. Yellow spots on the upper leaf surface and whitish discoloring on the underside of leaves are the most common damage symptoms. Infected leaves may drop prematurely, and leaves and shoots may become distorted, dwarfed, and discol-ored, such as oak terminals that form "witches' brooms." The type and severity of symptoms depend on the species or cultivar of host plant, the age of tissue when infected, environmental conditions, and the specific pathogen involved.

IDENTIFICATION AND BIOLOGY

Powdery mildew can develop on any susceptible green plant tissue or on flowers and fruits. The pathogen usually appears as a grayish or white powdery growth on leaves and other infected tissue. Spores are produced on vegetative strands in these fungal mats, and in some powdery mildews these spores form in chains and can be seen with a hand lens. Weblike russeting may appear on infected fruit. There are many powdery mildew species; some prefer new plant growth while others are more prevalent on old tissue. Some powdery mildew species have many different host plants, whereas others, such as *Microsphaera euonymi-japonici* on euonymus, grow only on host plants in one genus and are not known to spread to plant species in other genera.

Powdery mildew spreads as windblown spores. Spores do not need free water to germinate; they die in water. Powdery mildew survives only on plant tissue and in dormant buds and does not survive in the soil. It may overwinter on senescent and fallen leaves as little round structures (cleistothecia) that when viewed through a microscope look like grains of pepper with appendages (Figure 5-6).

Powdery mildews grow best at moderate temperatures and in shade, but they occur in humid, foggy areas as well as in dry locations. Powdery mildews are particularly severe in semiarid areas, such as most of California, and are less troublesome in high-rainfall areas. These fungi are favored by warm days and cool nights; at leaf temperatures above 90°F some powdery mildew spores and mycelia are killed. Rain and direct sunlight inhibit powdery mildew.

Powdery mildew is growing on these rose leaves and sepals, but it usually does not grow on the flower petals.

This coast live oak shoot has become distorted, dwarfed, and discolored by a powdery mildew infection, giving it a witches' broom appearance. Eriophyid mites, mistletoe, rust fungi, and viruses are among the other organisms that can cause witches' brooms on certain hosts.

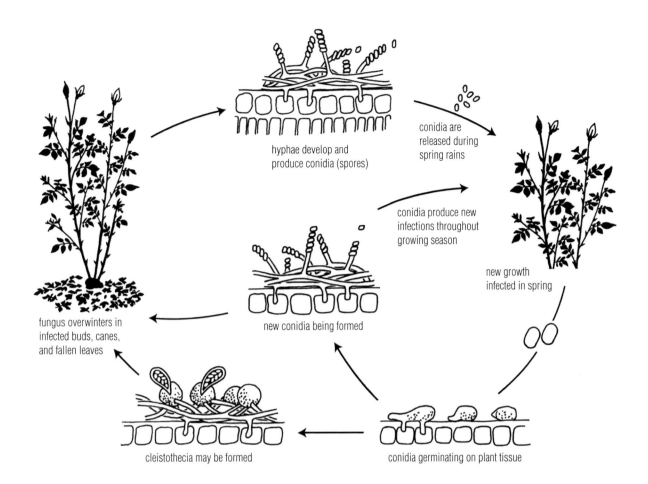

hyphae develop and
produce conidia (spores)

conidia are
released during
spring rains

conidia produce new
infections throughout
growing season

new growth
infected in spring

new conidia being formed

fungus overwinters in
infected buds, canes,
and fallen leaves

cleistothecia may be formed

conidia germinating on plant tissue

FIGURE 5-6. Stages and life cycle of a typical powdery mildew, illustrated by *Sphaerotheca pannosa* infecting rose. The fungus persists and overwinters in infected buds, canes, and fallen leaves (illustration at left). Hyphae develop and produce airborne ascospores or conidia spores (top) that land, germinate, and develop more spore-forming structures. Powdery fungal growth is often visible on infected surfaces. By V. Winemiller from Dreistadt 2001.

MANAGEMENT

Moderate levels of powdery mildew can be ignored on most plant species, but prevention and immediate control action should be taken to avoid damage to highly susceptible plants, such as certain cultivars of crape myrtle, euonymus, and rose. Manage powdery mildew through plant selection, altering the growing environment, using appropriate cultural practices, and applying fungicides to highly susceptible hosts when conditions favor disease development.

Use resistant cultivars where powdery mildew is a problem. *Platanus acerifolia* 'Columbia,' 'Liberty,' and 'Yarwood' are resistant in comparison with other sycamores. Powdery mildew–resistant

crape myrtle cultivars include many hybrids with Native American names, some of which are listed in Table 5-9. Many euonymus and some rose cultivars are resistant, although which cultivars are most resistant has apparently not been well documented. Variegated cultivars of euonymus tend to be more resistant to powdery mildew than nonvariegated types. Powdery mildew–resistant roses reportedly include many shrub roses such as all colors of 'Meidiland,' all colors of 'Simplicity' floribundas, *Rosa rugosa* cultivars, and many glossy-leafed hybrid tea, grandiflora cultivars. Contact the Cooperative Extension office in your county or a certified nurseryperson for current recommendations.

Plant susceptible species or cultivars in a sunny location with good air circulation. Pruning plants to improve air circulation and increase light penetration can reduce the incidence of powdery mildew. Pruning infected tissue and disposing of it away from plants can temporarily improve plant appearance. However, pruning often stimulates new growth that can promote pathogen development because many powdery mildews infect primarily young tissue. Avoid excessive fertilization or irrigation; these activities promote susceptible new growth. For example, witches' broom or powdery mildew (*Cystotheca =Sphaerotheca lanestris*) of oak often follows the

TABLE 5-9.

Some Crape Myrtle Cultivars Reported as Resistant to Powdery Mildew.

RESISTANT IN CALIFORNIA
Catawba, Cherokee, Natchez, Muskogee, Seminole, Tuscarora
RESISTANT IN THE EASTERN U.S.[1]
Acoma, Biloxi, Caddo, Choctaw, Comanche, Fantasy, Hope, Hopi, Lipan, Miami, Osage, Pecos, Sioux, Tonto, Tuskegee, Yuma

Most of these plants are *Lagerstroemia indica* × *L. faurei* hybrids. Cultivars resistant in California are also reported resistant in the eastern U.S. Cultivars resistant in the East presumably show some resistance in California, but this may not have not been documented.

1. Adapted from Cooke 1999, Knox 2000.

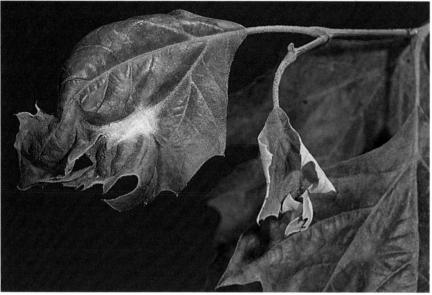

Powdery mildew (*Microsphaera alni*) caused white patches and distorted these sycamore leaves, which may die back.

stimulation of off-season growth resulting from summer irrigation or pruning.

Overhead sprinkling or syringing plants may reduce powdery mildew infection because spores cannot germinate, and some are killed, when plants are wet. Sprinkle plants during midday when most spores are formed; this allows plants to dry before nightfall, reducing the likelihood that sprinkling will promote other pathogens.

Fungicides. Bicarbonates, botanical and horticultural oils, and sulfur are widely used fungicides for powdery mildews in landscapes (Tables 5-3, 5-4). These primarily prevent infection of pesticide-covered foliage. Once powdery mildew growth is extensive, it is generally too late for fungicides to be very effective. Sulfur or sulfur combinations (such as products with both sulfur and soap) applied regularly can prevent powdery mildew from becoming a serious problem on plants that can be thoroughly sprayed.

Certain oils (e.g., JMS Stylet Oil, jojoba oil, neem oil) can cure slight to moderate powdery mildew infections. Potassium bicarbonate or sodium bicarbonate (baking soda) are protectants, but these are most effective if combined with oil. Professional applicators must use a registered product, but individuals spraying on their own private property can mix a solution of about 4 teaspoons of baking soda per gallon of water with a 1% solution of narrow-range oil. The best time to apply this solution to minimize problems with phytotoxicity is during cool weather. Sodium bicarbonate can undesirably raise soil pH, can be deleterious to soil structure, and may leave white foliar deposits. Avoid numerous applications with runoff. Potassium salts of fatty acids, also called soaps (M-Pede, Safer) can reduce powdery mildew development. Neem oil and soap have primarily curative properties, but also provide some protection. Be aware that oil and sulfur in combination can be highly phytotoxic and unless otherwise stated on the label should not be applied within 2 weeks or more of each other.

Certain fungicides that consist of beneficial microorganisms (such as *Ampelomyces quisqualis*) or were discovered as microorganism by-products then synthesized as pesticides (strobilurins) are registered for powdery mildew control, but these may be available only to professional applicators. *Ampelomyces quisqualis* is a beneficial fungus that acts as a hyperparasite or mycoparasite of powdery mildew fungi, reducing powdery mildew growth and eventually killing some colonies of the pathogen. When using this mycofungicide, apply it at the earliest signs of disease, before powdery mildew becomes extensive. More than one application is needed to establish a good population of this beneficial microorganism. Because it is a fungus, *Ampelomyces* is not compatible with certain fungicides, such as dithiocarbamates or EBDCs, soaps, strobilurins, and sulfur. Registration may be limited to relatively few plants, including grapes and roses. *Ampelomyces quisqualis* apparently is not as effective as certain other materials, such as oils and sulfur. It should not be used if powdery mildew is already abundant, if conditions are highly favorable to disease-development, or if sulfur has been applied within the past several weeks.

Cinnamaldehyde (also called cinnamic aldehyde) can be derived from the bark of several *Cinnamomum* species trees, but the cinnamaldehyde used in pesticides is synthesized. This powdery mildew curative may be available only to professional applicators. Cinnamaldehyde apparently is not as effective as the oils and sulfur discussed above. Test it on a limited area of foliage and wait at least a week before deciding whether to use it further; it has been phytotoxic to some plants.

Antitranspirants have provided some protectant control of powdery mildews in certain crops. However, antitranspirants may not be registered for use as fungicides, and they can be phytotoxic under certain growing conditions.

Myclobutanil has both curative and protectant action against powdery mildew and certain other pathogens such as rusts. Several other synthetic fungicides, mostly protectants, are also available (Table 5-4), but some of these are available only to professional applicators. Consult *Powdery Mildew on Ornamentals Pest Notes* (Raabe, Gubler, and Koike 2001) and *Rose Diseases and Abiotic Disorders Pest Notes* (Karlik and Flint 1999) for more information on fungicides and powdery mildew control.

Downy Mildews

Downy mildews, including *Peronospora* and *Plasmopara* species, are primarily foliage blights. They affect ornamentals and various fruit, grain, and vegetable crops, such as caneberries and rose.

Downy mildew is named for its soft and fluffy gray, purplish, or light brown sporulation on the underside of leaves and sometimes on stems or buds. Pale yellow areas or irregular purplish red to dark brown necrotic lesions are sometimes visible on the upper surface of infected leaves. In certain plant species, the fungus can become systemic when young shoots are infected, resulting in stunted, malformed, yellowish growth. Infected woody plants rarely, if ever, die, but sometimes they defoliate.

Downy mildew can be confused with powdery mildew. However, grayish downy mildew patches are almost always limited to the underside of leaves, while powdery mildew growth is common on both sides of the leaf; and in general, the whitish to gray growth is more extensive and prominent with powdery mildew than with downy mildew. The conditions conducive to development of these diseases are very different. Downy mildews are favored by low temperatures. High relative humidity (≥90%) or free moisture is required for downy mildew spores to germinate and infect plants. Powdery mildew development is retarded when foliage is wet.

Downy mildew spores are produced only on living plants. Spores usually are short-lived; under ideal cool, moist conditions, spores may persist for several days. Spores become airborne, and after landing on a susceptible host they germinate and infect within 8 to 12 hours if free water is present. In the absence of a live host, downy mildew fungi can produce persistent spores that resist drying. Infection is sometimes carried in seeds or bulbs.

To control downy mildew, provide good air circulation and maintain low humidity, such as by pruning canopies or nearby vegetation. Avoid wetting foliage; use drip instead of overhead irrigation where feasible. Promptly remove and dispose of infected foliage to reduce disease inoculum. Some fungicides are available, mostly to help prevent infections.

Sooty Mold

Sooty molds are dark, nonparasitic fungi that grow on plant surfaces that have become covered with insect honeydew. These Ascomycetes fungi, such as *Capnodium* and *Limacinula* species, are generally harmless to plants and can be ignored, except when they are extremely abundant and prevent enough light from reaching leaf surfaces, causing plants to become stressed.

Sooty molds can be distinguished from other fungi by the fact that their dark mycelial growth can be completely wiped from plant surfaces using moistened cloth, paper, or a hand, revealing a healthy-looking plant surface underneath. Even if sooty mold is extensive, do not apply fungicides. Wash sooty mold from plants with a forceful stream of water. Control insects that produce the honeydew on which sooty mold grows.

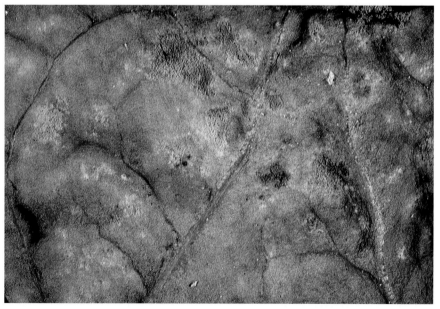

A magnified view of downy mildew on the underside of a leaf. Unlike powdery mildew, which commonly produces pale, powdery growth on extensive areas on both sides of leaves, the grayish patches caused by downy mildew are almost always limited to the underside of leaves, and the grayish growth is less extensive.

Blackish sooty mold on California bay infested with scale insects and aphids. Sooty mold is generally harmless, but if intolerable, it is managed by controlling insects that secrete the honeydew on which sooty mold grows.

Insecticidal soap controls most exposed-feeding, plant juice–sucking insects and helps to wash away honeydew and sooty mold. For more information, consult *Sooty Molds Pest Notes* (Laemmlen 2003).

RUSTS

Rusts infect many hosts, including birch, cottonwood, fuchsia, hawthorn, juniper, pear, pine, poplar, rhododendron, and rose. These parasitic fungi are named for the dry reddish, yellowish, or orange spore masses or pustules that many species form on infected tissue, commonly on the lower leaf surface of broadleaf plants or on the bark of conifers.

Moderate populations of rust pustules on lower leaf surfaces apparently do not harm plants. The upper surface of heavily infected leaves may turn yellow or brown, and infected leaves may drop prematurely. Orange, gelatinous masses appear on some infected evergreen hosts. Some rust species damage bark, causing tissue swellings or galls, colorful spots,

or cankers. These rust fungi can cause branch dieback and occasionally kill the entire plant.

Rusts are spread primarily by wind-blown spores and possibly by water-splashed spores. In addition to orangish pustules, many species also form black overwintering spores on leaves in the autumn, which start the disease cycle in the spring. Many species have complex life cycles, alternating generations between two host species. Others, such as the rose rust (*Phragmidium mucronatum*) are apparently restricted to one host genus. Each type of rust is specific to certain hosts.

MANAGEMENT OF RUST

Rust fungi infect under mild, moist conditions. Avoid overhead watering, which favors spore germination. Rake infected leaves or needles and clip and dispose of infected shoots and branches away from host plants as soon as infected parts appear. Prune and dispose of severely infected woody parts if pruning will not be so extensive that plants are seriously damaged. Eliminating nearby alternate hosts may help to control certain pine rusts. Fungicides applied in the spring

can prevent or reduce some rust diseases. The frequent applications required to provide good rust control may not be warranted in many landscape situations.

Chrysanthemum White Rust
Puccinia horiana

Chrysanthemums are infected by common rust (*Puccinia chrysanthemi*), which has been present throughout the United States for many years, and white rust (*P. horiana*), which has recently been found in coastal areas of the western United States. White rust has been the target of an eradication and quarantine programs that in certain areas prohibit growing landscape chrysanthemums.

White rust is named for the white (sometimes pinkish or brownish) pustules it causes on leaf undersides. It distorts, discolors, defoliates, and kills chrysanthemums. Before pustules form and foliar damage becomes extensive, careful inspection can reveal pale green, yellow, or white spots or lesions on the upper surfaces of infected leaves.

White rust usually does not damage chrysanthemums grown outdoors because direct sunlight and low humidity destroy white rust spores. However, outdoor residential chrysanthemum plantings in coastal areas of California, Oregon, and Washington can serve as a reservoir of infection that is difficult to eliminate. When infection spreads from outdoors to chrysanthemums in greenhouses, commercial crops can be devastated.

Report any suspected white rust infections to the county department of agriculture or other agricultural officials. Hosts include florist's chrysanthemum (*Dendranthema grandiflora*), hardy chrysanthemum (*Chrysanthemum morifolium*), and the perennial garden mum (*Chrysanthemum pacificum*). Growing, selling, or shipping any chrysanthemums from designated eradication zones may be prohibited during certain parts of the year. In order to break the disease cycle,

S. T. KOIKE

Light-colored white rust pustules on the underside of a Chrysanthemum leaf. Report any suspected infections of this quarantined pathogen to your county department of agriculture.

Rust, visible as dry, orangish spore masses on the leaf underside, also caused discoloring of the upper side of these rose leaves.

all chrysanthemums must be removed, bagged, and disposed of in the trash (not composted) during this period.

Western Gall Rust
Endocronartium (=Peridermium) *harknessii*

Western gall rust infects two-needle and three-needle pines in the western United States, including Aleppo, Bishop, lodgepole, and Monterey pine. The disease results in spherical swellings or galls on branches. In spring, galls develop orange spores, which are spread from pine to pine by wind and infect healthy shoots. Infection occurs only during spring and only if shoots are wet. Foliage beyond the galls may become stunted and bushy. Galled stems may exude sap. Sometimes galls become colonized by other fungi or insects, and plant tissue terminal to the gall may die.

Prune and dispose of infected branches during October to January, before spring.

Round western gall rust swellings, which in spring become covered with orange spores.

If western gall rust galls occur on the trunk where pruning is impractical, you can wrap galls with a sheet of plastic during spring through early summer to reduce spore dispersal and spread to other pines. Wrapping galls helps only in landscapes where trees are isolated from other pines, which may be infected. Large galls on major limbs or the trunk can lead to structural failure; consider removing and replacing trees that may be hazardous, as discussed in Chapter 3.

Gymnosporangium Rusts
Gymnosporangium spp.

Gymnosporangium rusts are also called cedar rusts, cypress rusts, and juniper rusts. They cause orange gelatinous masses, galls, stunted and bushy branches (witches' brooms), and stem dieback. They are uncommon in California, except for junipers in some urban areas and cedar, cypress, and juniper in the Sierra Nevada. They are more common in the Pacific Northwest and some areas of the eastern United States. Gymnosporangium rusts require a rosaceous plant such as fruit trees (apple or pear) or hawthorn to complete their life cycle. Gymnosporangium rusts on these alternate hosts can cause swellings and colorful spots on leaves, twigs, and fruit. Infected plant parts usually do not die.

Prune and dispose of infected twigs in the fall, before spores are produced in the spring. Remove galls by making cuts in healthy wood below swollen, infected tissue. Avoid overhead watering. Eliminating nearby rosaceous species that serve as alternate hosts may provide some control.

Pine Stem and Cone Rusts
Cronartium spp.

Pine stem and cone rusts are common throughout the Sierra Nevada and in the Lake Tahoe area of California. White pine blister rust (Cronartium ribicola) is the most important species. These rusts initially cause yellow or brown dead spots and blotches on pine needles. Later the infection spreads to twigs, where the fungus grows beneath bark and in wood. Infection of wood becomes visible in the spring when yellow to whitish, blister-like spore-forming bodies erupt through the bark. More serious damage includes galls, cankers, and branch and trunk dieback on pines. Seriously infected trees may be killed.

With white pine blister rust, resin may stream down the trunk around cankerous areas of infected, roughened bark. Sugar pines are most seriously affected by this introduced pathogen. Bristlecone, foxtail, whitebark, and western white pines are other hosts in California. Ribes species, such as currants and gooseberries, are alternate hosts on which white pine blister completes its development. These plants can serve as a source of inoculum that reinfects pines. Fungicide application or removing all Ribes species within 1,000 feet of pines are sometimes suggested as control methods, but these have not been demonstrated to be effective for this pathogen.

Cronartium coleosporioides is a complex of incompletely understood rust fungi also called by other names (e.g., Peridermium spp.). These include stalactiform rust (Peridermium stalactiforme), which causes trunk and branch cankers mostly on the lower trunk of Coulter pine, Jeffrey pine, lodgepole pine, and ponderosa pine. Its alternate hosts are figworts (family Scrophulariaceae), especially Indian paintbrush (Castilleja spp.). Because these rust cankers are often chewed by animals such as squirrels, cankered limbs can become especially weak and potentially hazardous.

Filamentous rust (P. filamentosum) infects mostly the middle and upper branches of Apache, Jeffrey, and ponderosa pines. Some forms of this pathogen alternate hosts on Castilleja species, while other forms apparently spread from pine to pine without an alternate host.

Pine Needle Rusts
Coleosporium spp.

Over 20 different species of needle rusts infect pines in the United States. They alternate generations with other hosts, often in the Asteraceae (=Compositae) family. Pine needle rusts cause brown, reddish, or yellow spots or bands to develop on partially green or yellow needles. Tiny, whitish bubblelike or tongue-shaped spore-forming bodies may also appear on needles, usually in winter or spring.

Coleosporium pacificum (=C. madiae) on Monterey pine is a common pine needle rust in California. Provide some control of it on pines by eliminating alternate hosts in the family Asteraceae within 1,000 feet of pines, especially Madia species such as Chile tarweed, coast tarweed, and gumweed.

Gray Mold or Botrytis Blight

Gray mold is named for the gray, brown, or tan fungal spores that develop on infected tissue when conditions are humid, making rotted tissue appear fuzzy when viewed by the naked eye. Botrytis cinerea is the most common causal organism, but other Botrytis species and related fungi such as Botryotinia species can also be involved. Succulent tissue of most plants is susceptible to gray mold, also called Botrytis blight. Landscape hosts include azalea, bird of paradise, cacti, coast redwood, fuchsia, giant sequoia, hydrangea, rhododendron, and rose.

DAMAGE

Gray mold causes brown, water-soaked spots or decay on leaves, petals, and succulent stems. Symptoms often start as tiny, almost translucent spots. Infected terminals and stems may be girdled and rot. Diseased tissue wilts and infected seedlings can die.

IDENTIFICATION AND BIOLOGY

Botrytis cinerea does not infect woody plant parts. Active green plant parts and healthy tissue other than petals are seldom infected directly. Only tender plant parts (such as petals), weakened tissue (tissue damaged by other pathogens), or injured, old, or dead nonwoody tissue is susceptible to infection. Once established, the fungus can move from an infected plant parts and invade healthy green tissue it contacts.

Moisture is the primary factor limiting this disease. Gray mold spores germinate

FIGURE 5-7. The infection cycle and stages of Botrytis blight or gray mold. Spores can initiate infections only when they contact tissue that is already injured or declining (top). However, healthy tissue can be infected if it contacts tissue that is already infected. Adapted from Agrios 1997 by V. Winemiller from Dreistadt 2001.

Labels in figure:
Old petals
Flower
Dead leaf tip
Conidia germinate and invade dead or inactive tissue.
Conidia (spores) on conidiophore
Airborne conidium (spore)
Infected cells collapse.
Mycelium produces conidiophore.
Any healthy tissue can become infected if it contacts infected tissues.
Sclerotium produces hyphae.
Hyphae
Conidiophores form on infected tissue.
Infected tissue softens and rots.
Hyphae and sclerotia carry over on plant debris and in soil.
Blossom blight
Decay of dying leaf

and produce new infections only after about 6 or more consecutive hours in contact with water, including free moisture from splashing, condensation, and exudation or when relative humidity is higher than about 90%. In California, humidity can be high any time of year in coastal areas and high inland during the rainy season (late fall through early spring). Gray mold can grow on almost any moist, decaying, herbaceous vegetation. Weeds and plant debris are common pathogen reservoirs producing gray mold spores. Spores are produced on

dark, hairlike stalks (conidiophores). They are readily dislodged and once airborne are the primary method of spreading the fungus (Figure 5-7).

Gray mold is particularly troublesome under moderate temperatures and high humidity. The optimal temperatures for its development are about 70° to 77°F. However, *Botrytis* is active over a broad temperature range.

MANAGEMENT

Good cultural practices, sanitation, and environmental modification where feasi-

ble are the most effective management strategies. Abundant airborne spores develop on old or dead plants. Promptly clip affected plant parts such as old blossoms, prunings, and fallen leaves and dispose of them in covered containers or a well-managed compost pile away from susceptible plants.

Avoid overhead irrigation, especially during bloom. If plants are sprinkled, do so early in the day so that plants dry as rapidly as possible and are not wet overnight. Increase the interval between irrigations to the maximum

Dead brown and watersoaked rose blossoms infected with gray mold. Changing from overhead watering to drip or flood irrigation would greatly reduce this problem.

Prominent brown veins that are darker than the surrounding petal tissue distinguish camellia petal blight from similar damage caused by Botrytis blight, frost, old age, and injury due to chemicals, mishandling, or wind.

extent consistent with good growth. Provide good air circulation, such as by pruning overly dense plants or nearby plants. Fungicides are probably not very effective in landscapes when conditions (primarily wet plants) favor gray mold development, and fungicides are only preventative and must be applied prior to infection.

Camellia Petal Blight
Ciborinia camelliae

Camellia petal blight fungus, also called Cibornia petal blight, infects all cultivars of *Camellia japonica*. *Camellia sasanqua* is infected less often in California. Camellia petal blight initially causes small, brown, irregularly shaped blotches. Spots enlarge rapidly until the entire flower is brown and dead. Except when wet, blighted petals are dry or leathery but do not crumble when handled. Blossoms drop prematurely to the ground, often as intact flowers. Prominent dark brown veins give infected petals a netted appearance. Damage resembling that of camellia petal blight is also caused by Botrytis blight,

frost, old age (overmature blossoms), and injury due to chemicals, mishandling, or wind. Symptoms that distinguish camellia petal blight from these other causes include petal veins darker than the surrounding tissue, infections beginning near the central part of the flower (not appearing first near petal margins), and symptoms that occur only on petals.

Ciborinia camelliae produces dark, hard, irregular-shaped sclerotia at the base of infected flowers, where they replace the calyx lobe. Depending on the extent to which nearby sclerotia unite, they typically range in size from $1/12$ to 1 inch. Sclerotia can lie dormant for several years on or near the soil surface. During winter and spring when camellias blossom, sclerotia produce light brown saucer-shaped apothecia (inverted mushroomlike bodies) about $1/5$ to $3/4$ inch in diameter. Apothecia forcibly discharge large numbers of spores that are carried by wind onto emerging blooms, where in the presence of condensed moisture they germinate and infect flowers.

Pathogen development is favored by wet, humid conditions and mild temperatures (about 59 to 70°F) during bloom. Outbreaks are initiated by sclerotia-

infested soil received with new plants and by sclerotia persisting beneath established plants that have previously been infected. Sclerotia continue to produce apothecia for 3 to 5 years after being introduced into soil.

The disease cannot be eradicated once present. The best control is prevention. Plant camellias in a well-ventilated location. Avoid overhead irrigation. Pull off infected flowers as they appear and collect fallen blossoms and dispose of them in a covered location away from camellias. Composting kills the fungus on infected plant parts if good techniques and a rapid composting method are used. However, regular composting is not recommended if the material will be used near camellia; it is very difficult to maintain the temperature of 140°F required to kill pathogen propagules. Do not add camellia petals or leaves to mulch that will be used around camellia.

Each year, when blossoms are no longer present, apply a fresh layer of pathogen-free organic mulch beneath plants. Apply and maintain a 4-inch layer of organic mulch beneath and somewhat beyond plants to interfere with pathogen spore production. Remove fallen petals and other camellia plant debris before applying fresh mulch, but otherwise avoid moving or disturbing existing mulch beneath plants where fungi may be present. Keep deep mulch several inches away from trunk.

Even with the most careful sanitation, some sclerotia may survive on the ground. Spraying the soil beneath plants with an appropriate fungicide during bloom can help to reduce infections. Depending on the fungicide used, reapplication may be needed every 10 to 14 days while conditions remain suitable for the pathogen. Use fungicides only in conjunction with recommended sanitation and cultural practices.

Azalea Petal and Rhododendron Petal Blight
Ovulinia azaleae

Azalea and rhododendron are highly susceptible to petal blight, also called flower blight or Ovulinia petal blight. Kalmia is also reported to be susceptible to this fungus. This fungus infects only petals, initially appearing as white to brownish spots that enlarge rapidly on blossoms. Petals become limp, droopy, slimy, and sometimes cling to leaves after they fall.

Ovulinia petal blight damage resembles that caused by Botrytis blight. However, Botrytis blight is a drier rot that also affects dying or inactive green tissue, while petal blight infects only blossoms. *Botrytis*-infected tissue develops numerous minute, stalked spores that give plants a gray fuzzy appearance when conditions are wet. *Botrytis* and *Ovulinia* produce similar sclerotia that are irregular, flattened, and black and about ⅛ to ½ inch long. Sclerotia from fallen flowers produce very small, brownish, inverted mushroomlike or wine glass–shaped apothecia about 1/12 inch diameter on stalks about ⅛ to ⅖ inch long.

The biology of Ovulinia blight is nearly identical to that of camellia petal blight discussed above. It infects wet blossoms

Ovulinia petal blight fungus caused these water-soaked blotches on an azalea flower. These early symptoms are largely indistinguishable from Botrytis blight damage unless symptoms also occur on green tissue (*Ovulinia* infects only petals) or the characteristic fungal reproductive structures are present.

when temperatures are mild, about 50° to 70°F. One difference is that in addition to sclerotia and apothecia produced on petals that drop to the ground, Ovulinia petal blight also produces colorless conidia (asexual spores) on infected petals. These spores spread in wind and also can be spread by flower-visiting insects, especially bumble bees. This allows the fungus to reproduce and spread from blossom to blossom within several days of an initial infection.

Removing and disposing of fallen, old, and infected flowers is the primary management method. Gently twist the flower stem and discard it in the trash. Otherwise manage Ovulinia petal blight the same ways discussed for camellia petal blight. Avoid overhead irrigation. Provide good air circulation. Use good sanitation practices. Apply and maintain a 4-inch layer of uncontaminated organic mulch. Application of appropriate fungicides prior to rainy weather can help to reduce infections, but use fungicides only in combination with the recommended sanitation and cultural practices.

Bacterial Blight and Canker
Pseudomonas syringae

Damage from bacterial blight and bacterial canker varies, depending on the host plant and strain of *Pseudomonas syringae* involved. The most common symptoms are elongated lesions on twigs and infected tissue that oozes during wet weather. On apricot, cherry, peach, and other stone fruit trees, bacterial blight commonly causes brown to black lesions on the flowers, fruits, and stems; branch cankers and brown streaks in the wood may also occur, seriously damaging trees. Shoots, leaves, and stems commonly discolor and shrivel on infected lilacs (*Syringa* spp.). Blossom and tip dieback, vein blackening, leaf spots, or stem cankers are common disease symptoms on oleander and many herbaceous ornamentals. Infected oleander and olive develop galls or swellings, as discussed on the next page.

Bacterial gall is infecting this oleander stem and leaves. This problem usually is not a serious threat to plant health and is especially difficult to control on oleander.

Bacterial blight caused by *Pseudomonas syringae* killed these apple shoots and blossoms.

Bacteria entered and killed the lower almond shoot and are causing the adjacent wet, gummy accumulation on bark.

Prune and dispose of infected twigs and branches. Prune during the dry season when infection is less likely to occur. Do not wet foliage with overhead irrigation. Determine whether resistant species or cultivars are available when planting or replacing plants and consider using these. For example, many cultivars of *Syringa vulgaris* are highly susceptible to

bacterial blight and canker, while lilacs such as *Syringa josikaea, S. komarowii, S. microphylla, S. pekinensis,* and *S. reflexa* are generally less susceptible to *Pseudomonas.*

Damage in California is usually not severe enough on ornamentals to warrant spraying. Bactericide applications have not been found to give reliable control on stone fruits, and spraying for bacterial canker is not recommended on fruit trees.

Bacterial Gall
Pseudomonas syringae pathovar *savastanoi*

Bacterial gall affects oleander and olive, but it is uncertain whether the same or different *P. syringae* pathovars infect these hosts. *Pseudomonas syringae* causes galls or knots on stems and bark; branches, flower buds, and leaves also become galled on oleander. Bacterial gall can cause twigs and branches to die back, but overall plant health is usually not seriously threatened.

Gall-inducing bacteria reproduce in fissured or galled bark and are spread by contaminated water, implements, or

hands. Healthy oleander and olive tissue is infected through fresh wounds during wet weather, such as sites of physical injury and frost cracks. Additionally, olive can become infected through any leaf scars on branches for several days after olive leaves have dropped.

Avoid overhead watering, which spreads the bacteria. Where practical, especially for small plants or in the nursery, prune and dispose of infected tissue during the dry season. Whole branches may be removed on olive trees. Sterilizing pruning tools before each cut using a commercial disinfectant has been suggested as a method of limiting pathogen spread if plants must be pruned during the rainy season. However, sterilizing tools is futile if bacteria have already been splashed on plant surfaces.

Severe infections on olive can be controlled by applying Bordeaux mixture or a fixed copper fungicide about twice during the fall. Depending on the situation, to obtain good control it may be necessary to periodically spray through the spring as new growth appears. Pruning all symptomatic tissue during late summer to fall followed by spraying fixed copper or Bordeaux mixture can provide some control on oleander. However, bacterial infection can be systemic and symptoms usually reappear. Regular careful monitoring and prompt retreatment (pruning followed by spraying) are necessary to minimize damage. Oleander and olive in most landscape situations are not of sufficient aesthetic quality to warrant such intensive treatments.

Drippy Oak and Drippy Nut Disease

Clear, brownish, or frothy viscous liquid sometimes drips from oak acorns, leaves, or twigs in California, including those of coast live oak (*Quercus agrifolia*), interior live oak (*Q. wislizenii*), and valley oak (*Q. lobata*). Dripping oaks have been an intermittent problem from spring through fall in coastal areas and the interior valleys of California. Drippy oak causes a sticky mess on cars, lawn furniture, sidewalks, and other surfaces beneath affected oaks. Drippy oak apparently does not threaten tree health.

Drippy oak is different from honeydew produced by certain plant juice–sucking insects, such as aphids, scales, and whiteflies. Drippy oak is caused by a bacterium (*Erwinia quercina*) that colonizes wounded oak tissue, producing clear liquid drips from wounds in nuts, the acorn cap after the nut has dropped, and other plant parts. Injured nuts may decay somewhat, resulting in a brownish ooze. Bacteria apparently enter developing acorns when nuts are injured by filbert weevils (*Curculio* spp.), filbertworm (*Cydia =Melissopus latiferreanus*), and certain other insects such as cynipid gall wasps. Certain oak gall wasps in the genera *Andricus, Disholcaspis,* and *Dryocosmus* also induce plants to secrete copious sticky nectar, which can occur separately or in combination with bacterial ooze. In addition to *Erwinia quercina*, insect honeydew, and oak nectar induced by certain gall wasps, oaks can ooze liquid due to sudden oak death, slime flux or bacterial wetwood, and several other maladies that are not well understood, such as alcoholic flux or foamy canker.

In addition to dripping from older acorns or retained acorn caps as de-

A stunted acorn (at the left) exuding liquid and a healthy acorn on a coast live oak. Drippy oak or drippy nut is a poorly understood malady that sometimes occurs after injuries allow *Erwinia quercina* bacteria to enter plant tissue.

scribed above, profuse dripping or frothy exudate apparently due to *Erwinia quercina* infection occurs from very young or barely developed acorns, from distortions where young acorns would be expected to occur, and from leaves or twigs where there are no acorns. Oviposition wounds from several species of cynipid gall wasps allow bacterial entry and dripping in at least certain situations. Cynipid species associated with drippy oak include a stem gall wasp (*Disholcaspis washingtonensis*) and leaf gall wasps (*Callirhytis flora* and *Dryocosmus minusculus*). Gall wasp presence may not be evident during spring when dripping occurs if plant tissue does not become distorted until wasp larvae mature later in the season. In some instances no insects or their damage have been definitely associated with drippy oak. Mechanically puncturing bacteria-covered twigs has also been found to induce profuse dripping.

Oak drip washes away readily if the dripping is relatively recent, so regularly wash away drippy liquid with water or soap and water. Pruning

branches to reduce canopy overhang in sensitive areas (e.g., patios, driveways) can reduce potential dripping. However, extensive pruning or removing large limbs injures trees and allows entry of decay organisms that can weaken trees, so pruning may not be an appropriate response to this temporary aesthetic problem.

If oak dripping is from nectar-producing gall wasps (certain cynipids in the genera *Andricus, Disholcaspis,* and *Dryocosmus*), controlling ants may gradually (over several years) help to reduce gall wasp populations and eventually reduce dripping. This is because ants help protect nectar-producing gall wasps from their invertebrate natural enemies. No method will eliminate *Erwinia quercina* bacteria from oak trees; the bacterium is ubiquitous to the oak environment. Controlling all types of insects that cause tiny injuries is also not feasible. In situations where most dripping is clearly associated with acorns, collecting or raking away and disposing of fallen nuts that can harbor acorn-damaging insects may help reduce reproduction and survival of nut-feeding insects. However, disposing of fallen nuts is time-consuming and would not reduce insect damage (and potential dripping) until the season after nuts are collected.

No methods have been demonstrated as effective in controlling bacterial-associated dripping from oaks. The problem may not reoccur during consecutive years even without control efforts, which are of uncertain effectiveness. Regular washing and tolerating dripping oaks are the primary recommendations.

Fasciation

Fasciation is an abnormal flattening of stems, often appearing as if several adjoining stems have fused. Small stems or leaves growing from distorted stems are abnormally abundant and undersized. Some fasciations are noninfectious, possibly caused by a genetic disorder. The bacterium *Rhodococcus fascians* is a common cause of infectious fasciation. Although the cause of many fasciations has not been identified,

manage fasciation as if it were a bacterial infection unless information is available indicating another cause.

Fasciation bacteria survive on infected plants and debris. They spread in water and may infect through wounds. Control bacterial fasciation primarily through good sanitation and use of pathogen-free plants. Avoid injuring the base of plants, especially when plants are wet, except to prune and dispose of distorted tissue. Keep the base of plants dry. To control fasciation due to all likely causes (bacterial and genetic), do not propagate or graft symptomatic plants. If affected plants are not removed, at least prune and dispose of distorted tissue.

SYMPTOMS ON TRUNKS AND BRANCHES

Damage to trunks and branches can be caused by many factors, including injuries, weather, wood-attacking insects, and disease-producing organisms. Some

diseases that affect roots or leaves also cause damage to trunks and branches, but are discussed elsewhere. Diseases causing cankers, galls on bark, and wood decay are discussed here.

Wood Decay in Trunks and Limbs

Several fungal diseases, sometimes called heart or sap rots, cause the wood in the center of trunks and limbs to decay. Under ideal conditions, certain rot fungi can decay extensive portions of the wood of living trees in a relatively short time (months to years). This significantly reduces wood strength and kills sapwood storage and conductive tissues. Almost all species of woody plants are subject to trunk and limb decay. Common wood decay-causing fungi include *Armillaria mellea* (discussed later), *Echinodontium tinctorium*, *Ganoderma applanatum*, *Laetiporus sulphureus*, *Phaeolus schweinitzii*, *Schizophyllum commune*, and various species in the genera *Cerrena*, *Fomes*, *Fomitopsis*, *Inonotus*, *Phanerochaete*, *Phellinus*, *Polyporus*, *Steccherinum*, and *Trametes*. For more information, consult *Wood Decay Fungi in Landscape Trees Pest Notes* (Hickman and Perry 2003).

DAMAGE

Decay fungi destroy the plant's internal supportive or structural tissues (cellulose, hemicellulose, and sometimes lignin). Decay is not visible on the outside of the plant, except where the bark has been cut or injured, when a cavity is present, or when the rot fungi produce reproductive structures. Wood decay makes trees hazardous because trunks and limbs become unable to support their own weight and can fall, especially when stressed by conditions such as heavy rain, snow, or wind.

IDENTIFICATION AND BIOLOGY

Many wood rot fungi can be identified by the distinctive shape, color, and tex-

P. SVIHRA

A curled, flattened green stem terminal and bushy foliage of fasciated Chinese pistache.

Seashell-shaped brackets on bark and mushrooms growing near the trunk indicate decay in this alder. Decayed trees can be hazardous because limbs or trunks may fail (fall).

The white underside of these *Ganoderma applanatum* basidiocarps turns dark where touched; they're sometimes called artist's conks. Shoots are not often seen growing through conks as shown here, but shoot growth demonstrates that the tree is alive but has internal decay. Basidiocarps of another *Ganoderma* species are pictured near the introduction to this chapter.

Avoid making large wounds. Fungi have entered where a large limb was pruned from this black walnut trunk, causing internal decay.

ture of the fruiting bodies they form on trees. These structures, called conks, or basidiocarps, are often located around wounds in bark, at branch scars, or around the root crown. Some decay fungi (such as *Armillaria mellea*) produce typical fleshy mushroom-shaped fruiting bodies. In other groups, the spore-forming bodies form groups of half-mushrooms or seashell-shapes called brackets. Some fruiting bodies are annual (for example, appearing soon after the beginning of seasonal rains), but most others are perennial and grow by adding a new layer each year.

Decay fungi often are divided into brown rots, white rots, and soft rots. White rots commonly cause rotted wood to feel moist, soft, spongy, or stringy and to appear white or yellow.

Brown rots primarily decay the cellulose and hemicellulose (carbohydrates) in wood, leaving behind the brownish wood lignin. Wood affected by brown rot is usually dry and fragile, readily crumbles into cubes because of longitudinal and transverse cracks, and commonly forms a solid column of rot in wood. Brown rot is generally more serious than white rot.

Soft rots are caused by both bacteria and fungi. They decay cellulose, hemicellulose, and lignin, but only in areas directly adjacent to their growth. Soft rots grow more slowly than brown and white rots and usually do not cause extensive structural damage to wood of living trees.

Fungi that decay limbs and trunks are spread by airborne spores, which infect trees through injuries and wounds, such as the stubs of freshly pruned branches. Injuries are often caused by people and include pruning wounds, vandalism, or damage from machinery or construction. Boring insects, extreme temperatures, fire, ice, lightning, and snow are among the other causes of wounds through which decay fungi infect wood. Some decay fungi, such as Annosus root disease and *Armillaria mellea*, discussed later in this chapter, infect principally the roots and can spread to nearby plants from the roots of infected hosts.

MANAGEMENT

Wood decay is usually a disease of old, large trees. It is very difficult to manage.

Provide proper cultural care to keep plants vigorous. Minimize wood decay by protecting plants from injuries, as discussed in Chapter 3. Properly prune young trees to promote good structure and to avoid the need to remove large limbs from older trees, which creates large wounds. Cut out dead or diseased limbs. Make pruning cuts properly; prune just outside the branch bark ridge, leaving a collar of cambial tissue around cuts on the trunk to facilitate wound closure, but avoid leaving stubs (see Figure 3-9). Make cuts so that rainwater will drain. Wound dressings are not recommended as they have not been found to hasten wound closure or prevent decay. Annosus root disease may be prevented by treating freshly cut stumps with borax, as discussed below.

Trees that may cause personal injury or property damage if they fall should be regularly inspected by a qualified expert for signs of wood decay and other structural weakness. Hazardous trees may need to be trimmed, cabled, braced, or removed (see Chapter 3).

CANKER DISEASES

A canker is a sunken area containing dead tissue on a woody stem or branch. It may not be clearly visible, or it may be a well-defined infection on woody parts that often becomes surrounded by layers of callus tissue. Cankerlike wounds can be caused by injuries such as sunburn or sunscald, as well as by disease-producing microorganisms (Table 5-10). Cankers can cause foliage on infected branches to turn yellow or brown and wilt. Infected bark often discolors and may exude copious sap or resin (on conifers). Cankers are a serious concern because the pathogens associated with them can girdle and kill limbs or the entire plant. Many different hosts are infected by certain canker diseases, including Cytospora canker and Nectria canker. Other canker diseases can be identified largely based on the species of host plant they infect, including canker diseases infecting Chinese elm, cypress, pine, and sycamore.

TABLE 5-10.

Selected Causes of Cankers.

CAUSE	COMMENTS	SEE PAGE
anthracnose	Associated with leaf spots and distorted terminals.	223
bacterial blight	Bark oozes during wet weather, elongated lesions may appear on twigs.	245
Botryosphaeria canker	Limbs and branches die back on many hosts, wounds ooze on some hosts.	255
canker stain	Infects only sycamore and London plane.	256
Chinese elm anthracnose	Affects only Chinese elm (*Ulmus parvifolia*).	255
cypress canker	Affects cypress and sometimes arborvitae, *Chamaecyparis,* and juniper.	254
Cytospora canker	Many hosts, often causes sunken, elliptical lesions.	250
fire blight	Preceded by twig and leaf damage, affects some plants in Rosaceae family.	229
Hypoxylon canker	Many hosts, but in California reported primarily on oaks and tanbark oak.	257
injuries	Many causes.	44, 287
Nectria canker	Many hosts; wilted foliage appearing first in the spring is a common symptom.	257
Phytophthora root and crown rot	Wilting, foliage discoloration, and premature defoliation are most common aboveground symptoms.	265
pitch canker	Pine branches also turn reddish, die back.	251
pine rusts	Causes blistered, oozing, or swollen pine bark; may discolor or spot needles.	241
pruning wounds	Caused by pruning large limbs or by improperly making cuts.	41, 287
Septoria canker	Affects poplars, leaf spots are present.	227
sunburn or sunscald	Young or severely pruned trees commonly are affected.	288
underwatering	Summer rainfall-adapted plants are most susceptible to sunburn from heat and light if they lack sufficient water.	34, 273

MANAGEMENT OF CANKER DISEASES

Pitch canker, Chinese elm anthracnose canker, and cypress canker of Leyland and Monterey cypress attack apparently vigorous trees. Planting other species or resistant cultivars is the primary strategy for managing these diseases. Most other canker diseases, including Botryosphaeria, Cytospora, and Hypoxylon canker, damage primarily debilitated plants. Avoid planting species that are poorly adapted for local conditions. Provide plants with proper cultural care to keep them vigorous and to limit these diseases.

Prune dead and dying branches when they are first observed. Make the cuts in healthy wood beyond any apparent cankers. Once the main trunk is infected, pruning is of little value. Provide plants with moderate amounts of (preferably slow-release) fertilizer to improve plant growth, except for pines (and possibly also fire blight-infected hosts), which should not be fertilized at all when suffering from cankers. Avoid heavy fertilization, which may promote disease development.

Cytospora Canker
Cytospora spp.

Cytospora canker occurs in many plants including aspen, birch, ceanothus, cypress (Italian, Leyland, and Monterey cypress), fir, fruit trees, maple, poplar, redbud, and willow. Cankers on major branches appear as slightly sunken, smooth, roughly elliptical, reddish brown areas. Cankers are somewhat restricted when new and usually have a sharp margin between healthy and infected bark. However, *Cytospora chrysosperma* on aspen and poplar causes sunken lesions that kill many small branches and twigs without forming any definite canker. Minute, pimplelike fungal fruiting bodies may appear imbedded in infected bark and produce yellow to red "tendrils" of spores during

Cytospora canker infection has caused this large sunken lesion on the main trunk of corkscrew willow (*Salix matsudana* 'Tortuosa').

TABLE 5-11.

Relative Susceptibility of Some Pines (*Pinus* spp.) and Other Conifers to Pitch Canker.

SUSCEPTIBLE AND NATURALLY INFECTED	
Aleppo pine	*Pinus halepensis*
Bishop pine	*P. muricata*
Canary Island pine	*P. canariensis*
Coulter pine	*P. coulteri*
gray (digger) pine	*P. sabiniana*
Italian stone pine	*P. pinea*
knobcone pine	*P. attenuata*
Monterey pine	*P. radiata*
ponderosa pine	*P. ponderosa*
shore pine	*P. contorta*
Torrey pine	*P. torreyana*
Douglas fir	*Pseudotsuga menziesii*
SUSCEPTIBLE, BUT NATURAL INFECTIONS NOT OBSERVED[1]	
Eldarica pine	*Pinus eldarica*
Jeffrey pine	*P. jeffreyi*
Mugo pine	*P. mugo*
Scotch pine	*P. sylvestris*
sugar pine	*P. lambertiana*
RESISTANT CONIFERS	
Brutia pine	*Pinus brutia*
white fir	*Abies concolor*
coast redwood	*Sequoia sempervirens*
giant sequoia	*Sequoiadendron giganteum*
incense-cedar	*Calocedrus decurrens*
Norfolk Island pine	*Araucaria excelsa*

1. Susceptible in laboratory tests.   *Source:* Storer et al. 1994.

moist weather. *Cytospora* fungi can cause infected branches to turn brick-red in the spring, then fade to brown or tan by the fall.

Heat and drought stress combine to increase the susceptibility of many plants to Cytospora canker. Provide appropriate water for species adapted to summer rainfall or riverbank environments if these species are planted where summer drought prevails; irrigation should be deep and infrequent. Grow species that are resistant or not susceptible. Avoid planting susceptible cypress in warm areas, Poplar hybrids that show some resistance to *Cytospora* include 'Nor,' 'Easter,' 'Platte,' and 'Mighty Mo.'

Pitch Canker
Fusarium circinatum

Pitch canker, formerly called pine pitch canker, results from infection by the fungus *Fusarium circinatum* (=*F. subglutinans* f. sp. *pini*). Monterey pine has been most widely affected, but most non-native and many native California pines are susceptible to the fungus (Table 5-11). Douglas-fir has been infected in at least one location. Other California conifers and hardwoods are not susceptible.

Pitch canker occurs in the southeastern United States and some other countries including Japan and Mexico. Since its discovery in central California in 1986 it has spread to coastal and adjacent inland counties and occurs from San Diego north to Mendocino County. Pitch canker is contributing to the premature death of many pines in native coastal stands and landscapes and may cause more widespread damage if the pathogen spreads to the Sierra Nevada.

DAMAGE

Seedlings and small pines up to about Christmas tree size are killed directly by pitch canker due to girdling of the lower trunk. Infection of larger trees predisposes them to attack by bark beetles, especially engraver beetles (*Ips* species), resulting in tree death. Bishop and Monterey pines are especially susceptible to pitch canker. However, some individual trees of susceptible pine species are apparently resistant, and some infected trees can recover and survive the disease.

Branch dieback in the upper canopy is often the first obvious symptom of pitch canker. Terminal needles wilt, turn light green, yellow, reddish, then drop beginning anytime of year. The death of scattered branch terminals is often followed by the death of entire large limbs or the treetop or both. Eventually the entire tree may die.

IDENTIFICATION AND BIOLOGY

The most conspicuous initial symptom of pitch canker usually is "flagging," the discoloring and death of all needles on the ends of some branches scattered throughout the tree. This terminal branch death differs from the natural shed of older needles throughout the tree during late summer and fall. Certain insects and other pathogens often in combination also cause flagging or other damage resembling that of pitch canker (Table 5-12).

Pitch canker is named for the copious resin that typically flows from infection sites. Any pine tissue can become infected and exude pitch, including branches, cones, exposed roots, the main trunk, and at the base of trees where roots and the trunk meet (root crown). Flagging branch ends are often the first place where pitch flow attracts attention. Cone whirls are another common early site for exudate because infections are often initiated here by cone-feeding beetles contaminated with fungal spores.

If pitch canker is suspected, inspect bark for resinous exudate around the junction between discolored and green needles. Pitchy cankers usually appear near the ends of flagging branches before cankers become visible on main limbs and trunks, but occasionally pitch canker-infected Monterey pine have several trunk cankers before branch flagging appears.

Cut under pitchy bark longitudinally and look to see if cankered wood is resin-soaked and amber-colored, which are key characteristics of pitch canker. Infection by a native Diplodia canker or Diplodia blight fungus (*Sphaeropsis sapinea =Diplodia pinea*) also results in resin-soaked wood resembling that of pitch canker. However, there usually is little or no resinous flow or exudate from Diplodia canker infection sites and pitch associated with Diplodia is usually darker than the light amber resin from pitch canker. Diplodia blight infection occurs only near branch ends while pitch canker infection can occur anywhere on pines. Positive

TABLE 5-12.

Comparison of Pine Tree Maladies with Similar Symptoms.

MALADY	SYMPTOMS							
	OOZING OR STREAMING PITCH	LUMPY, PROTUDING, OR TUBULAR MASSES	YELLOW TO RED WILTED TIP NEEDLES	YELLOW TO RED UNWILTED TIP NEEDLES	DEAD TIPS, NEEDLE DROP	CONES OR CONELETS ABORT	SWELLING ON BRANCHES	SILK WEBBING ON TIPS
pitch canker	■		■	■	■	■		
Diplodia canker and blight	□		■	□	■	□		
blight, Aleppo pine	□		■	□	■			
western gall rust, pine rusts	□			■	□	□	■	
dwarf mistletoe	□			□	□		■	
pine scales			□	□	■			
pitch moths	□	■	□		□		□	
tip moths				■	□			
weevils				□	■			
red turpentine beetle		■						
Ips bark beetles		□	□	■	□	□		
cone beetles		■				■		
twig beetles			□	■	■	□		
injuries, pruning wounds	■	□						
salt, wind, or drought dieback				■	■			
shade-suppressed branches			□	■	■			
caterpillars					■			■

Other abiotic disorders such as poor growing conditions and inappropriate cultural practices, as discussed in Chapter 3, also can cause many of these symptoms. Consult the "Tree and Shrub Pest Tables" at the end of this book for a more complete list of pests affecting pines.

KEY

□ Symptom occasionally occurs

■ Symptom usually occurs

Adapted from Adams, undated; Dallara et al. 1995.

identification of pitch canker requires diagnostic laboratory culture from symptomatic plant tissue.

The primary way infections in California are spread appears to be vectoring by insects, especially bark beetles (family Scolytidae), including cone beetles (*Conophthorus* spp.), engraver beetles (*Ips* spp.), and twig beetles (*Pityophthorus* spp.). Even normally innocuous insects such as twig beetles that feed and reproduce beneath bark in stressed pines can become disease vectors when they move from infected to healthy pines and create wounds. Infection can also occur through wounds, including injuries made by pruning tools and other equipment when tools used on infected trees become contaminated with spores that are moved when working on healthy pines.

MANAGEMENT

Learn to recognize symptoms of pitch canker. If a suspected infection is found in areas where pitch canker is not known to occur, contact the county department of agriculture or local forestry officials and request help to determine whether the pathogen is present. To help manage pitch canker, control pathogen inoculum, reduce breeding material for insect vectors, and avoid planting hosts. No pesticide treatment has been shown to control pitch canker. Infected trees cannot be cured by treatments, though some will recover and survive without any control effort. Certain individuals of susceptible species apparently resist the pathogen. Watch for the commercial availability of resistant cultivars.

Avoid spreading pitch canker as discussed below. Promptly remove and properly dispose of dead trees. Pruning infected limbs is unlikely to eliminate the disease and pruning is not recommended for pitch canker control. If diseased limbs are too unsightly to tolerate, completely removing infected limbs can improve tree appearance. Except for hazardous limbs, which should be removed whenever they appear, prune pines only during the late fall and winter when insects that spread the causal fungus are less active. After using tools on trees with resinous

Dark, reddish, resinous pitch on a Monterey pine limb infected with pitch canker.

Extensive branch dieback on Monterey pine infected with pitch canker. Sanitation and providing pines with good cultural care are the only practical strategies for managing this disease.

cankers, or while working on the same tree after making a cut that contacts resinous wood, carefully clean and sterilize the tools as described earlier in the sanitation section (Table 5-2).

Check with the county department of agriculture or University Cooperative Extension office for the latest information on the handling and disposing of

pine material. Unless otherwise recommended, chip infected cut branches and trees and spread chips thinly for use on site as mulch. Alternatively, split logs and tightly seal them under clear plastic in the sun for at least several weeks until dry, then use logs locally for firewood. Do not move pine chips or firewood, diseased wood, or pine Christmas trees out of infested counties. Do not collect or transport pines or pine seeds in infested areas for planting in uninfested locations even if trees appear healthy.

Do not fertilize infected or nearby conifers. Avoid planting Monterey pine in hot areas, because even if not infected with the canker, Monterey pine typically declines and dies within about 20 to 30 years no matter how good the cultural care provided. Consider planting only nonhost species in coastal areas of California (Table 5-11). For more information, consult the latest *Pitch Canker Pest Notes* (Wikler et al. 2003), *Pitch Canker Diseases of Pines* (Aegerter et al. 2003), or the Pitch Canker Task Force at its http://frap.cdf.ca.gov/pitch_canker/index .htm Web site.

Cypress Canker
Seiridium (=Coryneum) cardinale

Cypress canker, also called Coryneum canker, infects primarily cypress. Leyland cypress is especially susceptible, as are Italian and Monterey cypress when they are planted away from the coast.

The fungus occasionally damages arborvitae, *Chamaecyparis*, and junipers. Resinous lesions form on infected bark and cambium, and the fungus can girdle limbs. Infected branches or treetops turn conspicuously yellow or faded and then die. The fungus often progresses until the entire plant is killed. Coryneum canker fungus is moved by the wind and spread within plants by splashing water.

Cypress cankers frequently become colonized by larvae of the cypress bark moth. These insects are secondary invaders attracted to the cankers, and their control is generally not warranted. It is the fungus that kills branches and trees, not the insect.

Provide trees with proper care and prune diseased branches as discussed above. Plant cypress species that are well adapted to local conditions and less susceptible to canker (Table 5-13). Instead of cypress, consider planting arborvitae or *Thuja* species or (along the coast) incense cedar. These conifers resemble cypress but are immune to this pathogen

TABLE 5-13.

Susceptibility of Cypress and Conifers with Similar Foliage to Cypress Canker When Planted Away from Direct Local Influence of Cool Coastal Climate.

COMMON NAME	SCIENTIFIC NAME
HIGHLY SUSCEPTIBLE	
Leyland cypress[1]	*Cupressocyparis leylandii*
Italian cypress	*Cupressus sempervirens*
Monterey cypress	*C. macrocarpa*
LESS SUSCEPTIBLE	
arborvitate	*Platycladus orientalis, Thuja occidentalis*
Arizona cypress	*Cupressus arizonica*
Mexican cypress	*C. lusitanica* var. *benthamii*
Portuguese cypress	*C. lusitanica*
NOT SUSCEPTIBLE	
incense cedar	*Calocedrus decurrens*
western red cedar	*Thuja plicata*

1. Reportedly is more susceptible to cypress canker than other hosts even when planted along the coast.

Yellow and brown branches on a Leyland cypress infected with cypress canker. Even when planted near the coast, Leyland is more susceptible to canker disease than other cypress.

Cypress canker causes resinous lesions and discolored bark. Avoid planting susceptible cypress species in hot areas of California, as they will unavoidably become damaged by this pathogen.

(incense cedar and *Thuja* spp.) or are less susceptible to cypress canker (arborvitae). In California, avoid planting Leyland cypress. Do not plant Italian cypress or Monterey cypress in inland areas away from the direct local influence of the coastal climate, including the warmer areas bordering the San Francisco Bay, such as most locations beyond San Francisco and the adjacent portions of Marin and San Mateo counties. In warm locations, Italian and Monterey cypress are likely to become severely infected with cypress canker.

Chinese Elm Anthracnose Canker
Stegophora ulmea

Irregular, black, tarlike spots on leaves, premature leaf drop, and twig dieback are common symptoms of Chinese elm anthracnose, as discussed and illustrated earlier in the sections "Anthracnose" and "Leaf Spots." More serious damage is caused by cankers on the limbs and trunk. Even vigorous Chinese elms (*Ulmus parvifolia*) may become girdled and die from this fungal disease in coastal areas of California. Chinese elm anthracnose is rarely a problem in hot interior areas of California.

Prune infected branches to the next healthy lateral. Excise small cankers on the trunk and major limbs before they become large by cutting about ½ inch into healthy wood, which should allow wounds to close. Do not make large wounds. Consider replacing severely infected trees. Plant the Drake cultivar of Chinese elm, as it is less susceptible to anthracnose canker fungus.

Botryosphaeria Canker and Dieback
Botryosphaeria dothidea

Botryosphaeria canker and dieback is caused by several *Botryosphaeria species*, most commonly *B. dothidea*. Giant sequoia is a major host, but many other plants in landscapes also can be affected,

Giant sequoia planted in hot areas typically displays branch dieback due to Botryosphaeria canker throughout its life, no matter how good the cultural care provided.

These Chinese elm anthracnose cankers may grow, eventually girdling limbs and causing dieback.

The dry leaves on this madrone twig were killed by *Botryosphaeria dothidea*. At the base of the blackened twig, there is a well-defined margin between the sunken dead stem and the healthy stem, which is producing swollen callus tissue.

including incense cedar, coast redwood, and madrone. Scattered branches are killed by *Botryosphaeria*; recently killed or dying branches are reddish brown and often exude drops of yellowish pitch. Branches with an older infection are grayish brown and mostly bare on conifers. On madrone, dead leaves often appear to have been scorched, and they remain attached to dead bark that is gray, reddish, or black depending on how long it has been killed. Cankers can occur on large, infected limbs. *Botryosphaeria* typically infects giant sequoia and other hosts that are drought-stressed or grown away from their native habitat. Damage is more severe in warmer locations. The fungus is spread primarily by splashing water in the spring and may develop slowly for many months before symptoms become visible.

Giant sequoia planted in hot areas typically displays branch dieback due to *Botryosphaeria* throughout its life. No matter how good the cultural care provided, this species is not adapted to heat and does poorly where hot weather prevails. Plant species that are well adapted to local conditions and provide them with proper irrigation and other care, as discussed in Chapter 3.

Sycamore Canker Stain
Ceratocystis fimbriata

Sycamore and London plane trees are susceptible to infection by *Ceratocystis fimbriata* f. sp. *platani*. The resulting malady, also called Ceratocystis canker, canker stain, or sycamore canker, is lethal to *Platanus* species. The fungus occurs in the eastern United States and Europe and in California at least in Modesto in the northern San Joaquin Valley.

Hosts infected by *Ceratocystis fimbriata* display a sparse canopy of small chlorotic leaves. Elongated cankers develop in infected large limbs and trunks. Cankers usually have little obvious callus growth along their margins and commonly appear sunken, dark, and flattened, or covered with bark that is off-colored or flaky. Cutting into cankers reveals that cambium, phloem, and sapwood are darkly stained, typically a bluish black. In the hot Central Valley of California, sycamore and London plane usually die within 1 or 2 years after symptoms first appear. When the dead tree is cut and the trunk viewed in cross-section, wood is often stained in a pie or wedge shape with the tip of the stain pointing toward the center of the trunk or branch. Stained wood is not decayed although secondary wood rot pathogens may invade and cause wood rot.

Ceratocystis canker is a vascular wilt disease similar to Dutch elm disease, discussed earlier. Certain wood-boring insects such as sap- and fungus-feeding beetles (family Nitidulidae) can spread the pathogen. However, this fungus is unusual in that infections at new locations are almost always the result of pruning or other mechanical injuries to trees caused by people. Black fruiting structures form on the wound surface soon after infection. Fungal spores spread readily from one tree to another on tools or equipment, including pruning saws and brushes used to apply wound dressings. *Ceratocystis fimbriata* spores are able to infect wood only through fresh wounds, but even tiny wounds allow entry and development of pathogen spores, which can remain infective on equipment for more than a month. Once introduced, the fungus may spread via root grafts to nearby hosts.

No chemicals effectively control this disease. Good sanitation and cultural practices are the only management methods. If symptomatic trees are found in areas where the pathogen has not previously been reported, send samples of freshly infected wood to a diagnostic laboratory to determine whether Ceratocystis canker has been introduced, warranting the use of methods described below to limit its spread.

Employ stringent sanitation when working on or near sycamore or London plane that exhibit potential canker stain symptoms. When working in areas known to harbor the pathogen, clean and disinfect all tools and equipment im-

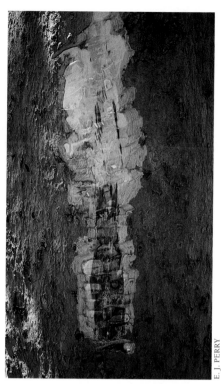

Chipping away bark with an ax reveals dark bluish cambial tissue in a dying sycamore infected with the canker stain fungus. This pathogen spreads on contaminated pruning tools and lawn mower blades that scalp shallow roots. Clean and disinfect equipment and tools that injure sycamore when working in areas where this pathogen occurs.

mediately after use on each sycamore, as described in the section "Disinfectants" earlier in this chapter. Do not wound trunks or shallow roots; for example, prevent injuries to bark from lawn mowers and string trimmers. Keep soil bare or use mulch within several feet of trunks to avoid the common problem of mower blades scraping wood in the crown area where roots and the trunk meet. Use good irrigation management of lawns and other ground covers beneath tree drip lines to encourage deeper root growth, such as relatively infrequent deep watering when needed instead of frequent shallow sprinkling.

Prune sycamore and London plane only during dry weather in December and January, except for hazardous or dead trees, which should be pruned or removed whenever they appear. When a tree is found to be infected, remove it promptly and dispose of the wood away from other *Platanus* species. Consider trenching at least 2 to 3 feet deep to eliminate any root contact between healthy hosts and infected *Platanus* species or where trees were recently removed because of Ceratocystis canker.

Nectria Canker
Nectria spp.

Many woody landscape plants are susceptible to Nectria canker, also called European canker when the disease occurs on fruit trees. *Nectria* species are primarily saprophytes, microorganisms that infect and decay dead plant tissue. *Nectria* infect through weakened or wounded tissue, such as leaf scars and pruning wounds. Less vigorous, injured, or otherwise unhealthy plants are most susceptible to infection, including young shrubs and trees stressed from recent planting.

The coral spot fungus (*N. cinnabarina*) may be most common of the several dozen species of *Nectria* infecting ornamentals. Hosts in California include apple, birch, ceanothus, California bay laurel, elm, maple, mulberry, oak, pear, quince, and rose. Damage symptoms include wilting of leaves and shoots, often beginning in spring. Infected twigs and branches may die back. Cankers (discolored, sunken, often elliptical areas) appear on infected woody plant parts. Although plants infected when young may die, *Nectria* fungi rarely, if ever, kill older plants. Callous tissue developing around wounds often limits the spread of perennial cankers, preventing cankers from girdling the trunk or limb. However, cankered limbs may be hazardous because they are more susceptible to wind breakage.

Nectria infection is often overlooked until clusters of the fungal fruiting bodies (the so-called coral spots) erupt from bark, usually during spring and summer. Each of these spherical, orange or red sporodochia and perithecia (spore-forming structures) are about $\frac{1}{50}$ to $\frac{1}{16}$

Nectria species are sometimes called coral spot fungi because of these orangish or red fruiting bodies, each $\geq \frac{1}{16}$ inch, that may appear in clusters on infected bark during spring or summer.

inch in diameter. Another type of spore-forming body that resembles white tufts may appear during wet conditions, typically from fall through spring. Cutting away bark on cankered limbs reveals a junction between dead (dark brown necrotic) and healthy (cream-colored) wood tissue. The green, living cambial layer found just beneath healthy bark is absent where cankers occur.

Plant only species well adapted to local conditions. Provide plants with proper cultural care, especially appropriate irrigation. Avoid wounding plants. Prune woody parts only if needed. Unless pruning must be seasonally timed to avoid other problems (Tables 4-20, 5-1), prune if needed during early summer to reduce chances of infection by *Nectria*.

Cultural practices are the most important management methods. There are no chemicals that cure plants infected with Nectria canker. If plants are heavily infected or susceptible species are newly planted, the frequency of new infections may be reduced if the plants are small enough to be sprayed thoroughly. Help

prevent infections by applying labeled rates of fixed copper or a freshly prepared Bordeaux mixture during early leaf fall just before rains begin. Where the disease is serious and leaf fall is prolonged by warm fall weather, make a second application when three-fourths of leaves have dropped.

Hypoxylon Canker
Hypoxylon spp.

Hypoxylon species are decay fungi that infect many different woody hosts. They are usually saprophytes, secondary pests that hasten the death of injured or severely stressed plants. In California, for example, Hypoxylon canker is often associated with active and older seeping areas on the lower portions of the trunk of true oaks and tanbark oaks infected with sudden oak death caused by *Phytophthora ramorum*. The most distinctive characteristic of *Hypoxylon* fungi are dark, hemispherical fruiting bodies, often about

Dark, hemispherical Hypoxylon canker fruiting bodies have developed on this oak bark. As with many other canker diseases, this pathogen primarily affects injured and severely stressed plants.

Trees infected with crown gall commonly have warty tumors on the lower trunk or large roots near the crown. A tree as large as this walnut usually tolerates the growths; however, trees infected when they are young may be seriously affected.

1 inch in diameter, that develop on the surface of infected bark or wood.

As with most other decay fungi, avoid Hypoxylon canker by planting species that are well adapted for conditions at that location; protecting plants from injury, stress, and other pests; and providing plants with proper cultural care, especially appropriate water.

Crown Gall
Agrobacterium tumefaciens

Agrobacterium tumefaciens bacteria commonly cause galls to form on the root crown at the soil line or just below the soil surface. Galls sometimes also develop on roots, limbs, and trunks. Many woody plants can be affected, especially euonymus, fruit trees, *Prunus* species, rose, and willow. Some herbaceous plants, such as chrysanthemums and daisies, also are susceptible.

DAMAGE

Agrobacterium tumefaciens usually does not seriously harm woody plants unless galls occur in the root crown area when plants are young. Infected young plants may become stunted and subject to wind damage and drought stress. Infrequently, if galls are large, water or nutrient transport can be inhibited to the extent that young plants are killed. Crown gall appears to have a relatively minor effect on most established host plants.

IDENTIFICATION AND BIOLOGY

Crown gall bacteria stimulate the plant to produce actively growing, disorganized tissue, which distorts the bark surface. Galls may resemble damage caused by some boring insects, woolly aphids, or certain other pests (Table 4-16). Certain boring insects may be attracted to gall tissue and colonize it, further complicating identification of the original causal agent. The surface of a crown gall is the same color as healthy bark, and galled wood has the same color as normal wood. However, when cut with a knife, crown galls are softer than normal wood and lack the typical pattern of annual growth rings. Galls can be tiny and smooth on young plants, but they are commonly rough and sometimes massive on mature trees.

Crown gall is caused by a bacterium that can survive for long periods in the soil. The bacterium enters plants through wounds, which are commonly infected by handling in the nursery or during transplanting. The bacteria can also enter established plants through growth cracks or wounds caused by cultivation, mowing, weed trimmers, or sucker removal. Certain natural wounds, such as where new roots emerge into bacteria-contaminated soil, also allow entry of the crown gall pathogen. After infection, the bacteria stimulate tissue to grow rapidly and form galls, which may slough off and return some bacteria to the soil.

MANAGEMENT

Purchase and plant only high-quality nursery stock. Avoid injuring trees during transplanting. Dipping seeds or roots in a solution containing a biological control agent, the K-84 or K-1026 (nonpathogenic) strains of *A. tumefaciens* (formerly called *Agrobacterium radiobacter* and marketed as Galltrol or Nogall) may reduce infection by most strains of pathogenic crown gall bacteria, but the strain commonly affecting grape is not prevented by these biological control agents. Solarization, covering moist, bare soil with clear plastic for 4 to 6 weeks during the sunny, dry season before planting (as detailed in Chapter 7), may reduce crown gall bacteria in the soil.

Crown gall bacteria are especially abundant where previously infected plants have grown. Where crown gall has been a problem, use only resistant plants, including birch, cedar, holly, incense cedar, magnolia, pine, redwood, spruce, tulip tree, and zelkova. Take care not to injure trees, especially around the soil line. Existing galls may be excised by cutting into healthy wood around galls, then exposing the tissue to drying. Cut out galls only during the dry season and minimize the amount of healthy tissue into which cuts are made. Research in certain tree crops such as almond, prune, and walnut demonstrates that after cutting out distorted tissue, gall regrowth is frequently avoided if a blowtorch is used to briefly heat and sterilize the edges of plant tissue where galls were cut from bark and wood. Do not cause plants to burn or char and use caution to avoid fire or injury if using this technique. If galls encompass much of the crown area, so that excising them may cause such extensive wounds that plants develop other problems or die, consider tree replacement. A bactericide, Gallex, may provide control when painted onto galls as directed on the product label.

Wetwood or Slime Flux

Wetwood is caused by several species of bacteria; yeast organisms may also be involved. Wetwood is especially common in elm and poplar, but it affects many other plants including box elder, fruitless mulberry, hemlock, magnolia, maple, and oak.

Trees affected with wetwood have stained areas of wood that exude fluid. Usually only trees about 10 years of age or older exhibit symptoms. Foliage wilt and branch dieback may occur on

severely infected trees, but the disease rarely causes serious harm to trees. Although it can be unsightly, limbs infected with wetwood may be as strong as healthy wood.

Wetwood causes a portion of the trunk or branches to appear discolored and watersoaked. A sour or rancid, reddish or brown fluid commonly seeps from infected bark cracks or wounds. Wetwood-causing microorganisms are common in soil and water. They infect trees through wounds, including sites where pesticides have been injected into trees. Alcoholic flux (see below) also causes wood to exude fluid, but only for a short time during the summer, and that fluid has a pleasant, fermentative odor.

Prevent wetwood bacteria and yeasts from infecting trees by avoiding injuries to bark and wood. Control wetwood infections if they are small by opening wounds so they are exposed to the air and so that liquids do not accumulate; avoid making large wounds. To reduce the spread of bacteria and yeasts in an infected tree, drill a ¼-inch hole several inches long until fluid begins flowing,

Stained wood exuding fluid around the crotch of this Siberian elm is a result of bacterial wetwood infection.

then install a copper tube to drain excess fluid and release the pressure of gases that form in infected wood. Do not insert the tube so far into the hole that the inside end becomes plugged. Leave the outside end of the tube protruding so that liquid drains away from the infected bark area. Check the tube opening regularly and clear it if it becomes plugged. Do not weaken the tree's structure by drilling drain holes at branch crotches.

Foamy Canker or Alcoholic Flux

White, frothy material sometimes exudes from cracks or holes in bark, commonly on elm, liquidambar, oak, sweet gum, and Victorian box. This foamy material appears for only a short time during warm weather, and it has a pleasant alcoholic or fermentative odor, unlike the rancid smell of wetwood fluids. In severely infected trees, the cambium beneath the bark may become rotten, white, mushy, and eventually turn brown and

This foamy material, or alcoholic flux, on almond has a pleasant fermentative odor, unlike the rancid smell of wetwood fluids.

die. The cause of this malady is unknown. Foamy canker was formerly attributed to *Zymomonas* species bacteria that sometimes are present on trees exhibiting this malady. However, *Zymomonas* are not always present, and the cause may be other bacteria, yeasts, or some combination of microorganisms and environmental conditions.

Preventing injuries to bark may help to prevent this malady. Prune infected tissue when it is limited to a small area of the bark to allow wounds to close; avoid making large wounds.

Pink Rot
Gliocladium vermoeseni

Pink rot fungus can kill infected fan palms (*Washingtonia* species), queen palms (*Arecastrum romanzoffianum* and *Syagrus* spp.), *Chamaedorea* species and many other palms. On *Syagrus* species, cankers form on trunks, which can become severely deformed and split. Dark material may ooze from wounds on severely infected tissue. Infection is most often observed around dying leaves and wounds and, in the case of *Chamaedorea* species, around the base of the plant near the soil. Pink rot is named for the pink mass of spores formed on infected tissue. The disease is most serious on plants of low vigor and on palms planted near the coast.

Plant Mexican fan palm (*Washingtonia robusta*), which is highly resistant to pink rot, instead of California fan palm (*W. filifera*), which is especially susceptible to pink rot along the coast. Provide proper cultural care to keep plants vigorous. Excessive moisture apparently promotes pink rot. Avoid overhead watering, do not overirrigate, and provide good drainage. Avoid wounding plants when removing old fronds. Remove only dead or dying fronds. Sterilize pruning tools with a commercial disinfectant before cutting on each new plant. Reciprocating power saws or hand tools should be used because these can be easily sterilized, unlike chain saws. Cut out trunk cankers if the rot is not extensive; avoid making large wounds. Replace severely infected palms. Applications of a systemic fungicide can control the fungus, but it should not be substituted for proper cultural care.

Sudden Oak Death
Phytophthora ramorum

Tanbark oak (also called chestnut oak or tanoak) and certain true oaks (*Quercus* spp.) have died in large numbers in California wildlands due to infection by *Phytophthora ramorum*. The cause of dying oaks was unknown for several years after it was first reported in Marin County in about 1995, and originally the malady was thought to affect only tanbark oak and true oaks. Sudden oak death (sometimes abbreviated as SOD), is now known to be caused by a *Phytophthora* species new to North America. Unlike most woody plant diseases caused by *Phytophthora* species, as discussed below in the section "Root and Crown Rots," *P. ramorum* primarily affects aboveground plant parts.

Phytophthora ramorum occurs in Europe, Oregon, and at least a dozen coun-

P. SVIHRA

The most reliable early symptom of sudden oak death is dark sap exuding from trunk base, as on this coast live oak. However, laboratory tests or DNA molecular techniques such as PCR (polymerase chain reaction) are the definitive way to diagnose infection by *Phytophthora ramorum*.

Pink rot spore mass on the trunk and under the rachis base of a stressed California fan palm. Minimize this problem by avoiding injuries and providing palms with appropriate cultural care.

ties in California within about 50 miles of the coast. The locations where *Phytophthora ramorum* occurs and the number of species affected are expected to expand. Plants in at least 11 families are known to be susceptible, including big leaf maple, California bay laurel, California black oak, California buckeye, California coffeeberry, California hazelnut, California honeysuckle, coast live oak, coast redwood, Douglas fir, huckleberry, madrone, manzanita, rhododendron, salmonberry, Shreve oak, tanbark oak, and toyon.

DAMAGE

Most of the plants killed by *Phytophthora ramorum* have been tanbark oak and true oaks in forests, wildlands, and urban-wildland interfaces (suburban development in wildlands). Other hosts exhibit leaf and twig injury, but usually are not seriously damaged or killed. In most landscape situations, symptoms resembling sudden oak death are due to other causes. Common causes of unhealthy landscapes include adverse soil conditions, inappropriate water (especially overirrigation), and pathogens such as Armillaria root rot, bacterial wetwood, and other *Phytophthora* species that have previously been known to affect these plants. The sections "Oak Branch Dieback" and "Oak Twig Blight" earlier in this chapter discuss other fungi that cause similar symptoms in tanbark oak and true oaks. Shoot dieback from oak twig girdlers, defoliation by caterpillars, and certain other problems summarized in the "Tree and Shrub Pest Tables" at the end of this book may also cause damage that resembles sudden oak death.

The severity of symptoms and damage varies greatly among plant species. Sudden simultaneous leaf death on a major stem, or leaf death on an entire tree, can indicate *Phytophthora ramorum* infection in tanbark oak and true oaks. On tanbark oak, discolored foliage, dead and green leaves intermixed, and branch tips and basal shoots that wilt and turn brown are often the first symptoms. On true oaks and often on tanbark oak, a common symptom is brown to red ooze or seeping

from the lower trunk. Lichens and moss on bark often become darkly stained from this ooze and die. Cutting under the ooze into the bark reveals discolored brown or reddish tissue separated from healthy green or whitish tissue by a distinct black zone line. Tanoak and true oak seeping from trunks usually occurs within 6 feet of the ground, but it occurs sometimes much higher. When oaks die, the foliage may become pale, then turn reddish brown and die. Bark sometimes develops dark hemispherical fruiting bodies of *Hypoxylon thouarsianum*, a decay fungus discussed in the section "Hypoxylon Canker." Western oak bark beetle (*Pseudopityophthorus pubipennis*) and oak ambrosia beetles (*Monarthrum scutellare* and *M. dentiger*) attack the dying oaks, producing red or white boring dust on bark.

On hosts other than true oaks and tanbark oak, the symptoms commonly are necrotic patches and spots on leaves, or leaf spots plus twig cankers and twig dieback. Certain hosts develop leaf wilting. Nurseries may be prohibited from selling and shipping certain plants to other states and countries because of quarantines prohibiting movement of host plants out of areas where *Phytophthora ramorum* occurs.

IDENTIFICATION AND BIOLOGY

Field symptoms are not sufficient for reliable diagnosis. Specific tests are the definitive way to diagnose sudden oak death. A fresh plant sample is cultured on special growing media in the laboratory, or the pathogen is identified using DNA molecular techniques such as PCR (polymerase chain reaction).

The pathogen's biology varies considerably among host species and is best understood for tanbark oak and true oaks. Inoculating mature oaks can produce cankers up to about 2 feet long within about 3 months after infection. Some trunks become completely girdled within this time. Foliage can become brown and die within 1 year of infection. On at least certain infected host plants (such as bay laurel, rhododendron, and tanbark oak), *Phytophthora ramorum*

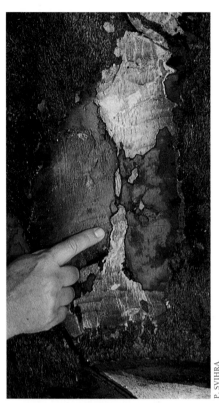

P. SVIHRA

Cutting beneath bark on this California black oak reveals discolored brown or reddish tissue separated from healthy cambium by a distinct black zone line. This discoloration is characteristic of infection by *Phytophthora ramorum*.

readily produces spores on the leaf surface. Spores from leaf and twig infections apparently move in air, splashing rain, and with infected plant material and soil. In true oaks and tanbark oak, infection apparently begins through bark. Infection in the other hosts may begin in the leaves or twigs.

The resting spores of other *Phytophthora* species can survive for years in soil, and this may be the case with *Phytophthora ramorum*. The pathogen may be spread inadvertently in contaminated soil by the activities of bikers, hikers, vehicles, and animals such as deer and horses. Plants from commercial nurseries in infected areas may also be a means of spread.

MANAGEMENT

Do not move host plants (foliage or wood) out of areas where *Phytophthora ramorum* is known to occur. Also minimize movement of host material within areas of infection. Promptly remove dead plants. Dead oaks will not recover. They serve as a breeding site for bark beetles that emerge and attack nearby healthy oaks. Dying limbs and trunks may be hazardous and may fall. Unless otherwise directed by agricultural officials, cut oak logs and cure them in the sun for several months under tightly sealed plastic to prevent bark beetle emergence before using logs for firewood. Alternatively, chip dead trees and use them on site as mulch.

Fungicides that help control other *Phytophthora* species in certain situations are being tested. However, in many landscape situations, large trees cannot be effectively treated with fungicide to control other *Phytophthora* species.

Meanwhile, provide oaks and other plants with proper cultural care and protect them from injuries. Be alert for new information on the diagnosis and management of sudden oak death. Consult the section "Tree and Shrub Pest Tables" at the end of this book to learn the maladies commonly affecting your plants and take steps to avoid these. For current information, consult publications such as the latest *Sudden Oak Death in California Pest Notes* (McPherson et al. 2002) and the online resources listed in that publication.

ROOT AND CROWN DISEASES

Several root and crown (root collar) diseases commonly affect landscape trees and shrubs. These include Armillaria root rot, Phytophthora root and crown rots, and Dematophora root rot. Because roots transport nutrients and water to the rest of the plant, any root disease is likely to affect other parts of the plant as well. Often the first observed symptoms of root disease in broadleaves is wilting foliage or leaf discoloring that resembles a nutrient deficiency. In conifers, chlorotic or faded green foliage is often the first obvious symptom. In advanced

Water around this trunk is promoting root and crown disease. Frequent, shallow irrigation (such as that applied to the surrounding lawn), is often incompatible with the long-term health and survival of trees, especially in poorly drained soil.

stages, leaves discolor and die, then branches and the entire plant are killed. Several abiotic disorders (see Chapter 6), including too much or too little water, mineral toxicity, and herbicides, can also damage roots and cause symptoms that may be confused with root and crown diseases. Because of their propensity to fall, root-damaged trees can be hazardous and may need to be removed if they are located where their failure could injure people or damage property.

Once fungi that cause root diseases become introduced in a location, they are often continuously present there in old roots, stumps, soil, or infected living or dead standing trees. In many landscape situations, fungicides are not available or effective in controlling root decay fungi. The most effective control is to provide trees with proper cultural care to keep them vigorous and to prevent conditions that promote disease development. Proper planting, as detailed in Chapter 3, and appropriate irrigation, as summarized earlier in this chapter (Figures 5-2 and 5-3), are critical to controlling root diseases. Purchase only high-

quality nursery stock (Table 3-1). Root rot diseases commonly develop in nurseries because potted plants are watered frequently, then these root rot fungi can then be introduced into landscapes on contaminated nursery stock.

Armillaria Root Rot
Armillaria mellea

Armillaria root rot, also known as oak root fungus disease or shoestring fungus disease, affects many broadleaf trees and conifers, as listed in Chapter 9. Bamboo and some herbaceous plants, such as amaryllis, bird of paradise, calla, carnation, daffodil, dahlia, geranium, jade plant, and peony are also susceptible. This native pathogen is most prevalent in landscapes established in areas of natural forests or where oaks or other native trees once grew.

DAMAGE

Armillaria infects and kills cambial tissue, causing major roots and the trunk near the ground to decay and die. The first aboveground symptoms are often undersized, discolored, and prematurely dropping leaves. Branches often begin dying first around the tops of deciduous trees or in the lower canopy of conifers. Eventually the entire plant can be killed. Young plants often die quickly; mature trees may die quickly or slowly, but they can recover, at least temporarily, if conditions become good for tree growth and poor for disease development.

IDENTIFICATION AND BIOLOGY

Armillaria forms characteristic white mycelial plaques between the bark and wood. These distinctive white fans have a mushroomlike odor when fresh and are visible when the bark is removed from infected roots and the lower trunk. *Dematophora* root rot also causes white growths that may be confused with *Armillaria* root rot, but *Dematophora* often is more tan to brown and tends to occur in smaller patches, as discussed below.

During cool rainy weather, usually in the fall or early winter, clusters of mushrooms may form at the base of *Armillaria*-infected trees. The honey yellow to brown mushrooms always occur in groups (never just one mushroom), and each mushroom ranges from 1 to 10 inches in diameter. They have a ring on the stalk just under the cap, and they shed white spores.

Armillaria frequently produces root-like structures (rhizomorphs) that attach to the surface of roots or the root crown of infected hosts and can infect roots of adjacent trees. Rhizomorphs have a black to dark reddish brown surface. When pulled from their host or pulled apart in the hands, their cottony interior becomes visible. When similar-sized roots are pulled apart for comparison, roots have a more solid, woody interior than rhizomorphs.

Armillaria thrives under warm, moist conditions, for example, when turf is planted around the roots of California native oaks and irrigated during warm weather. Plants become infected through root contact with infected plants, rhizomorphs attached to infected roots, or

Armillaria root rot fungus forms characteristic white mycelial fans between bark and wood in the root crown area. Armillaria root rot is promoted by summer irrigation of drought-adapted species such as oaks native to California.

During cool, rainy weather, clusters of mushrooms may form around the base of *Armillaria*-infected trees.

mycelium on dead roots in soil. Armillaria root rot can develop slowly, and symptoms may not appear until the fungus is well established. The fungus can survive for many years in dead or living tree roots.

MANAGEMENT

Prepare the site well before planting and provide appropriate cultural care, especially proper irrigation, as discussed in the introduction to this chapter and in Chapter 3. Plant only resistant species (Table 5-14) in locations where Armillaria root rot has been a problem. Be aware that even resistant species can become infected if they are poorly adapted for conditions at that site or receive inappropriate cultural care, such as irrigating too frequently. Because general tree health and care greatly decrease or

TABLE 5-14.

Landscape Plants Resistant to Armillaria Root Rot.

COMMON NAME	SCIENTIFIC NAME
acacia, black wattle	*Acacia mearnsii*
acacia, star	*Acacia verticillata*
acacia, Sydney golden wattle	*Acacia longifolia*
bald cypress	*Taxodium distichum*
bamboo, heavenly or sacred	*Nandina domestica*
boxwood	*Buxus sempervirens*
cherry, Catalina	*Prunus lyonii*
cherry, hollyleaf	*Prunus ilicifolia*
Chinese wisteria	*Wisteria sinensis*
cork tree	*Phellodendron amurense, P. chinense*
crabapple	*Malus floribunda, M. ioensis*
cryptomeria	*Cryptomeria japonica*
cypress, Leyland	*Cupressocyparis leylandii*
dawn redwood	*Metasequoia glyptostroboides*
eucalyptus, dollar leaf	*Eucalyptus cinerea*
eucalyptus, flooded	*Eucalyptus grandis*
hackberry, common	*Celtis occidentalis*
hackberry, European	*Celtis australis*
holly, American	*Ilex opaca*
holly, Dahoon	*Ilex cassine*
maidenhair tree	*Ginkgo biloba*
oak, holly	*Quercus ilex*
pine, black	*Pinus nigra*
pine, Scotch[1]	*Pinus sylvestris*
pine, Torrey	*Pinus torreyana*
pittosporum	*Pittosporum heterophyllum*
privet, Japanese	*Ligustrum tschonoskii*
smoke tree	*Cotinus coggygria*
sweet gum, Oriental	*Liquidambar orientalis*
tree-of-heaven	*Alianthus altissima*

This list provides only a guideline. Many of the species listed may be attacked if soil is highly contaminated with infected roots and if conditions are poor for plant growth and good for disease development, such as from irrigating too frequently.

1. There is disagreement regarding whether this is Armillaria-resistant.

Sources: Farr et al. 1989, Raabe 1979.

increase host susceptibility, Table 5-14 provides only a guideline.

Wood from *Armillaria*-infected trees can be chipped and used as mulch with little or no risk of spreading *Armillaria* if properly handled. Grind wood well to avoid large chunks and air-dry chips or leave them in a pile for about 2 weeks before using them around host plants to ensure that chips from *Armillaria*-infected plants are not a source of the pathogen. Before replanting where *Armillaria* has been a problem, remove from the soil as many roots as possible that are ½ inch in diameter or larger because these can harbor *Armillaria*. If infected roots remain, air-dry the soil before replanting if possible.

Soil fumigants may be available to professional applicators to treat a limited area of *Armillaria*-infested landscape soil before planting. However, fumigation of field soil usually does not kill the fungus in all roots, especially those deeper in soil. Fumigants can be highly toxic to people. They require stringent safety measures and their use is restricted. Consider alternatives before using a fumigant.

Dematophora Root Rot
Rosellinia (=*Dematophora*) *necatrix*

Dematophora root rot, also called white root rot, is less common than the other root diseases discussed here, but it quickly kills plants when it occurs. Its hosts include ceanothus, citrus, cotoneaster, fruit trees, holly, poplar, privet, and viburnum. The fungus is active whenever hosts are growing, especially during mild, wet weather. It infects primarily through healthy roots growing near infected plants.

The initial symptoms of canopy decline caused by Dematophora root rot may be exhibited throughout the entire plant or in just a portion of the canopy. Branches killed as a result of Dematophora root rot often retain dry foliage. A white mycelial mat may be visible on the lower trunk or in soil over infected roots. Minute white growths may also be visible beneath bark. These may extend down into wood of the root crown or roots. The whitish mycelial patches of *Rosellinia* are much smaller than *Armillaria* mycelia and lack the characteristic mushroomlike odor produced by *Armillaria*. If the soil is excavated, white strands can be observed growing from infected roots into the adjoining soil. A dark crust may also form over dead roots or around the root collar.

When *Rosellinia*-infected tissue is sealed in a moist chamber, such as a plastic bag or jar, it produces a distinctive white fluff within a few days. However, if Dematophora root rot is suspected, it is best to seek an expert to confirm its presence.

Minimize *Rosellinia*-caused disease by preparing the site well before planting and using quality nursery stock. Providing appropriate cultural care, such as proper irrigation as discussed in the introduction to this chapter and in Chapter 3, is especially important.

White, cobwebby patches of fungus in soil at the base of this apple tree are characteristic of Dematophora root rot.

Annosus Root Disease
Heterobasidion annosum (=*Fomes annosus*)

Annosus root disease can infect the roots or root crown of many conifers, and it occasionally occurs on some hardwoods. It infects through roots and primarily affects conifers in areas where they grow naturally. Pines are often killed within several years, and true firs are also highly susceptible. Other hosts, such Douglas fir, incense cedar, hemlock, larch, and spruce, are more tolerant and usually are not killed outright. However, because of infection, other conifers can develop decay in heartwood or sapwood that increases susceptibility to insect attack and wind damage.

The fungus can survive for several decades in the roots remaining from killed trees. Groups of trees often die in a gradually expanding clump as they are infected through root contact with the initial host. The fungus spreads long distances by airborne spores. Spores can germinate when they contact a freshly cut stump or fresh wound, creating a new infection center as the fungus spreads down through the stump into roots that contact nearby living trees.

Disease presence may be indicated by conks. These fleshy fruiting bodies vary in form, often forming a small button, seashell-like bracket, or amorphous whitish, gray, or light brown growth, usually around the root crown. Bark may separate readily from wood in infected trees; the separated surfaces are light brown, and the wood surface is often streaked with darker brown. Numerous silver or whitish flecks may also appear on the inner bark surface, and small whitish mycelial growths may occur between outer bark scales or on the bark surface.

Avoid wounding trees. Consider applying borax to freshly cut pine and true fir stumps in areas where these conifers grow naturally to prevent stumps from becoming infected by spores, which can spread *Heterobasidion annosum* from stumps through roots to nearby conifers. Apply borax (sodium borate) powder about ⅛ inch thick, for example, by sprinkling it with a salt shaker–type container, onto the stump surface within 2 days cutting.

Root and Crown Rot
Phytophthora spp.

Phytophthora cinnamomi and several other *Phytophthora* species commonly infect the roots and crowns of landscape plants. These root and crown rot fungi cause maladies that are also called collar rots, foot rots, and Phytophthora root rot. Certain other pathogens also cause root and crown rots, as discussed below in the section "Pythium Root Rot." *Phytophthora ramorum* primarily infects aboveground plant parts, so it is discussed separately above in the section "Sudden Oak Death." Hosts of Phytophthora root and crown rots in California include many species or cultivars of acacia, ceanothus, cedar, *Chamaecyparis*, chestnut, citrus, cypress, daphne, dogwood, eucalyptus, fir, *Fremontodendron*, fruit trees, hemlock, holly, juniper, larch, oak, pine, *Prunus*, redbud, redwood, *Rhamnus*, rhododendron, and walnut, as well as many other woody ornamental species.

DAMAGE

Phytophthora kills the roots and root crown area of infected plants and sometimes spreads upward into the stem. This causes plants to wilt and leaves to discolor, stunt, and drop prematurely. Infected mature plants grow slowly and may gradually decline. Twigs and branches die back and the entire plant can be killed. *Pythium* can cause similar damage and may occur along with *Phytophthora*, but *Pythium* is a much less common problem of woody landscape plants.

IDENTIFICATION AND BIOLOGY

The symptoms of a *Phytophthora* infection often vary with the environment,

Excess irrigation of nearby turf and compacted, poorly drained soil are promoting *Phytophthora cinnamomi* in this Irish yew, resulting in branch dieback.

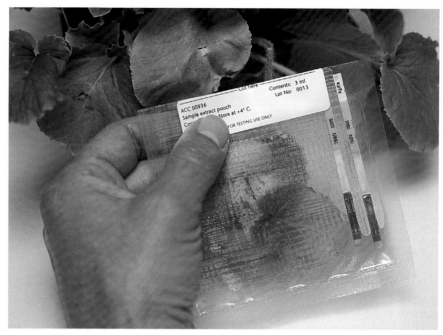

Several types of test kits are available for use in the field to determine whether plant tissue is infected with certain bacteria, fungi, or viruses. With the kit shown here, plant tissue is macerated in a pouch containing liquid, then detector strips are inserted through a slit. Certain color bands appear in the detector strips if the specific pathogen for which the test assays is present in plant tissue.

Gumming or a vertical streak, stain, or canker is often visible on the trunk of *Phytophthora*-infected trees, such as this citrus. However, certain plants often exude liquid when damaged, so this symptom can have other causes.

species of pathogen, and species of host plant. Often a vertical streak, stain, or canker becomes visible on infected trunk wood under bark. Black or reddish sap may ooze from darkened areas of infected bark. To confirm the presence of disease, cut away the outer bark around the stain streaks or canker. The concentric margins between the healthy whitish or yellowish wood and the reddish or brown infected wood in the trunk look like they are soaked with water. Woody roots decaying from *Phytophthora* are firm and brittle. In contrast, roots destroyed by excess water are soft, although *Phytophthora*-infected roots eventually soften because of the development of secondary decay organisms.

All *Phytophthora* species require high soil moisture to infect hosts, but temperature requirements vary. *Phytophthora cinnamomi,* an important species in California, spreads, infects plants, and develops rapidly during warm, moist conditions. In contrast, *P. cactorum* requires cool, moist weather. *Phytophthora* fungi can survive in the soil for many years and then enter susceptible plants through the

crown or roots. Depending on the species of *Phytophthora,* the pathogen may affect only small feeder roots or rootlets, major roots, or all roots and the crown. *Phytophthora ramorum,* the cause of sudden oak death as discussed above, infects through host trunks and leaves.

Phytophthora (and *Pythium*) species produce no fruiting bodies visible to the naked eye. Technically, *Phytophthora* and *Pythium* are not true fungi; they more closely resemble parasitic brown algae, which partly explains why the biology and management of *Phytophthora* and *Pythium* species differs some from that of soilborne fungi.

Confirmation of *Phytophthora* and *Pythium* species requires taking a sample from suspected infections, culturing it on laboratory medium, then examining this under a microscope. Test kits that employ the serological technique ELISA also are available. These can confirm the presence of *Phytophthora* in as little as 10 minutes with no need for specialized equipment or facilities. However, the use of test kits is limited primarily to nurseries and certain field crops where re-

Brownish streaks in roots indicate a *Phytophthora* infection.

search-based sampling recommendations have been developed. Caution must be exercised when using test kits, as several species of *Pythium* that apparently do not cause disease also react with the *Phytophthora* test kits. Samples must be collected from tissue having a viable infection. For more information on using ELISA test kits consult *Easy On-Site Tests for Fungi and Viruses in Nurseries and Greenhouses* (Kabashima et al. 1997).

MANAGEMENT

Prepare the site well before planting and provide appropriate cultural care, especially proper irrigation as discussed in the introduction to this chapter and in Chapter 3. Where Phytophthora root rot is a problem, such as where soils are compacted, drain poorly, or are usually damp, improve drainage and plant only species not reported to be susceptible. If you have identified *Phytophthora cinnamomi* as the cause of root disease, replant using species listed in Table 5-15. Some fungicides (for example, fosetyl-al) can be effective in managing certain *Phytophthora* species if combined with other practices, such as avoiding overirrigation and improving drainage. Their use may be warranted on some high-value specimen plants, but plants larger than medium-sized shrubs can be difficult to effectively treat in landscapes. Fungicides effective on *Phytophthora* or *Pythium* are often not effective against other root decay fungi such as *Rhizoctonia,* and vice versa. The genus of pathogen must definitely be known, and possibly the species may need to be identified, before applying a fungicide.

TABLE 5-15.

Trees and Shrubs Not Reported To Be Susceptible to *Phytophthora cinnamomi.*

COMMON NAME	GENUS NAME
albizia	*Albizia*
alder	*Alnus*
apple[1]	*Malus*
ash	*Fraxinus*
aspen	*Populus*
box elder	*Acer*
California bay[2]	*Umbellularia*
California buckeye[2]	*Aesculus*
cotoneaster[3]	*Cotoneaster*
cottonwood	*Populus*
coyote brush	*Baccharis*
elm	*Ulmus*
euonymus	*Euonymus*
honey locust	*Gleditsia*
linden	*Tilia*
madrone[1, 2]	*Arbutus*
magnolia	*Magnolia*
maidenhair tree	*Ginkgo*
mayten	*Maytenus*
oleander	*Nerium*
podocarpus	*Podocarpus*
poplar	*Populus*
sweet gum	*Liquidambar*
tamarisk	*Tamarix*
toyon[1, 2]	*Heteromeles*
tulip tree	*Liriodendron*
zelkova	*Zelkova*

This list provides only a guideline; host vigor and environmental conditions are important in disease development. Some hosts are susceptible to other *Phytophthora* species.

1. Susceptible to *Phytophthora cactorum.*
2. Susceptible to *Phytophthora ramorum.*
3. Susceptible to *Phytophthora cryptogea* and *P. parasitica.*

Sources: Farr et al. 1989, Ohr et al. 1980.

Applying the wrong material can do more harm than good by killing non-pathogen microorganisms that naturally help to limit certain pathogens.

Applying organic mulch and gypsum (calcium sulfate) beneath shallow-rooted shrubs and small trees (such as avocado and citrus) may help reduce survival of *Phytophthora* propagules (sporangia and zoospores), thereby reducing the incidence of new infections. The beneficial effect of organic mulch and gypsum is limited to within the mulch and the soil mulch interface where shallow roots occur; mulch and gypsum provide little if any benefit for large trees or plants with most of their roots deeper in the soil. Pathogen suppression may require several years to develop and probably affects only certain species of *Phytophthora*. Applying organic mulch and gypsum may only prevent new infections under certain circumstances and will not control Phytophthora root rots already infecting plants.

A general recommendation is to make a surface application of gypsum at a rate of about 25 pounds per 100 square feet and to maintain (periodically reapply after decomposition) organic mulch at a thickness of about 4 inches. Because mulch retards drying of soil and excess soil moisture greatly contributes to the development of root rots, improper or excessive use of mulch may actually promote root rot development. Most of the research on this method is from commercial orchards, such as avocado and citrus susceptible to *Phytophthora cinnamomi* and *P. citricola*. There is little information on the efficacy of gypsum and mulch for pathogen control in landscapes.

Pythium Root Rot

Although *Phytophthora* species are the more likely cause of root rot in woody landscape plants, *Pythium* species, and occasionally other soilborne pathogens such as *Rhizoctonia* species, can also cause basal stem decay and root rot of older, susceptible plants. *Pythium* and these others more often affect herbaceous species or cause "damping-off," the death of seedlings that collapse at the soil line under damp conditions. *Phytophthora* and *Pythium* species are closely related; both resemble parasitic brown algae and are not considered to be true fungi.

Prevent Pythium root rot and damping-off diseases by preparing the site well before planting and providing appropriate cultural care, especially proper irrigation and good drainage, as discussed earlier in this chapter and in Chapter 3. Manage Pythium root rot using the same techniques discussed above for Phytophthora root and crown rots.

Solarizing the soil before planting (see Chapter 7) can reduce *Pythium* fungi. Some fungicides available to professional applicators can be effective against *Pythium* (for example, fosetyl-al), and their use may be warranted on some high-value, specimen plants. However, fungicides effective on fungi such as *Rhizoctonia* are often not effective against *Phytophthora* or *Pythium,* and vice versa, so the genus of pathogen must definitely

Pythium infecting roots and overwatering are contributing to these aboveground symptoms, browning and decline of rose shoots.

be known before applying a fungicide. Applying the wrong material can do more harm than good by killing non-pathogen microorganisms that naturally help to limit certain pathogens.

VIRUSES

Viruses are submicroscopic noncellular particles that infect cells, changing some cell functions. Most viruses distort or discolor foliage. Viruses of abutilon, camellia, *Nandina* (heavenly bamboo), and rose are discussed here, but many other woody landscape plants may show similar viral symptoms on occasion.

DAMAGE

Viruses can slow plant growth, but most do not seriously harm woody landscape plants. Damage is usually noticeable only in flowers or foliage. Infected blossoms or leaves may become spotted, streaked, discolored, distorted, or stunted. The variegation or other appearance changes that viruses cause are sometimes considered to be attractive, such as abutilon mosaic virus.

IDENTIFICATION AND BIOLOGY

Most viral pathogens in landscape plants are named after the main or first-recognized host plant and a primary type of damage they cause. For example, apple mosaic virus and elm mosaic virus cause an irregular pattern of discolored leaves on apple and elm, respectively. Hibiscus chlorotic ringspot and prunus necrotic ringspot cause small yellow or brownish spots or blotches on the leaves of hibiscus or plants in the rose family, respectively.

Viruses can be transmitted by insects feeding on plant sap or mechanically in sap that is spread by hand or grafting tools. Viruses also commonly spread in seed, pollen, or in vegetative parts of plants used for propagation through budding and grafting. Once a plant becomes infected with virus, it usually remains infected throughout its life. Some viruses have a relatively narrow host range and apparently infect only one genus of plants, such as some that infect elms. Other viruses have a broad host range, such as impatiens necrotic spot virus and tomato spotted wilt virus, which are two members of the incompletely understood tospovirus complex that infects several hundred genera of mostly herbaceous plants, including many flowering ornamentals.

Rose Mosaic Virus

Rose mosaic virus, also called Prunus necrotic ringspot virus, may be a complex of more than one pathogen. Roses can also be infected by many other different viruses. Virus infection causes yellow to brownish lines, bands, rings, vein clearing or yellowing, oak-leaf patterns, or blotches on leaves, sometimes on only a portion of the plant. Virus-infected plants may grow more slowly, produce delayed or fewer flowers, and become more susceptible to frost damage. The severity of damage varies with the host cultivar, and some infected roses exhibit no damage. Rose mosaic and most other rose viruses are not spread by insects or pruning tools. These pathogens do not infect healthy roses except through grafting, budding, or rooting cuttings from infected plants. Roses infected during propagation can be symptomless until after they are planted and begin growing in landscapes.

Camellia Yellow Mottle Virus

Camellia yellow mottle virus causes an irregular yellow mottling of camellia leaves and a mottled whitish pattern in the blossoms. Camellia yellow mottle virus is sometimes deliberately introduced through grafting to produce an attractive leaf or flower variegation. It is spread only by budding, grafting, or rooting plants that are infected.

Vein clearing and yellow patterns on rose leaves caused by rose mosaic virus.

Camellia yellow mottle virus causes irregular yellow areas on foliage and pale blotches on petals (color break). Although discoloring may be aesthetically objectionable, most viruses do not seriously harm woody landscape plants.

Some virus infections may be considered attractive, like this nandina virus that causes reddish mottling on new leaves of heavenly bamboo.

Nandina Virus

Nandina virus causes a mottled red discoloration of the new leaves of heavenly bamboo. Nandina virus is apparently the same as cucumber mosaic virus, which infects a variety of agricultural and ornamental plants and annual and perennial weeds. Nandina virus is spread by aphids, especially the melon and green peach aphids. Aphids acquire the virus while feeding on infected plants and transmit it when they move and feed on other plants.

Abutilon Mosaic Virus

Abutilon mosaic virus causes vein-limited yellow blotches on leaves of Chinese lantern or Chinese bellflower. These leaf blotches are considered attractive; infected plants are commonly sold as variegated plants. The virus is deliberately spread by propagating with infected stock to produce the bright yellow variegation on leaves. More than one type of virus can infect abutilon, including abu-

tilon mosaic geminivirus, which is called a geminivirus because the virus particles, visible under extreme magnification, are formed in pairs (*gemini* is the Latin word for "twin"). See the section "Action Thresholds and Guidelines" near the beginning of Chapter 2 for a photograph of infected leaves.

MANAGEMENT

There is no cure or treatment for virus-infected plants in landscapes, and generally none is needed for woody ornamentals. Provide proper cultural care to improve plant vigor or replace infected plants if their growth is unsatisfactory. Purchase and plant only high-quality, certified virus-free, or virus-resistant nursery stock or seeds. Do not graft virus-infected plant parts onto virus-free plants unless you want to introduce the virus. Although certain viruses are spread by aphids and other insects that suck plant juices, controlling insects is generally not a recommended method of preventing virus infection in woody landscapes. It is very difficult to detect or control insects effectively at the low densities that can spread a virus, and to continually provide control through-

out the life of perennial plants, especially insects like the melon and green peach aphids that spread nandina virus and feed on many different plant species.

PHYTOPLASMAS

Phytoplasmas, formerly called mycoplasmas, are so minute they can be seen clearly only with an electron microscope. These single-cell organisms resemble bacteria, but they lack a cell wall. Phytoplasmas and phytoplasmalike organisms are often spread by leafhoppers. Yellowing, dwarfing, and abnormal leaves and shoots such as witches' brooms are common symptoms of phytoplasma infections. Some phytoplasmas cause severe decline and eventually the death of certain infected plants. Many phytoplasmas are poorly known, and their importance as pests of landscape plants may be underestimated.

Peach yellow leafroll and X-disease of cherry and peach are phytoplasma diseases that damage foliage, alter fruit flavor, and cause infected fruit trees to decline, as discussed in *Integrated Pest*

Diseases caused by phytoplasmas are often called "yellows" because chlorotic foliage is a common damage symptom. Peach yellow leafroll, caused by a phytoplasmalike organism, infects the leaf on the right, which is chlorotic, cupped, and has an enlarged midvein.

Management for Stone Fruits (Strand 1999). Ash yellows of ash and lilacs, elm yellows, and lethal yellowing of palm are important pathogens of woody landscape plants that so far in the United States have been found only in the East. Aster yellows, which is poorly understood and may be a complex of related phytoplasmas, is the most important phytoplasma infecting herbaceous flowering ornamentals, but it does not affect woody plants.

No chemicals are effective against phytoplasmas. Control them primarily through proper sanitation, excluding and controlling insect vectors, and using only pathogen-free stock. Sanitation primarily entails removing infected plants that are a source of pathogen that can spread, including certain weeds. For example, burclover (*Medicago polymorpha*), clovers (*Melilotus* and *Trifolium* spp.), and dandelion (*Taraxacum officinale*) host X-disease that spreads when certain leafhoppers feed on mycoplasma-infected plants and move to feed on cherry and peach. Cultivars often vary significantly in their susceptibility to phytoplasmas. Seek information on resistant cultivars and plant them where phytoplasmas are a problem.

Abiotic or Noninfectious Disorders

A N ABIOTIC (nonliving) or noninfectious disorder is plant damage caused by adverse environmental conditions. Many disorders result from human activity. For instance, injury may develop because the species planted is not well adapted to conditions at that location, the site was not well prepared before landscaping, or because of improper planting or inappropriate care. Causes of abiotic disorders include air pollution, herbicides or other pesticides, too little or too much water, mechanical injury, nutrient deficiencies or excesses, and poor drainage. Activities that compact soils, change soil grade, or injure trunks or roots also cause disorders.

The first step in remedying a noninfectious disorder is to identify the cause. Distinguish abiotic disorders from similar damage caused by pests such as insects, mites, pathogens, and vertebrates. Many noninfectious disorders can be recognized by distorted, discolored, or dying foliage. However, diagnosing the cause of disorders can be difficult. Different causes can produce the same symptoms. Often more than one cause is adversely affecting plants at the same time. In addition to directly damaging plants, abiotic disorders can predispose trees and shrubs to attack by insects and pathogens. Disorders and pests can act in combination to the extent of killing plants. Consult Table 6-1 to help you diagnose the cause of abiotic disorders based on symptoms. Consult publications such as *Abiotic Disorders of Landscape Plants: A Diagnostic Guide* (Costello et al. 2003) for more extensive discussion and photographs on this topic.

Cultural practices that cause or avoid abiotic disorders are discussed in Chapter 3. Causes of noninfectious disorders discussed here include air pollution, extreme light or temperatures, herbicides and other pesticides, gas, mechanical wounding, nutrient deficiencies and excesses, pH, and salts.

Water Deficiency and Excess

Inappropriate irrigation (often in combination with slow drainage) is probably the most common cause of landscape plant damage. Inadequate water causes foliage to wilt, discolor, and drop prematurely. Prolonged moisture stress results in smaller leaves, slower growth, dieback, and susceptibility to wood-boring insects and other pests, which eventually can kill plants. Irrigating too frequently (overirrigation) is more common than insufficient

273

This branch dieback on ash was caused by insufficient water. Irrigating too frequently also causes dieback. Too much water is more common in California landscapes than insufficient irrigation.

irrigation. Excess soil moisture deprives roots of oxygen and kills roots. As roots die, discolored and dying foliage appears in the aboveground portion of the plant. For more information on irrigation, see the section "Water Management" in Chapter 3 or consult publications such as "Water Management" (Hartin and Faber 2002).

Aeration Deficit

Aeration is the ability of roots to obtain adequate oxygen. Because roots require oxygen for metabolism, respiration, and uptake of nutrients and water, insufficient oxygen in the root zone is a serious, often life-threatening problem. Discolored or yellow leaves, premature leaf drop, stunted growth, wilting, and the gradual decline and death of plants are common aeration deficit symptoms. Air pollution, drought stress, excess salts, extreme light, herbicide toxicity, gas injury, overirrigation (irrigating too

frequently), and root pathogens cause similar damage symptoms. Excess soil moisture, insufficient oxygen, and root rot pathogens often act in combination to damage or kill plants.

Aeration deficit is especially common in irrigated landscapes. Excess soil moisture prevents adequate aeration because water occupies most of the pore spaces among soil particles, impeding oxygen diffusion (movement through soil) and leaving few water-free pore spaces for oxygen to occupy. Irrigating too frequently, especially when drainage is poor (slow), is the most common cause of aeration deficit. Compaction, flooding, hardpan (an impermeable soil layer), insufficient soil volume for root growth, poor soil structure and texture, a shallow water table, and surface barriers such as pavement are other causes of insufficient oxygen in soils.

Diagnose aeration deficit by investigating whether the causes listed above are present. Assess drainage, check soil moisture, determine whether the grade has been changed, and especially evalu-

ate irrigation practices. Measure soil bulk density (bulk density higher than critical levels for that soil texture indicates compaction). Send soil samples to a diagnostic laboratory to determine composition (soil aeration decreases with increasing percentage of clay). A percolation test, as described in the section "Prepare the Site" in Chapter 3, measures soil drainage (infiltration rate), which is one indicator of aeration. Instruments that directly measure soil oxygen and diffusion are used by researchers but generally are of little practical value to landscape managers because of the expense, skill, and time they require.

Prevent aeration deficit through good site preparation, appropriate planting, and proper cultural practices as discussed in the sections "Site Preparation and Planting" and "Irrigation" in Chapter 3. For more information, consult other publications such as *Arboriculture: Integrated Management of Landscape Trees, Shrubs, and Vines* (Harris, Clark, and Matheny 1999) and *Abiotic Disorders of Landscape Plants: A Diagnostic Guide* (Costello et al. 2003).

Nutrient Deficiencies

Plants require certain mineral nutrients for healthy growth. Deficiencies cause foliage to discolor, fade, distort, or become spotted, sometimes in a characteristic pattern that can help you identify the cause. Fewer leaves, flowers, and fruit may be produced, and these can develop later than normal and remain undersized. More severely deficient plants become stunted, exhibit dieback, are predisposed to other maladies, and can even die.

Nutrient deficiency symptoms in woody landscape plants usually are not due to a deficiency of nutrients in soil. Inadequate nitrogen, phosphorus, and potassium are especially rare in established landscape trees and shrubs, except in containers or planter boxes, fruit and nut trees, and palms. Nutrient defi-

TABLE 6-1.

Common Noninfectious Disorder Symptoms and Their Abiotic Causes.

SYMPTOMS	POSSIBLE CAUSE	MANAGEMENT
Bark is cracked or sunken, often on the south and west sides. Buds, flowers, limbs, and shoots may die back. Wood may be attacked by boring insects or decay fungi.	sunburn or sunscald	page 288
Bark or wood is dead, often in a streak or band on the trunk.	lightning	page 293
Foliage grows excessively or is overly succulent. Foliage may appear "burned" and die. Plant is infested with many aphids, mites, psyllids, or other invertebrates that suck plant juices.	nitrogen excess	page 280
Foliage is discolored, pale, or burned.	excess light	page 288
Foliage is darkened, pale, or yellowish. Shoots are long and spindly.	deficient light	page 289
Foliage is discolored, undersized, sparse, or distorted and may drop prematurely. Plant growth is slow. Limbs may die back	mineral deficiency	pages 40, 274, and Table 6-2
Foliage or shoots turn yellowish, are undersized, or distorted. Leaves may appear "burned" with dead margins and drop.	pesticide toxicity	page 284, Table 6-4
Foliage turns brown, dry, and crispy. Limbs may die back. Odor of ammonia, natural gas, or rotten eggs may be detectable.	gas injury	Contact utility company immediately if a natural gas leak is suspected.
Foliage wilts, droops, discolors, and drops prematurely. Foliage is undersized and plant grows slowly. Buds, flowers, limbs, and shoots may die back. Bark cracks and develops cankers. Plant may become attacked by wood-boring insects.	water deficiency	pages 234, 273, and Table 3-3
Foliage yellows and drops. Buds, limbs, and shoots die back. Root crown diseases develop. Mineral deficiency or toxicity symptoms develop.	water excess or poor (slow) drainage	pages 34, 273, and Table 3-4
Foliage, twigs, or limbs are injured. Small irregular depressions on stems. Cankers may develop.	hail or ice	page 292
Leaves develop yellow, brown, then white areas on upper side, beginning between veins. Foliage may die.	sunburn	page 288
Leaves or needles turn brownish, yellowish, or have discolored flecks. Foliage may be sparse, stunted, and drop prematurely.	air pollution	page 293
Leaves turn yellowish or brownish, especially along margins. Foliage may be undersized, distorted, or drop prematurely. Bark becomes corky.	mineral excess or salt toxicity	pages 40, 280
Shoots, buds, or flowers curl, darken, and die. Limbs and entire plant may die.	freezing or frost	page 291

Many of these symptoms can have other causes, including insects and pathogens. See the "Tree and Shrub Pest Tables" at the end of this book for a list of the pests commonly affecting each plant species.

ciency symptoms usually result from other causes, especially adverse soil conditions and anything that injures roots or restricts root growth. Common causes of deficiency symptoms include high pH, inappropriate irrigation, physical injury to roots, poor drainage, and root decay pathogens. With a few exceptions, such as fruit and nut trees and palms, fertilization of established woody plants is not recommended unless insufficient soil nutrients has definitely been diagnosed as the cause of unhealthy plants. Adding nutrients will not improve the appearance of foliage damaged by other causes and may divert attention from solving the true cause of unhealthy plants. Symptoms of common deficiencies are summarized in Table 6-2 and are discussed below. Consult publications such as *Abiotic Disorders of Landscape Plants: A Diagnostic Guide* (Costello et al. 2003) and *Fertilizing Landscape Trees* (Perry and Hickman 2001) for more detailed infor- mation on prevention, diagnosis, testing, and remediation of nutrient deficiencies.

NITROGEN

Uniform yellowing of leaves is usually the first symptom of nitrogen (N) deficiency. When deficient in nitrogen, plants grow slowly and in the spring produce fewer and smaller than normal leaves and shoots. Discolored foliage may drop prematurely or turn reddish during the fall.

Relatively uniform yellowing of leaves may indicate nitrogen deficiency in this rhododendron. Most deficiency symptoms are caused by adverse soil conditions and poor root health that prevent nutrient uptake. Symptoms due to these causes will not be remedied by soil fertilization.

Yellowish elemental sulfur has been spread on the ground beneath this tree's drip line. Once irrigated in, this sulfur can help to gradually remedy nutrient deficiencies caused by high soil pH. Because sulfur is relatively insoluble in water, it is more effective to mix sulfur with native soil and backfill the mix into shallow trenches. Alternatively, apply it in holes made using a soil probe, which requires many holes. The benefits may not be apparent for months.

When established woody plants exhibit nitrogen deficiency symptoms, the cause usually is not a lack of nitrogen in the soil. Exceptions are containers or planter boxes, fruit and nut trees, palms, and plants growing in very sandy soils. Symptoms resembling nitrogen deficiency can be caused by anything that impairs root health or restricts root growth. Common causes include adverse soil temperatures, compaction, low oxygen, poor drainage, root-feeding insects, root pruning, or root rot pathogens. These problems can produce chlorotic leaves, smaller and fewer leaves, and reduced shoot growth that resemble nitrogen deficiency. Adding nitrogen will not remedy these other causes. Excess nitrogen can pollute water, increase populations of certain sucking insects and mites, and promote diseases such as fire blight.

Visual observation of symptoms alone cannot diagnose nitrogen deficiency. Diagnose nitrogen deficiency by ruling out other potential causes and possibly by testing foliar nitrogen levels. There are no guidelines for appropriate nitrogen levels in most ornamentals, but conifer and broadleaf foliage typically has 1 to 3% total nitrogen. If testing foliage, con-

duct separate leaf analyses on current-season foliage of unhealthy and healthy plants of same species growing nearby and compare test results. Soil analyses are probably not useful because nitrogen availability in soil can change rather quickly and nitrogen availability to plants varies with soil conditions and plant rooting.

Nitrogen is provided to plants in nature by the decay of organic matter. Bacteria in soil or associated with roots also supply small amounts by converting nitrogen from air into forms usable by plants. Also, people supplement the nitrogen supply by applying fertilizers. Nitrogen availability to plants is reduced when nitrogen is absorbed by weeds, used by other organisms such as soil microbes decomposing organic matter low in nitrogen, or is leached from the root zone by water. Nitrogen availability is influenced by irrigation, pH, temperature, and the organisms present in soil. In the uncommon situations when it is appropriate to add nitrogen for established woody landscapes, nitrogen is commonly provided to plants as organic matter, as urea from either organic or synthetic sources, or as inorganic compounds of nitrate or ammonium.

Organic sources of nitrogen include blood, cottonseed, compost, fish meal, manures, and sewage sludge. Most organic forms of nitrogen must decompose before being absorbed by plants. Depending on soil conditions, decomposition takes weeks (when moist and warm) to months (when cool and dry). This slower availability of nitrogen is often desirable when growing woody plants. Organic material added to soil also improves soil tilth, increasing soil's water- and air-holding capacity and reducing compaction. However, compost and manure contain relatively little nitrogen, and manure is often high in salts, which can damage plants. Mixing excessive amounts of undecomposed organic matter into soil may actually increase nitrogen deficiency in plants because decomposer microorganisms can use up most of the available nitrogen. To avoid this problem, properly compost undecomposed organic matter and, before mixing it into soil, consider supplementing it by mixing in a more readily available form of nitrogen at a rate of about 1 pound of nitrogen per cubic yard of organic matter. If using ammonium sulfate, which is 21% nitrogen, a general recommendation would be to add 5 pounds of ammonium sulfate per cubic yard of organic matter before thoroughly mixing this into topsoil so that the organic amendment constitutes no more than about 20% of the soil volume in the upper 1 to 2 feet.

Commercially formulated slow-release fertilizers are also available (such as sulfur- or polymer-coated urea). They provide the easy handling of synthetic fertilizers and the preferred slow-release characteristics of organic materials. Although more expensive than other preparations, these can be a good choice for adding nitrogen to nutrient-poor soils.

If you determine that nitrogen is needed, consider what form is most appropriate for your situation. Fertilizers can undesirably alter soil pH, increase soil salinity, inhibit flowering, promote excess succulent growth that favors pests, kill leaves or roots, and pollute the environment. Use the correct type, rate, and method of fertilization for that situation.

PHOSPHORUS

Phosphorus deficiency is rare. Plants deficient in phosphorus (P) produce short, spindly shoots and grow slowly. Leaves can develop a bluish or purplish tint, and lower canopy leaves may turn light bronze with purple or brown spots. A plant may be deficient if current-season foliage of conifers or woody broadleaves is tested and found to contain less than 0.1% phosphorus, or if comparison testing reveals substantially less phosphorus in foliage from healthy versus nearby symptomatic plants of the same species.

Phosphorus occurs in soil in adequate amounts for most trees and shrubs. An exception is serpentine soils, such as in the Sierra Nevada foothills, where adding phosphorus can be beneficial. If phosphorus is deficient in

Pinched, undulating leaf margins on a phosphorus-deficient pear tree. These symptoms are typically due to poor soil conditions or unhealthy roots. Adding phosphorus to California soils is rarely beneficial to landscape plants.

leaves, the most likely causes are soil or root problems, as described above for nitrogen. Certain herbicides also cause leaf distortion and curling that resembles phosphorus deficiency symptoms. In unusual cases when soil is phosphorus-deficient, add a phosphorus fertilizer such as phosphoric acid. Relatively large amounts of chicken manure also provide this nutrient, but can be detrimental because manure often has a high salt content. Regardless of the form, adding phosphorus to most soils in California is rarely beneficial to landscape plants.

POTASSIUM

Potassium (K) deficiency causes leaf spotting and sparse leaf growth on shoots. Older leaves turn yellow and develop brown or yellow tips and margins or spots near the leaf edge. Palms develop yellow or orangish flecks or spots on older leaves. Potassium deficiency is rare in broadleaves and conifers in California landscapes. When present, deficiency symptoms are usually due to poor soil conditions and unhealthy roots, as

discussed above for nitrogen. Some sucking insects, foliar pathogens, and certain preemergence herbicides cause similar damage symptoms.

Fruit and nut trees grown in sandy soils occasionally suffer from a lack of potassium in soil. Palms are also susceptible to a deficiency of potassium, especially areca (*Dypsis* spp.), coconut, date, queen, royal, and sabal palms. Otherwise, potassium deficiency is rare in landscape trees and shrubs in California soils.

Foliage tests are unreliable for diagnosing this malady. Diagnose potassium deficiency based on visual symptoms, plant susceptibility (palms, and sometimes fruit and nut trees), and the presence of soil conditions that favor a deficiency (high leaching, sandy soil, sparse topsoil). To correct a deficiency, apply a slow-release potassium fertilizer if available (such as potassium silicate or sulfur- or polymer-coated products), then irrigate. Alternatively, apply potassium sulfate and water it in, spread organic mulch beneath plants, or both fertilize and mulch. Potassium nitrate may also be used, but this may result in the application of excess nitrogen unless nitrogen deficiency is also a problem. Do not use potassium chloride where chlorine or salt toxicity is a problem. Be aware that adding only potassium can cause an imbalance between potassium and magnesium because high potassium concentration reduces magnesium availability (and excess magnesium makes potassium unavailable).

It may be best to add both potassium and magnesium in combination, such as by using fertilizers formulated especially for palms. A slow-release fertilizer containing magnesium and with nitrogen, phosphorus, and potassium (NPK) in a ratio of 3-1-3 is good for palms. To avoid aggravating potassium deficiency, do not remove symptomatic leaves until they have turned entirely brown. Symptomatic palm foliage will not recover, and you must wait for new growth.

NITROGEN, PHOSPHORUS, AND POTASSIUM (NPK)

So-called complete fertilizers contain nitrogen (N), phosphorus (P), and potassium (K), listed by the percentage weight of NPK in that order. Except when growing palms or at very sandy or highly leached sites, soil around landscape trees and shrubs is rarely deficient in all three elements. Adding sufficient complete fertilizer to provide the deficient element can result in an excess of other nutrients and may contribute to salinity problems and water pollution. Established woody plants should be fertilized in response to specific needs. Complete fertilizers are generally not recommended for woody landscape plants, except for palms and possibly other woody monocots.

IRON

Iron deficiency causes new foliage to be bleached, chlorotic, or pale with green veins. Fading appears first around leaf margins, then spreads inward until only the veins are green. In contrast, nitrogen deficiency causes entire leaves, usually older leaves, to turn yellow. Brown spots can develop in leaves because iron deficiency inhibits plant metabolism and chlorophyll availability, making leaves susceptible to sunburn. Damaged leaves may dry and drop prematurely.

Insufficient iron is probably the most common deficiency in California landscapes even though sufficient iron is present in most soils. Many plants, such as azaleas, citrus, gardenias, and rhododendrons are adapted to acidic (low pH), well-drained, aerated soils high in organic matter. These plants are especially prone to iron deficiency because iron is less available and plants are unable to absorb iron if the soil is alkaline (high pH, as is common in California), high in calcium, poorly drained, waterlogged, too cool, or root health is impaired by pathogens or other causes.

Tissue analysis may not be reliable for diagnosing iron deficiency. Diagnose this malady based on visual symptoms, soil tests (for example, showing high pH or low organic matter), and knowledge of existing cultural practices, soil conditions, and whether iron deficiency is common in that species. Recognize that certain preemergence herbicides cause similar damage symptoms. However, preemergence herbicide damage occurs primarily on older leaves, while iron deficiency symptoms are most pronounced in new growth.

Remedy iron deficiency primarily by improving cultural practices and the soil environment. To improve aeration and reduce water logging, increase the interval between irrigations to the maximum extent that still provides adequate moisture to maintain good growth. If plants are small, consider digging them up and replanting them on a broad mound raised several inches to improve drainage. Amend soils to improve drainage, lower pH, and increase organic matter before planting or replanting species adapted to acidic soils.

If soil is alkaline, about 6 months before planting add 1 to 2 pounds of elemental sulfur per 100 square feet of soil surface, mix or rototill it in the top 6 inches, and irrigate. Bacteria slowly convert sulfur to sulfuric acid, which lowers soil pH and increases iron availability. This acidifying process may take several months, and soil must be moist, warm,

TABLE 6-2.

Common Mineral Deficiency Symptoms.

SYMPTOMS	DEFICIENCY
New foliage may be undersized and yellowish, except for green along veins. Brown dead spots may develop between veins. Leaves may be distorted or may dry and drop prematurely. Plants grow slowly, and branches may eventually die.	iron or manganese
Leaves or needles are uniformly pale green to yellowish. New growth is sparse and undersized but usually is green. Plants grow slowly and may drop foliage prematurely.	nitrogen
Foliage is abnormally dark green, bluish, purplish, or may develop spots. Shoots are short and spindly, and plant grows slowly. Phosphorus deficiency is rare in landscapes.	phosphorus
Foliage growth is sparse. Older foliage is yellowish and may have brown, orange, or yellow tips and margins or brownish spots near leaf edges or between veins. Uncommon in California landscapes except in palms and fruit or nut trees grown in sandy soils.	potassium
Leaves are uniformly yellowish and stunted, especially on new growth. Spring leaf flush and blossoming may be delayed. New leaves may be small, narrow, and grow in tufts. Foliage may turn purplish and die. Eventually, branches begin to die back.	zinc

These nutrient deficiency symptoms usually are not due to insufficient nutrients in soil; symptoms more commonly result from adverse soil conditions or anything that injures roots or restricts root growth, thereby inhibiting nutrient uptake.

Yellow new growth with distinctly green veins indicates an iron deficiency in this toyon. Sufficient iron is present in most soils. Deficiency symptoms typically are caused by adverse soil conditions such as high pH and poor drainage.

MANGANESE

Manganese (Mn) deficiency produces pale, chlorotic, sometimes stunted leaves with only the smallest veins remaining green. Brown dead spots can develop on leaves because manganese deficiency reduces chlorophyll production, making leaves susceptible to sunburn. Discoloration from manganese deficiency usually occurs only in new foliage, although older foliage is sometimes symptomatic in certain hosts such as mulberry and poinsettia. Some people believe you can visually distinguish the symptoms of iron deficiency from manganese deficiency, for example, by broader green veins or less severe discoloring when manganese deficiency is the cause. However, manganese deficiency symptoms are often nearly indistinguishable from iron deficiency, and any differences are too variable and unreliable to visually distinguish these maladies.

Diagnose this malady as described for iron deficiency. Manganese deficiency occurs primarily in certain species such as palms and in plants growing under adverse conditions such as in soils that are alkaline, cool, and poorly drained. Leaf symptoms can be remedied by lowering soil pH, increasing organic matter, and by otherwise improving the plant's cultural practices and growing environment, as discussed above for iron deficiency. Manganese chelates can be applied as labeled to newly emerging foliage as a quick, temporary remedy.

ZINC

Zinc deficiency, sometimes called little-leaf disease, most often occurs in fruit and nut trees, usually those grown in sandy soils or soils abnormally high in organic matter, such as former animal corral sites or old feed lots. Zinc deficiency is relatively uncommon in most other landscapes and is especially rare in palms. A mild deficiency of zinc (Zn) resembles iron or manganese deficiency; leaves are pale between the veins, may develop dead spots, and can be undersized. Symptoms are usually most apparent on new foliage in the spring.

and well aerated. Acidification is not effective if soil alkalinity is high (high in lime content, such as excess calcium carbonate). See the sections "pH" and "Alkalinity" below for an explanation of the differences between alkaline soils and alkalinity.

Alternatively, before planting, add acidic sphagnum peat or organic matter that has been well composted and mix it into the top 1 to 2 feet of soil at a rate not exceeding 20% of soil volume. Be aware that amended soils will settle as organic matter decomposes, causing new plants to settle in the planting hole and become subject to root and crown diseases. When planting in amended soil, compost organic matter well before use, form soil into a broad mound, place the rootball on solid soil, and plant about 2 inches or more above the native soil line.

One quick method is to spread an iron chelate evenly over the soil beneath the plant canopy or apply it to foliage according to the product label; check and compare labels to determine the percentage of iron before purchasing a product. Foliage appearance is only temporarily restored by chelates, so if used, apply them in combination with measures to improve the plant's culture, environment, and soil conditions. If applying inorganic fertilizers, switch from nitrate- to ammonium-based compounds; ammoniacal fertilizers such as ammonium nitrate gradually lower soil pH. Alternatively, use a soil probe to create holes in the soil around the drip line, then fill the holes with elemental sulfur or fill each hole with soil mixed with 2 or 3 teaspoons of sulfur. This will gradually lower soil pH and increase iron availability, but this method requires many holes and benefits may not become apparent until months later. Iron is also applied by trunk injections, but injections injure trunks.

Regularly placing composted organic matter as mulch on top of the roots of established plants will eventually (slowly) remedy iron deficiency; iron is taken up by roots as soil becomes more acidic and organic matter decays. Conifer needle mulch reportedly is more acidifying than mulch from broadleaf plants. Allow fallen leaves to remain on the soil over plant roots or gather and compost leaves and other organic debris, then spread this mulch over the soil. Mulch provides many benefits in addition to increasing nutrient availability.

Zinc-deficient trees can develop small, chlorotic leaves in tufts, like this almond. However, some zinc-deficient plants do not develop tufted foliage. Damage resembling this is also caused by glyphosate herbicide.

Severely deficient plants bloom and leaf out late, sometimes several weeks later than normal. When buds do open, leaves are small, mottled yellow, and may grow in tufts. Affected leaves may later turn purplish and die. When plants are severely affected, branches also die. Symptoms often resemble, and can be confused with, glyphosate herbicide injury.

Zinc is usually present in soils in adequate amounts. However, because zinc concentrations are naturally highest in surface soils, topsoil removal or grading can sometimes cause zinc deficiency in disturbed soils. Most commonly the problem is that plants cannot adequately absorb the zinc that is present. Zinc availability to plants is reduced by high soil pH, unhealthy roots, and by many of the same inappropriate cultural practices and adverse environmental conditions discussed for iron and nitrogen deficiencies.

Diagnose zinc deficiency based on characteristic foliar symptoms, laboratory soil analysis (which can reveal high pH or high phosphorus concentrations in soil that reduce zinc availability), and assessment of conditions that affect zinc availability. Remedy zinc deficiency by improving cultural practices and soil conditions to facilitate zinc uptake by plants.

If needed, apply zinc sulfate or chelates once a year according to the label; methods include applying the material to soil beneath plants and watering it in thoroughly or applying it as a foliar spray to newly emerging leaves.

MAGNESIUM

Magnesium (Mg) deficiency is extremely rare in broadleaves and conifers in landscape, but it is common in palms in southern California and the southwestern United States. In magnesium-deficient palms, individual leaf tips and the perimeter of fronds turn bright yellow, while leaf bases and frond tissue along the midrib remain green. Lower fronds may senesce prematurely.

This deficiency can be remedied by fertilizing soil with magnesium sulfate. Be aware that adding only magnesium sometimes leads to an imbalance between magnesium and potassium because high magnesium concentrations reduce potassium availability (and excess potassium makes magnesium unavailable). It may be best to add both potassium and magnesium in combination, such as by using fertilizers formulated especially for palms. To avoid aggravating this deficiency, do not remove symptomatic leaves until they have turned entirely brown. Symptomatic

leaves do not recover and must be replaced by new growth.

Nutrient and Mineral Excesses

Nutrients, salts, and pesticides can be toxic to plants if present in excess amounts or if applied incorrectly. Toxicity symptoms include leaf tip dieback, marginal leaf chlorosis, necrosis (or burn), branch dieback, and increased pest problems.

NITROGEN

Excess nitrogen kills small roots on plants and causes leaves to turn dark green, gray, or brown along the margins. Foliage may wilt temporarily or die. Plants given too much fertilizer grow excessively and develop succulent tissue, which promotes the development of certain pest problems, as discussed in Chapter 3. Apply only moderate amounts of fertilizer when needed. Slow-release fertilizers, as described in the nitrogen deficiency section above, are less likely to cause an excess in available nitrogen. Alleviate any drought stress before application and irrigate well after fertilizing.

SALINITY

Salts are compounds that separate into anions and cations in water or moist soil. Anions are negatively charged compounds or elements, such as chloride and sulfate. Cations, such as ammonium, calcium, and sodium, are positively charged. Plants normally obtain most nutrients from salts, and plants tolerate many different types of salts in low concentrations. However, roots and foliage can be injured by exposure to high concentrations of almost any salts, including those applied as fertilizer.

Soils with high salt concentrations are called saline soils. Saline soils can damage roots and prevent plants from absorbing nutrients and water. Saline soils may also contain specific ions, such as boron, that are toxic to plants at relatively low concentrations, even when overall measures of salinity are within acceptable limits. Soils high in exchangeable (readily available) sodium are called alkaline or sodic soils. Sodic soils are sometimes evident because of a white or dark crust on the soil surface and increasingly slow water penetration. Sodic soils may also damage roots and kill plants. Extreme levels of sodium can destroy the aggregate structure of fine- and medium-textured soils, preventing soil from holding air and water, so that plants cannot grow.

Root exposure to high salt concentrations causes wilting, stunted plant growth, and premature leaf drop. Margins of leaves or tips of needles commonly turn brown, reddish, or yellow, usually beginning with older foliage. Foliage exposed directly to water high in salts also discolors, beginning terminally and marginally, and may drop prematurely. Foliar salt exposure sometimes produces a distinct pattern of damage, such as only on lower foliage sprinkled with salty water or on the windward side of plants facing the ocean breeze. Symptoms are more severe in sensitive plant species and as the salt concentrations increase. Severely affected plants may die.

Salt toxicity is most common in some soils on the western side of the Central Valley of California, certain inland coastal areas such as northern California's Livermore Valley, parts of the Mojave Desert, and some coastal areas in southern California. Toxicity also occurs where plants are irrigated with water high in minerals, and it can occur along roadsides in cold regions where salt is used to dissolve snow and ice on the pavement. Root damage or direct injury to foliage can occur from overhead irrigation with water high in sodium or chloride, such as treated (reclaimed) municipal wastewater or swimming pool water. Excessive fertilization and frequent irrigation where drainage is poor also can result in salt damage. Table 6-3 summarizes conditions and locations where salt damage to plants is most likely to occur.

Evaluate potential salinity problems by testing soil and irrigation water. If irrigating with domestic water, contact the local municipal water agency to obtain results from its routine tests for salinity and specific ions. Diagnose soil salinity by testing the electrical conductivity (EC) of a combined sample (several subsamples mixed together) from the root zone, excluding all soil from the upper ½ inch, where salts often accumulate. A laboratory will mix soil with water before testing EC. Laboratories use different amounts of water to extract salt from media, and results considered to be acceptable vary depending on the method. For example, when using the saturated paste extract method, sensitive plants may be damaged if EC exceeds about 2 to 4 deciSiemans per meter (dS/m). EC may be reported in other units, such as millimhos per centimeter (mmhos/cm), where 1 dS/m = 1 mmhos/cm. The laboratory should provide guidelines on interpreting the test results in comparison with the specific method it used. Salinity in irrigation water is measured as total dissolved solids (TDS) or EC_w, and concentrations are expressed in parts per million (ppm) or dS/m, respectively. For landscape irrigation, values should generally be below about 1,000 ppm or 2 dS/m.

These basic salinity tests do not provide information on specific ions, such as boron, chloride, and sodium, which require separate laboratory tests. Depending on the specific suspected causes of problems, more than one test may be needed (such as for EC, sodium absorption ratio, and certain specific ions), and you may need to collect separately more than one type of sample (irrigation water, older plant leaves, and soil). The potential for problems caused by sodium in soil is based on the sodium absorption ratio (SAR), the ratio of sodium to calcium plus magnesium. If SAR exceeds about 6, soil permeability to water is likely to decrease, and the sodium levels in water may be directly toxic to plants. When testing foliage, collect separate samples from nearby plants with apparently healthy foliage for comparison testing.

This evergreen clematis exhibits terminal leaf necrosis because it is irrigated with salty water.

Salinity is common in arid regions where salts accumulate near the surface, as evidenced by the dark and white soil crust at the base of this stairway. Certain salt-tolerant species can be planted in saline soil to create an interesting, low-maintenance landscape.

TABLE 6-3.

Conditions and Locations Favoring Salt Damage to Plants.

- Animal manures or other salty amendments, or amendments of unknown salinity, were applied in excess amounts.
- Arid regions with salts accumulated near the surface, which may have a dark or white crust on soil.
- Coastal sites where plants are exposed to ocean spray.
- Drainage is poor, irrigation is frequent, or both.
- Fertilizers applied excessively, especially products with a high salt hazard or salt index.
- Irrigation with poor-quality salty water, such as reclaimed treated municipal wastewater or sources such as shallow wells or surface water flowing through arid agricultural areas.
- Low-lying area with salty water table near the surface.
- Snowy locations near pavement where deicing salts were applied.
- Soils were derived from weathering of salty minerals and rocks.

Adapted from Costello et al. 2003.

For more detailed information on salinity testing, consult publications such as *Abiotic Disorders of Landscape Plants: A Diagnostic Guide* (Costello et al. 2003), *Integrated Pest Management for Floriculture and Nurseries* (Dreistadt 2001), and *Western Fertilizer Handbook: Horticultural Edition* (California Fertilizer Association 1998).

Saline soils cannot be remedied by chemical amendments or fertilizers. Improve soil drainage so that salts can be leached below the root zone. Apply water that is low in minerals, such as rainwater, to leach salts away from roots. Leaching is not effective unless water is low in salts. Increase the application period (amount of time) and apply a greater volume of low-salt water each time so minerals are leached deeper into the soil and below roots; at the same time, increase the interval between irrigations to avoid overwatering. Apply mulch around plants to reduce evaporation; evaporation concentrates minerals near the soil surface where most roots occur. Minimize fertilizer applications where salinity is a problem because fertilizers add salts to the soil. If applying fertilizers, use formulations with a low salt hazard (salt index). Obtain an analysis or test the salinity of animal manures,

composts, and sewage sludge before deciding to apply them. Instead of rock salt to deice pavement, consider using alternatives such as calcium magnesium acetate (CMA) or sand. If foliage is exposed to salts, rinse leaves with good-quality water. Avoid using sprinklers if irrigating with salty water. Foliage is more sensitive to salt than roots. Reclaimed water such as treated municipal wastewater may be acceptable for use in drip or flood irrigation systems that do not apply water to foliage, especially when growing more salt-tolerant species. Plants vary greatly in their sensitivity to salt. When planting in locations or situations where salinity may be a problem, avoid plants with low salt tolerance and instead grow more salt-tolerant species. For extensive plant lists of salt tolerance, consult publications such as *Abiotic Disorders of Landscape Plants: A Diagnostic Guide* (Costello et al. 2003) and *Water Quality: Its Effects on Ornamental Plants* (Farnham, Hasek, and Paul 1985).

BORON

Boron (B) and certain other specific ions (such as ammonium, chloride) can be toxic to plants even when overall salt measures (such as EC, SAR, and TDS, as discussed above in the section "Salinity")

are within acceptable limits. Tiny amounts of boron are essential for plant growth, but there is a narrow acceptable range between sufficient and excess concentrations.

In many plants, boron accumulates in older foliage, causing the margins or tips of leaves and needles to turn yellow then brown or purplish brown. Discolored foliage may die and drop prematurely. In certain plants, including cotoneaster, gardenia, privet, pyracantha, rhaphiolepis, and syringa, boron accumulates mostly in new terminal growth and symptoms of toxicity appear in young expanding foliage. In apple, pear, and *Prunus* species such as stone fruits, boron toxicity symptoms appear in young expanding foliage and as misshapen fruit and cankering and dieback of petioles and young twigs. In any plant, bark can crack or become corky, and severely affected plants can die. Differences in the location of symptoms is apparently due to physiological differences among plants; this allows boron to be relatively mobile in the phloem of certain species (those showing damage to fruit, new leaves, or twigs) and not very mobile in others (plants that accumulate boron in old foliage).

Hazardous boron concentrations occur naturally in soils and water in many of the same locations described above in the section "Salinity." Diagnose boron toxicity based on visual symptoms on plants, knowledge of locations where boron typically is a problem, and ion-specific laboratory tests of soil or water. For most landscape plants, toxicity occurs when soil contains about 1 ppm or more of boron or irrigation water exceeds about 0.5 ppm boron.

Manage boron with the methods described for salinity, such as modifying irrigation to prevent sprinkling of foliage and especially by applying irrigation water low in boron. Improving drainage may gradually help to leach boron below roots, but only if water low in boron is used for irrigation. Boron salts are not very soluble, so excess concentrations will leach only over the long-term. Plant boron-tolerant species in locations where

Mineral toxicity is causing these ginkgo, or maidenhair tree, leaf margins to turn yellow, then brown and die. Laboratory testing of soil and water may be needed to diagnose the cause of damage such as this.

this toxicity is a problem. For lists of plant susceptibility to boron, consult publications such as *Abiotic Disorders of Landscape Plants: A Diagnostic Guide* (Costello et al. 2003) and *Water Quality: Its Effects on Ornamental Plants* (Farnham, Hasek, and Paul 1985).

pH

Hydrogen ion concentration (pH) affects the form and availability of nutrients and the ability of roots to absorb nutrients and water. Nutrient deficiency or toxicity symptoms commonly develop when plants grow in soil with adverse pH. The development of soil microorganisms and certain pathogens also depends partly on pH, but this may be of relatively minor importance in landscapes.

A scale from 0 to 14 is used to express pH. Low numbers represent acidic conditions; high numbers are alkaline (also called basic) conditions. Neutral pH is rated as 7. Because a negative logarithmic scale is used, ten times as many positively charged hydrogen ions are available at a pH 6 than at pH 7. A good range of soil pH for most landscapes is about 5.5 to 7.

Marginal or tip chlorosis and necrosis of leaves and interveinal chlorosis and bleaching of new growth are common symptoms in plants growing where pH is high. Damage is primarily a result of reduced availability of iron, manganese, and zinc, so any of the symptoms described earlier for those maladies may occur in alkaline soils. Alkaline (calcareous, typically fine-textured, light-colored) soils or highly alkaline (sodic, often crusty, poorly drained, high in sodium) soils are relatively common in the arid California locations listed earlier in the section "Salinity."

Chlorotic foliage, slow growth, and distorted and possibly necrotic new growth develop if soil is too acidic. In severe cases, affected roots can become discolored, short, and stubby. Symptoms result primarily from toxicity due to aluminum (and sometimes copper or manganese) or from deficiencies of calcium or magnesium due to changes in mineral availability resulting from low pH. Acidic soils are most common in regions with high average rainfall, and low pH is rarely a problem in California soils; a major exception is exposed subsoils in the coastal range, mostly from soil cuts and grading during development in coastal southern California.

Diagnose improper pH using knowledge of local soil conditions and plant species' susceptibility, and especially by testing the pH of soil from the root zone. Treated strips (pH paper) and portable meters are available for measuring pH. Laboratories can provide more accurate results and can conduct additional tests on the same sample. For example, if alkaline soils are suspected, obtain a separate test of alkalinity to measure soil buffering capacity (resistance to pH change), as discussed below.

Grow species more tolerant of the pH at that site. Learn what species naturally grow under local conditions, such as in acidic soils along California's north coast versus the alkaline soils of many desert locations. Resources such as *Sunset Western Garden Book* (Brenzel 2001) and *Abiotic Disorders of Landscape Plants: A Diagnostic Guide* (Costello et al. 2003), respectively, identify the native habitat and pH tolerance of many plants.

Mixing appropriate amounts of finely ground limestone into soil before planting (soil tests can provide specific rate recommendations) or fertilizing with calcium nitrate raises pH in the few California locations where pH is too low. To lower pH before planting, mix elemental sulfur or iron sulfate into topsoil or amend with organic matter as discussed earlier in the section "Iron." After planting, fertilizing with acidifying fertilizers such as ammonium sulfate may help to lower pH.

Alkalinity. The term *alkaline* (meaning basic or high pH) is often confused with the term *alkalinity*. High alkalinity usually results in high pH, but high pH does not always mean high alkalinity. A pH test by itself is not an indication of alkalinity. Alkalinity is a measure of the ability to neutralize or buffer acids. When alkalinity is low, the pH of soil or water readily changes to more closely resemble the acidity of fertilizers and other amendments that are added. If alkalinity is high, the pH tends to stay high (and become even higher after repeated irrigations) even when acidic chemicals are added.

Tests of alkalinity indicate the amount of acidifying amendments or fertilizers needed to lower soil pH, and how feasible it will be to remedy high alkalinity.

These two melaleuca exhibit extensive limb dieback and (when viewed close up) foliar symptoms of extreme iron deficiency. The cause is alkaline irrigation water and high soil pH, which inhibit adequate nutrient uptake.

If soils or water have high pH (are alkaline) but have relatively low alkalinity, addition of acidifying amendments or fertilizers as discussed earlier in the section "Iron" is likely to remedy the problem of high pH. If both pH and alkalinity are high in soil or water, it is generally not feasible to lower soil pH. An alternative, less-alkaline water source must be found for irrigating sensitive plant species. Only species more tolerant to alkalinity may grow there.

Simple on-site titration kits are available for estimating alkalinity. If alkalinity appears to be high, send samples to an outside laboratory for more accurate testing. Since bicarbonates and carbonates (such as calcium carbonate, $CaCO_3$) are usually the major contributors to alkalinity, most laboratories assume that total carbonates (carbonates plus bicarbonates) equals alkalinity. Alkalinity no higher than about 3 milliequivalents per liter of water (meq/l, where 1 meq/l = 60 ppm of carbonates) is considered suitable for most irrigation water.

Pesticides and Phytotoxicity

Phytotoxicity is the ability of materials, such as fertilizers and pesticides, to cause injury to plants. Herbicides are designed specifically to kill unwanted plants, but they can injure desirable species that are exposed to them. Fungicides, insecticides, and other pesticides can also cause phytotoxicity. Pesticides may cause foliage or shoots to become discolored, distorted, spotted, twisted, and die. Foliage may be undersized and drop prematurely, stunting plant growth. Plants exposed to certain herbicides in the fall or winter may not exhibit damage until months later in the spring when new growth occurs. Characteristic injury symptoms can often be used to determine the specific pesticide involved.

HERBICIDES

Herbicide use around landscapes sometimes injures desirable plants. Phytotoxicity is most likely when label directions are not followed, such as applying excessive rates or exposing plants not on the product label. Nearby landscapes can be injured as a result of weed control along rights-of-way or turf, or by vegetation control before paving. The most common symptoms of herbicide exposure are chlorosis, necrosis, or spotting of leaves, and distortion or stunting of leaves, shoots, and roots. Each kind of herbicide causes characteristic damage symptoms, as summarized in Table 6-4. Consult resources such as the UC Davis Weed Research and Information Center Web site at http://wric.ucdavis.edu for additional photographs and descriptions of herbicide injury symptoms.

Preemergence herbicides are generally tolerated by established woody plants, especially plants with healthy, well-developed root systems. Preemergent damage sometimes occurs if herbicide is incorporated too deeply into the root zone or material is applied near poorly rooted young plants or newly planted, shallow-rooted stock. Damage can also occur if roots of nearby plants grow into treated soil. For example, roots growing into fenceline areas or roadsides treated with preemergents such as atrazine or simazine can take up those translocated herbicides in their roots, resulting in damage to leaves or new buds.

The products most likely to damage landscapes are postemergence herbicides that are nonselective (such as glyphosate, glufosinate, pelargonic acid) or selective for (designed to kill) broadleaves (dicamba, triclopyr, and 2,4-D). Broadleaf and nonselective postemergence herbicides should be avoided in established landscapes or used only when exposure to desirable plants can absolutely be avoided.

Twisted shoots and leaf petioles are caused by broadleaf herbicides such as 2,4-D and triclopyr. Dicamba causes foliage to become dwarfed, distorted, and discolored. Dicamba and 2,4-D are phenoxy herbicides contained in some lawn "weed and feed" products and can severely damage or kill broadleaf trees and shrubs growing near treated lawns. They also can cause injury if droplets drift during application or when warm weather causes herbicides to vaporize after application. Spray equipment contaminated with minute quantities of phenoxy herbicides can damage plants when used to apply fertilizers, insecticides, or other chemicals.

Glyphosate (Roundup) contamination on basal buds, foliage, or thin or green bark causes leaves to turn yellow or mottled green and sometimes die. Plants contaminated with glyphosate in the fall may not exhibit symptoms until new growth appears in the spring. Plant growth is then retarded and leaves appear yellowish, undersized, puckered, and almost needlelike (resembling zinc deficiency). Oxyfluorfen (Goal) can cause new growth to be distorted and flecked with dead spots.

Herbicide damage can be difficult to diagnose because symptoms resemble injury caused by many other maladies. Inappropriate irrigation, foliar-applied fertilizers, nutritional disorders, unfavorable soil environment (compaction, pH, salinity), certain foliar or root pathogens, and virtually anything that contributes to unhealthy roots can cause symptoms resembling herbicide damage.

Learn what herbicides have been used nearby, what plants are susceptible to them, and the type of damage typically caused by those materials. Inspecting surrounding plants, including weeds, to observe where herbicide was applied may help you determine whether injury resulted from root absorption or aerial drift. Necrotic spots mostly on leaves of similar age may indicate drift of a contact postemergence herbicide. Chlorosis or necrosis mostly on older leaves on one side of a plant may have been caused by a systemic preemergence herbicide. Preemergence herbicide damage usually is most prominent in older foliage, while symptoms are often most prominent in new growth when inappropriate soil conditions or poor root health are the cause of damage.

You may be able to diagnose phytotoxicity by having a laboratory test soil for preemergence herbicides or by having it test foliage for systemic herbicides or spray residue. Samples should be tested soon after plant exposure. The laboratory may require you to identify the specific herbicides for which you want tests. Be aware that some soil-active herbicides can affect plants at concentrations that are below the minimum detection limit of the laboratory.

If soil-residual herbicides are suspected, bioassays may be useful. Collect soil from the upper 2 inches and separately from one or more deeper areas in the root zone. Separately collect uncontaminated soil that is otherwise similar. Plant seeds or transplant seedlings into small containers of these soils. Use species known to be susceptible to the suspect herbicides, such as target weeds listed on the label or sensitive desirable species the label warns applicators to avoid. Provide good growing conditions and appropriate cultural care and compare the emergence or growth of plants from the different soils. For more details on diagnosing phytotoxicity and a list of suggested herbicide indicator plants, consult *Abiotic Disorders*

In comparison with normal foliage, sycamore leaves on the right are twisted and cupped from exposure to 2,4-D. Broadleaf herbicides such as this are contained in some lawn "weed and feed" products and can severely damage trees and shrubs growing near treated lawns.

When glyphosate gets on trees in fall, symptoms the following spring include small, puckered needlelike leaves. Glyphosate injury can resemble symptoms of severe zinc deficiency.

of Landscape Plants: A Diagnostic Guide (Costello et al. 2003).

If phytotoxicity has occurred, be diligent about providing plants with proper cultural care, especially appropriate irrigation. Avoid fertilization and excess irrigation. Incorporating activated charcoal, compost, manure, or organic mulch into topsoil and keeping soil moist when temperatures are warm can help inactivate certain preemergence herbicides. Soluble herbicides can be removed by leaching soil with water, but plant injury may increase after irrigation. Do not leach unless you can definitely prevent offsite movement of herbicide-contaminated

soil and water. Usually it just takes time for herbicide residues to completely degrade.

Avoid phytotoxicity by applying pesticides carefully, as directed on the label. Because granular formulations of preemergence herbicides reduce the potential for foliar uptake, they are less likely to injury nearby landscapes than sprayable formulations. However, granules containing oxadiazon (Ronstar) or oxyfluorfen (Goal) will injure plants if they collect in the base of leaves or adhere to wet leaves. Do not spray herbicides during foggy weather. Do not allow spray or drift to contact desirable plants.

TABLE 6-4.

Some Common Symptoms of Herbicide Injury.

POSTEMERGENCE HERBICIDES		
INJURY SYMPTOMS	**MODE OF ACTION**	**EXAMPLES**
Chlorosis, necrosis. Plant turns yellow or brown within several days after exposure.	glutamine synthetase inhibitor[1]	glufosinate
Chlorosis, necrosis. Spotting, burning, or drying of foliage soon after foliar contact. Damaged leaves may appear to be watersoaked.	cell membrane disrupters (exact modes uncertain)[2]	fatty acids, pelargonic, salts
Chlorosis, necrosis. Spotting, burning, or drying of foliage soon after foliar contact.	photosynthesis inhibitor	diquat
Chlorosis, necrosis. Leaves turn reddish or yellow. Stems may be necrotic at nodes. Usually affects only grasses. Bamboos may be sensitive.	protein synthesis inhibitors (ACCase inhibition)[3]	clethodim, fluazifop, sethoxydim
Chlorosis, necrosis, distortion. Leaves turn yellow, brown, or mottled, usually within about 2 weeks after contact on foliage or green bark. If exposure occurs during fall, symptoms can be delayed until spring; new growth may then be reduced. Symptoms often most pronounced in growing points and new leaves.	amino acid synthesis inhibitor[4]	glyphosate
Chlorosis, distortion. Stems chlorotic, with shortened internodes. Plants stunted and may lack apical dominance. Leaves may be chlorotic or purplish. New growing points (e.g., buds) may be affected first, then plant dies back. Injury may not be apparent until months after exposure.	amino acid synthesis inhibitors[5]	imidazolinones (imazapyr), sulfonylureas (halosulfuron, sulfometuron)
Distortion. Young leaves and stems malformed, twisted. Leaves strap-shaped or cupped upwards. Stems may be brittle. Callus-like growth or swellings develop on young woody stems.	growth regulators[6]	2,4-D; clopyralid; triclopyr
Distortion, necrosis. Terminal growth distorted and necrotic. Petioles or stems twisted or bent downward. Leaves cupped upwards.	growth regulators[6]	dicamba
PREEMERGENCE HERBICIDES		
INJURY SYMPTOMS	**MODE OF ACTION**	**EXAMPLES**
Chlorosis. Leaves or their veins yellow or whitish. Pale and green areas within the same leaf often contrast sharply. Symptoms first appear in younger growth.	pigment synthesis inhibitor[7]	norflurazon
Chlorosis, necrosis. Leaves chlorotic between veins and sometimes necrotic along margins and tips. Symptoms most pronounced in older foliage, which may drop prematurely. Seedlings emerge, but leaf tips and margins turn yellow and may die.	photosynthesis inhibitors[8]	atrazine, bentazon, bromoxynil, simazine
Chlorosis, stunting. Leaves chlorotic. Shoots, roots, or entire plant short, stunted.	cell wall synthesis inhibitors	dichlobenil, isoxaben
Stunting, distortion. Shoots or entire plant stunted. Roots may be short. Lateral roots may be thick with swollen or clublike tips.	cell division inhibitor or protein synthesis inhibitors (not ACCase inhibition)[9]	benefin, bensulide, dithiopyr, napropamide, oryzalin, pendimethalin, prodiamine, trifluralin
Stunting, distortion. Shoots or roots distorted or stunted.	protein synthesis and cell division inhibitor[9]	metolachlor

1. Herbicide is not soil-active and is poorly translocated.

2. Foliar-applied herbicides that affect tissues only on contact.

3. Systemic, mostly foliar-active herbicides.

4. Translocated, foliar-active herbicide.

5. Slow-acting herbicides, which are active if sprayed on foliage or soil.

6. Translocated, mostly foliar-active herbicides with some soil activity.

7. Systemic, soil-applied herbicide.

8. Systemic, mostly soil-applied herbicides with some foliar activity.

9. Soil-applied herbicides with limited translocation.

Apply nonselective herbicides such as diquat, pelargonic acid, or glyphosate with low pressure and large droplets on a calm day. Trunk wraps may help protect green bark from herbicide drift. Use shielded sprayers if making applications around ornamentals to avoid contact with nontarget plants. Alternatively, special equipment such as low-pressure and wick-type applicators (Tables 2-4 to 2-6) can be used to avoid drift.

INSECTICIDES AND OTHER PESTICIDES

Fungicides, insecticides, and plant growth regulators (such as those used to prevent nuisance fruiting) occasionally cause leaves to burn, discolor, distort, spot, or drop prematurely. Injury can result from misapplication or when environmental conditions or cultural practices increase plants' susceptibility to phytotoxicity. Damage is common from applications during or just before hot weather (about 90°F) or if plants are stressed from drought or other factors. Emulsifiable concentrate (EC) formulations may be more likely to damage plants, whereas wettable powder (W or WP) formulations are generally less likely to cause phytotoxicity. Excess rates, conditions that do not favor rapid drying of spray, or treating during certain growth stages (such as young plants or during flowering) increase the risk of phytotoxicity.

Some plant species are sensitive to certain insecticides, such as insecticidal soap or horticultural oil. For example, although horticultural (narrow-range) oil is safe for foliage of most species when properly used, it discolors or spots foliage on some arborvitae, maple, palm, and spruce species. Check label precautions against use on certain species. *Managing Insects and Mites with Spray Oils* (Davidson et al. 1991) lists landscape species on which oil has safely been applied and species that may be damaged.

Pyrethroids such as cyfluthrin are reported to occasionally damage live oaks. Virtually any persistent, broad-spectrum insecticide (carbamate,

These rose leaves were burned along margins where oil collected after repeated spraying. Although narrow-range oil can safely be applied to most foliage, sequential insecticide applications of oil or other insecticides over relatively short periods can burn foliage.

organophosphate, pyrethroid) applied during warm weather can indirectly damage plants by inducing outbreaks of mites (by killing beneficial predatory mites, stimulating pest mite reproduction, or both), causing foliage to appear burned and possibly drop prematurely due to extensive feeding by these sucking pests.

Certain herbicides, drought stress, excess soil salinity, and some foliar pathogens are among the other causes that produce similar symptoms. If phytotoxicity is suspected, learn what chemicals were used, how and when they were applied, and their rates. Learn the history of cultural practices (especially irrigation) and environmental conditions (especially temperatures) to which plants were exposed. Look for patterns of injury, such as symptoms only on foliage of the age present at the time of application and damage limited to spots where spray was applied. Laboratory analysis of foliage may help if samples are collected soon after spraying and you tell the laboratory the specific pesticides for which you want tests.

Prevent phytotoxicity by using alternative control methods. Before any application, make sure environmental

conditions are appropriate and plants have been receiving proper cultural care, especially appropriate irrigation. When spraying, strictly follow all label directions. When in doubt as to whether the plant species is sensitive to that pesticide, spray one small plant or a small area of a large plant and observe it for about a week for any signs of damage before spraying any more. If phytotoxicity does occur, provide pesticide-damaged plants with good care, especially appropriate irrigation. Modify cultural methods, plant growing environment, and pest management practices to avoid phytotoxicity problems.

Mechanical Injury

Plants can be cut, crushed, punctured, rubbed, or struck due to accidental or deliberate physical actions. Mechanical injury can produce obvious wounds, such as broken limbs and stripped bark, or a wide range of decline symptoms such as discolored foliage, limb dieback, premature leaf drop, slow growth, wilting, and even plant death. Causes of mechanical injury include changing soil grade in the

These cankers developed as a result of mechanical injury from limbs rubbing against planting stakes. The stakes should have been removed within about 1 year after planting.

root zone, chewing by vertebrate pests, cutting roots during excavation or trenching, girdling from stakes or ties, impact from vehicle bumpers, operating heavy equipment or laying pavement over roots, pruning, vandalism, and weed or string trimmers that cut bark. Other causes that can produce symptoms resembling mechanical injury include canker diseases, chemical injury, extreme winds, inappropriate irrigation, poor soil conditions, root rot pathogens, vascular wilt disease, and wood-boring insects.

Sometimes the cause of injury is evident, such as ties or wires imbedded in bark, tooth marks of vertebrate pests, or a basal trunk of a mature tree that lacks basal flaring, indicating that soil grade has been raised. Historical knowledge can be helpful, such as whether weed trimmers were used without shielding trunks or potentially phytotoxic materials were applied. Mechanical injury to roots can be especially difficult to diagnose because wounds are hidden underground and aboveground symptoms

may not become obvious until months or years after root injury. Knowing the local history of construction or development helps to diagnose this cause, but usually you must excavate soil and inspect roots to determine whether they have been injured.

Prevent wounds to trees and shrubs through appropriate site design and good landscape maintenance. Protect plants by installing protective barriers and screens. For more information, consult the section "Injuries, Hazards, and Protecting Landscapes" in Chapter 3.

Sunlight

Too much or too little sunlight can damage plants. The amount of light required to cause damage varies with the species of plant, environmental conditions, and cultural practices, especially moisture availability. Sunburn and light deficiency are syndromes associated with adverse light conditions.

SUNBURN AND SUNSCALD

Sunburn is damage to bark, foliage, fruit, and other plant parts caused by exposure to solar radiation. Damage occurs from heat when solar radiation dehydrates tissue beyond a critical point. Sunburn usually is associated with high ambient temperatures and often with insufficient moisture availability. Similar foliar damage can occur even under cool conditions, such as when shade-adapted plants are directly exposed to bright sunlight. High light injury is discussed below in the section "Excess or Deficient Light."

Sunburned foliage develops yellow or brown areas, which may die beginning in areas between the veins. Sunburned conifer needles turn black, brown, or drop prematurely. Sunburned bark becomes cracked, sunken, and susceptible to attack by wood-boring insects and decay fungi. Sunburned trunks and limbs can become cankered or girdled and may be killed.

The terms "sunburn" and "sunscald" are used in different ways, and there is

disagreement regarding their definitions. Some people limit the definition of sunburn to damage to leaves and other herbaceous parts. They use sunscald or "summer sunscald" to describe bark damage from too much heat and insufficient moisture. "Winter sunscald" is freezing injury to bark that occurs during the winter primarily in the eastern United States and is uncommon in California except at high elevations. This freeze injury to bark is the only situation where certain people use the term "sunscald."

Sunburn injury to foliage is mostly aesthetic damage that rarely kills plants and can often be remedied by adequate irrigation, adding shade, and improving soil conditions. Sunburn or sunscald injury to bark cannot be reversed, and this bark damage contributes to tree decline and premature death.

Sunburned bark often occurs on young woody plants. Their bark is thin, and they may not tolerate being planted in exposed landscapes because before planting they were grown crowded together in nurseries where their trunks were shaded. Older trees can be damaged when bark is newly exposed to the sun because of extensive pruning or premature leaf drop. Removing structures or trees that provided shade or adding pavement or structures that reflect light or radiate heat around established plants can also lead to sunburn.

Moisture stress often contributes to sunburn, for example, in new plantings that lack a well-developed root system and cannot absorb adequate moisture. Restricted soil volumes, inappropriate soil moisture, or anything that makes roots unhealthy or prevents plants from absorbing adequate water may contribute to sunburn. Even in soil that is saturated with water, sunburn may occur if plants are unable to absorb sufficient moisture when it is sunny or temperatures are unusually hot or cold. Be aware that irrigating too frequently, especially when drainage is poor, is probably the most common cause of landscape damage in California. If plants are unhealthy due to prolonged excess soil moisture, increasing irrigation will increase damage.

Yellow and brown sunburned leaf areas developed on this rarely irrigated euonymus growing in California's hot, arid Central Valley. Appropriate irrigation can restore leaf color if sunburned foliage has not already been killed.

Sunburn or sunscald caused this cracked, sunken bark on the southwestern side of this toyon. Sunburn developed after overstory limbs that shaded the trunk were pruned out, increasing the bark's exposure to solar radiation.

Apply white *interior* latex paint, diluted 50% with water, to trunks where sunburn or sunscald may occur. White paint reflects light and reduces bark heating, thereby avoiding sunburn injury.

Management. Provide plants with proper cultural care, especially appropriate water, to prevent sunburn and sunscald. Appropriate changes in plant environment or cultural practices (especially appropriate irrigation) usually can restore the green color to sunburned foliage unless it has already been killed.

Avoid sunburn by choosing plants that are adapted to environmental conditions at the site where they are planted. When developing new landscapes, obtain plants that have been acclimated, such as by gradually increasing their spacing and sun exposure before leaving the nursery. Place plants at sites where roots will have adequate soil volume and sufficient growing space as they mature. Provide appropriate soil conditions and keep roots healthy. Avoid anything that damages roots or prevents them from absorbing sufficient nutrients or water, including irrigating too frequently. Where appropriate, modify the site to

provide partial shade and prevent bleached foliage in certain species such as camellia and rhododendron that are not adapted to prolonged full sunlight.

Apply white interior (not exterior) latex paint, diluted 50% with water, to the trunks of young trees and to older bark newly exposed to the sun if they are likely to be susceptible to sunburn. Encourage desired branch structure by properly pruning and training plants while they are young. Avoid removing more than about 20% of the plant canopy during any one year and avoid pruning during summer if possible. Apply and maintain appropriate mulch, which conserves soil moisture and reduces soil temperatures during summer. Mulch can also affect light around plants, depending on the location and type of material used (see Chapter 7). Minimize the changes to a plant's environment, unless deliberately done to improve conditions. Provide adequate irrigation.

EXCESS OR DEFICIENT LIGHT

Each plant is adapted to certain amounts of light, depending on its species, previous growing environment, and conditions prevailing where it is native. Plant growth can be retarded by either too much or too little light. Excess light can cause foliage to become chlorotic. Light can also injure leaves if iron or manganese deficiency reduces chlorophyll availability, causing foliage to become pale and susceptible to scorching. Unlike sunburn, high light injury can bleach foliage even when temperatures are cool.

Deficient light often causes elongated, spindly shoots so plants appear taller. Foliage can become pale or dark depending on the plant species. Leaves may become larger and thinner than normal, and leaves may drop prematurely beginning with the most shaded foliage.

Typical foliage color returns after plants receive appropriate light, but a

R. D. RAABE

Excess light discolored this foliage on camellia, which is adapted to partial shade. Overstory plantings to provide shade can help to restore the normal color of leaves damaged by high light.

These scabby blisters (edema) on eucalyptus leaves are apparently harmless to plants. No methods are definitely known to prevent edema in landscapes, but improving soil drainage and avoiding excess irrigation may be beneficial here.

prolonged light imbalance causes plants to become susceptible to other problems and possibly die. For example, artificial lights at night might alter the response of some plants sensitive to seasonal changes in natural light, increasing their susceptibility to frost damage.

Plant only species that are well adapted to the amount of light available at that location. At sites receiving full sun, do not plant light-sensitive species such as aralia, aucuba, camellia, cast iron plant, and vine maple (*Acer circinatum*). Avoid changing the environment in any way that significantly alters the amount of light received by established plants unless this is purposely done to remedy inappropriate light conditions. For example, planting overstory species can provide shade for plants sensitive to direct light. For a list of shade-tolerant species and directions on how to measure whether plants are receiving adequate light, consult publications such as *Abiotic Disorders of Landscape Plants: A Diagnostic Guide* (Costello et al. 2003).

Edema

Edema (formerly called oedema) is the development of raised, scabby areas on leaves. Although affected tissue is often brown and blisterlike, it is not necrotic. Damage is aesthetic and does not threaten plant health. The specific cause of this noninfectious disorder is not known. It often develops in the presence of light when soil is cool and wet and the air is relatively warm. These conditions apparently cause excess moisture to accumulate in leaves, damaging tissue and causing leaf blisters.

Injured tissue cannot be restored and no methods are known to prevent edema in landscapes. Excess soil moisture may promote edema, so avoid irrigating too frequently and improve drainage if these conditions are not appropriate. Avoiding prolonged excess soil moisture will at least help to prevent certain other common maladies.

Temperature Extremes

Low or high temperatures can damage plants. The temperature range tolerated varies by plant species and the previous growing conditions. Choose plants that are well-adapted to the local environment, such as native species and possibly mature specimens of exotic species that are growing well and have survived for many years in that area. Consult publications such as *Sunset Western Garden Book* (Brenzel 2001) for information on the temperature tolerances of plant species, which are presented in reference to plant climate zones developed by the U. S. Department of Agriculture.

HIGH TEMPERATURES

Plants are injured if temperatures become too high. Damage usually results from a combination of excessive heat and light and insufficient moisture, causing tissues to dehydrate. Symptoms of high temperature injury to aboveground plant parts are discussed in the section "Sunburn and Sunscald." In addition to the management methods discussed for sunburn, misting plants and screening them from wind where practical may reduce high temperature injury.

Root zone heat injury is common in plant containers exposed to direct sun, but it is uncommon in landscapes except in planter boxes and raised beds. Heat injury to roots results in the same aboveground symptoms as described for sunburn. Avoid high temperature injury to roots by planting properly, providing sufficient soil volume for root growth as plants mature, irrigating adequately, shading the sides of containers and planting boxes, and by applying organic mulch.

Organic matter decomposition by microorganisms can generate substantial heat, which can kill roots. Do not plant in soil that has recently been amended with a large percentage of undecomposed organic matter. If soil is amended with undecomposed organic matter at more than about 20% of topsoil volume, do not plant in it until after soil has been moist and warm for at least 2 months. This delayed planting provides time for decomposition. Organic matter stability is usually apparent based on appearance and texture before it is mixed into topsoil. If it is poorly composted or undecomposed, compost organic matter well before use.

"Thermal injury" refers to plant damage from fire and causes such as vented steam or combustion exhaust. Fire causes foliage or bark to become black, brown, charred, crisp, and scorched. This cause can be easy to diagnose because usually the fire event itself was observed and reported. Often it is apparent that fire was the cause based on surrounding damage, one-sided injury along edges, and distinct boundaries to the burn zone. See the section "Minimizing Fire Hazards" in Chapter 3 for more discussion.

FREEZING AND FROST

Cold temperature damage from frost or freezing causes buds, flowers, and shoots to curl, turn brown or black, and die. Bark and wood can crack or split. Whole branches or entire plants may be killed. Freeze injury to roots causes the same aboveground symptoms, but soil insulation usually prevents cold injury to roots, except in containers, planter boxes, and raised beds. Cold damage to foliage often resembles leaf anthracnose diseases—plants appear scorched because cold severely dehydrates plant tissue. Cold damage becomes most apparent after the temperature rises. Chemical injury, drought stress, natural gas injury, and unhealthy roots due to root cutting or rot fungi also cause symptoms resembling cold injury.

Frost and freezing cause the water in plant tissue or on plant surfaces to freeze. Frost and freezing produce the same symptoms but occur under different conditions, and some of their management strategies differ. Freezing occurs when air temperatures are below 32°F. Frost occurs when air is 32°F or warmer but plant tissues drop to below 32°F because plant surfaces radiate heat into the

Freezing weather killed this lemon foliage. Unless trees pose a hazard, such as falling limbs, do not prune freeze-damaged plants until after you are certain what tissues are dead, preferably by waiting until the subsequent spring.

atmosphere. During cool, clear nights, dust or bacteria, including some strains of *Pseudomonas syringae*, serve as particles on which moisture from the atmosphere can condense and freeze.

Cold injury is most likely during autumn and spring, the coldest times during winter, and when temperatures decline rapidly after warm weather. Minimum temperature, duration of cold, and the rate at which temperatures drop influence the severity of damage. Plants that are gradually exposed to increasingly cool weather, such as during the fall, become acclimated and tolerate more cold than during other times of the year. Broadleaf evergreens and plants not in dormancy generally are the most sensitive to cold. Buds, flowers, and younger leaves and shoots are the most susceptible to cold temperatures, especially succulent plant tissues in the spring. However, by the summer, new growth often replaces tissue damaged by cold during spring. Plants adapted to the local environment usually are not permanently harmed; however, they may occasionally suffer terminal dieback of new spring growth after late-season frost.

To avoid damage from frost or freezing, do not plant species adapted to mild climates in areas where adversely cold temperatures occur. Where terrain is uneven, grow the most cold-sensitive species on higher ground because colder air flows down to the lowest spots. In commercial situations (nurseries and orchards), frost may be avoided by using high-velocity fans to mix the cold surface-level air with warmer air higher above ground. Before frost or freezing is expected, provide soil with adequate moisture to increase its ability to retain heat. When frost is expected, cover sensitive plants overnight with cloth or similar material other than plastic to reduce heat loss to the atmosphere, but leave covers open at their bottom so heat radiating from soil can help warm the plant. Remove covers during the day.

During freezing temperatures, covering plants is of little help unless a heat source is also provided. Placing electric lights (household-size or Christmas lights) in the canopy may generate enough heat to prevent plants from freezing, but lights may of little help unless plants with lights are also covered. Be sure equipment is designed for outdoor use and not likely to create electrical shock or fire hazards. Operating misters or sprinklers continuously (such as all night) to wet foliage can reduce freeze damage because as water freezes, it gives off heat, causing slightly higher temperatures adjacent to the freezing water. Sprinkling can be effective only if it is begun when temperatures reach freezing, temperatures are not too extreme, and freezing conditions do not persist. To keep temperatures up, water must be applied continually during freezing conditions. This method should be used only with an irrigation system that will tolerate being covered with ice. Flooding underneath plants can also help to keep them warmer, but repeated flooding over a short time period can damage plants. Do not combine the use of outdoor lights and flooding or sprinkling.

Do not prune freeze-damaged plants until after you are certain what tissues are dead, preferably by waiting until the subsequent spring. An exception is limbs or trunks that are hazards and may fall (fail). Replant with more cold-tolerant species.

HAIL AND ICE

Hailstones usually only tear leaves and cause discolored pits or scars on fruit. Elliptical wounds in bark and broken bark and twigs sometimes also occur, and this bark injury may provide entry sites for certain pathogens. When serious, hail injury can girdle and kill branches. Where ice occurs on plants, limbs can break from the added weight.

Hail injury is relatively uncommon in California. It can be easy to diagnose because commonly the storm event is reported in the news. All exposed species at a site can show at least some damage. Wounds occur on the upper side of plants, especially on parts facing the direction from which storms come. Canker diseases or excess wind can cause similar symptoms. Pathogens such as shot hole cause fruit scars resembling hail damage. However, pathogens usually affect only certain species at a site;

for example, shot hole infects only *Prunus* species.

Prune out wood that is seriously damaged by hail or ice. Provide injured plants with proper cultural care, especially appropriate irrigation.

Wind

Wind causes foliage (and sometimes bark) to become dry. Flowers, foliage, and limbs can break. Leaves may become torn, shredded, and covered with irregular holes, sometimes called "tatters." Leaves may be necrotic along their margins and tips, and leaves may drop prematurely soon after exposure to dry or extreme winds. Windborne sand or soil can abrade tissue, for example, causing bark to appear sandblasted on plants in arid locations or near sandy beaches. Plants growing at windy sites often have smaller leaves and are stunted overall. Early abscission and wind breakage can cause plants to develop a highly "sculptured" structure, such as California's distinctive coastal Monterey cypress with their one-sided foliage and limb growth pointing away from the ocean.

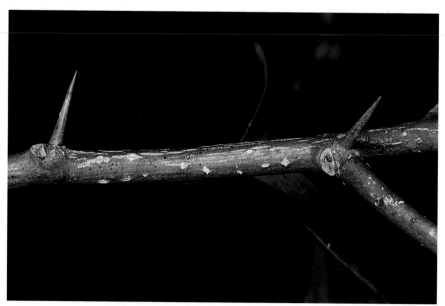

Hail made many small scars on this citrus twig. Unlike pathogens that are typically host-specific, adverse weather such as hail typically damages all exposed species at a site. The location of injury also aids in diagnosis, as these wounds all occur on the upper side of plants facing the direction from which storms come.

Provide plants with proper cultural care, especially appropriate irrigation, to reduce the adverse effects of wind. If needed during about their first year of growth, stake plants properly to allow young trunks to flex and become strong, as discussed in Chapter 3. Plant susceptible species in more sheltered locations and choose species carefully. Plants that grow fast, become tall, and have broad, thin leaves usually are less tolerant of wind. Smaller plants and those with narrow leaves with a thicker cuticle better tolerate wind. For lists of wind-sensitive species and tolerant plants suitable for living windbreaks, consult publications such as *Abiotic Disorders of Landscape Plants: A Diagnostic Guide* (Costello et al. 2003).

Lightning

Lightning most commonly strikes isolated, exposed, or tall trees, killing bark or wood in a long, vertical band. Lightning strikes sometimes cause plants to burn or explode. Lightning can seriously damage roots or internal tissues of trunks and limbs even though damage on the visible aboveground plant parts appears to be relatively minor. Abnormal wood growth beneath bark, galls, or roots growing from unexpected places on the trunk (adventitious roots) may develop after lightning injury.

Lightning is uncommon in urban California, occurring mostly at higher elevations and in eastern and northern regions of the state. Unless the event was actually observed or plants were inspected soon after lightning struck, suspect more common causes that produce damage resembling that from lightning, including adverse soil conditions, girdling injuries, mechanical wounding, and root rot pathogens. Where lightning is prevalent, lightning rods wired to the ground can be installed at the top of especially valuable, tall, specimen trees. The National Arborists Association and National Fire Protection Association publish standards for lightning rod systems.

Have a certified arborist or other expert inspect lightning-struck trees for limb, trunk, or root damage that may cause the tree to fail (fall). Immediate repairs generally should be limited to cleanup, pruning to reduce safety hazards, and tacking any loosened bark back into place over wounds, then periodically moistening loosened bark to reduce drying. Provide injured plants with proper cultural care, especially appropriate irrigation. Have lightning-struck trees periodically reinspected by an expert to determine whether hazard-reduction pruning, tree removal, or other remedies are appropriate.

Gas Injury

Landfills, natural gas lines, sewers, and wastewater disposal vents can emit or leak gases that injure or kill aboveground plant parts or roots. Initial injury symptoms can resemble damage from air pollution, compacted or poorly drained soil, herbicides, root rot pathogens, or stress from too little or too much water. Gas injury symptoms include slow plant growth, wilting, or foliage that turns brown, crispy, and dry. Affected roots may discolor, such as appearing bluish or watersoaked. Affected plants may only partially leaf out in spring. Limbs may die back and plants can be killed. Soil may be discolored black, bluish, or gray. Odor of ammonia, chlorine, natural gas, or rotten eggs may be detectable.

Contact the utility company immediately if a natural gas leak is suspected. After the leak has been repaired by professionals, leave the hole open, if possible, for several weeks to allow natural gas to dissipate from soil; take precautions so any holes are not a hazard. Depending on the situation, the local water agency, property owner, or persons causing damage are responsible for repairing sewer line breaks. If root growth is breaking sewer lines, consider whether nearby trees should be removed, landscape should be planted further from the sewer line, or soil conditions or cultural prac-

tices such as irrigation should be modified to reduce the likelihood of root damage. Prune landscaping away from plumbing vents or redirect vent outlets if their emissions are injuring foliage.

To diagnose whether the cause is gas emissions from garbage decaying beneath a former landfill, investigate the site's previous land use, test using special gas monitoring instruments, or send air samples to a laboratory. Add topsoil to plug leaks, increase the depth of the landfill cap layer, or install ventilation pipes in the ground. Grow shallow-rooted species, which generally are more tolerant of landfill conditions, or plant species that are more tolerant of landfill emissions. For a list of gas-tolerant plants, consult publications such as *Abiotic Disorders of Landscape Plants: A Diagnostic Guide* (Costello et al. 2003).

Air Pollution

Air pollution damage is caused by mostly invisible gases, especially ethylene, ozone, and sulfur oxides. A few inorganic chloride or fluoride compounds and acidic deposition (acid rain) can also damage plants. Damage is more likely when plants are located near sources of dirty air (such as certain industries) or where weather and topography concentrate local or distant sources of pollution in certain locations. Pollutants such as ozone develop through complex reactions among chemicals and light, so they are called secondary pollutants. Another secondary pollutant is peroxyacetyl nitrate (PAN), which results from ultraviolet radiation acting on nonoxidized hydrocarbons in photochemical smog.

Air pollution damage is difficult to diagnose. Many of its symptoms are similar to, and aggravated by, those resulting from other stresses including drought, nutrient disorders, pathogens, and sucking insects and mites. Typical symptoms from air pollution damage include leaf discoloration and dead or prematurely dropping leaves or needles. Symptoms may develop soon after

Air pollution like this causes plant damage that is difficult to diagnose because many symptoms with other causes are similar to, and are aggravated by, air pollution.

Ozone pollution damage can be subtle, such as the yellowish patches in this maple leaf.

OZONE

Ozone naturally occurring in the upper atmosphere (stratosphere) shields plants and animals from harmful solar radiation; ozone in the air near the ground (troposphere) damages plants. Ozone is produced in the lower atmosphere when nitrogen oxides and hydrocarbons react after being exposed to sunlight. Nitrogen oxides and hydrocarbons are primarily produced during combustion of fuels. In some locations, certain plants emit substantial amounts of hydrocarbons into the atmosphere.

Damaging levels of ozone occur near the ground during warm weather in summer and fall. In California, excess ozone occurs in major population centers (Los Angeles, San Diego, and San Francisco Bay Area), in the Central Valley, and in the Sierra Nevada and San Bernardino mountains up to elevations of about 6,000 feet.

Ozone causes bleaching, mottling, necrosis, pale flecks, or small dark patches to appear on needles and leaves, especially on upper surfaces. Discolored areas can enlarge and foliage may drop prematurely. Pine needle tips can turn brown, reddish, or yellow. Needles may become banded or shortened and die. Ozone retards growth and increases plants' susceptibility to certain insects and pathogens. Injury can result from long-term exposure to relatively low concentrations or incidents of short-term exposure to higher ozone levels. Younger plants and thin-leafed species generally are most sensitive, and damage is aggravated by other stresses, such as inappropriate cultural care. Leaf-feeding pests that suck sap (such as mites and thrips), foliar pathogens, and herbicides also cause injury resembling ozone damage.

SULFUR OXIDES

Sulfur oxides are produced by burning coal or oil and during refining of petroleum and some minerals. Sulfur oxides cause marginal and tip dieback and yellow or brown bands or streaks on conifer needles. Broadleaf foliage may become

short-term exposure to high concentrations of air pollutants, or after longer exposure to relatively lower pollution levels. The susceptibility of plants to air pollution damage varies greatly. Azalea, birch, fuchsia, pine, and sycamore are among the plants most readily damaged by air

pollution. Aside from ethylene, which is damaging mostly indoors such as in greenhouses, ozone currently is the most damaging air pollutant in California. Ethylene is discussed in publications such as *Integrated Pest Management for Floriculture and Nurseries* (Dreistadt 2001).

Shortened, chlorotic, and necrotic needles developed in this new pine growth affected by excess ozone levels. Management includes providing good cultural care and planting species less susceptible to ozone.

silvery, bleached, or appear watersoaked, beginning between the veins. Affected foliage may be sparse, stunted, or grow in tufts and may die. Industrial air pollution control measures and reductions in the sulfur content of fuels have greatly reduced the frequency of plant damage by sulfur oxides.

MANAGEMENT OF AIR POLLUTION INJURY

Provide proper cultural care and control other causes of stress to keep plants vigorous and increase their tolerance to pollution. Grow more plants because plants help to reduce many types of air pollutants in several ways. Particulates become trapped by foliage and are washed by precipitation from foliage to the soil.

Rinse plants with water where practical to remove particulates. Gaseous air pollutants are absorbed by bark and taken in through leaf stomata. Plant tolerant species in areas where air quality is especially poor. Lists of landscape species especially susceptible or tolerant to air pollution have been published in *Abiotic Disorders of Landscape Plants: A Diagnostic Guide* (Costello et al. 2003) and *Diseases of Trees and Shrubs* (Sinclair, Lyon, and Johnson 1987).

Air pollution is best controlled at its source. Reduce pollution by using alternative means of transportation and energy, properly maintaining vehicles and engines, conserving resources and materials, and supporting appropriate regulations.

CHAPTER SEVEN

Weeds

WEEDS ARE PLANTS growing where they are not wanted. The same plant species can be desirable in one setting and a weed in another situation. For example, turf and vigorous ground covers often invade areas under trees and shrubs, where they become weeds. In part because they produce abundant seeds that are dispersed widely, elm, oak, privet, and other trees and shrubs often grow where they were not planted and are not desired.

There are several key concerns with weeds around trees and shrubs. Turf, ground covers, and other low-growing species next to trunks are commonly trimmed with mowers or weed trimmers, which often injure trunks or roots around the crown; this damage makes plants susceptible to wood-boring insects, crown rot diseases, and other problems. Weeds compete with desirable landscape species for moisture and nutrients. Competition is especially detrimental to newly planted trees and shrubs, which can be stunted because of nearby competing vegetation. Herbaceous species around woody landscape plants can provide habitat for snails, rodents, and other pests and can contribute to the potential

for disease development by increasing humidity and moisture around trunks. Certain weeds are directly injurious to people, such as an irritating rash from exposure to poison oak and allergic reactions to weed pollen. Weeds can become eyesores in the landscape. Finally, certain introduced ornamentals such as blue gum eucalyptus, brooms, Himalayan blackberry, iceplant, and tamarisk have dispersed (escaped) from landscapes and become invasive pests in natural wildlands and parks. Information on invasive weeds that adversely affect native plants and wildlife is available from the California Exotic Pest Plant Council at www.caleppc.org and from the California Native Plant Society at www.cnps.org on the World Wide Web.

This chapter discusses preventing and managing weeds directly under and around woody plants in landscapes. Weed management of ornamentals in production is discussed in *Integrated Pest Management for Floriculture and Nurseries* (Dreistadt 2001). Management of weeds in turf, ground covers, and annual bedding plants is discussed in several publications listed in the Suggested Reading at the back of this book.

Tolerance Levels and Monitoring

A key concept of integrated pest management is that some level of weed infestation can be tolerated. Furthermore, it is generally not possible to completely and permanently eliminate all weeds from landscapes. The landscape manager must determine how many weeds are tolerable in each situation. For example, growth of young landscape plants can be greatly diminished by competition from weeds, so weeds should be well controlled in new plantings. In older plantings, weed impact on plant vigor may be minimal, but there can be diminished aesthetic quality. Aesthetic impacts vary depending on the observer and the visibility of the location. Weeds under roses in a home garden or in front of City Hall are more bothersome than in less-used areas. People may disagree on what species are weeds and where and at what densities they are bothersome.

Monitor weeds among widely spaced plants or in mulched beds or turf by walking a straight line, or transect, through the landscape. Record whether a weed, desirable plant, or substrate such as bare soil or mulch is at the tip of your toe after each step.

Inspect landscapes regularly for weeds to help you decide when and where weeds are a problem. Try to identify summer or winter annual species in the spring and fall when weeds germinate and are in their easier-to-control seedling stage. Establish tolerance levels by considering whether the species and abundance of weeds in an area are tolerable and when and where control is needed. Assess the potential of weeds to reproduce, spread, and cause problems. Tolerate fewer perennial weeds because they are more difficult to control.

Maintain written records of monitoring information, especially when managing commercial or large-scale landscapes. Good records include species of weeds, age (seedling or established), location, density, when weeds occurred, what action you took, and the approximate size of any area treated. Weed species and their abundance change seasonally and in response to your management actions. Careful records help you take timely action to control troublesome weeds before they spread. Written records also allow you to determine whether particular weed species are increasing, decreasing, or remaining about the same from year to year or after control actions have been taken.

Site Surveys. One monitoring method for weeds and other pests uses a landscape map. Draw a sketch of the landscape area and mark the location of landscape plants, mulch, bare soil, and other ground coverings at that location. Identify individual large plants or groups of smaller plants. Survey the landscape periodically (such as every fall and spring and before and after control actions) and use a copy of the map to record the location, date, and severity of any weed (or other pest) problems. Record any detailed monitoring information corresponding to these areas on a separate sheet of paper. You can employ a qualitative rating of weed severity for each area, as shown in Figure 7-1. For example, rate each different landscape area from 0 to 4, where 0 means very few weeds and 4

means a very heavy infestation. For greater detail, you can use the transect count method and assign quantitative weed ratings. Be sure to date all maps and notes.

Transect Counts. This method involves counting weeds at periodic intervals along a straight line, or transect. Tie a stake or pole on each end of a cord or rope of appropriate length for the size of your landscape area. A suggested length is about one-half or one-quarter as long as the area you intend to sample. Mark the line with paint, tape, or a permanent marker at regular intervals, such as every 1 or 2 feet. You can also use a tape measure and evaluate the area at 1- or 2-foot intervals. Adjust the length of your cord, the size of your sampling area, and the number of samples to the time available for monitoring each landscape. Stake the cord in a straight line running through your landscape. Be sure to include all the different areas of your landscape to get a representative sample. Try to sample in approximately the same area or areas on each date that you monitor that location so you can compare your results among sample dates.

Record the date, the species (weed or desirable landscape plant) or lack of vegetation (bare soil or mulch) and the age (seedling or established) of each plant touched by or underneath the mark on the cord. The percentage of samples with weeds is then determined by dividing the number of sample points with weeds by the total number of samples and multiplying by 100.

Another method for more widely spaced plants, mulched beds, or turf is to walk through the landscape and record whether or not a weed is at the tip of your toe after each step or set number of steps. You may want to relocate your cord (or walk-line) and take additional transect counts, especially if the sample area is large or the species counted are quite variable. Instead of simply noting weed absence or presence, you may want to record the specific substrate (such as desirable plant,

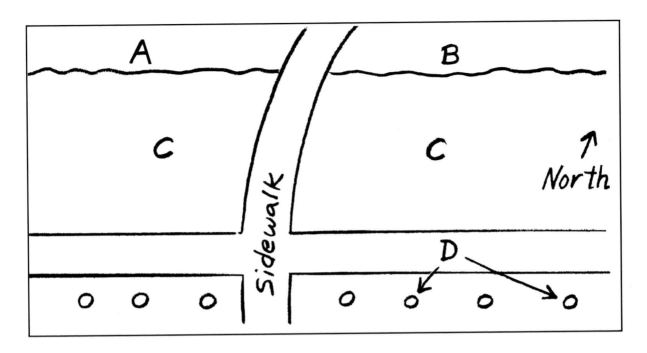

DATE <u>10 April 03</u>   LANDSCAPE MONITORED BY <u>Jane Smith</u>

LOCATION <u>400 Main St., City Hall</u>

Weed Infestation Level Ratings:

0   no weeds

1   light, ≤1–2% weeds

2   moderate, 3–10% weeds

3   heavy, 11–25% weeds

4   very heavy, > 25% weeds

Landscape Area	Weed Infestation Level	Management Actions Planned or Comments
A. Roses	1	Scattered annual weeds, hoe then apply more mulch
B. Roses	0	Apply more organic mulch
C. Turf	1	Dethatch, aerate, fertilize, overseed
D. Young trees	4	Remove and maintain turf 2 feet back from trunks

Notes: Monitor again in May after completing control actions.

FIGURE 7-1. Landscape map method of recording weed infestations, which can be modified to record areas or individual plants infested with other types of pests. Infestation level ratings and the number of weeds that are tolerable will vary, depending in part on weed species and the type of use for that area. Use a copy of your original map and record the above information each time you monitor as discussed in the text. Insects, diseases, or inadequate cultural care can also be recorded using landscape maps to document when and where these problems occurred.

mulch, or species of weed) in each sample. For example, a high proportion of samples with bare soil indicates the need to improve landscape plant vigor or reapply organic mulch to minimize future weed problems.

Figure 7-2 is an example of a form for recording transect monitoring information. You can use both a landscape map and transect monitoring at the same location until you become experienced enough at estimating weed cover that you can dispense with actual counts. It may be best to put weed counts and notes on the back of the landscape map. Use a new copy of the map on each monitoring date.

Managing Weeds

The best times for effective weed management are before planting, before weeds emerge, and before weeds mature (Figure 7-3). Prevent weed problems through good landscape planning and design and proper site preparation before planting. If you wait for weeds to mature and become a problem in landscapes and then try to cure these problems, your management options will be more limited and results will be less satisfactory than if you take preventive measures or act when weeds first appear.

Remove weeds and amend, loosen, and grade the soil before planting to provide for good landscape plant growth. Choose species that are well adapted to local conditions. Group together plants that require similar cultural care and environmental conditions, especially water and light. Separate plants with cultural care needs or growth characteristics that are incompatible with nearby plants. Plant correctly, take steps to prevent weed growth such as applying mulch, and adequately care for trees and shrubs, as discussed in chapter 3, so that desirable species outcompete, displace, and exclude weeds.

Prevent weed growth in established plantings by minimizing disturbance of the soil, using low-volume irrigation systems, and by carefully choosing, applying, and maintaining mulch. See Table 7-1 for a summary of weed IPM methods. If these preventive actions are taken, regular hand-pulling or hoeing of occasional weeds is all that will be needed in many situations once landscape plants become established.

DESIGNING AND REDESIGNING LANDSCAPES TO AVOID WEEDS

Avoid designing a new landscape that inadvertently encourages weeds. Consider redesigning and replanting landscapes with chronic problems. Weed-prone landscapes include those that are frequently reinfested with undesirable species or that have adjoining plants with different irrigation or other cultural care needs. Select landscape species that are well adapted to local soils, moisture, temperature, and light. Choose species or varieties that resist common insect and disease problems, as discussed in chapter 3 and Table 3-2. Plants that are appropriate for their location grow more vigorously and are less affected by competition from weeds.

DATE <u>13 Aug 03</u>　LANDSCAPE MONITORED BY <u>Joe Smith</u>

LOCATION <u>Community Park, Northeast shrub bed</u>

SAMPLE NO.	SUBSTRATE (e.g., SOIL, MULCH, ETC.) OR PLANT SPECIES	PLANT AGE (SEEDLING/ESTABLISHED) OR COMMENTS (e.g., CONTROL TAKEN)
1.	Rhaphiolepis	Mature Shrubs
2.	Mulch	
3.	Mulch	Mulch decomposing
4.	Spurge	
5.	Rhaphiolepis	
6.	Mulch	
7.	Euonymus	
8.	Mulch	
9.	Spurge	
10.	Euonymus	

NOTES: Low-growing spurge under mature shrubs is not very visible, tolerate or hand pull before seed production. Apply more mulch.

Total number of samples taken <u>10</u>

	Number	Percent[a]
Samples with desirable plants:	4	40
Samples with weeds:	2	20
Samples with bare soil, mulch, or other:	4	40

a. Percent is number of samples in that category, divided by total number of samples, multiplied times 100.

FIGURE 7-2. Keep records of your transect count weed monitoring using a form like this, which could be copied onto the back of a copy of the landscape map illustrated in Figure 7-1. An actual sampling program and record-keeping form should include more than ten samples.

Group together plants that have compatible cultural requirements. For instance, separate drought-tolerant species from those that are adapted to summer rainfall. The latter require regular irrigation where summer drought prevails, including most urban areas of California. Avoid planting together species with incompatible growth characteristics. For example, bermudagrass and kikuyugrass are hardy, drought-tolerant turfgrasses, but because they spread by rhizomes and stolons they can invade nearby shrubs. Do not plant spreading ground covers such as ivy or Mexican primrose or turf such as bermudagrass near trees and shrubs. If you do, minimize invasiveness by planting ground covers, trees, and shrubs in larger clusters rather than several smaller groups, each bordered by turf. Install deep barriers or headers between turf and planted areas.

Headers. Separate shrub areas from invasive ground covers or turf by using sidewalks, driveways, or headers. Headers are wood, metal, or concrete dividers buried 8 inches or more deep and projecting 2 to 3 inches above the soil (Figure 7-4). Wide cement or brick headers also serve as a mow strip, which allows lawn mowers to cut all the way to the edge of the turf and beyond, thereby reducing the chance that turf can spread into shrub beds. Flexible plastic or other temporary barriers can be used, then moved as the landscape matures or when portions are replanted. Instead of planting a mixture of turf, ground cover, and shrubs within the same median strip, header, or other area bordered by pavement, alternate plantings so that each area is entirely shrubs, ground cover, or turf. This reduces weed control efforts because the entire section can be managed the same and plantings are less likely to become weeds by overgrowing adjacent landscapes.

Competitive Plantings. Competitive plantings of ornamental species are an excellent method of weed control. Vigorous, densely growing annuals or ground

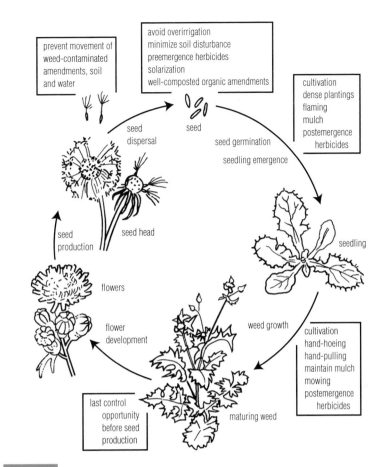

FIGURE 7-3. Methods and timing for annual weed control, illustrated here with annual sowthistle. The best times for effective weed management are before planting, before weeds emerge, and before weeds mature.

Use sidewalks, driveways, or headers to separate plants with different cultural requirements or to contain invasive species. If this is a running species of bamboo, unless it is contained by barriers that extend at least 18 inches below the surface, the bamboo will grow beneath pavement and become a weed in nearby plantings.

TABLE 7-1.

Summary of Weed IPM Methods.

FIGURE 7-4. Separate shrub areas from invasive lawns or ground covers by using headers. Headers are concrete, metal, plastic, or wood barriers extending 8 inches or more below ground and 2 to 3 inches above ground.

DESIGN OR REDESIGN SITES TO AVOID WEED PROBLEMS
• Select species that are well adapted to local climate and soil conditions.
• Group together plants that require similar cultural care, especially similar requirements for water and light.
• Separate plants with incompatible growth characteristics.
• Plan on installing a low-volume irrigation system.
• Consider using a professional landscape designer who is knowledgeable about pest prevention.
• Design features to contain vigorously spreading plants so that desirable species do not become weeds.
• Select plants that develop an overlapping canopy to shade out weeds.

BEFORE PLANTING PREPARE THE SITE THEN PLANT PROPERLY
• Eliminate any established weeds, especially perennial species.
• Grade and prepare the site for good drainage.
• Loosen and amend or add topsoil if needed, after making sure that new soil or amendments are free of seeds and other weed propagules.
• Irrigate and remove weeds that emerge and repeat this process if possible to reduce the weed seed bank before planting.
• Install any needed irrigation system.
• Plant trees and shrubs properly.
• Choose appropriate mulch and apply it correctly.

PROPERLY CARE FOR ESTABLISHED LANDSCAPES
• Provide desirable species with proper cultural care.
• Monitor regularly and frequently for weeds and keep written records of the species and when they appear.
• Determine which weeds can be tolerated and when control is warranted.
• Control weeds while they are seedlings, such as by hand-pulling or hoeing.
• Dig-out perennial weeds while they are small to remove persistent propagules.
• Effectively operate and maintain a low-volume irrigation system.
• Correctly maintain mulch depth.
• Minimize any disturbance to the soil.
• Use a preemergent herbicide, usually during fall or spring, or spot applications of a contact herbicide where appropriate.
• Consider redesigning and replanting problem-prone landscapes.

bare areas in between. Trim or remove some individual plants if needed as they become older and crowded. Interplanted landscape is more attractive and easier to care for than bare soil between landscape plants; bare soil is inevitably colonized by weeds and requires ongoing monitoring and weed removal.

Avoid planting turf and irrigated ground covers too close to tree trunks and shrubs. Turf, ground covers, or weeds near trunks dramatically retard growth of young trees and shrubs. Watering ground covers or turf near trunks can cause drought-adapted trees and shrubs to die from excess moisture or root and crown rot diseases. Conversely, woody plants adapted to summer rainfall may not get enough water and nutrients if turf and ground covers grow underneath them because these other plants can be more efficient at capturing water and nutrients near the soil surface. Although competition can be partially reduced by providing additional irrigation (and possibly fertilizer), better growth will occur if you mulch or maintain bare soil for several feet around the trunks of young woody landscape plants. Consider using mulch as an attractive ground cover where appropriate.

Allelopathy. Some plants, such as black walnut, certain aromatic shrubs, and many desert species such as sagebrush,

covers planted in bare spaces among trees and shrubs can rapidly grow together and shade out weeds. However, be aware that some aggressive ground covers, such as certain ivy species, can become weeds by crowding out and killing shrubs. Use species that have cultural requirements compatible with nearby plants. For example, Table 7-2 lists ground covers and perennials that require little or no irrigation after they are established and are therefore more compatible with native California oaks and other drought-adapted trees. Use enough plants so they form a dense canopy that shades the ground and excludes weeds; mulch any

Turf has stunted this tree's growth and invaded what was bare soil among the widely scattered shrubs in the background. Planting shrubs densely to shade the soil, applying and maintaining mulch, and keeping turf back while shrubs are young can minimize these weed problems.

TABLE 7-2.

Ground Covers or Shrubs Requiring Little or No Irrigation and Suitable for Around Mature, Drought-Adapted Trees in the Central Valley of California.

COMMON NAME	SCIENTIFIC NAME
FULL SUN (SOUTH OR WEST EXPOSURE)	
bush monkeyflower	*Mimulus aurantiacus*
California buckwheat	*Eriogonum fasciculatum*
California fuchsia	*Epilobium canum (=Zauschneria cana)*
deer grass	*Muhlenbergia rigens*
dwarf coyote brush	*Baccharis pilularis*
flannel bush	*Fremontodendron* spp.
purple needle grass	*Nassella (=Stipa) pulchra*
sage	*Salvia leucophylla*
silver bush lupine	*Lupinus albifrons*
yarrow	*Achillea millefolium*
yucca	*Yucca whipplei*
PARTIAL SHADE (EAST OR NORTH EXPOSURE)	
barberry, mahonia	*Mahonia fremontii, M. higginsiae, M. pinnata*
California fescue	*Festuca californica*
California wild rose	*Rosa californica*
Carpenteria	*Carpenteria californica*
ceanothus, wild lilac	*Ceanothus griseus, C. thyrsiflorus, C. maritimus*
coffeeberry	*Rhamnus californica*
evergreen viguiera	*Viguiera parishii*
gooseberry	*Ribes aureum, R. malvaceum, R. speciosum, R. sanguineum, R. viburnifolium*
holly-leaf cherry	*Prunus ilicifolia*
maritime ceanothus	*Ceanothus maritimus*
toyon	*Heteromeles arbutifolia*
western redbud	*Cercis occidentalis*
yerba de selva	*Whipplea modesta*

Once established, generally about 1 year after planting, these species require relatively little care. Many do best in hot, dry areas if irrigated once a month during the summer. For more information see the Literature Cited and Suggested Reading at the back of the book. *Sources:* Johnson undated, Zagory 1992.

produce compounds that retard the growth of nearby plants. This chemical suppression among plants is called allelopathy. Mature plants usually tolerate allelochemicals (compounds produced by plants that inhibit other plants), but germination and growth can be reduced in seedling plants such as annual flowers or weeds.

Certain species such as eucalyptus are assumed to be allelopathic because few plants grow around their trunks. However, a major reason few plants grow is the extreme competition for water and nutrients from the extensive shallow root system of eucalyptus. Ground eucalyptus is an excellent mulch and when properly used as mulch does not inhibit plant growth.

To date, little research has been conducted indicating that allelochemicals can be effectively used in landscapes. Applying certain fresh organic mulches may produce an effect similar to plant-

ing allelopathic species. In addition to preventing weed growth by excluding light, natural toxins leaching from uncomposted fresh bark or foliage of certain species applied as mulch may temporarily retard young plants (weeds), but they have little effect on mature, established plants. Composting the organic mulch or leaching it with a

heavy irrigation before use reduces or eliminates any phytotoxicity.

PREPARING THE PLANTING SITE

Prepare sites properly before planting, as discussed above and in chapter 3. Eliminate established weeds and reduce future weed growth before planting, such as by using proper irrigation and cultivation, solarization, or herbicides. It is especially important to reduce or eliminate perennial species, such as bermudagrass and yellow nutsedge, before planting or moving soil around the site. Loosen compacted soils and break up hardpan by ripping, chiseling, boring, or using other equipment. Soil may be amended by adding organic matter or changing pH if necessary, but the benefits of soil amendments are uncertain for most woody plants; it is better to choose species that are well adapted to conditions at that site. Properly grade soils or plant on berms or raised beds so that water drains well around roots, which helps to prevent root disease.

Irrigation. Avoid overwatering, which primarily results from irrigating too frequently. Weeds will establish in areas where water drains or puddles or where soil remains wet for a long time. Provide for any needed irrigation by installing drip irrigation or another efficient system that allows appropriate watering, as discussed in chapter 3. Unless the water source is high in minerals, irrigating beneath mulch with porous hoses or emitter heads can be especially good because this keeps water away from the surface and weed seeds near the surface are less likely to be wetted and germinate. Alternatively, use low-volume aboveground emitters to deliver water slowly near landscape plant roots. Sprinklers widely disperse water, much of which becomes available to weeds. Seasonally adjust irrigation schedules according to the weather and plants' changing need for water.

Cultivation. Cultivation cuts, uproots, or buries weeds. Rototill or manually cultivate before planting to kill young annual weeds. Reduce the number of weed seeds by irrigating the soil to promote germination, then cultivate again in about 1 to 3 weeks after seedlings emerge. Repeat these steps (water, wait, then cultivate) two or more times before planting. Avoid deep tilling, as this brings buried weed seeds to the surface where they are more likely to germinate.

Solarization before planting controls weeds and many soilborne diseases. To solarize, cover bare, moist, smooth soil with clear plastic for at least 4 to 6 weeks during hot, sunny weather.

Make each subsequent cultivation shallower than the last to minimize movement of buried seeds to the surface. To minimize any subsequent soil disturbance, the area must already be at final grade. If possible, install the irrigation system before beginning this "water, wait, then cultivate" system.

Although most effective against annuals, cultivation also controls perennial weed seedlings if it is conducted before they have stored much carbohydrate or produced tubers, stolons, or rhizomes. Plants should be cut before new top growth exceeds 6 inches and cultivation must be repeated when plants regrow. This repeated damage and disruption prevents perennial weeds from storing additional carbohydrate and requires them to continually draw on reserves, which are eventually depleted, killing the plant.

Some established perennials in dry inland valleys can be controlled by cultivating every 1 to 3 weeks during the summer without any irrigation, then allowing the soil and weeds to dry. This regime can control bermudagrass, johnsongrass, kikuyugrass, and purple nutsedge, but not yellow nutsedge. Repeated cultivation generally is required for more than 1 year to control field bindweed. Cultivation to control perennials is effective only when soil is warm and dry. Cultivating perennials generally does not give effective control in coastal areas or during cool, rainy weather; use other methods in these circumstances. Cultivating perennials when soil is moist or cultivation followed by irrigation or rain can increase the spread of perennials because individual pieces can develop into new plants.

Solarization. Solarization before planting can effectively control most annual and certain perennial weeds for 6 months to 1 year (see Table 7-3). Solarization, tarping soil to retain the sun's heat, also reduces nematodes and many soilborne diseases. For effective solarization, users must recognize and avoid its shortcomings (Table 7-4).

To solarize, cover bare, moist ground with clear (not black) plastic, 1.5 to 2 mils (0.0015–0.002 inch [0.038–0.05 mm]) thick, during the hottest part of the year. Thinner plastic is more economical and will allow greater heating, but 1 mil (0.001 inch [0.025 mm]) is not very resistant to tearing by wind or animals. Whenever possible, use plastic that contains additives to inhibit degradation by ultraviolet (UV) light. Although more expensive, UV inhibitors prevent plastic from becoming brittle and difficult to remove and often allow plastic to be reused unless it becomes excessively dirty. Using a double layer of plastic with an air space of at least ½ inch between layers can raise soil temperatures from 2° to 10°F higher than when using a single layer. Using a double layer requires more preparation and expense but can make solarization more feasible in areas with a cooler climate.

To solarize effectively:

- Clear any vegetation from the area to be solarized. Scrape vegetation off, mow weeds closely to ½ inch tall and rake the soil free of cuttings, or rototill no deeper than 4 inches.

- Grade soil and otherwise prepare it so it is ready for planting and any subsequent disturbance is minimized.

- Irrigate soil thoroughly just before covering it. Lightly work the soil surface to even it, then irrigate again if the soil surface has dried.

- Be sure the ground is smooth and free of clods and trash so that the plastic lies very close to the soil surface. Air gaps created by clods or air pores in dry soil are poor conductors of heat.

- Cover moist, smooth, debris-free soil with intact, clean, clear plastic tarps (preferably UV-inhibiting treated plastics).

- Seal any seams with clear plastic tape and seal the edges with soil to retain heat.

- Protect the tarp surface from punctures during solarization to achieve the highest soil temperatures. If holes form in the plastic while on the soil, seal them with clear patching tape.

- Plant soon after removing the plastic.

- After solarization, avoid deep cultivation. Working the soil deeper than about 3 inches may bring some weed seeds to the surface that were buried too deeply to have been exposed to temperatures high enough to kill them.

TABLE 7-3.

Weed Species Susceptibility to Soil Solarization.

COMMON NAME	SCIENTIFIC NAME	RELATIVE SUSCEPTIBILITY
barnyardgrass	*Echinochloa crus-galli*	S
Bermuda buttercup	*Oxalis pes-caprae*	S
bermudagrass	*Cynodon dactylon*	P
bindweed, field	*Convolvulus arvensis*	R
bittercress, lesser seeded	*Cardamine oligosperma*	S
bluegrass, annual	*Poa annua*	S
cheeseweed	*Malva parviflora*	S
chickweed, common	*Stellaria media*	S
crabgrass, large	*Digitaria sanguinalis*	P
creeping woodsorrel	*Oxalis corniculata*	S
fleabane, hairy	*Conyza bonariensis*	S
goosefoot, nettleleaf	*Chenopodium murale*	S
groundsel, common	*Senecio vulgaris*	S
henbit	*Lamium amplexicaule*	S
horseweed or marestail	*Conyza canadensis*	S
johnsongrass	*Sorghum halepense*	U
knotweed, common	*Polygonum arenastrum*	S
lambsquarter	*Chenopodium album*	S
lettuce, prickly	*Lactuca serriola*	S
lovegrass	*Eragrostis* spp.	P
mustard, black	*Brassica nigra*	S
nettles	*Urtica* spp.	S
nightshade, black	*Solanum nigrum*	S
nightshade, hairy	*Solanum sarrachoides*	S
nutsedge, purple	*Cyperus rotundus*	R
nutsedge, yellow	*Cyperus esculentus*	U
oat, wild	*Avena fatua*	P
pearlwort, birdseye	*Sagina procumbens*	S
pigweed, redroot	*Amaranthus retroflexus*	S
purslane, common	*Portulaca oleracea*	P
redmaids	*Calandrinia ciliata*	S
ryegrasses	*Lolium* spp.	S
shepherd's-purse	*Capsella bursa-pastoris*	S
sowthistle, annual	*Sonchus oleraceus*	S
spurges	*Chamaesyce (=Euphorbia)* spp.	S
sweetclover, white	*Melilotus alba*	R
willow herbs or fireweeds	*Epilobium* spp.	S

KEY

S   Susceptible: proper solarization can control all of this weed for one season if soil is undisturbed
P   Partially susceptible: many plants are killed, but some survival and regrowth may occur
R   Resistant: little or no control
U   Unpredictable, weed may or may not be controlled

Adapted from Elmore et al. 1997.

TABLE 7-4.

Advantages and Disadvantages of Solarization.

DISADVANTAGES
• Does not work well in cloudy, cool, windy areas.
• In the field, it requires a plant-free period of 4 to 6 weeks during a sunny time of year that is warm or calm or both.
• Effective use requires careful preparation (such as moist, smooth, debris-free soil) and adequate execution (such as tear-free plastic with sealed edges).
• Certain pests are resistant to solarization.
• Soil-contaminated plastic is often too dirty and damaged to reuse, many recyclers will not accept it, and used plastic in California is typically disposed of in landfills.

ADVANTAGES
• Safe, relatively simple, and scaleable for use in any size landscape.
• Is cheaper and less hazardous than chemical fumigation of soil.
• Often stimulates plant growth beyond that resulting solely from pest control, possibly because solarization increases nutrient availability and gives a competitive advantage to certain heat-tolerant beneficial soil microorganisms.
• Can improve soil texture and quality, facilitating planting.

Cover soil for about 4 to 6 weeks to solarize it. Solarization is most rapid and effective if conducted during a period of intense sunlight with little wind. Solarization requires more time and is less effective in cloudy, windy coastal areas. In California's Central Valley, soil can be solarized anytime from late May through September. In south coastal California, mid-July through August is usually the sunniest, calmest time of year. Along coastal areas of central and northern California, August to October and May through June are usually best; these are transitional periods when fog or wind can be at a minimum. Consult *Soil Solarization* (Elmore et al. 1997) for a more detailed discussion of solarization.

MULCH

Mulching is one of the most effective and desirable methods of preventing germination and growth of annual weeds. Mulch is a layer of material covering the soil to exclude sunlight. Many seeds require light to germinate, and all green plants need light to grow. Although effective mulching can require a significant initial investment, it provides long-term aesthetic benefits and greatly reduces on-

going weed management costs. When mulch is promptly applied to an area that has been adequately prepared, especially by removing perennial weeds and their propagules, regular hand-pulling or hoeing of weed seedlings and maintenance of the mulch may be the only weed management activities necessary. If perennials become established, other management practices such as herbicide use may be necessary.

Mulches include plant-derived materials such as bark, lawn clippings, wood chips, and greenwaste (Table 7-5). Effective nonorganic mulches include crushed rock and synthetic landscape fabrics (Table 7-6). In long-term plantings of trees and woody shrubs, landscape fabric covered with a bark, chip, or rock mulch is sometimes used to provide practical and long-lasting weed control. However, this combination can become a problem when landscape fabrics or plastic partially breaks down or is removed. Mulch can also be combined with a preemergence herbicide. The particle size of organic mulch, layer thickness, herbicide placement on top versus beneath mulch, and preemergence herbicide efficacy are among the important

considerations when combining organic mulch and preemergents. See *Weed Management in Landscapes Pest Notes* (Wilen and Elmore 2001) for specific herbicide recommendations for use with organic mulch.

In addition to good weed control, mulch conserves soil moisture by reducing evaporation and reducing water use by weeds. Mulch moderates the soil wetting and drying cycle between irrigations and reduces summer soil temperatures around roots, improving plant growth. Mulch also reduces compaction and erosion from irrigation, rainfall, and foot traffic.

Organic Mulch. Organic mulches have the major advantage of gradually improving soil quality as they decompose. The minerals and organic matter released from decaying mulch enrich deficient soils, replace nutrients taken up by roots as plants grow, and often enhance earthworm populations. Many organic mulches are attractive, contrasting nicely with foliage and flower colors and providing a pleasant "natural" appearance and aroma. Most organic mulches improve water penetration by reducing water runoff and increasing infiltration. Materials are often readily available onsite or are available free or at minimal cost from public parks departments, landfills, or private arborists and tree maintenance companies.

If not properly selected or used, organic mulches have some disadvantages. Organic mulches gradually decompose and must be periodically added to maintain a sufficiently deep layer to provide good weed control. Mushrooms sometimes grow in decaying mulch, and the appearance of these fungi can alarm people or pose a hazard if children are tempted to eat them. Unless consumed, mushrooms in mulch are generally harmless, and many are beneficial decomposers, as discussed in publications such as *Mushrooms and Other Nuisance Fungi in Lawns Pest Notes* (Le Strange, Frate, and Davis 2002).

Mulch may contain weed seeds or stolons; before applying it, consider prop-

TABLE 7-5.

Organic Mulches.

MATERIAL	COMMENTS
bark chips and ground bark	Attractive, slowly improves soil as it gradually decomposes. Often placed over plastics or landscape fabric as a decorative material, but plastic mulches can be difficult to remove once they begin to deteriorate.
compost[1]	Excellent source of organic matter, readily available or can be made. Because of its smaller particle size, applying and maintaining a 2-inch layer can be very effective. May harbor weed seeds, especially if not properly composted. May promote crown disease if applied to contact trunk.
grass clippings and leaves	Readily available, can be applied often. Fresh leaves may contain allelochemicals as discussed earlier; leach leaves well with water before using them around small or young plants. May contain weed propagules, e.g., seeds or bermudagrass stems. Mats and reduces water penetration, especially if not dried first. Better if composted before use.
greenwaste[2]	—
hay and straw	Allows good water penetration. Looks good. Usually contains grain seed, which may germinate.
leaf mold	Can add needed acidity to alkaline soils, and is attractive. Requires careful attention and substantial effort to prepare, or can be collected.
newspapers (shredded)	Readily available, inexpensive, no weed seeds. Can interfere with water penetration if not shredded. Not stable in windy conditions. Certain inks may be toxic, do not use around edible plants. Unattractive.
peat moss	Increases water-holding capacity if mixed into the soil. Adds acidity to alkaline soils. Contains few or no weeds. Blows away, especially if used alone. Resists wetting when dry. Expensive.
pine needles	Adds acidity, readily available. Slow to break down. Most suitable for plant species adapted to acidic soil.
pressed heavy fibrous paper for mulching (e.g., Hortopaper)[3]	Good water and air penetration, easy application. Must be purchased. Tends to break or tear after transplanting or if walked on.
rice hulls	Increases soil aeration and drainage if incorporated, slow to degrade. May contain weed seeds unless composted or rolled to crush seeds.
sawdust	Inexpensive or free. Will mat and inhibit water penetration. Blows away and decomposes rapidly. May contain allelochemicals; leach well with water before using around small or young landscape plants. Use only untreated wood.
wood chips	Long-lasting and resistant to wind movement. Sometimes inexpensive. May contain weed seeds. May not stay in place on slopes.

Mulch can increase populations of earwigs, sowbugs, and certain other soil-dwelling invertebrates that may be pests. Organic mulches can improve soil organic matter content as they decompose and become naturally incorporated into soil; for example, through the activities of soil-dwelling invertebrates such as earthworms and ants. Uncomposted organic mulches can reduce nitrogen availability to roots, but unless incorporated as a soil amendment, soil nitrogen deficiency from surface-applied mulch occurs slowly over the long term and may not be dramatic.

1. Commonly composed of greenwaste properly composted for 30 days or more.

2. Greenwaste, sometimes called yard waste, is uncomposted yard trimmings and untreated wood consisting of a variable mixture of bark, grass, ground wood, and leaves. See the table comments on these individual materials.

3. See Table 7-7 for how long this material remains effective.

erly composting organic mulch that may be contaminated. Hand-pull or otherwise control weeds during the seedling stage if they begin to grow in mulch. Mulch can harbor snails and slugs, earwigs and other insects, and rodents. Apply copper bands around tree trunks or planting areas to exclude snails and slugs. Use wire or plastic guards to protect trunks from gnawing rodents. Maintaining bare soil within about 1 foot of trunks also can reduce problems with these pests.

Although most organic mulches improve water penetration and retention, thick applications of certain materials such as sawdust or fresh grass clippings can reduce water penetration to roots. If sprinklers are used, apply more water during each irrigation so that moisture penetrates to soil and roots, but increase the interval between irrigations to avoid overwatering. If water runs off, suspend irrigation for about an hour to allow moisture to sink into the soil.

TABLE 7-6.

Nonorganic Mulches.

MATERIAL	COMMENTS
black plastic (polyethylene)	Very effective, easy to handle. Not permeable to air and water. Usually needs drip irrigation. Warms soil somewhat. Breaks down in a few months and is unattractive unless a top mulch is applied. Weeds can grow readily through tears or holes.
clear plastic (polyethylene)	Performs like black plastic, except that it encourages weed growth unless solarization procedures are followed. Cover with top mulch if not used for solarization. Weeds can grow readily through tears and holes.
crushed stone, gravel	Attractive as a top mulch for synthetics. Tends to become weed infested if used alone. May get too hot. Time-consuming to remove, may be expensive.
photodegradable plastic	May not need to be removed. Degradation has been inconsistent and may not be complete. Must be exposed to light to degrade. If exposed to light, not as long-lasting as some other materials.
roofing or building paper	Long-lasting and durable. Unattractive unless a top mulch is applied. Expensive. Certain materials containing petroleum products should not be used around herbaceous plants or small or young woody plants.
polypropylene and polyester (spun-bound, woven and nonwoven)	Very effective, long-lasting. Allows air and water penetration. Expensive, may be unattractive without a top mulch. Brands differ in effectiveness.

Some people recommend avoiding these materials as mulches in landscapes, especially in short-term plantings, because they can eventually contaminate soil and become difficult to remove. See Table 7-8 for information on how long some of these materials remain effective.

Water penetration problems are avoided if a low-volume irrigation system is used.

Certain fresh bark, foliage, and wood may contain naturally occurring toxic compounds (allelochemicals) that may damage herbaceous or young plants, but this will not affect established trees and shrubs. Before applying fresh organic mulch around herbaceous or young plants, compost the material well or leach it with a heavy irrigation to avoid this potential problem.

Synthetic Mulch. Certain plastics are widely used as weed block mulches. Synthetic mulches are often covered with gravel or organic mulch. Covering the plastic protects it from degradation by UV light, holds the material down when conditions are windy, reduces tearing from wind and foot traffic, covers a potentially slippery surface that can be hazardous, and improves appearance.

However, some people recommend that nonorganic materials such as gravel and plastic be avoided in landscapes because they can eventually contaminate soil and become difficult to remove. They do not improve soil quality and most are unattractive unless a top mulch is applied. Plastics are not recommended in beds that will be periodically replanted or where fabric would inhibit the rooting and spread of ground covers.

Certain plastics traditionally used for mulching, such as polyethylene, require special irrigation procedures because they are waterproof and prevent sprinklers from being used to water plants. These waterproof mulches can promote root and crown rot fungi and prevent adequate exchange of gasses (primarily carbon dioxide and oxygen) between plant roots and the atmosphere, especially if soils are poorly drained. Traditional black or clear polyethylene plastic

mulches are increasingly being replaced with specially designed polypropylene or polyester geotextiles, also called landscape fabrics or weed barriers. A major advantage of geotextiles is that most have some porosity that allows passage of air and water. These perforated, spunbound, or woven polyethylenes, polyesters, and other water-permeable geotextiles facilitate irrigation, allow water drainage, and reduce potential root decay problems caused by excess soil moisture. These products are more durable and effective than conventional plastic sheeting and should be used on long-term plantings instead of conventional plastics wherever possible.

Commercial geotextiles vary significantly in cost, performance, and special features. Depending on the product, some plastic mulches are impregnated with herbicide, incorporate compounds that resist degradation by UV light, or are designed to slowly decompose when exposed to light. Biodegradable plastics may avoid disposal problems and may be desirable where slow-growing shrubs or trees are expected to eventually shade out weeds. However, decomposition greatly reduces the length of time products are effective in controlling weeds; also, biodegradation has been inconsistent, and buried plastic remains in soil until it is brought to the surface and exposed to sunlight. Many geotextiles are currently not recyclable because of the type of plastic and presence of soil contamination. These plastics generally are disposed of in landfills.

Protecting plastic from degradation by UV light (either by covering it or using a product that incorporates UV protection chemicals, or both) greatly increases the life span of the mulch. Light-proof fabrics reduce the growth of weeds beneath the plastic better than clear, lightly colored, or thin plastics that allow passage of some light. Thicker fabrics are often more durable and better able to exclude all light. The method of manufacture also appears to affect fabric effectiveness. One study of polypropylene geotextiles found that woven fabrics and nonwoven spunbound products generally prevented weed penetration better than most non-woven meshed or nonwoven perforated fabrics (Table 7-7). Synthetic mulches or landscape fabrics vary in how long they remain effective (see Table 7-8). Shorter-lasting fabrics can be adequate where plants will soon grow together and shade the soil surface. Longer-lasting materials are preferable for use under slow-growing plants or where mulch alone is used as a ground cover between more widely spaced plants.

Proper Mulch Application and Maintenance. Use mulch whenever possible. Mulch is not appropriate in all situations, but its drawbacks can be minimized through proper use. Before applying mulch, be sure the soil is properly graded and weed-free and install any needed irrigation equipment. Keep organic mulch and waterproof synthetics several inches back from trunks, or apply only a thin layer of mulch near trunks to avoid promoting root and crown diseases. Weeds growing in a top mulch can damage the landscape fabrics underneath as their roots grow; regularly inspect mulch and remove any weeds soon after they appear.

Availability, cost, ease of application and maintenance, appearance, stability,

rate of decomposition, and penetration by water and air are considerations when selecting mulches. The characteristics of some common, effective mulches are listed in Tables 7-5, 7-6, 7-7, and 7-8. For more details on mulching, see

Arboriculture: Integrated Management of Landscape Trees, Shrubs, and Vines (Harris, Clark and Matheny 1999) and other publications listed in the Suggested Reading.

TABLE 7-8.

Selected Landscape Fabrics and the Approximate Effectiveness in Years when Used as Weed Barriers Under 2 to 3 Inches of Redwood Bark Chips.

MATERIAL	PRODUCT NAME	EFFECTIVENESS[1]
nonwoven polyester	Warren's Weed Arrest[2]	5+
nonwoven polyester	Terra Mat E	4
nonwoven polypropylene	Duon Weed Control Mat 2.5 oz[2]	3–5+
nonwoven polypropylene	Soil-check[2]	3–5+
nonwoven polypropylene	Typar (DuPont)[2]	3–5+
woven polypropylene	DeWitt Pro 5 Weed Barrier	3–5+
polyethylene	Black plastic, 4 mil not permeable[2]	3–5
polyethylene	Weed Block Landscape Fabric[2]	3–5
nonwoven polypropylene	Terra Mat P	2+
peat moss and cellulose fibers	Hortopaper[2]	½–1

1. Approximate length of time effective in years during field trials in Davis, California. Efficacy may vary, for example, due to local conditions or manufacturer changes in materials; + indicates that materials may last longer than indicated.

2. Materials require a top mulch to protect them from degradation by ultraviolet light and to provide the indicated longevity. If exposed to sunlight, these and some other materials may not last as long as indicated. In landscapes, certain materials may eventually contaminate soil and become difficult to remove.

TABLE 7-7.

Effectiveness of Some Synthetic Mulches in Preventing Weed Emergence.

WEED BARRIER FABRIC		NUMBER OF SHOOTS EMERGING THROUGH WEED BARRIER AFTER 30 DAYS			
POLYPROPYLENE TYPE	PRODUCT NAME	YELLOW NUTSEDGE	PIGWEED	JOHNSONGRASS	BERMUDAGRASS
nonwoven, spun-bound	DuPont Typar 307	0.0	0.0	0.0	2.5
nonwoven, spun-bound	DuPont Typar 312	0.0	0.3	0.0	0.8
woven	Weed Barrier Mat	0.3	0.0	0.3	0.0
woven	DeWitt Pro 5	1.0	0.5	2.3	1.5
nonwoven, meshed	Geoscape Landscape Fabric	0.8	0.0	0.3	9.3
nonwoven, meshed	Amoco Rit-a-Weed	2.5	8.3	7.0	17.5
nonwoven, meshed	Phillips Duon Fiber	3.3	7.8	6.5	12.0
nonwoven, perforated	Weedblock Fabric	1.8	20.3	8.0	72.6
	untreated	8.3	48.8	12.8	112.8

Weed seeds (0.3 tbs of seed per one-half flat) or nutsedge tubers (15 tubers per one-half flat) were planted in flats (shallow trays), covered with fabric, and irrigated to keep media moist. All fabrics completely suppressed emergence of sicklepod (*Cassia obtusifolia*) and smallflower morningglory (*Jacquemontia tamnifolia*) seedlings.

Source: Martin, Ponder, and Gilliam 1991.

Organic. Organic mulch must be applied to an adequate depth to prevent light from reaching soil and to assure suppression of most annual weeds. The larger the particle size of the mulch, the greater the depth required to effectively exclude light from the soil surface. Well-composted greenwaste, which typically has relatively fine particles, can provide excellent weed control when uniformly applied 2 to 3 inches thick. Many uncomposted mulches, such as medium-sized bark chips and ground wood with particle diameter sizes of about ⅕ to ½ inch, should be applied about 3 to 4 inches deep. Coarse chips or bark nuggets (particle sizes ½ to 2½ inches) need to be applied to a depth of about 4 inches or more. Organic mulches gradually break down and become mixed into the soil as they improve tilth, so additional mulch should be applied later unless plants grow together and shade the soil. Because decomposing organic mulch may temporarily reduce the nitrogen available to plants, consider adding nitrogen fertilizer if mulch is incorporated into soil. Adding nitrogen will promote more rapid mulch decomposition.

Synthetic. Avoid plastics that are not permeable to air and water. Smooth soil and remove any sharp objects before applying landscape fabrics. Dig and prepare the planting hole(s). Lay down the landscape

These photographs show the effectiveness of three weed control strategies in 15 × 15 foot plots of *Pittosporum tobira* 4 years after planting in Davis, California. Plants were drip-irrigated, with no weed control except at the time of planting. The top plot received a single postplant preemergent herbicide (oryzalin) application to bare soil. In the center plot, redwood chip mulch (2 to 3 inches deep) was applied once after planting. Landscape fabric (woven polypropylene) was applied to the bottom plot and covered with 2 to 3 inches of redwood chips. All plots are surrounded by unmanaged weeds, but *Pittosporum* within the bottom plot are larger and weed-free in comparison with the other plots because of the superior weed control and greater moisture availability provided by landscape fabric covered with chips.

fabric, mark the fabric to indicate the location where it will be cut for the planting hole, then make an X-shaped cut larger than the base of the plant. Place the plant through the fabric cut into the planting hole, and fold the cut fabric edges back around the plant base. Avoid leaving soil that may contain weed seeds on top the fabric and eliminate any gaps in the geotextile, such as by overlapping and tacking-down layers. Apply any top mulch to a depth of about 1 inch.

CONTROLLING WEEDS IN ESTABLISHED PLANTINGS

Good planning and preparation, correct planting, proper irrigation, and use of mulch minimize the need for ongoing weed control. Weeds that appear despite the above practices can be controlled with hand-weeding, hoeing, cultivation, weed trimmers, mowers, flamers, herbicides, or a combination of these methods.

Prevent Weed Reproduction. Control weeds before they produce seeds. If weeds were not controlled before planting or during the seedling stage, take action before flowers appear and before weeds produce seeds. Once they are produced, seeds can remain viable in the soil for many years, especially if they become buried.

Control perennial weeds as soon as possible, typically before they develop more than about one-half dozen true leaves. The longer perennials are permitted to develop, the more likely it becomes that they will form underground parts from which they can regrow after aboveground parts are removed.

Preventing Weed Introductions.
Weeds may be inadvertently introduced in landscape material and with plants. Topsoil, plants in containers, mulch, manure, and certain other soil amendments are often highly contaminated with weed seeds or plant propagules such as stolons, rhizomes, or tubers. Check to see if commercially obtained soil or mulch containing plant-derived material has been pasteurized, such as

Organic mulches can provide a pleasant, natural appearance and can improve plant growth as well as control weeds.

A covering layer of crushed rock can improve the appearance and protect landscape fabrics applied to control weeds.

by proper composting or steam treatment, to reduce their likelihood of being contaminated with weeds.

Mowers and other implements may be contaminated with weed seeds or vegetative parts. Clean equipment well before moving it from weedy areas. Inspect and avoid planting nursery stock that has weeds growing in the container soil. Surface water (from ponds or rivers) is often highly contaminated with weed seeds; filter surface water to reduce seeds before using it for irrigation.

Water and Fertilizer Management.
Evenly apply sufficient but not excessive irrigation water. Poor placement or

Use a dandelion knife or other specialized hand tool to remove scattered weeds and their roots like this sowthistle while minimizing soil disturbance.

Cut weeds near the soil surface when soil is dry by using a sharp scuffle hoe.

excessive applications of water reduces growth of desirable plants and promotes weed germination and growth. Improper nutrient conditions can also encourage weeds. Avoid fertilizing woody landscape plants unless a specific nutrient deficiency has been diagnosed.

Install a low-volume irrigation system around trees or shrubs to minimize weed growth. Maintain the irrigation equipment; many weed species can take advantage of extra moisture around leaky or improperly operating sprinkler heads. See chapters 3 and 6 for more details on appropriate fertilization and irrigation.

Hand-Pulling. Pulling weeds by hand is of great value in landscapes. Remove the entire crown and roots by pulling weeds when they are young and when soil is loose or wet. Removing the aboveground part temporarily improves landscape aesthetics, but established weeds often develop new shoots from the parts remaining underground. Irrigate dry soil the day before hand-pulling to make it easier to remove roots. Grasp weeds firmly near their base, rock weeds back and forth several times to loosen roots,

then steadily pull (do not jerk) weeds upwards. Place weeds into covered containers and dispose of them away from landscapes to prevent discarded weeds from rerooting (if conditions are moist) and to eliminate any seeds.

Weed poppers, dandelion knives, and similar specialized hand tools (Figure 7-5) are available for removing individual weeds and their roots while minimizing soil disturbance. To effectively control established perennial weeds, it may be necessary to dig up and destroy all underground stems (rhizomes) and tubers that can grow into new plants.

Hoeing. Cut weeds at the soil surface or slightly below the soil surface using a hoe. Keep the tool blade sharp so that weeds are easily cut. Do not use a hoe to cultivate or loosen earth by digging in soft soil. This exposes buried weed seeds, which may germinate. The best time to hoe is when the soil surface is dry and no rain is expected and no irrigation is planned for at least several days after hoeing. Allow 3 to 5 days for weeds to fully dry out before irrigating again. Hoeing is most effective against annual species, since perennial weeds can regrow from severed roots or stems. Young broadleaf weeds are easily controlled by cutting them at the soil surface. Grasses often have their growing point just beneath the soil surface. Before hoeing grasses, hand-pull several of them and determine the depth of their crown (the point where roots and stems meet). Cut weeds at or just below their crown, which is often about $\frac{1}{4}$ inch below the surface.

Scuffle hoes, also called shuffle or hula hoes (Figure 7-5), are used by scraping back and forth with a push-pull motion on the surface of dry soil to cut weeds off at their basal stem. Hoeing at the soil surface or no deeper than about 1 inch reduces the likelihood of injuring roots of desirable plants, minimizes damage to any layer of preemergence herbicide, and limits exposing new weed seeds to the surface for germination.

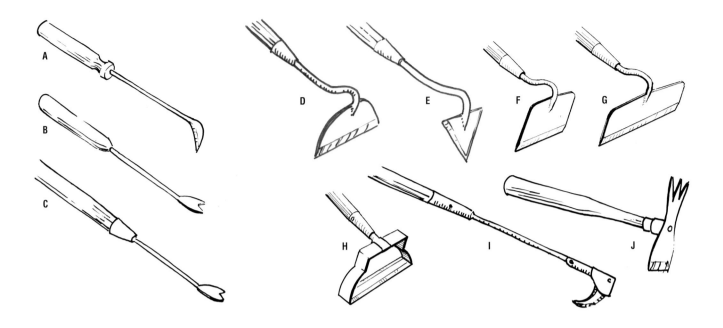

FIGURE 7-5. Hand-weeding is more effective and less work when performed with tools designed for that purpose. Available hand-weeding tools include. A. A weed knife for cutting and digging perennial weed roots. B–C. Short- and long-handled dandelion knives for prying tap roots out of the soil. D–G. Hoes for gently digging out weeds or chopping or cutting off their basal stems. H. A hula, scuffle, or shuffle hoe for scraping back and forth using a push-pull motion on the surface of dry soil to cut weeds. I. A briar hook for pulling weeds. J. A mattock, which has heads like an ax and pick for digging out roots and small stumps.

Cultivation. Cultivation around established landscapes controls primarily annual weeds. If mulches or other preventive measures are not applied, it may be necessary to cultivate about weekly when landscape plants are young to provide adequate control. However, cultivation, especially with rototillers or other motorized equipment, is generally not recommended in established plantings unless the entire area is being renovated and replanted. Mixing and disturbing the top several inches of soil brings previously buried weed seeds to the surface, where they can germinate in the freshly loosened earth. Cultivation or rototilling can also break up and spread vegetative parts of perennial plants, such as weed rhizomes, tubers, and stolons, which can develop into new plants. Cultivation can also injure surface roots of desirable plants. Consider methods other than cultivation if weeds appear in established landscapes.

Prior to planting a site, certain perennial weeds, such as bermudagrass,

Johnsongrass, and purple nutsedge, can be killed by cultivating the soil and allowing it to dry. This brings propagules (rhizomes or nutlets) to the surface, where they are dried by the sun and killed or use up their stored reserves by sprouting. Cultivate 3 or 4 times during dry summer weather and keep the soil dry at all times. Allow sufficient time between each cultivation so that the exposed propagules die and the sprouts have too few leaves to begin producing more propagules. Although the cultivation interval depends on prevailing conditions, it can be judged in part by feeling the soil to determine whether the top few inches have dried, by cutting or breaking open rhizomes or nutlets to assess whether their centers have dried completely, and by learning the maximum number of leaves on sprouts before they begin producing propagules. Keep soil dry at all times when cultivating or propagules will not die. Do not use dry cultivation of perennials unless it will be repeated as necessary;

otherwise, tillage can increase weed problems by breaking up and spreading propagules.

Mowing. If you choose to tolerate grasses or other tall herbaceous vegetation around trees and shrubs, mow or cut them before they bloom and form seeds. Be aware that repeated mowing without other control methods can induce weed shifts to low-growing broadleaf species and grasses that produce seed on plant parts below mowing levels.

Use a hand sickle or portable weed trimmer. Weed trimmers (also called string trimmers and weed flails) have a small motor that spins a short, flexible cord or hard plastic blade at high speeds to cut or break herbaceous species and small-diameter woody plants. Avoid damaging desirable plants, especially young or thin-barked plants. Trunk damage from flailing can girdle and kill young trees or promote attack by wood-boring insects. Before using a weed trimmer, place flexible metal or plastic shields around trunks, such as plastic drain tubing that is several inches in diameter and split lengthwise so it can be spread and temporarily placed around small trunks.

Flaming. Flaming controls weeds in bare earth, along fence rows, in pavement cracks, and in certain mulched areas. Special hand-held flamers are available for weed control, usually fueled with propane or kerosene. Many use an open flame, but other types, such as infrared devices, contain heating elements without an open flame. Although very useful in certain situations, weed flamers can cause a fire if not properly used. Do not flame weeds to the point where they char and burn; only brief contact with high temperatures is needed to disrupt cells. Kill weeds by moving the heating element over weeds or briefly touching the basal stem area of each plant with the tip of a hot flame. It is not necessary to flame the foliage because all aboveground parts die if the basal stem is killed. Flaming is best done in early morning or late evening when winds are low any open flame is more visible.

Plants may wilt, change color, or appear unaffected soon after flaming. Even if no change in the weeds is evident immediately, heating causes plants to yellow and die within several days. Broadleaf annuals and seedlings are most susceptible to flaming; grasses or estab-

Portable weed trimmers cut or break herbaceous species and small-diameter woody weeds.

Use trunk guards to protect young trees and thin-barked species when using weed trimmers or mowers nearby.

These weeds are being killed by flaming them before reapplying mulch to an area where mulch is too thin. Flaming also kills weeds in locations such as bare soil, along fence rows, and in pavement cracks. Do not flame weeds to the point where they char and burn. Keep fire suppression materials handy and use flamers properly to avoid causing a fire.

lished perennials are only partially controlled and often regrow. Work at a slower pace when flaming grasses because their growing points are somewhat protected because they are at or slightly below the soil surface. When flaming these less susceptible plants, it can be more effective to repeat flaming about a week after the initial treatment. Flame weeds when they are less than a few inches tall, especially less-susceptible species such as grasses.

Proper flaming produces little smoke or other emissions, so air quality impacts should not be a problem. Consider avoiding the practice during "spare the air days" because of the hydrocarbon emissions of the fuel and the small amount of smoke that occurs if weeds are inadvertently overheated. Do not flame close to trunks with dry leaves that may burn or smoulder and girdle the trunk. Avoid flaming mulches that may melt or burn, although flaming can be used with caution around damp or coarse chip and bark mulch if the flame is only briefly held near the surface as recommended.

Take care to avoid starting a fire. Use good judgment to identify hazardous situations where flaming should be avoided, such as immediately adjacent to structures and piles of dry debris. Do not use flames in dry areas where fire is a hazard. Keep fire suppression equipment handy, such as a fire extinguisher, shovel, and water, in case of accidents.

Hot Water. Weeds can be killed by applying hot water or steam to foliage and stems. Equipment ranges from relatively small, hand-held, plug-in electric water heaters to trailer, truck- or van-mounted, diesel-powered generators with a long hose and special application wand. Equipment includes general-purpose devices also used for cleaning or disinfecting surfaces to special systems (such as from Waipuna) that apply hot water with biodegradable foam composed of plant-derived compounds intended to increase heat retention and improve weed control.

Hot water treatment is most effective against annuals and young weeds. Established perennials can regrow from underground propagules, requiring re-treatment. Hot water application is most feasible for spot application, such as weeds growing along fence lines, right-of-way and path edges, or in pavement cracks. Treatment of large open areas is more time consuming than with certain other methods, such as herbicide application.

Biological Control. Many organisms feed on weed seeds, seedlings, or established plants. These biological control organisms are present in most landscapes and include microorganisms, invertebrates, and vertebrates. For example, microorganisms, seed-eating insects, birds, and other small animals feed on and destroy weed seeds remaining near the soil surface. Take advantage of these seed eaters by keeping seeds on or near the soil surface. Unless the purpose is to loosen compacted soils, avoid deeply turning soil, such as through spading, to prevent burying seeds where they cannot be attacked by seed predators and decomposers.

Microbial herbicides (mycoherbicides) consisting of diseases that affect only specific weeds have been used in a few nonlandscape situations. Introduced insects have been effective in controlling primarily aquatic and rangeland weeds, such as Klamathweed beetle as discussed in chapter 4. Introduced insects also help to control certain weeds in wildlands, such as brooms (*Cytisus* spp.), puncturevine, and yellow star-thistle (*Centaurea solstitialis*). The most common species on yellow starthistle are two weevils (*Bangasternus orientalis* and *Eustenopus villosus*) and a tephritid fly (*Urophora sirunaseva*). They feed on yellow starthistle buds, flower heads, and developing seed, reducing reproduction and retarding the spread of this roadside and wildland weed. Consult *Yellow Starthistle Pest Notes* (DiTomaso et al. 1999) for more information.

Two introduced *Microlarinus* species weevils help control puncturevine (*Tribulus terrestris*). This weed's spiny seed capsules injure people and puncture tires.

Two introduced weevils (*Microlarinus* spp.) provide complete biological control of puncturevine in Hawaii and partial control in some areas of California. Weevil presence can be recognized by feeding scars (lighter patches on the stem and brownish areas on the green seed capsule) or by larvae, pupae, or frass in plant crowns, stems, or seed capsules (it may be necessary to dissect the plants to find these). An adult weevil emerged from the hole in this stem (top left) after feeding inside.

The small grayish to brown weevils mine puncturevine seeds and stems, reducing weed reproduction and eventually killing the plants, retarding the spread of this weed into growing areas. Increase the effectiveness of puncturevine biological control by avoiding application of broad-spectrum persistent insecticides around puncturevine. Prevent irrigation water from running off onto areas infested with puncturevine because the weevils provide much better control of puncturevine if the weeds are not irrigated.

Domesticated animals, including ducks, geese, and goats, are used in some weed-control situations. Because of the difficulty in maintaining, protecting, and confining these animals, they have limited applications in landscapes. Goats are used to control weeds and create fire-breaks, for example, on steep hillsides that cannot be mowed or easily sprayed. Goats can also be used to clear weeds before planting new landscapes. They eat many different plants and prefer woodier species, including poison oak, bamboo, and blackberry. Goats may be rented and confined to a weedy location using portable fences or herd dogs. Goats are most effective when temporarily crowded into a comparatively small area where they consume nearly all available vegetation before being moved to a new location. Provide goats with water and protection from dogs and vandals.

Biological control is most effectively used in landscapes to control certain invertebrates, as discussed in chapter 4. There are no biological control agents available for application to control most weeds in landscapes. For more discussion of biological control, consult *Natural Enemies Handbook* (Flint and Dreistadt 1998).

Chemical Control. Herbicides are a convenient and generally inexpensive and effective way to control weeds in certain landscape situations. They are frequently used in larger, institutional landscapes to save labor costs. Properly applied herbicides reduce competition from weeds and enhance desirable plant growth. They allow landscape plants to grow more vigorously and outcompete and eventually

shade out weeds. Herbicides are especially useful during the establishment of new plantings, particularly at sites infested with perennial weeds that should be controlled before planting.

A well-designed, mature landscape should require little or no ongoing use of herbicides. There are several good reasons to rely on nonchemical methods where possible and to minimize herbicide use in established landscapes. Herbicides can damage desirable plants due to drift during application, runoff in irrigation or rainwater, volatilization and movement in air after application, or improper use. Examples of herbicide toxicity symptoms are illustrated in chapter 6 in the section "Pesticides and Phytotoxicity." Certain herbicides can persist in the soil and may injure species planted later or may damage nearby plants whose roots grow into treated soils. Repeated use of the same herbicide encourages buildup of species that tolerate certain herbicides. For example, common groundsel, bristly oxtongue, prickly lettuce, and bermudagrass tend to become more common where more-susceptible species have been killed by repeated applications of dinitroaniline herbicides, such as trifluralin. Furthermore, some herbicides may pose health or environmental risks, such as by contaminating water.

Given the time and energy involved in training and supervising personnel, reading pesticide labels, deciding on the proper chemical, checking and calibrating sprayers, measuring out the proper amount of chemical to use, applying the herbicide, washing out equipment after use, and the potential problems associated with storage, clean-up, disposal, and record-keeping, herbicides often may not be the preferred method of weed control in small landscapes. When used, herbicides should be integrated with the nonchemical methods described earlier. For example, after spraying to kill weeds, apply mulch to reduce new weed growth or plant and care for desirable species to increase competition that reduces reinvading weeds. See *Weed Management in Landscapes Pest Notes* (Wilen and Elmore 2001) and other *UC IPM Pest Notes* that

are listed in the Suggested Reading and available online for more specific herbicide recommendations.

Safe Use and Handling of Herbicides. If you decide to use herbicides, use them only where needed. Good landscape design, proper planting, and good management of desirable species can eliminate or at least reduce any need for herbicides. Persons who handle herbicides or other pesticides as part of their job must be trained and may need to be certified or licensed by the state or supervised by a certified or licensed person.

Strictly follow the label instructions of any herbicide or other pesticide that you use. The label is a legal document; you are responsible to follow it. Do not expose other people and minimize exposing yourself to pesticides. Wear proper protective equipment as indicated on the label; eye protective wear is required when handling or applying any pesticide in California. Avoid using pesticides or application methods that might injure nontarget organisms, property, or the environment.

Minimize the potential for herbicides to move off-site and contaminate water, for example, by avoiding excess irrigation and runoff into storm drains or surface water. Read the section "Pesticides Can Contaminate Water" in chapter 2 for more discussion of this problem. For preemergence herbicides that must be activated by irrigation, apply only enough water, about $\frac{1}{2}$ inch, to move herbicide into soil during the first irrigation after application. Consult *Integrated Pest Management for Floriculture and Nurseries* (Dreistadt 2001) or go to the pesticides and water quality information on the UC IPM Web site at www.ipm.ucdavis.edu or the pesticide leaching and runoff risk information at the UC Riverside Cooperative Extension "Pesticide Wise" Web site at www.pw.ucr.edu for more suggestions on avoiding pesticide contamination of water.

Carefully read the product label each time before you use a herbicide. Know how much to use, how and when to use it, how long it lasts, which ornamental plants or locations it is registered for, and what weeds it kills. Be aware that herbicides are hazardous even though many have low acute toxicity (high oral LD_{50} values, as listed in Table 2-2), and by this measure would be considered to be relatively "safe." For example, the commonly used herbicide glyphosate can severely damage or kill desirable plants if it is not carefully used. Certain glyphosate formulations are highly irritating to eyes and skin.

Use accurate rates; overdosing even with "selective" herbicides may injure desirable plants or the environment. Keep children and pets out of treated areas until the herbicide is mixed or irrigated into the soil, or has dried. Do not use herbicide spray equipment to apply any other pesticides. Some herbicides (especially phenoxy herbicides) leave difficult-to-remove residues in spray tanks or hoses that can damage desirable plants. Purchase only the amount of herbicide needed. Store herbicides and other pesticides in their original labeled container in a **locked** cabinet out of the reach of children and pets. Store herbicides separately from food, seeds, fertilizers, and other pesticides such as insecticides. Consult Table 7-9 or your local Cooperative Extension office for help in selecting the proper herbicide for your situation. For more information, also see chapter 2 of this book, *Residential, Industrial, and Institutional Pest Control* (Marer 1991), *The Safe and Effective Use of Pesticides* (O'Connor-Marer 2000), and other publications listed in the Suggested Reading.

Herbicide Resistance. Tolerance and resistance prevent some herbicides from controlling certain weeds. Tolerant plant species have a natural lack of susceptibility to certain herbicides. Tolerance can be desirable because it allows the use of selective herbicides, such as those that control either grasses or broadleaf weeds but not both types of plants. However, because of a lack of competition from susceptible species, repeated application of selective herbicides can allow tolerant weeds to increase unless other methods are used to control them.

TABLE 7-9.

Checklist for Selecting the Appropriate Herbicide.

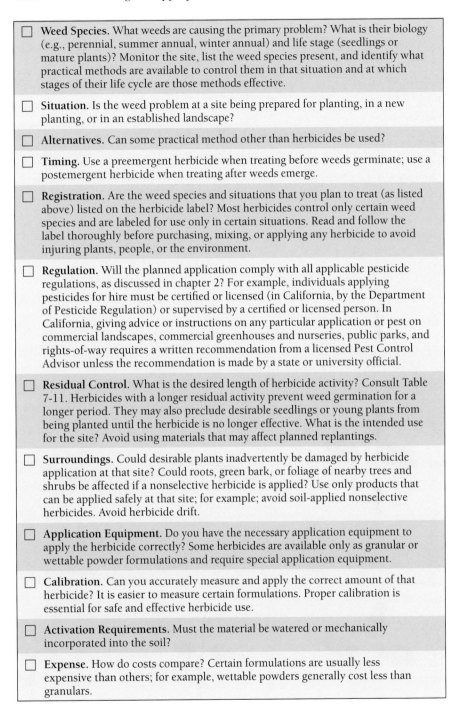

☐ **Weed Species.** What weeds are causing the primary problem? What is their biology (e.g., perennial, summer annual, winter annual) and life stage (seedlings or mature plants)? Monitor the site, list the weed species present, and identify what practical methods are available to control them in that situation and at which stages of their life cycle are those methods effective.

☐ **Situation.** Is the weed problem at a site being prepared for planting, in a new planting, or in an established landscape?

☐ **Alternatives.** Can some practical method other than herbicides be used?

☐ **Timing.** Use a preemergent herbicide when treating before weeds germinate; use a postemergent herbicide when treating after weeds emerge.

☐ **Registration.** Are the weed species and situations that you plan to treat (as listed above) listed on the herbicide label? Most herbicides control only certain weed species and are labeled for use only in certain situations. Read and follow the label thoroughly before purchasing, mixing, or applying any herbicide to avoid injuring plants, people, or the environment.

☐ **Regulation.** Will the planned application comply with all applicable pesticide regulations, as discussed in chapter 2? For example, individuals applying pesticides for hire must be certified or licensed (in California, by the Department of Pesticide Regulation) or supervised by a certified or licensed person. In California, giving advice or instructions on any particular application or pest on commercial landscapes, commercial greenhouses and nurseries, public parks, and rights-of-way requires a written recommendation from a licensed Pest Control Advisor unless the recommendation is made by a state or university official.

☐ **Residual Control.** What is the desired length of herbicide activity? Consult Table 7-11. Herbicides with a longer residual activity prevent weed germination for a longer period. They may also preclude desirable seedlings or young plants from being planted until the herbicide is no longer effective. What is the intended use for the site? Avoid using materials that may affect planned replantings.

☐ **Surroundings.** Could desirable plants inadvertently be damaged by herbicide application at that site? Could roots, green bark, or foliage of nearby trees and shrubs be affected if a nonselective herbicide is applied? Use only products that can be applied safely at that site; for example; avoid soil-applied nonselective herbicides. Avoid herbicide drift.

☐ **Application Equipment.** Do you have the necessary application equipment to apply the herbicide correctly? Some herbicides are available only as granular or wettable powder formulations and require special application equipment.

☐ **Calibration.** Can you accurately measure and apply the correct amount of that herbicide? It is easier to measure certain formulations. Proper calibration is essential for safe and effective herbicide use.

☐ **Activation Requirements.** Must the material be watered or mechanically incorporated into the soil?

☐ **Expense.** How do costs compare? Certain formulations are usually less expensive than others; for example, wettable powders generally cost less than granulars.

Resistance occurs when weeds are no longer controlled by herbicides that previously provided control (Figure 2-3). It develops because individuals in a species vary in their susceptibility to pesticides. Repeated applications that expose several generations of weeds to the same herbicide or other herbicides with the same mode of action causes the resistant biotypes to dominate the population. A different type of herbicide or other measures must be substituted to control that weed species. Take steps to avoid development of herbicide resistance, for example, by using methods recommended by the Weed Science Society of America (Table 7-10).

TABLE 7-10.

Steps for Avoiding Herbicide Resistance.

- Scout landscapes before applying any herbicide to determine what weed species are present.

- Consider the use of alternatives, such as cultivation, mulches, or solarization.

- Limit herbicide application and minimize use of a single herbicide, or herbicides with the same site of action, during a growing season.

- Learn herbicide modes of action and vary herbicides by using mixtures or making sequential applications of herbicides that have different modes of action.

- Scout landscapes after applying herbicides and note weed escapees or species shifts.

- Avoid spreading weed seeds from infested areas, for example, by controlling runoff water and cleaning equipment before moving to another site.

Adapted from Retzinger and Mallory-Smith 1997.

The growth and survival of young trees such as this redwood can be greatly improved by selective herbicides that kill only grasses and preemergence herbicides that prevent new weeds from developing.

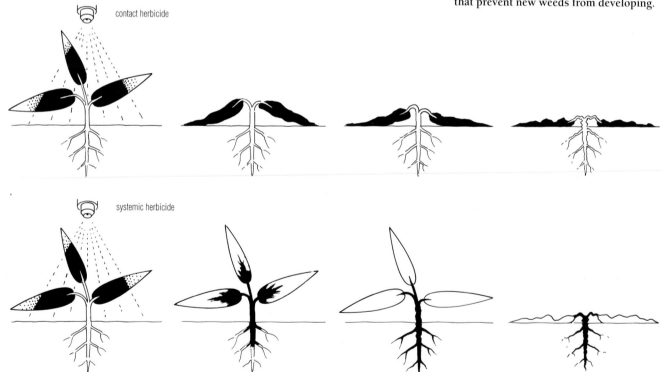

FIGURE 7-6. Contact herbicides usually kill only those green plant parts on which spray is deposited. Thorough coverage is vital for good control using contact herbicides, and even then certain weeds (e.g., established perennials) may regrow from underground plant parts. Systemic herbicides are taken up by green plant parts and are transported to the growing tips of roots and shoots. Because they are systemic, translocated herbicides can better control perennial weeds, as illustrated for the systemic herbicide that moves within the plant (black color) from sprayed leaves to roots. By David Kidd from Marer 1991.

Herbicide Classifications. Herbicides are classified in several ways, including according to when they are applied relative to plant growth, how they control weeds, and the product formulation. Different types of herbicide formulations may be appropriate for different situations or require different application equipment. Common formulations are granules (typically applied dry, then watered in) and wettable powders, flowables, and emulsifiable concentrates (mixed with water and sprayed).

Herbicides are also classified according to how they control weeds (mode of action). Many herbicides selectively affect certain physiological systems unique to plants, so they pose relatively little hazard to animals. Herbicide modes of action include amino acid synthesis inhibitors (such as glyphosate) and plant cell division inhibitors (many preemergents). Knowing the herbicide's mode of action is important for preserving its effectiveness by rotating among materials as discussed above in the section "Herbicide Resistance." Consult Tables 7-11 and 7-12 for the mode of action of herbicides used in landscapes.

Preemergence herbicides kill germinating weeds for several weeks or months after application. They must be applied before weed seeds germinate. Some preemergence herbicides must be mechanically mixed into the soil to place them at the proper location to control weeds. Others may be placed on the surface and followed with sprinkler irrigation or rainfall.

Preemergence herbicides generally do not kill established weeds (they often have no effect on them) and are relatively safe for application around existing landscapes. However, if applied before transplanting or soon after planting and before soil is settled around roots, some preemergence herbicides may retard the root growth of desirable plants, especially when plants are young. Because some materials are persistent (see Table 7-11), they may affect plants that are placed into a treated site for up to a year or more after application.

Postemergence herbicides are applied to emerged weeds (Table 7-12). *Contact*

TABLE 7-11.

Approximate Residual Control Provided by Selected Preemergent Herbicides.

COMMON NAME	TRADE NAME	MODE OF ACTION	PERSISTENCE (MONTHS)[1]
benefin	Balan	CDI	1–2
bensulide	Betasan	PSInA	8–10
corn gluten meal	Bio-Weed	?	≤0.5
DCPA	Dacthal	CDI	2–4
dichlobenil	Casoron	CWSI	3–12
dithiopyr	Crabgrass Preventer, Dimension	CDI	1–6
EPTC	Eptam	PSInA	1–2
isoxaben	Gallery, Green Light Portrait	CWSI	1–4
napropamide	Devrinol	PSInA	2–8
norflurazon	Predict	PSI	3–12
oryzalin	Surflan, Weed Stopper	CDI	4–6
oxadiazon[2]	Ronstar	CMD	4–6
oxyfluorfen[2]	Goal	CMD	4–6
oxyfluorfen[2] + oryzalin	Rout	CMD + CDI	4–8
pendimethalin	Halts, Pendulum, Pre-M	CDI	4–6
prodiamine	Barricade, Bayer Crabgrass Preventer, Endurance, Factor	CDI	3–12
simazine	Princep	PIPII	6–20
trifluralin	Treflan, Weed Stopper II	CDI	3–12

KEY

?	uncertain mode of action
CDI	cell division inhibitor
CMD	cell membrane disrupter
CWSI	cell wall synthesis inhibitor
PIPII	photosynthesis inhibitor, photosystem II
PSI	pigment synthesis inhibitor
PSInA	protein synthesis inhibitor (not ACCase inhibition)

Laws, regulations, and information concerning pesticides change frequently. Certain of these materials may not be registered (legal) for use in your situation, or are available only to professionals applicators. Consult a current label and the local department of agriculture for details on legal pesticide use. Consult *Weed Management in Landscapes* (Wilen and Elmore 2001) and *UC IPM Pest Notes* on specific weeds available online at the UC IPM Web site (www.ipm.ucdavis.edu) for more information on specific herbicides.

1. Approximate persistence in months on susceptible weed species. Actual persistence is influenced by many factors, including soil, irrigation, rainfall, and weather.

2. Herbicide effectiveness is reduced if soil is disturbed after application.

Adapted from Ahrens 1994, Herbicide Resistance Action Committee 2000, Weller and Hess 1997.

TABLE 7-12.

Some Postemergence Herbicides for Use in Landscapes.

COMMON NAME	TRADE NAME	MODE OF ACTION	ACTIVITY	SELECTIVITY[1]
2,4-D		GR	translocated	broadleaves
bentazon	Basagran, Nutgrass Nihilator	PIPII	contact	broadleaves
bromoxynil	Buctril	PIPII	contact	broadleaves
clethodim	Envoy	PSIA	translocated	grasses
dicamba	Banvel	GR	translocated	broadleaves
diquat	Reward	PIPI	contact	nonselective
fluazifop-p-butyl	Fusilade, Grass-B-Gone	PSIA	translocated	grasses
glufosinate	Finale	GSI	contact mostly	nonselective
glyphosate	Roundup Pro, others	AASI	translocated	nonselective
MCPA		GR	translocated	broadleaves
pelargonic acid, fatty acids	H01, Quick Weed Killer, Scythe	?	contact	nonselective, especially broadleaves
sethoxydim	Grass Getter, Poast	PSIA	translocated	grasses
triclopyr	Brush-B-Gon, Turflon	GR	translocated	broadleaves

KEY

?	uncertain mode of action
AASI	amino acid synthesis inhibitor
GR	growth regulator
GSI	glutamine synthetase inhibitor
PIPI	photosynthesis inhibitor, photosystem I
PIPII	photosynthesis inhibitor, photosystem II
PSIA	protein synthesis inhibitor (ACCase inhibition)

Avoid hazards to desirable plants by minimizing use of postemergence herbicides (especially broad-spectrum and broadleaf herbicides) in existing landscapes. For example, broadleaf herbicides commonly are for use only in turf because they injure shrubs and trees. Laws, regulations, and information concerning pesticides change frequently. Certain of these materials may not be registered (legal) for use in your situation, or are available only to professionals applicators. Consult a current label and the local department of agriculture for details on legal pesticide use.

1. Nonselective herbicides are toxic to many different plants, usually both broadleaves and grasses. The plant types primarily affected (broadleaves, grasses, or sedges) are listed for selective herbicides.

Adapted from Ahrens 1994, Herbicide Resistance Action Committee 2000, Weller and Hess 1997.

postemergence herbicides usually kill only those green plant parts on which spray is deposited, usually leaves and stems, so thorough coverage is important for good control (Figure 7-6). For example, certain fatty acids (soaplike herbicides) are effective against many weeds, especially young broadleaves. However, under certain circumstances, many postemergence herbicides (nonselective and broadleaf herbicides) can cause damage (phytotoxicity) to established desirable plants.

Translocated (systemic) herbicides are taken up by green parts of the plant and are transported to the growing tips of roots and shoots, so it may not be necessary to spray all of the plant to kill it. The principal advantage of translocated herbicides is that they can control perennial weeds. For best control, perennial weeds should be growing vigorously and have an abundance of mature leaves when they are sprayed. Depending on the season and stage of plant growth, the effect of some translocated herbicides may not be apparent until some time well after they are applied. For example, the effect of glyphosate may not be apparent until 2 or 3 weeks after application.

Selectivity. Some herbicides are nonselective or broad-spectrum; they can kill both weeds and desirable plants that are sprayed. Nonselective herbicides, such as glyphosate, are used where there are no desirable plants nearby or under certain circumstances where they can be applied so that the material contacts only weeds and not the green bark or foliage of desirable plants. Do not apply nonselective herbicides or broadleaf herbicides around desirable landscapes, except possibly when you can apply them very carefully, such as by using a special wick, wiper, or low-pressure applicator, as illustrated in Tables 2-4 and 2-5. Landscape plants may be damaged by direct spraying or from herbicides that reach plants through drift, volatilization after application, or by contacting roots in treated soils, as discussed in chapter 6 in the section "Pesticides and Phytotoxicity."

Selective herbicides kill only certain types of plants and can be used around some desirable plants, as directed on the label. For example, fluazifop and sethoxydim can be used as directed to selectively control most annual grasses and bermudagrass without injury to trees or shrubs. Phenoxy herbicides such as MCPA or 2,4-D are used in lawns because they kill most broadleaf weeds but not grasses when used as directed. However, phenoxy herbicides can injure nearby trees and shrubs if the material drifts onto leaves or volatilizes after application and is moved by air.

Fumigants are nonselective pesticides applied to soil before planting to kill weeds such as yellow nutsedge, seeds, nematodes, and soilborne disease-causing organisms. Fumigants are rarely applied in landscapes because of health hazards, regulatory restrictions, and toxicity to nearby plants. Solarization, as discussed earlier in this chapter, is a broad-spectrum pest control alternative to soil fumigation in certain circumstances.

Organically Acceptable Herbicides. Some people prefer pesticides used by growers of organic crops. Organically acceptable herbicides include certain salts of fatty acids, commonly called soaps and corn gluten meal. Herbicidal soaps are nonselective and effect mostly young or succulent plant tissue. Annual weeds can be killed on contact, but perennials may regrow from persistent propagules. Keep spray away from desirable succulent plant parts.

Corn gluten meal, a byproduct of milling corn, contains low concentrations of natural chemicals that apparently inhibit seedling root formation. It is also a relatively high source of nitrogen (about 10% N by weight). A fertilization effect contributes to its efficacy in lawns because a more vigorous (fertilized) turfgrass better out-competes weeds such as crabgrass. Results of using corn gluten meal may be disappointing in ornamental areas lacking established, desirable plants that can be stimulated to outcompete weeds. Users should not expect the material to be as effective as synthetic herbicides. Using it at recommended rates can be expensive and may attract birds or certain pests such as ants. High rates may result in an unpleasant odor and potential nitrogen pollution of water.

TYPES OF WEEDS

Plant species can be grouped according to their life cycle as annuals, biennials, or perennials. Annual plants begin each growing season as seeds and complete their life cycle in one year, often producing great quantities of seed before they die. Annual weeds are classified as summer annuals or winter annuals, depending on when they most commonly grow. Summer annuals germinate in the spring or early summer. They flower and produce seed in the fall before dying in the winter. Major species of summer annuals include crabgrass, pigweed, purslane, and spotted spurge. Winter annuals normally germinate in the fall, grow during the winter, flower and produce seed in the spring, and die by early summer. Annual bluegrass, annual ryegrass, annual sowthistle, common chickweed, and common groundsel are examples of winter annual weeds. In coastal areas with a moderate climate, winter annuals may germinate whenever water is present. Certain annuals such as annual bluegrass or cheeseweed can behave as biennials or short-lived perennials in some areas of California. Most annuals can be controlled in mature landscape plantings by an integrated program of mulching, hoeing, and hand-weeding or spot application of a herbicide.

Biennial weeds complete their life cycle in two growing seasons. They produce vegetative parts in the first growing season, and flowers and seeds develop during the second year. Bristly oxtongue and milk thistle are biennials.

Perennial plants can live for three years or longer. Perennials may be woody, such as trees and shrubs, or they may be herbaceous. The aboveground portion of herbaceous perennials may die back during the winter then regrow during the spring or early summer from underground roots, tubers, or rhizomes (underground stems). Although they produce seeds, many of the weedy perennial species spread and reproduce primarily by vegetative parts, such as stolons (stems that creep along the ground) or rhizomes (belowground stems), as illustrated in Figure 7-7. For example, a single tuber of yellow nutsedge can grow and reproduce so that hundreds of plants and several thousand tubers are produced within a year. When controlling weeds by digging them out, roots of broadleaves and rhizomes, stolons, and tubers of perennials must be removed to prevent weed regrowth.

Common perennial weeds are bamboo, bermudagrass, blackberry, field bindweed, kikuyugrass, nutsedges, oxalis, and poison oak. Because of their underground food reserves, established perennials are more difficult to control than annual weeds. *Preventing establishment of perennial weeds should be an important focus of your weed management program.*

WEED IDENTIFICATION

Learn the identity of plants in the landscape. Determine which ones can be weeds and what special problems are associated with their management. For example, some species spread aggressively and are difficult to control once they mature beyond the four- or five-leaf stage. Learn about the life cycle of particular weeds and consider available controls so you can choose effective and appropriate management methods should control action be warranted. Flowers are the primary structures used to reliably identify the species of plants. Because weeds should be controlled before they flower, the shape and arrangement of vegetative plant parts such as

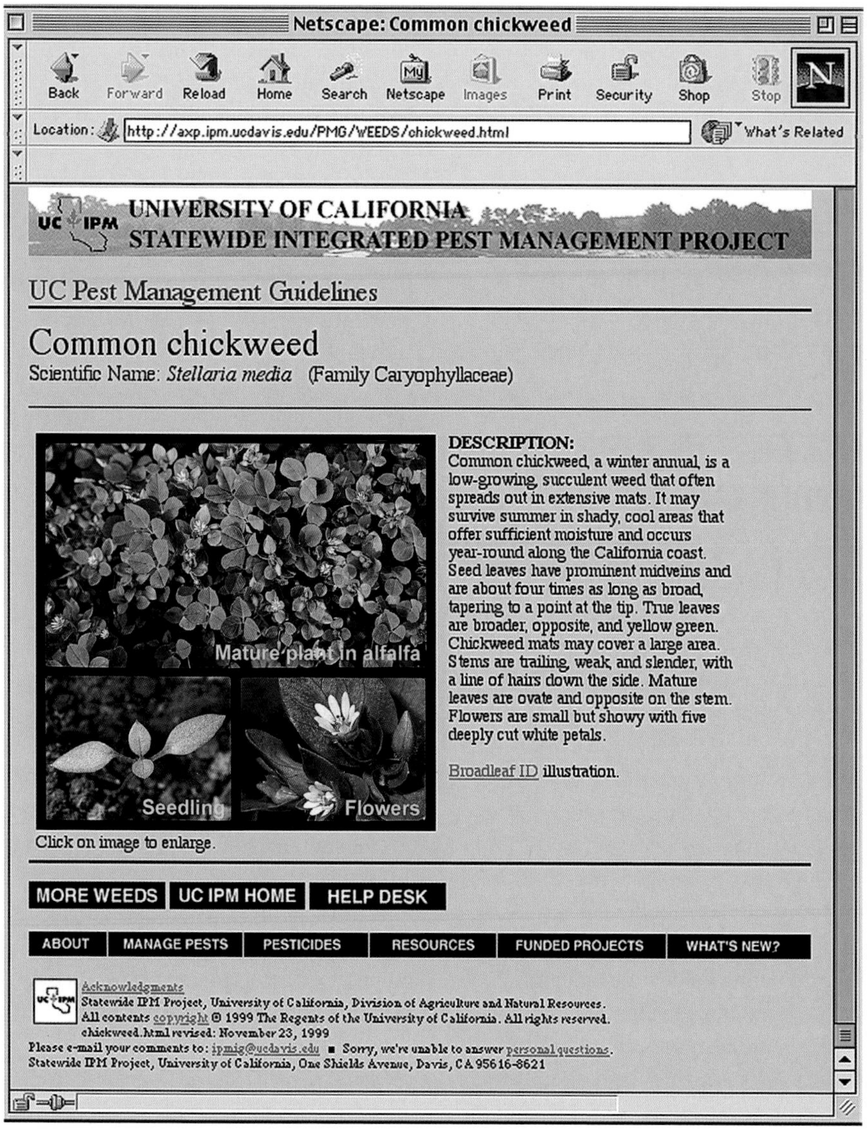

An example of pest identification information accessible through the Internet. The UC IPM Program's World Wide Web site at http://www.ipm.ucdavis.edu and other online sources provide a wealth of information on pest identification and management. Information includes herbicide recommendations in *Weed Management in Landscapes Pest Notes* (Wilen and Elmore 2001) and *UCIPM Pest Notes* on individual weeds available online.

leaves, stems, and veins are key characteristics used to identify weeds. Most broadleaf weeds have showy flowers and netlike veins in their leaves. Grasses and sedges resemble each other, but they are very different. Grass leaves have parallel veins, leaves are longer than they are wide, and the leaves alternate on each side of the stem; sedge leaves are joined to the stem in groups of three. Grass stems are hollow, rounded, and have nodes (joints) that are hard and closed; sedges have a solid stem that is triangular in cross-section.

Vegetative plant parts used in identifying weeds are illustrated in Figure 7-7. Proper species identification is essential when choosing certain management options. For example, most herbicides do not control all species, so if weeds are not identified accurately, herbicide applications may be ineffective and wasteful.

Many different weeds can infest woody landscapes. The species present depends mostly on what weeds and plants have grown in and around the landscape and the extent to which weed-contaminated equipment, plants, and soil have been brought into the growing area. Some common troublesome weeds are described below. To obtain more detailed help for identifying weeds, consult www.ipm.ucdavis.edu or the State of California's Noxious Weeds Web site at http://pi.cdfa.ca.gov/weedinfo and refer to publications such as *Weeds of the West* (Whitson et al. 1991) listed in the Suggested Reading. Cooperative Extension advisors, county agricultural commissioners, knowledgeable pest control advisers, certified nurserymen, and botanical garden and arboretum personnel can also help you identify weeds.

ANNUAL GRASSES

Annual bluegrass and crabgrasses are probably the most common annual grasses (family Poaceae) infesting California landscapes. Ryegrasses (*Lolium* spp.), wild barley or hare barley (*Hordeum murinum* ssp. *leporinum*), and wild oats (*Avena fatua*) are other pest species.

Annual Bluegrass

Poa annua

Annual bluegrass grows 3 to 12 inches tall at maturity. Its flower heads are branched with clusters of 3 to 6 flowers at the tip of each branch. It is a winter annual adapted to cool, moist sites. It can grow anytime of year in coastal areas of California if water is present, and it is deliberately grown as turfgrass in some golf courses along the central coast of California. In ornamental plantings annual bluegrass can form a dense mat that is aesthetically distracting, but probably has little detrimental effect on established woody

Annual bluegrass has light green, short, smooth leaf blades. Leaves are often folded at the tip, resembling the prow of a boat, especially on young plants. Seedlings such as this germinate in the fall or anytime where warm soil is frequently irrigated.

shrubs and trees. For information on identification and management, consult *Annual Bluegrass Pest Notes* (Cudney, Elmore, and Gibeault 2003).

Crabgrasses
Digitaria spp.

Large or hairy crabgrass (*Digitaria sanguinalis*), commonly called crabgrass, is a pale green summer annual. It usually has many branches at the base and spreads from roots growing at swollen joints in the stem. Leaves are 2 to 5 inches long. Smooth crabgrass (*D. ischaemum*) is similar to large crabgrass but is smaller and is not hairy. The bract covering the grain is brownish black compared with pale yellow in large crabgrass. Seed begin germinating about February or March, when soil at a depth of 1 to 2 inches is 50° to 55°F for 3 to 7 days. Crabgrass flower

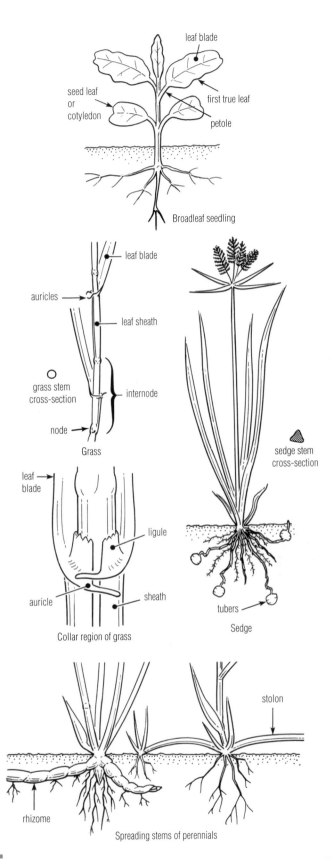

FIGURE 7-7. Vegetative parts of weeds and terms used in identification. Note that not all sedges have tubers (sometimes called nutlets). For the most effective control, the species should be identified and control action taken before weeds mature beyond the seedling stage.

stalks resemble the long claws of a bird. Flower stalks arise in a group near the stem tip, but unlike bermudagrass, often there are additional flower spikes branching from beneath the stem tip. Crabgrass thrives under hot conditions, often where there is frequent irrigation or poor drainage.

Manage crabgrass with a regular program of cultivation, hand-weeding, mulching, and avoiding excess irrigation. Vigilance is required as plants are difficult to remove once they grow and develop an extensive root system. Crabgrass seed is only partially controlled with solarization, but it is easily controlled by many preemergence herbicides. For more information and specific herbicide recommendations, see *Crabgrass Pest Notes* (Elmore 2002).

ANNUAL BROADLEAVES

Annual Sowthistle
Sonchus oleraceus

Sowthistle (family Asteraceae) is a winter annual commonly found in California's Central Valley and coastal areas where it grows year-round. In addition to being a direct pest, annual sowthistle is undesirable around herbaceous plants because it is an overwintering host of the silverleaf whitefly.

Annual sowthistle seed leaves are stalked and covered with a powdery, gray bloom. They have smooth edges and are spoon-shaped. True leaves have wavy edges and prickles. Upper leaf bases clasp the stems with clawlike lobes. Mature plants may reach a height of 3 to 6 feet. Its hollow stems secrete milky juice when cut or crushed. The yellow flowers of sowthistle mature into white, fluffy seed heads.

Annual sowthistle superficially resembles certain other weeds, including common groundsel and dandelion. However, dandelion is a perennial that regroups from a taproot, and it has only basal leaves that all grow from very near the ground. In addition to basal leaves, older annual sowthistle and common groundsel plants have leaves that arise on stems well above ground. Common groundsel can be distinguished by the conspicuous

Most large crabgrass flower stalks arise in a group near the stem tip, but often there are additional flower spikes branching from beneath the stem tip, as shown here. This summer annual reproduces from seed. Its flowers and seedheads resemble bermudagrass (pictured later). However, bermudagrass spreads primarily by rhizomes and stolons, which are lacking in crabgrass.

Annual sowthistle seed leaves have smooth edges and are spoon-shaped, while true leaves have wavy edges and prickles that become more prominent on older leaves.

This common groundsel can be confused with other sunflowers or thistles (family Asteraceae), such as annual sowthistle and prickly lettuce. Common groundsel can be distinguished by the conspicuous black tips on the green bracts surrounding groundsel's yellow flower clusters (lower right).

Annual sowthistle develops yellow flowers that mature into fluffy, white seedheads. Because these windblown seed germinate in decaying organic matter, organic mulch requires regular maintenance (such as periodic reapplication) and spot treatments (such as hoeing or hand-pulling) to control sowthistle.

black tips on the green bracts surrounding the yellow flower clusters; black tipped-bracts are absent in sowthistle.

Annual sowthistle seed germinate only in the top ½ inch of soil, so cultivation, plowing, or solarization before planting provide control. Mulching is effective, but regular maintenance (such as periodic reapplication of organic mulch) and spot treatments (such as hoeing or hand-pulling) are usually required. Because seeds of annual sowthistle and related species (such as common groundsel and prickly lettuce) are easily dispersed by wind, these weeds frequently germinate in decaying organic mulch or soil that accumulates on top of synthetic mulch. For more information, see publications such as *Dandelions Pest Notes* (Cudney and Elmore 2000).

Common Purslane
Portulaca oleracea

Common purslane (family Portulacaceae) is a prostrate, succulent, summer annual. It infests gardens, low-maintenance lawns, and ornamental plantings. Common purslane produces copious seed and rapidly colonizes warm, moist sites.

Common purslane has reddish stems that originate from a central rooting point and radiate out up to 1 foot, resembling the spokes of a wheel. Leaves are oval, smooth, and succulent and are ½ to 2 inches long. The yellow, five-petalled flowers are about ⅜ inch long. Flowers occur singly and open only in sunshine. They mature into small pods containing reddish brown to black, oval seed, each about 1/64 to 1/32 inch long. Lifting mature purslane in late summer can reveal thousands of seed on the soil surface. Seed germinate after irrigation or rain, beginning when soil temperatures reach about 60°F, from February to March in the southern desert to late spring in cooler areas of California.

Prevention is the primary control method. Make sure new plants and soil are weed-free before bringing them into uninfested areas. Clean mowers, cultivation equipment, and other tools before moving them from infested sites. Monitor landscapes and promptly destroy weed seedlings before they produce

seeds. In residential landscapes, control purslane primarily by cultural methods, especially hand-weeding and mulching.

Solarization before planting kills purslane, but do not disturb the soil or cultivate after solarization to avoid bringing new seed to the surface. Organic mulch provides control if it is at least 3 inches thick and evenly applied to prevent all light from reaching soil.

Irrigating then cultivating small seedlings can reduce the weed population. However, cultivation can bring more weed seeds to the surface, so carefully monitor after each irrigation and cultivate new seedlings while weeds are small. When cultivating, hand-pulling, or hoeing larger plants, do so before plants produce seed. Remove plants or allow them to thoroughly dry before irrigation. Purslane's fleshy stems can remain viable for several days, allowing pieces to reroot after cultivation if conditions are moist.

Common purslane seed leaves are elongate, smooth, and succulent with a reddish tinge. The first three true leaves, also seen here, have rounded tips that are broader than the leaf base.

Common purslane has yellow flowers and oval, smooth, stalkless, succulent leaves. Prevention is the primary control method. Make sure that infested material, such as this weedy potted plant, are not brought into landscapes.

Cudweed flower heads are crowded and densely arranged on the stem or at the base of leaf stalks. The fruit bear bristly, tuftlike projections that are shed at maturity.

these postemergents can be used around existing landscapes only when contact with desirable plants can absolutely be avoided. For more information and specific herbicide recommendations, see *Common Purslane Pest Notes* (Cudney and Elmore 1999).

Cudweeds
Gnaphalium spp.

Cudweeds (family Asteraceae) are usually annuals, but some plants survive into a second year before maturing. Mature cudweed is sparsely branched, mostly erect, and 8 to 20 inches tall. Plants develop many dense tufts of long woolly hairs. They can be controlled by cultivating, excluding windblown seed, flaming, hand-pulling, hoeing, mulching, and applying certain herbicides.

Little Mallow
Malva parviflora

Little mallow is one of several *Malva* species (family Malvaceae) that infest landscapes. In addition to being a direct pest, mallows host thrips and several viruses affecting herbaceous plants, including impatiens necrotic spot virus and tomato spotted wilt virus.

Purslane sawfly (*Schizocerella pilicornis*) mines purslane leaves and reduces the vigor and seed production of common purslane. However, biological control is not satisfactory, in part because plants still produce some seed and most sawfly damage occurs late in the growing season.

Chemical control of common purslane is generally not necessary in residential landscapes. Herbicides combined with cultural methods are used primarily in commercial landscapes and large-scale plantings. Many preemergents are effective if present at the soil surface during the time of seedling emergence. Postemergent broadleaf and nonselective herbicides control seedlings. However, control is erratic if plants are mature, and

Mallows are also called cheeseweeds because their fruit are disk-shaped or button-shaped with flattened lobes resembling an uncut block of cheese. True leaves are roundish and crinkled with wavy, shallow-toothed margins, and they often have a red spot at the leaf base. The mature plant forms dense bushes that trail along the ground or grow upright, 1 to 4 feet tall. It has a tough, woody stem and develops a deep taproot. Its flowers are white with a bluish or pinkish tinge and are held in clusters in the leaf axils. Depending on location and weather, little mallow is an annual (primarily a winter annual) or biennial.

Cultivating, flaming, hand-pulling, and hoeing are effective against mallows during the seedling stage. Mallows are susceptible to solarization and mulching before plants emerge. Certain preemergence and postemergence herbicides can provide control if applied while the weeds are young. However, mallows often escape preemergence herbicide application because seed can persist for years and germinate even though buried 1 to 2 inches deep. Control mallow before plants are about 4 to 6 inches tall,

after which their taproots make management increasingly difficult.

Spurges
Chamaesyce (=Euphorbia) spp.

About two dozen species of spurge (family Euphorbiaceae) occur in California. Spotted spurge (*Chamaesyce maculata*) is the major weedy spurge, but about five other species also occur in landscapes, including creeping spurge (*C. serpens*) and ground spurge (*C. prostrata*).

Spotted spurge is a many-branched, low-growing, mat-forming summer annual. Seed leaves are oval and about one and one-half to two times as long as wide, with a rounded tip and smooth margins. Seed leaves are bluish green, powdery or mealy on the upper surface, and have a reddish tinge underneath. Leaves on mature plants grow oppositely on short stalks. Spotted spurge has milky, sticky sap and small, inconspicuous flowers. The plant is named for the dark, reddish spots often found in the middle of the leaves.

Seed germinate around February or March. Each plant can produce 600 to 3,500 seed, which can survive for up to 12 years in the soil. Spotted spurge often thrives in areas of mostly bare soil. It also sprouts in cracks in pavement, along edges, and in bare spots, where it survives even very close mowing. Because it has a low-growing habit, some landscape managers tolerate spurge growing under woody plants in comparison with more visible weed species, which can grow up through or over shrubs.

Apply mulch before seedlings germinate to prevent spurge. Hoe or otherwise cultivate seedlings when small. Larger plants are easy to hand-pull if soil is moist and spurge is not too abundant; grasp a mat of stems and pull slowly to remove the whole plant, including its short roots. Because spurge is capable of setting seed within a few weeks of emergence, regularly monitor landscapes and promptly remove weeds before they produce seed. Preemergence herbicides applied in early spring are effective, and they are especially useful where infestations and seed production have been heavy. For more information, including

Little mallow has heart-shaped seed leaves. True leaves are more roundish with indented edges, and they often have a red spot at the base of the blade where the leaf joins the petiole. Take control action when mallow is young. Mature plants have a deep taproot and produce persistent seed.

Spotted surge is named for the dark reddish area in the center of true leaves. Milky, sticky sap exuding from the broken stem is characteristic of plants in the family Euphorbiaceae.

Mature spotted surge is low-growing. Leaves grow opposite on short stalks, are finely toothed on the margin, and are covered with soft hairs.

Northern willowherb develops tiny pinkish flowers on the end of short stalks. Each of these stalked flowers will mature into ½-inch-long brown seed pods.

specific herbicide recommendations, see *Spotted Spurge Pest Notes* (Cudney, Elmore, and Sanders 1997).

Willow Herbs
Epilobium spp.

Northern willow herb, also called fringed willowherb (*Epilobium ciliatum*), and panicle-leaf willow herb, also called panicled willowherb or panicle willowweed (*E. brachycarpum* =*E. paniculatum*), are two similar-looking weeds that infest landscapes. These members of the evening primrose family (Onagraceae) are also called fireweeds. These willow herbs are usually annuals that vary at maturity from about ½ to 6 feet tall. Their white, pink, or purplish flowers occur from about June through September.

Control willow herbs before they flower or produce seed. Each seed is attached to a tuft of long white hairs, so seed are easily dispersed by wind. Provide good drainage and maintain irrigation systems to prevent water puddles where windblown seed often collect and germinate. Cultivating, hand-weeding, mulching, solarizing soil, and applying certain preemergence herbicides can

control willow herbs. Flaming is effective on seedling or annual willow herbs.

SEDGES

Sedges resemble grasses but have solid stems that are triangular in cross-section (see Figure 7-7) and leaves that usually radiate out in three directions from the stem. True grasses have hollow, round stems. The sedge family (Cyperaceae) includes both annual and perennial species. Green kyllinga and nutsedges are important perennial sedges infesting landscapes.

Green Kyllinga
Kyllinga brevifolia

Green kyllinga is a weedy sedge that is a relatively recent introduction in California. It infests ornamentals and turf and is often confused with yellow or purple nutsedge because it is similar in size and growth habits. However, green kyllinga flowers and the absence of underground tubers distinguish it from nutsedge.

Green kyllinga is a perennial that grows best during warm weather and in moist or wet areas that receive full sun. If unmanaged, it can reach a height of about 18 inches. Its leaves are long and narrow, ranging from 1 to 5 inches or more in length. Flowering usually occurs from May to October, sometimes earlier in warm locations. Flower stalks are triangular in cross-section, 2 to 8 inches in length, and terminate in a globular, green flower about ⅜ inch in diameter. Directly below the flower are three leaves that radiate out. Green kyllinga seed are oval, flat in cross-section, and about 1/16 to ⅛ inch wide. Seed germinate at or very near the soil surface when soil temperatures reach about 65°F.

Seedlings may require several weeks to become established, after which they develop a vigorous system of underground stems or rhizomes. If mowed, green kyllinga grows prostrate, develop-

Green kyllinga is a relatively low-growing sedge that spreads from rhizomes (underground stems). It is distinguished from nutsedges by the absence of underground tubers, as seen in this plant removed from landscape.

Green kyllinga produces a globular green flower immediately above three leaves that radiate outward.

ing into thick mats. If chopped into pieces, new plants can be produced from each node or stem section. Seed and rhizomes are spread by cultivation, foot traffic, mowing, and in infested soil or container plants that are moved.

Maintain landscapes to promote vigorous, dense turfgrass and ornamentals; this will exclude weeds and shade the soil surface, making if difficult for green kyllinga seedlings to establish. Prevent new infestations by thoroughly cleaning mowers and cultivation equipment before moving from infested to weed-free areas. Inspect new plants and soil to be sure they are weed-free. If solitary green kyllinga plants appear, promptly remove the entire plant, including roots. Mark, isolate, and monitor the area for several months to make sure that removal was complete. Hand-pulling or cultivation to remove established green kyllinga is usually futile and may spread this weed unless done repeatedly over a long time.

Geotextile mulches combined with hand-removal can provide adequate control in home landscapes. Geotextiles can be effective if they are overlapped and no light is allowed to penetrate to

the soil. Wood chips or bark may be placed on top. Organic mulches alone may not be effective because green kyllinga may grow through the mulch. However, burying seed as little as 1/3 inch below the soil surface greatly reduces germination.

Certain preemergent herbicides can be effective if green kyllinga is not already established. Spot treatment with glyphosate can reduce growth, but do not let the spray come in contact with desirable plants. For more information, see *Green Kyllinga Pest Notes* (Cudney et al. 2003).

Nutsedges
Cyperus spp.

Nutsedges are common weeds in the coastal valleys, Central Valley, and southern areas of California. Yellow nutsedge (*Cyperus esculentus*) has tan or yellowish flowers and light brown seeds. Purple nutsedge (*C. rotundus*) has purplish flowers and blackish brown seeds. Nutsedges spread primarily from tubers

This young nutsedge resembles grass, but its leaves are thicker and stiffer than most grasses. Nutsedge leaves are V-shaped in cross-section and grow from the base in sets of three; grass leaves are opposite in sets of two.

or "nutlets" that form on rhizomes growing as deep as 8 to 12 inches below the surface. Yellow nutsedge tubers are formed at the ends of rhizomes and have an almond taste when eaten. Purple nutsedge tubers are formed like beads on a chain and have a bitter taste. Tubers can remain viable for several years, even in dry soil.

Do not confuse yellow or purple nutsedge with tall umbrella sedge (*C. eragrostis*). Tall umbrella sedge is a large, light green sedge that does not produce tubers. It spreads by seed or by new plants that form on short, thick rhizomes around the base of the mother plant. It can be distinguished from yellow nutsedge by its wider leaves and stems, its short, thick rhizomes, its lack of tubers, and its tendency to grow in tight clumps that are less than 1 foot in diameter. If uncut, umbrella sedge also grows taller than yellow nutsedge.

Nutsedges thrive in waterlogged soil, indicating that drainage is poor, irrigation is too frequent, or sprinklers are leaky. Irrigate properly, maintain irrigation equipment, and provide for good drainage. Cultivate or hand-weed when plants are young. Control individual plants before they produce 5 or 6 leaves or when they are less than 6 inches tall; older plants produce tubers from which they can resprout. Planting competing species that grow tall quickly can reduce the establishment of yellow nutsedge because it does not grow well in shade. Purple nutsedge can be controlled with repeated summer tillage of dry soil because its tubers are readily killed by drying. Tubers are not killed if soil is moist or has large clods. Mulching, solarization, or using the herbicides glyphosate, halosulfuron, or MSMA can reduce nutsedge populations somewhat. Herbicides alone generally do not provide good control. It is extremely difficult to control nutsedge without an integrated program involving several tactics. Consult *Nutsedge Pest Notes* (Wilen, McGiffen, and Elmore 2003) for more information.

Three long, leaflike bracts develop at the base of each nutsedge flower head. This plant will spread to form a dense, weedy clump that becomes increasingly difficult to control as the plant develops more underground propagules.

The running *Phyllostachys* species of bamboo in the background is sprouting new plants from rhizomes that spread from the main clump into turf and shrubs.

PERENNIAL GRASSES

Bermudagrass, kikuyugrass, and various species of bamboo are important perennial grasses (family Poaceae) infesting landscapes.

Bamboo

Bamboos (many genera) are evergreen grasses that grow as woody perennials. Their stems are divided into sections by obvious joints, and plants reproduce via rhizomes.

Bamboos are often planted, but frequently they become weeds. Some "running" species (e.g., *Pleioblastus* and *Phyllostachys* species) spread beyond where they are desired unless they are regularly trimmed and their root zone is confined. In most situations, plant only clumping bamboos (e.g., *Bambusa* and *Fargesia* species). If running species are used, provide a barrier to spreading bamboo rhizomes by planting only in areas bordered by pavement or fences that extend beneath the soil. Install headers (narrow concrete, wood, or metal barriers extending 18 inches or more below the soil surface) to help confine rhizomes.

Eliminate established clumps of bamboo or reduce their spread by regularly cutting back aboveground parts to near the ground, digging up and removing underground parts, applying an appropriate herbicide to foliage or freshly cut stumps, or a combination of these methods. Persistent effort and repeated control action against any regrowth is needed to provide good control.

Bermudagrass
Cynodon dactylon

Bermudagrass is used as a hardy turf species that is well adapted to drought and alkaline soils. Because it spreads readily, bermudagrass is often a weed in planting beds, shrubs, and lawns where

Bermudagrass spreads as a mat of prostrate stolons and rhizomes. The slender spikes of flower heads usually branch from the same point on the stem tip, in contrast with crabgrass, which often has flower spikes that branch from more than one point, as pictured earlier.

other grass species are preferred. It is common along roadsides, sidewalks, and in vacant urban lots, but it is generally absent from California's inland valley and foothill slopes that are dry during the summer. Bermudagrass becomes dormant and turns brown during the winter in cold areas and is not as aggressive in dense shade.

Mature bermudagrass plants form a dense mat with spreading, branching stolons and rhizomes. Stems grow 4 to 18 inches tall. Bermudagrass has a conspicuous ring or fringe of short, whitish hairs at the base of each blade. Plants produce inflorescences consisting of three to seven slender spikes radiating from one point. Bermudagrass reproduces from seed as well as rhizomes and stolons.

With persistent effort, bermudagrass can be controlled by consistently removing plants as they emerge and by preventing additional seed and stems from being introduced. Rhizomes are readily killed when exposed to the sun so repeated cultivation can provide control if soil is dry and remains dry for a week or more after each cultivation. Although

mulch can reduce growth, bermudagrass can grow through most organic mulches. Thick geotextiles can be effective if the plastic is handled and maintained to prevent holes.

Proper solarization, as discussed earlier, controls bermudagrass in warmer areas of California, but carry out the solarization for at least 6 weeks during the hottest time of the summer. Closely mow bermudagrass to about ½ inch and rake the soil free of cuttings and trash before irrigating and tarping. Alternatively, rototill then irrigate soil before tarping it. Do not rototill deeper than 4 inches, as deeper cultivation may bury rhizomes too deeply to be effectively controlled. For more information, see the section "Solarization" earlier in this chapter.

Well-timed herbicide applications can control bermudagrass, but retreatments will be necessary. Follow all label instructions and absolutely avoid nonselective herbicide contact with desirable plants. Glyphosate is most effective during bermudagrass flowering or soon after seedheads form, if sufficient leaves are present to allow good spray coverage.

Fluazifop-butyl or sethoxydim are most effective if applied when new growth is about 4 to 6 inches long. Cultivating 1 week after application and keeping soil dry greatly improves control. Once mature plants are controlled, monitor regularly and cultivate, apply mulch, or use other methods to control seedlings that will emerge when irrigation resumes. Once you have removed bermudagrass, avoid reinfestation with infested soil, mulch, sod, compost, or contaminated mowers and tools. For more information, consult *Bermudagrass Pest Notes* (Elmore and Cudney 1998).

Kikuyugrass
Pennisetum clandestinum

Kikuyugrass, which is sometimes grown as a hardy turfgrass, is also an invasive perennial in ornamental plantings, rights-of-way, and non-kikuyugrass lawns. It interferes with irrigation equipment, overgrows fences and shrubs, and invades ground covers and flower beds, where it is unattractive and competes for light, nutrients, and water, causing infested ornamentals to decline.

Kikuyugrass has light green leaves about 1 to 10 inches long. It has pointed leaf tips and flat leaf blades that are about ⅛ to ¼ inch wide. An identifying characteristic of kikuyugrass is the long fringe of hairs that parallels the stem in the leaf collar region.

Kikuyugrass spreads primarily by thick, fleshy stems (stolons) that can form a mat on the surface and by buried stems (rhizomes) 1 to 4 inches deep in the soil. It can also spread by seed.

The best way to control kikuyugrass is to prevent its introduction into new areas. Small stem pieces can produce new shoots and roots, so clean equipment and tools such as mowers to remove any kikuyugrass seed and stems before moving from infested areas. Make sure that incoming soil, sod, and planting stock are weed-free. Regularly inspect landscapes and adjoining areas for invading weeds and take prompt action to control them.

Mulching with a strong landscape fabric (such as polypropylene or polyester geotextiles) can be effective if it is overlapped and no light is allowed to penetrate to the soil. Organic mulches alone may not be effective because plants sprouting from rhizomes can grow through the mulch. Dense turfgrass and ornamental plantings shade the soil surface, making the establishment of kikuyu-grass more difficult. Avoid irrigation runoff and overwatering, as kikuyugrass thrives with excess moisture and nitrogen.

Hand-pulling is the primary method of control when kikuyugrass appears in residential landscapes. Cultivation or hoeing, although sometimes possible, is often detrimental because it breaks rhizomes and transplants them to new areas, especially if followed by irrigation.

Certain preemergent herbicides applied in about March can limit germination of kikuyugrass seed. Preemergents are of little benefit if kikuyugrass is already established. Because this weed spreads primarily by regrowth from stem sections, multiple applications of postemergent grass herbicides are required to control established infestations. Careful spot-spraying with nonselective herbicides may be feasible for solitary plants, but this can be very difficult in established landscapes where contact with desirable plants absolutely must be avoided. For more information and specific herbicide recommendations, see *Kikuyugrass Pest Notes* (Cudney, Elmore, and Gibeault 2003).

These thick, fleshy kikuyugrass stolons are overgrowing a Natal plum hedge. Prevent kikuyugrass spread beyond turfgrass because infestations established in other ornamentals are difficult to manage.

PERENNIAL BROADLEAVES

Many different broadleaf perennials can infest landscapes, including certain planted species that commonly spread where they are not desired. Blackberries, dodder, field bindweed, ivy, mistletoe, *Oxalis* species, periwinkle, poison oak, and mistletoes are discussed below.

Bermuda Buttercup and Creeping Woodsorrel
Oxalis spp.

Bermuda buttercup or buttercup oxalis (*Oxalis pes-caprae*) and creeping woodsorrel (*O. corniculata*) are pests in lawns, planting beds, and nurseries. These weeds (family Oxalidaceae) have yellow, five-petalled flowers and compound leaves. Each leaf consists of three heart-shaped leaflets resembling clover leaves. *Oxalis* species prefer moist, shady situations, but grow in full sun in cool, coastal locations. Creeping woodsorrel is more tolerant of sun even in hot areas if soil remains moist, and it is more invasive than Bermuda buttercup.

Bermuda buttercup is attractive when flowering, but some people consider this *Oxalis* species to be a nuisance when it spreads into shrubs like this juniper.

Creeping woodsorrel flowers are about ¼ inch in diameter and develop throughout much of the year. Flowers mature into hairy, cylindrical, pointed pods about ⅓ to 1 inch long. Each pod contains 10 to 50 reddish seed, each about 1⁄25 inch long. Creeping woodsorrel reproduces primarily by seed, which are forcefully ejected up to several feet by the pods. Seed germinate whenever conditions are warm and moist. Seedlings develop rapidly, forming a fleshy taproot and a prostrate mass of foliage and shallow roots that spread outward. If plants are pulled, roots often break and remain in the soil, allowing plants to regrow.

Bermuda buttercup reproduces primarily by small, whitish bulblets, which may grow 8 to 12 inches deep beneath soil. Plants spread when bulb-contaminated soil is moved to uninfested areas. Bermuda buttercup leaves are often spotted with purple, and they are larger and thicker than creeping woodsorrel leaves. Its bright yellow flowers are ¾ to 1½ inch in diameter, and they develop from late fall through spring. These flowers are wider and have taller stalks than those of creeping woodsorrel. Bermuda buttercup is sometimes grown as an ornamental because these hardy plants can flower profusely.

Hand-pull young *Oxalis* plants before flowers form. Use shallow cultivation to kill young seedlings. Landscape fabric (geotextiles) or thick organic mulch prevents most growth; young *Oxalis* growing in the mulch can be hand-pulled. Solarization before planting provides partial control of creeping woodsorrel. Multiple applications of a herbicide such as glyphosate may be needed to eliminate well-established Bermuda buttercup (because of its bulbs) and creeping woodsorrel (because of its tenacious root system). Absolutely avoid broad-spectrum and nonselective herbicide contact with desirable landscape plants. For more information, consult *Clovers Pest Notes* (Elmore and Cudney 2001) and *Creeping Woodsorrel and Bermuda Buttercup Pest Notes* (Elmore and Cudney 2002).

Blackberries
Rubus spp.

Blackberries (family Rosaceae) have long, trailing, somewhat woody canes. Leaves are up to several inches wide and are compound, with 3 to 5 leaflets. The blackberry species found in California produce white to reddish flowers and have thorny stems and leaves. The juicy, tasty, roundish, red to shiny black fruit are enjoyed by people and wildlife. Blackberry hedges can provide an effective barrier to restrict access by people and pets, but they can overgrow surrounding vegetation and sometimes harbor rats.

Keep desired hedges well pruned. Kill established clumps by repeatedly pruning

Creeping woodsorrel infests these container plants. Because pods forcefully eject tiny seed up to several feet, this weed is readily spread in new plants and soil that have been near mature weeds such as these.

Blackberry leaflets grow in clusters of 3 to 5 on long, thorny, somewhat woody canes. Wild blackberry can spread aggressively over shrubs like this flowering rhaphiolepis.

stems until root reserves are exhausted. New canes are produced each year from the crown (base of plant), so established clumps can be killed by digging crowns from soil and allowing then to dry in the sun. Alternatively, apply an appropriate herbicide to foliage at bloom stage, before berries form. For more information and specific herbicide recommendations, consult *Wild Blackberries Pest Notes* (DiTomaso 2002).

Dodder
Cuscuta spp.

Dodder (family Convolvulaceae) is a parasitic weed that can infest many herbaceous and woody broadleaf plants. Dodder grows by penetrating host plant tissues to obtain water and nutrients. Seedlings must attach to a suitable host within a few days of germination or the seedlings die. Once attached, dodder "roots" die and the weed is no longer connected to the ground. Spaghettilike, leafless dodder stems twine around their host, covering it with a tangled yellow or orangish net or mat. Flowers and seed capsules are about ⅛ inch long and develop in clusters. Each dodder plant can produce thousands of hard seed that can remain dormant in the soil for years.

Dodder is difficult to manage, so eliminate isolated patches as soon as they appear, before dodder reproduces and spreads. Cultivation, flaming, hand-pulling, mulching, or applying nonselective herbicides kills seedlings before they attach to hosts. Certain preemergent herbicides control dodder if applied before seedlings emerge (beginning in mid-February in most of central and southern California). More than one application a season may be necessary as dodder continues to germinate through most of the growing season.

A dense landscape plant canopy discourages dodder, as the parasite requires sunlight to twine and grow vigorously. Isolated patches on woody plants may be removed by pruning off infested host tissue below the point of dodder attachment. However, to eliminate established dodder it may be necessary to remove infested host plants and take ongoing action over several years until the soil seed bank is depleted. In soil heavily infested with dodder seed, rotating the site for several years into nonhost plants such as turfgrass may be an efficient strategy. Dodder seedlings try to attach to the first plant they encounter, and seedlings die if that plant is not a suitable host. Consult *Dodder Pest Notes* (Lanini et al. 2002) for more information.

Field Bindweed
Convolvulus arvensis

Mature field bindweed, or perennial morningglory, (family Convolvulaceae) has slender, twining stems up to 5 feet long. Leaves vary greatly in shape, but are often rounded with a blunt tip and shaped like an arrow point. The white, pink, or reddish funnel-shaped flowers open only on sunny mornings. Seed pods are roundish and light brown. Plants produce abundant seed, which can remain dormant in the soil for many

Spaghettilike dodder stems are growing as a tangled yellow or orangish mat in this California pepper tree. Dodder grows by penetrating host plant tissues to obtain water and nutrients.

Dodder seed capsules and stems shown close up. Each dodder plant can produce thousands of hard seed that can remain dormant in the soil for years, so eliminate isolated patches as soon as they appear.

Field bindweed seed leaves are nearly square with an indented tip (top left). The variable true leaves often resemble blunt-tipped arrowheads. Cultivate seedlings before they mature beyond about 5 leaves; mature plants are very difficult to control.

Field bindweed infests this juniper. Field bindweed has slender twining stems and white to reddish funnel-shaped flowers that open on sunny mornings.

years. Many new plants can develop from field bindweed's extensive root system, which grows to a depth of 10 feet or more and spreads several feet wide. Plants often occur in heavy soils, in hardpan or crusty soils, and less often in sandy soils.

Field bindweed can be easily controlled with cultivation while it is a seedling, before young plants develop beyond the five-leaf stage. Once plants begin to mature they are very difficult to control. Repeated cultivation of dry soil at about 3-week intervals for more than 1 year can provide control of established plants, but lack of persistence in cultivation only spreads the weed as it sprouts from severed pieces of root. Solarization for 6 to 9 weeks reduces, but does not eliminate, field bindweed, as bindweed seed is relatively heat-resistant. Rototill no deeper than 4 inches, then smooth and irrigate the soil well before tarping it. A systemic herbicide used properly can provide good control. Glyphosate is effective if applied when bindweed is growing vigorously but before full bloom. Plants must be well irrigated and dust-free for the maximum effect. Multiple treatments are often necessary to control a well-established infestation.

For more information, see *Field Bindweed Pest Notes* (Elmore and Cudney 2003).

Ivy
Hedera spp.

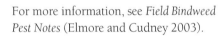

Some ornamental *Hedera* species (family Araliaceae) become weeds unless they are well maintained. These vigorous vines overgrow nearby structures and plants and can gradually kill trees by shading them and physically injuring hosts with their twining stems and aerial roots. Ivy often harbors rats, snails, and slugs.

Algerian ivy (*Hedera canariensis*) and English ivy (*H. helix*) are the common pest species. Do not confuse these with less invasive plants that are also called ivy, including Boston ivy (*Parthenocissus tricuspidata*), grape ivy (*Cissus rhombifolia*), and Swedish ivy (*Plectranthus australis*). Algerian and English ivy are evergreen, woody vines with self-clinging branches. These vines climb vertical objects and can reach heights of 25 to 50 feet above ground. Cultivated varieties vary in leaf color, size, and shape, and juvenile and adult ivy foliage differ markedly in appearance. Juvenile

foliage occurs on flexible stems and develops into palmate leaves with three to five shallow lobes. Adult foliage occurs on stiff stems with leaves that generally are not lobed; when present, adult foliage is often at the terminals of tall vines where it is not readily observed. Mature foliage produces clusters of small greenish flowers, which develop into bluish or black berries about ¼ inch in diameter.

Consider planting less vigorous species as ground covers instead of Algerian or English ivy. If there's any chance that plants will not be pruned regularly, remove the ivy within a couple years of planting, after which it becomes increasingly invasive. Regularly shear terminals to contain their spread, clip off flowers or fruit if any are seen, and remove seedlings that appear where ivy is not desired. To maintain ivy's appearance, do most pruning in spring when new growth will more quickly cover bare stems.

Retard growth of unwanted ivy by increasing its exposure to light and decreasing its access to water, to the extent compatible with the needs of surrounding landscapes. Remove ivy by pulling up vines and digging out the roots. Repeat this until ivy no longer resprouts. Where ivy climbs trees, cut stems as high

Most English ivy growth is juvenile foliage, which has palmate leaves on flexible, reddish stems, as shown here. Unless well maintained, these vigorous vines often overgrow and gradually kill nearby trees and shrubs.

Vinca major has purplish blossoms and round to ovate leaves. Sometimes grown as a ground cover, this vigorous plant can spread undesirably in landscapes, along roadsides, and in woodlands.

above ground as you can reach and remove them. Ivy readily develops from cuttings, which may already have aerial roots. Dispose of ivy in a manner that does not allow prunings to develop into new infestations.

Some broadleaf and nonselective herbicides control ivy, but it can be difficult to use them in landscapes without damaging desirable plants. Cutting stems and promptly (within minutes) applying an appropriate herbicide to fresh wounds with a brush, wick, or wiper applicator may be the most effective technique.

Periwinkle

Vinca major

Periwinkle (family Apocynaceae), is a perennial, trailing evergreen sometimes planted as a ground cover. Also called blue periwinkle, large periwinkle, or myrtle, this vigorous plant can spread undesirably in landscapes, along roadsides, and in woodlands. It is also a host of *Xylella fastidiosa*, a bacterium spread by leafhoppers that causes plant dis-

eases, as discussed in chapter 5 in the section "Bacterial Leaf Scorch and Oleander Scorch."

Periwinkle often grows in dense patches or mats around the base of trees and in low, shaded areas. It is most vigorous in partial shade and moist, well-drained soil high in organic matter, but it tolerates substantial drought and sun. Plants have erect flowering stems about 10 to 20 inches long and trailing non-flowering stems about 3 feet long. Stems root at the nodes and tips where roots touch the ground. The shiny, dark green leaves are 1 to 3 inches long, opposite, and round-ovate. The violet or blue, solitary flowers appear in spring and are about 1 to 2 inches wide with 5 petals. Periwinkle apparently does not reproduce by seed in California.

Vinca major closely resembles dwarf periwinkle, or dwarf running myrtle (*Vinca minor*). In comparison with *Vinca major*, *Vinca minor* has comparatively smaller features, is less invasive, and has light blue or white flowers. Milky stem latex and dark green leaves usually distinguish these periwinkles from other California species they resemble.

Grow alternative species as ground covers instead of periwinkle. For example, *Vinca* is sometimes confused with creeping cultivars of Madagascar periwinkle (*Catharanthus roseus* =*Vinca rosea*), but Madagascar periwinkle is not invasive because individual plants do not spread more than about 1 or 2 feet. Alternative ground covers that resemble periwinkle include perennial bellflowers (*Campanula* spp.) and ground morning glory (*Convolvulus mauritanicus*). Consult Table 7-2 and publications in the Suggested Reading for other plant recommendations.

Hand-pulling periwinkle is effective in small areas or with isolated plants. Raising the runners with a rake and mowing them closely or digging them out by hand can be effective, but likely must be repeated after regrowth from established infestations. Where compatible with surrounding landscapes, increasing light exposure and reducing irrigation will suppress periwinkle, increasing the effectiveness of other control methods. Certain broadleaf or nonselective herbicides can be effective; however, applications may need to be repeated. Chemical control can be difficult, in part because postemergent herbicide contact with desirable plants must absolutely be avoided and periwinkle's waxy leaves repel liquids. Cutting stems and promptly (within minutes) applying herbicide to fresh wounds with a brush, wick, or wiper applicator may be the most effective technique.

Poison Oak
Toxicodendron toxicarium

Contact with poison oak or its oil, which rubs off onto clothing or pets, causes many people to develop a very bothersome skin rash. Poison oak (also called western poison oak) occurs throughout the western United States. In California it is common from sea level to elevations of about 5,000 feet. It occurs in open chaparral and woodlands, coniferous forests, and grassy hillsides. It is common along fence rows and under utility wires and trees where birds roost and excrete seeds. A related species, poison ivy (*Toxicodendron radicans =Rhus radicans*), occurs primarily in the midwestern and eastern United States.

Poison oak (family Anacardiaceae) is an erect, deciduous shrub or vine that often climbs trees and shrubs. Its leaves are green or light red in the spring, glossy green in late spring and summer, and yellow or red in the fall. Leaves are clusters of three leaflets, each 1 to 4 inches long and resembling an individual leaf. The most terminal or central leaflet has a petiole or stem; the side leaflets have no distinct stem. The leaves of true oaks grow singly, and each leaf has a distinct petiole. In spring, poison oak produces clusters of small white flowers that develop into white, waxy berries.

Poison oak in high-use areas warrants aggressive control action because of its severe skin hazard. However, because it can be an important food for wildlife such as birds, deer, and rabbits, and because control of established plants is difficult, consider tolerating poison oak in natural areas and locations not frequented by people or pets. Infested areas can be posted with a warning sign and description of the plant to educate people and restrict access to sites.

Goats can be very effective in reducing poison oak if they are confined in infested areas and are excluded from landscapes to prevent them from feeding on desirable plants. Physical removal can effectively control a few plants. Carefully cut and remove all top growth, then grub or dig out roots to a depth of 8 to 10 inches and remove horizontal runners. Wear tightly woven protective clothing, including washable cotton gloves worn over plastic gloves. Wash tools, rinse them in alcohol, then oil and dry tools to prevent rust. Separately launder all clothing thoroughly and shower immediately after working around poison oak; use a soap recommended for washing away poison oak. Do not burn poison oak: burning causes hazardous oils to be transported with the smoke. Breathing smoke from poison oak causes severe respiratory irritation.

Poison oak can be controlled with glyphosate or certain other herbicides applied as a foliar spray to actively growing plants, but do not allow spray to contact desirable plants. Full foliage to flowering is the optimal time for a foliar spray; spraying anytime before leaves change color in the fall can be effective. However, the soil must be moist or control will be poor. Follow all label directions carefully.

Herbicides, grubbing, or a combination of chemical and physical control

Poison oak has small, whitish flowers. Leaves are clusters of three leaflets, each 1 to 4 inches long and resembling an individual leaf. The most terminal leaflet has a stem; the side leaflets have no distinct stem.

may be needed more than once on well-established clumps of poison oak. Once an area has been cleared of poison oak, plant and provide proper care to desirable species to exclude reinfestation. See *Poison Oak Pest Notes* (DiTomaso and Lanini 2001) for further control measures.

Mistletoes

Mistletoes are parasitic perennials that grow on woody plants, extracting moisture and nutrients from their host. The most common species in California landscapes are broadleaf mistletoes (*Phoradendron* spp.), also called large leaf or leafy mistletoes. An otherwise healthy tree can tolerate a few broadleaf mistletoes, but individual branches may be killed. Bark often swells or galls around where mistletoe attaches to its host. Host plants can suffer reduced vigor or become stunted, especially if they are stressed by other problems such as drought or disease. Dwarf mistletoes (*Arceuthobium* spp.)

have more severe impact, often slowly killing their conifer hosts.

At least seven *Phoradendron* species occur in California. Oak mistletoe (*Phoradendron villosum*) occurs primarily on *Quercus* species and less often on other hosts including California bay laurel and manzanita. Big leaf mistletoe (*P. macrophyllum*) does not attack oak, but it infects many landscape plants, especially ash. Other hosts of big leaf mistletoe include alder, birch, black walnut, box elder, California buckeye, cottonwood, fruit and nut trees, locust, maple, mesquite, and willow. Other *Phoradendron* species occur only on conifers, including fir, incense cedar, and juniper. European mistletoe (*Viscum album*) resembles *Phoradendron macrophyllum*. European mistletoe in the United States occurs only in Sonoma County, California, primarily on alder, apple, black locust, cottonwood, and maple. Dwarf mistletoes attack primarily conifers and are a problem in landscapes in forests, such as in California's Sierra Nevada foothills.

Broadleaf and European mistletoes have succulent green stems that become

woody at the base. The green leaves are thick and nearly oval. Plants often develop a roundish form up to 2 feet or more in diameter. Dwarf mistletoes are smaller plants with mature stems less than 6 to 8 inches long. Dwarf mistletoe shoots are nonwoody, segmented, and have small scale-like leaves. Broadleaf mistletoe seeds are dispersed by birds, which feed on the plant's small, sticky, white to orangish berries. Birds excrete the indigestible seeds on branches, which is why these mistletoes often are most abundant around the tree tops. Dwarf mistletoe seeds are spread mostly by their forcible discharge from fruit, which can propel seeds horizontally into trees up to 30 to 40 feet away. All mistletoe seeds are sticky and can be spread attached to animals or tree-trimming equipment. Only female plants produce seed because male and female flowers occur on different mistletoe plants.

Some tree species appear resistant to mistletoe. Although resistance may vary among locations, resistant species should be planted in problem areas. Chinese pistache, crape myrtle, eucalyptus,

Large-leaf mistletoes are evergreen plants. Roundish clumps of mistletoe infesting deciduous trees are most apparent during the host plant's dormant season.

Large-leaf mistletoe leaves are thick and nearly oval. The small, sticky orangish to white berries are spread by birds or on tree-trimming equipment.

Dwarf mistletoe stems and seeds are growing from a swollen area of a pine branch.

Lichens are growing harmlessly on this hackberry bark. Algae, lichens, or mosses often develop as green, gray, or orangish tissue growing on or hanging from older bark.

ginkgo, golden rain tree, liquidambar, and sycamore are rarely infested. Conifers are also less often attacked by broadleaf mistletoes, but white fir (*Abies concolor*) is significantly infested in the southern Sierra. Consider replacing severely infested trees with resistant species, although there is no guarantee that mistletoe could not become a pest of these species in some locations.

The most effective control is to prune out infested branches as soon as mistletoe appears. Cut infected limbs at least 1 foot below the point of mistletoe attachment, but make pruning cuts properly, near crotches but leaving the branch bark ridge intact (Figure 3-9). Severe heading (topping) is often used to remove heavy tree infestations; however, such pruning weakens a tree's structure and destroys its natural form. In some cases it is best to remove severely infested trees entirely because they are a source of mistletoe seed.

Mistletoe infesting a main branch or trunk where it cannot be pruned may be controlled by cutting off the mistletoe flush with the limb or trunk of its host, then covering bark. Wrap the attachment point with several layers of wide, black polyethylene or landscape fabric. Tie it with twine or flexible tape to exclude light. Large-leaf mistletoes require light and die within a year or more after they are cut and wrapped. It may be necessary to repeat this treatment, especially if the plastic becomes detached. If mistletoe is cut but not covered, it will grow back. However, cutting can reduce the spread of mistletoe and may reduce damage to its host.

The plant growth regulator ethephon may be used during the dormant season as directed on the label to control mistletoe on some species of severely infested deciduous trees. To be effective, spray must thoroughly wet the mistletoe foliage. By treating when trees are dormant, the tree foliage will not get in the way of the spray and the mistletoe clumps are more visible than when leaves are on the tree. Spraying often provides only temporary control by causing some mistletoe plants to fall off, and mistletoe may soon regrow at the same point. For more information, consult *Mistletoe Pest Notes* (Perry and Elmore 2001).

ALGAE, LICHENS, AND MOSS

Woody plants sometimes have greenish, gray, or orangish tissue growing on or hanging from bark. Algae, lichens, or moss are common causes of these bark growths. Algae and moss are relatively simple (primitive) green plants. Lichens are a mutually beneficial association between certain algae and fungi.

These organisms are generally harmless to trees. Many are epiphytes, green plants that derive their nutrients and moisture from the air and grow on the host surface only for support. Some are saprophytes, absorbing nutrients from soil and dead organic debris that lodge in bark crevices, and minimally consuming the outer, dead bark surface. Heavy growth is common on older trees in part because the more rapidly expanding bark on younger trees spreads and "dilutes" the appearance of these surface growths. However, profuse epiphytes or saprophytes on bark may indicate that a host plant is growing more slowly than desired and would benefit from improved environmental conditions and appropriate cultural care. Abundant algae and moss sometimes indicate that soil drains poorly or landscapes are being overwatered, and these poor growing conditions can seriously damage plants.

Moss and algae thrive under damp conditions; their growth may be retarded by reducing humidity (such as preventing sprinklers from hitting bark), improving air circulation around host plants (such as by trimming branches), improving soil drainage, and increasing the frequency between irrigations to the extent compatible with healthy plant growth. Moss prefers partly shaded locations, so it may be retarded by increasing light around plants, such as by thinning branches and nearby plants. Conversely, growth of lichens and sometimes algae is stimulated by increased light.

Some people consider epiphytes and saprophytes in landscapes to be interesting and desirable. Where growths are not aesthetically tolerable, herbicidal soaps or certain copper sprays may be applied to provide control. Keep certain of these sprays away from desirable, succulent plant parts, which may be damaged.

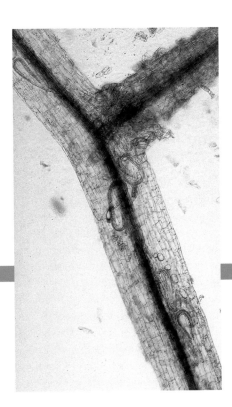

CHAPTER EIGHT

Nematodes

N EMATODES ARE TINY (usually
microscopic) unsegmented roundworms that feed on a wide variety of organisms. Many species are free-living in
soil or water and feed on bacteria and
fungi. Others feed on plants or parasitize
humans and animals (e.g., heartworms,
hookworms, and pinworms). Some nematodes are beneficial because they kill
pest nematodes or insects. For example,
nematodes in the genus *Mononchus* feed
on other nematodes. Insect-parasitic *Heterorhabditis* and *Steinernema* species nematodes can be purchased and applied
to control certain insects that feed on
roots or bore in wood, as discussed in
Chapter 4 in the section "Entomopathogenic Nematodes."

Most species of pest nematodes feed in
or on roots. The most important are root
knot nematodes (*Meloidogyne* spp.),
which attack many woody and herbaceous ornamentals, fruit and nut trees,
and vegetables. Other root-feeding
species include citrus, cyst, dagger, ring,
root lesion, and stunt nematodes.
Pinewood nematode and foliar nematodes attack above-ground plant parts
but appear to be relatively uncommon
pests in landscapes. Consult *Nematodes
Pest Notes* (Perry 2001) or *UCIPM Pest*

Management Guidelines listed in the
Suggested Reading and available online through the UC IPM Web site at
www.ipm.ucdavis.edu for more regularly
updated information on pest nematodes.

Damage

The extent to which nematodes damage
woody landscape plants is not well
known. Their microscopic size, hidden
feeding habits, and sometimes subtle
damage makes it difficult to diagnose
nematode infestations. Much of what is
known about nematodes is extrapolated
from agricultural crops. Nematodes affect woody crops primarily by reducing
fruit or nut yields and slowing plant
growth. These effects may not be a serious concern in landscapes.

Pest nematodes feed by inserting their
entire body or only their spearlike
mouthparts into plant tissue and consuming cell contents. This feeding directly injures or kills plant cells and inhibits the
plant's ability to obtain nutrients and
water. Nematode damage symptoms that
are visible aboveground include slow
growth or yellow foliage that may drop a

341

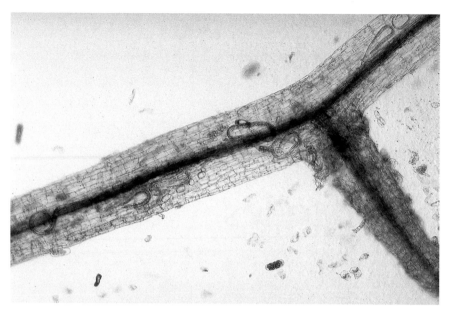

Adult root lesion nematodes are visible within this root.

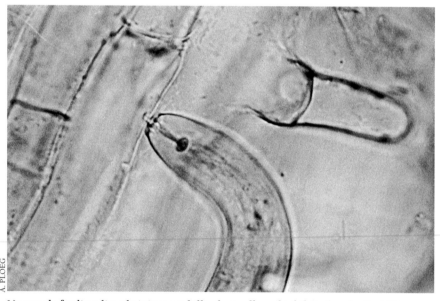

Nematode feeding directly injures or kills plant cells and inhibits the plant's ability to obtain nutrients and water. An adult root lesion nematode (*Pratylenchus penetrans*) is shown here attached to the outside of a root by its mouthparts, which have punctured the cell wall to suck out root contents.

herbaceous and annual plants nearby because nematodes have become so prevalent in the soil.

Identification and Biology

Plant-feeding nematodes go through six stages: egg, four juvenile stages, and adult. Many species can develop from egg to egg-laying adult in as little as 3 or 4 weeks during warm weather. Juveniles and adult males are long, slender worms. The mature adult females of some species, such as root knot nematode, change to a swollen, pearlike shape, whereas females of other species such as lesion nematode remain slender worms. In some, such as root knot nematodes, only adult males and second-stage juveniles are mobile in soil or roots (Figure 8-1); the other juvenile stages and adult females are immobile. Most plant-feeding nematodes are less than $\frac{1}{20}$ inch long (about the thickness of a dime) and are too small to be seen without the aid of a microscope.

Nematodes require moist environments to feed and reproduce. During adverse conditions, such as dry soil, cold temperatures, or the lack of host plants, some species develop resistant stages. Root knot nematodes are believed to survive primarily as an egg in the soil when host plants are not present. Resistant stages of cyst nematodes are typically eggs or first-stage juveniles within eggs, which become inactive and can survive for a year or more.

Nematode infestations should be suspected whenever a general decline of a particular plant species is observed, including stunting or yellow leaves. If no other causes for the unhealthy plant are obvious, remove soil from around some roots and examine them for signs of nematodes. Ease the roots out of the soil gently so that the smaller feeder roots are not broken off and can be examined. Nematodes can cause root galls or stubby, stunted, or proliferating roots. Roots that

few weeks prematurely. Plant tip dieback may be visible on infected trees and shrubs that are not regularly pruned. Similar decline symptoms can be caused by root or vascular wilt diseases, certain insects or mites, and a lack of proper cultural care, such as inappropriate irrigation or fertilization. Nematodes can also act in combination with other pests by creating wounds that provide entry for

microorganisms. Certain nematodes vector pathogenic microorganisms.

Damage usually results only from heavy populations on the nematode-parasitized roots. Nematode feeding causes plant stress, but established woody plants are rarely killed by nematodes. However, if woody plants become heavily infected with nematodes, it may be difficult to grow certain are darkened or have lesions and plants with fewer roots than normal can also indicate a nematode infestation.

Not all nematodes produce obvious symptoms on roots. To confirm a nematode infestation, collect roots and soil from plants showing poor growth and send them to a laboratory that can identify any nematodes present.

Sampling. Unless your laboratory recommends other procedures, take several soil subsamples from locations scattered around the roots of affected plants. Each subsample can contain about 1 pint of soil. Soil can be dug with a shovel or collected using a soil sampling tube. Collect moist (not soggy) soil from the root zone or the upper 6 to 18 inches of soil. Thoroughly mix the subsamples to make a composite sample and send about 1 quart of soil to be tested. Also dig up several small plants or several root parts from one large plant, including the surrounding soil, and seal them in a bag for testing. If possible, collect separately one or two small, apparently healthy plants or root pieces from one large healthy plant of the same species growing nearby and send them along with surrounding soil for comparison testing.

Label each sample with location, plant species, symptoms observed, and your name, address, and phone number. Seal samples in plastic to prevent them from drying out and keep them cool at about 50° to 60°F until the material reaches the laboratory. Laboratories report sampling results as the genus of nematode found, the number of nematodes per unit of soil (usually per pint or liter), and the extraction efficiency. It is important to know the laboratory's method (and the method's efficiency) for extracting nematodes from soil. Certain methods are not adequate for identifying the presence of certain genera of pest nematodes. Some tests provide only qualitative results, which tell you that nematodes are present but do not provide a quantitative measure of nematode abundance. Quantitative tests are preferred because they measure the

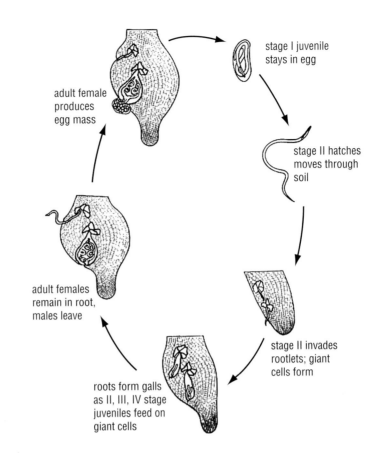

FIGURE 8-1. Root knot nematodes spend most of their active life cycle in galls on roots. Second-stage juveniles invade new sites, usually near root tips, causing root cells to grow into giant cells where the nematodes feed. As feeding continues, the plant produces a gall around the infected area. Mature females produce eggs in a small gelatinous mass on the root surface (as shown) or inside the root.

number of certain genera or species of pest nematodes per volume of soil.

Thresholds. For nearly all landscape plant species there are no threshold guidelines for comparison with test results to determine whether nematodes are abundant enough to cause damage. It is doubtful that thresholds suggested for plants such as fruit trees apply in landscapes, as these guidelines were developed for commercial orchards. However, laboratory tests can help you diagnose whether nematodes are a likely cause of unhealthy plants. Quantitative tests reveal whether nematodes are more abundant, or whether the nematode genera or species are different, around symptomatic plants in comparison with test results from healthy plants. Also, comparison of results from quantitative

tests repeated over time can indicate whether nematode populations are increasing, decreasing, or remaining relatively constant.

Management of Nematodes

Prevention, sanitation, and growing different plants where practical are the most important nematode management strategies. To avoid introducing nematodes into landscapes, use only pest-free amendments, soil, and plants obtained from a reliable supplier (see Table 3-1). Nematode-free plants for certain species can be obtained from participants in the California Certification Nursery program. Consider replacing severely infested

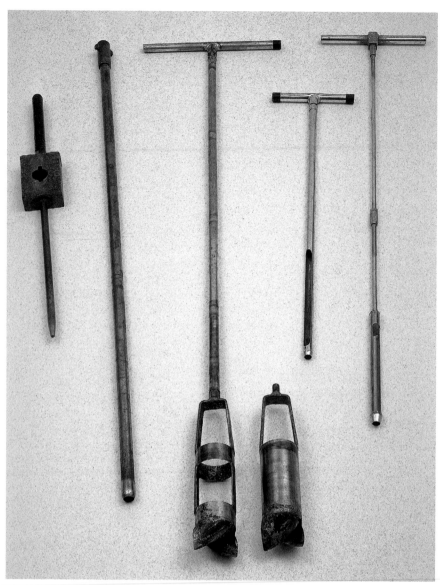

Various tools are available for collecting samples to test for nematodes or to monitor soil type or moisture. The two-piece Veihmeyer tube (left) has a slotted hammer for driving the tube into soil and removing it. Soil augers (center) have a variety of bits for taking different soil samples. Oakfield soil tubes (right) may be the easiest to use for sampling down to about 2 feet.

Composted greenwaste, manure, peat, or other organic amendments can be added to soil to improve plant growth by reducing the impact of nematodes, especially in sandy soils. The amendments are useful because they increase the water- and nutrient-holding capacity of the soil and possibly encourage greater numbers of nematode predators and parasites in soil. Incorporating modest amounts of animal manures, composted greenwaste, cole crop residue, or inorganic fertilizers into the soil before applying clear plastic can increase the effectiveness of preplant solarization.

Do not allow irrigation water from around infested plants to run off onto soil around healthy plants as this spreads nematodes. Do not transfer soil from around infested plants to healthy plants. Thoroughly wash soil and plant parts from all tools and equipment used around infested plants before working around healthy landscapes.

Provide proper cultural care so that plants are vigorous and better able to tolerate feeding by nematodes and other pests. More frequent irrigation of drought-stressed plants can reduce damage caused by root knot nematodes but does not reduce the population levels of nematodes.

Certain marigolds (*Tagetes* spp.) suppress root knot and lesion nematodes. French marigolds (including Nemagold, Petite Blanc, Queen Sophia, and Tangerine) are most effective. Signet marigolds (*Tagetes tenuifolia* =*T. signata*) should be avoided because nematodes will feed and reproduce on these. Marigolds do not work well against the northern root knot nematode (*Meloidogyne hapla*), a species common in areas with cool winters. The effect of marigolds is greatest when they are grown as a solid planting for an entire season prior to landscaping that site. Nematode populations may rapidly increase as soon as susceptible plants are grown. Leaving marigolds in the soil, either through cultivation or by mowing the tops and leaving the roots underground, can improve nematode control, but phytotoxicity (such as slower growth) may be observed when other

plants; replant with species or cultivars more tolerant of the specific nematodes present. Do not plant susceptible species in locations where nematodes have previously been a problem; for example, do not replant the same plant genera into the old site. If you intend to grow susceptible woody plants in a nematode-infested area, consider fallowing the soil for 4 years before planting. Remove and dispose of dead and dying conifers, which host pinewood nematodes and the wood-boring beetles that spread them.

Solarization before planting, covering moist, bare soil with clear plastic for 4 to 6 weeks during hot weather, as discussed in Chapter 7, temporarily reduces nematode populations in the upper 12 inches of soil. Solarization before planting reduces nematode damage to annual plants and may help young woody plants to become established before nematode populations increase. Solarization is of little or no help to deeply rooted plants, and any nematode control is temporary.

plants are grown soon after incorporating marigolds into the soil. When marigolds are grown under shrubs or trees (intercropping), nematode control is usually not very good. To prevent marigold seed from getting in the soil, cut or mow the plants before flowers open.

At least one nematode-killing biological pesticide has been registered for nematode control in California. This beneficial fungus, *Myrothecium verrucaria* (Ditera), may be available only to professional applicators, and there is little information on its effectiveness in landscapes. Various microbial products not registered as pesticides are sold with the implication that these products can control nematodes. In comparison with registered pesticides, there is often little reliable information on largely unregulated soil amendments or inoculants.

Chemical nematicides or soil fumigants are not available to home gardeners for nematode control in gardens and landscapes. A soil fumigant before planting or postplant nematicide for around established plants may be available to certified applicators for use in certain commercial situations, but these are costly, rarely used, and generally are not warranted or recommended in landscapes. Use alternatives, such as planting species or cultivars tolerant to the nematodes present at that location and planting susceptible species only in locations where nematode populations are low and where soil or conditions are not conducive to nematode buildup.

Root Knot Nematodes
Meloidogyne spp.

Root knot nematodes are the most common species attacking annual and perennial landscape plants, especially in warm, irrigated, coarse-textured soils (sand, sandy loam, and loamy sand). Woody landscape plants occasionally stunted by root knot nematodes are listed in Table 8-1. Other plants may be attacked, and the host list for many ornamental species is incomplete. A plant

A heavy root knot nematode infestation has caused these numerous galls. Beneficial nitrogen-fixing bacteria nodules also grow on some roots, but bacterial nodules rub off and a thumbnail can be pressed into them easily, while root knot nematodes cause a firm swelling of the root.

species resistant to one or more species of root knot nematode may be susceptible to other *Meloidogyne* species, and more than one *Meloidogyne* species can occur at the same site.

Root knot nematodes (Figure 8-1) cause galls or swellings on roots of many broadleaf plants. Some infected plants, especially annual grasses and certain legumes, may exhibit no galls. When roots infected with root knot nematodes are washed they may appear gnarled and restricted. Severely infected roots may become attacked by a variety of decay or disease organisms, including those causing crown gall, root and crown rots, and certain vascular wilt diseases.

Many common weeds also host root knot nematodes. One way to determine if soils are heavily infested with root knot nematodes is to dig up weeds around poorly growing landscape plants and examine their roots for infestation. Alternatively, you can plant several different species of quick-growing, susceptible annual plants underneath and around woody plants suspected of being in-

fested; squash and tomatoes that are not resistant to nematodes (non-N or non-VFN) are good choices. Dig the plants up after they have grown for about 4 to 6 weeks in soil above 65°F. Wash or gently tap the soil from their roots and examine the roots for swellings. Gently cut open any galls and use a dissecting binocular microscope to examine them for the presence of pinhead-sized, shiny white females that look like tiny pearls.

Beneficial nitrogen-fixing bacteria often form nodules on the roots of beans and other legumes, but these rub off roots easily, while galls caused by root knot nematodes are truly swellings of the roots. Also, a thumbnail can be pressed into a bacterial gall easily, but not into a root knot gall. Other causes of plant galls are summarized in Table 4-16.

To confirm a root knot nematode infestation, you must collect root and soil samples, as described above, and send the material to a laboratory that can provide positive identification of the infesting species.

Root Lesion Nematodes
Pratylenchus spp.

Damaging population levels of root lesion nematodes (such as *Pratylenchus penetrans* and *P. vulnus*) can occur on many plants (Table 8-1). In the early stages of infestation, a lack of small and large roots may be detectable. The lack of feeder roots and well-developed major roots can be seen if you remove soil around roots of healthy plants and compare these to roots from around unhealthy plants. On roses and some other hosts, infected plants are stunted, leaves are yellow, and roots are smaller and darker than on healthy plants.

Root lesion nematodes occasionally cause brown or black lesions to appear on roots. Lesions are usually apparent only on the larger roots of older trees, especially on walnut. Lesions, when present, become apparent when roots are scraped with a knife. However, apparent lesions can develop on roots for other reasons unrelated to nematodes, for example, on walnuts if they are given too much water.

Many plant species may be infected with high populations of root lesion nematodes without any evidence of necrosis (dead tissue) or lesions. A laboratory analysis of samples is the only sure method of diagnosing root lesion nematodes.

Pin nematodes (*Paratylenchus* spp.) are related species that have been reported to cause lesions and death of some plum and prune roots. Although pin nematodes are frequently found in these fruit trees, they currently are not thought to significantly stunt plant growth or reduce fruit yield.

Dagger Nematodes
Xiphinema spp.

Grapes, roses, true firs (*Abies* spp.), and occasionally stone fruits are reported to be damaged by dagger nematodes in California. Dagger nematodes (such as

TABLE 8-1.

Woody Landscape Plants Known or Suspected of Being Damaged by Nematodes in California.

HOST PLANT		PEST NEMATODES		
COMMON NAME	SCIENTIFIC NAME	ROOT KNOT	ROOT LESION	OTHER
abelia, glossy	*Abelia grandiflora*	■		
albizia	*Albizia*	■		
alder	*Alnus*	■		
almond[1]	*Prunus*	■	■	ring
apple	*Malus*	■	■	ring
apricot[2]	*Prunus*	■	■	ring
aralia	*Fatsia (=Aralia)*	■		
azalea, rhododendron	*Rhododendron*	■		foliar, spiral, stubby root, stunt
bird of paradise	*Strelitzia*	■		spiral
boxwood	*Buxus*	■		
cactus	several genera	■		cyst
camellia	*Camellia japonica*			spiral, stunt
catalpa	*Catalpa*	■		
cedar	*Cedrus*	■		pinewood
cherry	*Prunus*	■		
citrus[3]	*Citrus*		■	citrus
cryptomeria	*Cryptomeria japonica*	■	■	
dracaena	*Cordyline*	■		
echium	*Echium*	■		
euonymus	*Euonymus*	■		
ferns	many genera			foliar
fig	*Ficus*			foliar
fir	*Abies*			dagger
gardenia	*Gardenia jasminoides*	■		
grape[4]	*Vitis*	■	■	citrus, dagger, ring, stubby root
hibiscus	*Hibiscus*	■		foliar
hydrangea	*Hydrangea*	■	■	foliar
juniper	*Juniperus*	■		
larch	*Larix*			pinewood
lilac	*Syringa*			citrus
maidenhair	*Ginkgo*	■		
melaleuca	*Melaleuca*	■		
mulberry	*Morus*	■		
nectarine[1]	*Prunus*	■	■	ring
oak	*Quercus*	■		

TABLE 8-1.

Woody Landscape Plants Known or Suspected of Being Damaged by Nematodes in California *(continued)*.

HOST PLANT		PEST NEMATODES		
COMMON NAME	SCIENTIFIC NAME	ROOT KNOT	ROOT LESION	OTHER
olive	*Olea*	■	■	citrus
orchid tree	*Bauhinia*	■		
palm	several genera	■		
peach[1]	*Prunus*	■	■	ring
pear	*Pyrus*		■	
persimmon	*Diospyros*			citrus
pine	*Pinus*			pinewood
pittosporum	*Pittosporum*	■		
plum	*Prunus*		■	ring
poinsettia	*Euphorbia*	■		
rose	*Rosa*	■	■	dagger
saltbush	*Atriplex*	■		
spruce	*Picea*			pinewood
sweet shade	*Hymenosporum flavum*	■		
tamarisk	*Tamarix*	■		
tea tree	*Leptospermum*	■		
walnut	*Juglans*	■	■	ring

KEY

citrus	*Tylenchulus semipenetrans*	root knot	*Meloidogyne* spp.
cyst	*Cactodera cacti*	root lesion	*Pratylenchus* spp.
dagger	*Xiphinema* spp.	spiral	*Heliocotylenchus* spp.
foliar	*Aphelenchoides* spp.	stubby root	*Paratrichodorus, Trichodorus* spp.
pinewood	*Bursaphelenchus xylophilus*	stunt	*Tylenchorhynchus* spp.
ring	*Criconemoides xenoplax*		

1. Nemaguard and Nemared rootstocks are resistant to root knot nematodes.
2. Royal Blenheim rootstock is resistant to root knot and root lesion nematodes.
3. Trifoliate and Troyer rootstocks are resistant to the citrus nematode.
4. Freedom and Harmony rootstocks are resistant to root knot nematodes.

Consult *Integrated Pest Management for Floriculture and Nurseries* (Dreistadt 2001) for the nematode susceptibility of herbaceous and flowering ornamentals.

Xiphinema index) can vector a virus and can cause a sparseness of feeder roots, but this is difficult to recognize. Terminal galls can form on the roots of grapes, each with hundreds of dagger nematodes of the same species feeding on it. A laboratory analysis of soil surrounding affected roots is usually needed to confirm the presence of this pest, which mostly lives in soil and feeds from outside of roots.

Ring Nematode
Criconemoides (=Criconemella) xenoplax

Ring nematode is named for its annulated (ringed) body, which is visible under a microscope; most nematode species have a relatively smooth body.

Ring nematode prunes the smallest roots on many woody plants. If extensive, this damage weakens trees and can predispose *Prunus* and occasionally *Malus* species to branch dieback and springtime death by bacterial canker disease.

Stunt Nematodes
Tylenchorhynchus spp.

Stunt nematode hosts include azalea, camellia, and rhododendron. Infestations cause roots and aboveground plant parts to grow slowly and be undersized. Leaves may turn yellow, die back, or drop prematurely. Iron deficiency symptoms, primarily leaf yellowing, may be aggravated on infested plants.

Citrus Nematode
Tylenchulus semipenetrans

A citrus nematode infestation can reduce fruit size and number on infested host plants (Table 8-1). Serious infestations cause undersized leaves and twig dieback. Provide trees with proper cultural care so that they are better able to tolerate nematode feeding. Purchase trees from a nursery that sells nematode-free plants. Use resistant rootstock, especially when replanting in soil known to be nematode-infested. Orange rootstocks such as Trifoliate and Troyer are resistant to citrus nematode. Citrus nematode biology and management is detailed in *Integrated Pest Management for Citrus* (UCIPM 1991).

Pinewood Nematode
Bursaphelenchus xylophilus

Pinewood nematode feeds in the vascular tissue of conifer trunks, twigs, and stems. Pines are most seriously affected, but other conifers including cedar, larch, and spruce are also hosts. Branch dieback is the most common symptom in native pines infested with pinewood nematodes. Pinewood nematodes are widespread in exotic conifers, such as Japanese black pine, Japanese red pine, and Scotch pine, that have been introduced into the United States.

Pinewood nematodes are spread primarily by juveniles "hitchhiking" on adult roundheaded borers or long-horned beetles, including *Monochamus* spp. The beetles feed as larvae beneath bark and pupate in wood, then emerge from dead or dying trees as adults contaminated with nematodes. Before laying their eggs in unhealthy trees, adult beetles may fly to other pines to feed on foliage; nematodes can leave the beetles then and infect the new tree. If beetles feed on the foliage of healthy plants, the introduced nematodes may eventually contribute to the decline of that plant as they reproduce within the tree.

Foliar Nematodes
Aphelenchoides spp.

Foliar nematodes (*Aphelenchoides fragariae* and *A. ritzemabosi*) are leaf-infesting species that attack ferns, tropical foliage plants, vegetatively propagated ornamentals, and strawberries. They are relatively unimportant in California, with damage occurring mostly in certain greenhouses and outdoors along coastal areas where ornamental hosts and strawberries are grown.

Foliar nematodes cause vein-limited blotches and lesions on leaves, which typically start near the leaf base and spread outward. Infested young leaves or shoots may remain undersized, become bushy or distorted, and produce little or no foliage or flowers. Damaged foliage may become brittle or shrivel and then drop. Damage usually appears beginning in spring (or winter in coastal areas) and becomes most severe by summer. Foliar nematode damage can be confused with damage caused by bacteria, fungi, viruses, nutrient deficiencies, or chemical injuries, and infestations must be confirmed by sending samples to a diagnostic laboratory staffed with a trained nematologist.

Foliar nematodes are typically introduced in vegetatively propagated material, so use only nematode-free plants. Employ good sanitation practices by removing plant debris, promptly disposing of all infested plants, and eliminating nearby weed hosts (such as goldenrod, groundsel, and sneezeweed). Avoid crowding plants and, where foliar nematodes have been a problem, use irrigation methods other than overhead water to reduce the risk that foliar nematodes will spread by traveling in a water film on plant surfaces. Consult *Integrated Pest Management for Floriculture and Nurseries* (Dreistadt 2001) for more information.

CHAPTER NINE

Problem-Solving Tables

THIS CHAPTER contains two compli-
mentary tables that **must** be used
together when diagnosing problems. If
you are not certain of the cause of a problem and do not know which chapter to
consult for solutions, go to the "Problem-
Solving Guide." This briefly summarizes
common damage symptoms that can
occur on many woody landscape plants
and directs you to the section(s) of the
book that discuss these problems. "Tree
and Shrub Pest Tables" are more extensive
and are organized according to host plants.
These list problems of about 200 genera of
landscape plants, **excluding** many common problems (primarily abiotic or noninfectious disorders) that affect many
different species. To conserve space and
avoid repetition, problems such as too
much or too little water that affect many
different plants are usually included only
in the Problem-Solving Guide. Use **both**
tables when diagnosing problems.

Check the index at the back of the book
to find where in the Tree and Shrub Pest
Tables the plant species of interest to you
is located. The Tree and Shrub Pest Tables
are organized alphabetically, usually by the
common name of the plant. Some plants
have several common names, and related
species or genera are grouped together.
Check the index for the page numbers.

The Problem-Solving Guide and Tree
and Shrub Pest Tables refer you to other
parts of the book where you can find more

information on identification, biology, and
management. For pests not specifically
discussed elsewhere in the book, or for
unique information, a brief description of
management practices is provided in these
tables; for more information the reader is
often referred to earlier sections on similar
pests or maladies. Scientific names of pests
are not listed in the tables if those names
are prominently presented in major text
sections earlier in the book.

Because of the broad scope of this publication, its California and Pacific Northwest emphasis, and because new plant and
pest species are often introduced from elsewhere, some of the pests you encounter
may not be pictured or described here.
For identification and biology of pests
affecting herbaceous and nonwoody flowering ornamentals, consult publications
such as *Integrated Pest Management for
Floriculture and Nurseries* (Dreistadt 2001).
For vertebrate pests, see publications such
as *Wildlife Pest Control Around Gardens and
Homes* (Salmon and Lickliter 1984). Other
sources of information are listed in the
"Suggested Reading." Some pest problems
can be diagnosed reliably only with the use
of special tools such as laboratory tests or
by experienced professionals. Your Cooperative Extension advisor, certified arborist,
certified nurseryperson, or qualified horticultural consultant may be able to diagnose the cause of problems or direct you
to other professional diagnostic services.

Problem-Solving Guide

Common disorder symptoms and pest damage on many woody plant species, by plant part on which they frequently appear

Entire Plant May Exhibit Symptoms

WHAT THE PROBLEM LOOKS LIKE	PROBABLE CAUSE	COMMENTS
Foliage fades, discolors, then wilts, often in scattered portions of the canopy. Foliage drops prematurely. Branches, treetop, or entire plant may die.	Root and crown rots.	May have bark cankers or ooze. *See 262.*
	Verticillium wilt.	Discoloring often scattered throughout canopy. Vascular tissue may turn brown. *See 232.*
	Armillaria root rot.	Possible mushrooms near trunk in fall and white mycelia fan beneath bark. *See 262.*
	Dematophora root rot.	May be minute white growths beneath bark or white strands on soil. *See 264.*
	Annosus root disease.	Affects mostly conifers in locations where conifers grow naturally. *See 265.*
	Fusarium wilt.	*See 233.*
	Too much or too little water.	*See 34, 273.*
	Nematodes.	*See 341.*
	Scale insects.	*See 130.*
	Moth larvae that bore in tissues.	*See 166, 185–196.*
	Gall makers.	*See 160.*
	Wood-boring beetles.	*See 171.*
	Twig blight fungi.	*See 223, 228.*
	Freeze damage.	*See 291.*
	Sunburn or sunscald.	*See 288.*
Older needles or leaves drop. Lower or inner branches may die back.	Normal maturation, not a disease, may be aggravated by poor pruning or improper irrigation.	Evergreen plants periodically drop old foliage. Lower and inner, shaded branches naturally die and drop. Certain plants become dormant during summer or naturally drop foliage sooner than others.
Yellow, dead, or prematurely dropping leaves or needles. Foliage discolored, flecked, sparse, stunted, distorted, or may have irregular yellow patterns. Plant grows slowly.	Air pollution.	*See 293.*
	Mineral deficiency.	*See 274.*
	Salt damage.	*See 280.*
	Herbicide toxicity.	*See 284.*
	Viruses.	*See 268.*
Leaves, blossoms, or fruit have black or brown lesions or spots. Leaf veins may darken. Terminals may die back. Bleeding cankers or lesions may occur on stems.	Bacterial blight and canker.	*See 245.*
Grayish, yellowish, or brownish encrustations form on plant. Leaves may yellow, branches may die back.	Scale insects.	*See 130.*
Leafless, orangish stems entangle host plant. Clusters of small, white flowers in summer yield seeds that germinate from soil next season.	Dodder, *Cuscuta* spp., parasitic annual plants sprouting from seeds and requiring sunny locations.	*See 334.*

Bark, Limb, and Trunk Symptoms, Primarily

WHAT THE PROBLEM LOOKS LIKE	PROBABLE CAUSE	COMMENTS
Fleshy or woody growths occur on bark, often mushroom- or seashell-shaped.	Trunk and limb rots, fungi decaying internal supportive wood tissue.	Decay often undetected except where bark cut or injured. Limbs or tree may fail (fall). *See 248.*
Bulging bark outgrowths or galls form.	Crown gall, a bacterial infection. Woolly apple aphid. Western gall rust, a fungal disease. Mistletoe, a parasitic plant.	Damage often around root crown. *See 258.* *See 105.* Affects only pines. *See 241.* *See 338.*
Bark splits or cracks.	Inappropriate water. Sunburn or sunscald. Lightning damage. Freeze damage. Wind damage. Rapid growth.	*See 34, 273.* *See 288.* *See 293.* *See 291.* *See 292.* Provide proper cultural care; *see Chapter 3.*
Areas of dead bark (canker) may be surrounded by callus tissue layers. Material may ooze from bark. Limbs or entire plant may die back.	Inappropriate water. Pruning wound. Sunburn. Injuries. Canker diseases, fungal infections.	*See 34, 273.* *See 41, 287.* *See 288.* *See 287.* *See Table 5-10, 250.*
Stained bark exudes dark liquid, often around crotches, or whitish frothy material, often from holes or cracks.	Wetwood or slime flux. Foamy canker or alcoholic flux.	Liquid odor, typically rancid. *See 259.* Liquid has pleasant alcoholic or fermentative odor. *See 259.*
Pitchy masses form on bark.	Moth larvae, insects bore under bark. Canker diseases, fungal infections.	*See 185–196.* *See 250.*
Holes, pitch tubes, boring dust, or stains occur on bark. Foliage may discolor and branches or entire plant may die.	Twig-, branch-, and trunk-boring insects. Pinewood nematode.	*See 171.* *See 347.*
Green plants with smooth stems and thick roundish leaves infest branches.	Broadleaf mistletoe, a parasitic, evergreen plant on host.	*See 338.*
Small, leafless, orangish, upright plants grow on host stems. Distorted and slow plant growth. Branches die back.	Dwarf mistletoe, *Arceuthobium* spp., host-specific parasitic plants that infect only conifers and extract nutrients from host plant.	Prune out infected branches. Replace heavily infected plants with species from other genera; dwarf mistletoes won't spread to unrelated species. *See 338.*
Grayish, greenish, or orangish tissue grows on or hangs from bark.	Lichens, mosses, and algae.	Often grow on older trees. Generally harmless to host plant, but may indicate overwatering of the landscape. *See 339.*

Foliage and Terminal Symptoms, Primarily

WHAT THE PROBLEM LOOKS LIKE	PROBABLE CAUSE	COMMENTS
Sudden wilting, blackening or browning of shoots, blossoms, or fruit. Plant appears scorched.	Fire blight, a bacterial disease.	Affects only rose family plants. *See 229.*
Conspicuous spots or irregular dead areas form on leaves. Foliage or flowers curl, turn brown or black, may drop prematurely.	Sunburn.	Damage often starts between veins. *See 288.*
	Frost damage.	*See 291.*
	Wind or hot weather damage.	*See 292.*
	Rust fungi.	*See 240.*
	Leaf spots.	*See* Table 5-5, *223.*
	Anthracnose, many different species of fungi.	Affects many deciduous plants, especially ash, oak, sycamore, and Chinese elm in California. Lower branch foliage often more affected than upper foliage. Cankers on twigs or branches. *See 223.*
	Too much or too little water.	*See 34, 273.*
	Root rots.	*See 262.*
	Root injury.	*See 44, 262, 287.*
Small, well-defined, tan, reddish, or black blotches form on leaves, often with yellowish border. Leaves may drop prematurely.	Leaf spot fungi.	*See 223.*
Foliage is flecked, yellowed, bleached, or bronzed by pests that suck plant juices.	Mites.	*See 197.*
	Thrips.	*See 156.*
	Leafhoppers.	*See 148.*
	True bugs.	*See 152.*
	Sycamore scale.	*See 143.*
Dark, varnishlike specks form on leaves.	True bugs.	*See 152.*
	Greenhouse thrips.	*See 158.*
	House flies and certain other flies.	
Light-colored powdery growth on plant. Leaves distort, discolor, or drop prematurely.	Powdery mildew, a fungal disease.	*See 236.*
Dry, orangish or yellowish pustules occur, usually on leaf undersides.	Rust fungi.	*See 240.*
Dark sooty growth on leaves and stems, washes from plant.	Sooty mold, a fungus growing on honeydew excreted by insects on that plant or nearby plants.	*See 239.*
Clear, sticky substance appears on plant. May be white to clear cast skins on foliage or twigs. On oaks, liquid may be brownish.	Honeydew, excreted by plant-sucking insects, including aphids, scales, leafhoppers, mealybugs, psyllids, and whiteflies.	Identify insect, then see that section. If on oaks, *also see Drippy Oak and Nut Disease, 247.*
Copious, misty, nonsticky liquid raining from plant. Surfaces covered with whitish residue.	Glassy-winged sharpshooter.	*See 148.*
Whitish, frothy material on foliage.	Spittlebugs.	*See 151.*

Foliage and Terminal Symptoms, Primarily (continued)

WHAT THE PROBLEM LOOKS LIKE	PROBABLE CAUSE	COMMENTS
Whitish, cottony, waxy material occurs on plant.	Adelgids. Mealybugs. Woolly aphids. Whiteflies. Cottony cushion scales, some others.	*See 112.* *See 126.* *See 106* *See 121.* *See 142.*
Winding or blotched tunnels or mines in foliage.	Leafminers or shield bearers.	*See 166–169.*
Chewed, tattered, or scraped foliage, shoots, or blossoms.	Moth or butterfly larvae. Sawfly larvae. Leaf beetles or flea beetles. Weevils. Snails or slugs. Grasshoppers or katydids.	*See 71.* *See 82.* *See 84.* Adult weevils feed at night. *See 92.* Slimy or clear trails present. *See 205.* *See 99.*
Silken tents, mats, or webbing occur on chewed foliage or terminals.	Tent caterpillars, webworms, or leafrollers.	*See 77–82.*
Discolored foliage. Excessive or spindly growth.	Excess or deficient light. Herbicide phytotoxicity. Nutrient deficiencies.	*See 289.* *See 284.* *See 40, 274.*
Distorted, curled, swollen, or galled leaves, flowers, stems, or branches.	Gall mites. Thrips. Moth larvae. Psyllids. Gall makers. Aphids. *Taphrina* spp. fungi. Herbicide phytotoxicity. Nutrient deficiencies.	*See 203.* *See 156.* *See 165.* *See 114.* *See 160.* *See 103.* *See Table 5-5, 204.* *See 284.* *See 40, 274.*

Tree and Shrub Pest Tables
Common Problems and their Causes, by Plant

WHAT THE PROBLEM LOOKS LIKE	PROBABLE CAUSE	COMMENTS
ABELIA (*Abelia* spp.)		
Galls or swellings on roots. Plants may grow slowly.	**Root knot nematodes.** Tiny root-feeding roundworms.	*See 345.*
ABUTILON (*Abutilon* spp.), Chinese bellflower, Chinese lantern, Flowering maple		
Leaves with yellowish blotches.	**Abutilon mosaic virus.** Virus that is mechanically spread during propagation.	Considered attractive. Infected plants cannot be cured. *See 8, 270.*
Leaves or blossoms chewed.	**Fuller rose beetle.** Pale brown adult snout weevils, about ⅜ inch long.	Adults hide during day and feed at night. Larvae feed on roots. *See 94.*
Sticky honeydew and blackish sooty mold on foliage. Twigs or branches may decline or die back.	**Black scale, Brown soft scale.** Black, brown, or yellowish, bulbous or flattened insects.	*See 136–137.*
Sticky honeydew and blackish sooty mold on foliage. Leaves may yellow and wither.	**Whiteflies**, including **Bandedwinged whitefly,** *Tetraleurodes abutilonea*; **Silverleaf whitefly**. Tiny, whitish, mothlike adult insects.	*See 121.*
Brownish, grayish, tan, or white encrustations on twigs.	**Oleander scale.** Tiny, flattened, circular insects, ≤1⁄16 inch long.	Rarely if ever causes serious damage to plants. *See 134.*
ACACIA (*Acacia* spp.)		
Leaves discolored, wilted, stunted, may drop prematurely. Discolored bark may ooze sap. Branches or plant may die.	**Root and crown rots.** Decay fungi favored by excess soil moisture and poor drainage.	*See 265.*
Leaves turn brown or yellow, especially along margins and at tip. Leaves may drop prematurely.	**Leaf burn** or **Scorch.** Abiotic disorders commonly caused by frost, inappropriate irrigation, or poor drainage, but many other potential causes.	Provide plants with a good growing environment and proper cultural care. *See 273.*
Sticky or waxy honeydew and possibly blackish sooty mold on foliage. Terminals may brown or die.	**Acacia psyllid.** Tiny brown, green, or orange, flattened or winged insects on new growth.	*See 114.*
Sticky honeydew and blackish sooty mold on plant. May be cottony bodies (egg sacs) on bark.	**Cottony cushion scale.** Orangish, flat immatures or cottony females on bark.	Normally controlled by natural enemies. *See 142.*
Copious, misty, nonsticky liquid raining from plant. Surfaces covered with whitish residue.	**Glassy-winged sharpshooter.** Active, dark brown or gray leafhoppers, ≤½ inch long, suck xylem fluid.	Vectors pathogens of oleander and certain crops, especially grapes. Report suspected glassy-winged sharpshooters to agricultural officials if found in areas where this pest is not known to occur. *See 148.*
Wet, white, frothy masses on foliage.	**Spittlebugs**, including *Clastoptera arizonica*. Greenish bugs in spittle, suck sap.	Tolerate, does not damage plants. Hose plants with water. *See 151.*
Stippled, flecked, or bleached foliage.	**Leafhopper,** *Kunzeana kunzii*. Green insects, ≤1⁄16 inch long, suck sap.	Damage commonly minor, tolerate. Apply soap, oil, or botanical insecticide. *See 148.*
Chewed leaves. Foliage may be rolled and tied together with silk.	**Omnivorous looper.** Yellow, green, or pink larvae, ≤1½ inches long, with green, yellow or black stripes.	*See 79.*

ACACIA (*Acacia* spp.), continued

WHAT THE PROBLEM LOOKS LIKE	PROBABLE CAUSE	COMMENTS
Chewed leaves webbed with silk.	**Orange tortrix**, *Argyrotaenia citrana* (family Tortricidae). Larvae whitish with brown head and dark "shield" on back. Adults orangish to gray moths, ≤¼ inch long.	Larvae wiggle vigorously when touched. Vigorous plants tolerate moderate defoliation. Prune out webbing. Apply *Bacillus thuringiensis* or another insecticide. *See Foliage-Feeding Caterpillars, 71.*
Chewed leaves or blossoms.	**Fuller rose beetle.** Pale brown adult snout weevils, about ⅜ inch long.	Adults hide during day and feed at night. Larvae feed on roots. *See 94.*
Brownish, gray, tan, orangish, or white immobile encrustations (insects) on bark. Rarely, declining or dead twigs or terminals.	**California red scale, Greedy scale, Latania scale, Oleander scale, San Jose scale.** Tiny circular to oval, flattened insects.	*See 131–135.*
Dieback of occasional twigs. Tunnels in twigs or branches, often at crotch.	**Leadcable borer**, *Scobicia declivis* (family Bostrichidae). Black or brown beetles, ¼ inch long.	Prune out affected parts. Eliminate nearby dead wood in which beetles breed.

AGAVE (*Agave* spp.); YUCCA (*Yucca* spp.)

WHAT THE PROBLEM LOOKS LIKE	PROBABLE CAUSE	COMMENTS
Leaves discolor, stunt, wilt, or drop prematurely. Plants grow slowly and may die. Roots or plant base dark, decayed.	**Root and crown rot, Pythium root rot.** Pathogens promoted by excess soil moisture and poor drainage.	*See 265, 268.*
Leaves with discolored or dead blotches or spots. Leaves may wilt and die prematurely if severe.	**Leaf spots** and **Leaf blights**, including *Kellermania* spp., *Leptosphaeria* sp., *Microsphaeropsis concentrica*, *Stagonospora gigantea*. Fungi, some of which are secondary invaders of dead or injured tissue.	*See 223.*
Leaves turn brown or yellow, especially along margins and at tip. Leaves may wilt and die prematurely.	**Leaf burn** or **Scorch.** Abiotic disorders with many potential causes, including frost, overirrigation, or poor drainage.	Provide plants with a good growing environment and proper cultural care. *See 273.*
Sticky honeydew, blackish sooty mold, and cottony waxy material on plant.	**Large yucca mealybug**, *Puto yuccae.* Powdery, white oval insects, ≤⅛ inch long.	Conserve natural enemies that provide control. Apply soap, oil, or another insecticide if not tolerable. *See Mealybugs, 126.*
Sticky honeydew and blackish sooty mold on foliage. Possible yellowing and dieback of foliage.	**Hemispherical scale**, *Saissetia coffeae.* Yellowish or brown, oval, flattened, or bulbous insects.	Conserve natural enemies. Tolerate moderate populations or monitor and apply oil or other insecticide if crawlers numerous. *See Scales, 130.*
Brownish, grayish, tan, or white encrustations on bark. May be declining or dead plant parts.	**Oleander scale, Oystershell scale.** Tiny circular to elongate insects.	*See 134–135.*
Decline of plant. Holes punctured in leaves.	**Yucca weevil**, *Scyphophorus yuccae.* Adult is black snout weevil about ½ inch long. Larva is white grub that tunnels in base of green flower stalks and heart of plant.	Provide plants with proper cultural care. No other management known.

ALBIZIA (*Albizia* spp.), Mimosa, Silk tree

WHAT THE PROBLEM LOOKS LIKE	PROBABLE CAUSE	COMMENTS
Leaves yellowing and may die, with older foliage affected first. Browning of vascular tissue. Limbs may die back.	**Mimosa wilt**, *Fusarium* spp. Fungi infect plants through spores in soil.	Avoid injuring living tissue. Provide good drainage and appropriate irrigation. *See Fusarium Wilt, 233.*
Leaves turn yellow and drop prematurely.	**Natural senescence.** Leaves often naturally drop sooner than on other species.	Providing trees with a good growing environment and appropriate cultural care may delay leaf drop.
Sticky or waxy honeydew and possibly blackish sooty mold on foliage. Terminals may brown or die.	**Acacia psyllid.** Tiny orange, green, or brown, flattened or winged insects on new growth.	*See 114.*

WHAT THE PROBLEM LOOKS LIKE	PROBABLE CAUSE	COMMENTS
Chewed leaves. Silk tents in trees.	**Mimosa webworm.** Gray to brown larvae, ≤½ inch long, with white stripes.	*See 82.*
Holes in wood. Boring dust on bark. Branches may break and fall. Tree may decline.	**Carpenterworm.** Dark whitish larvae, ≤2½ inches long, boring in wood.	*See 194.*

ALDER (*Alnus* spp.)

WHAT THE PROBLEM LOOKS LIKE	PROBABLE CAUSE	COMMENTS
Leaves with whitish, powdery growth. Shoots or leaves may be stunted and distorted.	**Powdery mildews,** including *Erysiphe aggregata, Microsphaera penicillata, Phyllactinia guttata.* Fungi favored by moderate temperatures, shade, and poor air circulation.	*See 236.*
Leaves with brown to yellow blotches or spots and orangish pustules. Leaves may die and drop prematurely.	**Rusts,** including *Melampsora betulinum* =*M. alni.* Fungi infect and develop when leaves are wet.	*See 240.*
Leaves may discolor and wilt, usually in spring. Branches may die back. Stems may have dark cankers, callus tissue, or coral-colored pustules.	**Nectria canker,** *Nectria* spp. Fungi primarily affect injured or stressed trees.	*See 257.*
Leaves may discolor and wilt. Dieback of branches. Gnarled, ridged bark with wet spots and D-shaped, ⅛-inch-diameter emergence holes.	**Flatheaded borers,** including **Flatheaded alder borer.** Whitish larvae, ≤½ inch long, beneath bark.	*See 179.*
Leaves may discolor and wilt. Branches wilted or dying. Boring dust, swellings, or holes on trunk or branches.	**Redbelted clearwing,** *Synanthedon culiciformis.* White larvae, ≤1 inch long, with brown head. Adult are wasplike moths.	*See similar Ash Borer, 187.*
Leaves may discolor and wilt. Bark may have boring frass, elliptical holes, or oozing liquid. Branches and entire tree may die.	**Longhorned borers,** including **Banded alder borer,** *Rosalia funebris.* White larvae are ≤1 inch long. Adult *Rosalia* are whitish with black.	Usually secondary pests that attack injured or severely stressed trees. *See 183.*
Leaves cupped, curled, folded, or thickened (galled) along edges or midvein.	**Alder gall midge,** *Dasineura* sp. Tiny whitish to pink larvae in distorted tissue.	Apparently harmless to plant. Tolerate or prune out affected tissue. *See Gall Midges, 164.*
Leaves or catkin scales curl, enlarge, or twist and turn reddish or purplish. Shiny or pale fungal spores may cover infected tissue.	**Catkin Hypertrophy** or **Leaf curl,** *Taphrina japonica, T. occidentalis.* Fungi favored by wet conditions during spring.	Apparently harmless to plants. No control recommended.
Sticky honeydew, blackish sooty mold, and whitish cast skins on leaves.	**Aphids,** including *Euceraphis gillettei, Pterocallis alni.* Yellowish green, tiny insects on leaves, suck sap.	*See 103.*
Sticky honeydew and blackish sooty mold on leaves. Plant decline or dieback may occur.	**Cottony maple scale,** *Pulvinaria innumerabilis.* Females cottony. **European fruit lecanium scale.** Flat to bulbous, brown, ≤¼ inch long.	Plants tolerate moderate populations. *See 139.*
Cottony white, waxy tufts on leaves.	**Cottony alder psyllid,** *Psylla alni.* Yellow to green, 1⁄16 inch long insects beneath wax, suck sap.	Vigorous plants tolerate moderate populations. *See Psyllids, 114.*
Stippled or bleached leaves. Dark, varnish-like specks and cast skins on undersides of leaves.	**Lace bugs,** *Corythucha* spp. Adults ≤⅛ inch long, wings lacy. Nymphs spiny.	*See 154.*

| --- | --- | --- |

ALDER (*Alnus* spp.), continued

WHAT THE PROBLEM LOOKS LIKE	PROBABLE CAUSE	COMMENTS
Leaves skeletonized.	**Alder flea beetle**, *Altica ambiens*. Metallic blue adults, ¼ inch long. Larvae are brown to black.	Vigorous trees tolerate moderate defoliation. Provide plants proper cultural care. Apply oil or other insecticide to larvae on foliage if needed. *See Leaf Beetles and Flea Beetles, 84.*
Webbing or tents on branch terminals. Chewed foliage.	**Fall webworm.** Larvae white to yellow, hairy, ≤1 inch long.	*See 81.*
Brown to gray encrustations on bark. May be stunting or dieback of woody parts.	**Oystershell scale.** Immobile, tiny, oyster-shaped insects, often in colonies.	*See 135.*
Galls or swellings on roots.	**Root knot nematode**, *Meloidogyne* sp. Tiny root-feeding roundworms.	*See 345.*

ALMOND (*Prunus dulcis*)[1]

WHAT THE PROBLEM LOOKS LIKE	PROBABLE CAUSE	COMMENTS
Leaves discolor, stunt, wilt, or drop prematurely. Stems discolor, canker, and die. Minute white fungus growths may be visible beneath bark or on soil.	**Armillaria root rot.** Present in many soils. Favored by warm, wet soil. Persists for years in infected roots.	*See 262.*
Leaves discolor, stunt, wilt, or drop prematurely. Plants grow slowly and may die. Roots dark, decayed.	**Root and crown rot**, *Phytophthora* spp. Pathogens promoted by excess soil moisture and poor drainage.	*See 265.*
Leaves discolor, stunt, wilt, or drop prematurely, often on one side of plant. Stem xylem discolored. Stems or entire plant may die.	**Verticillium wilt**, *Verticillium* spp. Fungi persist in soil, infect through roots.	*See 232.*
Cankers or oozing gum on bark. Stems, flowers, or nuts may have dark lesions.	**Bacterial blight and canker; Band canker**, *Botryosphaeria dothidea*; **Ceratocystis canker**, *Ceratocystis fimbriata*. Fungal pathogens. **Foamy canker.** Undiagnosed cause, possibly a bacterium.	*See 245, 255.*
Small brownish leaf spots, may have tan centers. Holes in leaf from dropped, infected tissue. Concentric lesions on branch.	**Shot hole.** A fungal disease promoted by moist spring weather or splashing irrigation water.	*See 226.*
Leaves or nut hulls have black, brown, gray, tan, orange, or yellow circular spots or blotches. Leaf tips die. Foliage may yellow or wilt. Blossoms may darken and die. Shoots may die back.	**Alternaria leaf spot**, *Alternaria alternata*; **Almond scab**, *Fusicladium carpophilum*; **Anthracnose**, *Colletotrichum acutatum*. Fungi that persist in infected tissue. Spores spread by splashing water. Favored by wet conditions.	*See 223.*
Circular brown decay develops on nuts. Blossoms and twigs may turn brown and die.	**Brown rot**, *Monilinia fructicola, M. laxa*. Windborne fungal pathogens that infect wet tissue.	Avoid wounding trees. Remove any infected nuts ("mummies") left on trees.
Brown to gray encrustations on bark. May be declining or dead twigs or branches.	**Olive scale**, *Parlatoria oleae*; **San Jose scale.** Circular to oval insects, <¹⁄₁₆ inch long, on twigs and branches.	*See 132.*
Stippled, bleached, or reddened foliage.	**Brown mite**; *Bryobia rubrioculus*; **European red mite; Pacific spider mite; Twospotted spider mite.** Brown, green, reddish, or yellow specks.	*See 197.*

1. For more information on pest identification and biology, see publications such as *Almond Pest Management Guidelines* (Teviotdale et al. 2002) and *Integrated Pest Management for Almonds* (Strand 2002).

ALMOND (*Prunus dulcis*), continued

WHAT THE PROBLEM LOOKS LIKE	PROBABLE CAUSE	COMMENTS
Stippled, flecked, or bleached leaves with whitish cast skins on undersides. Leaves may drop prematurely.	**Leafhoppers**, including **Appletree leafhopper**, *Empoasca maligna*; **White apple leafhopper**, *Typhlocyba pomaria*. Pale green, yellow, or white, wedgelike insects ≤⅛ inch long.	Plants generally tolerate, control rarely warranted. *See 148.*
Spotted or yellow foliage. Nuts may exude gum or shrivel.	**Boxelder bugs; Leaffooted bug**, *Leptoglossus clypealis*. Brown, gray, or red adults, ≤1 inch long.	Adults invading houses may be a problem. *See 153.*
Sticky honeydew and blackish sooty mold on leaves and twigs. Dieback of twigs or branches possible.	**Black scale, European fruit lecanium.** Black, brown, or yellow, flattened or bulbous insects, ≤⅕ inch long.	*See 136, 139.*
Leaves chewed. Single branches or entire plant may be defoliated. Foliage may be rolled and tied together with silk.	**Fruittree leafroller; Obliquebanded leafroller**, *Choristoneura rosaceana*; **Tent caterpillars.** Moth larvae ≤½ inch long.	*See 79–81.*
Galls or swellings on roots. Plants may grow slowly.	**Root knot nematodes.** Tiny root-feeding roundworms.	*See 341.*
Galls or swellings on trunk and roots, usually near soil.	**Crown gall.** Bacterium that infects plant via wounds.	*See 258.*
Dead twigs or branches. Plant declines, may die. Tiny "BB shot"-sized holes in bark.	**Shothole borer.** Small brown bark beetles and whitish larvae tunnel beneath bark.	*See 176.*
Roughened bark, reddish brown granular material (frass) at base of trunk and main limbs. May be dark ooze from bark.	**American plum borer; Peachtree borer; Prune limb borer**, *Bondia comonana* (family Gelechiidae). Brown to pink larvae that bore under bark.	Prevent injuries to bark. Provide proper cultural care. *See 187, 193.*
Dieback of woody plant parts. Tunnels and larvae in wood.	**Pacific flatheaded borer.** Whitish larvae ≤¾ inch long with enlarged head.	*See 179.*

APPLE, CRABAPPLE (*Malus* spp.)[2]

WHAT THE PROBLEM LOOKS LIKE	PROBABLE CAUSE	COMMENTS
Foliage yellows and wilts. Branches or entire plant may die. May be minute white fungus growths beneath bark or on soil.	**Armillaria root rot.** Present in many soils. Favored by warm, wet soil. Persists for years in infected roots.	*See 262.*
Leaves discolor, stunt, wilt, and remain dead on tree or drop prematurely. Plants grow slowly and may die. Root crown dark, decayed.	**Root and crown rots**, *Phytophthora* spp. Pathogens promoted by excess soil moisture and poor drainage.	*See 265.*
Sudden wilting then shriveling and blackening of shoots, blossoms, and fruit. Plant appears scorched.	**Fire blight.** Bacterium enters plants through blossoms.	Plant less-susceptible cultivars. *See 229.*
Black to dark olive spots on fruit, leaves, or stems. Fruit may have scabby blotches or become misshapen.	**Scab**, *Venturia inaequalis*. A fungal disease spread by water from infected leaves and twigs.	*See 227.*
Flower buds, fruit, petals, or stems turn brown and papery, die, and drop prematurely. Fruit spurs and sometimes twigs may darken and die.	**Bacterial blight and canker** or **Blossom blast.** Disease favored by wet conditions.	*See 245.*
Shoots die back. Branches develop reddish brown lesions or cankers. Fruit may rot around calyx.	**European canker**, *Nectria galligena*. Fungus persists in cankered wood and infects through leaf scars when plant is wet.	Prune out infected wood. Apply copper spray in fall just before leaves drop and again when most leaves have dropped. *See Nectria Canker, 257.*

2. For more information on pest identification and biology, see publications such as *Apple Pest Management Guidelines* (Teviotdale et al. 2002) and *Integrated Pest Management for Apples and Pears* (Ohlendorf 1999).

WHAT THE PROBLEM LOOKS LIKE	PROBABLE CAUSE	COMMENTS
APPLE (*Malus* spp.), continued		
Gray or whitish patches on foliage. Shoots may be stunted or distorted. Fruit may be mottled, russetted, or scabby.	**Powdery mildews**, including *Podosphaera leucotricha*. Fungal diseases favored by moderate temperatures, shade, and poor air circulation.	*See 236.*
Sticky honeydew, blackish sooty mold, and whitish cast skins on foliage. May be pale wax on leaves and twigs. Growth may be stunted.	**Aphids**, including **Green apple aphid**, *Aphis pomi;* **Rosy apple aphid**, *Dysaphis plantaginea;* **Woolly apple aphid**, *Eriosoma lanigerum.* Small black, gray, green, purplish, yellow, or waxy insects in groups on leaves and terminals.	*See 103.*
Leaves bleached. May be dark excrement specks and sticky honeydew on fruit and leaves.	**Leafhoppers**, including **White apple leafhopper**, *Typhlocyba pomaria;* **Rose leafhopper**, *Edwardsiana rosae.* Pale green, yellow, or white, wedgelike insects ≤⅛ inch long.	Leafhoppers do not feed on fruit and do not seriously threaten plant health. *See 148.*
Stippled, bleached, or reddened foliage. May be fine webbing on leaves or terminals. Leaves may drop prematurely. Fruit may be small and poorly colored.	**European red mite; McDaniel spider mite**, *Tetranychus mcdanieli;* **Pacific spider mite; Twospotted spider mite.** Brown, green, reddish, or yellow specks.	*See 197.*
Pale blotches, spots, or winding tunnels in leaves. Leaves may drop prematurely.	**Leafminers**, *Phyllonorycter* spp. Pale larvae tunnel in leaves. Adults are brownish moths with silver or white.	Plants tolerate extensive mining. Conserve parasites, which usually control leafminers unless biological control is disrupted.
Fruit with discolored spots or pits. Fruit with hard pithy areas or brown patches in flesh. Flower buds may exude gum, shrivel and die, or drop prematurely.	**Lygus bugs**, *Lygus elisus* and *L. hesperus;* **Stink bugs**, including **Conchuela**, *Chlorochroa ligata;* **Consperse stink bug**, *Euschistus conspersus;* **Redshouldered stink bug**, *Thyanta pallidovirens.* True bugs with sucking mouthparts.	*See True Bugs, 152.*
Brown to gray encrustations on bark. May be declining or dead twigs or branches.	**Italian pear scale**, *Epidiaspis leperii;* **San Jose scale.** Tiny circular to elongate insects.	Italian pear scale survives only under shelter such as lichens and moss on bark. The female's body is reddish purple beneath its cover. *See 132.*
Foliage notched or clipped. Bark chewed or stripped around basal trunks and root crown.	**Cribrate weevil**, *Otiorhynchus cribricollis.* Adults are black or gray snout beetles, about ⅛ inch long. Larvae are white grubs with brown head.	Bark girdling and extensive leaf chewing of young trees are the problems. Root feeding and any injury to older trees is apparently not serious. *See similar Black Vine Weevil, 92.*
Leaves or blossoms chewed. Single branches or entire plant may be defoliated. Foliage may be rolled and tied together with silk. Fruit may have small gouges or brownish scars.	**Apple pandemis**, *Pandemis pyrusana;* **Fruittree leafroller; Humped green fruitworm**, *Amphipyra pyramidoides;* **Obliquebanded leafroller**, *Choristoneura rosaceana;* **Omnivorous leafroller**, *Platynota stultana;* **Orange tortrix**, *Argyrotaenia citrana;* **Speckled green fruitworm**, *Orthosia hibisci;* **Western tussock moth.** Moth larvae ≤1½ inches long.	*See 71.*
Fruit brown, decayed, or tunneled. Brown tunnels beneath skin may be visible from outside.	**Apple maggot**, *Rhagoletis pomonella.* Cream-colored maggots feed in fruit. Adults are dark- and-light-banded flies.	Eliminate alternate hosts and use good sanitation to help reduce populations. Pest is difficult to control without insecticide sprays, which must be well-timed by trapping adults.
Fruit brown, decayed, or tunneled, including around center. Dark oviposition marks on fruit.	**Codling moth**, *Cydia pomonella.* Pale larvae with dark head bore in fruit. Adults are small, brown, coppery moths.	Bagging fruit individually when young will avoid infestation. Consult *Codling Moth Pest Notes* (Bentley et al. 1999) for more information.

APRICOT (*Prunus* spp.)[3]

WHAT THE PROBLEM LOOKS LIKE	PROBABLE CAUSE	COMMENTS
Leaves discolor, stunt, wilt, or drop prematurely. Stems discolor, canker, and die. May be white mycelial growths beneath bark or on soil.	**Armillaria root rot.** Present in many soils. Favored by warm, wet soil. Persists for years in infected roots.	*See 262.*
Leaves discolor, stunt, wilt, or drop prematurely. Plants grow slowly and may die. Roots dark, decayed.	**Root and crown rots,** *Phytophthora* spp. Pathogens promoted by excess soil moisture and poor drainage.	*See 265.*
Leaves discolor, stunt, wilt, or drop prematurely, often on one side of plant. Stem xylem discolored. Stems or entire plant may die.	**Verticillium wilt,** *Verticillium* spp. Fungi persist in soil, infect through roots.	*See 232.*
Leaves yellow and wilt. Dead leaves may remain on tree through winter. Branches canker and die back. Wood discolors.	**Eutypa dieback,** *Eutypa lata.* Fungus infects through wounds, persists in infected tissue. Spreads during wet conditions.	In California most serious along coast. Avoid wounding plants, except to prune off infected tissue during July and August, making cuts in healthy tissue. Provide a good growing environment and appropriate cultural care.
Stems, flowers, or fruit with dark lesions. Cankers possible on branches.	**Bacterial blight and canker.** Disease favored by wet conditions.	*See 245.*
Small brownish leaf spots, may have tan centers. Holes in leaf from dropped, infected tissue. Concentric lesions on branch.	**Shot hole.** A fungal disease promoted by moist spring weather or splashing irrigation water.	*See 226.*
Circular brown decay develops on fruit. Blossoms and twigs may turn brown and die.	**Brown rot,** *Monilinia fructicola, M. laxa.* Windborne fungal pathogens that infect wet tissue.	Avoid wounding fruit and trees. Remove any infected fruit ("mummies") left on trees.
Powdery white growth and yellow blotches on leaves and sometimes on terminals and fruit. Shoots and leaves may be undersized or distorted.	**Powdery mildews,** *Podosphaera* spp., *Sphaerotheca pannosa.* Fungal diseases favored by moderate temperatures, shade, and poor air circulation.	*See 236.*
Sticky honeydew, blackish sooty mold, and whitish cast skins on plant.	**Aphids,** including **Mealy plum aphid,** *Hyalopterus pruni.* Small, black, brown, green, yellowish, or waxy, pear-shaped insects, often in groups.	*See 103.*
Sticky honeydew and blackish sooty mold on leaves and twigs. Possible dieback.	**Kuno scale.** Adult scales beadlike and dark shiny brown.	*See 140.*
Leaves chewed. Single branches or entire plant may be defoliated. Foliage may be rolled and tied together with silk.	**Fruittree leafroller, Omnivorous looper, Redhumped caterpillar, Tent caterpillars, Tussock moths.** Moth larvae ≤1½ inches long.	*See 77–81.*
Galls or swellings on roots. Plants may grow slowly.	**Root knot nematodes.** Tiny root-feeding roundworms.	*See 345.*
Galls or swellings on trunk and roots, usually near soil.	**Crown gall.** Bacterium that infects plant via wounds.	*See 258.*
Dead twigs or branches. Plant declines, may die. Tiny "BB shot"-sized holes in bark.	**Shothole borer.** Small brown bark beetles and whitish larvae tunnel beneath bark.	*See 176.*
Roughened bark, reddish brown granular material (frass) at base of trunk and main limbs. May be dark ooze from bark.	**American plum borer; Peachtree borer; Prune limb borer,** *Bondia comonana* (family Gelechiidae). Brown to pink larvae that bore under bark.	Prevent injuries to bark. Provide proper cultural care. *See 187, 193.*

3. For more information on pest identification and biology, see publications such as *Apricot Pest Management Guidelines* (Teviotdale et al. 2002) and *Integrated Pest Management for Stone Fruits* (Strand 1999).

WHAT THE PROBLEM LOOKS LIKE	PROBABLE CAUSE	COMMENTS

ARALIA (Fatsia japonica =Aralia sieboldii); ANGELICA

WHAT THE PROBLEM LOOKS LIKE	PROBABLE CAUSE	COMMENTS
Conspicuous spots or irregular dead areas on leaves. Foliage or flowers curl and turn brown or black.	**Sunburn.** Abiotic disorder most prevalent under bright, hot, water-stressed conditions.	*See 288.*
Brown to yellow blotches or spots on upper surface and orange or yellowish pustules on underside of leaves.	**Rust,** *Nyssopsora clavellosa.* Fungus favored by wet conditions.	*See 240.*
Sticky honeydew and blackish sooty mold on foliage. Twig or branch decline or dieback.	**Black scale; Brown soft scale; Hemispherical scale,** *Saissetia coffeae.* Small black, brown, or yellowish insects, flattened or bulbous.	*See 136–137.*
Plant has sticky honeydew and blackish sooty mold. Plant grows slowly. Foliage may yellow.	**Pyriform scale,** *Protopulvinaria pyriformis.* Triangular, ⅛-inch-long, brown, yellow, or mottled red insects. May be small white egg sacs.	Common in Florida and also occurs in southern California. *See Soft Scales, 136.*
Sticky honeydew, blackish sooty mold, and copious white waxy material on plant. Leaves may yellow, wither, and drop prematurely.	**Giant whitefly.** Adults are tiny, whitish, mothlike insects. Nymphs and pupae are flattened, oval, translucent, and greenish or yellow.	*See 122.*
Blackish sooty mold, sticky honeydew, and whitish cast skins on plant.	**Aphids.** Small, pear-shaped insects on leaves, often in groups.	*See 103.*
Brownish, grayish, tan, or white encrustations on bark. Rarely, plant parts may die back.	**Greedy scale, Latania scale, Oleander scale.** Tiny, circular, flattened insects, usually in groups.	*See 133–135.*
Leaves chewed. Leaves may be tied together with silk.	**Orange tortrix,** *Argyrotaenia citrana* (family Tortricidae); **Omnivorous looper.** Caterpillars ≤1½ inch long.	Vigorous plants tolerate moderate leaf damage. Prune out infested foliage. Apply *Bacillus thuringiensis* or another insecticide when young larvae are feeding. *See 79.*
Galls or swellings on roots. Plants may grow slowly.	**Root knot nematodes.** Tiny root-feeding roundworms.	*See 345.*

ARAUCARIA (Araucaria spp.), Bunya-Bunya tree, Monkey puzzle tree, Norfolk Island pine

WHAT THE PROBLEM LOOKS LIKE	PROBABLE CAUSE	COMMENTS
Gray to reddish encrustations on shoots or needles (scale insect bodies). Plant may decline and die back.	**Dictyospermum scale,** *Chrysomphalus dictyospermi.* Tiny, immobile, flattened insects suck plant juices, have several generations per year.	Occasional problem in California, mostly in the south. Conserve introduced natural enemies, which can provide excellent biological control. *See Armored Scales, 131.*
Black, dark brown, or gray encrustations on shoots or needles. Needles may yellow. More a problem in California in south.	**Black araucaria scale,** *Lindingaspis rossi.* Tiny circular to oval armored scales.	Conserve natural enemies that provide control. Monitor and apply narrow-range oil or another insecticide when crawlers numerous in spring. *See Armored Scales, 131.*
Needles discolored. Sticky honeydew, blackish sooty mold, and grayish, flocculent material on plant. Plant growth may slow.	**Golden mealybug,** *Nipaecoccus aurilanatus.* Females globular, ⅒ inch long, purplish with felty, golden band marginally and on back.	Several generations occur each year. Natural enemies or soap or oil sprays can help to control. *See Mealybugs, 126.*
Sticky honeydew and blackish sooty mold on plant. Elongate, whitish material (mature female egg sacs) at leaf axils.	**Araucaria scale,** *Eriococcus araucariae* (family Eriococcidae). A scale with orangish eggs in elongate, whitish females.	Vigorous plants tolerate moderate populations. Monitor and if needed apply oil when crawlers are active. *See similar Cottony Cushion Scale, 142.*

ARBORVITAE (Platycladus orientalis, thuja occidentalis); WESTERN RED CEDAR (Thuja plicata)

WHAT THE PROBLEM LOOKS LIKE	PROBABLE CAUSE	COMMENTS
Chewed needles.	**Conifer sawflies, Cypress sawfly.** Greenish larvae, ≤1 inch long, on needles.	*See 83–84.*
Sticky honeydew and blackish sooty mold on foliage.	**Arborvitae aphid,** *Dilachnus tujafilinus.* Brown to gray insects, ⅛ inch long, on leaves and twigs.	Vigorous plants tolerate moderate populations. Hose forcefully with water. Tolerate or apply insecticidal soap or oil. *See Aphids, 103.*

ARBORVITAE (*Platycladus orientalis, thuja occidentalis*); WESTERN RED CEDAR (*Thuja plicata*), continued

WHAT THE PROBLEM LOOKS LIKE	PROBABLE CAUSE	COMMENTS
Discolored or dying foliage. Tiny oval to circular bodies on foliage.	**Juniper scale**, *Carulaspis juniperi*; **Minute cypress scale.** Tiny armored scales.	Populations in California seldom warrant control, except on Italian cypress or in nurseries. *See 136.*
Foliage turns brown at base of branches, evenly scattered throughout canopy, during summer or fall. Needles may drop prematurely.	**Flagging.** Abiotic disorders with many potential causes, commonly caused by injury to roots, drought stress, and hot weather.	Protect trees from injury. Avoid disturbing soil around roots. Provide good cultural care, such as appropriate irrigation during prolonged drought.
Brown or yellow dying foliage on branches. Cankers and resinous exudate on limbs or trunk.	**Cypress canker.** A fungal disease.	Arborvitae is occasionally infected. Primarily affects *Cupressus* spp. *See 254.*
Browning of tips beginning in fall, browning worst late winter to spring.	**Cypress tip miner.** Greenish larvae, ≤⅛ inch long, tunnel in foliage.	*See 167.*
Terminals distorted, wilting, or dead.	**Leaffooted bugs.** Mostly brown bug with yellow or bright colors and enlarged, flattened hind legs. Suck plant juices.	Control not investigated. Plants probably tolerate. *See True Bugs, 152.*
Dead twigs on tree. Lateral twigs killed about 6 inches from tip.	**Cedar bark beetles** or **Cypress bark beetles.** Adults are small, dark beetles that feed on twigs. Larvae and adults bore under bark.	*See 175.*
Branches killed, sometimes to trunk. Coarse boring dust at trunk wounds and branch crotches.	**Cypress bark moth**, *Laspeyresia cupressana* (family Tortricidae). Larvae, ≤½ inch long, under bark of trunk and limbs.	Provide plants with proper cultural care. Avoid excess water and fertilizer that promote rapid growth and thin bark. Avoid wounding bark, as insects colonize wounds.
Needles are chewed. Roots or the basal trunk may be cankered or injured.	**Conifer twig weevils.** Small black to brown weevils that chew needles and shoots. Pale larvae bore in the root crown of dying or injured conifers.	Except for white pine weevil, most are secondary pests of minor importance. *See 93.*

ARTEMISIA (*Artemisia* spp.), Mugwort, Sagebrush, Tarragon, Wormwood

WHAT THE PROBLEM LOOKS LIKE	PROBABLE CAUSE	COMMENTS
Sticky honeydew and blackish sooty mold on leaves or twigs. Plants may decline.	**Black scale.** Brown to black, bulbous to flattened insects, ≤³⁄₁₆ inch long. Raised H-shape often on back.	*See 136.*
Sticky honeydew, blackish sooty mold, and whitish cast skins on plant.	**Aphids.** Small green, orange, or black insects, often in groups on leaves or stems.	*See 103.*
Chewed foliage. Plant may be defoliated.	**Leaf beetles**, *Trirhabda flavolimbata, T. pilosa.* Black to brown larvae, ≤½ inch long, overwinter as eggs in soil. Larvae crawl up trunk in spring and begin feeding. Adults are metallic, blue to green beetles, head yellowish.	One generation each year. Adults drop when disturbed. Vigorous plants tolerate damage. Sticky material around trunk may exclude larvae if foliage is trimmed back from ground. Foliar insecticide can be applied in spring if severe. *See 84.*
Leaves or stems thickened, distorted, galled, or have felty patches.	**Eriophyid mites**, *Aceria* spp. Microscopic mites living in groups.	*See Gall Mites, 203.*

ASH (*Fraxinus* spp.)

WHAT THE PROBLEM LOOKS LIKE	PROBABLE CAUSE	COMMENTS
Foliage fades, yellows, browns, or wilts, often scattered throughout canopy. Branches die. Entire plant may die.	**Verticillium wilt.** A soil-dwelling fungus that infects through roots.	*See 232.*
Foliage fades, yellows, browns, or wilts, often scattered throughout canopy. Branches die. Entire plant may die.	**Ash dieback.** Unexplained malady primarily affecting Raywood ash.	Provide a good growing environment and appropriate cultural care. No known specific remedy.
Leaves and branches wilt in spring. Stems may have dark cankers, callus tissue, or coral-colored pustules.	**Nectria canker**, *Nectria* sp. Fungus primarily affects injured or stressed trees.	*See 257.*

ASH (*Fraxinus* spp.), continued

WHAT THE PROBLEM LOOKS LIKE	PROBABLE CAUSE	COMMENTS
Leaves with irregular brown, tan, or white areas. Premature leaf drop. Twigs die back. Large branches may die if repeatedly defoliated.	**Ash anthracnose**, *Discula fraxinea* =*Gloeosporium aridum*. Fungus infects leaves and twigs. Splashing rain spreads spores.	Affects only flowering ash (*Fraxinus ornus*) and Modesto ash (*F. velutina* var. *glabra*). Prune out and dispose of infected twigs before spring. Provide deep irrigation about monthly during periods of prolonged drought. Fungicide sprays offer some protection if properly applied. *See 223.*
Leaves with brown spots with pale or yellow borders. Leaves may drop prematurely.	**Leaf spots**, including *Mycosphaerella effigurata*, *M. fraxinicola*. Fungi promoted and spread by wet conditions.	*See 223.*
Leaves turn brown or yellow, especially along margins and at tip. Leaves may drop prematurely.	**Leaf burn** or **Scorch**. Abiotic disorders. Causes include drought, dry wind, excess fertilization, excess light, and saline irrigation water or soil.	Provide plants with a good growing environment and proper cultural care. *See 273.*
Leaves brown around edges and sometimes between veins.	**Bacterial leaf scorch**, *Xylella fastidiosa*. A bacterium spread by leafhoppers that occurs in the eastern U.S., but there is disagreement whether *X. fastidiosa* strains in California affect ash.	Providing deep irrigation may help to relieve symptoms. *See Bacterial Leaf Scorch and Oleander Leaf Scorch, 230.*
Leaves or shoots with powdery growth. Shoots or leaves may be stunted and distorted.	**Powdery mildews**, including *Erysiphe cichoracearum*, *Phyllactinia guttata*. Fungi favored by moderate temperatures, shade, and poor air circulation.	*See 236.*
Leaves may discolor and wilt. Branches wilted or dying. Boring dust, ooze, or holes on trunk or branches.	**Ash borer, Redbelted clearwing**. White larvae ≤1 inch long, head brown.	Adult moths wasplike. *See 187.*
Leaves may discolor and wilt. Holes, ≤½ inch in diameter, in wood. Boring dust. Limbs may die and drop.	**Carpenterworm**. Dark whitish larvae, ≤2½ inches long, bore in wood.	*See 194.*
Sticky honeydew, blackish sooty mold, and whitish wax on foliage. Leaves curl, gall, and distort. Leaves may drop prematurely.	**Ash leaf curl aphids**, *Prociphilus* spp. Gray to green, waxy insects in distorted leaves.	*See 107.*
Sticky honeydew and blackish sooty mold on leaves and twigs. Tiny, white, mothlike adult insects.	**Ash whitefly**. Tiny oval nymphs are flattened and clear. Older nymphs have a band of white wax on the back.	Under good biological control and rarely a problem unless natural enemies are disrupted. *See 121.*
Sticky honeydew, blackish sooty mold, or whitish wax on foliage. Leaves or terminals curled or distorted.	**Ash psyllid**, *Psyllopsis fraxinicola*. Aphidlike insects, suck sap.	*See Psyllids, 114.*
Sticky honeydew and blackish sooty mold on plant.	**Frosted scale**. Bulbous or flattened, brown or whitish insects, may be waxy, ≤¼ inch long, suck sap.	*See 139.*
Copious, misty, nonsticky liquid raining from plant. Surfaces covered with whitish residue.	**Glassy-winged sharpshooter**. Active, dark brown or gray leafhoppers ≤½ inch long, suck xylem fluid.	Vectors pathogens of oleander, certain crops (especially grapes), and (possibly) ash. Report suspected glassy-winged sharpshooters to agricultural officials if found in areas where this pest is not known to occur. *See 148.*
Coarse, yellow stippling (flecking) of leaves. Dark, varnishlike excrement on undersides of leaves. Leaves may drop prematurely.	**Ash plant bugs**. Brown, green, or yellowish true bugs ≤³⁄₁₆ inch long.	*See 153.*
Stippled, bleached leaves with dark specks of excrement on undersides.	**Arizona ash tingid**, *Leptoypha minor*. Pale brown insect, ≤⅛ inch long, wings lacelike.	*See 154.*

ASH (*Fraxinus* spp.), continued

WHAT THE PROBLEM LOOKS LIKE	PROBABLE CAUSE	COMMENTS
Leaves scraped, skeletonized, may be slime-covered.	**Pear sawfly** or **Pearslug**. Green, slimy, sluglike insects, ≤½ inch long.	*See 83.*
Leaves chewed in spring, usually only on inner canopy near bark where the night-feeding larvae hide during the day.	**Ash moth** or **Bentley Ash moth**, *Oncocnemis punctilinea*. Dark gray to brown larvae, ≤½ inch long, with lighter longitudinal stripe. Head dark with light patterns.	Pest in Central Valley and southern deserts of California. One generation per year. Ash generally tolerates damage. Apply *Bacillus thuringiensis* if intolerable.
Leaves chewed, scraped, covered with silken strands, or webbed together.	**Moths**, including **Fall webworm**; **Omnivorous leafroller**, *Platynota stultana* (family Tortricidae); *Zelleria* sp. (Yponomeutidae). Larvae are brownish, greenish orangish, tan, or dirty whitish with a dark head.	Vigorous plants tolerate moderate defoliation. *See Foliage-Feeding Caterpillars, 71.*
Tan or gray encrustations on bark. May be dead or declining twigs and branches.	**Oystershell scale, Walnut scale**. Tiny round to elongate insects, often in colonies.	*See 135.*
Roughened twig bark. Possible twig dieback.	**Treehoppers**, including **Buffalo treehopper**, *Stictocephala bisonia*. Bright yellow to green insects, horny or spiny.	*See 151.*
Green plants with smooth stems, thick roundish leaves infesting branches.	**Broadleaf mistletoe**, *Phoradendron* sp. Parasitic evergreen plant on host.	*See 338.*

AUCUBA (*Aucuba japonica*), Gold-dust plant, Gold spot aucuba, Japanese aucuba

WHAT THE PROBLEM LOOKS LIKE	PROBABLE CAUSE	COMMENTS
Leaves with black spots, blotches, or terminals. Black cannot be scraped off as with sooty mold.	**Leaf spot**. Abiotic disorders due to excess light and high temperature, may be aggravated by drought stress.	Provide appropriate growing environment and cultural care. Provide some shade. Plant tall species and darken light-colored surfaces nearby.
Yellowish or brownish spots on leaves, leaves may drop prematurely if severe.	**Phyllosticta leaf spot**, *Phyllosticta aucubae*. A fungal disease promoted by wet foliage.	Avoid overhead watering. *See Leaf Spots, 223.*
Brownish, grayish, tan, reddish, yellowish, or whitish encrustations (insect bodies) on twigs or leaves. Plant may decline or die back.	**Dictyospermum scale**, *Chrysomphalus dictyospermi*; **False oleander scale**, *Pseudaulacaspis cockerelli*; **Greedy scale**; **Oleander scale**; **Yellow scale**, *Aonidiella citrina*. Small, flattened, oval to round insects.	Narrow-range oil or another insecticide can provide control when crawlers are active. Monitor crawlers to effectively time sprays. *See 131.*
Sticky honeydew and blackish sooty mold on plant. Waxy, cottony material on leaves or twigs.	**Obscure mealybug**. Powdery, whitish insects ≤⅛ inch long with filaments, longest at tail. Suck sap.	*See 127.*
Sticky honeydew and blackish sooty mold on plant. Leaves distorted, may drop prematurely. Plant growth slow.	**Foxglove aphid**, *Aulacorthum solani*. Small dull greenish or brownish to shiny yellowish insects, usually in groups.	*See Aphids, 103.*

AUSTRALIAN WILLOW (*Geijera parviflora*)

WHAT THE PROBLEM LOOKS LIKE	PROBABLE CAUSE	COMMENTS
Leaves stunt, yellow, wilt, or drop prematurely. Plants grow slowly and may die. Roots dark, decayed.	**Root and crown rot**. Pathogen promoted by excess soil moisture and poor drainage.	*See 265.*
Sticky honeydew and blackish sooty mold on plant. Bulbous, irregular, brown, gray, or white bodies (scales) on twigs.	**Chinese wax scale**. Bulbous to hemispherical, waxy insects, suck sap.	*See 141.*

AUSTRALIAN WILLOW MYRTLE (*Agonis* spp.), Juniper willow myrtle, Peppermint tree

No serious invertebrate or pathogen pests have been reported in California. If plants are unhealthy, investigate whether they have been injured or lack good growing conditions or appropriate cultural care.

WHAT THE PROBLEM LOOKS LIKE	PROBABLE CAUSE	COMMENTS

AVOCADO *(Persea* spp.)[4]

WHAT THE PROBLEM LOOKS LIKE	PROBABLE CAUSE	COMMENTS
Leaves stunt, yellow, wilt, or drop prematurely. Stems discolor, canker, and die. Minute white fungus growths may be visible beneath bark or on soil.	**Armillaria root rot.** Present in many soils. Favored by warm, wet soil. Persists for years in infected roots.	*See 262.*
Leaves stunt, yellow, wilt, or drop prematurely. Plants grow slowly and may die. Roots dark, decayed.	**Root and crown rots,** *Phytophthora citricola, P. cinnamomi.* Pathogens promoted by excess soil moisture and poor drainage.	*See 265.*
Leaves wilt, turn brown, and die, often on one side of plant. Dead leaves may remain on stems. Stem xylem discolored. Stems or entire plant may die.	**Verticillium wilt,** *Verticillium albo-atrum.* Fungus that persists in soil and infects through roots.	*See 232.*
Leaves yellow. Growth stunted. Roots smaller, darker than on healthy plants.	**Root lesion nematode,** *Pratylenchus vulnus.* Tiny root-feeding roundworms.	*See 346.*
Twigs with elongated lesions. Bark splits. Necrotic streaks in wood.	**Bacterial blight and canker.** Disease favored by wet conditions.	*See 245.*
Brownish, gray, orange, reddish, tan, or white encrustations on bark. May be stunted, declining, or dead branches.	**California red scale; Dictyospermum scale,** *Chrysomphalus dictyospermi;* **Greedy scale; Latania scale.** Tiny, circular, flattened insects.	*See 131.*
Leaves bleached, blotched, discolored, or stippled. May be fine webbing on foliage. Leaves may drop prematurely.	**Avocado brown mite,** *Oligonychus punicae;* **Avocado sixspotted mite,** *Eotetranychus sexmaculatus;* **Persea mite.** Tiny sand-sized specks on leaves.	*See 197.*
Leaves bleached, discolored, or stippled. Leaf underside has dark, varnishlike excrement.	**Greenhouse thrips.** Tiny, slender black, brown, or yellowish insects.	*See 158.*
Irregular brownish or leathery scarring on leaves and fruit.	**Avocado thrips.** Tiny, slender, yellow insects.	Damage is aesthetic and does not harm tree or affect internal fruit quality. *See Thrips, 156.*
Sticky honeydew and blackish sooty mold on foliage. Possible decline or dieback of twigs and branches.	**Black scale; Brown soft scale; European fruit lecanium; Hemispherical scale,** *Saissetia coffeae.* Yellow, orange, brown, or black, flattened or bulbous insects, often in groups.	*See 136–139.*
Sticky honeydew and blackish sooty mold on foliage. Copious white waxy material present with certain species. Leaves may yellow and wither.	**Giant whitefly; Greenhouse whitefly; Mulberry whitefly,** *Tetraleurodes mori;* **Nesting whitefly,** *Paraleyrodes minei;* **Redbanded whitefly,** *Tetraleurodes perseae.* Tiny, whitish, mothlike adult insects.	*See 121.*
Sticky honeydew and blackish sooty mold on foliage. Cottony or waxy material on plant.	**Mealybugs,** including **Pink hibiscus mealybug, Vine mealybug.** Powdery grayish insects, ≤¼ inch long, may have waxy filaments.	Vigorous plants tolerate moderate populations. Conserve natural enemies that help in control. *See 128.*
Leaves chewed. Leaves may be tied together with silk.	**Omnivorous looper; Orange tortrix,** *Argyrotaenia citrana* (family Tortricidae); **Fruittree leafroller; Western avocado leafroller,** *Amorbia cuneana* (Tortricidae). Naked larvae, ≤1½ inch long.	Vigorous plants tolerate moderate leaf damage. Prune out infested foliage. Apply *Bacillus thuringiensis* or another insecticide when young larvae are feeding. *See 71.*

4. For more information on pest identification and biology, see publications such as *Avocado Pest Management Guidelines* (Faber et al. 2001).

AZALEA (*Rhododendron* spp.)[5]

WHAT THE PROBLEM LOOKS LIKE	PROBABLE CAUSE	COMMENTS
New foliage yellows beginning along margins, but **veins green**. Leaves may develop brown **blotches**.	**Iron deficiency** or **Manganese deficiency**. Abiotic disorders usually caused by poor soil conditions or unhealthy roots.	*See 278–279.*
New foliage yellow overall. Plants may grow **slowly** and produce fewer and smaller than normal leaves and shoots. Discolored foliage may drop prematurely.	**Nitrogen deficiency**. Abiotic disorder usually caused by poor soil conditions or unhealthy roots.	*See 275.*
Leaves **turn brown** or yellow, especially along margins and at tip. Leaves may drop prematurely.	**Leaf burn** or **Scorch**. Abiotic disorders. Causes include drought, dry wind, excess fertilization, excess light, frost, saline irrigation water or soil, or transplant shock.	Provide plants with a good growing environment and proper cultural care. *See 273.*
Foliage yellows and wilts. Branches or entire plant dies.	**Root and crown rots**, *Phytophthora* spp., *Pythium* spp. Pathogens promoted by excess soil moisture and poor drainage.	*See 265.*
Foliage may yellow, wilt, die back, or drop prematurely. Plant grows slowly. May be galls or swellings on roots.	**Root knot nematodes, Stubby root nematodes, Stunt nematode**. Tiny root-feeding roundworms.	*See 341.*
Leaves with brown, light green, or yellow spots or dead blotches. Twigs and stems may canker or ooze. Plant may die.	**Sudden oak death**, *Phytophthora ramorum*. Pathogen spreads via air and contaminated soil. Apparently can infect through bark or leaves.	Primarily a problem in wildlands, killing many oaks there. Do not move infected plant material. Report to agricultural officials if found outside areas where pathogen is known to occur. *See 260.*
Brownish to reddish spots and yellowing on leaves. Leaves may drop prematurely.	**Septoria leaf spot** or **Leaf scorch**, *Septoria azaleae*. A fungal disease promoted and spread by wet conditions.	Keep foliage dry. Dispose of fallen leaves. *See 227.*
Leaves with pale green to yellow spots on upper surface and brown to purple spots on underside. Leaf undersides with blisters or orangish pustules. Leaves may drop prematurely.	**Rusts**, including *Chrysomyxa ledi, C. piperiana*. Pathogens favored by wet conditions. Fungal spores persist in plant debris.	Avoid overhead watering. Remove and dispose of infected leaves. Plants tolerate moderate populations. *See 240.*
Brown, purple, or yellow blotches on leaves. Powdery, whitish growth on leaves and possibly other tissue.	**Powdery mildews**, including *Erysiphe polygoni, Microsphaera azaleae, Microsphaera penicillata*. Fungi develop on living tissue, favored by moderate temperatures, shade, and poor air circulation.	*See 236.*
Small round to larger spots on flowers. Flowers collapse, become slimy and soft, and cling to leaves or stems.	**Azalea petal blight** or **Ovulinia petal blight**. Fungus favored by cool, wet weather during flowering. Spores spread by splashing water.	*See 245.*
Soft, brown decay on flowers, buds, or leaves. May be woolly gray growth (spores) on dead tissue.	**Gray mold** or **Botrytis petal blight**. Fungus develops in plant debris or inactive tissue. Favored by high humidity and moderate temperatures. Spores airborne.	Unlike Ovulinia petal blight, infected flowers do not become slimy. *See 242.*
Leaves partly or all crisp, distorted, thickened, and brown or white. White or pinkish spores cover infected tissue.	**Leaf gall** or **Kinnikinnick**, *Exobasidium vaccinii*. Fungus spreads by air only during wet weather.	Avoid overhead watering. Prune only when dry. Improve air circulation. Vigorous plants tolerate extensive leaf galling. Handpick or prune out galls. Rake and dispose of fallen leaves.
Sticky honeydew and blackish sooty mold on foliage. Tiny, whitish, mothlike insects (adult whiteflies) on foliage.	**Azalea whitefly**, *Pealius azaleae*; **Greenhouse whitefly**; **Rhododendron whitefly**, *Massileurodes* (=*Dialeurodes*) *chittendeni*; **Silverleaf whitefly**. Nymphs oval, flattened, yellowish to greenish, suck sap.	Cultivars vary greatly in susceptibility to these pests, which rarely cause serious damage to plants. *See 121.*

5. Also see Rhododendron.

| --- | --- | --- |

AZALEA *(Rhododendron* spp.), continued

WHAT THE PROBLEM LOOKS LIKE	PROBABLE CAUSE	COMMENTS
Sticky honeydew and blackish sooty mold on plant. Whitish cottony bodies on bark. Bark rough. Branches may deform. Possible dieback.	**Azalea bark scale** or **Woolly azalea scale,** *Acanthococcus (=Eriococcus) azaleae* (family Eriococcidae). Dark, reddish, oval insects underneath white wax, on bark crevices and in crotches.	Occurs in the eastern U.S. and in Oregon and Washington. If found in California, report to county department of agriculture. *See Other Common Scales, 142.*
Sticky honeydew and blackish sooty mold on leaves and twigs. Whitish cast skins on undersides of leaves.	**Aphids,** including *Illinoia* spp.; **Spirea aphid,** *Aphis citricola.* Tiny pear-shaped insects, often brownish, green, or yellowish.	*See 103.*
Leaves bleached, stippled, may turn brown and drop prematurely. Terminals may be distorted. Plant may have fine webbing.	**Mites,** including **Southern red mite, Two-spotted spider mite.** Tiny, often green, pink, or red pests; may have 2 dark spots.	*See 197.*
Stippled or bleached leaves with dark, varnishlike excrement specks on undersides.	**Greenhouse thrips.** Tiny, slender blackish adults or yellowish nymphs.	*See 158.*
Leaf edges notched or ragged, including on nearby hosts. Wilted or dying plants. Roots missing, debarked, girdled near soil surface.	**Black vine weevil; Obscure root weevil,** *Sciopithes obscurus;* **Woods weevil,** *Nemocestes incomptus.* Adults dark brown to black or grayish snout weevils, ≤½ inch long. Larvae white grubs in soil.	*See 92.*
Browning of leaves or leaves tied together with silk. Leaves curled.	**Azalea leafminer,** *Caloptilia azaleella.* Greenish larvae, ≤½ inch long, secretive. Young larvae mine leaves, older larvae feed externally.	Vigorous plants tolerate extensive leaf damage. Control difficult. Clip and dispose of infested leaves. If needed, apply oil to mature larvae or systemic insecticide for all larval stages.
Copious, misty, nonsticky liquid raining from plant. Surfaces covered with whitish residue.	**Glassy-winged sharpshooter.** Active, dark brown or gray leafhoppers ≤½ inch long, suck xylem fluid.	Vectors pathogens of oleander and certain crops, especially grapes. Report suspected glassy-winged sharpshooters to agricultural officials if found in areas where this pest is not known to occur. *See 148.*

BAMBOO *(Bambusa, Fargesia, Pleioblastus, Phyllostachys* spp.)*

WHAT THE PROBLEM LOOKS LIKE	PROBABLE CAUSE	COMMENTS
Stems die back. Entire plant may die. Minute white fungus growths may be visible in stems or on soil.	**Armillaria root rot.** Present in many soils. Favored by warm, wet soil. Persists for years in infected roots.	*See 262.*
New foliage yellows beginning along margins, but veins green. Leaves may develop brown blotches.	**Iron deficiency.** Abiotic disorder usually caused by poor soil conditions or unhealthy roots.	*See 278.*
Pale, brown, or purplish blotches or streaks on foliage. Foliage may drop prematurely.	**Spider mites,** including **Bamboo spider mites,** *Schizotetranychus* spp.; **Persea mite.** Tiny green to yellow mites, often with dark spots.	*See 197.*
Yellowing leaves. Sticky honeydew, blackish sooty mold, and tiny whitish cast skins on leaves.	**Bamboo aphids,** *Takecallis* spp. Pale yellow insects about ⅟₁₆ inch long with black marks.	Vigorous plants tolerate many aphids. Hose forcefully with water. Tolerate or apply soap or narrow-range oil. *See Aphids, 103.*
Sticky honeydew and blackish sooty mold on plant. Cottony material in leaf axils. Dead foliage.	**Noxious bamboo mealybug,** *Antonina pretiosa.* Black, brown, or reddish, elongate to round insects that secrete grayish wax.	Plants tolerate moderate populations. Apply soap or oil if needed. *See Mealybugs, 126.*
Groups of dark to pale, flattened insects encrusting plant. Possible dieback of plant parts.	**Bamboo scale,** *Asterolecanium bambusae.* Black, orange, or yellow, circular to oval insects, ≤⅟₁₆ inch long, on leaves, stems, or under sheaths.	Usually unimportant in landscapes. If severe, apply oil when crawlers are active. *See Other Common Scales, 142.*

*Some species are invasive weeds. Other species may be better choices when planting.

BAMBOO (*Bambusa, Fargesia, Pleioblastus, Phyllostachys* spp.), continued

Foliage discolors and wilts. Stems die back. Seashell-shaped fruiting bodies may develop on stems.	**Decay** or **Sapwood rot**, *Schizophyllum commune*. A decay fungus that aggressively invades injured tissue and unhealthy plants.	Protect plants from injuries and stress. Provide good growing conditions and appropriate cultural care. *See Wood Decay in Trunks and Limbs, 248.*

BEECH (*Fagus* spp.)

Sticky honeydew, blackish sooty mold, and whitish cast skins on foliage.	**Woolly beech leaf aphid**, *Phyllaphis fagi*. Small, greenish insects in groups on underside of leaves.	Plants tolerate abundant aphids. Tolerate or apply insecticidal soap or oil if populations bothersome. *See Aphids, 103.*

BEEFWOOD (*Casuarina* spp.), Coast Beefwood, She-oak

Foliage may discolor and wilt. Branches or entire tree may die. Minute white fungus growths may be visible under bark or on soil.	**Armillaria root rot.** Present in many soils. Favored by warm, wet soil. Persists for years in infected roots.	*See 262.*
Grayish encrustations on bark. Rarely, dead or declining branches.	**Latania scale.** Individuals circular, ≤1/16 inch long, usually in groups.	*See 133.*
Sticky honeydew and blackish sooty mold on plant. Popcornlike bodies (egg sacs) on bark.	**Cottony cushion scale.** Orangish, flat immatures or cottony females on bark.	Normally controlled by natural enemies. *See 142.*
Leaves discolored, wilted, stunted, may drop prematurely. Discolored bark may ooze sap. Branches or plant may die. Trees may fall over.	**Wood decay** or **Heart rots**, including *Ganoderma* sp. Fungi that attack injured or stressed trees. *Ganoderma* produces large, fan-shaped basidiocarps on lower trunks.	*See Wood Decay in Trunks and Limbs, 248.*

BIRCH (*Betula* spp.)

Leaves discolor, wilt, stunt, or drop prematurely. Stems discolored, cankered, may ooze sap and die. Minute white fungus growths may be visible beneath bark or on soil.	**Armillaria root rot.** Present in many soils. Favored by warm, wet soil. Persists for years in infected roots.	*See 262*
Leaves discolor and wilt. Branches or treetop dying. Branches may have cankers or brownish ooze.	**Botryosphaeria canker and dieback, Cytospora canker, Hypoxylon canker, Nectria canker.** Fungi primarily affect injured or drought-stressed trees.	*See 250.*
Leaves with irregular brown to yellow blotches. Leaves may die and drop prematurely.	**Anthracnose.** Fungal pathogen favored by cool, wet, conditions. Persists in plant debris.	*See 223.*
Leaves spotted, may yellow and drop prematurely. Reddish yellow pustules on lower leaf surface (spores that reinfect birch).	**Rust**, *Melampsoridium betulinum*. Fungal spores overwinter around bud scales.	Rake and dispose of all birch leaves in the fall. *See 240.*
Leaves discolor and wilt. Branches wilted or dying. Boring dust, ooze, holes on trunk or branches.	**Borers**, including **Bronze birch borer, Carpenterworm, Redbelted clearwing, Western poplar clearwing.** Whitish larvae ≤2½ inches long, head brown, bore under bark.	*See 179–195.*
Brown, gray, or tan encrustations on bark. May be dead or declining twigs and branches.	**Oystershell scale, Walnut scale.** Individuals elongate to round, ≤3/16 inch diameter, often in colonies.	*See 135.*
Sticky honeydew, blackish sooty mold, and tiny whitish cast skins on leaves.	**Aphids.** Yellow to green insects, ≤1/16 inch long on leaf undersides.	*See 103.*
Sticky honeydew and blackish sooty mold on plant.	**Frosted scale.** Hemispherical to flattened, brown or whitish insects, may be waxy, ≤¼ inch long, suck sap.	*See 139.*

BIRCH (*Betula* spp.), continued

WHAT THE PROBLEM LOOKS LIKE	PROBABLE CAUSE	COMMENTS
Chewed leaves. Foliage may be webbed or contain silken tents.	**Fall webworm, Redhumped caterpillar, Tent caterpillars.** Larvae ≤1½ inch long, may be hairy.	*See 71.*
Stippled, flecked, or bleached leaves with whitish cast skins on undersides.	**Leafhoppers,** including *Empoasca* sp.; *Alebra albostriella.* Green, wedgelike insects ≤⅛ inch long.	Quick insects, often on leaf underside. Plants generally tolerate, control rarely warranted. *See 148.*
Leaves stippled or bleached, with cast skins and varnishlike specks.	**Lace bug,** *Corythucha* sp. Brown adults, ≤⅛ inch long, wings lacelike.	*See 154.*
Leaves with large blotchy or irregular mines. Larvae may be visible through leaf surface. Foliage turns brown, wilts, and may drop prematurely.	**Leafminers,** including **Birch leafminer sawfly,** *Fenusa pusilla.* Larvae feed in leaf tissue. Adults are black, broad-waisted, stout wasps.	Consider planting less-susceptible black birch (*Betula lenta*), monarch birch (*B. maximowicziana*), river birch (*B. nigra*), or yellow birch (*B. alleghaniensis*). If problem has been severe, apply systemic insecticide during spring.
Leaves chewed along edges. Entire branches may be defoliated.	**Sawflies,** including **Birch sawfly,** *Arge pectoralis;* **Dusky birch sawfly,** *Croesus latitarsus.* Green, orangish, or yellow larvae with black dots, often feed in groups on leaves. Adults are black, stout wasps.	*See 82.*

BIRD OF PARADISE (*Strelitzia* spp.), Giant bird of paradise

WHAT THE PROBLEM LOOKS LIKE	PROBABLE CAUSE	COMMENTS
Leaves discolor, wilt, stunt, or drop prematurely. Plants stunted. Root system reduced, small roots rotted.	**Pythium root rot.** Soilborne fungus favored by excess soil moisture and poor drainage.	*See 268.*
Leaves discolor, wilt, stunt, or drop prematurely. Stems discolored, cankered, may ooze sap and die. Minute white fungus growths may be visible beneath bark or on soil.	**Armillaria root rot.** Present in many soils. Favored by warm, wet soil. Persists for years in infected roots.	*See 262.*
Petals or leaves have brown, water-soaked spots or decay. Dead tissue may have woolly gray growth (spores). Stem may be girdled.	**Gray mold.** Fungus develops in plant debris or inactive tissue. Favored by wet conditions and moderate temperatures. Spores airborne.	*See 242.*
Sticky honeydew and blackish sooty mold on foliage. Foliage may yellow. Plant may have cottony material (egg sacs).	**Citrus mealybug,** *Planococcus citri;* **Long-tailed mealybug,** *Pseudococcus longispinus;* **Obscure mealybug.** Powdery gray insects with waxy filaments.	*See 127.*
Sticky honeydew and blackish sooty mold on foliage. Copious white waxy material may be on plant. Leaves may yellow and wither.	**Greenhouse whitefly; Giant whitefly; Iris whitefly,** *Aleyrodes spiraeoides.* Nymphs and pupae are flattened, oval, and pale. Adults are tiny mothlike insects.	*See 122–123.*
Sticky honeydew, blackish sooty mold, and whitish cast skins on plant. Foliage may yellow.	**Aphids.** Tiny pear-shaped insects, often green, yellowish, or blackish.	*See 103.*
Sticky honeydew and blackish sooty mold on foliage. Foliage may yellow and plant may die back.	**Brown soft scale,** *Coccus hesperidum;* **Nigra scale,** *Parasaissetia nigra.* Orange, black, brown or yellow, flattened to bulbous, oval insects.	*See Scales, 137.*
Stems or leaves have brown, gray, tan, reddish, orange, or white encrustations. Foliage may yellow. Rarely, plant may decline or die back.	**California red scale; Cycad scale; Dictyospermum scale,** *Chrysomphalus dictyospermi;* **Greedy scale; Latania scale; Oleander scale.** Oval to round, flattened insects, ≤¹⁄₁₆ inch long.	*See 131.*

BIRD OF PARADISE (*Strelitzia* spp.), Giant bird of paradise, continued

WHAT THE PROBLEM LOOKS LIKE	PROBABLE CAUSE	COMMENTS
Plants may stunt, decline, or, rarely, die. Powdery waxy material may be visible on roots and around crown.	**Ground mealybugs,** *Rhizoecus* spp. Small, slender, pale insects, may be lightly covered with powdery wax, but lack marginal filaments.	*See 130.*
Foliage yellows, wilts, and dies. Basal stem has holes or decay.	**Crown borer,** *Opogona omoscopa* (family Tineidae). Dark, brownish moth. Grayish larva ≤¾ inch long, head dark, bores in plant.	Probably a secondary pest attracted to decaying tissue. Avoid wounding plants. Provide good cultural care. Avoid excess irrigation. Use good sanitation; remove debris and dying plants.

BOTTLEBRUSH (*Callistemon* spp.)

WHAT THE PROBLEM LOOKS LIKE	PROBABLE CAUSE	COMMENTS
Gray to reddish encrustations on shoots or needles (scale insect bodies). Plant may decline and die back.	**Dictyospermum scale,** *Chrysomphalus dictyospermi.* Tiny, immobile, flattened insects that suck plant juices. Several generations per year.	Occasional problem in California, mostly in south. Conserve introduced natural enemies, which can provide excellent biological control. *See Armored Scales, page 131.*
Foliage or flowers curl, turn brown or black, and die. Terminals die back.	**Leaf burn** or **Scorch.** Abiotic disorders with many potential causes, including freeze or cold damage.	Provide plants with a good growing environment and proper cultural care. *See 273.*

BOTTLETREE (*Brachychiton* spp.)

No serious invertebrate or pathogen pests have been reported in California. If plants are unhealthy, investigate whether they have been injured or lack good growing conditions or appropriate cultural care.

BOUGAINVILLEA (*Bougainvillea* spp.)

WHAT THE PROBLEM LOOKS LIKE	PROBABLE CAUSE	COMMENTS
Foliage or flowers curl, turn brown or black, and die. Branches may die back.	**Leaf burn** or **Scorch.** Abiotic disorders with many potential causes, including freeze or cold damage.	*See 273.*
Sticky honeydew and blackish sooty mold on foliage. Cottony or waxy material on plant.	**Citrus mealybug, Longtailed mealybug.** Powdery, grayish, ≤¼ inch long, with waxy filaments.	Vigorous plants tolerate moderate populations. Conserve natural enemies that help in control. *See 127.*
Sticky honeydew and blackish sooty mold on foliage. Leaves cupped, curled, or twisted.	**Cowpea aphid,** *Aphis craccivora;* **Melon aphid.** Brown, black, or green, pear-shaped insects, usually in groups.	Conserve natural enemies that provide control. Hose forcefully with water. Tolerate or apply soap or oil if severe. *See 103.*
Sticky honeydew and blackish sooty mold on foliage. Possibly twig or branch decline or dieback.	**Brown soft scale.** Small brown, orangish, or yellowish insects, flattened or bulbous.	*See 137.*

BOX ELDER (*Acer negundo* spp.)

WHAT THE PROBLEM LOOKS LIKE	PROBABLE CAUSE	COMMENTS
Foliage fades, yellows, browns, or wilts, often scattered throughout canopy. Branches die. Entire plant may die.	**Verticillium wilt.** A soil-dwelling fungus that infects through roots.	*See 232.*
Discolored leaf spots, often between veins. Large spots chlorotic, then tan or brown.	**Sunburn** or **Summer leaf scorch.** Noninfectious disorder, appears during or after drought stress and high temperatures.	*See 273.*
Small discrete spots to irregular, large blotches or holes over most of leaf surface. Leaves may drop prematurely if severe.	**Leaf spots,** including *Cylindrosporium, Phyllosticta, Septoria* spp. Fungi spread by air or splashing water. Favored by wet conditions.	*See 223.*
Oval or irregular, glossy black, thick tarlike raised spots on upper leaf surface.	**Tar spot,** *Rhytisma punctatum.* Fungus most prevalent in moist environments.	Rake and dispose of leaves in the fall. *See Leaf Spots, 223.*
Powdery white growth on leaves. Tiny, black overwintering bodies may develop later.	**Powdery mildew,** *Phyllactinia guttata* = *P. corylea.* Fungal disease favored by moderate temperatures, shade, and poor air circulation.	Generally not severe enough to warrant control. *See 236.*

BOX ELDER (*Acer negundo* spp.), continued

WHAT THE PROBLEM LOOKS LIKE	PROBABLE CAUSE	COMMENTS
Chewed leaves. Foliage may be rolled and tied together with silk.	**Caterpillars**, including **Fruittree leafroller, Omnivorous looper.** Moth larvae ≤1½ inches long.	*See 71.*
Chewed leaves or blossoms.	**Fuller rose beetle.** Pale brown adult snout weevils, about ⅜ inch long.	Adults hide during day and feed at night. Larvae feed on roots. *See 94.*
Foliage discolored, stippled, or bleached, and may drop prematurely. Terminals may distort. Plant may have fine webbing.	**Mites,** including *Oligonychus* sp., **Two-spotted spider mite.** Tiny greenish or yellowish arthropods, may have two dark spots.	*See 197*
Spotted or yellow foliage, usually severe only on female trees.	**Boxelder bugs.** Gray and red adults, about ½ inch long. Nymphs red.	Trees tolerate damage. Adults invading houses are the primary problem. *See 153.*
Sticky honeydew, blackish sooty mold, and whitish cast skins on leaves.	**Aphids.** Tiny pear-shaped insects, often brown, green, or yellowish, clustered on leaves.	*See 103.*
Sticky honeydew and blackish sooty mold on foliage. White popcornlike material on twigs (female scale egg sacs.)	**Cottony maple scale,** *Pulvinaria innumerabilis.* Immatures flattened, yellow to tan, ≤1/16 inch long, on leaves, suck sap.	Vigorous plants tolerate moderate populations. Monitor and if needed apply narrow-range oil or another insecticide when crawlers are active. *See Scales and Monitoring of Scales, 130.*
Sticky honeydew and blackish sooty mold on foliage.	**Calico scale.** Adults globular, black with white or yellow spots.	*See 138.*
Brown to gray encrustations on bark. Twigs or limbs may die back.	**Oystershell scale.** Individuals about 1/16 inch long, oyster-shaped, suck sap.	*See 135.*
Woody parts die back. Wet spots or sawdustlike frass on bark.	**Flatheaded appletree borer.** Whitish larvae ≤¾ inch long.	*See 179.*
Bark stained brownish, exudes rancid fluid, often around crotches, wounds.	**Wetwood** or **Slime flux.** Bacterial infection.	Usually does not cause serious harm to trees. *See 259.*

BOXWOOD (*Buxus* spp.), Box

WHAT THE PROBLEM LOOKS LIKE	PROBABLE CAUSE	COMMENTS
Foliage discolors, wilts, stunts, and may drop prematurely. Branches or plant may die. Plant base or roots dark or decayed.	**Root and crown rots, Foliage blights, Stem necrosis,** *Phytophthora* spp., *Pythium* spp. Decay fungi favored by excess soil moisture and poor drainage.	*See 265–268.*
Leaves on branch terminals turn red, then bronze, and finally yellow. Branches may have loose bark, girdling cankers, or dieback.	**Canker** or **Stem blights,** *Pseudonectria rousseliana =Volutella buxi.* Fungal pathogen persists in infected wood, is favored by wet conditions.	Prune out infected branches during dry weather. Remove fallen leaves. If severe, copper sprays or lime sulfur applied just before new growth and again when new leaves stop flushing can reduce new infections. *See similar Nectria Canker, 257.*
Leaves with discolored blotches or spots, which may be dotted with dark, fungal fruiting bodies.	**Leaf spots,** including *Macrophoma candollei, Phyllosticta* sp. Fungal diseases that infect and develop when foliage is wet.	*See 223.*
Foliage bleached, discolored, stippled, or streaked. Plant may have fine webbing.	**Spider mites,** including **Boxwood mite,** *Eurytetranychus buxi.* Tiny greenish, reddish, or yellowish arthropods.	*See 197.*
Brownish, grayish, orange, tan, or white encrustations on bark. Rarely, twigs or branches die back or growth is stunted.	**California red scale, Greedy scale, Oleander scale, Oystershell scale.** Tiny circular to elongate insects.	*See 131.*

BOXWOOD (*Buxus* spp.), Box, continued

WHAT THE PROBLEM LOOKS LIKE	PROBABLE CAUSE	COMMENTS
Leaves have blisters, blotchy mines, or yellow spots. Foliage sparse. Leaves drop prematurely. Shoots may die back. Plant growth may be stunted.	**Boxwood leafminer,** *Monarthropalpus flavus* =*M. buxi* (family Cecidomyiidae). Greenish or orange fly larvae mine leaves. Adults are tiny, delicate, and resemble mosquitoes.	*Buxus harlandii, B. microphylla,* and some *B. sempervirens* cultivars can be heavily damaged. Consider replacing susceptible species. Resistant plants include *Buxus sempervirens* 'Argenteo-variegata,' 'Pendula,' and 'Suffruticosa.' Rake and dispose of infested fallen leaves, which may contain fly pupae.
Sticky honeydew and blackish sooty mold on foliage. Popcornlike bodies (egg sacs) on bark.	**Cottony cushion scale.** Orangish, flat immatures or cottony females on bark.	Normally controlled by natural enemies. *See 142.*
Cupping of leaves.	**Boxwood psyllid.** Greenish adults, ⅛ inch long, nymphs flattened.	American boxwood more susceptible than English boxwood. Tolerate, psyllids apparently do not harm shrubs. *See Psyllids, 114.*
Plants stunted, decline, may die. Powdery, waxy material may be visible on roots and around crown.	**Ground mealybug,** *Rhizoecus falcifer.* Small, slender, pale insects, which may have powdery wax covering but no marginal filaments.	*See 130.*

BROOM (*Cytisus* spp.)*

WHAT THE PROBLEM LOOKS LIKE	PROBABLE CAUSE	COMMENTS
Sticky honeydew and blackish sooty mold on foliage. May be distorted terminals.	**Bean aphid.** Dull black or green insects, <⅛ inch long.	Plants tolerate moderate populations. Hose forcefully with water. Tolerate or apply soap or oil. *See 104.*
Brownish, grayish, tan, or white encrustations on bark. Twigs or limbs may die back.	**Greedy scale, Oleander scale, Oystershell scale.** Tiny circular to elongate individuals. Suck sap.	*See 133–135.*
Chewed leaves. Plants may be defoliated.	**Genista caterpillar,** *Uresiphita reversalis* (family Pyralidae). Caterpillars ≤1¼ inches long, green to orange with black and white hairs.	Introduced to control brooms, which are often considered weeds. In California more common in south than north. Apply *Bacillus thuringiensis* or another insecticide if broom are desirable.

BUCKWHEAT (*Eriogonum* spp.)

WHAT THE PROBLEM LOOKS LIKE	PROBABLE CAUSE	COMMENTS
Chewed flowers. Leaves chewed or surfaces scraped.	**Common hairstreak butterfly,** *Strymon melinus* (family Hesperiidae). Larvae greenish with short brown hairs. Adult 1 inch long, gray above with marginal red wing spot.	Plants tolerate extensive feeding by larvae, which mature into attractive butterflies. *See Foliage-Feeding Caterpillars, 71.*
Flowers chewed.	**Tumbling flower beetle,** *Mordella* sp. (family Mordellidae). Dark, ⅛ inch long, narrow adults with tapered abdomen.	Feed mostly on pollen, damage usually minor. Adults often become very active when disturbed. No known controls.
Sticky honeydew, blackish sooty mold, or whitish cast skins. Flowers may drop prematurely or distort.	**Aphids,** *Braggia* spp. Small grayish green to black insects in groups.	Plants tolerate many aphids. Flowers and seed can be reduced. *See 103.*

BUDDLEIA (*Buddleia* spp.)

WHAT THE PROBLEM LOOKS LIKE	PROBABLE CAUSE	COMMENTS
Leaves webbed, skeletonized. Leaves and terminal buds chewed.	**Buddleia budworm,** *Pyramidobela angelarum* (family Gelechiidae). Yellow to green larvae, ≤⅛ inch long. Adult is tiny grayish moth.	Prune out infested foliage. Vigorous plants tolerate moderate defoliation. *See Foliage-Feeding Caterpillars, 71.*

BUSH ANEMONE (*Carpenteria californica*)

WHAT THE PROBLEM LOOKS LIKE	PROBABLE CAUSE	COMMENTS
Sticky honeydew, blackish sooty mold, or whitish cast skins. Leaves and shoots may curl or distort.	**Aphids.** Small green, brown, black, or yellowish insects, often in groups.	Inspect new growth regularly and hose aphids forcefully with water. Apply insecticidal soap or oil before damage occurs. *See 103.*

*Some species are invasive weeds. Other species may be better choices when planting.

BUSH ANEMONE (*Carpenteria californica*), continued

WHAT THE PROBLEM LOOKS LIKE	PROBABLE CAUSE	COMMENTS
Thickening of sections of twigs. Shoots may be killed or distorted.	**Pit-making pittosporum scale,** *Planchonia* (=*Asterolecanium*) *arabidis* (family Asterolecaniidae). Brown to white insects, ≤⅛ inch long, on twigs.	Occasional problem only. No known management. *See Other Common Scales, 142.*

BUSH MORNING GLORY (*Convolvulus cneorum*), Silver bush

WHAT THE PROBLEM LOOKS LIKE	PROBABLE CAUSE	COMMENTS
Leaf undersides with orangish pustules. Leaves may be spotted, drop prematurely.	**Rust,** *Puccinia convolvuli.* Pathogen favored by wet conditions. Fungal spores persist in plant debris.	Avoid overhead watering. Plants tolerate moderate populations. *See 240.*
Sticky honeydew or blackish sooty mold on leaves or twigs. Plants may decline.	**Black scale.** Brown to black, bulbous to flattened insects, ≤³⁄₁₆ inch long. Raised H-shape often on back.	*See 136.*

CACTUS (*Cereus* spp., *Echinocactus* spp., *Echinopsis* =*Lobivia* spp., *Epiphyllum* spp., *Mammillaria* spp.); **PRICKLY-PEAR** (*Opuntia* spp.); **SAGUARO** (*Carnegiea gigantea*)

WHAT THE PROBLEM LOOKS LIKE	PROBABLE CAUSE	COMMENTS
Leaves or stems discolor, wilt, and may die back. Plant base or roots dark, decayed, or discolored.	**Root and Crown rots** and **Stem rots,** *Phytophthora* spp., *Pythium* spp. Decay fungi favored by excess soil moisture and poor drainage.	*See 265.*
Leaves or stems discolor, wilt, or die. Minute white fungus growths may be visible beneath bark or on soil.	**Armillaria root rot.** Present in many soils. Favored by warm, wet soil. Persists for years in infected roots.	*See 262.*
Leaves or stems discolor, wilt, and may die back. Tissue browns and may decay.	**Leaf burn** or **Scorch.** Abiotic disorders with many potential causes, including frost, too much or too little water, and sunburn, which kill tissue.	Provide proper growing conditions and good cultural practices. *See 273.*
Leaves or stems with brown to yellow spots or blotches. Foliage or stems may shrivel and die.	**Anthracnose, Blights,** and **Leaf spots,** including *Alternaria, Cercospora, Colletotrichum,* and *Phyllosticta* spp. Fungal pathogens favored by cool, wet, conditions. Persist in plant debris.	*See 223.*
Leaves or stems with brown or yellow spots. Basal stem or roots may brown and rot. Plant may yellow, wilt, and die.	**Fusarium wilt, Basal stem rot,** and **Leaf spot,** *Fusarium oxysporum, Fusarium* sp. Fungi persist in soil and infect through roots or spores on wounded leaves or stems.	Avoid injuring live tissue. Provide good drainage. *See 233.*
Flowers, fruit, leaves, or stems are soft, brown, or decayed. May be woolly gray growth (spores) on dead tissue.	**Gray mold.** Fungus develops in injured or inactive tissue and is favored by wet conditions and moderate temperatures.	*See 242.*
Foliage or stems yellow and wilt. Branches or entire plant may die. Fungal fruiting bodies may be on wood or around roots.	**Decay** or **Heart rots,** including *Phanerochaete* spp. Fungi that attack injured or stressed plants.	*See Wood Decay in Trunks and Limbs, 248.*
Whitish to brownish encrustations on plant. May be dieback of plant parts.	**Armored scales,** including **Cactus scale,** *Diaspis echinocacti.* Tiny oval to circular, flattened insects.	Apply narrow-range oil or another insecticide when crawlers are abundant in spring or summer. *See 131.*
Sticky honeydew and blackish sooty mold on plant. Waxy, cottony material on plant.	**Mealybugs,** including **Longtailed mealybug.** Powdery, whitish insects ≤⅛ inch long with filaments longest at tail, suck sap.	*See 126.*
Stunting of plant. Pinhead-sized white, yellow, or brown projections on roots.	**Cyst nematode,** *Heterodera cacti.* Microscopic root-feeding roundworms.	*See Chapter 8, Nematodes.*
Stunting of plant. Galls or swellings on roots.	**Root knot nematode,** *Meloidogyne* sp. Tiny root-feeding roundworms.	*See 345.*

CALIFORNIA BAY (*Umbellularia californica*), Bay, California bay laurel, Oregon myrtle, Pepperwood

WHAT THE PROBLEM LOOKS LIKE	PROBABLE CAUSE	COMMENTS
Leaves discolor and wilt, usually in spring. Stems may have dark, sunken cankers. May be small, coral-colored pustules on infected wood.	**Cankers**, including **Nectria canker**, *Nectria cinnabarina, N. coccinea, N. peziza.* Fungi primarily attack injured or stressed trees.	*See 250.*
Foliage yellows and wilts. Branches or entire plant may die. Fungal fruiting bodies may be on wood or around roots.	**Wood decay** or **Heart rots**, including *Ganoderma* spp., *Phellinus* spp., *Schizophyllum commune.* Fungi that attack injured or stressed trees.	*See Wood Decay in Trunks and Limbs, 248.*
Small, black, angular spots and large, irregular, brown spots on leaves.	**Leaf blights, Anthracnose**, *Pseudomonas* sp., *Kabatiella* sp., *Gloeosporium* sp. Bacterial and fungal pathogens favored by prolonged rainy springs.	Usually not serious enough to threaten tree health or warrant control effort. No controls known to be effective. *See 223.*
Leaves with brown, light green, or yellow lesions or dead spots.	**Sudden oak death**, *Phytophthora ramorum.* Pathogen spreads via air and contaminated soil.	Primarily a problem in wildlands, killing many oaks there. Do not move infected plant material. Report to agricultural officials if found outside areas where pathogen is known to occur. *See 260.*
Sticky honeydew and blackish sooty mold on leaves or twigs.	**California laurel aphid**, *Euthoracaphis umbellulariae.* Grayish insects, $\frac{1}{16}$ inch long, resembling immature whiteflies or scales on undersides of leaves.	Ignore, even heavy populations apparently do not harm tree. Hose forcefully with water. Tolerate or apply soap or oil. *See 108.*
Sticky honeydew and blackish sooty mold on leaves or twigs. Plants may decline.	**Black scale.** Brown to black, bulbous to flattened insects, $\leq\frac{3}{16}$ inch long. Raised H-shape often on back.	*See 136.*
Sticky honeydew and blackish sooty mold on plant. Bulbous, irregular, brown, gray, or white bodies (scales) on twigs.	**Wax scales.** Bulbous to hemispherical, waxy insects, suck sap.	*See 141.*
Brownish, grayish, tan, or white encrustations on twigs. Rarely, twig or branch dieback.	**Greedy scale, Oleander scale.** Oval to circular insects, $\leq\frac{1}{16}$ inch long. Rarely if ever cause serious damage to plants.	*See 133, 134.*
Dieback of occasional twigs.	**Branch and twig borers**, including **Lead-cable borer**, *Scobicia declivis* (family Bostrichidae); *Melalgus* (=*Polycaon*) *confertus* (family Cerambycidae). Adults $\frac{1}{4}$ to $\frac{1}{2}$ inch long, tunnel in twigs.	Keep plants vigorous, provide proper cultural care. Prune out affected parts. Eliminate nearby dead hardwood where beetles breed. *See Longhorned Borers, 183.*

CAESALPINIA (*Caesalpinia, Poinciana* spp.), Bird of paradise bush, Dwarf poinciana, Barbados pride

WHAT THE PROBLEM LOOKS LIKE	PROBABLE CAUSE	COMMENTS
Foliage discolors and wilts. Branches develop cankers and die back. Seashell-shaped fruiting bodies may develop on injured tissue.	**Sapwood rot**, *Schizophyllum commune.* A decay fungus that aggressively invades injured tissue and unhealthy plants.	Protect plants from injuries and stress. Provide good growing conditions and appropriate cultural care. *See 248.*

CALIFORNIA BUCKEYE (*Aesculus californica*), Horse chestnut

WHAT THE PROBLEM LOOKS LIKE	PROBABLE CAUSE	COMMENTS
Leaves yellow and brown. Dead leaves may hang on tree.	**Blight.** Normal dormancy, leaves die during summer or sooner under drought conditions.	Early leaf drop is normal drought adaptation. No control.
Leaves and leaf petioles with brown, light green, or yellow lesions or dead spots.	**Sudden oak death**, *Phytophthora ramorum.* Pathogen spreads via air and contaminated soil. Apparently can infect through leaves.	Primarily a problem in wildlands, killing many oaks there. Do not move infected plant material. Report to agricultural officials if found outside areas where pathogen is known to occur. *See 260.*
Leaves with pale blisters, spots, or felty masses of pale spores.	**Yellow leaf blister**, *Taphrina aesculi.* Fungus favored by wet conditions during spring.	Rarely serious enough to threaten tree health or warrant control effort.

CALIFORNIA BUCKEYE *(Aesculus californica)*, Horse chestnut, continued

WHAT THE PROBLEM LOOKS LIKE	PROBABLE CAUSE	COMMENTS
Powdery white growth on leaves, tiny, black, overwintering bodies may develop later.	**Powdery mildew,** *Phyllactinia guttata.* Fungal disease favored by moderate temperatures, shade, and poor air circulation.	Generally not severe enough to warrant control. *See 236.*
Chewed leaves. Foliage may be rolled and tied together with silk.	**Omnivorous looper.** Yellow, green, or pink larvae, ≤1½ inches long, with green, yellow, or black stripes.	Larvae crawl in "looping" manner. *See 79.*

CAMELLIA *(Camellia spp.)*

WHAT THE PROBLEM LOOKS LIKE	PROBABLE CAUSE	COMMENTS
Leaves discolor, wilt, stunt, and may drop prematurely. Discolored bark or cankers may ooze sap. Branches or plants may die.	**Root and Crown rots,** *Phytophthora* spp., *Pythium* sp. Pathogens favored by excess soil moisture and poor drainage.	*See 265.*
Leaves turn brown or yellow, especially along margins and at tip. Leaves may drop prematurely.	**Leaf burn** or **Scorch.** Abiotic disorders. Causes include boron toxicity, excess light, frost, overfertilization, poor soil conditions, saline irrigation water or soil, or too much or too little water.	Provide plants with a good growing environment and proper cultural care.
New leaves and shoots chlorotic, except for green veins. Plants may be stunted.	**Iron deficiency.** Abiotic disorder usually caused by poor soil conditions or unhealthy roots.	*See 278.*
New leaves light green to yellow, especially at sunny sites.	**Light damage.** Noninfectious disorder caused by high-intensity light.	Plant overstory species or otherwise provide partial shade. *See 289.*
Leaves with irregular, yellow mottling. Blossoms mottled whitish.	**Variegation** or **Viruses,** including **Camellia yellow mottle virus.** Introduced during plant propagation, not spread by insects.	Generally harmless to plants and often considered attractive. Infected plants cannot be "cured." *See 269.*
Leaf underside has pimplelike blisters or water-soaked spots. Leaves brown, harden, appear corky, especially on underside. Foliage yellows and drop prematurely.	**Edema** or **Oedema.** Abiotic disorder. Leaves accumulate excess water when soil is warm and moist and air is cool and moist. Exact cause unknown.	Irrigate only in morning. Avoid irrigation if cool and cloudy. Provide good air circulation. Keep humidity low. Provide good drainage. *See 290.*
Leaves or shoots cupped, distorted, or swollen, and whitish or reddish. Galled tissue may develop discolored blotches.	**Leaf gall,** *Exobasidium camelliae.* Fungus infects and spreads when plant is wet.	Avoid overhead watering. Prune only when dry. Improve air circulation. Vigorous plants tolerate extensive leaf galling. Hand-pick or prune out galls. Rake and dispose of fallen leaves.
Flower bud edges turn brown, then entire bud browns and drops. Petals turn brown or drop prematurely.	**Camellia bud mite,** *Cosetacus* (=*Aceria*) *camelliae.* Translucent to white eriophyids, ≤¹⁄₁₀₀ inch long, that infest inner surface of bud scales or petals.	*See Gall Mites, 203.*
Buds drop prematurely.	**Premature bud drop.** Abiotic disorder caused by poor cultural practices.	Provide appropriate irrigation and good drainage. Current spring's bud drop is caused by inadequate cultural care the previous summer and fall when buds were developing.
Blossoms rot. Brown lesions develop on petals, centers discolor first. Blossoms drop prematurely.	**Camellia petal blight,** *Cibornia camelliae.* Fungal disease promoted by rainy weather.	Apply 4 inches of organic mulch beneath plants to reduce spore survival. Pick and dispose of all blighted blossoms. Avoid overhead irrigation. *See 244.*
Sticky honeydew and blackish sooty mold on foliage. Leaves may be cupped, curled, or twisted.	**Aphids,** including **Black citrus aphid,** *Toxoptera aurantii;* **Green peach aphid;** **Melon aphid.** Brown, black, or green insects in groups on growing points.	Conserve natural enemies that provide control. Hose forcefully with water. Tolerate or apply soap or oil if severe. *See 103.*

WHAT THE PROBLEM LOOKS LIKE	PROBABLE CAUSE	COMMENTS
CAMELLIA (*Camellia* spp.), continued		
Sticky honeydew or cottony material on plant and blackish sooty mold on foliage. Twigs or branches may decline or die back.	**Black scale, Brown soft scale, Green shield scale.** Small brown, green, yellowish, or blackish insects, flattened or bulbous.	*See 136–139.*
Sticky honeydew, blackish sooty mold, and cottony waxy material on plant.	**Mealybugs**, including **Longtailed mealybug, Obscure mealybug.** Grayish, waxy, slow-moving insects.	*See 126.*
Sticky honeydew and blackish sooty mold on plant. Plant has elongate, slender, cottony material (egg sacs).	**Cottony camellia scale**, *Pulvinaria floccifera.* Oval, flattened, yellow or brown insects and cottony eggs.	*See similar Cottony Cushion Scale, 142.*
Sticky honeydew and blackish sooty mold on plant. Leaves yellow and wither. Tiny, whitish, mothlike adult insects.	**Whiteflies**, including **Greenhouse whitefly.** Oval, flattened, yellow to greenish nymphs and pupae with waxy filaments.	*See 121.*
Copious, misty, nonsticky liquid raining from plant. Surfaces covered with whitish residue.	**Glassy-winged sharpshooter.** Active, dark brown or gray leafhoppers ≤½ inch long, suck xylem fluid.	Vectors pathogens. Report to agricultural officials if found where this pest is not known to occur. *See 148.*
Brownish, grayish, tan, or white encrustations on bark. Plants may grow slowly, stunt or die back.	**Greedy scale, Oleander scale, Oystershell scale.** Individuals oval to elongate, ≤¹⁄₁₆ inch long.	*See 133–135.*
Chewed leaves and blossoms. Plants may decline or grow slowly.	**Black vine weevil, Fuller rose beetle.** Adults black, pale brown, or gray, ⅜-inch-long beetles with a snout.	*See 92.*
Foliage may yellow, wilt, die back, or drop prematurely. Plant grows slowly.	**Spiral nematode, Stunt nematode.** Tiny root-feeding roundworms.	*See 347.*
CAMPHOR TREE (*Cinnamomum camphora*)		
Foliage fades, yellows, browns, or wilts, often scattered throughout canopy. Branches die. Entire plant may die.	**Verticillium wilt.** A soil-dwelling fungus that infects through roots.	*See 232.*
Sticky honeydew and blackish sooty mold on plant.	**California laurel aphid**, *Euthoracaphis umbellulariae.* Gray insects resemble immature whiteflies on leaves.	Ignore; even heavy populations do not harm tree. Hose forcefully with water. Tolerate or apply soap or oil. *See 108.*
CANEBERRIES (*Rubus* spp.), Blackberry, Raspberry, Thimbleberry[6]*		
Foliage fades, yellows, browns, or wilts, often scattered throughout canopy. Fruiting canes may darken. Symptoms sometimes appear first on only one side of the plant. Canes die. Entire plant may die.	**Verticillium wilt.** A soil-dwelling fungus that infects through roots.	*See 232.*
Foliage discolors and wilts. Canes wilt and die back. Entire plant may die. Minute white fungus growths may be visible in canes or on soil.	**Armillaria root rot.** Present in many soils. Favored by warm, wet soil. Persists for years in infected roots.	*See 262.*
Leaves with brown, light green, or yellow spots or dead blotches.	**Sudden oak death**, *Phytophthora ramorum.* Pathogen spreads via air and contaminated soil. Apparently can infect through bark or leaves.	Infects at least *Rubus spectabilis.* Primarily a problem in wildlands, killing many oaks there. Do not move infected plant material. Report to agricultural officials if found outside areas where pathogen is known to occur. *See 260.*
Flowers or fruit covered with powdery growth or whitish strands or develop watery decay.	**Botrytis blight.** A fungal disease that thrives under moist conditions and cool to moderate temperatures.	*See 242.*

6. For more information on pest identification and biology, see publications such as *Caneberries Pest Management Guidelines* (Gubler et al. 2002) and *Wild Blackberries Pest Notes* (DiTomaso 2002).

*Some species are invasive weeds. Other species may be better choices when planting.

CANEBERRIES (*Rubus* spp.), Blackberry, Raspberry, Thimbleberry, continued

WHAT THE PROBLEM LOOKS LIKE	PROBABLE CAUSE	COMMENTS
Purplish, red, or yellow blotches on leaves. Leaf undersides covered with downy fungal growth. Leaves may die and drop prematurely.	**Downy mildew,** *Peronospora sparsa.* Spores produced only on living plants. Resistant spores carry fungus over unfavorable periods. Favored by moist, humid conditions.	Prune plants to improve air circulation. Reduce humidity around plants, such as through drip or low-volume irrigation. Avoid overhead watering. *See 239.*
Powdery white growth on underside and yellow blotches on upperside of leaves. Terminals and fruit may be covered with whitish growth. Shoots and leaves may be undersized or distorted.	**Powdery mildew,** *Sphaerotheca macularis.* Fungal disease favored by moderate temperatures, shade, and poor air circulation.	Thin canes and otherwise improve air circulation. Remove late-forming, infected suckers. Plant resistant caneberry varieties. *See 236.*
Orange or yellow pustules on canes or leaves. Foliage discolors and may drop prematurely.	**Rusts,** including *Arthuriomyces peckianus, Gymnoconia nitens,* and *Phragmidium rubi-idaei.* Fungal diseases favored by wet conditions.	Remove and dispose of infected canes and leaves. Avoid overhead irrigation. Provide good air circulation. *See 240.*
Blackish sooty mold, sticky honeydew, and whitish cast skins on plant.	**Aphids.** Small green, brown, black, or yellowish insects on leaves or fruit, especially under calyx.	*See 103.*
Copious, misty, nonsticky liquid raining from plant. Surfaces covered with whitish residue.	**Glassy-winged sharpshooter.** Active, dark brown or gray leafhoppers ≤½ inch long, suck xylem fluid.	Vectors pathogens of oleander and certain crops, especially grapes. Report suspected glassy-winged sharpshooters to agricultural officials if found in areas where this pest is not known to occur. *See 148.*
Leaves bleached. May be dark excrement specks on fruit.	**Leafhoppers,** including **White apple leafhopper,** *Typhlocyba pomaria;* **Rose leafhopper,** *Edwardsiana rosae.* Pale green, yellow, or white, wedgelike insects ≤⅙ inch long.	Leafhoppers do not feed on fruit and do not seriously threaten plant health. *See 148.*
Tips of canes wilt in the spring and die back in summer. Spiral girdling (by larvae) in canes.	**Raspberry horntail,** *Hartigia cressoni.* Segmented white larvae ≤1 inch long. Adult sawflies black or black and yellow, ½ inch long, wasplike.	In California, mostly in interior valleys. *See 196.*
Wilting or dead plants. Some roots stripped of bark or girdled near soil. Foliage may be notched or clipped.	**Black vine weevil, Cribrate weevil, Fuller rose beetle, Woods weevil.** Adults are black, brown, or gray snout beetles, ≤½ inch long. Larvae are white grubs with brown head.	Leaf chewing does not harm plants. Larvae of some species feeding on roots can seriously damage plants. *See 92.*
Grayish encrustations on bark. Rarely, dead or declining branches.	**Latania scale.** Individuals circular, <1/16 inch long, usually in groups.	*See 133.*

CAPE CHESTNUT (*Calodendrum capense*)

No serious invertebrate or pathogen pests have been reported in California. If plants are unhealthy, investigate whether they have been injured or lack good growing conditions or appropriate cultural care.

CAPE HONEYSUCKLE (*Tecomaria capensis*)

WHAT THE PROBLEM LOOKS LIKE	PROBABLE CAUSE	COMMENTS
Foliage or flowers curl, turn brown or black, may die.	**Leaf burn** or **Scorch.** Abiotic disorders with many potential causes, including freeze or cold damage.	*See 273.*

CAROB (*Ceratonia siliqua*)

WHAT THE PROBLEM LOOKS LIKE	PROBABLE CAUSE	COMMENTS
Brownish, grayish, tan, or white encrustations on twigs or foliage.	**Oleander scale.** Tiny, oval, immobile, tan to yellow insects.	Rarely if ever causes serious damage to plants. *See 134.*

CASSIA (*Cassia* spp.), Gold medallion tree, Senna

WHAT THE PROBLEM LOOKS LIKE	PROBABLE CAUSE	COMMENTS
Stippled or bleached leaves, varnishlike excrement specks on undersides.	**Thrips.** Tiny, slender, blackish or yellowish insects.	*See 156.*

CATALPA (*Catalpa* spp.)

WHAT THE PROBLEM LOOKS LIKE	PROBABLE CAUSE	COMMENTS
Sticky honeydew, blackish sooty mold, and whitish cast skins on foliage.	**Melon aphid.** Small, greenish, blackish, or yellowish insects in groups.	*See 104.*
Sticky honeydew and blackish sooty mold on foliage. Cottony or waxy material on plant.	**Grape mealybug,** *Pseudococcus maritimus.* Powdery, grayish insects ≤¼ inch long with waxy filaments.	Vigorous plants tolerate moderate populations. Conserve natural enemies that help in control. *See 126.*
Foliage fades, yellows, browns, or wilts, often scattered throughout canopy. Branches die. Entire plant may die.	**Verticillium wilt.** A soil-dwelling fungus that infects through roots.	*See 232.*
Galls or swellings on roots.	**Root knot nematode,** *Meloidogyne* sp. Tiny root-feeding roundworms.	*See 345.*

CEANOTHUS (*Ceanothus* spp.), Wild lilac

WHAT THE PROBLEM LOOKS LIKE	PROBABLE CAUSE	COMMENTS
Leaves discolor, stunt, wilt, or drop prematurely. Stems discolor, canker, and die. Minute white fungus growths may be visible beneath bark or on soil.	**Armillaria root rot.** Present in many soils. Favored by warm, wet soil. Persists for years in infected roots.	*See 262.*
Leaves discolor, stunt, wilt, or drop prematurely. Plants grow slowly and may die. Roots dark, decayed.	**Root and crown rots,** *Phytophthora* spp. Pathogens promoted by excess soil moisture and poor drainage.	*See 265.*
Leaves wilted, discolored, may drop prematurely. Branches or entire plant may die. May be white fungal growth or dark crust on basal trunk, roots, or soil.	**Dematophora root rot.** Fungus favored by mild, wet conditions. Infects primarily through roots growing near infested plants.	Less common than Armillaria or Phytophthora. *See 264.*
Leaves turn red, brown, then fade. May be cankers or oozing sap on bark.	**Cankers** including **Botryosphaeria canker and dieback, Cytospora canker.** Fungal diseases that primarily attack injured or stressed plants.	*See 250.*
Leaves or shoots turn reddish, then yellow, brown, and drop prematurely. Powdery growth on tissue. Shoots or leaves may be stunted and distorted.	**Powdery mildews,** including *Erysiphe polygoni, Microsphaera penicillata.* Fungi develop on living tissue, are favored by moderate temperatures, shade, and poor air circulation.	*See 236.*
Leaves with brown to yellow spots or blotches. Spots may have dark or yellowish margins. Foliage may shrivel and drop prematurely.	**Leaf spots,** including *Cercospora ceanothi, C. macclatchieana, Phloeosporella ceanothi, Phyllosticta* sp. Spread by air or splashing water. Favored by prolonged cool, wet conditions.	*See 223.*
Leaves turn brown or yellow, especially along margins and at tip. Leaves may drop prematurely.	**Leaf burn** or **Scorch.** Abiotic disorders with many causes. Too much water after establishment or poor drainage are most common causes.	Provide plants with a good growing environment and proper cultural care. *See 273.*
Leaves may discolor and drop prematurely. Trunk or limbs with roughened, wet, or oozing area. Cracked bark and dieback.	**Flatheaded borers.** Larvae under bark, whitish with enlarged head. Adults are bullet-shaped, metallic, coppery, gray, greenish, or bluish.	*See 179.*
Spindle-shaped swellings (galls) on green stems. Reduced flowering.	**Ceanothus stem gall moth.** Gray larvae, ≤¼ inch long, inside gall.	*See 165.*
Stippled or bleached leaves with dark specks of excrement on undersides.	**Ceanothus tingid,** *Corythucha obliqua.* Adults brown, ³⁄₁₆ inch long, wings lacelike. Nymphs smaller, flattened.	*See Lace Bugs, 154.*
Brownish, gray, tan, or white encrustations on bark. Rarely, dieback of twigs or branches.	**Greedy scale, Oystershell scale.** Tiny, flattened, round or elongate insects.	*See 133, 135.*

CEANOTHUS (*Ceanothus* spp.), Wild lilac, continued

WHAT THE PROBLEM LOOKS LIKE	PROBABLE CAUSE	COMMENTS
Sticky honeydew, blackish sooty mold, and whitish cast skins on foliage. Reduced shoot growth.	**Ceanothus aphid**, *Aphis ceanothi*. Small black to reddish brown insects.	Vigorous plants tolerate. Conserve beneficials. Tolerate or apply soap or oil. *See Aphids, 103.*
Sticky honeydew, blackish sooty mold, and waxy, cottony material on plant.	**Mealybugs.** Powdery, elongate to oval insects, ≤⅛ inch long.	*See 126.*
Cottony spots ≤¼ inch long on underside of leaves.	**Psyllid**, *Euphalerus vermiculosus*. Small greenish nymphs beneath cottony material. Suck sap.	Apparently do not damage plants. *See 114.*
Leaves chewed, drop prematurely. May be silken webbing on plants.	**Tent caterpillars.** Hairy, colorful larvae ≤2 inches long.	*See 80.*

CEDAR (*Cedrus* spp.), Atlas cedar, Deodar cedar; **INCENSE CEDAR** (*Calocedrus decurrens*)

WHAT THE PROBLEM LOOKS LIKE	PROBABLE CAUSE	COMMENTS
Stunted, bushy branches. Orangish, gelatinous masses or galls on bark. Stems may die back.	**Gymnosporangium rusts.** Fungi that infect and thrive under wet conditions.	*See 242.*
Foliage pinkish tan, then browns, dies, and drops prematurely. Shoots die back.	**Needle blights**, including *Kabatina sp.*, *Sirococcus conigenus*. Fungi spread by splashing water, favored by cool, wet springs.	Prune out and destroy infected tissue during dry weather. Rake and dispose of plant debris in and beneath limbs.
Foliage discolors, wilts, stunts, may drop prematurely. Discolored bark or cankers may ooze sap. Branches or plant may die.	**Root and crown rots.** Decay fungi favored by excess soil moisture and poor drainage.	*See 262.*
Branches, treetop dying. Some branches reddish, pitchy or grayish, bare. Wood cankered.	**Botryosphaeria canker and dieback**, **Phomopsis canker.** Fungi primarily affect injured and drought-stressed trees.	Provide proper irrigation. *See 255.*
White, waxy threads on bark. Foliage may redden, yellow, and eventually die. Treetop or entire tree may die.	**Cypress bark mealybug** or **Cypress bark scale**; **Incense cedar scale** or **Monterey cypress scale**, *Xylococculus macrocarpae* (family Margarodidae). Tiny, immobile, reddish, waxy insects on bark beneath wax.	Primarily pests on Monterey cypress and incense cedar. Only heavily infested young trees may be harmed. Apply oil to bark if necessary. *See 127.*
Sticky honeydew and blackish sooty mold on plant.	**Giant conifer aphids**, *Cinara* spp. Small, black, long-legged insects.	Often infest only a single branch. More common in California in south than in north. *See 105.*
Brownish, gray, or tan encrustations on bark or foliage.	**Latania scale.** Tiny, circular, flattened insects on stems or leaves.	*See 133.*

CHASTE TREE (*Vitex agnus-castus*)

WHAT THE PROBLEM LOOKS LIKE	PROBABLE CAUSE	COMMENTS
Leaves discolor, stunt, wilt, or drop prematurely. Plants grow slowly and may die. Roots dark, decayed.	**Root and crown rots**, *Phytophthora* spp. Pathogens promoted by excess soil moisture and poor drainage.	*See 265.*
Leaves turn brown or yellow, especially along margins and at tip. Leaves may drop prematurely.	**Leaf burn** or **Scorch.** Abiotic disorders with many causes, including excess salinity, frost, poor drainage, and too much or too little water.	Provide plants with a good growing environment and proper cultural care. *See 273.*
Twigs distorted, swollen, and pitted. Leaves dwarfed. Shoots may die back.	**Pit-making pittosporum scale**, *Planchonia* (=*Asterolecanium*) *arabidis* (family Asterolecaniidae). Brown to white insects, ≤⅛ inch long, on twigs, often in pits.	In California, an occasional problem in the north. Management not investigated. *See Other Common Scales, 142.*
Brownish, grayish, tan, or white encrustations on twigs.	**Oleander scale.** Tiny, flattened, circular insects, ≤1/16 inch long.	Rarely if ever causes serious damage to plants. *See 134.*
Sticky honeydew, blackish sooty mold, and whitish cast skins on plant.	**Aphids.** Small pear-shaped insects, commonly black, brown, green, or yellowish, often in groups.	*See 103.*

CHERRY (*Prunus* spp.)[7]

WHAT THE PROBLEM LOOKS LIKE	PROBABLE CAUSE	COMMENTS
Leaves discolor, stunt, wilt, or drop prematurely. Stems discolored, cankered, and die. Minute white fungus growths may be visible beneath bark or on soil.	**Armillaria root rot.** Present in many soils. Favored by warm, wet soil. Persists for years in infected roots.	*See 262.*
Leaves discolor, stunt, wilt, or drop prematurely. Plants grow slowly and may die. Roots dark, decayed.	**Root and crown rot,** *Phytophthora* spp. Pathogens promoted by excess soil moisture and poor drainage.	*See 265.*
Leaves discolor, stunt, wilt, or drop prematurely, often on one side of plant. Stem xylem discolored. Stems or entire plant may die.	**Verticillium wilt,** *Verticillium* spp. Persist in soil, infect through roots.	*See 232.*
Leaves yellow and wilt. Dead leaves may remain on tree through winter. Branches canker and die back. Wood discolors.	**Eutypa dieback,** *Eutypa lata.* Fungus infects through wounds, persists in infected tissue. Spreads during wet conditions.	In California most serious along coast. Avoid wounding plants, except to prune off infected tissue during July and August, making cuts in healthy tissue. Provide a good growing environment and appropriate cultural care.
Stems, flowers, or fruit with dark lesions. Cankers possible on branches.	**Bacterial blight and canker.** Disease favored by wet conditions.	*See 245.*
Reddened, distorted foliage in spring. Shoots thickened, distorted, may die. Leaves may drop prematurely.	**Leaf curl** or **Plum pockets,** *Taphrina* spp. Fungal diseases promoted by moist spring weather or splashing irrigation water.	Apply calcium polysulfides (lime sulfur) or fungicide with at least 50% copper or synthetic fungicide in fall after leaf drop, repeat when buds swell.
Circular brown decay develops on fruit. Blossoms and twigs may turn brown and die.	**Brown rot,** *Monilinia fructicola, M. laxa.* Windborne fungal pathogens that infect wet tissue.	Avoid wounding fruit and trees. Remove any infected fruit ("mummies") left on trees.
Powdery white growth and yellow blotches on leaves and sometimes on terminals and fruit. Shoots and leaves may be undersized or distorted.	**Powdery mildews,** *Podosphaera* spp., *Sphaerotheca pannosa.* Fungal diseases favored by moderate temperatures, shade, and poor air circulation.	*See 236.*
Sticky honeydew, blackish sooty mold, and whitish cast skins on plant.	**Aphids.** Small green, black, brown, or yellowish, pear-shaped insects, often in groups.	*See 103.*
Leaves chewed. Single branches or entire plant may be defoliated. Foliage may be rolled and tied together with silk.	**Fruittree leafroller, Omnivorous looper, Redhumped caterpillar, Tent caterpillars, Tussock moths.** Moth larvae ≤1½ inches long.	*See 71.*
Galls or swellings on roots. Plants may grow slowly.	**Root knot nematodes.** Tiny root-feeding roundworms.	*See 345.*
Galls or swellings on trunk or roots, usually near soil.	**Crown gall.** Bacterium that infects plant via wounds.	*See 258.*
Dead twigs or branches. Plant declines, may die. Tiny "BB shot"-sized holes in bark.	**Shothole borer.** Small brown bark beetles and whitish larvae tunnel beneath bark.	*See 176.*
Roughened bark. Reddish brown granular material (frass) at base of trunk and main limbs. May be dark ooze from bark.	**American plum borer; Peachtree borer; Prune limb borer,** *Bondia comonana* (family Gelechiidae). Brown to pink larvae that bore under bark.	Prevent injuries to bark. Provide proper cultural care. *See 187, 193.*

7. For more information on pest identification and biology, see publications such as *Cherry Pest Management Guidelines* (Teviotdale et al. 2002) and *Integrated Pest Management for Stone Fruits* (Strand 1999).

WHAT THE PROBLEM LOOKS LIKE	PROBABLE CAUSE	COMMENTS
CHESTNUT (*Castanea* spp.)		
Leaves discolored, wilted, stunted, may drop prematurely. Discolored bark may ooze sap. Branches or plant may die.	**Root and crown rots.** Decay fungi favored by excess irrigation and poor drainage.	*See 262.*
Leaves turn yellow or brown on scattered branches, which die. Foliage drops prematurely. Orange cankers develop on limbs and the trunk. Bark splits. Trunk becomes girdled and the tree dies.	**Chestnut blight,** *Cryphonectria* (=*Endothia*) *parasitica.* An introduced fungus that infects through bark wounds and has killed many thousands of chestnuts.	Primarily affects American chestnut (*C. dentata*) and European chestnut (*C. sativa*) in the eastern U.S. Apparently eradicated from the western U.S. In the West, promptly report suspected infections to agricultural officials.
Leaves turn yellow or brown on scattered branches. Foliage dies and may drop prematurely. Cankers or lesions may develop on limbs and possibly on the trunk.	**Cankers, Stem blight,** including *Amphiporthe castanea;* **Botryosphaeria canker and dieback;** *Coryneum* sp. Fungal diseases most often affecting injured or stressed trees.	Protect trees from injury and provide good cultural care, especially appropriate irrigation. *See 250.*
Chewed leaves. Foliage may be rolled and tied together with silk.	**Omnivorous looper.** Yellow, green, or pink larvae, ≤1½ inches long, with green, yellow or black stripes.	*See 79.*
Sticky honeydew and blackish sooty mold on foliage. Tiny mothlike adults.	**Crown whitefly.** Black, oval nymphs with spreading, whitish, waxy plates.	*See 122.*
Holes in nuts. Tunnels inside nuts may contain whitish larvae.	**Acorn moth, Filbertworm.** Adults are tiny bronze, coppery, or reddish brown moths.	May reduce natural tree regeneration, but established trees are not damaged. *See Filbert Weevils and Acorn Worms, 93.*
CHILOPSIS (*Chilopsis linearis*), Desert catalpa, Desert willow		
Sticky honeydew, blackish sooty mold, and whitish cast skins on foliage.	**Aphids.** Small, pear-shaped insects, usually in groups.	*See 103.*
Foliage fades, yellows, browns, or wilts, often scattered throughout canopy or first on one side of the plant. Branches die. Entire plant may die.	**Verticillium wilt.** A soil-dwelling fungus that infects through roots.	*See 232.*
CHINABERRY (*Melia azedarach*), Texas umbrella tree		
Brownish, grayish, tan, or white encrustations on bark. Possibly decline or dieback of woody parts.	**Greedy scale.** Insects are circular to flattened, <1/16 inch long.	*See 133.*
CHINESE PISTACHE (*Pistacia chinesis*), Pistache [8]		
Leaves discolor, stunt, wilt, or drop prematurely. Plants grow slowly and may die. Roots dark, decayed.	**Root and crown rots,** *Phytophthora* spp. Pathogens promoted by excess soil moisture and poor drainage.	*See 265.*
Leaves discolor and wilt. Branches die back. Entire tree may die. Minute white fungus growths may be visible in wood or on soil.	**Armillaria root rot.** Fungus present in many soils. Favored by warm, wet soil. Persists for years in infected roots.	*See 262.*
Leaves brown, fade, yellow, or wilt, often scattered throughout canopy. Foliage may appear sparse, undersized. Plants may grow slowly. Branches die. Entire plant may die.	**Verticillium wilt,** *Verticillium albo-atrum, V. dahliae.* Soil-dwelling fungi that infect through roots.	*See 232.*
Leaves have black, brown, or yellow blotches. Leaves appear scorched and may drop prematurely.	**Alternaria leaf spot** or **Alternaria blight,** *Alternaria* spp. Spores spread by splashing water. Disease favored by wet conditions.	Mostly a problem on pistachio nut (*Pistacia vera*). Drip or subirrigation instead of sprinkling may reduce disease development. *See Leaf Spots, 223.*

8. For more information on pest identification and biology, see publications such as *Pistachio Pest Management Guidelines* (Teviotdale et al. 2002).

CHINESE PISTACHE (*Pistacia chinesis*), Pistache, continued

WHAT THE PROBLEM LOOKS LIKE	PROBABLE CAUSE	COMMENTS
Leaves turn yellow or reddish and drop prematurely.	**Natural senescence.** Leaves often naturally drop sooner than on other species.	Providing trees with a good growing environment and appropriate cultural care may delay leaf drop.
Leaves, buds, or shoots blacken or brown and die. Branches or twigs may develop cankers or die.	**Botryosphaeria canker and dieback.** Pathogen persists in twigs and dead tissue and is favored by wet conditions.	*See 255.*
Leaves and blossoms brown, dry, shrivel, wilt, and die. Dead shoots may remain on plant. May be woolly gray growth (spores) on dead tissue.	**Gray mold,** *Botryotinia fuckeliana, Botrytis cinerea.* Fungi favored by wet conditions and moderate temperatures.	Mostly a problem on pistachio nut (*Pistacia vera*). *See 242.*
Leaves and shoots brown, yellow, and may die. Foliage may be distorted, undersized, or be covered with powdery white.	**Powdery mildew,** *Oidium* sp. Fungal disease favored by moderate temperatures, shade, and poor air circulation.	*See 236.*
Leaves chewed. Foliage webbed with silk.	**Obliquebanded leafroller,** *Choristoneura* (=*Archips*) *rosaceana.* Greenish yellow larvae ≤1½ inches long. Adults are a small orangish moth with brown and white.	*See Foliage-Feeding Caterpillars, 71.*
Leaves chewed, may be tied with silk. Plant may be defoliated.	**Western tussock moth.** Dark, hairy larvae, ≤2 inches long, with red and yellow spots. Adults are grayish moth with black and white.	*See 77.*
Sticky honeydew and blackish sooty mold on foliage. Possible decline or dieback of twigs and branches.	**Black scale, Brown soft scale, European fruit lecanium, Frosted scale.** Black, brown, orange, yellow, or waxy whitish, flattened or bulbous insects.	*See 136–139.*
Sticky honeydew, blackish sooty mold, and whitish cast skins on foliage.	**Aphids.** Small insects, usually in groups, often pale yellowish, waxy, or white.	*See 103.*

CHINESE TALLOW TREE (*Sapium* spp.), Japanese tallow tree*

WHAT THE PROBLEM LOOKS LIKE	PROBABLE CAUSE	COMMENTS
Leaves discolor and wilt. Branches die back. Entire tree may die. Minute white fungus growths may be visible beneath bark or on soil.	**Armillaria root rot.** Present in many soils. Favored by warm, wet soil. Persists for years in infected roots.	*See 262.*
Twig terminals die back in fall. Foliage curls, turns brown or black, and dies.	**Leaf burn** or **Scorch.** Abiotic disorders with many potential causes, including freeze or cold damage.	Avoid excess fertilization, irrigation, and pruning that stimulate excess growth, especially in fall. Provide plants with a good growing environment and proper cultural care. *See 273.*

CHOISYA (*Chosiya ternata*), Mexican orange, Mock orange

WHAT THE PROBLEM LOOKS LIKE	PROBABLE CAUSE	COMMENTS
Sticky honeydew and blackish sooty mold on leaves and twigs. Plant may grow slowly.	**Black scale.** Brownish, orangish, or yellow, flattened (immature) or blackish, bulbous (adults) insects.	*See 136.*
Stippled, flecked, or bleached leaves. Leaves may drop prematurely.	**Mites,** including **Citrus red mite.** Tiny sand-sized specks on leaves, often reddish. Suck sap.	*See Red Mites, 197.*

CISTUS (*Cistus* spp.), Rock rose

WHAT THE PROBLEM LOOKS LIKE	PROBABLE CAUSE	COMMENTS
Sticky honeydew, blackish sooty mold, and whitish cast skins on foliage.	**Aphids.** Small insects, usually in groups, often black.	*See 103.*

*Some species are invasive weeds. Other species may be better choices when planting.

WHAT THE PROBLEM LOOKS LIKE	PROBABLE CAUSE	COMMENTS

CITRUS (*Citrus* spp.), Lemon, Lime, Grapefruit, Orange, Tangerine[9]

WHAT THE PROBLEM LOOKS LIKE	PROBABLE CAUSE	COMMENTS
Leaves discolor, stunt, wilt, or drop prematurely. Plant grows slowly. Shoots may die back. Minute white fungus growths may be visible beneath bark or on soil.	**Armillaria root rot.** Present in many soils. Favored by warm, wet soil. Persists for years in infected roots.	*See 262.*
Foliage discolors, wilts, stunts, may drop prematurely. Discolored bark or cankers may ooze sap. Plant slowly declines. Branches or plant may die.	**Root and crown rots,** *Phytophthora citrophthora, P. parasitica.* Decay fungi favored by excess soil moisture and poor drainage.	Symptoms are often difficult to distinguish from nematode, salt, or flooding damage; laboratory analysis may be required to diagnose damage cause. *See 265.*
Bark cracks and oozes discolored sap. Bark eventually dries and sloughs off. Foliage discolors and wilts as trunk becomes girdled. Tree may die.	**Phytophthora gumosis,** *Phytophthora* spp. Decay fungi infect through wounds on trunk during moist conditions.	*Manage as discussed in Root and Crown Rots, 265.*
Blossoms, leaves, and terminals turn brown, wilt, and die. Dark lesions or blotches at base of leaves or on fruit. Cankers or lesions may occur on twigs. Shoots may die back.	**Bacterial blight and canker** or **Bacterial blast.** Disease favored by wet conditions.	On citrus in California, primarily a problem in the Sacramento Valley after cool, wet winter or spring. *See 245.*
Fruit develop water-soaked spots, which turn soft, tan to olive brown, and develop a pungent odor. Blossoms, leaves, or twigs may turn brown and die.	**Citrus brown rots,** *Phytophthora* spp. Fungi develop on lower fruit and infect from rain-splashed spores on the soil.	Prune lower branches at least 2 feet up off the ground. If previously severe, apply copper spray during October or November and possibly again January or February to foliage within 4 feet of the ground.
Fruit, leaves, or twigs develop small brown, reddish, or tan spots.	**Septoria leaf spot,** *Septoria* spp. Fungal diseases promoted and spread by wet conditions.	Keep foliage dry. If previously severe, a copper spray during late fall or early winter may prevent malady. *See 227.*
Buds, blossoms, fruit, or leaves are scabby or scared, and possibly distorted. Fruit may have blackish, brown, or silvery discolored patches.	**Citrus bud mite,** *Eriophyes* (=*Aceria*) *sheldoni;* **Citrus broad mite,** *Polyphagotarsonemus latus;* **Citrus flat mite,** *Brevipalpus lewisi;* **Citrus rust mite,** *Phyllocoptruta oleivora.* Tiny elongate eriophyid mites.	These mites do not seriously harm trees. Cosmetic injury to rinds usually does not harm the internal quality of fruit. No control is recommended in landscapes. *See Gall Mites, 203.*
Stippled, flecked, or bleached leaves. Leaves may drop prematurely. Fruit may be scabby or silvery if mites have been very numerous.	**Mites,** including **Citrus red mite, Twospotted spider mite; Yuma spider mite,** *Eotetranychus yumensis.* Tiny sand-sized specks on leaves.	Fruit damage is cosmetic. Does not harm internal quality of fruit. *See 197.*
Fruit blotchy grayish, dirty spotted, scabby, or scarred, usually where fruit touch or in a ring around the stem.	**Citrus thrips, Greenhouse thrips.** Tiny, slender, black, orangish, yellow, or whitish insects.	Fruit damage is cosmetic. Does not harm internal quality of fruit. *See 156.*
Fruit with brown to yellowish, roundish scars. Leaflets may be bleached or stippled.	**Potato leafhopper,** *Empoasca fabae.* Greenish to whitish, wedge-shaped insects, ≤⅛ inch long.	Cosmetic injury to rinds usually does not harm the internal quality of fruit. Plants tolerate moderate leaf stippling. *See Leafhoppers, 148.*
Fruit may be scabby or scarred. Leaves or shoots are chewed.	**Katydids,** including **Angularwinged katydid,** *Microcentrum retinerve;* **Forktailed bush katydid,** *Scudderia furcata.* Elongate, green, grasshopperlike insects.	Usually not serious enough to warrant control in landscapes. *See 99.*
Fruit may be scabby, scarred, or chewed. Leaves, buds, or flowers are chewed. Leaves may be tied together with silk.	**Citrus cutworm,** *Egira* (=*Xylomyges*) *curialis;* **Omnivorous looper; Orange tortrix,** *Argyrotaenia citrana;* **Fruittree leafroller; Pink scavenger caterpillar,** *Pyroderces rileyi;* **Western avocado leafroller,** *Amorbia cuneana;* **Western tussock moth.** Naked to hairy larvae, ≤1½ inch long.	Vigorous plants tolerate moderate leaf damage. Prune out infested foliage. Apply *Bacillus thuringiensis* or another insecticide when young larvae are feeding. *See 71.*

9. For more information on pest identification and biology, see publications such as *Citrus Pest Management Guidelines* (Ohr et al. 2002) and *Integrated Pest Management for Citrus* (UCIPM 1991).

WHAT THE PROBLEM LOOKS LIKE	PROBABLE CAUSE	COMMENTS
CITRUS (*Citrus* spp.), Lemon, Lime, Grapefruit, Orange, Tangerine, *continued*		
Leaves are chewed.	**Anise swallowtail** or **California orange-dog**, *Papilio zelicaon* (family Papilionidae). Larvae ≤1½ inches long, green with black and yellow bands. Adults 2 inches long, yellow with black.	Caterpillars mature into attractive butterflies. Control not recommended. Young larvae are killed by *Bacillus thuringiensis*. *See Foliage-Feeding Caterpillars, 71.*
Fruit may be chewed. Foliage or shoots chewed, ragged, or clipped. May be slimy or silvery trails on or around plants.	**Brown garden snail.** Snails move slowly on slimy, muscular foot and have a spiraled shell.	Snails may feed in citrus at night then hide on ground during the day. *See 205.*
Whitewash or chalky residue on foliage and fruit. Nonsticky liquid or mist drops from trees. Citrus is otherwise undamaged, except possibly lemon if pest populations are very high.	**Glassy-winged sharpshooters.** Active, dark brownish leafhoppers ≤½ inch long.	Vectors pathogens that damage oleander and certain crops, especially grapes. Report suspected glassy-winged sharpshooters to agricultural officials if found in areas where this pest is not known to occur. *See 148.*
Sticky honeydew and blackish sooty mold on fruit, leaves, and twigs. Whitish cast skins on undersides of leaves.	**Spirea aphid,** *Aphis citricola*; **Black citrus aphid,** *Toxoptera aurantii.* Tiny green to brownish insects in groups.	In California, mostly in coastal areas. Conserve natural enemies that help control. Tolerate or apply soap or oil if needed. *See Aphids, 103.*
Sticky honeydew and blackish sooty mold on fruit, leaves, and twigs. Plant growth may be slow. Branches may die back.	**Black scale, Brown soft scale, Citricola scale, Cottony cushion scale.** Black, brown, cottony, gray, orange, yellow, or whitish, bulbous or flattened insects.	*See 136–142.*
Sticky honeydew and blackish sooty mold on fruit, leaves, and twigs. Cottony or waxy material on plant.	**Citrus mealybug; Citrophilus mealybug,** *Pseudococcus calceolariae*; **Comstock mealybug,** *Pseudococcus comstocki*; **Long-tailed mealybug.** Powdery gray insects, ≤¼ inch long, with waxy filaments.	Conserve natural enemies that provide control. *See 126.*
Sticky honeydew and blackish sooty mold on fruit, leaves, and twigs. Tiny, whitish, mothlike insects (adult whiteflies).	**Whiteflies,** including **Ash whitefly; Bayberry whitefly,** *Parabemisia myricae*; **Citrus whitefly; Greenhouse whitefly; Woolly whitefly.** Nymphs oval, flattened, yellowish to greenish.	*See 121.*
Leaves or blossoms chewed.	**Fuller rose beetle.** Pale brown adult snout weevils, about ⅜ inch long.	Adults hide during day and feed at night. Larvae feed on roots. *See 94.*
Brownish, grayish, or orange encrustations on bark or fruit. Stunted, declining, or dead branches.	**California red scale, Purple scale, San Jose scale, Yellow scale.** Tiny circular to elongate insects.	*See 131.*
Growth slow. Fruit may be few in number and undersized. Roots may be darker or fewer than normal. Soil may cling to roots and be difficult to wash off.	**Citrus nematode; Root lesion nematode; Sheath nematode,** *Hemicycliophora arenaria.* Tiny root-feeding roundworms.	*See 341.*
CLEMATIS (*Clematis* spp.)		
Leaves chlorotic and necrotic and may be undersized.	**Alkaline soil.** Symptoms of various mineral deficiencies and toxicities develop if irrigation water or soil has high pH.	*See 283.*
Conspicuous spots or irregular dead areas form on leaves. Foliage or flowers curl and turn brown or black.	**Sunburn.** Abiotic disorder most prevalent under bright, hot, water-stressed conditions.	*See 288.*
Leaves and stems have brown to yellow spots or blotches. Spots may have dark or yellowish margins. Foliage may shrivel and drop prematurely.	**Leaf and stem spots,** *Cercospora squalidula, Ramularia clematidis.* Fungi spread by air or splashing water. Disease favored by prolonged wet conditions. Pathogens persist in plant debris.	Avoid wetting foliage. Use drip irrigation where feasible. Promptly remove and dispose of plant debris and infected leaves. *See Leaf Spots, 223.*

CLEMATIS *(Clematis* spp.), continued

WHAT THE PROBLEM LOOKS LIKE	PROBABLE CAUSE	COMMENTS
Reddish yellow pustules on lower leaf surface. Leaves discolor, spot, and may drop prematurely.	**Rusts**, *Puccinia pulsatillae, P. recondita.* Pathogens favored by wet conditions. Fungal spores persist in plant debris.	*See 240.*
Foliage or shoots turn reddish, then yellow, brown, and drop prematurely. Powdery growth on tissue. Shoots or leaves may be stunted and distorted.	**Powdery mildew**, *Erysiphe polygoni.* Fungus develops on living tissue, favored by moderate temperatures, shade, and poor air circulation.	*See 236.*
Sticky honeydew, blackish sooty mold, and whitish cast skins on foliage.	**Aphids**, including **Green peach aphid.** Groups of small insects, often green or yellowish.	*See 103.*
Sticky honeydew and blackish sooty mold on foliage. Possibly twig or branch decline or dieback.	**Brown soft scale.** Small brown, orangish, or yellowish insects, flattened or bulbous.	*See 137.*
Sticky honeydew and blackish sooty mold on foliage. Tiny, whitish, mothlike insects (adult whiteflies) on foliage.	**Whiteflies**, including **Greenhouse whitefly.** Nymphs oval, flattened, yellowish to greenish, suck sap.	*See 121.*
Chewed leaves. Foliage may be webbed. Plant may be defoliated.	**Omnivorous looper.** Yellow, green, or pink larvae, ≤1½ inches long, with green, yellow, or black stripes.	Larvae crawl in "looping" manner. *See 79.*
Brown to gray encrustations on bark. Twigs or limbs may die back.	**Oystershell scale.** Individuals about ⅟₁₆ inch long, oyster-shaped, suck sap.	*See 135.*

COAST REDWOOD *(Sequoia sempervirens),* Redwood, Sequoia

WHAT THE PROBLEM LOOKS LIKE	PROBABLE CAUSE	COMMENTS
Foliage discolors, wilts, stunts, may drop prematurely. Discolored bark may ooze sap. Branches or plant may die.	**Root and crown rots.** Decay fungi favored by excess soil moisture and poor drainage.	*See 265.*
Needles and shoots turn brown, tan, or yellow and may die. Dead, dying, and falling branchlets.	**Needle blight** or **Scorch.** Abiotic disorders. Causes include alkaline water, drought stress, dry wind, high temperatures, and salty spray onto foliage.	Some needles and branchlets are shed naturally. Provide trees with a good growing environment and appropriate cultural care.
Needles turn brown, tan, or yellow, beginning in inner, lower canopy. Affected needles and shoots drop, leaving only green terminals.	**Cercospora needle blight**, *Cercospora sequoiae.* Fungal disease favored by warm, wet conditions.	Avoid sprinkling foliage. Improve air circulation. Copper sprays can help to prevent infection on small plants.
Needles discolor and die on branch terminals. Cankers on branches. Twigs or small branches may die.	**Sudden oak death**, *Phytophthora ramorum.* Pathogen spreads via air and contaminated soil. Apparently can infect through bark or foliage.	May not be a serious pathogen of redwoods. Primarily a problem in wildlands, killing many oaks there. Do not move infected plant material. Report to agricultural officials if found outside areas where pathogen is known to occur. *See 260.*
Dead or dying branches. Cankers on trunk or limbs. Dying branches with resinous lesions.	**Botryosphaeria canker and dieback, Cytospora canker.** Fungal diseases, often affecting drought-stressed trees.	Provide good growing conditions and appropriate cultural care, especially adequate irrigation. *See 250.*
Resinous lesions or cankers on bark, branches or treetop die back.	**Redwood canker**, *Coryneum* sp. Fungal disease, usually at warm, dry sites.	Prune out and dispose of diseased branches. Irrigate adequately. *See similar Cypress Canker, 254.*
Terminals die back. Twigs may develop brown sunken cankers. May be woolly gray growth (spores) on tissue.	**Gray mold.** Fungus favored by wet conditions. Spreads by airborne spores.	*See 242.*

COAST REDWOOD (*Sequoia sepervirens*), Redwood, Sequoia, continued

WHAT THE PROBLEM LOOKS LIKE	PROBABLE CAUSE	COMMENTS
Black, dark brown, or gray encrustations on shoots or needles. Needles may yellow.	**Black araucaria scale,** *Lindingaspis rossi;* **Redwood scale,** *Aonidia shastae.* Tiny circular to oval armored scales.	More a problem in California in the south. Vigorous trees tolerate moderate populations. Conserve natural enemies. Tolerate or monitor and apply oil if needed. *See Scales, 130.*
Browning of tips, beginning in fall, worst in late winter and spring.	**Cypress tip miner.** Silvery tan moths, green larvae, about ¼ inch long.	*See 167.*
Terminals brown and die several inches back from tip.	**Redwood bark beetle,** *Phloeosinus sequoiae.* Adults are tiny, dark reddish bark beetles.	Terminal feeding doesn't seriously harm trees. Provide trees proper cultural care, especially adequate water. Prune out and dispose of nearby dead cypress, *Chamaecyparis,* and redwood where beetles breed. *See Bark Beetles, 173.*
Older foliage dark in color, stippled, may contain fine webbing.	**Spruce spider mite.** Sand-sized specks on needles.	Mites feed during cool weather. *See Pine and Spruce Spider Mites, 200.*
Globular galls, up to several inches in diameter on branches.	**Unidentified cause.** Believed to be a genetic disorder. Tree vigor not seriously affected.	No control except to eliminate tree. Tolerate, does not spread to other trees.

COCCULUS (*Cocculus laurifolius*)

WHAT THE PROBLEM LOOKS LIKE	PROBABLE CAUSE	COMMENTS
Sticky honeydew and blackish sooty mold on plant. Popcornlike bodies (egg sacs) on bark.	**Cottony cushion scale.** Orangish, flat immatures or cottony females on bark.	Can be a severe pest on *Cocculus* planted away from the coast. Vedalia lady beetle important in biological control inland avoids this plant. *See 142.*

COFFEE TREE (*Gymnocladus dioica*), Kentucky coffee tree

WHAT THE PROBLEM LOOKS LIKE	PROBABLE CAUSE	COMMENTS
Tan or gray encrustations on bark. May be dead or declining twigs and branches.	**Walnut scale.** Individuals ≤³⁄₁₆ inch diameter, often in colonies.	*See similar San Jose Scale, 132.*

CORAL TREE (*Erythrina* spp.)

WHAT THE PROBLEM LOOKS LIKE	PROBABLE CAUSE	COMMENTS
Foliage discolors and wilts. Branches die back. Entire tree may die. Minute white fungus growths may be visible beneath bark or on soil.	**Armillaria root rot.** Present in many soils. Favored by warm, wet soil. Persists for years in infected roots.	*See 262.*
Foliage fades, yellows, browns, or wilts, often scattered throughout canopy or first on one side of plant. Branches die. Entire plant may die.	**Verticillium wilt.** A soil-dwelling fungus that infects through roots.	*See 232.*
Sticky honeydew and blackish sooty mold on plant. Elongated, whitish material (egg sacs) on twigs or leaves.	**Cottony cushion scale.** Females brown, orange, red, or yellow, with elongated, white, fluted egg sacs when mature.	Natural enemies usually provide good control. *See 142.*
Sticky honeydew and blackish sooty mold on foliage. Cottony or waxy material on plant.	**Obscure mealybug.** Powdery, grayish, insects ≤¼ inch long, with waxy filaments.	Vigorous plants tolerate moderate populations. Conserve natural enemies that help in control. *See 127.*

COTONEASTER (*Cotoneaster* spp.)*

WHAT THE PROBLEM LOOKS LIKE	PROBABLE CAUSE	COMMENTS
Leaves with tiny reddish to brown spots, may have yellow halos. Larger, dark areas on leaves. Leaves may drop prematurely.	**Entomosporium leaf spot.** A fungal disease promoted by wet foliage.	*See 227.*
Leaves or fruit with dark scabby or velvety spots.	**Scab,** *Venturia* sp. A fungal disease promoted by wet foliage.	*See 227.*
Leaves or shoots with powdery white growth and yellow blotches. Shoots and leaves may be undersized or distorted.	**Powdery mildew,** *Podosphaera* sp. Fungal disease favored by moderate temperatures, shade, and poor air circulation.	*See 236.*

*Some species are invasive weeds. Other species may be better choices when planting.

COTONEASTER (*Cotoneaster* spp.), continued

WHAT THE PROBLEM LOOKS LIKE	PROBABLE CAUSE	COMMENTS
Leaves discolor, stunt, wilt, or drop prematurely. Stems discolored, cankered, and die. Minute white fungus growths may be visible beneath bark or on soil.	**Armillaria root rot.** Present in many soils. Favored by warm, wet soil. Persists for years in infected roots.	*See 262.*
Leaves wilted, discolored, may drop prematurely. Branches or entire plant may die. May be white fungal growth or dark crust on basal trunk, roots, or soil.	**Dematophora root rot.** Fungus favored by mild, wet conditions. Infects primarily through roots growing near infested plants.	Less common than *Armillaria. See 264.*
Sudden wilting then shriveling and blackening of shoots, blossoms, and fruit. Plant appears scorched.	**Fire blight.** Bacterium enters plants through blossoms.	*See 229.*
Flower buds, petals, or stems turn brown and die. Shoots and stems may darken, canker, exude resin, and die.	**Bacterial blight.** Pathogen infects through wounds. Disease favored by wet conditions.	*See 245.*
Leaves wilted, discolored, may drop prematurely. Trunk or limbs with roughened, wet, or oozing area. Cracked bark and dieback.	**Flatheaded borers.** Whitish larvae with enlarged head, under bark. Adults are bullet-shaped, metallic, coppery, gray, greenish, or bluish beetles.	*See 179.*
Bronzing, darkening, or spotting of fruit or leaves. Buds or fruit may blacken or fail to develop and drop prematurely.	**Pearleaf blister mite,** *Phytoptus pyri.* A microscopic elongate eriophyid mite.	*See Gall Mites, 203.*
Leaves bleached, discolored, or stippled. Terminals may distort. Plant may have fine webbing.	**Spider mites.** Tiny greenish, reddish, or yellowish mites; may have 2 dark spots.	*See 197.*
Leaves bleached, discolored, or stippled with dark varnishlike specks on undersides.	**Lace bug,** *Corythucha* sp. Pale brown adults, ≤⅛ inch long, wings lacelike. Nymphs flattened.	*See 154.*
Brownish, grayish, tan, or white encrustations on bark. May be declining and dead twigs.	**Greedy scale, Oystershell scale, San Jose scale.** Tiny circular to elongate individuals, often in colonies.	*See 131.*
Sticky honeydew, blackish sooty mold, and whitish cast skins on plant.	**Aphids,** including **Apple aphid,** *Aphis pomi.* Tiny insects, often green, clustered on new growth.	Plants tolerate moderate aphid populations. *See 103.*
Sticky honeydew and blackish sooty mold on leaves and twigs. Possible dieback.	**Kuno scale.** Adult scales beadlike and dark shiny brown.	*See 140.*
Foliage covered with silken webs. Leaves skeletonized.	**Cotoneaster webworm,** *Athrips rancidella* (family Gelechiidae). Larvae brownish black. Tiny grayish moths active at night.	Vigorous plants tolerate moderate defoliation. Prune out infested foliage. Tolerate or spray if larvae abundant. *See Foliage-Feeding Caterpillars, 71.*

COYOTE BUSH (*Baccharis pilularis*)

WHAT THE PROBLEM LOOKS LIKE	PROBABLE CAUSE	COMMENTS
Leaves with dark or yellow spots. Leaf undersides with orangish pustules. Leaves may drop prematurely.	**Rusts,** *Pucciniastrum baccharidis, P. evadens.* Fungi infect and develop when foliage is wet.	Avoid overhead watering. Plants tolerate moderate populations. *See 240.*
Leaves or shoots with powdery growth. Shoots or leaves may be stunted and distorted.	**Powdery mildews,** including *Erysiphe cichoracearum, Phyllactinia guttata.* Fungi favored by moderate temperatures, shade, and poor air circulation.	*See 236.*
Leaves and stems have dark to yellow spots. Foliage may shrivel and drop prematurely.	**Leaf and stem spots,** including *Cercospora baccharidis.* Fungi spread by air or splashing water. Disease favored by prolonged wet conditions.	Avoid wetting foliage. Use drip irrigation where feasible. Promptly remove and dispose of plant debris and infected leaves. *See Leaf Spots, 223.*

COYOTE BUSH (Baccharis pilularis), continued

WHAT THE PROBLEM LOOKS LIKE	PROBABLE CAUSE	COMMENTS
Chewed foliage. Plant may be defoliated.	**Baccharis leaf beetle**, *Trirhabda flavolimbata*. Larvae are brown to black, ≤½ inch long. Adults are metallic, blue to green beetles, with yellowish head.	Insect has one generation each year. Adults drop when disturbed. Vigorous plants tolerate moderate damage. Insecticide can be applied in the spring. *See Leaf Beetles and Flea Beetles, 84.*
Chewed foliage. Plant may be defoliated.	**Looper**, *Prochoerodes truxaliata* (family Gracillariidae). Brown to purplish caterpillars, ≤½ inch long, hide on ground during day.	Vigorous plants tolerate moderate damage. If needed, apply *Bacillus thuringiensis* or other insecticide when young larvae are abundant.
Chewed leaves. Foliage may be webbed. Plant may be defoliated.	**Omnivorous looper.** Yellow, green, or pink larvae, ≤1½ inches long, with green, yellow, or black stripes.	Larvae crawl in "looping" manner. *See 79.*
Fleshy, knoblike swellings (galls) on shoot tips. Galled shoots stop growing.	**Gall fly**, *Rhopalomyia californica*. Orange maggots, ≤¹⁄₁₆ inch long, in galls. Adults tiny, delicate flies, lay tiny reddish eggs on terminals.	Plants are not killed. Tolerate galling. No known artificial controls. Many species of beneficial parasites attack gall fly larvae. Conserve natural enemies. *See Gall Midges, 164.*
Bead galls on leaves, open on leaf underside. Leaves may be deformed.	**Baccharis gall mite**, *Aceria baccharices*. A tiny elongate eriophyid mite.	Plants apparently tolerate extensive galling. Control difficult. *See Gall Mites, 203.*
Sticky honeydew and blackish sooty mold on leaves or twigs. Plants may decline.	**Black scale.** Brown to black, bulbous to flattened insects, ≤³⁄₁₆ inch long. Raised H-shape often on back.	*See 136.*
Sticky honeydew and blackish sooty mold on plant. Bulbous, irregular, brown, gray, or white bodies (scales) on twigs.	**Wax scales.** Bulbous to hemispherical waxy insects, suck sap.	*See 141.*
Copious, misty, nonsticky liquid raining from plant. Surfaces covered with whitish residue.	**Glassy-winged sharpshooter.** Active, dark brown or gray leafhoppers ≤½ inch long, suck xylem fluid.	Vectors pathogens of oleander and certain crops, especially grapes. Report suspected glassy-winged sharpshooters to agricultural officials if found in areas where this pest is not known to occur. *See 148.*
Leaves stippled or bleached, with cast skins and varnishlike specks.	**Lace bug**, *Corythucha* sp. Brown adults, ≤⅛ inch long, wings lacelike.	*See 154.*
Dead or declining branches or plant. Tunneling in wood.	**Flatheaded borer**, *Chrysobothris* sp. Whitish larvae ≤1¼ inches long with enlarged head, tunnel in wood.	*See 179.*
Brownish, grayish, tan, or white encrustations on bark. Rarely, dead or declining branches.	**Greedy scale.** Individuals circular, <¹⁄₁₆ inch long, suck sap.	*See 133.*

CRAPE MYRTLE (Lagerstroemia spp.)

WHAT THE PROBLEM LOOKS LIKE	PROBABLE CAUSE	COMMENTS
Foliage covered with whitish growth. Shoots may be stunted, distorted.	**Powdery mildews**, including *Erysiphe lagerstroemiae*. Fungal diseases favored by moderate temperatures, shade, and poor air circulation.	Plant resistant cultivars. *See 236.*
Sticky honeydew, blackish sooty mold, and whitish cast skins on plant.	**Crapemyrtle aphid.** Yellowish green, pear-shaped insects with black wing markings.	*See 105.*
Copious, misty, nonsticky liquid raining from plant. Surfaces covered with whitish residue.	**Glassy-winged sharpshooter.** Active, dark brown or gray leafhoppers ≤½ inch long, suck xylem fluid.	Vectors pathogens of oleander and certain crops, especially grapes. Report suspected glassy-winged sharpshooters to agricultural officials if found in areas where this pest is not known to occur. *See 148.*

CRYPTOMERIA (*Cryptomeria japonica*)

WHAT THE PROBLEM LOOKS LIKE	PROBABLE CAUSE	COMMENTS
Leaves turn yellow, then brown, beginning at the tip. Lower, older foliage is most affected.	**Blight**, *Pestalotiopsis funerea*. Fungal disease that affects stressed and weakened plants.	Provide good growing conditions and appropriate cultural care.
Foliage may yellow or wilt. Roots may be darker or fewer than normal. Galls or swellings may be on roots. Plants may grow slowly.	**Root lesion nematode, Root knot nematodes.** Tiny root-feeding roundworms.	*See 341.*

CUPANIOPSIS (*Cupaniopsis anacardioides*), Carrot wood

No serious invertebrate or pathogen pests have been reported in California. If plants are unhealthy, investigate whether they have been injured or lack good growing conditions or appropriate cultural care.

CYPRESS (*Cupressus* spp.); MONTEREY CYPRESS (*Cupressus macrocarpa*); FALSE CYPRESS (*Chamaecyparis* spp.)

WHAT THE PROBLEM LOOKS LIKE	PROBABLE CAUSE	COMMENTS
Foliage brown or yellow and dying. Cankers and resinous exudate on limbs or trunk.	**Cankers,** including **Cypress canker,** *Cytospora cardinale;* **Cytospora canker,** *Cytospora cenisia; Phomopsis* sp. Fungi that infect cypress bark.	Primarily infect *Cupressus* spp., especially Italian, Leyland, and Monterey cypress. *See 250.*
Foliage discolors, wilts, stunts, may drop prematurely. Discolored bark or cankers may ooze sap. Branches or plant may die.	**Root and crown rots,** *Phytophthora* spp. Decay fungi infect through wounds or roots in moist soils.	*See 265.*
Foliage discolors, wilts, stunts, and dies prematurely. Inner bark brown. Bark may ooze. Tree dies.	**Port Orford cedar root disease,** *Phytophthora lateralis.* Fungus spreads in water and by equipment or people moving contaminated soil or infected plant material.	Introduced and widespread at least in Oregon and Washington. Infects only *Chamaecyparis,* primarily Lawson cypress or Port Orford cedar (*C. lawsoniana*). Do not move *Chamaecyparis* or soil in areas where pathogen occurs. *See Root and Crown Rots, 265.*
Stunted, bushy branches or witches' brooms. Orange masses or gall on bark. Stems die back.	**Gymnosporangium rusts.** Fungi infect and develop during wet conditions.	Occur on *Cupressus* spp. *See 242.*
Foliage browning at tips beginning in fall, worst late winter to spring.	**Cypress tip miner.** Adults are small, silvery tan moths. Green larvae, ≤⅛ inch long, tunnel in foliage.	*See 167.*
Foliage yellow or brown. Whitish to brownish encrustations on foliage.	**Juniper scale,** *Carulaspis juniperi;* **Minute cypress scale.** Circular to elongate insects, ≤¹⁄₁₆ inch long.	Populations in California rarely warrant control, except on Italian cypress or in nurseries. Minute cypress scale not on *Chamaecyparis. See 136.*
Stippled, flecked, or yellow foliage.	**Spruce spider mite.** Tiny green specks, may be fine webbing on foliage.	Occurs on *Chamaecyparis* spp. *See Pine and Spruce Spider Mites, 200.*
Stickiness and blackening of foliage from honeydew and sooty mold.	**Arborvitae aphid,** *Dilachnus tujafilinus.* Brown to gray insects, about ⅛ inch long. Suck sap.	Plants tolerate moderate populations. Hose with forceful water. Tolerate or apply soap or oil if severe. *See Aphids, 103.*
Chewed needles.	**Conifer sawflies, Cypress sawfly.** Green larvae, ≤1 inch long, on needles.	*See 82.*
Dead and living foliage tied together with silk. Foliage may turn brown.	**Cypress leaf tier,** *Epinotia subviridis* (family Tortricidae); **Cypress webber,** *Herculia phoezalis* (Pyralidae). Pink to dark larvae ≤¾ inch long, feed singly (*Epinotia*) or grouped in "nests" (*Herculia*).	More common in California in south than north. Vigorous plants tolerate moderate defoliation. Prune out infested foliage or tolerate. Apply broad-spectrum insecticide at high pressure in March or April if problem severe.
Twigs killed back about 6 inches from tips. Dead foliage hanging on tree.	**Cedar and Cypress bark beetles.** Adults small, dark beetles. Whitish larvae and adults bore beneath bark.	*See 175.*

CYPRESS *(Cupressus* spp.); MONTEREY CYPRESS *(Cupressus macrocarpa);* FALSE CYPRESS *(Chamaecyparis* spp.), continued

WHAT THE PROBLEM LOOKS LIKE	PROBABLE CAUSE	COMMENTS
Foliage discolors. Branches may be killed, sometimes to trunk. Coarse boring dust at trunk wounds and branch crotches.	**Cypress bark moths,** *Laspeyresia cupressana; Epinotia hopkinsana.* Larvae ≤½ inch long (family Tortricidae), feed under bark, in cones, or on foliage.	Provide plants proper cultural care. Avoid excess water and fertilizer, which promote rapid growth and susceptible thin bark. Avoid wounding bark. Control is generally not warranted. Insects are secondary, not cause of dieback. Often colonize cypress cankers.
Branches dead or dying. Holes about ¼ inch diameter in wood. May be large larvae boring beneath bark.	**Western horntail,** *Sirex areolatus* (family Siricidae). Dark, metallic blue, broad-waist adult wasps and yellowish or white larvae, both ≤1½ inches long.	Attacks only dead, dying, or injured trees. Protect plants from injury. Provide plants with a good growing environment and appropriate cultural care.
White waxy threads or tufts on bark. Foliage may redden, yellow, and eventually die. Treetop or entire tree may die.	**Cypress bark mealybug** or **Cypress bark scale; Incense cedar scale** or **Monterey cypress scale,** *Xylococculus macrocarpae* (family Margarodidae). Tiny, immobile, reddish, waxy insects on bark beneath wax.	On Monterey cypress and incense cedar. Only heavily infested young trees may be damaged. Tolerate or monitor crawlers then apply oil to bark. *See 127.*
Bright orange bark, mostly along the coast on the bark side facing the ocean.	**Lace lichen,** *Trentepohlia aurea.* A non-parasitic green algae containing orange carotenoid pigments. Organism thrives in salty California coastal winds.	Mostly on Monterey cypress, but also on downed wood, rocks, and other surfaces. Tolerate as it is harmless to trees.

DAPHNE *(Daphne* spp.)

WHAT THE PROBLEM LOOKS LIKE	PROBABLE CAUSE	COMMENTS
Leaves discolored, wilted, stunted, may drop prematurely. Discolored bark may ooze sap. Branches or plant may die.	**Root and crown rots.** Decay fungi favored by excess soil moisture and poor drainage.	*See 265.*
Yellowing of foliage. Decline and death of branches or entire plant.	**Euonymus scale.** Tiny, elongate, white male and purplish, oyster-shaped female insects encrusting leaves and stems.	Primarily a pest of euonymus. *See 135.*

DAWN REDWOOD *(Metasequoia glyptostroboides)*

No serious invertebrate or pathogen pests have been reported in California. If plants are unhealthy, investigate whether they have been injured or lack good growing conditions or appropriate cultural care.

DODONAEA *(Dodonaea viscosa),* Hopbush, Hopseed tree

WHAT THE PROBLEM LOOKS LIKE	PROBABLE CAUSE	COMMENTS
Foliage fades, yellows, browns, or wilts, often scattered throughout canopy. Branches die. Entire plant may die.	**Verticillium wilt.** A soil-dwelling fungal disease, infects through roots.	*See 232.*
Sticky honeydew and blackish sooty mold on leaves or twigs. Twigs and branches may die back.	**Black scale.** Brown to black, bulbous to flattened insects, ≤³⁄₁₆ inch long. Raised H-shape often on back.	*See 136.*

DOGWOOD *(Cornus* spp.)

WHAT THE PROBLEM LOOKS LIKE	PROBABLE CAUSE	COMMENTS
Leaves with large, irregular brown or purplish blotches. Infected leaves may drop prematurely or dead gray leaves may remain on twigs overwinter. Infected twigs develop discolored, sunken spots, cankers, then die back.	**Dogwood anthracnose,** *Discula destructiva.* A fungal disease favored by wet conditions.	Serious disease in the Pacific Northwest and parts of the eastern U.S. Plant resistant cultivars and species. *See 223.*
Leaves, flowers, or young shoots with small, circular, dirty yellow spots with purple margins.	**Spot anthracnose,** *Elsinoe corni.* A fungal disease favored by wet conditions.	Generally not a serious problem and is tolerated by plants. *See 223.*

DOGWOOD (*Cornus* spp.), continued

WHAT THE PROBLEM LOOKS LIKE	PROBABLE CAUSE	COMMENTS
Leaves with brown, gray, reddish, yellow, or whitish, circular to angular spots.	**Leaf spots**, including *Phyllosticta, Ramularia*, and *Septoria* spp. Fungal diseases that infect and develop when foliage is wet.	*See 223.*
Leaves discolored, wilted, stunted, may drop prematurely. Discolored bark may ooze sap. Branches or plant may die.	**Root and crown rots.** Decay fungi favored by excess soil moisture and poor drainage.	*See 265.*
Leaves discolor and wilt. Branches die back. Entire tree may die. Minute white fungus growths may be visible beneath bark or on soil.	**Armillaria root rot.** Present in many soils. Favored by warm, wet soil. Persists for years in infected roots.	*See 262.*
Leaves or shoots turn yellow or brown and wilt. Leaves drop prematurely. Limbs may canker or die back.	**Cankers**, including *Cytospora, Nectria, Phoma*, and *Phomopsis* spp. Fungal diseases that primarily affect injured or stressed trees.	Protect trees from injury. Provide good cultural care, especially appropriate irrigation. *See Cytospora Canker, Nectria Canker, 250.*
Leaves turn brown at the margins and tip. Leaves may be curled or puckered. Leaves may drop prematurely.	**Leaf burn** or **Scorch.** Abiotic disorders. Causes include drought, excess heat, injury, overirrigation, and poor drainage.	Protect trees from injury. Provide good cultural care, especially appropriate irrigation. *See 273.*
Leaves or shoots turn yellow, then brown. Powdery, whitish growth on blossoms, buds, leaves, or shoots. Shoots or leaves may be stunted and distorted.	**Powdery mildews**, *Microsphaera penicillata, Phyllactinia guttata.* Fungi favored by moderate temperatures, shade, and poor air circulation.	*See 236.*
Soft, brown decay on flowers, buds, or leaves. May be woolly gray growth (spores) on dead tissue.	**Gray mold.** Fungus develops in plant debris or inactive tissue. Favored by wet conditions and moderate temperatures.	*See 242.*
Stippled, flecked, or bleached leaves with whitish cast skins on undersides. Leaves may drop prematurely.	**Leafhoppers.** Pale green, yellow, or white, wedgelike insects ≤⅛ inch long.	Plants generally tolerate, control rarely warranted. *See 148.*
Sticky honeydew and blackish sooty mold on foliage. Possible decline or dieback of twigs or branches.	**Brown soft scale, European fruit lecanium scale.** Flattened to hemispherical, brown to yellow insects, suck sap.	*See 137–139.*
Sticky honeydew and blackish sooty mold on foliage. Tiny, powdery white, mothlike adult insects.	**Greenhouse whitefly.** Immatures are green to yellow, flattened and oval.	*See 123.*
Sticky honeydew, blackish sooty mold, and whitish cast skins on foliage.	**Aphids.** Small green, yellowish, brown or blackish insects, often in groups.	*See 103.*
Trunk or limbs with roughened, wet, or oozing area. Cracked bark and dieback.	**Flatheaded borers.** Whitish larvae with enlarged head, under bark. Adults are bullet-shaped, metallic, coppery, gray, greenish, or bluish.	*See 179.*
Brown to gray encrustations on bark. May be declining or dead twigs or branches.	**Oystershell scale.** Tiny elongate to oval insects on bark.	*See 135.*

DOUGLAS-FIR (*Pseudotsuga menziesii*)

WHAT THE PROBLEM LOOKS LIKE	PROBABLE CAUSE	COMMENTS
Foliage discolors and wilts. Branches die back. Entire tree may die. Minute white fungus growths may be visible beneath bark or on soil.	**Armillaria root rot.** Present in many soils. Favored by warm, wet soil. Persists for years in infected roots.	*See 262.*
Foliage discolors, wilts, stunts, and may drop prematurely. Branches or plant may die. Plant base or roots dark or decayed.	**Root and crown rots, Foliage blights**, or **Stem necrosis**, *Fusarium* sp.; *Phytophthora* spp. Decay fungi that persist in soil and infect roots.	Fusarium rot is primarily a problem in the eastern U.S. and Pacific Northwest. *See 265.*

DOUGLAS-FIR (*Pseudotsuga menziesii*), continued

WHAT THE PROBLEM LOOKS LIKE	PROBABLE CAUSE	COMMENTS
Foliage discolors and wilts. Branches die back. Treetop or entire plant may die. Cankers on bark.	**Phomopsis canker,** *Phomopsis lokoyae.* A fungal disease that primarily affects young, stressed trees.	Provide appropriate water and cultural care.
Foliage browns, yellows, wilts, and drops prematurely. Branches die back. Entire plant may die.	**Annosus root disease.** Decay fungus that spreads through roots and airborne spores.	*See 265.*
Foliage or new shoots turn brown and droop or wilt. May be grayish growth on terminals.	**Botrytis blight.** Fungal disease promoted by wet spring weather.	Improve air flow around plants as discussed below for Needle Blights. *See 242.*
Needles discolor and die on branch terminals. Cankers on branches. Twigs or small branches may die.	**Sudden oak death,** *Phytophthora ramorum.* Pathogen spreads via air and contaminated soil. Apparently can infect through bark or foliage.	May not be a serious pathogen of Douglas-fir. Primarily a problem in wildlands, killing many oaks there. Do not move infected plant material. Report to agricultural officials if found outside areas where pathogen is known to occur. *See 260.*
Needles light green, yellow, or pale-spotted. Orangish to yellow to pustules on underside of needles. If severe, shoots develop reddish cankers and die back.	**Rusts,** including *Melampsora occidentalis.* Fungal diseases promoted by wet conditions.	*See 240.*
Needles brown, light green, yellow, or pale-spotted, often beginning at tips. Needles drop prematurely. Plant growth slow. Tiny black (if *Phaeocryptopus*) or orangish (*Rhabdocline*) fruiting bodies along underside of needles.	**Needle blights,** including **Douglas-fir needle cast,** *Rhabdocline pseudotsugae, R. weirii;* **Swiss needle cast,** *Phaeocryptopus gaeumannii.* Fungi favored by cool, wet conditions in spring.	Remove nearby plants and weeds. Thin canopy and prune off lower branches to reduce humidity and improve air circulation.
Branch terminals turn brown and die. Tree deformed. Growth retarded.	**Douglas-fir twig weevil,** *Cylindrocopturus furnissi.* Adults black to gray. Pale larvae mine twigs. Primarily attacks small, stressed trees.	Provide appropriate irrigation and other cultural care. Prune and dispose of infested shoots during fall.
Yellow mottling or dieback of needles.	**Pine needle scale,** *Chionaspis pinifoliae;* **Black pineleaf scale,** *Nuculaspis californica.* White, gray, or black armored scales, $\frac{1}{16}$ inch long, on needles.	Scales have several generations a year in warm areas, only one at cool sites. Plants tolerate moderate populations. Conserve natural enemies. If damaging, monitor and apply oil. *See Armored Scales, 131.*
Interior needles turn brown or yellow and drop prematurely, leaving only young terminal needles. Tree may die.	**Spruce aphid,** *Elatobium abietinum.* Small pear-shaped insects, dark to light green, in groups on older foliage.	Usually abundant only on spruce, where it can be a serious pest. *See Aphids, 103.*
Pale greenish or yellow needles. Foliage stippled. May be fine webbing at foliage base.	**Spider mites,** including **Spruce spider mite.** Tiny pests, often greenish specks.	*See Pine and Spruce Spider Mites, 200.*
Sticky honeydew, blackish sooty mold, and whitish cast skins on needles. Brown to purplish insects clustered on foliage.	**Giant conifer aphids.** Dark, long-legged, $\leq \frac{1}{5}$-inch-long insects.	Apparently harmless to trees. *See 105.*
Sticky honeydew, blackish sooty mold, and whitish cast skins on needles.	**Aphids,** including **Monterey pine aphids,** *Essigella californica.* Small pear-shaped insects, usually green, may or may not be in groups.	*See 103.*
Cottony white tufts on needles. Needles have yellow spots.	**Adelgids,** including **Cooley spruce gall adelgid.** Tiny purplish insects beneath cottony tufts.	*See 112.*
Wet, white, frothy masses on needles or twigs.	**Spittlebugs,** including **Western pine spittlebug,** *Aphrophora permutata.* Green to black sucking insects secrete spittle.	Tolerate; spittlebugs cause no apparent harm to trees. *See 151.*

WHAT THE PROBLEM LOOKS LIKE	PROBABLE CAUSE	COMMENTS
DOUGLAS-FIR (*Pseudotsuga menziesii*), continued		
Pitchy masses 1 to 4 inches in diameter protruding from trunks and limbs. Limbs occasionally break.	**Douglas-fir pitch moth.** Dirty whitish larvae, ≤1 inch long, in pitch.	*See Pitch Moths, 191.*
Globular growths ½ to 12 inches in diameter on stems. Shoots may die back.	**Bacterial gall,** possibly *Agrobacterium pseudotsugae.* Disease of crowded, stressed trees under wet conditions.	*See similar Crown Gall, 258.*
Needles galled or swollen. Possible needle drop and twig dieback.	**Needle and twig midges,** *Contarinia* spp. White larvae in swollen needles. Tiny mosquitolike adults emerge from pupae in soil.	Apparently do not harm landscape trees. Prune out damaged shoots. New shoots on especially valuable (nursery) trees may be sprayed if well-timed when adults are laying eggs. *See Gall Midges, 164.*
Buds or terminals curled, distorted, or swollen. Shoots may grow crookedly.	**Douglas fir bud mite,** *Trisetacus* sp. Tiny elongate eriophyid mites that suck bud tissue.	*See Gall Mites, 203.*
Needles are chewed. Roots or the basal trunk may be cankered or injured.	**Conifer twig weevils.** Small black to brown weevils chew needles and shoots. Pale larvae bore in the root crown of dying or injured conifers.	Except for white pine weevil, most are secondary pests of minor importance. *See 93.*
Needles chewed or notched. Branches may yellow or die. Some roots stripped of bark or girdled near soil.	**Black vine weevil.** Adults are black or grayish snout beetles, about ⅜ inch long. Larvae are white grubs with brown head.	*See 92.*
Needles chewed. Foliage browns. May be silk webbing on needles.	**Douglas-fir tussock moth,** *Orgyia pseudotsugata;* **Silverspotted tiger moth,** *Lophocampa argentata* (family Arctiidae). Caterpillars hairy, brownish with orange, red, or yellow.	Vigorous trees tolerate moderate damage. Apply *Bacillus thuringiensis* to control young larvae, if needed. *See Tussock Moths, 74, 77.*
DRACAENA (*Cordyline, Dracaena* spp.), Corn plant, Dragon tree, Ti tree		
Leaves yellow and wilt. Entire plant may die. Minute white fungus growths may be visible beneath bark or on soil.	**Armillaria root rot.** Present in many soils. Favored by warm, wet soil. Persists for years in infected roots.	*See 262.*
Leaves fade, yellow, brown, or wilt, often scattered throughout canopy or first on one side of plant. Branches die. Entire plant may die.	**Verticillium wilt.** A soil-dwelling fungus that infects through roots.	*See 232.*
Leaves have tan to brown circular spots or blotches. Leaf tips die. Plants turn slightly yellow, wilt.	**Anthracnose,** *Glomerella cingulata.* Fungus persists in infected tissue. Spores spread by splashing water. Favored by wet conditions.	*See 223.*
Plants may stunt, decline, or (rarely) die. Powdery waxy material may be visible on roots and around crown.	**Ground mealybug,** *Rhizoecus falcifer.* Small, slender, pale insects; may have powdery wax covering but no marginal filaments.	*See 130.*
Sticky honeydew and blackish sooty mold on plant. Foliage may yellow. Plants may grow slowly.	**Mealybugs,** including **Longtailed mealybug.** Powdery gray insects with waxy marginal filaments.	*See 126.*
Sticky honeydew and blackish sooty mold on plant. Elongated, whitish material (egg sacs) on stems or leaves.	**Cottony cushion scale.** Females brown, orange, red, or yellow with elongated, white, fluted egg sacs when mature.	Natural enemies usually provide good control. *See 142.*
Leaves chewed.	**Fuller rose beetle.** Pale brown adult snout weevils, about ⅜ inch long.	Adults hide during day and feed at night. Larvae feed on roots. *See 94.*
Foliage discolored, stippled, or bleached. Terminals may distort. Plant may have fine webbing.	**Spider mites.** Tiny greenish, reddish, or yellowish mites; may have 2 dark spots.	*See 197.*

WHAT THE PROBLEM LOOKS LIKE	PROBABLE CAUSE	COMMENTS

DRACAENA (Cordyline, Dracaena spp.), Corn plant, Dragon tree, Ti tree, continued

Foliage discolored, bleached, or stippled. Leaf underside has dark, varnishlike excrement.	**Dracaena thrips**, *Parthenothrips dracaenae*; **Greenhouse thrips**. Tiny, slender, black, brown, or yellowish insects.	*See 156.*

ECHIUM (Echium spp.), Pride of Madeira

No serious invertebrate or pathogen pests have been reported in California. If plants are unhealthy, investigate whether they have been injured or lack good growing conditions or appropriate cultural care.

ELDERBERRY (Sambucus spp.)

Foliage yellows and wilts. Stems may have dark, sunken cankers. Limbs or entire tree may die.	**Cankers**, including **Botryosphaeria canker and dieback**, *Botryosphaeria* spp.; **Diaporthe stem canker and dieback**, *Diaporthe sociabilis*; **Nectria canker**, *Nectria* spp.; *Sphaeropsis* spp. Fungi primarily affect injured or stressed trees.	Avoid wounding plants, except to prune off infected limbs. Provide a good growing environment and appropriate cultural care. *See 250.*
Foliage yellows and wilts. Branches or entire plant may die. Fungal fruiting bodies may be on wood or around roots.	**Wood decay** or **Heart rots**, including *Ganoderma* spp., *Phellinus igniarius*, *Schizophyllum commune*. Fungi that attack injured or stressed trees.	*See Wood Decay in Trunks and Limbs, 248.*
Foliage and stems have brown to yellow spots or blotches. Spots may have dark or yellowish margins. Foliage may shrivel and drop prematurely.	**Leaf and stem spots**, including *Cercospora* sp., *Ramularia glauca, R. sambucina, Septoria sambucina, Stigmina* spp. Fungi spread by air or splashing water. Diseases favored by prolonged wet conditions. Pathogens persist in plant debris.	Avoid wetting foliage. Use drip irrigation where feasible. Promptly remove and dispose of plant debris and infected leaves. *See Leaf Spots, 223.*
Bark with wet spots or sawdustlike boring material. Limbs may decline and die.	**Elder borers**, *Desmocerus* spp. Adult longhorned beetles bluish, greenish, or blackish with gold or orange and feed on elderberry flowers. Larvae bore in living trees, which usually are not killed.	Attack stressed trees and dying limbs. Valley elderberry longhorn beetle (*D. californicus*) may be threatened species and its habitat (dying elderberry) may be protected by law. *See Longhorned Borers, 183.*
Sticky honeydew, blackish sooty mold, and whitish cast skins on plant.	**Aphids**, including **Bean aphid**. Small green or black insects in groups.	*See 103.*
Sticky honeydew and blackish sooty mold on leaves and twigs. May be dieback of twigs or branches.	**European fruit lecanium**. Black, brown, or yellow, bulbous or flattened insects ≤⅛ inch long.	*See 139.*

ELM (Ulmus spp.)

Foliage yellows then wilts, usually first in one part of canopy. Curled, dead brown leaves remain on tree.	**Dutch elm disease**. Fungus spread by bark beetles and root grafts.	Do not confuse with elm leaf beetle feeding that causes skeletonized leaves. *See 234.*
Foliage fades, yellows, browns, or wilts, often scattered throughout canopy. Branches die. Entire plant may die.	**Verticillium wilt**. A soil-dwelling fungal disease, infects through roots.	*See 232.*
Foliage with irregular, black, tarlike spots. Premature leaf drop. Perennial cankers on limbs and trunk. Dieback.	**Chinese elm anthracnose**. A fungal disease affecting only Chinese (evergreen) elm (*Ulmus parvifolia*).	In California usually a problem only near the coast. Plant resistant cultivars or species. *See 223, 255.*
Foliage wilts and branches die back. Stems may have dark cankers, callus tissue, or coral-colored pustules.	**Nectria canker**, *Nectria cinnabarina*. Fungus primarily affects injured or stressed trees.	On elm most common on Chinese elm (*Ulmus parvifolia*). *See 257.*
Foliage brown or yellow, especially along leaf margins and tips. Leaves may drop prematurely.	**Leaf burn** or **Scorch**. Abiotic disorders with many potential causes. Too little water may be most common cause when summer-rainfall-adapted elms are planted in arid California.	Provide plants with a good growing environment and proper cultural care, especially appropriate irrigation. *See 273.*

ELM (*Ulmus* spp.), continued

WHAT THE PROBLEM LOOKS LIKE	PROBABLE CAUSE	COMMENTS
Leaves discolored with irregular, yellowish pattern. Abnormal leaf size.	**Viruses,** including **Elm mosaic virus,** which may be same organism as **Cherry leaf roll virus.** Spread mechanically in sap or seed. Certain elm viruses are apparently spread by certain nematodes.	May slow growth, but otherwise harmless to elms. Provide proper cultural care, especially proper water. No other treatment. *See 268.*
Leaves with powdery white growth. May be tiny, black overwintering bodies later.	**Powdery mildew,** *Phyllactinia guttata.* A fungal disease favored by moderate temperatures, shade, and poor air circulation.	Generally not severe enough to warrant control. *See 236.*
Sticky honeydew, blackish sooty mold, and whitish cast skins on leaves. Leaves may curl.	**Aphids,** including **Elm leaf aphid,** *Tinocalis ulmifolii;* **Woolly aphids,** *Eriosoma spp.* Tiny green insects clustered on leaves.	Trees are not damaged by aphids. Tolerate or apply soap or oil (on small trees) or systemic insecticide. *See 103.*
Sticky honeydew and blackish sooty mold on plant. Possible dieback.	**European elm scale.** Dark, reddish, oval insects with white, waxy fringe.	Commonly at twig crotches or on undersides of limbs, especially on Chinese elm (*Ulmus parvifolia*). *See 144.*
Sticky honeydew and blackish sooty mold on leaves and twigs. Possible plant dieback.	**Citricola scale, European fruit lecanium scale, Frosted scale.** Brown, gray, yellow, white, or waxy, flattened to bulbous insects on twigs or leaves.	*See 137.*
Copious, misty, nonsticky liquid raining from plant. Surfaces covered with whitish residue.	**Glassy-winged sharpshooter.** Active, dark brown or gray leafhoppers ≤½ inch long, suck xylem fluid.	Vectors pathogens of oleander and certain crops, especially grapes. Report suspected glassy-winged sharpshooters to agricultural officials if found in areas where this pest is not known to occur. *See 148.*
Stippled, bleached leaves and whitish cast skins. Sticky honeydew and blackish sooty mold may be present.	**Leafhoppers,** including *Empoasca* sp.; **Rose leafhopper.** Pale green to white, ≤⅛ inch long, wedge-shaped insects.	Tolerate, apparently do not harm elms. Apply insecticidal soap or oil if not tolerable. *See 148.*
Leaves skeletonized, some small holes. Leaves turn yellow, brown, and fall. Yellowish pupae around tree base.	**Elm leaf beetle.** Adults greenish with black, longitudinal stripes. Larvae black to green, ≤¼ inch long.	*See 85.*
Leaves chewed. Often only a single branch is defoliated.	**Spiny elm caterpillar** or **Mourningcloak butterfly; Western tiger swallowtail,** *Papilio rutulus* (family Papilionidae). Dark, hairy caterpillars, ≤1½ inch long.	Ignore, they do not harm tree, or prune out infested branches. *Bacillus thuringiensis* kills young larvae. *See Foliage-Feeding Caterpillars, 80.*
Chewed leaves. Foliage may be webbed or contain silken tents.	**Fall webworm, Fruittree leafroller, Omnivorous looper.** Larvae ≤1 inch long. May be in webbed foliage.	*See 71.*
Woody swellings (galls), or cottony, waxy material on branches or roots.	**Woolly apple aphid,** *Eriosoma lanigerum.* Tiny, reddish, cottony, or waxy insects.	Conserve natural enemies that help control. Apply insecticidal soap or another insecticide. *See Woolly Aphids, 106.*
Decline of branches or entire tree. Canopy yellowing but leaves not chewed. Tiny "shot holes" in bark.	**European elm bark beetle.** Small, dark, stout adults. Whitish larvae tunnel beneath bark.	Beetles can transmit Dutch elm disease. *See 176, 234.*
Large holes, ≤½ inch diameter, in trunks and limbs. Limbs may die back or drop. Slow tree growth.	**Carpenterworm.** Whitish larvae, ≤2½ inches long, with brown head, tunnel in wood.	*See 194.*
Bark exudes white, frothy material, often around wounds, has pleasant odor.	**Foamy canker.** Unidentified cause, possibly a bacterium.	Foamy material appears for only short time during warm weather. *See 259.*
Bark stained brownish, exudes rancid fluid, often around crotches, wounds.	**Wetwood** or **Slime flux.** Bacterial infection.	Usually does not cause serious harm to trees. *See 259.*

ESCALLONIA (*Escallonia* spp.)

WHAT THE PROBLEM LOOKS LIKE	PROBABLE CAUSE	COMMENTS
Sticky honeydew and blackish sooty mold on plant. Bulbous, irregular, brown, gray, or white bodies (scales) on twigs.	**Chinese wax scale.** Bulbous to hemispherical, waxy insects, suck sap.	*See 141.*
Foliage yellows, browns, and wilts. Branches die. Entire plant may die.	**Escallonia dieback.** Unexplained malady affecting *Escallonia* 'Fradesii.'	Provide a good growing environment and appropriate cultural care. No known specific remedy.

EUCALYPTUS (*Eucalyptus* spp.), Gum*

WHAT THE PROBLEM LOOKS LIKE	PROBABLE CAUSE	COMMENTS
Leaves yellow and wilt. Branches or entire plant dies. Roots may be dark or decayed.	**Root and crown rots,** *Phytophthora* spp. Pathogens promoted by excess soil moisture and poor drainage.	*See 265.*
Leaves brown or yellow. Branches die back. Entire plant may die. Minute white fungus growths may be visible beneath bark or on soil.	**Armillaria root rot.** Present in many soils. Favored by warm, wet soil. Persists for years in infected roots.	*See 262.*
Leaves yellow and wilt. Stems may have dark, sunken cankers. Limbs or entire tree may die.	**Cankers,** including **Botryosphaeria canker and dieback; Diaporthe stem canker and dieback,** *Diaporthe eucalypti; Harknessia* spp.; **Nectria canker,** *Nectria eucalypti.* Fungi primarily affect injured or stressed trees.	Avoid wounding plants, except to prune off infected limbs. Provide a good growing environment and appropriate cultural care. *See 250.*
Leaves and twigs with small to large discolored blotches, spots, or streaks. Leaves may drop prematurely. Cankers may develop on twigs.	**Anthracnose, Leaf spots,** and **Tar spots,** including *Colletotrichum gloeosporioides, Heterosporium eucalypti, Mycosphaerella molleriana, Phyllachora eucalypti, Septoria* spp. Fungi infect and develop on wet tissue.	*See 223.*
Leaves turn brown or yellow, especially along margins and at tip. Leaves may drop prematurely.	**Leaf burn** or **Scorch.** Abiotic disorders with many potential causes, including direct injury to trunks or roots, frost, poor soil conditions, and too much or too little water.	Provide plants with a good growing environment and proper cultural care. *See 273.*
Leaves yellow and wilt. Branches or entire plant may die. Trees may fall over. May be fleshy or woody fungal growths on bark or around roots.	**Wood decay** or **Heart rot,** including *Ganoderma applanatum, Laetiporus sulphureus, Phellinus* spp. Fungi that infect injured or severely stressed trees.	*See Wood Decay in Trunks and Limbs, 248.*
Leaves or shoots with powdery growth. Shoots or leaves may be stunted and distorted.	**Powdery mildews,** including *Erysiphe cichoracearum, Phyllactinia guttata.* Fungi favored by moderate temperatures, shade, and poor air circulation.	*See 236.*
Leaves may discolor, wilt, or drop prematurely. Dead tree or dying limbs have broad galleries beneath bark.	**Eucalyptus longhorned borers.** Adults reddish brown with yellow on the back. Larvae whitish. Both about 1 inch long.	*See 183.*
Leaf underside has pimplelike blisters or water-soaked spots. Leaves brown, harden, appear corky, especially on underside. Foliage may yellow, drop prematurely.	**Edema** or **Oedema.** Noninfectious disorder. Leaves accumulate excess water when soil is warm and moist and air is cool and moist. Exact cause unknown.	May not be manageable in landscapes. Provide good air circulation. Provide good drainage. *See 290.*
Leaves with tiny black, purple, red, or tan bumps or wartlike swellings on blades or midvein. Leaves develop a roughened appearance.	**Eucalyptus gall wasps,** *Epichrysocharis* (=*Aprostocetus*) *burwelli, Epichrysocharis* sp. (family Eulophidae). Tiny black and yellow or brown and yellow wasps with pale larvae that feed within leaves.	Only occur on lemon gum (*E. citriodora*). Cause only minor aesthetic damage and do not threaten plant health. No control known or recommended.

*Some species are invasive weeds. Other species may be better choices when planting.

EUCALYPTUS (*Eucalyptus* spp.), Gum, continued

WHAT THE PROBLEM LOOKS LIKE	PROBABLE CAUSE	COMMENTS
Sticky honeydew and blackish sooty mold on foliage. May be tiny whitish caps or funnel-shaped waxiness on leaves. New shoots may be distorted, covered with whitish, waxy strands.	**Psyllids,** including **Blue gum psyllid,** *Ctenary-taina eucalypti;* **Lemongum lerp psyllid,** *Eucalyptolyma maideni;* **Redgum lerp psyllid; Spottedgum psyllid,** *Cryptoneossa triangula.* Tiny gray, green, or orange nymphs. Adults like tiny cicadas. Some species feed beneath waxy covers on leaves.	*See 114.*
Copious, misty, nonsticky liquid raining from plant. Surfaces covered with whitish residue.	**Glassy-winged sharpshooter.** Active, dark brown or gray leafhoppers ≤½ inch long, suck xylem fluid.	Vectors pathogens of oleander and certain crops, especially grapes. Report suspected glassy-winged sharpshooters to agricultural officials if found in areas where this pest is not known to occur. *See 148.*
Leaves chewed. Trees may drop leaves prematurely.	**Eucalyptus tortoise beetle.** Adults hemispherical, brown and darkly mottled, larvae greenish, both ≤⅜ inch long.	Insects may be overlooked as they often feed at night and hide beneath bark during the day. *See 90.*
Leaves chewed. Leaves with scraped surface, winding discolored trails, or elongate holes.	**Eucalyptus snout beetle,** *Gonipterus scutellatus.* Reddish brown adult weevils and legless, yellowish green larvae with a slimy coating.	Uncommon as under good biological control from *Anaphes nitens* egg parasite. Holes in leaves distinguish this species from tortoise beetle (above), which only chews along leaf edges.
Chewed leaves. Foliage may be rolled and tied together with silk.	**Caterpillars,** including **Omnivorous looper; Orange tortrix;** *Argyrotaenia citrana* (family Tortricidae). Yellow, green, pink, or whitish larvae, ≤1½ inches long.	*See 71.*
Distorted bark, galls or swellings around trunk base.	**Ligno-tubers.** Abiotic disorder. Galls are latent buds from which shoots sprout in response to stress.	Protect trees from injury. Provide good growing conditions and proper cultural care. Ligno-tubers are not harmful, but may indicate tree stress or injury.

EUGENIA (*Syzygium paniculatum*), Australian brush cherry, Brush cherry

WHAT THE PROBLEM LOOKS LIKE	PROBABLE CAUSE	COMMENTS
Foliage or flowers curl, turn brown or black, and die. Branches may die back.	**Abiotic disorders.** Common causes include freeze or cold damage, poor drainage, and too much or too little water.	*See 273.*
Sticky honeydew and blackish sooty mold on foliage. Leaves and terminals pitted, distorted, and discolored.	**Eugenia psyllid.** Adults are tiny leafhopperlike insects. Nymphs feed in pits on lower leaf surface.	*See 115.*
Sticky honeydew and blackish sooty mold on foliage. Tiny, whitish, mothlike adult insects.	**Woolly whitefly.** Nymphs are oval, waxy or cottony insects.	Usually under good biological control unless natural enemies are disrupted. *See 124.*
Sticky honeydew and blackish sooty mold on foliage. May be cottony material (egg sacs) on plant.	**Green shield scale.** Brownish, green, or yellowish convex or flattened insects on bark or leaves.	*See 139.*
Copious, misty, nonsticky liquid raining from plant. Surfaces covered with whitish residue.	**Glassy-winged sharpshooter.** Active, dark brown or gray leafhoppers ≤½ inch long, suck xylem fluid.	Vectors pathogens of oleander and certain crops, especially grapes. Report suspected glassy-winged sharpshooters to agricultural officials if found in areas where this pest is not known to occur. *See 148.*
Grayish, orange, or brownish encrustations on bark or foliage. Rarely, stunted, declining, or dead branches.	**California red scale.** Tiny, circular, flattened insects on stems or leaves.	Rarely if ever causes significant damage to eugenia. *See 131.*

EUONYMUS (*Euonymus* spp.)

WHAT THE PROBLEM LOOKS LIKE	PROBABLE CAUSE	COMMENTS
Discolored leaf blotches, often between veins. Large spots chlorotic, then tan or brown.	**Sunburn** or **Summer leaf scorch.** Non-infectious disorder, appears during or after drought stress and high temperatures.	*See 273.*

EUONYMUS (*Euonymus* spp.), continued

WHAT THE PROBLEM LOOKS LIKE	PROBABLE CAUSE	COMMENTS
Yellowing of foliage. Decline and death of branches or entire plant.	**Euonymus scale.** Tiny, elongate, white male and purplish, oyster-shaped female insects encrusting leaves and stems.	*See 135.*
Brownish, gray, tan or orange encrustations on bark or foliage. Rarely, stunted, declining, or dead branches.	**California red scale, Greedy scale, Latania scale.** Tiny, circular, flattened insects on stems or leaves.	Rarely if ever cause serious damage to euonymus. *See 131.*
Whitish patches of growth on foliage. Leaves may yellow, distort, or drop prematurely.	**Powdery mildew,** *Microsphaera euonymi-japonici.* A fungal disease favored by moderate temperatures, shade, and poor air circulation.	*See 236.*
Copious, misty, nonsticky liquid raining from plant. Surfaces covered with whitish residue.	**Glassy-winged sharpshooter.** Active, dark brown or gray leafhoppers ≤½ inch long, suck xylem fluid.	Vectors pathogens of oleander and certain crops, especially grapes. Report suspected glassy-winged sharpshooters to agricultural officials if found in areas where this pest is not known to occur. *See 148.*
Sticky honeydew, blackish sooty mold, or whitish cast skins on plant.	**Aphids,** including **Melon aphid, Bean aphid.** Groups of small green, black, or yellow insects.	*See 103.*
Wilting or dead plants. Some roots stripped of bark or girdled near soil. Foliage may be chewed, ragged.	**Black vine weevil.** Adults are black or grayish snout beetles, about ⅜ inch long. Larvae are white grubs with brown head.	*See 92.*
Galls or swellings on trunk and roots, usually near soil, may be on branches. Branches or entire plant may die.	**Crown gall.** Bacteria that infect plant via wounds.	*See 258.*
Galls or swellings on roots.	**Root knot nematode,** *Meloidogyne* sp. Tiny root-feeding roundworms.	*See 345.*

EVERGREEN PEAR (*Pyrus calleryana*)[10]

WHAT THE PROBLEM LOOKS LIKE	PROBABLE CAUSE	COMMENTS
Sudden wilting then shriveling and blackening of shoots, blossoms, and fruit. Plant appears scorched.	**Fire blight.** Bacterium enters plants through blossoms.	Plant cultivars such as Bradford or Chanticleer, which are less susceptible. *See 229.*
Stems or flowers with dark lesions. Cankers possible on branches.	**Bacterial blight and canker.** Disease favored by wet conditions.	*See 245.*
Tiny reddish to brown leaf spots, may have yellow halos. Larger, dark areas on leaves. Leaves may drop prematurely.	**Entomosporium leaf spot.** A fungal disease promoted by wet foliage.	*See 223.*

FICUS (*Ficus* spp.), Fig, Indian laurel, Laurel fig*

WHAT THE PROBLEM LOOKS LIKE	PROBABLE CAUSE	COMMENTS
Foliage yellows and wilts. Branches or entire plant dies. Roots or plant base may be dark or decayed.	**Root and crown rots,** *Phytophthora* spp. Pathogens promoted by excess soil moisture and poor drainage.	*See 265.*
Foliage browns or yellows. Branches die back. Entire plant may die. Minute white fungus growths may be visible beneath bark or on soil.	**Armillaria root rot.** Present in many soils. Favored by warm, wet soil. Persists for years in infected roots.	*See 262.*
Foliage bleaches out to yellow or almost white, especially in bright, hot locations.	**Excess light.** Abiotic disorder induced by excess light or changes in lighting.	Avoid changing light conditions around established plants. Provide partial shade. *See 289.*

10. Also see Pear (fruiting pear) for additional pests that may occur on evergreen pear.

*Some species are invasive weeds. Other species may be better choices when planting.

FICUS (*Ficus* spp.), Fig, Indian laurel, Laurel fig, continued

WHAT THE PROBLEM LOOKS LIKE	PROBABLE CAUSE	COMMENTS
Foliage drops prematurely. Dropped leaves may be yellow or a healthy-looking green. Entire plant may defoliate.	**Abiotic disorders.** Caused by any severe environmental change, including extreme light or temperature, inappropriate irrigation, and root injury.	Protect plants from injury. Avoid rapid environmental changes. Provide a good growing environment and appropriate cultural practices.
Leaves with warty blisters or swellings. Leaves yellow, curl, and drop prematurely.	**Ficus gall wasp.** Tiny brown introduced wasp oviposits in leaves, where pale maggots feed and cause swellings.	Affects new growth of *Ficus microcarpa.* Does not threaten tree health. *See 160.*
Foliage underside has pimplelike blisters or water-soaked spots. Leaves brown, harden, appear corky, especially on underside. Foliage may yellow and drop prematurely.	**Edema** or **Oedema.** Abiotic disorder. Leaves accumulate excess water when soil is warm and moist and air is cool and moist. Exact cause unknown.	Irrigate only in morning. Avoid irrigation if cool and cloudy. Provide good air circulation. Keep humidity low. Provide good drainage. *See 290.*
Sticky honeydew, blackish sooty mold, and cottony waxy material on plant.	**Mealybugs,** including **Citrus mealybug, Longtailed mealybug, Pink hibiscus mealybug, Vine mealybug.** Grayish, oval, waxy, and slow-moving insects, may have waxy filaments.	*See 126.*
Sticky honeydew and blackish sooty mold on foliage. Tiny, whitish, mothlike adults.	**Whiteflies,** including **Citrus whitefly, Greenhouse whitefly, Silverleaf whitefly.** Nymphs oval, flat, green to yellow.	*See 121.*
Sticky honeydew and blackish sooty mold on foliage. May be cottony material (egg sacs) on plant.	**Green shield scale.** Brownish, green, orange, red, or yellowish convex or flattened insects on bark or leaves.	*See 139.*
Sticky honeydew and blackish sooty mold on leaves and twigs. May be dieback of twigs or branches.	**Black scale.** Black, brown, or yellow, flattened or bulbous insects, ≤⅕ inch long.	*See 136.*
Gray to reddish encrustations on shoots or needles (scale insect bodies). Plant may decline and die back.	**Dictyospermum scale,** *Chrysomphalus dictyospermi.* Tiny, immobile, flattened insects that suck plant juices. Several generations per year.	Occasional problem in California, mostly in south. Conserve introduced natural enemies, which can provide excellent biological control. *See Armored Scales, 131.*
Curling and purple pitting of terminal leaves. In California, problem mostly in south.	**Cuban laurel thrips.** Slender, black adults, or yellow nymphs ≤⅕ inch long, in curled leaves.	Ficus microcarpa, also sometimes called *F. nitida* or *F. retusa,* is preferred host. *See 157.*

FILBERT (*Corylus* spp.), California Hazel, Hazelnut

WHAT THE PROBLEM LOOKS LIKE	PROBABLE CAUSE	COMMENTS
Foliage yellows and wilts. Entire plant may die. Minute white fungus growths may be visible beneath bark or on soil.	**Armillaria root rot.** Present in many soils. Favored by warm, wet soil. Persists for years in infected roots.	*See 262.*
Treetop or branches dying. Some branches reddish, pitchy or grayish, bare.	**Botryosphaeria canker and dieback,** *Botryosphaeria obtusa.* Fungus primarily affects injured or stressed trees.	*See 255.*
Blossoms, leaves, and terminals turn brown, wilt, and die. Cankers or lesions may occur on twigs.	**Bacterial blight and canker.** Disease favored by wet conditions.	*See 245.*
Blossoms, leaves, and terminals turn brown, wilt, and die. Leaves discolor and drop prematurely. Cankers or lesions may occur on limbs or twigs. Cambial tissue darkens.	**Bacterial blight,** *Xanthomonas campestris* pv. *corylina.* Disease favored by wet conditions.	*See similar Bacterial Blight and Canker, 245.*
Blossoms, leaves, and terminals turn brown, wilt, and die. Leaves discolor and drop prematurely. Cankers or lesions may occur on limbs or twigs, especially in upper canopy.	**Eastern filbert blight,** *Anisogramma anomala.* A fungus that infects buds and young leaves and shoots via airborne spores produced during wet conditions.	Occurs in Oregon and the eastern U.S. Prune out infected limbs during dry weather. Remove escaped seedlings. Plant resistant cultivars and species, such as *Corylus cornuta* var. *californica.*

FILBERT (*Corylus* spp.), California hazel, Hazelnut, continued

WHAT THE PROBLEM LOOKS LIKE	PROBABLE CAUSE	COMMENTS
Discolored blotches on foliage, often brown, reddish, or yellow. Leaves may drop prematurely.	**Leaf spots**, *Anguillospora coryli*, *Gnomonia gnomon*, *Mamianiella coryli*, *Septoria ostryae*. Fungal pathogens favored by wet conditions.	*See 223.*
Powdery white growth on leaves, tiny, black overwintering bodies later.	**Powdery mildew**, *Phyllactinia guttata*. Fungal disease favored by moderate temperatures, shade, and poor air circulation.	Generally not severe enough to warrant control. *See 236.*
Sticky honeydew and blackish sooty mold on foliage.	**Aphids**, including **Filbert aphid**, *Myzocallis coryli*; *Macrosiphum* spp. Pear-shaped, greenish to yellow insects, usually in groups on leaves and terminals.	Conserve effective natural enemies, including the filbert aphid parasite, *Trioxys pallidus*. *See 103.*
Leaves chewed. Foliage webbed with silk.	**Caterpillars**, including **Filbert leafroller**, *Archips rosanus*; **Obliquebanded leafroller**, *Choristoneura* (=*Archips*) *rosaceana* (family Tortricidae); Tent caterpillars. Naked or hairy larvae, ≤1½ inches long.	Vigorous plants tolerate moderate defoliation. *See 71.*
Holes in nuts. Tunnels inside nuts may contain whitish larvae.	**Filbertworm**. Adults are tiny bronze, coppery, or reddish brown moth. Larvae bore in oak acorns and nut crops.	Established trees are not damaged. *See Filbert Weevils and Acorn Worms, 93.*

FIR (*Abies* spp.)

WHAT THE PROBLEM LOOKS LIKE	PROBABLE CAUSE	COMMENTS
Foliage discolors, wilts, stunts, or may drop prematurely. Discolored bark or cankers may ooze sap. Branches or plant may die.	**Root and crown rots**. Decay fungi favored by excess soil moisture and poor drainage.	*See 265.*
Foliage turns red, brown, then fades. May be small, pimplelike growths or brownish cankers on bark. Limbs die back.	**Cytospora canker**. Fungal disease primarily affecting injured or stressed trees.	*See 250.*
Foliage browns and needles drop prematurely. Slow plant growth.	**Needle casts**, *Virgella robusta*, *Lirula abietis-concoloris*. Fungal diseases favored by cool, wet conditions in spring.	Remove nearby plants and weeds, thin canopy, and prune off lower branches to improve air circulation and reduce humidity.
Foliage browns, yellows, wilts, and needles drop prematurely. Branches die back. Entire plant may die.	**Annosus root disease**. Fungal disease spreads through roots and airborne spores.	*See 265.*
Foliage browns or yellows and needles drop prematurely. Treetop or entire tree dies.	**Engraver beetles**. Adults are small, brown bark beetles. White larvae bore under bark.	*See 173.*
Brown to purplish insects clustered on foliage. Sticky honeydew and blackish sooty mold may be on foliage.	**Giant conifer aphids**. Dark, long-legged, ≤⅛ inch long.	Apparently harmless to trees. *See 105.*
Chewed foliage. Tree may be defoliated.	**Rusty tussock moth**, *Orgyia antiqua*; **Douglas-fir tussock moth**. Hairy caterpillars, ≤1 inch long.	*See 71.*
Chewed needles.	**Conifer sawflies**. Green larvae ≤1 inch long, on needles.	*See 83.*
Bleached or stippled foliage. Foliage color abnormally light green or yellowish. May be in fine webbing at foliage base.	**Spider mites**, including **Spruce spider mite**. Tiny pests, often greenish specks.	*See Pine and Spruce Spider Mites, 200.*
Interior needles turn brown or yellow and drop prematurely, leaving only young terminal needles. Tree may die.	**Spruce aphid**, *Elatobium abietinum*. Small pear-shaped insects, dark to light green, in groups on older foliage.	Unlike most aphids, this can be a serious pest on spruce. *See Aphids, 103.*

FIR (*Abies* spp.), continued

WHAT THE PROBLEM LOOKS LIKE	PROBABLE CAUSE	COMMENTS
Needles are chewed. Roots or the basal trunk may be cankered or injured.	**Conifer twig weevils.** Small black to brown weevils chew needles and shoots. Pale larvae bore in the root crown of dying or injured conifers.	Except for white pine weevil, most are secondary pests of minor importance. *See 93.*
Powdery white or grayish material on cones, limbs, needles, or the trunk.	**Adelgids.** Aphidlike insects suck sap and alternative hosts with other conifers.	*See 112.*
Wet, white, frothy masses on needles or twigs.	**Spittlebugs**, including **Western pine spittlebug** (*Aphrophora permutata*). Green to black sucking insects secrete spittle.	Tolerate; spittlebugs cause no apparent harm to trees. *See 151.*
Pitchy masses 1 to 4 inches in diameter on trunks and limbs.	**Douglas-fir pitch moth.** Dirty whitish larvae, ≤1 inch long, in pitch.	*See 191.*
Distorted, stunted twigs or needles. Needles may drop prematurely.	**Balsam twig aphid**, *Mindarus abietinus*. Tiny, greenish yellow, powdery insects.	Vigorous plants tolerate. Control generally not warranted except on high value (nursery) trees. *See Aphids, 103.*
Bark stained brownish, exudes rancid fluid, often around crotches, wounds.	**Wetwood or Slime flux.** Bacterial infection.	Usually does not cause serious harm to trees. *See 259.*
Small leafless, orangish, upright, plants on host stems. Distorted and slow plant growth. Branches die back.	**Dwarf mistletoe**, *Arceuthobium* spp. Host-specific parasitic plants that extract nutrients from host plant.	Prune out infected branches. Replace heavily infected plants with broadleaf species or conifers from other genera; dwarf mistletoes don't spread to unrelated host species. *See 338.*

FLANNEL BUSH (*Fremontodendron* =*Fremontia* spp.)

WHAT THE PROBLEM LOOKS LIKE	PROBABLE CAUSE	COMMENTS
Brownish, grayish, tan, or white bark encrustations. May be decline or dieback of branches, twigs.	**Greedy scale.** Tiny circular to elongate individuals on twigs, branches.	*See 133.*
Foliage yellows and wilts. Branches or entire plant dies.	**Root and crown rots**, *Phytophthora* spp. Fungal diseases favored by wet, poorly drained soil.	*See 265.*

FORSYTHIA (*Forsythia* spp.)

WHAT THE PROBLEM LOOKS LIKE	PROBABLE CAUSE	COMMENTS
Leaves yellow and wilt. Plants wilt and may die, often suddenly. Roots and stem near soil dark, decayed. Leaves may have dark blotches.	**Root and crown rots**, *Phytophthora* spp. Diseases favored by wet, poorly drained soil.	*See 265.*
Leaves with black, brown, tan, or yellow spots or blotches. Foliage may die and drop prematurely.	**Leaf spots**, including *Alternaria* spp., *Phyllosticta* spp. Fungi spread by air or splashing water. Favored by prolonged cool, wet, conditions.	*See 223.*
Buds, flowers, leaves, or shoots darken or wilt and die.	**Bacterial blight.** Disease favored by wet conditions.	*See Bacterial Blight and Canker, 245.*
Galls or swellings on roots or stems, usually near the soil.	**Crown gall.** Bacterium that infects plant via wounds.	*See 258.*
Galls or swellings on twigs or stems, often high on the plant in comparison with crown galls. Twigs or stems may die back.	**Stem gall**, *Phomopsis* sp. A fungal disease most damaging to injured or stressed plants.	Protect plants from injury. Provide a good growing environment and appropriate cultural care.

FRINGE TREE (*Chionanthus virginicus*); **CHINESE FRINGE TREE** (*Chionanthus retusus*)

No serious invertebrate or pathogen pests have been reported in California. If plants are unhealthy, investigate whether they have been injured or lack good growing conditions or appropriate cultural care.

FUCHSIA (*Fuchsia* spp.)

WHAT THE PROBLEM LOOKS LIKE	PROBABLE CAUSE	COMMENTS
Leaves brown, fade, yellow, or wilt, often scattered throughout canopy. Branches die. Entire plant may die.	**Verticillium wilt.** A soil-dwelling fungal disease, infects through roots.	*See 232.*
Leaves yellow. Plants wilt and die, often suddenly. Roots and stem near soil dark, decayed, girdled by lesions. Leaves may have dark blotches.	**Pythium root rot; Root and crown rots,** *Phytophthora* spp. Fungi survive in soil. Diseases favored by wet, poorly drained soil.	*See 265, 268.*
Leaves discolor, wilt, stunt, or drop prematurely. Stems discolored, cankered, and die. Minute white fungus growths may be visible beneath bark or on soil.	**Armillaria root rot.** Present in many soils. Favored by warm, wet soil. Persists for years in infected roots.	*See 262.*
Leaves, buds, or flowers brown, decayed, and may be covered with woolly gray growth (spores).	**Botrytis blight** or **Gray mold.** Fungus develops in plant debris or inactive tissue. Favored by high humidity and moderate temperatures. Spores airborne.	*See 242.*
Leaves yellow or with yellow blotches, lines, or intricate patterns. Leaves may distort. Plants may be stunted.	**Bean yellow mosaic virus, Cucumber mosaic virus.** Spread by aphids or in infected plants. **Impatiens necrotic spot virus** and **Tomato spotted wilt virus.** Spread by thrips or in infected plants.	Usually not damaging or important in landscapes. Once infected, there is no control except to replace plants. *See 268.*
Leaf undersides with orangish pustules. Leaves may be spotted, drop prematurely.	**Rust,** *Pucciniastrum pustulatum.* Fungus requires moisture to develop.	Avoid overhead watering. Plants tolerate moderate populations. *See 240.*
Leaves and shoots distorted, galled, or thickened.	**Fuchsia gall mite.** Microscopic, wormlike eriophyid mite.	*See 205.*
Leaves blotched or dark streaked. Leaves or terminals distorted. Flowers small. Plants stunted. Buds may darken or drop.	**Cyclamen mite,** *Phytonemus pallidus.* A pinkish orange mite, $\leq\frac{1}{100}$ inch long, which feeds protected in buds and distorted tissue.	Primarily a problem during propagation and in greenhouses. Relatively uncommon in landscapes. *See Broad Mites and Cyclamen Mite, 203.*
Stippled or bleached leaves with varnishlike specks on undersides.	**Greenhouse thrips.** Tiny, slender, black adults or yellow nymphs.	*See 158.*
Leaves discolored, stippled, or bleached, and may drop prematurely. Terminals may distort. Plant may have fine webbing.	**Mites,** including **Privet mite,** *Brevipalpus obovatus;* **Twospotted spider mite.** Greenish or yellowish, tiny arthropods, which may have two dark spots.	*See 197.*
Sticky honeydew and blackish sooty mold on foliage. Tiny, whitish, mothlike adult insects.	**Bandedwinged whitefly,** *Trialeurodes abutilonea;* **Giant whitefly; Greenhouse whitefly; Iris whitefly,** *Aleyrodes spiraeoides.* Nymphs oval, flattened, yellow to greenish.	*See 121.*
Sticky honeydew, blackish sooty mold, and whitish cast skins on foliage.	**Aphids,** including **Crescent-marked lily aphid,** *Aulacorthum circumflexum;* **Green peach aphid; Potato aphid,** *Macrosiphum euphorbiae.* Groups of small, black, green, or yellowish insects on succulent foliage and shoots.	*See 103.*
Sticky honeydew and blackish sooty mold on foliage. Waxy, cottony material on plant.	**Citrus mealybug; Longtailed mealybug; Mexican mealybug,** *Phenacoccus gossypii.* Oblong, waxy, slow-moving insects, $\leq\frac{1}{8}$ inch long.	*See 126.*
Sticky honeydew and blackish sooty mold on foliage. Possible decline or dieback of twigs and branches.	**Black scale.** Black, brown, orange, or yellow, flattened or bulbous insects on leaves or twigs.	*See 136.*

WHAT THE PROBLEM LOOKS LIKE	PROBABLE CAUSE	COMMENTS
FUCHSIA (*Fuchsia* spp.), continued		
Chewed or notched leaves or blossoms.	**Fuller rose beetle.** Pale brown adult snout weevils, about ⅜ inch long. Larvae feed on roots.	Adults hide during day and feed at night. *See 94.*
Brownish, grayish, tan, or white encrustations on bark. Rarely, dead or declining branches.	**Greedy scale, Latania scale.** Individuals circular, flattened ≤1⁄16 inch long, usually in groups.	*See 133.*
GARDENIA (*Gardenia augusta*), Cape jasmine		
Foliage yellows. Plants wilt and die, often suddenly. Roots and stem near soil dark, decayed, girdled by lesions. Leaves may have large dark spots.	**Root and crown rots,** *Phytophthora* spp. Fungi survive in soil, favored by wet, poorly drained soil.	*See 265.*
Leaves discolor, wilt, stunt, or drop prematurely. Stems discolored, cankered, and die. Minute white fungus growths may be visible beneath bark or on soil.	**Armillaria root rot.** Present in many soils. Favored by warm, wet soil. Persists for years in infected roots.	*See 262.*
New growth chlorotic, except for green veins. Plants may be stunted.	**Iron deficiency.** Abiotic disorder usually caused by poor soil conditions or unhealthy roots.	*See 278.*
Buds or leaves drop prematurely. Fewer flowers than normal.	**Leaf drop** and **Bud blast.** Noninfectious disorder caused by poor cultural practices and poor growing conditions.	Provide appropriate irrigation and good drainage. Bud drop in spring is caused by poor conditions and practices the previous summer and fall, when buds developed.
Leaves bleached, stippled, may turn brown and drop prematurely. Terminals may be distorted. Plant may have fine webbing.	**Spider mites,** *Tetranychus* spp. Tiny, often green, pink, or red pests; may have 2 dark spots.	*See 197.*
Sticky honeydew, blackish sooty mold, and whitish cast skins on foliage.	**Aphids,** including **Green peach aphid, Melon aphid.** Groups of small, pear-shaped insects, commonly green, on succulent foliage.	*See 103.*
Sticky honeydew and blackish sooty mold on foliage. Cottony or waxy material on plant.	**Mealybugs,** including **Citrus mealybug, Longtailed mealybug, Obscure mealybug.** Powdery grayish insects, ≤¼ inch long with waxy filaments.	Vigorous plants tolerate moderate populations. Conserve natural enemies that help in control. *See 126.*
Sticky honeydew and blackish sooty mold on foliage. Leaves may yellow and wither. Tiny, whitish, mothlike adult insects.	**Whiteflies,** including **Bayberry whitefly,** *Parabemisia myricae;* **Citrus whitefly; Greenhouse whitefly; Silverleaf whitefly.** Oval, flattened, translucent, yellow to greenish nymphs and pupae.	*See 121.*
Sticky honeydew and blackish sooty mold on foliage. Possible decline or dieback of twigs and branches. May be cottony whitish material (egg sacs) on bark.	**Black scale; Brown soft scale; Cottony cushion scale; Green shield scale; Hemispherical scale,** *Saissetia coffeae;* **Wax scales.** Black, brown, gray, green, orange, yellow, waxy, or whitish, flattened or bulbous insects, on leaves or twigs.	*See 136–141.*
Plant has sticky honeydew and blackish sooty mold. Plant grows slowly. Foliage may yellow.	**Pyriform scale,** *Protopulvinaria pyriformis.* Triangular insects, ⅛ inch long, brown, yellow, or mottled red. May be small white egg sacs.	Common in Florida and also occurs in southern California. *See Soft Scales, 136.*
Sticky honeydew and blackish sooty mold on leaves. Twigs and limbs may die back.	**Tuliptree scale.** Females ≤⅓ inch, irregularly hemispherical, and variably colored brown to gray with other-colored blotches.	Primarily a pest of tulip tree and deciduous magnolias. Widespread in eastern U.S. In California present at least in south and eastern San Francisco Bay Area. *See 141.*

GARDENIA (*Gardenia augusta*), Cape jasmine, continued

WHAT THE PROBLEM LOOKS LIKE	PROBABLE CAUSE	COMMENTS
Foliage chewed or notched around margins. May be wilting or dieback of young plants. Some roots stripped of bark or girdled near soil.	**Black vine weevil, Cribrate weevil, Fuller rose beetle.** Adults are black, brown, or grayish snout beetles, ≤½ inch long. Larvae are white grubs with brown head.	*See 92.*
Galls or swellings on roots. Plants may grow slowly.	**Root knot nematodes.** Tiny root-feeding roundworms.	*See 345.*

GERMANDER (*Teucrium* spp.)

No serious invertebrate or pathogen pests have been reported in California. If plants are unhealthy, investigate whether they have been injured or lack good growing conditions or appropriate cultural care.

GIANT SEQUOIA (*Sequoiadendron giganteum*), Big tree, Sierra redwood

WHAT THE PROBLEM LOOKS LIKE	PROBABLE CAUSE	COMMENTS
Stippled foliage. Foliage color abnormally light green or yellowish.	**Spruce spider mite.** Greenish specks, often in fine webbing at foliage base.	Highest populations occur during spring and fall. *See Pine and Spruce Spider Mites, 200.*
Terminals die back. Twigs may develop brown sunken cankers. May be woolly gray growth (spores) on tissue.	**Gray mold.** Fungus favored by wet conditions. Spreads by airborne spores.	*See 242.*
Needles turn brown, tan, or yellow, beginning in inner, lower canopy. Affected needles and shoots drop, leaving only green terminals.	**Needle blight,** *Cercospora sequoiae.* Fungal disease favored by warm, wet conditions.	Avoid wetting foliage. Improve air circulation. Copper sprays can help to prevent infection on small plants.
Brownish or grayish encrustations on foliage. Foliage may yellow.	**Redwood scale,** *Aonidia shastae.* Oval to circular insects, each ≤¹⁄₁₆ inch long, often in colonies.	Conserve natural enemies that provide control. Vigorous plants tolerate moderate populations. Monitor for crawlers and apply oil if severe. *See Scales, 131.*
Treetop, branches dying. Some branches reddish, pitchy or grayish, bare.	**Botryosphaeria canker and dieback.** Fungus primarily affecting injured or stressed trees.	Avoid planting sequoia in hot areas outside of native range. Affects drought-stressed trees. Provide proper irrigation. *See 255.*

GOLDEN-CHAIN TREE (*Laburnum* spp.)

WHAT THE PROBLEM LOOKS LIKE	PROBABLE CAUSE	COMMENTS
Foliage yellows and wilts. Limbs may have lesions and die back.	**Diaporthe stem canker and dieback,** *Diaporthe rudis.* Fungus infects through wounds, persists in infected tissue.	Avoid wounding plants, except to prune off infected limbs. Provide a good growing environment and appropriate cultural care.
Sticky honeydew and blackish sooty mold on foliage. Cottony or waxy material on plant.	**Grape mealybug,** *Pseudococcus maritimus.* Powdery grayish insects, ≤¼ inch long, with waxy filaments.	Vigorous plants tolerate moderate populations. Conserve natural enemies that help in control. *See Mealybugs, 126.*
Chewed leaves. Plants may be defoliated.	**Genista caterpillar,** *Uresiphita reversalis* (family Pyralidae). Caterpillars ≤1¼ inches long, green to orange with black and white hairs.	Introduced to control brooms, which are often considered weeds. In California more common in south than north. Apply *Bacillus thuringiensis* or another insecticide.

GRAPE (*Vitis* spp.)[11]

GRECIAN LAUREL (*Laurus nobilis*), Sweetbay

WHAT THE PROBLEM LOOKS LIKE	PROBABLE CAUSE	COMMENTS
Stippled or bleached leaves with varnish-like specks on undersides.	**Greenhouse thrips.** Tiny, slender, black adults or yellow nymphs.	*See 158.*
Leaf margins cupped or rolled inward, forming galls, which turn red then brown.	**Laurel psyllid,** *Trioza alacris.* Nymphs about ¹⁄₁₆ inch long, powdery insects, within galls.	Conserve natural enemies that help control. Vigorous plants tolerate. If not tolerable, well-timed, repeated shearing of terminals may provide some control. *See Psyllids, 114.*
Grayish encrustations on leaves or bark. Rarely, declining or dead twigs.	**Oleander scale.** Tiny circular to oval insects on twigs, branches, and leaves.	Rarely if ever cause serious damage to plants. *See 134.*

11. For information on grape pest identification and biology, see publications such as *Grape Pest Management Guidelines* (Gubler et al. 2000) and *Grape Pest Management* (Flaherty et al. 1992).

WHAT THE PROBLEM LOOKS LIKE	PROBABLE CAUSE	COMMENTS
GREVILLEA (*Grevillea* spp.), Silk oak		
Sticky honeydew and blackish sooty mold on plant. Elongated, whitish material (egg sacs) on bark.	**Cottony cushion scale.** Females brown, orange, red, or yellow with elongated, white, fluted egg sacs when mature.	Natural enemies usually provide good control. *See 142.*
Sticky honeydew, blackish sooty mold, and cottony or waxy material on plant.	**Mealybugs,** including **Pink hibiscus mealybug.** Powdery grayish insects, ≤¼ inch long, may have waxy filaments.	*See 126.*
Grayish encrustations on bark. Rarely, dead or declining branches.	**Scales,** including **Latania scale.** Individuals circular, ≤¹⁄₁₆ inch long, usually in groups	*See 130.*
GOLDEN RAIN TREE (*Koelreuteria* spp.), Chinese flame tree		
Trunk or limbs with roughened, wet, or oozing area. Cracked bark and dieback.	**Flatheaded borers.** Whitish larvae with enlarged behind head, tunneling under bark.	*See 179.*
HACKBERRY (*Celtis* spp.)		
Foliage yellows beginning along margins, but veins green. Leaves may be undersized or necrotic.	**Iron deficiency.** Abiotic disorder usually caused by poor soil conditions or unhealthy roots, often from excess irrigation and poor drainage.	*See 278.*
Foliage brown, yellow, undersized, or sparse. Limbs dieback. Vascular tissue may be dark, stained. Tree may die.	**Hackberry dieback.** Unexplained malady. Symptoms resemble those of a vascular wilt disease.	Reported only on *Celtis sinensis,* occurs at least around Davis, California. Provide appropriate cultural care and a good growing environment, especially adequate drainage. Avoid excess irrigation. Where problem occurs, sterilize tools after working on each hackberry, as malady may be mechanically spread.
Foliage wilts, discolors, and may drop prematurely. Branches die back. Entire tree may die. Minute white fungus growths may be visible beneath bark or on soil.	**Armillaria root rot.** Present in many soils. Favored by warm, wet soil and frequent irrigation. Persists for years in infected roots.	Hackberry is resistant but not immune to *Armillaria* if conditions are highly conducive to disease development. *See 262.*
Sticky honeydew and blackish sooty mold on foliage. Plant growth may slow. Foliage may yellow.	**Citricola scale, European fruit lecanium.** Brownish or grayish, flattened or bulbous insects.	Avoid injecting or implanting roots or trunks with systemic insecticide for scale control as this may mechanically spread the unexplained hackberry dieback. *See 138, 139.*
Sticky honeydew and blackish sooty mold on foliage. Cottony bluish white wax or small fuzzy balls on underside of leaves.	**Asian woolly hackberry aphid,** *Shivaphis celti.* Tiny insects suck phloem sap from the underside of leaves. Overwinter as eggs on hackberry twigs.	An introduced pest occurring in California and in the southeastern U.S. Does not threaten survival of otherwise healthy hackberry. Avoid injecting or implanting roots or trunks with systemic insecticide for scale control as this may mechanically spread the unexplained hackberry dieback. *See Woolly Aphids, 106.*
HAWTHORN (*Crataegus* spp.)		
Sudden wilting then shriveling and blackening of shoots, blossoms, and fruit. Plant appears scorched.	**Fire blight.** Bacterium enters plants through blossoms.	*See 229.*
Tiny reddish to brown leaf spots, may have yellow halos. Larger, dark areas on leaves. Leaves may drop prematurely.	**Entomosporium leaf spot.** A fungal disease promoted by wet foliage.	*See 227.*
Leaves yellow, spotted, and may have orangish pustules. Leaves may drop prematurely. Swellings possible on leaves, twigs.	**Rusts,** *Gymnosporangium* spp. Fungi alternate hosts, often on juniper or cedar, and spread by windblown or water-splashed spores.	Avoid overhead watering. Vigorous plants tolerate moderate populations. Clip infected shoots, rake fallen leaves, and dispose of them. *See 240.*

HAWTHORN (*Crataegus* spp.), continued

WHAT THE PROBLEM LOOKS LIKE	PROBABLE CAUSE	COMMENTS
Powdery white growth on leaves. Tiny, black overwintering bodies may develop later.	**Powdery mildews**, including *Phyllactinia guttata*. Fungal diseases favored by moderate temperatures, shade, and poor air circulation.	*See 236.*
Black to dark olive spots on fruit, leaves, or stems. Fruit may have scabby blotches or become misshapen.	**Scab**, *Venturia inaequalis*. A fungal disease spread by water from infected leaves and twigs.	*See 227.*
Leaves chewed, may be tied with silk. Plant may be defoliated.	**Caterpillars**, including **Fruittree leafroller, Tent Caterpillars, Tussock moths.** Green or hairy larvae, ≤1½ inch long.	*See 71.*
Leaves scraped, skeletonized, and webbed together with silk.	**Leafminers**, including **Apple-and-thorn skeletonizer**, *Choreutis pariana* (family Choreutidae). Adult *Choreutis* is a dark brown moth <½ inch long. Larvae are ≤1 inch long and greenish or yellow.	*Choreutis* occurs throughout the northern U.S., reportedly including northern California. Plants usually tolerate damage. Prune off infested foliage or apply *Bacillus thuringiensis*.
Leaves scraped, skeletonized, may be slime-covered.	**Pear sawfly** or **Pearslug**. Green, slimy, sluglike insects, ≤½ inch long.	*See 83.*
Roughened twig bark. Possible twig dieback.	**Treehoppers**, including **Buffalo tree-hopper**, *Stictocephala bisonia*. Bright yellow to green insects, horny or spiny.	*See 151.*
Sticky honeydew, blackish sooty mold, and whitish cast skins on foliage. May be flocculent wax on plant. Leaves may curl or distort.	**Aphids**, including **Apple aphid**, *Aphis pomi*; *Eriosoma crataegi*; **Woolly apple aphid**, *Eriosoma lanigerum*. Groups of small, gray, green, pinkish, yellowish, white, or waxy insects on leaves.	*See 103.*
Sticky honeydew and blackish sooty mold on foliage. May be whitish cottony bodies on bark.	**Cottony maple scale**, *Pulvinaria innumerabilis*; **Frosted scale.** Brown, yellow, white, or waxy, flattened to bulbous insects.	*See 139.*
Sticky honeydew and blackish sooty mold on plant. Whitish cottony bodies on bark. Bark rough. Branches may deform. Possible dieback.	**Azalea bark scale** or **Woolly azalea scale**, *Acanthococcus* (=*Eriococcus*) *azaleae* (family Eriococcidae). Dark, reddish, oval insects underneath white wax, on bark crevices and in crotches.	Occurs in the eastern U.S. and in Oregon and Washington. If found in California, report to county department of agriculture. *See Other Common Scales, 142.*
Leaves bleached. May be sticky honeydew or dark excrement specks on foliage.	**Leafhoppers**, including **White apple leaf-hopper**, *Typhlocyba pomaria*; **Rose leafhopper**, *Edwardsiana rosae*. Greenish to whitish, wedge-shaped insects, ≤⅛ inch long.	Leafhoppers do not seriously threaten plant health, tolerate them. *See 148.*
Stippled, bleached, or reddened foliage.	**Mites**, including **European red mite**; *Oligonychus* spp. Tiny green, reddish, or yellow arthropods.	*See 197.*
Grayish encrustations on bark or twigs. Rarely, declining or dead twigs or branches.	**San Jose scale**. Circular, flattened, ≤1/16 inch long, often in colonies.	Usually harmless to hawthorn. *See 132.*
Trunk or limbs with roughened, wet, or oozing area. Bark cracks. Limbs dieback.	**Flatheaded borers, Longhorned borers.** Whitish larvae tunneling under bark.	*See 179.*
Dead branches, limbs, or twigs. Plant declines, may die. Tiny "BB shot"-sized holes in bark, which may ooze.	**Shothole borer.** Small brown adults, whitish larvae, tunnel beneath bark.	*See 176.*

HEATH (*Erica* spp.); **HEATHER** (*Calluna vulgaris*)

WHAT THE PROBLEM LOOKS LIKE	PROBABLE CAUSE	COMMENTS
Leaves discolored, wilted, stunted, or may drop prematurely. Discolored bark may ooze sap. Branches or plant may die.	**Root and crown rots.** Decay fungi favored by excess soil moisture and poor drainage.	*See 265.*

WHAT THE PROBLEM LOOKS LIKE	PROBABLE CAUSE	COMMENTS

HEATH (*Erica* spp.); HEATHER (*Calluna vulgaris*), continued

WHAT THE PROBLEM LOOKS LIKE	PROBABLE CAUSE	COMMENTS
Leaves discolor, wilt, stunt, or drop prematurely. Stem bases discolor and die. Minute white fungus growths may be visible beneath bark or on soil.	**Armillaria root rot.** Present in many soils. Favored by warm, wet soil. Persists for years in infected roots.	*See 262.*
Leaves or shoot tips turn brown, reddish, yellow, and may drop prematurely. Shoots may be bushy, distorted, or stunted. Leaves or shoots may be covered with whitish growth.	**Powdery mildew,** *Erysiphe polygoni.* Fungus develops on living tissue, favored by moderate temperatures, shade, and poor air circulation.	Infects *Erica persoluta. See 236.*
Leaves have brown or yellow blotches and may drop prematurely. Leaves have powdery orange pustules.	**Rust,** *Uredo ericae.* Spores from foliage may be carried for miles by wind. Favored by low temperatures, dew, and rain.	Infects *Erica hirtiflora* and *E. persoluta* var. *alba. See 240.*
Foliage discolored, stippled, brownish, or bleached, and may drop prematurely. Terminals may distort. Plant may have fine webbing.	**Spider mites,** including **Twospotted mite.** Tiny greenish, reddish, or yellowish mites, may have two dark spots.	*See 197.*
Bark or leaves have gray, brown, tan, or yellow encrustations (colonies of scales). Foliage may yellow. Rarely, plant dies back.	**Greedy scale, Oleander scale, Oystershell scale.** Circular flat or elongate to oval insects ≤¹⁄₁₆ inch long.	*See 133–135.*
Sticky honeydew and blackish sooty mold on foliage. Possible plant decline or dieback.	**European fruit lecanium.** Brown or yellow, flat or bulbous, immobile scale insects.	*See 139.*
Foliage notched around margins. Wilting or dead plants. Some roots stripped of bark or girdled near soil.	**Black vine weevil.** Adults are black or grayish snout beetles, about ⅜ inch long. Larvae are white grubs with brown head.	Larvae feed on roots. Adults hide during day and feed at night. *See 92.*

HEBE (*Hebe, Veronica* spp.)

WHAT THE PROBLEM LOOKS LIKE	PROBABLE CAUSE	COMMENTS
Leaves with reddish, brownish, or yellowish spots or blotches.	**Septoria leaf spot.** A fungal disease favored by wet foliage.	Avoid overhead irrigation. *See 227.*
Foliage fades, yellows, browns, or wilts, often scattered throughout canopy. Branches die. Entire plant may die.	**Verticillium wilt.** A soil-dwelling fungal disease, infects through roots.	*See 232.*
Yellowing and death of foliage, older foliage affected first. Browning of vascular tissue.	**Fusarium wilt,** *Fusarium oxysporum.* Fungus persists in soil and infects plant through roots.	Avoid injuring live tissue. Provide proper drainage, irrigation, and fertilization. Avoid planting hebe where *Fusarium* was previously a problem. *See 233.*
Twigs distorted, swollen, and pitted. Leaves dwarfed. Shoots may die back.	**Pit-making pittosporum scale,** *Planchonia* (=*Asterolecanium*) *arabidis* (family Asterolecaniidae). Brown to white insects, ≤⅛ inch long, on twigs, often in pits.	In California, an occasional problem in the north. Management not investigated. *See Other Common Scales, 142.*

HEMLOCK (*Tsuga* spp.)

WHAT THE PROBLEM LOOKS LIKE	PROBABLE CAUSE	COMMENTS
Foliage discolors, wilts, stunts, or may drop prematurely. Discolored bark or cankers may ooze sap. Branches or plant may die.	**Root and crown rots.** Decay fungi favored by excess soil moisture and poor drainage.	*See 265.*
Foliage browns. Needles drop prematurely. Lower limbs die back.	**Needle blights,** including **Brown Felt Blight** or **Snow blight,** *Herpotrichia juniperi.* Fungal pathogens favored by wet conditions and injured or stressed plants.	Keep foliage dry. Use drip irrigation and provide good air circulation. Provide plants with good growing conditions and proper cultural care.
Foliage brown, reddish, yellow, or wilted. Shoots die back. Shoots may be bushy, stunted, or form witches' brooms.	**Twig blights,** including *Kabatina juniperi, Phomopsis juniperovora.* Fungal pathogens that infect wet foliage through wounds.	Avoid wounding twigs, except to prune out and dispose of infected shoots during dry conditions. Keep foliage dry. Use drip irrigation and provide good air circulation. Avoid fertilization.

HEMLOCK (*Tsuga* spp.), continued

WHAT THE PROBLEM LOOKS LIKE	PROBABLE CAUSE	COMMENTS
Foliage browns, yellows, or wilts. Branches or entire plant may die. Fungal fruiting bodies may be on wood or around roots.	**Wood decay** or **Heart rots**, including *Fomitopsis pinicola*; **Indian paint fungus**, *Echinodontium tinctorium*; *Phaeolus schweinitzii*; *Phellinus pini*. Decay fungi that infect injured or stressed trees.	*See Wood Decay in Trunks and Limbs, 248.*
Foliage browns, yellows, wilts, and drops prematurely. Branches die back. Entire plant may die.	**Annosus root disease.** Decay fungus that spreads through roots and airborne spores.	*See 265.*
Foliage browns. Scattered twig dieback. Limbs may ooze or have boring dust or holes.	**Twig beetles**, *Pityophthorus* spp. Adults are brown bark beetles, ≤⅛ inch long, that chew twig bark. White larvae tunnel beneath bark.	Generally harmless to plants. No recommended control, except to provide a good growing environment and proper cultural care. *See Bark Beetles, 173.*
Bleeding or frothy material bubbling from tiny holes in trunk or limbs. Fine boring dust may surround holes. Limbs or entire tree may die.	**Bark beetles**, including *Pseudohylesinus* spp., *Scolytus* spp. Adults brown, ≤⅛ inch long. White larvae tunnel beneath bark.	*See 173.*
Bark stained brownish, exudes rancid fluid, often around crotches, wounds.	**Wetwood** or **Slime flux.** Bacterial infection.	Rarely causes serious harm to trees. *See 259.*
Pale greenish or yellow needles. Foliage stippled.	**Spruce spider mite.** Tiny pests, often greenish specks, may be in fine webbing at foliage base.	*See Pine and Spruce Spider Mites, 200.*
Yellow spots or cottony white tufts on needles. White encrustations on bark. Trees may decline or die if severely infested.	**Hemlock adelgid**, *Adelges tsugae*. Tiny aphidlike insects that suck sap and may alternate hosts on other conifers.	*See Adelgids, 112.*
Wet, white, frothy masses on needles or twigs.	**Spittlebugs**, including **Western pine spittlebug**, *Aphrophora permutata*. Green to black sucking insects secrete spittle.	Tolerate. Spittlebugs cause no apparent harm to trees. *See 151.*
Brown to gray encrustations on needles. Branches or twigs may decline or die.	**Hemlock scale**, *Abgrallaspis ithacae*. Tiny circular to oblong armored scales.	Primarily a pest on Colorado blue spruce in the Pacific Northwest. Also occurs in the eastern U.S. *See Armored Scales, 131.*
Brown to purplish insects clustered on foliage. May be sticky honeydew and blackish sooty mold.	**Giant conifer aphids.** Dark, long-legged insects, ≤⅛ inch long.	Apparently harmless to trees. *See 105.*
Needles chewed.	**Conifer sawflies.** Green larvae, ≤1 inch long, on needles.	*See 83.*
Needles chewed and may drop prematurely.	**Caterpillars**, including **Rusty tussock moth.** Caterpillars, ≤2 inches long, may be hairy and brown or colorful.	*See 71.*
Needles chewed or notched around margins. Roots or basal trunk may be stripped of bark. Plants may wilt or die back.	**Black vine weevil.** Adults are black or grayish snout beetles, about ⅜ inch long. Larvae are white grubs with brown head.	Larvae feed on roots. Adults hide during day and feed at night. *See 92.*

HIBISCUS (*Hibiscus* spp.)

WHAT THE PROBLEM LOOKS LIKE	PROBABLE CAUSE	COMMENTS
Leaves yellow. Plant grows slowly. Plants wilt and die. Roots and stem near soil dark and decayed.	**Root and crown rots**, *Pythium* spp., *Phytophthora* spp. Fungi persist in soil. Favored by wet, poorly drained soil.	*See 265.*
Leaves discolor, wilt, stunt, or drop prematurely. Stems discolored, cankered, and die. Minute white fungus growths may be visible beneath bark or on soil.	**Armillaria root rot.** Present in many soils. Favored by warm, wet soil. Persists for years in infected roots.	*See 262.*

HIBISCUS (Hibiscus spp.), continued

WHAT THE PROBLEM LOOKS LIKE	PROBABLE CAUSE	COMMENTS
Leaves have brown to yellow spots or blotches, mostly on older foliage. Spots may have dark or yellowish margins. Foliage may shrivel, drop.	**Leaf spots**, including *Cercospora* spp. Spread by air or splashing water. Favored by prolonged wet conditions. Uncommon on hibiscus in western U.S.	Avoid overhead irrigation. Don't overwater. Don't crowd plants. Use good sanitation. *See 223.*
Leaves have dark, angular spots or blotches, may have reddish margin or yellow border. Foliage may yellow and drop.	**Bacteria leaf spots**, *Pseudomonas* spp., *Xanthomonas* spp. Spread by air and splashing water.	Avoid overhead irrigation. Don't overwater. Don't crowd plants. Use good sanitation. *See 223.*
Leaves with yellow to brownish blotches, rings, spots, or vein-banding.	**Hibiscus chlorotic ringspot virus.** Mechanically spread pathogen, not insect-vectored. Often introduced with new plant.	Keep plants vigorous by providing proper cultural care. No other treatment. *See 268.*
Flowers or flower head have soft brown decay. Lower leaves, growing points may decay. May be woolly gray growth (spores) on dead tissue.	**Gray mold.** Fungus favored by mild, wet conditions. Spreads by airborne spores.	*See 242.*
Chewed leaves or blossoms.	**Fuller rose beetle.** Pale brown adult snout weevils, about ⅜ inch long.	Adults hide during day and feed at night. Larvae feed on roots. *See 94.*
Foliage has sticky honeydew and blackish sooty mold. May be copious white waxy on plant.	**Whiteflies**, including **Bandedwinged whitefly**, *Trialeurodes abutilonea*; **Giant whitefly**; **Greenhouse whitefly**; **Nesting whitefly**, *Paraleyrodes minei*; **Silverleaf whitefly**. Nymphs are oval and flattened. Adults are tiny, whitish, mothlike insects.	*See 121.*
Sticky honeydew and blackish sooty mold on foliage. May be cottony material (egg sacs) on plant.	**Black scale, Brown soft scale, Green shield scale.** Brownish, black, green, orange, red, or yellowish, convex or flattened insects on bark or leaves.	*See 136–139.*
Sticky honeydew and blackish sooty mold on foliage. Waxy, cottony material on plant.	**Mealybugs** including **Longtailed mealybug, Pink hibiscus mealybug.** Powdery grayish insects, ≤⅛ inch long, may have waxy filaments.	*See 126.*
Sticky honeydew, blackish sooty mold, and whitish cast skins on foliage.	**Aphids**, including **Melon aphid**. Small greenish, blackish, or yellowish insects in groups.	*See 103.*
Copious, misty, nonsticky liquid raining from plant. Surfaces covered with whitish residue.	**Glassy-winged sharpshooter.** Active, dark brown or gray leafhoppers ≤½ inch long, suck xylem fluid.	Vectors pathogens of oleander and certain crops, especially grapes. Report suspected glassy-winged sharpshooters to agricultural officials if found in areas where this pest is not known to occur. *See 148.*
Galls or swellings on roots.	**Root knot nematode**, *Meloidogyne* sp. Tiny root-feeding roundworms.	*See 345.*

HOLLY (Ilex spp.)

WHAT THE PROBLEM LOOKS LIKE	PROBABLE CAUSE	COMMENTS
Leaves discolored, wilted, stunted, may drop prematurely. Discolored bark may ooze sap. Branches or plant may die.	**Root and crown rots.** Decay fungi favored by excess soil moisture and poor drainage.	*See 265.*
Leaves wilted, discolored, may drop prematurely. Branches or entire plant may die. May be white fungal growth or dark crust on basal trunk, roots, or soil.	**Dematophora root rot.** Fungus favored by mild, wet conditions. Infects primarily through roots growing near infested plants.	Less common than *Phytophthora*. *See 264.*
Sticky honeydew and blackish sooty mold on foliage. Possible decline or dieback of twigs and branches.	**Black scale, Brown soft scale.** Yellow, orange, brown, or black, flattened or bulbous insects, often in groups.	*See 136, 137.*

WHAT THE PROBLEM LOOKS LIKE	PROBABLE CAUSE	COMMENTS
HOLLY (*Ilex* spp.), continued		
Sticky honeydew and blackish sooty mold on plant. Bulbous, irregular, brown, gray, or white bodies (scales) on twigs.	**Wax scales.** Bulbous to hemispherical, waxy insects, suck sap.	*See 141.*
Leaves bleached, stippled, may turn brown and drop prematurely. Terminals may be distorted. Plant may have fine webbing.	**Mites,** including **Southern red mite.** Tiny arthropods, often green, pink, or red.	*See 197.*
Brownish, grayish, or tan encrustations on twigs, branches, or leaves. May be dead or declining twigs or branches.	**Greedy scale, Oleander scale, Oystershell scale.** Tiny circular to oval insects, often in colonies.	*See 133–135.*
Slender winding or blotched mines. Pin-pricklike scars in leaves. Mines occur in American holly, puncture scars on American and Japanese holly.	**Native holly leafminer,** *Phytomyza ilicicola* (family Agromyzidae). Adults are tiny black flies, active about April to June. Flattened, pale larvae are in mines in leaves.	Ignore or prune out damage. Plants tolerate abundant mines. Can apply certain insecticides if not tolerable.
Galls or swellings on trunk and roots, usually near soil.	**Crown gall.** Bacterium that persists in soil and infects plant via wounds.	*See 258.*
HONEY LOCUST (*Gleditsia triacanthos*)		
Leaflets turn yellow and drop prematurely.	**Leaf drop,** normal senescence. Leaves often drop in fall sooner than on other species.	Providing trees with a good growing environment and appropriate cultural care may delay leaf drop.
Leaflets turn brown or yellow, especially along margins and at tip. Leaflets may drop prematurely.	**Leaf burn** or **Scorch.** Abiotic disorders, commonly caused by extreme temperature, inappropriate irrigation, poor drainage, and sunburn.	Provide plants with a good growing environment and proper cultural care. *See 273.*
Leaflets yellow, wilt, and drop prematurely. Stems may have dark, sunken cankers. May be orangish, red, or yellow fungal fruiting bodies on wood.	**Cankers,** including **Nectria canker,** *Nectria cinnabarina; Phomopsis* sp. Fungi primarily affect injured or stressed trees.	*See 250.*
Leaflets or shoots with white powdery growth. Leaflets may drop prematurely. Terminals may be distorted or stunted.	**Powdery mildew,** *Microsphaera ravenelii.* A fungal disease favored by moderate temperatures, shade, and poor air circulation.	*See 236.*
Leaflets brown, yellow, stippled, or distorted and may drop prematurely. Branch tips may die back.	**Honeylocust plant bug,** *Diaphnocoris chlorionis.* Greenish or yellow bugs ≤³⁄₁₆ inch long.	*See similar Ash Plant Bugs, 153.*
Leaflets bleached or stippled with spots larger than mite stippling. Cast skins on underside of leaflets.	**Leafhoppers,** including **Potato leafhopper,** *Empoasca fabae.* Greenish to whitish, wedge-shaped insects, ≤⅛ inch long.	Plants tolerate moderate stippling. Apply insecticidal soap or another insecticide if severe. *See 148.*
Leaflets terminate in podlike galls. Foliage browns and drops prematurely.	**Honeylocust pod gall midge.** Adult is tiny fly. White larvae occur in pods.	*See 164.*
Leaflets discolored, stippled, or bleached. Terminals may distort. Plant may have fine webbing.	**Spider mites.** Tiny greenish, reddish, or yellowish mites; may have 2 dark spots.	*See 197.*
Chewed leaflets. Silken tents in tree.	**Mimosa webworm.** Larvae gray to brown with white stripes, ≤½ inch long.	*See 82.*
Sticky honeydew and blackish sooty mold on foliage. Tiny, whitish mothlike adult insects.	**Greenhouse whitefly.** Nymphs are oval, flattened, yellow to greenish insects.	*See 123.*
Sticky honeydew and blackish sooty mold on foliage. Twigs or branches may decline or die back.	**Black scale, European fruit lecanium.** Black, brown, or yellow, flattened or bulbous insects.	*See 136, 139.*

HONEY LOCUST (*Gleditsia triacanthos*), continued

WHAT THE PROBLEM LOOKS LIKE	PROBABLE CAUSE	COMMENTS
Roughened twig bark. Possible twig dieback.	**Treehoppers**, including **Buffalo treehopper**, *Stictocephala bisonia*. Bright yellow to green insects, horny or spiny.	*See 151.*
Dieback of branches. Gnarled, ridged bark with wet spots. Oval to D-shaped emergence holes in wood.	**Flatheaded borer**, *Agrilus* spp.; **Longhorned borers**, including **Locust borer**, *Megacyllene robiniae*. Whitish larvae ≤1 inch long beneath bark.	*See 179, 183.*
Branches or entire plant may die. Foliage yellows and wilts. Fungal fruiting bodies may be on wood or around roots.	**Wood decay** or **Heart rots**, including *Ganoderma applanatum, Phellinus* spp., *Schizophyllum commune*. Fungi that attack injured or stressed trees.	*See Wood Decay in Trunks and Limbs, 248.*

HONEYSUCKLE (*Lonicera* spp.), California honeysuckle

WHAT THE PROBLEM LOOKS LIKE	PROBABLE CAUSE	COMMENTS
Foliage yellows and wilts. Stems may have decay or lesions and die back.	**Diaporthe stem canker and dieback**, *Diaporthe eres*; **Eutypa dieback**, *Eutypa lata*; **Phoma stem and leaf blight**, *Phoma xylostei*. Fungi infect through wounds, persist in infected tissue. Spread during wet conditions.	Avoid wounding plants, except to prune off infected tissue only during prolonged dry weather, making cuts in healthy tissue. Provide a good growing environment and appropriate cultural care.
Foliage discolors and wilts. Branches develop cankers and die back. Dark hemispherical fruiting bodies develop on bark or wood.	**Hypoxylon canker**, *Hypoxylon rubiginosum*. A decay fungus that attacks injured or stressed trees.	*See 257.*
Leaves with brown, light green, yellow, or dead spots or blotches.	**Sudden oak death**, *Phytophthora ramorum*. Pathogen spreads via air and contaminated soil. Apparently can infect through leaves.	On honeysuckle, hosts include at least *L. hispidula*. Primarily a problem in wildlands, killing many oaks there. Do not move infected plant material. Report to agricultural officials if found outside areas where pathogen is known to occur. *See 260.*
Foliage or shoots turn reddish, then yellow, brown, and drop prematurely. Powdery growth on tissue. Shoots or leaves may be stunted and distorted.	**Powdery mildew**, *Erysiphe polygoni*. Fungus develops on living tissue, favored by moderate temperatures, shade, and poor air circulation.	*See 236.*
Brownish, grayish, tan, or white encrustations on bark or twigs. Rarely, declining or dead twigs or branches.	**Greedy scale**. Circular, flattened, ≤1/16 inch long, often in colonies.	Rarely if ever causes serious damage to plants. *See 133.*
Sticky honeydew, blackish sooty mold, and whitish cast skins on plant. Blossoms may be distorted.	**Aphids**, including **Potato aphid**, *Macrosiphum euphorbiae*. Small, pear-shaped insects in groups, often greenish, but may be pink to yellow.	*See 103.*
Chewed leaves. Plants may be defoliated.	**Genista caterpillar**, *Uresiphita reversalis* (family Pyralidae). Caterpillars ≤1¼ inches long, green to orange with black and white hairs.	Introduced to control brooms, which are often considered weeds. In California more common in south than north. Apply *Bacillus thuringiensis* or another insecticide.

HORNBEAM (*Carpinus caroliniana*)

WHAT THE PROBLEM LOOKS LIKE	PROBABLE CAUSE	COMMENTS
Powdery white growth on leaves. Leaves or shoots may distort.	**Powdery mildews**, including *Phyllactinia guttata, Microsphaera penicillata*. Fungal diseases favored by moderate temperatures, shade, and poor air circulation.	*See 236.*
Foliage yellows and wilts. Branches or entire plant may die. Trees may fall over. Fungal fruiting bodies may develop on wood.	**Heart rot** or **Decay fungi**, including *Ganoderma applanatum*, which produces large, fan-shaped basidiocarps on bark. Fungi that infect injured or stressed trees.	*See Wood Decay in Trunks and Limbs, 248.*

WHAT THE PROBLEM LOOKS LIKE	PROBABLE CAUSE	COMMENTS

HORNBEAM (*Carpinus caroliniana*), continued

Foliage discolors and wilts. Branches develop cankers and die back. Dark hemispherical fruiting bodies develop on bark or wood.	**Hypoxylon canker,** *Hypoxylon mammatum.* A decay fungus that attacks injured or stressed trees.	*See 257.*
Sticky honeydew and blackish sooty mold on foliage. Possible plant decline or dieback.	**European fruit lecanium.** Brown or yellow, flat or bulbous, immobile scale insects.	*See 139.*

HYDRANGEA (*Hydrangea* spp.)

Plants stunted. Root system reduced, small roots rotted.	**Pythium root rot,** *Pythium* spp. Soilborne fungi. Spread by spores in soil and water. Favored by excess soil moisture and poor drainage.	*See 268.*
Leaves discolor, wilt, stunt, or drop prematurely. Stems discolored, cankered, and die. Minute white fungus growths may be visible beneath bark or on soil.	**Armillaria root rot.** Present in many soils. Favored by warm, wet soil. Persists for years in infected roots.	*See 262.*
Brown to yellow spots or blotches on leaves. Spots may have dark or yellowish margins. Foliage may shrivel and drop prematurely.	**Leaf spots,** including *Cercospora hydrangeae, Phyllosticta hydrangeae, Septoria hydrangeae.* Spread by air or splashing water. Favored by prolonged cool, wet, conditions. Persist in plant debris. Not reported on hydrangea in California.	Avoid wetting foliage. Use drip irrigation if feasible. Use good sanitation; promptly remove and dispose of debris and infected leaves. *See 223.*
Brown to orangish powdery pustules and yellowish spots on leaves. Leaves may yellow and drop prematurely.	**Rust,** *Pucciniastrum hydrangeae.* Fungus survives on living tissue. Spores are airborne. Favored by high humidity and water.	*See 240.*
Soft, brown decay on flowers, buds, or leaves. May be woolly gray growth (spores) on dead tissue.	**Gray mold.** Fungus develops in plant debris or inactive tissue. Favored by wet conditions and moderate temperatures.	*See 242.*
White powdery patches on leaves and stems. Brown patches may be on upper surface of leaves. Basal leaves may yellow, then brown, and die. Flowers may be deformed or spotted.	**Powdery mildew,** *Erysiphe polygoni.* Fungus survives on living plants. Spores spread by splashing water. Favored by moderate temperatures, shade, and crowding.	*See 236.*
Foliage may yellow or wilt. Roots may be darker or fewer than normal. Galls or swellings may be on roots. Plants may grow slowly.	**Root lesion nematode, Root knot nematodes.** Tiny root-feeding roundworms.	*See 341.*
New growth chlorotic, except for green veins. Plants may be stunted.	**Iron deficiency.** Abiotic disorder usually caused by poor soil conditions or unhealthy roots.	*See 278.*
Sticky honeydew, blackish sooty mold, and whitish cast skins on plant. Foliage may yellow.	**Aphids,** including *Aulacorthum circumflexum;* **Green peach aphid, Melon aphid.** Pear-shaped, often green or yellowish insects.	*See 103.*
Sticky honeydew and blackish sooty mold on plant. Copious white waxy material may be present. Leaves may yellow and wither. Tiny, whitish, mothlike adult insects.	**Whiteflies,** including **Giant whitefly, Greenhouse whitefly, Silverleaf whitefly.** Oval, flattened, translucent, yellow to greenish nymphs and pupae.	*See 121.*

HYDRANGEA (*Hydrangea* spp.), continued

WHAT THE PROBLEM LOOKS LIKE	PROBABLE CAUSE	COMMENTS
Sticky honeydew and blackish sooty mold on plant. Elongate, slender, cottony material (egg sacs) on plant.	**Cottony hydrangea scale**, *Pulvinaria hydrangeae.* Oval, flattened, yellow or brown insects and cottony eggs.	*See Soft Scales, 136.*
Dark brown encrustations on bark. Foliage may yellow. May be decline or dieback of plant.	**Oystershell scale**, *Lepidosaphes ulmi.* Elongate to oval insects, ≤1/16 inch long.	*See 135.*
Unusual branching. Premature flower bud formation. Distorted flowers. Delayed or no flowers. Dead leaf patches. Leaf tips may wilt.	**Plant bugs**, *Lygus* spp. Brown, green, or yellowish bugs, ≤1/4 inch long, suck plant juices.	*See 155.*
Leaves bleached, stippled, may turn brown and drop prematurely. Terminals may be distorted. Plant may have fine webbing.	**Spider mites**, *Tetranychus* spp. Tiny, often green, pink, or red pests; may have 2 dark spots.	*See 197.*
Foliage chewed and webbed together with silk. Stems may be mined. Larvae wriggle vigorously when touched.	**Caterpillars**, including **Greenhouse leaftier**, *Udea rubigalis* (family Pyralidae). *Udea* larvae are yellowish green with three longitudinal green to white stripes, adults are reddish brown with black wavy lines on wings, both are ≤3/4 inch long.	*Udea* has about 6 generations per year. *See Foliage-Feeding Caterpillars, 71.*

HYPERICUM (*Hypericum* spp.), Gold flower, St. Johnswort

WHAT THE PROBLEM LOOKS LIKE	PROBABLE CAUSE	COMMENTS
Leaves wilted, discolored, may drop prematurely. Branches or entire plant may die. May be white fungal growth or dark crust on basal trunk, roots, or soil.	**Dematophora root rot.** Fungus favored by mild, wet conditions. Infects primarily through roots growing near infested plants.	*See 264.*
Leaves with orangish powder or pustules. Leaves spotted, discolored, and may drop prematurely.	**Rusts**, including *Melampsora hypericorum, Uromyces triquetrus.* Fungal diseases favored by wet foliage.	*Hypericum calycinum* is especially susceptible. Avoid overhead watering. Vigorous plants tolerate moderate rust infections. *See 240.*
Chewed leaves. Entire plant may be defoliated.	**Klamathweed beetle.** Adults metallic, oval, bluish, about 1/4 inch long.	*See 91.*
Leaves stippled, bleached, with varnishlike specks on undersides.	**Greenhouse thrips.** Tiny, slender, black adults or yellowish nymphs.	*See 158.*

IRONWOOD (*Lyonothamnus floribundus*), Catalina ironwood

WHAT THE PROBLEM LOOKS LIKE	PROBABLE CAUSE	COMMENTS
Leaves chlorotic and necrotic and may be undersized.	**Alkaline soil.** Symptoms of various mineral deficiencies and toxicities develop when grown in soil with high pH.	*See 283.*
Sticky honeydew and blackish sooty mold on leaves. White popcornlike bodies on bark.	**Cottony cushion scale.** Orangish, flat immatures or cottony females on bark.	Usually under good biological control. *See 142.*

IVY (*Hedera* spp.), Algerian ivy, English ivy*

WHAT THE PROBLEM LOOKS LIKE	PROBABLE CAUSE	COMMENTS
Leaves have black, brown, tan, or yellow blotches. Spots usually angular and vein-limited where veins are large, round where veins are absent. Spots may have yellowish halo. Leaves may drop prematurely.	**Bacterial leaf spots and blight**, *Pseudomonas cichorii, Xanthomonas campestris* pv. *hederae.* Bacteria spread by water. Favored by cool, wet conditions. Persist in plant debris.	Avoid overhead irrigation. Improve air circulation. Plant resistant English ivy cultivars.
Leaves have brown to yellow spots or blotches. Spots may have dark or yellowish margins. Foliage may shrivel and drop prematurely.	**Leaf spots or blight, Anthracnose**, *Alternaria, Colletotrichum, Phyllosticta* spp. Fungi spread by air or splashing water. Favored by wet conditions.	Spots often less angular and have less of a chlorotic halo than with bacterial caused spots. *See 223.*

*Some species are invasive weeds. Other species may be better choices when planting.

IVY (*Hedera* spp.), Algerian ivy, English ivy, continued

WHAT THE PROBLEM LOOKS LIKE	PROBABLE CAUSE	COMMENTS
Discolored spots between veins. Large spots chlorotic, then tan or brown.	**Leaf burn** or **Sunburn.** Abiotic disorders commonly cause by high temperatures, inadequate irrigation, poor soil conditions, or unhealthy roots.	*See 288.*
Foliage yellows. Plants wilt and die, often suddenly. Roots and stem near soil dark, decayed, girdled by lesions. Leaves have large dark spots.	**Root and crown rots,** *Pythium, Phytophthora* spp. Fungi survive in soil, favored by wet, poorly drained soil.	*See 265, 268.*
Foliage discolored, stippled, or bleached, and may drop prematurely. Terminals may distort. Plant may have fine webbing.	**Spider mites,** including **Privet mite, Two-spotted spider mite.** Greenish, yellowish, or red, tiny arthropods; may have 2 dark spots.	*See 197.*
Plant has sticky honeydew and blackish sooty mold. Plant grows slowly. Foliage may yellow.	**Pyriform scale,** *Protopulvinaria pyriformis.* Triangular, ⅛ inch long, brown, yellow, or mottled red. May be small white egg sacs.	Common in Florida and also occurs in southern California. *See Soft Scales, 136.*
Foliage yellows. Rarely, plant may decline or die back. Bark or leaves have gray, brown, tan, white, or yellow encrustations.	**Dictyospermum scale,** *Chrysomphalus dictyospermi;* **Greedy scale; Latania scale; Oleander scale; Yellow scale.** Circular, flattened insects, <¹⁄₁₆ inch long.	*See 131.*
Plant has sticky honeydew and blackish sooty mold. Foliage may yellow.	**Nigra scale,** *Parasaissetia nigra;* **Brown soft scale.** Oval, flat or convex, black, brown, orange, or yellow insects ≤⅜ inches long.	*See 137.*
Plant has sticky honeydew, blackish sooty mold, and whitish cast skins. Foliage may yellow from aphids sucking sap.	**Aphids,** including **Bean aphid; Green peach aphid; Ivy aphid,** *Aphis hederae.* Small pear-shaped insects, often green, yellowish, or blackish.	*See 103.*
Plant has sticky honeydew, blackish sooty mold, and cottony material (egg sacs). Foliage may yellow.	**Grape mealybug,** *Pseudococcus maritimus.* Oval, soft, powdery, waxy insects, ≤⅛ inch long.	*See 126.*
Foliage has sticky honeydew and blackish sooty mold. Leaves may yellow and wither. Tiny, whitish, mothlike adult insects.	**Whiteflies,** including **Citrus whitefly.** Oval, flattened, translucent, yellow to greenish nymphs and pupae.	*See 121.*
Leaves chewed. Foliage may be rolled or tied together with silk.	**Omnivorous looper.** Tan to brownish adult moths and yellow, green, or pink larvae, ≤1½ inches long, with green, yellow or black stripes.	*See 79.*
Foliage or shoots chewed, ragged, or clipped. May be slimy or silvery trails on or around plants.	**Brown garden snail.** Mollusk moves slowly on slimy, muscular foot and has a spiraled shell.	*See 205.*

JACARANDA (*Jacaranda* spp.)

WHAT THE PROBLEM LOOKS LIKE	PROBABLE CAUSE	COMMENTS
Leaves with blackish sooty mold, sticky honeydew, and whitish cast skins.	**Aphids,** including **Bean aphid.** Small green or black insects in groups.	*See 103.*

JAPANESE PAGODA TREE (*Sophora japonica*)

WHAT THE PROBLEM LOOKS LIKE	PROBABLE CAUSE	COMMENTS
Leaves discolor and wilt. Branches die back. Entire tree may die. Minute white fungus growths may be visible beneath bark or on soil.	**Armillaria root rot.** Present in many soils. Favored by warm, wet soil. Persists for years in infected roots.	*See 262.*
Chewed leaves. Plants may be defoliated.	**Genista caterpillar,** *Uresiphita reversalis* (family Pyralidae). Caterpillars ≤1¼ inches long, green to orange with black and white hairs.	Introduced to control brooms, which are often considered weeds. In California more common in south than north. Apply *Bacillus thuringiensis* or another insecticide.

WHAT THE PROBLEM LOOKS LIKE	PROBABLE CAUSE	COMMENTS
JASMINE (*Jasminum* spp.), Star jasmine		
Sticky honeydew and blackish sooty mold on plant. Waxy, cottony material on plant.	**Mealybugs,** including **Longtailed mealybug.** Powdery grayish insects, ≤⅛ inch long, with waxy filaments.	*See 126.*
Sticky honeydew and blackish sooty mold on leaves or twigs. Plants may decline.	**Scales,** including **Black scale.** Bulbous to flattened insects, black, brown, or yellowish. May be H-shape on back.	*See 136.*
JUNIPER (*Juniperus* spp.)	Juniper (Juniperus spp.)	
Foliage yellows and wilts. Branches or entire plant dies. Roots may be dark or decayed.	**Root and crown rots,** *Phytophthora* spp. Pathogens promoted by excess soil moisture and poor drainage.	*See 265.*
Foliage brown, reddish, yellow, or wilted. Shoots die back. Shoots may be bushy, stunted, witches' brooms.	**Twig blights,** including *Kabatina juniperi, Phomopsis juniperovora.* Fungal pathogens that infect wet foliage through wounds.	Avoid wounding twigs, except to prune out and dispose of infected shoots. Keep foliage dry. Use drip irrigation and provide good air circulation. Avoid fertilization.
Foliage browns or yellows. Branches die back. Entire plant may die. Minute white fungus growths may be visible beneath bark or on soil.	**Armillaria root rot.** Present in many soils. Favored by warm, wet soil. Persists for years in infected roots.	*See 262.*
Brown or yellow dying foliage on branches. Cankers and resinous exudate on limbs or trunk.	**Cypress canker.** A fungal disease.	Not common on juniper. Primarily infects cypress. *See 250.*
Browning of shoot tips beginning in fall, worst late winter to spring.	**Cypress tip miner.** Adults are small, silvery tan moths. Green larvae, ≤⅛ inch long, tunnel in foliage.	*See 167.*
Browning of shoot tips. Plant appears brown most of the year.	**Juniper needle miner,** *Stenolechia bathrodyas* (family Gelechiidae). Green larvae, ≤⅛ inch long, mine leaflets. Adults are silvery moths, about ¼ inch long.	In California, a problem along the south coast. Plants tolerate extensive needle mining. If not tolerable, adults may be sprayed during three annual flights of moths. Shake foliage regularly March–October, spray only if moths abundant. *See similar Cypress Tip Miner, 167.*
Browning and webbing of needles, initially in patches and then overall if severe.	**Juniper webworm,** *Dichomeris marginella* (family Gelechiidae). Brown, reddish, purplish, or yellowish larvae, mine needles when young and feed externally in webbing when mature. Adults are small coppery brown and white moths.	Plants tolerate extensive needle mining. If not tolerable, may be sprayed using high-pressure sprayer to penetrate webbing during early spring and late fall when large larvae or adults are observed. *See similar Cypress Tip Miner, 167.*
Foliage turns brown or yellow. Needles may drop prematurely.	**Leaf burn** or **Scorch.** Abiotic disorders with many potential causes, including inappropriate irrigation, poor drainage, saline water, unfavorable soil pH.	Older, inner needles are unavoidable shed naturally. Provide plants with a good growing environment and proper cultural care. *See 273.*
Pale greenish or yellow needles. Foliage stippled.	**Spider mites,** including **Spruce spider mite.** Tiny pests, often greenish specks, may be in fine webbing at foliage base.	*See Pine and Spruce Spider Mites, 200.*
Yellow or brown foliage. Whitish to brownish encrustations on foliage.	**Juniper scale,** *Carulaspis juniperi;* **Minute cypress scale.** Circular to elongate insects, ≤1/16 inch long.	Populations in California rarely warrant control, except on Italian cypress or in nurseries. *See 136.*
Yellow or brown foliage on scattered dying or dead branches. Entire plant never dead.	**Juniper twig girdler.** Off-white larva with brown head, ≤⅜ inch long, occurs in tunnel beneath twig bark.	*See 195.*

JUNIPER (*Juniperus* spp.), continued

WHAT THE PROBLEM LOOKS LIKE	PROBABLE CAUSE	COMMENTS
Yellow or brown foliage. Dieback of branches.	**Flatheaded borer,** *Chrysobothris* sp. Whitish larva ≤1¼ inches long with enlarged head, tunnels in wood.	In California affects mostly *Juniperus chinensis* 'Kaizuka' or 'Torulosa' in San Joaquin Valley. Keep plants vigorous. *See 179.*
Orangish, gelatinous masses or galls on bark. Stem dieback. Shoots may be discolored, bushy, or stunted.	**Juniper rusts,** *Gymnosporangium* spp. Fungi favored by wet conditions, alternate on deciduous hosts.	*See Gymnosporangium Rusts, 242.*
Tufts of cottony material protruding from bark. Foliage may redden, yellow, and eventually die. Treetop or entire tree may die.	**Cypress bark mealybug; Incense cedar scale** or **Monterey cypress scale,** *Xylococcus macrocarpae* (family Margarodidae). Reddish insects ≤¹⁄₁₆ inch long under cottony wax.	*See 127.*
Brown to purplish insects clustered on foliage. May be sticky honeydew or blackish sooty mold on foliage.	**Giant conifer aphids.** Dark, long-legged, ≤⅛ inch long.	Apparently harmless to trees. *See 105.*
Chewed needles.	**Conifer sawflies, Cypress sawfly.** Green larvae ≤1 inch long, on needles.	*See 83, 84.*
Galls or swellings on roots.	**Root knot nematode,** *Meloidogyne* sp. Tiny root-feeding roundworms.	*See 345.*

KATSURA TREE (*Cercidiphyllum japonicum*)

Brown to gray encrustations on bark. Possibly declining or dead twigs or branches.	**Purple scale,** *Lepidosaphes beckii*. Small elongate insects, often in colonies.	Plants tolerate moderate populations. Conserve beneficials. Tolerate or monitor and apply oil if damaging. *See 131.*

LANTANA (*Lantana montevidensis*)

Flowers, leaves, and shoots discolor, wilt, decay, and drop prematurely.	**Botrytis blight.** A fungal disease favored by moist conditions and mild temperatures.	Avoid overhead watering. Thin canopy to improve air circulation. Provide proper care. Prune out dying tissue, make cuts in healthy stems. *See 242.*
Sticky honeydew and blackish sooty mold on foliage. Tiny, whitish, mothlike adult insects.	**Greenhouse whitefly, Silverleaf whitefly.** Nymphs oval, flattened, yellowish to translucent.	*See 123, 124.*
Leaves with brown to gray irregular roundish botches. Heavily infested leaves may drop prematurely.	**Lantana leafblotch miner,** *Liriomyza* sp. (family Agromyzidae). Yellow to orange larvae feed within leaves, then drop and pupate in soil. Adults are small, black and bright yellow flies.	Occurs in south coastal California. No documented control. Insecticides that have translaminar movement may control larvae.

LARCH (*Larix* spp.)

Foliage discolors and drops.	**Normal dormancy.**	Larch are deciduous conifers that normally drop all needles in the fall.
Foliage discolors, wilts, stunts, drops prematurely. Discolored bark or cankers may ooze sap. Branches or plant may die.	**Root and crown rots.** Decay fungi favored by excess soil moisture and poor drainage.	*See 265.*
Powdery white or grayish material on cones, limbs, needles, or the trunk.	**Adelgids.** Aphidlike insects suck sap and alternative hosts with other conifers.	*See 112.*
Chewed needles.	**Conifer sawflies.** Green larvae, ≤1 inch long, on needles.	*See 83.*

LAUREL (*Prunus* spp.); CAROLINA LAUREL CHERRY (*P. caroliniana*); CATALINA CHERRY (*P. lyonii*); ENGLISH LAUREL (*P. laurocerasus*); HOLLYLEAF CHERRY (*P. ilicifolia*)

Foliage yellows and wilts. Entire plant may die. Minute white fungus growths may be visible beneath bark or on soil.	**Armillaria root rot.** Present in many soils. Favored by warm, wet soil. Persists for years in infected roots.	*See 262.*

LAUREL (*Prunus* spp.); **CAROLINA LAUREL CHERRY** (*P. caroliniana*); **CATALINA CHERRY** (*P. lyonii*); **ENGLISH LAUREL** (*P. laurocerasus*); **HOLLYLEAF CHERRY** (*P. ilicifolia*), continued

WHAT THE PROBLEM LOOKS LIKE	PROBABLE CAUSE	COMMENTS
Foliage yellows and wilts. Branches or entire plant dies.	**Root and crown rots**, *Phytophthora* spp. Fungal pathogens favored by wet soil and poor drainage.	*See 265.*
Leaves with brown, reddish, or yellow discolored blotches. Infected blotches may drop, leaving holes in leaves. Leaves may drop prematurely.	**Leaf spots**, including the bacterium *Pseudomonas syringae* and fungi such as *Blumeriella* sp., *Cercospora* sp. Pathogens favored by wet conditions.	*See 223.*
Small brownish, purplish, or reddish leaf spots, centers tan. Holes in leaf from dropped, infected tissue. Concentric lesions on branch.	**Shot hole.** A fungal disease favored by prolonged wet conditions.	*See 226.*
Leaves with necrotic blotches or spots. Spots may have reddish or yellow margins. Leaves may drop prematurely.	**Physiological leaf spot.** Abiotic disorders with many potential causes, including boron toxicity, direct injury to bark or roots, high temperatures, poor drainage, and too much or too little water.	Provide plants with good growing conditions and proper cultural care. *See 273.*
Powdery white growth and brown or yellow blotches on leaves and sometimes on stems. Shoots and leaves may be undersized or distorted.	**Powdery mildews**, *Podosphaera* spp., *Sphaerotheca pannosa*. Fungal diseases favored by moderate temperatures, shade, and poor air circulation.	*See 236.*
Brownish, grayish, tan, or white encrustations on bark.	**Greedy scale, Oleander scale.** Insects are circular to flattened, <¹⁄₁₆ inch long.	Rarely if ever cause serious damage to plants. *See 133, 134.*
Dead twigs or branches. Plant declines, may die. Tiny "shot holes" in bark.	**Shothole borer.** Small brown adults, whitish larvae, tunnel beneath bark.	*See 176.*
Sticky honeydew, blackish sooty mold, and whitish cast skins on foliage.	**Aphids.** Small blackish, brown, green, or yellowish insects, usually in groups.	*See 103.*
Sticky honeydew and blackish sooty mold on plant. Woody parts may decline and die back.	**Brown soft scale, Frosted scale.** Oval, flat or bulbous insects, brown, orangish, yellow, whitish or waxy insects.	*See 137, 138.*
Stippled or bleached leaves, varnishlike excrement specks on undersides.	**Greenhouse thrips.** Tiny, slender, blackish adults or yellowish nymphs.	*See 158.*
Stippled, flecked, or bleached leaves. Leaves may drop prematurely.	**Mites**, including **Citrus red mite.** Tiny, sand-sized specks on leaves, often reddish, suck sap.	*See 197.*

LINDEN (*Tilia* spp.)

WHAT THE PROBLEM LOOKS LIKE	PROBABLE CAUSE	COMMENTS
Sticky honeydew, blackish sooty mold, and whitish cast skins on leaves.	**Linden aphid**, *Eucallipterus tiliae*. Small yellowish insects, with black.	Conserve *Trioxys curvicaudus* parasites and other natural enemies. Plant *Tilia platyphyllos* or other species with more hairy leaf undersides. Avoid more susceptible, *T. cordata* and *T. europaea*. *See Aphids, 103.*
Sticky honeydew and blackish sooty mold on leaves. Twigs and limbs may die back.	**Tuliptree scale.** Females ≤¹⁄₃ inch, irregularly hemispherical, and variably colored brown to gray with other-colored blotches.	Primarily a pest of tulip tree and deciduous magnolias. *See 141.*
Leaves with elongate or pointed growths on upper surface.	**Linden gall mite**, *Eriophyes tiliae*. Microscopic, wormlike eriophyid mites that induce leaf galls.	These mites do not seriously harm trees. No control is recommended. *See Gall Mites, 203.*
Leaves may discolor and wilt. Bark may have boring frass, elliptical holes, or oozing liquid. Branches or entire tree may die.	**Borers**, including **Longhorned borers**, *Saperda* spp. White larvae, ≤1½ inches long, that bore beneath bark.	Usually secondary pests that attack injured or severely stressed trees. *See 171, 183.*

LIQUIDAMBAR (*Liquidambar* spp.), Sweet gum

WHAT THE PROBLEM LOOKS LIKE	PROBABLE CAUSE	COMMENTS
Limbs drop, usually during or after hot weather.	**Summer limb drop.** Abiotic disorders caused by tree injury or stress, such as drought.	Protect trees from injury. Provide good growing conditions and appropriate cultural care. Have tree inspected by arborist.
Leaves discolor and wilt. Branches or tree-top dying. Branches may canker or exude reddish pitchy.	**Botryosphaeria canker and dieback.** Fungus primarily affects injured or drought stressed trees.	Provide proper irrigation. *See 255.*
Leaves with dark or discolored blotches. Leaves may drop prematurely.	**Leaf spots,** including *Cercospora* spp. Fungi favored by wet conditions.	*See 223.*
Leaves with brown or purplish blotches or streaks. Foliage may drop prematurely.	**Persea mite.** Tiny green to yellow mites, often with dark spots.	*See 199.*
Sticky honeydew and blackish sooty mold on foliage. Trees may decline and eventually die.	**Calico scale.** Adults globular, black with white or yellow spots.	Can be a serious pest on liquidambar. *See 138.*
Chewed foliage. Webbing or tents on branch terminals.	**Fall webworm.** Larvae white to yellow, hairy, ≤1 inch long	*See 81.*
Leaves chewed, may be tied with silk. Plant may be defoliated.	**Fruittree leafroller, Tussock moths.** Larvae green or hairy, ≤1½ inches long.	*See 77, 79.*
Chewed foliage. Typically only single branches are defoliated.	**Redhumped caterpillar.** Larvae, ≤1 inch long, with red head, body yellowish with reddish and black stripes.	*See 78.*
Foliage may be notched around margins. Some roots stripped of bark or girdled near soil. Young trees may wilt or die.	**Black vine weevil.** Adults are black or grayish snout beetles, about ⅜ inch long. Larvae are white grubs with brown head.	Larvae feed on roots. Adults hide during day and feed at night. *See 92.*
Bark exudes white, frothy material, often around wounds, has pleasant odor.	**Foamy canker.** Unidentified cause, possibly a bacterium.	Foamy material appears for only short time during warm weather. *See 259.*

LOCUST (*Robinia* spp.), Black locust

WHAT THE PROBLEM LOOKS LIKE	PROBABLE CAUSE	COMMENTS
Leaves or shoots with powdery growth. Shoots or leaves may be stunted and distorted.	**Powdery mildews,** including *Erysiphe polygoni.* Fungi favored by moderate temperatures, shade, and poor air circulation.	*See 236.*
Leaves and branches wilt in spring. Stems may have callus tissue, dark or sunken cankers, or coral-colored pustules.	**Nectria canker.** Fungus primarily affects injured or stressed trees.	*See 257.*
Leaves yellow and wilt. Branches or entire plant may die. Trees may fall over.	**Heart rot** or **Decay fungi,** including *Ganoderma applanatum,* which produces large, fan-shaped basidiocarps on bark. Fungi that infect injured or stressed trees.	*See Wood Decay in Trunks and Limbs, 248.*
Limbs dying or dead. Large holes, ≤½ inch diameter, in trunks and limbs. Slow tree growth.	**Carpenterworm.** Whitish larvae, ≤2½ inches long, with brown head, tunnel in wood.	*See 194.*
Limbs dying or dead. Bark has many tiny round holes, which may ooze.	**Bark beetles,** including *Chramesus* spp. Adults ¹⁄₁₀ inch long, dark, cylindrical. Whitish maggotlike larvae under bark.	Attack only severely stressed trees and dying limbs. Prune out infested wood. Provide trees proper care. *See 173.*
Bark discolored, oozing, or swollen. Boring dust in crevices, at tree base. Dying limbs. Tree may decline.	**Black locust borer,** *Megacyllene robiniae.* Whitish larvae bore under bark. Adult is yellow and black longhorned beetle.	Attacks primarily stressed trees. Provide trees proper cultural care. *See Longhorned Borers, 183.*
Roughened twig bark. Possible twig dieback.	**Treehoppers,** including **Buffalo treehopper,** *Stictocephala bisonia.* Bright yellow to green insects, horny or spiny.	*See 151.*

LOCUST (*Robinia* spp.), Black locust, continued

WHAT THE PROBLEM LOOKS LIKE	PROBABLE CAUSE	COMMENTS
Copious, misty, nonsticky liquid raining from plant. Surfaces covered with whitish residue.	**Glassy-winged sharpshooter.** Active, dark brown or gray leafhoppers ≤½ inch long, suck xylem fluid.	Vectors pathogens of oleander and certain crops, especially grapes. Report suspected glassy-winged sharpshooters to agricultural officials if found in areas where this pest is not known to occur. *See 148.*
Sticky honeydew and blackish sooty mold on plant.	**Frosted scale.** Hemispherical to flattened, brown, yellowish, or waxy insects, ≤¼ inch long, suck sap.	*See 139.*
Leaves chewed and may be tied with silk. Plant may be defoliated.	**Fruittree leafroller.** Green larvae, ≤1½ inches long, with black head.	*See 79.*
Leaves stippled, bleached, or reddened.	**Spider mites,** including **European red mite.** Tiny reddish to yellow arthropods, suck sap.	*See 197.*
Leaflets galled, margins rolled, or terminals podlike. Foliage may brown and drop prematurely.	**Pod gall midges,** including *Dasineura* sp., *Obolodiplosis robiniae.* Adults are tiny flies. Pale larvae occur in galled or rolled leaflets, then drop and pupate beneath plant.	Plants tolerate extensive galling. Foliar oil sprays during oviposition in spring may control. *See Gall Midges, 164.*

LOQUAT (*Eriobotrya japonica*)

WHAT THE PROBLEM LOOKS LIKE	PROBABLE CAUSE	COMMENTS
Sudden wilting then shriveling and blackening of shoots, blossoms, and fruit. Plant appears scorched.	**Fire blight.** Bacterium enters plants through blossoms.	*See 229.*
Black to dark olive spots on fruit and sometimes on leaves. Leaves yellow and may drop prematurely.	**Scab,** *Spilocaea pyracanthae.* A fungal disease spread by water from infected leaves and twigs.	Avoid overhead watering. Prune out infected twigs in fall, make the cuts in healthy wood. Rake and dispose of infected leaves. *See 227.*
Tiny reddish to brown leaf spots, may have yellow halos. Larger, dark areas on leaves. Leaves may drop prematurely.	**Entomosporium leaf spot.** A fungal disease promoted by wet foliage.	*See 227.*
Leaves stippled and may become bleached.	**Spider mites,** including **Sycamore spider mite.** Green specks, suck sap.	In California, a problem mostly in interior valleys. *See 197.*

MADRONE (*Arbutus menziesii*); **STRAWBERRY TREE** (*Arbutus unedo*)

WHAT THE PROBLEM LOOKS LIKE	PROBABLE CAUSE	COMMENTS
Leaves discolor, stunt, or drop prematurely. Cankers may develop on basal stems. Plants grow slowly and may die. Roots or basal stem may be dark or decayed.	**Root and crown rot,** *Phytophthora cactorum.* Pathogen promoted by excess soil moisture and poor drainage.	*See 265.*
Leaves brown, yellow, and wilt. Scorched leaves may remain on plant. May be dying and dead branches or cankers on large branches and the trunk. Dead branches may turn black.	**Cankers, Twig dieback,** including *Botryosphaeria dothidea, Fusicoccum aesculi, Nattrassia mangiferae, Phomopsis* spp. Fungi that primarily attack injured or weakened trees.	Prune out dead and diseased branches in summer. Provide appropriate water and other cultural care to improve tree vigor. Manage as with *Botryosphaeria Canker and Dieback, 250, 255.*
Leaves yellow, wilt and drop prematurely. Branches die back and entire plant may die.	**Annosus root disease.** Decay fungus that spreads through roots and airborne spores.	*See 265.*
Leaves with brown, light green, yellow, or dead spots or blotches. Twigs and stems may canker, ooze, or die back. Plants may die.	**Sudden oak death,** *Phytophthora ramorum.* Pathogen spreads via air and contaminated soil. Apparently can infect through bark or leaves.	Primarily a problem in wildlands, killing many oaks there. Do not move infected plant material. Report to agricultural officials if found outside areas where pathogen is known to occur. *See page 260.*
Leaves with small discrete spots to irregular, large blotches or holes over most of surface. Tree may defoliate if severe.	**Leaf spots,** including *Cryptostictis arbuti, Mycosphaerella arbuticola, Phyllosticta fimbriata, Sphaceloma* sp. Fungi spread in water and favored by cool, wet, conditions.	Diseases apparently promoted by wet winters. Plants tolerate extensive leaf spotting. Little or no effective controls in landscapes or wildlands. *See 223.*

MADRONE (*Arbutus menziesii*); STRAWBERRY TREE (*Arbutus unedo*), continued

WHAT THE PROBLEM LOOKS LIKE	PROBABLE CAUSE	COMMENTS
Leaves with oval or irregular, glossy black, thick tarlike raised spots on upper surface.	**Tar spot**, *Rhytisma arbuti*. Fungus most prevalent in moist environments.	Rake and dispose of leaves in the fall. *See Leaf Spots, 223.*
Leaves with mined blotches or dead patches. Lower leaf surface scraped.	**Leafblotch miner**, *Gelechia panella* (family Gelechiidae). Moth larva ≤⅔ inch long.	Does not harm plant. Tolerate or clip and dispose of infested leaves. *See Foliage Miners, 166.*
Leaves with elliptical blotches or holes, ⅛ to ¼ inch long, or winding tunnels.	**Madrone shield bearer**, *Coptodisca arbutiella*. Larvae, ≤¼ inch long, mine leaves. Adult is tiny moth.	Vigorous plants tolerate moderate leaf damage. No management known. *See Shield Bearers, 169.*
Leaves with winding, silvery or whitish tunnels.	**Leafminer**, *Marmara arbutiella* (family Geometridae). Moth larva feed within leaves.	Does not harm plant. Tolerate or clip and dispose of infested leaves. *See Foliage Miners, 166.*
Leaves have pinkish to pale blisters. Leaves are partly or all crisp, distorted, thickened, and brown or white. White or pinkish spores may cover infected tissue.	**Blister blight** or **Leaf gall**, *Exobasidium vaccinii*. Fungus spreads by air only during wet weather.	Avoid overhead watering. Prune only when dry. Improve air circulation. Vigorous plants tolerate extensive leaf galling. Hand-pick or prune out galls. Rake and dispose of fallen leaves.
Sticky honeydew and blackish sooty mold on foliage. Dark, immobile bodies (pupae) about 1/16 inch long on underside of leaves.	**Madrone whitefly**, *Trialeurodes madroni*. Fringe of white filaments on sides of dark pupal cases.	Tolerate. Apparently does not damage plants. *See Whiteflies, 121.*
Sticky honeydew and blackish sooty mold on foliage. White felty sacs mostly on twigs.	**Madrone psyllid**, *Euphyllura arbuti*. Tiny, reddish, winged adults or flattened, gray to whitish, waxy nymphs.	After initial abundance, populations decline due to natural enemies including lady beetles, predaceous bugs, and parasitic wasps such as *Psyllaephagus arbuticola*. Conserve natural enemies. If severe, a fall or spring oil spray may provide control. *See Psyllids, 114.*
Sticky honeydew and blackish sooty mold on foliage. Twigs or branches may decline or die back.	**Black scale, Brown soft scale.** Black, brown, orangish, or yellow, flattened or bulbous insects.	*See 136, 137.*
Sticky honeydew, blackish sooty mold, and whitish cast skins on plant.	**Aphids.** Small green, black, brown, or yellowish, pear-shaped insects, often in groups.	*See 103.*
Leaves stippled, bleached. Varnishlike specks on underside.	**Greenhouse thrips.** Tiny, slender, black adults or yellowish nymphs.	*See 158.*
Chewed leaves. Tents or mats of silk on leaves.	**Western tent caterpillar.** Hairy larva, mostly brown, ≤2 inches long.	*See 80.*
Trunk or limbs with roughened, wet, or oozing area. Cracked bark and dieback.	**Flatheaded borers.** Larvae whitish, with enlarged head, under bark. Adults bullet-shaped, metallic, coppery, gray, greenish, or bluish.	*See 179.*
Brownish, grayish, tan, or white encrustations on twigs or bark. Rarely, declining or dead twigs or branches.	**Greedy scale, San Jose scale.** Circular, flattened, ≤1/16 inch long, often in colonies.	Rarely if ever causes serious damage to trees. *See 132, 133.*

MAGNOLIA (*Magnolia* spp.), Tulip tree

WHAT THE PROBLEM LOOKS LIKE	PROBABLE CAUSE	COMMENTS
Leaves and blossoms with dark blotches. Blossoms, leaves, and terminals turn brown, wilt, and die. Cankers or lesions may occur on twigs.	**Bacterial blight and canker.** Disease favored by wet conditions.	*See 245.*
Leaves and branches wilt in spring. Stems may have dark cankers, callus tissue, or coral-colored pustules.	**Nectria canker**, *Nectria* spp. Fungi primarily affect injured or stressed trees.	*See 257.*

WHAT THE PROBLEM LOOKS LIKE	PROBABLE CAUSE	COMMENTS
MAGNOLIA (*Magnolia* spp.), Tulip tree, continued		
Brown, black, tan, or yellow spots or blotches on leaves. Spots may have dark or yellowish margins. Foliage may die and drop prematurely.	**Leaf spots**, including *Cladosporium* sp., *Phyllosticta* sp. Fungi spread in water and are favored by prolonged cool, wet, conditions.	*See 223*
Leaves yellowish, except along veins. Leaves may be small or drop prematurely.	**Iron deficiency.** Abiotic disorder usually caused by poor soil conditions or unhealthy roots.	*See 278.*
Leaves turn brown or yellow, especially along margins and at tip. Leaves may drop prematurely.	**Leaf burn** or **Scorch.** Abiotic disorders with many potential causes, commonly caused by high temperatures, inappropriate irrigation, or poor drainage.	Provide plants with a good growing environment and proper cultural care. *See 273.*
White powdery growth on leaves or shoots. Terminals may be distorted or stunted.	**Powdery mildew**, possibly *Microsphaera* sp. Fungal disease favored by moderate temperatures, shade, and poor air circulation.	*See 236.*
Sticky honeydew and blackish sooty mold on leaves. White popcornlike bodies on bark.	**Cottony cushion scale.** Orangish, flat immatures or cottony females on bark.	Usually under good biological control. *See 142.*
Sticky honeydew and blackish sooty mold on leaves.	**Obscure mealybug.** Powdery gray insects with waxy filaments.	Conserve natural enemies that help in control. *See 127.*
Sticky honeydew and blackish sooty mold on leaves. Twigs and limbs may die back.	**Tuliptree scale.** Females ≤⅓ inch wide, irregularly hemispherical, and variably colored brown to gray with other-colored blotches.	Primarily a pest of *Liriodendron tulipifera* and deciduous magnolias. *See 141.*
Leaves stippled, bleached. Varnishlike specks on underside.	**Greenhouse thrips.** Tiny, slender, black adults or yellowish nymphs.	*See 158.*
Chewed leaves. Foliage may be rolled and tied together with silk.	**Omnivorous looper.** Yellow, green, or pink larvae, ≤1½ inches long, with green, yellow or black stripes.	Larvae crawl in "looping" manner. *See 79.*
Brownish, grayish, tan, orange, or white bark encrustations. Rarely, dead or dying twigs or branches.	**California red scale, Greedy scale, Oleander scale.** Tiny circular to oval individuals, often in colonies.	*See 131–135.*
Galls or swellings on trunk and roots, usually near soil.	**Crown gall.** Bacterium persists in soil and infects plant via wounds.	*See 258.*
Bark stained brownish, exudes rancid fluid, often around crotches, wounds.	**Wetwood** or **Slime flux.** Bacterial infection.	Usually does not cause serious harm to trees. *See 259.*
MAHONIA (*Mahonia, Berberis* spp.), Barberry, Oregon grape		
Leaves stippled, bleached. Varnishlike specks on underside.	**Greenhouse thrips.** Tiny, slender, black adults or yellowish nymphs.	*See 158.*
Leaves chewed. Plants may be defoliated.	**Barberry looper**, *Coryphista meadii* (family Gracillariidae). Green caterpillars, ≤1 inch long.	Vigorous plants tolerate moderate defoliation. Tolerate or apply *Bacillus thuringiensis* or another insecticide. *See Foliage-Feeding Caterpillars, 71.*
Foliage discolored, reddening with irregular brown to black dead spots. Orangish pustules or coating on leaves.	**Mahonia rusts**, *Cumminsiella mirabilissima, Puccinia* spp. Fungal diseases favored by wet foliage.	Avoid overhead watering. Vigorous plants tolerate moderate infection. *See Rusts, 240.*
Sticky honeydew and blackish sooty mold on plant. Tiny mothlike insects (adult insects) on foliage. May be poor plant growth.	**Deer brush whitefly**, *Aleurothrixus interrogationis.* Oval, yellow, or tan nymphs and black pupae that suck sap on undersides of leaves.	Plants tolerate moderate densities. If severe, insecticidal soap may be applied. *See Whiteflies, 121.*

WHAT THE PROBLEM LOOKS LIKE	PROBABLE CAUSE	COMMENTS
MAHONIA (*Mahonia, Berberis* spp.), Barberry, Oregon grape, *continued*		
Sticky honeydew and blackish sooty mold on plant. Leaves may yellow and drop prematurely.	**Chinese wax scale.** Bulbous, irregular, brown, gray, or white waxy bodies (scales) on twigs.	*See 141.*
Sticky honeydew, blackish sooty mold, and whitish flocculent material on leaves or stems.	**Mealybug,** *Pseudococcus fragilis.* Oval, powdery grayish or whitish insects with waxy filaments.	*See 126.*
Brownish, grayish, tan, or white encrustations on bark. Rarely, dead or declining twigs or branches.	**Greedy scale.** Nearly circular insects, <¹⁄₁₆ inch long.	*See 133.*
MAIDENHAIR TREE (*Ginkgo biloba*), Ginkgo		
Chewed leaves.	**Omnivorous looper.** Yellow, green, or pink larvae, ≤1½ inches long, with green, yellow or black stripes.	Larvae crawl in "looping" manner. *See 79.*
Galls or swellings on roots.	**Root knot nematode,** *Meloidogyne* sp. Tiny root-feeding roundworms.	*See 345.*
MANZANITA (*Arctostaphylos* spp.), Bearberry, Kinnikinnick		
Leaves discolor, stunt, wilt, or drop prematurely. Plants grow slowly and may die. Roots or basal stem dark, decayed.	**Root and crown rots,** *Phytophthora* spp. Pathogens promoted by excess soil moisture and poor drainage.	*See 265.*
Leaves discolor and wilt. Branches or treetop dying. Branches may canker or exude reddish pitch. Branches may blacken.	**Cankers** or **Dieback,** including **Botryosphaeria canker and dieback,** *Botryosphaeria arctostaphyli*; *Fusicoccum* spp. Fungi primarily affect injured or stressed trees.	Prune out dead and diseased branches in summer. Provide appropriate water and other cultural care to improve tree vigor. *See 250.*
Leaves with brown, light green, yellow, or dead spots or blotches. Twigs and stems may canker, ooze, or die back.	**Sudden oak death,** *Phytophthora ramorum.* Pathogen spreads via air and contaminated soil. Apparently can infect through bark or leaves.	Primarily a problem in wildlands, killing many oaks there. Do not move infected plant material. Report to agricultural officials if found outside areas where pathogen is known to occur. *See 260.*
Leaves with dark or discolored blotches. Leaves may yellow and drop prematurely.	**Leaf spots,** including *Phyllosticta amicta, Cryptosporium candidum.* Fungal diseases that infect and develop when foliage is wet.	*See 223.*
Leaves have black or yellow blotches. Leaves may yellow overall and drop prematurely. Terminals may die back.	**Bacterial leaf spot and blight,** *Xanthomonas* sp. Bacteria spread by water. Favored by cool, wet conditions. Persist in plant debris.	Avoid overhead irrigation. Improve air circulation. Rake and dispose of fallen leaves. *See Leaf Spots, 223*
Leaves with dark or yellow spots. Leaf undersides with orangish pustules. Leaves may drop prematurely.	**Rusts,** *Chrysomyxa arctostaphyli, Pucciniastrum sparsum, P. evadens.* Fungi infect and develop when foliage is wet.	Avoid overhead watering. Plants tolerate moderate populations. *See 240.*
Leaves, buds, or shoots bushy, distorted, galled, reddish, or thickened. Leaves with red blisters.	**Leaf gall** or **Kinnikinnick,** *Exobasidium vaccinii, E. vaccinii-uliginosi.* Fungi infect and develop in wet new growth.	Avoid overhead watering. Prune only when dry. Improve air circulation. Vigorous plants tolerate extensive leaf galling. Hand-pick or prune out galls. Rake and dispose of fallen leaves.
Fleshy red galls on leaves. Plants may grow slowly.	**Manzanita leaf gall aphid.** Tiny gray or greenish insects in leaf galls.	*See Aphids, page 103.*
Leaves with elliptical blotches or holes, ⅛ to ¼ inch long, or winding tunnels.	**Madrone shield bearer,** *Coptodisca arbutiella.* Larvae, ≤¼ inch long, mine leaves. Adult is tiny moth.	Vigorous plants tolerate extensive leaf damage. *See Shield Bearers, 169.*
Leaves chewed, drop prematurely. May be silken webbing on plant.	**Tent caterpillar, Western tussock moth.** Hairy brown or colorful caterpillars ≤2 inches long.	*See 77, 80.*

MANZANITA (*Arctostaphylos* spp.), Bearberry, Kinnikinnick, *continued*

WHAT THE PROBLEM LOOKS LIKE	PROBABLE CAUSE	COMMENTS
Sticky honeydew, blackish sooty mold, whitish cast skins on leaves. Shoots may die back.	**Aphids**, including *Wahlgreniella nervata*. Pink to green insects in colonies on leaves and terminals.	Plants tolerate moderate populations. Hose forcefully with water. Apply soap or oil if not tolerable. *See 103.*
Sticky honeydew and blackish sooty mold on foliage. Possible twig and branch dieback.	**Brown soft scale.** Yellow to brown, flattened insects in groups.	*See 137.*
Sticky honeydew and blackish sooty mold on foliage. May be whitish wax.	**Psyllids**, including **Manzanita psyllid,** *Neophyllura* (=*Euphyllura*) *arctostaphyli*. Adult *Neophyllura* are brown, reddish, and yellow insects resembling leafhoppers.	Usually not abundant and rarely if ever harmful to manzanita. *See 114.*
Sticky honeydew and blackish sooty mold on foliage. Immobile, dark or pale, oval bodies (immatures) ≤¹⁄₁₆ inch long on leaf undersides.	**Whiteflies**, including **Crown whitefly; Greenhouse whitefly; Iridescent whitefly,** *Aleuroparadoxus iridescens*. Tiny moth-like adults.	Conserve natural enemies that help control. *See 121.*
Sticky honeydew and blackish sooty mold on foliage. Cottony waxy material on plant.	**Mealybugs**, including **Manzanita mealy-bug,** *Puto arctostaphyli*; **White mealybug,** *Puto albicans*. Powdery white insects, ≤¼ inch long, with waxy fringe.	Apply soap or oil if intolerable. *See 126.*
Brownish, grayish, tan, or white encrustations on twigs and branches. Possible dead or dying twigs or branches.	**Greedy scale; Manzanita scale,** *Diaspis manzanitae*; **Oleander scale.** Tiny oval to circular insects.	Vigorous plants tolerate moderate populations. If needed, monitor and apply oil in the spring or early summer when crawlers are abundant. *See 131.*
Trunk or limbs with roughened, wet, or oozing area. Cracked bark and dieback.	**Flatheaded borers** including *Chrysobothris* spp. Larvae whitish with enlarged head, under bark. Adults are bullet-shaped.	*See 179.*

MAPLE (*Acer* spp.)

WHAT THE PROBLEM LOOKS LIKE	PROBABLE CAUSE	COMMENTS
Foliage fades, yellows, browns, or wilts, often scattered throughout canopy. Branches die. Entire plant may die.	**Verticillium wilt.** A soil-dwelling fungus that infects through roots.	*See 232.*
Foliage turns red, brown, then fades. Leaves drop prematurely. Cankers develop on bark.	**Botryosphaeria canker and dieback, Cytospora canker, Hypoxylon canker, Nectria canker.** Fungal diseases that commonly infect injured or stressed trees.	*See 250.*
Foliage yellows and wilts. Branches or entire plant dies.	**Root and crown rots,** *Phytophthora* spp. Fungal diseases caused by too much water or poor drainage.	*See 265.*
Powdery white growth on leaves. Tiny, black overwintering bodies may develop later.	**Powdery mildews,** *Phyllactinia guttata, Sphaerotheca fuliginea*. Fungal diseases favored by moderate temperatures, shade, and poor air circulation.	*See 236.*
Discolored leaf spots, often between veins. Large spots chlorotic, then tan or brown.	**Summer leaf scorch** or **Sunburn.** Non-infectious disorder, commonly appears during or after drought stress and high temperatures.	*See 288.*
Oval or irregular, glossy black, thick tarlike raised spots on upper leaf surface.	**Tar spot,** *Rhytisma punctatum*. Fungus most prevalent in moist environments.	Rake and dispose of leaves in the fall. *See Leaf Spots, 223.*
Small discrete spots to irregular, large blotches or holes over most of leaf surface. Leaves may drop prematurely if severe.	**Leaf spots,** including *Cylindrosporium, Phyllosticta, Septoria* spp. Fungi spread by air or splashing water. Favored by wet conditions.	*See 223.*

MAPLE (*Acer* spp.), continued

WHAT THE PROBLEM LOOKS LIKE	PROBABLE CAUSE	COMMENTS
Leaves with brown, light green, or yellow lesions or dead spots, especially along leaf margins.	**Sudden oak death**, *Phytophthora ramorum*. Pathogen spreads via air and contaminated soil.	On maple, hosts include at least *Acer acrophyllum*. Primarily a problem in wildlands, killing many oaks there. Do not move infected plant material. Report to agricultural officials if found outside areas where pathogen is known to occur. *See 260.*
Leaves with dark blotches or black veins. Leaves may drop prematurely. Terminals may die back.	**Bacterial leaf blight** or **Bacterial leaf spot**. Bacteria persist in bark and infect wet leaves and small twigs.	*See Bacterial Blight and Canker, 245.*
Leaves with irregular dark blotches. Blotches may follow veins. Leaves may drop prematurely. Twig cankers possible.	**Anthracnose**, *including Apiognomonia* sp.; *Discula* spp.; *Aureobasidium apocryptum* =*Kabatiella apocrypta*. Fungi persist in infected twigs. Favored by wet conditions.	Common on maple in the Pacific Northwest and eastern U.S. *See 223.*
Leaves with black to brown blotches. Bulges or blisters on upper leaf surface. Leaves curled, may drop prematurely.	**Leaf blight** or **Leaf curl**, *Taphrina* spp. Fungal diseases promoted by wet foliage during leaf flush.	Provide proper cultural care. Usually does not seriously harm trees. No control generally recommended.
Leaves stippled, bleached, or reddened. May be fine webbing on leaves or terminals. Leaves may drop prematurely.	**Spider mites**, including **Pacific spider mite**, **Twospotted spider mite**. Tiny arthropods, commonly greenish or yellowish, may have two dark spots.	*See 197.*
Leaves crumpled or with swollen galls, often along midvein. Leaves may brown and drop prematurely.	**Pod gall midge**, *Dasineura communis*. Adults are tiny flies. Pale larvae occur in galls, then drop and pupate beneath plant.	Plants tolerate extensive galling. *See Gall Midges, 164.*
Leaves with many small, green, red, or yellowish blisters or warty growths on upper surface and discolored patches on underside.	**Maple bladdergall mite**, *Vasates quadripedes*. Tiny elongate eriophyid mites that induce leaf galls.	Occurs in the Pacific Northwest and eastern U.S. These unsightly mites do not seriously harm trees. No control is recommended. *See Gall Mites, 203.*
Leaves with reddish, felty patches on underside. May be yellow blotches on upper surface.	**Eriophyid mites**, *Aceria* and *Vasates* spp. Tiny elongate eriophyid mites that feed on underside of leaves.	These mites do not seriously harm trees. No control is recommended. *See Gall Mites, 203.*
Spotted or yellow foliage, usually severe only on female trees.	**Boxelder bugs**. Gray and red adults, ½ inch long. Nymphs red.	Trees tolerate damage. Adults invading houses is the primary problem. *See 153.*
Leaves bleached or stippled with spots larger than mite stippling. Cast skins on underside of leaves. May be sticky or whitish honeydew on foliage.	**Leafhoppers**, including **Rose leafhopper**, *Edwardsiana rosae*; **Potato leafhopper**, *Empoasca fabae*. Greenish, yellow, or whitish wedge-shaped insects, ≤⅙ inch long.	Plants tolerate moderate stippling. Apply insecticidal soap or another insecticide if severe. *See 148.*
Sticky honeydew, blackish sooty mold, and whitish cast skins on leaves.	**Aphids**, including *Periphyllus* spp.; **Painted maple aphid**, *Drepanaphis acerifolii*. Tiny green insects clustered on leaves.	*See 103.*
Sticky honeydew and blackish sooty mold on foliage. May be dead or dying twigs and branches. Cottony white material (*Pulvinaria* egg sacs) on plant.	**Black scale; Calico scale; Cottony maple scale**, *Pulvinaria innumerabilis*. Yellow, brown, black, or white with spots, flattened to bulbous.	*See 136–138.*
Brownish, grayish, tan, or white encrustations on twigs and branches. Rarely, dead or dying twigs or branches.	**Oleander scale, Oystershell scale, San Jose scale**. Tiny circular to elongate individuals, often in groups.	*See 131.*
Dieback of woody plant parts. Tunnels and larvae in wood.	**Flatheaded appletree borer, Pacific flatheaded borer**. Whitish larvae ≤1 inch long with enlarged head.	*See 179.*

MAPLE (Acer spp.), continued

WHAT THE PROBLEM LOOKS LIKE	PROBABLE CAUSE	COMMENTS
Leaves chewed. Foliage may be webbed, defoliated, or contain silk tents.	**Fall webworm, Fruittree leafroller, Omnivorous looper.** Caterpillars ≤1½ inch long.	*See 71.*
Bark stained brownish, exudes rancid fluid, often around crotches, wounds.	**Wetwood** or **Slime flux.** Bacterial infection.	Usually does not cause serious harm to trees. *See 259.*

MAYTEN (Maytenus boaria)

Mayten (Maytenus boaria)

WHAT THE PROBLEM LOOKS LIKE	PROBABLE CAUSE	COMMENTS
Leaves discolor, wilt, stunt, and may drop prematurely. Branches or entire plant may die.	**Verticillium wilt.** Soil-dwelling fungus, infects through roots.	*See 232.*
Leaves discolor. Bark may canker or ooze. Limbs or entire plant may die.	**Borers,** including **Flatheaded appletree borer, Pacific flatheaded borer.** Whitish larvae with enlarged head in tunnels.	*See 179.*
Sticky honeydew and blackish sooty mold on foliage.	**Black scale, Nigra scale.** Yellowish to brown, flattened oval insects or black and elongate or bulbous.	*See 136.*
Sticky honeydew and blackish sooty mold on plant. Bulbous, irregular, brown, gray or white bodies (scales) on twigs.	**Chinese wax scale.** Bulbous to hemispherical waxy insects, suck sap.	*See 141.*
Sticky honeydew, blackish sooty mold, and whitish cast skins on plant.	**Aphids.** Small, greenish to black, pear-shaped insects often in groups on leaves and stems.	*See 103.*

MELALEUCA (Melaleuca spp.), Black tea tree, Granite bottlebrush, Myrtle, Paperbark

WHAT THE PROBLEM LOOKS LIKE	PROBABLE CAUSE	COMMENTS
Branches die back. Entire tree may die. Minute white fungus growths may be visible beneath bark or on soil.	**Armillaria root rot.** Present in many soils. Favored by warm, wet soil. Persists for years in infected roots.	*See 262.*
Galls or swellings on roots. Plants may grow slowly.	**Root knot nematodes.** Tiny root-feeding roundworms.	*See 345.*

MESQUITE (Prosopis spp.)

WHAT THE PROBLEM LOOKS LIKE	PROBABLE CAUSE	COMMENTS
Swollen growths on stems, may produce orange powdery or sticky material. Foliage may distort, gall, or form stunted witches' brooms.	**Stem gall rust,** *Ravenelia holwayi.* Fungal disease infects through bark wounds.	Pruning and disposing of infected stems during dry conditions may provide some control. *See similar Western Gall Rust, 241.*
Black, brown, or tan encrustations on leaves or twigs. Rarely, declining or dead twigs or branches.	**Candidula scale,** *Hemiberlesia candidula;* **Mesquite scale,** *Xerophilaspis prosopidis.* Tiny, flattened, oval to circular insects.	Rarely if ever cause serious damage to plants. *See Armored Scales, 131.*
Sticky honeydew, blackish sooty mold, and cottony or waxy material on plant.	**Mealybugs,** including **Vine mealybug.** Powdery grayish insects, ≤¼ inch long, with waxy filaments.	*See 126.*
Dead tree or dying limbs. Broad galleries beneath bark.	**Borers,** including **Flatheaded appletree borer; Mesquite girdler,** *Oncideres rhodosticta;* **Oldman longhorn,** *Schizax senex;* **Roundheaded mesquite borer,** *Megacylene antennatus.* Pale larvae that tunnel beneath bark.	*See Flatheaded Borers, Longhorned Borers, 179, 183.*

METROSIDEROS (Metrosideros spp.), Iron tree, New Zealand Christmas tree

WHAT THE PROBLEM LOOKS LIKE	PROBABLE CAUSE	COMMENTS
Leaves discolor, stunt, wilt, or drop prematurely. Plants grow slowly and may die. Roots dark, decayed.	**Root and crown rot,** *Phytophthora* sp. Pathogen promoted by excess soil moisture and poor drainage.	*See 265.*
Leaves discolor and wilt. Dead tree or dying limbs. Broad galleries beneath bark.	**Eucalyptus longhorned borers.** Adults reddish brown with yellow on the back. Larvae whitish. Both ≤1 inch long.	Primarily pests of eucalyptus. *See 183.*

WHAT THE PROBLEM LOOKS LIKE	PROBABLE CAUSE	COMMENTS

METROSIDEROS (*Metrosideros* spp.), Iron tree, New Zealand Christmas tree, *continued*

WHAT THE PROBLEM LOOKS LIKE	PROBABLE CAUSE	COMMENTS
Brown, black, tan or yellow spots or blotches on leaves. Spots may have dark or yellowish margins. Foliage may die and drop prematurely.	**Anthracnoses, Blights,** and **Leaf spots.** Fungal diseases favored by cool, wet, conditions.	*See 223.*
Sticky honeydew and blackish sooty mold on foliage. Leaves and terminals pitted, distorted, and discolored.	**Eugenia psyllid.** Adults are tiny leaf-hopperlike insects. Nymphs feed in pits on lower leaf surface.	Primarily a pest of eugenia. In southern California, young foliage of *Metrosideros excelsus* may be infested during winter. *See 115.*

MONKEY FLOWER (*Diplacus, Mimulus* spp.)

WHAT THE PROBLEM LOOKS LIKE	PROBABLE CAUSE	COMMENTS
Leaves have brown to yellow spots or blotches. Spots may have dark or yellowish margins. Foliage may shrivel and drop prematurely.	**Leaf spots,** including *Ramularia mimuli, Septoria mimuli.* Fungal diseases favored by prolonged wet conditions. Pathogens persist in plant debris.	*See 223.*
Leaves with dark or yellow spots and orangish pustules. Leaves may drop prematurely.	**Rusts.** Fungal pathogens favored by wet conditions.	Avoid overhead watering. Remove and dispose of infected leaves. *See 240.*
Leaves or shoots with powdery growth. Shoots or leaves may be stunted and distorted.	**Powdery mildews,** including *Erysiphe cichoracearum.* Fungi favored by moderate temperatures, shade, and poor air circulation.	*See 236.*
Leaves stippled or bleached. Leaves and shoots may die back.	**Seed bugs,** *Kleidocerys* spp. (family Lygaeidae). Small, brown, oval insects, suck plant juices.	No known controls. *See True Bugs, 152.*
Stippled or bleached leaves, varnishlike excrement specks on undersides.	**Thrips.** Tiny, slender, blackish or orangish insects.	*See 156.*
Flower buds mined or distorted. Flowering reduced. Insect pupal skins (exuviae) attached to flower buds.	**Gall midges,** *Asphondylia* spp. Larvae maggotlike, often several per bud. Adults tiny flies.	No known controls. Larvae reduce seeds, but established plants are not threatened. Several generations per year. *See Gall Midges, 164.*
Sticky honeydew, blackish sooty mold, and grayish, flocculent material on plant. Foliage discolored. Plant growth slow.	**Golden mealybug,** *Nipaecoccus aurilanatus.* Females globular, 1/10 inch long, purplish with felty, golden band marginally and on back.	Several generations occur each year. Natural enemies or soap or oil sprays can help to control. *See Mealybugs, 126.*

MOUNTAIN ASH (*Sorbus* spp.)

WHAT THE PROBLEM LOOKS LIKE	PROBABLE CAUSE	COMMENTS
Sudden wilting then shriveling and blackening of blossoms or shoots. Plant appears scorched. Shoots may develop cankers, which may ooze.	**Fire blight.** Bacterium enters plants through blossoms.	Plant less-susceptible cultivars. *See 229.*
Brownish, sunken lesions on trunk and large limbs. Small branches and twigs may be killed without any apparent canker.	**Cankers,** including **Cytospora canker, Nectria canker.** Fungal diseases primarily affecting injured or severely stressed trees.	*See 250.*
Leaves with orangish pustules or light to dark spots. Leaves may drop prematurely. Terminals may die back.	**Rusts,** *Gymnosporangium* spp. Fungi that infect and develop during moist conditions.	Avoid overhead watering. Vigorous plants tolerate moderate infection. *See 240.*
Leaves may discolor and wilt. Bark may be holey, roughened, or ooze dark liquid. May be reddish brown granular material (frass) on trunk or limbs.	**Borers,** including **American plum borer; Flatheaded appletree borer; Longhorned borer,** *Saperda* sp. Brown, pink, or whitish larvae ≤2 inches long that bore under bark.	*See 179, 193.*
Stippled, bleached, or reddened foliage.	**Spider mites,** including **European red mite;** *Oligonychus* sp. Tiny reddish to yellow arthropods, suck sap.	*See 197.*

WHAT THE PROBLEM LOOKS LIKE	PROBABLE CAUSE	COMMENTS

MOUNTAIN ASH (*Sorbus* spp.), continued

WHAT THE PROBLEM LOOKS LIKE	PROBABLE CAUSE	COMMENTS
Sticky honeydew, blackish sooty mold, and whitish cast skins on plant. May be whitish wax on plant.	**Apple aphid**, *Aphis pomi*; **Melon aphid**; **Woolly apple aphid.** Bright green to grayish insects on terminals or leaves.	Conserve natural enemies that provide control. Tolerate or apply soap or oil. *See Aphids, 103.*
Sticky honeydew and blackish sooty mold on foliage. Possible decline or dieback of twigs or branches.	**Frosted scale.** Brown, yellow, or waxy insects, bulbous or flattened, on leaves or twigs.	*See 139.*
Grayish or brown encrustations on bark. May be declining or dead twigs or branches.	**Oystershell scale; San Jose scale; Walnut scale,** *Diaspidiotus* (=*Quadraspidiotus*) *juglansregiae.* Tiny oval to circular insects on bark.	*See 132, 135.*
Leaves or blossoms chewed. Single branches or entire plant may be defoliated. Foliage may be rolled and tied together with silk.	**Caterpillars,** including **Obliquebanded leafroller,** *Choristoneura rosaceana* (family Tortricidae). Moth larvae ≤1½ inches long.	*See Foliage-Feeding Caterpillars, 71.*
Leaves scraped, skeletonized, and webbed together with silk.	**Leafminers,** including **Apple-and-thorn skeletonizer,** *Choreutis pariana* (family Choreutidae). Adult *Choreutis* is dark brown moth, <½ inch long. Larvae are ≤1 inch long and greenish or yellow.	*Choreutis* occurs throughout the northern U.S., reportedly including northern California. Plants usually tolerate damage. Prune off infested foliage or apply *Bacillus thuringiensis.*

MOUNTAIN MAHOGANY (*Cercocarpus* spp.)

WHAT THE PROBLEM LOOKS LIKE	PROBABLE CAUSE	COMMENTS
Powdery white growth and yellow blotches on leaves or shoots. Leaves or shoots may be undersized or distorted.	**Powdery mildew,** *Sphaerotheca macularis.* Fungus favored by moderate temperatures, shade, and poor air circulation.	*See 236.*
Leaves with small discrete spots to irregular, large blotches. Leaves may drop prematurely.	**Anthracnose, Leaf spots,** including *Phloeospora cercocarpi, Sphaceloma cercocarpi.* Fungi spread in water and are favored by cool, wet, conditions.	Diseases apparently promoted by wet winters. Plants tolerate extensive leaf spotting. Little or no effective controls in landscapes or wildlands. *See 223.*
Leaves discolor and wilt. Branches or treetop may die. Bark may canker or ooze.	**Cankers,** including *Hypoxylon mori, H. rubiginosum.* Fungi primarily affect injured or drought-stressed trees.	*See 250.*
Foliage yellows and wilts. Branches or entire plant may die. May be fleshy or woody fungal growths around roots or on wood.	**Wood decays** or **Heart rots,** including *Phellinus* spp., *Trametes* spp. Fungi that infect injured or severely stressed trees.	*See Wood Decay in Trunks and Limbs, 248.*
Leaves yellow, wilt, and drop prematurely. Branches die back and entire plant may die.	**Annosus root disease.** Decay fungus that spreads through roots and airborne spores.	*See 265.*
Leaves discolor and wilt. Trunk or limbs with cankered, roughened, wet, or oozing area. May be cracked bark and dieback.	**Flatheaded borers,** including **Flatheaded appletree borer.** Pale larvae ≤½ inch long, with enlarged head, bore under bark.	*See 179.*
Blackish sooty mold, sticky honeydew, and whitish cast skins on plant.	**Aphids.** Small, greenish to black insects, often in groups on leaves and stems.	*See 103.*

MULBERRY (*Morus* spp.)

WHAT THE PROBLEM LOOKS LIKE	PROBABLE CAUSE	COMMENTS
Angular blackened areas on leaves. Young leaves and shoots distorted. Elongated lesions may occur on twigs.	**Bacterial blight and canker.** Disease favored by wet conditions.	*See 245.*
Leaves discolor, stunt, wilt, or drop prematurely. Basal trunk discolored. Minute white fungus growths may be visible beneath bark or on soil.	**Armillaria root rot.** Present in many soils. Favored by warm, wet soil. Persists for years in infected roots.	*See 262.*
Leaves discolor and wilt. Bark may have dark, sunken cankers or coral-colored pustules.	**Nectria canker.** Fungus that primarily affects injured or stressed trees.	*See 257.*

WHAT THE PROBLEM LOOKS LIKE	PROBABLE CAUSE	COMMENTS

MULBERRY (*Morus* spp.), continued

WHAT THE PROBLEM LOOKS LIKE	PROBABLE CAUSE	COMMENTS
Sticky honeydew and blackish sooty mold on leaves. Blackish to gray, oval bodies with white waxy fringe (nymphs) on leaves.	**Whiteflies**, including **Giant whitefly**; **Mulberry whitefly**, *Tetraleurodes mori*. Small mothlike adults and oval nymphs, suck sap.	Conserve natural enemies that help to control. *See 121.*
Sticky honeydew and blackish sooty mold on foliage. Cottony or waxy material on plant.	**Mealybugs**, including **Pink hibiscus mealybug**. Powdery grayish insects, ≤¼ inch long.	*See 126.*
Copious, misty, nonsticky liquid raining from plant. Surfaces covered with whitish residue.	**Glassy-winged sharpshooter**. Active, dark brown or gray leafhoppers ≤½ inch long, suck xylem fluid.	Vectors pathogens of oleander and certain crops, especially grapes. Report suspected glassy-winged sharpshooters to agricultural officials if found in areas where this pest is not known to occur. *See 148.*
Brownish, grayish, tan, or white encrustations on leaves, twigs, or branches. Rarely, declining or dead twigs or branches.	**California red scale, Oleander scale, San Jose scale**. Circular to oval insects, <¹⁄₁₆ inch long.	*See 131.*
Webbing or silk tents on ends of branches. Chewed leaves.	**Fall webworm**. Hairy, white to yellow larvae, ≤1 inch long, in colonies.	*See 81.*
Bark stained brownish, exudes rancid fluid, often around crotches, wounds.	**Wetwood** or **Slime flux**. Bacterial infection.	Usually does not cause serious harm to trees. *See 259.*
Galls or swellings on roots.	**Root knot nematode**, *Meloidogyne* sp. Tiny root-feeding roundworms.	*See 345.*

MYOPORUM (*Myoporum* spp.), Lollipop tree*

WHAT THE PROBLEM LOOKS LIKE	PROBABLE CAUSE	COMMENTS
Leaves brown or yellow, wilted, and may drop prematurely. Branches or plant may die.	**Pythium root rot**, *Pythium* sp. Decay fungus common in moist, poorly drained soils.	*See 268.*
Leaves bleached or stippled with spots. Cast skins on underside of leaves.	**Blue-green sharpshooter**, *Graphocephala atropunctata*. Greenish, wedge-shaped insects, ≤⅛ inch long.	Plants tolerate moderate stippling. Apply insecticidal soap or another insecticide if severe. *See 148.*

NANDINA (*Nandina domestica*), Heavenly bamboo, Sacred bamboo

WHAT THE PROBLEM LOOKS LIKE	PROBABLE CAUSE	COMMENTS
Whitish, cottony material on bark or underside of leaves.	**Comstock mealybug**, *Pseudococcus comstocki*. Oblong, soft, powdery, waxy insects with filaments.	Control ants, reduce dust, avoid persistent pesticides that disrupt effective natural enemies. *See Mealybugs, 126.*
Sticky honeydew and blackish sooty mold on foliage. Popcornlike bodies (egg sacs) on bark.	**Cottony cushion scale**. Orangish, flat immatures or cottony females on bark.	Normally controlled by natural enemies. *See 142.*
Foliage mottled, reddish.	**Nandina virus**. Disease spread by aphids.	Plants usually tolerate. No control. *See 270.*

NATAL PLUM (*Carissa grandiflora, C. macrocarpa*)

WHAT THE PROBLEM LOOKS LIKE	PROBABLE CAUSE	COMMENTS
Foliage yellows and wilts. Leaves may drop prematurely. Branches or entire plant dies. Roots or basal stem dark, decayed.	**Root and crown rots**, *Phytophthora* spp., **Pythium root rot**. Fungal diseases favored by excess soil moisture and poor drainage.	*See 265, 268.*
Brown, black, tan, or yellow spots or blotches on leaves. Spots may have dark or yellowish margins. Foliage may die and drop prematurely.	**Leaf spots**, including *Alternaria* sp. Spread by air or splashing water. Favored by prolonged cool, wet, conditions. Persist in plant debris.	*See 223.*
Sticky honeydew, blackish sooty mold, and cottony or waxy material on plant.	**Mealybugs**, including **Pink hibiscus mealybug**. Powdery grayish insects, ≤¼ inch long.	*See 126.*
Sticky honeydew and blackish sooty mold on foliage. May be declining or dead twigs or branches.	**Black scale; Hemispherical scale**, *Saissetia coffeae*. Small black, brown, or yellowish, flattened or bulbous insects.	*See 136.*

*Some species are invasive weeds. Other species may be better choices when planting.

WHAT THE PROBLEM LOOKS LIKE	PROBABLE CAUSE	COMMENTS

OAK (*Quercus* spp.)

Leaves or shoots covered with white, powdery growth. Shoots brown or reddish, bushy, short, or shriveled.	**Witches' broom** or **Powdery mildew,** *Sphaerotheca lanestris.* Fungal disease attacks new growth, is favored by moderate temperatures, shade, and poor air circulation.	Avoid cultural practices that stimulate excess growth, such as summer irrigation and heavy pruning. Prune out infected growth in winter. Rake and dispose of infected leaves. *See 236.*
Leaves discolor, stunt, wilt, or drop prematurely. Basal trunk discolored and may die. Minute white fungus growths may be visible beneath bark or on soil.	**Armillaria root rot** or **Oak root fungus.** Present in many soils. Favored by warm, wet soil. Persists for years in infected roots.	*See 262.*
Leaves discolor, stunt, wilt, or drop prematurely. Plants grow slowly and may die. Roots dark, decayed.	**Root and crown rots,** *Phytophthora* spp. Pathogens promoted by excess soil moisture and poor drainage.	*See 265.*
Leaves yellow and wilt. Branches or entire plant may die. Trees may fall over.	**Heart rot** or **Decay fungi,** including *Ganoderma applanatum,* which produces large, fan-shaped basidiocarps on bark. Fungi that infect injured or severely stressed trees.	*See Wood Decay in Trunks and Limbs, 248.*
Leaves brown, light green, yellow, or wilted. Trunks ooze, usually near the ground. Limbs and eventually entire tree dies. Trees become heavily colonized by bark beetles.	**Sudden oak death,** *Phytophthora ramorum.* Pathogen spreads via air and contaminated soil. Apparently can infect through trunk bark.	On *Quercus,* hosts include at least *Q. agrifolia, Q. kelloggii,* and *Q. parvula* var. *shrevei.* Primarily a problem in wildlands, killing many oaks there. Do not move infected plants. Report to agricultural officials if found outside areas where pathogen is known to occur. *See 260.*
Leaves discolor and wilt. Branches develop cankers and die back. Dark, hemispherical fruiting bodies develop on bark.	**Cankers,** including **Hypoxylon canker,** *Hypoxylon fuscum, H. mediterraneum, H. thouarsianum, H. vogesiacum;* **Nectria canker,** *Nectria peziza.* Decay fungi that attack injured or stressed trees.	*See 250.*
Leaves yellowish, except along veins. Leaves small, drop prematurely. Branches die back.	**Iron deficiency.** Abiotic disorder usually caused by poor soil conditions or unhealthy roots.	Especially common in pin oak, *Quercus palustris. See 278.*
Leaves brown, dead areas along veins. Leaves on lower branches commonly are more severely affected.	**Anthracnose,** *Apiognomonia errabunda.* Fungal disease active in the spring.	Commonly infects *Quercus kelloggii.* Usually not serious enough to warrant control. *See 223.*
Leaves brown, dead areas along veins. Leaves on lower branches commonly are more severely affected. Can cause severe defoliation.	**Anthracnose,** *Gloeosporium quercuum.* Fungal disease active in the spring.	Commonly infects *Quercus agrifolia.* No controls are known. Fungicide applications are ineffective. *See 223.*
Leaves wilt, turn yellow, then entirely brown in large groups. Wood is stained brown. Bark, branches, cambium, and sapwood die.	**Branch dieback,** *Diplodia quercina.* A fungal disease often associated with oak pit scales.	*See 228.*
Leaves brown or white. Groups of entirely dead leaves remain on twigs, scattered throughout canopy. Death of current season's twigs.	**Twig blights,** *Cryptocline cinerescens, Discula quercina.* Fungal diseases more severe if oak pit scale present.	Infect primarily *Quercus agrifolia. See 229.*
Leaves turn brown or yellow, especially along margins and at tip. Leaves may drop prematurely.	**Leaf burn** or **Scorch.** Abiotic disorders with many potential causes, including watering near trunks, injuring trunks or roots, irrigating too frequently, planting irrigated landscapes beneath oaks, poor drainage, or salty soil or water.	Provide plants with a good growing environment and proper cultural care. *See 273.*

OAK (*Quercus* spp.), continued

WHAT THE PROBLEM LOOKS LIKE	PROBABLE CAUSE	COMMENTS
Leaves brown or scorched along margins and veins. Partially brown and entirely green leaves occur side-by-side on same twigs.	**Leaf scorch** or **Twohorned oak gall wasp.** Galls cause portion of leaf to die terminal to where wasp larvae fed. Small oblong galls or brown scars left by dropped galls occur on underside of leaf along vein.	Infests *Quercus agrifolia* and *Q. wislizenii.* Damage is apparently harmless to oaks. *See 163.*
Bulges on upper leaf surface. Leaves galled, curled, may drop prematurely. Pale growth on either leaf surface.	**Oak leaf blister,** *Taphrina caerulescens.* Fungal disease promoted by wet foliage during leaf flush.	Provide oaks proper cultural care. No control generally recommended. *See 204.*
Raised blisters on upper leaf surface. Orange to pale felty depressions on leaf underside.	**Live oak erineum mite.** Tiny elongate erio-phyid mites.	No management known. *See Gall Mites, 204.*
Leaves, branches, flowers, or twigs with distorted growths or swellings (galls), which may be colorful.	**Cynipid gall wasps.** Adults tiny wasps. Larvae whitish maggots in galls. Hundreds of species occur on oaks.	Most galls apparently do not harm trees. No control known for most oak galls, except pruning. *See 161.*
Twigs with black, brown, green, or red spherical swellings ≤4 inches in diameter.	**California gallfly** or **Oak apple gall wasp,** *Andricus californicus.* Adults are ⅛ inch long, brown or reddish wasps. Larvae are pale maggots.	Galls do not harm trees. No control is recommended. Prune off galls if intolerable. *See 161.*
Leaves stippled or bleached. Severely infested leaves may brown and drop prematurely.	**Spider mites,** including **Sycamore spider mite.** Tiny arthropods, often green, suck sap.	Problem in California mostly in interior valleys, especially after insecticide spray during hot weather. *See 197.*
Leaves with many tiny, round, brown and yellow spots. Tiny brown to yellow, round growths on underside of leaves.	**Jumping oak gall wasp,** *Neuroterus salta-torius.* Galls drop from leaves in summer and may be seen hopping on ground beneath oaks due to larva moving inside.	Occurs on various oaks, in California especially on *Quercus lobata* in the Central Valley. Damage is harmless to oaks. *See 161.*
Leaves with many tiny, irregular, brown and yellow spots. Young plants most susceptible.	**Oak leaf phylloxera** (family *Phylloxeridae*). Tiny, yellowish aphidlike insects on underside of leaves, suck sap.	Plants apparently not damaged. Tolerate or thoroughly apply soap to leaf underside when nymphs present, before severe spotting.
Sticky honeydew and blackish sooty mold on foliage. Globular gall-like bodies (mature scales) on leaves or twigs.	**Kermes scales,** including **Black-punctured kermes,** *Kermes nigropunctatus* (family Kermesidae). Spherical scales, ≤¼ inch diameter. Most species are mostly brownish.	Usually not abundant enough to warrant control. *See Scales, 130.*
Sticky honeydew and blackish sooty mold on foliage.	**Oak lecanium scale,** *Parthenolecanium quercifex.* Flattened orangish nymphs to bulbous brown adults on twigs.	Scale has one generation a year. Control usually not warranted. If severe, monitor in spring, apply oil when crawlers are abundant. *See Lecanium Scales, 139.*
Sticky honeydew and blackish sooty mold on foliage. Dark, oval bodies (nymphs), about ¹⁄₁₆ inch long on underside of leaves, often with white, waxy fringe.	**Stanford whitefly,** *Tetraleurodes stanfordi;* **Gelatinous whitefly,** *Aleuroplatus gelatinosus;* **Crown whitefly.** Adults tiny moth-like insects that suck phloem sap.	Ignore insects, they apparently do not damage trees. *See 121.*
Sticky honeydew and blackish sooty mold on foliage.	**Aphids,** including *Myzocallis* spp. Tiny green to yellow insects, clustered on leaves.	Plants tolerate moderate aphid populations. Conserve natural enemies. Hose forcefully with water. Apply soap or oil if not tolerable. *See 103.*
Sticky honeydew and blackish sooty mold on foliage. Leaves may curl or have rolled margins.	**Woolly oak aphids,** including *Stegophylla quercicola.* Small, greenish to bluish, cottony wax-covered insects.	Plants tolerate moderate aphid densities. *See Aphids, 106.*
Sticky honeydew, blackish sooty mold, and whitish wax on foliage.	**Obscure mealybug.** Powdery gray insects with waxy filaments.	Conserve natural enemies that help in control. *See 127.*
Twig bark roughened. Terminals may die back. May be sticky honeydew and blackish sooty mold on foliage.	**Oak treehopper.** Adults green to brown with red dots and horn on head, often on twigs with group of nymphs.	*See 151.*

OAK (*Quercus* spp.), continued

WHAT THE PROBLEM LOOKS LIKE	PROBABLE CAUSE	COMMENTS
White, frothy material exudes from bark, often around wounds. Material has pleasant odor.	**Foamy canker.** Unidentified cause, possibly a bacterium.	Foamy material appears for only short time during warm weather. *See 259.*
Brownish, sometimes rancid fluid exudes from bark, often around crotches or wounds. Bark stained.	**Wetwood** or **Slime flux.** Bacterial infection.	Usually does not cause serious harm to trees. *See 259.*
Brownish to clear sticky material dripping from acorns, leaves, or twigs.	**Drippy Oak and Drippy Nut Disease.** A bacterium that causes injured acorns, leaves, and twigs to exude viscous liquid.	Associated with filbertworm, filbert weevils, gall wasps, and virtually any injury that allows bacteria to colonize. *See 247.*
Brownish, clear, frothy, or sticky liquid dripping from leaves, nuts, or twigs.	**Oak gall wasp nectar.** Certain *Andricus, Disholcaspis,* and *Dryocosmus* spp. cynipids induce oak galls that secrete nectar, which attracts ants that protect gall wasps from their natural enemies.	Control ants; over several years this can allow natural enemies to dramatically reduce populations of nectar-inducing gall wasps. *See 161.*
Copious, misty, nonsticky liquid raining from plant. Surfaces covered with whitish residue.	**Glassy-winged sharpshooter.** Active, dark brown or gray leafhoppers ≤½ inch long, suck xylem fluid.	Vectors pathogens of oleander and certain crops, especially grapes. Report suspected glassy-winged sharpshooters to agricultural officials if found in areas where this pest is not known to occur. *See 148.*
Chewed leaves. Tree may be defoliated.	**California oakworm.** Dark to greenish larvae, ≤1¼ inches long, with yellow stripes.	In California, on oaks near coastal areas. *See 75.*
Leaves chewed, tied together with silk. Tree may be defoliated.	**Fruittree leafroller.** Green larvae, with black head and "shield" behind head. Larvae ≤¾ inch long, wriggle vigorously when touched.	In California, a common oak defoliator in warmer interior areas. *See 79.*
Chewed leaves. Silken mats or "tents" sometimes seen in trees. Tree may be defoliated.	**Pacific tent caterpillar, Western tent caterpillar, Tussock moths.** Hairy, brownish to colorful caterpillars.	*See 77, 80.*
Chewed leaves or blossoms.	**Fuller rose beetle.** Pale brown adult snout weevils, about ⅜ inch long.	Adults hide during day and feed at night. Larvae feed on roots. *See 94.*
Leaf surface etched. These "windows" may turn brown. White, ribbed, cigar-shaped cocoons on leaves or bark.	**Oak ribbed casemaker.** Larvae are ≤¼ inch long.	*See 168.*
Leaves with elliptical blotches or holes, ⅛ to ¼ inch long, or winding tunnels.	**Shield bearers.** Tiny larvae cut mined foliage from leaf.	*See 169.*
Gouged and etched leaves. Leaves may turn brown. Most new leaf damage appears from April to June.	**Live oak weevil,** *Deporaus glastinus.* Adults are dark, metallic-blue snout beetles, about ¼ inch long.	Most common on *Quercus agrifolia.* Tolerate as damage does not threaten tree health. *See Weevils, 92.*
Patches of dead leaves at end of branches of live oaks.	**Oak twig girdler; Roundheaded oak twig borer,** *Styloxus fulleri.* Adult cylindrical, metallic beetle, larvae whitish.	*See 182.*
Gray, pinkish, or whitish encrustations on bark, usually on the limb underside of evergreen oaks, especially in southern California.	**Ehrhorn's oak scale,** *Mycetococcus ehrhorni* (family Asterolecaniidae). A ¹⁄₂₅-inch reddish scale that occurs in symbiotic colonies with the fungus *Septobasidium canescens.*	Heavy infestations may slow oak growth, but populations are often innocuous. *See Scales, 130.*
Gray encrustations on bark. May be declining or dead twigs or branches.	**Obscure scale.** Tiny, grayish, circular to oval insects on or under bark.	Occurs in the eastern U.S. and in California at least in Sacramento. If found outside areas where it is known to occur, report this to agricultural officials. *See 134.*

OAK (*Quercus* spp.), continued

WHAT THE PROBLEM LOOKS LIKE	PROBABLE CAUSE	COMMENTS
Rough bark, ring-shaped swellings. Dead twigs and branches. Dead leaves persist over winter on deciduous oak.	**Oak pit scales.** Pinhead-sized, brown to green insects, on bark in roundish swellings.	*See 144.*
Greatly roughened bark on lower trunk or major limb crotches. Slow growth.	**Sycamore borer.** Pink larvae ≤¾ inch long, bore in bark or wood.	*See 188.*
Large holes, ≤½ inch diameter, in trunks and limbs. Slow tree growth. Limbs may fall.	**Carpenterworm.** Whitish larvae, ≤2½ inches long, with brown head, tunnel in wood.	*See 194.*
Bleeding or frothy material bubbling from tiny holes in trunk or limbs. Fine boring dust may surround holes. Limbs or entire tree may die.	**Oak bark beetles, Ambrosia beetles.** Adults brown, ⅛ inch long bark beetles. White larvae tunnel beneath bark.	*See 177.*
Trunk or limbs with roughened, wet, or oozing area. Cracked bark and dieback. Foliage may discolor and wilt.	**Flatheaded borers,** including **Flatheaded appletree, Pacific flatheaded borer.** Larvae whitish with enlarged head, under bark. Adults bullet-shaped.	*See 179.*
Holes in acorns. Tunnels inside acorns may contain insect larvae.	**Acorn moth, Filbert weevils, Filbertworm.** Yellow to whitish grubs or maggots that tunnel in nuts.	Acorns on shady tree side more likely attacked. May reduce natural oak regeneration, but established trees are not damaged. *See Filbert Weevils and Acorn Worms, 93.*
Green plants with smooth stems, thick roundish leaves infesting branches.	**Broadleaf mistletoe,** *Phoradendron villosum.* Parasitic, evergreen plant on host.	*See 338.*

OLEANDER (*Nerium oleander*)

WHAT THE PROBLEM LOOKS LIKE	PROBABLE CAUSE	COMMENTS
Leaves turn brown or yellow, especially along margins and at tip. Leaves and shoots die. Entire plant dies rapidly or slowly over several years.	**Oleander leaf scorch,** *Xylella fastidiosa.* Bacteria spread by certain leafhoppers. Only molecular ELISA test can confidently diagnose this cause of damage.	Many infected hosts are symptomless, but oleander and certain crops such as grapes are severely damaged or killed. *See Bacterial Leaf Scorch and Oleander Leaf Scorch, 230.*
Leaves brown, yellow, and wilt. Terminals may die back. Stems die back. Stems may have cankers, decay, or lesions, which can help distinguish this malady from oleander leaf scorch.	**Phoma stem and leaf blight,** *Phoma exigua.* Fungus infects through wounds, persists in infected tissue, and spreads during wet conditions.	Avoid wounding plants, except to prune off infected tissue only during prolonged dry weather, making cuts in healthy tissue. Provide a good growing environment and appropriate cultural care.
Leaves turn brown or yellow, especially along margins and at tip. Leaves may drop prematurely.	**Leaf burn** or **Scorch.** Abiotic disorders with many potential causes, including frost, inappropriate irrigation, pesticide phytotoxicity, poor drainage, or saline soil or water.	Provide plants with a good growing environment and proper cultural care. *See 273.*
Leaves, blossoms, or stems with black to brown lesions, spots, or streaks. Wood may be cankered, dark, or die back.	**Bacterial blight and canker.** Disease favored by wet conditions.	*See 245.*
Leaves with brown, black, tan, or yellow spots or blotches. Spots may have dark or yellowish margins.	**Leaf spots,** including *Alternaria* sp., *Septoria oleandrina.* Favored by prolonged cool, wet, conditions. Persist in plant debris.	*See 223.*
Sticky honeydew and blackish sooty mold on foliage.	**Black scale.** Orangish flat immatures or brown to black bulbous adults with raised H-shape on back.	*See 136.*
Sticky honeydew and blackish sooty mold on foliage. May be cottony or waxy material on plant.	**Mealybugs,** including **Longtailed mealybug, Obscure mealybug, Pink hibiscus mealybug.** Grayish, powdery waxy insects.	*See 126.*

OLEANDER (*Nerium oleander*), continued

WHAT THE PROBLEM LOOKS LIKE	PROBABLE CAUSE	COMMENTS
Sticky honeydew, blackish sooty mold, and whitish cast skins on leaves and terminals. New growth may be deformed.	**Oleander aphid**, *Aphis nerii*. Orangish or yellow insects with black, clustering on leaves, shoots, and flowers.	Water and prune less to reduce new growth that promotes aphids. Conserve natural enemies that help control. Hose forcefully with water. Tolerate or apply soap. *See Aphids, 103.*
Copious, misty, nonsticky liquid raining from plant. Surfaces covered with whitish residue.	**Glassy-winged sharpshooter.** Active, dark brown or gray leafhoppers ≤½ inch long, suck xylem fluid.	Vectors pathogens of oleander and certain crops, especially grapes. Report suspected glassy-winged sharpshooters to agricultural officials if found in areas where this pest is not known to occur. *See 148 and Bacterial Leaf Scorch and Oleander Leaf Scorch, 230.*
Brownish, grayish, tan, or white encrustations on leaves or twigs.	**Armored scales**, including **Greedy scale, Oleander scale.** Tiny, flattened, circular insects, ≤1/16 inch long.	Rarely if ever cause serious damage to oleander. *See 131.*
Galls or knots on stems, bark, and occasionally on leaves. Twigs may die back.	**Bacterial gall.** Bacterium infects wet tissue through wounds.	*See 246.*
Galls or swellings on trunk and roots, usually near soil.	**Crown gall.** Bacterium that infects plant via wounds.	*See 258.*

OLIVE (*Olea europaea*)[12]

WHAT THE PROBLEM LOOKS LIKE	PROBABLE CAUSE	COMMENTS
Foliage fades, yellows, browns, or wilts, often scattered throughout canopy. Branches die. Entire plant may die.	**Verticillium wilt.** A soil-dwelling fungus that infects through roots.	Xylem discolors little or not at all in olive infected with Verticillium wilt. *See 232.*
Leaves discolor, stunt, wilt, or drop prematurely. Plants grow slowly and may die. Roots dark, decayed.	**Root and crown rots**, *Phytophthora* spp. Pathogens promoted by excess soil moisture and poor drainage.	*See 265.*
Leaves discolor and wilt at branch tips. Dieback of some twigs. Tunnels under bark.	**Branch and twig borer**, *Melalgus* (=*Polycaon*) *confertus* (family Bostrichidae). Adults black to brown beetles, ≤½ inch long. Larvae whitish.	Prune out affected parts. Eliminate nearby dying hardwoods in which beetles breed. Provide trees with proper cultural care.
Bark has boring dust or holes or oozes. Slow tree growth. Branches may wilt or die back.	**American plum borer, Ash borer.** Brown, green, pink, or white larvae, ≤1 inch long, bore beneath bark.	Distinguish between these differently managed species. *See 187 and 193.*
Sticky honeydew and blackish sooty mold on foliage.	**Black scale.** Orangish flat immatures or brown to black bulbous adults, may have raised H-shape on back.	*See 136.*
Sticky honeydew and blackish sooty mold on foliage. Cottony or popcornlike bodies (egg sacs) on bark.	**Cottony cushion scale.** Orangish, flat immatures or cottony females on bark.	Normally controlled by natural enemies. *See 142.*
Sticky honeydew and blackish sooty mold on foliage. Tiny, whitish, mothlike adults.	**Citrus whitefly.** Nymphs oval, flattened, green to yellow.	*See 121.*
Brown, gray, or orangish encrustations on bark. Rarely, declining or dead twigs and branches.	**California red scale; Olive scale**, *Parlatoria oleae*; **Oleander scale.** Circular to oval, ≤1/16 inch long, on twigs and branches.	Rarely if ever cause serious damage to olive. Conserve natural enemies. Monitor in spring and apply oil when crawlers are abundant if populations are damaging. *See Scales, 131.*

12. For information on pest identification and biology, see publications such as *Olive Pest Management Guidelines* (Teviotdale et al. 2000).

OLIVE (*Olea europaea*), continued

WHAT THE PROBLEM LOOKS LIKE	PROBABLE CAUSE	COMMENTS
Copious, misty, nonsticky liquid raining from plant. Surfaces covered with whitish residue.	**Glassy-winged sharpshooter.** Active, dark brown or gray leafhoppers ≤½ inch long, suck xylem fluid.	Vectors pathogens of oleander and certain crops, especially grapes. Report suspected glassy-winged sharpshooters to agricultural officials if found in areas where this pest is not known to occur. *See 148.*
Leaves develop blackish or green circular blotches, ≤½ inch in diameter. Spots may have a faint yellow halo. Leaves fall prematurely and twigs may die due to leaf drop.	**Olive peacock spot,** *Spilocaea oleaginea*. Fungus infects during wet winter weather and is most severe in lower canopy.	Usually harmless to trees. Where problem has been severe, copper fungicides can help to prevent disease. *See Scabs, 227.*
Leaves turn yellow, brown, and drop prematurely. Limbs die back.	**Branch dieback.** Abiotic disorder with many potential causes, commonly caused by excess soil moisture and poor drainage, especially around the root crown.	Avoid wetting trunk or root crown. Avoid overhead irrigation around olive. Do not plant olive in frequently irrigated landscapes, such as lawns.
Decaying, prematurely dropping fruit beneath trees. Discoloring, tunnels, and yellowish maggots in fruit.	**Olive fruit fly,** *Bactrocera oleae* (family Tephritidae). Adults are brown, yellow, and white flies with clear wings that lay eggs in olives.	Promptly disposing of dropped fruit may help to control. Yellow sticky trap monitoring, mass trapping, and insecticide baits are key management methods.
Decaying, dropped fruit and dark or oily stains beneath trees.	**Messy fruit.** Unharvested fruit naturally drop, which can create a slippery hazard beneath trees.	Plant fruitless olive such as Majestic Beauty, Mother, and Swan Hill. Knock fruit onto tarps beneath trees. Prune off limbs overhanging surfaces such as pavement. Spray flowers with growth regulator before fruit set as directed on product label.
Galls or knots on stems, bark, and occasionally on leaves. Twig dieback.	**Bacterial gall** or **Olive knot.** Bacterium infects wet tissue through wounds.	*See 246.*
Galls or swellings on roots. Plants may grow slowly.	**Root knot nematode,** *Meloidogyne* sp. Tiny root-feeding roundworms.	*See 345.*

ORCHID TREE (*Bauhinia* spp.), Brazilian butterfly tree

WHAT THE PROBLEM LOOKS LIKE	PROBABLE CAUSE	COMMENTS
Leaves with black, brown, tan, or yellow blotches or spots. Spots may have dark or yellowish margins. Foliage may die and drop prematurely.	**Anthracnoses, Blights,** and **Leaf spots.** Fungi spread in water and are favored by cool, wet, conditions.	*See 223.*
Foliage has sticky honeydew and blackish sooty mold. May be copious white waxy material. Leaves may yellow, wither, and drop prematurely.	**Whiteflies,** including **Giant whitefly, Silverleaf whitefly.** Adults are tiny, whitish, mothlike insects. Nymphs and pupae are flattened and oval.	*See 121.*
Sticky honeydew, blackish sooty mold, and cottony or waxy material on plant.	**Mealybugs,** including **Pink hibiscus mealybug.** Powdery grayish insects, ≤¼ inch long.	*See 126.*
Galls or swellings on roots. Plants may grow slowly.	**Root knot nematodes.** Tiny root-feeding roundworms.	*See 345.*

PALM (*Archontophoenix, Arecastrum, Brahea, Butia, Caryota, Chamaedorea, Dypsis, Hedyscepe, Howea, Jubaea, Livistona, Phoenix, Rhapis, Sabal, Syagrus, Trachycarpus, Washingtonia* spp.)

WHAT THE PROBLEM LOOKS LIKE	PROBABLE CAUSE	COMMENTS
Fronds bend downward. Crinkled, deformed fronds. Trunks bend.	**Eriophyid mites.** Tiny arthropods feed in buds and growing tips.	*See Gall Mites, 203.*
Fronds bend downward. New leaves deformed, twisted. Entire leaf crown curves downward.	**Leaning crown syndrome** or **Palm bending.** Cause unknown.	Effective treatment unknown. Provide palms with good growing conditions and appropriate cultural care.

PALM (*Archontophoenix, Arecastrum, Brahea, Butia, Caryota, Chamaedorea, Dypsis, Hedyscepe, Howea, Jubaea, Livistona, Phoenix, Rhapis, Sabal, Syagrus, Trachycarpus, Washingtonia* spp.), continued

WHAT THE PROBLEM LOOKS LIKE	PROBABLE CAUSE	COMMENTS
Yellowing of fronds. Leaf crown and upper portion of trunk decay. Entire top drops suddenly.	**Crown drop** or **Inflorescence rot**, *Thielaviopsis* spp. Fungal pathogens, which can be spread by contaminated climbing equipment and pruning tools.	Primarily attacks *Phoenix* spp., especially Canary Island date palm. Avoid wounding trunk, especially when removing fronds. Disinfect tools after working on each palm. Do not prune palms with chain saws.
Yellowing and death of fronds, often older fronds or leaflets on one side die first. Vascular tissue brown.	**Dothiorella wilt, Fusarium wilt.** *Fusarium* infects through roots and contaminated pruning tools.	Attack *Phoenix* spp., primarily Canary Island palm. Avoid injuring living tissue. Disinfect tools after working on each palm. Obtain a laboratory test to distinguish these causes. *See 234.*
Premature yellowing of lower fronds.	**Abiotic disease.** Many potential causes, including excess or deficient water; magnesium, nitrogen, or potassium deficiency; and pesticide or other chemical injury.	Provide a good growing environment and proper cultural care. Apply special palm fertilizer to prevent or remedy symptoms due to true nutrient deficiency.
Yellow and dark mottling and necrosis of fronds. Black or greasy, diamond-shaped or elongate fungal bodies on fronds. Fronds may die back.	**Diamond scale**, *Sphaerodothis neowashingtoniae*. A fungal disease. Symptoms superficially resemble nutrient disorders such as magnesium or potassium deficiency.	Primarily affects California fan palm, *Washingtonia filifera*. Plant *W. robusta* or other species. *See 211.*
Leaf stalk bases rot and die. Terminal bud dies. Infected tissue may be covered with pink spores. Trunk cankers on Queen palm (*Syagrus romanzoffianum*).	**Pink Rot**, *Gliocladium vermoeseni*. Fungal disease most serious on plants of low vigor and when fronds are wet.	Most serious near the coast and on plants of low vigor. Select species appropriate for that location. Provide good growing conditions and appropriate cultural care. *See 260.*
Yellowing of main shoots. Odorous rot.	**Bud rot**, *Phytophthora cactorum*. Fungus most severe during warm, moist, or humid weather.	Provide good soil drainage and proper cultural care. Bordeaux spray helps to prevent further infection if applied at first signs of damage. *See Root and Crown Rots, 265.*
Yellowing fronds and plant death. Tissue may contain tunnels or boring insects.	**Giant palm borer**, *Dinapate wrighti* (family Bostrichidae). Brown to black adult beetles and stout, yellowish larvae, both ≤1½ inches long, tunnel in wood.	Primarily a secondary pest attacking dead and dying palms. Provide good growing conditions and proper cultural care. Dispose of dead palms in which beetles breed.
Brownish, grayish, tan, orange, or white encrustations on fronds. May be yellowing or dieback of fronds.	**Boisduval scale**, *Diaspis boisduvalii*; **California red scale**; **Greedy scale**; **Oleander scale**. Tiny, circular to oval, flattened insects.	*See 131.*
Browning and scraping of upper surface of fronds. Fronds webbed and covered with reddish frass.	**Palm leafskeletonizer**, *Homaledra sabalella* (family Coleophoridae). Creamy, orangish to whitish larvae, ≤½ inch long, in groups or within silken tube, chew leaf surface. Adults are small tan moths.	Attacks many palms, including *Phoenix* and *Washingtonia* spp. Palms are seldom killed, but become unsightly. Remove, bag, and dispose of infested fronds. *See Foliage-Feeding Caterpillars, 71.*
Sticky honeydew and blackish sooty mold on fronds.	**Black scale; Brown soft scale; Hemispherical scale**, *Saissetia coffeae*. Flattened to bulbous, black, brown, or yellowish insects.	*See 136, 137.*
Sticky honeydew, blackish sooty mold, and cottony waxy material on plants.	**Mealybugs**, including **Longtailed mealybug, Obscure mealybug, Pink hibiscus mealybug, Vine mealybug**. Powdery gray insects.	*See 126.*
Sticky honeydew and blackish sooty mold may occur on fronds. Small, flattened, dark disks with pale, waxy fringes (insects) on fronds.	**Palm aphid** or **Lantana aphid**, *Cerataphis brasiliensis =C. fransseni =C. palmi*. Atypical aphid resembles immature form of certain whiteflies, usually occurs in groups.	*See Aphids, 103.*
Foliage discolored, stippled, bleached, or reddened. Fronds may decline prematurely. Plant may have fine webbing.	**Mites**, including *Oligonychus* spp. Tiny greenish, red, or yellowish mites, suck sap.	*See 197.*

PALM (Archontophoenix, Arecastrum, Brahea, Butia, Caryota, Chamaedorea, Dypsis, Hedyscepe, Howea, Jubaea, Livistona, Phoenix, Rhapis, Sabal, Syagrus, Trachycarpus, Washingtonia spp.), continued

WHAT THE PROBLEM LOOKS LIKE	PROBABLE CAUSE	COMMENTS
Stippled or bleached fronds with varnish-like specks on undersides.	**Greenhouse thrips.** Tiny, slender, black adults or yellow nymphs. On palm reported only on *Chamaedorea* spp.	*See 158.*
Plants stunted and may decline or slowly die. Powdery, waxy material may be visible on roots and around crown.	**Ground mealybugs,** *Rhizoecus* spp. Small, slender, pale insects, may be lightly covered with powdery wax, but lack marginal filaments.	*See 130.*
Galls or swellings on roots.	**Root knot nematode,** *Meloidogyne* sp. Tiny root-feeding roundworms.	*See 345.*

PALO VERDE (Cercidium spp.)

WHAT THE PROBLEM LOOKS LIKE	PROBABLE CAUSE	COMMENTS
Foliage discolors and wilts and may drop prematurely. Decline or death of limbs. Bark discolored or bleeding.	**Flatheaded borers,** including **Flatheaded appletree borer.** Whitish larvae ≤1 inch long with enlarged head in tunnels.	Keep plants vigorous. Remove and dispose of damaged limbs. *See 179.*
Foliage discolors and wilts and may drop prematurely. Limbs or tree may decline and die. Basal roots have elliptical holes ≤¾ inch in diameter.	**Palo Verde root borer,** *Derobrachus geminatus.* Pale larvae ≤5 inches long bore in roots and basal trunk. Adults are dark longhorned borers ≤3½ inches long.	Attacks unhealthy trees. Protect trees from injury. Provide plants with good growing environment and appropriate cultural care. No direct control known to be effective. *See Longhorned Borers, 183.*
Leaves chewed and webbed with silk. Leaves may drop prematurely.	**Palo Verde webworm** (family Gelechiidae). Adults are ¼ inch long tan moths. Larvae, ≤½ inch long, feed mostly hidden in silk tubes or webs.	Otherwise healthy Palo Verde tolerate extensive leaf chewing. *See Foliage-Feeding Caterpillars, 71.*
Leaves may dry up and drop prematurely. Shoots may be brown or yellow, bushy, or distorted into witches' brooms.	**Spider mites.** Tiny arthropods, often greenish or yellowish, suck sap.	*See 197.*
Green plants with smooth stems, thick roundish leaves infesting branches. Shoots may distort into witches' brooms.	**Broadleaf mistletoe.** Parasitic, evergreen plant on host.	*See 338.*

PEACH, NECTARINE (Prunus persica)[13]

WHAT THE PROBLEM LOOKS LIKE	PROBABLE CAUSE	COMMENTS
Leaves discolor, stunt, wilt, or drop prematurely. Stems discolored, cankered, and die. Minute white fungus growths may be visible beneath bark or on soil.	**Armillaria root rot.** Present in many soils. Favored by warm, wet soil. Persists for years in infected roots.	*See 262.*
Leaves discolor, stunt, wilt, or drop prematurely. Plants grow slowly and may die. Roots dark, decayed.	**Root and crown rots,** *Phytophthora* spp. Pathogens promoted by excess soil moisture and poor drainage.	*See 265.*
Leaves discolor, stunt, wilt, or drop prematurely, often on one side of plant. Stem xylem discolored. Stems or entire plant may die.	**Verticillium wilt,** *Verticillium* spp. Persist in soil, infect through roots.	*See 232.*
Stems, flowers, or fruit with dark lesions. Cankers possible on branches.	**Bacterial blight and canker.** Disease favored by wet conditions.	*See 245.*
Small brownish leaf spots, may have tan centers. Holes in leaf from dropped, infected tissue. Concentric lesions on branch.	**Shot hole.** A fungal disease promoted by moist spring weather or splashing irrigation water.	*See 226.*
Reddened, distorted foliage in spring. Shoots thickened, distorted, may die. Leaves may drop prematurely.	**Leaf curl** or **Plum pockets,** *Taphrina* spp. Fungal diseases promoted by moist spring weather or splashing irrigation water.	*See Leaf Curl Pest Notes* (Ohlendorf and Flint 2000).

13. For information on pest identification and biology, see publications such as *Nectarine Pest Management Guidelines* (Teviotdale et al. 2000), *Peach Pest Management Guidelines* (Teviotdale et al. 2002), and *Integrated Pest Management for Stone Fruits* (Strand 1999).

PEACH, NECTARINE *(Prunus persica)*, continued

WHAT THE PROBLEM LOOKS LIKE	PROBABLE CAUSE	COMMENTS
Circular brown decay develops on fruit. Blossoms and twigs may turn brown and die.	**Brown rot,** *Monilinia fructicola, M. laxa.* Windborne fungal pathogens that infect wet tissue.	Avoid wounding fruit and trees. Remove any infected fruit ("mummies") left on trees.
Powdery white growth and yellow blotches on leaves and sometimes on terminals and fruit. Shoots and leaves may be undersized or distorted.	**Powdery mildews,** *Podosphaera* spp., *Sphaerotheca pannosa.* Fungal diseases favored by moderate temperatures, shade, and poor air circulation.	*See 236.*
Sticky honeydew and blackish sooty mold on leaves and twigs. Possible dieback.	**Kuno scale.** Adult scales beadlike and dark shiny brown.	*See 140.*
Leaves chewed. Single branches or entire plant may be defoliated. Foliage may be rolled and tied together with silk.	**Fruittree leafroller, Omnivorous looper, Redhumped caterpillar, Tent caterpillars, Tussock moths.** Moth larvae ≤1½ inches long.	*See 71.*
Galls or swellings on roots. Plants may grow slowly. Roots may be darker or fewer than normal. Branch tips may die back.	**Ring nematode, Root knot nematodes, Root lesion nematode.** Tiny root-feeding roundworms.	*See 341.*
Galls or swellings on trunk and roots, usually near soil.	**Crown gall.** Bacterium that infects plant via wounds.	*See 258.*
Dead twigs or branches. Plant declines, may die. Tiny "BB shot"-sized holes in bark.	**Shothole borer.** Small brown bark beetles and whitish larvae tunnel beneath bark.	*See 176.*
Roughened bark, reddish brown granular material (frass) at base of trunk and main limbs. May be dark ooze from bark.	**American plum borer; Peachtree borer; Prune limb borer,** *Bondia comonana* (family Gelechiidae). Brown to pink larvae that bore under bark.	Prevent injuries to bark. Provide good growing conditions and proper cultural care. *See 187, 193.*

PEAR *(Pyrus communis)*[14]

WHAT THE PROBLEM LOOKS LIKE	PROBABLE CAUSE	COMMENTS
Foliage yellows and wilts. Branches or entire plant may die. Minute white fungus growths may be visible beneath bark or on soil.	**Armillaria root rot.** Present in many soils. Favored by warm, wet soil. Persists for years in infected roots.	*See 262.*
Sudden wilting then shriveling and blackening of shoots, blossoms, and fruit. Plant appears scorched.	**Fire blight.** Bacterium enters plants through blossoms.	*See 229.*
Shoots die back. Plants may grow slowly. Leaves may drop prematurely. Leaves and fruit may be undersized.	**Pear decline.** A phytoplasma or mycoplasmalike organism vectored by pear psylla.	Use resistant rootstock, which includes most currently available rootstocks except *Pyrus calleryana.* Control pear psylla. Provide trees with good cultural care. *See 270.*
Black to dark olive spots on fruit, leaves, or stems. Leaves may distort, tear, yellow, or drop prematurely.	**Scab,** *Venturia pirina.* A fungal disease spread by water from infected leaves and twigs.	*See 227.*
Brown, reddish, or purple blotches or spots on leaves, may have yellow halos. Leaves may drop prematurely.	**Entomosporium leaf spot.** A fungal disease promoted by wet foliage.	*See 227.*
Brown or yellow spots on upperside and orangish pustules on underside of leaves. Leaves may drop prematurely.	**Rusts,** including *Gymnosporangium asiaticum, G. fuscum, G. libocedri.* Fungi that infect and develop during moist conditions.	Avoid overhead watering. Vigorous plants tolerate moderate infection. *See 240.*
Flower buds brown, die, and drop. Dark spots may appear on fruit or leaves. Stems or flowers with dark lesions. Cankers or lesions may develop on stems.	**Bacterial blight and canker** or **Blossom blast.** Disease favored by wet conditions.	*See 245.*

14. For information on pest identification and biology, see publications such as *Pear Pest Management Guidelines* (Elkins et al. 2001), and *Integrated Pest Management for Apples and Pears* (Ohlendorf 1999).

PEAR (*Pyrus communis*), continued

WHAT THE PROBLEM LOOKS LIKE	PROBABLE CAUSE	COMMENTS
Leaves discolor and wilt. Stems may have callus tissue, dark cankers, or coral-colored pustules.	**Cankers**, including *Nectria cinnabarina*, *N. galligena*, *Phomopsis* spp. Fungi that primarily affect injured or stressed trees.	*See Nectria Canker, 257.*
Sticky honeydew and blackish sooty mold on leaves and twigs. Dieback of twigs or branches possible.	**Black scale, Calico scale, European fruit lecanium.** Black, brown, yellow, white, or mottled, flattened or bulbous insects ≤⅛ inch long.	*See 136–139.*
Sticky honeydew and blackish sooty mold on foliage.	**Bean aphid, Green peach aphid, Melon aphid.** Small black, gray, green, or yellow insects on leaves and terminals.	*See 104.*
Sticky honeydew and blackish sooty mold on foliage. Slow growth and possible premature leaf drop.	**Pear psylla**, *Cacopsylla* (=*Psylla*) *pyricola*. Tiny orangish nymphs in honeydew droplets. Brown to reddish adults look like tiny cicadas.	Conserve natural enemies that help in control. Apply narrow-range oil in dormant season, thoroughly covering terminals where eggs occur. *See Psyllids, 114.*
Sticky honeydew and blackish sooty mold on foliage. Cottony or waxy material on plant.	**Grape mealybug, Obscure mealybug.** Powdery, grayish insects, ≤¼ inch long with waxy filaments.	*See 127.*
Sticky honeydew and blackish sooty mold on leaves and twigs. Tiny, white, mothlike insects (adults) present.	**Ash whitefly.** Tiny, oval, flattened nymphs, pale colored, often with white wax on back.	Conserve natural enemies, which generally provide effective biological control. *See 121.*
Stippled, bleached, or reddened foliage. May be fine webbing on leaves or terminals. Leaves may drop prematurely.	**Brown mite**; *Bryobia rubrioculus*; **European red mite**; **McDaniel spider mite**, *Tetranychus mcdanieli*; **Pacific spider mite**; **Two-spotted spider mite.** Brown, green, reddish, or yellow specks.	*See 197.*
Pale blotches, spots, or winding tunnels in leaves. Leaves may drop prematurely.	**Leafminers**, *Phyllonorycter* spp. (family Geometridae). Pale larvae tunnel in leaves. Adults are brownish moths with silver or white.	Plants tolerate extensive mining. Conserve parasites, which usually control leafminers unless biological control is disrupted.
Bronzing or darkening of fruit or leaves. Plant growth may slow.	**Pear rust mite**, *Epitrimerus pyri*. A tiny elongate eriophyid mite.	Usually not important as damage is cosmetic. *See Gall Mites, 203.*
Bronzing, darkening, or spotting of fruit or leaves. Buds may blacken or fail to develop and drop. Fruit may be distorted.	**Pearleaf blister mite**, *Phytoptus pyri*. A tiny elongate eriophyid mite.	*See Gall Mites, 203.*
Fruit scabby, bronzed, deformed, or has slight depressions. Flower buds may exude gum, shrivel and die, or drop prematurely.	**Pear thrips**, *Taeniothrips inconsequens*; **Western flower thrips.** Tiny, slender, black, brown, or yellow insects.	*See 157.*
Fruit with discolored spots or irregularly shaped depressions. Fruit with hard, pithy areas or brown patches in flesh. Flower buds may exude gum, shrivel and die, or drop prematurely.	**Bordered plant bug**, *Euryophthalmus convivus*; **Boxelder bug; Leaffooted plant bug**, *Leptoglossus clypealis*; **Lygus bugs**, *Lygus elisus* and *L. hesperus*; **Stink bugs**, including **Conchuela**, *Chlorochroa ligata*; **Consperse stink bug**, *Euschistus cons, persus*; **Redshouldered stink bug**, *Thyanta pallidovirens*. True bugs with sucking mouthparts.	*See True Bugs, 152.*
Brown to gray encrustations on bark. May be declining or dead twigs or branches.	**Italian pear scale**, *Epidiaspis leperii*; **San Jose scale.** Tiny circular to elongate insects.	Italian pear scale survives only under shelter such as lichens and moss on bark. The female's body is reddish purple beneath its cover. *See 132.*

PEAR (*Pyrus communis*), continued

WHAT THE PROBLEM LOOKS LIKE	PROBABLE CAUSE	COMMENTS
Leaves or blossoms chewed. Single branches or entire plant may be defoliated. Foliage may be rolled and tied together with silk. Fruit may have small gouges or brownish scars.	**Fruittree leafroller; Humped green fruitworm,** *Amphipyra pyramidoides;* **Oblique-banded leafroller,** *Choristoneura rosaceana;* **Omnivorous leafroller,** *Platynota stultana;* **Orange tortrix,** *Argyrotaenia citrana;* **Speckled green fruitworm,** *Orthosia hibisci.* Moth larvae ≤1½ inches long.	*See 71.*
Leaves holey, scraped, or skeletonized and may be slime-covered.	**California pear sawfly,** *Pristiphora abbreviata;* **Pearslug.** Green to dark, slimy or smooth caterpillar or sluglike insects, ≤½ inch long.	*See 83.*
Fruit brown, decayed, or tunneled. Brown tunnels beneath skin may be visible from outside.	**Apple maggot,** *Rhagoletis pomonella* (family Tephritidae). Cream colored maggots feed in fruit. Adults are dark and light banded flies.	Eliminate alternate hosts and use good sanitation to help reduce populations. Pest is difficult to control without insecticide sprays, which should be well-timed by trapping adults.
Fruit brown, decayed, or tunneled, including around center. Dark oviposition marks on fruit.	**Codling moth,** *Cydia pomonella* (family Tortricidae). Pale larvae with dark head bore in fruit. Adults are small, brown and coppery moths.	Bagging fruit individually when young will avoid infestation. Consult *Codling Moth Pest Notes* (Bentley et al. 1999) for more information.

PECAN (*Carya illinoensis*)[15]

WHAT THE PROBLEM LOOKS LIKE	PROBABLE CAUSE	COMMENTS
Leaves brown, yellow, or die. Branches may die back. Wood may canker or ooze.	**Cankers,** including **Botryosphaeria canker and dieback.** Fungi primarily affect injured and stressed plants.	*See 250.*
Yellowish to brown angular patches, sticky honeydew, and blackish sooty mold on leaves. Premature leaf drop.	**Aphids,** including **Black pecan aphid,** *Melanocallis caryaefoliae.* Black, green, or yellowish insects.	Feeding may cause portions of leaves to die. *See 103.*

PEPPER TREE (*Schinus molle*), California pepper tree

WHAT THE PROBLEM LOOKS LIKE	PROBABLE CAUSE	COMMENTS
Leaves discolor, stunt, wilt, or drop prematurely. Stems discolored, cankered, and die. Minute white fungus growths may be visible beneath bark or on soil.	**Armillaria root rot.** Present in many soils. Favored by warm, wet soil. Persists for years in infected roots.	*See 262.*
Leaves discolor, stunt, wilt, or drop prematurely, often on one side of plant. Stem xylem discolored. Stems or entire plant may die.	**Verticillium wilt.** Fungus persists in soil, infects through roots.	*See 232.*
Leaves turn brown or yellow, especially along margins and at tip. Leaves may drop prematurely.	**Leaf burn** or **Scorch.** Abiotic disorders with many potential causes, including frost, inappropriate irrigation, or poor drainage.	Provide plants with a good growing environment and proper cultural care. *See 273.*
Chewed leaves. Foliage may be rolled and tied together with silk.	**Omnivorous looper.** Yellow, green, or pink larvae, ≤1½ inches long, with green, yellow or black stripes.	*See 79.*
Roundish pits in leaflets, petioles, and twigs. Trees grayish green with sparse foliage.	**Peppertree psyllid.** Tiny green adults, ¹⁄₁₆ inch long. Nymphs flattened and in pits, suck sap.	*See 116.*
Stippled, bleached foliage.	**Citrus thrips.** Tiny, slender, yellow.	Rarely if ever seriously damages pepper tree. *See 156.*

15. For information on pest identification and biology, see publications such as *Pecan Pest Management Guidelines* (Sibbett et al. 2000).

WHAT THE PROBLEM LOOKS LIKE	PROBABLE CAUSE	COMMENTS

PEPPER TREE *(Schinus molle)*, California pepper tree, continued

| Sticky honeydew and blackish sooty mold on foliage. May be declining or dead twigs or branches. | **Barnacle scale,** *Ceroplastes cirripediformis;* **Black scale; Green shield scale; Hemispherical scale,** *Saissetia coffeae;* **Wax scales.** Small, black, brown, green, yellowish, waxy, or whitish, flattened or bulbous insects. | *See 136.* |
| Brownish, grayish, tan, or white encrustations on bark. Rarely, declining or dead twigs or branches. | **Greedy scale, Oleander scale.** Tiny oval to circular insects on bark. | Rarely if ever cause serious damage to plants. *See 133, 134.* |

PERIWINKLE *(Vinca roseus =Catharanthus roseus)*, Myrtle

Shoots, leaves, and stems yellow and wilt. Plants grow slowly and may die. Roots dark, decayed.	**Root, stem and crown rot,** *Phytophthora* sp. Pathogen promoted by excess soil moisture and poor drainage.	*See 265.*
Foliage fades, yellows, browns, and wilts, often on one side of plant. Stem xylem has reddish discoloration. Stems or entire plant may die.	**Verticillium wilts,** *Verticillium dahliae, V. albo-atrum.* Fungi persist in soil, infect through roots.	*See 232.*
Stems yellow, wilt, blacken, and die. Shoots and runners have sunken or decayed lesions that girdle stems or trunks. Stems may enlarge. Leaf spots possible.	**Stem rot,** *Phoma exigua.* Fungus invades through wounds. Spreads in water. Favored by high soil moisture. Prefers stressed plants.	Avoid overhead watering or reduce frequency. Provide good drainage.
Discolored spots and orangish pustules on leaves. Leaves may drop prematurely.	**Rusts,** *Puccinia vincae.* Pathogen favored by wet conditions. Fungal spores persist in plant debris.	Avoid overhead watering. Plants tolerate moderate populations. *See 240.*
New growth chlorotic, except for green veins.	**Iron deficiency.** Abiotic disorder usually caused by poor soil conditions or unhealthy roots.	*See 278.*
Foliage discolored, stippled, bleached, or reddened; may distort or drop prematurely. Plant may have fine webbing.	**Spider mites.** Tiny greenish, red, or yellowish mites, often with 2 darker spots.	*See 197.*
Stems or leaves have brownish gray, tan, white, or purplish encrustations. Foliage may yellow.	**Greedy scale, Oleander scale.** Circular to elongate, flattened armored scale insects, <¹⁄₁₆ inch long.	Rarely if ever cause serious damage to periwinkle. *See 133, 134.*
Foliage or stems have blackish sooty mold. Plant may wilt, decline, or die back.	**Black scale.** Orange, black, or brown, flattened to bulbous insects.	*See 136.*
Foliage has sticky honeydew and blackish sooty mold. Leaves yellow and wither. Tiny, whitish, mothlike adult insects present.	**Whiteflies,** including **Citrus whitefly, Silverleaf whitefly.** Oval, flattened, yellow to greenish nymphs.	*See 121.*
Foliage has sticky honeydew, blackish sooty mold, and whitish cast skins. Foliage may yellow.	**Aphids,** including **Cresentmarked lily aphid,** *Aulacorthum (=Myzus) circumflexum;* **Green peach aphid; Leaf curl plum aphid,** *Brachycaudus (=Aphis) helichrysi.* Pear-shaped insects, often green, yellowish, or blackish.	*See 103.*
Leaves and blossoms chewed (edges notched).	**Fuller rose beetle.** Rarely seen adult pale brown weevil feeds at night. Larvae (whitish maggots) live in soil and eat roots.	*See 94.*

PERSIMMON *(Diospyros spp.)*

| Leaves with black, brown, tan, or yellow blotches or spots. Spots may have dark or yellowish margins. Foliage may die and drop prematurely. | **Leaf spots** and **Blights,** including *Cladosporium* sp. Fungi spread in water and favored by prolonged cool, wet, conditions. | *See 223.* |

PERSIMMON (*Diospyros* spp.), continued

WHAT THE PROBLEM LOOKS LIKE	PROBABLE CAUSE	COMMENTS
Leaves yellow and wilt. Branches or entire plant may die. Minute white fungus growths may be visible beneath bark or on soil.	**Armillaria root rot.** Present in many soils. Favored by warm, wet soil. Persists for years in infected roots.	*See 262.*
Leaves yellow and wilt. Branches or entire plant dies.	**Root and crown rot,** *Phytophthora cinnamomi.* Pathogen favored by wet soil and poor drainage.	*See 265.*
Foliage yellows and wilts. Branches or entire plant may die. Fungal fruiting bodies may be on wood or around roots.	**Wood decay** or **Heart rots,** including *Ganoderma applanatum.* Fungi that attack injured or stressed trees. *Ganoderma* produces large, fan-shaped basidiocarps on bark.	*See Wood Decay in Trunks and Limbs, 248.*
Dieback of branches. Foliage yellows and wilts. Gnarled, ridged bark with wet spots and D-shaped, ⅛-inch-diameter emergence holes.	**Flatheaded borer,** *Agrilus* sp. Whitish larvae ≤½ inch long beneath bark.	*See 179.*
Growth slow. Fruit may be few in number and undersized. Foliage may yellow. Soil clings to roots and is difficult to wash off.	**Citrus nematode,** *Tylenchulus semipenetrans.* Microscopic root-feeding roundworms.	*See 347.*
Soft, brown decay on flowers, buds, or leaves. May be woolly gray growth (spores) on dead tissue.	**Gray mold.** Fungus favored by mild, wet conditions. Spreads by airborne spores.	*See 242.*
Sticky honeydew and blackish sooty mold on leaves. Whitish, cottony material on bark or leaves. Terminals may distort.	**Mealybugs,** including **Comstock mealybug,** *Pseudococcus comstocki;* **Longtailed mealybug.** Oblong, soft, powdery, waxy insects with filaments.	*See 126.*
Sticky honeydew and blackish sooty mold on foliage. Possible plant decline or dieback.	**Lecanium scale,** *Parthenolecanium* sp. Brown, flat or bulbous, immobile insects.	*See 139.*
Brownish, grayish, tan, or white encrustations on bark or leaves. Rarely, plant parts die back.	**Greedy scale.** Tiny circular, flattened insects, usually in groups.	*See 133.*
Leaves with brown or purplish blotches or streaks. Foliage may drop prematurely.	**Persea mite.** Tiny green to yellow mites, often with dark spots.	*See 199.*
Fruit brown or scabby, especially around stem. Fruit may distort or drop prematurely if severe. Flower bud edges or entire bud browns and may drop. Petals may turn brown or drop prematurely.	**Brown lace collar** or **Persimmon bud mite,** *Aceria diospyri.* Translucent to white eriophyids, ≤¹⁄₁₀₀ inch long, that infest inner surface of bud scales and under the fruit button.	*See Gall Mites, 203.*
Chewed leaves. Silken tents may occur on terminals. Single branches may be defoliated.	**Fall webworm, Redhumped caterpillar.** Smooth to hairy caterpillars, ≤1½ inches long.	*See 78, 81.*
Chewed leaves or blossoms. Leaf margins notched, ragged.	**Fuller rose beetle.** Pale brown adult snout weevils, about ⅜ inch long.	Adults hide during day and feed at night. Larvae feed on roots. *See 94.*

PHOTINIA (*Photinia* spp.), Red tips

WHAT THE PROBLEM LOOKS LIKE	PROBABLE CAUSE	COMMENTS
Foliage yellows and wilts. Branches or entire plant dies. Rootlets decayed or sparse.	**Root and crown rot,** *Phytophthora* sp. Pathogen favored by wet soil and poor drainage.	*See 265.*
New foliage yellows, beginning along margins, but veins green. Leaves may develop brown blotches.	**Iron deficiency.** Abiotic disorder usually caused by poor soil conditions or unhealthy roots.	*See 278.*

WHAT THE PROBLEM LOOKS LIKE	PROBABLE CAUSE	COMMENTS
PHOTINIA *(Photinia* spp.), Red tips, continued		
Sudden wilting then shriveling and blackening of shoots and blossoms. Plants appear scorched.	**Fire blight.** Bacterium infects plants through blossoms.	*See 229.*
Powdery white growth and yellow blotches on leaves and sometimes on terminals and fruit. Shoots and leaves may be undersized or distorted.	**Powdery mildews**, *Podosphaera leucotricha, Sphaerotheca pannosa.* Fungal diseases favored by moderate temperatures, shade, and poor air circulation.	*See 236.*
Tiny brown, reddish, or purple leaf spots, may have yellow halos. Larger, dark areas on leaves. Leaves may drop prematurely.	**Entomosporium leaf spot.** A fungal disease promoted by wet foliage.	*See 227.*
Black to dark olive spots on leaves. Leaves yellow and may drop prematurely.	**Scab**, *Spilocaea* sp. A fungal disease spread by water from infected leaves and twigs.	Avoid overhead watering. Prune out infected twigs and leaves in fall. *See 227.*
Tiny brown, reddish, or purple leaf spots. Unlike Entomosporium leaf spot, spots lack dark centers. Leaves may drop prematurely.	**Physiological leaf spot.** Abiotic disorders with many potential causes. Cold stress is a common cause of damage, especially if plants are low-lying or shaded.	Apparently harmless to plants. Plant in full sun. Do not plant in low-lying spots were cold air settles. Provide good growing conditions and proper cultural care.
Stippled, bleached, or reddened leaves with varnishlike specks on undersides.	**Greenhouse thrips.** Slender black adults or yellow nymphs.	Look for insects to distinguish from similar damage caused by lace bugs. *See 158.*
Stippled or bleached leaves with varnishlike specks on undersides.	**Lace bug**, *Corythucha* spp. Adults ≤⅙ inch long, wings lacy. Nymphs spiny.	Look for insects to distinguish from similar damage caused by thrips. *See 154.*
Blackish sooty mold, sticky honeydew, and whitish cast skins on plants.	**Aphids.** Small green, brown, black, or yellowish insects, often in groups.	*See 103.*
Leaf margins chewed, notched. Young plants may decline.	**Weevils**, including **Fuller rose beetle;** *Otiorhynchus* spp. Adults chew foliage. Larvae chew roots.	*See 94.*
PIERIS *(Pieris, Andromeda* spp.)		
Foliage yellows and wilts. Branches or entire plant dies.	**Root and crown rot**, *Phytophthora* sp. Pathogen favored by wet soil and poor drainage.	*See 262.*
Brown, black, tan or yellow spots or blotches on leaves. Spots may have dark or yellowish margins. Foliage may die and drop prematurely.	**Leaf spots**, *Alternaria* sp., *Phyllosticta* sp. Spread by air or splashing water. Favored by prolonged cool, wet, conditions. Persist in plant debris.	*See 223.*
Wilting or dead plants. Some roots stripped of bark or girdled near soil. Foliage may be notched around margins.	**Black vine weevil.** Adults are black or grayish snout beetles, about ⅜ inch long. Larvae are white grubs with brown head.	Larvae feed on roots. Adults hide during day and feed at night. *See 92.*
Stippled or bleached leaves. Leaves may dry up and drop prematurely.	**Spider mites**, *Tetranychus* spp. Greenish specks, suck sap.	Conserve natural enemies that help control. *See 197.*
Leaves stippled or bleached, with cast skins or varnishlike specks on underside.	**Andromeda lace bug**, *Stephanitis takeyai.* Black and clear insects, ≤⅙ inch long with lacy wings.	*See Lace Bugs, 154.*
PINE *(Pinus* spp.)		
Needles discolor, stunt, wilt, or drop prematurely. Stems discolored, cankered, and die. Minute white fungus growths may be visible beneath bark or on soil.	**Armillaria root rot.** Present in many soils. Favored by warm, wet soil. Persists for years in infected roots.	Certain pines are resistant, including *Pinus nigra, P. sylvestris, P. torreyana. See 262.*
Needles discolor, stunt, wilt, or drop prematurely. Plants grow slowly and may die. Roots dark, decayed.	**Root and crown rots**, *Phytophthora* spp. Pathogens promoted by excess soil moisture and poor drainage.	*See 265.*

PINE (*Pinus* spp.), continued

WHAT THE PROBLEM LOOKS LIKE	PROBABLE CAUSE	COMMENTS
Needles discolor, wilt, stunt, and may drop prematurely. Branches may canker or die back. Plant base or roots dark or decayed. Plant may die.	**Root and crown rot, Foliage blight,** or **Stem necrosis,** *Fusarium* sp. Fungus that persists in soil and infects roots.	This Fusarium rot is primarily a problem in the eastern U.S. and Pacific Northwest. *See similar Root and Crown Rots, 265.*
Needles yellow, wilt and drop prematurely. Branches die back and entire plant may die.	**Annosus root disease.** Decay fungus that spreads through roots and airborne spores.	*See 265.*
Slightly raised reddish or yellow spots on needles. Cankers, galls, or oozing on stems. Needles may drop prematurely. Terminals brown and die.	**Pine stem and cone rusts,** including **White pine blister rust,** *Cronartium ribicola.* Fungi persist in infected bark. Disease is favored by cool, wet conditions.	*See 242.*
Brown, reddish, or yellow bands or spots on needles. Needles drop prematurely, especially on lower branches.	**Pine needle rusts,** *Coleosporium* spp. Fungal diseases.	*See 242.*
Black, brown, reddish, or yellow lesions, spots, or streaks on needles or stems. Shoots may be bushy or distorted. Needles drop prematurely. Plants grow slowly. Branches may die back.	**Needle blight, Needle cast,** and **Needle spot,** including *Elytroderma deformans, Lophodermella* spp., *Lophodermium* spp., *Mycosphaerella* spp., Fungal diseases favored by cool, wet conditions in spring.	Moist conditions favor fungi. Remove nearby plants and weeds, thin canopy, and prune off lower limbs to reduce humidity. Remove and dispose of fallen, infected needles.
Brown or yellow needles, especially at branch tips. Dead needles may persist on branches. Terminals or branches may dieback.	**Blight** or **Aleppo pine blight.** Abiotic disorders with many causes, including dry winds, excess light, fertilizer toxicity, low humidity, high temperatures, root injury, soil compaction, or too much or too little water.	Aleppo pine (*Pinus halepensis*) is commonly affected. Provide trees with a good growing environment and proper cultural care.
Needles wilt, turn yellow, then entirely brown in large groups. Twigs and tree top may die. Wood is stained black or brown.	**Diplodia canker,** *Sphaeropsis sapinea* =*Diplodia pinea.* A fungal disease that primarily affects injured or weakened pine.	*See similar Oak Branch Dieback, 228.*
Dead branches with clinging needles, mostly in upper canopy. Trunk cankers and branches exuding copious pitch.	**Pitch canker** or **Pine pitch canker.** A fungal disease.	Occurs in the southeastern U.S. and coastal areas of California. If found where not known to occur, report this to agricultural officials. *See 250.*
Stunted, bushy foliage, possible dieback. Round swellings on branches, orangish (spore covered) in spring.	**Western gall rust.** Fungus that infects 2- and 3-needle pines.	*See 241.*
Pitchy masses 1 to 4 inches in diameter protruding from trunks and limbs. Limbs occasionally break.	**Douglas-fir pitch moth, Sequoia pitch moth.** Dirty, whitish larvae, ≤1 inch long, in pitch. Adults wasplike.	Avoid injuring pines, wounds attract moths. Plants tolerate these insects that feed shallowly beneath bark. *See 191.*
Sticky honeydew and blackish sooty mold on foliage. Whitish wax may cover needles. Possible yellowing of needles.	**Aphids,** including *Essigella californica;* **Woolly pine needle aphid,** *Schizolachnus piniradiatae.* Tiny green to gray insects.	*See 103.*
Cottony white or grayish material on bark or needles. Slow pine growth.	**Pine bark adelgids,** *Pineus* spp. Tiny purplish insects under cottony wax.	*See 112.*
Sticky honeydew, blackish sooty mold, and waxy, whitish material on needles and twigs.	**McKenzie pine mealybug,** *Dysmicoccus pinicolus;* **Obscure mealybug.** Oval, waxy-fringed insect, ≤⅙ inch long.	Conserve natural enemies. Plants tolerate moderate populations. Insecticidal soap can be applied. *See Mealybugs, 126.*
Sticky honeydew and blackish sooty mold on foliage. Brown to purplish insects clustered on foliage.	**Giant conifer aphids.** Dark, long-legged insects, ≤⅙ inch long.	Apparently harmless to trees. *See 105.*
Sticky honeydew and blackish sooty mold on foliage. Possible yellowing of older needles. Male scales resemble rice grains on needles.	**Monterey pine scale,** *Physokermes insignicola.* **Irregular pine scale.** Females, ¼ inch long, resemble chips of marble or dark, shiny, beads on twigs.	Vigorous trees tolerate moderate populations. *See 140.*

PINE (*Pinus* spp.), continued

WHAT THE PROBLEM LOOKS LIKE	PROBABLE CAUSE	COMMENTS
Interior needles turn brown or yellow and drop prematurely, leaving only young terminal needles. Tree may die.	**Spruce aphid**, *Elatobium abietinum*. Small pear-shaped insects, dark to light green, in groups on older foliage.	Usually abundant only on spruce, where it can be a serious pest. *See Aphids, 103.*
Yellow mottling or dieback of needles.	**Pine needle scale**, *Chionaspis pinifoliae*; **Black pine leaf scale**, *Nuculaspis californica*. White, gray, or black armored scales, ¹⁄₁₆ inch long, on needles.	Scales have several generations a year in warm areas, only one at cool sites. Plants tolerate moderate populations. Conserve natural enemies. If damaging, monitor and apply oil. *See Armored Scales, 131.*
Stippled or bleached needles, more common on young pines.	**Spider mites**, *Oligonychus* spp. Green to pink specks on needles, suck sap.	*See Pine and Spruce Spider Mites, 200.*
Needles chewed, notched along length. Needles turn brown in late winter or spring. Damaged needles drop prematurely.	**Pine needle weevils**, *Scythropus* spp. Adults ¼-inch-long, brownish snout beetles.	Adult damage to needles and larvae feeding on roots appear not to harm trees. No control known. *See Weevils, 92.*
Chewed needles.	**Conifer sawflies**, *Neodiprion* spp. Green larvae, ≤1 inch long, on needles.	*See 83.*
Chewed needles, may be webbed with silk.	**Silverspotted tiger moth**, *Lophocampa argentata* (family Arctiidae); **Tussock moths**. Dark, hairy larvae, ≤1¼ inches, may have colorful hairs or spots. Adults brownish to tan moths and may have silvery spots.	*See 74, 77.*
Mined buds and shoot tips. Killed tips give tree red or brown appearance. Foliage becomes bunchy-looking.	**Monterey pine tip moth**, **Nantucket pine tip moth**, **Ponderosa pine tip moth**. Adults ⅓ inch long yellow, gray, to brown moths. Orangish larvae in mines.	Pines tolerate extensive tip mining. *See 170.*
Terminals distorted, chewed, dead. Foliage may become busy, crooked. Roots or the basal trunk may be injured.	**Conifer twig weevils** or **Pine weevils**, including **White pine weevil**. Small black to brown weevils chew needles and shoots. Depending on the species, larvae chew on or within needles and shoots or bore in the root crown.	Grublike larvae of damaging species mine shoots. Tolerate or prune out damage. On high aesthetic value (nursery) trees, a foliar insecticide spray in the spring may be applied when adults feed and lay eggs. *See 93.*
Terminals brown, dead, or webbed with silk. Needles are clipped, mined, pale streaked, or wilted and drop prematurely. Foliage may be sparse. Plant growth stunted.	**Pine needle sheathminer**, *Zelleria haimbachi* (family Yponomeutidae). Tiny moths with larvae that feed inside needles.	Where previously severe, a spring application to new growth of an insecticide registered for this use may provide control.
Needles mined or with pale streaks. Foliage may be webbed, sparse, and drop prematurely. Plant growth stunted. Trees may die.	**Pine needle miners**, *Chionodes* spp., *Coleotechnites* spp. (family Gelechiidae). Tiny moths with larvae that feed inside needles.	Where previously severe, a spring application to new growth of an insecticide registered for this use may provide control.
Needles distorted, short, twisted, yellow, and may drop prematurely. Plants may grow slowly.	**Pine bud mite**, *Trisetacus* sp. Tiny elongate eriophyid mites that suck bud tissue.	*See Gall Mites, 203.*
Sections of shoot with greatly shortened needles with swollen bases.	**Monterey pine midge**, *Thecodiplosis piniradiatae*. White or orangish larvae in swollen needles.	Control generally not warranted. No management known. *See Gall Midges, 164.*
Wet, white, frothy masses of spittle on twigs or cones.	**Spittlebugs**, including **Western pine spittlebug**. Green to black insects in spittle.	Tolerate, spittlebugs cause no apparent harm to pines. *See 151.*
Tips of Monterey pine mined, but only for 1 or 2 inches. Tips die, often in crooked position.	**Monterey pine bud moth**, *Exoteleia burkei* (family Gelechiidae). Larvae brownish yellow, ≤³⁄₁₆ inch long, in mines.	Damage very localized and unlikely to harm tree. Prune out and dispose of affected tips, no other control known.
Small, leafless, orangish, upright plants on host stems. Distorted and slow plant growth. Branches die back.	**Dwarf mistletoe**, *Arceuthobium* spp. Host-specific parasitic plants that extract nutrients from host plant.	Prune out infected branches. Replace heavily infected plants with broadleaf species or conifers from other genera; *See 338.*

WHAT THE PROBLEM LOOKS LIKE	PROBABLE CAUSE	COMMENTS

PINE (*Pinus* spp.), continued

WHAT THE PROBLEM LOOKS LIKE	PROBABLE CAUSE	COMMENTS
Tree declining or dead. Boring dust or coarse granular material around tree base or on bark plates or branch crotches. Pitch tubes on bark.	**Bark beetles.** Brown to black, stout beetles ≤¼ inch long. Larvae white grubs under bark.	*See 173.*
Tree dead, sometimes dying quickly.	**Pinewood nematode,** *Bursaphelenchus xylophilus.* Microscopic roundworms that feed inside limbs.	*See 347.*
Foliage discolors. Tree or limbs declining or dead.	**Flatheaded** and **Longhorned borers.** Whitish larvae, ≤1 inch long tunneling beneath bark.	*See 179, 183.*
Plants stunted, decline, may die. Powdery, waxy material may be visible on roots and around crown.	**Ground mealybugs,** *Rhizoecus* spp. Small, slender, pale insects, may be lightly covered with powdery wax, but lack marginal filaments.	*See 130.*

PITTOSPORUM (*Pittosporum* spp.), Mock orange, Tobira, Victorian box

WHAT THE PROBLEM LOOKS LIKE	PROBABLE CAUSE	COMMENTS
Leaves discolor, stunt, wilt, and remain dead on plant or drop prematurely. Plants grow slowly and may die. Root crown dark, decayed.	**Root and crown rots.** Pathogens promoted by excess soil moisture and poor drainage.	*See 265.*
Flower buds, leaves, petals, or stems turn brown and die. Stems may ooze or be cankered.	**Bacterial blight and canker** or **Blossom blast.** Disease favored by wet conditions.	*See 245.*
Twigs distorted, swollen, and pitted. Leaves dwarfed. Shoots may die back.	**Pit-making pittosporum scale,** *Planchonia* (=*Asterolecanium) arabidis* (family Asterolecaniidae). Brown to white insects, ≤⅛ inch long, on twigs, often in pits.	In California, an occasional problem in the north. Management not investigated. *See Other Common Scales, 142.*
Sticky honeydew, blackish sooty mold, and whitish cast skins on plant.	**Apple aphid,** *Aphis pomi;* **Melon aphid; Woolly apple aphid.** Bright green insects on terminals or leaves.	Conserve natural enemies that provide control. Tolerate or apply soap or oil. *See Aphids, 103.*
Sticky honeydew and blackish sooty mold on plant. May be cottony whitish material (egg sacs) on bark.	**Cottony cushion scale, Green shield scale.** Brownish, green, orange, red, or yellowish convex or flattened insects on bark or leaves.	*See 139, 142.*
Sticky honeydew, blackish sooty mold, and cottony waxy material on plant.	**Longtailed mealybug, Obscure mealybug.** Powdery, grayish, segmented insects with fringe filaments, longer at tail.	*See 127.*
Brownish, grayish, tan, or white encrustations on bark. Rarely, declining or dead twigs or branches.	**Greedy scale.** Nearly circular insects, ¹⁄₁₆ inch long, on bark.	*See 133.*
Leaves discolored, wilted, stunted, may drop prematurely. Discolored bark may ooze sap. Branches or plant may die. Trees may fall over.	**Heart rot** or **Wood decay,** including *Ganoderma applanatum.* Decay fungi that infect injured or severely stressed plants. *Ganoderma* produces large, fan-shaped basidiocarps on lower trunks.	*See Wood Decay in Trunks and Limbs, 248.*
Galls or swellings on roots.	**Root knot nematode,** *Meloidogyne* sp. Tiny root-feeding roundworms.	*See 345.*

PLUM, PRUNE (*Prunus* spp.)[16]

WHAT THE PROBLEM LOOKS LIKE	PROBABLE CAUSE	COMMENTS
Leaves discolor, stunt, wilt, or drop prematurely. Stems discolored, cankered, and die. Minute white fungus growths may be visible beneath bark or on soil.	**Armillaria root rot.** Present in many soils. Favored by warm, wet soil. Persists for years in infected roots.	*See 262.*

16. For more information on pest identification and biology, see publications such as *Plum Pest Management Guidelines* (Teviotdale et al. 2000) and *Integrated Pest Management for Stone Fruits* (Strand 1999).

WHAT THE PROBLEM LOOKS LIKE	PROBABLE CAUSE	COMMENTS
PLUM, PRUNE (*Prunus* spp.), continued		
Leaves discolor, stunt, wilt, or drop prematurely. Plants grow slowly and may die. Roots dark, decayed.	**Root and crown rots,** *Phytophthora* spp. Pathogens promoted by excess soil moisture and poor drainage.	*See 265.*
Leaves discolor, stunt, wilt, or drop prematurely, often on one side of plant. Stem xylem discolored. Stems or entire plant may die.	**Verticillium wilts,** *Verticillium* spp. Persist in soil, infect through roots.	*See 232.*
Leaves discolor and die. Stems, flowers, or fruit with dark lesions. Cankers possible on branches.	**Bacterial blight and canker.** Disease favored by wet conditions.	*See 245.*
Leaves reddened, distorted in spring. Shoots thickened, distorted, may die. Leaves may drop prematurely.	**Leaf curl** or **Plum pockets,** *Taphrina* spp. Fungal diseases promoted by moist spring weather or splashing irrigation water.	Apply calcium polysulfides (lime sulfur), fungicide with at least 50% copper, or synthetic fungicide in fall after leaf drop, repeat when buds swell.
Leaves with small brownish spots, which may have tan centers. Leaves have small holes. May be concentric lesions on branches.	**Shot hole.** A fungal disease promoted by moist spring weather or splashing irrigation water.	Does not affect prune and is uncommon on fruiting plum. *See 226.*
Circular brown decay develops on fruit. Blossoms and twigs may turn brown and die.	**Brown rot,** *Monilinia fructicola, M. laxa.* Windborne fungal pathogens that infect wet tissue.	Avoid wounding fruit and trees. Remove any infected fruit ("mummies") left on trees.
Powdery white growth and yellow blotches on leaves and sometimes on terminals and fruit. Shoots and leaves may be undersized or distorted.	**Powdery mildews,** *Podosphaera* spp., *Sphaerotheca pannosa.* Fungal diseases favored by moderate temperatures, shade, and poor air circulation.	*See 236.*
Sticky honeydew, blackish sooty mold, and whitish cast skins on plant. Leaves may curl or be covered with whitish wax.	**Aphids,** including **Green peach aphid; Leaf curl plum aphid,** *Brachycaudus helichrysi*; **Mealy plum aphid,** *Hyalopterus pruni.* Small brownish, green, or yellowish, pear-shaped insects.	*See 103.*
Sticky honeydew and blackish sooty mold on leaves and twigs. Possible dieback.	**Kuno scale.** Adult scales beadlike and dark shiny brown.	*See 140.*
Leaves chewed. Single branches or entire plant may be defoliated. Foliage may be rolled and tied together with silk.	**Fruittree leafroller, Omnivorous looper, Redhumped caterpillar, Tent caterpillars, Tussock moths.** Moth larvae ≤1½ inches long.	*See 71.*
Galls or swellings may be on roots. Foliage may yellow or wilt. Roots may be darker or fewer than normal. Plants may grow slowly.	**Pin nematode, Ring nematode, Root lesion nematode, Root knot nematodes.** Tiny root-feeding roundworms.	*See 341.*
Galls or swellings on trunk and roots, usually near soil.	**Crown gall.** Bacterium that infects plant via wounds.	*See 258.*
Dead twigs or branches. Plant declines, may die. Tiny "BB shot"-sized holes in bark.	**Shothole borer.** Small brown bark beetles and whitish larvae tunnel beneath bark.	*See 176.*
Roughened bark, reddish brown granular material (frass) at base of trunk and main limbs. May be dark ooze from bark.	**American plum borer; Peachtree borer; Prune limb borer,** *Bondia comonana* (family Gelechiidae). Brown to pink larvae that bore under bark.	Prevent injuries to bark. Provide proper cultural care. *See 187, 193.*
PODOCARPUS (*Podocarpus* spp.), African fern pine, Yew pine		
Brownish to orangish encrustations on bark.	**California red scale.** Circular to oval insects, <¹⁄₁₆ inch long.	Rarely if ever causes serious damage. *See 131.*

WHAT THE PROBLEM LOOKS LIKE	PROBABLE CAUSE	COMMENTS

PODOCARPUS *(Podocarpus* spp.*)*, African fern pine, Yew pine, *continued*

WHAT THE PROBLEM LOOKS LIKE	PROBABLE CAUSE	COMMENTS
Sticky honeydew, blackish sooty mold, and whitish cast skins on leaves. Bluish white bloom covering foliage.	**Podocarpus aphid**, *Neophyllaphis podocarpi.* Grayish insects, about $\frac{1}{16}$ inch long, grouped on stems or leaves.	Plants tolerate extensive aphid feeding. Hose with forceful water. Tolerate or apply soap or oil if damaging. *See Aphids, 103.*

POMEGRANATE *(Punica granatum)* — Pomegranate (Punica granatum)

WHAT THE PROBLEM LOOKS LIKE	PROBABLE CAUSE	COMMENTS
Leaves discolor and wilt. Limbs die back. Entire plant may die. Minute white fungus growths may be visible beneath bark or on soil.	**Armillaria root rot.** Present in many soils. Favored by warm, wet soil. Persists for years in infected roots.	*See 262.*
Flowers or fruit develop watery decay, may be covered with grayish woolly growth.	**Botrytis blight.** A fungal disease that thrives under moist conditions and cool to moderate temperatures.	*See 242.*
Sticky honeydew and blackish sooty mold on foliage. Tiny, whitish, mothlike insects (adult whiteflies).	**Whiteflies,** including **Ash whitefly, Citrus whitefly.** Nymphs oval, flattened, yellowish to greenish.	Conserve natural enemies, which usually provide good biological control. *See 121.*
Sticky honeydew and blackish sooty mold on foliage. Cottony or waxy material on plant.	**Mealybugs,** including **Vine mealybug.** Powdery, grayish insects, ≤¼ inch long, with waxy filaments.	Vigorous plants tolerate moderate populations. Conserve natural enemies that help in control. *See 126.*
Sticky honeydew and blackish sooty mold on plant. Foliage may yellow.	**Citricola scale.** Brownish or grayish flattened or bulbous insects.	Rarely occurs and generally is not a pest on pomegranate. *See 138.*

POPLAR, COTTONWOOD, ASPEN *(Populus* spp.*)*

WHAT THE PROBLEM LOOKS LIKE	PROBABLE CAUSE	COMMENTS
Leaves or terminals with powdery white growth and yellow blotches. Shoots and leaves may be undersized or distorted.	**Powdery mildew,** *Uncinula adunca.* Fungal disease favored by moderate temperatures, shade, and poor air circulation.	*See 236.*
Leaves yellow, wilt, and may drop prematurely. Branches die back. Entire tree may die. Minute white fungus growths may be visible beneath bark or on soil.	**Armillaria root rot.** Present in many soils. Favored by warm, wet soil. Persists for years in infected roots.	*See 262.*
Leaves wilted, discolored, may drop prematurely. Branches or entire plant may die. May be white fungal growth or dark crust on basal trunk, roots, or soil.	**Dematophora root rot.** Fungus favored by mild, wet conditions. Infects primarily through roots growing near infested plants.	Less common than *Armillaria. See 264.*
Black to brown lesions, spots or streaks on blossoms, leaves, and stems. Cankers and brown streaks on wood. Limbs may die back.	**Bacterial blight and canker.** Disease favored by wet conditions.	*See 245.*
Leaves may discolor and wilt. Brownish, sunken lesions on trunk and large limbs. Small branches and twigs may be killed without apparent canker.	**Cankers,** including *Cytospora chrysosperma, Hypoxylon mediterraneum.* Fungal diseases most serious on low vigor trees. Often infect through wounds.	Provide moderate fertilizer, adequate water, and proper cultural care. Prune out dead and diseased branches. *See 250.*
Leaves with circular to irregular tan or darker blotches or spots on leaves. Terminals may die back. Branches may canker on some hosts.	**Leaf spots** and **Shoot blights,** including *Mycosphaerella populorum* (on cottonwood), *Marssonina* spp. (aspen and poplar), *Septoria* sp. (cottonwood and poplar), *Venturia* spp. (on all). Fungal diseases promoted and spread by water.	*See 223.*
Leaves turn brown at the margins and tip. Leaves may be curled or puckered. Leaves may drop prematurely.	**Leaf burn** or **Scorch.** Abiotic disorders. Common causes include drought, excess heat, injury to trunks or roots, overirrigation, and poor drainage.	Protect trees from injury. Provide good cultural care, especially appropriate irrigation. *See 273.*
Leaves with light to dark spots and orangish pustules. Leaves may drop prematurely.	**Rusts,** *Melampsora* spp. Fungi require moist conditions.	Avoid overhead watering. Vigorous plants tolerate moderate infection. *See 240.*

POPLAR, COTTONWOOD, ASPEN (*Populus* spp.), continued

WHAT THE PROBLEM LOOKS LIKE	PROBABLE CAUSE	COMMENTS
Leaves with pale blisters, spots, or felty masses of pale spores.	**Yellow leaf spot**, *Taphrina populi-salicis*. Fungus favored by wet conditions during spring.	Rarely serious enough to threaten tree health or warrant control effort.
Leaves with brown or dead patches. Leaves or terminals distorted, malformed.	**Lygus bugs**, *Lygus elisus, L. hesperus*. Brown, green, or yellowish bugs, ≤¼ inch long, suck plant juices.	*See 155.*
Leaves stippled or bleached, with cast skins and varnishlike specks.	**Lace bug**, *Corythucha* sp. Brown adults, ≤⅛ inch long, wings lacelike.	*See 154.*
Leaves chewed. Tree may be defoliated. Leaves may be tied together with silk. May be silken tents in tree.	**Caterpillars**, including **Fall webworm**; **Fruittree leafroller**; **Satin moth**, *Leucoma salicis* (family Lymantriidae); **Silver spotted tussock moth**, *Lophocampa maculata* (family Arctiidae); **Tent caterpillars**. *Leucoma* and *Lophocampa* larvae are ≤1½ inches long, hairy, and black with yellow, white, or reddish.	*See 71.*
Leaves chewed on scattered terminals. Caterpillars feeding in groups on shoots.	**Redhumped caterpillar**; **Spiny elm caterpillar**; **Western tiger swallowtail**, *Papilio rutulus* (family Papilionidae). *Papilio* larvae are bright green with eyespots and black and yellow markings. Adult *Papilio* are ≤2 inches long and yellow with black.	Spiny elm caterpillars and *Papilio* mature into attractive butterflies. Control not recommended. Clip infested shoots or apply *Bacillus thuringiensis* to larvae if intolerable. *See 71.*
Leaves chewed along edges. Entire branches may be defoliated.	**Sawflies**, including *Nematus* spp., *Trichiocampus* spp. Larvae often feed in groups and commonly are greenish or yellowish with black. Adults are black, stout wasps.	Occasional pests of *Populus* spp. in the Pacific Northwest and eastern U.S. *See 82.*
Leaves with elliptical blotches or holes, ⅛ to ¼ inch long, or winding tunnels.	**Poplar shield bearer**, *Coptodisca* sp. Moth larvae mine foliage.	*See 169.*
Skeletonized leaf surfaces. No silk.	**Leaf beetles**, **Flea beetles**, *Altica* spp., *Chrysomela* spp., *Plagiodera* spp. Adults dark or metallic, oval, ≤⅜ inch long. Larvae are dark, ≤½ inch long.	*See 84.*
Sticky honeydew, blackish sooty mold, and whitish cast skins on leaves.	**Aphids**, including **Cloudywinged cottonwood aphid**, *Periphyllus populicola*; *Chaitophorus* spp. Brownish, gray, green, or yellowish pear-shaped insects, suck sap.	Plants tolerate abundant aphids. Hose forcefully with water. If severe, soap or oil may be applied. *See 103.*
Sticky honeydew and blackish sooty mold on foliage. Possible decline or dieback of twigs or branches.	**Black scale**; **Brown soft scale**; **Cottony maple scale**, *Pulvinaria innumerabilis*; **European fruit lecanium scale**. Oval, yellow to brown, and flattened; or black, brown, or cottony and bulbous.	*See 136–139.*
Swellings (galls), often globular or purse-like, on leaves and leaf petioles.	**Poplar gall aphids**. Tiny, grayish, waxy insects in galls.	*See 106.*
Brown to gray encrustations on bark. May be declining or dead twigs or branches.	**Oystershell scale**, **San Jose scale**. Tiny oval to circular insects on bark.	*See 132, 135.*
Dieback of branches or sometimes entire tree. Wet or dark spots on bark. Bark galled or gnarled.	**Carpenterworm**; **Clearwing moths**, including **American hornet moth** and **Western poplar clearwing**; **Flatheaded borers**, including the **Bronze birch borer** and **Bronze poplar borer**; **Longhorned borers**, including *Saperda* spp. Whitish larvae ≤2 inches long, mine beneath bark or in wood.	*See 179–195.*

POPLAR, COTTONWOOD, ASPEN (*Populus* spp.), continued

WHAT THE PROBLEM LOOKS LIKE	PROBABLE CAUSE	COMMENTS
Roughened twig bark. Possible twig dieback.	**Treehoppers**, including **Buffalo treehopper**, *Stictocephala bisonia*. Bright yellow to green insects, horny or spiny.	*See 151.*
Warty, woody swellings on twigs around buds. Terminals may be crooked.	**Cottonwood gall mite**, *Eriophyes parapopuli*. Tiny elongate eriophyid mites in galls.	Plants tolerate extensive galling. *See Gall Mites, 203.*
Green plants with smooth stems, thick roundish leaves infesting branches.	**Broadleaf mistletoe.** Parasitic, evergreen plant on host.	*See 338.*
Bark stained brownish, exudes rancid fluid, often around crotches, wounds.	**Wetwood** or **Slime flux.** Bacterial infection.	Usually does not cause serious harm to trees. *See 259.*

PRIVET (*Ligustrum* spp.)

WHAT THE PROBLEM LOOKS LIKE	PROBABLE CAUSE	COMMENTS
Leaves yellow, wilt, and may drop prematurely. Branches die back. Entire tree may die. Minute white fungus growths may be visible beneath bark or on soil.	**Armillaria root rot.** Present in many soils. Favored by warm, wet soil. Persists for years in infected roots.	*Ligustrum tschonskii* reportedly is resistant to Armillaria root rot. *See 262.*
Leaves wilted, discolored, may drop prematurely. Branches or entire plant may die. May be white fungal growth or dark crust on basal trunk, roots, or soil.	**Dematophora root rot.** Fungus favored by mild, wet conditions. Infects primarily through roots growing near infested plants.	Less common than *Armillaria. See 264.*
Leaves fade and wilt, often scattered throughout canopy. Branches die. Boring dust, ooze, or holes on trunk or branches.	**Ash borer** or **Lilac borer.** White larvae ≤1 inch long bore in wood. Adults are wasplike moths.	*See 187.*
Leaves or shoots stunted, brown. Buds distorted, galled, dead.	**Privet rust mite**, *Aceria ligustri*; **Privet bud mite**, *Vasates ligustri*. Microscopic eriophyids, suck plant juice.	Vigorous plants tolerate mite feeding. Eriophyid mites are difficult to control. *See Gall Mites, 203.*
Leaves discolored, stippled, or bleached. Foliage may drop prematurely. Terminals may distort. Plant may have fine webbing.	**Spider mites**, including **Privet mite**, *Brevipalpus obovatus*. Greenish or yellowish tiny arthropods, which may have two dark spots.	*See 197.*
Sticky honeydew and blackish sooty mold on foliage.	**Black scale.** Orangish, flattened, and oval or bulbous, black, with H-shape on back.	*See 136.*
Brown, gray, or orangish encrustations on bark. Rarely, declining or dead twigs or branches.	**Armored scales**, including **California red scale, San Jose scale.** Tiny circular to oval insects on bark.	Rarely if ever cause serious damage to privet. *See 131.*
Foliage chewed or notched around margins. May be wilting or dieback of young plants. Some roots stripped of bark or girdled near soil.	**Black vine weevil.** Adults are black or grayish snout beetles, about ⅜ inch long. Larvae are white grubs with brown head.	*See 92.*
Twigs distorted, swollen, and pitted. Leaves dwarfed. Shoots may die back.	**Pit-making pittosporum scale**, *Planchonia* (=*Asterolecanium*) *arabidis* (family Asterolecaniidae). Brown to white insects, ≤⅛ inch long, on twigs, often in pits.	In California, an occasional problem in the north. Management not investigated. *See Other Common Scales, 142.*

PYRACANTHA (*Pyracantha* spp.)

WHAT THE PROBLEM LOOKS LIKE	PROBABLE CAUSE	COMMENTS
Leaves yellow, wilt, and may drop prematurely. Branches die back. Entire tree may die. Minute white fungus growths may be visible beneath bark or on soil.	**Armillaria root rot.** Present in many soils. Favored by warm, wet soil. Persists for years in infected roots.	*See 262.*
Leaves brown, yellow, and die, often beginning with older foliage. Browning of vascular tissue.	**Fusarium wilt**, *Fusarium oxysporum*. Fungus infects plant through roots.	Avoid injuring live tissue. Provide adequate drainage and appropriate irrigation. *See 233.*

PYRACANTHA (*Pyracantha* spp.), continued

WHAT THE PROBLEM LOOKS LIKE	PROBABLE CAUSE	COMMENTS
Sudden wilting, shriveling, blackening of shoots, blossoms, fruits. Plant appears scorched.	**Fire blight.** Bacteria enter plant through blossoms.	*See 229.*
Black to dark olive spots on fruit and sometimes on leaves. Leaves yellow and may drop prematurely.	**Scab,** *Spilocaea pyracanthae.* A fungal disease spread by water from infected leaves and twigs.	Avoid overhead watering. Prune out infected twigs and leaves in fall. *See 227.*
Tiny reddish to brown leaf spots, may have yellow halos. Larger, dark areas on leaves. Leaves may drop prematurely.	**Entomosporium leaf spot.** A fungal disease promoted by wet foliage.	*See 227.*
Powdery white growth and yellow blotches on leaves and sometimes on terminals and fruit. Shoots and leaves may be undersized or distorted.	**Powdery mildews,** including *Podosphaera* sp. Fungal diseases favored by moderate temperatures, shade, and poor air circulation.	*See 236.*
Reddening or bronzing of foliage.	**Spider mites,** including **Southern red mite, Sycamore spider mite.** Tiny brownish, green, or reddish arthropods on leaves.	*See 197.*
Stippled or bleached leaves. Dark, varnish-like specks and cast skins on undersides of leaves.	**Hawthorn lace bugs,** *Corythucha cydoniae.* Adults ≤⅛ inch long, wings lacy. Nymphs spiny.	*See Lace Bugs, 154.*
Sticky honeydew, blackish sooty mold, and whitish cast skins on plant.	**Aphids,** including **Apple aphid,** *Aphis pomi;* **Bean aphid.** Small green or black insects grouped on leaves or terminals.	Conserve natural enemies that provide control. Hose with forceful water. Tolerate or apply soap or oil if severe. *See 103.*
Sticky honeydew and blackish sooty mold on plant. Slow plant growth.	**European fruit lecanium, Kuno scale.** Brown or yellowish, beadlike, bulbous, or flattened insects on leaves or twigs.	Tolerate or monitor and apply oil or another insecticide when crawlers abundant. *See 139, 140.*
Sticky honeydew and blackish sooty mold on foliage. Popcornlike bodies (egg sacs) on bark.	**Cottony cushion scale.** Orangish, flat immatures or cottony females on bark.	Normally controlled by natural enemies. *See 142.*
Brownish, grayish, tan, or white encrustations on bark. Rarely, declining or dead twigs or branches.	**Greedy scale, San Jose scale.** Tiny, circular to oval, flattened insects, often in colonies.	Rarely if ever cause serious damage to pyracantha. *See 132, 133.*
Chewed leaves. Plant may be defoliated.	**Tussock moths.** Hairy larvae, ≤1 inch long, may have colorful spots.	*See 77.*
Wood swellings (galls), cottony, waxy material on branches and roots.	**Woolly apple aphid,** *Eriosoma lanigerum.* Tiny, reddish, cottony or waxy insects.	Conserve natural enemies that help control. Tolerate or apply soap or another insecticide if severe. *See Aphids, 106.*

QUINCE (*Chaenomeles* spp.)

WHAT THE PROBLEM LOOKS LIKE	PROBABLE CAUSE	COMMENTS
Gray or whitish patches on foliage. Shoots may be stunted or distorted. Fruit may be mottled, russetted, or scabby.	**Powdery mildews,** including *Podosphaera leucotricha.* Fungal diseases favored by moderate temperatures, shade, and poor air circulation.	*See 236.*
Sudden wilting then shriveling and blackening of blossoms, fruit, and shoots. Plant appears scorched.	**Fire blight.** Bacterium enters plants through blossoms.	*See 229.*
Circular brown decay develops on fruit. Blossoms may turn brown and die.	**Brown rot,** *Monilinia fructicola, M. laxa.* Windborne fungal pathogens that infect wet tissue.	Avoid wounding fruit and trees. Remove any infected fruit ("mummies") left on trees.
Tiny reddish to brown leaf spots, may have yellow halos. Larger, dark areas on leaves. Leaves may drop prematurely.	**Entomosporium leaf spot.** A fungal disease promoted by wet foliage.	*See 227.*

QUINCE (*Chaenomeles* spp.), continued

Leaves with orangish pustules, light to dark spots. Leaves may drop prematurely. May be orange masses or galls on bark. Stems may die back.	**Rusts,** *Gymnosporangium* spp. Fungi that infect and develop during moist conditions.	Avoid overhead watering. Vigorous plants tolerate moderate infection. *See 240.*
Leaves discolor and wilt. Stems may have dark cankers, callus tissue, or coral-colored pustules.	**Nectria canker,** *Nectria cinnabarina.* Fungus primarily affects injured or stressed trees.	*See 257.*
Sticky honeydew and blackish sooty mold on leaves. Twigs may die back and plants may decline.	**Black scale.** Brown to black, bulbous to flattened insects, ≤³⁄₁₆ inch long. Raised H-shape often on back.	*See 136.*
Sticky honeydew, blackish sooty mold, and whitish cast skins on plant.	**Aphids.** Small green, orange, or black insects, often in groups on leaves or stems.	*See 103.*
Sticky honeydew, blackish sooty and waxy material on plants.	**Grape mealybug, Obscure mealybug.** Oval, soft, powdery, waxy insects, ≤⅛ inch long.	*See 127.*
Sticky honeydew and blackish sooty mold on leaves. Popcornlike bodies (egg sacs) or cottony material on bark.	**Cottony cushion scale.** Orangish, flat immatures or cottony females on bark.	Normally controlled by natural enemies. *See 142.*
Stippled or bleached leaves. Dark, varnish-like specks and cast skins on undersides of leaves.	**Hawthorn lace bugs,** *Corythucha cydoniae.* Adults ≤⅛ inch long, wings lacy. Nymphs spiny.	*See 154.*
Chewed leaves. Foliage may be rolled and tied together with silk.	**Fruittree leafroller.** Greenish larvae with black shiny head.	*See 79.*
Brownish, grayish, tan, or white encrustations on bark or twigs. Rarely, declining or dead twigs or branches.	**Greedy scale.** Circular, flattened, ≤¹⁄₁₆ inch long, often in colonies.	Rarely if ever causes serious damage to trees. *See 133.*
Dieback of woody plant parts. Tunnels beneath bark and in wood.	**Roundheaded appletree borer,** *Saperda candida.* Whitish, larvae ≤1 inch long beneath bark.	*See Longhorned Borers, 179.*

REDBUD (*Cercis* spp.)

Leaves fade, yellow, brown, or wilt, often scattered throughout canopy. Branches die. Entire plant may die.	**Verticillium wilt.** A soil-dwelling fungus that infects through roots.	*See 232.*
Leaves discolor, stunt, wilt, or drop prematurely. Plants grow slowly and may die. Roots dark, decayed.	**Root and crown rot,** *Phytophthora* sp. Pathogen promoted by excess soil moisture and poor drainage.	*See 265.*
Leaves turn red, brown, then fade. May be small, pimplelike growths or brownish cankers on bark.	**Cytospora canker.** Fungal disease that primarily affects injured or stressed trees.	*See 250.*
Leaves with discolored spots or irregular blotches. Leaves may drop prematurely.	**Anthracnose,** Leaf spots, including *Mycosphaerella cercidicola.* Fungi infect and develop on wet tissue.	*See 223.*
Brownish, grayish, tan, or white encrustations on bark. Rarely, declining or dead twigs and branches.	**Greedy scale, Oleander scale.** Tiny oval insects, often in colonies.	Rarely if ever cause serious damage to redbud. *See 133, 134.*
Sticky honeydew and blackish sooty mold on foliage. Tiny, powdery white mothlike insects.	**Whiteflies,** including **Ash whitefly, Greenhouse whitefly.** Flat, oval, yellow to green nymphs on leaf undersides.	*See 121.*

| --- | --- | --- |
REDBUD (*Cercis* spp.), continued		
Chewed leaves. May be silken tents or mats on plants.	**Tussock moths, Tent caterpillars, Red-humped caterpillar.** Larvae ≤2 inches long, may be hairy or colorful.	*See 77–81.*
Leaves chewed, tied together with silk. Tree may be defoliated.	**Fruittree leafroller.** Green larvae, ≤¼ inch long, with black head.	*See 79.*
RHAMNUS (*Rhamnus* spp.), Buckthorn, Coffeeberry, Redberry		
Leaves discolor, stunt, wilt, or drop prematurely. Plants grow slowly and may die. Roots dark, decayed.	**Root and crown rot,** *Phytophthora* sp. Pathogen promoted by excess soil moisture and poor drainage.	*See 265.*
Leaves with brown, light green, or yellow lesions or dead spots.	**Sudden oak death,** *Phytophthora ramorum.* Pathogen spreads via air and contaminated soil. Apparently can infect through bark or leaves.	On *Rhamnus*, hosts include at least *R. californica*. Primarily a problem in wildlands, killing many oaks there. Do not move infected plant material. Report to agricultural officials if found outside areas where pathogen is known to occur. *See 260.*
Leaves or shoots turn yellow or brown and wilt. Leaves drop prematurely. Terminals die back. Branches may be cankered.	**Blight** or **Twig dieback** including *Diplodia frangulae, Phoma rhamnicola, Phomopsis communis.* Fungal diseases that primarily affect injured or stressed plants.	Protect plants from injury. Provide good cultural care, especially appropriate irrigation. Avoid overhead irrigation. *See similar Botryosphaeria Canker and Dieback, 255.*
Leaves with brown to yellow blotches or scabby spots. Foliage may shrivel and drop prematurely.	**Leaf spots** including *Cylindrosporium rhamni, Septoria blasdalei.* Fungal pathogens favored by prolonged cool, wet, conditions.	Avoid wetting foliage. Use drip irrigation if feasible. Use good sanitation; promptly remove and dispose of debris and infected leaves. *See 223.*
Leaves of fruit with dark scabby or velvety spots.	**Scab,** *Venturia rhamni.* Fungal disease promoted by moist spring weather.	*See 227.*
Leaves with discolored spots and orangish pustules. Leaves may drop prematurely.	**Rusts,** including *Puccinia mesnieriana.* Pathogens favored by wet conditions. Fungal spores persist in plant debris.	Avoid overhead watering. Plants tolerate moderate populations. *See 240.*
Leaves or shoots with powdery white growth or yellow blotches. Shoots and leaves may be undersized or distorted.	**Powdery mildews,** including *Stictis radiata.* Fungal diseases favored by moderate temperatures, shade, and poor air circulation.	*See 236.*
Sticky honeydew, blackish sooty mold, and whitish cast skins on plant.	**Aphids,** including *Aphis* sp., *Sitobion* sp. Colonies of small, pear-shaped insects, often greenish.	*See 103.*
Sticky honeydew and blackish sooty mold on plant. Tiny, white mothlike adults.	**Grape whitefly,** *Trialeurodes vittata.* Tiny, yellowish to translucent, oval nymphs. Mature nymphs (pupae) dark brown or mottled dark and yellowish.	Usually most severe on *Rhamnus californica* near grapes, especially in fall when insects move from senescent grape leaves. *See Whiteflies, 121.*
RHAPHIOLEPIS (*Rhaphiolepis* spp.), Indian hawthorn		
Tiny reddish to brown leaf spots, may have yellow halos. Larger, dark areas on leaves. Leaves may drop prematurely.	**Entomosporium leaf spot.** A fungal disease promoted by wet foliage.	*See 227.*
Sudden wilting then shriveling and blackening of shoots and blossoms. Plants appear scorched.	**Fire blight.** Bacterium infects plants through blossoms.	*See 229.*
Leaves discolor, stunt, wilt, or drop prematurely. Plants grow slowly and may die. Roots dark, decayed.	**Root and crown rot,** *Phytophthora* sp. Pathogen promoted by excess soil moisture and poor drainage.	*See 265.*

WHAT THE PROBLEM LOOKS LIKE	PROBABLE CAUSE	COMMENTS

RHAPHIOLEPIS (*Rhaphiolepis* spp.), Indian hawthorn, continued

Leaves wilt, turn brown, and die, often first on one side of plant. Dead leaves may remain on stems. Stem xylem discolored. Stems or entire plant may die.	**Verticillium wilt**, *Verticillium albo-atrum*. Fungus that persists in soil and infects through roots.	*See 232.*
Blackish sooty mold, sticky honeydew, and whitish cast skins on plant.	**Aphids**. Small, pear-shaped insects, often brownish, green, or yellowish, in groups.	*See 103.*
Leaf margins chewed, notched. Young plants may decline.	**Weevils**, including **Fuller rose beetle;** *Otiorhynchus* or *Brachyrhinus* sp. Adults chew foliage. Larvae chew roots.	*See 92.*
Trunk or limbs with roughened, wet, or oozing area. Cracked bark and dieback.	**Borers** including **Flatheaded borers,** *Chrysobothris* spp. Flatheaded borer larvae are whitish with enlarged head and bore under bark.	*See 179.*

RHODODENDRON (*Rhododendron* spp.)[17]

New foliage yellows beginning along margins, but veins green. Leaves may develop brown blotches.	**Iron deficiency** or **Manganese deficiency**. Abiotic disorders usually caused by poor soil conditions or unhealthy roots.	*See 278–279.*
New foliage yellow overall. Plants may grow slowly and produce fewer and smaller than normal leaves and shoots. Discolored foliage may drop prematurely.	**Nitrogen deficiency**. Abiotic disorder usually caused by poor soil conditions or unhealthy roots.	*See 275.*
Leaves turn brown or yellow, especially along margins and at tip. Leaves may drop prematurely.	**Leaf burn** or **Scorch**. Abiotic disorders. Common causes include drought, dry wind, excess fertilization, excess light, frost, poor soil conditions, saline irrigation water or soil, too much or too little water, or transplant shock.	Provide plants with a good growing environment and proper cultural care. *See 273.*
Leaves with brown, light green, or yellow spots or dead blotches. Twigs and stems may canker or ooze. Plant may die.	**Sudden oak death**, *Phytophthora ramorum*. Pathogen spreads via air and contaminated soil. Apparently can infect through bark or leaves.	Primarily a problem in wildlands, killing many oaks there. Do not move infected plant material. Report to agricultural officials if found outside areas where pathogen is known to occur. *See 260.*
Leaves discolored, wilted, stunted, may drop prematurely. Discolored bark may ooze sap. Branches or plant may die.	**Root and crown rots**, *Phytophthora* spp., *Pythium* spp. Decay fungi favored by excess soil moisture and poor drainage.	*See 265.*
Leaves with pale green to yellow spots on upper surface and brown to purple spots on underside. Leaf undersides with blisters or orangish pustules. Leaves may drop prematurely.	**Rusts**, including *Chrysomyxa ledi, C. piperiana*. Pathogens favored by wet conditions. Fungal spores persist in plant debris.	Avoid overhead watering. Remove and dispose of infected leaves. Plants tolerate moderate populations. *See 240.*
Flowers with blotches or round spots. Flowers collapse, become slimy and soft and cling to leaves or stems.	**Rhododendron petal blight** or **Ovulinia petal blight**, *Ovulinia azaleae*. Fungus favored by cool, wet weather during flowering. Spores spread by splashing water.	Remove and dispose of diseased blossoms. Don't overhead water. Improve air circulation. *See 245.*
Flowers, buds, or leaves with soft, brown decay. May be woolly gray growth (spores) on dead tissue.	**Gray mold** or **Botrytis petal blight**. Fungus develops in plant debris or inactive tissue. Favored by high humidity and moderate temperatures. Spores airborne.	Unlike Ovulinia petal blight, infected flowers do not become slimy. *See 242.*
Leaves stippled or bleached with varnish-like specks on undersides.	**Greenhouse thrips**. Tiny, slender, black adults or yellow nymphs.	*See 158.*

17. Also see Azalea.

RHODODENDRON (*Rhododendron* spp.), continued

WHAT THE PROBLEM LOOKS LIKE	PROBABLE CAUSE	COMMENTS
Leaves bleached, stippled, may turn brown and drop prematurely. Terminals may be distorted. Plant may have fine webbing.	**Mites**, including **Southern red mite, Two-spotted spider mite**. Tiny, often green, pink, or red pests; may have 2 dark spots.	*See 197.*
Sticky honeydew and blackish sooty mold on foliage. Tiny, whitish, mothlike insects (adult whiteflies) on foliage.	**Whiteflies**, including **Azalea whitefly**, *Pealius azaleae;* **Greenhouse whitefly; Rhododendron whitefly**, *Massilieurodes (=Dialeurodes) chittendeni;* **Silverleaf whitefly**. Nymphs oval, flattened, yellowish to greenish, suck sap.	Cultivars vary greatly in susceptibility to these pests, which rarely cause serious damage to plants. *See 121.*
Sticky honeydew and blackish sooty mold on plant. Whitish cottony bodies on bark. Bark rough. Branches may deform. Possible dieback.	**Azalea bark scale** or **Woolly azalea scale**, *Acanthococcus (=Eriococcus) azaleae* (family Eriococcidae). Dark, reddish, oval insects underneath white wax, on bark crevices and in crotches.	Occurs in the eastern U.S. and in Oregon and Washington. If found in California, report to county department of agriculture. *See Other Common Scales, 142.*
Sticky honeydew and blackish sooty mold on leaves and twigs. Whitish cast skins on underside of leaves.	**Aphids**, including *Illinoia* spp.; **Spirea aphid**, *Aphis citricola*. Tiny, pear-shaped insects, often brownish, green, or yellowish.	*See 103.*
Wilted or dying plants. Roots missing, debarked, girdled near soil surface. Notched or ragged leaves, including on nearby hosts.	**Black vine weevil; Obscure root weevil**, *Sciopithes obscurus;* **Woods weevil**, *Nemocestes incomptus*. Adults dark brown to black or grayish snout weevils, ≤½ inch long. Larvae white grubs in soil.	*See 92.*
Foliage may yellow, wilt, die back, or drop prematurely. Plant grows slowly. May be galls or swellings on roots.	**Root knot nematodes, Stubby root nematodes, Stunt nematode**. Tiny root-feeding roundworms.	*See 341.*

RHUS (*Rhus* spp.), Lemonade berry, Sugarbush, Sumac, Wax tree

WHAT THE PROBLEM LOOKS LIKE	PROBABLE CAUSE	COMMENTS
Leaves discolor, stunt, wilt, or drop prematurely. Stems discolor, canker, and die. Minute white fungus growths may be visible beneath bark or on soil.	**Armillaria root rot**. Present in many soils. Favored by warm, wet soil. Persists for years in infected roots.	*See 262.*
Leaves discolor and wilt. Stems may have dark, sunken cankers and dieback. May be small, coral-colored pustules on infected wood.	**Cankers**, including **Nectria canker**, *Nectria cinnabarina*. Fungi primarily attack injured or stressed trees.	*See 250.*
Leaves with black, brown, tan, or yellow spots or blotches. Foliage may die and drop prematurely. Twigs may die back.	**Leaf spots**, including *Cladosporium aromaticum, Gloeosporium toxicodendri, Phyllosticta* spp., *Pseudocercospora rhoina*. Fungi spread in water and are favored by prolonged cool, wet, conditions.	*See 223.*
Leaves or shoots with powdery growth. Shoots or leaves may be stunted and distorted.	**Powdery mildews**, including *Erysiphe cichoracearum, Phyllactinia guttata*. Fungi favored by moderate temperatures, shade, and poor air circulation.	*See 236.*
Sticky honeydew and blackish sooty mold on leaves or twigs. Whitish, waxy material on leaves and shoots.	**Sumac psyllids**, *Calophya* spp. Nymphs flattened, brown, orangish, or greenish. Eggs tiny, black.	Plants tolerate abundant psyllids. Conserve natural enemies, no other management recommended. *See Psyllids, 114.*
Sticky honeydew and blackish sooty mold on leaves or twigs. Terminals may die back and plants may decline.	**Black scale**. Brown to black, bulbous to flattened insects, ≤³⁄₁₆ inch long. Raised H-shape often on back.	*See 136.*
Sticky honeydew, blackish sooty mold, and whitish cast skins on plant.	**Aphids**. Small green, brownish or yellowish insects, often in groups.	*See 103.*

WHAT THE PROBLEM LOOKS LIKE	PROBABLE CAUSE	COMMENTS
RIBES (*Ribes* spp.), Currant, Gooseberry		
Sticky honeydew, blackish sooty mold, and whitish cast skins on plant.	**Aphids.** Small green, brown, black or yellowish insects, often in groups.	*See 103.*
Slightly raised, yellowish spots on undersides of leaves and young stems. Leaves may drop prematurely.	**White pine blister rust.** Alternate host stage of fungal disease that primarily damages pines.	*See 242.*
ROSE (*Rosa* spp.)[18]		
White to gray growth, often powdery, on leaves, shoots, and buds. Leaves may become distorted and may drop prematurely.	**Powdery mildew.** A fungal disease favored by moderate temperatures, shade, and poor air circulation.	Grow resistant cultivars. *See 236.*
Small orange pustules, primarily on leaf undersides. Upper leaf surface may discolor. Leaves may drop prematurely.	**Rust,** *Phragmidium disciflorum.* Fungus favored by cool, moist weather. Spores airborne.	Avoid overhead watering and condensation. Fungicides help to prevent damage. *See 240.*
Dark spots with fringed margins on upper surface of leaves and succulent stems. Yellow areas develop around spots. Leaves may drop prematurely.	**Black spot,** *Diplocarpon rosae.* Fungal spores spread by splashing water.	Avoid wetting foliage. Prune out and dispose of infected tissue. Remove fallen leaves. Fungicides help to prevent.
Purplish, red, or dark brown spots on leaves. Leaf undersides covered with downy fungal growth. Leaves may yellow and drop prematurely.	**Downy mildew,** *Peronospora sparsa.* Spores produced only on living plants. Resistant spores carry fungus over unfavorable periods. Favored by moist, humid conditions.	Prune plants to improve air circulation. Reduce humidity around plants, such as through drip or low-volume irrigation. Avoid overhead watering. Fungicide applications help prevent damage. *See 239.*
Leaves yellow or with yellow blotches, lines, or intricate patterns. Leaves may distort. Plants may be stunted.	**Viruses,** including **Rose mosaic** or **Prunus necrotic ringspot.** The most common virus or complex of viruses affecting landscape roses.	Usually does not threaten plant health. Severity of symptoms varies greatly with rose variety. Many infected varieties exhibit few symptoms. *See 268.*
Leaves curl downward and canes die. Leaves readily drop from new shoots, which are typically pointed with a broad base.	**Rose leaf curl.** Probably a virus.	Obtain virus-free stock. No known treatment. Tolerate or replace infected plants.
Leaves emerging in spring are balled or curved on very short shoots with conspicuous vein clearing. Slow plant growth. Symptoms tend to disappear later in season.	**Rose spring dwarf.** Probably a virus.	Obtain virus-free plants. No known treatment. Tolerate or replace infected plants.
Black to brown spots or streaks on leaves or stems. Blossoms, buds, or leaves darken and shrivel. Oozing lesions on twigs.	**Bacterial blight and canker.** Pathogen infects through wounds. Disease favored by wet conditions.	*See 245.*
Soft, brown decay on flowers, buds, or leaves. May be woolly gray growth (spores) on dead tissue.	**Gray mold.** Fungus develops in plant debris or inactive tissue. Favored by wet conditions and moderate temperatures.	*See 242.*
Foliage discolors and wilts. Shoots die back. Brown cankers, sometimes with gray centers, on stems. Small, black, spore-producing structures (pycnidia) on dead tissue.	**Cankers** and **Dieback,** including *Botryosphaeria dothidea, Coniothyrium fuckelii, Cryptosporella umbrina, Nectria cinnabarina.* Fungi that primarily affect injured or stressed plants.	Provide proper cultural care to keep plants vigorous. Prune off diseased or dead tissue, making cuts at an angle in healthy tissue and just above a node. Avoid otherwise wounding tissue. Avoid overhead water. *See Botryosphaeria Canker and Dieback, Nectria Canker, 250.*
Foliage fades, yellows, browns, or wilts, often scattered throughout canopy. Branches die. Entire plant may die.	**Verticillium wilt.** A soil-dwelling fungus that infects through roots.	*See 232.*

18. For more information, see publications such as *Healthy Roses* (Flint and Karlik 2000), *Rose Diseases and Abiotic Disorders Pest Notes* (Karlik and Flint 1999), and *Rose Insect and Mite Pests and Beneficials Pests Notes* (Flint and Karlik 1999).

WHAT THE PROBLEM LOOKS LIKE	PROBABLE CAUSE	COMMENTS
ROSE (*Rosa* spp.), continued		
Leaves yellow, wilt, and may drop prematurely. Branches die back. Entire tree may die. Minute white fungus growths may be visible beneath bark or on soil.	**Armillaria root rot.** Present in many soils. Favored by warm, wet soil. Persists for years in infected roots.	*See 262.*
Leaves discolor, stunt, wilt, or drop prematurely. Plants grow slowly and may die. Roots dark, decayed.	**Root and crown rot,** *Phytophthora* sp. Pathogen promoted by excess soil moisture and poor drainage.	*See 265.*
Small discrete spots to irregular, large blotches or holes over most of leaf surface. Leaves may drop prematurely.	**Leaf spots,** including *Mycosphaerella* spp., *Sphaceloma* spp. Fungi promoted and spread by wet conditions.	*See 223.*
Leaves bleached or stippled. Foliage may be finely webbed. Leaves may dry and drop prematurely.	**Spider mites,** including **Persea mite, Twospotted spider mite.** Tiny greenish or yellowish arthropods, may have 2 dark spots.	Plants tolerate extensive leaf stippling, especially on older foliage. *See 197.*
Leaves bleached or stippled. Cast skins on underside of leaves.	**Rose leafhopper,** *Edwardsiana rosae.* Greenish to whitish, wedge-shaped insects, ≤⅛ inch long.	Plants tolerate extensive leaf stippling. Apply insecticidal soap or another insecticide if severe. *See Leafhoppers, 148.*
Sticky honeydew, blackish sooty mold, and whitish cast skins on plant. Blossoms may be distorted.	**Aphids,** including **Melon aphid; Rose aphid;** *Macrosiphum euphorbiae; Wahlgreniella nervata.* Tiny green to pink insects on terminals and buds.	*See 103.*
Sticky honeydew and blackish sooty mold on foliage. May be whitish wax or cottony material on plant. Possible decline or dieback of canes.	**Black scale, Brown soft scale, Cottony cushion scale, European fruit lecanium, Frosted scale, Kuno scale.** Flattened or bulbous and black, brownish, orangish, or yellow insects, may be cottony or waxy.	*See 136–140.*
Sticky honeydew and blackish sooty mold on foliage. Tiny, powdery white, mothlike insects.	**Greenhouse whitefly, Silverleaf whitefly.** Flat, oval, tiny, yellow to green insects on leaf undersides.	*See 123, 124.*
Sticky honeydew and blackish sooty mold on foliage. Cottony or waxy material on plant.	**Mealybugs,** including **Citrus mealybug, Pink hibiscus mealybug.** Powdery grayish insects, ≤¼ inch long, may have waxy filaments.	Vigorous plants tolerate moderate populations. Conserve natural enemies that help in control. *See 126.*
Blossom petals or sepals streaked with brown.	**Thrips,** including **Madrone thrips,** *Thrips madroni;* **Western flower thrips.** Tiny, slender, yellow or black insects in blossoms.	Damage occurs before buds open. Thrips present in flowers may be pollen-feeders, not petal-damaging species. *See 156.*
Chewed leaves or blossoms. Leaf margins notched, ragged.	**Fuller rose beetle.** Pale brown adult snout weevils, about ⅜ inch long.	Adults hide during day and feed at night. Larvae feed on roots. *See 94.*
Chewed blossoms, especially white and yellow flowers.	**Hoplia beetle.** Adult beetles about ¼ inch long, mostly reddish brown with silver, black, or white.	Larvae feed on roots. Larvae not known to damage rose roots. *See 97.*
Leaf undersides scraped, skeletonized. Large holes may be eaten in leaves.	**Roseslugs,** including **Bristly roseslug.** Green to yellowish larvae, ≤⅝ inch, may be bristly.	*See 84.*
Holes punched in flowers and canes. Blossoms ragged.	**Rose curculios.** Red to black snout weevils, ¼ inch long. Small, whitish larvae in buds.	*See 94.*
Chewed leaves. Buds may be mined or have holes. Leaves may be tied together with silk.	**Caterpillars,** including **Orange tortrix,** *Argyrotaenia citrana* (family Tortricidae); **Tussock moths; Fruittree leafroller; Tent caterpillars; Omnivorous looper.** Hairy to naked larvae ≤1½ inches long.	*See 71.*

ROSE (*Rosa* spp.), continued

WHAT THE PROBLEM LOOKS LIKE	PROBABLE CAUSE	COMMENTS
Semicircular holes cut in margins of leaves or blossoms.	**Leafcutting bees,** *Megachile* spp. (family Megachilidae). About ½ inch long, robust bees.	Bees line their nests with cut plant parts. Bees are important pollinators and should not be killed. No effective nonchemical controls known.
Flower petals spotted. Buds rot. Twig dieback and cane canker. Woolly, gray fungal spores on decaying tissue.	**Botrytis blight.** Favored by high humidity. Spores are airborne.	Remove and dispose of fallen leaves and debris around plants. Reduce humidity around plants by modifying irrigation, pruning, reducing ground cover. Fungicides are not very effective in landscapes. *See 242.*
Brownish, grayish, tan, orange, or white encrustations on canes. Rarely, canes may decline or die back.	**California red scale; Greedy scale; Latania scale; Rose scale,** *Aulacaspis rosae;* **San Jose scale.** Tiny circular to oval insects, often in colonies.	Rarely if ever cause serous damage to rose in California. *See 131.*
Decline or death of canes or entire plant. Larvae, ≤1 inch long, tunneling in canes.	**Flatheaded appletree borer, Pacific flatheaded borer.** Whitish larvae with enlarged head in tunnels.	Keep plants vigorous. Prevent sunburn or sunscald. Remove and dispose of cane stubs from earlier pruning. *See 179.*
Tips of canes wilt in the spring and die back in summer. Spiral girdling (by larvae) in canes.	**Raspberry horntail.** Segmented white larvae ≤1 inch long. Adult sawflies black or black and yellow, ½ inch long, wasplike.	In California, mostly in interior valleys. *See 196.*
Tips of canes bend, darken, distort, or wither and die. Flower buds darken and drop. Blossoms appear scorched.	**Rose midge,** *Dasineura rhodophaga.* Adults are tiny flies. Pale larvae occur between petals and sepals at flower bud base.	In Pacific Northwest and eastern U.S. In California reported only in Sonoma County. Distinguish from similar-looking beneficial predaceous aphid midges. Prune and dispose of infested tissue. If severe, apply systemic insecticide in spring.
Galls or swellings on roots. Foliage may yellow and plants may grow slowly.	**Root knot nematode,** *Meloidogyne* sp.; **Dagger nematode,** *Xiphinema index.* Tiny root-feeding roundworms.	*See 345, 346.*
Roots smaller, darker than on healthy plants. Leaves may yellow. Growth may be stunted.	**Root lesion nematode,** *Pratylenchus* sp. Tiny root-feeding roundworms.	*See 346.*
Galls or enlarged, distorted tissue on stems and roots.	**Crown gall.** Bacteria persist in soil, spread in water, and infect through wounds.	*See 258.*
Swollen root tips with dense clusters of small rootlets. Foliage may yellow. Plants may grow slowly and die prematurely.	**Hairy root,** *Agrobacterium rhizogenes.* Bacteria persist in soil, spread in water, and infect through wounds.	Purchase high-quality plants. Avoid injuring plants during transplanting. Solarize soil before planting. *See similar Crown Gall, 258.*

ROSEMARY (*Rosmarinus officinalis*)

WHAT THE PROBLEM LOOKS LIKE	PROBABLE CAUSE	COMMENTS
Brown, yellow, or wilted leaves. Roots or basal stem may be dark, decayed. Plant may die.	**Root and crown rot,** *Phytophthora* sp. Pathogen favored by excess soil moisture and poor drainage.	*See 265.*
Powdery, whitish growth on leaves or shoots. Foliage or shoots may distort or turn yellow or brown.	**Powdery mildew,** *Sphaerotheca* sp. Fungus favored by moderate temperatures, shade, and poor air circulation.	*See 236.*
Blackish sooty mold, sticky honeydew, and whitish cast skins on plant.	**Aphids.** Small green, brown, black or yellowish insects, often in groups.	*See 103.*
Blackish sooty mold and sticky honeydew on plant. Tiny, white, mothlike insects on plant.	**Whiteflies,** including **Greenhouse whitefly.** Nymphs and pupae are flattened, oval, and pale.	*See 121.*

WHAT THE PROBLEM LOOKS LIKE	PROBABLE CAUSE	COMMENTS
ROSEMARY (*Rosmarinus officinalis*), continued		
Wet, white, frothy masses of spittle on leaves or stems.	**Spittlebugs.** Insects covered in spittle, suck plant juices.	Tolerate, as they do not threaten plant health. Wash with forceful water. *See 151.*
SAGO PALM (*Cycas* spp.)[19], Cycad		
Brown, yellow, or wilted leaves. Roots or basal stem may be dark, decayed. Fronds or entire plant may die.	**Root and crown rots,** *Phytophthora* sp., *Pythium* sp. Fungal pathogens favored by excess soil moisture and poor drainage.	*See 265.*
Brown, yellow, or wilted leaves. Fronds or entire plant may die.	**Leaf burn** or **Scorch.** Abiotic disorders with many potential causes, including excess light, overirrigation, poor drainage, and sunburn.	Provide plants with a good growing environment and proper cultural care. *See 273.*
Sticky honeydew, blackish sooty mold, and pale, waxy material on leaves.	**Mealybugs,** including **Longtailed mealybug.** Powdery, whitish insects ≤⅛ inch long with filaments, suck sap.	*See 126.*
Mottling or yellowing of leaves. White to tan encrustations on plant. Growth stunted. Plants may die back.	**Cycad scale, Oleander scale.** Scales feed on the underside and base of fronds and on the basal trunk.	Distinguish between these species. Oleander scale is innocuous, but cycad scale is a serious pest. *See 132, 134.*
SALTBUSH (*Atriplex* spp.)*		
Discolored spots and orangish pustules on leaves. Leaves may drop prematurely.	**Rusts,** *Puccinia* sp., *Uromyces shearianus.* Pathogens favored by wet conditions. Fungal spores persist in plant debris.	Avoid overhead watering. Plants tolerate moderate populations. *See 240.*
Stems have brownish cankers, sometimes with grayish centers. Dead tissue has small, black, spore-forming fungal pycnidia.	**Coniothyrium stem blight and canker,** *Microsphaeropsis olivaceae.* Fungus infects through wounds. Spread and favored by wet conditions.	Provide plants with proper cultural care and good growing conditions to keep them vigorous. Prune off and dispose of diseased tissue; otherwise avoid wounding plants, especially when wet.
Sticky honeydew and blackish sooty mold on plant. Bulbous, irregular, brown, gray, or white bodies (scales) on twigs.	**Wax scales.** Bulbous to hemispherical waxy insects, suck sap.	*See 141.*
SALVIA (*Salvia* spp.), Sage		
Leaves or shoots with powdery growth. Shoots or leaves may be distorted or stunted.	**Powdery mildews,** including *Erysiphe cichoracearum, Phyllactinia guttata.* Fungi favored by moderate temperatures, shade, and poor air circulation.	*See 236.*
Leaves with brown or yellow spots and orangish pustules. Leaves may drop prematurely.	**Rusts,** including *Puccinia mellifera.* Fungi favored by wet conditions.	Avoid overhead watering. Plants tolerate moderate populations. *See 240.*
Leaves with brown, gray, reddish, yellow, or whitish blotches or spots. Leaves may drop prematurely.	**Leaf spots,** including *Mycosphaerella audibertiae, Septoria rhabdocarpa.* Fungal diseases that infect and develop when foliage is wet.	*See 223.*
Blackish sooty mold, sticky honeydew, and whitish cast skins on plant.	**Aphids.** Small green, brown, black, or yellowish insects, often in groups.	*See 103.*
Stippled or bleached leaves, varnishlike excrement specks on undersides.	**Thrips.** Tiny, slender, blackish or yellowish insects.	*See 156.*

19. For more information, see publications such as *Sago Palms in the Landscape* (Geisel, Unruh, and Lawson 2001).

*Some species are invasive weeds. Other species may be better choices when planting.

WHAT THE PROBLEM LOOKS LIKE	PROBABLE CAUSE	COMMENTS

SERVICEBERRY (*Amelanchier* spp.), Shadbush

Leaves, blossoms, or shoots suddenly blacken, brown, shrivel, or wilt. Plant appears scorched.	**Fire blight.** Bacterium infects plants through blossoms.	*See 229.*
Leaves with tiny brown, reddish, or purple blotches or spots, may have yellow halos. Leaves may drop prematurely.	**Entomosporium leaf spot.** A fungal disease promoted by wet foliage.	*See 227.*
Leaves with brown to yellow blotches and orangish pustules. Leaves may drop prematurely.	**Rusts,** *Gymnosporangium species.* Fungi favored by wet foliage.	Avoid overhead watering. Vigorous plants tolerate moderate infection. *See 240.*
Leaves discolor and wilt. Woody parts die back. Wet spots or sawdustlike frass on bark.	**Borers,** including **Flatheaded appletree borer.** Whitish larvae ≤¾ inch long.	*See 179.*
Leaves discolor and wilt. Dead branches, limbs, or twigs. Plant declines, may die. Tiny "BB shot"-sized holes in bark, which may ooze.	**Shothole borer.** Small brown adults, whitish larvae, tunnel beneath bark.	*See 176.*
Leaves stippled, bleached, or reddened. May be fine webbing on leaves or terminals. Leaves may drop prematurely.	**Spider mites,** including **McDaniel spider mite.** Brown, green, reddish, or yellow specks.	*See 197.*
Leaves scraped, skeletonized, may be slime-covered.	**Pear sawfly** or **Pearslug.** Green, slimy, sluglike larvae, ≤½ inch long.	*See 83.*
Sticky honeydew, blackish sooty mold, and whitish cast skins on leaves.	**Aphids,** including **Bean aphid.** Small pear-shaped insects, often green, yellowish, or blackish.	*See 103.*

SOUR GUM (*Nyssa* spp.), Tupelo, Tupelo gum

Chewed foliage. Leaves may be webbed with silk.	**Tent caterpillars, Redhumped caterpillar.** Larvae hairy or colorful, ≤1 inch long.	*See 78, 80.*
Sticky honeydew and blackish sooty mold on foliage. Possible plant decline or dieback.	**European fruit lecanium.** Brown or yellow, flat or bulbous, immobile scale insects.	*See 139.*

SPIREA (*Spirea* spp.)

Sudden wilting then shriveling and blackening of shoots and blossoms. Plants appear scorched.	**Fire blight.** Bacterium infects plants through blossoms.	*See 229.*
Powdery white growth and yellow blotches on leaves and sometimes on terminals. Shoots and leaves may be undersized or distorted.	**Powdery mildews,** including *Podosphaera clandestina, Microsphaera* sp., *Stictis* spp. Fungal diseases favored by moderate temperatures, shade, and poor air circulation.	*See 236.*
Sticky honeydew, blackish sooty mold, and whitish cast skins on leaves. Leaves curled.	**Spirea aphid,** *Aphis citricola.* Green insects, <⅛ inch long, clustered on growing leaves and tips.	Vigorous plants tolerate moderate populations. Hose with forceful water. Tolerate or apply soap or oil. *See Aphids, 103.*
Leaves bleached, stippled, may turn brown and drop prematurely. Terminals may be distorted. Plant may have fine webbing.	**Spider mites,** including *Eotetranychus* sp. Tiny arthropods, often green, pink, red, or yellowish.	*See 197.*
Needles mottled brown, light green, or yellow. Needles die and drop prematurely, often beginning with lower canopy. Plant growth slow.	**Needle casts, Needle blights,** and **Tar spots,** including *Lirula* sp., *Lophodermium piceae, Rhizosphaera kalkhoffii.* Fungi favored by cool, wet conditions in spring.	Remove nearby plants and weeds. Thin canopy and prune off lower branches to reduce humidity and improve air circulation. *See Leaf Spots, 223.*

SPRUCE (Picea spp.)

WHAT THE PROBLEM LOOKS LIKE	PROBABLE CAUSE	COMMENTS
Needles with dark or yellow spots. Shoots brown or yellow, bushy witches' brooms. Orangish pustules or pale growth on foliage. Needles may drop prematurely.	**Rusts**, including *Chrysomyxa arctostaphyli, Chrysomyxa* spp. Fungi infect and develop when foliage is wet. Some infect alternate hosts, such as *C. arctostaphyli* on manzanita.	Avoid overhead watering. Plants tolerate moderate damage. Eliminating nearby alternate hosts may help in control. *See 240.*
Needles and terminals brown, yellow, and wilt. Roots or basal stem may be dark, decayed. Branches or entire plant dies.	**Root and crown rots,** *Phytophthora* spp. Fungal pathogens favored by excess soil moisture and poor drainage.	*See 265.*
Needles brown, yellow, or drop prematurely. Treetop or entire tree dies.	**Engraver beetles.** Adults are small, brown bark beetles. White larvae bore under bark.	*See 175.*
Needles turn brown or yellow on branch interiors and drop prematurely, leaving only young terminal needles. Tree may die.	**Spruce aphid,** *Elatobium abietinum.* Small pear-shaped insects, dark to light green, in groups on older foliage.	Most common late winter to early spring. Can be a serious pest of spruce. *See Aphids, 103.*
Needles pale, mottled, or chlorotic.	**Pine needle scale,** *Chionaspis pinifoliae.* White, immobile armored scales about 1/16 inch long. Suck sap.	Vigorous plants tolerate moderate populations. Conserve beneficials and tolerate. Monitor; if damaging, apply soap to crawlers. *See Armored Scales, page 131.*
Needles bleached, stippled. Foliage color abnormally light green or yellowish.	**Spider mites,** including **Spruce spider mite.** Greenish specks, often in fine webbing at foliage base.	Highest populations occur during spring and fall. *See 197.*
Needles with brown to gray encrustations. Branches or twigs may decline or die. Plant may die.	**Hemlock scale,** *Abgrallaspis ithacae.* Tiny oblong armored scales.	Primarily a pest on Colorado blue spruce in the Pacific Northwest. Also occurs in the eastern U.S. *See Armored Scales, 131.*
Needles chewed. Foliage browns. May be silk webbing on needles.	**Caterpillars,** including **Douglas-fir tussock moth,** *Orgyia pseudotsugata;* **Silverspotted tiger moth,** *Lophocampa argentata* (family Arctiidae). Caterpillars hairy, brownish with orange, red, or yellow.	Vigorous trees tolerate moderate damage. Apply *Bacillus thuringiensis* to control young larvae, if needed. *See Tussock Moths, 74, 77.*
Needles chewed.	**Conifer sawflies.** Green larvae, ≤1 inch long, on needles.	*See 83.*
Terminals distorted, chewed, dead. Foliage may become busy, crooked. Roots or the basal trunk may be injured.	**Conifer twig weevils** or **Pine weevils,** including **White pine weevil.** Small black to brown weevils chew needles and shoots. Depending on the species, larvae chew on or within needles and shoots or bore in the root crown.	Grublike larvae of damaging species mine shoots. Tolerate or prune out damage. On high aesthetic value (nursery) trees, a foliar insecticide spray in the spring may be applied when adults feed and lay eggs. *See 93.*
Wet, white, frothy masses on needles or twigs.	**Spittlebugs,** including **Western pine spittlebug,** *Aphrophora permutata.* Green to black sucking insects, secrete spittle.	Tolerate; spittlebugs cause no apparent harm to trees. *See 151.*
Terminals galled, brown, light green, or purplish. Needles may have yellow spots. May be cottony or waxy material on bark or needles.	**Adelgids,** including **Cooley spruce gall adelgid.** Tiny aphidlike insects feed on bark, at needle bases, and within galls.	*See 112.*
Sticky honeydew and blackish sooty mold on foliage. Brown to purplish insects clustered on foliage.	**Giant conifer aphids,** *Cinara* spp. Small, black, long-legged insects.	Often infest only a single branch. In California, more common in south than in north. *See 105.*
Plants stunted, decline, may die. Powdery, waxy material may be visible on roots and around crown.	**Ground mealybugs,** *Rhizoecus* spp. Small, slender, pale insects, may be lightly covered with powdery wax, but lack marginal filaments.	*See 130.*

SPRUCE (*Picea* spp.), continued

WHAT THE PROBLEM LOOKS LIKE	PROBABLE CAUSE	COMMENTS
Pitchy masses 1 to 4 inches in diameter protruding from trunks and limbs. Limbs occasionally break.	**Douglas-fir pitch moth.** Dirty whitish larvae, ≤1 inch long, in pitch.	*See Pitch Moths, 191.*
Galls or swellings on trunk and roots, usually near soil, may be on branches.	**Crown gall.** Bacteria infect plant via wounds.	*See 258.*

SWEET SHADE (*Hymenosporum flavum*)

No serious invertebrate or pathogen pests have been reported in California. If plants are unhealthy, investigate whether they have been injured or lack good growing conditions or appropriate cultural care.

SYCAMORE (*Platanus* spp.), London plane, Plane tree

WHAT THE PROBLEM LOOKS LIKE	PROBABLE CAUSE	COMMENTS
Leaves or shoots with white powdery growth. Terminals may be distorted or stunted.	**Powdery mildew,** *Microsphaera alni.* A fungal disease favored by moderate temperatures, shade, and poor air circulation.	Disease most damaging on severely pruned trees. Plant resistant Yarwood cultivar. *See 236.*
Leaves smaller and fewer in number than normal. Rapid decline and death of entire tree.	**Sycamore canker stain.** Fungus enters wounds and spreads by contaminated equipment or tools or root grafts.	Pathogen occurs in eastern U.S. and in California at least in the San Joaquin Valley. *See 256.*
Leaves spotted, brown, or yellow, and may distort or drop prematurely. Cottony material in bark crevices overwinter.	**Sycamore scale.** Bulbous insects, ≤¹⁄₁₆ inch long, in center of yellow spot on lower leaf surface.	*See 143.*
Leaves, buds, and shoots distorted and discolored. Irregular brown dead areas along leaf veins. Twigs die back. Branches may grow crookedly or be bent from regrowth after dieback.	**Anthracnose,** *Apiognomonia veneta =Discula veneta.* A fungal disease favored by wet conditions.	Grow resistant cultivars. *See 223.*
Leaves with brown to tan spots. Infected tissue may drop, leaving leaf holes. Leaves may drop prematurely.	**Leaf spot,** *Stigmina platani-racemosae.* A fungal disease promoted by moist spring weather or splashing irrigation water.	*See similar Shot Hole, 226.*
Leaves with discolored spots, often between veins. Large spots chlorotic, then tan or brown.	**Summer leaf scorch** or **Sunburn.** Noninfectious disorders, commonly appear during or after drought stress or high temperatures.	*See 288.*
Leaves with irregular brown or yellow blotches or spots. Leaves may become holey or tattered. Dark, varnishlike excrement may be on undersides of leaves. Leaves may drop prematurely.	**Sycamore plant bug,** *Plagiognathus albatus.* Brown, greenish, or yellow bugs ≤³⁄₁₆ inch long.	*See similar Ash Plant Bugs, 153.*
Leaves stippled, bleached, and have cast skins and varnishlike specks. May be sticky honeydew on plant.	**Western sycamore lace bug.** *Corythucha confraterna.* Adults ≤⅛ inch long, wings lacy. Nymphs spiny.	*See 154.*
Leaves stippled and may become bleached.	**Sycamore spider mite.** Green specks, suck sap.	Problem in California mostly in interior valleys. *See 197.*
Sticky honeydew and blackish sooty mold on plant.	**European fruit lecanium, Frosted scale.** Hemispherical to flattened, brown, yellow, or whitish insects, suck sap.	*See 139.*
Sticky honeydew, blackish sooty mold, and whitish cast skins on foliage.	**Aphids,** including **Melon aphid.** Small, greenish, blackish, or yellowish insects in groups.	*See 103.*
Webbing or silk tents on ends of branches. Chewed leaves.	**Fall webworm.** Hairy, white to yellow larvae, ≤1 inch long, in colonies.	*See 81.*

SYCAMORE *(Platanus* spp.), London plane, Plane tree, continued

WHAT THE PROBLEM LOOKS LIKE	PROBABLE CAUSE	COMMENTS
Young leaves skeletonized. Holes in leaves.	**Sycamore leaf skeletonizer,** *Gelechia desiliens* (family Gelechiidae). Greenish larvae, ≤½ inch long, in tubular nest on leaves.	Plants tolerate extensive skeletonization. Tolerate or apply *Bacillus thuringiensis* if young moth larvae are abundant.
Brown to gray encrustations on bark. Possible stunting or dieback of woody parts.	**Oystershell scale.** Tiny oyster-shaped insects, often in colonies.	*See 135.*
Decline or death of canes or entire plant. Larvae, ≤1 inch long, tunneling in canes.	**Flatheaded appletree borer, Pacific flatheaded borer.** Whitish larvae with enlarged head in tunnels.	*See 179.*
Greatly roughened bark and boring dust on lower trunk and branch crotches. Slow tree growth. May be dark ooze from bark.	**American plum borer, Sycamore borer.** Brown to pink larvae that bore under bark.	Distinguish between these differently managed species. Trees are not seriously harmed by sycamore borer. *See 188, 193.*

SYRINGA *(Syringa* spp.), Japanese tree lilac, Lilac

WHAT THE PROBLEM LOOKS LIKE	PROBABLE CAUSE	COMMENTS
Leaves or stems with black to brown spots and streaks. Blossoms, buds, or leaves darken and shrivel. Oozing lesions on twigs.	**Bacterial blight and canker.** Pathogen infects through wounds. Disease favored by wet conditions.	Grow resistant plants. *Syringa josikaea, S. komarowii, S. microphylla, S. pekinensis,* and *S. reflexa* are less susceptible than many *S. vulgaris* cultivars. *See 245.*
Leaves yellow and wilt. Branches die back. Entire plant may die. Minute white fungus growths may be visible beneath bark or on soil.	**Armillaria root rot.** Present in many soils. Favored by warm, wet soil. Persists for years in infected roots.	*See 262.*
Leaves fade, yellow, brown, wilt, often scattered throughout canopy or first on one side of plant. Branches die. Entire plant may die.	**Verticillium wilt.** A soil-dwelling fungus that infects through roots.	*See 232.*
Leaves fade and wilt, often scattered throughout canopy. Branches die. Boring dust, ooze, or holes on trunk or branches.	**Lilac borer** or **Ash borer.** White larvae ≤1 inch long bore in wood. Adults are wasplike moths.	*See 187.*
Leaves turn brown or yellow, especially along margins and at tip. Leaves may drop prematurely.	**Leaf burn** or **Scorch.** Abiotic disorders with many potential causes, including extreme temperatures, excess light, inappropriate irrigation, or poor drainage.	Provide plants with a good growing environment and proper cultural care. *See 273.*
Leaves or shoots with gray or white powdery growth. Leaves or terminals may distort.	**Powdery mildew,** *Microsphaera* sp. A fungal disease favored by moderate temperatures, shade, and poor air circulation.	Usually does no serious harm to lilac. *See 236.*
Soft, brown decay on buds, flowers, or leaves. May be woolly gray growth (spores) on dead tissue.	**Gray mold.** Fungus develops in plant debris or inactive tissue. Favored by high humidity and moderate temperatures. Spores airborne.	*See 242.*
Leaves with brown, black, tan, or yellow spots or blotches. Spots may have dark or yellowish margins. Foliage may die and drop prematurely.	**Leaf spots,** including *Alternaria* sp. Spread by air or splashing water. Favored by prolonged cool, wet, conditions. Persist in plant debris.	*See 223.*
Leaves with brown, yellow, or whitish blotches. Leaves may be rolled at edges or tip.	**Leafminers,** including **Lilac leafminer,** *Caloptilia syringella* (family Gracillariidae). Greenish larvae tunnel in leaves. Adults are small brownish moths.	Plants tolerate extensive mining. If problem has been severe, apply systemic insecticide during spring.
Sticky honeydew and blackish sooty mold on foliage. Possible plant decline or dieback.	**European fruit lecanium.** Brown to yellow, flat or bulbous, immobile scale insects.	*See 139.*

SYRINGA (Syringa spp.), Japanese tree lilac, Lilac, continued

WHAT THE PROBLEM LOOKS LIKE	PROBABLE CAUSE	COMMENTS
Brown to gray encrustations on twigs or branches. May be stunted or dying woody parts.	**Oystershell scale.** Individuals resemble miniature oysters, ¹⁄₁₆ inch long.	*See 135.*
Chewed leaves or blossoms.	**Fuller rose beetle.** Pale brown adult snout weevils, about ⅜ inch long.	Adults hide during day and feed at night. Larvae feed on roots. *See 94.*
Plants stunted, decline, may die. Powdery waxy material may be visible on roots and around crown.	**Ground mealybugs,** *Rhizoecus* spp. Small, slender, pale insects, may be lightly covered with powdery wax, but lack marginal filaments.	*See 130.*

TAMARISK (Tamarix spp.)*

WHAT THE PROBLEM LOOKS LIKE	PROBABLE CAUSE	COMMENTS
Gray to brown encrustations on bark. May be stunted or dead twigs and branches.	**Oystershell scale.** Insects resemble small oysters, in colonies on bark.	*See 135.*
Wilting or dead plants. Some roots stripped of bark or girdled near soil. Foliage may be notched or clipped.	**Black vine weevil.** Adults are black or grayish snout beetles, about ⅜ inch long. Larvae are white grubs with brown head.	Larvae feed on roots. *See 92.*
Galls or swellings on roots.	**Root knot nematode,** *Meloidogyne* sp. Tiny root-feeding roundworms.	*See 345.*

TANBARK OAK (Lithocarpus densiflorus), Tanoak, Tan oak

WHAT THE PROBLEM LOOKS LIKE	PROBABLE CAUSE	COMMENTS
Terminals bend downwards. Leaves and shoots brown, light green, yellow, or wilted. Trunks ooze, usually near the ground. Leaves, shoots, and eventually entire tree die. Trees become heavily colonized by bark beetles.	**Sudden oak death,** *Phytophthora ramorum.* Pathogen spreads via air and contaminated soil. Apparently can infect through trunk bark.	Primarily a problem in wildlands, killing many oaks there. Do not move infected plants. Report to agricultural officials if found outside areas where pathogen is known to occur. *See 260.*
Foliage discolors, stunts, wilts, or drops prematurely. Plants grow slowly and may die. Roots dark, decayed.	**Root and crown rots,** *Phytophthora* spp. Pathogens promoted by excess soil moisture and poor drainage.	*See 265.*
Foliage yellows and wilts. Branches or entire plant may die. Trees may fall over. May be fleshy or woody fungal growths on bark or around roots.	**Wood decay** or **Heart rot,** including *Phellinus ferreus, Steccherinum* spp. Fungi that infect injured or severely stressed trees.	*See Wood Decay in Trunks and Limbs, 248.*
Foliage discolors and wilts. Branches develop cankers and die back. Dark hemispherical fruiting bodies develop on bark or wood.	**Hypoxylon canker.** A decay fungus that attacks injured or stressed trees.	*See 257.*
Foliage or shoots turn yellow, then brown. Shoots may be bushy, short, or shriveled. Powdery, whitish growth on leaves or shoots.	**Powdery mildews,** including *Brasiliomyces trina, Microsphaera penicillata, Sphaerotheca lanestris.* Fungi favored by moderate temperatures, shade, and poor air circulation.	*See 236.*
Bleeding or frothy material bubbling from tiny holes in trunk or limbs. Fine boring dust may surround holes.	**Ambrosia beetles, Oak bark beetles.** Adults brown, ⅛ inch long. White larvae tunnel beneath bark.	*See 177.*
Sticky honeydew and blackish sooty mold on foliage.	**Aphids,** including *Myzocallis* sp. Pear-shaped, greenish to yellow insects, usually in groups on leaves and terminals.	*See 103.*
Sticky honeydew and blackish sooty mold on foliage. Cottony or waxy material on plant.	**Mealybugs,** including *Pseudococcus* sp. Powdery grayish insects, ≤¼ inch long, with waxy filaments.	*See 126.*

*Some species are invasive weeds. Other species may be better choices when planting.

TANBARK OAK (Lithocarpus densiflorus), Tanoak, Tan oak, continued

WHAT THE PROBLEM LOOKS LIKE	PROBABLE CAUSE	COMMENTS
Sticky honeydew and blackish sooty mold on foliage. Black, brown, or yellow oval bodies (nymphs) often with white, waxy, fringe, on leaves.	**Stanford whitefly**, *Tetraleurodes stanfordi*. Adults tiny, mothlike.	Ignore insects, they apparently do not damage trees. *See Whiteflies, 121.*
Gray, pinkish, or whitish encrustations on bark, usually on the limb underside.	**Ehrhorn's oak scale**, *Mycetococcus ehrhorni*. A ⅟₂₅-inch red scale (family Asterolecaniidae) that occurs in symbiotic colonies with the fungus *Septobasidium canescens*.	Heavy infestations may slow tree growth, but populations are often innocuous. *See Other Common Scales, 142.*
Brown, gray, tan, or white encrustations on bark or leaves. Rarely, declining or dead twigs or branches.	**Greedy scale; Tanoak scale**, *Aspidaspis densiflorae*. Tiny oval to circular insects on bark.	Rarely if ever cause serious damage to plants. *See 133.*
Patches of dead leaves at end of branches.	**Oak twig girdler.** Adult cylindrical, metallic beetle, larvae whitish, in tunnels.	*See 182.*

TEA TREE (Leptospermum spp.)

WHAT THE PROBLEM LOOKS LIKE	PROBABLE CAUSE	COMMENTS
Branches die back. Entire tree may die. Minute white fungus growths may be visible beneath bark or on soil.	**Armillaria root rot.** Present in many soils. Favored by warm, wet soil. Persists for years in infected roots.	*See 262.*
Galls or swellings on roots. Plants may grow slowly.	**Root knot nematodes.** Tiny root-feeding roundworms.	*See 345.*

TOYON (Heteromeles arbutifolia), Christmas berry

WHAT THE PROBLEM LOOKS LIKE	PROBABLE CAUSE	COMMENTS
Sudden wilting then shriveling and blackening of shoots and blossoms. Plants appear scorched.	**Fire blight.** Bacteria enter plants through blossoms.	*See 229.*
Leaves with brown, light green, yellow, or dead spots or blotches. Twigs and stems may canker, ooze, or die back.	**Sudden oak death**, *Phytophthora ramorum*. Pathogen spreads via air and contaminated soil. Apparently can infect through bark or leaves.	Primarily a problem in wildlands, killing many oaks there. Do not move infected plant material. Report to agricultural officials if found outside areas where pathogen is known to occur. *See 260.*
Foliage discolored, wilted, stunted, drops prematurely. Discolored bark may ooze sap. Branches or plant may die.	**Root and crown rot**, *Phytophthora cactorum*. Decay fungus favored by excess irrigation and poor drainage.	Toyon resists *Phytophthora cinnamomi*, but is susceptible to *P. cactorum*. *See 265.*
Tiny reddish to brown leaf spots, may have yellow halos. Larger, dark areas on leaves. Leaves may drop prematurely.	**Entomosporium leaf spot.** A fungal disease promoted by wet foliage.	*See 227.*
Dark scabby or velvety spots on leaves or fruit.	**Scab**, *Spilocaea photinicola*. Fungal disease promoted by moist spring.	*See 227.*
Foliage may discolor and wilt. Dieback of branches or entire plant.	**Pacific flatheaded borer.** Whitish larvae with enlarged head in tunnels.	*See 179.*
Terminal leaves severely curled and twisted. Damage occurs early in season.	**Toyon thrips**, *Rhyncothrips ilex*. Tiny, slender, black (adult) and orangish (immature) insects in new terminals.	Insect has one annual generation. Tolerate damage. Keeping soil bare beneath plants or applying oil or soap to new growth may reduce damage. *See 156.*
Stippled, bleached leaves, with varnishlike specks on undersides.	**Greenhouse thrips.** Tiny, slender, black adults or yellowish nymphs.	*See 158.*
Stippled, bleached leaves with varnishlike specks on undersides.	**Lace bugs**, *Corythucha* spp. Adults ≤ ⅛ inch long, wings lacy. Nymphs spiny.	*See 154.*
Sticky honeydew and blackish sooty mold on leaves and twigs. Tiny, white, mothlike insects (adults) present.	**Ash whitefly; Crown whitefly; Iridescent whitefly**, *Aleuroparadoxus iridescens*. Tiny, oval, flattened nymphs, often white wax on fringe or back.	Conserve natural enemies, no other control generally recommended, plants tolerate. Soap spray provides some control. *See 121.*

TOYON (*Heteromeles arbutifolia*), Christmas berry, continued

WHAT THE PROBLEM LOOKS LIKE	PROBABLE CAUSE	COMMENTS
Sticky honeydew and blackish sooty mold on foliage. Possible plant decline or dieback.	**European fruit lecanium.** Brown to yellow, flat or bulbous, immobile scale insects on leaves and twigs.	*See 139.*
Chewed leaves. May be silken tents or mats of silk in plant.	**Western tent caterpillar, Western tussock moth.** Hairy caterpillars, ≤2 inches long, dark or colorful.	*See 77, 80.*
Chewed leaves.	**Fuller rose beetle.** Pale brown adult snout weevils, about ⅜ inch long.	Adults hide during day and feed at night. Larvae feed on roots. *See 94.*

TRISTANIA (*Lophostemon =Tristania conferta*), Brisbane box; (*Tristaniopsis =Tristania laurina*), Water gum

No serious invertebrate or pathogen pests have been reported in California. If plants are unhealthy, investigate whether they have been injured or lack good growing conditions or appropriate cultural care.

TULIP TREE (*Liriodendron tulipifera*), Tulip poplar, Yellow poplar

WHAT THE PROBLEM LOOKS LIKE	PROBABLE CAUSE	COMMENTS
Leaves wilt, discolor, and may drop prematurely. Branches die back. Entire tree may die. Minute white fungus growths may be visible beneath bark or on soil.	**Armillaria root rot.** Present in many soils. Favored by warm, wet soil. Persists for years in infected roots.	Tuliptree is resistant but not immune to *Armillaria* if conditions are highly conducive to disease development. *See 262.*
Leaves discolor, stunt, wilt, or drop prematurely, often on one side of plant. Stem xylem discolored. Stems or entire plant may die.	**Verticillium wilt.** Fungus persists in soil, infects through roots.	*See 232.*
Leaves yellow and wilt. Branches die back.	**Cylindrocladium root rot,** *Cylindrocladium* spp. Fungi persist in soil. Disease is favored by excess soil moisture and poor drainage.	Usually affect only young trees. Provide good drainage. Reduce irrigation if disease develops. *See similar Root and Crown Rots, 265.*
Black, raised, tarlike blotches on leaves.	**Tarspot,** *Rhytisma liriodendron.* Fungus most prevalent in moist environments.	Occasional problem that does not threaten tree health. Rake and dispose of fallen leaves. *See Leaf Spots, 223.*
Dark spots on leaves. Leaves may yellow and drop prematurely.	**Physiological leaf spotting** or **Leaf Burn.** Abiotic disorders, commonly caused by drought stress, dry wind, excess heat, low humidity, or poor cultural care.	Provide a good growing environment and appropriate cultural care, especially good drainage and adequate summer irrigation in areas with rainless summers. *See 273.*
Foliage turns reddish, then yellow, brown, and may drop prematurely. Powdery growth on tissue. Shoots or leaves may be stunted and distorted.	**Powdery mildew,** *Erysiphe polygoni.* Fungal disease favored by moderate temperatures, shade, and poor air circulation.	*See 236.*
Sticky honeydew, blackish sooty mold, and whitish cast skins on leaves. Possible premature leaf yellowing.	**Tuliptree aphid,** *Macrosiphum (=Illinoia) liriodendri.* Tiny green insects in colonies on underside of leaves.	Plants tolerate extensive aphid populations. *See 103.*
Sticky honeydew and blackish sooty mold on leaves. Twigs and limbs may die back.	**Tuliptree scale.** Females ≤⅕ inch, irregularly hemispherical, and variably colored brown to gray with other-colored blotches.	Widespread in eastern U.S. In California present at least in southern and eastern San Francisco Bay Area. *See 141.*
Galls or swellings on trunk and roots, usually near soil, may be on branches.	**Crown gall.** Bacteria infect plant via wounds.	*See 258.*

VIBURNUM (*Viburnum* spp.), Cranberry bush

WHAT THE PROBLEM LOOKS LIKE	PROBABLE CAUSE	COMMENTS
Foliage yellows and wilts. Branches or entire plant dies.	**Root and crown rot,** *Phytophthora* sp. Pathogen favored by wet soil and poor drainage.	*See 265.*
Leaves wilted, discolored, may drop prematurely. Branches or entire plant may die. May be white fungal growth or dark crust on basal trunk, roots, or soil.	**Dematophora root rot.** Fungus favored by mild, wet conditions. Infects primarily through roots growing near infested plants.	Less common than *Phytophthora*. *See 264.*

WHAT THE PROBLEM LOOKS LIKE	PROBABLE CAUSE	COMMENTS

VIBURNUM (*Viburnum* spp.), Cranberry bush, continued

WHAT THE PROBLEM LOOKS LIKE	PROBABLE CAUSE	COMMENTS
Leaves and stems with brown, water-soaked lesions. Shoots and stems may darken and die back.	**Bacterial blight and canker.** Pathogen infects through wounds. Disease favored by wet conditions.	*See 245.*
Leaves with dark or discolored blotches. Leaves may drop prematurely.	**Leaf spots,** *Cercospora* spp., *Phyllosticta* sp. Fungi favored by wet conditions.	*See 223.*
Stems with lesions or discoloring. Leaves discolor and wilt. Stems may die back.	**Sudden oak death,** *Phytophthora ramorum.* Pathogen spreads via air and contaminated soil. Apparently can infect through bark or leaves.	Primarily a problem in wildlands, killing many oaks there. Do not move infected plant material. Report to agricultural officials if found outside areas where pathogen is known to occur. *See 260.*
Powdery, whitish growth on leaves and shoots. Terminals may distort.	**Powdery mildews,** including *Microsphaera sparsa, Microsphaera penicillata.* Fungi develop on living tissue, favored by moderate temperatures, shade, and poor air circulation.	*See 236.*
Stippled, bleached leaves with varnishlike specks on undersides.	**Greenhouse thrips.** Tiny, slender, black adults or yellow immatures.	*See 158.*
Leaves bleached, stippled, may turn brown and drop prematurely. Terminals may be distorted. Plant may have fine webbing.	**Mites,** including **Southern red mite.** Tiny arthropods, often green, pink, or red.	*See 197.*
Sticky honeydew and blackish sooty mold on foliage. May be distorted terminals.	**Aphids,** including **Bean aphid.** Dull black or green insects, <⅛ inch long.	*See 103.*
Brown encrustations on bark. May be stunting or dieback of woody parts.	**Oystershell scale.** Tiny immobile insects, resembling miniature oysters.	*See 135.*
Foliage chewed or notched around margins. Some roots stripped of bark or girdled near soil. Young plants may wilt or die.	**Weevils,** including **Black vine weevil, Woods weevil.** Adults are dark snout beetles, ≤½ inch long. Larvae are white grubs with brown head.	*See 92.*

WALNUT (*Juglans* spp.)[20]

WHAT THE PROBLEM LOOKS LIKE	PROBABLE CAUSE	COMMENTS
Leaves discolor, wilt, stunt, may drop prematurely. Discolored bark may ooze sap. Branches or plant may die.	**Root and crown rots.** Decay fungi favored by excess soil moisture and poor drainage.	*See 265.*
Leaves discolor, wilt, stunt, may drop prematurely. Branches die back. Entire tree may die. Minute white fungus growths may be visible beneath bark or on soil.	**Armillaria root rot.** Present in many soils. Favored by warm, wet soil. Persists for years in infected roots.	*See 262.*
Leaves discolor and wilt. Branches die. Bark may have cankers or brownish ooze.	**Cankers, Twig dieback,** including *Botryosphaeria dothidea, Diplodia juglandis, Nectria cinnabarina.* Fungi primarily affect injured or stressed trees.	*See 250.*
Leaves with irregular brown, tan, yellow, or white blotches or spots. Leaves may die and drop prematurely.	**Anthracnose, Blight, Leaf spots,** including *Cylindrosporium juglandis, Marssonia californica, M. juglandis.* Fungi favored by wet conditions and persist in infected leaves and twigs.	*See 223.*
Leaves may yellow or wilt. Roots may be darker or fewer than normal. Galls or swellings may be on roots. Plants may grow slowly.	**Ring nematode, Root lesion nematode, Root knot nematodes.** Tiny root-feeding roundworms.	*See 341.*

20. For more information on pest identification and biology, see publications such as *Walnut Pest Management Guidelines* (Teviotdale et al. 2000) and *Integrated Pest Management for Walnuts* (Strand 2003).

WALNUT (*Juglans* spp.), continued

WHAT THE PROBLEM LOOKS LIKE	PROBABLE CAUSE	COMMENTS
Leaves discolor or wilt. Dieback of woody plant parts. Tunnels and larvae in wood.	**Pacific flatheaded borer.** Whitish larvae ≤1 inch long with enlarged head.	*See 179.*
Leaves discolor or wilt. Brown to gray encrustations on bark. May be declining or dead twigs or branches.	**Italian pear scale,** *Epidiaspis leperii;* **Walnut scale,** *Diaspidiotus* (=*Quadraspidiotus*) *juglansregiae;* **Oystershell scale; San Jose scale.** Tiny circular to elongate insects.	Italian pear scale survives only under shelter such as lichens and moss on bark. The female's body is reddish purple beneath its cover. *See Armored Scales, 131.*
Sticky honeydew, blackish sooty mold, and whitish cast skins on foliage.	**Walnut aphid,** *Chromaphis juglandicola;* **Duskyveined aphid,** *Callaphis juglandis.* Tiny yellowish to brown insects on either leaf surface.	Conserve natural enemies that provide control. Plants tolerate aphids, control is rarely needed. If severe, apply insecticidal soap or oil. *See Aphids, 103.*
Sticky honeydew and blackish sooty mold on foliage. Woody parts may decline and die back.	**Black scale, Calico scale, Citricola scale, European fruit lecanium, Frosted scale, Kuno scale.** Oval, flat or bulbous insects, brown, yellow, spotted, or whitish waxy insects.	*See 136–140.*
Sticky honeydew and blackish sooty mold on foliage. Cottony or waxy material on plant.	**Obscure mealybug.** Powdery, grayish insects, ≤¼ inch long with waxy filaments.	Conserve natural enemies that help in control. *See 127.*
Copious, misty, nonsticky liquid raining from plant. Surfaces covered with whitish residue.	**Glassy-winged sharpshooter.** Active, dark brown or gray leafhoppers ≤½ inch long, suck xylem fluid.	Vectors pathogens of oleander and certain crops, especially grapes. Report suspected glassy-winged sharpshooters to agricultural officials if found in areas where this pest is not known to occur. *See 148.*
Leaves stippled, bleached, or reddened.	**European red mite, Pacific spider mite, Twospotted spider mite.** Tiny greenish, reddish, or yellowish specks.	*See 197.*
Leaves with raised blisters on upper surface and pale, hairy or felty patches on underside. Leaves may curl or distort.	**Walnut blister mite,** *Eriophyes erinea* =*Aceria erinea.* Tiny elongate eriophyid mites.	Occurs on English or Persian walnut (*Juglans regia*). Harmless to walnut. No control recommended. *See Gall Mites, 203.*
Leaves with swollen, globular growths on upper surface and small pits on underside. Leaves may curl or distort.	**Walnut purse gall mite** or **Walnut pouch gall mite,** *Eriophyes brachytarsus* =*Aceria brachytarsus.* Tiny elongate eriophyid mites.	Occurs on California black walnut (*Juglans californica*) and its cultivars (e.g., *J. hindsii*). Harmless to walnut. No control recommended. *See Gall Mites, 203.*
Chewed leaves. Silken tents may occur on terminals. Single branch or entire tree may be defoliated.	**Fall webworm, Redhumped caterpillar, Tussock moths.** Smooth to hairy caterpillars, ≤1½ inches long.	*See 77–81.*
Catkins develop black lesions. Green husks have dark, sunken lesions on tip or sides. Leaflets have irregular dark blotches or lesions.	**Walnut blight,** *Xanthomonas campestris* p.v. *juglandis.* Bacterium overwinters in buds and twig lesions and during wet conditions, infects through blossoms.	Control effort generally not warranted in landscapes. If problem has been severe and nuts will be harvested, Bordeaux or fixed copper sprays at 7- to 14-day intervals during blossoming can prevent infection.
Husks have dark scars or spots (egg-laying stings). Inner husk is dark and soft. Hull and shell are difficult to separate. Nut shell is stained.	**Walnut husk fly,** *Rhagoletis completa* (Family Tephritidae). Larvae are yellow or white maggots. Adults are orange and yellow flies with black and clear wings.	Nut meat usually is not affected, but sometimes will decay, mold, or shrivel. *See Walnut Husk Fly Pest Notes* (Ohlendorf 2000) for more information.
Husks have oily appearance or appear normal. Nuts inside are eaten and contain frass, webbing, or one or several larvae.	**Navel orangeworm,** *Amyelois transitella* (family Pyralidae). Adult moths are grayish with black. Larvae are pink, reddish, or dirty white and (unlike codling moth) have a pair of brown, crescent-shaped marks on the second segment behind the head.	Prevent infestation by harvesting nuts before husks split. After harvest, remove and dispose of all old nuts on and beneath trees, as pest overwinters inside these.

WHAT THE PROBLEM LOOKS LIKE	PROBABLE CAUSE	COMMENTS

WALNUT (*Juglans* spp.), continued

WHAT THE PROBLEM LOOKS LIKE	PROBABLE CAUSE	COMMENTS
Husks exude brownish frass from blossom end of nut. Kernels brown, decayed, or tunneled and may contain maggot.	**Codling moth**, *Cydia pomonella* (family Tortricidae). Pale larvae with dark head bores in nut. Adults are small, brown, coppery moths.	Pest difficult to manage. Control effort generally not warranted in landscapes Consult *Codling Moth Pest Notes* (Bentley et al. 1999) for more information.
Galls or swellings on trunk and roots, usually near soil, may be on branches.	**Crown gall.** Bacteria infect plant via wounds.	*See 258.*

WAX MYRTLE (*Myrica* spp.), Bayberry, California wax myrtle

Irregular brown, tan, or white blotches or spots on leaves. Leaves may die and drop prematurely.	**Anthracnose**, *Gnomonia myricae*; **Leaf spots and Blight**, *Cronartium comptoniae, Lophodermium foliicola, Phyllosticta myricae.* Fungi favored by wet conditions and persist in infected leaves and twigs.	*See 223.*
Sticky honeydew and blackish sooty mold on leaves and twigs. Stems may die back.	**European fruit lecanium.** Brown or yellowish, flattened to bulbous scale insects on twigs.	*See 139.*
Sticky honeydew and blackish sooty mold on leaves. Blackish, oval bodies with white waxy fringe (nymphs) on leaves.	**Mulberry whitefly**, *Tetraleurodes mori.* Tiny adults, white or yellowish and mothlike.	Conserve natural enemies that help to control. Difficult to control with sprays. Soap or oil can reduce populations. *See Whiteflies, 121.*
Sticky honeydew, blackish sooty mold, and copious white waxy material on plant. Leaves may yellow, wither, and drop prematurely.	**Giant whitefly.** Adults are tiny, whitish, mothlike insects. Nymphs and pupae are flattened, oval, translucent, and greenish or yellow.	*See 122.*
Leaves discolored, wilted, and may drop prematurely. Branches or plant may die.	**Limb and trunk rot**, *Phellinus ferreus.* Decay fungus may produce bracts or fruiting bodies on bark.	*See Wood Decay in Trunks and Limbs, 248.*

WEIGELA (*Weigela* spp.)

Whitish, cottony material on bark or underside of leaves.	**Comstock mealybug**, *Pseudococcus comstocki.* Oblong, soft, powdery, waxy insects with filaments.	Control ants, reduce dust, avoid persistent pesticides that disrupt effective natural enemies. *See Mealybugs, 126.*

WILLOW (*Salix* spp.)

Leaves with yellow spots and yellow to orangish powdery pustules on lower surface. Leaves may drop prematurely.	**Rusts**, *Melampsora* spp. Fungal diseases that infect and develop when leaves are wet.	Damage usually not severe enough to warrant control action. *See 240.*
Leaves with oval or irregular, glossy black, thick, tarlike raised spots on upper leaf surface.	**Tar spot**, *Rhytisma salicinum.* Fungus most prevalent in moist environments.	Rarely if ever threatens plant health. Rake and dispose of leaves in the fall. *See Leaf Spots, 223.*
Leaves or twigs with irregular, small to large, black or brown blotches. Spots may have pale centers. Leaves may drop prematurely. Twigs may develop small cankers and dieback.	**Leaf and twig spots**, including *Marssonina apicalis, M. kriegeriana* spp.; **Gray scab**, *Sphaceloma murrayae.* Fungi promoted and spread by wet conditions.	Rarely if ever threatens plant health. *See Leaf Spots, 223.*
Leaves with black, brown, or dark olive spots in early spring. Leaves yellow and may drop prematurely. Twigs may develop small cankers or dieback.	**Scab** or **Twig blight**, *Venturia chlorospora, V. saliciperda.* Fungal diseases spread by water from infected leaves and twigs.	Avoid overhead watering. Prune out infected twigs and leaves in fall. *See 227.*
Leaves brown, yellow, or drop prematurely. Terminals may die back. Branches or limbs may develop cankers. Infected wood is streaked brown.	**Bacterial blight and canker.** Disease favored by wet conditions.	*See 245.*

WILLOW (*Salix* spp.), continued

WHAT THE PROBLEM LOOKS LIKE	PROBABLE CAUSE	COMMENTS
Leaves or shoots with powdery white growth and yellow blotches. Shoots and leaves may be undersized or distorted.	**Powdery mildews**, including *Uncinula adunca*. Fungal diseases favored by moderate temperatures, shade, and poor air circulation.	*See 236.*
Leaves may yellow and wilt. Brownish, sunken lesions on limbs, trunk, or twigs. Small branches or twigs may die without any definite canker evident.	**Cankers, Twig blights**, including *Botryosphaeria ribis, Cytospora chrysosperma, Nectria* spp., *Valsa salicina, V. sordida*. Fungal diseases most serious on injured or low vigor trees.	*See 250.*
Leaves turn brown or yellow, especially along margins and at tip. Leaves may drop prematurely.	**Leaf burn** or **Scorch**. Abiotic disorders with many causes, including frost, inappropriate irrigation, poor drainage, or sunburn.	Provide plants with a good growing environment and proper cultural care. *See 273.*
Leaves discolor and wilt. Decline or dieback of some branches or entire tree. Roughened bark may have dark or wet spots.	**Borers**, including **American hornet moth; Carpenterworm; Flatheaded appletree borer; Pacific flatheaded borer; Poplar borer**, *Saperda calcarata*; **Western poplar clearwing**. Whitish larvae ≤2 inches long, tunnel beneath bark or in wood.	*See 179–194.*
Bark stained brownish, exudes rancid fluid, often around crotches, wounds.	**Wetwood** or **Slime flux**. Bacterial infection.	Usually does not cause serious harm to trees. *See 259.*
Sticky honeydew and blackish sooty mold on plant. Twigs and branches may die.	**Giant bark aphid**, *Longistigma caryae*. Relatively large aphids, ≤¼ inch long, grayish and black, in groups on bark.	Unlike most aphids, can be a serious pest, causing dieback. *See Aphids, 103.*
Sticky honeydew and blackish sooty mold on plant.	**Aphids**, including *Chaitophorus* spp.; **Giant willow aphid**, *Lachnus salignus*; **Melon aphid**. Green to brown insects, ≤⅛ inch long, clustered on leaves or twigs.	Plants tolerate moderate aphid populations. Conserve natural enemies. Hose forcefully with water. Tolerate or apply soap or oil in spring. *See 103.*
Sticky honeydew and blackish sooty mold on foliage. May be pale waxiness on plants.	**Psyllids**, including *Psylla alba, P. americana*. Aphidlike insects, often brown, green, orangish, reddish, or white.	*See 114.*
Sticky honeydew and blackish sooty mold on foliage. Cottony or waxy material on plant.	**Mealybugs**, including **Obscure mealybug, Vine mealybug**. Powdery, grayish insects, ≤¼ inch long, with waxy filaments.	Conserve natural enemies that help in control. *See 126.*
Sticky honeydew and blackish sooty mold on foliage. Tiny, whitish, mothlike adult insects.	**Silverleaf whitefly**. Nymphs oval, flattened, yellowish to translucent.	*See 121.*
Sticky honeydew and blackish sooty mold on plant. Possible decline and dieback of woody parts. May be cottony material on plant.	**Brown soft scale; Cottony maple scale**, *Pulvinaria innumerabilis*. Yellow to brown, oval, flattened insects or cottony white, popcornlike bodies.	Cottony maple scale has one generation a year. Conserve natural enemies and tolerate moderate populations or monitor and apply oil in spring when crawlers are abundant. *See 137.*
Leaves stippled or bleached, with cast skins and varnishlike specks.	**Lace bug**, *Corythucha* sp. Brown adults, ≤⅛ inch long, wings lacelike.	*See 154.*
Leaves bleached, blotched, discolored, or stippled. May be fine webbing on foliage. Leaves may drop prematurely.	**Spider mites**, including **Persea mite**. Tiny arthropods, often green or yellowish.	*See 197.*
Brownish, grayish, tan, or white encrustations on bark. May be decline or dieback of twigs or branches.	**Greedy scale, Latania scale, Oystershell scale, San Jose scale**. Tiny circular to elongate insects on twigs and branches.	*See 132–135.*

WILLOW (*Salix* spp.), continued

WHAT THE PROBLEM LOOKS LIKE	PROBABLE CAUSE	COMMENTS
Leaves skeletonized.	**Leaf beetles**, including *Altica bimarginata;* **California willow beetle**, *Melasomida californica; Chrysomela aeneicollis;* **Cottonwood leaf beetle**; *Syneta albida.* Brown to metallic black adults; larvae are dark, elongate.	Vigorous plants tolerate moderate leaf damage. Provide proper cultural care, including adequate water for willows, which are adapted to moist soils. Tolerate or apply oil or another insecticide to kill eggs and larvae. *See 84.*
Leaves chewed. May be silken tents in tree.	**Fall webworm; Fruittree leafroller; Omnivorous looper; Redhumped caterpillar; Tent caterpillars; Tussock moths; Satin moth**, *Leucoma salicis* (family Lymantriidae). Naked, spiny or hairy larvae, ≤2 inches long.	Vigorous plants tolerate moderate defoliation. Prune out colonies of caterpillars confined to a few branches. Apply *Bacillus thuringiensis* or other insecticide when caterpillars are young if damage not tolerable. *See 71.*
Leaves chewed.	**Cerisyi's sphinx, Eyed sphinx,** or **One-eyed sphinx**, *Smerinthus cerisyi* (family Sphingidae). Adult mostly brown, tan, and reddish moth. Caterpillar green with pink anal horn. Both ≤2 inches long.	*See Foliage-Feeding Caterpillars, 71.*
Leaves chewed, often on scattered branches. Larvae present may be feeding in groups.	**Spiny elm caterpillar** or **Mourningcloak butterfly; Western tiger swallowtail**, *Papilio rutulus* (family Papilionidae). *Papilio* larvae are bright green with eyespots, black and yellow markings; adult is ≤2 inches long, yellow with black.	Caterpillars mature into highly attractive butterflies. Control not recommended. *Bacillus thuringiensis* kills young larvae. *See 80.*
Prominent red globular or elongate swellings (galls) on leaves, terminals, or twigs.	**Willow gall sawflies.** Tiny whitish larvae feed in galls. Adults are small, stout wasps.	Galls do not harm plant. *See 166.*
Roundish brown, reddish, or green galls with pointed end on shoots.	**Willow beaked-gall midge**, *Mayetiola* (=*Rabdophaga*) *rigidae.* Larva feeding in new buds causes distortion.	Galls do not harm plant. *See Gall Midges, 164.*
Roundish, grayish to red blisters, beadlike swellings, or fuzzy growths on leaves.	**Blister gall mites**, including *Vasates laevigatae.* Microscopic eriophyid mites living in groups.	*See Gall Mites, 203.*
Galls or swellings on trunk and roots, usually near soil, may be on branches.	**Crown gall.** Bacteria infect plant via wounds.	*See 258.*

WISTERIA (*Wisteria* spp.)

WHAT THE PROBLEM LOOKS LIKE	PROBABLE CAUSE	COMMENTS
Leaves brown, yellow or die. Branches may die back. Wood may canker or ooze.	**Cankers**, including **Botryosphaeria canker and dieback, Phomopsis canker.** Fungi primarily affect injured and stressed plants.	*See 250.*
Leaves have pale blotches, mottling, spots, or line patterns.	**Tobacco mosaic virus.** Virus spread by thrips, infects wide host range.	Rarely if ever threatens plant health. Infected landscape plants cannot be cured.
Sticky honeydew, blackish sooty mold, and whitish cast skins on plant.	**Aphids.** Small green, black, brown, or yellowish pear-shaped insects, often in groups.	*See 103.*
Sticky honeydew and blackish sooty mold on foliage.	**Calico scale.** Adults globular, black with white or yellow spots.	Rarely if ever threatens plant health. *See 138.*
White encrustations on woody parts and leaves.	**Wisteria scale**, *Chionaspis wistariae.* Elongate, <1/16 inch long.	Effect of scale on plant unknown. *See Armored Scales, 131.*
Decline of plant. Dying branches.	**Spotted tree borer**, *Synaphaeta guexi.* Larvae are whitish grubs ≤¾ inch long, tunnel in woody parts. Adults are mostly grayish with black, orange, and white.	Borer attacks injured and dying wisteria. Provide proper cultural care to keep plants vigorous. Prune out and dispose of damaged plant parts, no other management known. *See Longhorned Borers, 183.*

WHAT THE PROBLEM LOOKS LIKE	PROBABLE CAUSE	COMMENTS

XYLOSMA (*Xylosma congestum*)

WHAT THE PROBLEM LOOKS LIKE	PROBABLE CAUSE	COMMENTS
Leaves with dark, brown circular blotches, ≤¼ inch in diameter. Orangish pustules on leaf underside. Leaves may drop prematurely.	**Xylosma rust**, *Melampsora medusae.* Fungal disease favored by wet foliage.	Avoid overhead watering. Vigorous plants can tolerate a moderate infection. *See Rusts, 240.*
Branches die back. Entire plant may die. Minute white fungus growths may be visible beneath bark or on soil.	**Armillaria root rot.** Present in many soils. Favored by warm, wet soil. Persists for years in infected roots.	*See 262.*
Foliage has sticky honeydew, blackish sooty mold, and copious white waxy material. Leaves may yellow, wither, and drop prematurely.	**Giant whitefly.** Adults are tiny, whitish, mothlike insects. Nymphs and pupae are flattened, oval, translucent, and greenish or yellow.	*See 123.*
Leaves bleached, stippled, may turn brown and drop prematurely. Terminals may be distorted. Plant may have fine webbing.	**Spider mites**, *Tetranychus* spp. Tiny, often green, pink, or red pests; may have 2 dark spots.	*See 197.*

YEW (*Taxus* spp.)

WHAT THE PROBLEM LOOKS LIKE	PROBABLE CAUSE	COMMENTS
Foliage discolored, wilted, stunted, drops prematurely. Discolored bark may ooze sap. Branches or plant may die.	**Root and crown rots.** Decay fungi favored by excess soil moisture and poor drainage.	*See 265.*
Sticky honeydew and blackish sooty mold on foliage. Cottony waxy material on plant.	**Obscure mealybug.** Powdery, grayish, waxy insects with fringe filaments.	*See 127.*
Brown, gray, or purplish encrustations on bark. Rarely, declining or dead twigs or branches.	**Purple scale**, *Lepidosaphes beckii*; **Oleander scale.** Tiny circular to elongate insects, often in colonies.	Rarely if ever cause serious damage to yew. *See 134.*
Needles notched or clipped. Foliage may yellow or wilt. General decline of plant may occur.	**Black vine weevil.** Adults ½ inch long, black or grayish snout beetles, active at night.	Larvae feed on roots. *See 92.*

ZELKOVA (*Zelkova serrata*), Japanese zelkova

WHAT THE PROBLEM LOOKS LIKE	PROBABLE CAUSE	COMMENTS
Foliage yellows then wilts, usually first in one part of canopy. Curled, dead, brown leaves remain on tree.	**Dutch elm disease.** Fungus spread by bark beetles and root grafts.	Zelkova is moderately resistant to this pathogen. *See 234.*
Leaves discolor, stunt, wilt, or drop prematurely. Stems discolored, cankered, and die. Minute white fungus growths may be visible beneath bark or on soil.	**Armillaria root rot.** Present in many soils. Favored by warm, wet soil. Persists for years in infected roots.	*See 262.*
Leaves and branches wilt in spring. Stems may have dark cankers, callus tissue, or coral-colored pustules.	**Nectria canker**, *Nectria cinnabarina.* Fungus primarily affects injured or stressed trees.	*See 257.*
Pale blotches or irregular, black, tar-like spots on leaves. Leaves may drop prematurely.	**Anthracnose** or **Chinese elm anthracnose.** A fungal disease.	In California usually severe only on Chinese elm, *Ulmus parvifolia,* near the coast. *See 223.*
Sticky honeydew and blackish sooty mold on leaves and twigs.	**Calico scale.** Black, brown, and white, mottled, flattened to bulbous insects on twigs.	Rarely if ever threatens plant health. *See 138.*
Leaves skeletonized, some small holes. Leaves turn yellow, brown, and drop prematurely.	**Elm leaf beetle.** Adults greenish with black, longitudinal stripes. Larvae black to green, ≤¼ inch long.	Pest is unable to complete development on zelkova. A problem only when beetles move from nearby favored *Ulmus* spp., where control should be targeted. *See 85.*
Galls or swellings on trunk and roots, usually near soil.	**Crown gall.** Bacterium that infects plant via wounds.	*See 258.*

Suppliers

CERTAIN INDUSTRY publications and industry- and university-sponsored World Wide Web sites provide regularly updated guides or lists of IPM product manufacturers and suppliers. Also consult the section "World Wide Web Sites" for more current information on IPM product suppliers.

BENEFICIAL ORGANISMS

Beneficial Organism Suppliers in North America
www.cdpr.ca.gov/docs/ipminov/bensuppl.htm

Biological-based Product Commercial Producers
www.nal.usda.gov/bic/Misc_pubs/bioprod.html

Plant Pathogen Commercial Biocontrol Products
http://www.oardc.ohio-state.edu/apsbcc/productlist.htm

Insect Parasitic Nematodes
http://www2.oardc.ohio-state.edu/nematodes

MONITORING AND DIAGNOSTIC EQUIPMENT

BioQuip Products
2321 Gladwick St.
Rancho Dominiguez, CA 90220
(310) 667-8800
www.bioquip.com

Donegan Optical Company
(Optivisor hands-free magnifier)
15549 West 108th St.
Lenexa, KS 66219
(913) 492-2500
www.doneganoptical.com

Forestry Suppliers, Inc.
P.O. Box 8397
Jackson, MS 39284-8397
(601) 354-3565
www.forestry-suppliers.com

Gempler's
P.O. Box 270
Mt. Horeb, WI 53527
(800) 382-8473
www.gemplers.com

Great Lakes IPM
10220 Church Road NE
Vestaburg, MI 48891
(989) 268-5693
www.greatlakesipm.com

IPM Laboratories, Inc.
Main Street
Locke, NY 13092-0300
(315) 497-2063
www.ipmlabs.com

Phero Tech, Inc.
7572 Progress Way
Delta, British Columbia V4G 1E9
Canada
(800) 665-0076
www.pherotech.com

Praxis
2723 116th Avenue
Allegan, MI 49010
(616) 673-2793
www.praxis-ibc.com

Seabright Laboratories
4026 Harlan Street
Emeryville, CA 94608-3604
(800) 284-7363
www.seabrightlabs.com

Spraying Systems Co.
(water-sensitive papers)
P.O. Box 7900
Wheaton, IL 60189-7900
(630) 665-5000
www.spray.com or www.teejet.com

The Tanglefoot Co.
314 Straight Ave., SW
Grand Rapids, MI 49504
(616) 459-4139
www.tanglefoot.com

Trece, Inc.
P.O. Box 129
Adair, OK 74330
(918) 785-3061
www.trece.com

Whitmire Micro-Gen
3568 Tree Court Industrial Blvd.
St. Louis, MO 63122
(800) 777-8570
www.wmmg.com

World Wide Web Sites

THE WORLD WIDE WEB portion of the Internet is a vast source of information on crop production and pest management. Among the many resources available online through the Web are color photographs of crop damage, pests, and natural enemies; information on biology; management recommendations; decision-making models; and communication with pest control experts and practitioners. Although any printed list of online sites is immediately out of date, some relevant sites and their online addresses or URLs include:

Agdia plant pathogen diagnostic testing
www.agdia.com

Beneficial Organism Suppliers in North America
www.cdpr.ca.gov/docs/ipminov/bensuppl.htm

Biological Control News, Midwest
www.entomology.wisc.edu/mbcn/mbcn.html

Biological-based Product Commercial Producers
www.nal.usda.gov/bic/Misc_pubs/bioprod.html

Environmental Protection Agency, U. S.
www.epa.gov

Environmental Protection Agency, Western United States
www.epa.gov/region09

Exotic Pest Plant Council, California
www.caleppc.org

Factsheet, Ohio State (database for all university sites)
www.hcs.ohio-state.edu

Fungicide Resistance (Management) Action Committee
http://www.frac.info

Glassy-winged Sharpshooter Information
http://danr.ucop.edu/news/MediaKit/GWSS.shtml

Herbicide Resistance (Management) Action Committee
http://plantprotection.org/HRAC

Insecticide Resistance (Management) Action Committee
http://PlantProtection.org/IRAC

Integrated Pest Management Program, University of California Statewide
www.ipm.ucdavis.edu

IPM Resources (Database)
www.ippc.orst.edu

Material Safety Data Sheet (MSDS), UC Management System
www.ucmsds.com

Native Plant Society, California
www.cnps.org

Nematodes, Insect Parasitic
http://www2.oardc.ohio-state.edu/nematodes

Ornamental Horticulture Research & Information Center, UC
http://ohric.ucdavis.edu

Pesticide Regulation, California Department of
www.cdpr.ca.gov

Pesticide Information, Extension Toxicology Network (EXTOXNET)
http://ace.orst.edu/info/extoxnet

Pesticide Wise (pesticide properties and water quality risk)
www.pw.ucr.edu

Pitch Canker Task Force Web site
http://frap.cdf.ca.gov/pitch_canker/index.htm

Tree Selection Guide, California Polytechnic State University
http://selectree.calpoly.edu

Waste Management Board, California Integrated (composting information)
www.ciwmb.ca.gov/organics

Water Resources Control Board, California State
www.swrcb.ca.gov/index.html

Water Resources, California Department of
http://wwwdwr.water.ca.gov

Weed Research and Information Center, UC Davis
http://wric.ucdavis.edu

Weeds, California's
http://pi.cdfa.ca.gov/

Suggested Reading

THESE PUBLICATIONS are referred to in text as sources of further information. For publications cited in figures and tables as the sources of information and illustrations, see the Literature Cited.[1]

Abiotic Disorders of Landscape Plants: A Diagnostic Guide. 2003. L. R. Costello, E. J. Perry, N. P. Matheny, J. M. Henry, and P. M. Geisel. Calif. Agric. Nat. Res. Publ. 3420. Oakland.

Almond Pest Management Guidelines. 2002. B. L. Teviotdale, W. D. Gubler, and J. J. Stapleton (Diseases); F. G. Zalom, R. A. Van Steenwyk, W. J. Bentley, R. L. Coviello, R. E. Rice, L. C. Hendricks, C. Pickel, M. W. Freeman (Insects and Mites); and M. V. McKenry (Nematodes). University of California Statewide Integrated Pest Management Program. Univ. Calif. Agric. Nat. Res. Publ. 3431. Oakland.

An Annotated Checklist of Woody Ornamental Plants of California, Oregon, and Washington. 1979. E. McClintock and T. Leiser. Univ. Calif. Agric. Nat. Res. Publ. 4091. Oakland.

Ants Pest Notes. 2000. M. Rust and J. Klotz. University of California Statewide Integrated Pest Management Program. Univ. Calif. Agric. Nat. Res. Publ. 7411. Oakland.

Annual Bluegrass Pest Notes. 2003. D. W. Cudney, C. L. Elmore, and V. A. Gibeault. University of California Statewide Integrated Pest Management Program. Univ. Calif. Agric. Nat. Res. Publ. 7464. Oakland.

Anthracnose Pest Notes. 1999. P. Gouveia, B. Ohlendorf, and M. L. Flint. University of California Statewide Integrated Pest Management Program. Univ. Calif. Agric. Nat. Res. Publ. 7420. Oakland.

Aphids Pest Notes. 2000. M. L. Flint. University of California Statewide Integrated Pest Management Program. Univ. Calif. Agric. Nat. Res. Publ. 7404. Oakland.

Apple Pest Management Guidelines. 2002. B. L. Teviotdale, W. D. Gubler (Diseases); J. Caprile, L. Varela, C. Pickel, W. W. Coates, W. J. Bentley, P. M. Vossen (Insects and Mites); B. B. Westerdahl, and U. C. Kodira (Nematodes). University of California Statewide Integrated Pest Management Program. Univ. Calif. Agric. Nat. Res. Publ. 3432. Oakland.

Apple Scab Pest Notes. 2001. B Ohlendorf and M. L. Flint, eds. University of California Statewide Integrated Pest Management Program. Univ. Calif. Agric. Nat. Res. Publ. 7413. Oakland.

Apricot Pest Management Guidelines. 2002. B. L. Teviotdale, J. E. Adaskaveg, W. D. Gubler, W. W. Coates, J. J. Stapleton (Diseases); R. A. Van Steenwyk, W. W. Coates, L. C. Hendricks (Insects and Mites); and B. B. Westerdahl (Nematodes). University of California Statewide Integrated Pest Management Program. Univ. Calif. Agric. Nat. Res. Publ. 3433. Oakland.

Arboriculture: Integrated Management of Landscape Trees, Shrubs, and Vines. 3rd ed. 1999. R. W. Harris, J. R. Clark, and N. P. Matheny. Prentice-Hall. Englewood Cliffs, NJ.

Avocado Pest Management Guidelines. 2001. B. A. Faber, L. J. Marais (Diseases); B. A. Faber, P. A. Phillips (Insects and Mites); B. B. Westerdahl, and U. C. Kodira (Nematodes). University of California Statewide Integrated Pest Management Program. Univ. Calif. Agric. Nat. Res. Publ. 3436. Oakland.

Bark Beetles Pest Notes. 2000. D. Dahlsten, S. Dreistadt, and T. Paine. University of California Statewide Integrated Pest Management Program. Univ. Calif. Agric. Nat. Res. Publ. 7421. Oakland.

Bermudagrass Pest Notes. 2002. C. L. Elmore and D. W. Cudney. University of California Statewide Integrated Pest Management Program. Univ. Calif. Agric. Nat. Res. Publ. 7453. Oakland.

Biological Control of Insect Pests and Weeds. 1964. P. DeBach and E. I. Schlinger, eds. Reinhold Publishing Corp., New York.[2]

Bordeaux Mixture Pest Notes. 2000. D. R. Donaldson, W. H. Olson, and R. D. Raabe. University of California Statewide Integrated Pest Management Program. Univ. Calif. Agric. Nat. Res. Publ. 7481. Oakland.

California Ground Squirrel Pest Notes. 2002. T. P. Salmon and W. P. Gorenzel. University of California Statewide Integrated Pest Management Program. Univ. Calif. Agric. Nat. Res. Publ. 7438. Oakland.

California Insects. 1979. J. A. Powell and C. L. Hogue. Univ. Calif. Press. Berkeley.

California Master Gardener Handbook. 2002. D. R. Pittenger, ed. Univ. Calif. Agric. Nat. Res. Publ. 3382. Oakland.

California Oakworm Pest Notes. 2000. P. Gouveia, B. Ohlendorf, and M. L. Flint, eds. University of California Statewide Integrated Pest Management Program. Univ. Calif. Agric. Nat. Res. Publ. 7422. Oakland.

Caneberries Pest Management Guidelines. 2002. W. D. Gubler, E. J. Perry, L. J. Bettiga (Diseases); E. J. Perry, L. J. Bettiga, and B. M. Tyler (Insects and Mites). University of California Statewide Integrated Pest Management Program. Univ. Calif. Agric. Nat. Res. Publ. 3437. Oakland.

Carpenter Ants Pest Notes. 2000. M. Rust and J. Klotz. University of California Statewide Integrated Pest Management Program. Univ. Calif. Agric. Nat. Res. Publ. 7416. Oakland.

Carpenter Bees Pest Notes. 2000. B. Ohlendorf, ed. University of California Statewide Integrated Pest Management Program. Univ. Calif. Agric. Nat. Res. Publ. 7407.

Carpenterworm Pest Notes. 2003. P. Geisel. University of California Statewide Integrated Pest Management Program. Univ. Calif. Agric. Nat. Res. Publ. 74105. Oakland.

Cherry Pest Management Guidelines. 2002. B. L. Teviotdale, J. E. Adaskaveg, and W. D. Gubler (Diseases); R. A. Van Steenwyk, K. M. Daane, J. A. Grant (Insects and Mites); and B. B. Westerdahl (Nematodes). University of California Statewide Integrated Pest Management Program. Univ. Calif. Agric. Nat. Res. Publ. 3440. Oakland.

Citrus Pest Management Guidelines. 2002. H. D. Ohr, J. A. Menge (Diseases); E. E. Grafton-Cardwell, J. G. Morse, N. V. O'Connell, P. A. Phillips (Insects, Mites, and Snails); and B. B. Westerdahl (Nematodes). University of California Statewide Integrated Pest Management Program. Univ. Calif. Agric. Nat. Res. Publ. 3441. Oakland.

Clearwing Moth Pest Notes. 2000. S. H. Dreistadt and E. J. Perry. University of California Statewide Integrated Pest Management Program. Univ. Calif. Agric. Nat. Res. Publ. 7477. Oakland.

Cliff Swallows Pest Notes. 2000. T. P. Salmon and W. P. Gorenzel. University of California Statewide Integrated Pest Management Program. Univ. Calif. Agric. Nat. Res. Publ. 7482. Oakland.

Clovers Pest Notes. 2001. C. L. Elmore and D. W. Cudney. University of California Statewide Integrated Pest Management Program. Univ. Calif. Agric. Nat. Res. Publ. 7490. Oakland.

Codling Moth Pest Notes. 1999. W. Bentley, J. Caprile, R. Elkins, B. Olson, C. Pickel, S. Swezey, P. Vossen, and F. Zalom, University of California Statewide Integrated Pest Management Program. Univ. Calif. Agric. Nat. Res. Publ. 7412. Oakland.

Color-Photo and Host Keys to the Armored Scales of California. 1982. R. J. Gill. Scale and Whitefly Key #5. Calif. Dept. Food Agric., Sacramento, CA.[2]

Color-Photo and Host Keys to California Whiteflies. 1982. R. J. Gill. Scale and Whitefly Key #2. Calif. Dept. Food Agric., Sacramento, CA.[2]

Color-Photo and Host Keys to the Mealybugs of California. 1982. R. J. Gill. Scale and Whitefly Key #3. Calif. Dept. Food Agric., Sacramento, CA.[2]

Color-Photo and Host Keys to the Soft Scales of California. 1982. R. J. Gill. Scale and Whitefly Key #4. Calif. Dept. Food Agric., Sacramento, CA.[2]

Common Names of Arachnids. 1995. R. G. Breene. American Tarantula Society. South Padre Island, TX.

Common Names of Insects and Related Organisms 1997. 1997. J. J. Bosik, ed. Entomological Society of America. Lanham, MD.

Common Purslane Pest Notes. 1999. D. Cudney and C. Elmore. University of California Statewide Integrated Pest Management Program. Univ. Calif. Agric. Nat. Res. Publ. 7461. Oakland.

Common-Sense Pest Control. 1991. W. Olkowski, S. Daar, and H. Olkowski. The Tauton Press. Newton, CT.

Compatible Plants Under and Around Oaks. 1991. B. W. Hagen, B. D. Coate, and G. Keater. California Oak Foundation. Oakland, CA.

Compendium of Rose Diseases. 1989. R. K. Horst. American Phytopathological Society. St. Paul, MN.

Composite List of Weeds. 1989. J. F. Alex, G. A. Bozarth, C. T. Bryson, J. W. Everest, E. P. Flint, F. Forcella, D. W. Hall, H. F. Harrison, Jr., L. W. Hendrick, L. G. Holm, D. E. Seaman, V. Sorensen, H. V. Strek, R. H. Walker, and D. T. Patterson. Weed Science Society of America. Champaign, IL.

Conenose Bugs Pest Notes. 2002. L. Greenberg and J. H. Klotz. University of California Statewide Integrated Pest Management

Program. Univ. Calif. Agric. Nat. Res. Publ. 7455. Oakland.

Cottony Cushion Scale Pest Notes. 1998. B. Ohlendorf and M. L. Flint, eds. University of California Statewide Integrated Pest Management Program. Univ. Calif. Agric. Nat. Res. Publ. 7456. Oakland.

Crabgrass Pest Notes. 2002. C. L. Elmore. University of California Statewide Integrated Pest Management Program. Univ. Calif. Agric. Nat. Res. Publ. 7456. Oakland.

Creeping Woodsorrel and Bermuda Buttercup Pest Notes. 2002. C. L. Elmore and D. W. Cudney. University of California Statewide Integrated Pest Management Program. Univ. Calif. Agric. Nat. Res. Publ. 7444. Oakland.

Dandelions Pest Notes. 2000. D. Cudney and C. Elmore. University of California Statewide Integrated Pest Management Program. Univ. Calif. Agric. Nat. Res. Publ. 7469. Oakland.

Destructive and Useful Insects. Fifth Edition. 1993. R. L. Metcalf and R. A. Metcalf. McGraw-Hill, New York.

Determining Daily Reference Evapotranspiration (Eto). 1987. R. L. Snyder, W. O. Pruitt, and D. A. Shaw. Univ. Calif. Agric. Nat. Res. Publ. 21426. Oakland.

Diseases of Forest and Shade Trees of the United States. 1971. G. H. Hepting. U. S. Dept. Agric. Handb. 386. Washington, D.C.

Diseases of Pacific Coast Conifers. 1993. R. F. Scharpf, ed. U. S. Dept. Agric. Handb. 521. Washington, D.C.

Diseases of Trees and Shrubs. 1987. W. A. Sinclair, H. H. Lyon, and W. T. Johnson. Cornell Univ. Press. Ithaca, NY.

Dodder Pest Notes. 2002. W. T. Lanini, D. W. Cudney, G. Miyao, and K. J. Hembree. University of California Statewide Integrated Pest Management Program. Univ. Calif. Agric. Nat. Res. Publ. 7496. Oakland.

Drip Irrigation in the Home Landscape. 1999. L. Schwankl and T. Prichard. Univ. Calif. Agric. Nat. Res. Publ. 21579. Oakland.

Drywood Termites Pest Notes. 2002. V. R. Lewis. University of California Statewide Integrated Pest Management Program. Univ. Calif. Agric. Nat. Res. Publ. 7440. Oakland.

Easy On-Site Tests for Fungi and Viruses in Nurseries and Greenhouses. 1997. J. N. Kabashima, J. D. MacDonald, S. H. Dreistadt, and D. E. Ullman. Univ. Calif. Div. Agric. Nat. Res. Publ. 8002. Oakland.

Elm Leaf Beetle Pest Notes. 2001. S. H. Dreistadt, D. L. Dahlsten, and A. B. Lawson. University of California Statewide Integrated Pest Management Program. Univ. Calif. Agric. Nat. Res. Publ. 7403. Oakland.

Eucalyptus Longhorned Borers Pest Notes. 2000. T. D. Paine, J. G. Millar, and S. H. Dreistadt. University of California Statewide Integrated Pest Management Program. Univ. Calif. Agric. Nat. Res. Publ. 7425. Oakland.

Eucalyptus Redgum Lerp Psyllid Pest Notes. 2003. D. L. Dahlsten, S. H. Dreistadt, R. W. Garrison, and R. Gill. University of California Statewide Integrated Pest Management Program. Univ. Calif. Agric. Nat. Res. Publ. 7460. Oakland.

Eucalyptus Tortoise Beetle Pest Notes. 2003. J. G. Millar, T. D. Paine, K. A. Campbell, R. W. Garrison, and S. H. Dreistadt. University of California Statewide Integrated Pest Management Program. Univ. Calif. Agric. Nat. Res. Publ. 74104. Oakland.

Evaluation of Hazard Trees in Urban Areas. 1991. N. P. Matheny and J. R. Clark. International Society of Arboriculture. Urbana, IL.

Evapotranspiration and Irrigation Water Requirements. 1990. M. E. Jensen, R. D. Burman, and R. G. Allen, eds. American Society of Civil Engineers. New York.

Extension Toxicology Network. Oregon State University. http://ace.orst.edu/info/extoxnet

Fertilizing Landscape Trees. 2001. E. Perry and G. W. Hickman. Univ. Calif. Agric. Nat. Res. Publ. 8045. Oakland.

Field Bindweed Pest Notes. 2003. C. L. Elmore and D. W. Cudney. University of California Statewide Integrated Pest Management Program. Univ. Calif. Agric. Nat. Res. Publ. 7462. Oakland.

Fire Blight Pest Notes. 1999. B. Ohlendorf and M. L. Flint, eds. University of California Statewide Integrated Pest Management Program. Univ. Calif. Agric. Nat. Res. Publ. 7414. Oakland.

Floriculture and Ornamental Nurseries Pest Management Guidelines. 2002. R. D. Raabe, M. E. Grebus, C. A. Wilen, A. H. McCain (Diseases); K. L. Robb, H. S. Costa, J. A. Bethke, R. S. Cowles, M. P. Parrella (Insects and Mites); C. L. Elmore, and C. A. Wilen (Weeds). University of California Statewide Integrated Pest Management Program. Univ. Calif. Agric. Nat. Res. Publ. 3392. Oakland.

Fruittree Leafroller on Ornamental and Fruit Trees Pest Notes. 2000. W. J. Bentley, C. Pickel, R. E. Rice, and R. Van Steenwyk. University of California Statewide Integrated Pest Management Program. Univ. Calif. Agric. Nat. Res. Publ. 7473. Oakland.

Fungi on Plants and Plant Products in the United States. 1989. D. F. Farr, G. F. Bills, G. P. Chamuris, and A. Y. Rossman. 1989. American Phytopathological Society. St. Paul, MN.

Generalized Plant Climate Map of California. 1988. Sunset Western Garden Book. Univ. Calif. Agric. Nat. Res. Publ. 3328. Oakland.

Generalized Soil Map of California. 1988. R. E. Storie. Univ. Calif. Agric. Nat. Res. Publ. 3327. Oakland.

Giant Whitefly Pest Notes. 2002. T. S. Bellows, J. N. Kabashima, and K. Robb. University of California Statewide Integrated Pest Management Program. Univ. Calif. Div. Agric. Nat. Res. Publ. 7400. Oakland.

Glassy-Winged Sharpshooter Pest Notes. 2001 P. A. Phillips, C. A. Wilen, and L. G. Varela. University of California Statewide Integrated Pest Management Program. Univ. Calif. Agric. Nat. Res. Publ. 7492. Oakland.

Grape Pest Management. 2d ed. 1992. D. L. Flaherty, L. P. Christensen, W. T. Lanini, J. J. Marois, P. A. Phillips, and L. T. Wilson, eds. Univ. Calif. Div. Agric. Nat. Res. Publ. 3343. Oakland.

Grape Pest Management Guidelines. 2000. D. Gubler, J. Stapleton, G. Leavitt, A. Purcell, L. Varela, R. J. Smith (Diseases); W. J. Bentley, F. Zalom, J. Granett, R. J. Smith, L. Varela, A. Purcell (Insects and Mites); U. C. Kodira, and B. B. Westerdahl (Nematodes). University of California Statewide Integrated Pest Management Program. Univ. Calif. Agric. Nat. Res. Publ. 3448. Oakland.

Grasshoppers Pest Notes. 2002. M. L. Flint. University of California Statewide Integrated Pest Management Program. Univ. Calif. Agric. Nat. Res. Publ. 74103. Oakland.

Green Kyllinga Pest Notes. 2003. D. W. Cudney, C. L. Elmore, D. A. Shaw, and C. A. Wilen. University of California Statewide Integrated Pest Management Program. Univ. Calif. Agric. Nat. Res. Publ. 7459. Oakland.

A Guide to Estimating Irrigation Water Needs of Landscape Plantings in California. 2000. Calif. Dept. Water Resources. Sacramento. http://wwwdpla.water.ca.gov/urban/ conservation/landscape/wucols/wucols_ 2000.pdf

A Guide to Shrubs for Coastal California. 1980. H. M. Butterfield and W. B. Davis. Univ. Calif. Agric. Nat. Res. Publ. 2584. Oakland.

Handbook of Turfgrass Insect Pests. 1995. R. L. Brandenburg and M. G. Villani. Entomological Society of America. Lanham, MD.

Healthy Roses: Environmentally Friendly Ways to Manage Pests and Disorders in Your Garden and Landscape. M. L. Flint and J. F. Karlik. 2000. Univ. Calif. Div. Agric. Nat. Res. Publ. 21589. Oakland.

Hoplia Beetle Pest Notes. 2002. E. J. Perry. University of California Statewide Integrated Pest Management Program. Univ.

Calif. Div. Agric. Nat. Res. Publ. 7499. Oakland.

House Mouse Pest Notes. 2000. R. M. Timm. University of California Statewide Integrated Pest Management Program. Univ. Calif. Agric. Nat. Res. Publ. 7483. Oakland.

How Can We Live with Wildland Fire? 1998. T. E. Adams, L. Huntsinger, and J. Wright. Univ. Calif. Agric. Nat. Res. Publ. 21582. Oakland.

Insects Affecting Ornamental Conifers in Southern California. 1967. L. R. Brown and C. O. Eads. Calif. Experiment Sta. Bull. 834.[2]

Insect Pest Management Guidelines for California Landscape Ornamentals. 1987. C. S. Koehler. Univ. Calif. Agric. Nat. Res. Publ. 3317. Oakland.[2]

Insects and Diseases of Woody Plants of the Central Rockies. 2000. W. Cranshaw, D. Leatherman, B. Kondratieff, R. Stevens, and R. Wawrzynski. Colorado State Univ. Ft. Collins.

Insects of the Los Angeles Basin. C. L. Hogue. 1993. Natural History Museum of Los Angeles County. Los Angeles.

Insects That Feed on Trees and Shrubs. 1988. W. J. Johnson, and H. H. Lyon. Cornell Univ. Press. Ithaca, NY.

Insects and Mites of Western North America. 1958. E. O. Essig. MacMillan. New York.[2]

Integrated Pest Management for Almonds. 2d ed. 2002. L. L. Strand. University of California Statewide Integrated Pest Management Program. Univ. Calif. Div. Agric. Nat. Res. Publ. 3303. Oakland.

Integrated Pest Management for Apples and Pears. 2d ed. 1999. B. L. P. Ohlendorf. University of California Statewide Integrated Pest Management Program. Univ. Calif. Agric. Nat. Res. Publ. 3340. Oakland.

Integrated Pest Management for Citrus. 2d ed. 1991. University of California Statewide Integrated Pest Management Program. Univ. Calif. Div. Agric. Nat. Res. Publ. 3303. Oakland.

Integrated Pest Management for Floriculture and Nurseries. 2001. S. H. Dreistadt. University of California Statewide Integrated Pest Management Program. Univ. Calif. Agric. Nat. Res. Publ. 3402. Oakland.

Integrated Pest Management for Stone Fruits. 1999. L. L. Strand. University of California Statewide Integrated Pest Management Program. Univ. Calif. Agric. Nat. Res. Publ. 3389. Oakland.

Integrated Pest Management for Walnuts. 3d ed. 2003. University of California Statewide Integrated Pest Management Program. Univ. Calif. Agric. Nat. Res. Publ. 3270. Oakland.

An Introduction to Biological Control. 1982. R. van den Bosch, P. S. Messenger, and A. P. Gutierrez. Plenum Press. New York.

Introduction to Integrated Pest Management. 1981. M. L. Flint and R. van den Bosch. Plenum Press. New York, NY.

IPM in Practice: Principles and Methods of Integrated Pest Management. 2001. M. L. Flint and P. Gouveia. University of California Statewide Integrated Pest Management Program. Univ. Calif. Agric. Nat. Res. Publ. 3418. Oakland.

The IPM Practitioner. Bio-Integral Resource Center. Berkeley, CA.

The Jepson Manual: Higher Plants of California. 1993. J. C. Hickman, ed. Univ. Calif. Press. Berkeley.

Key to Identifying Common Household Ants. 2001. C. A. Reynolds, M. L. Flint, M. K. Rust, P. S. Ward, R. L. Coviello, and J. H. Klotz. Univ. Calif. Statewide Integrated Pest Management Program. www.ipm.ucdavis.edu/TOOLS/ANTKEY/

A Key to the Most Common and/or Economically Important Ants of California with Color Photographs. 1983. P. Haney. P. A. Philips, and R. Wagner. Univ. Calif. Agric. Nat. Res. Publ. 21433. Oakland.

Kikuyugrass Pest Notes. 2003. D. W. Cudney, C. L. Elmore, and V. A. Gibeault. University of California Statewide Integrated Pest Management Program. Univ. Calif. Agric. Nat. Res. Publ. 7458. Oakland.

Lace Bugs Pest Notes. 2000. S. H. Dreistadt and E. J. Perry. University of California Statewide Integrated Pest Management Program. Univ. Calif. Agric. Nat. Res. Publ. 7428. Oakland.

Landscape for Fire Protection. 1976. Univ. Calif. Agric. Nat. Res. Publ. 2401. Oakland.

Landscape Plant Problems: A Pictorial Diagnostic Manual. 2000. R. S. Byther, C. R. Foss, A. L. Antonelli, R. R. Maleike, and V. M. Bobbitt. Washington State Univ. Pullman.

Landscape Trees for the Great Central Valley of California. 1979. W. B. Davis. Univ. Calif. Agric. Nat. Res. Publ. 2580. Oakland.

Leaf Curl Pest Notes. 2000. B. Ohlendorf and M. L. Flint, eds. University of California Statewide Integrated Pest Management Program. Univ. Calif. Agric. Nat. Res. Publ. 7426. Oakland.

Life Stages of California Red Scale and Its Parasitoids. 1995. L. D. Forster, R. F. Luck, and E. E. Grafton-Cardwell. Univ. Calif. Div. Agric. Nat. Res. Publ. 21529. Oakland.

Living Among the Oaks: A Management Guide for Homeowners. Undated. S. G. Johnson. Univ. Calif. Agric. Nat. Res. Publ. 21538. Oakland.

Managing Insects and Mites with Spray Oils. 1991. N. J. Davidson, J. E. Dibble, M. L. Flint, P. J. Marer, and A. Guye. Univ. Calif. Agric. Nat. Res. Publ. 3347. Oakland.

Mealybugs in California Vineyards. 2002. K. E. Godfrey, K. M. Daane, W. J. Bentley, R. J. Gill, and R. Malakar-Kuenen. Univ. Calif. Agric. Nat. Res. Publ. 21612. Oakland.

Mistletoe Pest Notes. 2001. E. J. Perry and C. L. Elmore. University of California Statewide Integrated Pest Management Program. Univ. Calif. Agric. Nat. Res. Publ. 7437. Oakland.

Mushrooms and Other Nuisance Fungi in Lawns Pest Notes. 2002. M. Le Strange, C. A. Frate, and R. M. Davis. University of California Statewide Integrated Pest Management Program. Univ. Calif. Agric. Nat. Res. Publ. 74100. Oakland.

Natural Enemies Are Your Allies! 1990. M. L. Flint and J. K. Clark. Poster. Univ. Calif. Div. Agric. Nat. Res. Publ. 21497. Oakland.

Natural Enemies Handbook: The Illustrated Guide to Biological Pest Control. 1998. M. L. Flint and S. H. Dreistadt. Univ. Calif. Div. Agric. Nat. Res. Publ. 3386. Oakland.

Nematodes Pest Notes. 2001. E. J. Perry. University of California Statewide Integrated Pest Management Program. Univ. Calif. Agric. Nat. Res. Publ. 7489. Oakland.

Nectarine Pest Management Guidelines. 2002. B. L. Teviotdale, W. D. Gubler, J. E. Adaskaveg (Diseases); W. J. Bentley, K. R. Day (Insects and Mites); and B. B. Westerdahl (Nematodes). University of California Statewide Integrated Pest Management Program. Univ. Calif. Agric. Nat. Res. Publ. 3451. Oakland.

Nutsedge Pest Notes. 2003. C. A. Wilen, M. E. McGiffen, and C. L. Elmore. University of California Statewide Integrated Pest Management Program. Univ. Calif. Agric. Nat. Res. Publ. 7432. Oakland.

Oak Pit Scales Pest Notes. 2000. P. Geisel and E. Perry. University of California Statewide Integrated Pest Management Program. Univ. Calif. Agric. Nat. Res. Publ. 7470. Oakland.

Oleander Leaf Scorch Pest Notes. 2000. C. Wilen, J. Hartin, M. Henry, H. Costa, M. Blua, and A. Purcell. University of California Statewide Integrated Pest Management Program. Univ. Calif. Agric. Nat. Res. Publ. 7480. Oakland.

Olive Pest Management Guidelines. 2000. B. L. Teviotdale and L. Ferguson (Diseases); G. S. Sibbett, R. A. Van Steenwyk, and L. Ferguson (Insects and Mites); M. V. McKenry (Nematodes). University of California Statewide Integrated Pest Management Program. Univ. Calif. Agric. Nat. Res. Publ. 3452. Oakland.

Ornamental Trees: An Illustrated Guide to Their Selection and Care. 1955. E. Maino and F. Howard. Univ. Calif. Press. Berkeley.[2]

Pacific Northwest Landscape Integrated Pest Management (IPM) Manual. Culture of Key Trees and Shrubs, Problem Diagnosis and Management Options. 2002. V. M. Bobbitt, A. L. Antonelli, C. R. Foss, R. M. Davidson Jr., R. S. Byther, and R. R. Maleike. Washington State University. Pullman.

Peach Pest Management Guidelines. 2002. B. L. Teviotdale, W. D. Gubler, J. E. Adaskaveg (Diseases); C. Pickel, W. J. Bentley, J. K. Hasey, K. R. Day (Insects and Mites); and B. B. Westerdahl (Nematodes). University of California Statewide Integrated Pest Management Program. Univ. Calif. Agric. Nat. Res. Publ. 3454. Oakland.

Pear Pest Management Guidelines. 2001. R. B. Elkins, W. D. Gubler (Diseases); R. B. Elkins, R. A. Van Steenwyk, L. G. Varela, and C. Pickel (Insects and Mites). University of California Statewide Integrated Pest Management Program. Univ. Calif. Agric. Nat. Res. Publ. 3455. Oakland.

Pecan Pest Management Guidelines. 2000. G. S. Sibbett, R. A. Van Steenwyk (Insects and Mites); B. B. Westerdahl, and U. C. Kodira (Nematodes). University of California Statewide Integrated Pest Management Program. Univ. Calif. Agric. Nat. Res. Publ. 3456. Oakland.

Pesticides: Theory and Application. G. W. Ware. 1983. W. H. Freeman. San Francisco.

Pesticide Wise. J. Gan and P. X. Pang. University of California, Riverside. www.pw.ucr.edu

Pests of the Garden and Small Farm. 2d ed. 1998. M. L. Flint. University of California Statewide Integrated Pest Management Program. Univ. Calif. Div. Agric. Nat. Res. Publ. 3332. Oakland.

Pests of the West. 1998. W. Cranshaw. Colorado State University. Fort Collins.

Pistachio Pest Management Guidelines. 2002. B. L. Teviotdale, T. J. Michailides (Diseases); W. J. Bentley, R. E. Rice, R. H. Beede, K. Daane (Insects and Mites); B. B. Westerdahl, and U. C. Kodira (Nematodes). University of California Statewide Integrated Pest Management Program. Univ. Calif. Agric. Nat. Res. Publ. 3461. Oakland.

Pitch Canker Diseases of Pines: A Technical Review. 2003. B. Aegerter, T. Gordon, A. Storer, and D. Wood. Univ. Calif. Agric. Nat. Res. Publ. 21616. Oakland.

Pitch Canker Pest Notes. 2003. K. Wikler, T. R. Gordon, A. J. Storer, and D. L. Wood. University of California Statewide Integrated Pest Management Program. Univ. Calif. Agric. Nat. Res. Publ. 74107. Oakland.

Plant Health Care for Woody Ornamentals. 1997. J. E. Lloyd, ed. International Society of Arboriculture. Champaign, IL

Plants Resistant or Susceptible to Verticillium Wilt. 1981. A. H. McCain, R. D. Raabe, and S. Wilhelm. Univ. Calif. Agric. Nat. Res. Publ. 2703. Oakland.

Planting Landscape Trees. 2001. G. W. Hickman and P. Svihra. Univ. Calif. Agric. Nat. Res. Publ. 8046. Oakland.

Plum Pest Management Guidelines. 2000. B. L. Teviotdale, W. D. Gubler, J. E. Adaskaveg (Diseases); W. J. Bentley, R. E. Rice, K. R. Day (Insects and Mites); M. V. McKenry, and B. B. Westerdahl (Nematodes). University of California Statewide Integrated Pest Management Program. Univ. Calif. Agric. Nat. Res. Publ. 3462. Oakland.

Pocket Gophers Pest Notes. 2002. T. P. Salmon and W. P. Gorenzel. University of California Statewide Integrated Pest Management Program. Univ. Calif. Agric. Nat. Res. Publ. 7433. Oakland.

Poison Oak Pest Notes. 2001. J. M. DiTomaso and W. T. Lanini. University of California Statewide Integrated Pest Management Program. Univ. Calif. Agric. Nat. Res. Publ. 7431. Oakland.

Powdery Mildew on Ornamentals Pest Notes. 2001. R. D. Raabe, W. D. Gubler, and S. T. Koike. University of California Statewide Integrated Pest Management Program. Univ. Calif. Agric. Nat. Res. Publ. 7493. Oakland.

Principles of Weed Control. Third Edition. California Weed Science Society. 2002. Thompson. Fresno, CA.

A Property Owner's Guide to Reducing Wildfire Threat. D. S. Farnham. 1995. Univ. Calif. Agric. Nat. Res. Publ. 21539. Oakland.

Protecting Trees When Building on Forested Land. 1983. C. S. Koehler, R. H. Hunt, D. F. Lobel, and J. Geiger. Univ. Calif. Agric. Nat. Res. Publ. 21348. Oakland.

Psyllids Pest Notes. 2001. S. H. Dreistadt and D. L. Dahlsten. University of California Statewide Integrated Pest Management Program. Univ. Calif. Agric. Nat. Res. Publ. 7423. Oakland.

Questions and Answers About Tensiometers. 1981. A. W. Marsh. Univ. Calif. Agric. Nat. Res. Publ. 2264. Oakland.

Rabbits Pest Notes. 2002. T. P. Salmon and W. P. Gorenzel. University of California Statewide Integrated Pest Management Program. Univ. Calif. Agric. Nat. Res. Publ. 7447. Oakland.

Rebugging Your Home and Garden: A Step By Step Guide to Modern Pest Control. 1996. R. Troetschler, A. Woodworth, S. Wilcomer, J. Hoffmann, and M. Allen. PTF Press. Palo Alto, CA.

Recognizing Tree Hazards: A Photographic Guide for Homeowners. 1999. L. R. Costello, B. Hagen, and K. S. Jones. Univ. Calif. Agric. Nat. Res. Publ. 21584. Oakland.

Red Imported Fire Ant Pest Notes. 2001. L. Greenberg, J. Klotz, and J. Kabashima. University of California Statewide Integrated Pest Management Program. Univ. Calif. Agric. Nat. Res. Publ. 7487. Oakland.

Redhumped Caterpillar Pest Notes. 2000. R. E. Rice and R. Van Steenwyk. University of California Statewide Integrated Pest Management Program. Univ. Calif. Agric. Nat. Res. Publ. 7474. Oakland.

Residential, Industrial, and Institutional Pest Control. 1991. P. J. Marer. University of California Statewide Integrated Pest Management Program. Univ. Calif. Agric. Nat. Res. Publ. 3334. Oakland.

Resistance or Susceptibility of Certain Plants to Armillaria Root Rot. 1979. R. D. Raabe. Univ. Calif. Agric. Nat. Res. Publ. Publ. 2591. Oakland.

Rose Diseases and Abiotic Disorders Pest Notes. 1999. J. Karlik and M. L. Flint. University of California Statewide Integrated Pest Management Program. Univ. Calif. Agric. Nat. Res. Publ. 7463. Oakland.

Rose Insect and Mite Pests and Beneficials Pest Notes. 1999. M. L. Flint and J. Karlik. University of California Statewide Integrated Pest Management Program. Univ. Calif. Agric. Nat. Res. Publ. 7466. Oakland.

The Safe and Effective Use of Pesticides. 2d ed. 2000. P. J. O'Connor-Marer. University of California Statewide Integrated Pest Management Program. Univ. Calif. Div. Agric. Nat. Res. Publ. 3324. Oakland.

Sago Palms in the Landscape. 2001. P. M. Geisel, C. L. Unruh, and P. M. Lawson. Univ. Calif. Agric. Nat. Res. Publ. 7466. Oakland.

The Scale Insects of California Part 1: The Soft Scales. R. J. Gill. 1988. Calif. Dept. of Food and Agric. Sacramento.

The Scale Insects of California Part 2: The Minor Families. R. J. Gill. 1993. Calif. Dept. of Food and Agric. Sacramento.

The Scale Insects of California Part 3: The Armored Scales. R. J. Gill. 1997. Calif. Dept. of Food and Agric. Sacramento.

Scales Pest Notes. 2001. S. H. Dreistadt, R. J. Gill, J. G. Morse, P. A. Phillips, and R. E. Rice. University of California Statewide Integrated Pest Management Program. Univ. Calif. Div. Agric. Nat. Res. Publ. 7408. Oakland.

SelecTree: A Tree Selection Guide. 2001. J. L. Reimer and W. Mark. Calif. State Univ. San Luis Obispo. http://selectree.calpoly.edu

Sequoia Pitch Moth Pest Notes. 2000. P. Svihra and S. H. Dreistadt. University of California Statewide Integrated Pest Management Program. Univ. Calif. Agric. Nat. Res. Publ. 7479. Oakland.

Snails and Slugs Pest Notes. 2003. M. L. Flint. University of California Statewide Integrated Pest Management Program. Univ. Calif. Div. Agric. Nat. Res. Publ. 7427. Oakland.

Soil Solarization: A Natural Mechanism of Integrated Pest Management. 1995. J. J. Stapleton and J. E. DeVay. In *Novel Approaches to Integrated Pest Management,* R. Reuveni, ed. Lewis Publishers. Boca Raton, FL.

Sooty Molds Pest Notes. 2003. F. F. Laemmlen. University of California Statewide Integrated Pest Management Program. Univ. Calif. Div. Agric. Nat. Res. Publ. 74108. Oakland.

Specification Guidelines for Container-Grown Trees. 2002. R. Harris, M. Ozonoff, D. Burger, R. Crudup, B. D. Coate, L. Costello, B. Kempf, B. Hagen, B. Ludekins, J. Wick, J. Geiger, E. Perry, M. Roberts, S. Jones, J. Koch, E. Murdock, and G. McPherson. Urban Tree Foundation. Visalia, CA. www.urbantree.org/newspecs.asp

Spider Mites Pest Notes. 2000. B. Ohlendorf and M. L. Flint, eds. University of California Statewide Integrated Pest Management Program. Univ. Calif. Agric. Nat. Res. Publ. 7405. Oakland.

Spotted Spurge Pest Notes. 2002. D. W. Cudney, C. L. Elmore, and A. Sanders. University of California Statewide Integrated Pest Management Program. Univ. Calif. Agric. Nat. Res. Publ. 7445. Oakland.

Stages of the Cottony Cushion Scale (Icerya purchasi) *and its Natural Enemy, the Vedalia Beetle* (Rodolia cardinalis). 2002. B. Grafton-Cardwell. Univ. Calif. Agric. Nat. Res. Publ. 8051. Oakland.

Staking Landscape Trees. 1982. R. W. Harris, A. T. Leiser, and W. B. Davis. Univ. Calif. Agric. Nat. Res. Publ. 2576. Oakland.

Sticky Trap Monitoring of Insect Pests. 1998. S. H. Dreistadt, J. P. Newman, and K. L. Robb. Univ. Calif. Agric. Nat. Res. Publ. 21572. Oakland.

Sudden Oak Death in California Pest Notes. 2002. B. A. McPherson, D. M. Rizzo, M. Garbelotto, P. Svihra, D. L. Wood, A. J. Storer, N. M. Kelly, N. Palkovsky, S. A. Tjosvold, R. B. Standiford, and S. T. Koike. University of California Statewide Integrated Pest Management Program. Univ. Calif. Agric. Nat. Res. Publ. 7498. Oakland.

Sunset Western Garden Book. 2001. Seventh ed. K. N. Brenzel, ed. Sunset Publishing Co. Menlo Park, CA.

Sycamore Scale Pest Notes. 2000. B. Ohlendorf and M. L. Flint, eds. University of California Statewide Integrated Pest Management Program. Univ. Calif. Agric. Nat. Res. Publ. 7409. Oakland.

A Technical Study of Insects Affecting the Elm Tree in Southern California. 1966. L. R. Brown and C. O. Eads. Calif. Agric. Experiment Stat. Bull. 821.[2]

A Technical Study of Insects Affecting the Oak Tree in Southern California. 1965. L. R. Brown and C. O. Eads. Calif. Agric. Experiment Stat. Bull. 810.[2]

A Technical Study of Insects Affecting the Sycamore Tree in Southern California. 1965. L. R. Brown and E. O. Eads. Calif. Agric. Experiment Stat. Bull. 818.[2]

Termites Pest Notes. 2001. V. R. Lewis. University of California Statewide Integrated Pest Management Program. Univ. Calif. Agric. Nat. Res. Publ. 7415. Oakland.

Thrips Pest Notes. 2001. S. H. Dreistadt and P. A. Phillips. University of California Statewide Integrated Pest Management Program. Univ. Calif. Agric. Nat. Res. Publ. 7429. Oakland

Training Young Trees for Structure and Form. 1999. L. R. Costello. Univ. Calif. Agric. Nat. Res. Video V99A. Oakland.

Trees and Development: A Technical Guide to Preservation of Trees During Land Development. 1998. N. Matheny and J. Clark. International Society of Arboriculture. Champaign, IL.

Trees and Shrubs of California. 2001. J. D. Stuart and J. O. Sawyer. Univ. Calif. Press. Berkeley.

Trees for Saving Energy. 1991. R. Thayer. Univ. Calif. Agric. Nat. Res. Publ. 21485. Oakland.

Trees Under Power Lines: A Homeowner's Guide. 1989. L. R. Costello, A. M. Berry, F. J. Chan, and R. R. Novembri. Univ. Calif. Agric. Nat. Res. Publ. 21470. Oakland.

Turfgrass Insects of the United States and Canada. 2nd ed. 1999. P. J. Vittum, M. G. Villani, and H. Tashiro. Cornell Univ. Press. Ithaca, NY.

Turfgrass Pests. 1989. A. D. Ali and C. L. Elmore, eds. Univ. Calif. Agric. Nat. Res. Publ. 4053. Oakland.

Twig Blight and Branch Dieback of Oaks in California. 1989. L. R. Costello, E. I. Hecht-Poinar, and J. R. Parmeter. Univ. Calif. Agric. Nat. Res. Publ. 21462. Oakland.

UC Guide to Solving Garden and Landscape Problems. 2000. M. L. Flint, P. Geisel, J. Strand, and C. A. Reynolds. University of California Statewide Integrated Pest Management Program. Univ. Calif. Agric. Nat. Res. Publ. 3400. CD-ROM. Oakland.

Urban Entomology. 1978. W. Ebeling. Univ. Calif. Div. Agric. Sci. Berkeley.[2]

Voles (Meadow Mice) Pest Notes. 2002. T. P. Salmon and W. P. Gorenzel. University of California Statewide Integrated Pest Management Program. Univ. Calif. Agric. Nat. Res. Publ. 7439. Oakland.

Walnut Husk Fly Pest Notes. 2000. B. Ohlendorf, ed. University of California Statewide Integrated Pest Management Program. Univ. Calif. Agric. Nat. Res. Publ. 7430. Oakland.

Walnut Pest Management Guidelines. 2000. B. L. Teviotdale, W. D. Gubler (Diseases); W. J. Bentley, W. W. Coates, J. Hasey, L. C. Hendricks, W. H. Olson, C. Pickel, G. S. Sibbett, R. A. Van Steenwyk (Insects and Mites); B. B. Westerdahl, and U. C. Kodira (Nematodes). University of California Statewide Integrated Pest Management Program. Univ. Calif. Agric. Nat. Res. Publ. 3471. Oakland.

Water Conservation Tips for the Home Lawn and Garden. 2001. P. M. Geisel and C. L. Unruh. Univ. Calif. Agric. Nat. Res. Publ. 8036. Oakland.

Water Management. 2002. J. Hartin and B. Faber. In *California Master Gardener Handbook,* D. R. Pittenger, ed. Univ. Calif. Agric. Nat. Res. Publ. 3382. Oakland.

Water Quality: Its Effects on Ornamental Plants. 1985. D. S. Farnham, R. F. Hasek, and J. L. Paul. Univ. Calif. Div. Agric. Nat. Res. Leaflet 2995. Oakland.

Weed Management in Landscapes Pest Notes. 2001. C. Wilen and C. L. Elmore. University of California Statewide Integrated Pest Management Program. Univ. Calif. Agric. Nat. Res. Publ. 7441. Oakland.

Weeds of California. 1970. W. Robbins, M. Bellue, and W. Ball. State of California Documents and Publications. North Highlands, CA.

Weeds of the West. 1991. T. D. Whitson, L. C. Burrill, S. A. Dewey, D. W. Cudney, B. E. Nelson, R. D. Lee, and R. Parker. Wyoming Agric. Extension. Jackson, WY. Available as Univ. Calif. Agric. Nat. Res. Publ. 3350. Oakland.

Western Fertilizer Handbook: 2nd Horticultural Edition. 1998. California Fertilizer Association. Interstate. Danville, IL.

Western Forest Insects. 1977. R. L. Furniss and V. M. Carolin. U. S. Dept. Agric. Misc. Pub. 1339. Washington, DC.[2]

Wild Blackberries Pest Notes. 2002. J. M. DiTomaso. University of California Statewide Integrated Pest Management Program. Univ. Calif. Agric. Nat. Res. Publ. 7434. Oakland.

Whiteflies Pest Notes. 2002. M. L. Flint. University of California Statewide Integrated Pest Management Program. Univ. Calif. Agric. Nat. Res. Publ. 7401. Oakland.

Wildlife Pest Control around Gardens and Homes. 1984. T. P. Salmon and R. E. Lickliter. Univ. Calif. Agric. Nat. Res. Publ. 21385. Oakland.

Wood Decay Fungi in Landscape Trees Pest Notes. 2003. G. W. Hickman and E. J. Perry. University of California Statewide Integrated Pest Management Program. Univ. Calif. Agric. Nat. Res. Publ. 74109. Oakland.

Wood Preservation. 1992. P. J. Marer and M. Grimes. University of California Statewide Integrated Pest Management Program. Univ. Calif. Agric. Nat. Res. Publ. 3335. Oakland.

Wood Wasps and Horntails Pest Notes. 2000. E. C. Mussen. University of California Statewide Integrated Pest Management Program. Univ. Calif. Agric. Nat. Res. Publ. 7407. Oakland.

Woody Landscape Plants. 2002. D. R. Hodel and D. R. Pittenger. In *California Master Gardener Handbook,* D. R. Pittenger, ed. Univ. Calif. Agric. Nat. Res. Publ. 3382. Oakland.

Yellow Starthistle Pest Notes. 1999. J. M. DiTomaso, W. Thomas Lanini, C. D. Thomsen, T. S. Prather, C. E. Turner, M. J. Smith, C. L. Elmore, M. P. Vayssieres, and W. A. Williams. University of California Statewide Integrated Pest Management Program. Univ. Calif. Agric. Nat. Res. Publ. 7402. Oakland.

1. University of California Publications are available for free download (in certain instances) or can be purchased by visiting the http://anrcatalog.ucdavis.edu or www.ipm.ucdavis.edu World Wide Web sites.

2. Publications out of print. Copies may be available for reference at libraries.

Names of Pests and Plants

BOTH COMMON and scientific names are used to identify organisms. Because different humans (*Homo sapiens*) may use different names for the same organism, names are often a source of confusion.

Scientists use a unique two-word combination for each animal, plant, and microorganism. This scientific name provides the surest identification because scientific names are used according to agreed-upon rules. Although scientific names are sometimes changed based on new information, each organism has only one valid scientific name, which is used throughout the world. If a scientific name has recently been changed, both names may be printed: *Cotesia* (=*Apanteles*), with the currently correct name listed first followed by an equal sign and the former name (sometimes in parentheses).

The first word of a scientific name, the genus or generic name, is capitalized. The second word, the species or specific name, is not. Both words are italicized and are also Latinized so scientists can understand what plant or animal others are referring to, regardless of nationality and native language. After its first use in the text, the genus name is often abbreviated; for example, *Eucalyptus globulus* is shortened to *E. globulus*. When several species within the same genus are discussed together, species may be abbreviated as "spp." (e.g., *Eucalyptus* spp.). When referring to only one species, "sp." is used. A third scientific name, subspecies (abbreviated ssp.), may also be used: *Bacillus thuringiensis* subspecies *tenebrionis*, or *B. thuringiensis* ssp. *tenebrionis*. Subspecies are especially common among microorganisms. Other subspecies-type categories used by plant pathologists for certain organisms listed in this book include special forms, or *forma specialis* (f. sp.), and pathovar (pv). For example, *Ceratocystis fimbriata* f. sp. *platani* is a wilt fungus that causes canker stain of sycamore. *Xanthomonas campestris* pv. *hederae* is a leaf spot bacterium that infects ivy.

Scientific names are used in a hierarchical organization that includes the order and family names. These hierarchical names show relationships among organisms, as illustrated here for the common convergent lady beetle:

Kingdom: Animalia (animals)
Class: Insecta (insects)
Order: Coleoptera (beetles)
Family: Coccinellidae
(lady beetles)
Genus: *Hippodamia*
Species: *convergens*

Besides the two-part scientific name, many plants, insects, and diseases also have common names. Common names are familiar to more people than scientific names, and they are often easier to pronounce and remember. However, there are serious problems with common names. There are no clear rules for deciding what is the correct common name of most organisms. A single common name is often used to refer to several distinctly different organisms. The same organism can have several common names, some of which may be known and used only by people in certain locations. Common names may also be inaccurate; pineapple refers to a plant that is very unlike pines and apples. Ladybug refers to certain beetles, which are very different from the insects that scientists call true bugs. The sequoia pitch moth (*Synanthedon sequoiae*) infests only pines; sequoia pitch moth never attacks giant sequoia (*Sequoiadendron giganteum*) or coast redwood (*Sequoia sempervirens*). Many important organisms, including most species of beneficial predators, parasites, and pathogens, have no common name, often because they are tiny or known mostly only to scientists.

Both common and scientific names are used in this book. Pest scientific and common names are given in the index, and both names are used together in the major section discussing that pest as listed in the table of contents. Scientific names and common names are also used in the "Tree and Shrub Pest Tables" for pests not detailed elsewhere.

Plant scientific names are generally avoided, except in the index and tables. Common names are more widely known for most plants and can be found in other references, such as the *Sunset Western Garden Book* (Brenzel 2001) and *Trees and Shrubs of California* (Stuart and Sawyer 2001). Some plants are mentioned so often that using their scientific names in this book would consume much space and be awkward. For many plants, such as camellia, citrus, and rhododendron, the genus name and common name are the same, except that the common name is not capitalized or italicized. Exceptions include plants named after people, such as Douglas-fir, which is capitalized because the tree is named for the nineteenth-century botanist David Douglas.

Sources for names used in this book include: *An Annotated Checklist of Woody Ornamental Plants of California, Oregon, and Washington* (McClintock and Leiser 1979), *Common Names of Arachnids* (Breene 1995), *Common Names of Insects and Related Organisms 1997* (Bosik 1997), *Composite List of Weeds* (Alex et al. 1989), *Fungi on Plants and Plant Products in the United States* (Farr et al. 1989), and *The Jepson Manual: Higher Plants of California* (Hickman 1993).

Glossary

abdomen. The posterior body division of an arthropod.

abiotic disorder. A disease caused by factors other than a pathogen, such as adverse environmental conditions or inappropriate cultural practices.

alkaline. Basic, having a high pH or pH greater than 7.

alkalinity. A measure of the ability to neutralize or buffer acids; sometimes used to mean alkaline or having a high pH, but high alkalinity and high pH are not the same.

allelopathy. The ability of a plant species to produce substances that are toxic to certain other plants.

annual. A plant that normally completes its life cycle of seed germination, vegetative growth, reproduction, and death in a single year.

antenna (pl., **antennae**). The paired segmented sensory organs on each side of the head.

ascospores. A spore produced within the saclike cell of the sexual state of a fungus.

auricle. A small earlike projection from the base of a leaf or petal.

available water. The amount of water held in the soil that can be extracted by plants.

B.t. or **Bt.** Abbreviations for *Bacillus thuringiensis*.

***Bacillus thuringiensis*.** A bacterium that causes disease in certain insects, most commonly caterpillars; formulations of the several subspecies of B.t. are used as insecticides.

bacterium (pl., **bacteria**). A single-celled, microscopic organism that lacks a nucleus. Some bacteria cause plant or animal diseases.

biofix. An identifiable event that signals when to begin degree-day accumulation.

biological control. The action of parasites, predators, or pathogens in maintaining another organism's population density at a lower average level than would occur in their absence. Biological control may occur naturally in the field or result from manipulation or introduction of biological control agents (natural enemies) by people.

biotic disease. Disease caused by a pathogen, such as a bacterium, fungus, phytoplasma, or virus.

botanical. Derived from plants or plant parts, as with pyrethrin insecticides.

broad-spectrum pesticide. A pesticide that kills a large number of unrelated species.

cambium. Thin layer of undifferentiated, actively growing plant tissue between the phloem and the xylem.

canker. A dead, discolored, often sunken area (lesion) on a branch, root, stem, or trunk.

canopy. The leafy parts of vines or trees.

caterpillar. The immature stage of butterflies and moths.

chlorophyll. The green pigment of plants that captures the energy from sunlight necessary for photosynthesis.

chlorosis. Yellowing or bleaching of normally green plant tissue.

cornicle. Two tubular structures projecting from the rear of an aphid's abdomen.

cotyledon. A leaf formed within the seed and present on a seedling at germination; seed leaf. Cotyledons typically have a different appearance than true leaves, which develop entirely after a seed germinates.

crawler. The active first instar of certain types of insects, such as scales and mealybugs.

crochets. Tiny hooks on the prolegs of caterpillars.

cross resistance. In pest management, resistance of a pest population to a pesticide to which it has not been exposed that accompanies the development of resistance to a pesticide to which it has been exposed.

crown. The plant part near the soil surface where the main stem (trunk) and roots join. Also used in forestry to refer to the topmost limbs on a tree or shrub.

cultivar. An identifiable strain within a plant species that is specifically bred for particular properties; sometimes used synonymously with *variety*.

degree-day. A unit combining temperature and time that is used in monitoring growth and development of organisms. Also called heat unit.

delayed dormant. The treatment period beginning when buds begin to swell and ending with the beginning of green tip development or just before the emergence of new leaves.

developmental threshold. The lowest temperature at which growth occurs in a given species.

diapause. A period of physiologically controlled inactivity or dormancy in insects.

disease. Any disturbance of a plant that interferes with its normal structure, function, or economic value; unhealthy conditions that result from an interaction among the host plant, its environment, and causal agents such as pathogenic microorganisms.

dormant. Inactive during periods of adverse environmental conditions, commonly during winter or cold weather.

drift. The aerial dispersal of a substance such as a pesticide beyond the intended application area.

dwarfing. Stunting of normal growth characterized in plants by smaller-than-normal leaves and stems.

entomopathogenic nematodes. Nematodes that, in combination with symbiotic bacteria, kill insects.

evapotranspiration. The loss of soil moisture due to evaporation from the soil surface and transpiration by plants.

field capacity. The amount of water held in soil after saturation and the drainage and runoff of excess water.

frass. Solid fecal material produced by certain insects.

fruiting bodies. In fungi, reproductive structures containing spores.

fungicide. A pesticide used to control fungi.

fungus (pl., **fungi**). A multicellular, generally microscopic organism lacking chlorophyll, such as mildew, mold, rust, or smut. The fungus body normally consists of filamentous strands called mycelium and reproduces through dispersal of spores.

gall. Localized swelling or outgrowth of plant tissue, often formed by the plant in response to the action of an insect, pathogen, or other pest.

girdle. Damage that completely encircles a stem or root, often resulting in death of plant parts above or below the girdle.

ground cover. Any of various low, dense-growing plants, such as ivy and pachysandra, used for covering the ground, as in places where it is difficult to grow grass.

hazard. The risk of danger from pesticides. Hazard, or risk, is a function of two factors—toxicity and potential exposure to the toxic substance.

heat unit. *See* **degree-day**.

herbicide. A pesticide used to control weeds.

honeydew. An excretion from insects, such as aphids, mealybugs, whiteflies, and soft scales, consisting of modified plant sap and composed mostly of water and sugars.

horticultural oils. Highly refined petroleum (or plant-derived) oils that are manufactured specifically to control pests on plants.

host. A plant or animal that provides sustenance for another organism.

hypha. (pl., **hyphae**). One of the filaments forming the body (vegetative, nonreproductive structure), or mycelium, of a fungus.

inorganic. Containing no carbon; generally used to indicate materials (for example, fertilizers) that are of mineral origin.

instar. The larval or nymphal stage of an immature insect between successive molts.

integrated pest management (IPM). A pest management strategy that focuses on long-term prevention or suppression of pest problems through a combination of techniques such as encouraging biological control, using resistant varieties, and adopting alternate cultural practices such as modifying irrigation or pruning to make the habitat less conducive to pest development. Pesticides are used only when careful monitoring indicates they are needed according to preestablished guidelines or treatment thresholds, or to prevent pests from significantly interfering with the purposes for which plants are being grown.

invertebrate. An animal having no internal skeleton, such as an earthworm or insect.

juvenile. Immature form of a nematode that hatches from an egg and molts several times before becoming an adult.

larva (pl., **larvae**). The immature form of insects that develop through complete metamorphosis including egg, several larval stages, pupa, and adult. In mites, the first-stage immature is also called a larva.

lesion. Localized area of diseased or discolored tissue.

ligule. In many grasses, a short membranous projection on the inner side of the leaf blade at the point where the leaf blade and leaf sheath meet.

mandibles. Jaws; the forward-most pair of mouthparts of an insect.

metamorphosis. The change in form that takes place as insects grow from an immature to adult.

microbial pesticides. Bacteria, fungi, viruses, or other microorganisms that are commercially produced for control of invertebrates, plant pathogens, or weeds.

microorganism. An organism of microscopic size, such as a bacterium, fungus, phytoplasma, or virus.

molt. In insects and other arthropods, the forming of a new cuticle (skin) that precedes shedding of the old skin (ecdysis), part of the process of development into a larger and older instar or metamorphosis into the next life stage.

monitoring. Carefully watching and recording information on the abundance, activities, development, and growth of organisms or other factors on a regular basis over a period of time, often utilizing very specific procedures.

mulch. A layer of material placed on the soil surface to prevent weed growth and improve plant health.

mummy. The crusty skin of an aphid whose inside has been consumed by a parasite. An unharvested nut remaining on the tree.

mycelium. A mass of branching or interwoven hyphae that are the vegetative (nonreproductive) structure on most true fungi.

mycoplasma. Living organisms smaller than bacteria, now called phytoplasmas; they have a unit membrane but no cell wall as do bacteria.

mycorrhizae. Beneficial associations between plant roots and fungi.

narrow-range oil. A highly refined petroleum or plant-derived oil that is manufactured specifically to control pests on plants; also called superior, supreme, or horticultural oil.

natural enemies. Predators, parasites, or pathogens that are considered beneficial because they attack and kill pests. The organisms are used in the biological control of pests.

necrosis. Death of tissue accompanied by dark discoloration, usually occurring in a well-defined part of a plant, such as the portion of a leaf between leaf veins or the xylem or phloem in a stem or tuber.

nymph. Immature stage of insects that develop through incomplete metamorphosis, such as aphids, grasshoppers, leafhoppers, mealybugs, and true bugs that hatch from eggs and gradually acquire adult form through a series of molts without passing through a pupal stage.

organic. A material (e.g., a pesticide) whose molecules contain carbon and hydrogen atoms. Also refers to plants or animals that are grown without the use of synthetic fertilizers or pesticides.

oviposit. To lay or deposit eggs.

parasite. An organism that lives and feeds in or on a larger organism (the host) without killing the host directly. Also, an insect that spends its immature stages in or on the body of a host that dies just before the parasite emerges (this type is more accurately called a parasitoid). Unlike many other parasites, adult parasitoids are free-living.

pathogen. A disease-causing organism.

perennial. A plant that can live 3 or more years and flower at least twice.

pest resurgence. Rapid rebound of a pest population after it has been controlled.

pesticide. Any substance or mixture intended for preventing, destroying, repelling, killing, or mitigating problems caused by fungi, insects, nematodes, rodents, weeds, or other pests; and any other substance or mixture intended for use as a plant growth regulator, defoliant, or desiccant.

pesticide resistance. The ability of an organism to survive a pesticide application at doses that once killed most individuals of the same species, an ability acquired by subsequent generations through genetic selection.

petiole. The stalk connecting a leaf to a stem.

pH. A value used to express the relative degree of acidic or basic conditions; the hydrogen ion concentration as expressed in a negative logarithmic scale ranging from 0 to 14.

pheromone. A substance secreted by an organism to affect the behavior or development of other members of the same species. Sex pheromones that attract the opposite sex for mating are used in monitoring or management of certain insects.

phloem. The food-conducting tissue of a plant, made up of sieve tubes, companion cells, phloem parenchyma, and fibers.

photosynthesis. The process by which plants convert sunlight into energy.

phytoplasma. Living organisms smaller than bacteria, formerly called mycoplasmas or mycoplasmalike organisms; they have a unit membrane but no cell wall, as do bacteria.

phytotoxicity. Ability of a material such as a pesticide or fertilizer to cause injury to plants.

postemergence herbicide. Herbicide applied after the emergence of weeds.

predator. Organism (including certain insects and mites) that attacks, kills, and feeds on several or many other individuals (its prey) during its lifetime.

preemergence herbicide. Herbicide applied before emergence of weeds.

presence/absence sampling. A sampling method that involves recording only whether members of the population being sampled (such as an insect pest) are present or absent on a sample unit (such as a leaf), rather than counting the numbers of individuals. Also called binomial sampling.

proleg. A fleshy, unsegmented leglike appendage, as on the abdomen of caterpillars; the presence, location, and number of these appendages help to distinguish among larvae of different types of insects, such as larvae of moths in comparison with those of beetles or sawflies.

propagules. Any part of an organism from which progeny can grow, including bulbs, tubers, and seeds of plants, and sclerotia and spores of fungi.

prothorax. The anterior of the three thoracic segments of an insect.

pupa (pl., **pupae**). Nonfeeding stage between larva and adult in insects with complete metamorphosis.

pupate. To develop from the larval stage to the pupa.

resistant. Able to tolerate conditions (such as pesticide sprays or pest damage) harmful to other species or other strains of the same species, but not immune to such conditions.

rhizome. A horizontal, underground shoot, especially one that forms roots at the nodes to produce new plants.

rogue. To remove diseased or undesirable plants.

sanitation. Activity that reduces the spread of pathogen inoculum, such as removal and destruction of infected plant parts or cleaning of contaminated tools and equipment.

sclerotium (pl., **sclerotia**). A compact mass of hardened mycelium that serves as a dormant stage in some fungi.

secondary outbreak. The increase in the number of a nontarget species to harmful (pest) levels following a pesticide application to control a different species that was the target pest; caused by destruction of natural enemies that normally control the nontarget species.

sedges. Group of grasslike herbaceous plants that, unlike grasses, have unjointed stems. Stems are usually solid and often triangular in cross-section.

seed leaf. Leaf formed in a seed and present on a seedling at germination; cotyledon.

selective pesticide. Pesticides that are toxic primarily to the target pest (and often related species), leaving most other organisms, including natural enemies, unharmed.

sign. Presence of pathogen reproductive structures (e.g., mushrooms or rust pustules) or vegetative structures (hyphae, mycelium) that indicate that plants may be diseased.

solarization. Heating soil to temperatures that are lethal to pests by applying clear plastic to the soil surface for 4 to 6 weeks to capture solar energy during warm, sunny weather.

sooty mold. Dark coating on foliage or fruit formed by the mycelia of fungi that live on honeydew secreted by certain insects.

spore. Seedlike reproductive structure produced by certain fungi and other organisms that is capable of growing into a new individual under proper conditions.

stolon. Trailing aboveground stem or shoot, often rooting at the nodes and forming new plants.

symptom. Outward expression by a host that it is unhealthy, such as chlorosis, necrosis, or wilting that occurs in diseased plants.

synthetic organic pesticides. Manufactured pesticides produced from petroleum and containing largely carbon and hydrogen atoms in their basic structure.

systemic. Capable of moving throughout a plant or other organism, usually in the vascular system.

target pest. A pest species that a control action is intended to manage.

tensiometer. Device for measuring soil moisture, such as a mechanical device consisting of a buried tube of water that develops a partial vacuum as surrounding soil dries out.

terminal. The growing tip of a stem, especially the main stem.

thorax. The second of three major divisions in the body of an insect, and the one bearing the legs and (if present) wings.

tolerance. Inherent lack of susceptibility to a pesticide. Also, the ability of a plant to grow in spite of infection by a pathogen.

translocated herbicide. Herbicide that is able to move throughout a plant after being applied to leaf surfaces.

transpiration. Evaporation of water vapor from plants, mostly through tiny leaf openings (stomata).

tuber. An enlarged, fleshy, underground stem with buds capable of producing new plants.

vascular system. The system of plant tissues that conducts water, mineral nutrients, and products of photosynthesis through the plant, consisting of the xylem and phloem.

vector. Organism able to transport and transmit a pathogen to a host.

virus. Noncellular, submicroscopic particle that can multiply only within living cells of other organisms and is capable of producing disease symptoms in some plants and animals.

xylem. Plant tissue that conducts water and nutrients from the roots up through the plant.

Literature Cited

THESE PUBLICATIONS are cited in figures and tables as the sources of information and illustrations. For publications referred to in text as sources of further information, see the Suggested Reading.[1]

Adams, D. Undated. *Pitch Canker–An Introduced Disease*. Davis, CA: Calif. Dept. Forestry Fire Protection. Unpublished.

Agrios, G. N. 1997. *Plant Pathology*. 4th ed. San Diego: Academic Press.

Ahrens, W. H., ed. 1994. *Herbicide Handbook*. 7th ed. Champaign, IL: Weed Science Society of American.

Anonymous. 1990. *Western Fertilizer Handbook: 2nd Horticulture Edition*. Danville, IL: Interstate.

Antonelli, A. L., and R. L. Campbell. 1984. *Root Weevil Control on Rhododendrons*. Pullman: Washington State Univ. Extension. Bull. 0970.

Bosik, J. J., ed. 1997. *Common Names of Insects and Related Organisms 1997*. Lanham, MD: Entomological Society of America.

Brennan, E. B., G. F. Hrusa, S. A. Weinbaum, and W. Levison. 2001. Resistance of *Eucalyptus* species to *Glycaspis brimblecombei* (Homoptera: Psyllidae) in the San Francisco Bay Area. *Pan-Pacific Entomologist* 77: 249–253.

Cooke, A., ed. 1999. *Powdery Mildew: Crapemyrtle Cultivars*. Carthage: North Carolina State Univ. Coop. Extension Moore County. HortNews 7(4).

Costello, L. R., C. S. Koehler, and W. W. Allen. 1987. *Fuchsia Gall Mite*. Oakland: Univ. Calif. Agric. Nat. Res. Publ. 7179.

Croft, B. A. 1990. *Arthropod Biological Control Agents and Pesticides*. New York: Wiley.

Dahlsten, D., S. Dreistadt, and T. Paine. 2000. *Bark Beetles Pest Notes*. University of California Statewide Integrated Pest Management Program. Oakland: Univ. Calif. Agric. Nat. Res. Publ. 7421.

Dahlsten, D. L., S. M. Tait, D. L. Rowney, and B. J. Gingg. 1993. A monitoring system and development of ecologically sound treatments for elm leaf beetle. *J. Arboriculture* 19: 181–186.

Dallara, P. L., A. J. Storer, T. R. Gordon, and D. L. Wood. 1995. *Current Status of Pitch Canker Disease in California*. Sacramento: Calif. Dept. For. Fire Protection. Tree Notes 20.

Davidson, N. A., J. E. Dibble, M. L. Flint, P. J. Marer, and A. Guye. 1991. *Managing Insects and Mites with Spray Oils*. University of California Statewide Integrated Pest Management Program. Oakland: Univ. Calif. Agric. Nat. Res. Publ. 3347.

Derr, J. F., J. C. Neal, L. J. Kuhns, R. J. Smeda, L. A. Weston, C. Elmore, C. A. Wilen, J. Ahrens, A. Senesac, and T. Mervosh. 1997. Weed Management in Landscape and Nursery Plantings. In *Weed Management in Horticultural Crops*, M. E. McGiffen, ed. Alexandria, VA: American Society for Horticultural Science.

Dreistadt, S. H. 2001. *Integrated Pest Management for Floriculture and Nurseries*. University of California Statewide Integrated Pest Management Program. Oakland: Univ. Calif. Agric. Nat. Res. Publ. 3402.

Dreistadt, S. H., and D. L. Dahlsten. 2001. *Psyllids Pest Notes*. University of California Statewide Integrated Pest Management Program. Oakland: Univ. Calif. Agric. Nat. Res. Publ. 7423.

Dreistadt, S. H., and M. L. Flint. 1996. Melon aphid (Homoptera: Aphididae) control by inundative convergent lady beetle (Coleoptera: Coccinellidae) release on chrysanthemum. *Environ. Entomol.* 25: 688–697.

Easterbrook, M. A. 1992. The possibilities for control of two-spotted spider mite *Tetranychus urticae* on field-grown strawberries in the UK by predatory mites. *Biocontrol Sci. Tech.* 2: 235–245.

Elmore, C. L., J. J. Stapleton, C. E. Bell, and J. E. DeVay. 1997. *Soil Solarization: A Nonpesticidal Method for Controlling Diseases, Nematodes, and Weeds*. Oakland: Univ. Calif. Agric. Nat. Res. Publ. 21377.

Fan, Y., and F. L. Petitt. 1994. Biological control of broad mite, *Polyphagotarsonemus latus* (Banks), by *Neoseiulus barkeri* Hughes on pepper. *Biol. Control* 4: 390–395.

Farnham, D. S., R. F. Hasek, and J. L. Paul. 1985. *Water Quality: Its Effects on Ornamental Plants*. Oakland: Univ. Calif. Agric. Nat. Res. Publ. 2995.

Farr, D. F., G. F. Bills, G. P. Chamuris, and A. Y. Rossman. 1989. *Fungi on Plants and Plant Products in the United States*. St. Paul, MN: American Phytopathological Society.

Frankie, G. W., J. B. Fraser, and J. F. Barthell. 1986. Geographic distribution of *Synanthedon sequoia* and host plant susceptibility on Monterey pine in adventive and native stands in California (Lepidoptera: Sesiidae). *Pan-Pacific Entomologist* 62:29–40.

Garrison, R. W. 1993. New Agricultural Pest For Southern California: Black Vine Weevil (*Otiorhynchus sulcatus*). El Monte, CA: Los Angeles County Department of Agriculture.

Gouveia, P., B. Ohlendorf, and M. L. Flint, eds. 1999. *Anthracnose Pest Notes*. University of California Statewide Integrated Pest Management Program. Oakland: Univ. Calif. Agric. Nat. Res. Publ. 7420.

Hanks, L. M., T. D. Paine, J. G. Millar, and J. L. Hom. 1995. Variation among *Eucalyptus* species in resistance to eucalyptus longhorned borer in southern California. *Entomologia Experimentalis et Applicata* 74: 185–194.

Hassan, S. A., F. Bigler, H. Bogenschütz, E. Boller, J. Brun, J. N. M. Calis, J. Coremans-Pelseneer, C. Duso, A. Grove, U. Heimbach, N. Helyer, H. Hokkanen, G. B. Lewis, F. Mansour, L. Moreth, L. Polgar, L. Samsøe-Petersen, B. Sauphanor, A. Stäubli, G. Sterk, A. Vainio, M. van de Veire, G. Viggiani, and H. Vogt. 1994. Results of the sixth joint pesticide testing programme of the IOBC/WPRS working group-pesticides and beneficial organisms. *Entomophaga* 39: 107–119.

Herbicide Resistance Action Committee. 2000. *Classification of Herbicides According to Mode of Action*. http://plantprotection.org/HRAC/MOA.html

Hickman, G. W., and P. Svihra. 2001. *Planting Landscape Trees*. Oakland: Univ. Calif. Agric. Nat. Res. Publ. 8046.

Horst, R. K. 1985. *Compendium of Rose Diseases*. St. Paul, MN: APS Press.

Jepson, P. C., ed. 1989. *Pesticides and Nontarget Invertebrates*. Wimborne, UK: Intercept.

Johnson, S. G. Undated. *Living Among the Oaks*. Berkeley: Univ. Calf. Coop. Extension Nat. Resource Program. Available as Univ. Calif. Agric. Nat. Res. Publ. 21538.

Kabashima, J. N., J. D. MacDonald, S. H. Dreistadt, and D. E. Ullman. 1997. *Easy On-Site Tests for Fungi and Viruses in Nurseries and Greenhouses.* Oakland: Univ. Calif. Agric. Nat. Res. Publ. 8002.

Kaya, H. K. 1993. Contemporary issues in biological control with entomopathogenic nematodes. Taipei City, Taiwan: *Food and Fertilizer Technology Center Extension Bull.* 375.

Knox, G. W. 2000. *Crape Myrtle in Florida.* Monticello: Florida Coop. Extension Serv. Fact Sheet ENH-52.

Koehler, C. S., W. W. Allen, and L. R. Costello. 1985. Fuchsia gall mite management. *Calif. Agric.* 39(7, 8): 10–12.

Koehler, C. S., and W. W. Moore. 1983. Resistance of several members of the Cupressaceae to the cypress tip miner, *Argyresthia cupressella.* J. Environ. Hort. 1: 87–88.

Koehler, C. S., W. S. Moore, and B. Coate. 1983. Resistance of *Acacia* to the acacia psyllid, *Psylla uncatoides.* J. Environ. Hort. 1: 65–67.

Marer, P. J. 1991. *Residential, Industrial, and Institutional Pest Control.* University of California Statewide Integrated Pest Management Program. Oakland: Univ. Calif. Div. Agric. Nat. Res. Publ. 3334.

Marer, P. J., M. Grimes, and R. Cromwell. 1995. *Forest and Right-of-Way Pest Control.* University of California Statewide Integrated Pest Management Program. Oakland: Univ. Calif. Div. Agric. Nat. Res. Publ. 3336.

Martin, C. A., H. G. Ponder, and C. H. Gilliam. 1991. Evaluation of landscape fabrics in suppressing growth of weed species. *J. Environ. Hort.* 9: 38–40.

McCain, A. H., R. D. Raabe, and S. Wilhelm. 1981. *Plants Resistant or Susceptible to Verticillium Wilt.* Oakland: Univ. Calif. Agric. Nat. Res. Publ. 2703.

Munro, J. A. 1963. Biology of the ceanothus stem-gall moth, *Periploca ceanothiella,* with consideration of its control. *J. Res. Lepid.* 1: 183–190.

O'Connor-Marer, P. J. 2000. *The Safe and Effective Use of Pesticides.* 2d ed. University of California Statewide Integrated Pest Management Program. Oakland: Univ. Calif. Div. Agric. Nat. Res. Publ. 3324.

Ohlendorf, B., and M. L. Flint, eds. 1999. *Fire Blight Pest Notes.* University of California Statewide Integrated Pest Management Program. Oakland: Univ. Calif. Agric. Nat. Res. Publ. 7414.

Ohr, H. D., J. A. Menge (Diseases); E. E. Grafton-Cardwell, J. G. Morse, N. V. O'Connell, P. A. Phillips (Insects, Mites, and Snails); and B. B. Westerdahl (Nematodes). *Citrus Pest Management Guidelines.* 2002. Oakland: Univ. Calif. Agric. Nat. Res. Publ. 3441.

Ohr, H. D., G. A. Zentmyer, E. C. Pond, and L. J. Klure. 1980. *Plants in California Susceptible to Phytophthora cinnamomi.* Oakland: Univ. Calif. Agric. Nat. Res. Publ. 21178.

Osborne, L. S., L. E. Ehler, and J. R. Nechols. 1985. *Biological Control of Twospotted Spider Mite in Greenhouses.* Gainesville: Univ. Florida Agric. Exp. Sta. Bull. 853.

Peterson, A. 1956. *Larvae of Insects.* Part 1. Ann Arbor, MI: Edwards Brothers.

———. 1960. *Larvae of Insects.* Part 2. Ann Arbor, MI: Edwards Brothers.

Raabe, R. D. 1979. *Resistance or Susceptibility of Certain Plants to Armillaria Root Rot.* Oakland: Univ. Calif. Agric. Nat. Res. Publ. Publ. 2591.

Retzinger, E. J., and C. Mallory-Smith. 1997. Classification of herbicides by site of action for weed resistance management strategies. *Weed Technology* 11: 384–393.

Scriven, G. T., and R. F. Luck. 1980. Susceptibility of pines to attack by the Nantucket pine tip moth in southern California. *J. Econ. Entomol.* 73: 318–320.

Smith, R. F., and K. S. Hagen. 1956. Enemies of spotted alfalfa aphid. *Calif. Agric.* 10(4): 8–10.

Stapleton, J. J., and J. E. DeVay. 1995. Soil solarization: A Natural Mechanism of Integrated Pest Management. In R. Reuveni, ed. *Novel Approaches to Integrated Pest Management.* Boca Raton, FL: Lewis Publ. 309–322.

Storer, A. J., T. R. Gordon, P. L. Dallara, and D. L. Wood. 1994. Pitch canker kills pines, spreads to new species and regions. *Calif. Agric.* 48(6): 9–13.

Svihra, P. 1994. Principles of eradicative pruning. *J. Arboriculture* 20: 262–272.

———. 1999. Sudden Death of Tanoak, *Lithocarpus densiflorus.* Novato, CA: Univ. Calif. Coop. Ext. Marin County Pest Alert 1.

Svihra, P., and B. Duckles. 1999. Bronze Birch Borer. Novato, CA: Univ. Calif. Coop. Ext. Marin County. Pest Alert 2.

Teviotdale, B. L. 1991. Further Tests on Effectiveness of Disinfectants for Preventing Transmission of Fireblight. Kearney: Univ. Calif. Plant Protection Quarterly 1(2): 5–6.

———. 1992. Efficacy of Trisodium Phosphate and Sodium Hypochlorite as Disinfectants to Prevent Transmission of Fire Blight. Kearney: Univ. Calif. Plant Protection Quarterly 2(2): 9–10.

Teviotdale, B. L., M. F. Wiley, and D. H. Harper. 1991. How disinfectants compare in preventing transmission of fire blight. *Calif. Agric.* 45(4): 21–23.

Ware, G. W. 1983. *Pesticides: Theory and Application.* San Francisco: W. H. Freeman.

Weller, S. C., and F. D. Hess. 1997. Herbicide use and mode of action. In M. E. McGriffen, ed. *Weed Management in Horticultural Crops.* Alexandria, VA: American Society for Horticultural Science. 74–115.

Whitson, T. D., L. C. Burrill, S. A. Dewey, D. W. Cudney, B. E. Nelson, R. D. Lee, and R. Parker. 1991. *Weeds of the West.* Jackson, WY: University of Wyoming. Available as Univ. Calif. Agric. Nat. Res. Public. 3350.

Yang, J., and C. S. Sandof. 1995. Variegation in *Coleus blumei* and life history of citrus mealybug (Homoptera: Pseudococcidae). *Environ. Entomol.* 24: 1650–1655.

Zagory, E. 1992. Plants to Use Under Old Oaks. Davis: University of California. Arboretum Review (winter) p. 2.

1. University of California Publications are available for free download (in certain instances) or can be purchased by visiting the http://anrcatalog.ucdavis.edu or www.ipm.ucdavis.edu World Wide Web sites.

Lists of Figures and Tables

Lists of Figures and Tables (continued)

Index

ANR COMMUNICATION SERVICES

To order this or any of our other publications,
visit the ANR Communication Services online catalog at
http://anrcatalog.ucdavis.edu or contact us at:

University of California
Agriculture and Natural Resources
Communication Services
6701 San Pablo Avenue, 2nd Floor
Oakland, California 94608-1239

TELEPHONE 1-800-994-8849
(510) 642-2431
FAX (510) 643-5470
E-MAIL: danrcs@ucdavis.edu

Order by web, phone, or FAX.
We accept checks, money orders (payable to UC Regents),
VISA, MasterCard, American Express, and Discover.

Pests of Landscape Trees and Shrubs: An Integrated Pest Management Guide,
Second Edition. Publication 3359

Our indispensable products include:

- *UC IPM Pest Notes* (available online at www.ipm.ucdavis.edu)
- *Abiotic Disorders of Landscape Plants: A Diagnostic Guide* #3420
- *Natural Enemies Handbook* #3386
- *IPM for Floriculture and Nurseries* #3402
- *Pests of the Garden and Small Farm,* Second Edition #3332
- *Integrated Pest Management Manuals for: Alfalfa Hay* (#3312);
  Almonds, Second Edition (#3308); *Apples and Pears,* Second Edition (#3340);
  Citrus, Second Edition (#3303); *Cole Crops and Lettuce* (#3307);
  Cotton, Second Edition (#3305); *Rice,* Second Edition (#3280);
  Small Grains (#3333); *Stone Fruits* (#3389); *Tomatoes,* Fourth Edition (#3274);
  Walnuts, Third Edition (#3270)

- *UC IPM Pest Management Guidelines* for the above crops
  and more available online at www.ipm.ucdavis.edu

Also visit our Web sites:
UC Statewide IPM Program:
http://www.ipm.ucdavis.edu
UC ANR Communication Services:
http://anrcatalog.ucdavis.edu